PHILIP'S

ROAD ATLAS

2025 BIG ATLAS BRITAIN & IRELAND

CONTENTS

www.philips-maps.co.uk

First published in 2009 by Philip's
a division of Octopus Publishing Group Ltd
www.octopusbooks.co.uk
Carmelite House, 50 Victoria Embankment
London EC4Y 0DZ
An Hachette UK Company
www.hachette.co.uk

Sixteenth edition 2024
First impression 2024

ISBN 978-1-84907-664-7 spiral-bound
ISBN 978-1-84907-663-0 paperback

Cartography by Philip's

Copyright © 2024 Philip's

Ordnance Survey Licensed Data

This product includes mapping data licensed from Ordnance Survey®, with the permission of the Controller of His Majesty's Stationery Office. © Crown copyright 2024. All rights reserved. Licence number AC0000851689

ORDNANCE SURVEY® OF NORTHERN IRELAND

The map of Ireland on pages XII–XIII is based upon the Crown Copyright and is reproduced with the permission of Land & Property Services under delegated authority from the Controller of His Majesty's Stationery Office, © Crown Copyright and database right 2024, PMLPA No 100503, and on Ordnance Survey Ireland by permission of the Government © Ordnance Survey Ireland / Government of Ireland Permit number 9296.

No part of this publication may be reproduced, stored in a retrieval system or transmitted in any form or by any means, electronic, mechanical, photocopying, recording or otherwise, without the permission of the Publishers and the copyright owner.

While every reasonable effort has been made to ensure that the information compiled in this atlas is accurate, complete and up-to-date at the time of publication, some of this information is subject to change and the Publisher cannot guarantee its correctness or completeness.

The information in this atlas is provided without any representation or warranty, express or implied and the Publisher cannot be held liable for any loss or damage due to any use or reliance on the information in this atlas, nor for any errors, omissions or subsequent changes in such information.

The representation in this atlas of any road, drive or track is no evidence of the existence of a right of way.

Information for National Parks, National Landscapes, National Trails and Country Parks in Wales supplied by the Countryside Council for Wales.

Information for National Parks, National Landscapes, National Trails and Country Parks in England supplied by Natural England. Data for Regional Parks, Long Distance Footpaths and Country Parks in Scotland provided by Scottish Natural Heritage.

Gaelic name forms used in the Western Isles provided by Comhairle nan Eilean.

Data for the National Nature Reserves in England provided by Natural England. Data for the National Nature Reserves in Wales provided by Countryside Council for Wales. Darparwyd data'n ymwneud â Gwarchodfeydd Natur Cenedlaethol Cymru gan Gyngor Cefn Gwlad Cymru.

Information on the location of National Nature Reserves in Scotland was provided by Scottish Natural Heritage.

Data for National Scenic Areas in Scotland provided by the Scottish Government. Crown copyright material is reproduced with the permission of the Controller of HMSO and the King's Printer for Scotland. Licence number C02W0003960.

Printed in China

*Data from Nielsen Total Consumer Market 2023 weeks 1–52

T0271293

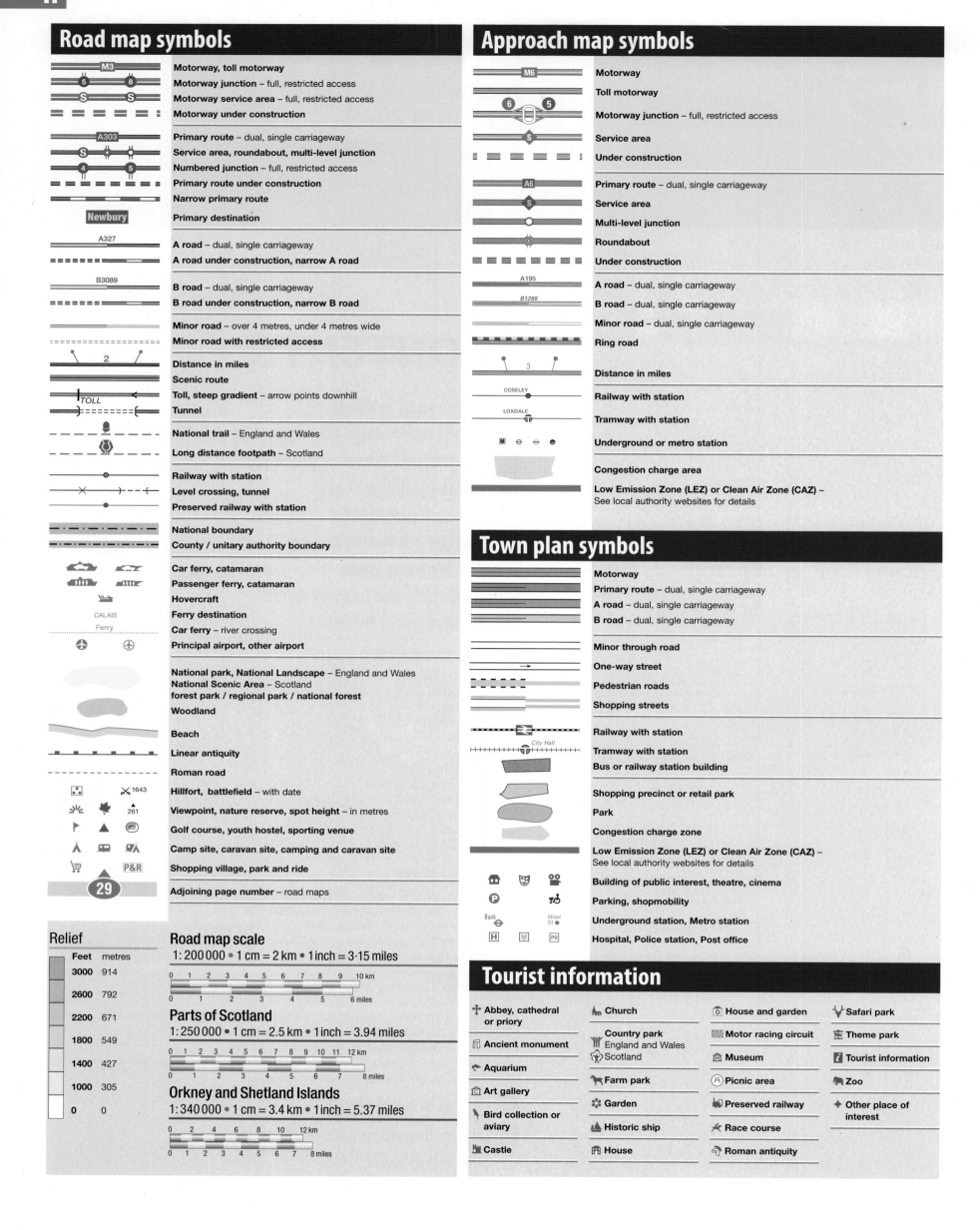

Road map symbols

M3 Motorway, toll motorway
Motorway junction – full, restricted access
Motorway service area – full, restricted access
Motorway under construction

A303 Primary route – dual, single carriageway
Service area, roundabout, multi-level junction
Numbered junction – full, restricted access
Primary route under construction
Narrow primary route
Newbury Primary destination

A327 A road – dual, single carriageway
A road under construction, narrow A road

B3089 B road – dual, single carriageway
B road under construction, narrow B road

Minor road – over 4 metres, under 4 metres wide
Minor road with restricted access

Distance in miles
Scenic route
TOLL Toll, steep gradient – arrow points downhill
Tunnel

National trail – England and Wales
Long distance footpath – Scotland

Railway with station
Level crossing, tunnel
Preserved railway with station

National boundary
County / unitary authority boundary

Car ferry, catamaran
Passenger ferry, catamaran
Hovercraft
CALAIS Ferry — Ferry destination
Car ferry – river crossing
Principal airport, other airport

National park, National Landscape – England and Wales
National Scenic Area – Scotland
forest park / regional park / national forest
Woodland

Beach
Linear antiquity
Roman road
1643 Hillfort, battlefield – with date
261 Viewpoint, nature reserve, spot height – in metres
Golf course, youth hostel, sporting venue
Camp site, caravan site, camping and caravan site
P&R Shopping village, park and ride

29 Adjoining page number – road maps

Relief

Feet	metres
3000	914
2600	792
2200	671
1800	549
1400	427
1000	305
0	0

Road map scale

1: 200 000 • 1 cm = 2 km • 1 inch = 3·15 miles

0 1 2 3 4 5 6 7 8 9 10 km
0 1 2 3 4 5 6 miles

Parts of Scotland

1: 250 000 • 1 cm = 2.5 km • 1 inch = 3.94 miles

0 1 2 3 4 5 6 7 8 9 10 11 12 km
0 1 2 3 4 5 6 7 8 miles

Orkney and Shetland Islands

1: 340 000 • 1 cm = 3.4 km • 1 inch = 5.37 miles

0 2 4 6 8 10 12 km
0 1 2 3 4 5 6 7 8 miles

Approach map symbols

M6 Motorway
Toll motorway
Motorway junction – full, restricted access
Service area
Under construction

A6 Primary route – dual, single carriageway
Service area
Multi-level junction
Roundabout
Under construction

A195 A road – dual, single carriageway
B1288 B road – dual, single carriageway
Minor road – dual, single carriageway
Ring road

Distance in miles

COSELEY Railway with station
LOXDALE Tramway with station
Underground or metro station

Congestion charge area
Low Emission Zone (LEZ) or Clean Air Zone (CAZ) – See local authority websites for details

Town plan symbols

Motorway
Primary route – dual, single carriageway
A road – dual, single carriageway
B road – dual, single carriageway

Minor through road
One-way street
Pedestrian roads
Shopping streets

Railway with station
City Hall — Tramway with station
Bus or railway station building

Shopping precinct or retail park
Park
Congestion charge zone
Low Emission Zone (LEZ) or Clean Air Zone (CAZ) – See local authority websites for details

Building of public interest, theatre, cinema
Parking, shopmobility
Bank, West St — Underground station, Metro station
Hospital, Police station, Post office

Tourist information

- Abbey, cathedral or priory
- Ancient monument
- Aquarium
- Art gallery
- Bird collection or aviary
- Castle
- Church
- Country park England and Wales / Scotland
- Farm park
- Garden
- Historic ship
- House
- House and garden
- Motor racing circuit
- Museum
- Picnic area
- Preserved railway
- Race course
- Roman antiquity
- Safari park
- Theme park
- Tourist information
- Zoo
- Other place of interest

Smart motorways and motorway service areas

Smart motorways

M1	
Juncs 6a–10	Controlled motorway, 4-lane
Juncs 10–13	Dynamic hard shoulder
Juncs 16–13	All lane running
Juncs 19–16	All lane running
Juncs 23a–24	Controlled motorway, 4-lane
Juncs 24–25	All lane running
Juncs 25–28	Controlled motorway, 4-lane
Juncs 28–31	All lane running
Juncs 31–32	Controlled motorway, 4-lane
Juncs 32–35a	All lane running
Juncs 39–42	All lane running

M3	
Juncs 2–4a	All lane running

M4	
Juncs 3–12	All lane running

M4–M5 interchange	
M4 juncs 19–20	Dynamic hard shoulder
M5 juncs 15–16	Controlled motorway
M5 juncs 16–17	Dynamic hard shoulder

M5	
Juncs 4a–6	All lane running

M6	
Juncs 2–3a	All lane running
Juncs 3a–4	Controlled motorway, 3-lane
Juncs 4–4a	
Northbound	Dynamic hard shoulder
Southbound	Controlled motorway, 3-lane
Juncs 4a–8	Dynamic hard shoulder
Juncs 8–10a	Dynamic hard shoulder
Juncs 10a–11a	Controlled motorway, 3-lane
Juncs 11a–13	All lane running
Juncs 13–15	All lane running
Juncs 16–19	All lane running
Juncs 20a–26	All lane running (undergoing conversion)

M20	
Juncs 3–5	All lane running
Juncs 5–6	Controlled motorway, 3-lane
Juncs 6–7	Controlled motorway, 4-lane

M23	
Juncs 8–10	All lane running

M25	
Juncs 2–3	Controlled motorway, 4-lane
Juncs 5–6	All lane running
Juncs 6–7	
Eastbound	Controlled motorway, 4-lane
Westbound	All lane running
Juncs 7–12	Controlled motorway, 4-lane
Juncs 12–14	Controlled motorway, 5-lane
Juncs 14–15	Controlled motorway, 6-lane
Juncs 15–23	Controlled motorway, 4-lane
Juncs 23–27	All lane running
Juncs 27–30	Controlled motorway, 4-lane

M27	
Juncs 4–11	All lane running

M42	
Juncs 3a–7	Dynamic hard shoulder
Juncs 7–9	Controlled motorway, 4-lane

M56	
Juncs 6–8	All lane running

M60	
Juncs 8–12	Controlled motorway, 3-lane
Juncs 12–17	Controlled motorway, 4-lane

M62	
Juncs 10–12	All lane running
Juncs 18–20	All lane running
Juncs 25–26	All lane running
Juncs 26–28	Dynamic hard shoulder
Juncs 28-29	Controlled motorway, 4-lane
Juncs 29-30	
Eastbound	Dynamic hard shoulder
Westbound	All lane running

Undergoing conversion to smart motorway

Information for smart motorways supplied by National Highways

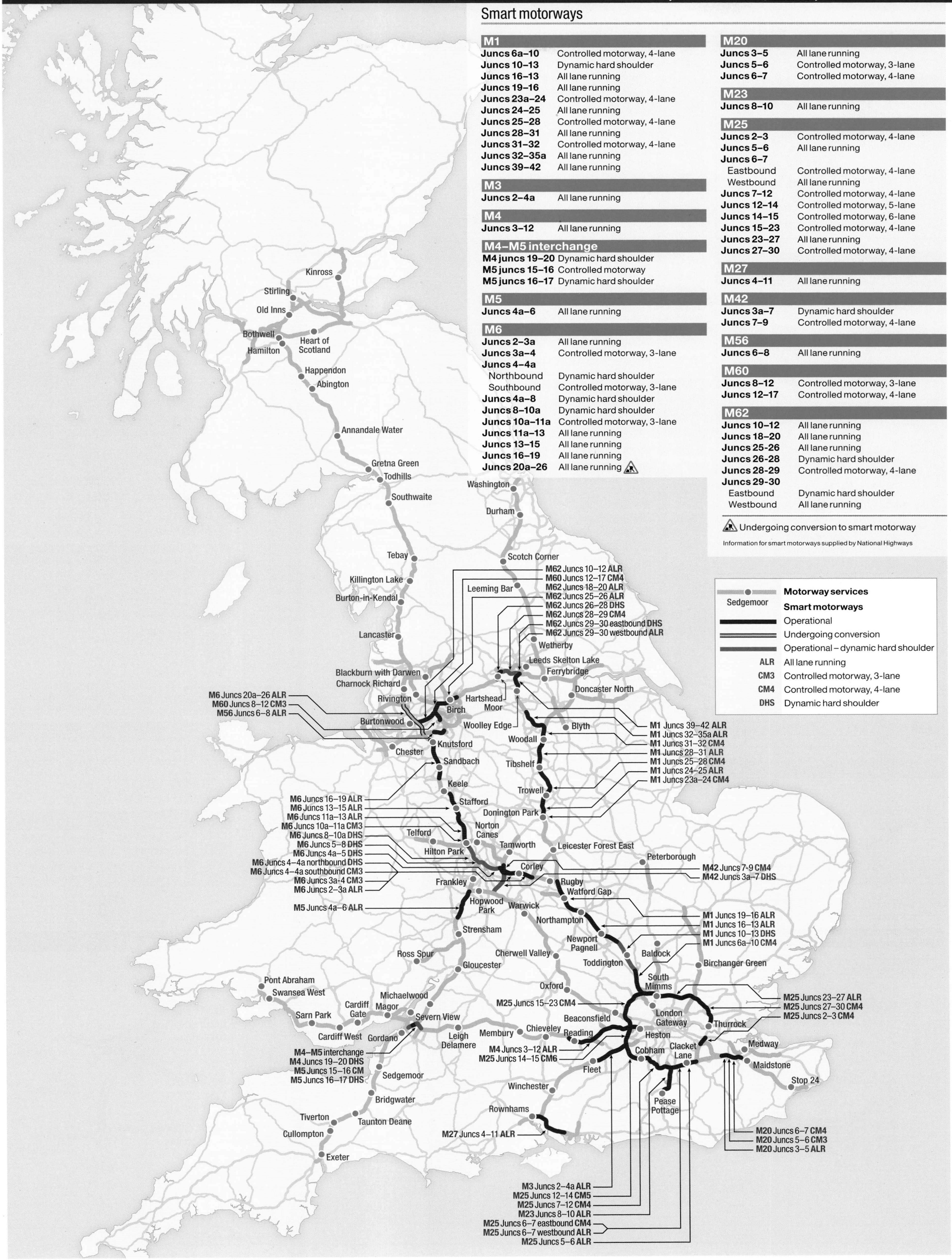

Motorway services
Sedgemoor
Smart motorways
Operational
Undergoing conversion
Operational – dynamic hard shoulder
ALR All lane running
CM3 Controlled motorway, 3-lane
CM4 Controlled motorway, 4-lane
DHS Dynamic hard shoulder
Kinross
Stirling
Old Inns
Bothwell
Hamilton
Heart of Scotland
Happendon
Abington
Annandale Water
Gretna Green
Todhills
Southwaite
Washington
Durham
Tebay
Scotch Corner
Killington Lake
Burton-in-Kendal
Leeming Bar
Lancaster
Wetherby
Leeds Skelton Lake
Ferrybridge
Blackburn with Darwen
Charnock Richard
Rivington
Hartshead Moor
Birch
Doncaster North
Burtonwood
Woolley Edge
Blyth
Woodall
Knutsford
Chester
Sandbach
Tibshelf
Keele
Trowell
Stafford
Donington Park
Norton Canes
Telford
Tamworth
Leicester Forest East
Hilton Park
Peterborough
Corley
Frankley
Rugby
Watford Gap
Hopwood Park
Warwick
Northampton
Strensham
Newport Pagnell
Baldock
Ross Spur
Cherwell Valley
Toddington
Birchanger Green
Gloucester
South Mimms
Pont Abraham
Swansea West
Oxford
Michaelwood
Cardiff Gate
Magor
London Gateway
Sarn Park
Severn View
Beaconsfield
Thurrock
Cardiff West
Gordano
Leigh Delamere
Membury
Chieveley
Reading
Heston
Clacket Lane
Medway
Cobham
Fleet
Maidstone
Sedgemoor
Winchester
Stop 24
Bridgwater
Pease Pottage
Rownhams
Tiverton
Taunton Deane
Cullompton
Exeter
M62 Juncs 10–12 ALR
M60 Juncs 12–17 CM4
M62 Juncs 18–20 ALR
M62 Juncs 25–26 ALR
M62 Juncs 26–28 DHS
M62 Juncs 28–29 CM4
M62 Juncs 29–30 eastbound DHS
M62 Juncs 29–30 westbound ALR
M6 Juncs 20a–26 ALR
M60 Juncs 8–12 CM3
M56 Juncs 6–8 ALR
M1 Juncs 39–42 ALR
M1 Juncs 32–35a ALR
M1 Juncs 31–32 CM4
M1 Juncs 28–31 ALR
M1 Juncs 25–28 CM4
M1 Juncs 24–25 ALR
M1 Juncs 23a–24 CM4
M6 Juncs 16–19 ALR
M6 Juncs 13–15 ALR
M6 Juncs 11a–13 ALR
M6 Juncs 10a–11a CM3
M6 Juncs 8–10a DHS
M6 Juncs 5–8 DHS
M6 Juncs 4a–5 DHS
M6 Juncs 4–4a northbound DHS
M6 Juncs 4–4a southbound CM3
M6 Juncs 3a-4 CM3
M6 Juncs 2–3a ALR
M5 Juncs 4a–6 ALR
M42 Juncs 7-9 CM4
M42 Juncs 3a–7 DHS
M1 Juncs 19–16 ALR
M1 Juncs 16–13 ALR
M1 Juncs 10–13 DHS
M1 Juncs 6a–10 CM4
M25 Juncs 15–23 CM4
M25 Juncs 23–27 ALR
M25 Juncs 27–30 CM4
M25 Juncs 2–3 CM4
M4–M5 interchange
M4 Juncs 19–20 DHS
M5 Juncs 15–16 CM
M5 Juncs 16–17 DHS
M4 Juncs 3–12 ALR
M25 Juncs 14–15 CM6
M27 Juncs 4–11 ALR
M20 Juncs 6–7 CM4
M20 Juncs 5–6 CM3
M20 Juncs 3–5 ALR
M3 Juncs 2–4a ALR
M25 Juncs 12–14 CM5
M25 Juncs 7–12 CM4
M23 Juncs 8–10 ALR
M25 Juncs 6–7 eastbound CM4
M25 Juncs 6–7 westbound ALR
M25 Juncs 5–6 ALR

Restricted motorway junctions

M1 Junction 34

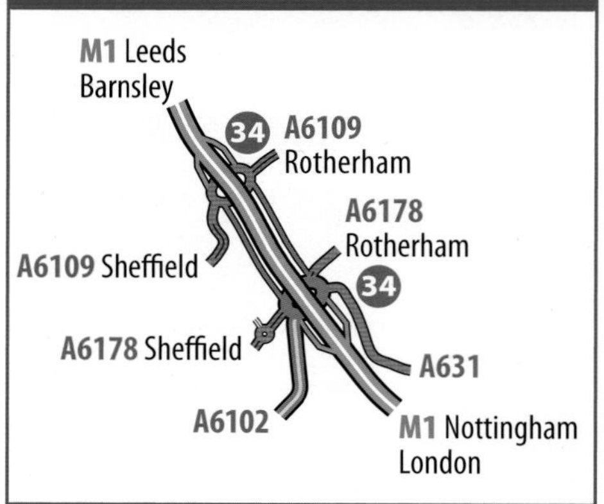

M1 Junctions 6, 6A
M25 Junctions 21, 21A

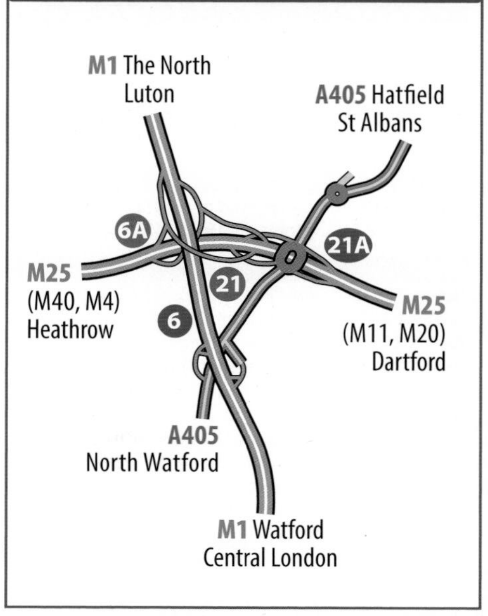

M4 Junctions 25, 25A, 26

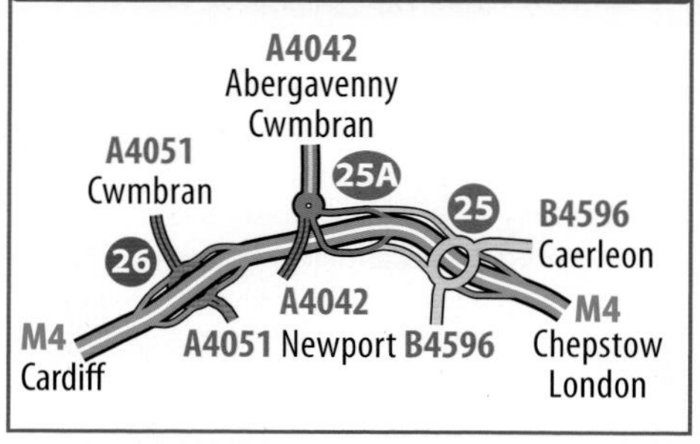

M5 Junction 11A

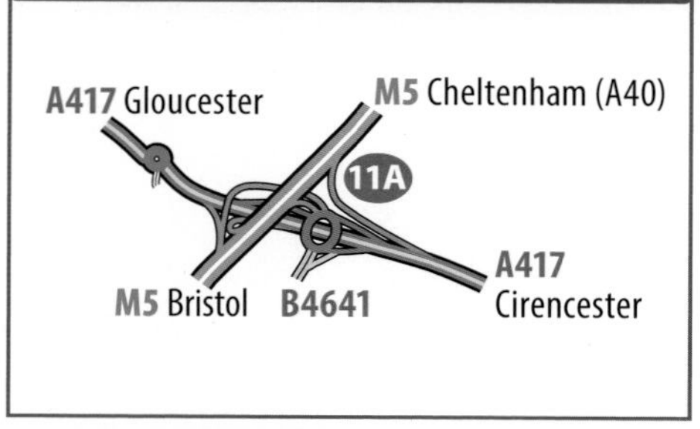

M1	Northbound	Southbound
2	No exit	No access
4	No exit	No access
6A	No exit. Access from M25 only	No access. Exit to M25 only
7	No exit. Access from A414 only	No access. Exit to A414 only
17	No access. Exit to M45 only	No exit. Access from M45 only
19	No exit to A14	No access from A14
21A	No access	No exit
23A		Exit to A42 only
24A	No exit	No access
35A	No access	No exit
43	No access. Exit to M621 only	No exit. Access from M621 only
48	No exit to A1(M) southbound	

M3	Eastbound	Westbound
8	No exit	No access
10	No access	No exit
13	No access to M27 eastbound	
14	No exit	No access

M4	Eastbound	Westbound
1	Exit to A4 eastbound only	Access from A4 westbound only
2	Access from A4 eastbound only	Access to A4 westbound only
21	No exit	No access
23	No access	No exit
25	No exit	No access
25A	No exit	No access
29	No exit	No access
38		No access
39	No exit or access	No exit
42	Access from A483 only	Exit to A483 only

M5	Northbound	Southbound
10	No exit	No access
11A	No access from A417 eastbound	No exit to A417 westbound

M6	Northbound	Southbound
3A	No access.	No exit. Access from M6 eastbound only
4A	No exit. Access from M42 southbound only	No access. Exit to M42 only
5	No access	No exit
10A	No access. Exit to M54 only	No exit. Access from M54 only
11A	No exit. Access from M6 Toll only	No access. Exit to M6 Toll only
20	No exit to M56 eastbound	No access from M56 westbound
20A	No exit	No access
24	No exit	No access
25	No access	No exit
30	No exit. Access from M61 northbound only	No access. Exit to M61 southbound only
31A	No access	No exit
45	No access	No exit

M6 Toll	Northbound	Southbound
T1		No exit
T2	No exit, no access	No access
T5	No exit	No access
T7	No access	No exit
T8	No access	No exit

M8	Eastbound	Westbound
6	No exit	No access
6A	No access	No exit
7	No Access	No exit
7A	No exit. Access from A725 northbound only	No access. Exit to A725 southbound only
8	No exit to M73 northbound	No access from M73 southbound
9	No access	No exit
13	No exit southbound	Access from M73 southbound only
14	No access	No exit
16	No exit	No access
17	No exit	
18		No exit
19	No exit to A814 eastbound	No access from A814 westbound
20	No exit	No access
21	No access from M74	No exit
22	No exit. Access from M77 only	No access. Exit to M77 only
23	No exit	No access
25	Exit to A739 northbound only. Access from A739 southbound only	
25A	No exit	No access
28	No exit	No access
28A	No exit	No access
29A	No exit	No access

M9	Eastbound	Westbound
2	No access	No exit
3	No exit	No access
6	No access	No exit
8	No exit	No access

M11	Northbound	Southbound
4	No exit	No access
5	No access	No exit
8A	No access	No exit
9	No access	No exit
13	No access	No exit
14	No exit to A428 westbound	No exit. Access from A14 westbound only

M20	Eastbound	Westbound
2	No access	No exit
3	No exit Access from M26 eastbound only	No access Exit to M26 westbound only
10	No access	No exit
11A	No access	No exit

M23	Northbound	Southbound
7	No exit to A23 southbound	No access from A23 northbound
10A	No exit	No access

M25	Clockwise	Anticlockwise
5	No exit to M26 eastbound	No access from M26 westbound
19	No access	No exit
21	No exit to M1 southbound. Access from M1 southbound only	No exit to M1 southbound. Access from M1 southbound only
31	No exit	No access

M27	Eastbound	Westbound
10	No exit	No access
12	No access	No exit

M40	Eastbound	Westbound
3	No exit	No access
7	No exit	No access
8	No exit	No access
13	No exit	No access
14	No access	No exit
16	No access	No exit

M42	Northbound	Southbound
1	No exit	No access
7	No access Exit to M6 northbound only	No exit. Access from M6 northbound only
7A	No access. Exit to M6 southbound only	No exit
8	No exit. Access from M6 southbound only	Exit to M6 northbound only. Access from M6 southbound only

M45	Eastbound	Westbound
M1 J17	Access to M1 southbound only	No access from M1 southbound
With A45	No access	No exit

M48	Eastbound	Westbound
M4 J21	No exit to M4 westbound	No access from M4 eastbound
M4 J23	No access from M4 westbound	No exit to M4 eastbound

M8 Junctions 8, 9 · M73 Junctions 1, 2 · M74 Junctions 2A, 3, 3A, 4

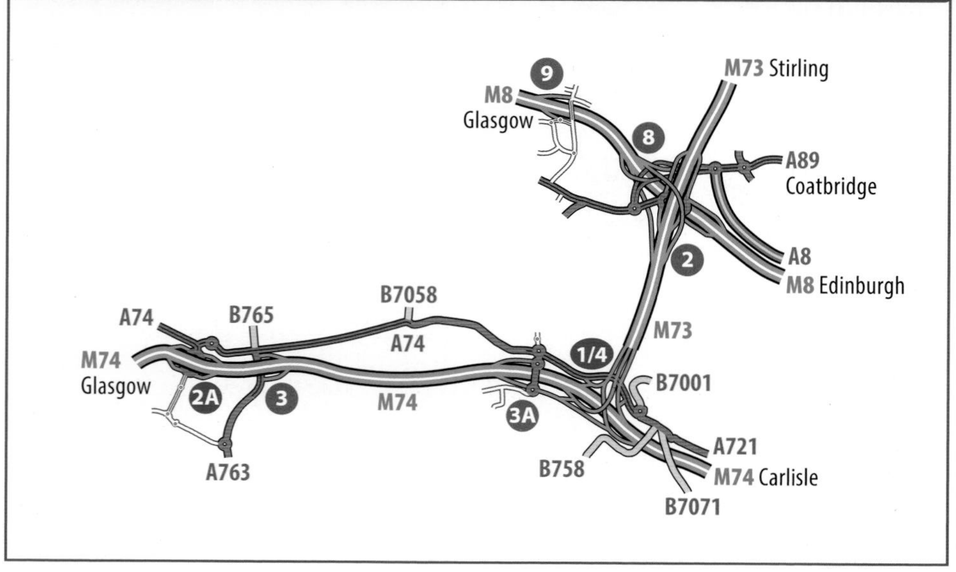

M11 Junctions 13, 14

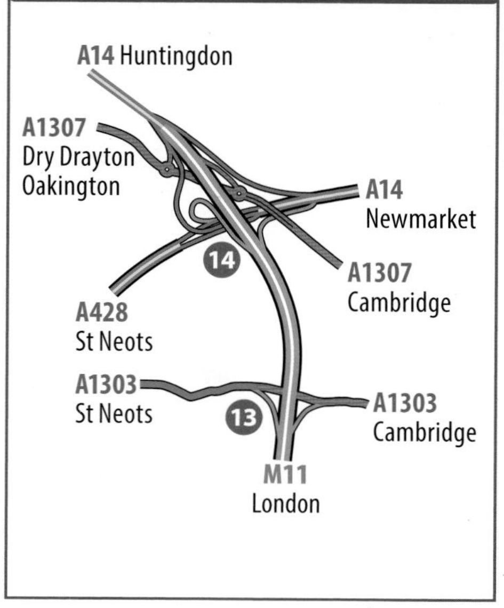

M49	Southbound	Northbound
18A	No exit to M5 northbound	No access from M5 southbound

M53	Northbound	Southbound
11	Exit to M56 eastbound only. Access from M56 westbound only	Exit to M56 eastbnd only. Access from M56 westbound only

M56	Eastbound	Westbound
2	No exit	No access
3	No access	No exit
4	No exit	No access
7		No access
8	No exit or access	No exit
9	No access from M6 northbound	No access to M6 southbound
15	No exit to M53	No access from M53 northbound

M57	Northbound	Southbound
3	No exit	No access
5	No exit	No access

M60	Clockwise	Anticlockwise
2	No exit	No access
3	No exit to A34 northbound	No exit to A34 northbound
4	No access from M56	No exit to M56
5	No exit to A5103 southbound	No exit to A5103 northbound
14	No exit	No access
16	No exit	No access
20	No access	No exit
22		No access
25	No access	
26		No exit or access
27	No exit	No access

M61	Northbound	Southbound
2	No access from A580 eastbound	No exit to A580 westbound
3	No access from A580 eastbound. No access from A666 southbound	No exit to A580 westbound
M6 J30	No exit to M6 southbound	No access from M6 northbound

M62	Eastbound	Westbound
23	No access	No exit

M65	Eastbound	Westbound
9	No access	No exit
11	No exit	No access

M66	Northbound	Southbound
1	No access	No exit

M67	Eastbound	Westbound
1A	No access	No exit
2	No exit	No access

M69	Northbound	Southbound
2	No exit	No access

M73	Northbound	Southbound
2	No access from M8 eastbound	No exit to M8 westbound

M74	Northbound	Southbound
3	No access	No exit
3A	No exit	No access
7	No exit	No access
9	No exit or access	No access
10		No exit
11	No exit	No access
12	No access	No exit

M77	Northbound	Southbound
4	No exit	No access
6	No exit	No access
7	No exit	
8	No access	No access

M80	Northbound	Southbound
4A	No access	No exit
6A	No exit	No access
8	Exit to M876 northbound only. No access	Access from M876 southbound only. No exit

M90	Northbound	Southbound
1	Access from A90 northbound only	No access. Exit to A90 southbound only
2A	No access	No exit
7	No exit	No access
8	No access	No exit
10	No access from A912	No exit to A912

M180	Eastbound	Westbound
1	No access	No exit

M621	Eastbound	Westbound
2A	No exit	No access
4	No exit	
5	No exit	No access
6	No access	No exit

M876	Northbound	Southbound
2	No access	No exit

A1(M)	Northbound	Southbound
2	No access	No exit
3		No access
5	No exit	No exit, no access
14	No exit	No access
40	No access	No exit
43	No exit. Access from M1 only	No access. Exit to M1 only
57	No access	No exit
65	No access	No exit

M3 Junctions 13, 14 · M27 Junction 4

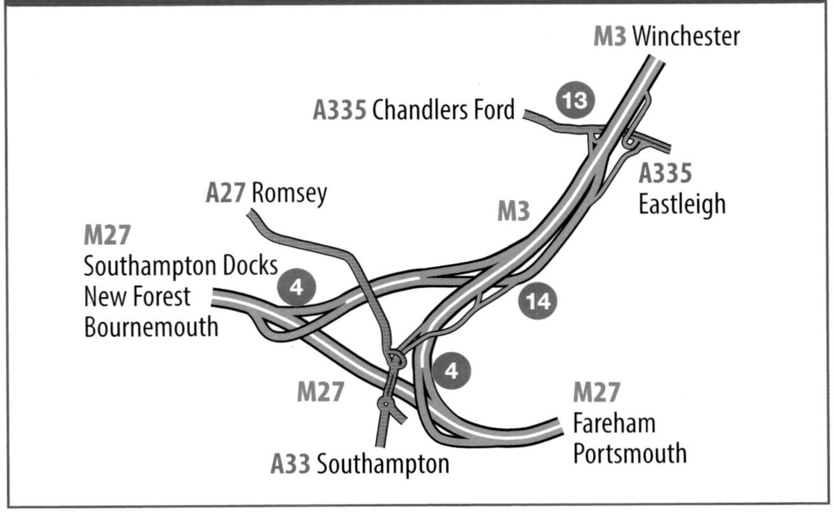

A3(M)	Northbound	Southbound
1	No exit	No access
4	No access	No exit

A38(M) with Victoria Rd, (Park Circus) Birmingham	
Northbound	No exit
Southbound	No access

A48(M)	Northbound	Southbound
M4 Junc 29	Exit to M4 eastbound only	Access from M4 westbound only
29A	Access from A48 eastbound only	Exit to A48 westbound only

A57(M)	Eastbound	Westbound
With A5103	No access	No exit
With A34	No access	No exit

A58(M)	Southbound
With Park Lane and Westgate, Leeds	No access

A64(M)	Eastbound	Westbound
With A58 Clay Pit Lane, Leeds	No access from A58	No exit to A58

A74(M)	Northbound	Southbound
18	No access	No exit
22		No exit to A75

A194(M)	Northbound	Southbound
A1(M) J65 Gateshead Western Bypass	Access from A1(M) northbound only	Exit to A1(M) southbound only

M6 Junctions 3A, 4A · M42 Junctions 7, 7A, 8, 9
M6 Toll Junctions T1, T2

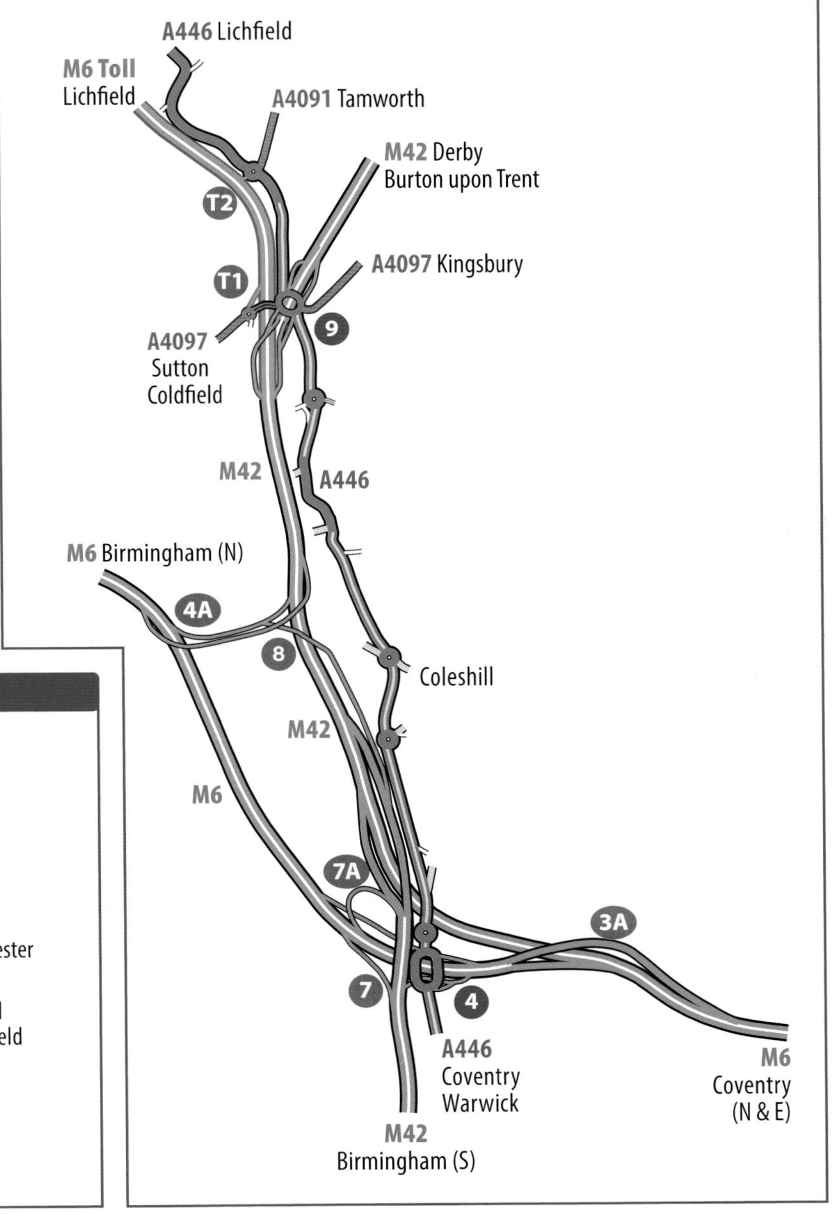

M62 Junctions 32A, 33 · A1(M) Junctions 40, 41

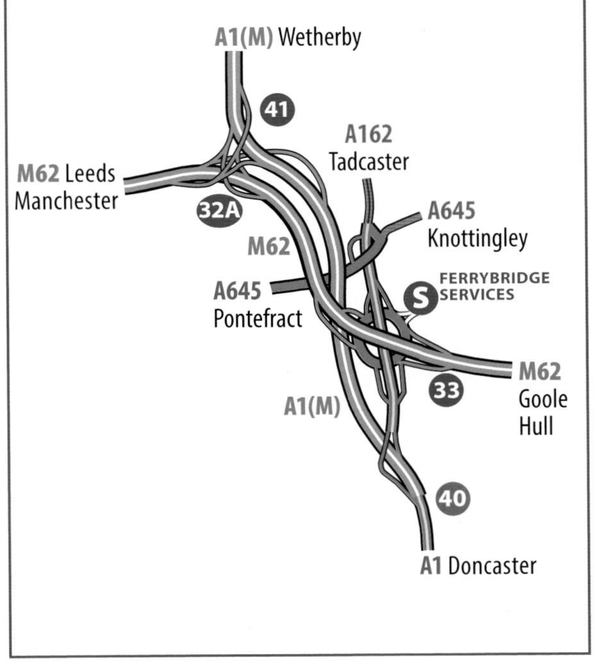

M6 Junction 20, 20A · M56 Junction 9

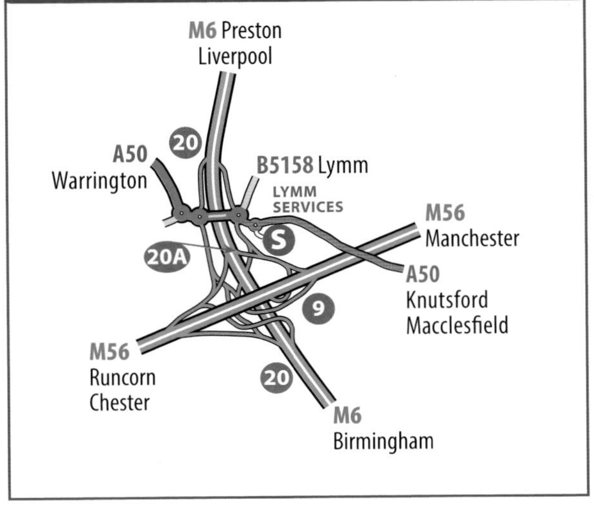

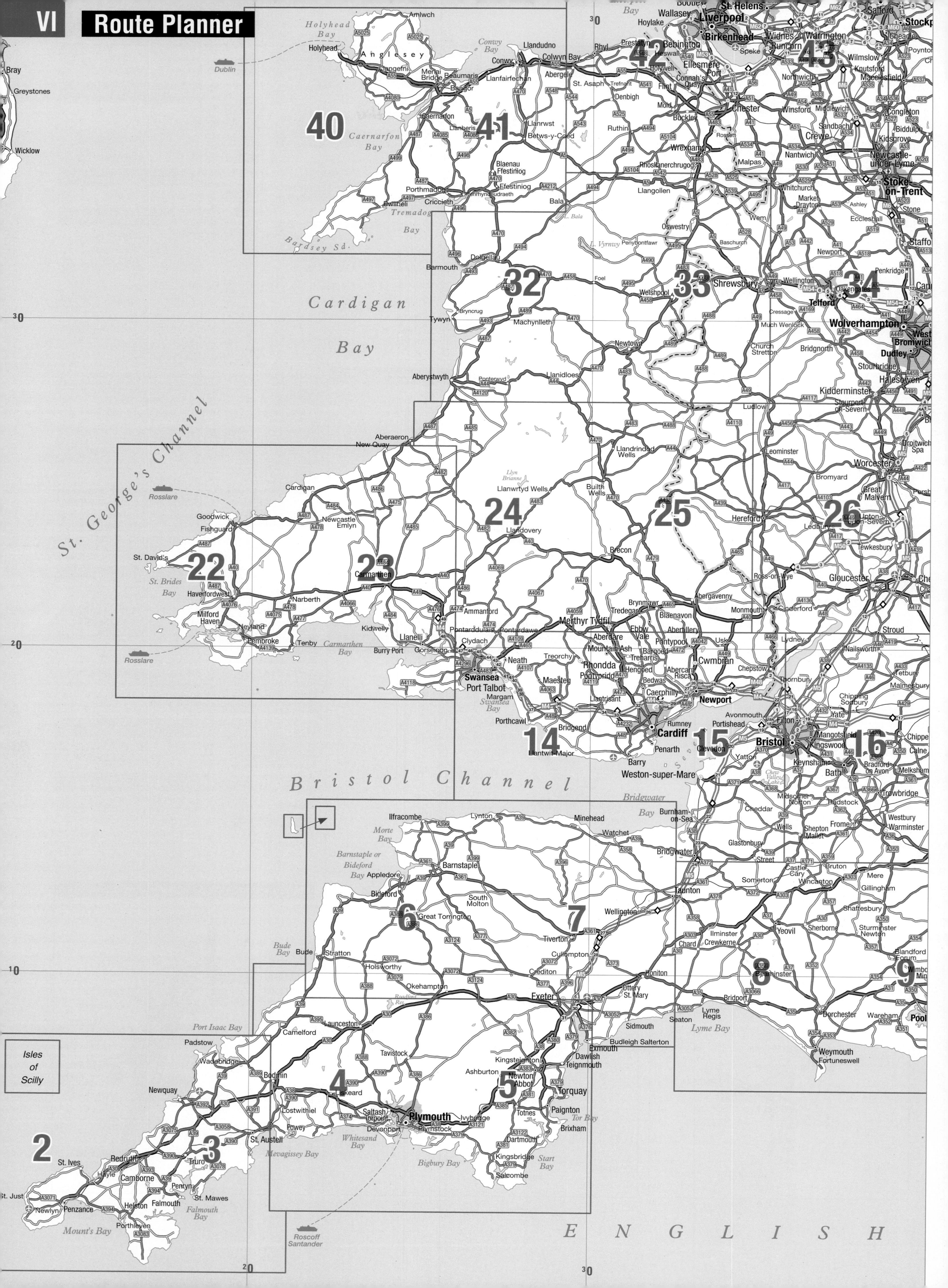
Holyhead Bay
Amlwch
Holyhead
Anglesey
Beaumaris
Bangor
Dublin
Conwy Bay
Llandudno
Conwy
Colwyn Bay
Abergele
Rhyl
Prestatyn
Liverpool
Birkenhead
St. Helens
Wallasey
Hoylake
Bebington
Ellesmere Port
Runcorn
Widnes
Warrington
Salford
Stockport
Wilmslow
Knutsford
Macclesfield
Northwich
Chester
Flint
Mold
Winsford
Middlewich
Congleton
Sandbach
Crewe
Kidsgrove
Nantwich
Newcastle-under-Lyme
Stoke-on-Trent
Wrexham
Buckley
Ruthin
Denbigh
St. Asaph
Llanrwst
Betws-y-Coed
Caernarfon
Llanberis
Caernarfon Bay
Blaenau Ffestiniog
Ffestiniog
Porthmadog
Criccieth
Pwllheli
Tremadog Bay
Bardsey Sd.
Bala
Llangollen
Whitchurch
Market Drayton
Stone
Eccleshall
Stafford
Oswestry
Wem
Newport
Penkridge
Shrewsbury
Wellington
Telford
Wolverhampton
West Bromwich
Dudley
Stourbridge
Halesowen
Kidderminster
Stourport-on-Severn
Bridgnorth
Much Wenlock
Church Stretton
Welshpool
Newtown
Dolgellau
Barmouth
Tywyn
Machynlleth
Llanidloes
Aberystwyth
Cardigan Bay
Aberaeron
New Quay
Cardigan
St. George's Channel
Rosslare
Goodwick
Fishguard
Newcastle Emlyn
St. David's
St. Brides Bay
Haverfordwest
Milford Haven
Neyland
Pembroke
Tenby
Narberth
Carmarthen
Carmarthen Bay
Kidwelly
Llanelli
Burry Port
Gorseinon
Ammanford
Llandovery
Llanwrtyd Wells
Builth Wells
Llandrindod Wells
Ludlow
Leominster
Worcester
Droitwich Spa
Bromyard
Great Malvern
Hereford
Ledbury
Upton-upon-Severn
Tewkesbury
Gloucester
Ross-on-Wye
Brecon
Abergavenny
Monmouth
Cinderford
Stroud
Merthyr Tydfil
Tredegar
Brynmawr
Ebbw Vale
Blaenavon
Abertillery
Pontypool
Usk
Cwmbran
Chepstow
Lydney
Nailsworth
Tetbury
Malmesbury
Thornbury
Aberdare
Mountain Ash
Treorchy
Rhondda
Pontypridd
Maesteg
Neath
Swansea
Port Talbot
Swansea Bay
Porthcawl
Bridgend
Llantrisant
Caerphilly
Newport
Cardiff
Penarth
Barry
Llantwit Major
Bristol Channel
Weston-super-Mare
Clevedon
Portishead
Avonmouth
Filton
Bristol
Kingswood
Keynsham
Bath
Bradford-on-Avon
Melksham
Trowbridge
Chipping Sodbury
Yate
Mangotsfield
Midsomer Norton
Radstock
Frome
Westbury
Warminster
Cheddar
Wells
Shepton Mallet
Glastonbury
Street
Bridgwater Bay
Burnham-on-Sea
Bridgwater
Minehead
Watchet
Lynton
Ilfracombe
Morte Bay
Barnstaple
Barnstaple or Bideford Bay
Appledore
Bideford
Great Torrington
South Molton
Tiverton
Wellington
Taunton
Somerton
Castle Cary
Bruton
Wincanton
Mere
Gillingham
Shaftesbury
Sherborne
Sturminster Newton
Blandford Forum
Wimborne Minster
Yeovil
Ilminster
Crewkerne
Chard
Beaminster
Bridport
Lyme Regis
Lyme Bay
Seaton
Honiton
Ottery St. Mary
Sidmouth
Budleigh Salterton
Exmouth
Dorchester
Wareham
Poole
Weymouth
Fortuneswell
Bude Bay
Bude
Stratton
Holsworthy
Okehampton
Crediton
Cullompton
Exeter
Dawlish
Teignmouth
Kingsteignton
Newton Abbot
Torquay
Paignton
Tor Bay
Brixham
Totnes
Dartmouth
Kingsbridge
Start Bay
Salcombe
Bigbury Bay
Ivybridge
Plymouth
Plymstock
Devonport
Saltash
Torpoint
Whitesand Bay
Roscoff Santander
Launceston
Camelford
Tavistock
Ashburton
Port Isaac Bay
Padstow
Wadebridge
Bodmin
Liskeard
Lostwithiel
Fowey
Newquay
St. Austell
Mevagissey Bay
Truro
Redruth
Camborne
Hayle
St. Ives
Penryn
Falmouth
Falmouth Bay
St. Mawes
Helston
Porthleven
Mount's Bay
Penzance
Newlyn
St. Just
Isles of Scilly
Bray
Greystones
Wicklow
ENGLISH
2
3
4
5
6
7
8
9
14
15
16
22
23
24
25
26
32
33
34
40
41
42
43

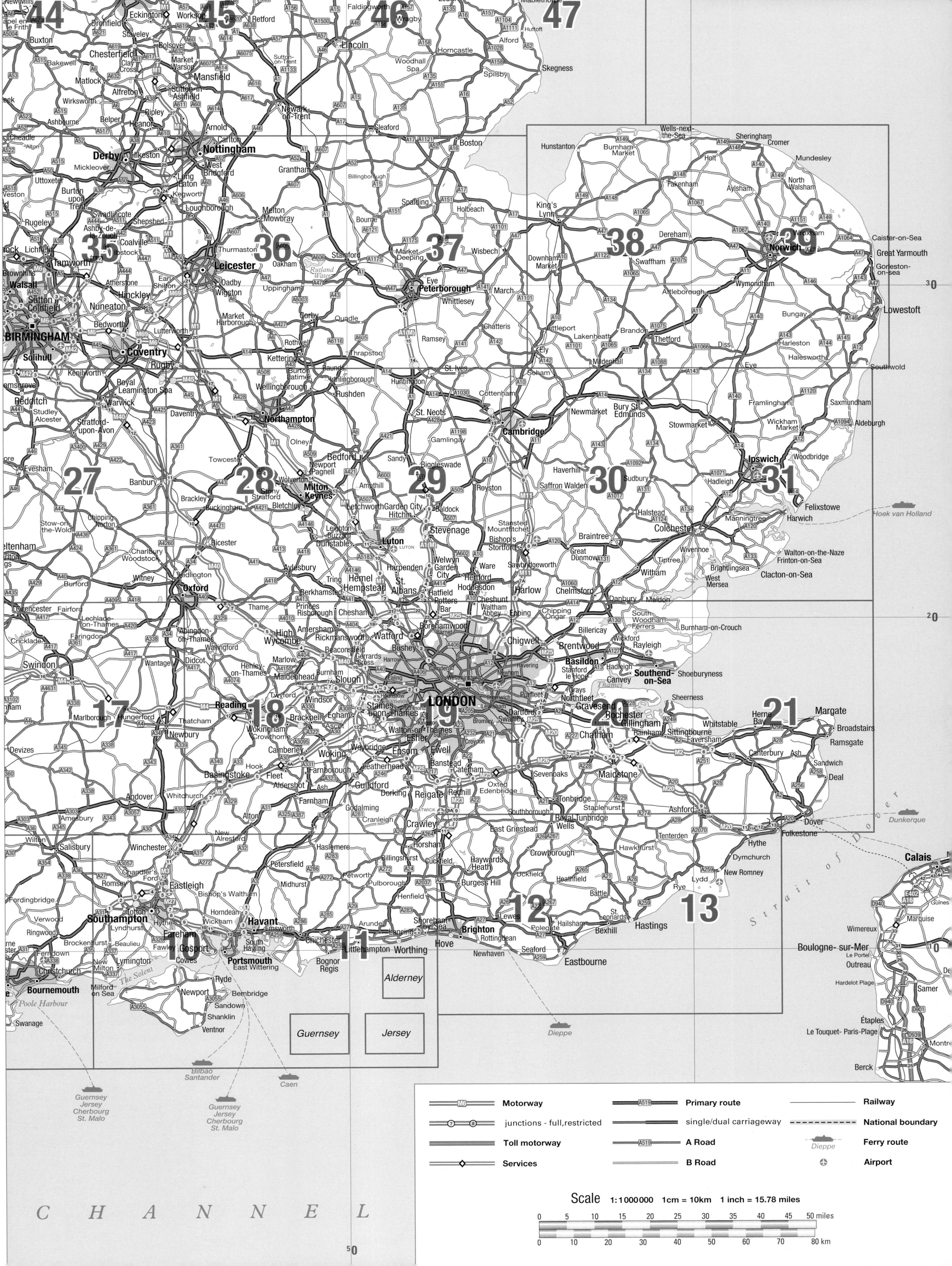
Motorway
junctions - full,restricted
Toll motorway
Services
Primary route
single/dual carriageway
A Road
B Road
Railway
National boundary
Ferry route
Airport
Scale 1:1000000 1cm = 10km 1 inch = 15.78 miles
0 5 10 15 20 25 30 35 40 45 50 miles
0 10 20 30 40 50 60 70 80 km
C H A N N E L
Strait of Dover
Alderney
Guernsey
Jersey

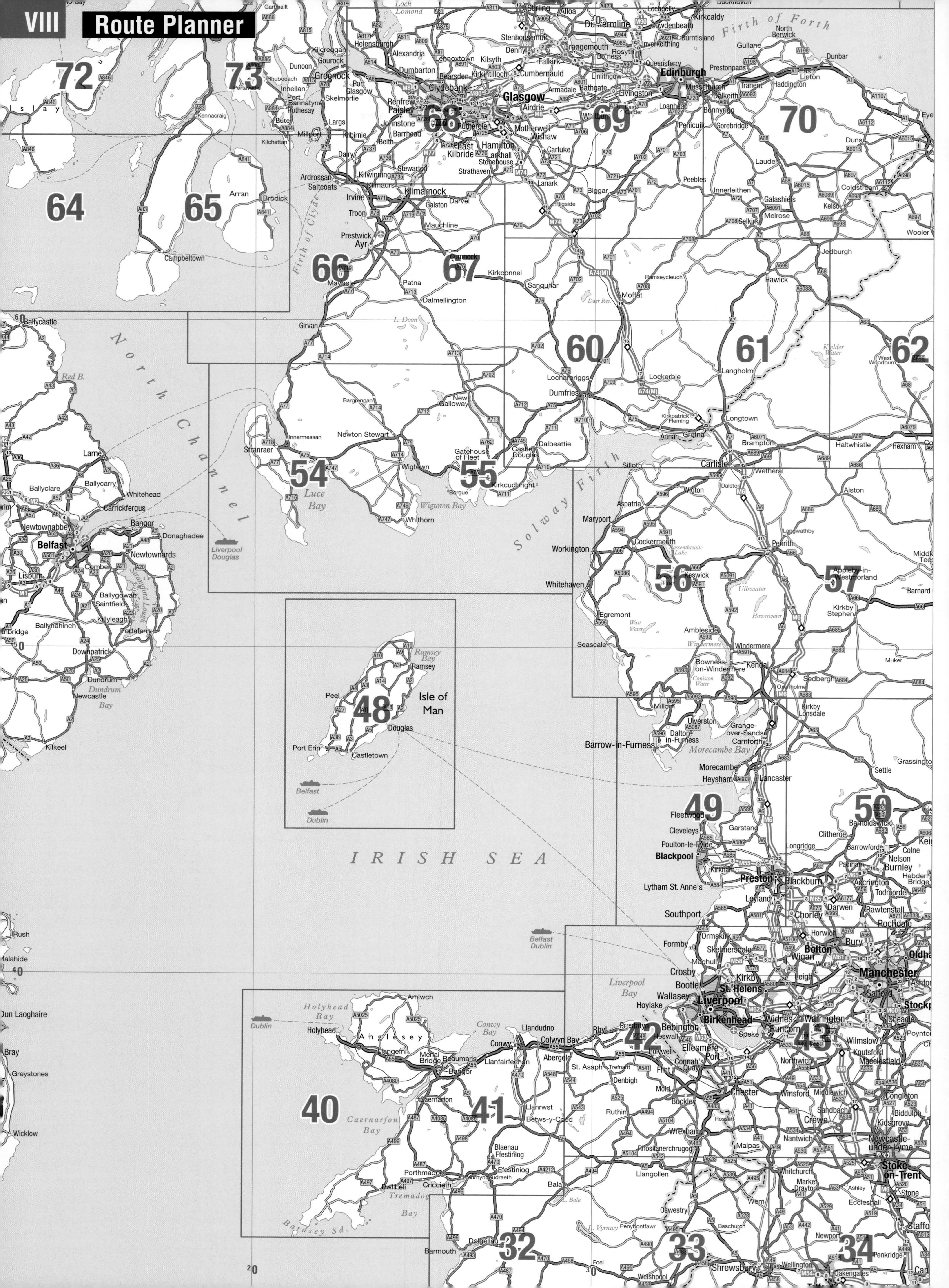
72
73
64
65
66
67
68
69
70
60
61
62
54
55
56
57
48
49
50
40
41
42
43
32
33
34
Islay
Arran
Brodick
Campbeltown
Kennacraig
Firth of Clyde
Loch Lomond
Stirling
Alloa
Dunfermline
Kirkcaldy
Firth of Forth
North Berwick
Dunbar
Edinburgh
Musselburgh
Dalkeith
Haddington
Falkirk
Grangemouth
Linlithgow
Livingston
Bathgate
Cumbernauld
Kilsyth
Glasgow
Clydebank
Paisley
Renfrew
Greenock
Gourock
Helensburgh
Dumbarton
Alexandria
Dunoon
Rothesay
Largs
Airdrie
Motherwell
Wishaw
Hamilton
East Kilbride
Rutherglen
Lanark
Carluke
Biggar
Peebles
Penicuik
Galashiels
Melrose
Selkirk
Kelso
Coldstream
Jedburgh
Hawick
Wooler
Ardrossan
Saltcoats
Irvine
Kilmarnock
Troon
Prestwick
Ayr
Maybole
Cumnock
Kirkconnel
Sanquhar
Moffat
Girvan
Dalmellington
Patna
Stranraer
Newton Stewart
Wigtown
Whithorn
Gatehouse of Fleet
Kirkcudbright
Castle Douglas
Dalbeattie
Dumfries
Lockerbie
Langholm
Longtown
Annan
Gretna
Carlisle
Brampton
Haltwhistle
Hexham
Luce Bay
Wigtown Bay
Solway Firth
North Channel
IRISH SEA
Ballycastle
Larne
Ballyclare
Whitehead
Carrickfergus
Newtownabbey
Belfast
Bangor
Donaghadee
Newtownards
Lisburn
Comber
Ballygowan
Saintfield
Killyleagh
Ballynahinch
Portaferry
Strangford Lough
Downpatrick
Dundrum
Newcastle
Kilkeel
Isle of Man
Ramsey
Peel
Douglas
Port Erin
Castletown
Liverpool
Dublin
Belfast
Maryport
Workington
Whitehaven
Cockermouth
Keswick
Penrith
Appleby-in-Westmorland
Egremont
Seascale
Ambleside
Windermere
Kendal
Sedbergh
Kirkby Lonsdale
Ulverston
Barrow-in-Furness
Grange-over-Sands
Morecambe Bay
Morecambe
Heysham
Lancaster
Fleetwood
Cleveleys
Poulton-le-Fylde
Blackpool
Garstang
Clitheroe
Preston
Blackburn
Burnley
Lytham St. Anne's
Leyland
Chorley
Southport
Ormskirk
Bolton
Wigan
Formby
Crosby
Bootle
St. Helens
Manchester
Salford
Liverpool Bay
Wallasey
Hoylake
Birkenhead
Widnes
Runcorn
Warrington
Holyhead
Anglesey
Amlwch
Llandudno
Conwy
Colwyn Bay
Abergele
Rhyl
Prestatyn
Bangor
Menai Bridge
Beaumaris
Caernarfon
Caernarfon Bay
Llanrwst
Betws-y-Coed
Denbigh
Ruthin
Mold
Flint
Chester
Ellesmere Port
Wrexham
Llangollen
Oswestry
Bala
Blaenau Ffestiniog
Porthmadog
Criccieth
Pwllheli
Tremadog Bay
Bardsey Sd.
Barmouth
Dolgellau
Welshpool
Shrewsbury
Whitchurch
Nantwich
Crewe
Macclesfield
Congleton
Newcastle-under-Lyme
Stoke-on-Trent
Market Drayton
Stone
Wellington
Newport

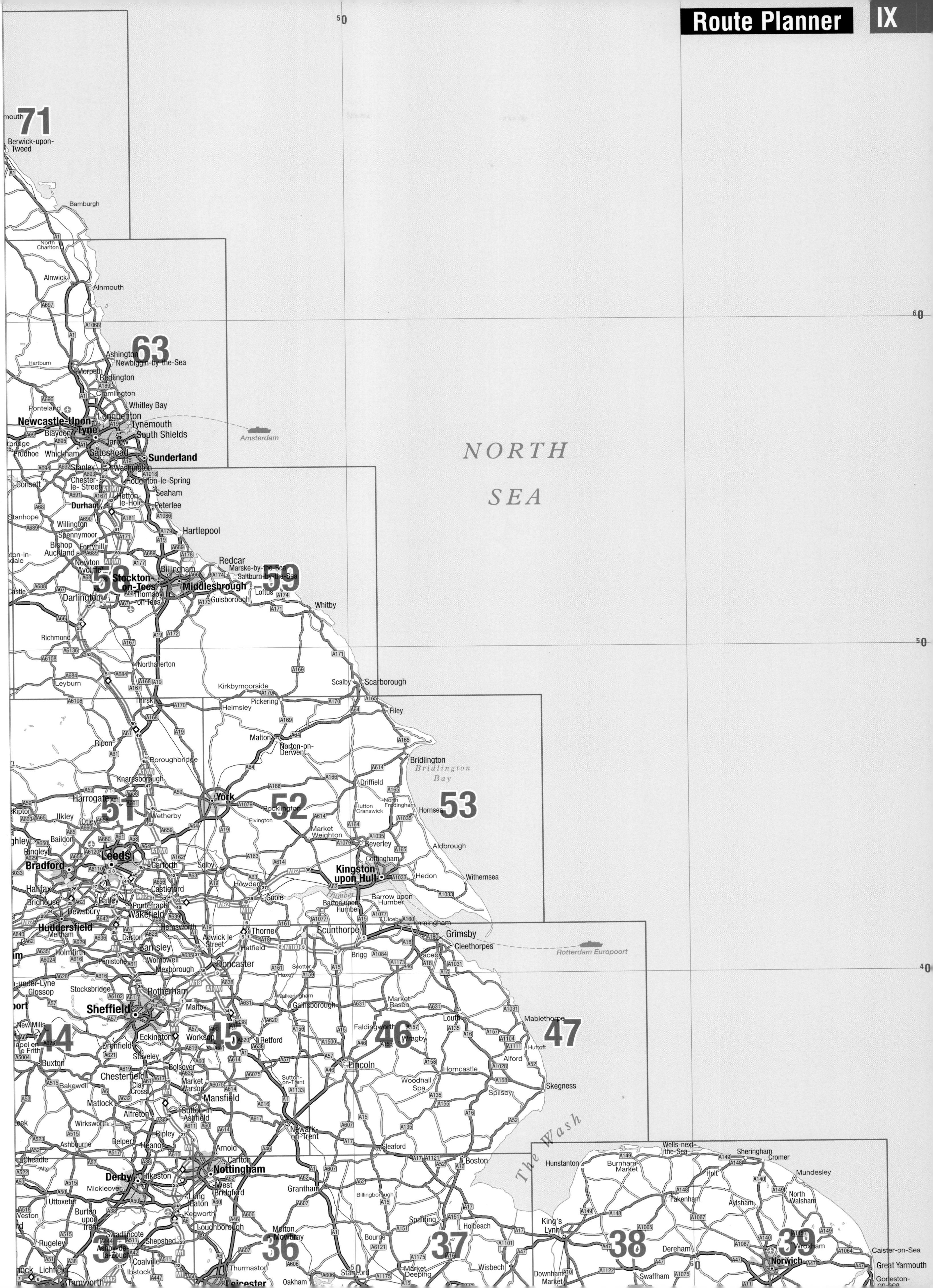

NORTH
SEA
71
Berwick-upon-Tweed
Bamburgh
North Charlton
Alnwick
Alnmouth
63
Ashington
Newbiggin-by-the-Sea
Hartburn
Morpeth
Bedlington
Cramlington
Whitley Bay
Ponteland
Longbenton
Newcastle-Upon-Tyne
Tynemouth
South Shields
Amsterdam
Blaydon
Jarrow
Prudhoe
Whickham
Gateshead
Sunderland
Stanley
Washington
Consett
Chester-le-Street
Houghton-le-Spring
Seaham
Durham
Hetton-le-Hole
Peterlee
Stanhope
Willington
Hartlepool
Spennymoor
Bishop Auckland
Ferryhill
Redcar
Newton Aycliffe
Billingham
Marske-by-the-Sea
Saltburn-by-the-Sea
58
59
Stockton-on-Tees
Middlesbrough
Loftus
Darlington
Thornaby on Tees
Guisborough
Whitby
Richmond
Northallerton
Leyburn
Kirkbymoorside
Scalby
Scarborough
Thirsk
Helmsley
Pickering
Filey
Malton
Ripon
Norton-on-Derwent
Boroughbridge
Bridlington
Bridlington Bay
Knaresborough
Driffield
Harrogate
York
52
51
53
Hutton Cranswick
North Frodingham
Hornsea
Ilkley
Wetherby
Pocklington
Otley
Elvington
Market Weighton
Baildon
Beverley
Aldbrough
Bingley
Leeds
Cottingham
Bradford
Garforth
Selby
Kingston upon Hull
Hedon
Withernsea
Halifax
Howden
Castleford
Humber
Brighouse
Batley
Goole
Barrow upon Humber
Barton-upon-Humber
Dewsbury
Pontefract
Wakefield
Huddersfield
Hemsworth
Thorne
Scunthorpe
Immingham
Grimsby
Meltham
Darton
Adwick le Street
Cleethorpes
Barnsley
Hatfield
Rotterdam Europoort
Holmfirth
Penistone
Wombwell
Brigg
Doncaster
Mexborough
Scotter
Laceby
Glossop
Stocksbridge
Rotherham
Walkeringham
Market Rasen
Sheffield
Maltby
Gainsborough
Louth
Mablethorpe
New Mills
44
45
46
47
Eckington
Worksop
Retford
Faldingworth
Wragby
Huttoft
Bronfield
Staveley
Alford
Buxton
Lincoln
Chesterfield
Bolsover
Horncastle
Bakewell
Clay Cross
Market Warsop
Sutton-on-Trent
Woodhall Spa
Skegness
Matlock
Mansfield
Spilsby
Alfreton
Sutton-in-Ashfield
Wirksworth
Ripley
Newark-on-Trent
The Wash
Ashbourne
Belper
Heanor
Arnold
Sleaford
Wells-next-the-Sea
Sheringham
Cromer
Boston
Hunstanton
Burnham Market
Holt
Mundesley
Derby
Ilkeston
Carlton
Nottingham
Mickleover
West Bridgford
Grantham
Fakenham
Aylsham
North Walsham
Uttoxeter
Long Eaton
Billingborough
Burton upon Trent
Kegworth
Spalding
Holbeach
King's Lynn
Loughborough
Melton Mowbray
Bourne
Swadlincote
35
36
37
38
39
Rugeley
Shepshed
Ashby-de-la-Zouch
Dereham
Wroxham
Caister-on-Sea
Coalville
Norwich
Great Yarmouth
Lichfield
Thurmaston
Market Deeping
Wisbech
Downham Market
Swaffham
Gorleston-on-Sea
Tamworth
Ibstock
Leicester
Oakham
Stamford

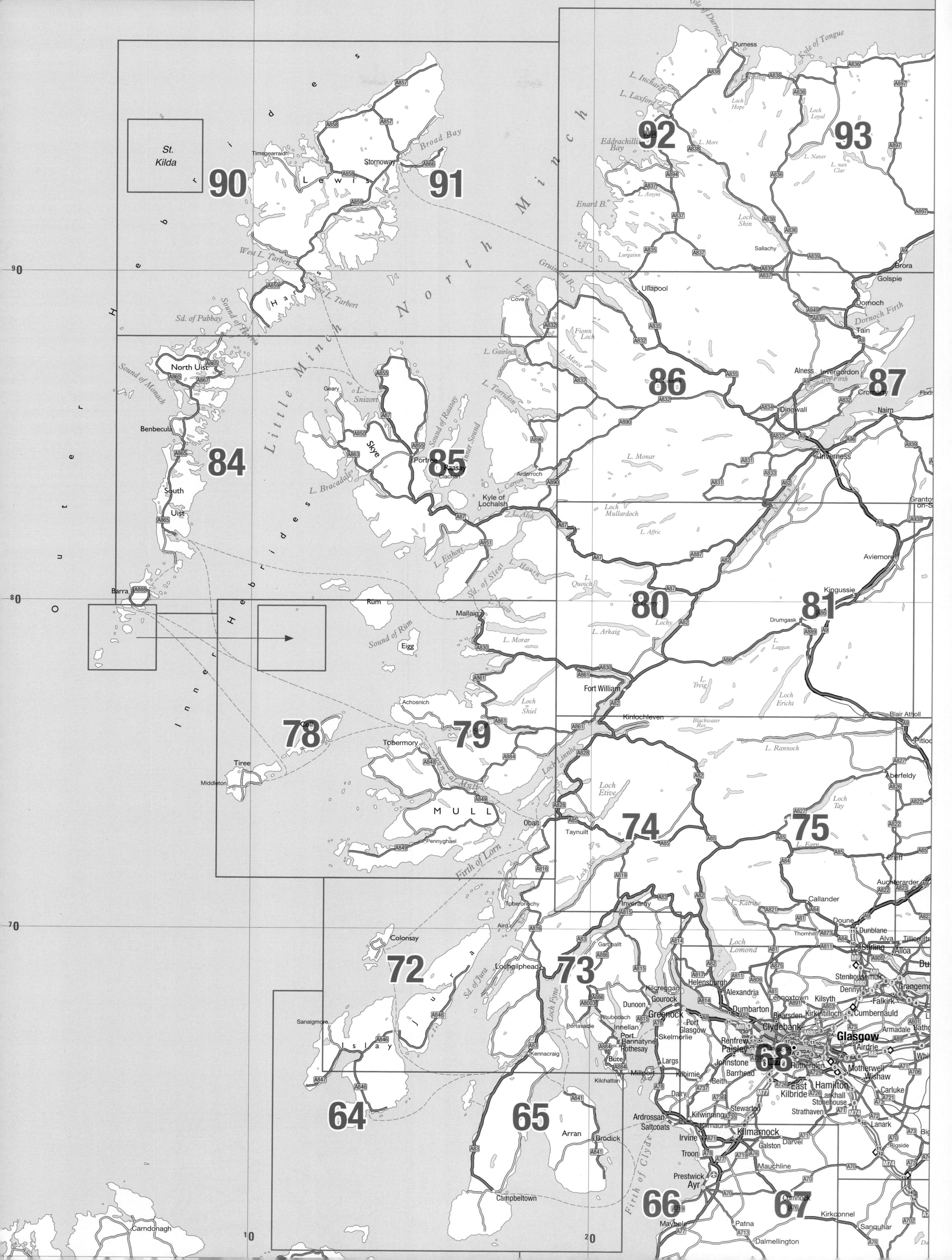

90
91
92
93
84
85
86
87
80
81
78
79
74
75
72
73
64
65
66
67
68
St. Kilda
Outer Hebrides
Inner Hebrides
North Minch
Little Minch
Lewis
Harris
Stornoway
Timsgearraidh
Broad Bay
West L. Tarbert
East L. Tarbert
Sd. of Pabbay
Sound of Harris
North Uist
Sound of Monach
Benbecula
South Uist
Barra
Rum
Eigg
Sound of Rum
Coll
Tiree
Middleton
Tobermory
Achosnich
MULL
Pennyghael
Oban
Taynuilt
Firth of Lorn
Colonsay
Jura
Sd. of Jura
Islay
Sanaigmore
Skye
Geary
L. Snizort
Portree
Raasay
Clachan
Sound of Raasay
Inner Sound
L. Bracadale
Kyle of Lochalsh
L. Alsh
L. Eishort
Sd. of Sleat
L. Hourn
L. Nevis
Mallaig
L. Morar
Ardarroch
L. Carron
L. Torridon
L. Gairloch
L. Maree
L. Ewe
Cove
Gruinard B.
Fionn Loch
Ullapool
L. Lurgainn
Enard B.
L. Assynt
Eddrachillis Bay
L. Laxford
L. Inchard
Kyle of Durness
Durness
Kyle of Tongue
Loch Hope
L. More
Loch Loyal
L. Naver
L. nan Clar
Loch Shin
Sallachy
Brora
Golspie
Dornoch
Dornoch Firth
Tain
Alness
Invergordon
Cromarty Firth
Cromarty
Dingwall
Nairn
Inverness
L. Fannich
L. Monar
Loch Mullardoch
L. Affric
Loch Ness
Aviemore
Kingussie
Drumgask
L. Laggan
L. Quoich
L. Lochy
L. Arkaig
Fort William
L. Treig
Loch Ericht
Loch Shiel
Loch Linnhe
Kinlochleven
Blackwater Res.
L. Rannoch
Blair Atholl
Aberfeldy
Loch Tay
Loch Etive
Loch Awe
L. Earn
Crieff
Auchterarder
Callander
L. Katrine
Doune
Dunblane
Stirling
Alloa
Alva
Falkirk
Grangemouth
Denny
Stenhousemuir
Kilsyth
Cumbernauld
Kirkintilloch
Lennoxtown
Bearsden
Clydebank
Glasgow
Airdrie
Coatbridge
Motherwell
Wishaw
Hamilton
East Kilbride
Rutherglen
Larkhall
Stonehouse
Strathaven
Carluke
Lanark
Inveraray
Loch Lomond
Helensburgh
Alexandria
Dumbarton
Kilcreggan
Gourock
Greenock
Port Glasgow
Dunoon
Rothesay
Port Bannatyne
Innellan
Skelmorlie
Largs
Millport
Bute
Renfrew
Paisley
Johnstone
Barrhead
Kilbirnie
Beith
Dalry
Kilwinning
Stewarton
Kilmaurs
Ardrossan
Saltcoats
Irvine
Kilmarnock
Galston
Darvel
Troon
Prestwick
Ayr
Mauchline
Cumnock
Maybole
Patna
Dalmellington
Kirkconnel
Sanquhar
Firth of Clyde
Arran
Brodick
Campbeltown
Kennacraig
Kilchattan
Portavadie
Tighnabruaich
Lochgilphead
Loch Fyne
Garbhallt
Aird
Toberonochy
Carndonagh

Shetland Islands
St. Magnus Bay
Yell Sound
Colgrave Sd.
Yell
Norwick
Unst
Fetlar
Funzie
Isbister
Whalsay
Neap
Dale
Lerwick
Scalloway
West Burra
Foula
Fair Isle
Sumburgh
Aberdeen Kirkwall
96
Orkney Islands
Westray
N. Ronaldsay
The North Sound
Burness
Midbea
Calfsound
Eday
Sanday
Store
Sanday Sound
Rousay
Veness
Odie
Stronsay
Stronsay Firth
Shapinsay
Kirkwall
Stromness
Mainland
Linksness
Scapa Flow
Hoy
Longhope
South Ronaldsay
Aberdeen Lerwick
95
Scrabster
Thurso
Halkirk
Wick
Stromness
Longhope
94
Lybster
Helmsdale
Moray Firth
Lossiemouth
Spey B.
Findochty
Portknockie
Buckie
Portsoy
Banff
Macduff
Fraserburgh
Elgin
Forres
Rothes
Keith
Aberchirder
Turriff
Peterhead
88
89
Charlestown of Aberlour
Marypark
Dufftown
Huntly
Ellon
Oldmeldrum
Inverurie
Kintore
Dyce
Alford
Kirkwall Lerwick
Bridge of Don
Aberdeen
Westhill
Cults
Peterculter
82
83
Braemar
Ballater
Aboyne
Banchory
Stonehaven
Inverbervie
Laurencekirk
Kirkton of Glenisla
Brechin
Montrose
Kirriemuir
Alyth
Rattray
Blairgowrie
Forfar
Lunan B.
Meigle
Coupar Angus
Monikie
Arbroath
Carnoustie
Monifieth
Dundee
76
77
Perth
Scone
Firth of Tay
Tayport
Newport-on-Tay
Newburgh
Cupar
St. Andrews
Auchtermuchty
Ladybank
Falkland
Crail
Kinross
Leslie
Markinch
Anstruther
Glenrothes
Leven
St. Monance
Buckhaven
Elie
Lochgelly
Kirkcaldy
Cowdenbeath
Dunfermline
Burntisland
Inverkeithing
Rosyth
Bo'ness
Queensferry
North Berwick
Gullane
Dunbar
Prestonpans
East Linton
Edinburgh
Haddington
Tranent
Musselburgh
Dalkeith
Livingston
Loanhead
Bonnyrigg
Eyemouth
69
70
71
Penicuik
Gorebridge
Duns
Berwick-upon-Tweed
Lauder
Peebles
Innerleithen
Coldstream
Galashiels
Kelso
Melrose
Selkirk
Bamburgh
Wooler
Jedburgh
North Charlton
Ramseycleuch
Hawick
Alnwick
Alnmouth
Moffat

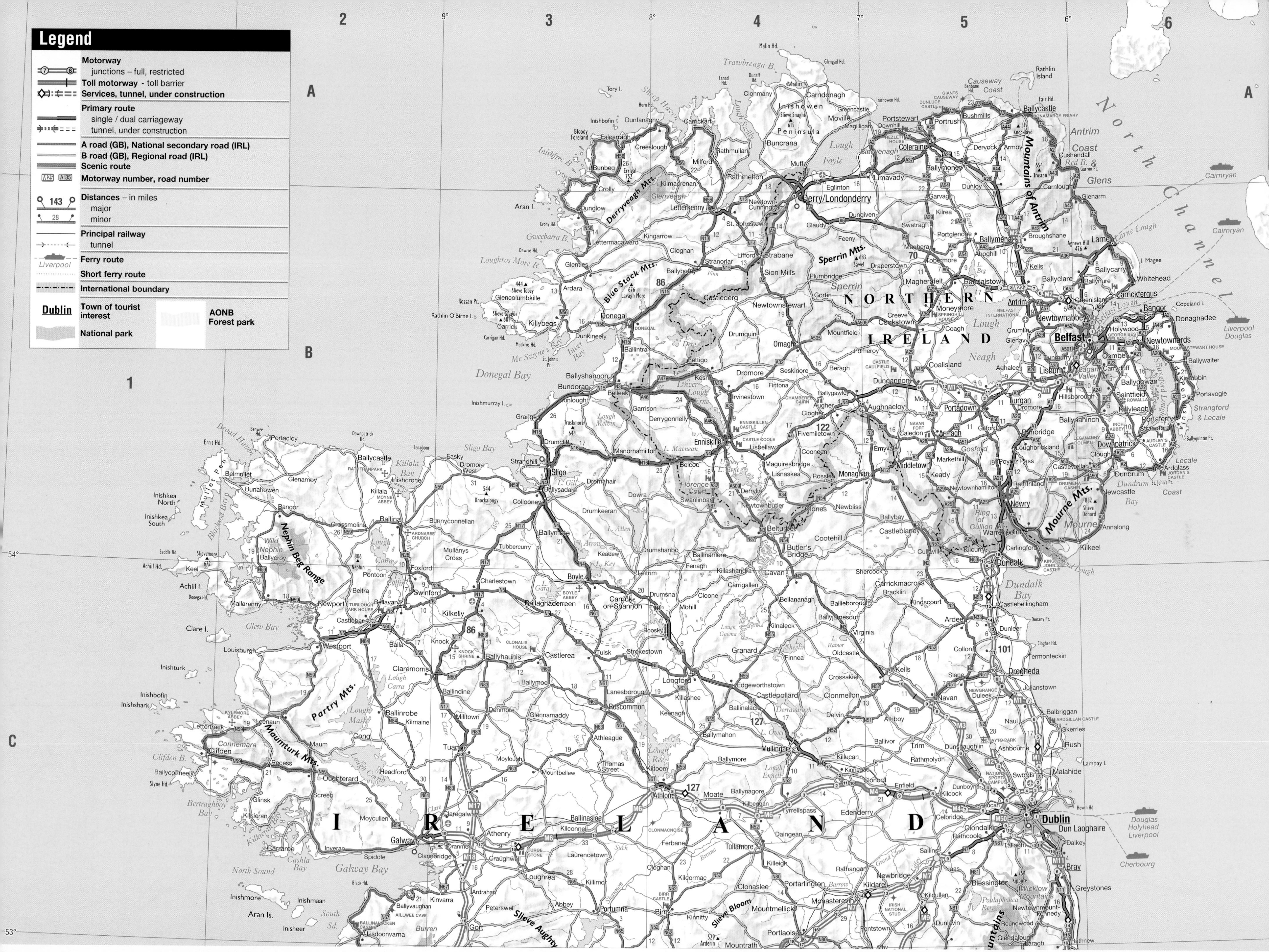
Legend
Motorway
junctions – full, restricted
Toll motorway - toll barrier
Services, tunnel, under construction
Primary route
single / dual carriageway
tunnel, under construction
A road (GB), National secondary road (IRL)
B road (GB), Regional road (IRL)
Scenic route
Motorway number, road number
Distances – in miles
major
minor
Principal railway
tunnel
Ferry route
Short ferry route
International boundary
Dublin
Town of tourist interest
National park
AONB
Forest park
NORTHERN IRELAND
IRELAND
North Channel
Donegal Bay
Galway Bay
Dundalk Bay
Mountains of Antrim
Sperrin Mts.
Mourne Mts.
Blue Stack Mts.
Derryveagh Mts.
Nephin Beg Range
Partry Mts.
Maumturk Mts.
Slieve Bloom
Slieve Aughty
Belfast
Dublin
Derry/Londonderry
Galway
Sligo
Donegal
Letterkenny
Enniskillen
Armagh
Newry
Dundalk
Drogheda
Athlone
Mullingar
Westport
Castlebar
Ballina
Clifden
Aran Is.
Achill I.
Rathlin Island
Liverpool
Douglas
Holyhead
Cherbourg
Cairnryan

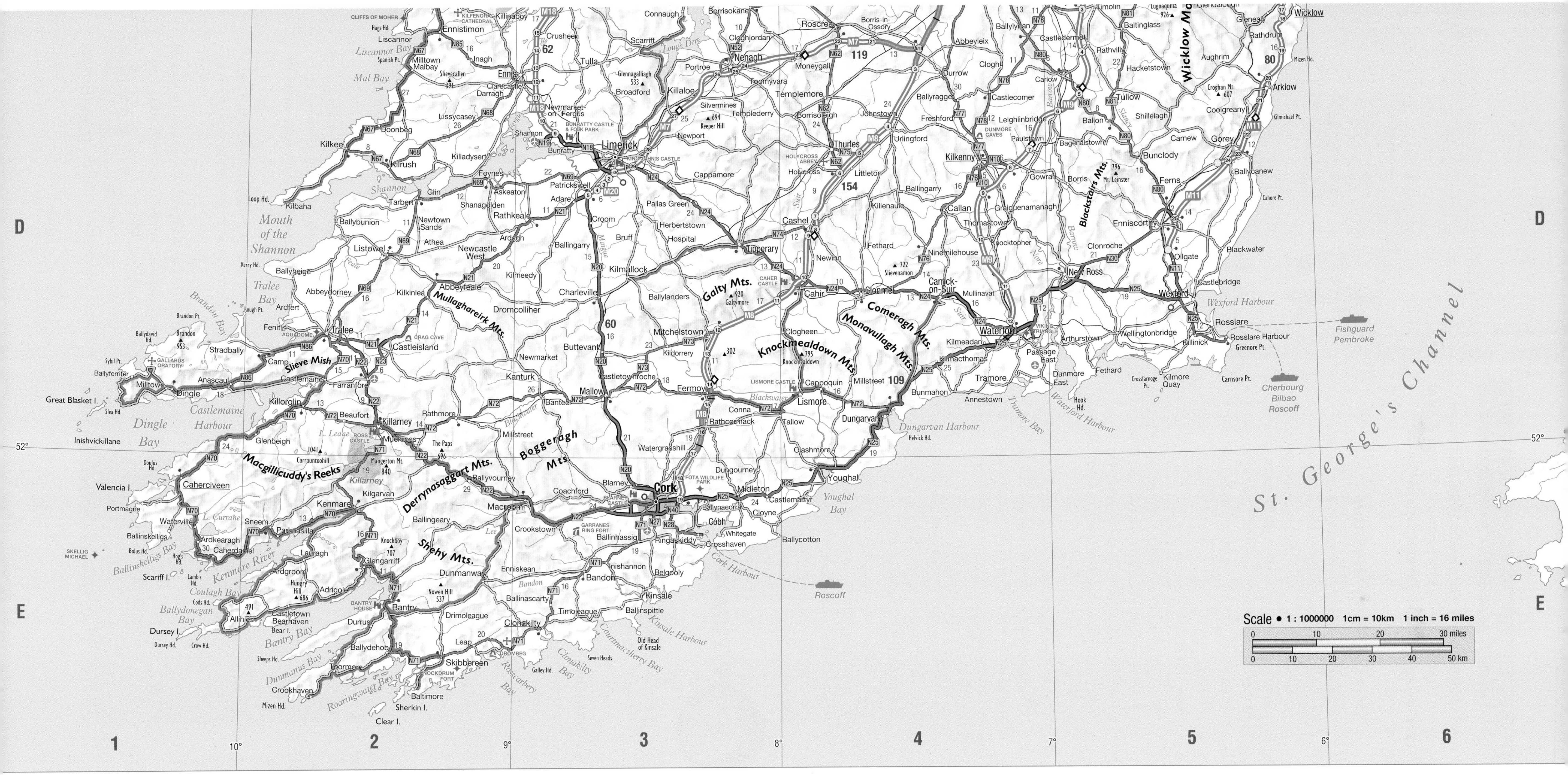

Index to Ireland

Top tips for better driving

iAM RoadSmart is the UK's largest road safety charity. Formed in 1956, they have spent more than 60 years making our roads safer by improving driver and rider skills through coaching and education. They recommend the following tips for better driving. For more details see www.iamroadsmart.com

Check your tyres

Tyres play a huge part in road safety, including steering, braking, and acceleration.

Pressure Make sure your tyres have the correct pressure. You can find this information in the vehicle handbook and on the inside of the fuel filler cap or driver's door sill. Having the correct pressure in your tyres will ensure even wear and will also help with handling and fuel efficiency.

Tread Ensure that your tyres have a tread depth of at least 1.6mm. Remember that this is a legal minimum, but a newer tyre with deeper tread will perform much better in wet conditions. Use the wear indicators on the tyre itself, or a tyre tread depth gauge, to check if your tyres are safe. If you're unsure, take them to a specialist.

Condition Cracks and bulges in a tyre's sidewalls indicate damage and this means that the tyre should be replaced, even if the tread depth is still within the legal limit. A damaged tyre can be a ticking timebomb; it's best to get it replaced as soon as possible.

Overloading your vehicle can cause excessive heat and wear on your tyres. Ensure that your vehicle's overall weight does not exceed its Gross Vehicle Weight (GVW) rating – this can be found on your VIN plate. Heavy loads can also lead to poor braking and stability, so even if the weight is below the GVW rating, it's important to adjust your driving style to match these decreases in vehicle performance.

Driving safely in winter

Driving safely during any season is essential but is especially important when faced with the challenges of winter. During severe winter weather, there may be snow and ice around which makes driving difficult. Consider if your journey is necessary, and only travel when there is no other option.

Have a safe TRIP

Top-up your fuel/electricity charge, oil and screen-wash. Many breakdowns can be avoided simply by doing some easy vehicle checks. They'll help you to have a safer journey and save you time and money.

Rest the day before you're due to make a long journey. Before you set out, plan where you will take a break. It's important to break every two hours. You could stretch your legs at a motorway service area.

Inspect your tyres. It takes around 10 minutes to check tyre pressures and treads – a small amount of time to invest in your big trip.

Prepare for severe weather. If severe weather is expected, consider delaying your journey until it clears. Check your route in advance of setting out to see if there are any incidents or roadworks to be aware of.

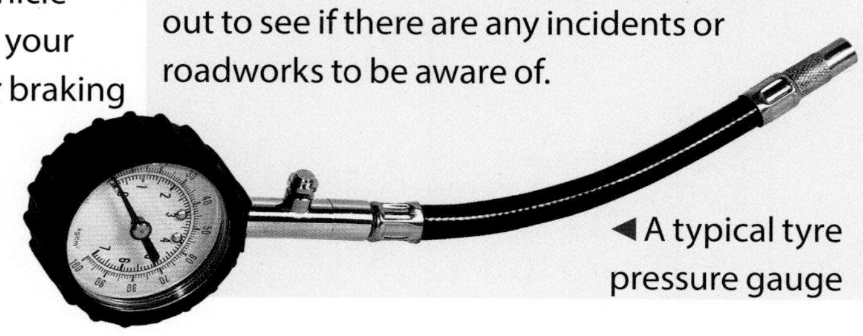

◄ A typical tyre pressure gauge

Pack a winter kit of essentials

Consider carrying a winter kit especially if there's a forecast of severe weather. This should include an ice-scraper, snow shovel, torch, blanket, de-icer and a first aid kit, just in case. Packing water and snacks is also a good idea, should you find yourself waiting for a recovery truck.

When you're on the road

- Follow this advice when travelling in winter weather when icy and snowy conditions can be a challenge:
- Stick to main roads where you can and only travel if necessary.
- Slow down – it can take 10 times longer to stop in icy conditions.
- Use a high gear to avoid spinning your wheels.
- Accelerate gently, using low revs. You may need to start in second gear to avoid skidding.
- You may need up to 10 times the normal gap between your car and the car in front.
- Avoid sudden braking, it may lock up your wheels and you could skid further.
- Be extra cautious at road junctions where road markings may not be visible.

Improve your parking

Being able to park well is an essential part of being a responsible and confident driver.

Can I park here? Before choosing a spot make sure it's safe and legal to park there. You can usually tell by the road markings and road signs. Can you get in and out of the parking space easily and confidently? If you must drive in, take extra care when reversing out. When parallel parking, ensure that you choose a space that is large enough for you to manoeuvre into and out of again. Adjusting your nearside mirror downwards will help you check the kerb – just remember to adjust it back again.

Concentration Firstly, avoid any distractions. Turn the music down, don't get distracted by the tech in your vehicle. Doing these things mean you're more likely to hear other vehicles and pedestrians, including children who could be running around the area where are you trying to park.

Take your time Don't feel pressured, many drivers feel the watchful eye of other drivers and pedestrians when they try to park.

Know your neighbours Choose your parking neighbours and space carefully; a car which is looked after and in good condition is less likely to have a door open into yours. Also, although never on purpose, a car with child seats in it might have children who are not quite as careful when in charge of the door.

Parking manoeuvres For those new to driving, and even the most experienced, parallel parking can be a source of anxiety at the best of times. It involves a lot of hand-eye coordination, judgement, and vehicle control.

How to parallel park There is no one correct way to parallel park, but here are some useful guidelines. Take your time and keep watching and listening throughout all your manoeuvres.

- Select a space that is one and a half times the length of your vehicle or more.
- In your direction of travel, on a two-way street, line up parallel to the kerb, with your near side mirror just past the farthest end of the vehicle you intend parking behind.
- Check, indicate and select reverse gear.
- Reverse until the top of your backseat is in line with the nearest end of the vehicle you intend parking behind before steering towards the kerb.
- Turn the steering wheel one full turn towards the kerb. Keep looking around as the back of your car edges towards the kerb and the front edges out into the road.
- When the line of the kerb appears just under the nearside door handle, as seen in the near side mirror, turn the steering wheel two complete turns away from the kerb.
- As soon as the car is parallel to the kerb, make one final turn towards the kerb to straighten the wheels.
- At the end of the manoeuvre your vehicle should be neatly parked parallel to the kerb and if you are not straight it's OK to shunt back and forwards to straighten the vehicle.

iAM RoadSmart

Robert Stainforth / Alamy Stock Photo

The aim of The Highway Code is to promote safety on the road, whilst also supporting a healthy, sustainable and efficient transport system. The new edition of The Highway Code published in 2022 introduced a new section covering the 'hierarchy of road users'.

Hierarchy of road users

The 'hierarchy of road users' is a concept that places those road users most at risk in the event of a collision at the top of the hierarchy. The hierarchy does not remove the need for everyone to behave responsibly. The road users most likely to be injured in the event of a collision are pedestrians, cyclists, horse riders and motorcyclists, with children, older adults and disabled people being more at risk. The following H rules clarify this concept.

Rule H1

It is important that ALL road users are aware of The Highway Code, are considerate to other road users and understand their responsibility for the safety of others.

Everyone suffers when road collisions occur, whether they are physically injured or not. But those in charge of vehicles that can cause the greatest harm in the event of a collision bear the greatest responsibility to take care and reduce the danger they pose to others. This principle applies most strongly to drivers of large goods and passenger vehicles, vans/minibuses, cars/taxis and motorcycles.

Cyclists, horse riders and drivers of horse-drawn vehicles likewise have a responsibility to reduce danger to pedestrians.

None of this detracts from the responsibility of ALL road users, including pedestrians, cyclists and horse riders, to have regard for their own and other road users' safety.

Always remember that the people you encounter may have impaired sight, hearing or mobility and that this may not be obvious.

Rule H2

Rule for drivers, motorcyclists, horse-drawn vehicles, horse riders and cyclists

At a junction you should give way to pedestrians crossing or waiting to cross a road into which or from which you are turning.

You **MUST** give way to pedestrians on a zebra crossing, and to pedestrians and cyclists on a parallel crossing.

Pedestrians have priority when on a zebra crossing, on a parallel crossing or at light controlled crossings when they have a green signal.

You should give way to pedestrians waiting to cross a zebra crossing, and to pedestrians and cyclists waiting to cross a parallel crossing.

Horse riders should also give way to pedestrians on a zebra crossing, and to pedestrians and cyclists on a parallel crossing.

Cyclists should give way to pedestrians on shared-use cycle tracks and to horse riders on bridleways.

Only pedestrians may use the pavement. Pedestrians include wheelchair and mobility scooter users.

Pedestrians may use any part of the road and use cycle tracks as well as the pavement, unless there are signs prohibiting pedestrians.

Rule H3

Rule for drivers and motorcyclists

You should not cut across cyclists, horse riders or horse-drawn vehicles going ahead when you are turning into or out of a junction or changing direction or lane, just as you would not turn across the path of another motor vehicle. This applies whether they are using a cycle lane, a cycle track, or riding ahead on the road and you should give way to them.

Do not turn at a junction if to do so would cause the cyclist, horse rider or horse-drawn vehicle going straight ahead to stop or swerve.

You should stop and wait for a safe gap in the flow of cyclists if necessary. This includes when cyclists are:

- approaching, passing or moving off from a junction
- moving past or waiting alongside stationary or slow-moving traffic
- travelling around a roundabout

▲ **Rule H2** Wait for the pedestrian to cross the junction before turning. This applies if you are turning right or left into the junction.

▲ **Rule H3** Wait for the cyclist to pass the junction before turning. This also applies if there is a cycle lane or cycle track and if you are turning right or left into the junction.

To access the full Highway Code:

Print The Official Highway Code ISBN 978-0-11-553995-4
Online The Highway Code – Guidance – GOV.UK (www.gov.uk)

Distances and journey times

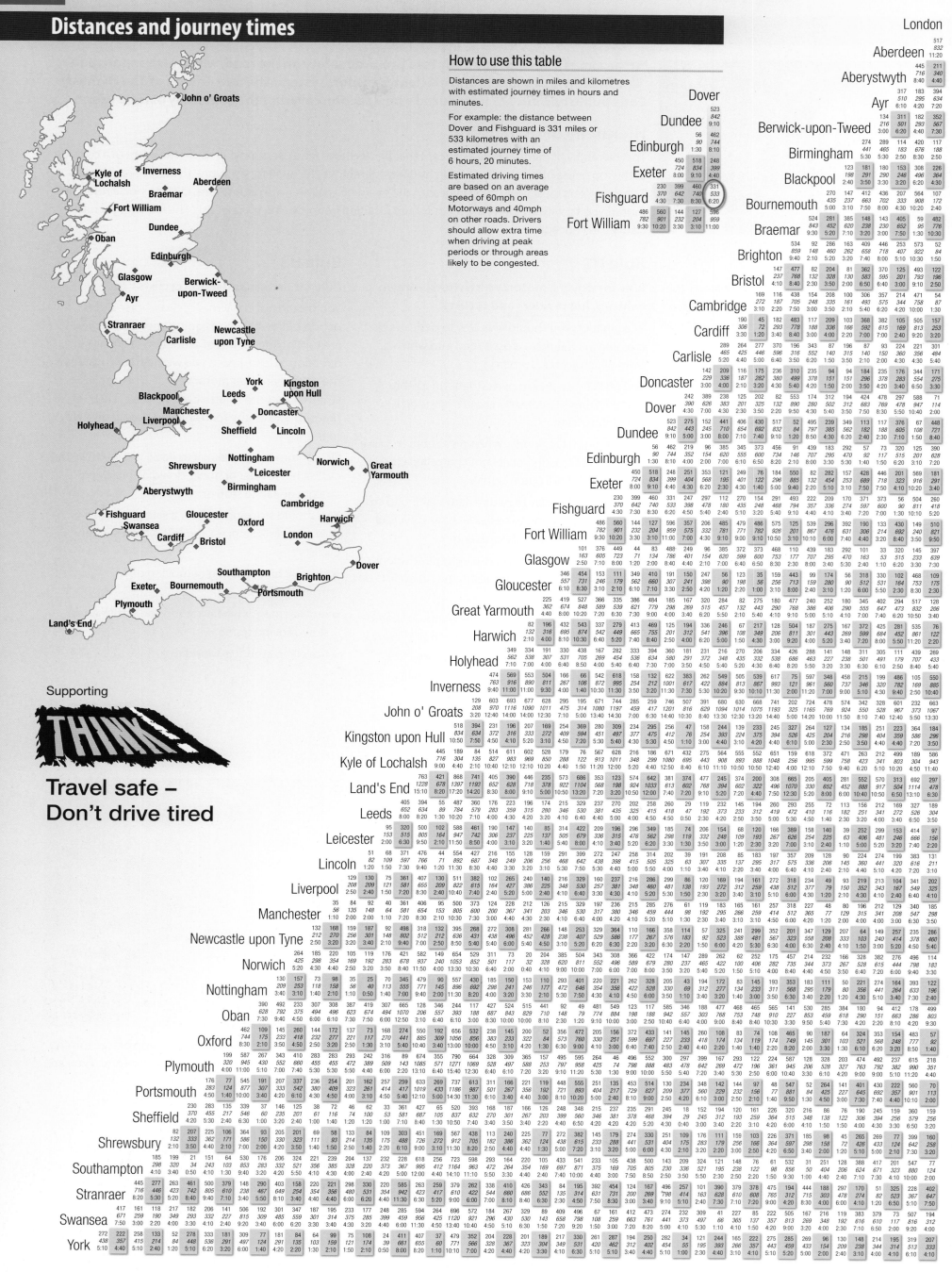

How to use this table

Distances are shown in miles and kilometres with estimated journey times in hours and minutes.

For example: the distance between Dover and Fishguard is 331 miles or 533 kilometres with an estimated journey time of 6 hours, 20 minutes.

Estimated driving times are based on an average speed of 60mph on Motorways and 40mph on other roads. Drivers should allow extra time when driving at peak periods or through areas likely to be congested.

Dover					
Dundee					523 842 9:10
Edinburgh				56 90 1:30	462 744 8:10
Exeter			450 724 8:00	518 834 9:10	248 399 4:40
Fishguard		230 370 4:30	399 642 7:30	460 740 8:30	331 533 6:20
Fort William	486 782 9:30	560 901 10:20	144 232 3:30	127 204 3:10	596 959 11:00

London																																																
Aberdeen																																																517 832 11:20
Aberystwyth																																															445 716 8:40	211 340 4:40
Ayr																																														317 510 6:10	183 295 4:20	394 634 7:20
Berwick-upon-Tweed																																													134 216 3:00	311 501 6:20	182 293 4:40	352 567 7:30
Birmingham																																												274 441 5:30	289 465 5:30	114 183 2:50	420 676 8:30	117 188 2:50
Blackpool																																											123 198 2:40	181 291 3:50	180 290 3:30	153 246 3:20	308 496 6:20	226 364 4:30
Bournemouth																																										270 435 5:00	147 237 3:10	412 663 7:50	436 702 8:00	207 333 4:30	564 908 10:20	107 172 2:40
Braemar																																									524 843 9:30	281 452 5:20	385 620 7:10	148 238 3:20	143 230 3:00	405 652 7:50	59 95 1:30	482 776 10:30
Brighton																																								534 859 9:40	92 148 2:10	286 460 5:20	163 262 3:20	409 658 7:40	446 718 8:00	253 407 5:10	573 922 10:30	52 84 1:50
Bristol																																							147 237 4:10	477 768 8:40	82 132 2:30	204 328 3:50	81 130 2:00	362 583 6:50	370 595 6:40	125 201 3:00	493 793 9:10	122 196 2:50
Cambridge																																						169 272 3:10	116 187 2:20	438 705 7:50	154 248 3:00	208 335 3:50	100 161 2:10	306 493 5:40	357 575 6:20	214 344 4:20	471 758 10:00	54 87 1:30
Cardiff																																					190 306 3:30	45 72 1:20	182 293 3:40	483 778 8:40	117 188 3:00	209 336 4:00	103 166 2:20	368 592 7:00	382 615 7:00	105 169 2:40	505 813 9:20	157 253 3:20
Carlisle																																				289 465 5:20	264 425 4:40	277 446 5:00	370 596 6:40	196 316 3:50	343 552 6:20	87 140 1:50	196 315 3:50	87 140 2:10	93 150 2:00	224 360 4:30	221 356 4:30	301 484 5:40
Doncaster																																			142 229 3:00	209 336 4:00	116 187 2:10	175 282 3:20	236 380 4:30	310 499 5:40	235 378 4:20	94 151 1:50	94 151 2:00	184 296 3:50	235 378 4:20	176 283 3:40	344 554 6:50	171 275 3:30
Dover																																		242 390 4:30	389 626 7:00	238 383 4:30	125 201 2:30	202 325 3:50	82 132 2:20	553 890 9:50	174 280 4:30	312 502 5:40	194 312 3:50	424 683 7:50	478 769 8:30	297 478 5:50	588 947 10:40	71 114 2:00
Dundee																																	523 842 9:10	275 443 5:00	152 245 3:00	441 710 8:00	406 654 7:10	430 692 7:40	517 832 9:10	52 84 1:20	495 797 8:50	239 385 4:30	349 562 6:20	113 182 2:40	117 188 2:30	376 605 7:10	67 108 1:50	448 721 8:40
Edinburgh																																56 90 1:30	462 744 8:10	219 352 4:00	96 154 2:00	385 620 7:00	345 555 6:10	373 600 6:50	456 734 8:20	91 146 2:10	439 707 8:00	183 295 3:30	292 470 5:30	57 92 1:40	73 117 1:50	320 515 6:20	125 201 3:10	390 628 7:20
Exeter																															450 724 8:00	518 834 9:10	248 399 4:40	251 404 4:30	353 568 6:20	121 195 2:30	249 401 4:30	76 122 1:40	184 296 5:00	550 885 9:40	82 132 2:20	282 454 5:10	157 253 3:10	428 689 7:50	446 718 7:50	201 323 4:10	569 916 10:20	181 291 3:40
Fishguard																														230 370 4:30	399 642 7:30	460 740 8:30	331 533 6:20	247 398 4:50	297 478 5:40	112 180 2:40	270 435 5:10	154 248 3:20	291 468 5:40	493 794 9:10	222 357 4:40	209 336 4:10	170 274 3:40	371 597 7:20	373 600 7:00	56 90 1:30	504 811 10:10	260 418 5:20
Fort William																													486 782 9:30	560 901 10:20	144 232 3:30	127 204 3:10	596 959 11:00	357 575 7:00	206 332 4:30	485 781 9:10	479 771 9:00	486 782 9:10	575 926 10:50	125 201 3:10	539 867 10:10	296 476 6:00	392 631 7:40	190 306 4:40	133 214 3:20	430 692 8:40	149 240 3:50	510 821 9:50
Glasgow																												101 163 2:50	376 605 7:10	449 723 8:00	44 71 1:20	83 134 2:00	488 786 8:40	249 401 4:40	96 154 2:10	385 620 7:00	372 599 6:40	373 600 6:50	468 753 8:30	110 177 2:30	439 707 8:00	183 295 3:40	292 470 5:30	101 163 2:40	33 53 1:10	320 515 6:20	145 233 3:30	397 639 7:30
Gloucester																											346 557 6:10	454 731 8:30	153 246 3:10	111 179 2:10	349 562 6:10	410 660 7:10	191 307 3:30	150 241 2:50	247 398 4:20	56 90 1:20	123 198 2:20	35 56 1:00	159 256 3:10	443 713 8:00	99 159 2:40	174 280 3:10	56 90 1:20	318 512 6:00	330 531 5:50	102 164 2:30	468 753 8:30	109 175 2:30
Great Yarmouth																										225 362 4:40	419 674 8:00	527 848 10:20	366 589 7:20	335 539 6:30	386 621 7:30	484 779 9:00	185 298 4:00	167 269 3:40	320 515 6:20	284 457 5:50	82 132 2:10	275 443 5:40	180 290 4:10	477 768 9:10	240 386 5:00	252 406 5:10	180 290 4:10	345 555 7:00	402 647 7:40	294 473 6:20	517 832 10:50	128 206 3:40
Harwich																									82 132 2:10	196 316 4:00	432 695 8:10	543 874 10:30	337 542 6:40	279 449 5:20	413 665 7:40	469 755 8:40	125 201 2:50	194 312 4:00	336 541 6:20	246 396 5:00	67 108 1:50	217 349 4:30	128 206 3:00	504 811 9:20	187 301 4:00	275 443 5:20	167 269 3:40	372 599 7:20	425 684 8:00	281 452 5:50	535 861 11:20	76 122 2:20
Holyhead																								349 562 7:10	334 538 7:00	191 307 4:00	330 531 6:40	438 705 8:50	167 269 4:00	282 454 5:40	333 536 6:40	394 634 7:30	360 580 7:00	181 291 3:50	231 372 4:50	216 348 5:40	270 435 5:20	206 332 4:30	334 538 6:40	426 686 8:20	288 463 5:50	141 227 3:20	148 238 3:30	311 501 6:30	305 491 6:10	111 179 2:50	439 707 8:40	269 433 5:40
Inverness																							474 763 9:40	569 916 11:00	553 890 11:00	504 811 9:30	166 267 4:00	66 106 1:40	542 872 10:30	618 995 11:30	158 254 3:50	132 212 3:20	622 1001 11:30	383 617 7:30	262 422 5:30	549 884 10:20	505 813 9:30	539 867 10:10	617 993 11:30	75 121 2:00	597 961 11:20	348 560 7:00	458 737 9:00	215 346 5:10	199 320 4:30	486 782 9:40	105 169 2:50	550 885 10:40
John o' Groats																						129 208 3:20	603 970 12:40	693 1116 14:00	677 1090 14:00	628 1011 12:30	295 475 7:10	195 314 5:00	671 1080 13:40	744 1197 14:30	285 459 7:00	259 417 6:30	746 1201 14:40	507 816 10:30	391 629 8:40	680 1094 13:30	630 1014 12:30	668 1075 13:20	741 1193 14:40	202 325 5:00	724 1165 14:20	478 769 10:00	574 924 11:50	342 550 8:10	328 528 7:40	601 967 12:40	232 373 5:50	663 1067 13:30
Kingston upon Hull																					518 834 10:50	394 634 7:50	231 372 4:50	196 316 4:10	207 333 5:20	169 272 3:10	254 409 4:50	369 594 7:20	280 451 5:30	309 497 5:40	234 377 4:30	295 475 5:30	256 412 4:50	47 76 1:10	158 254 3:00	244 393 4:40	139 224 3:10	233 375 4:20	245 394 4:40	327 526 6:10	264 425 5:00	127 204 2:30	134 216 2:50	185 298 3:50	251 404 4:40	223 359 4:40	364 586 7:20	184 296 3:50
Kyle of Lochalsh																				445 716 9:00	189 304 4:40	84 135 2:10	514 827 10:40	611 983 12:10	602 969 12:10	528 850 10:20	179 288 4:40	76 122 1:50	567 913 11:20	628 1011 12:00	216 348 5:20	186 299 4:40	671 1080 12:50	432 695 8:40	275 443 6:10	564 908 11:10	555 893 10:50	552 888 10:50	651 1048 12:40	159 256 4:00	618 995 12:10	372 599 7:50	471 758 9:40	263 423 6:20	212 341 5:10	499 803 10:20	189 304 4:50	586 943 11:40
Land's End																			763 1228 15:10	421 678 8:20	868 1397 17:20	741 1193 14:20	405 652 8:30	390 628 8:00	446 718 9:10	235 378 5:00	573 922 10:50	686 1104 13:20	353 568 7:20	123 198 3:20	574 924 10:50	642 1033 12:00	381 613 7:40	374 602 7:20	477 768 9:10	245 394 5:20	374 602 7:20	200 322 4:40	308 496 7:50	665 1070 12:30	205 330 5:20	405 652 8:00	281 452 6:00	552 888 10:40	570 917 10:50	313 504 6:50	692 1114 13:10	297 478 6:30
Leeds																		405 652 8:00	394 634 8:20	55 89 1:30	487 784 10:20	360 579 7:10	176 283 4:00	223 359 4:30	196 315 4:20	174 280 3:20	215 346 4:10	329 530 6:40	237 381 4:40	270 435 5:00	202 325 4:00	258 415 4:50	260 418 4:50	29 47 0:50	119 192 2:30	232 373 4:20	145 233 2:50	194 312 3:50	260 419 5:00	293 472 5:30	255 410 4:50	72 116 1:40	113 182 2:30	156 251 3:20	212 341 4:00	169 272 3:40	327 526 6:50	189 304 3:50
Leicester																	95 153 2:00	320 515 6:30	500 805 9:50	102 164 2:10	588 947 11:50	461 742 8:50	190 306 4:00	147 237 3:10	140 225 3:20	85 137 1:40	314 505 5:40	422 679 8:00	209 336 4:10	196 315 3:40	296 476 5:20	349 562 6:20	185 298 3:30	74 119 1:30	206 332 3:50	154 248 3:00	68 109 1:20	120 193 2:30	166 267 3:20	389 626 7:00	158 254 3:10	140 225 2:40	39 63 1:10	252 406 5:00	299 481 5:20	153 246 3:20	414 666 7:40	97 156 2:20
Lincoln																51 82 1:20	68 109 1:50	371 597 7:30	476 766 9:40	44 71 1:20	554 892 11:30	427 687 8:30	216 348 4:40	155 249 3:30	128 206 3:20	159 256 3:10	291 468 5:30	399 642 7:50	272 438 5:30	247 398 4:40	258 415 5:00	314 505 5:50	202 325 4:00	39 63 1:10	191 307 3:40	208 335 4:10	85 137 2:20	183 295 3:40	197 317 4:00	357 575 6:40	209 336 4:10	128 206 2:40	90 145 2:10	224 360 4:40	274 441 5:10	199 320 4:20	383 616 7:20	131 211 3:10
Liverpool															129 208 2:50	130 209 2:40	75 121 1:50	361 581 7:20	407 655 8:30	130 209 2:40	511 822 10:40	382 615 7:40	102 164 2:40	265 427 5:20	240 386 5:00	140 225 2:40	216 348 4:10	329 530 6:40	160 257 3:30	237 381 4:30	216 348 4:10	286 460 5:20	299 481 5:30	86 138 1:50	120 193 2:30	169 272 3:20	194 312 3:40	161 259 3:10	272 438 5:10	318 512 6:00	234 377 4:30	49 79 1:20	93 150 2:10	219 352 4:30	213 343 4:10	104 167 2:40	341 549 6:40	202 325 4:10
Manchester														35 56 1:10	84 135 2:00	92 148 2:00	40 64 1:10	361 581 7:20	406 654 8:30	95 153 2:10	500 805 10:30	373 600 7:30	124 200 3:00	228 367 4:40	212 341 4:30	126 203 2:30	215 346 4:10	329 530 6:40	197 317 4:00	236 380 4:20	215 346 4:10	285 459 5:20	276 444 5:10	61 98 1:30	119 192 2:30	183 295 3:40	165 266 3:10	161 259 3:10	257 414 4:50	318 512 6:00	227 365 4:20	48 77 1:20	80 129 2:00	196 315 4:00	212 341 4:00	129 208 3:00	340 547 6:30	185 298 3:50
Newcastle upon Tyne													132 212 2:50	168 270 3:20	159 256 3:20	187 301 3:40	92 148 2:10	498 802 9:40	318 512 7:00	132 212 2:50	395 636 8:50	268 431 5:40	272 438 5:40	308 496 6:00	281 452 5:40	266 428 4:50	148 238 3:10	253 407 5:20	329 529 6:20	364 586 6:30	110 177 2:20	166 267 3:20	358 576 6:30	114 183 2:20	57 92 1:50	325 523 6:00	241 388 4:20	299 481 5:30	352 567 6:30	201 323 4:00	347 558 6:30	129 208 2:40	207 333 4:10	64 103 1:50	149 240 3:00	257 414 5:20	235 378 4:50	286 460 5:40
Norwich												264 425 5:20	185 298 4:30	220 354 4:40	105 169 2:50	119 192 3:20	176 283 3:50	421 678 8:40	582 937 11:50	149 240 4:00	654 1053 13:30	529 852 10:30	311 501 6:40	73 117 2:00	20 32 0:40	204 328 4:10	385 620 9:00	504 811 10:00	343 552 7:00	308 496 6:00	366 589 7:00	422 679 8:00	174 280 3:50	147 237 3:20	289 465 5:40	262 422 5:20	62 100 1:50	252 406 5:10	175 282 4:00	457 735 8:40	214 344 4:40	232 373 4:50	166 267 3:50	328 528 6:40	382 615 7:20	276 444 6:00	496 798 9:40	114 183 3:30
Nottingham											130 209 3:40	157 253 3:10	73 118 1:40	98 158 2:10	35 56 1:10	25 40 0:50	70 113 1:40	345 555 7:00	479 771 9:40	90 145 2:00	557 896 11:30	430 692 8:20	185 298 4:00	150 241 3:20	153 246 3:30	110 177 2:10	293 472 5:30	401 646 7:50	220 354 4:30	221 356 4:10	262 422 4:50	328 528 6:00	205 330 3:50	43 69 1:10	194 312 3:40	172 277 3:20	83 134 1:40	145 233 3:00	193 311 3:50	353 568 6:30	183 295 3:40	111 179 2:20	50 80 1:20	221 356 4:30	274 441 5:10	164 264 3:40	393 633 7:30	122 196 2:40
Oban										390 628 7:30	492 792 9:40	233 375 4:50	307 494 6:00	308 496 6:10	387 623 7:30	419 674 7:50	307 494 6:00	665 1070 12:50	128 206 3:10	346 557 6:40	244 393 6:10	117 188 3:00	427 687 8:30	524 843 10:00	515 829 10:00	441 710 8:10	92 148 2:30	49 79 1:20	481 774 9:10	549 884 10:00	123 198 3:00	117 188 2:50	585 942 10:40	346 557 6:40	188 303 4:00	477 768 9:00	468 753 8:40	465 748 8:40	565 910 10:30	141 227 3:30	530 853 9:50	285 459 5:40	384 618 7:30	180 290 4:20	94 151 2:20	412 663 8:10	178 286 4:20	499 803 9:30
Oxford									462 744 8:30	109 175 2:10	145 233 3:50	260 418 4:50	144 232 2:50	172 277 3:20	137 221 2:50	73 117 1:30	168 270 3:10	274 441 5:40	550 885 10:40	192 309 3:40	656 1056 13:00	532 856 10:00	238 383 4:50	145 233 3:10	200 322 4:20	52 84 1:30	356 573 6:30	472 760 9:00	205 330 4:10	156 251 3:00	372 599 6:40	433 697 7:40	141 227 2:50	145 233 2:40	260 418 4:40	108 174 2:20	83 134 1:40	74 119 1:40	108 174 2:20	465 749 8:20	90 145 2:00	187 301 3:30	64 103 1:30	324 521 6:10	353 568 6:20	154 248 3:20	483 777 8:50	57 92 1:40
Plymouth								199 320 4:00	587 945 11:00	267 430 5:10	343 552 7:00	410 660 7:40	283 455 5:30	283 455 5:30	293 472 5:50	242 389 4:40	316 509 6:00	89 143 2:20	674 1085 13:10	355 571 6:40	790 1271 15:40	664 1069 12:30	328 528 6:40	309 497 6:10	365 588 7:20	157 253 3:20	495 797 9:10	595 958 11:20	264 425 5:30	46 74 1:30	496 798 9:00	552 888 10:00	300 483 5:50	297 478 5:40	399 642 7:20	167 269 3:40	293 472 5:30	122 196 2:50	224 361 6:00	587 945 10:40	128 206 3:30	328 528 6:10	203 327 4:20	474 763 9:00	492 792 9:00	237 382 5:10	615 990 11:20	218 351 4:40
Portsmouth							176 283 4:50	77 124 1:40	545 877 10:00	191 307 3:40	207 333 4:20	337 542 6:10	236 380 4:30	254 409 4:50	201 323 4:00	162 261 3:10	257 414 4:50	259 417 5:40	633 1019 12:10	269 433 5:00	737 1186 14:30	613 987 11:30	311 501 6:10	166 267 3:40	221 356 4:40	119 192 3:00	448 721 8:10	555 893 10:20	251 404 5:00	135 217 2:40	453 729 8:10	514 827 9:00	130 209 2:50	234 377 4:20	348 560 6:10	142 229 3:00	144 232 2:50	97 156 2:10	48 77 1:40	547 881 9:50	52 84 1:30	264 425 4:50	141 227 3:00	401 645 7:30	430 692 7:40	222 357 4:40	560 901 10:10	70 113 2:00
Sheffield						230 370 4:20	283 455 5:30	135 217 2:40	339 546 6:30	37 60 1:00	146 235 3:20	125 201 2:40	38 61 1:00	72 116 1:40	46 74 1:20	62 100 1:20	33 53 1:00	361 581 7:10	427 687 8:40	65 105 1:30	520 837 10:50	393 632 7:40	168 270 3:40	187 301 3:50	166 267 3:40	126 203 2:20	248 399 4:40	348 560 6:50	215 346 4:20	237 381 4:20	235 378 4:20	291 468 5:20	245 394 4:30	18 29 0:40	152 245 3:00	194 312 3:40	120 193 2:20	161 259 3:10	226 364 4:20	320 515 6:00	216 348 4:10	86 138 1:50	76 122 1:50	190 306 4:00	245 394 4:30	159 256 3:30	360 579 6:50	159 256 3:20
Shrewsbury					82 132 2:10	207 333 3:50	225 362 4:40	106 171 2:10	364 586 7:00	93 150 2:00	205 330 4:20	201 323 3:50	69 111 1:40	58 93 1:50	133 214 2:50	84 135 1:40	109 175 2:20	303 488 6:10	451 726 9:00	169 272 3:10	567 912 11:30	438 705 8:20	113 182 2:50	240 386 4:40	225 362 4:40	77 124 1:30	272 438 5:00	382 615 7:20	145 233 3:10	179 288 3:20	274 441 5:00	330 531 6:00	251 404 4:30	109 175 2:10	176 283 3:20	111 179 2:20	159 256 3:00	103 166 2:50	226 364 4:20	371 597 6:50	185 298 3:40	98 158 2:00	45 72 1:20	265 426 5:10	269 433 5:00	77 124 2:10	399 642 7:30	160 258 3:20
Southampton				185 298 4:10	199 320 3:40	21 34 0:50	151 243 4:10	64 103 1:30	530 853 9:40	176 283 3:20	206 332 4:20	324 521 5:50	221 356 4:10	239 385 4:30	204 328 4:00	137 220 2:40	232 373 4:20	228 367 5:00	618 995 12:00	256 412 4:40	723 1164 14:10	598 963 11:10	293 472 5:50	164 264 3:30	220 354 4:40	105 169 2:40	433 697 7:40	541 871 10:00	233 375 4:40	105 169 3:00	438 705 7:50	500 805 8:50	143 230 2:50	209 336 3:50	324 521 5:50	121 195 2:30	148 238 2:50	76 122 2:20	61 98 1:50	532 856 9:30	31 50 1:00	251 404 4:40	128 206 2:40	388 624 7:10	417 671 7:30	201 323 4:10	547 880 10:00	77 124 2:00
Stranraer			445 716 8:20	277 446 5:30	263 423 5:20	461 742 8:40	500 805 9:40	379 610 7:10	148 238 3:40	290 467 5:50	403 649 8:10	158 254 3:40	220 354 4:40	221 356 4:40	298 480 6:00	330 531 6:20	220 354 4:40	585 942 11:30	263 423 6:30	259 417 5:20	379 610 9:00	262 422 6:00	338 544 7:00	410 660 8:10	426 686 8:40	343 552 6:30	84 135 2:30	195 314 4:50	392 631 7:50	454 731 8:30	124 200 3:00	167 269 3:40	496 798 9:10	257 414 5:10	101 163 2:40	390 628 7:30	379 610 7:10	378 608 7:20	475 765 9:00	194 312 4:20	444 715 8:30	188 303 4:00	297 478 6:00	170 274 4:10	51 82 1:20	325 523 6:50	228 367 5:10	402 647 7:50
Swansea		417 671 7:50	161 259 3:00	118 190 2:20	217 349 4:00	182 293 3:30	206 332 4:10	141 227 2:40	506 815 9:20	192 309 3:40	301 485 6:00	347 559 6:20	187 301 3:30	195 314 3:40	233 375 4:30	177 285 3:20	248 399 4:40	285 459 6:00	594 956 11:30	264 425 4:50	696 1120 13:40	572 921 10:40	184 296 4:50	267 430 5:10	329 530 6:30	89 143 1:50	409 658 7:20	496 798 9:20	67 108 1:50	161 259 3:00	412 663 7:20	473 761 8:20	274 441 5:00	232 373 4:10	309 497 5:30	41 66 1:10	227 365 4:10	85 137 1:50	222 357 4:20	505 813 9:00	167 269 3:20	216 348 4:00	119 192 2:30	383 616 7:10	379 610 6:50	73 117 2:00	507 816 9:20	194 312 4:00
York	272 438 5:10	222 357 4:40	258 415 5:10	133 214 2:40	52 84 1:20	278 448 5:10	333 536 6:20	181 291 3:20	309 497 6:00	77 124 1:40	181 291 4:20	84 135 2:20	64 103 1:30	99 159 2:10	75 121 1:50	108 174 2:10	24 39 0:50	411 661 8:00	407 655 8:20	37 60 1:10	479 771 10:10	352 566 7:00	204 328 4:20	228 367 4:40	201 323 4:20	189 304 3:30	217 349 4:10	330 531 6:30	261 420 5:10	287 462 5:10	194 312 3:40	250 402 4:40	282 454 5:10	34 55 1:00	121 195 2:30	244 393 4:40	165 266 3:10	222 357 4:10	275 443 5:10	285 459 5:20	269 433 5:00	96 154 2:00	130 209 2:40	148 238 3:10	214 344 4:00	195 314 4:10	319 513 6:10	207 333 4:10

Supporting

THINK!

Travel safe – Don't drive tired

Key to road map pages

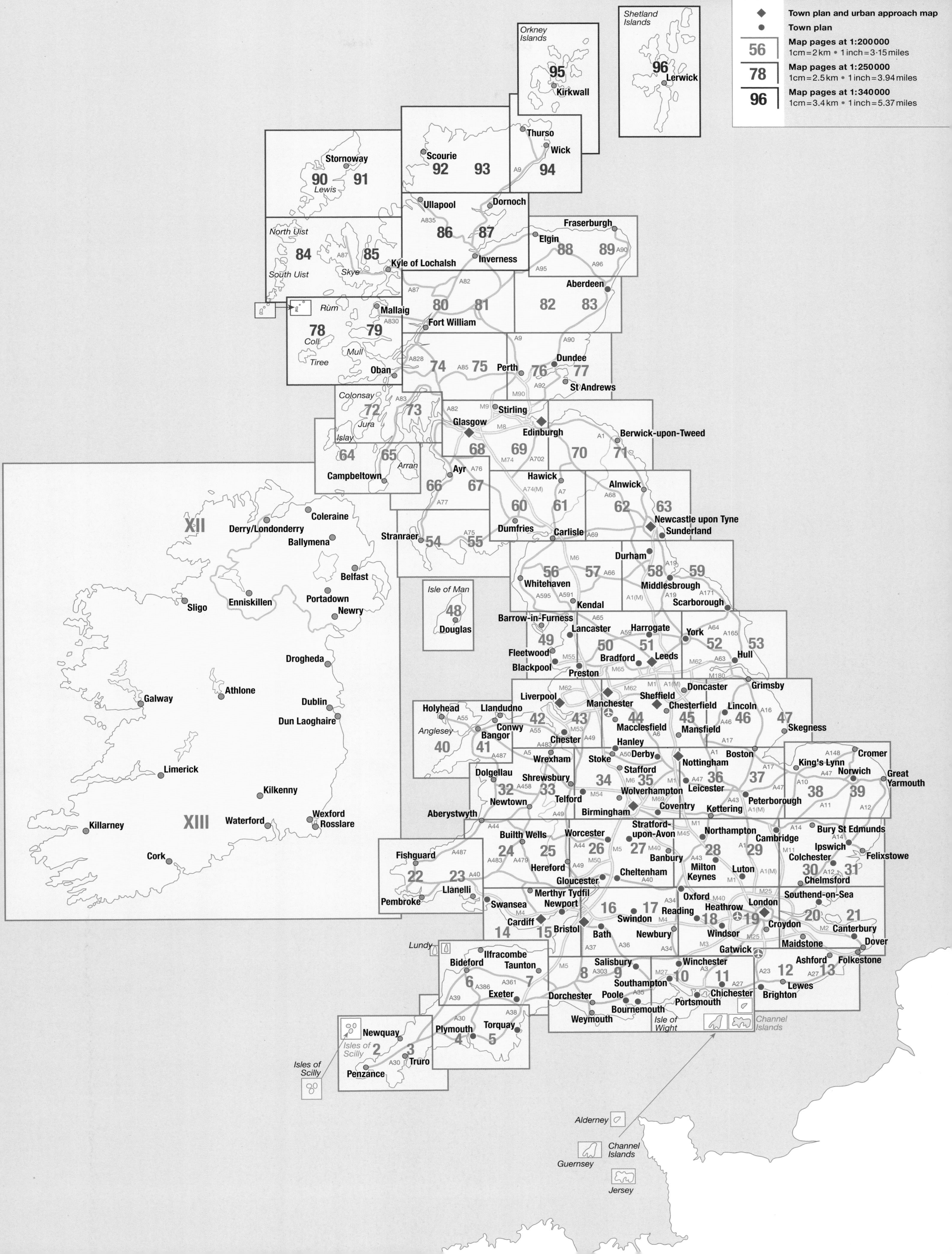
Town plan and urban approach map
Town plan
56 Map pages at 1:200000
1cm=2km • 1inch=3·15miles
78 Map pages at 1:250000
1cm=2.5km • 1inch=3.94miles
96 Map pages at 1:340000
1cm=3.4km • 1inch=5.37miles
Shetland Islands
96
Lerwick
Orkney Islands
95
Kirkwall
Thurso
Wick
94
Scourie
92
93
Stornoway
90
91
Lewis
Ullapool
Dornoch
86
87
Inverness
Fraserburgh
Elgin
88
89
North Uist
84
85
Skye
South Uist
Kyle of Lochalsh
Aberdeen
80
81
82
83
Rùm
Mallaig
78
79
Coll
Tiree
Mull
Fort William
Oban
74
75
Perth
76
Dundee
77
St Andrews
Colonsay
72
73
Jura
Islay
Stirling
Glasgow
Edinburgh
68
69
70
71
Berwick-upon-Tweed
64
65
Arran
Campbeltown
Ayr
66
67
Hawick
Alnwick
60
61
62
63
Newcastle upon Tyne
Sunderland
Dumfries
Carlisle
Stranraer
54
55
Durham
56
57
58
59
Whitehaven
Middlesbrough
Kendal
Scarborough
Isle of Man
48
Douglas
Barrow-in-Furness
Lancaster
Harrogate
York
49
50
51
52
53
Fleetwood
Blackpool
Bradford
Leeds
Hull
Preston
Grimsby
Doncaster
Liverpool
Manchester
Sheffield
Chesterfield
Lincoln
Holyhead
Llandudno
Anglesey
Conwy
Bangor
40
41
42
43
44
45
46
47
Skegness
Macclesfield
Mansfield
Chester
Hanley
Boston
Cromer
Wrexham
Stoke
Derby
Nottingham
King's Lynn
Norwich
Great Yarmouth
Dolgellau
Shrewsbury
Stafford
32
33
34
35
36
37
38
39
Newtown
Telford
Wolverhampton
Leicester
Peterborough
Aberystwyth
Birmingham
Coventry
Kettering
Builth Wells
Worcester
Stratford-upon-Avon
Northampton
Cambridge
Bury St Edmunds
Ipswich
Felixstowe
Fishguard
24
25
26
27
28
29
Colchester
22
23
Hereford
Banbury
Milton Keynes
Luton
30
31
Chelmsford
Gloucester
Cheltenham
Pembroke
Llanelli
Merthyr Tydfil
Oxford
Southend-on-Sea
Swansea
Newport
Heathrow
London
Cardiff
16
17
Reading
18
19
20
21
14
15
Bristol
Swindon
Croydon
Canterbury
Bath
Newbury
Windsor
Maidstone
Dover
Lundy
Ilfracombe
Gatwick
Bideford
Taunton
Salisbury
Winchester
Ashford
Folkestone
6
7
8
9
10
11
12
13
Exeter
Southampton
Lewes
Dorchester
Poole
Chichester
Brighton
Bournemouth
Portsmouth
Weymouth
Isle of Wight
Channel Islands
Newquay
Plymouth
Torquay
Isles of Scilly
2
3
4
5
Truro
Penzance
Isles of Scilly
XII
Coleraine
Derry/Londonderry
Ballymena
Belfast
Sligo
Enniskillen
Portadown
Newry
Drogheda
Galway
Athlone
Dublin
Dun Laoghaire
Limerick
Kilkenny
XIII
Killarney
Waterford
Wexford
Rosslare
Cork
Alderney
Channel Islands
Guernsey
Jersey

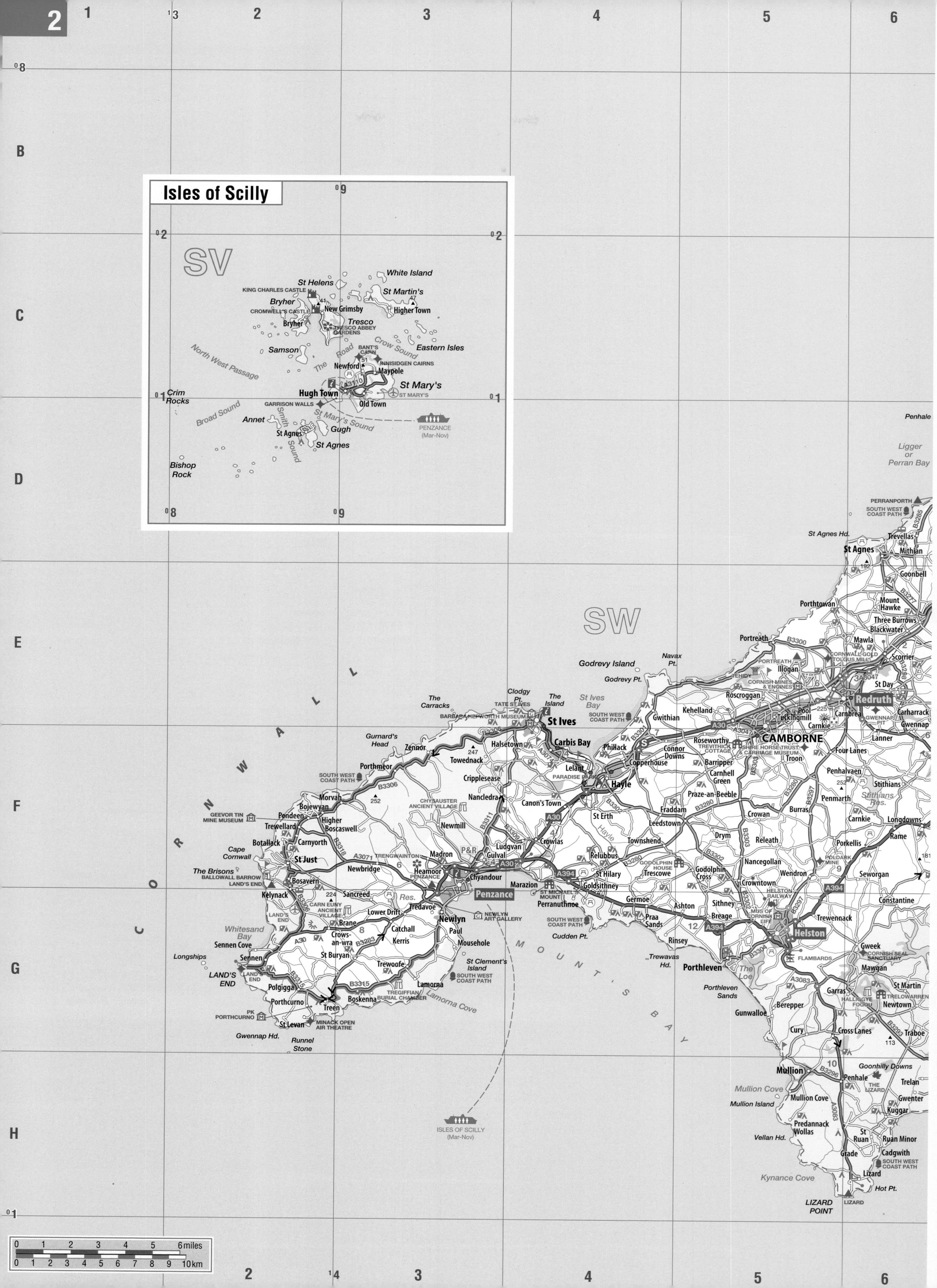
Isles of Scilly
SV
White Island
St Helens
St Martin's
KING CHARLES CASTLE
Bryher
Higher Town
CROMWELL'S CASTLE
New Grimsby
Tresco
TRESCO ABBEY GARDENS
Eastern Isles
Samson
North West Passage
Crow Sound
BANT'S CARN
INNISIDGEN CAIRNS
Newford
Maypole
St Mary's
Crim Rocks
Hugh Town
ST MARY'S
GARRISON WALLS
Old Town
Broad Sound
Smith Sound
St Mary's Sound
Annet
St Agnes
Gugh
PENZANCE (Mar-Nov)
Bishop Rock
SW
CORNWALL
Penhale
Ligger or Perran Bay
PERRANPORTH
SOUTH WEST COAST PATH
St Agnes Hd.
St Agnes
Trevellas
Mithian
Goonbell
Porthtowan
Mount Hawke
Three Burrows
Blackwater
Portreath
Mawla
Scorrier
Illogan
St Day
Godrevy Island
Godrevy Pt.
Navax Pt.
Redruth
Carnbrea
Carharrack
Gwennap
Lanner
CAMBORNE
Pool
Tuckingmill
Roscroggan
Kehelland
Gwithian
St Ives Bay
St Ives
Carbis Bay
Clodgy Pt.
TATE ST IVES
BARBARA HEPWORTH MUSEUM
The Island
The Carracks
Gurnard's Head
Zennor
Towednack
Halsetown
Lelant
Phillack
Hayle
Copperhouse
Connor Downs
Roseworthy
Barripper
Carnhell Green
Troon
Four Lanes
Penhalvaen
Stithians
Porthmeor
Cripplesease
Nancledra
Canon's Town
Praze-an-Beeble
Penmarth
Morvah
Bojewyan
Pendeen
GEEVOR TIN MINE MUSEUM
Trewellard
Higher Boscaswell
CHYSAUSTER ANCIENT VILLAGE
Newmill
St Erth
Fraddam
Leedstown
Crowan
Burras
Carnkie
Longdowns
Rame
Botallack
Carnyorth
Cape Cornwall
St Just
The Brisons
BALLOWALL BARROW
Bosavern
Kelynack
Newbridge
Madron
Heamoor
Ludgvan
Gulval
Chyandour
Crowlas
Townshend
Relubbus
St Hilary
Drym
Releath
Nancegollan
Porkellis
Penzance
Marazion
Goldsithney
ST MICHAEL'S MOUNT
Perranuthnoe
Trescowe
Godolphin Cross
Crowntown
Wendron
Seworgan
Sancreed
Tredavoe
Newlyn
NEWLYN ART GALLERY
Lower Drift
Brane
Catchall
Kerris
Paul
Mousehole
Germoe
Praa Sands
Ashton
Sithney
Breage
Helston
Trewennack
Constantine
Whitesand Bay
Sennen Cove
Sennen
LAND'S END
St Buryan
Crows-an-wra
Trewoofe
St Clement's Island
Cudden Pt.
Rinsey
Trewavas Hd.
Porthleven
FLAMBARDS
Gweek
Mawgan
Longships
Polgigga
Porthcurno
PK PORTHCURNO
Treen
Boskenna
Lamorna
Lamorna Cove
TREGIFFIAN BURIAL CHAMBER
MINACK OPEN AIR THEATRE
St Levan
Gwennap Hd.
Runnel Stone
MOUNT'S BAY
The Loe
Porthleven Sands
Gunwalloe
Berepper
Garras
St Martin
Newtown
Cury
Cross Lanes
Traboe
Goonhilly Downs
Mullion
Penhale
Trelan
Mullion Cove
Mullion Island
Gwenter
Kuggar
Predannack Wollas
Vellan Hd.
St Ruan
Ruan Minor
Grade
Cadgwith
Kynance Cove
Lizard
Hot Pt.
LIZARD POINT
ISLES OF SCILLY (Mar-Nov)
0 1 2 3 4 5 6 miles
0 1 2 3 4 5 6 7 8 9 10 km

Camelford
Delabole
Valley Truckle
Helstone
Port Isaac Bay
Port Isaac
Port Quin Bay
Port Quin
Port Gaverne
Pendoggett
Pentire Pt.
New Polzeath
Padstow Bay
Polzeath
Trebetherick
Trelights
St Endellion
Trelill
St Teath
Treveighan
Michaelstow
St Minver
Pityme
Trewethern
Chapel Amble
St Kew
St Kew Highway
St Tudy
St Breward
Wenfordbridge
Blisland
Gulland Rock
Gunver Hd.
TREVOSE HEAD
Crugmeer
Trevone
Constantine Bay
Treyarnon
St Merryn
Padstow
Rock
Bodieve
Trevanson
Wadebridge
Egloshayle
Burlawn
Little Petherick
Whitecross
St Breock
St Issey
Tredinnick
Rumford
St Jidgey
Shop
Porthcothan
Penrose
St Ervan
Park Hd.
St Eval
Mawgan Porth
Trenance
Berryl's Pt.
Trevarrian
St Mawgan
Talskiddy
WATERGATE BAY
Tregurrian
St Columb Major
Newquay Bay
Towan Hd.
Fistral Bay
Porth
St Columb Minor
Kelsey Hd.
Pentire
West Pentire
Newquay
Crantock
Nansledan
Colan
Quintrell Downs
Trebudannon
Mountjoy
Lane
Kestle Mill
St Columb Road
Fraddon
Penhale
Indian Queens
Trevarren
Ruthvoes
Belowda
Victoria
Tregoss
Roche
Trezaise
Bugle
Bilberry
Lockengate
Lanivet
Bodmin
Nanstallon
St Lawrence
Rutherbridge
Withiel
Rosenannon
St Wenn
Tregonetha
St Mabyn
Helland
Washaway
Bodmin Forest
Cardinham
Warleggan
Temple
Millpool
Maidenwell
Bradford
BODMIN MOOR
Dozmary Pool
Colliford Lake
High Moor
Altarnun
Trewint
St Clether
Laneast
Polyphant
Lewannick
Codda
Bolventor
Congdon's Shop
Trebartha
North Hill
Bathpool
Henwood
Rilla Mill
Upton Cross
Minions
Darite
Commonmoor
St Neot
Mount
Ley
St Cleer
Tremar
Merrymeet
Dobwalls
Doublebois
Liskeard
East Taphouse
West Taphouse
St Pinnock
Trebyan
Sweethouse
Redmoor
Lostwithiel
Braddock
Herodsfoot
St Keyne
Trewidland
Duloe
Lanlivery
Luxulyan
Couch's Mill
Milltown
Bocaddon
Lerryn
St Veep
Penpoll
Lanreath
Sandplace
Morval
Muchlarnick
Pelynt
St Martin
Looe
East Looe
West Looe
Looe Bay
Talland Bay
Polperro
Lansallos
Trenewan
Lanteglos Highway
Bodinnick
Fowey
Polruan
Golant
Tywardreath
Par
St Blazey
Penwithick
Stenalees
Trethurgy
Carclaze
Boscoppa
St Austell
Holmbush
Charlestown
Polkerris
Menabilly
Gribbin Hd.
Pencarrow Hd.
ST. AUSTELL BAY
Porthpean
Polgooth
Trenarren
Black Hd.
Pentewan
Mevagissey Bay
Mevagissey
Portmellon
Chapel Pt.
Gorran Churchtown
Gorran Haven
Boswinger
Penare
Dodman Pt.
St Michael Caerhays
Trevarrick
Portholland
Veryan Bay
Portloe
Veryan
Carne
Gerrans Bay
Nare Hd.
Kestle
St Ewe
Polmassick
Hewas Water
Sticker
St Mewan
Trewoon
Coombe
St Stephen
Grampound Road
Grampound
Creed
Tregony
Probus
Tresillian
Tresawle
Truro
Kenwyn
Merther
St Clement
Ruan Lanihorne
Lamorran
St Michael Penkevil
Malpas
Old Kea
Kea
Playing Place
Trelissick
Philleigh
Treworga
Treworlas
Trewithian
Portscatho
Gerrans
St Just in Roseland
St Mawes
Bohortha
Greeb Pt.
Zone Pt.
Carrick Roads
Feock
Devoran
Penpol
Carnon Downs
Bissoe
Baldhu
Threemilestone
Chacewater
Twelve Heads
Perranarworthal
Ponsanooth
Burnthouse
Mylor Bridge
Flushing
Penryn
Falmouth
Mabe Burnthouse
Budock Water
Treverva
Pendennis Pt.
Penjerrick
Falmouth Bay
Mawnan Smith
Rosemullion Hd.
Mawnan
Porth Navas
Helford Passage
Helford River
Helford
St Anthony-in-Meneage
Nare Pt.
Manaccan
Porthallow
Tregidden
Porthoustock
Manacle Pt.
The Manacles
St Keverne
Lowland Pt.
Coverack
Chynhalls Pt.
Black Hd.
Summercourt
Brighton
Mitchell
Newlyn Downs
Carland Cross
Trelassick
New Mills
Ladock
St Erme
Trispen
St Allen
Zelah
Callestick
Marazanvose
Allet
Shortlanesend
Perranporth
Bolingey
Perranzabuloe
Goonhavern
Mount
Rose
Rejerrah
Cubert
Holywell
Carines
Penhale Sands
St Newlyn East
Gummow's Shop
St Enoder
St Dennis
Whitemoor
Retew
Treviscoe
Trethosa
Nanpean
Foxhole
High Street
Carthew
Hensbarrow Downs
CORNWALL
SX
4

BUDE BAY
CORNWALL
Widemouth Bay
Widemouth Sand
Dizzard Pt.
Millook
Poundstock
Coppathorne
Marhamchurch
Bridgerule
Pyworthy
Derril
Derriton
Holsworthy
Whimble
Chasty
Brandis Corner
Hollacombe
Highampton
Chilla
Graddon Moor
Halwill Junction
Halwill
Beaworthy
Northlew
Ashbury
Patchacott
BROADBURY
Leworthy
Clawton
Quoditch
Ashwater
Henford
Eworthy
Germansweek
Boasley Cross
Thorndon Cross
Virginstow
Chapmans Well
Roadford Res.
Grinacombe Moor
Bratton Clovelly
Sourton Cross Services
Budd's Titson
Whitstone
North Tamerton
Tetcott
Lana
Luffincott
Treskinnick Cross
Week St Mary
Penhallam
Tregole
Trewint
Rosecare
St Gennys
South West Coast Path
Cambeak
Crackington Haven
Jacobstow
Wainhouse Corner
South Wheatley
West Curry
Maxworthy
Bennacott
Boyton
Northcott
East Panson
St Giles on the Hth.
Gridley Corner
Broadwoodwidger
Bridestowe
Fire Beacon Pt.
Tresparrett Posts
Beeny
Marshgate
Boscastle
Tresparrett
Lesnewth
Otterham
Canworthy Water
Brazacott
Tamar Otter & Wildlife Centre
Langdon
Bridgetown
Cross Green
Thrushelton
Werrington
Trevalga
Tintagel Hd.
Castle
Old Post Office
Tintagel
Bossiney
Trelash
Warbstow
Tremaine
North Petherwin
Treneglos
Hallworthy
Tresmeer
Yeolmbridge
Langore
Stowford
Lewdown
Shortacombe
Dingle's Fairground Heritage Centre
Trewarmett
Treknow
Start Pt.
Davidstow
Trewassa
Tremail
The Vale of Avalon
Cornwall at War
Davidstow Moor
Trebarwith
Cold Northcott
Tregeare
Egloskerry
St Stephen's
Dutson
Liftondown
Lifton
Tinhay
Portgate
Lewtrenchard
Lydford
Lydford Gorge
Coryton
Trelligga
Delabole
Valley Truckle
Camelford
Crowdy Res.
The Hidden Valley Discovery Park
Piper's Pool
Trethorne Leisure Park
Tregadillett
Launceston
Launceston Steam Railway
St Clether
Laneast
Trewen
Daw's House
Lawhitton
Kelly
Port Isaac Bay
Helstone
High Moor
Rough Tor
Brown Willy
Wesley Cottage
Altarnun
Polyphant
South Petherwin
North Brentor
Black Down
Chillaton
Bradstone
Port Gaverne
St Teath
Pendoggett
Treveighan
Trewint
Lewannick
Lezant
Milton Abbot
Mary Tavy
Horndon
Cudliptown
Trelill
Michaelstow
Garrow Tor
Codda
Congdon's Shop
Trebartha
Dunterton
Trekenner
Rezare
Treburley
Trebullett
Peter Tavy
St Kew
St Tudy
St Breward
Row
Museum of Smuggling (Jamaica Inn)
Bolventor
North Hill
Coad's Green
Sydenham Damerel
Lamerton
Wilminstone
St Kew Highway
Bradford
Wenfordbridge
BODMIN MOOR
Dozmary Pool
Kilmar Tor
Henwood
Bathpool
Bray Shop
Stoke Climsland
Horsebridge
Tavistock
Blisland
Temple
Colliford Lake
Rilla Mill
Upton Cross
Linkinhorne
South Hill
Luckett
Latchley
Downgate
Chilsworthy
Gunnislake
Gulworthy
Whitchurch
Grenofen
St Mabyn
Pencarrow House
Helland
Millpool
Maidenwell
The Hurlers Stone Circles
Minions
Caradon Hill
Siblyback Lake
Pensilva
Golberdon
Haye
Kelly Bray
Kit Hill
St Ann's Chapel
Drakewalls
Higher Walreddon
Washaway
Bodmin Forest
Warleggan
Commonmoor
Golitha Falls
King Doniert's Stone
Darite
Trethevy Quoit
Trevigro
Callington
Harrowbarrow
Dupath Well House
Albaston
Calstock
Cotehele
Horrabridge
Buckland Monachorum
The Garden House
Yelverton
Nanstallon
Bodmin
Cardinham
Mount
St Neot
St Cleer
Tremar
Gang
St Ive
Newbridge
St Dominick
TAMAR VALLEY
Crapstone
Bodmin Town Museum
St Lawrence
Bodmin and Wenford Railway
Ley
Carnglaze Slate Caverns
Merrymeet
Pengover Green
Bere Alston
Buckland Abbey
Milton Combe
Lanivet
Lanhydrock House
Fowey
East Taphouse
Dobwalls
Doublebois
Liskeard
Quethiock
St Mellion
Weir Quay
Lopwell
Clearbrook
West Taphouse
St Pinnock
Trebyan
Restormel Castle
Menheniot
Pillaton
Cargreen
Bere Ferrers
Bickleigh
Cornwall Services
Lockengate
Sweetshouse
Redmoor
Braddock
Herodsfoot
St Keyne
Blunts
Tideford Cross
Hatt
Botusfleming
Landulph
Tamerton Foliot
Roborough
Bilberry
Lostwithiel
Trewidland
Landrake
Saltash Services
Crownhill Fort
Bugle
Lanlivery
Couch's Mill
Duloe
Tideford
Trematon
Saltash
Toll
Crownhill
Eggbuckland
Plym Valley
Stenalees
Luxulyan
Milltown
Bocaddon
Widegates
Trerulefoot
Hessenford
St Erney
St Stephens
Mary Newman's Cottage
St Budeaux
Penwithick
Penpillick
Lerryn
Sandplace
Morval
St Germans
Antony House
Trethurgy
Golant
Lanreath
Muchlarnick
Polbathic
Sheviock
Torpoint
Devonport
Plymouth
Merchant's House
Eden Project
St Blazey
Tywardreath
St Veep
Penpoll
Pelynt
Looe
St Martin
Monkey Sanctuary
Seaton
Downderry
Crafthole
Antony
Saltram
Carclaze
Boscoppa
Par
Lanteglos Highway
Trenewan
East Looe
West Looe
Old Guildhall
Portwrinkle
St John
Cremyll
Mount Edgcumbe
Royal Citadel
Plymstock
Elburton
Holmbush
Shipwreck Treasure Mus
Polkerris
Menabilly
Fowey
Bodinnick
Porthallow
Looe Bay
South West Coast Path
Freathy
Millbrook
Drake's I.
The Sound
Hooe
Staddiscombe
Charlestown
St Austell Brewery
St Catherine's Castle
Polruan
Lansallos
Talland Bay
St George's or Looe I.
Whitsand Bay
Kingsand
Porthpean
St. Austell Bay
South West Coast Path
Pencarrow Hd.
Polperro
Heritage Mus of Smuggling & Fishing
Cawsand
Rame
Bovisand Bay
Down Thomas
Knighton
Trenarren
Gribbin Hd.
Penlee Pt.
Rame Hd.
Heybrook Bay
Wembury
Wembury Bay
Black Hd.
Pentewan
Mevagissey Bay
(Apr-Oct)
Great Mew Stone
Worswell
Mevagissey
World of Model Railways
Chapel Pt.
Gorran Haven
Penare
Dodman Pt.
Roscoff Santander (Mar-Nov)
A30
A39
A38
A388
A390
A386
A395
A3072
A3079
A387
A374
B3254
B3257
B3266
B3263
B3314
B3267
B3268
B3269
B3359
B3252
B3253
B3247
B3249
B3271
B3362
B3357
B3373
B3413
0 1 2 3 4 5 6 miles
0 1 2 3 4 5 6 7 8 9 10 km

Okehampton
Exeter
Crediton
DARTMOOR
DARTMOOR
NATIONAL
FOREST
PARK
Exmouth
Teignmouth
Dawlish
NEWTON ABBOT
Kingsteignton
Torquay
Paignton
TORBAY
TOR BAY
Brixham
Dartmouth
Totnes
Ashburton
Buckfastleigh
Ivybridge
Kingsbridge
Salcombe
Modbury
Moretonhampstead
Chagford
Bovey Tracey
Chudleigh
Topsham
Budleigh Salterton
Princetown
Two Bridges
Postbridge
Widecombe in the Moor
South Brent
Dartmeet
Lympstone
Starcross
Powderham
Cockwood
Dawlish Warren
Shaldon
Babbacombe
Maidencombe
Goodrington
Galmpton
Kingswear
Stoke Fleming
Blackpool
Strete
Slapton
Torcross
Beesands
Hallsands
START POINT
Prawle Pt.
Bolt Hd.
Bolt Tail
Hope
Bigbury on Sea
Burgh I.
BIGBURY BAY
Thurlestone
Aveton Gifford
Loddiswell
Yealmpton
Noss Mayo
Stoke Pt.
Sharkham Pt.
Berry Head
Straight Pt.
Hope's Nose
Start Bay
Slapton Sands
Lannacombe Bay
Mew Stone
Scabbacombe Hd.
BABBACOMBE BAY
S O U T H D E V O N
Cosdon Hill
High Willhays
Yes Tor
Cut Hill
Sittaford Tor
Hameldown Tor
Rippon Tor
Rough Tor
Ryder's Hill
Shell Top
Burrator Res.
Ugborough Moor
Exeter International
Crealy Great Adventure Park
Castle Drogo
Canonteign Falls
Powderham Castle
Buckfast Abbey
Dartington Hall
Berry Pomeroy Castle
Compton Castle
Kent's Cavern Prehistoric Caves
Model Village
Dartmouth Castle
Coleton Fishacre
Overbecks Museum and Garden
Woodlands Family Theme Park
South West Coast Path
A30
A38
A380
A381
A385
A379
A3122
A377
A386
A376
M5
6
7
8
9
10
11
D
E
F
G
H

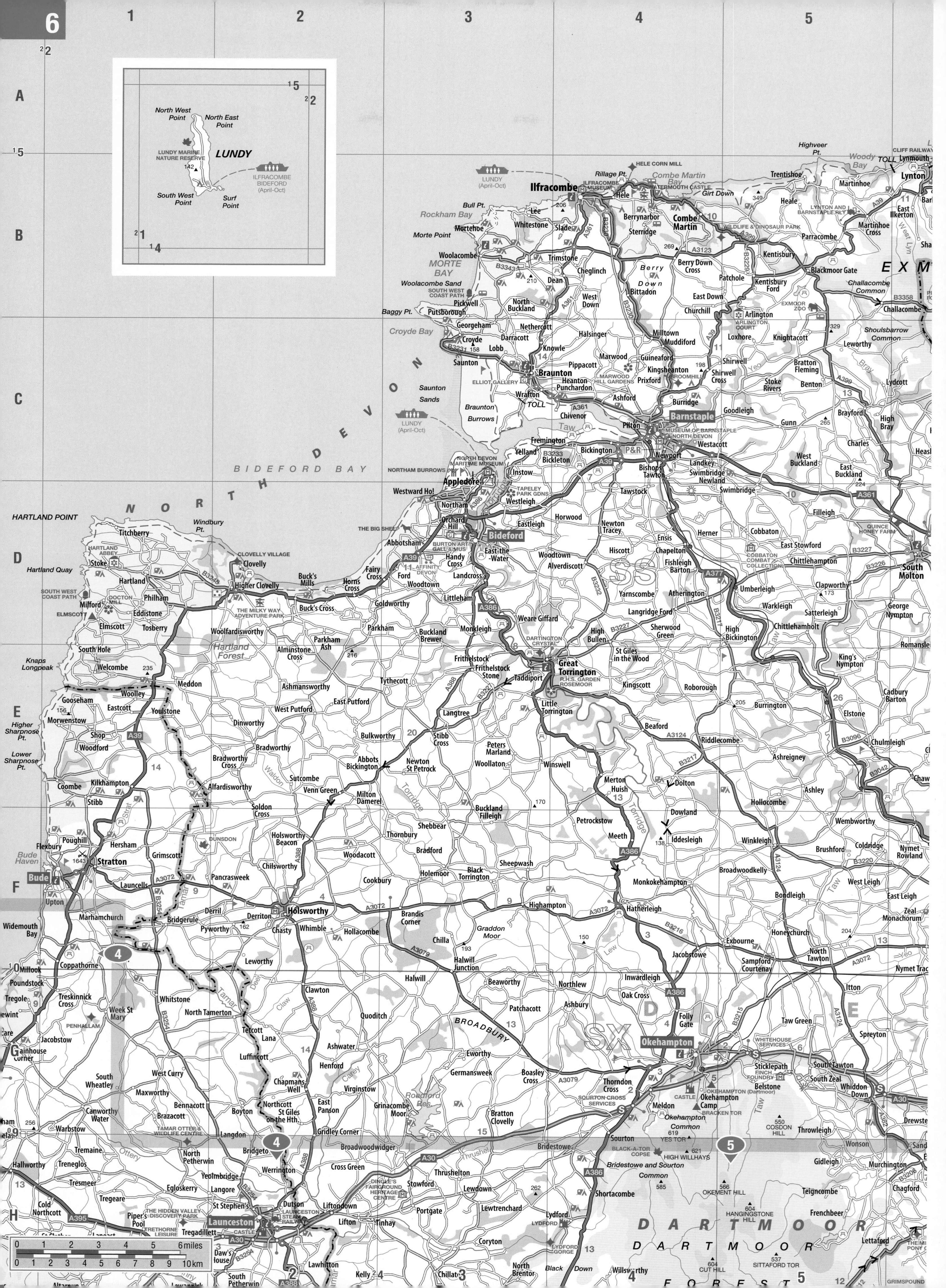
North West Point
North East Point
LUNDY
LUNDY MARINE NATURE RESERVE
South West Point
Surf Point
ILFRACOMBE BIDEFORD (April-Oct)
LUNDY (April-Oct)
HELE CORN MILL
Rillage Pt.
Ilfracombe
ILFRACOMBE MUSEUM
Combe Martin Bay
WATERMOUTH CASTLE
Hele
Berrynarbor
Combe Martin
Sterridge
Girt Down
WILDLIFE & DINOSAUR PARK
Highveer Pt.
Woody Bay
CLIFF RAILWAY
Lynmouth
Lynton
Trentishoe
Martinhoe
Heale
LYNTON AND BARNSTAPLE RLY
East Ilkerton
Martinhoe Cross
Parracombe
Kentisbury
Blackmoor Gate
EXMOOR
Challacombe Common
Challacombe
Bull Pt.
Rockham Bay
Lee
Whitestone
Slade
Mortehoe
Morte Point
Woolacombe
MORTE BAY
Trimstone
Cheglinch
Berry Down
Bittadon
Berry Down Cross
Patchole
Kentisbury Ford
Dean
Woolacombe Sand
SOUTH WEST COAST PATH
Pickwell
North Buckland
West Down
East Down
Churchill
Arlington
ARLINGTON COURT
EXMOOR ZOO
Baggy Pt.
Putsborough
Croyde Bay
Georgeham
Darracott
Nethercott
Halsinger
Milltown
Muddiford
Loxhore
Knightacott
Shoulsbarrow Common
Leworthy
Croyde
Lobb
Knowle
Saunton
Marwood
Guineaford
Kingsheanton
Shirwell
Shirwell Cross
Bratton Fleming
Benton
Lydcott
Pippacott
MARWOOD HILL GARDENS
Prixford
BROOMHILL
Stoke Rivers
Braunton
ELLIOT GALLERY
Heanton Punchardon
Saunton Sands
Wrafton
TOLL
Ashford
Burridge
Goodleigh
Braunton Burrows
Chivenor
Barnstaple
Pilton
MUSEUM OF BARNSTAPLE & NORTH DEVON
Gunn
Brayford
High Bray
Charles
NORTH DEVON
Fremington
Yelland
Bickleton
Bickington
Newport
Westacott
Landkey
Swimbridge Newland
West Buckland
East Buckland
BIDEFORD BAY
NORTHAM BURROWS
NORTH DEVON MARITIME MUSEUM
Instow
Bishops Tawton
Swimbridge
Appledore
Westward Ho!
TAPELEY PARK GDNS
Tawstock
Northam
Westleigh
Filleigh
HARTLAND POINT
Windbury Pt.
THE BIG SHEEP
Orchard Hill
Eastleigh
Horwood
Newton Tracey
Cobbaton
QUINCE HONEY FARM
Titchberry
Abbotsham
BURTON ART GALL & MUS
Bideford
Herner
HARTLAND ABBEY
CLOVELLY VILLAGE
Handy Cross
East-the-Water
Hiscott
Ensis
Chapelton
East Stowford
COBBATON COMBAT COLLECTION
Hartland Quay
Stoke
Clovelly
Fairy Cross
Ford
AFFINITY DEVON
Woodtown
Alverdiscott
Fishleigh Barton
Chittlehampton
South Molton
Hartland
Higher Clovelly
Buck's Mills
Horns Cross
Landcross
SS
SOUTH WEST COAST PATH
Philham
DOCTON MILL
Milford
Eddistone
ELMSCOTT
THE MILKY WAY ADVENTURE PARK
Buck's Cross
Goldworthy
Littleham
Yarnscombe
Atherington
Umberleigh
Clapworthy
Warkleigh
George Nympton
Elmscott
Tosberry
Woolfardisworthy
Parkham Ash
Parkham
Buckland Brewer
Monkleigh
Weare Giffard
Langridge Ford
Sherwood Green
High Bickington
Satterleigh
Chittlehamholt
Hartland Forest
Alminstone Cross
DARTINGTON CRYSTAL
High Bullen
Knaps Longpeak
South Hole
Frithelstock
Frithelstock Stone
Great Torrington
St Giles in the Wood
King's Nympton
Romansleigh
Welcombe
Meddon
Tythecott
Taddiport
R.H.S. GARDEN ROSEMOOR
Kingscott
Roborough
Ashmansworthy
East Putford
Cadbury Barton
Gooseham
Woolley
Eastcott
Youlstone
Morwenstow
West Putford
Langtree
Little Torrington
Burrington
Elstone
Higher Sharpnose Pt.
Shop
Dinworthy
Bulkworthy
Stibb Cross
Beaford
Riddlecombe
Chulmleigh
Woodford
Bradworthy
Peters Marland
Lower Sharpnose Pt.
Bradworthy Cross
Abbots Bickington
Newton St Petrock
Woollaton
Winswell
Ashreigney
Alfardisworthy
Waldon
Sutcombe
Merton
Huish
Dolton
Coombe
Kilkhampton
Venn Green
Milton Damerel
Torridge
Ashley
Hollocombe
Stibb
Soldon Cross
Buckland Filleigh
Dowland
Petrockstow
Holsworthy Beacon
Shebbear
Thornbury
Iddesleigh
Wembworthy
DUNSDON
Meeth
Poughill
Flexbury
Hersham
Bradford
Winkleigh
Brushford
Coldridge
Nymet Rowland
Bude Haven
Stratton
Grimscott
Woodacott
Chilsworthy
Sheepwash
Bude
Pancrasweek
Holemoor
Black Torrington
Monkokehampton
Broadwoodkelly
West Leigh
Launcells
Upton
Cookbury
Bondleigh
East Leigh
Marhamchurch
Derril
Derriton
Holsworthy
Brandis Corner
Highampton
Hatherleigh
Zeal Monachorum
Widemouth Bay
Bridgerule
Pyworthy
Chasty
Whimble
Hollacombe
Graddon Moor
Chilla
Exbourne
Honeychurch
Halwill Junction
Jacobstowe
North Tawton
Millook
Coppathorne
Leworthy
Sampford Courtenay
Nymet Tracey
Poundstock
Halwill
Beaworthy
Inwardleigh
Itton
Clawton
Northlew
Tregole
Treskinnick Cross
Week St Mary
Whitstone
North Tamerton
Oak Cross
Ashbury
PENHALLAM
Quoditch
Patchacott
BROADBURY
Folly Gate
Taw Green
Jacobstow
Tetcott
Lana
Ashwater
SX
Okehampton
WHITEHOUSE SERVICES
Spreyton
Gainhouse Corner
Luffincott
Henford
Eworthy
South Tawton
Sticklepath
FINCH FOUNDRY
South Zeal
West Curry
Germansweek
Boasley Cross
Thorndon Cross
Belstone
South Wheatley
Maxworthy
Chapmans Well
Virginstow
SOURTON CROSS SERVICES
OKEHAMPTON (Dartmoor)
CASTLE
Okehampton Camp
Whiddon Down
Bennacott
Northcott
St Giles on the Hth.
East Panson
Grinacombe Moor
Roadford Res.
Bratton Clovelly
Meldon
BRACKEN TOR
Drewsteignton
Canworthy Water
Brazacott
Boyton
Okehampton Common
COSDON HILL
Throwleigh
Warbstow
TAMAR OTTER & WILDLIFE CENTRE
Langdon
Gridley Corner
Sourton
YES TOR
Tremaine
Ottery
North Petherwin
Bridgetown
Broadwoodwidger
Thrushel
Bridestowe
BLACK-A-TOR COPSE
HIGH WILLHAYS
Wonson
Hallworthy
Treneglos
Werrington
Cross Green
Bridestowe and Sourton Common
Gidleigh
Murchington
Tresmeer
Yeolmbridge
Thrushelton
Chagford
Egloskerry
Langore
DINGLE'S FAIRGROUND HERITAGE CENTRE
Stowford
Lewdown
Shortacombe
OKEMENT HILL
Teigncombe
Tregeare
St Stephen's
Dutson
Cold Northcott
Piper's Pool
THE HIDDEN VALLEY DISCOVERY PARK
LAUNCESTON STEAM RAILWAY
Liftondown
Portgate
Lewtrenchard
HANGINGSTONE HILL
Frenchbeer
Launceston
TRETHORNE LEISURE
Tregadillett
CASTLE
Lifton
Tinhay
Lydford
LYDFORD
DARTMOOR
Coryton
Lettaford
Daw's House
LYDFORD GORGE
Lawhitton
North Brentor
Black Down
CUT HILL
SITTAFORD TOR
South Petherwin
Kelly
Chillaton
Willsworthy
DARTMOOR FOREST
GRIMSPOUND
0 1 2 3 4 5 6 miles
0 1 2 3 4 5 6 7 8 9 10km

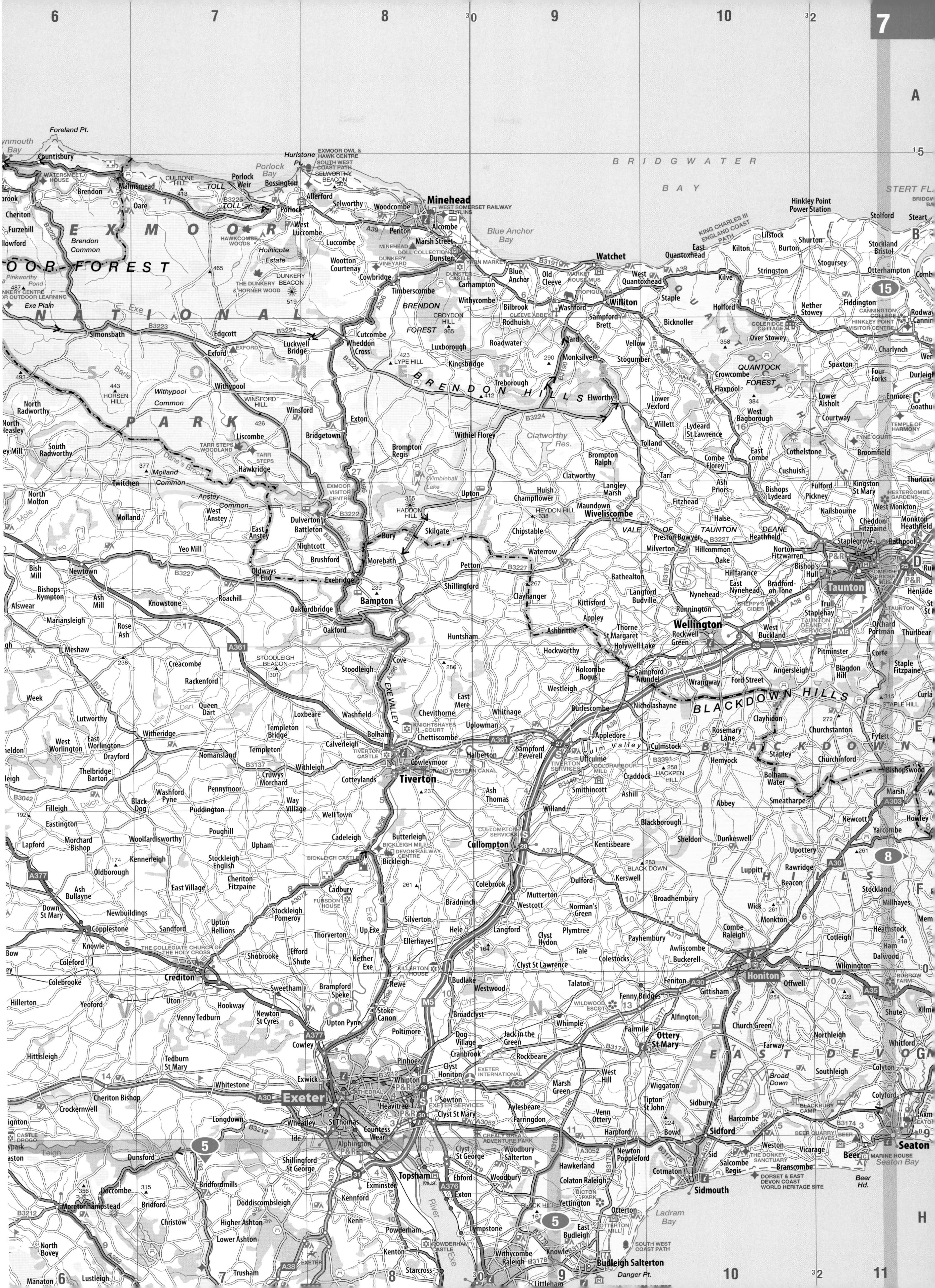

Foreland Pt.
Countisbury
Brendon
Malmsmead
Oare
Porlock Weir
Porlock
Bossington
Hurlstone Pt.
EXMOOR OWL & HAWK CENTRE
SOUTH WEST COAST PATH
SELWORTHY BEACON
Allerford
Selworthy
Woodcombe
Minehead
WEST SOMERSET RAILWAY
BUTLINS
Alcombe
Periton
Marsh Street
Dunster
DUNSTER CASTLE
Blue Anchor Bay
Blue Anchor
Carhampton
West Luccombe
Luccombe
Wootton Courtenay
Cowbridge
Timberscombe
DUNKERY BEACON
THE DUNKERY & HORNER WOOD
Holnicote Estate
HAWKCOMBE WOODS
Cheriton
Furzehill
Brendon Common
EXMOOR
EXMOOR FOREST
NATIONAL
PARK
SOMERSET
Pinkworthy Pond
Exe Plain
Simonsbath
Edgcott
Exford
Luckwell Bridge
Cutcombe
Wheddon Cross
BRENDON FOREST
CROYDON HILL
Luxborough
LYPE HILL
Kingsbridge
BRENDON HILLS
Withypool
Withypool Common
HORSEN HILL
WINSFORD HILL
Winsford
North Radworthy
North Heasley
South Radworthy
Liscombe
TARR STEPS WOODLAND
TARR STEPS
Hawkridge
Molland Common
Twitchen
North Molton
Molland
West Anstey
Anstey Common
East Anstey
EXMOOR VISITOR CENTRE
Dulverton
Battleton
Bridgetown
Exton
Brompton Regis
Wimbleball Lake
HADDON HILL
Upton
Skilgate
Bury
Morebath
Nightcott
Brushford
Exebridge
Oldways End
Yeo Mill
Bish Mill
Newtown
Bishops Nympton
Ash Mill
Alswear
Knowstone
Roachill
Oakfordbridge
Bampton
Oakford
Mariansleigh
Rose Ash
Meshaw
STOODLEIGH BEACON
Stoodleigh
Creacombe
Rackenford
Queen Dart
Week
Lutworthy
Witheridge
West Worlington
East Worlington
Drayford
Nomansland
Templeton
Templeton Bridge
Loxbeare
Washfield
Calverleigh
Thelbridge Barton
Cruwys Morchard
Pennymoor
Washford Pyne
Black Dog
Puddington
Way Village
Well Town
Cadeleigh
Fillеigh
Eastington
Lapford
Morchard Bishop
Kennerleigh
Woolfardisworthy
Poughill
Upham
Stockleigh English
Cheriton Fitzpaine
Oldborough
East Village
Ash Bullayne
Down St Mary
Newbuildings
Copplestone
Sandford
Upton Hellions
Knowle
THE COLLEGIATE CHURCH OF THE HOLY CROSS
Crediton
Coleford
Colebrooke
Shobrooke
Efford
Shute
Thorverton
Stockleigh Pomeroy
FURSDON HOUSE
Cadbury
Up Exe
Nether Exe
Hillerton
Yeoford
Uton
Hookway
Venny Tedburn
Newton St Cyres
Sweetham
Brampford Speke
Rewe
Stoke Canon
Upton Pyne
Cowley
Hittisleigh
Tedburn St Mary
Whitestone
Cheriton Bishop
Crockernwell
Longdown
Exeter
Exwick
Whitley
St Thomas
Ide
CASTLE DROGO
Dunsford
Bridfordmills
Doccombe
Bridford
Moretonhampstead
Christow
Doddiscombsleigh
Higher Ashton
Lower Ashton
North Bovey
Manaton
Lustleigh
Trusham
Shillingford St George
Alphington
Countess Wear
Exminster
Kennford
Kenn
Powderham
POWDERHAM CASTLE
Kenton
Starcross
Topsham
Ebford
Exton
Lympstone
Woodbury
Woodbury Salterton
Clyst St George
Clyst St Mary
Sowton
Clyst Honiton
EXETER INTERNATIONAL
Whipton
Heavitree
Pinhoe
Poltimore
Broadclyst
Dog Village
Cranbrook
Jack in the Green
Rockbeare
Aylesbeare
Farringdon
Marsh Green
West Hill
Whimple
Talaton
Fenny Bridges
Feniton
Gittisham
Honiton
Offwell
Alfington
Fairmile
Ottery St Mary
Wiggaton
Tipton St John
Venn Ottery
Harpford
Bowd
Sidbury
Sidford
Sidmouth
Newton Poppleford
Colaton Raleigh
Hawkerland
Yettington
Otterton
East Budleigh
Budleigh Salterton
Knowle
Withycombe Raleigh
Littleham
Danger Pt.
Ladram Bay
Salcombe Regis
Branscombe
Weston
Vicarage
Beer
Beer Hd.
Seaton
Seaton Bay
Colyford
Colyton
Southleigh
Farway
Northleigh
Church Green
Whitford
Shute
Wilmington
Dalwood
Cotleigh
Heathstock
Stockland
Millhayes
Monkton
Wick
Combe Raleigh
Buckerell
Awliscombe
Payhembury
Broadhembury
Plymtree
Norman's Green
Westcott
Mutterton
Colebrook
Bradninch
Hele
Langford
Clyst Hydon
Clyst St Lawrence
Tale
Colestocks
Cullompton
Kentisbeare
Dulford
Kerswell
Blackborough
Sheldon
Dunkeswell
Luppitt
Upottery
Rawridge
Yarcombe
Newcott
Smeatharpe
Abbey
Bolham Water
Hemyock
Culmstock
Churchstanton
Churchinford
Clayhidon
Rosemary Lane
Stapley
BLACKDOWN HILLS
Ashill
Craddock
Smithincott
Uffculme
Sampford Peverell
Halberton
Willand
Ash Thomas
Tiverton
Cowleymoor
Bolham
Chettiscombe
Chevithorne
KNIGHTSHAYES COURT
Uplowman
Whitnage
East Mere
Burlescombe
Appledore
Westleigh
Holcombe Rogus
Hockworthy
Huntsham
Cove
Butterleigh
Bickleigh
Bickleigh Castle
Sampford Arundel
Wrangway
Ford Street
Nicholashayne
Holywell Lake
Thorne St Margaret
Ashbrittle
Appley
Kittisford
Greenham
Clayhanger
Shillingford
Petton
Waterrow
Chipstable
Wiveliscombe
Maundown
Huish Champflower
Langley Marsh
Clatworthy
Clatworthy Res.
Brompton Ralph
Withiel Florey
Treborough
Elworthy
Monksilver
Yard
Roadwater
Rodhuish
Bilbrook
CLEEVE ABBEY
Washford
Old Cleeve
Watchet
West Quantoxhead
Williton
Sampford Brett
Bicknoller
Vellow
Stogumber
Staple
Kilve
Holford
Lower Vexford
Willett
Tolland
Lydeard St Lawrence
Combe Florey
Ash Priors
Tarr
Fitzhead
Halse
Bishops Lydeard
Cothelstone
Cushuish
Heathfield
Milverton
Preston Bowyer
Hillcommon
Oake
Langford Budville
Bathealton
Runnington
Nynehead
Wellington
Rockwell Green
Hillfarance
East Nynehead
Bradford-on-Tone
Norton Fitzwarren
Staplegrove
Taunton
Bishop's Hull
Trull
Staplehay
West Buckland
Orchard Portman
Thurlbear
Pitminster
Corfe
Angersleigh
Blagdon Hill
Staple Fitzpaine
VALE OF TAUNTON DEANE
BRIDGWATER BAY
Hinkley Point Power Station
Lilstock
Kilton
Shurton
Burton
Stogursey
Stockland Bristol
Stolford
Steart
Otterhampton
East Quantoxhead
Stringston
Nether Stowey
Over Stowey
Fiddington
Charlynch
Spaxton
QUANTOCK FOREST
QUANTOCK HILLS
Crowcombe
Flaxpool
West Bagborough
Lower Aisholt
Courtway
Four Forks
Durleigh
Enmore
East Combe
Broomfield
Kingston St Mary
Fulford
Pickney
Nailsbourne
West Monkton
Monkton Heathfield
Cheddon Fitzpaine
Bathpool
Henlade
EAST DEVON

Bridgwater
Street
Taunton
Chard
Ilminster
Crewkerne
Yeovil
Sherborne
Somerton
Castle Cary
Wincanton
Bruton
Milborne Port
Merriott
South Petherton
Beaminster
Axminster
Lyme Regis
Seaton
Beer
Bridport
Dorchester
Weymouth
Fortuneswell
Easton
PORTLAND
Bill of Portland
Melcombe Regis
Wyke Regis
Preston
Abbotsbury
Charmouth
Chideock
Seatown
West Bay
Burton Bradstock
Evercreech
Glastonbury Tor
Langport
Muchelney
Martock
Montacute
Stoke sub Hamdon
Ilchester
Sparkford
Wraxall
Kingsbury Episcopi
Curry Rivel
Hatch Beauchamp
Broadwindsor
Netherbury
Maiden Newton
Cerne Abbas
Charminster
Poundbury
Winterborne Monkton
Upwey
Radipole
Portesham
Rodden
Langton Herring
Chickerell
Charlestown
Westham
Weston
Southwell
Grove
Kilmington
Musbury
Uplyme
Combpyne
Rousdon
Axmouth
Colyton
Shute
Whitford
Chardstock
Thorncombe
Drimpton
Mosterton
Misterton
South Perrott
Corscombe
Evershot
Halstock
Melbury Osmond
Yetminster
Leigh
Chetnole
Holnest
Hermitage
Batcombe
Minterne Magna
Up Cerne
Up Sydling
Sydling St Nicholas
Godmanstone
Piddletrenthide
Frampton
Grimstone
Stratton
Bradford Peverell
Winterbourne Abbas
Long Bredy
Littlebredy
Martinstown
Puncknowle
Swyre
West Bexington
Kingston Russell
Askerswell
Loders
Uploders
Powerstock
Nettlecombe
West Milton
Salwayash
Dottery
Symondsbury
Morcombelake
Whitchurch Canonicorum
Ryall
Wootton Fitzpaine
Marshwood
Pilsdon
Bettiscombe
Hawkchurch
Holditch
Membury
Stockland
Yarcombe
Wambrook
Whitestaunton
Buckland St Mary
Donyatt
Horton
Broadway
Ashill
Ilton
Puckington
Stocklinch
Shepton Beauchamp
Barrington
Kingstone
Dinnington
Hinton St George
Chillington
Cudworth
Chaffcombe
Cricket St Thomas
Hewish
Wayford
Winsham
Clapton
Seaborough
Chedington
Odcombe
Brympton
West Coker
East Coker
North Coker
Barwick
Stoford
Bradford Abbas
Thornford
Over Compton
Nether Compton
Trent
Mudford
Yeovil Marsh
Chilthorne Domer
Tintinhull
Ash
Stapleton
Long Load
Long Sutton
Huish Episcopi
Pitney
Low Ham
High Ham
Aller
Othery
Middlezoy
Westonzoyland
Chedzoy
Moorlinch
Greinton
Shapwick
Ashcott
Walton
Butleigh
Compton Dundon
Kingweston
Keinton Mandeville
Barton St David
Charlton Adam
Charlton Mackerell
Kingsdon
Podimore
Queen Camel
West Camel
Marston Magna
Rimpton
Sandford Orcas
Adber
Poyntington
Oborne
Goathill
Purse Caundle
Stalbridge Weston
Stalbridge
Stourton Caundle
Bishop's Caundle
Holwell
Lyon's Gate
Buckland Newton
Alton Pancras
Plush
Piddlehinton
Charlton Down
Stinsford
Kingston Maurward
Whitcombe
Broadmayne
Poxwell
Osmington
Osmington Mills
Littlemoor
Bincombe
Overcombe
Nottington
Broadwey
LYME BAY
Charlton Bay
Seaton Bay
Portland Harbour
West Bay
CHESIL BEACH
SY
DEVON
DORSET
SOMERSET
BLACKMOOR VALE
0 1 2 3 4 5 6 miles
0 1 2 3 4 5 6 7 8 9 10 km

CRANBORNE CHASE AND WEST WILTSHIRE DOWNS
Maiden Bradley
Mere
Gillingham
Shaftesbury
Sturminster Newton
Blandford Forum
Wimborne Minster
Corfe Mullen
Poole
Hamworthy
Bournemouth
BOURNEMOUTH, CHRISTCHURCH & POOLE
CHRISTCHURCH
Christchurch Bay
Highcliffe
New Milton
Barton on Sea
Milford on Sea
Ringwood
Fordingbridge
Salisbury
Wilton
Verwood
Ferndown
West Parley
Wareham
Wool
Swanage
Swanage Bay
Studland
Studland Bay
Sandbanks
Brownsea Island
Poole Harbour
POOLE BAY
Hengistbury Head
Durlston Head
Peveril Pt.
Tilly Whim Caves
St Alban's Head
Kimmeridge Bay
Worbarrow Bay
Lulworth Cove
Durdle Door
Chaldon Down
ISLE OF PURBECK
PURBECK HILLS
Nine Barrow Down
Corfe Castle
Kimmeridge
Tyneham
Worth Matravers
Langton Matravers
Harman's Cross
East Lulworth
West Lulworth
Winfrith Newburgh
Owermoigne
Warmwell
Crossways
Moreton
Bovington Camp
Wareham Forest
Lytchett Minster
Lytchett Matravers
Upton
Broadstone
Canford Heath
Kinson
Bear Cross
Wimborne St Giles
Cranborne
Alderholt
Tarrant Hinton
Tarrant Gunville
Pimperne
Stourpaine
Winterborne Whitechurch
Winterborne Kingston
Milton Abbas
Milborne St Andrew
Bere Regis
Puddletown
Tolpuddle
Affpuddle
Fiddleford
Child Okeford
Shillingstone
Okeford Fitzpaine
Ibberton
Durweston
Bryanston
Blandford St Mary
Charlton Marshall
Spetisbury
Sturminster Marshall
Shapwick
Witchampton
Cashmoor
Farnham
Tollard Royal
Ashmore
Donhead St Andrew
Donhead St Mary
Semley
Tisbury
Hindon
Fonthill Bishop
Chicklade
Great Ridge
Vale of Wardour
Grovely Wood
Wylye Valley
Wylye
Stapleford
Broad Chalke
Bishopstone
Coombe Bissett
Stratford Tony
Martin Drove End
Martin Down
Rockbourne
Damerham
Breamore
Downton
Redlynch
Bodenham
Alderbury
West Grimstead
Whiteparish
Landford
Nomansland
Fritham
Minstead
Burley
Bransgore
Sopley
Hurn
Ashley Heath
St Ives
St Leonards
Three Legged Cross
West Moors
Ibsley
Blashford
Sway
Hordle
NEW FOREST NATIONAL PARK
Ringwood Forest
Stourhead
Stourton
Zeals
Kilmington
Cann
Melbury Abbas
Compton Abbas
Fontmell Magna
Sutton Waldron
Iwerne Minster
Hambledon Hill
Motcombe
Kingston Lacy
Knowlton
Moor Crichel
Long Crichel
Gussage All Saints
Sixpenny Handley
Woodcutts
Pentridge
Winterbourne Dauntsey
Winterbourne Gunner
Old Sarum
Bemerton
Laverstock
Milford
Britford
CHERBOURG
GUERNSEY JERSEY ST. MALO
The Needles
SU
SZ

Winchester
Southampton
Portsmouth
EASTLEIGH
HAVANT
GOSPORT
LYMINGTON
NEWPORT
RYDE
Romsey
Totton
Fareham
Chandler's Ford
Kings Worthy
New Alresford
Bishop's Waltham
Hedge End
West End
Waterlooville
Horndean
Emsworth
Hayling Island
Southsea
Cowes
East Cowes
Yarmouth
Totland
Freshwater
Sandown
Shanklin
Ventnor
Bembridge
Brading
Niton
Lyndhurst
Brockenhurst
Beaulieu
Hythe
Fawley
Netley
Wickham
Twyford
Stockbridge
New Milton
Milford on Sea
Barton on Sea
THE SOLENT
SPITHEAD
SOUTHAMPTON WATER
ISLE OF WIGHT
NEW FOREST NATIONAL PARK
HAMPSHIRE
Christchurch Bay
Osborne Bay
Sandown Bay
Brighstone Bay
Chale Bay
The Needles
St Catherine's Point
SZ
0 1 2 3 4 5 6 miles
0 1 2 3 4 5 6 7 8 9 10 km

Cranleigh
Haslemere
Liphook
Bordon
Petersfield
Midhurst
Petworth
Pulborough
Billingshurst
Horsham
Crawley
Storrington
Steyning
Henfield
Arundel
Chichester
Bosham
Southbourne
Angmering
Rustington
LITTLEHAMPTON
Middleton-on-Sea
Bognor Regis
Worthing
Lancing
SHOREHAM-BY-SEA
Southwick
Portslade-by-Sea
BRIGHTON AND HOVE
Selsey
SELSEY BILL
East Wittering
West Wittering
S O U T H D O W N S
N A T I O N A L P A R K
W E S T S U S S E X
S O U T H D O W N S
TV
CAEN
ST. MALO
CHERBOURG (SEASONAL)
Alderney
31/2 miles to 1 inch
ALDERNEY
Braye
St Anne
Quesnard Pt.
Longis Bay
Clonque Bay
Telegraph Bay
Brehou
DIÉLETTE ST. PETER PORT (Apr-Sept)
Guernsey
31/2 miles to 1 inch
GUERNSEY
St Peter Port
St Sampson
Herm
Jethou
L'Ancresse Bay
Le Plomb
La Fontenelle
Grand Havre
L'Islet
Cobo Bay
Vazon Bay
Le Villocq
Belle Greve Bay
Lihou I.
Mont Saint
Rocquaine Bay
Pleinmont Pt.
Le Planel
La Planque
Carmel
Fort George
Mouilpied
St Martin's Pt.
Pointe de la Moye
Icart Pt.
Moulin Huet Bay
POOLE
PORTSMOUTH
SARK
SHELL BEACH
CASTLE CORNET
ST. HELIER
ST. HELIER ST. MALO
DIÉLETTE ALDERNEY (Apr-Sept)
Jersey
31/2 miles to 1 inch
JERSEY
St Helier
St Aubin
St Ouen
St Mary
St John
Trinity
Rozel
St Martin
Gorey
Grouville
St Clement
St Brelade
St Peter
Carrefour Selous
Five Oaks
Grosnez Pt.
Plémont Pt.
Sorel Pt.
Ronez Pt.
St John's Bay
Belle Hougue Pt.
Bouley Bay
Tour de Rozel
La Coupe Pt.
St Ouen's Bay
Corbière Pt.
St Brelades Bay
St Aubin's Bay
Noirmont Pt.
Le Nez Pt.
St Clements Bay
La Rocque Pt.
Royal Bay of Grouville
St Catherine's Bay
MONT ORGUEIL CASTLE
ELIZABETH CASTLE
CARTERET
SARK (Apr-Sept)
ST. PETER PORT POOLE
ST. PETER PORT PORTSMOUTH
ST. MALO
GRANVILLE ST. PETER PORT CARTERET (Apr-Sept)
6
7
8
9
10
11
E
F
G
H

Merstham
REDHILL
Nutfield
Reigate
Betchworth
Buckland
Earlswood
South Nutfield
Bletchingley
Godstone
Oxted
Limpsfield
Westerham
Tandridge
Crockham Hill
Brasted Chart
Toy's Hill
Ide Hill
Sevenoaks Weald
Ivy Hatch
Plaxtol
Mereworth
Teston
Wateringbury
West Farleigh
Underriver
Oakhurst
Coldharbour
Shipbourne
West Peckham
Nettlestead
Hadlow
Yalding
Hunton
Hildenborough
Hilden Park
Higham Wood
Golden Green
East Peckham
Hale Street
Laddingford
Chainhurst
Salfords
Sidlow
South Godstone
Crowhurst Lane End
Crowhurst
Marlpit Hill
Four Elms
Pootings
Chiddingstone Causeway
Crouch House Green
Edenbridge
Blindley Heath
How Green
Bough Beech
Hever
Chiddingstone
Leigh
Brook Street
TONBRIDGE
Tudeley
Barnes Street
Whetsted
Queen Street
Collier Street
Paddock Wood
Claygate
19
20
Outwood
Horne
Lingfield
Marsh Green
Horley
Smallfield
Weatherhill
Meath Green
Norwood Hill
Hookwood
Charlwood
GATWICK AIRPORT
LONDON GATWICK
Burstow
Newchapel
Felcourt
Dormansland
Markbeech
Penshurst
Bidborough
Southborough
High Brooms
Matfield
Brenchley
Castle Hill
Pembury
Speldhurst
Chiddingstone Hoath
Cowden
Copthorne
Felbridge
Lullenden
Hammerwood
Blackham
Fordcombe
Rusthall
Petteridge
Horsmonden
Blackwell
East Grinstead
Ashurst
Langton Green
Royal Tunbridge Wells
Hawkenbury
Lamberhurst Quarter
Goudhurst
Hazel Street
County Oak
Ifield
Three Bridges
Crawley
Pound Hill
Worth
Lambs Green
Crawley Down
Sunnyside
Ashurstwood
Hartfield
Forest Row
Groombridge
Bells Yew Green
Lamberhurst
Iden Green
Turners Hill
Saint Hill
Withyham
Eridge Green
Frant
Hook Green
Kilndown
Broadfield
Tilgate
Selsfield Common
West Hoathly
Coleman's Hatch
Upper Hartfield
Lye Green
Cousley Wood
Wood's Green
Bedgebury Forest
Pease Pottage
Colgate
Tilgate Forest Row
Balcombe Lane
Sharpthorne
Wych Cross
Friar's Gate
Boarshead
Durgates
Wadhurst
Three Leg Cross
Flimwell
St Leonard's Forest
11
Balcombe
Highbrook
Chelwood Gate
ASHDOWN FOREST
Crowborough
Poundfield
Mark Cross
Town Row
Riseden
Bestbeech Hill
Shover's Green
Wallcrouch
Ticehurst
Union Street
Ashfold Crossways
Handcross
Staplefield
Ardingly
Horsted Keynes
Chelwood Common
Nutley
Duddleswell
Jarvis Brook
Rotherfield
Tidebrook
Stonegate
Swiftsden
Monk's Gate
Slaugham
Lower Beeding
Warninglid
Slough Green
Brook Street
Danehill
Cackle Street
Fairwarp
High Hurstwood
Coggins Mill
Mayfield
Witherenden Hill
Etchingham
Cuckfield
Whitemans Green
Lindfield
HAYWARDS HEATH
Sheffield Green
Splayne's Green
Fletching
Maresfield
Butcher's Cross
Hadlow Down
Five Ashes
Burwash Common
Burwash
Northbridge Street
Bolney
Ansty
Scayne's Hill
Pound Green
Buxted
Ringles Cross
Cross in Hand
Broad Oak
Burwash Weald
Robertsbridge
Kent Street
Wineham
Hickstead
Twineham
Wivelsfield
Wivelsfield Green
North Chailey
Newick
Grisling Common
Uckfield
Framfield
Blackboys
Heathfield
Cade Street
Punnett's Town
Three Cups Corner
Brightling
Oxley's Green
BURGESS HILL
Sayers Common
Chailey
South Street
Ridgewood
Waldron
Little London
Old Heathfield
Maynard's Green
Rushlake Green
Dallington
Darwell Hole
Mountfield
Netherfield
Blackstone
Albourne
Hurstpierpoint
Hurst Wickham
Plumpton Green
Spithurst
Isfield
Little Horsted
Foxhunt Green
Horam
Vine's Cross
Warbleton
Penhurst
Canada
Battle
Woodmancote
Hassocks
Keymer
Ditchling
Streat
East Chiltington
Chiltington
Barcombe Cross
Barcombe
Rose Hill
Halland
East Hoathly
Shortgate
Whitesmith
Burlow
Foul Mile
Ponts Green
Bodle Street Green
Catsfield
Small Dole
Fulking
Poynings
Clayton
Pyecombe
Westmeston
Plumpton
Cooksbridge
Offham
Hamsey
Broyle Side
Laughton
Chiddingly
Gun Hill
Cowbeech
Herstmonceux
Windmill Hill
Ninfield
Henley's Down
Edburton
Saddlescombe
DITCHLING BEACON
MT. HARRY
Lewes
South Malling
Ringmer
Glyndebourne
Mark Cross
Golden Cross
Hellingly
Lower Horsebridge
Lower Dicker
Upper Dicker
Upper Horsebridge
Hailsham
Magham Down
Boreham Street
Lunsford's Cross
Hooe Common
Hooe
Wartling
Patcham
Stanmer
Falmer
Wallands Park
Glynde
Ripe
Chalvington
Arlington
Selmeston
Mile Oak
Westdene
Withdean
Coldean
Kingston near Lewes
Beddingham
West Firle
Alciston
Berwick
Polegate
Sidley
Little Common
Cooden
Portslade
West Blatchington
Preston
Moulsecoomb
Bevendean
Iford
Rodmell
Southease
Woodingdean
Ovingdean
Pevensey Levels
Hankham
Norman's Bay
Kingston by Sea
Southwick
Portslade-by-Sea
SHOREHAM-BY-SEA
Hove
Brighton
Kemp Town
Rottingdean
Saltdean
Telscombe
Telscombe Cliffs
Peacehaven
Piddinghoe
Newhaven
Tarring Neville
South Heighton
Denton
Norton
Bishopstone
Wilmington
Folkington
Alfriston
Lullington Heath
Litlington
Westdean
Willingdon
Jevington
Stone Cross
Westham
Pevensey
Friday Street
Hampden Park
Langney
Pevensey Bay
St Anthony's Hill
Roselands
East Blatchington
Seaford
Friston
East Dean
Eastbourne
Holywell
Birling Gap
BEACHY HEAD
DIEPPE
SOUTH DOWNS
WEALD
TQ
TV
0 1 2 3 4 5 6 miles
0 1 2 3 4 5 6 7 8 9 10 km

Otham
Leeds
Harrietsham
Stalisfield Green
Leaveland
Chilham
Garlinge Green
Lower Hardres
Bishopsbourne
Aylesham
Nonington
Snowdown
Tilmanstone
Elvington
Boughton Monchelsea
Langley
Langley Heath
Leeds Castle
Broomfield
Lenham
Sandway
Warren Street
Molash
Petham
Upper Hardres Court
Kingston
Barham
Derringstone
Womenswold
Barfrestone
Eythorne
Warmlake
Kingswood
Lenham Heath
Charing
Challock
Godmersham
Sole Street
Waltham
Bossingham
Chart Corner
Chart Sutton
Sutton Valence
Ulcombe
Grafty Green
Boughton Malherbe
Charing Heath
Westwell Leacon
Westwell
Boughton Aluph
Bilting
Crundale
Elham Valley Vineyard
Woolage Green
Shepherdswell
Coxhill
Rabbit's Cross
Egerton
Little Chart
Ram Lane
Goat Lees
Boughton Lees
Hassell Street
Wye
Stelling Minnis
Denton
Wingmore
Lydden
Coldred
Cross-at-Hand
Southernden
Egerton Forstal
Pluckley
Hothfield
Kennington
Bodsham
Elmsted
Wootton
Selsted
Lydden
Milebush
Hawkenbury
Headcorn
Pluckley Thorne
Godinton House
Brook
Hastingleigh
Elham
St John's Commandery
Temple Ewell
Ewell Minnis
Swingfield Street
Staplehurst
Marden Thorn
Sinkhurst Green
Smarden Bell
Maltman's Hill
Great Chart
Ashford
Conningbrook Lakes
Lymbridge Green
Rhodes Minnis
Swingfield Minnis
Crabble Corn Mill
Buckland
Knox Bridge
Iden Croft Herbs
Frittenden
Smarden
Haffenden Quarter
Wissenden
Willesborough
Sevington
Hinxhill
Willesborough Lees
Brabourne
Ottinge
Alkham
Drellingore
Densole
Kent Battle of Britain Museum
Lashenden
Bethersden
Brabourne Lees
Stowting
Lymínge
Paddlesworth
West Hougham
Farthingloe
Cranbrook Common
Three Chimneys
Standen
Stubbs Cross
Kingsnorth
Mersham
Smeeth
Postling
Etchinghill
Hawkinge
Capel le Ferne
Sissinghurst Castle
Biddenden
Tanden
Shadoxhurst
Cheeseman's Green
Sellindge
Sellindge Lees
Stop 24 Services
Beachborough
Channel Tunnel
Newington
East Cliff & Warren
East Wear Bay
Wilsley Pound
Cranbrook Museum
Union Mill
Sissinghurst
High Halden
Bromley Green
Aldington Frith
Clap Hill
Aldington
E. Stour
Stanford
Newingreen
Pedlinge
Elham Valley Rly Mus
Cheriton
Folkestone
Biddenden Vineyards
Henghurst
Cranbrook
East End
St Michael's
Shirkoak
Orlestone
Ham Street Woods
Bonnington
Court-at-Street
Port Lympne Wild Animal Park and Gardens
Lympne
Saltwood
Sandgate
Cliff Lift
Kent & East Sussex Railway
Parkgate
Woodchurch
South of England Rare Breeds Cen
Ruckinge
Bilsington
Brockhill
Hythe
Tenterden
Benenden
CM'Booth Collection
Leigh Green
Brook Street
Kenardington
Hamstreet
Military Canal
Royal
West Hythe
Palmarsh
Gill's Green
Colonel Stephens Railway Museum
Warehorne
Burmarsh
Iden Green
Dingleden
Rolvenden
Newchurch
Hawkhurst
Four Throws
Small Hythe
Reading Street
Appledore Heath
Horne's Place Chapel
Snave
Romney, Hythe and Dymchurch Railway
The Moor
Rolvenden Layne
Smallhythe Place
Isle of Oxney
Appledore
Romney Marsh
Dymchurch
Martello Tower
Sandhurst
Linkhill
Peening Quarter
Snargate
St Mary in the Marsh
Sandhurst Cross
Newenden
Wittersham
Stone
Brenzett
Ivychurch
Aeronautical Museum
Romney Warren
St Mary's Bay
Bodiam
Rother
Great Dixter
Ham Green
The Stocks
Rother Levels
Romney Marsh Visitor Centre
Brookland
Old Romney
Littlestone on Sea
TR
Salehurst
Rother Valley Rly
Ewhurst Green
Northiam
Beckley
Four Oaks
Iden
Houghton Green
New Romney
Romney Sands
Millcorner
Clayhill
Walland Marsh
Staple Cross
Peasmarsh
Rye Foreign
Greatstone on Sea
Horns Cross
Cripp's Corner
Playden
East Guldeford
Lydd
Lydd (London Ashford)
Vinehall Street
Tillingham
Rye
Denge Marsh
Lydd on Sea
Broad Oak
Broadland Row
Udimore
Rye Heritage Centre
Camber
Lydd International Raceway
Sedlescombe
Rye Harbour
Dungeness
Denge Beach
Sedlescombe Street
Brede
Brede Steam Giants
Winchelsea
Camber Castle
Dungeness
The Old Lighthouse
Guestling Thorn
Rye Bay
Icklesham
Winchelsea Court Hall Museum
Winchelsea Beach
Kent Street
Three Oaks
Westfield
Telham
Pett
Baldslow
Guestling Green
Cliff End
Crowhurst
Hollington
St Helen's
Ore
Fairlight
Hastings
Fairlight Cove
Combe Valley
Silverhill
St Clement's Caves
Fishermen's & Shipwreck Museums
Hastings Aquarium
St Leonards
Hastings
Bulverhythe
West Marina
Bexhill
English Channel
A229
A274
B2163
A20
M20
A252
A28
A251
A2
A260
B2068
A2070
A262
A268
B2086
B2082
B2080
B2067
A259
B2075
B2165
B2089
A21
A2100
A2036
B2092
B2244
A261
A256
A20
20
21
21
C
D
E
F
G
H
6
7
8
9
10
11

SN
SS
SWANSEA
NEATH
PORT TALBOT
(CASTELL-NEDD PORT TALBOT)
RHONDDA CYNON TAF
(RHONDDA CYNON TAF)
BRIDGEND
(PEN-Y-BONT AR OGWR)
VALE OF GLAMORGAN
(BRO MORGANNWG)
SWANSEA BAY
BAE ABERTAWE
MÔR HAFREN
BRISTOL CHANNEL
EXMOOR
EXMOOR FOREST
NATIONAL PARK
BRENDON HILLS
BRENDON FOREST
Swansea
(ABERTAWE)
Neath
(CASTELL-NEDD)
Port Talbot
Bridgend
(Pen-y-bont ar Ogwr)
Porthcawl
MAESTEG
ABERDARE
(ABERDÂR)
MOUNTAIN ASH
(ABERPENNAR)
RHONDDA
PONTYPRIDD
Merthyr Tydfil
(Merthyr Tudful)
Pontarddulais
Gorseinon
Clydach
Pontardawe
Ystalyfera
Glyn-neath
(Glynedd)
Hirwaun
Baglan
Margam
Pyle
(Y Pîl)
Pencoed
Llantrisant
Cowbridge
(Y Bont-Faen)
Llantwit Major
(Llanilltud Fawr)
Rhoose
(Y Rhws)
Ogmore-by-Sea
St Brides Major
The Mumbles
(Y Mwmbwls)
Mumbles Hd.
Trwyn yr Mwmbwls
Pwlldu Hd.
Pen Pwlldu
Nash Pt.
Trwyn yr As
Breaksea Pt.
Trwyn Breaksea
Tusker Rock
Foreland Pt.
Highveer Pt.
Lynmouth
Lynton
Countisbury
Porlock
Porlock Bay
Hurlstone Pt.
Minehead
Dunster
Watchet
Williton
Blue Anchor Bay
Combe Martin
Barnstaple
Simonsbath
Exford
Withypool
Winsford
Dunkery Beacon
Wheddon Cross
6 miles
10km

MONMOUTHSHIRE
SIR FYNWY
TORFAEN
(TOR-FAEN)
CAERPHILLY
(CAERFFILI)
NEWPORT
(CASNEWYDD)
NORTH SOMERSET
BRISTOL
ABER HAFREN
MOUTH OF THE SEVERN
ST
SO
BRIDGWATER BAY
MENDIP HILLS
POLDEN HILLS
QUANTOCK HILLS
Blaina
Rhymney
(Rhymni)
Tredegar
Abertillery
(Abertyleri)
Abersychan
PONTYPOOL
(PONT-Y-PWL)
Usk
(Brynbuga)
Raglan
Bargoed
Blackwood
(Coed Duon)
Cwmbran
(Cwmbrân)
Risca
(Rhisga)
Caerleon
(Caerllion)
Newport
(Casnewydd)
Chepstow
(Cas-gwent)
Caldicot
Lydney
Thornbury
CAERPHILLY
(CAERFFILI)
CARDIFF
(CAERDYDD)
PENARTH
BARRY
(Y BARRI)
Portishead
Clevedon
Avonmouth
FILTON
Bristol
Nailsea
Yatton
Keynsham
Weston-super-Mare
Cheddar
Wells
Burnham-on-Sea
Highbridge
Bridgwater
Glastonbury
Street
Shepton Mallet
Steep Holm
Flat Holm
Sully Island
Ynys Sili
Hinkley Point
Power Station
Severn Beach
PRINCE OF WALES BRIDGE
SEVERN ROAD BRIDGE
PONT HAFREN
25
16
7
8

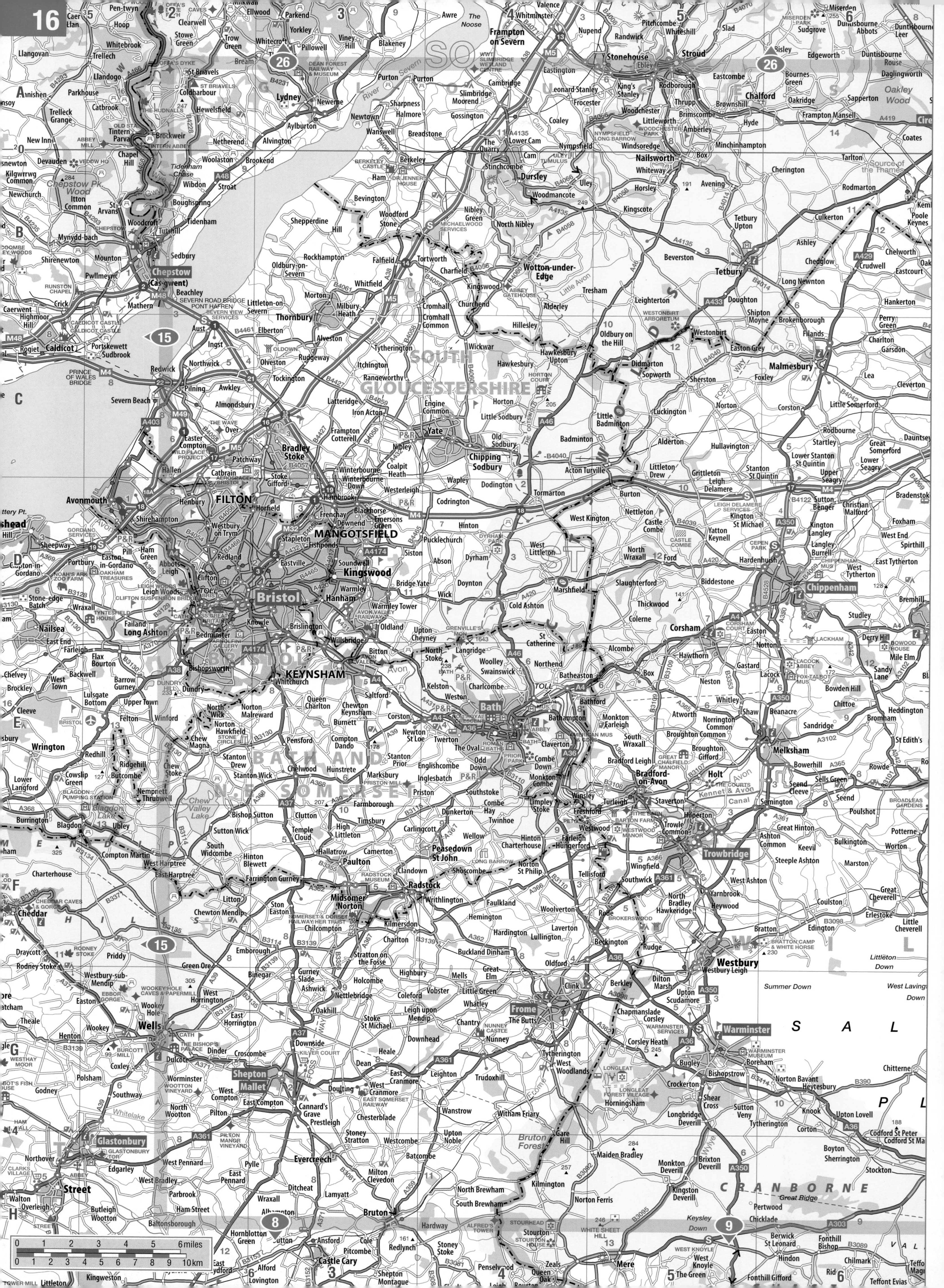
Stroud
Stonehouse
Dursley
Nailsworth
Tetbury
Malmesbury
Chepstow (Cas-gwent)
Lydney
Thornbury
Wotton-under-Edge
SOUTH GLOUCESTERSHIRE
Yate
Chipping Sodbury
FILTON
Bradley Stoke
MANGOTSFIELD
Kingswood
Bristol
Avonmouth
Portishead
Nailsea
KEYNSHAM
Bath
Chippenham
Corsham
Melksham
Bradford-on-Avon
Trowbridge
Westbury
Warminster
Frome
Radstock
Midsomer Norton
Paulton
BATH AND N.E. SOMERSET
Cheddar
Wells
Shepton Mallet
Glastonbury
Street
Bruton
Castle Cary
Mere
Caldicot
CRANBORNE
0 1 2 3 4 5 6 miles
0 1 2 3 4 5 6 7 8 9 10km

Carterton
Oxford
ABINGDON-ON-THAMES
Fairford
Lechlade-on-Thames
Faringdon
Highworth
Cricklade
South Cerney
Swindon
Stratton St Margaret
Royal Wootton Bassett
Wantage
Didcot
VALE OF WHITE HORSE
LAMBOURN DOWNS
Lambourn
Calne
Marlborough
Hungerford
Newbury
Thatcham
MARLBOROUGH DOWNS
Savernake Forest
Devizes
Pewsey
VALE OF PEWSEY
Pewsey Down
Tidworth
Ludgershall
Collingbourne Forest
Andover
Whitchurch
Overton
Durrington
Amesbury
Bulford
Stockbridge
Kings Worthy
Harewood Forest
Doles Wood
WILTSHIRE
BERKSHIRE
SALISBURY PLAIN
Swindon
Marlborough
Newbury
Andover

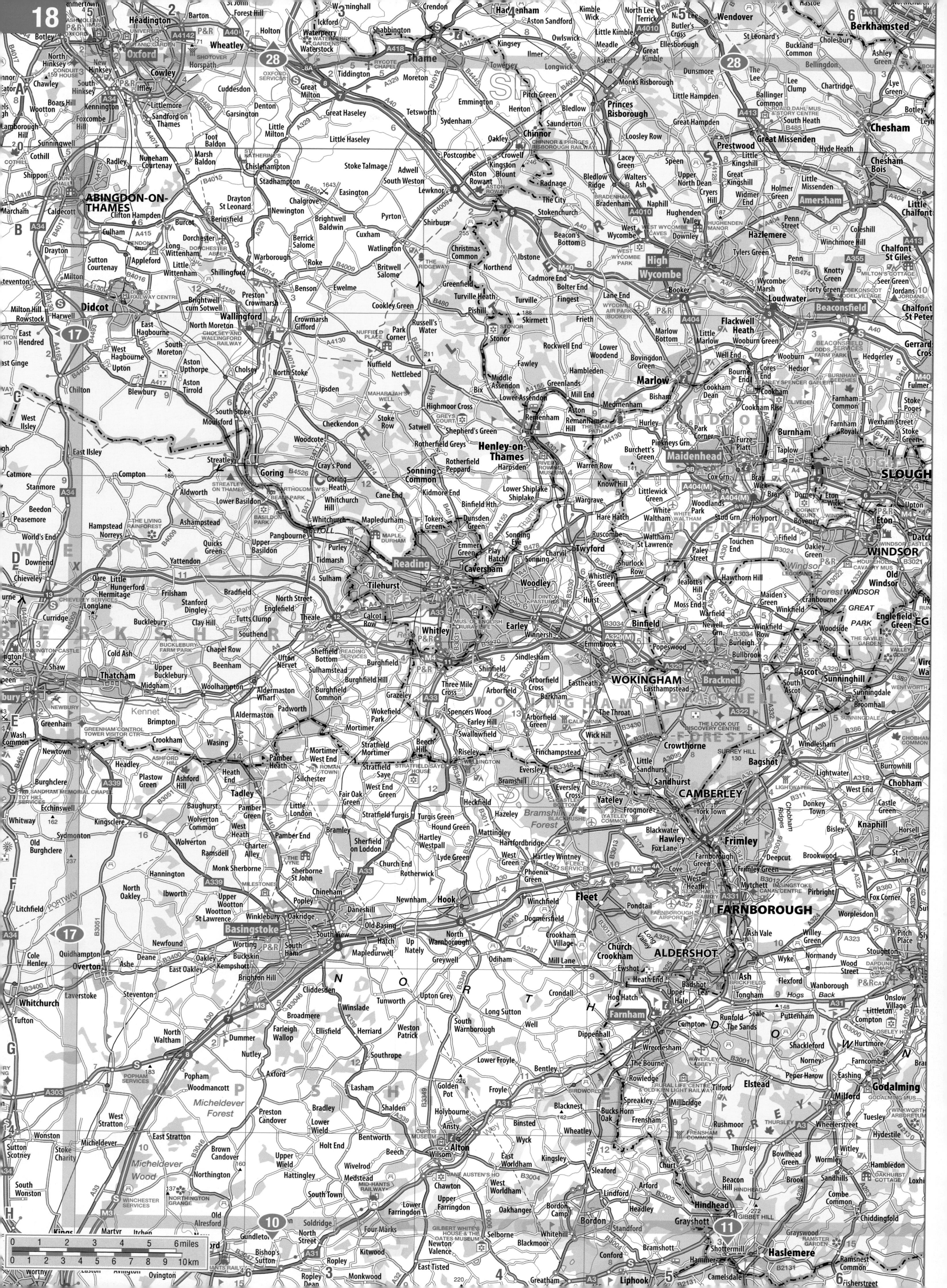
Headington
Oxford
Botley
Cowley
North Hinksey
Iffley
Littlemore
Kennington
Sandford on Thames
Wheatley
Holton
Forest Hill
Barton
Horspath
Cuddesdon
Garsington
Denton
Toot Baldon
Marsh Baldon
Nuneham Courtenay
Radley
Sunningwell
Abingdon-on-Thames
Culham
Clifton Hampden
Drayton
Sutton Courtenay
Appleford
Long Wittenham
Little Wittenham
Dorchester
Berinsfield
Drayton St Leonard
Chislehampton
Stadhampton
Milton
Didcot
Harwell
East Hagbourne
West Hagbourne
Brightwell cum Sotwell
Wallingford
North Moreton
South Moreton
Aston Upthorpe
Aston Tirrold
Blewbury
Cholsey
North Stoke
South Stoke
Moulsford
Streatley
Goring
East Ilsley
West Ilsley
Chilton
Compton
Aldworth
Hampstead Norreys
Yattendon
Ashampstead
Upper Basildon
Pangbourne
Purley
Tidmarsh
Sulham
Bradfield
Frilsham
Hermitage
Chieveley
Curridge
Bucklebury
Stanford Dingley
Englefield
Theale
Calcot Row
Tilehurst
Reading
Caversham
Earley
Woodley
Whitley
Shinfield
Three Mile Cross
Thatcham
Midgham
Woolhampton
Aldermaston
Aldermaston Wharf
Padworth
Burghfield
Burghfield Common
Mortimer
Stratfield Mortimer
Mortimer West End
Silchester
Pamber Heath
Tadley
Baughurst
Kingsclere
Headley
Greenham
Newtown
Crookham
Brimpton
Wasing
Burghclere
Old Burghclere
Ecchinswell
Sydmonton
Whitway
Hannington
North Oakley
Ibworth
Wolverton
Ramsdell
Monk Sherborne
Charter Alley
Sherborne St John
Chineham
Basingstoke
Popley
Oakridge
Winklebury
Worting
South Ham
Old Basing
Hatch
Up Nately
North Warnborough
Hook
Newnham
Odiham
Greywell
Mapledurwell
Cliddesden
Winslade
Tunworth
Upton Grey
Herriard
Ellisfield
Farleigh Wallop
Dummer
North Waltham
Nutley
Axford
Preston Candover
Bradley
Lower Wield
Upper Wield
Bentworth
Lasham
Shalden
Alton
Holybourne
Chawton
Four Marks
Ropley
Medstead
Selborne
Newton Valence
East Tisted
Bordon
Whitehill
Headley
Arford
Lindford
Grayshott
Hindhead
Haslemere
Liphook
Greatham
Frensham
Churt
Tilford
Elstead
Milford
Godalming
Farncombe
Puttenham
Seale
Tongham
Farnham
Aldershot
Ash
Farnborough
Fleet
Church Crookham
Crondall
Hartley Wintney
Yateley
Sandhurst
Camberley
Frimley
Bagshot
Lightwater
Windlesham
Chobham
Knaphill
Worplesdon
Sunninghill
Ascot
Bracknell
Wokingham
Binfield
Crowthorne
Finchampstead
Arborfield
Eversley
Riseley
Swallowfield
Windsor
Old Windsor
Eton
Slough
Maidenhead
Cookham
Bourne End
Marlow
Henley-on-Thames
Twyford
Wargrave
Sonning
Hurst
Sonning Common
Woodcote
Checkendon
Nettlebed
Benson
Ewelme
Watlington
Chalgrove
Thame
Chinnor
Princes Risborough
Wendover
Great Missenden
Prestwood
Chesham
Amersham
Beaconsfield
High Wycombe
Hazlemere
Stokenchurch
Lewknor
Tetsworth
Great Haseley
Great Milton
Berkhamsted
Kingsey
Haddenham
Wokingham
Reading
Windsor Great Park
Micheldever Forest
Micheldever Wood
Stratton
East Stratton
Sutton Scotney
South Wonston
Overton
Whitchurch
Laverstoke
Tufton
Steventon
Oakley
Deane
Popham
Woodmancott
Brown Candover
Northington
Old Alresford
Bishop's Sutton
Oxford
Didcot
Basingstoke
Farnham
Bracknell
Maidenhead
High Wycombe
Amersham
Beaconsfield
0 1 2 3 4 5 6 miles
0 1 2 3 4 5 6 7 8 9 10 km

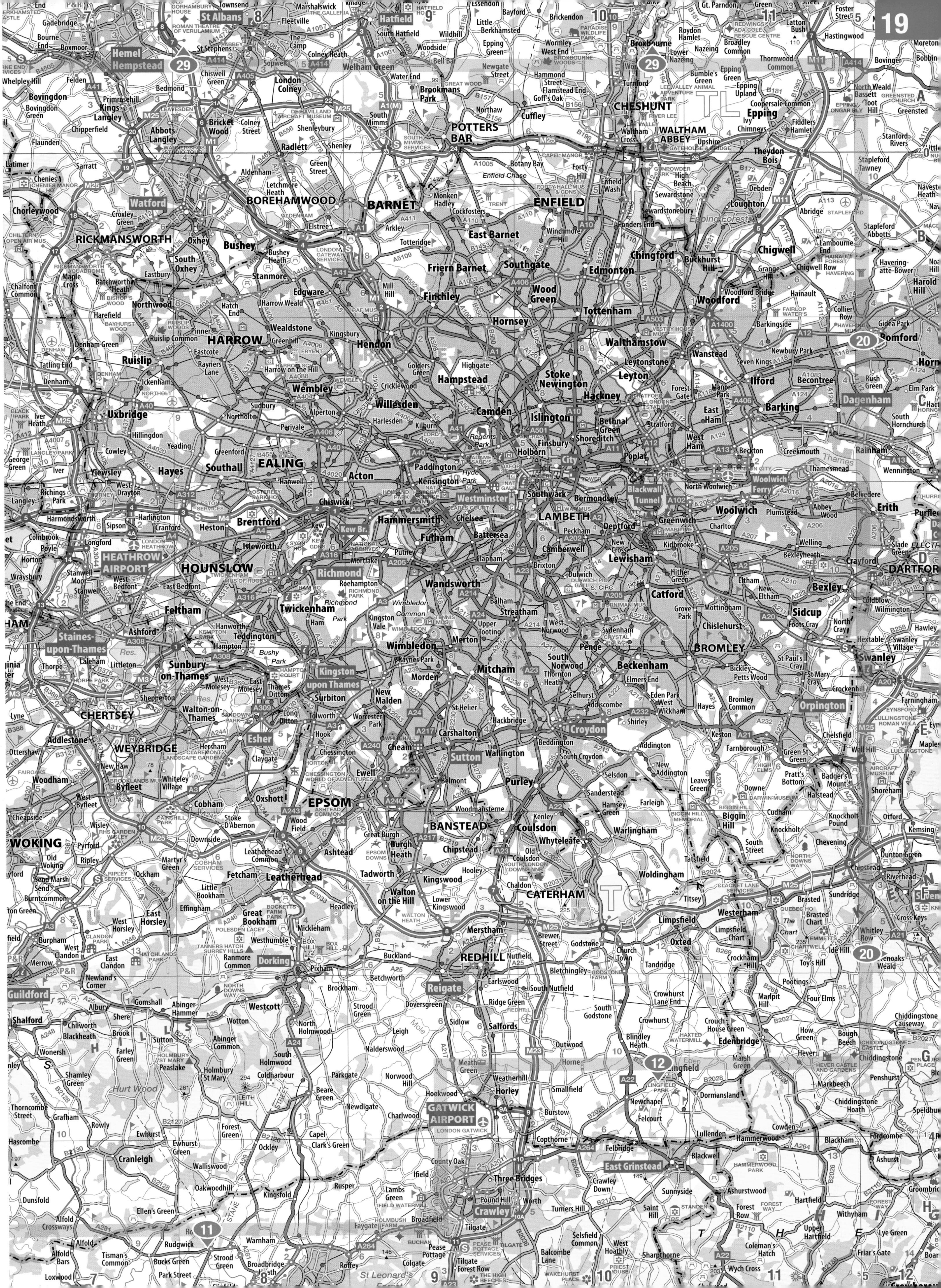
St Albans
Hatfield
Hemel Hempstead
Watford
BOREHAMWOOD
BARNET
ENFIELD
CHESHUNT
WALTHAM ABBEY
POTTERS BAR
Epping
Loughton
RICKMANSWORTH
HARROW
Ruislip
Uxbridge
Wembley
Hendon
Finchley
Edgware
Tottenham
Walthamstow
Woodford
Chingford
Edmonton
Hornsey
Hampstead
Camden
Islington
Hackney
Stoke Newington
Ilford
Barking
Romford
Dagenham
EALING
Southall
Hayes
Acton
Willesden
Paddington
Westminster
City
Kensington
Hammersmith
Fulham
Chelsea
Battersea
Southwark
LAMBETH
Bermondsey
Deptford
Greenwich
Woolwich
Lewisham
Catford
Blackwall Tunnel
Erith
Bexley
Sidcup
DARTFORD
HEATHROW AIRPORT
HOUNSLOW
Brentford
Richmond
Twickenham
Feltham
Staines-upon-Thames
Wandsworth
Streatham
Wimbledon
Merton
Mitcham
BROMLEY
Beckenham
Swanley
Orpington
Kingston upon Thames
Sunbury-on-Thames
Surbiton
CHERTSEY
WEYBRIDGE
Esher
Croydon
Sutton
EPSOM
Purley
Coulsdon
BANSTEAD
WOKING
Leatherhead
CATERHAM
Dorking
REDHILL
Reigate
Guildford
Oxted
Edenbridge
Horley
GATWICK AIRPORT
Crawley
East Grinstead
Cranleigh
Sevenoaks

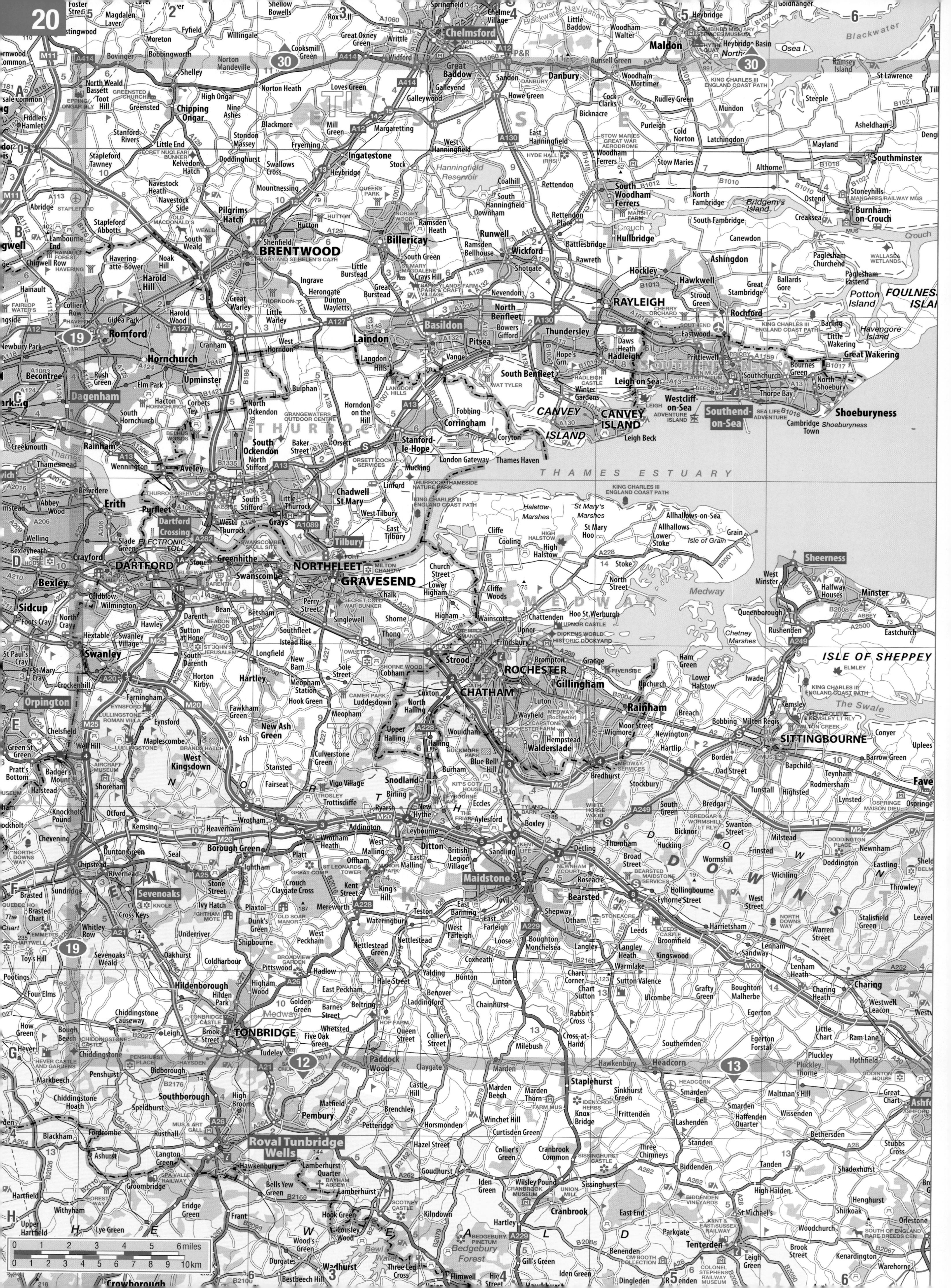
Chelmsford
Maldon
Great Baddow
Danbury
Heybridge
Osea I.
Blackwater
Chipping Ongar
Ingatestone
Billericay
BRENTWOOD
Wickford
Runwell
South Woodham Ferrers
Burnham-on-Crouch
Southminster
Hullbridge
Hockley
Hawkwell
Ashingdon
RAYLEIGH
Rochford
FOULNESS ISLAND
Romford
Hornchurch
Upminster
Dagenham
Laindon
Basildon
Pitsea
Thundersley
Hadleigh
SOUTHEND-ON-SEA
Leigh on Sea
Westcliff-on-Sea
Southend-on-Sea
Shoeburyness
Great Wakering
CANVEY ISLAND
Stanford-le-Hope
Corringham
Rainham
South Ockendon
Aveley
Purfleet
Erith
Grays
Tilbury
Dartford Crossing
DARTFORD
Bexley
Sidcup
Swanley
Orpington
Greenhithe
Swanscombe
NORTHFLEET
GRAVESEND
THAMES ESTUARY
Allhallows-on-Sea
Isle of Grain
Sheerness
Minster
Queenborough
ISLE OF SHEPPEY
Eastchurch
Strood
ROCHESTER
CHATHAM
Gillingham
Rainham
SITTINGBOURNE
Faversham
Snodland
Walderslade
Sevenoaks
Borough Green
West Malling
Maidstone
Bearsted
Lenham
Charing
TONBRIDGE
Paddock Wood
Headcorn
Staplehurst
Marden
Southborough
Royal Tunbridge Wells
Pembury
Cranbrook
Biddenden
Tenterden
Hawkhurst
Wadhurst
Crowborough
Ashford
Bedgebury Forest
1 2 3 4 5 6 miles
0 1 2 3 4 5 6 7 8 9 10 km

TM
TR
Bradwell Waterside
Bradwell on Sea
St Peter's on the Wall
Dengie
Ray Sand
King Charles III England Coast Path
Montsale
Deal Hall
Foulness Sand
Foulness Pt.
Courtsend
Churchend
Maplin Sands
Warden Pt.
Warden
Leysdown-on-Sea
Shell Ness
Isle of Harty
The Swale
WHITSTABLE
HERNE BAY
Tankerton
Swalecliffe
Seasalter
Chestfield
Greenhill
Herne
Beltinge
Broomfield
Hillborough
Reculver
Reculver Towers and Roman Fort
Minnis Bay
Birchington
Westgate on Sea
Margate
Turner Contemporary
The Shell Grotto
Cliftonville
Foreness Pt.
Dreamland
Kingsgate
North Foreland
Northdown
St Peter's
BROADSTAIRS
Dickens House Museum
Dumpton
Newington
Ramsgate
Maritime Museum
Manston
Northwood
Spitfire and Hurricane Mem
Powell-Cotton Museum
Isle of Thanet
Acol
St Nicholas at Wade
Sarre
Monkton
Minster
Cliffsend
Pegwell
Pegwell Bay
Sandwich & Pegwell Bay
St. Augustine's Cross
Boyden Gate
Hoath
Chislet
South Street
Yorkletts
Calcott
Upstreet
West Stourmouth
East Stourmouth
Westmarsh
Ware
Richborough Castle
Amphitheatre
Great Stonar
Sandwich
Sandwich Bay
Royal St. George's
Stone Cross
Graveney
Goodnestone
Dargate
Hernhill
Blean Woods
Mount Ephraim
Blean
Honey Hill
Broadoak
Hersden
Grove
Stodmarsh
Preston
Westbere
Sturry
Fordwich
Tyler Hill
Hales Place
Rough Common
Boughton Street
Dunkirk
Canterbury
Harbledown
Thanington
St. Augustine's Abbey
Wickhambreux
Wingham Wildlife Park
Elmstone
Hoaden
Ash
Guilton
Ickham
Littlebourne
Wingham
Marshborough
Woodnesborough
Howletts Wild Animal Park
Bekesbourne
Bramling
Staple
Gore
Eastry
Worth
Ham
Finglesham
Betteshanger
Sholden
Maritime and Local History Museum
DEAL
Deal Castle
The Downs
Walmer
Walmer Castle and Gardens
Kingsdown
Faversham
Preston
North Street
South Street
Oversland
Chartham Hatch
Selling
Old Wives Lees
Chartham
Shottenden
Badlesmere
Chilham
Shalmsford Street
Nackington
Street End
Patrixbourne
Adisham
Goodnestone
Goodnestone Park
Knowlton
Chillenden
Bridge
Lower Hardres
Garlinge Green
Bishopsbourne
Aylesham
Nonington
Easole Street
Snowdown
Tilmanstone
Elvington
Northbourne
Great Mongeham
Ripple
Sutton
East Studdal
Molash
Petham
Upper Hardres Court
Kingston
Barham
Womenswold
Barfrestone
East Kent Rly
Eythorne
Shepherdswell
Ringwould
Martin
Martin Mill
Challock
Godmersham
Sole Street
Crundale
Waltham
Derringstone
Bossingham
Woolage Green
Coxhill
West Langdon
East Langdon
Whitfield
Guston
St Margaret's at Cliffe
St Margaret's Mus
West Cliffe
The Pines Garden
St Margaret's Bay
Bilting
Boughton Aluph
Boughton Lees
Hassell Street
Wye Crown
Wye
Goat Lees
Elham Valley Vineyard
Stelling Minnis
Denton
Lydden
Wootton
Wingmore
Coldred
Lydden Temple Ewell
Temple Ewell
Ewell Minnis
St John's Commandery
Selsted
Swingfield Street
Kennington
Brook
Bodsham
Elmsted
Elham
North Downs Way
Conningbrook Lakes
Hinxhill
Willesborough Lees
Willesborough
Sevington
Lymbridge Green
Brabourne
Stowting
Brabourne Lees
Rhodes Minnis
Lyminge Forest
Ottinge
Lyminge
Swingfield Minnis
Alkham
Buckland
Crabble Corn Mill
Roman Painted House
Maxton
Drellingore
Farthingloe
West Hougham
Hawkinge
Densole
Kent Battle of Britain Museum
Paddlesworth
DOVER
Castle & Hellfire Corner
White Cliffs
South Foreland
Calais Dunkerque
Aycliff
Samphire Hoe
De Bradelei Wharf
Capel le Ferne
East Cliff & Warren
East Wear Bay
Kingsnorth
Mersham
Smeeth
Cheeseman's Green
Sellindge
Sellindge Lees
Stop 24 Services
Postling
Etchinghill
Beachborough
Stanford
CHANNEL TUNNEL
Newington
Aldington Frith
Clap Hill
Aldington
E. Stour
Bonnington
Court-at-Street
Newingreen
Lympne
Pedlinge
Elham Valley Rly Mus
Cheriton
Folkestone
Saltwood
Sandgate
Cliff Lift
Channel Tunnel
Ham Street Woods
Bilsington
Port Lympne Wild Animal Park and Gardens
Brockhill
Hythe
Ruckinge
West Hythe
Royal Military Canal
Hamstreet
Palmarsh
Burmarsh
Newchurch
Kent
North Downs
7
8
9
10
11
12
A
B
C
D
E
F
G
H
31
13
M2
M20
A2
A20
A28
A252
A256
A257
A258
A259
A261
A290
A299
A2990
A253
A255
B2231
B2068
B2046
B2050
B2190
B2052
B2011
B2067

SM
SR
PEMBROKESHIRE COAST
ARFORDIR PENFRO
PEMBROKESHIRE COAST PATH
LLWYBR ARFORDIR PENFRO
PEMBROKESHIRE (SIR BENFRO)
MYNYDD PRESELI
ST. BRIDES BAY
BAE SAIN FFRAID
ROSSLARE
Cardigan I. Ynys Aberteifi
Cemaes Head Pen Cemaes
Gwbert
Y Ferwig
MWNT
POPPIT SANDS
Cippyn
Cardigan (Aberteifi)
St Dogmaels
ABBEY
Bridgend
Moylgrove
Monington
Croft
Pen-y-bryn
Glanrhyd
Bridell
Llantood
Pontgareg
Rhos
Newport Bay
Bae Trefdraeth
Dinas Head
Berry Hill
Nevern
Felindre Farchog
PENGELLI FOREST
CASTELL HENLLYS FORT
Eglwyswrw
DYFED SHIRE HORSE FARM
Llanfair-Nant-Gwyn
Aton Nevern
Blae
Strumble Head Pen Caer
Tresinwen
PWLL DERI
Llanwnda
Fishguard Bay
Bae Abergwaun
Brynhenllan
NEWPORT PEMBROKESHIRE
Parrog
Goodwick (Wdig)
Lower Town
Dinas Cross
Newport (Trefdraeth)
CARNINGLI
Cilgwyn
TY CANOL
Crosswell
Pontyglasier
Eglwyswen
Penygroes
Trefasser
Penbwchdy
Dyffryn
Fishguard (Abergwaun)
Manorowen
St Nicholas
PEMBROKESHIRE COAST PATH LLWYBR ARFORDIR PENFRO
TREGWYNT WOOLLEN MILL
Llanychaer
Brynberian
Scleddau
Pontfaen
Ynysduellyn
Abercastle
Granston
Trecwn
Crymych
Penclegyr
Porthgain
Trefin
Mathry
Newbridge
FOEL-CWMCERWYN
Abereiddy
Llanrhian
Penparc
Castlemorris
CORSYDD LLANGLOFFAN
Pentre-galar
Croes-goch
New Inn
Rosebush
Mynachlog-ddu
ST. DAVID'S HEAD
PENMAEN DEWI
Tretio
Treffynnon
Treddiog
Letterston
Little Newcastle
Puncheston
Castlebythe
Glandwr
Treleddyd-fawr
Carnhedryn
Treglemais
Llanreithan
Welsh Hook
Tufton
Henry's Moat
Maenclochog
Hebron
Whitesand Bay
Porth-mawr
ST DAVID'S
BISHOP'S PALACE
Rhodiad
Caerfarchell
Llandeloy
St Dogwells
Glandy Cross
Llanglydwen
Rhosson
Whitchurch
Middle Mill
Trefgarn Owen
Hayscastle
Pont-yr-hafod
Wolf's Castle
Ambleston
Woodstock
Llangolman
Pant-y-Caws
CATHEDRAL
St David's (Tyddewi)
Nine Wells
Solva
Brimaston
Rinaston
Wallis
New Moat
Efailwen
Cefn
Ramsey Island
Ynys Dewi
Ramsey Sound
RAMSEY ISLAND
Hayscastle Cross
Mountain Water
Treffgarne
Triffleton
LLYS-Y-FRAN RESERVOIR
Llys-y-frân
Llanycefn
Maesgwyn
Penycwm
DUDWELL MT.
Leweston
Spittal
Walton East
Pen-ffordd
Login
Cross-hands
Newgale
SCOLTON MANOR
Llandissilio
Roch
Wolfsdale
Clarbeston
Hiraeth
Roch Gate
Camrose
Rudbaxton
Clarbeston Road
Bletherston
Henllan Amgoed
Llanfallteg
Keeston
Nolton Haven
Simpson Cross
Tangiers
Gelli
Clunderwen
Nolton
Pelcomb Cross
Crundale
Wiston
LLAWHADEN CASTLE
Bethesda
Druidston
Lambston
Slade
Haverfordwest (Hwlffordd)
Llawhaden
Robeston Wathen
Llanddewi Velfrey
Pelcomb Bridge
Portfield Gate
HAVERFORDWEST TOWN MUSEUM
The Rhos
Narberth (Arberth)
MUSEUM
Lampeter Velfrey
Haroldston West
BROAD HAVEN
Dreenhill
Uzmaston
Blackpool
Crinow
Broad Haven
Merlin's Bridge
Millin Cross
PICTON CASTLE & GARDENS
Little Haven
Broadway
Pope Hill
Boulston
Minwear
OAKWOOD
Cross Hands
Cold Blow
Princes Gate
Tavernspite
Talbenny
Walton West
North Johnston
Landshipping
Templeton
Tower Point
Trwyn Twr
Walwyn's Castle
Freystrop
Hook
Martletwy
St Bride's
Ludchurch
Llanteg
NATIONAL NATURE RESERVE
Wooltack Point
Trwyn Wooltack
Johnston
Landshipping Quay
Longstone
Skomer Island
Ynys Skomer
MARLOES SANDS
SKOMER ISLAND
Marloes
Hasguard
Tiers Cross
Robeston Cross
Llangwm
Black Tar
Yerbeston
FOLLY FARM
Reynalton
Broad Sound
Thornton
Rosemarket
Hill Mountain
Port Lion
Loveston
Thomas Chapel
Stepaside
COLBY WOODLAND GARDEN
Herbrandston
Steynton
Houghton
Cresswell Quay
Begelly
Gateholm Island
Ynys Gateholm
St Ishmael's
Sandy Haven
Milford Haven (Aberdaugleddau)
Honeyborough
Lawrenny
Cresselly
Jeffreyston
Kilgetty
Amroth
Dale
Hakin
Waterston
Neyland
Burton
West Williamston
Broadmoor
MILFORD HAVEN
ABERDAUGLEDDYF
Llanstadwell
UPTON CASTLE GARDENS
Carew Newton
East Williamston
Saundersfoot
Skokholm Island
Ynys Skokholm
Pembroke Dock (Doc Penfro)
Cosheston
CAREW CASTLE
Redberth
Carew
Broadfield
Angle
Angle Bay
Bae Angle
Pwllcrochan
PEMBROKE DOCK SUNDERLAND TRUST
Pennar
Milton
Carew Cheriton
Sageston
THE DINOSAUR PARK
New Hedges
St Ann's Hd.
Pentir St. Ann
Sheep Island
Ynys y Defaid
Rhoscrowther
Monkton
Pembroke (Penfro)
LAMPHEY BISHOP'S PALACE
MANOR WILDLIFE PARK
TUDOR MERCHANT'S HOUSE
Hundleton
Lamphey
St Florence
Gumfreston
Tenby (Dinbych-y-Pysgod)
Freshwater West
Maiden Wells
Jameston
Penally
Hodgeston
Freshwater East
Lydstep
Giltar Pt.
Castlemartin
St Twynnells
Caldey Sound
Warren
Cheriton or Stackpole Elidor
MANORBIER CASTLE
Manorbier
MANORBIER
Caldey Island
Ynys Bŷr
Linney Hd.
Pentir Linney
Merrion
St Petrox
Trewent Pt.
Trwyn Trewent
Old Castle Hd.
Stackpole
Chapel Pt.
Trwyn Capel
ELEGUG STACKS
Bosherston
STACKPOLE
Stackpole Hd.
Pen Stackpole
The Wash
St Govan's Hd.
Pen St Gofan
A40
A487
A478
A477
A4076
A4075
A4115
A4139
B4313
B4329
B4330
B4331
B4327
B4341
B4320
B4319
B4322
B4325
B4318
B4316
B4314
B4328
B4546
B4548
B4582
B4583
B4584
B4585
B4586
B4327
213
191
347
468
536
197
289
164
178
181
145
108
82
79
71
0 1 2 3 4 5 6 miles
0 1 2 3 4 5 6 7 8 9 10 km

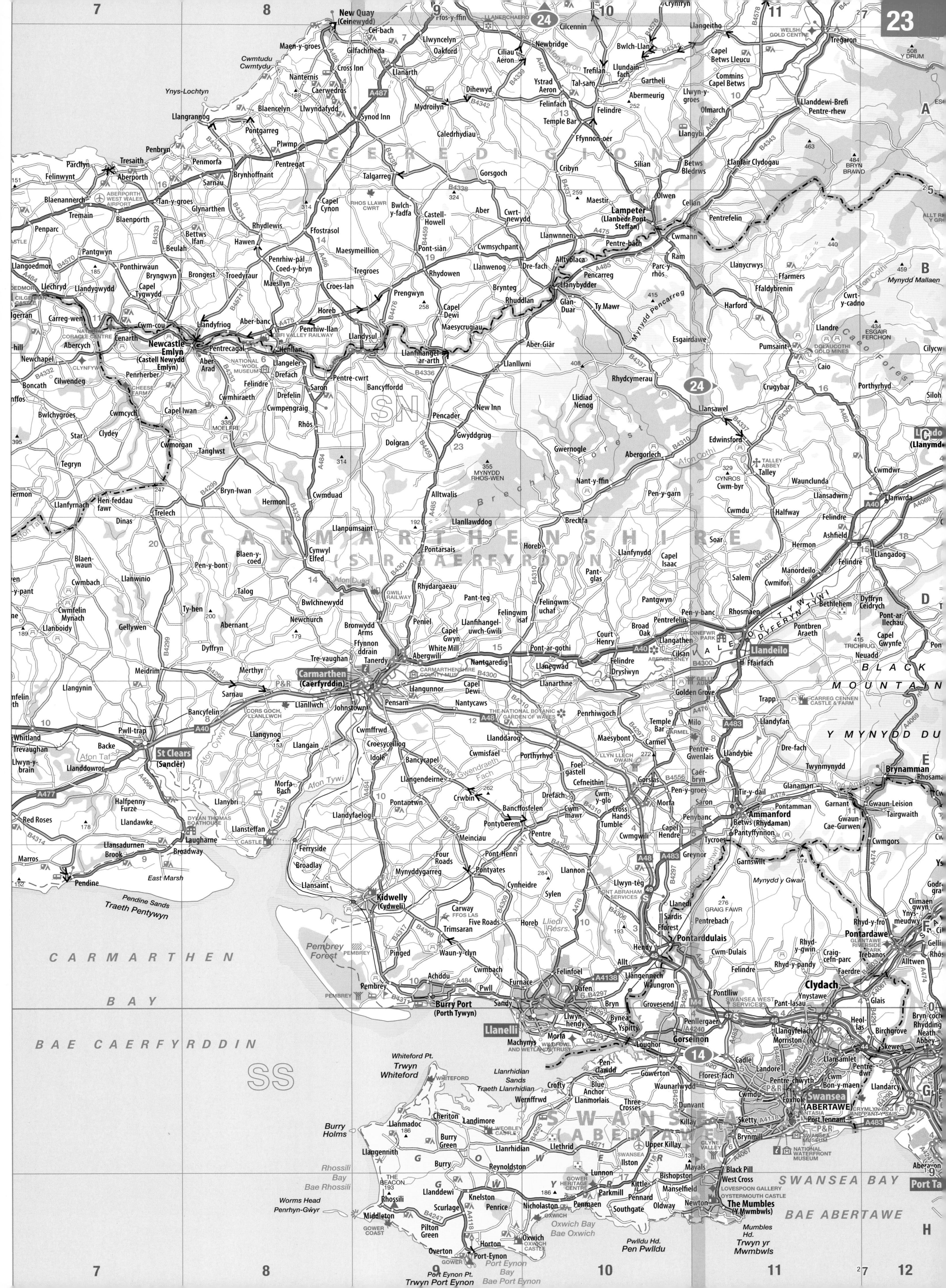
CEREDIGION
CARMARTHENSHIRE
(SIR GAERFYRDDIN)
SWANSEA
(ABERTAWE)
CARMARTHEN BAY
BAE CAERFYRDDIN
SWANSEA BAY
BAE ABERTAWE
BLACK MOUNTAIN
Y MYNYDD DU
SN
SS
New Quay
(Ceinewydd)
Aberaeron
Lampeter
(Llanbedr Pont Steffan)
Newcastle Emlyn
(Castell Newydd Emlyn)
Carmarthen
(Caerfyrddin)
St Clears
(Sanclêr)
Llandeilo
Ammanford
(Rhydaman)
Kidwelly
(Cydweli)
Burry Port
(Porth Tywyn)
Llanelli
Pontarddulais
Gorseinon
Swansea
(ABERTAWE)
The Mumbles
(Y Mwmbwls)
Pontardawe
Clydach
Brynamman
Tregaron
Llandysul
Aberporth
Llangrannog
Synod Inn
Llanybydder
Pencader
Brechfa
Talley
Llangadog
Llanwrda
Laugharne
Pendine
Ferryside
Llansteffan
Rhossili
Port-Eynon
Oxwich
Worms Head
Penrhyn-Gŵyr
Whiteford Pt.
Trwyn Whiteford
Burry Holms
Mumbles Hd.
Trwyn yr Mwmbwls
Port Eynon Pt.
Trwyn Port Eynon
Pwlldu Hd.
Pen Pwlldu
Pendine Sands
Traeth Pentywyn
Pembrey Forest
Llanrhidian Sands
Traeth Llanrhidian
Oxwich Bay
Bae Oxwich
Port Eynon Bay
Bae Port Eynon
Rhossili Bay
Bae Rhossili
Brechfa Forest
Caeo Forest
Mynydd Pencarreg
Mynydd Mallaen
Mynydd y Gwair
Afon Tywi
Afon Aeron
Afon Cothi
Afon Taf
A40
A48
A483
A484
A485
A487
A475
A476
A477
A4138
M4
24
14
7
8
9
10
11
12

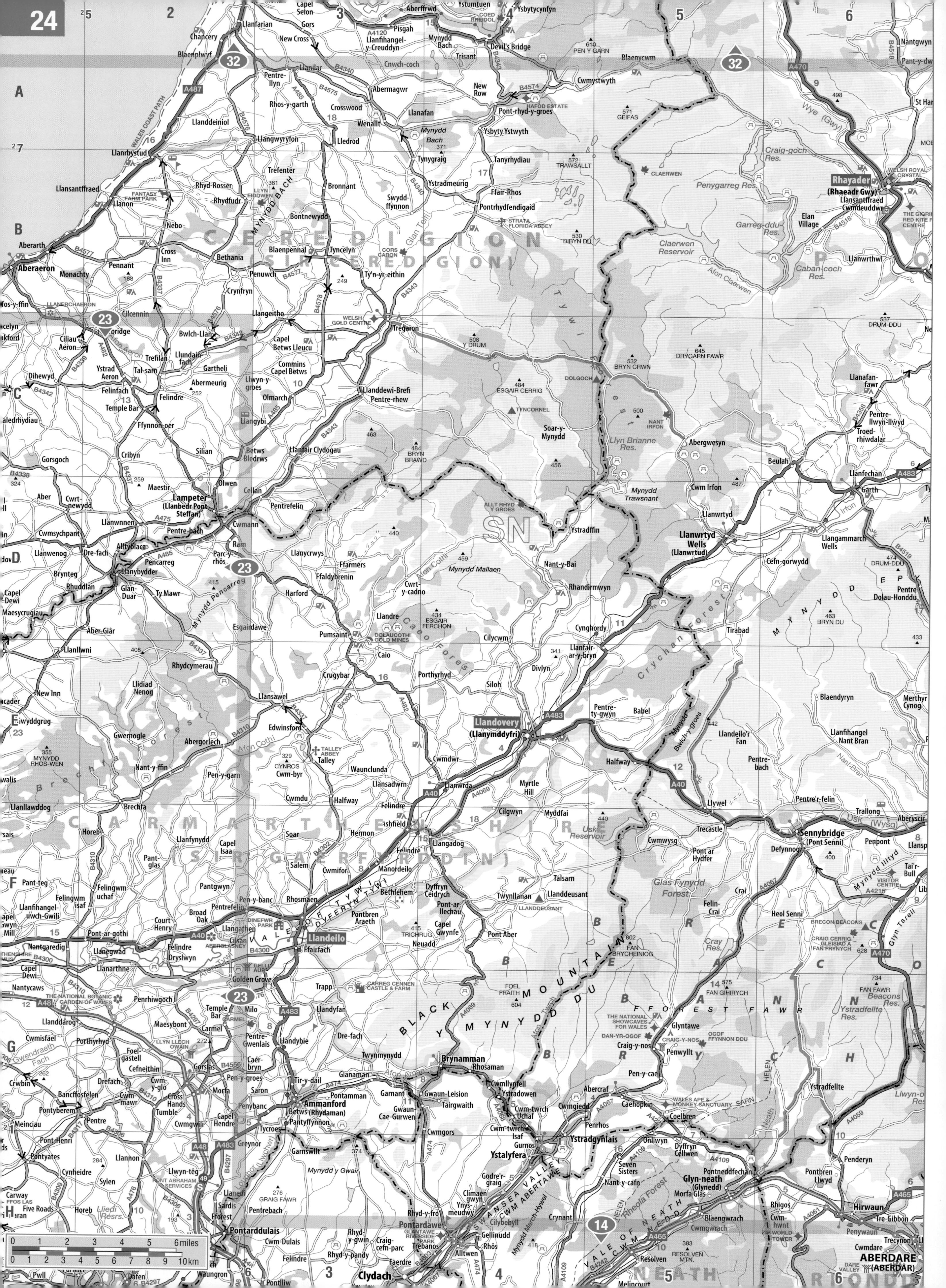
Llanfarian
Chancery
Blaenplwyf
Gors
New Cross
Aberffrwd
Pisgah
Llanfihangel-y-Creuddyn
Mynydd Bach
Trisant
Devil's Bridge
Ysbyty Cynfyn
Ystumtuen
Cnwch-coch
Llanilar
Pentre-llyn
Abermagwr
Rhos-y-garth
Crosswood
Llanafan
Wenallt
New Row
Pont-rhyd-y-groes
Hafod Estate
Cwmystwyth
Blaenycwm
Pen y Garn
Geifas
Llanddeiniol
Llangwyryfon
Lledrod
Ysbyty Ystwyth
Tynygraig
Tanyrhydiau
Trawsallt
Claerwen
Craig-goch Res.
Penygarreg Res.
Rhayader
(Rhaeadr Gwy)
Llansantffraed Cwmdeuddwr
Elan Village
Garreg-ddu Res.
Claerwen Reservoir
Caban-coch Res.
Afon Claerwen
Llanwrthwl
Wye (Gwy)
Nantgwyn
Pant-y-dwr
St Harmon
Llanrhystud
Trefenter
Rhyd-Rosser
Rhydfudr
Llyn Eiddwen
Mynydd Bach
Bronnant
Swydd-ffynnon
Ystradmeurig
Ffair-Rhos
Pontrhydfendigaid
Strata Florida Abbey
Dibyn Du
Llansantffraed
Fantasy Farm Park
Llanon
Nebo
Bontnewydd
Glan Teifi
Aberarth
Aberaeron
Monachty
Pennant
Cross Inn
Bethania
Blaenpennal
Tyncelyn
Cors Caron
Penuwch
Ty'n-yr-eithin
CEREDIGION
(SIR CEREDIGION)
Crynfryn
Llanerchaeron
Cilcennin
Llangeitho
Welsh Gold Centre
Tregaron
Ciliau Aeron
Bwlch-Llan
Capel Betws Lleucu
Y Drum
Bryn Crwn
Drygarn Fawr
Drum-ddu
Afon Aeron
Trefilan
Llundain-fach
Gartheli
Commins Capel Betws
Dolgoch
Dihewyd
Ystrad Aeron
Tal-sarn
Abermeurig
Llwyn-y-groes
Esgair Cerrig
Llanafan-fawr
Felinfach
Felindre
Olmarch
Llanddewi-Brefi
Pentre-rhew
Tyncornel
Nant Irfon
Pentre-llwyn-llwyd
Temple Bar
Ffynnon-oer
Llangybi
Soar-y-Mynydd
Llyn Brianne Res.
Abergwesyn
Troed-rhiwdalar
Silian
Betws Bledrws
Llanfair Clydogau
Bryn Brawd
Beulah
Gorsgoch
Cribyn
Maestir
Lampeter
(Llanbedr Pont Steffan)
Olwen
Cellan
Cwm Irfon
Mynydd Trawsnant
Llanfechan
Garth
Aber
Cwrt-newydd
Pentrefelin
Allt Rhyd y Groes
Llanwrtyd
Irfon
Llanwnnen
Cwmann
Pentre-bach
SN
Ystradffin
Llanwrtyd Wells
(Llanwrtud)
Llangammarch Wells
Cwmsychpant
Llanwenog
Dre-fach
Alltyblaca
Pencarreg
Llanybydder
Ram
Parc-y-rhôs
Llanycrwys
Ffarmers
Mynydd Mallaen
Nant-y-Bai
Cefn-gorwydd
Brynteg
Rhuddlan
Glan-Duar
Ty Mawr
Mynydd Pencarreg
Ffaldybrenin
Harford
Cwrt-y-cadno
Rhandirmwyn
Mynydd Epynt
Pentre Dolau-Honddu
Capel Dewi
Maesycrugiau
Esgairdawe
Llandre
Esgair Ferchon
Caeo Forest
Cynghordy
Bryn Du
Tirabad
Aber-Giâr
Pumsaint
Dolaucothi Gold Mines
Cilycwm
Llanfair-ar-y-bryn
Crychan Forest
Llanllwni
Rhydcymerau
Caio
Divlyn
Llidiad Nenog
Crugybar
Porthyrhyd
Siloh
New Inn
Llansawel
Llandovery
(Llanymddyfri)
Pentre-ty-gwyn
Babel
Blaendyryn
Merthyr Cynog
Gwyddgrug
Edwinsford
Mynydd Bwlch-y-groes
Llandeilo'r Fan
Llanfihangel Nant Bran
Gwernogle
Abergorlech
Afon Cothi
Cynros
Talley Abbey
Talley
Cwm-byr
Cwmdwr
Halfway
Pentre-bach
Mynydd Rhos-wen
Nant-y-ffin
Pen-y-garn
Waunclunda
Llansadwrn
Llanwrda
Myrtle Hill
Nant-Bran
Brechfa Forest
Cwmdu
Llywel
Pentre'r-felin
Trallong
Aberyscir
Llanllawddog
Brechfa
Felindre
Cilgwyn
Myddfai
Usk Reservoir
Trecastle
Sennybridge
(Pont Senni)
Penpont
Usk (Wysg)
Horeb
CARMARTHENSHIRE
(SIR GAERFYRDDIN)
Soar
Hermon
Ishfield
Llangadog
Cwmwysg
Defynnog
Llanfynydd
Capel Isaac
Pont ar Hydfer
Pant-glas
Salem
Cwmifor
Manordeilo
Talsarn
Mynydd Illtyd
Visitor Centre
Tai'r-Bull
Pant-teg
Felingwm uchaf
Pantgwyn
Rhosmaen
Bethlehem
Dyffryn Ceidrych
Twynllanan
Llanddeusant
Glas Fynydd Forest
Crai
Felingwm isaf
Pen-y-banc
Pentrefelin
Pontbren Araeth
Capel-ar-llechau
Felin-Crai
Llanfihangel-uwch-Gwili
Broad Oak
Court Henry
Llangathen
Dinefwr Park
Vale of Tywi
Dyffryn Tywi
Capel Gwynfe
Trichrug
Heol Senni
Brecon Beacons
Craig Cerrig Gleisiad a Fan Frynych
Pont-ar-gothi
Cilsan
Llandeilo
Pont Aber
Fan Brycheiniog
Cray Res.
Glyn Tarell
Nantgaredig
Llanegwad
Felindre
Dryslwyn
Aberglasney
Ffairfach
Neuadd
Capel Dewi
Llanarthne
Golden Grove
Carreg Cennen Castle & Farm
Foel Fraith
Black Mountain
Y Mynydd Du
Fan Gihirych
Fan Fawr
Beacons Res.
Ystradfellte Res.
Nantycaws
The National Botanic Garden of Wales
Penrhiwgoch
Trapp
Fforest Fawr
Temple Bar
Milo
Llandyfan
The National Showcaves for Wales
Dan-yr-Ogof
Glyntawe
Craig-y-nos
Ogof Ffynnon Ddu
Llanddarog
Maesybont
Carmel
Llandybie
Dre-fach
Penwyllt
Cwmisfael
Porthyrhyd
Llyn Llech Owain
Pentre-Gwenlais
Foel-gastell
Cefneithin
Twynmynydd
Brynamman
Rhosaman
Gorslas
Caer-bryn
Pen-y-groes
Pen-y-cae
Helen
Ystradfellte
Crwbin
Drefach
Cwm-y-glo
Glanaman
Afon Aman
Tir-y-dail
Cwmllynfell
Ystradowen
Abercraf
Llwyn-on
Bancffosfelen
Cwm-mawr
Cross Hands
Saron
Pontamman
Garnant
Gwaun-Leision
Tairgwaith
Cwmgiedd
Caehopkin
Wales Ape & Monkey Sanctuary
Sarn Helen
Neath
Pontyberem
Tumble
Penybanc
Ammanford
Betws (Rhydaman)
Gwaun-Cae-Gurwen
Cwm-twrch Uchaf
Coelbren
Meinciau
Pentre
Cwmgwili
Capel Hendre
Pantyffynnon
Tycroes
Cwmgors
Cwm-twrch Isaf
Gurnos
Ystradgynlais
Ystalyfera
Onllwyn
Dyffryn Cellwen
Pont-Henri
Pontyates
Greynor
Garnswllt
Mynydd y Gwair
Seven Sisters
Nant-y-cafn
Pontneddfechan
Glyn-neath
(Glynedd)
Morfa Glas
Penderyn
Pontbren Llwyd
Cynheidre
Sylen
Llannon
Llwyn-teg
Pont Abraham Services
Godre'r-graig
Swansea Valley
Cwm Abertawe
Rheola Forest
Rhigos
Hirwaun
Carway
Ffos Las
Five Roads
Horeb
Lliedi Resrs.
Llanedi
Graig Fawr
Pentrebach
Sardis
Fforest
Climaen gwyn
Ynys-meudwy
Rhyd-y-fro
Cilybebyll
Crynant
Vale of Neath
Cwm Nedd
Blaengwrach
Cwmgwrach
Cwm-hwnt
Zip World Tower
Tre-Gibbon
Penywaun
Trecynon
Cwmdare
Aberdare
(Aberdâr)
Pontarddulais
Cwm-Dulais
Rhyd-y-gwin
Craig-cefn-parc
Rhyd-y-pandy
Pontardawe
Glantawe Riverside Park
Trebanos
Gellinudd
Rhôs
Alltwen
Mynydd March-Hywel
Resolven
Resolven Mtn.
Felindre
Faerdre
Pontlliw
Clydach
Pwll
Dafen
Waungron
Melincourt
Neath
Wales Coast Path
0 1 2 3 4 5 6 miles
0 1 2 3 4 5 6 7 8 9 10 km

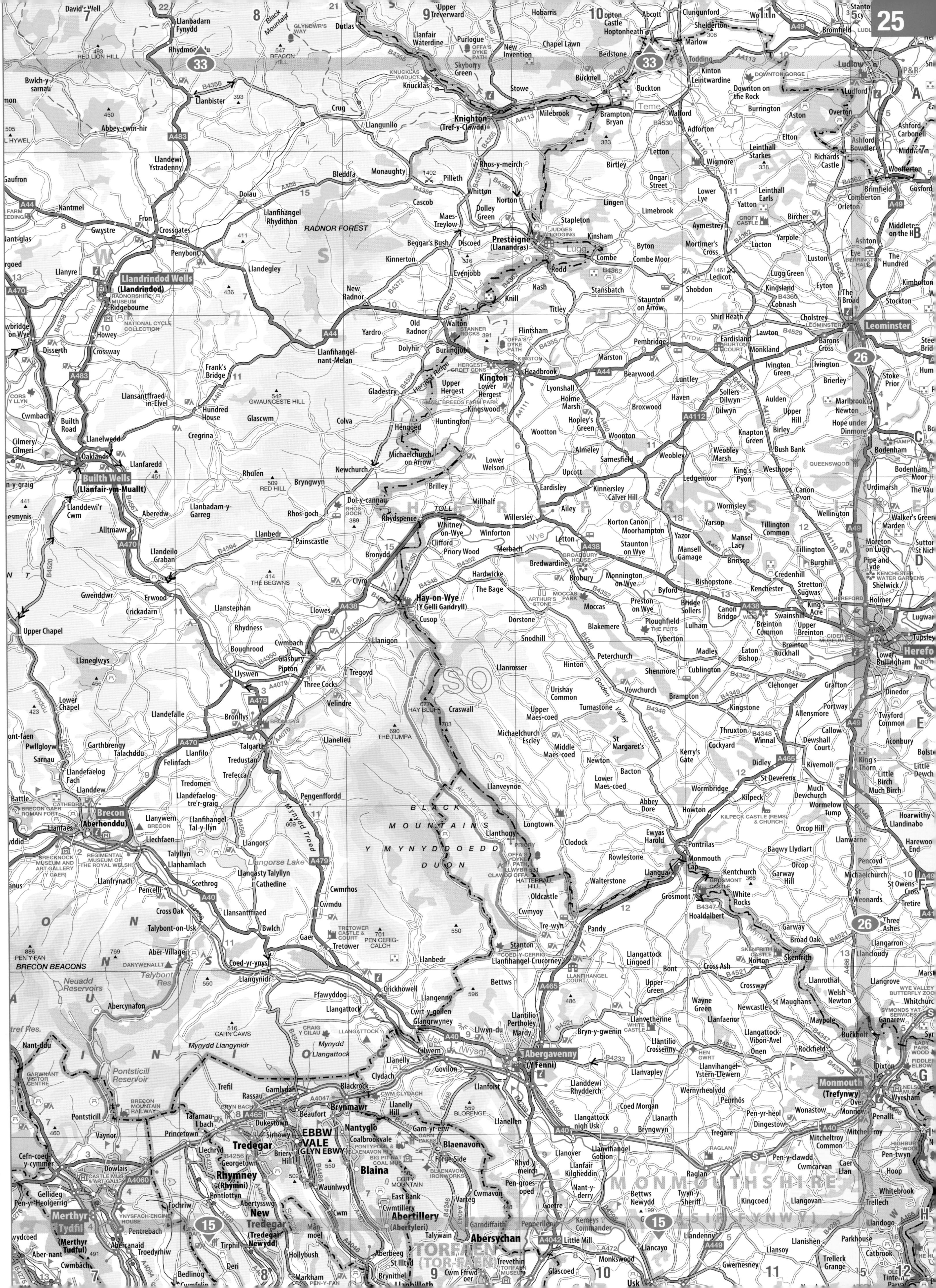

David's Well
Llanbadarn Fynydd
Rhydmeirionydd
RED LION HILL
Black Mountain
GLYNDWR'S WAY
BEACON HILL
Dutlas
Upper Treverward
Llanfair Waterdine
Purlogue
OFFA'S DYKE PATH
Hobarris
New Invention
Chapel Lawn
Clungunford
Shelderton
Marlow
Opton Castle
Hoptonheath
Abcott
Bedstone
Bucknell
Bromfield
Ludlow
Skyborry Green
KNUCKLAS VIADUCT
Knucklas
Stowe
Buckton
Todding
Kinton
Leintwardine
DOWNTON GORGE
Downton on the Rock
Ludford
Bwlch-y-sarnau
Llanbister
Crug
Llangunllo
Knighton (Tref-y-Clawdd)
Milebrook
Brampton Bryan
Walford
Burrington
Aston
Overton
Abbey-cwm-hir
Ashford Carbonell
Ashford Bowdler
Adforton
Elton
Letton
Leinthall Starkes
Richards Castle
Middleton
Llandewi Ystradenny
Monaughty
Pilleth
Rhos-y-meirch
Birtley
Ongar Street
Wigmore
Woofferton
Gaufron
Bleddfa
Whitton
Norton
Lingen
Lower Lye
Leinthall Earls
Yatton
Brimfield
Comberton
Orleton
Gosford
Nantmel
Dolau
Cascob
Dolley Green
Limebrook
Fron
Llanfihangel Rhydithon
Maes-Treylow
Stapleton
Aymestrey
CROFT CASTLE
Bircher
Middleton on the Hill
Gwystre
Crossgates
RADNOR FOREST
Presteigne (Llanandras)
JUDGES LODGING
Kinsham
Yarpole
Penybont
Beggar's Bush
Discoed
Mortimer's Cross
Byton
Lucton
Luston
Ashton
Llanyre
Llandegley
Kinnerton
Lugg
Combe
Combe Moor
Ledicot
Eye
BERRINGTON HALL
The Hundred
Llandrindod Wells (Llandrindod)
RADNORSHIRE MUSEUM
Ridgebourne
Evenjobb
Rodd
Nash
Stansbatch
Shobdon
Lugg Green
Kingsland
Eyton
Kimbolton
New Radnor
Knill
Titley
Staunton on Arrow
Cobnash
The Broad
Stockton
NATIONAL CYCLE COLLECTION
Howey
Old Radnor
Walton
STANNER ROCKS
Flintsham
Shirl Heath
Cholstrey
Leominster
Disserth
Yardro
Llanfihangel-nant-Melan
Dolyhir
Burlingjobb
OFFA'S DYKE PATH
Pembridge
Arrow
Eardisland
BURTON COURT
Lawton
Monkland
Barons Cross
Crossway
Frank's Bridge
HERGEST CROFT GDNS
Kington
Headbrook
Marston
Bearwood
Ivington Green
Ivington
Stoke Prior
Hergest Ridge
Upper Hergest
Lower Hergest
Gladestry
Lyonshall
Luntley
Sollers Dilwyn
Brierley
Aulden
Marlbrook
Newton
Llansantffraed-in-Elvel
GWAUNCESTE HILL
Hundred House
SMALL BREEDS FARM PARK
Kingswood
Holme Marsh
Broxwood
Haven
Dilwyn
Upper Hill
Hope under Dinmore
Cwmbach
Builth Road
Glascwm
Colva
Hengoed
Huntington
Hopley's Green
Wootton
Woonton
Knapton Green
Birley
Bodenham
Cilmery
Llanelwedd
Oaklands
Cregrina
Almeley
Sarnesfield
Weobley
Weobley Marsh
Bush Bank
Llanfaredd
Builth Wells (Llanfair-ym-Muallt)
Rhulen
RED HILL
Bryngwyn
Newchurch
Michaelchurch-on-Arrow
Lower Welson
Upcott
Ledgemoor
King's Pyon
Westhope
QUEENSWOOD
Bodenham Moor
Llanddewi'r Cwm
Aberedw
Llanbadarn-y-Garreg
Rhos-goch
Dol-y-cannau
Brilley
Eardisley
Kinnersley
Calver Hill
Canon Pyon
Urdimarsh
The Vauld
Alltmawr
RHOS GOCH
Rhydspence
TOLL
Millhalf
Aile
HEREFORDSHIRE
Wormsley
Wellington
Walker's Green
Marden
Llanbedr
Painscastle
Whitney-on-Wye
Clifford
Winforton
Willersley
Norton Canon
Moorhampton
Yarsop
Tillington Common
Moreton on Lugg
Llandeilo Graban
Bronydd
Priory Wood
Merbach
Wye
Letton
Staunton on Wye
Yazor
Mansell Lacy
Mansell Gamage
Brinsop
Tillington
Burghill
Pipe and Lyde
KENCHESTER WATER GARDENS
Shelwick
Erwood
THE BEGWNS
Clyro
Hardwick
The Bag
Bredwardine
BROADBURY HOUSE
Brobury
Monnington on Wye
Credenhill
Gwenddwr
Crickadarn
Llanstephan
Llowes
Hay-on-Wye (Y Gelli Gandryll)
Cusop
ARTHUR'S STONE
MOCCAS PARK
Moccas
Preston on Wye
Byford
Bishopstone
Kenchester
Stretton Sugwas
King's Acre
Holmer
Hereford
Upper Chapel
Rhydness
Dorstone
Blakemere
Ploughfield
THE FLITS
Bridge Sollers
Canon Bridge
Swainshill
Breinton Common
Upper Breinton
Breinton
CIDER MUSEUM
Lulham
Tyberton
Llaneglwys
Boughrood
Cwmbach
Glasbury
Pipton
Llanigon
Snodhill
Peterchurch
Madley
Eaton Bishop
Ruckhall
Lower Bullingham
Llyswen
Three Cocks
Tregoyd
Llanrosser
Hinton
Shenmore
Cublington
Clehonger
Grafton
Lower Chapel
Velindre
SO
HAY BLUFF
Craswall
Urishay Common
Vowchurch
Brampton
Kingstone
Dinedor
Llandefalle
Bronllys
BRONLLYS
Talgarth
THE TUMPA
Turnastone
Golden Valley
Upper Maes-coed
Michaelchurch Escley
Middle Maes-coed
St Margaret's
Thruxton
Winnal
Allensmore
Portway
Callow
Twyford Common
Garthbrengy
Talachddu
Felinfach
Llanfilo
Tredustan
Trefecca
Llanelieu
Newton
Kerry's Gate
Cockyard
Dewshall Court
Aconbury
Didley
Kivernoll
King's Thorn
Little Dewchurch
Little Birch
Much Birch
Pwllgloyw
Sarnau
Llandefaelog Fach
Llanddew
Tredomen
Llandefaelog-tre'r-graig
Pengenffordd
Llanveynoe
Lower Maes-coed
Bacton
St Devereux
Wormbridge
Kilpeck
Much Dewchurch
Wormelow Tump
Hoarwithy
Llandinabo
Battle
BRECON GAER ROMAN FORT
CATHEDRAL
Brecon (Aberhonddu)
Llanfaes
Llanywern
Llanfihangel Tal-y-llyn
Mynydd Troed
BLACK MOUNTAINS
Y MYNYDDOEDD DUON
Afon Honddu
Llanthony
PRIORY
Longtown
Abbey Dore
Howton
KILPECK CASTLE (REMS) & CHURCH
Orcop Hill
Llanwarne
Harewood End
Llechfaen
BRECKNOCK MUSEUM AND ART GALLERY (Y GAER)
REGIMENTAL MUSEUM OF THE ROYAL WELSH
Talyllyn
Llanhamlach
Llangors
Llangorse Lake
Llangasty Talyllyn
Cathedine
Llanfrynach
Pencelli
Scethrog
Clodock
Ewyas Harold
Pontrilas
Monmouth Cap
Rowlestone
Kentchurch
Bagwy Llydiart
Orcop
Pencoyd
Garway Hill
Michaelchurch
St Owens Cross
OFFA'S DYKE PATH
LLWYBR CLAWDD OFFA
HATTERRALL HILL
Oldcastle
Walterstone
Llangua
GROSMONT CASTLE
Grosmont
White Rocks
St Weonards
Tretire
Cross Oak
Talybont-on-Usk
Llansantffraed
Cwmrhos
Cwmdu
Cwmyoy
Tre-wyn
Pandy
Hoaldalbert
Garway
Broad Oak
Three Ashes
Llangarron
Llancloudy
Bwlch
TRETOWER CASTLE & COURT
PEN CERIG-CALCH
Stanton
COED-Y-CERRIG
Llanfihangel-Crucorney
Llangattock Lingoed
SKENFRITH CASTLE
Skenfrith
Norton
Cross Ash
Bont
PEN Y FAN
BRECON BEACONS
Aber-Village
DANYWENALLT
Talybont Res.
Coed-yr-ynys
Gaer
Tretower
Llanbedr
Bettws
LLANFIHANGEL COURT
Upper Green
Crossway
Llanrothal
Welsh Newton
Langrove
WYE VALLEY BUTTERFLY ZOO
Whitchurch
Neuadd Reservoirs
Llangynidr
Crickhowell
Ffawyddog
Llangattock
Llangenny
Cwrt-y-gollen
Glangrwyney
Wayne Green
Newcastle
St Maughans
Llanfaenor
Maypole
Abercynafon
GARN CAWS
Mynydd Llangynidr
CRAIG Y CILAU
LLANGATTOCK
Mynydd Llangattock
Llwyn-du
Llantilio Pertholey
Mardy
Bryn-y-gwenin
Llanvetherine
WHITE CASTLE
Llantilio Crossenny
Llangattock-Vibon-Avel
Onen
Rockfield
Buckholt
Ganarew
SYMONDS YAT SERVICES
Nant-ddu
Pontsticill Reservoir
GARWNANT VISITOR CENTRE
Usk (Wysg)
Gilwern
Llanelly
Clydach
Govilon
Abergavenny (Y Fenni)
Llanvapley
HEN GWRT
Llanvihangel-Ystern-Llewern
Trothi
Dixton
LADY PARK WOOD
FIDDLER ELBOW
Trefil
BRECON MOUNTAIN RAILWAY
Rassau
Garnlydan
Blackrock
CWM CLYDACH
Llanelly Hill
BLORENGE
Llanfoist
Llanddewi Rhydderch
Wernyrheolydd
Penrhôs
Monmouth (Trefynwy)
NELSON MUS
Wyesham
Over Monnow
Penallt
Pontsticill
Vaynor
Tafarnau-bach
BRYN BACH
Dukestown
Sirhowy
EBBW VALE (GLYN EBWY)
Beaufort
Brynmawr
Nantyglo
Garn-yr-erw
Coalbrookvale
PONTYPOOL & BLAENAVON RLY
BIG PIT NAT COAL MUS
Blaenavon
Llanellen
Llangattock nigh Usk
Coed Morgan
Llanarth
Bryngwyn
Pen-yr-heol
Dingestow
Wonastow
Tregare
Mitchel Troy
Mitchel Troy Common
HIGHBURY WOOD
Cefn-coed-y-cymmer
Princetown
Tredegar
Georgetown
Llechryd
Briery Hill
Blaina
COITY MOUNTAIN
Forge Side
BLAENAVON IRONWORKS
Llanover
Llanvihangel Gobion
Llanfair Kilgheddin
RAGLAN
Raglan
Pen-y-clawdd
Cwmcarvan
Caer Llan
Pen-twyn
Hoop
Dowlais
CASTLE MUS & ART GALL
Rhymney (Rhymni)
Pontlottyn
Abertysswg
Waunlwyd
East Bank
Cwmtillery
Varteg
Cwmavon
Rhyd-y-meirch
Pen-groes-oped
Nant-y-derry
MONMOUTHSHIRE
SIR FYNWY
Bettws Newydd
Twyn-y-Sheriff
Kingcoed
Llangovan
Whitebrook
Trellech
Gellideg
Pen-yr-Heolgerrig
YNYSFACH ENGINE HOUSE
Fochriw
New Tredegar (Tredegar Newydd)
Cwm
Abertillery (Abertyleri)
Goetre
Kemeys Commander
Llandenny
Llandogo
Merthyr Tydfil (Merthyr Tudful)
Pentrebach
Abercanaid
Troedyrhiw
Aber-nant
Cwmbach
Tirphil
Mân-moel
Talywain
Garndiffaith
Abersychan
Pennerlleni
Little Mill
Llancayo
Llanishen
Parkhouse
Catbrook
Deri
Hollybush
Aberbeeg
St Illtyd
TORFAEN (TOR-FAEN)
Trevethin
TORFAEN MUSEUM
Monkswood
Gwernesney
Llansoy
Trelleck Grange
Bedlinog
Markham
Brynithel
Cwm Ffrwd-oer
Glascoed
Usk
Tintern Parva

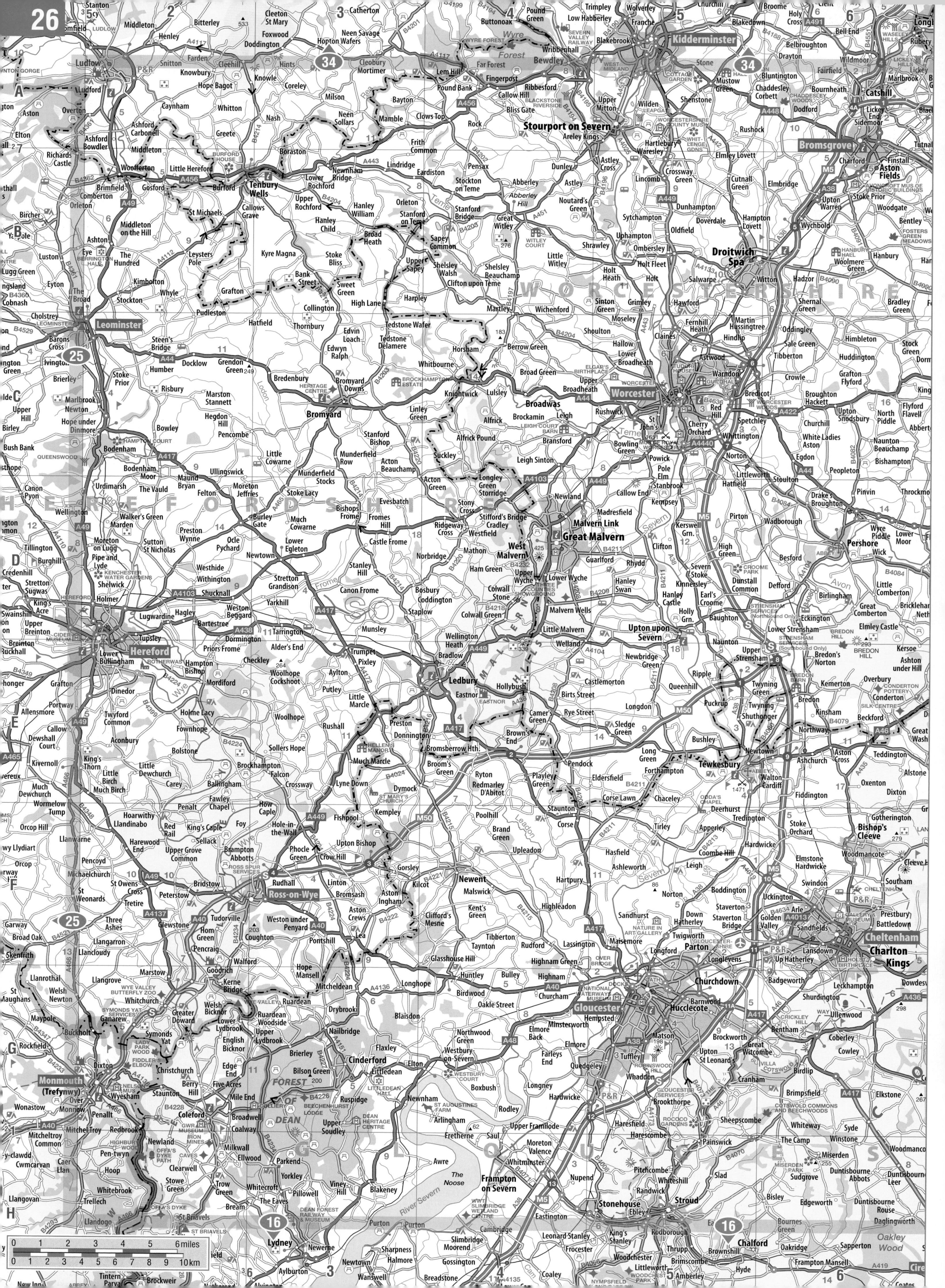

Ludlow
Middleton
Henley
Bitterley
Cleeton St Mary
Catherton
Buttonoak
Pound Green
Trimpley
Wolverley
Low Habberley
Franche
Blakedown
Broome
Holy Cross
Belbroughton
Bell End
Rubery
Foxwood
Doddington
Neen Savage
Hopton Wafers
Wyre Forest
Wribbenhall
Blakebrook
Kidderminster
Farden
Cleehill
Snitton
Hints
Cleobury Mortimer
Far Forest
Bewdley
Stone
Drayton
Wildmoor
Knowbury
Hope Bagot
Knowle
Coreley
Milson
Lem Hill
Pound Bank
Fingerpost
Callow Hill
Ribbesford
Bliss Gate
Upper Mitton
Wilden
Shenstone
Mustow Green
Chaddesley Corbett
Bluntington
Fairfield
Marlbrook
Catshill
Bournheath
Dodford
Lickey End
Sidemoor
Ludford
Caynham
Whitton
Bayton
Mamble
Clows Top
Rock
Stourport on Severn
Areley Kings
Hartlebury
Waresley
Rushock
Bromsgrove
Finstall
Aston Fields
Charford
Overton
Aston
Nash
Neen Sollars
Elton
Ashford Carbonell
Ashford Bowdler
Greete
Boraston
Frith Common
Elmley Lovett
Richards Castle
Middleton
Woofferton
Little Hereford
Tenbury Wells
Burford
Newnham Bridge
Lindridge
Eardiston
Pensax
Dunley
Astley Cross
Crossway Green
Cutnall Green
Elmbridge
Brimfield
Gosford
Comberton
Orleton
Lower Rochford
Upper Rochford
Stockton on Teme
Abberley
Astley
Lincomb
Noutard's Green
Dunhampton
Hampton Lovett
Upton Warren
Stoke Prior
Woodgate
Bircher
St Michaels
Callows Grave
Hanley William
Hanley Child
Orleton
Stanford on Teme
Stanford Bridge
Great Witley
Abberley Hill
Sytchampton
Doverdale
Oldfield
Wychbold
Bentley
Middleton on the Hill
Yarpole
Ashton
Luston
Eye
The Hundred
Leysters Pole
Kyre Magna
Broad Heath
Stoke Bliss
Sapey Common
Upper Sapey
Shelsley Walsh
Witley Court
Little Witley
Shrawley
Uphampton
Ombersley
Holt Fleet
Droitwich Spa
Hanbury
Woolmere Green
Lugg Green
Eyton
Kimbolton
Whyle
Bank Street
Sweet Green
Shelsley Beauchamp
Clifton upon Teme
Holt Heath
Holt
Salwarpe
Witton
Hadzor
Kingsland
Cobnash
The Broad
Stockton
Grafton
High Lane
Harpley
WORCESTERSHIRE
Pudleston
Collington
Martley
Wichenford
Sinton Green
Grimley
Hawford
Fernhill Heath
Martin Hussingtree
Sheral Green
Bradley Green
Cholstrey
Leominster
Hatfield
Thornbury
Tedstone Wafer
Moseley
Shoulton
Claines
Hindlip
Oddingley
Himbleton
Barons Cross
Ivington
Steen's Bridge
Docklow
Grendon Green
Edvin Loach
Tedstone Delamere
Edwyn Ralph
Horsham
Berrow Green
Hallow
Lower Broadheath
Astwood
Sale Green
Tibberton
Stock Green
Humber
Stoke Prior
Bredenbury
Bromyard Downs
Whitbourne
Broad Green
Upper Broadheath
Warndon
Huddington
Brierley
Risbury
Marston Stannett
Bromyard
Brockhampton Estate
Knightwick
Lulsley
Broadwas
Worcester
Crowle
Grafton Flyford
Marlbrook
Newton
Hegdon Hill
Linley Green
Alfrick
Brockamin
Leigh
Rushwick
St John's
Red Hill
Bredicot
Broughton Hackett
Flyford Flavell
Upper Hill
Hope under Dinmore
Bowley
Pencombe
Stanford Bishop
Alfrick Pound
Bransford
Cherry Orchard
Spetchley
Upton Snodsbury
North Piddle
Birley
Hampton Court
Bodenham
Little Cowarne
Munderfield Row
Acton Beauchamp
Suckley
Leigh Sinton
Bowling Green
Powick
Whittington
Churchill
White Ladies Aston
Naunton Beauchamp
Bush Bank
Queenswood
Bodenham Moor
Maund Bryan
Ullingswick
Munderfield Stocks
Acton Green
Longley Green
Storridge
Callow End
Pole Elm
Stanbrook
Norton
Littleworth
Egdon
Bishampton
Peopleton
Canon Pyon
Urdimarsh
The Vault
Felton
Moreton Jeffries
Stoke Lacy
Evesbatch
Stony Cross
Newland
Madresfield
Kempsey
Hatfield
Stoulton
Pinvin
Throckmorton
HEREFORDSHIRE
Wellington
Walker's Green
Marden
Burley Gate
Much Cowarne
Bishops Frome
Fromes Hill
Ridgeway Cross
Stifford's Bridge
Cradley
Westfield
Malvern Link
Great Malvern
West Malvern
Kerswell Grn.
Pirton
Wadborough
Drake's Broughton
Wyre Piddle
Pershore
Lower Moor
Tillington
Moreton on Lugg
Preston Wynne
Sutton St Nicholas
Ocle Pychard
Lower Egleton
Castle Frome
Norbridge
Mathon
Clifton
High Green
Besford
Wick
Burghill
Pipe and Lyde
Kenchester Water Gardens
Newtown
Westhide
Withington
Stanley Hill
Ham Green
Upper Wyche
Lower Wyche
Guarlford
Rhydd
Severn Stoke
Kinnersley
Croome Park
Dunstall Common
Defford
Little Comberton
Credenhill
Stretton Sugwas
Shelwick
Shucknall
Stretton Grandison
Canon Frome
Bosbury
Coddington
Colwall Stone
Three Counties Showground
Hanley Swan
Hanley Castle
Earl's Croome
Birlingham
King's Acre
Holmer
Hereford
Lugwardine
Hagley
Weston Beggard
Yarkhill
Colwall Green
Malvern Wells
Holly Grn.
Baughton
Eckington
Great Comberton
Elmley Castle
Swainshill
Upper Breinton
Bartestree
Dormington
Tarrington
Staplow
Munsley
Wellington Heath
Little Malvern
Upton upon Severn
Strensham Services
Lower Strensham
Bredon Hill
Breinton
Ruckhall
Priors Frome
Alder's End
Trumpet
Pixley
Bradlow
Welland
Naunton
Upper Strensham
Bredon's Norton
Kersoe
Ashton under Hill
Lower Bullingham
Hampton Bishop
Checkley
Woolhope Cockshoot
Aylton
Ledbury
Hollybush
Eastnor
Newbridge Green
Ripple
Overbury
Conderton
Grafton
Dinedor
Mordiford
Putley
Little Marcle
Castlemorton
Birts Street
Queenhill
Twyning Green
Kemerton
Allensmore
Twyford Common
Holme Lacy
Woolhope
Preston
Camer's Green
Rye Street
Longdon
Puckrup
Twyning
Shuthonger
Bredon
Kinsham
Beckford
Callow
Fownhope
Rushall
Donnington
Brown's End
Sledge Green
Northway
Great Washbourne
Dewsall Court
Aconbury
Sollers Hope
Hellens Manor
Bromsberrow Hth.
Pendock
Bushley
Newtown
Aston Cross
Teddington
Kivernoll
Bolstone
Little Dewchurch
King's Thorn
Brockhampton
Much Marcle
Broom's Green
Long Green
Forthampton
Tewkesbury
Ashchurch
Alstone
Little Birch
Much Birch
Carey
Ballingham
Falcon
Crossway
Ryton
Redmarley D'Abitot
Playley Green
Eldersfield
Walton Cardiff
Oxenton
Dixton
Much Dewchurch
Fawley Chapel
Lyne Down
Dymock
St Mary's Church
Corse Lawn
Chaceley
Odda's Chapel
Fiddington
Wormelow Tump
Penalt
How Caple
Kempley
Poolhill
Staunton
Deerhurst
Tredington
Hoarwithy
Llandinabo
Red Rail
King's Caple
Foy
Fishpool
Brand Green
Corse
Tirley
Apperley
Stoke Orchard
Gotherington
Orcop Hill
Llanwarne
Harewood End
Sellack
Hole-in-the-Wall
Upton Bishop
Upleadon
Hasfield
Hardwicke
Bishop's Cleeve
Wormbridge
Upper Grove Common
Brampton Abbotts
Phocle Green
Crow Hill
Coombe Hill
Woodmancote
Kilpeck
Orcop
Pencoyd
Ross Spur Services
Gorsley
Newent
Ashleworth
Leigh
Elmstone Hardwicke
Michaelchurch
St Owens Cross
Bridstow
Rudhall
Linton
Malswick
Hartpury
Norton
Boddington
Uckington
Southam
Cheltenham
St Weonards
Tretire
Peterstow
Ross-on-Wye
Bromsash
Kilcot
Aston Ingham
Kent's Green
Highleadon
Sandhurst
Down Hatherley
Staverton
Staverton Bridge
Arle
Golden Valley
Prestbury
Garway
Three Ashes
Glewstone
Tudorville
Aston Crews
Weston under Penyard
Clifford's Mesne
Nature in Art Gallery
Twigworth
Sandfields
Battledown
Broad Oak
Llangarron
Hom Green
Coughton
Pontshill
Lea
Tibberton
Taynton
Rudford
Lassington
Maisemore
Longford
Parton
Lansdown
Charlton Kings
Skenfrith
Llancloudy
Pencraig
Walford
Glasshouse Hill
Highnam Green
Over Bridge
Longlevens
Up Hatherley
Llanrothal
Llangrove
Marstow
Goodrich
Hope Mansell
Huntley
Bulley
Highnam
Churchdown
Leckhampton
St Maughans
Welsh Newton
Wye Valley Butterfly Zoo
Whitchurch
Kerne Bridge
Mitcheldean
Longhope
Birdwood
Churcham
National Waterways Museum
Gloucester
Barnwood
Hucclecote
Badgeworth
Dowdeswell
Symonds Yat Services
Ganarew
Greater Doward
Welsh Bicknor
Lower Lydbrook
Ruardean
Ruardean Woodside
Drybrook
Blaisdon
Oakle Street
Elmore Back
Minsterworth
Hempsted
Shurdington
Ullenwood
Maypole
Buckholt
Symonds Yat
English Bicknor
Upper Lydbrook
Nailbridge
Northwood Green
Westbury-on-Severn
Elmore
Matson
Brockworth
Crickley Hill
Bentham
Coberley
Rockfield
Lady Park Wood
Fiddler's Elbow
Christchurch
Edge End
Brierley
Cinderford
Flaxley
Farleys End
Quedgeley
Tuffley
Upton St Leonard's
Great Witcombe
Cowley
Dixton
Monmouth (Trefynwy)
Berry Hill
Five Acres
Bilson Green
Littledean
Elton
Westbury Court
Robinswood Hill
Whaddon
Cranham
Birdlip
Wonastow
Over Monnow
Wyesham
Staunton
Mile End
Forest of Dean
Ruspidge
Newnham
Boxbush
Longney
Hardwicke
Brookthorpe
Brimpsfield
Elkstone
Penallt
Mitchel Troy
Redbrook
Coleford
Broadwell
Coalway
Beechenhurst Lodge
Upper Soudley
Dean Heritage Centre
Littledean Hall
St Augustines Farm
Arlingham
Rodley
Upper Framilode
Haresfield
Harescombe
Rococo Gardens
Cotswold Commons and Beechwoods
Sheepscombe
Whiteway
Syde
Mitcheltroy Common
Highbury Wood
Newland
Offa's Dyke Path
Clearwell Caves
Milkwall
Ellwood
Parkend
Fretherne
Saul
Moreton Valence
Whitminster
Painswick
The Camp
Winstone
Woodmancote
Cwmcarvan
Pen-twyn
Caer Llan
Clearwell
Stowe Green
Yorkley
Awre
The Noose
Frampton on Severn
Nupend
Pitchcombe
Whiteshill
Slad
Miserden
Miserden Park
Sudgrove
Duntisbourne Abbots
Duntisbourne Leer
Hoop
Whitebrook
Trellech
Llangovan
Trow Green
Bream
Whitecroft
Pillowell
Viney Hill
Blakeney
River Severn
Randwick
Stroud
Stonehouse
Ebley
Eastington
Bisley
Edgeworth
Duntisbourne Rouse
Daglingworth
The Eaves
Dean Forest Railway Museum
Slimbridge Wetland Centre
Llandogo
St Briavels
Offa's Dyke
Lydney
Purton
Cambridge
Slimbridge
Moorend
Leonard Stanley
King's Stanley
Rodborough
Thrupp
Chalford
Bournes Green
Oakridge
Sapperton
Oakley Wood
Newerne
Sharpness
Halmore
Gossington
Frocester
Woodchester
Brimscombe
Brownshill
Frampton Mansell
Tintern Parva
Brockweir
Aylburton
Newtown
Wanswell
Breadstone
Coaley
Nympsfield
Littleworth
Woodchester Park
Amberley
Hyde
Coates
0 1 2 3 4 5 6 miles
0 1 2 3 4 5 6 7 8 9 10 km

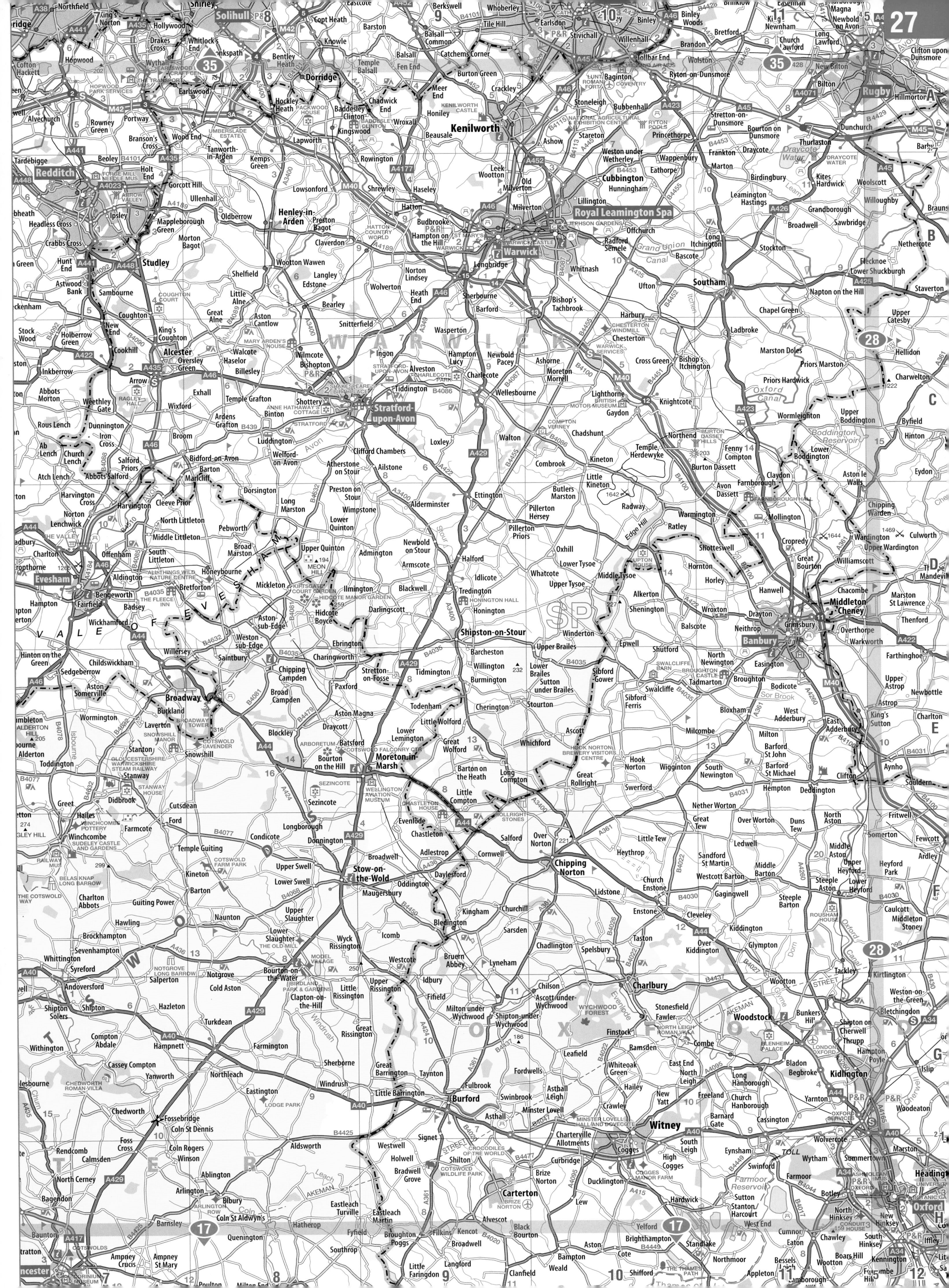
Solihull
Redditch
Kenilworth
Warwick
Royal Leamington Spa
Rugby
Cubbington
Southam
Studley
Alcester
Henley-in-Arden
Stratford-upon-Avon
Evesham
Broadway
Chipping Campden
Shipston-on-Stour
Moreton-in-Marsh
Stow-on-the-Wold
Chipping Norton
Banbury
Middleton Cheney
Charlbury
Woodstock
Kidlington
Burford
Witney
Carterton
Oxford
Dorridge
Knowle
Hockley Heath
Lapworth
Wellesbourne
Kineton
Ettington
Hook Norton
Deddington
Bicester
Northleach
Bourton-on-the-Water
Winchcombe
Fairford
Lechlade
Bampton
Eynsham
Kirtlington
Fenny Compton
Cropredy
Adderbury
Bloxham
Steeple Aston
Enstone
Blockley
Mickleton
Bidford-on-Avon
Alveston
Tiddington
Snitterfield
Wootton Wawen
Coventry
Dunchurch
Long Itchington
Harbury
Bishop's Itchington
Napton on the Hill
Priors Marston
Wormleighton
Warmington
Radway
Shenington
Tadmarton
Sibford Gower
Long Compton
Little Compton
Adlestrop
Kingham
Churchill
Chadlington
Shipton-under-Wychwood
Milton under Wychwood
Ascott-under-Wychwood
Minster Lovell
Brize Norton
Ducklington
Hailey
Freeland
Long Hanborough
Bladon
Yarnton
Wolvercote
Botley
Cumnor
Standlake
Aston
Northmoor
Kennington
Sandford St Martin
Great Tew
Little Tew
Swerford
Wigginton
Kiddington
Tackley
Upper Heyford
Lower Heyford
Middle Aston
North Aston
Somerton
Fritwell
Aynho
Souldern
Clifton
Kings Sutton
Charlton
Newbottle
Farthinghoe
Upper Astrop
Marston St Lawrence
Thenford
Overthorpe
Warkworth
Grimsbury
Neithrop
Drayton
Hanwell
Horley
Hornton
Wroxton
Balscote
Great Bourton
Williamscott
Wardington
Chacombe
Claydon
Mollington
Farnborough
Avon Dassett
Burton Dassett
Gaydon
Lighthorne
Moreton Morrell
Charlecote
Hampton Lucy
Wasperton
Barford
Sherbourne
Longbridge
Hatton
Haseley
Shrewley
Rowington
Lowsonford
Claverdon
Wolverton
Norton Lindsey
Langley
Bearley
Aston Cantlow
Wilmcote
Shottery
Luddington
Welford-on-Avon
Clifford Chambers
Atherstone on Stour
Preston on Stour
Alderminster
Halford
Tredington
Honington
Ilmington
Ebrington
Hidcote Boyce
Aston-sub-Edge
Weston-sub-Edge
Saintbury
Willersey
Snowshill
Stanton
Stanway
Didbrook
Temple Guiting
Guiting Power
Naunton
Upper Slaughter
Lower Slaughter
Upper Swell
Lower Swell
Broadwell
Donnington
Longborough
Condicote
Oddington
Maugersbury
Daylesford
Icomb
Bledington
Westcote
Idbury
Fifield
Little Rissington
Great Rissington
Great Barrington
Little Barrington
Taynton
Windrush
Sherborne
Farmington
Hampnett
Turkdean
Hazleton
Salperton
Notgrove
Cold Aston
Clapton-on-the-Hill
Eastington
Aldsworth
Coln St Aldwyn's
Bibury
Ablington
Arlington
Barnsley
Quenington
Hatherop
Southrop
Filkins
Broughton Poggs
Kencot
Langford
Little Faringdon
Eastleach Turville
Eastleach Martin
Westwell
Holwell
Bradwell Grove
Shilton
Signet
Asthall
Swinbrook
Fulbrook
Asthall Leigh
Leafield
Ramsden
Finstock
Fawler
Stonesfield
Combe
Wootton
Glympton
Tackley
Cassington
Church Hanborough
Barnard Gate
South Leigh
High Cogges
Curbridge
Lew
Yelford
Cote
Shifford
Brighthampton
Hardwick
Sutton
Stanton Harcourt
Appleton
Eaton
Farmoor
Swinford
Wytham
Summertown
Marston
Iffley
Kennington
Boars Hill
Wootton
Sunningwell
Cirencester
Chedworth
Yanworth
Fossebridge
Coln St Dennis
Coln Rogers
Winson
Rendcomb
Calmsden
North Cerney
Bagendon
Baunton
Ampney Crucis
Ampney St Mary
Withington
Compton Abdale
Cassey Compton
Shipton
Andoversford
Syreford
Whittington
Sevenhampton
Brockhampton
Charlton Abbots
Kineton
Barton
Farmcote
Ford
Cutsdean
Buckland
Laverton
Wormington
Aston Somerville
Childswickham
Sedgeberrow
Hinton on the Green
Badsey
Bretforton
Honeybourne
Offenham
Aldington
Bengeworth
Hampton
Wickhamford
Harvington
Norton
Lenchwick
Church Lench
Atch Lench
Rous Lench
Abbots Morton
Inkberrow
Dunnington
Iron Cross
Salford Priors
Abbots Salford
Cleeve Prior
North Littleton
Middle Littleton
South Littleton
Pebworth
Broad Marston
Long Marston
Dorsington
Marlcliff
Barton
Temple Grafton
Ardens Grafton
Binton
Exhall
Wixford
Broom
Arrow
Oversley Green
Haselor
Walcote
Billesley
Kings Coughton
Coughton
Sambourne
Astwood Bank
Cookhill
New End
Great Alne
Little Alne
Shelfield
Morton Bagot
Oldberrow
Ullenhall
Mappleborough Green
Gorcott Hill
Ipsley
Headless Cross
Crabbs Cross
Hunt End
Beoley
Holt End
Tanworth-in-Arden
Wood End
Portway
Rowney Green
Alvechurch
Hopwood
Hollywood
Wythall
Earlswood
Kings Norton
Northfield
Balsall Common
Berkswell
Tile Hill
Burton Green
Crackley
Honiley
Beausale
Leek Wootton
Old Milverton
Milverton
Lillington
Offchurch
Radford Semele
Whitnash
Bishop's Tachbrook
Ufton
Stockton
Birdingbury
Marton
Frankton
Eathorpe
Hunningham
Weston under Wetherley
Wappenbury
Princethorpe
Stretton-on-Dunsmore
Bourton on Dunsmore
Draycote
Thurlaston
Ryton-on-Dunsmore
Baginton
Stoneleigh
Ashow
Bubbenhall
Brandon
Wolston
Binley
Willenhall
Stivichall
Earlsdon
Whoberley
Bretford
Church Lawford
Long Lawford
King's Newnham
Newbold on Avon
Clifton upon Dunsmore
Hillmorton
Bilton
Barby
Kites Hardwick
Woolscott
Willoughby
Grandborough
Sawbridge
Leamington Hastings
Broadwell
Flecknoe
Lower Shuckburgh
Nethercote
Staverton
Upper Catesby
Hellidon
Charwelton
Byfield
Upper Boddington
Lower Boddington
Hinton
Aston le Walls
Eydon
Chipping Warden
Culworth
Upper Wardington
Chesterton
Ladbroke
Marston Doles
Priors Hardwick
Knightcote
Northend
Temple Herdewyke
Chadshunt
Combrook
Little Kineton
Butlers Marston
Pillerton Hersey
Pillerton Priors
Oxhill
Lower Tysoe
Middle Tysoe
Upper Tysoe
Whatcote
Idlicote
Alkerton
Ratley
Shotteswell
Epwell
Shutford
Winderton
Upper Brailes
Lower Brailes
Sutton under Brailes
Barcheston
Willington
Burmington
Cherington
Stourton
Whichford
Ascott
Great Rollright
Over Norton
Salford
Cornwell
Sibford Ferris
Swalcliffe
Broughton
North Newington
Easington
Bodicote
Milcombe
Barford St John
Barford St Michael
South Newington
Hempton
Nether Worton
Over Worton
Duns Tew
Heythrop
Church Enstone
Westcott Barton
Steeple Barton
Ledwell
Gagingwell
Cleveley
Over Kiddington
Lidstone
Spelsbury
Taston
Chilson
Sarsden
Lyneham
Bruern Abbey
Chastleton
Evenlode
Todenham
Little Wolford
Great Wolford
Barton on the Heath
Lower Lemington
Batsford
Bourton on the Hill
Sezincote
Draycott
Aston Magna
Paxford
Blockley
Stretton-on-Fosse
Tidmington
Charingworth
Broad Campden
Admington
Upper Quinton
Lower Quinton
Wimpstone
Newbold on Stour
Armscote
Blackwell
Darlingscott
Loxley
Walton
Hampton on the Hill
Budbrooke
Wroxall
Chadwick End
Baddesley Clinton
Kingswood
Copt Hearth
Barston
Balsall
Temple Balsall
Fen End
Meer End
Catchems Corner
Bentley Heath
Drakes Cross
Whitlock's End
VALE OF EVESHAM
WARWICK
OXFORD
COTSWOLD

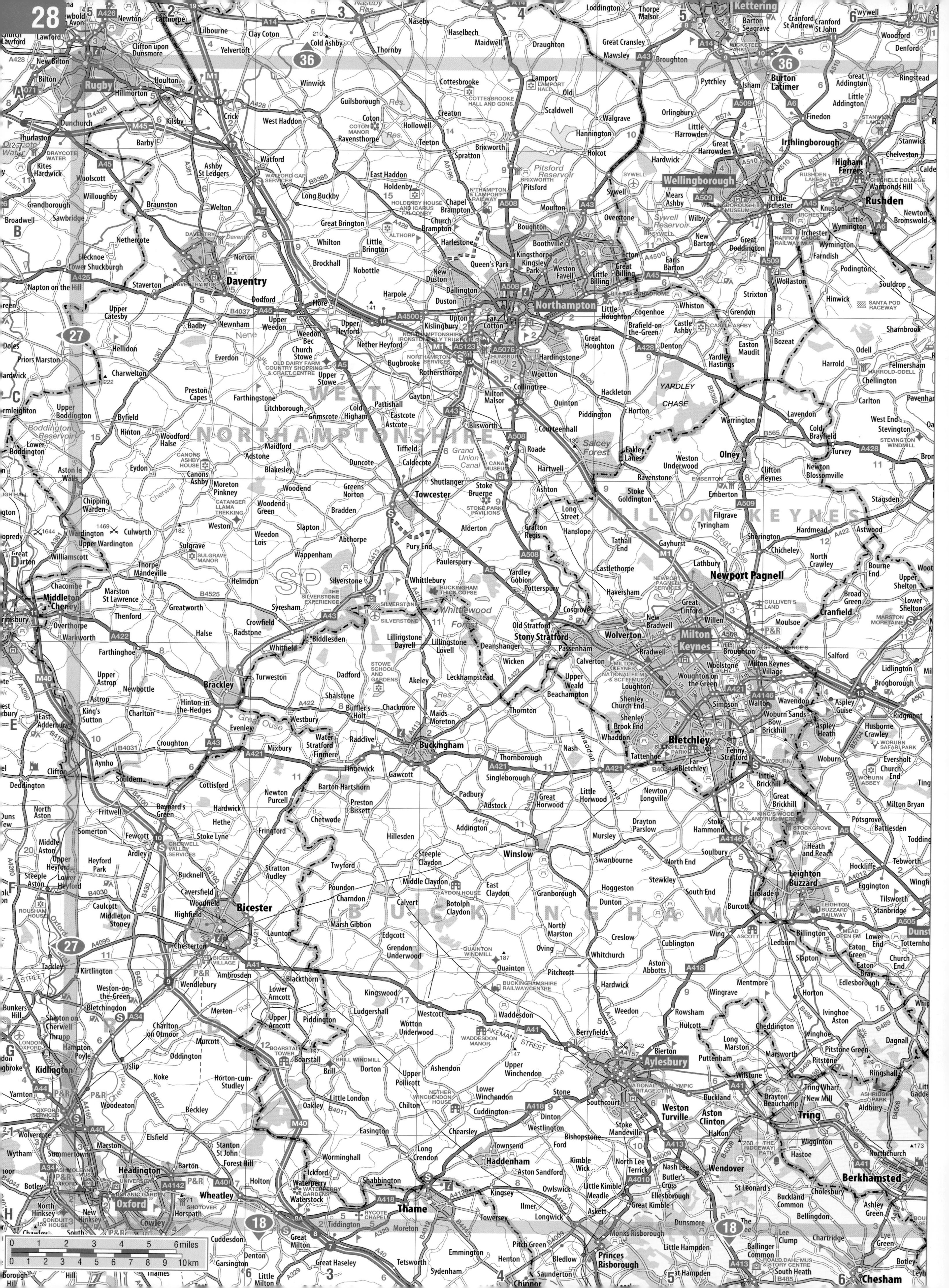
Rugby
Daventry
Northampton
Kettering
Wellingborough
Rushden
Higham Ferrers
Irthlingborough
Burton Latimer
Finedon
Olney
Newport Pagnell
Milton Keynes
Wolverton
Stony Stratford
Bletchley
Towcester
Brackley
Buckingham
Winslow
Bicester
Leighton Buzzard
Aylesbury
Tring
Berkhamsted
Wendover
Princes Risborough
Thame
Haddenham
Oxford
Headington
Kidlington
Wheatley
Middleton Cheney
Chesham
WEST NORTHAMPTONSHIRE
MILTON KEYNES
BUCKINGHAM
SP
Pitsford Reservoir
Salcey Forest
Whittlewood Forest
Yardley Chase
Grand Union Canal
SILVERSTONE
SANTA POD RACEWAY
WOBURN SAFARI PARK
0 1 2 3 4 5 6 miles
0 1 2 3 4 5 6 7 8 9 10 km
27
36
18

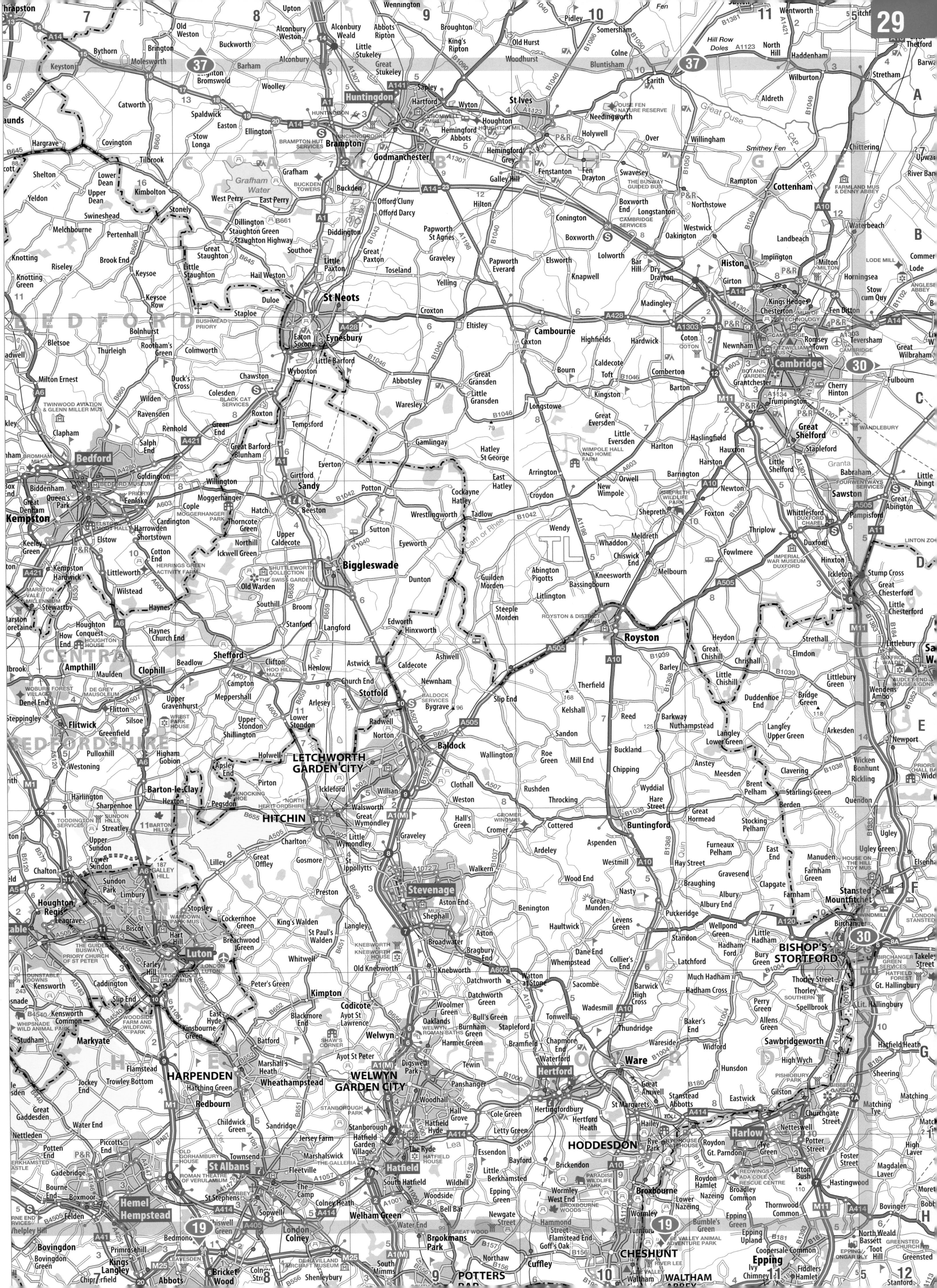
Upton
Wennington
Pidley
Somersham
Wentworth
Thetford
Old Weston
Alconbury Weston
Alconbury Weald
Abbots Ripton
Broughton
King's Ripton
Old Hurst
Woodhurst
Colne
Bluntisham
Earith
Hill Row
Doles
North Hill
Haddenham
Bythorn
Brington
Buckworth
Alconbury
Little Stukeley
Great Stukeley
Keyston
Molesworth
Barham
Leighton Bromswold
Woolley
Huntingdon
Sapley
Hartford
Wyton
St Ives
Houghton
Hemingford Abbots
Hemingford Grey
Needingworth
Holywell
Over
Willingham
Wilburton
Stretham
Aldreth
Catworth
Spaldwick
Easton
Ellington
Stow Longa
Brampton
Godmanchester
Covington
Hargrave
Tilbrook
Shelton
Lower Dean
Upper Dean
Kimbolton
Grafham
Grafham Water
Buckden
Offord Cluny
Offord Darcy
Fenstanton
Fen Drayton
Swavesey
Galley Hill
Hilton
Rampton
Cottenham
Yeldon
Swineshead
Stonely
West Perry
East Perry
Dillington
Staughton Green
Staughton Highway
Melchbourne
Pertenhall
Diddington
Papworth St Agnes
Papworth Everard
Conington
Boxworth
Boxworth End
Longstanton
Northstowe
Westwick
Oakington
Landbeach
Waterbeach
Great Staughton
Little Staughton
Southoe
Little Paxton
Great Paxton
Toseland
Graveley
Yelling
Elsworth
Knapwell
Lolworth
Bar Hill
Dry Drayton
Histon
Impington
Girton
Milton
Horningsea
Stow cum Quy
Knotting
Knotting Green
Riseley
Brook End
Keysoe
Keysoe Row
Hail Weston
Duloe
St Neots
Croxton
Eltisley
Madingley
Kings Hedges
Chesterton
Fen Ditton
Teversham
Great Wilbraham
BEDFORD
Staploe
Bolnhurst
Bushmead Priory
Eaton Socon
Eynesbury
Cambourne
Caxton
Highfields
Hardwick
Coton
Newnham
Cambridge
Romsey Town
Bletsoe
Thurleigh
Rootham's Green
Colmworth
Little Barford
Wyboston
Chawston
Abbotsley
Great Gransden
Little Gransden
Bourn
Caldecote
Toft
Comberton
Barton
Kingston
Grantchester
Cherry Hinton
Fulbourn
Trumpington
Milton Ernest
Duck's Cross
Colesden
Roxton
Waresley
Longstowe
Great Eversden
Little Eversden
Haslingfield
Hauxton
Great Shelford
Stapleford
Wandlebury
Clapham
Wilden
Ravensden
Renhold
Salph End
Green End
Tempsford
Gamlingay
Hatley St George
Harlton
Harston
Little Shelford
Babraham
Bedford
Great Barford
Blunham
Everton
East Hatley
Arrington
Orwell
Barrington
Newton
Sawston
Great Abington
Pampisford
Biddenham
Queen's Park
Goldington
Willington
Moggerhanger
Girtford
Sandy
Potton
Cockayne Hatley
Croydon
New Wimpole
Shepreth
Foxton
Whittlesford
Great Denham
Kempston
Fenlake
Cople
Cardington
Hatch
Beeston
Wrestlingworth
Tadlow
Wendy
Thriplow
Duxford
Harrowden
Shortstown
Thorncote Green
Upper Caldecote
Sutton
Eyeworth
Whaddon
Meldreth
Fowlmere
Hinxton
Elstow
Keeley Green
Cotton End
Northill
Ickwell Green
Biggleswade
Dunton
Guilden Morden
Abington Pigotts
Chiswick End
Kneesworth
Melbourn
Ickleton
Stump Cross
Great Chesterford
Kempston Hardwick
Littleworth
Wilstead
Old Warden
Bassingbourn
Litlington
Little Chesterford
Stewartby
Haynes
Southill
Broom
Steeple Morden
Houghton Conquest
How End
Stanford
Langford
Edworth
Hinxworth
Royston
Heydon
Strethall
Haynes Church End
Ashwell
Great Chishill
Chrishall
Elmdon
Littlebury
Ampthill
Clophill
Shefford
Clifton
Henlow
Astwick
Caldecote
Barley
Little Chishill
Maulden
Beadlow
Campton
Church End
Stotfold
Newnham
Therfield
Littlebury Green
Denel End
Meppershall
Upper Gravenhurst
Arlesey
Baldock Services
Bygrave
Slip End
Kelshall
Duddenhoe End
Bridge Green
Wendens Ambo
Steppingley
Flitwick
Flitton
Silsoe
Upper Stondon
Lower Stondon
Radwell
Norton
Reed
Barkway
Nuthampstead
Langley Upper Green
Arkesden
Greenfield
Shillington
Sandon
Langley Lower Green
Newport
BEDFORDSHIRE
Pulloxhill
Higham Gobion
Holwell
LETCHWORTH GARDEN CITY
Baldock
Wallington
Buckland
Wicken Bonhunt
Westoning
Apsley End
Roe Green
Mill End
Chipping
Anstey
Meesden
Clavering
Rickling
Pirton
Clothall
Wyddial
Brent Pelham
Starlings Green
Quendon
Harlington
Barton-le-Clay
Ickleford
Willian
Weston
Rushden
Throcking
Hare Street
Berden
Sharpenhoe
Hexton
Pegsdon
Walsworth
Great Wymondley
Hall's Green
Cottered
Buntingford
Great Hormead
Stocking Pelham
Streatley
HITCHIN
Cromer
Toddington Services
Upper Sundon
Charlton
Little Wymondley
Graveley
Ardeley
Aspenden
Furneaux Pelham
East End
Ugley
Lower Sundon
Lilley
Great Offley
Gosmore
St Ippolyts
Walkern
Westmill
Hay Street
Manuden
Ugley Green
Chalton
Sundon Park
Limbury
Wood End
Gravesend
Braughing
Clapgate
Farnham Green
Houghton Regis
Leagrave
LUTON
Preston
Stevenage
Aston End
Nasty
Great Munden
Albury
Albury End
Farnham
Stansted Mountfitchet
Stopsley
Cockernhoe Green
King's Walden
Langley
Shephall
Benington
Levens Green
Puckeridge
Wellpond Green
Little Hadham
Birchanger
Biscot
Hart Hill
Luton
Breachwood Green
St Paul's Walden
Broadwater
Aston
Haultwick
Standon
Hadham Ford
Bury Green
BISHOP'S STORTFORD
Farley Hill
Whitwell
Bragbury End
Dane End
Collier's End
Whempstead
Latchford
Kensworth
Caddington
Old Knebworth
Knebworth
Datchworth
Watton at Stone
Sacombe
Much Hadham
Hadham Cross
Thorley Street
Thorley
Gt. Hallingbury
Slip End
Peter's Green
Kimpton
Codicote
Datchworth Green
Barwick
High Cross
Wadesmill
Perry Green
Spellbrook
Lit. Hallingbury
Kensworth Common
East Hyde
Kinsbourne Green
Blackmore End
Ayot St Lawrence
Woolmer Green
Oaklands
Bull's Green
Burnham Green
Tonwell
Thundridge
Baker's End
Allens Green
Sawbridgeworth
Studham
Markyate
Batford
Welwyn
Harmer Green
Stapleford
Bramfield
Chapmore End
Wareside
Widford
Hatfield Heath
Flamstead
Marshall's Heath
Wheathampstead
Ayot St Peter
Digswell Park
Tewin
Waterford
Hertford
Ware
Hunsdon
High Wych
Sheering
Jockey End
Trowley Bottom
HARPENDEN
Hatching Green
Redbourn
WELWYN GARDEN CITY
Panshanger
Woodhall
Great Amwell
Stanstead Abbotts
Eastwick
Gilston
Matching
Matching Tye
Great Gaddesden
Water End
Childwick Green
Sandridge
Hall Grove
Cole Green
Hertingfordbury
St Margarets
Hertford Heath
Hailey
Netteswell
Churchgate Street
Nettleden
Potten End
Piccotts End
Jersey Farm
Stanborough
Hatfield Hyde
Letty Green
Rye Park
Harlow
Tye Green
Potter Street
High Laver
Townsend
Hatfield Garden Village
The Ryde
Essendon
Bayford
HODDESDON
Roydon
Gt. Parndon
Foster Street
Magdalen Laver
Gadebridge
St Albans
Marshalswick
Fleetville
Hatfield
Little Berkhamsted
Brickendon
Roydon Hamlet
Latton Bush
Hastingwood
Bourne End
Boxmoor
St Stephens
The Camp
South Hatfield
Wildhill
Epping Green
Wormley West End
Broxbourne
Lower Nazeing
Nazeing
Broadley Common
Hemel Hempstead
Felden
Sopwell
Colney Heath
Woodside
Welham Green
Newgate Street
Wormley
Epping Green
Thornwood Common
Bovinger
Bell Bar
Water End
Hammond Street
Flamstead End
Turnford
Bumble's Green
Epping Upland
North Weald Bassett
Toot Hill
Bovingdon
Bovingdon Green
Primrosehill
Kings Langley
Abbots
Bedmond
London Colney
Brookmans Park
Northaw
Goff's Oak
Cuffley
CHESHUNT
Waltham
Ivy Chimney
Epping
Coopersale Common
Fiddlers Hamlet
Greensted
Stanford
Bricket Wood
Colney Street
Shenleybury
South Mimms
POTTERS BAR
WALTHAM ABBEY
Chipperfield
Leavesden

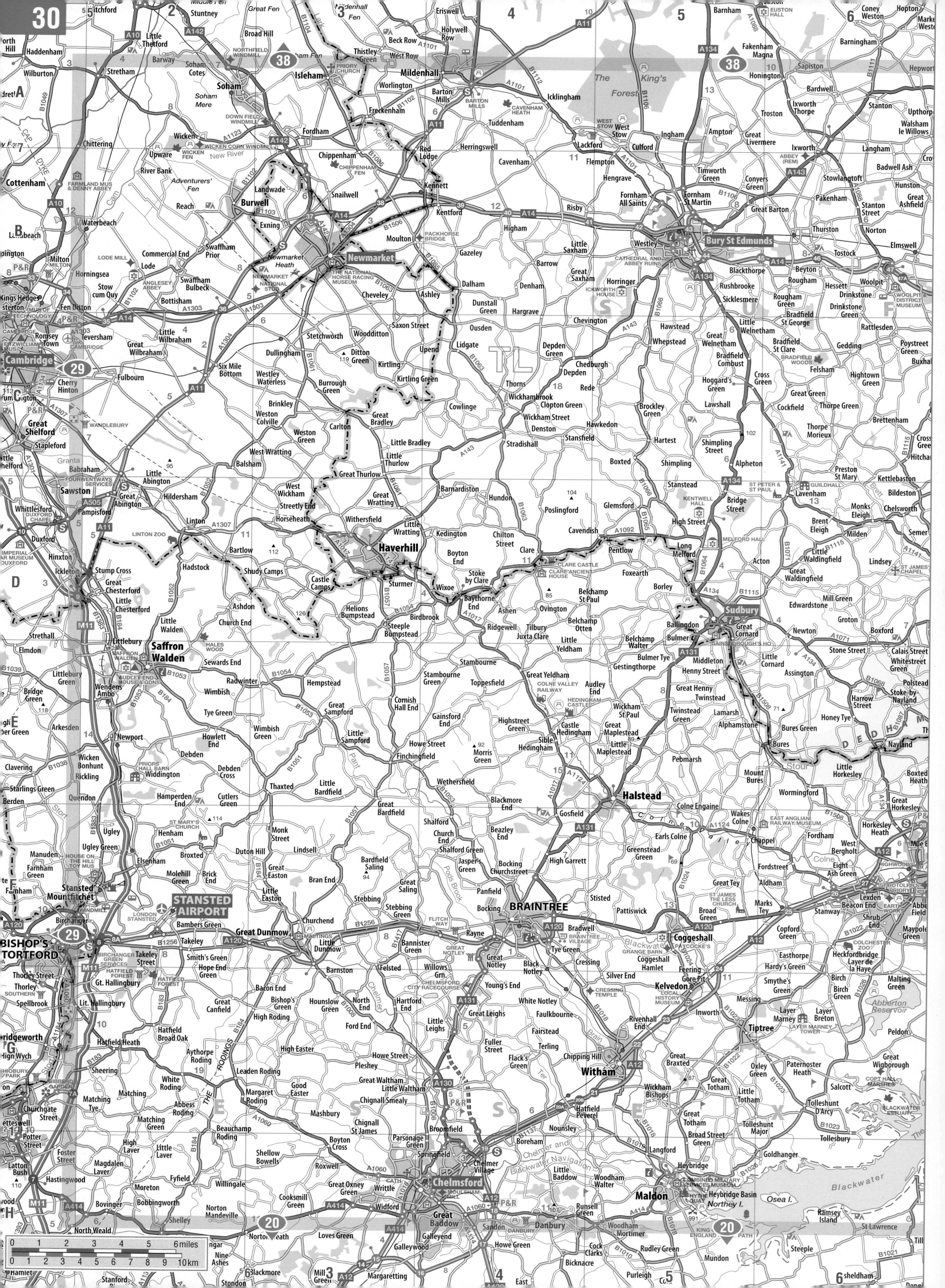
Soham
Isleham
Mildenhall
Barton Mills
Icklingham
The King's Forest
Fakenham Magna
Honington
Ixworth
Ixworth Thorpe
Stanton
Fordham
Freckenham
Red Lodge
Herringswell
Cavenham
Lackford
Flempton
Culford
Ingham
Ampton
Great Livermere
Wicken
Upware
Chippenham
Kennett
Cottenham
Landwade
Burwell
Snailwell
Kentford
Risby
Fornham All Saints
Fornham St Martin
Great Barton
Pakenham
Thurston
Waterbeach
Exning
Newmarket
Moulton
Higham
Gazeley
Little Saxham
Westley
Bury St Edmunds
Milton
Horningsea
Lode
Swaffham Prior
Swaffham Bulbeck
Stow cum Quy
Bottisham
Cheveley
Ashley
Dalham
Barrow
Denham
Great Saxham
Horringer
Rushbrooke
Rougham
Woolpit
Drinkstone
Fen Ditton
Teversham
Cambridge
Cherry Hinton
Fulbourn
Little Wilbraham
Great Wilbraham
Six Mile Bottom
Stetchworth
Dullingham
Woodditton
Saxon Street
Ousden
Hargrave
Chevington
Hawstead
Whepstead
Great Welnetham
Bradfield St George
Rattlesden
Gedding
Kirtling
Kirtling Green
Lidgate
Depden
Chedburgh
Brockley
Felsham
Westley Waterless
Burrough Green
Brinkley
Cowlinge
Thorns
Wickhambrook
Rede
Lawshall
Cockfield
Great Shelford
Stapleford
Weston Colville
Carlton
Great Bradley
Little Bradley
Stradishall
Denston
Stansfield
Hawkedon
Hartest
Shimpling Street
Thorpe Morieux
Brettenham
Balsham
West Wratting
Little Thurlow
Great Thurlow
Boxted
Shimpling
Alpheton
Babraham
Little Abington
Great Abington
Sawston
Hildersham
West Wickham
Barnardiston
Hundon
Poslingford
Glemsford
Stanstead
Lavenham
Kettlebaston
Bildeston
Whittlesford
Pampisford
Linton
Horseheath
Withersfield
Haverhill
Kedington
Chilton Street
Clare
Cavendish
Long Melford
Bridge Street
Chelsworth
Duxford
Hinxton
Bartlow
Hadstock
Shudy Camps
Castle Camps
Sturmer
Boyton End
Stoke by Clare
Pentlow
Foxearth
Acton
Lindsey
Ickleton
Great Chesterford
Little Chesterford
Ashdon
Helions Bumpstead
Steeple Bumpstead
Birdbrook
Baythorne End
Ashen
Ovington
Belchamp St Paul
Belchamp Otten
Borley
Sudbury
Ballingdon
Great Cornard
Edwardstone
Groton
Boxford
Littlebury
Saffron Walden
Little Walden
Ridgewell
Tilbury Juxta Clare
Little Yeldham
Great Yeldham
Belchamp Walter
Bulmer
Middleton
Newton
Elmdon
Sewards End
Radwinter
Hempstead
Stambourne
Toppesfield
Gestingthorpe
Henny Street
Little Cornard
Assington
Wendens Ambo
Wimbish
Great Sampford
Little Sampford
Cornish Hall End
Gainsford End
Castle Hedingham
Sible Hedingham
Great Maplestead
Little Maplestead
Wickham St Paul
Twinstead
Lamarsh
Alphamstone
Bures
Nayland
Newport
Debden
Thaxted
Little Bardfield
Great Bardfield
Finchingfield
Wethersfield
Halstead
Pebmarsh
Colne Engaine
Wakes Colne
Earls Colne
Chappel
Wormingford
Clavering
Widdington
Ugley
Henham
Elsenham
Broxted
Lindsell
Shalford
Gosfield
Greenstead Green
Fordham
West Bergholt
Manuden
Stansted Mountfitchet
Stansted Airport
Great Easton
Little Easton
Bardfield Saling
Great Saling
Stebbing
Panfield
Bocking
Braintree
Stisted
Coggeshall
Great Tey
Aldham
Marks Tey
Stanway
Bishop's Stortford
Great Dunmow
Little Dunmow
Rayne
Takeley
Felsted
Great Notley
Black Notley
Cressing
Kelvedon
Feering
Copford Green
Birchanger
Barnston
Young's End
White Notley
Faulkbourne
Inworth
Tiptree
Layer Marney
Birch
Messing
Hatfield Broad Oak
High Roding
Ford End
Little Leighs
Fairstead
Terling
Rivenhall End
Sawbridgeworth
Hatfield Heath
Aythorpe Roding
Leaden Roding
High Easter
Pleshey
Howe Street
Great Waltham
Little Waltham
Witham
Chipping Hill
Great Braxted
Tolleshunt D'Arcy
Sheering
White Roding
Good Easter
Margaret Roding
Abbess Roding
Matching
Chignall St James
Broomfield
Hatfield Peverel
Wickham Bishops
Great Totham
Little Totham
Tolleshunt Major
Salcott
Peldon
Harlow
Beauchamp Roding
High Laver
Little Laver
Shellow Bowells
Boyton Cross
Boreham
Nounsley
Langford
Heybridge
Tollesbury
Goldhanger
Magdalen Laver
Roxwell
Springfield
Chelmer Village
Chelmsford
Little Baddow
Woodham Walter
Maldon
Heybridge Basin
Northey I.
Osea I.
Blackwater
Moreton
Fyfield
Willingale
Writtle
Bobbingworth
Norton Mandeville
Cooksmill Green
Widford
Great Baddow
Sandon
Danbury
Woodham Mortimer
Ramsey Island
St Lawrence
North Weald
Loves Green
Galleywood
Howe Green
Cock Clarks
Rudley Green
Mundon
Steeple
Margaretting
Bicknacre
Purleigh
0 1 2 3 4 5 6 miles
0 1 2 3 4 5 6 7 8 9 10 km

Thelnetham
Hinderclay
Redgrave
Wortham
Palgrave
Stuston
Thrandeston
Billingford Windmill
Oakley
Hoxne
Syleham
Fressingfield
Little Whittingham Green
Linstead Parva
Chediston
Halesworth
Holton
Blyford
Wangford
Reydon
Southwold Museum
Southwold
Botesdale
Rickinghall
Burgate
Brome
Brome Street
Langton Green
Cross Street
Heckfield Green
Wingfield
Battlesea Green
Chippenhall Green
Silverley's Green
Cratfield
Cookley
Wenhaston
Blackheath
Blythburgh
Hen Reedbed Nature Reserve
Walberswick
Mellis
Yaxley
Eye
Denham
Stradbroke
Pixey Green
Swan Green
Ashfield Green
Banyard's Green
Huntingfield
Walpole
Thorington
Bramfield
Wattisfield
Allwood Green
Cranmer Green
Gislingham
Thornham Parva
Thornham Magna
Braiseworth
Cranley
Denham Street
Redlingfield
Horham
Wilby
Wootten Green
Russel's Green
Laxfield
Heveningham
Sibton Green
High Street
Suffolk Coast
Dunwich
Dunwich Forest
Dunwich Museum
Four Ashes
Wickham Street
Stoke Ash
Thorndon
Occold
Athelington
Fingal Street
Stanway Green
Foals Green
Brundish Street
Crown Corner
Ubbeston Green
Hemp Green
Darsham
Westhorpe
Long Thurlow
Finningham
Wickham Skeith
Rishangles
Southolt
Brundish
Owl's Green
Peasenhall
Sibton
Yoxford
Westleton Heath
Westleton
Minsmere RSPB Nature Reserve
Wyverstone
Wyverstone Street
Bacton
Cotton
Thwaite
Brockford Street
Bedingfield
Worlingworth
Tannington
Badingham
Rotten End
Middleton Moor
Middleton
Earl's Green
Bacton Green
Ford's Green
Wetheringsett
Mid Suffolk Light Rly & Mus
Blacksmith's Green
Bedfield
Kenton
Maypole Green
Dennington
Bruisyard
North Green
Theberton
Eastbridge
Haughley Green
Ward Green
Canham's Green
Mendlesham
Mendlesham Green
Monk Soham
Saxtead Green Post Mill
Saxtead
Brabling Green
Cransford
Curlew Green
Rendham
Kelsale
Carlton
Leiston Abbey
Saxmundham
Wetherup Street
Debenham
Saxtead Green
Framlingham
Sweffling
Great Glemham
Leiston
Sizewell
Wetherden
Haughley Park
Haughley
Gipping
Saxham Street
Middlewood Green
Mickfield
Ashfield
Earl Soham
Winston
Lampardbrook
Cole's Green
Benhall Street
Sternfield
Knodishall
Long Shop Mus
Aldringham
Thorney Green
Stowupland
Little Stonham
Winston Green
Peats Corner
Brandeston
Cretingham
Kettleburgh
Parham
Stratford St Andrew
Benhall Green
Coldfair Green
Friston
Thorpeness
Harleston
Buxhall Fen Street
Forward Green
Stonham Aspal
Pettaugh
Framsden
Easton
Easton Farm Park
Hacheston
Farnham
Gromford
Snape
North Warren RSPB Nature Reserve
The Museum of Food
Stowmarket
Earl Stonham
Creeting St Mary
Creeting Bottoms
Helmingham Hall Gardens
Helmingham
Monewden
Letheringham
Marlesford
Little Glemham
Blaxhall
Snape Maltings
Iken
Aldeburgh
Great Finborough
Combs Ford
Combs
Crowfield
Charsfield
Wickham Market
Lower Hacheston
Campsey Ash
Aldeburgh Bay
High Street Green
Moats Tye
Beacon Hill Services
Gosbeck
Otley
Clopton Corner
Dallinghoo
Debach
Pettistree
Tunstall
Tunstall Forest
High Street
Little Finborough
Battisford
Needham Market
Coddenham
Ashbocking
Rendlesham
Sudbourne
Charles Tye
Battisford Tye
Ringshall
Needham Lake
Barking
Hemingstone
Swilland
Clopton
Bredfield
Ufford
Chillesford
Wattisham Station Heritage Mus
Barking Tye
Baylham
Eyke
Butley
Wattisham
Ringshall Stocks
Barham
Henley
Witnesham
Burgh
Grundisburgh
Hasketon
Melton
Bromeswell
Rendlesham Forest
Orford Castle
Orford
Great Bricett
Willisham Tye
Great Blakenham
Claydon
Nedging Tye
Offton
Little Blakenham
Akenham
Tuddenham St Martin
Culpho
Boot Street
Great Bealings
Woodbridge
Sutton Hoo
Butley High Corner
Orford Ness
Orfordness-Havergate
Naughton
Somersham
Westerfield
Playford
Maidensgrave
Capel St Andrew
Flowton
Whitton
Rushmere St Andrew
Little Bealings
Ash Street
Elmsett
Martlesham
Boyton
Whatfield
Bramford
Christchurch Mansion
Waldringfield Heath
Sutton
Stores Corner
Sproughton
Westbourne
Ipswich
Ipswich Mus
Martlesham Heath
Waldringfield
Duck Corner
Shottisham
Hollesley Bay
TM
Aldham
Kesgrave
Martlesham Heath Control Tower
Wolves Wood RSPB Reserve
Burstall
Rose Hill
Hollesley
Kersey
Hintlesham
Chantry
Stoke
Warren Heath
Brightwell
Newbourne
Hadleigh
Chattisham
Maidenhall
Bucklesham
Shingle Street
Copdock
Gainsborough
Hemley
Alderton
Coles Green
Layham
Mace Green
Belstead
Wherstead
Orwell
Nacton
Bawdsey
Kirton
Raydon
Freston
Falkenham
Great Wenham
Capel St Mary
Woolverstone
Levington
Deben
Shelley
Pin Mill
Thorpe Common
Trimley St Martin
Holton St Mary
Chelmondiston
Trimley Lower Street
Felixstowe Ferry
Tattingstone
Alton Water Reservoir
Holbrook
Bentley
The Heath
Trimley St Mary
Trimley Marshes Nature Reserve
Walton
Old Felixstowe
Higham
East Bergholt
Lower Holbrook
Erwarton
Shotley
Stratford St Mary
Stutton
Harkstead
Shotley Gate
Felixstowe
Boxted
Dedham
Brantham
Upper Street
Stour Valley
Holbrook Bay
Shop Corner
Stour
Harwich
Bridge Cottage
Cattawade
Mistley Towers
Boxted Cross
The Munnings Art Museum
Dedham Heath
Mistley
Parkeston
Harwich Redoubt Fort
Langham
Lawford
Manningtree
Bradfield
Wrabness
Ramsey
Upper Dovercourt
Dovercourt
Bradfield Heath
Ardleigh
Little Bromley
Horsleycross Street
Little Oakley
Horsley Cross
Wix
Parson's Heath
Fox Street
Crockleford Heath
Great Bromley
Stone's Green
Great Oakley
Little Bentley
Tendring Green
Colchester
Elmstead Market
Beaumont
Hoek van Holland
Hare Green
Balls Green
Horsey Island
The Naze
Old Heath
Wivenhoe Cross
Tendring
Thorpe Green
Hamford Water
Beth Chatto Gdns
Bourne Mill
Frating Green
Great Bentley
Thorpe-le-Soken
Kirby-le-Soken
Blackheath
Wivenhoe
Weeley
Weeley Heath
Walton-on-the-Naze
Rowhedge
Aingers Green
Alresford
Kirby Cross
Frinton-on-Sea
Fingringhoe
Row Heath
Thorrington
Little Clacton
Clacton Village
Great Holland
Abberton
Holland Haven
Langenhoe
River Colne
St Osyth Heath
Brightlingsea
St Osyth Priory
St Osyth
Holland-on-Sea
Great Clacton
Mersea Island
East Mersea
Cudmore Grove
Point Clear
Clacton-on-Sea
Blue Row
Colne Estuary
Jaywick
West Mersea
Mersea Museum
Colne Pt.
Nass
Virley Channel
Sales Pt.
St Peter's on the Wall
Bradwell Waterside
King Charles III England Coast Path
Bradwell on Sea
Dengie
A143
A140
A14
A12
A1120
A1094
A1071
A1214
A1156
A137
A120
A133
A134
A1152
B1117
B1118
B1113
B1077
B1078
B1079
B1116
B1119
B1120
B1121
B1122
B1125
B1069
B1353
B1084
B1083
B1438
B1070
B1080
B1456
B1068
B1029
B1027
B1028
B1025
B1035
B1033
B1034
B1032
B1352
B1414
B1336
B1123
B1126
B1387
B1094
B1078
39
21
7
8
9
10
11
12
A
B
C
D
E
F
G
H

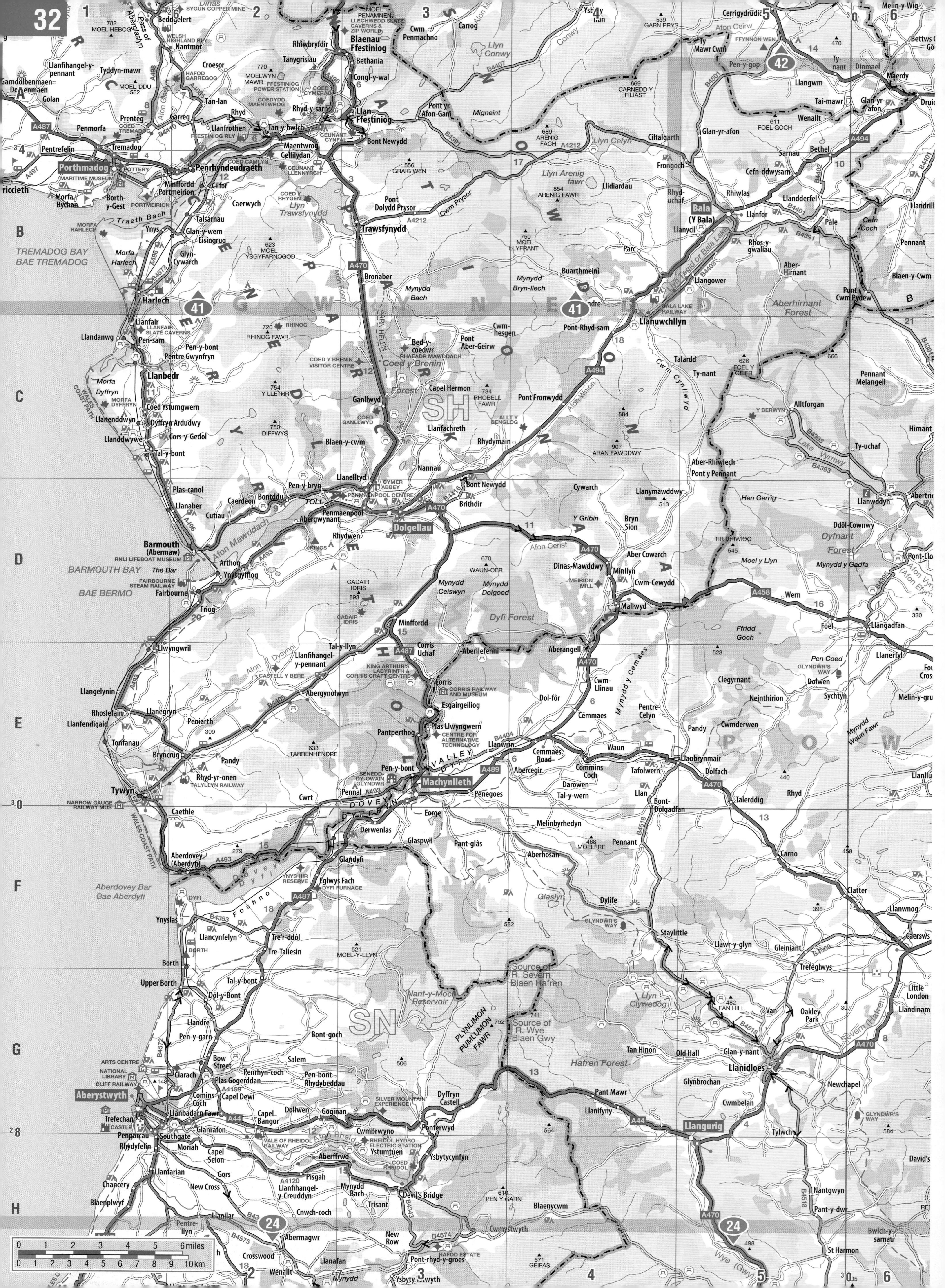

Beddgelert
Pass of Aberglaslyn
782 MOEL HEBOG
SYGUN COPPER MINE
WELSH HIGHLAND RLY
Nantmor
Llanfihangel-y-pennant
Tyddyn-mawr
Garndolbenmaen
Golan
MOEL-DDU 552
Croesor
HAFOD GARREGOG
770 MOELWYN MAWR
FFESTINIOG POWER STATION
COEDYDD MAENTWROG
Tan-lan
Rhyd
Prenteg
Garreg
Llanfrothen
FFESTINIOG RLY
Tan-y-bwlch
Penmorfa
Tremadog
Pentrefelin
Porthmadog
POTTERY
MARITIME MUSEUM
Criccieth
Morfa Bychan
Borth-y-Gest
Minffordd
Portmeirion
PORTMEIRION
Penrhyndeudraeth
COED CAMLYN
Maentwrog
Gellilydan
CEUNANT LLENNYRCH
Cilfor
Caerwych
COED RHYGEN
Llyn Trawsfynydd
Talsarnau
Glan-y-wern
Eisingrug
Ynys
Traeth Bach
MORFA HARLECH
TREMADOG BAY
BAE TREMADOG
Morfa Harlech
Glyn-Cywarch
623 MOEL YSGYFARNOGOD
Harlech
Llanfair
LLANFAIR SLATE CAVERNS
Llandanwg
Pen-sarn
Pen-y-bont
Pentre Gwynfryn
720 RHINOG
RHINOG FAWR
Llanbedr
Morfa Dyffryn
MORFA DYFFRYN
WALES COAST PATH
Coed Ystumgwern
Llanenddwyn
Dyffryn Ardudwy
Llanddwywe
Cors-y-Gedol
754 Y LLETHR
750 DIFFWYS
Tal-y-bont
Plas-canol
Llanaber
Caerdeon
Bontddu
Cutiau
Barmouth (Abermaw)
RNLI LIFEBOAT MUSEUM
Afon Mawddach
Arthog
BARMOUTH BAY
The Bar
BAE BERMO
Ynysgyfflog
FAIRBOURNE STEAM RAILWAY
Fairbourne
Friog
Llwyngwril
Llangelynin
Rhoslefain
Llanfendigaid
Llanegryn
Peniarth
Tonfanau
Bryncrug
Pandy
Rhyd-yr-onen
TALYLLYN RAILWAY
Tywyn
NARROW GAUGE RAILWAY MUS
Caethle
WALES COAST PATH
Aberdovey (Aberdyfi)
Aberdovey Bar
Bae Aberdyfi
Dovey
Dyfi
Ynyslas
Fochno
Llancynfelyn
BORTH
Borth
Tre'r-ddôl
Tre-Taliesin
521 MOEL-Y-LLYN
Upper Borth
Tal-y-bont
Dôl-y-Bont
Llandre
Pen-y-garn
Bont-goch
Bow Street
Salem
ARTS CENTRE
NATIONAL LIBRARY
CLIFF RAILWAY
Clarach
Penrhyn-coch
Pen-bont Rhydybeddau
Plas Gogerddan
Aberystwyth
Comins Coch
Capel Dewi
Trefechan
CASTLE
Llanbadarn Fawr
Penparcau
Southgate
Glanrafon
Capel Bangor
Dollwen
Goginan
SILVER MOUNTAIN EXPERIENCE
Rhydyfelin
Moriah
Capel Seion
VALE OF RHEIDOL RAILWAY
Cwmbrwyno
RHEIDOL HYDRO ELECTRIC STATION
Ystumtuen
Aberffrwd
Afon Rheidol
COED RHEIDOL
Llanfarian
Gors
Pisgah
Chancery
New Cross
Llanfihangel-y-Creuddyn
Mynydd Bach
Devil's Bridge
Blaenplwyf
Trisant
Llanilar
Cnwch-coch
Pentre-llyn
Abermagwr
New Row
Crosswood
Llanafan
Pont-rhyd-y-groes
HAFOD ESTATE
Wenallt
Ysbyty Ystwyth
Dyffryn Castell
Ponterwyd
Ysbytycynfyn
610 PEN Y GARN
Blaenycwm
Cwmystwyth
571 GEIFAS
PLYNLIMON PUMLUMON FAWR
752
741
Source of R. Wye Blaen Gwy
Source of R. Severn Blaen Hafren
Nant-y-Moch Reservoir
506
564
Hafren Forest
Tan Hinon
Old Hall
Glan-y-nant
Llanidloes
Glynbrochan
Pant Mawr
Llanifyny
Cwmbelan
Llangurig
Newchapel
Tylwch
GLYNDWR'S WAY
584
Nantgwyn
Pant-y-dwr
Bwlch-y-sarnau
St Harmon
498
Wye (Gwy)
MOEL PENAMNEN
LLECHWEDD SLATE CAVERNS & ZIP WORLD
Blaenau Ffestiniog
Rhiwbryfdir
Bethania
Tanygrisiau
Congl-y-wal
CEUNANT CYMERAU
COED CYMERAU
Rhyd-y-sarn
Llan Ffestiniog
CEUNANT CYNFAL
Bont Newydd
Cwm Penmachno
Carrog
Llyn Conwy
Pont yr Afon-Gam
Migneint
556 GRAIG WEN
689 ARENIG FACH
Llyn Celyn
Pont Dolydd Prysor
Cwm Prysor
Trawsfynydd
Llyn Arenig fawr
854 ARENIG FAWR
750 MOEL LLYFRANT
Bronaber
Afon Eden
Mynydd Bach
Mynydd Bryn-llech
SARN HELEN
Bed-y-coedwr
RHAEADR MAWDDACH
COED Y BRENIN VISITOR CENTRE
Coed y Brenin Forest
Cwm-hesgen
Pont Aber-Geirw
Capel Hermon
734 RHOBELL FAWR
Ganllwyd
COED GANLLWYD
SH
Llanfachreth
ALLT Y BENGLOG
Rhydymain
Blaen-y-cwm
Nannau
Llanelltyd
CYMER ABBEY
Pen-y-bryn
PENMAENPOOL CENTRE
TOLL
Penmaenpool
Abergwynant
Dolgellau
Rhydwen
KINGS
Bont Newydd
Brithdir
CADAIR IDRIS 893
CADAIR IDRIS
670 WAUN-OER
Mynydd Ceiswyn
Mynydd Dolgoed
Dyfi Forest
Minffordd
Tal-y-llyn
Afon Dysynni
Llanfihangel-y-pennant
CASTELL Y BERE
Corris Uchaf
KING ARTHUR'S LABYRINTH & CORRIS CRAFT CENTRE
Corris
CORRIS RAILWAY AND MUSEUM
Abergynolwyn
Esgairgeiliog
309
633 TARRENHENDRE
Pantperthog
Plas Llwyngwern
CENTRE FOR ALTERNATIVE TECHNOLOGY
Pen-y-bont
SENEDD-DY-OWAIN GLYNDWR
Machynlleth
Pennal
Cwrt
DOVEY
DYFFRYN
Derwenlas
Forge
Glaspwll
Pant-glâs
Glandyfi
YNYS HIR RESERVE
Eglwys Fach
DYFI FURNACE
DYFI
Aberllefenni
Aberangell
VALLEY DYFI
Llanwrin
Cemmaes Road
Abercegir
Penegoes
Commins Coch
Darowen
Tal-y-wern
Melinbyrhedyn
468 MOELFRE
Aberhosan
Glaslyn
Dylife
GLYNDWR'S WAY
582
Nant-y-Moch
Ciltalgarth
Frongoch
Llidiardau
Rhyd-uchaf
Bala (Y Bala)
Llanycil
Llyn Tegid or Bala Lake
Parc
Buarthmeini
Llangower
BALA LAKE RAILWAY
Llanuwchllyn
Pont-Rhyd-sarn
Talardd
Ty-nant
Cwm Cynllwyd
Afon Wnion
Pont Fronwydd
884
907 ARAN FAWDDWY
Cywarch
Llanymawddwy
513
Y Gribin
Bryn Sion
Afon Cerist
Aber Cowarch
Dinas-Mawddwy
Minllyn
MEIRION MILL
Cwm-Cewydd
Mallwyd
Mynydd y Cemaes
Cwm-Llinau
Dol-fôr
Cemmaes
Pentre-Celyn
Waun
Llanbrynmair
Tafolwern
Llan
Bont-Dolgadfan
Pennant
Cerrigydrudion
539 GARN PRYS
Afon Ceirw
Ty Mawr Cwm
FFYNNON WEN
Pen-y-gop
669 CARNEDD Y FILIAST
Glan-yr-afon
611 FOEL GOCH
Wenallt
Llangwm
Tai-mawr
Sarnau
Cefn-ddwysarn
Rhiwlas
Llandderfel
Llanfor
Rhos-y-gwaliau
Aber-Hirnant
Aberhirnant Forest
626 FOEL Y GEIFR
Y BERWYN
Alltforgan
Lake Vyrnwy
Aber-Rhiwlech
Pont y Pennant
Hen Gerrig
TIR RHIWIOG 545
Moel y Llyn
Wern
Ffridd Goch
523
Clegyrnant
Neinthirion
Cwmderwen
Pandy
Dolfach
Talerddig
Rhyd
440
Carno
458
Clatter
398
Staylittle
Llawr-y-glyn
Gleiniant
Trefeglwys
Llyn Clywedog
482 FAN HILL
Van
Oakley Park
Melin-y-Wig
Bettws Gwerfil Goch
Ty-nant
Dinmael
Maerdy
Glan-yr-afon
Bethel
Llandrillo
Pale
Cefn Coch
Pennant
Blaen-y-Cwm
Pont Cwm Pydew
666
Pennant Melangell
Hirnant
Ty-uchaf
Llanwddyn
Abertridwr
Ddôl-Cownwy
Dyfnant Forest
Pont-Llogel
Mynydd y Gadfa
Afon Efyrnwy
330
Foel
Llangadfan
Pen Coed
GLYNDWR'S WAY
Llanerfyl
Dolwen
Sychtyn
Melin-y-grug
Mynydd Waun Fawr
Llanllugan
Llanwnog
Caersws
Little London
Llandinam
307
Severn (Hafren)
GWYNEDD
SNOWDONIA
CEREDIGION
POWYS
SN
41
42
24
0 1 2 3 4 5 6 miles
0 1 2 3 4 5 6 7 8 9 10 km

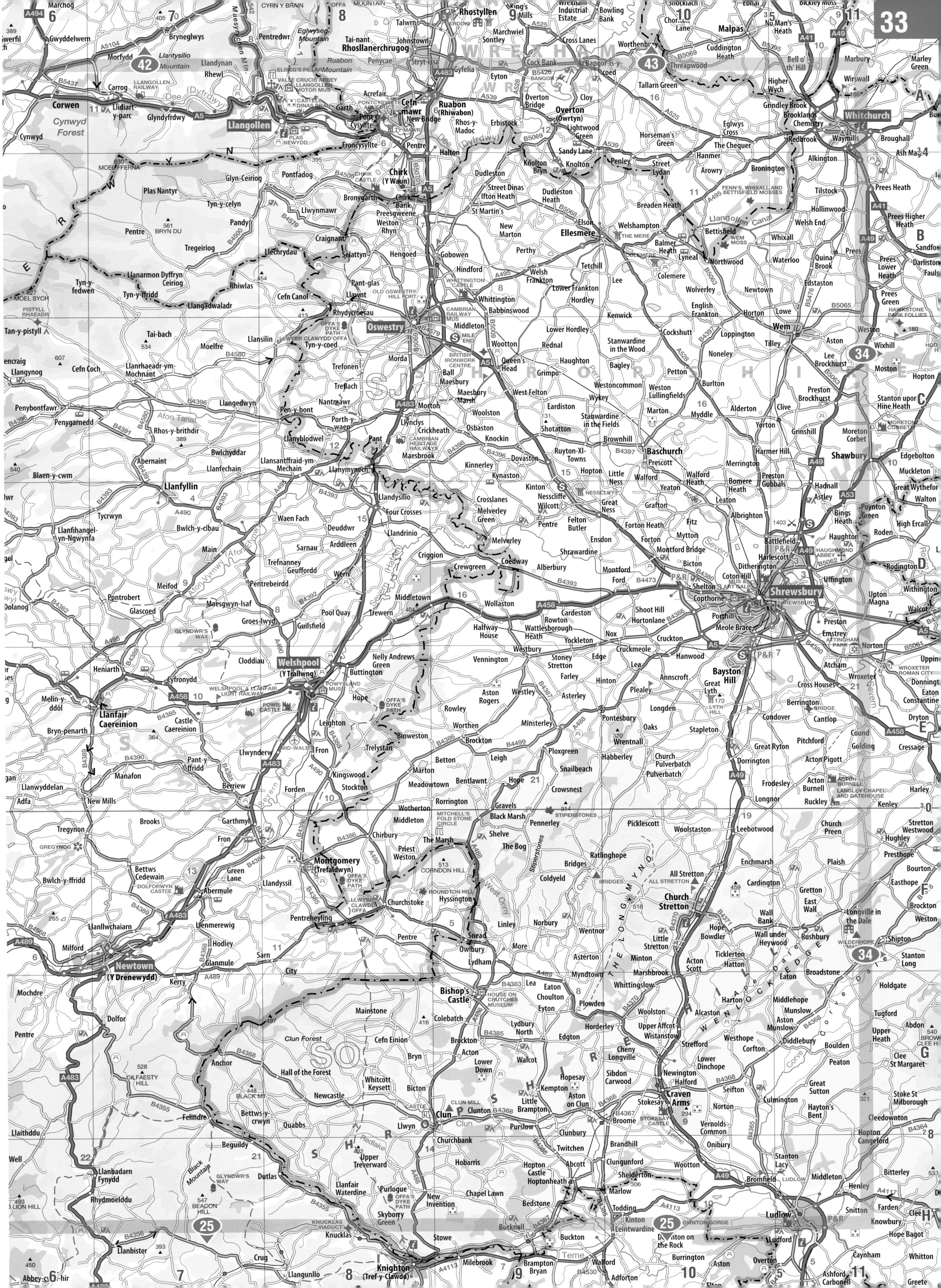
Corwen
Llangollen
Rhosllanerchrugog
Ruabon
Cefn-mawr
Chirk (Y Waun)
Overton
Malpas
Whitchurch
Ellesmere
Wem
Oswestry
Llanfyllin
Welshpool (Y Trallwng)
Shrewsbury
Baschurch
Shawbury
Llanfair Caereinion
Montgomery (Trefaldwyn)
Newtown (Y Drenewydd)
Church Stretton
Bishop's Castle
Craven Arms
Clun
Ludlow
Knighton (Tref-y-Clawdd)
Bayston Hill
Dorrington
Pontesbury
Minsterley
Chirbury
Clun Forest
Cynwyd Forest
Black Mountain
Offa's Dyke Path
Llangollen Canal
W R E X H A M
S H R O P S H I R E
Wenlock Edge
The Long Mynd
Stiperstones
Corndon Hill
Dee (Dyfrdwy)
Severn (Hafren)
Teme
Afon Tanat
Afon Vyrnwy (Afon Efyrnwy)
A5
A483
A458
A49
A41
A488
A489
A495
A528
A4113
A4117
42
43
34
25

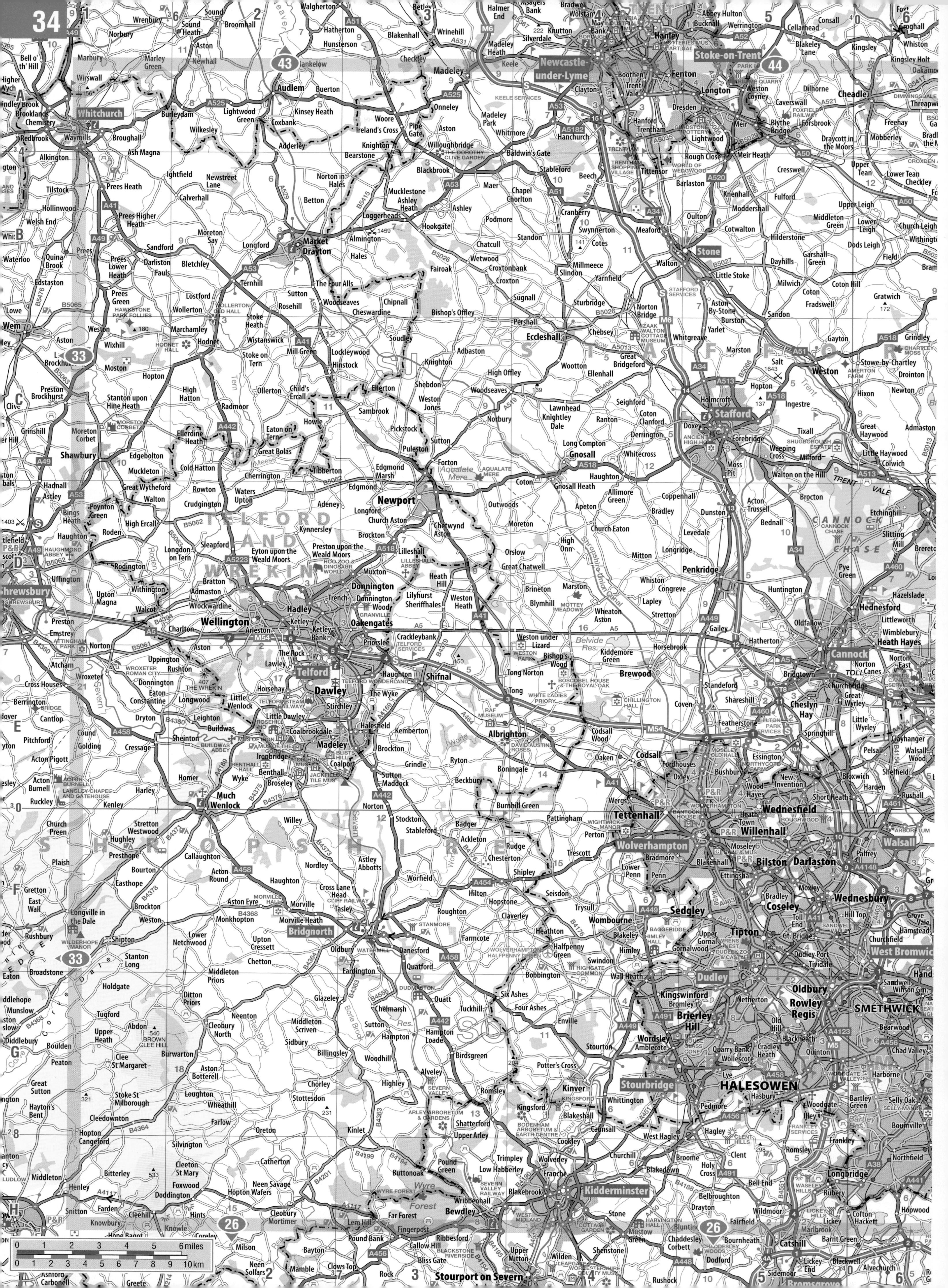
Whitchurch
Audlem
Madeley
Newcastle-under-Lyme
Stoke-on-Trent
Hanley
Fenton
Longton
Cheadle
Market Drayton
Stone
Wem
Hodnet
Eccleshall
Stafford
Shawbury
Newport
Gnosall
Penkridge
Cannock
Hednesford
Shrewsbury
Wellington
Hadley
Oakengates
Donnington
Telford
Dawley
Madeley
Shifnal
Albrighton
Codsall
Much Wenlock
Tettenhall
Wolverhampton
Wednesfield
Willenhall
Walsall
Bilston
Darlaston
Wednesbury
Sedgley
Coseley
Tipton
West Bromwich
Dudley
Bridgnorth
Wombourne
Kingswinford
Brierley Hill
Oldbury
Rowley Regis
SMETHWICK
Stourbridge
HALESOWEN
Kinver
Kidderminster
Bewdley
Stourport on Severn
Longbridge
TELFORD AND WREKIN
SHROPSHIRE
STAFFORDSHIRE
CANNOCK CHASE
M6
M54
M5
A5
A41
A49
A53
A442
A458
A449
A34
A51
0 1 2 3 4 5 6 miles
0 1 2 3 4 5 6 7 8 9 10km

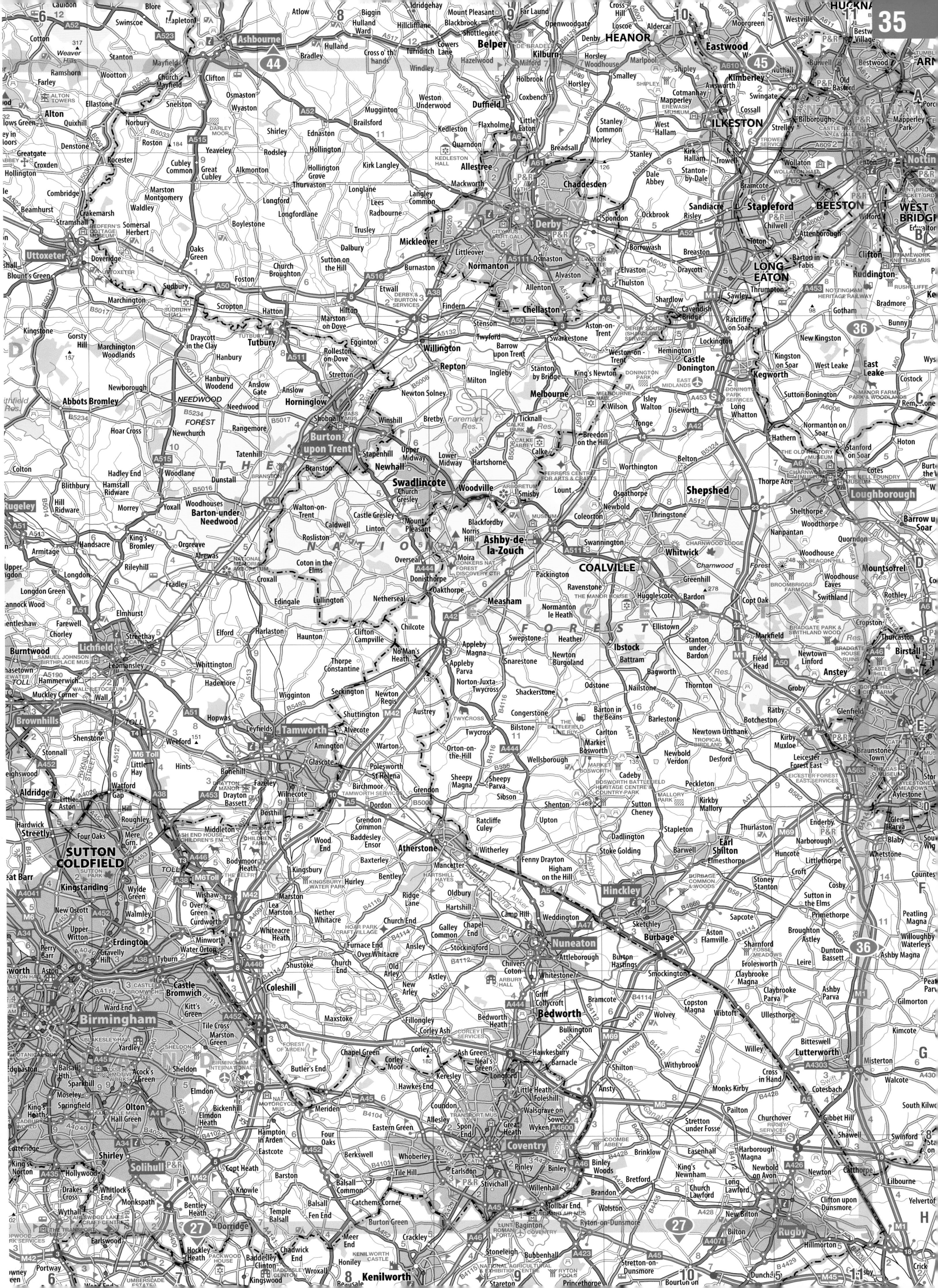
Ashbourne
Belper
HEANOR
Eastwood
Hucknall
Kimberley
ILKESTON
NOTTINGHAM
Uttoxeter
Derby
DERBY
Stapleford
BEESTON
WEST BRIDGFORD
LONG EATON
Tutbury
Burton upon Trent
Swadlincote
Ashby-de-la-Zouch
COALVILLE
Shepshed
Loughborough
Rugeley
Lichfield
Brownhills
Tamworth
Atherstone
Hinckley
Nuneaton
Bedworth
SUTTON COLDFIELD
Birmingham
Solihull
Coventry
Kenilworth
Rugby
Lutterworth
Leicester
NATIONAL FOREST
LEICESTERSHIRE
44
45
36
27

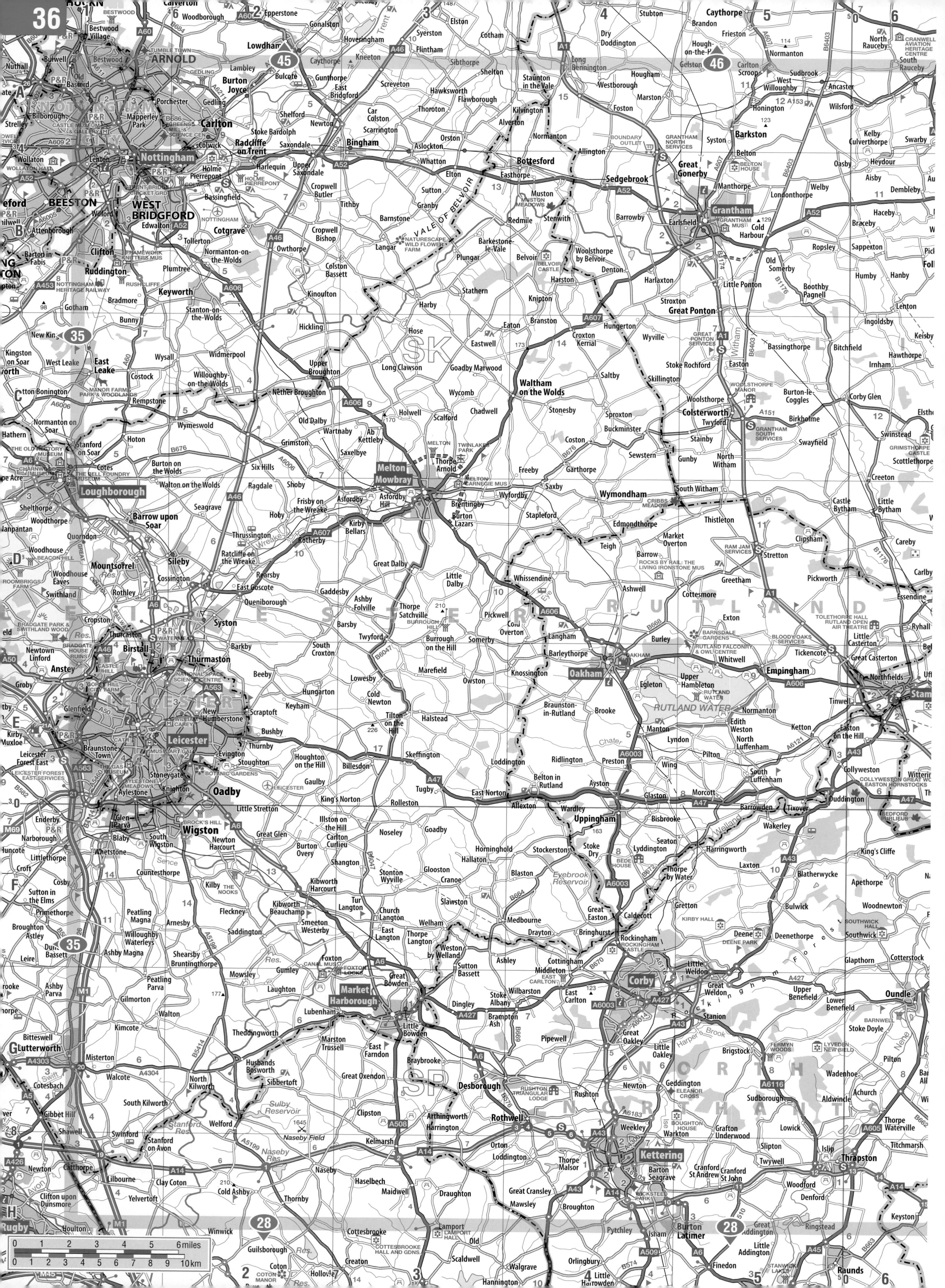
Nottingham
Arnold
Beeston
West Bridgford
Carlton
Bingham
Bottesford
Sedgebrook
Grantham
Great Gonerby
Barkston
Caythorpe
Lowdham
Burton Joyce
Gedling
Radcliffe on Trent
Cotgrave
Keyworth
Ruddington
Clifton
Gotham
East Leake
Loughborough
Barrow upon Soar
Sileby
Mountsorrel
Syston
Birstall
Thurmaston
Anstey
Leicester
Oadby
Wigston
Melton Mowbray
Waltham on the Wolds
Wymondham
Colsterworth
Great Ponton
Oakham
Uppingham
Empingham
Stamford
Rutland Water
Market Harborough
Corby
Kettering
Desborough
Rothwell
Burton Latimer
Thrapston
Oundle
Raunds
Lutterworth
Rugby
Vale of Belvoir
Belvoir Castle
Rutland
Northants
Leicestershire
SK
SP
Long Clawson
Asfordby
Frisby on the Wreake
Kirby Bellars
Great Dalby
Tilton on the Hill
Billesdon
Great Glen
Kibworth Harcourt
Kibworth Beauchamp
Husbands Bosworth
Welford
Great Oakley
Geddington
Rushton
Harringworth
Morcott
Cottesmore
Greetham
Exton
Langham
Barleythorpe
Whissendine
Ketton
Easton on the Hill
Collyweston
Duddington
Glaston
Lyddington
Rockingham
Cottingham
Middleton
Weldon
Brigstock
Stanion
Little Oakley
Newton
Thorpe Malsor
Broughton
Mawsley
Great Cransley
Maidwell
Naseby
Kelmarsh
Clipston
Sibbertoft
Lubenham
Little Bowden
Great Bowden
Foxton
Gumley
Laughton
Mowsley
Saddington
Fleckney
Arnesby
Shearsby
Peatling Magna
Peatling Parva
Gilmorton
Kimcote
Walton
Misterton
Cotesbach
Swinford
Stanford on Avon
Clay Coton
Yelvertoft
Lilbourne
Catthorpe
Clifton upon Dunsmore
Cosby
Blaby
Enderby
Narborough
Whetstone
Countesthorpe
Kilby
Broughton Astley
Ashby Magna
Ashby Parva
Dunton Bassett
Leire
Bitteswell
Welham
Slawston
Medbourne
Drayton
Bringhurst
Great Easton
Caldecott
Blaston
Hallaton
Horninghold
Stockerston
Stoke Dry
Loddington
Skeffington
East Norton
Allexton
Belton in Rutland
Ayston
Wardley
Preston
Wing
Manton
Lyndon
Pilton
Edith Weston
North Luffenham
South Luffenham
Normanton
Tinwell
Tickencote
Great Casterton
Little Casterton
Pickworth
Clipsham
Stretton
Thistleton
Market Overton
Teigh
Barrow
Ashwell
Burley
Egleton
Hambleton
Braunston-in-Rutland
Brooke
Knossington
Owston
Somerby
Pickwell
Cold Overton
Burrough on the Hill
Twyford
Marefield
Lowesby
Cold Newton
Halstead
Hungarton
Keyham
Scraptoft
Bushby
Thurnby
Houghton on the Hill
Stoughton
Evington
Gaulby
King's Norton
Rolleston
Illston on the Hill
Noseley
Goadby
Carlton Curlieu
Burton Overy
Shangton
Stonton Wyville
Glooston
Cranoe
Church Langton
East Langton
Tur Langton
Thorpe Langton
Smeeton Westerby
Marston Trussell
East Farndon
Theddingworth
North Kilworth
South Kilworth
Walcote
Great Oxendon
Braybrooke
Arthingworth
Harrington
Orton
Draughton
Haselbech
Thornby
Cold Ashby
Winwick
Guilsborough
Cottesbrooke
Lamport
Old
Scaldwell
Walgrave
Hannington
Orlingbury
Little Harrowden
Pytchley
Isham
Finedon
Great Addington
Little Addington
Ringstead
Woodford
Denford
Islip
Twywell
Slipton
Cranford St Andrew
Cranford St John
Grafton Underwood
Warkton
Weekley
Barton Seagrave
Lowick
Sudborough
Aldwincle
Titchmarsh
Thorpe Waterville
Achurch
Wadenhoe
Pilton
Stoke Doyle
Lower Benefield
Upper Benefield
Glapthorn
Cotterstock
Southwick
Deenethorpe
Deene
Bulwick
Blatherwycke
Laxton
Gretton
Wakerley
Barrowden
Tixover
Apethorpe
Woodnewton
King's Cliffe
Rockingham Forest
Welland
Eye Brook Reservoir
Sulby Reservoir
Naseby Field
Carlby
Essendine
Ryhall
Little Bytham
Castle Bytham
Creeton
Swinstead
Corby Glen
Bitchfield
Irnham
Ingoldsby
Boothby Pagnell
Little Ponton
Old Somerby
Ropsley
Sapperton
Humby
Hanby
Lenton
Keisby
Hawthorpe
Bassingthorpe
Burton-le-Coggles
Birkholme
Swayfield
Grimsthorpe Castle
Scottlethorpe
North Witham
South Witham
Stainby
Gunby
Twyford
Woolsthorpe
Skillington
Stoke Rochford
Easton
Wyville
Hungerton
Croxton Kerrial
Branston
Knipton
Eaton
Eastwell
Goadby Marwood
Harby
Hose
Stathern
Plungar
Barkestone-le-Vale
Redmile
Muston
Easthorpe
Stenwith
Woolsthorpe by Belvoir
Denton
Harlaxton
Stroxton
Harston
Belvoir
Allington
Normanton
Kilvington
Alverton
Staunton in the Vale
Long Bennington
Foston
Marston
Hougham
Westborough
Dry Doddington
Stubton
Brandon
Hough-on-the-Hill
Gelston
Frieston
Carlton Scroop
Normanton
North Rauceby
South Rauceby
Sudbrook
Ancaster
West Willoughby
Honington
Wilsford
Kelby
Culverthorpe
Swarby
Heydour
Aisby
Oasby
Dembleby
Welby
Londonthorpe
Belton
Syston
Manthorpe
Barrowby
Earlsfield
Cold Harbour
Haceby
Braceby
Elston
Cotham
Syerston
Flintham
Sibthorpe
Shelton
Hawksworth
Flawborough
Thoroton
Orston
Aslockton
Whatton
Elton
Sutton
Granby
Barnstone
Langar
Tithby
Cropwell Butler
Cropwell Bishop
Colston Bassett
Kinoulton
Hickling
Upper Broughton
Nether Broughton
Old Dalby
Holwell
Scalford
Wycomb
Chadwell
Ab Kettleby
Wartnaby
Grimston
Saxelbye
Thorpe Arnold
Freeby
Saxby
Garthorpe
Coston
Sproxton
Buckminster
Sewstern
Wyfordby
Brentingby
Burton Lazars
Stapleford
Edmondthorpe
Six Hills
Ragdale
Shoby
Hoby
Rotherby
Thrussington
Ratcliffe on the Wreake
Rearsby
Cossington
East Goscote
Queniborough
Gaddesby
Ashby Folville
Barsby
Thorpe Satchville
Little Dalby
South Croxton
Beeby
Barkby
Seagrave
Walton on the Wolds
Burton on the Wolds
Cotes
Hoton
Prestwold
Wymeswold
Rempstone
Costock
Wysall
Widmerpool
Willoughby-on-the-Wolds
Stanton-on-the-Wolds
Bunny
Bradmore
Plumtree
Normanton-on-the-Wolds
Tollerton
Owthorpe
Colston
Scarrington
Car Colston
Newton
Saxondale
Shelford
East Bridgford
Gunthorpe
Kneeton
Hoveringham
Caythorpe
Epperstone
Gonalston
Woodborough
Lambley
Bulcote
Stoke Bardolph
Colwick
Holme Pierrepont
Bassingfield
Edwalton
Wilford
Attenborough
Barton in Fabis
Bilborough
Strelley
Wollaton
Lenton
Bulwell
Nuthall
Bestwood Village
Mapperley
Porchester
Stanford on Soar
Normanton on Soar
Sutton Bonington
Kingston on Soar
West Leake
Shelthorpe
Woodthorpe
Quorndon
Woodhouse
Woodhouse Eaves
Swithland
Rothley
Cropston
Thurcaston
Newtown Linford
Glenfield
Groby
Kirby Muxloe
Leicester Forest East
Braunstone Town
New Humberstone
Humberstone
Stoneygate
Knighton
Aylestone
Glen Parva
South Wigston
Newton Harcourt
Little Stretton
Littlethorpe
Croft
Sutton in the Elms
Primethorpe
Gibbet Hill
Shawell
Newton
Houlton
Sutton Bassett
Weston by Welland
Ashley
Wilbarston
Stoke Albany
Dingley
Brampton Ash
Pipewell
East Carlton
0 1 2 3 4 5 6 miles
0 1 2 3 4 5 6 7 8 9 10 km

Leasingham
Evedon
Ewerby
Ewerby Thorpe
South Kyme Fen
Holdingham
Kirkby la Thorpe
Howell
Sleaford
Asgarby
Quarrington
Silk Willoughby
Heckington
Great Hale
Little Hale
Heckington Windmill
Burton Pedwardine
Northbeck
Helpringham
Scredington
Aswarby
Osbournby
Spanby
Swaton
Threekingham
Bridge End
Horbling
Billingborough
Stow
Birthorpe
Pointon
Laughton
Aslackby
Millthorpe
Dowsby
Graby
Kirkby Underwood
Rippingale
Dunsby
Bulby
Stainfield
Haconby
Hanthorpe
Morton
Cawthorpe
Dyke
Edenham
Bourne
Twenty
Tongue End
Northorpe
Thurlby
Toft
Manthorpe
Thetford
Obthorpe
Wilsthorpe
Braceborough
Greatford
Baston
Langtoft
Barholm
Towngate
Market Deeping
Frognall
Deeping St James
Deeping Gate
Tallington
West Deeping
Maxey
Northborough
Etton
Peakirk
Glinton
Bainton
Barnack
Ufford
Pilsgate
Helpston
Southorpe
Werrington
Gunthorpe
Marholm
Walton
Upton
Dogsthorpe
Newark
Peterborough
Wansford
Stibbington
Ailsworth
Castor
Longthorpe
Sutton
Water Newton
Alwalton
Orton Longueville
Orton Waterville
Old Fletton
Fengate
Stanground
Hampton
Farcet
Chesterton
Elton
Haddon
Yaxley
Morborne
Eaglethorpe
Warmington
Tansor
Norman Cross
Folksworth
Stilton
Caldecote
Ashton
Polebrook
Lutton
Denton
Holme
Conington
Glatton
Barnwell St Andrew
Hemington
Luddington in the Brook
Sawtry
Great Gidding
Little Gidding
Thurning
Steeple Gidding
Winwick
Hamerton Zoo Park
Coppingford
Clopton
Hamerton
Upton
Old Weston
Alconbury Weston
Alconbury Weald
Alconbury
Brington
Bythorn
Molesworth
Buckworth
Barham
Leighton Bromswold
Woolley
Catworth
Spaldwick
Easton
Ellington
Huntingdon
Little Stukeley
Great Stukeley
Abbots Ripton
Wennington
Broughton
King's Ripton
Sapley
Hartford
Wyton
Houghton
Hemingford Abbots
St Ives
Holywell
Needingworth
Bluntisham
Colne
Somersham
Earith
Old Hurst
Woodhurst
Pidley
Fenton
Warboys
Little Raveley
Great Raveley
Wistow
Upwood
Bury
Ramsey
Ramsey Heights
Ramsey Hollow
Ramsey Forty Foot
Ramsey St Mary's
Ramsey Mereside
Church End
Wood Walton
Woodwalton Fen
Holme Fen
Monks Wood
Whittlesey Mere
Farcet Fen
Pondersbridge
Middle Moor
Benwick
Whittlesey
King's Delph
Inham's End
Eastrea
Coates
Turves
North Side
Eldernell
Stone Bridge Corner
Thorney
Eye
Eye Green
Newborough
Thorney Toll
Nene Terrace
Crowland
Dowsdale
North Fen
Throckenholt
Parson Drove
Church End
Murrow
Rogue's Alley
Guyhirn Gull
Guyhirn
Ring's End
Tholomas Drove
Wisbech St Mary
Wisbech
Walsoken
New Walsoken
Emneth
Elm
Friday Bridge
Waldersey
Coldham
Chainbridge
Westry
Norwoodside
March
Town End
Wimblington
Doddington
Flood's Ferry
Manea
Chatteris
Horseway
Welches Dam
Purls Bridge
Ferry Hill
Chapel Head
Tick Fen
Pidley Fen
Mepal
Sutton
Witcham
Wentworth
Witchford
Coveney
Wardy Hill
Ely
Queen Adelaide
Prickwillow
Chettisham
Little Downham
Pymoor
Littleport
Stuntney
Little Thetford
Barway
Soham Cotes
Soham
Stretham
Wilburton
Haddenham
North Hill
Aldreth
Hill Row
Doles
Welney
Lakesend
Christchurch
Tipsend
Upwell
Three Holes
Nordelph
Outwell
Stow Bardolph
Barroway Drove
West Head
Emneth Hungate
Holly End
Marshland St James
Marshland Fen
St John's Fen End
St John's Highway
Tilney St Lawrence
Walpole Highway
Walpole St Peter
Walpole St Andrew
Walpole Marsh
West Walton
West Walton Highway
Ingleborough
Terrington St John
Terrington St Clement
Tilney High End
Tilney All Saints
Hay Green
Walpole Cross Keys
Orange Row
Clenchwarton
Sutton Bridge
Long Sutton
Little London
Chapelgate
Guy's Head
Terrington Marsh
Gedney Drove End
Gedney Marsh
Dawsmere
Gedney Dyke
Gedney
Fleet Hargate
Fleet
Gedney Broadgate
Lutton
Sutton Crosses
Tydd St Mary
Tydd Gote
Four Gotes
Tydd St Giles
Newton
Fitton End
Leverington
Gorefield
Sutton St Edmund
Sutton St James
Holbeach St Johns
Holbeach Drove
Gedney Hill
Shepeau Stow
Whaplode Drove
Moulton Eaugate
Moulton Chapel
Cowbit
Brotherhouse Bar
Deeping St Nicholas
Deeping Fen
Hop Pole
Pode Hole
Little London
Clay Lake
Spalding
Low Fulney
Weston Hills
Austendike
Whaplode St Catherine
Moulton
Weston
Whaplode
Holbeach
Holbeach Clough
Holbeach Bank
Saracen's Head
Halesgate
Holbeach Hurn
Holbeach St Marks
Holbeach St Matthew
Holbeach Marsh
Moulton Seas End
Pinchbeck
Pinchbeck West
Pinchbeck Bars
Northgate
Crossgate
Surfleet
Surfleet Seas End
Risegate
Gosberton
Gosberton Clough
Westhorpe
Quadring
Church End
Donington
Donington South Ing
Northorpe
Wigtoft
Sutterton
Algarkirk
Fosdyke
Bicker
Asperton
Kirton
Kirton End
Drayton
Swineshead
Swineshead Bridge
Fenhouses
North End
Kirton Holme
Frampton West End
Frampton
Wyberton
Skirbeck Quarter
Hubbert's Bridge
Chain Bridge
Boston
Boston West
Skirbeck
Fishtoft
Scrane End
Freiston
Butterwick
Sandholme
Skeldyke
Seadyke
Bucklegate
East Heckington
Holland Fen
Amber Hill
Brothertoft
Langrick
Anton's Gowt
Frith Bank
Hill Dyke
Boston Long Hedges
Cowbridge
Haltoft End
Benington
Leverton
Leverton Outgate
Leverton Highgate
Leverton Lucasgate
Boston Deeps
Lynn Deeps
The Wash
Lynn Channel
Bicker Haven
Great Ouse
New Bedford River
Old Bedford River
Sixteen Foot Drain
Twenty Foot River
Forty Foot Drain
Bedford Level (North)
Bedford Level (Middle)
Isle of Ely
Lincoln
Peterborough
Cambridge
Norfolk
TF
TL
46
47
38
29

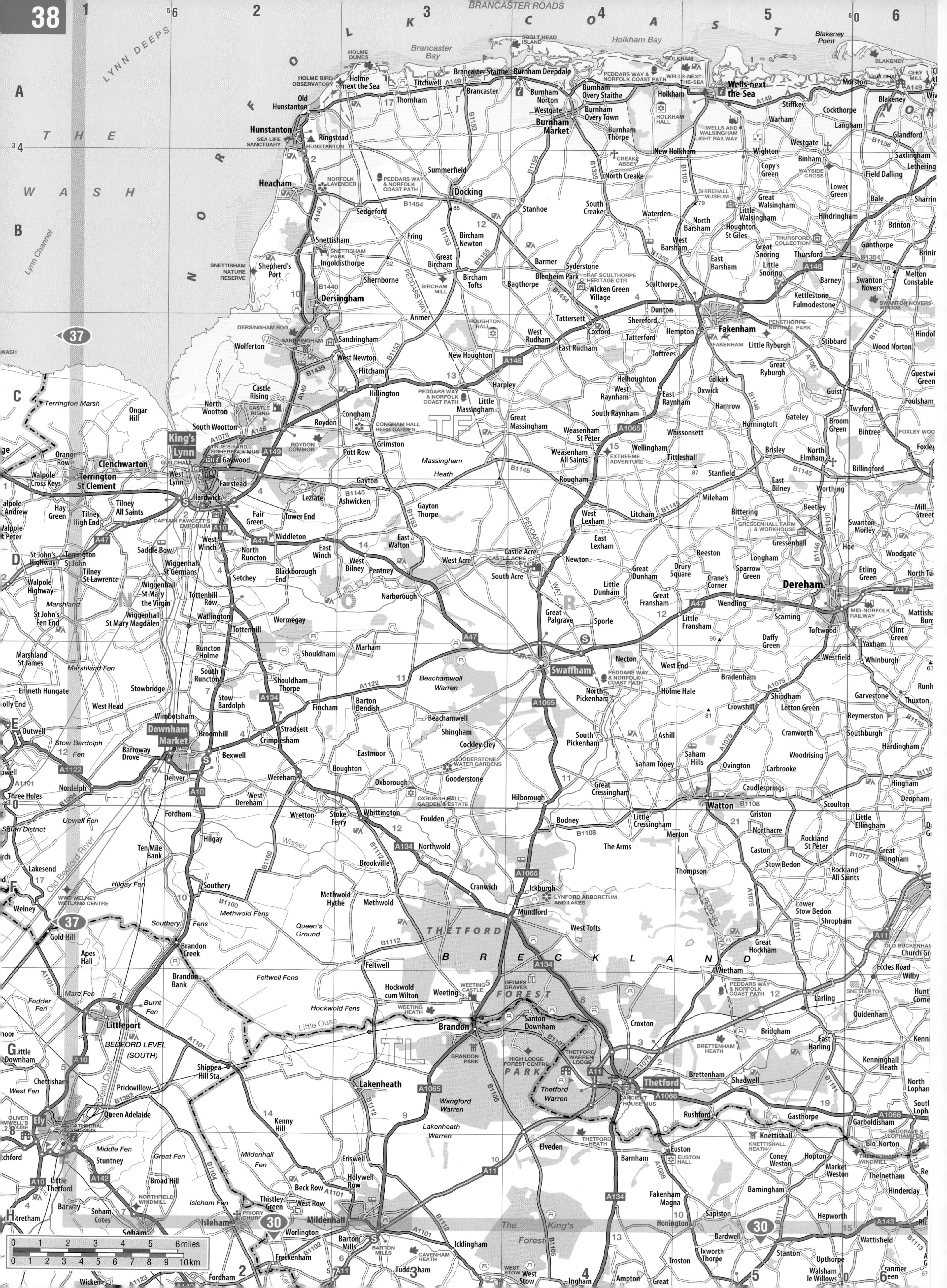

BRANCASTER ROADS
LYNN DEEPS
N O R F O L K   C O A S T
T H E   W A S H
N O R F O L K
Lynn Channel
Holkham Bay
Blakeney Point
Brancaster Bay
HOLME DUNES
SCOLT HEAD ISLAND
HOLME BIRD OBSERVATORY
Holme next the Sea
Titchwell
Brancaster Staithe
Burnham Deepdale
Brancaster
Burnham Norton
Burnham Overy Staithe
Holkham
Wells-next-the-Sea
Morston
Blakeney
Cley next the Sea
Old Hunstanton
Thornham
Burnham Westgate
Burnham Market
Burnham Overy Town
Burnham Thorpe
HOLKHAM HALL
WELLS AND WALSINGHAM LIGHT RAILWAY
Stiffkey
Cockthorpe
Langham
Glandford
Hunstanton
SEA LIFE SANCTUARY
Ringstead
CREAKE ABBEY
New Holkham
Wighton
Westgate
Binham
Saxlingham
Letheringsett
Copy's Green
WAYSIDE CROSS
Field Dalling
Heacham
NORFOLK LAVENDER
PEDDARS WAY & NORFOLK COAST PATH
Summerfield
Docking
North Creake
SHIREHALL MUSEUM
Great Walsingham
Lower Green
Bale
Sharrington
Sedgeford
Stanhoe
South Creake
Waterden
North Barsham
Little Walsingham
Houghton St Giles
Hindringham
Brinton
Snettisham
SNETTISHAM PARK
Fring
Bircham Newton
West Barsham
THURSFORD COLLECTION
Thursford
Gunthorpe
SNETTISHAM NATURE RESERVE
Shepherd's Port
Ingoldisthorpe
Great Bircham
Barmer
Syderstone
East Barsham
Great Snoring
Little Snoring
Briningham
Melton Constable
Shernborne
BIRCHAM MILL
Bircham Tofts
Bagthorpe
Blenheim Park
RAF SCULTHORPE HERITAGE CTR
Wicken Green Village
Sculthorpe
Barney
Swanton Novers
Dersingham
Kettlestone
Fulmodestone
SWANTON NOVERS WOODS
DERSINGHAM BOG
Anmer
HOUGHTON HALL
Tattersett
Dunton
Shereford
Hempton
Fakenham
PENSTHORPE NATURAL PARK
Hindolveston
Wolferton
SANDRINGHAM
Sandringham
West Rudham
Coxford
Tatterford
Little Ryburgh
Stibbard
Wood Norton
West Newton
New Houghton
East Rudham
Toftrees
Great Ryburgh
Flitcham
Harpley
Helhoughton
Colkirk
Guestwick Green
Terrington Marsh
Castle Rising
Hillington
Little Massingham
West Raynham
East Raynham
Oxwick
Guist
Foulsham
North Wootton
Ongar Hill
CASTLE RISING
Congham
CONGHAM HALL HERB GARDEN
Great Massingham
South Raynham
Hamrow
Twyford
South Wootton
Roydon
Horningtoft
Gateley
Broom Green
Bintree
FOXLEY WOOD
King's Lynn
TRUE'S YARD FISHERFOLK MUS
Gaywood
ROYDON COMMON
Grimston
Weasenham St Peter
Whissonsett
Foxley
Orange Row
Clenchwarton
GUILDHALL
Pott Row
Massingham Heath
Weasenham All Saints
EXTREME ADVENTURE
Wellingham
Tittleshall
Brisley
North Elmham
Walpole Cross Keys
Terrington St Clement
West Lynn
Fairstead
Gayton
Rougham
Stanfield
Billingford
Hardwick
Leziate
Ashwicken
East Bilney
Worthing
Walpole St Andrew
Hay Green
Tilney High End
Tilney All Saints
CAPTAIN FAWCETT'S EMPORIUM
Fair Green
Tower End
Gayton Thorpe
West Lexham
Litcham
Mileham
Bittering
Beetley
Mill Street
Walpole St Peter
West Winch
Middleton
GRESSENHALL FARM & WORKHOUSE
Swanton Morley
St John's Highway
Terrington St John
Saddle Bow
North Runcton
East Winch
East Walton
East Lexham
Gressenhall
Hoe
Tilney St Lawrence
Wiggenhall St Germans
West Bilney
Pentney
West Acre
Castle Acre
CASTLE ACRE PRIORY
Newton
Beeston
Longham
Woodgate
Walpole Highway
Wiggenhall St Mary the Virgin
Setchey
Blackborough End
South Acre
Great Dunham
Drury Square
Crane's Corner
Sparrow Green
Etling Green
North Tuddenham
Marshland
Tottenhill Row
Little Dunham
Great Fransham
Dereham
St John's Fen End
Wiggenhall St Mary Magdalen
Watlington
Narborough
Wendling
MID-NORFOLK RAILWAY
Mattishall Burgh
Wormegay
Tottenhill
Great Palgrave
Sporle
Little Fransham
Scarning
Toftwood
Clint Green
Marshland St James
Runcton Holme
Shouldham
Marham
Swaffham
Necton
Daffy Green
Yaxham
Marshland Fen
South Runcton
Beachamwell Warren
PEDDARS WAY & NORFOLK COAST PATH
West End
Westfield
Whinburgh
Emneth Hungate
Stowbridge
Shouldham Thorpe
North Pickenham
Holme Hale
Bradenham
Runhall
Holly End
West Head
Stow Bardolph
Fincham
Barton Bendish
Shipdham
Garvestone
Thuxton
Wimbotsham
Beachamwell
Crowshill
Letton Green
Reymerston
Outwell
Downham Market
Broomhill
Stradsett
Shingham
South Pickenham
Ashill
Cranworth
Southburgh
Stow Bardolph Fen
Barroway Drove
Bexwell
Crimplesham
Cockley Cley
Saham Hills
Woodrising
Hardingham
Eastmoor
GOODERSTONE WATER GARDENS
Saham Toney
Ovington
Carbrooke
Nordelph
Denver
Wereham
Boughton
Oxborough
Gooderstone
Great Cressingham
Caudlesprings
Hingham
Three Holes
West Dereham
OXBURGH HALL, GARDEN & ESTATE
Hilborough
Watton
Scoulton
Deopham
Upwell Fen
Fordham
Wretton
Stoke Ferry
Whittington
Foulden
Bodney
Little Cressingham
Griston
Little Ellingham
South District
Hilgay
Wissey
Northwold
Merton
Northacre
Rockland St Peter
Ten Mile Bank
The Arms
Caston
Great Ellingham
Lakesend
Old Bedford River
Brookville
Stow Bedon
Thompson
Rockland All Saints
WWT WELNEY WETLAND CENTRE
Hilgay Fen
Southery
Cranwich
Ickburgh
LYNFORD ARBORETUM AND LAKES
Welney
Methwold Hythe
Methwold
Methwold Fens
Mundford
Lower Stow Bedon
Shropham
Gold Hill
Southery Fens
Queen's Ground
THETFORD
West Tofts
Apes Hall
Brandon Creek
B R E C K L A N D
Great Hockham
OLD BUCKENHAM
Church Green
Feltwell
Wretham
Eccles Road
Wilby
Brandon Bank
Feltwell Fens
Hockwold cum Wilton
Weeting
WEETING CASTLE
GRIMES GRAVES
FOREST
PEDDARS WAY & NORFOLK COAST PATH
SNETTERTON
Hunt's Corner
Fodder Fen
Mare Fen
Burnt Fen
Hockwold Fens
WEETING HEATH
Larling
Littleport
Little Ouse
Brandon
Santon Downham
Croxton
Quidenham
BEDFORD LEVEL (SOUTH)
Bridgham
Kenninghall
Little Downham
BRANDON PARK
HIGH LODGE FOREST CENTRE
PARK
THETFORD WARREN LODGE
BRETTENHAM HEATH
East Harling
Shippea Hill Sta.
Kenninghall Heath
Chettisham
Great Ouse
Prickwillow
Lakenheath
Thetford Warren
Brettenham
Shadwell
North Lopham
West Fen
Thetford
ANCIENT HOUSE MUS
South Lopham
Ely
CATHEDRAL AND MUS
OLIVER CROMWELL'S HOUSE
Queen Adelaide
Kenny Hill
Wangford Warren
Rushford
Gasthorpe
Garboldisham
Lakenheath Warren
Knettishall
KNETTISHALL HEATH
REDGRAVE & LOPHAM FEN
Middle Fen
Stuntney
Mildenhall Fen
Elveden
THETFORD HEATH
Euston
EUSTON HALL
Blo' Norton
Stretham
Great Fen
Broad Hill
Eriswell
Barnham
Coney Weston
Hopton
Market Weston
THELNETHAM WINDMILL
Thelnetham
Redgrave
Little Thetford
Holywell Row
Beck Row
Isleham Fen
NORTHFIELD WINDMILL
Thistley Green
West Row
Fakenham Magna
Barningham
Hinderclay
Barway
Soham Cotes
Isleham
PRIORY CHURCH
Mildenhall
Worlington
Sapiston
Honington
Hepworth
Rickinghall
Soham
The King's Forest
Bardwell
Wattisfield
Barton Mills
BARTON MILLS
Icklingham
Freckenham
CAVENHAM HEATH
Ixworth Thorpe
Stanton
Upthorpe
Walsham le Willows
Troston
Wicken
Fordham
Tuddenham
West Stow
Ingham
Ampton
Great
Cranmer Green
TF
TL
37
30
0 1 2 3 4 5 6 miles
0 1 2 3 4 5 6 7 8 9 10 km

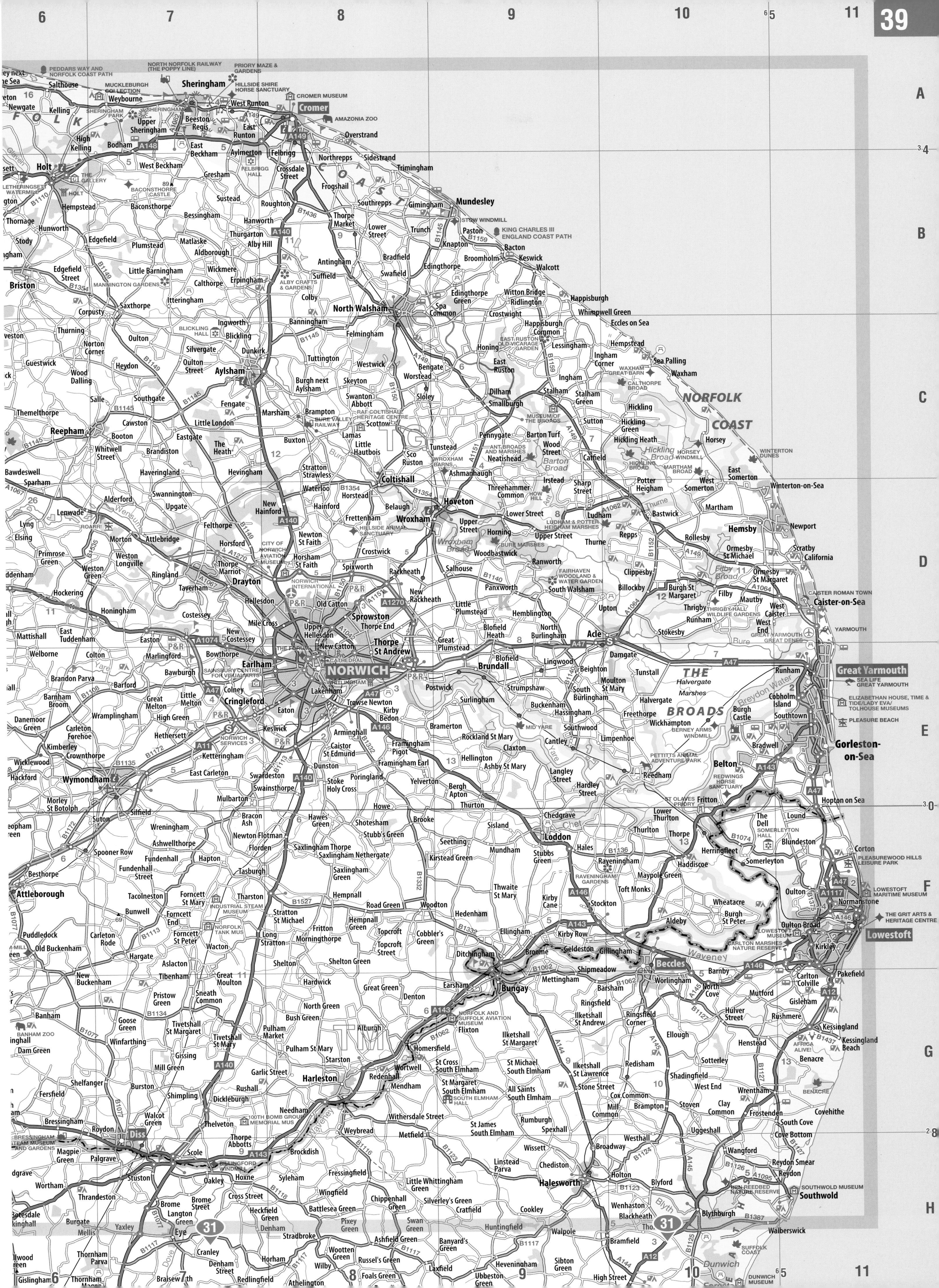
Sheringham
Cromer
Holt
Mundesley
North Walsham
Aylsham
Reepham
Coltishall
Wroxham
Hoveton
Drayton
NORWICH
Earlham
Cringleford
Wymondham
Attleborough
Diss
Eye
Harleston
Bungay
Beccles
Loddon
Acle
Halesworth
Southwold
Lowestoft
Great Yarmouth
Gorleston-on-Sea
Caister-on-Sea
Hemsby
Happisburgh
Stalham
Ludham
Horning
Brundall
Sprowston
Thorpe St Andrew
Costessey
Taverham
Hellesdon
Belton
Kessingland
Wrentham
Blythburgh
Walberswick
Dunwich
NORFOLK COAST
THE BROADS
Breydon Water
Hickling Broad
Filby Broad
Barton Broad
Wroxham Broad
Waveney
Yare
Bure
Thurne
Chet
Blyth
PEDDARS WAY AND NORFOLK COAST PATH
NORTH NORFOLK RAILWAY (THE POPPY LINE)
PRIORY MAZE & GARDENS
MUCKLEBURGH COLLECTION
HILLSIDE SHIRE HORSE SANCTUARY
CROMER MUSEUM
AMAZONIA ZOO
FELBRIGG HALL
BACONSTHORPE CASTLE
LETHERINGSETT WATERMILL
MANNINGTON GARDENS
ALBY CRAFTS & GARDENS
BLICKLING HALL
STOW WINDMILL
KING CHARLES III ENGLAND COAST PATH
EAST RUSTON OLD VICARAGE GARDEN
WAXHAM GREAT BARN
CALTHORPE BROAD
MUSEUM OF THE BROADS
RAF COLTISHALL HERITAGE CENTRE
BURE VALLEY RAILWAY
ANT BROADS AND MARSHES
WROXHAM BARNS
HOW HILL
LUDHAM & POTTER HEIGHAM MARSHES
BURE MARSHES
HORSEY WINDMILL
HICKLING BROAD
MARTHAM BROAD
WINTERTON DUNES
HILLSIDE ANIMAL SANCTUARY
CITY OF NORWICH AVIATION MUSEUM
NORWICH INTERNATIONAL
ROARR!
FAIRHAVEN WOODLAND & WATER GARDEN
THRIGBY HALL WILDLIFE GARDENS
CAISTER ROMAN TOWN
YARMOUTH
GREAT YARMOUTH GREAT DENES
SEA LIFE GREAT YARMOUTH
ELIZABETHAN HOUSE, TIME & TIDE/LADY EVA/TOLHOUSE MUSEUMS
PLEASURE BEACH
SAINSBURY CENTRE FOR VISUAL ARTS
THE FORUM
CATHEDRAL
NORWICH SERVICES
MID YARE
BERNEY ARMS WINDMILL
PETTITTS ANIMAL ADVENTURE PARK
REDWINGS HORSE SANCTUARY
ST OLAVES PRIORY
SOMERLEYTON HALL
PLEASUREWOOD HILLS LEISURE PARK
LOWESTOFT MARITIME MUSEUM
THE GRIT ARTS & HERITAGE CENTRE
LOWESTOFT MUSEUM
CARLTON MARSHES NATURE RESERVE
RAVENINGHAM GARDENS
INDUSTRIAL STEAM MUSEUM
NORFOLK TANK MUS
NORFOLK AND SUFFOLK AVIATION MUSEUM
SOUTH ELMHAM HALL
100TH BOMB GROUP MEMORIAL MUS
BILLINGFORD WINDMILL
BRESSINGHAM STEAM MUSEUM AND GARDENS
BANHAM ZOO
AFRICA ALIVE!
BENACRE
HEN REEDBED NATURE RESERVE
SOUTHWOLD MUSEUM
SUFFOLK COAST
DUNWICH MUSEUM
A140
A149
A148
A1067
A1074
A47
A11
A146
A143
A144
A145
A12
A1270
A1151
A1062
A1064
A1117
A1095
31

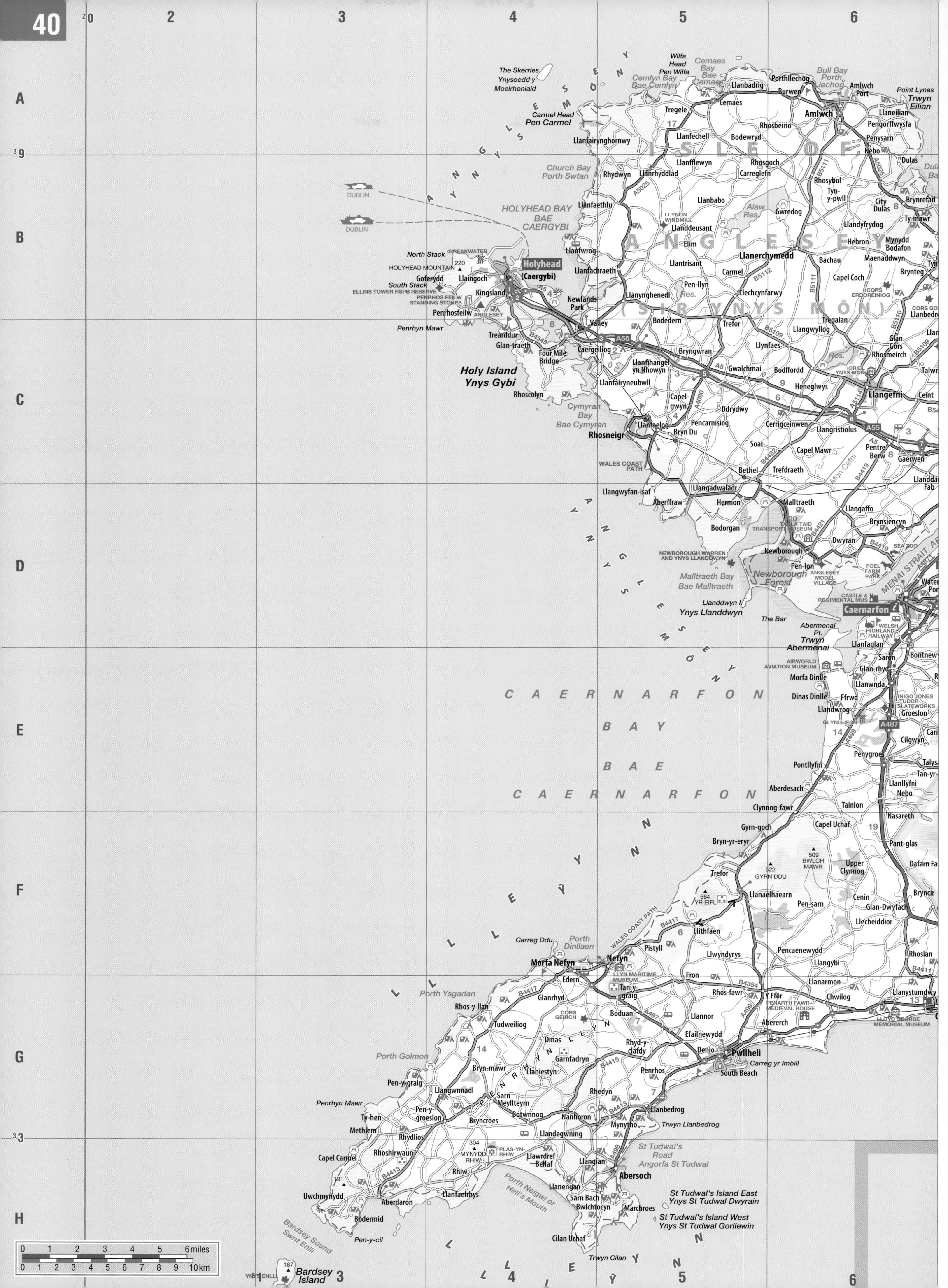

ISLE OF ANGLESEY (SIR YNYS MÔN)
Holy Island Ynys Gybi
CAERNARFON BAY BAE CAERNARFON
PENRHYN LLŶN
The Skerries Ynysoedd y Moelrhoniaid
Carmel Head Pen Carmel
Church Bay Porth Swtan
HOLYHEAD BAY BAE CAERGYBI
Cemlyn Bay Bae Cemlyn
Cemaes Bay Bae Cemaes
Wilfa Head Pen Wilfa
Bull Bay Porth Llechog
Point Lynas Trwyn Eilian
North Stack
South Stack
HOLYHEAD MOUNTAIN
ELLINS TOWER RSPB RESERVE
PENRHOS FEILW STANDING STONES
Holyhead (Caergybi)
Penrhyn Mawr
Cymyran Bay Bae Cymyran
WALES COAST PATH
NEWBOROUGH WARREN AND YNYS LLANDDWYN
Malltraeth Bay Bae Malltraeth
Newborough Forest
Llanddwyn I. Ynys Llanddwyn
The Bar
Abermenai Pt. Trwyn Abermenai
MENAI STRAIT
Caernarfon
AIRWORLD AVIATION MUSEUM
INIGO JONES TUDOR SLATEWORKS
Amlwch
Cemaes
Llanerchymedd
Llangefni
Rhosneigr
Valley
Trearddur
Rhoscolyn
Aberffraw
Newborough
Malltraeth
Dwyran
Bodorgan
Nefyn
Morfa Nefyn
Porth Dinllaen
Carreg Ddu
Porth Ysgadan
Porth Golmon
Tudweiliog
Trefor
Llanaelhaearn
Clynnog-fawr
Pwllheli
South Beach
Carreg yr Imbill
Llanbedrog
Trwyn Llanbedrog
Abersoch
St Tudwal's Road Angorfa St Tudwal
St Tudwal's Island East Ynys St Tudwal Dwyrain
St Tudwal's Island West Ynys St Tudwal Gorllewin
Porth Neigwl or Hell's Mouth
Aberdaron
Uwchmynydd
Bardsey Sound Swnt Enlli
Bardsey Island
Trwyn Cilan
Cilan Uchaf
Penrhyn Mawr
LLŶN MARITIME MUSEUM
PENARTH FAWR MEDIEVAL HOUSE
LLOYD GEORGE MEMORIAL MUSEUM
DUBLIN
0 1 2 3 4 5 6 miles
0 1 2 3 4 5 6 7 8 9 10 km

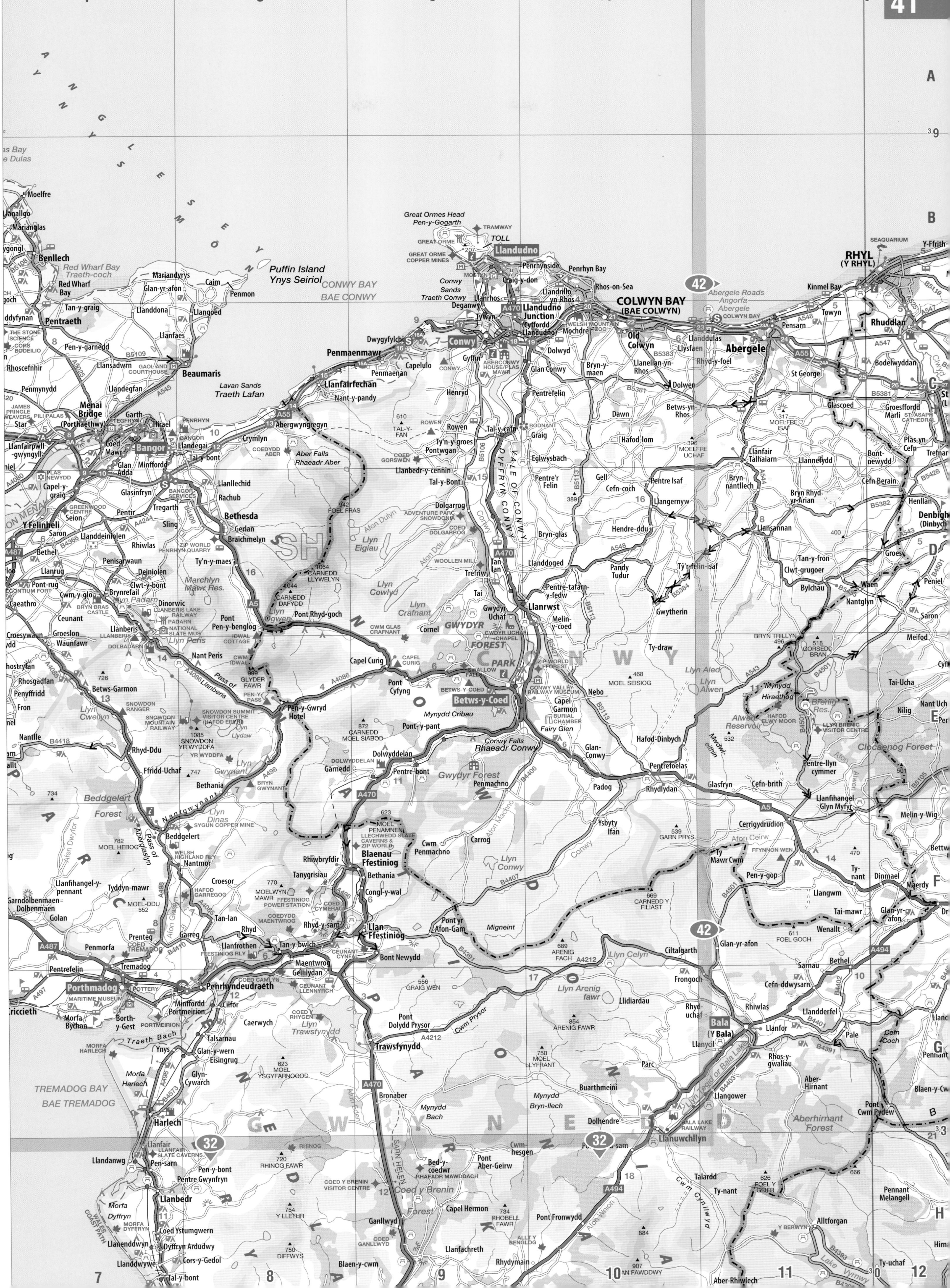
7
8
9
10
11
A
B
C
D
E
F
G
H
12
ANGLESEY
YNYS MÔN
Moelfre
Benllech
Red Wharf Bay
Traeth-coch
Puffin Island
Ynys Seiriol
CONWY BAY
BAE CONWY
Great Ormes Head
Pen-y-Gogarth
Llandudno
Llandudno Junction
(Cyffordd Llandudno)
Craig-y-don
Penrhyn Bay
Rhos-on-Sea
COLWYN BAY
(BAE COLWYN)
Old Colwyn
Llysfaen
Llanddulas
Abergele
Abergele Roads
Pensarn
Towyn
Kinmel Bay
RHYL
(Y RHYL)
Rhuddlan
Bodelwyddan
St George
Denbigh
(Dinbych)
Conwy
Deganwy
Penmaenmawr
Llanfairfechan
Abergwyngregyn
Beaumaris
Lavan Sands
Traeth Lafan
Pentraeth
Menai Bridge
(Porthaethwy)
Bangor
Y Felinheli
Llandegai
Tal-y-bont
Bethesda
Rachub
Llanberis
Dinorwic
Deiniolen
Llanrug
Caeathro
Waunfawr
Betws-Garmon
Rhyd-Ddu
Nant Peris
Pass of Llanberis
Pen-y-Gwryd Hotel
Capel Curig
SNOWDON
YR WYDDFA
1085
Beddgelert
Nantgwynant
Pass of Aberglaslyn
Nantmor
Croesor
Tremadog
Porthmadog
Penrhyndeudraeth
Minffordd
Portmeirion
Criccieth
Morfa Bychan
Borth-y-Gest
Maentwrog
Gellilydan
Tan-y-bwlch
Blaenau Ffestiniog
Llan Ffestiniog
Bont Newydd
Dolwyddelan
Pentre-bont
Betws-y-Coed
Pont-y-pant
Penmachno
Gwydyr Forest
Llanrwst
Trefriw
Tal-y-Bont
Dolgarrog
Rowen
Tal-y-cafn
Eglwysbach
Glan Conwy
Llangernyw
Llansannan
Pentrefoelas
Rhydlydan
Cerrigydrudion
Glasfryn
Ysbyty Ifan
Trawsfynydd
Llyn Trawsfynydd
Harlech
Talsarnau
Ynys
Llanbedr
Llanfair
Pen-sarn
TREMADOG BAY
BAE TREMADOG
Bronaber
Bala
(Y Bala)
Llyn Tegid or Bala Lake
Llanuwchllyn
Llangower
Llanfor
Frongoch
Rhiwlas
Llandderfel
Sarnau
Bethel
Llyn Celyn
Llyn Arenig fawr
Arenig Fawr
854
Capel Hermon
Coed y Brenin
Ganllwyd
Llanfachreth
Rhydymain
Dyffryn Ardudwy
Tal-y-bont
Llanddwywe
Alltforgan
Lake Vyrnwy
SNOWDONIA
NATIONAL PARK
PARC CENEDLAETHOL ERYRI
CONWY
GWYNEDD
Clocaenog Forest
Alwen Reservoir
Llyn Brenig
A5
A55
A470
A494
A487
A4212
42
32

SC
I R I S H
S E A
LIVERPOOL BAY
SH
Southport
Formby
HOYLAKE
West Kirby
Wallasey
Birkenhead
Bootle
BEBINGTON
Heswall
Neston
Flint (Y Fflint)
Connah's Quay
Queensferry
Mold (Yr Wyddgrug)
Buckley (Bwcle)
Holywell (Treffynnon)
Prestatyn
RHYL (Y RHYL)
COLWYN BAY (BAE COLWYN)
Abergele
Rhuddlan
St Asaph (Llanelwy)
Denbigh (Dinbych)
Ruthin (Rhuthun)
Wrexham (WRECSAM)
Llangollen
Corwen
FLINTSHIRE (SIR Y FFLINT)
DENBIGHSHIRE (SIR DDINBYCH)
CONWY
River Dee Afon Dyfrdwy
West Hoyle Bank
Welsh Channel
Point of Ayr Yr Parlwr Du
Clocaenog Forest
Llyn Brenig
Alwen Reservoir
BELFAST
DOUGLAS (Nov-March) DUBLIN
DOUGLAS (March-Nov)
41
49
32
33
0 1 2 3 4 5 6 miles
0 1 2 3 4 5 6 7 8 9 10 km

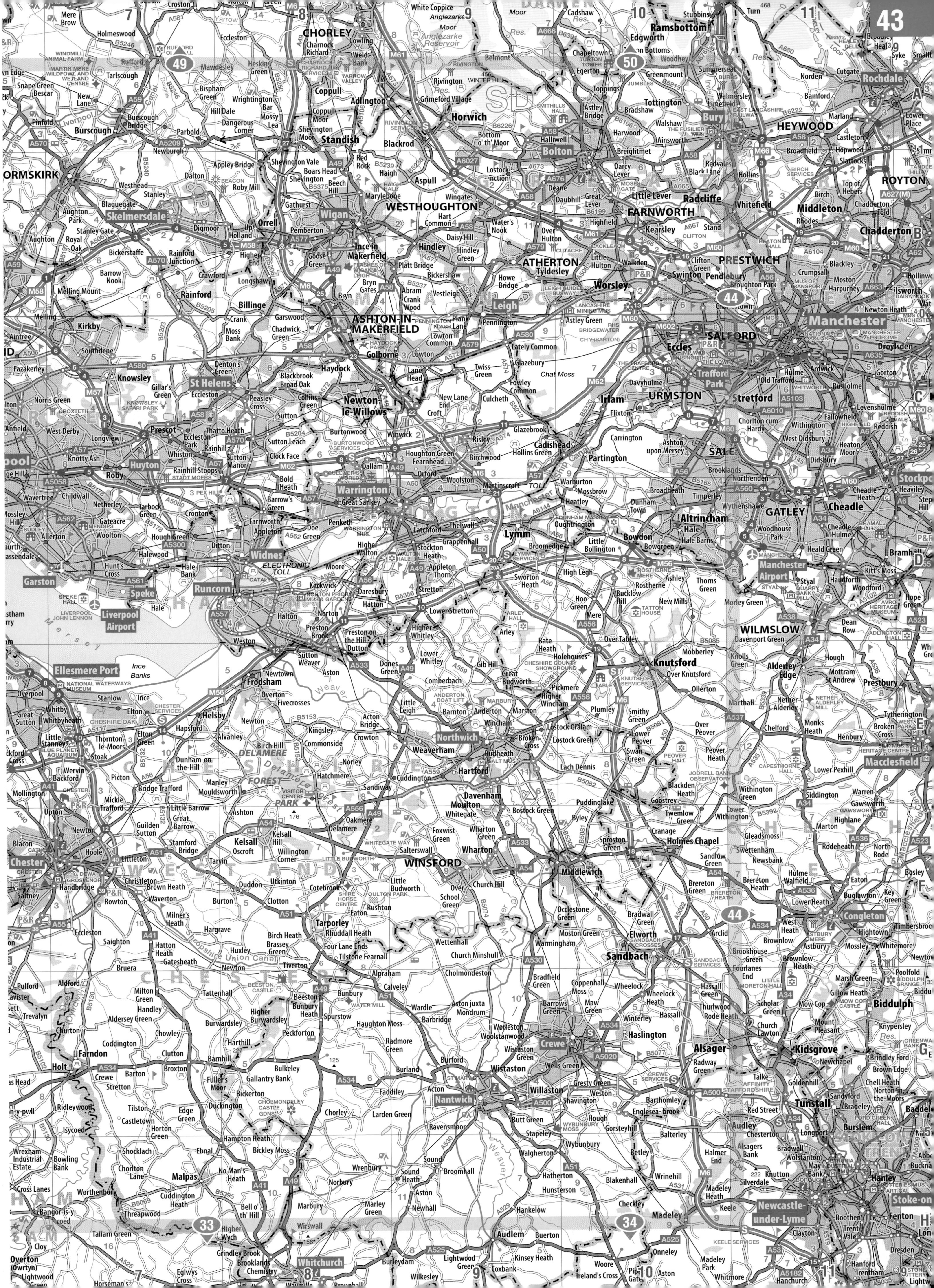
CHORLEY
Ramsbottom
Edgworth
Rochdale
HEYWOOD
Bury
ROYTON
Horwich
Bolton
Standish
Adlington
Wigan
WESTHOUGHTON
Skelmersdale
ORMSKIRK
Burscough
Orrell
Radcliffe
FARNWORTH
Little Lever
Middleton
Chadderton
PRESTWICH
ATHERTON
Tyldesley
Worsley
Swinton
Pendlebury
Leigh
ASHTON-IN-MAKERFIELD
Golborne
Haydock
Kirkby
Knowsley
St Helens
Rainford
Billinge
SALFORD
Eccles
Manchester
Trafford Park
URMSTON
Irlam
Stretford
Droylsden
Prescot
Huyton
Roby
Newton-le-Willows
Warrington
Partington
SALE
Cadishead
Widnes
Runcorn
Garston
Speke
Liverpool Airport
Lymm
Altrincham
Hale
Bowdon
GATLEY
Cheadle
Stockport
Manchester Airport
WILMSLOW
Knutsford
Alderley Edge
Prestbury
Macclesfield
Ellesmere Port
Frodsham
Helsby
Northwich
Weaverham
Hartford
Chester
WINSFORD
Middlewich
Holmes Chapel
Tarporley
Sandbach
Congleton
Biddulph
Crewe
Alsager
Kidsgrove
Tunstall
Burslem
Nantwich
Wistaston
Willaston
Audley
Newcastle-under-Lyme
Stoke-on-Trent
Hanley
Fenton
Farndon
Holt
Malpas
Audlem
Whitchurch
Bangor-is-y-coed
Overton
M6
M56
M60
M62
M61
M58
M57
M53
M602
M66
A49
A50
A51
A54
A556
A34
A41
A534
A530
A500
A580
A5020
A523
A536
A538
A555
A556
A560
A34
A627(M)
49
50
44
33
34

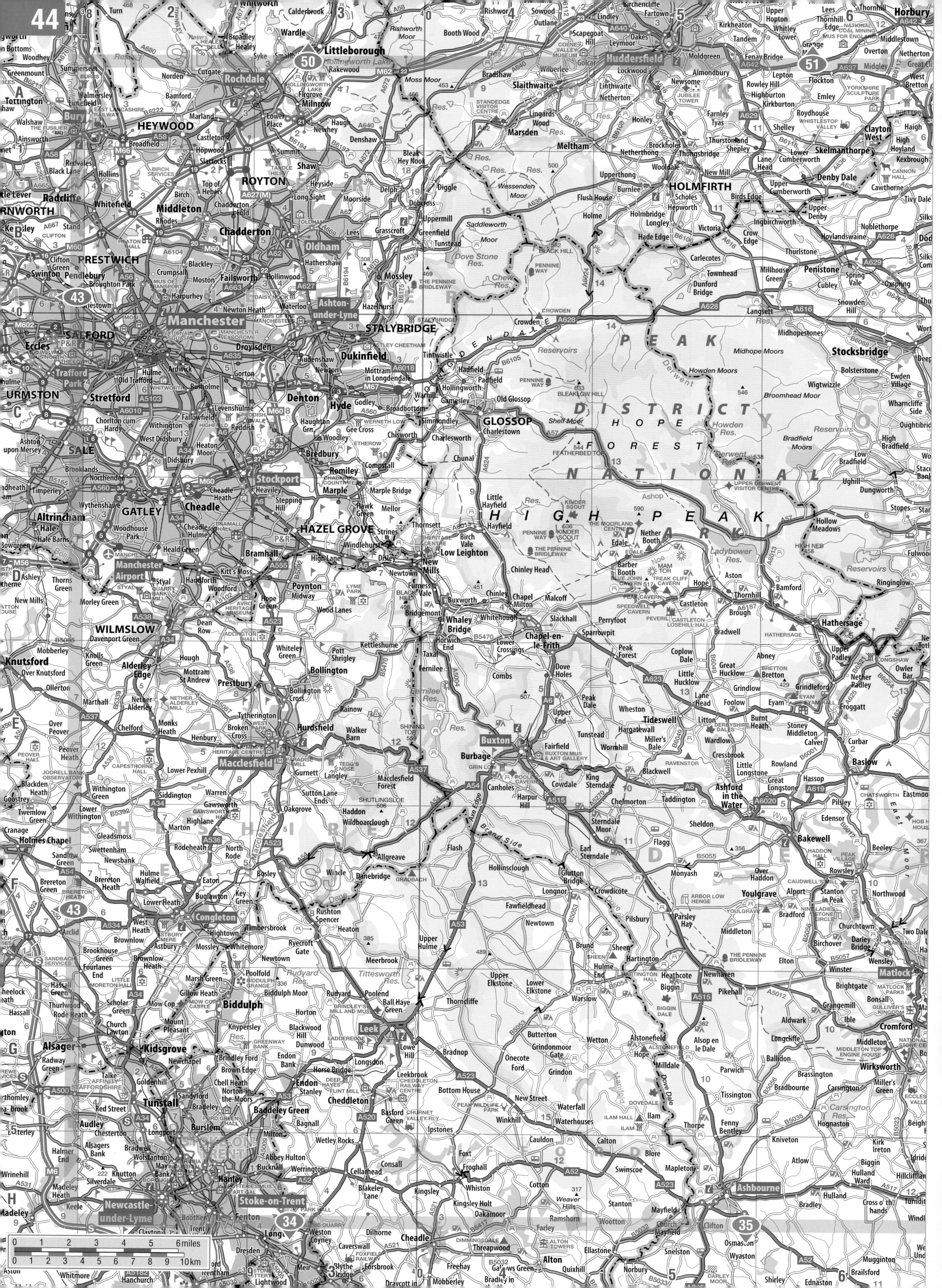
Rochdale
Littleborough
Huddersfield
Bury
HEYWOOD
ROYTON
Middleton
Chadderton
Oldham
PRESTWICH
Radcliffe
Manchester
SALFORD
Eccles
Trafford Park
URMSTON
Stretford
SALE
Ashton-under-Lyne
STALYBRIDGE
Dukinfield
Denton
Hyde
GLOSSOP
Stockport
Cheadle
GATLEY
Altrincham
HAZEL GROVE
Bramhall
Manchester Airport
WILMSLOW
Knutsford
Alderley Edge
Macclesfield
Bollington
Buxton
Chapel-en-le-Frith
Whaley Bridge
New Mills
Low Leighton
Congleton
Biddulph
Kidsgrove
Alsager
Holmes Chapel
Tunstall
Burslem
Hanley
Stoke-on-Trent
Newcastle-under-Lyme
Leek
Cheadle
Ashbourne
Bakewell
Matlock
Wirksworth
Cromford
Hathersage
Stocksbridge
Penistone
HOLMFIRTH
Meltham
Marsden
Slaithwaite
Denby Dale
Skelmanthorpe
Clayton West
Horbury
PEAK DISTRICT NATIONAL PARK
HIGH PEAK
HOPE FOREST
Tideswell
Ashford in the Water
Youlgrave
Hartington
Alton
Alton Towers
Dove Dale
Ladybower Res.
Howden Moors
Broomhead Moor
Edale
Castleton
Hope
Bamford
CHESHIRE
STAFFORDSHIRE
DERBYSHIRE
YORKSHIRE
0 1 2 3 4 5 6 miles
0 1 2 3 4 5 6 7 8 9 10 km

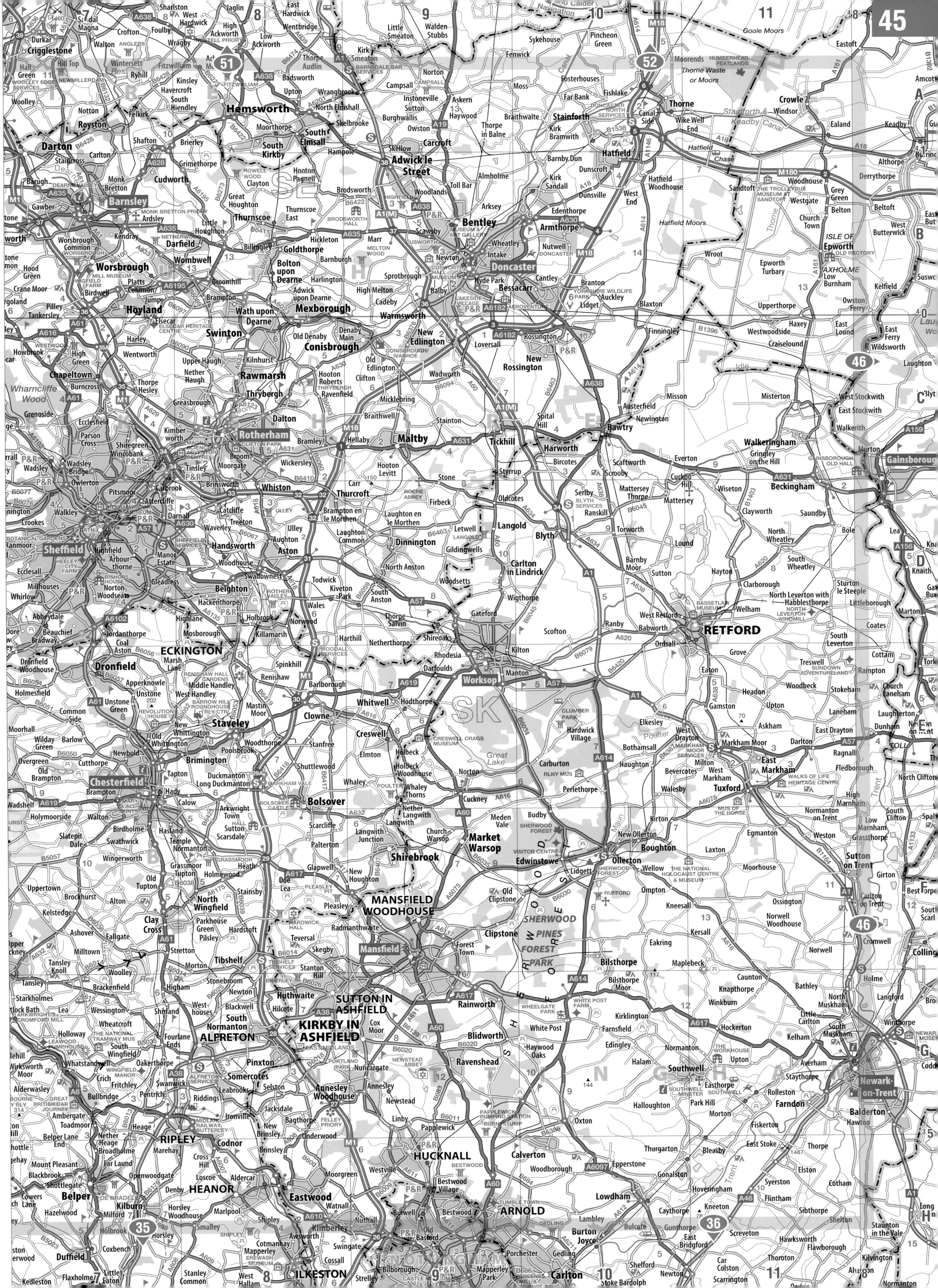
Hemsworth
Darton
Royston
Barnsley
Cudworth
Thurnscoe
Adwick le Street
Bentley
Doncaster
Armthorpe
Stainforth
Thorne
Hatfield
Crowle
Epworth
Darfield
Wombwell
Worsbrough
Hoyland
Mexborough
Conisbrough
Swinton
Goldthorpe
Rawmarsh
Rotherham
Sheffield
Chapeltown
Maltby
Tickhill
Harworth
Bawtry
New Rossington
Beckingham
Gainsborough
Dinnington
Aston
Beighton
Langold
Blyth
Carlton in Lindrick
RETFORD
Worksop
ECKINGTON
Dronfield
Staveley
Chesterfield
Bolsover
Clowne
Creswell
Tuxford
Shirebrook
Market Warsop
Ollerton
Boughton
Edwinstowe
MANSFIELD WOODHOUSE
Mansfield
Clipstone
SHERWOOD PINES FOREST PARK
SHERWOOD FOREST
Rainworth
Bilsthorpe
North Wingfield
Clay Cross
Tibshelf
SUTTON IN ASHFIELD
KIRKBY IN ASHFIELD
ALFRETON
Southwell
Newark-on-Trent
Farndon
Balderton
Ravenshead
Blidworth
Pinxton
Somercotes
Annesley Woodhouse
RIPLEY
Codnor
HUCKNALL
Calverton
Belper
HEANOR
Eastwood
ARNOLD
Lowdham
Burton Joyce
Carlton
Duffield
ILKESTON
NOTTINGHAM
Kimberley

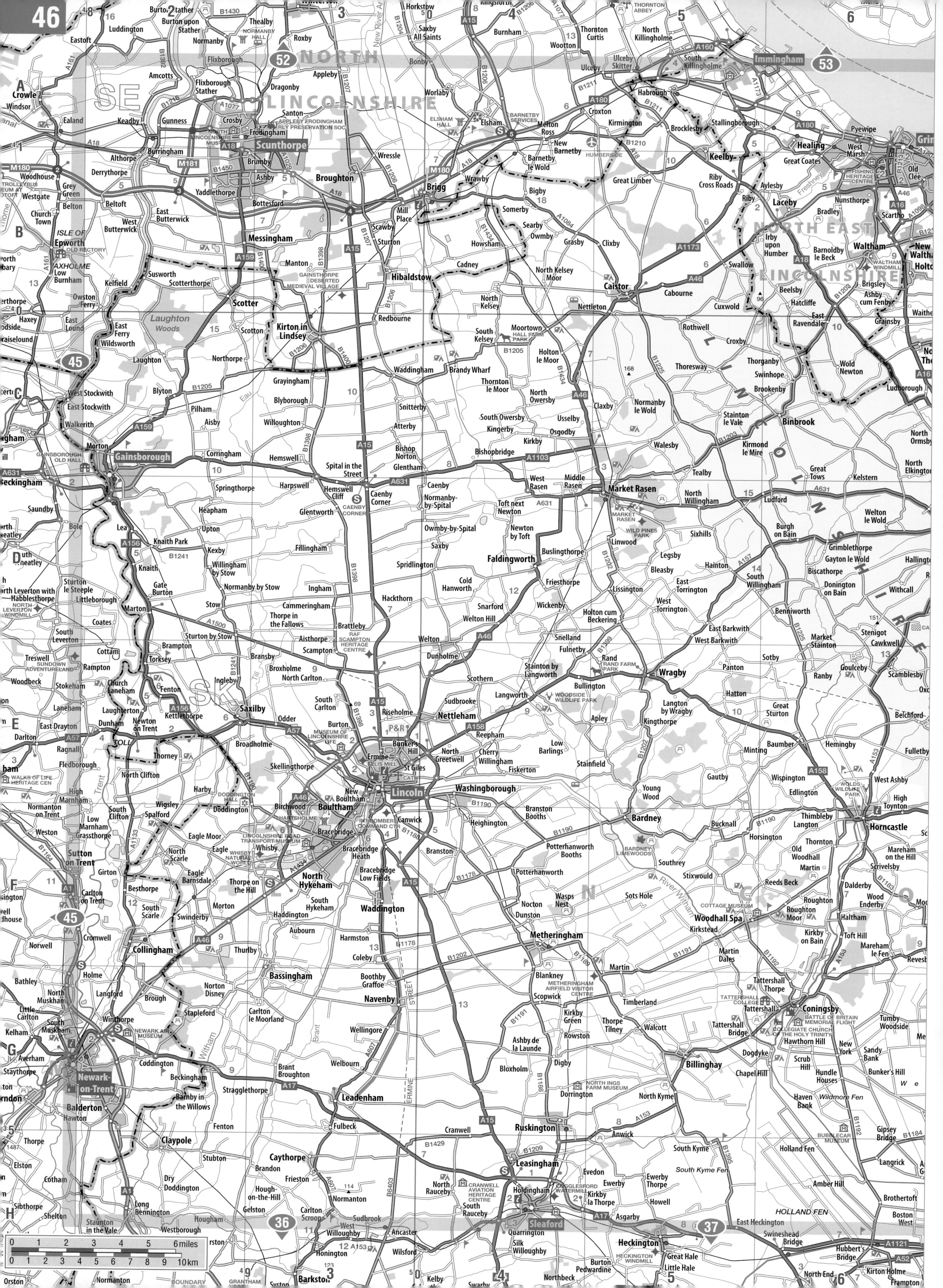
NORTH LINCOLNSHIRE
NORTH EAST LINCOLNSHIRE
LINCOLNSHIRE
SE
52
53
45
36
37
Luddington
Eastoft
Burton upon Stather
Thealby
Normanby
Roxby
Winterton
Horkstow
Saxby All Saints
Bonby
Burnham
Thornton Curtis
Wootton
North Killingholme
Thornton Abbey
Ulceby
Ulceby Skitter
South Killingholme
Immingham
Crowle
Amcotts
Flixborough
Flixborough Stather
Dragonby
Appleby
Worlaby
Habrough
Keadby
Gunness
Crosby
Santon
Frodingham
Scunthorpe
Elsham
Melton Ross
Croxton
Kirmington
Brocklesby
Stallingborough
Pyewipe
Healing
Great Coates
West Marsh
Old Clee
Ealand
Althorpe
Burringham
Brumby
Ashby
Wressle
Broughton
New Barnetby
Barnetby le Wold
Keelby
Riby Cross Roads
Woodhouse
Derrythorpe
Yaddlethorpe
Bottesford
Brigg
Wrawby
Great Limber
Aylesby
Laceby
Nunsthorpe
Scartho
Grey Green
Westgate
Belton
Beltoft
Church Town
East Butterwick
West Butterwick
Messingham
Mill Place
Scawby
Sturton
Bigby
Somerby
Searby
Owmby
Grasby
Clixby
Bradley
Irby upon Humber
Barnoldby le Beck
Waltham
Isle of Epworth
Epworth
Axholme
Low Burnham
Kelfield
Susworth
Scotterthorpe
Manton
Hibaldstow
Cadney
Howsham
North Kelsey Moor
Caistor
Cabourne
Swallow
Cuxwold
Brigsley
Beelsby
Ashby cum Fenby
Hatcliffe
East Ravendale
Haxey
Owston Ferry
East Lound
Laughton Woods
Scotter
Scotton
Kirton in Lindsey
Redbourne
North Kelsey
Nettleton
Rothwell
Croxby
Grainsby
East Ferry
Wildsworth
Laughton
Northorpe
South Kelsey
Moortown
Holton le Moor
Thoresway
Thorganby
Swinhope
Wold Newton
Brookenby
Ludborough
Waddingham
Brandy Wharf
Grayingham
Blyborough
Thornton le Moor
North Owersby
Claxby
Normanby le Wold
West Stockwith
East Stockwith
Blyton
Pilham
Aisby
Willoughton
Snitterby
Atterby
South Owersby
Kingerby
Usselby
Osgodby
Kirkby
Stainton le Vale
Binbrook
Walkerith
Morton
Gainsborough
Corringham
Hemswell
Bishop Norton
Glentham
Bishopbridge
Walesby
Kirmond le Mire
North Ormsby
Spital in the Street
West Rasen
Middle Rasen
Market Rasen
Tealby
Great Tows
Kelstern
North Elkington
Beckingham
Springthorpe
Harpswell
Hemswell Cliff
Caenby Corner
Caenby
Normanby-by-Spital
Toft next Newton
North Willingham
Ludford
Saundby
Heapham
Glentworth
Newton by Toft
Welton le Wold
Upton
Owmby-by-Spital
Linwood
Sixhills
Burgh on Bain
Lea
Knaith Park
Kexby
Fillingham
Saxby
Faldingworth
Buslingthorpe
Legsby
Hainton
Gayton le Wold
Biscathorpe
Knaith
Willingham by Stow
Spridlington
Bleasby
South Willingham
Donington on Bain
Withcall
Sturton le Steeple
Gate Burton
Normanby by Stow
Ingham
Cold Hanworth
Friesthorpe
Lissington
East Torrington
North Leverton with Habblesthorpe
Littleborough
Hackthorn
Snarford
Wickenby
West Torrington
Benniworth
Marton
Stow
Cammeringham
Welton Hill
Holton cum Beckering
Coates
Thorpe in the Fallows
Brattleby
East Barkwith
West Barkwith
Stenigot
South Leverton
Sturton by Stow
Aisthorpe
Scampton
Welton
Snelland
Market Stainton
Cawkwell
Cottam
Brampton
Torksey
Bransby
Dunholme
Fulnetby
Rand
Wragby
Panton
Sotby
Goulceby
Treswell
Rampton
Broxholme
North Carlton
Stainton by Langworth
Bullington
Ranby
Scamblesby
Woodbeck
Stokeham
Church Laneham
Ingleby
Fenton
Scothern
Langworth
Hatton
Saxilby
South Carlton
Sudbrooke
Langton by Wragby
Great Sturton
Laneham
Laughterton
Newton on Trent
Kettlethorpe
Odder
Burton
Riseholme
Nettleham
Apley
Kingthorpe
Belchford
East Drayton
Dunham
Darlton
Ragnall
Broadholme
Reepham
Low Barlings
Minting
Baumber
Hemingby
Fulletby
Thorney
Bunkers Hill
North Greetwell
Cherry Willingham
Stainfield
Fledborough
North Clifton
Skellingthorpe
Ermine
St Giles
Fiskerton
Gautby
Wispington
West Ashby
Harby
Lincoln
Washingborough
Young Wood
Edlington
High Toynton
High Marnham
Wigsley
Spalford
Doddington
Birchwood
New Boultham
Boultham
Branston Booths
Bardney
Bucknall
Thimbleby
Langton
Horncastle
Normanton on Trent
Low Marnham
South Clifton
Canwick
Heighington
Horsington
Weston
Grassthorpe
Eagle Moor
Bracebridge
Thornton
Eagle
Whisby
Bracebridge Heath
Branston
Potterhanworth Booths
Southrey
Old Woodhall
Mareham on the Hill
Sutton on Trent
North Scarle
Stixwould
Martin
Scrivelsby
Girton
Eagle Barnsdale
Thorpe on the Hill
North Hykeham
Bracebridge Low Fields
Potterhanworth
Reeds Beck
Dalderby
Carlton on Trent
Besthorpe
South Hykeham
Nocton
Wasps Nest
Sots Hole
Roughton
Wood Enderby
South Scarle
Morton
Haddington
Waddington
Dunston
Woodhall Spa
Roughton Moor
Haltham
Swinderby
Aubourn
Kirkstead
Kirkby on Bain
Toft Hill
Cromwell
Collingham
Thurlby
Harmston
Metheringham
Martin Dales
Mareham le Fen
Norwell
Coleby
Bassingham
Boothby Graffoe
Martin
Holme
Bathley
North Muskham
Langford
Norton Disney
Brough
Navenby
Blankney
Scopwick
Tattershall Thorpe
Timberland
Coningsby
Little Carlton
South Muskham
Stapleford
Carlton le Moorland
Kirkby Green
Thorpe Tilney
Walcott
Tattershall
Tattershall Bridge
Tumby Woodside
Kelham
Winthorpe
Wellingore
Rowston
Ashby de la Launde
Dogdyke
Hawthorn Hill
New York
Sandy Bank
Averham
Coddington
Welbourn
Bloxholm
Digby
Billinghay
Chapel Hill
Scrub Hill
Hundle Houses
Bunker's Hill
Staythorpe
Newark-on-Trent
Beckingham
Brant Broughton
Stragglethorpe
Leadenham
Dorrington
North Kyme
Haven Bank
Wildmore Fen
Balderton
Hawton
Barnby in the Willows
Fenton
Fulbeck
Cranwell
Ruskington
Anwick
Gipsey Bridge
Thorpe
Claypole
Caythorpe
South Kyme
Holland Fen
Elston
Stubton
Brandon
Leasingham
Evedon
Langrick
Cotham
Dry Doddington
Frieston
North Rauceby
Holdingham
Ewerby
Ewerby Thorpe
Kirkby la Thorpe
Amber Hill
Brothertoft
Sibthorpe
Shelton
Long Bennington
Hough-on-the-Hill
Gelston
Normanton
South Rauceby
Howell
Asgarby
Holland Fen
Boston West
Staunton in the Vale
Westbrough
Carlton Scroop
Sudbrook
Sleaford
East Heckington
Swineshead Bridge
West Willoughby
Ancaster
Quarrington
Silk Willoughby
Heckington
Great Hale
Little Hale
Hubbert's Bridge
Honington
Wilsford
Burton Pedwardine
Northbeck
North End
Kirton Holme
Frampton
Orston
Normanton
Barkston
Kelby
Swarby
Syston
0 1 2 3 4 5 6 miles
0 1 2 3 4 5 6 7 8 9 10 km

NORTH SEA
TA
TF
Kilnsea
SPURN DISCOVERY CENTRE
SPURN
SPURN HEAD
ROTTERDAM EUROPOORT
CLEETHORPES
MOUTH OF THE HUMBER
CLEETHORPES COAST LIGHT RAILWAY
Humberston
Tetney Lock
North Cotes
Tetney
Donna Nook
Marshchapel
Eskham
Wragholme
Grainthorpe
North Somercotes
DONNA NOOK
Skidbrooke North End
Fulstow
LINCOLNSHIRE WOLDS RLY
Covenham St Bartholomew
Conisholme
South Somercotes
Saltfleet
Covenham St Mary
Utterby
Yarburgh
Skidbrooke
Fotherby
Little Grimsby
Alvingham
North Cockerington
Saltfleetby St Clements
SALTFLEETBY THEDDLETHORPE
RUSHMOOR
Saltfleetby All Saints
Theddlethorpe St Helen
South Elkington
South Cockerington
Saltfleetby St Peter
Louth
Keddington
Grimoldby
Theddlethorpe All Saints
SEAL SANCTUARY & WILDLIFE CENTRE
ST JAMES
Stewton
Manby
Meers Bridge
Mablethorpe
Little Carlton
Great Carlton
Legbourne
Trusthorpe
South Reston
Gayton le Marsh
Little Cawthorpe
North Reston
Strubby
Sutton on Sea
Tathwell
Thorpe
Haugham
Muckton
Tothill
Withern
Maltby le Marsh
Sandilands
Authorpe
Beesby
Maidenwell
Burwell
Woodthorpe
Hannah
KING CHARLES III ENGLAND COAST PATH
Belleau
CLAYTHORPE WATER MILL AND WILDFOWL GARDENS
Saleby
Markby
Farforth
Ruckland
White Pit
Aby
Swaby
Asserby
Ketsby
South Thoresby
Bilsby
Huttoft
ALFORD MANOR HOUSE
Alford
South Ormsby
Rigsby
Haugh
Anderby
WOLDS
Tetford
Calceby
Farlesthorpe
Mumby
Authorpe Row
Brinkhill
Driby
Well
Cumberworth
Salmonby
Somersby
Ulceby
Helsey
Chapel St Leonards
Sutterby
Bonthorpe
Hogsthorpe
Claxby
Bag Enderby
Harrington
Willoughby
Ashby Puerorum
Langton
Sloothby
HARDY'S ANIMAL FARM
Greetham
Aswardby
Skendleby
Ingoldmells
Hagworthingham
Sausthorpe
Addlethorpe
FANTASY ISLAND
SNIPE DALES
Partney
Lusby
Welton le Marsh
Raithby
Scremby
BUTLINS SKEGNESS
Hameringham
Mavis Enderby
Candlesby
Orby
Orby Marsh
Asgarby
Spilsby
Ashby by Partney
GUNBY HALL
Burgh le Marsh
Winthorpe
Seathorne
Old Bolingbroke
Hundleby
NORTHCOTE HEAVY HORSE CENTRE
Great Steeping
Bratoft
Hareby
BOLINGBROKE
Halton Holegate
NATURELAND SEAL SANCTUARY
Miningsby
West Keal
Toynton All Saints
Irby in the Marsh
BURGH LE MARSH WINDMILL
THE VILLAGE CHURCH FARM
Skegness
East Keal
THE LIFEBOAT STATION
AQUARIUM
East Kirkby
Toynton St Peter
Firsby
Toynton Fen Side
Little Steeping
LINCOLNSHIRE AVIATION HERITAGE CENTRE
Keal Cotes
Thorpe Culvert
Thorpe St Peter
Croft
Seacroft
Croft Marsh
Revesby Bridge
Thorpe Fendykes
Wainfleet All Saints
Stickford
Wainfleet Bank
MAGDALEN COLL MUS
New Bolingbroke
Fen Side
GIBRALTAR POINT
Midville
New Leake
Wainfleet Tofts
Wainfleet St Mary
Stickney
Eastville
LINCOLNSHIRE WILDLIFE PARK
Friskney Eaudike
Wainfleet Sand
East Fen
Friskney
Carrington
Lade Bank
Wrangle Bank
Friskney Tofts
Northlands
Leake Commonside
SIBSEY TRADER MILL
Sibsey
Wrangle Lowgate
Friskney Flats
Frithville
Old Leake
Wrangle
Fishtoft Drove
Hurn's End
Boston Long Hedges
Leverton Outgate
Hill Dyke
Frith Bank
Leverton Highgate
BOSTON DEEPS
Cowbridge
Leverton
Leverton Lucasgate
Benington
MAUD FOSTER MILL
Haltoft End
LYNN DEEPS
Boston
GUILDHALL
Butterwick
Freiston
Chain Bridge
Skirbeck
Skirbeck Quarter
Fishtoft
Scrane End
THE WASH
BRANCASTER ROADS
Brancaster Bay
SCOLT HEAD ISLAND
HOLME DUNES
HOLME BIRD OBSERVATORY
Holme next the Sea
Titchwell
Brancaster Staithe
Burnham Deepdale
Brancaster
Burnham Norton
Burnham Westgate
Burnham Market
Old Hunstanton
Thornham
Hunstanton
A1031
B1201
A16
A157
A1104
B1373
A157
A1111
B1449
A52
A1104
A1028
B1196
A158
B1195
A155
B1183
B1184
A52
A149
B1153
B1200
53
38
37
7
8
9
10
11
A
B
C
D
E
F
G
H

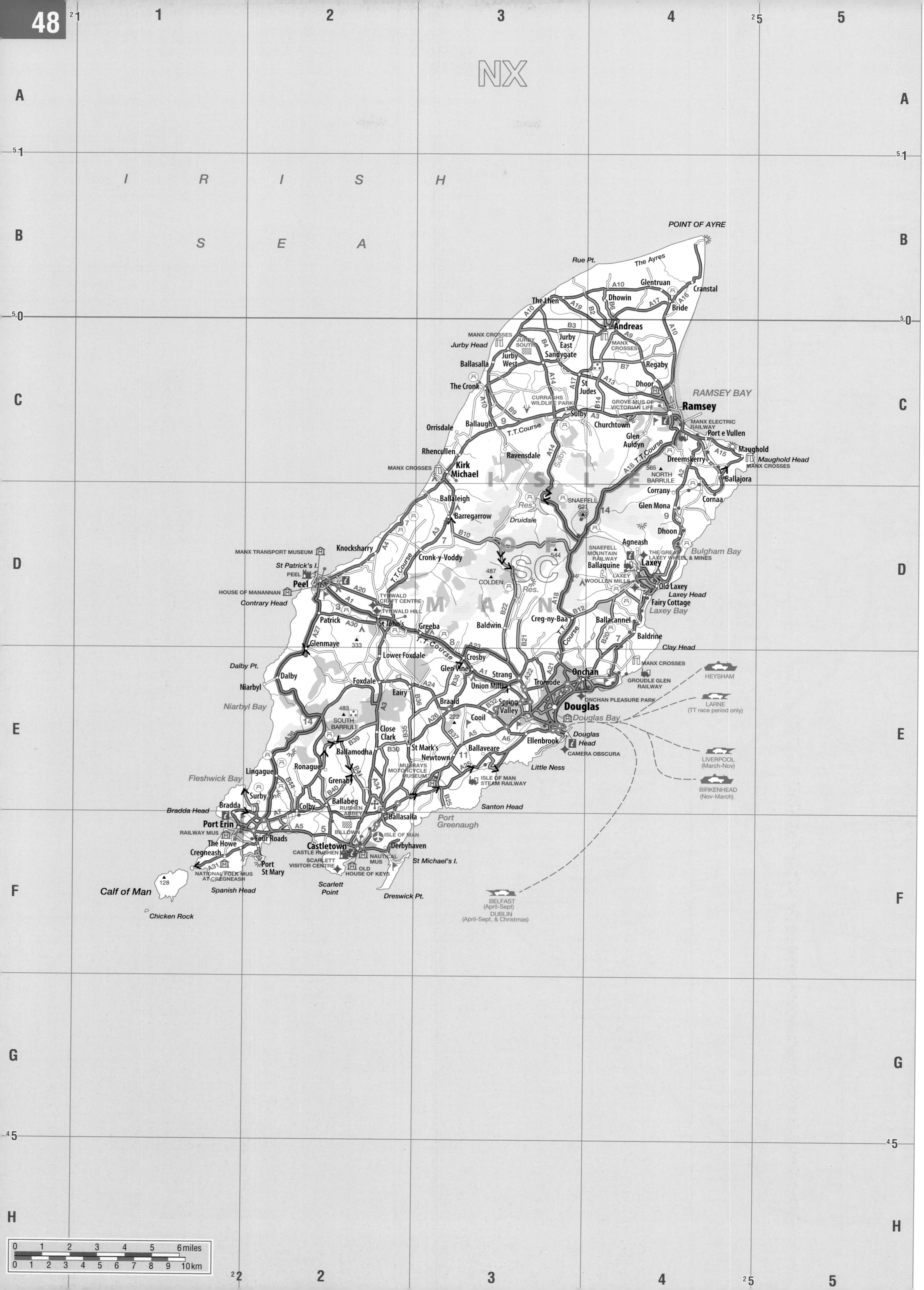
NX
SC
IRISH SEA
ISLE OF MAN
POINT OF AYRE
Rue Pt.
The Ayres
Glentruan
Cranstal
Dhowin
The Lhen
Bride
Andreas
MANX CROSSES
Jurby Head
Jurby South
Jurby East
Jurby West
Sandygate
Ballasalla
Regaby
Dhoor
The Cronk
CURRAGHS WILDLIFE PARK
St Judes
GROVE MUS OF VICTORIAN LIFE
RAMSEY BAY
Ramsey
MANX ELECTRIC RAILWAY
Port e Vullen
Orrisdale
Ballaugh
Sulby
Churchtown
Glen Auldyn
Maughold
Maughold Head
Rhencullen
Ravensdale
Dreemskerry
Kirk Michael
NORTH BARRULE
Ballajora
Corrany
Cornaa
Ballaleigh
SNAEFELL
Glen Mona
Barregarrow
Druidale
Res.
Dhoon
T.T. Course
Agneash
MANX TRANSPORT MUSEUM
Knocksharry
SNAEFELL MOUNTAIN RAILWAY
THE GREAT LAXEY WHEEL & MINES
Bulgham Bay
Cronk-y-Voddy
Ballaquine
Laxey
St Patrick's I.
PEEL
COLDEN
LAXEY WOOLLEN MILLS
Old Laxey
Peel
Laxey Head
HOUSE OF MANANNAN
TYNWALD CRAFT CENTRE
Fairy Cottage
Contrary Head
TYNWALD HILL
Laxey Bay
Patrick
St John's
Baldwin
Creg-ny-Baa
Ballacannel
Greeba
Baldrine
Glenmaye
Clay Head
Lower Foxdale
Crosby
Dalby Pt.
Glen Vine
MANX CROSSES
Strang
Onchan
HEYSHAM
Niarbyl
Dalby
Foxdale
Union Mills
Tromode
GROUDLE GLEN RAILWAY
Eairy
Spring Valley
ONCHAN PLEASURE PARK
LARNE (TT race period only)
Niarbyl Bay
SOUTH BARRULE
Braaid
Douglas
Cooil
Douglas Bay
Close Clark
Ellenbrook
Douglas Head
Ballamodha
St Mark's
Ballaveare
CAMERA OBSCURA
Newtown
LIVERPOOL (March-Nov)
Lingague
Ronague
MURRAYS MOTORCYCLE MUSEUM
Little Ness
Fleshwick Bay
Grenaby
ISLE OF MAN STEAM RAILWAY
BIRKENHEAD (Nov-March)
Surby
Ballabeg
Bradda Head
Bradda
Colby
RUSHEN ABBEY
Santon Head
Ballasalla
Port Greenaugh
Port Erin
BILLOWN
ISLE OF MAN
RAILWAY MUS
Four Roads
The Howe
Castletown
Derbyhaven
Cregneash
CASTLE RUSHEN
NAUTICAL MUS
SCARLETT VISITOR CENTRE
St Michael's I.
Port St Mary
NATIONAL FOLK MUS AT CREGNEASH
OLD HOUSE OF KEYS
Calf of Man
Spanish Head
Scarlett Point
Dreswick Pt.
BELFAST (April-Sept)
DUBLIN (April-Sept, & Christmas)
Chicken Rock
0 1 2 3 4 5 6 miles
0 1 2 3 4 5 6 7 8 9 10 km

Bootle
Duddon Bridge
Broughton in Furness
Lower Hawthwaite
Blawith
Nibthwaite
Rusland
Stott Park Bobbin Mill
Satterthwaite
Cartmel Fell
Bridge
Row
The Howe
Sizergh
Cotes
Sedgwick
Barrows Green
Old Hutton
Black Combe
Hallthwaites
Lowick Bridge
Colton
Oxen Park
Fells
Lakeside
Lakes Aquarium
Fell Foot
Lowick Green
Grizebeck
Foxfield
Duddon Mosses
Gawthwaite
Spark Bridge
Bouth
Lakeside and Haverthwaite Railway
Newby Bridge
Staveley
Whitbarrow
Sampool Bridge
Levens
Stainton
Gatebeck
Whitbeck
The Green
Backbarrow
Witherslack
Levens Hall
Mill Side
Heversham
Endmoor
Crooklands
Kirkby-in-Furness
Penny Bridge
Haverthwaite
Ayside
High Newton
Low Newton
Town End
Leasgill
Silecroft
Whicham
The Hill
Beck Side
Broughton Beck
Greenodd
Field Broughton
Milnthorpe
Lupton
Kirksanton
Millom
Millom Heritage & Arts Centre
Soutergate
Arrad Foot
Roudsea Wood and Mosses
Meathop
Farleton
Haverigg
Mansriggs
Laurel & Hardy Mus
Cartmel Priory
Lindale
Storth
Heron Corn Mill
Beetham
Clawthorpe Fell
King Charles III England Coast Path
Duddon Sands
Askam in Furness
Ulverston
Pennington
Cartmel
Holker Hall
Grange-over-Sands
Arnside
Lakeland Wildlife Oasis
Holme
Hutton Roof
Clawthorpe
Burton-in-Kendal
Whittington
Ireleth
Lindal in Furness
Swarthmoor
Conishead Priory & Manjushri Kadampa Meditation Centre
Cark
Holker
Allithwaite
Flookburgh
Kents Bank
Gait Barrows
Arnside and Silverdale
Yealand Redmayne
Yealand Conyers
Burton-in-Kendal Services (Northbound Only)
Sandscale Haws
Safari Zoo Cumbria
Great Urswick
Cartmel Sands
Ravenstown
Silverdale
Leighton Hall
Priest Hutton
Dalton-in-Furness
Dalton Castle
Little Urswick
Bardsea
Humphrey Head Pt.
Warton Sands
Warton
Borwick
Capernwray
Arkholme
North Walney
Barrow (Walney Island)
Stainton with Adgarley
Scales
Hawcoat
Bow Bridge
Baycliff
Old Rectory
Millhead
Melling
Ormsgill
Newbarns
Newton
Furness Abbey
Gleaston Watermill
Aldingham
Barrow-in-Furness
Dendron
Gleaston
Carnforth
North Scale
Yarlside
Custom Ho
Newbiggin
Morecambe
Over Kellet
Gressingham
Hornby
The Dock Museum
Vickerstown
Barrow Island
Leece
Roosebeck
Bolton-le-Sands
Nether Kellet
Biggar
Rampside
Bay
Hest Bank
Bolton Town End
Aughton
Farleton
Claughton
Roa Island
Slyne
Bare
Morecambe
Halton
Caton
Caton Green
Brookhouse
Caton Moor
Foulney Island
Piel Island
South End
Isle of Walney
Sandylands
Torrisholme
Skerton
Maritime Mus
Crossgill
South Channel
South End Point
White Lund
Heysham
Lancaster
Priory Church
Ashton Memorial
Aldcliffe
City Mus
Hayloft Fell
Heaton
Scotforth
Clougha
Douglas
Middleton
Overton
Quernmore
Ward's Stone
Lee Fell
Glasson
Conder Green
Galgate
Sunderland Pt.
Shoulder of Lune
Thurnham
Smith Green
Ortner
Lee
Abbeystead
Wyre
SD
Dolphinholme
Cockerham Sands
Cockerham
Lancaster (Forton) Services
Hawthornthwaite Fell
Braides
Forton
Street
Fell Top
Irish Sea
Hollins Lane
Knott End-on-Sea
Dam Side
Fleetwood
Pilling Lane
Pilling
Scorton
Bleasdale Moors
Rossall Point
Preesall
Stake Pool
Winmarleigh
Cabus
Oakenclough
Affinity Lancashire
Fair Snape Fell
Eagland Hill
Garstang
Calder Vale
Bleasdale
Stalmine
Staynall
Nateby
Bowgreave
Marsh Mill-in-Wyre
Wyre Estuary
Cleveleys
Trunnah
Hambleton
Moss Edge
Churchtown
Catterall
Claughton
Beacon Fell
Anchorsholme
Thornton
Out Rawcliffe
Ratten Row
Whitechapel
Norbreck
Little Eccleston
Toll
St Michael's on Wyre
Bilsborrow
Skippool
Little Singleton
Inglewhite
Bispham
Carleton
Great Eccleston
Blackpool
Warbreck
Poulton-le-Fylde
Singleton
Elswick
Crossmoor
Myerscough
North Shore
Thistleton
Inskip
Cuddy Hill
Queenstown
Normoss
Esprick
Roseacre
Barton
Goosnargh
Layton
Staining
Lancashire
Catforth
Blackpool Tower
Sea Life Centre
Madame Tussaud's Blackpool
Blackpool Zoo
Great Marton
Corner Row
Wharles
Woodplumpton
Broughton
Chingle Hall
Weeton
Haighton Green
Hawes Side
Mereside
Little Plumpton
Great Plumpton
Wesham
Treales
Lower Bartle
Higher Bartle
Sharoe Green
South Shore
Blackpool Pleasure Beach
Common Edge
Kirkham
Cottam
Ingol
Fulwood
Ribbleton
Squires Gate
Westby
Dowbridge
Lancaster Canal
Cadley
Moss Side
Wrea Green
Lea Town
Preston
Higher Ballam
Newton
Scales
Clifton
Royal Lytham & St Annes
Ansdell
Lytham Hall
Lytham
Ribble Steam Railway
Freckleton
St Annes
Lytham St Anne's
Fairhaven
Warton
Higher Penwortham
Walton-le-Dale
Bottom of Hutton
Salters Bank
Hutton
Middleforth Green
Bamber Bridge
Higher Walton
Gregson Lane
Ribble
Ribble Estuary
Longton
Lostock Hall
Banks Sands
Ribble Marshes
West Lancashire Light Railway
Walmer Bridge
New Longton
Farington
British Commercial Vehicle Mus
Clayton Green
Hesketh Bank
Midge Hall
Great Bank
Becconsall
Much Hoole
Leyland
Clayton-le-Woods
King Charles III England Coast Path
Hundred End
Broadfield
South Ribble Museum & Exhibition Centre
Worden Park
Banks
Tarleton
Horse Bank
Bretherton
Buckshaw Village
Euxton
Marshside
Crossens
Sollom
Croston
Ulnes Walton
Shaw Green
Eco Visitor Centre
Churchtown
Mere Brow
Yarrow
Southport
The Atkinson
Holmeswood
Eccleston
Chorley
Blowick
Windmill Animal Farm
Rufford Old Hall
Rufford
Martin Mere Wildfowl and Wetland Centre
Tarlscough
Mawdesley
Heskin Green
Charnock Richard
Charnock Richard Services
Birkdale
Brown Edge
Snape Green
Bescar
Bispham Green
Wrightington Bar
Coppull
Hillside
Royal Birkdale
Scarisbrick
New Lane
Hill Dale
Mossy Lea
Ainsdale-on-Sea
Ainsdale
Shirdley Hill
Pinfold
Burscough Bridge
Dangerous Corner
Coppull Moor
Woodvale
Burscough
Parbold
Shevington Moor
0 1 2 3 4 5 6 miles
0 1 2 3 4 5 6 7 8 9 10 km

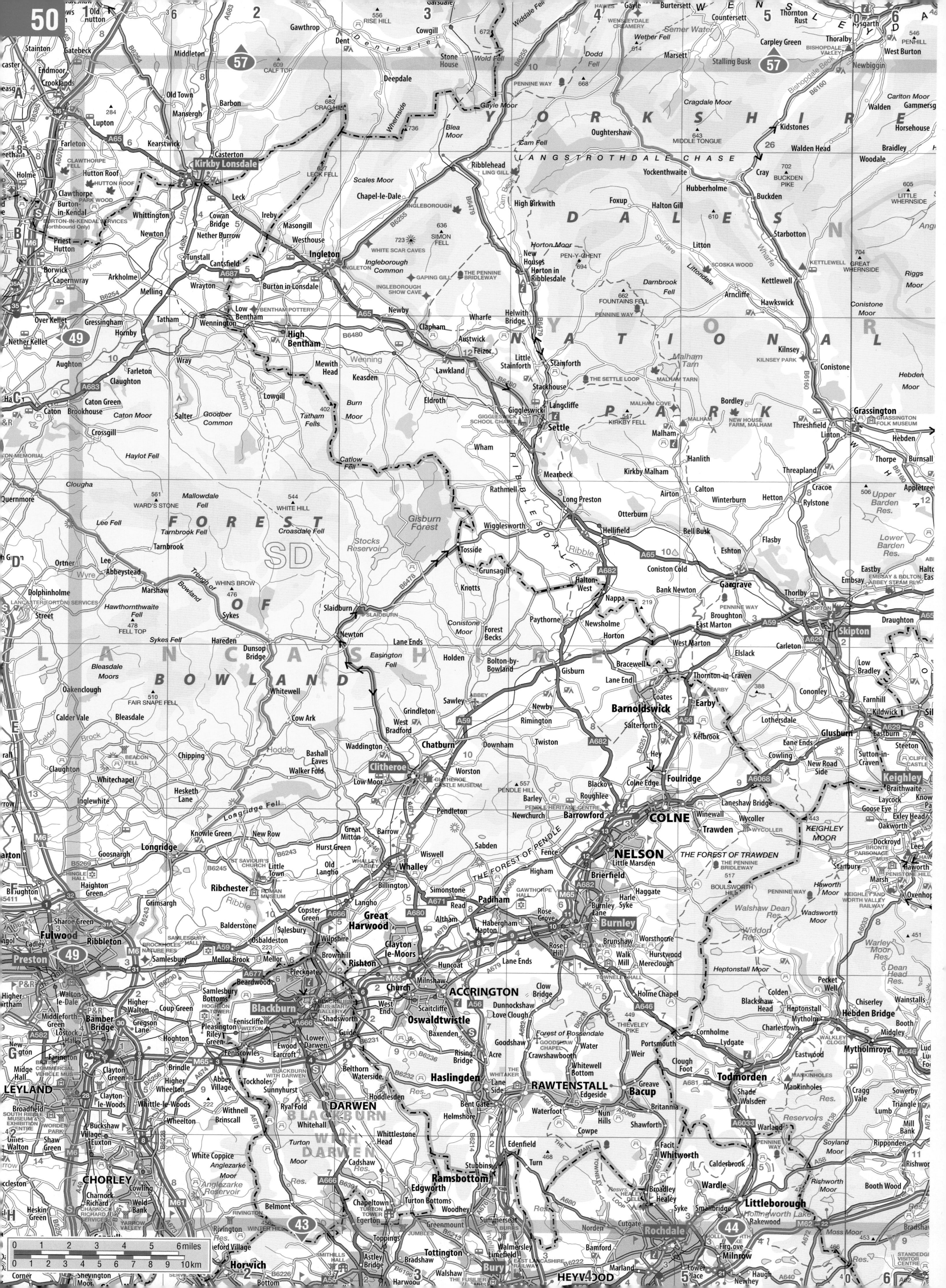

YORKSHIRE DALES NATIONAL PARK
FOREST OF BOWLAND
LANCASHIRE
SD
LANGSTROTHDALE CHASE
WENSLEYDALE
RIBBLESDALE
THE FOREST OF PENDLE
THE FOREST OF TRAWDEN
BLACKBURN WITH DARWEN
Kirkby Lonsdale
Ingleton
Settle
Giggleswick
Skipton
Keighley
Clitheroe
Barnoldswick
COLNE
NELSON
Burnley
Preston
Blackburn
ACCRINGTON
Oswaldtwistle
Great Harwood
Clayton-le-Moors
Haslingden
RAWTENSTALL
Bacup
Todmorden
Hebden Bridge
Mytholmroyd
DARWEN
CHORLEY
LEYLAND
Fulwood
Longridge
Whalley
Padiham
Ramsbottom
Edgworth
Horwich
Bury
Rochdale
HEYWOOD
Littleborough
Milnrow
Whitworth
Wardle
Grassington
Kettlewell
Malham
Long Preston
Hellifield
Gargrave
Earby
Foulridge
Barrowford
Brierfield
Sabden
Chatburn
Slaidburn
Newton
Dunsop Bridge
Chipping
Ribchester
Bentham
High Bentham
Low Bentham
Wennington
Hornby
Clapham
Austwick
Horton in Ribblesdale
Ribblehead
Dent
Sedbergh
Gawthrop
Cowgill
Deepdale
Barbon
Casterton
Whittington
Burton-in-Kendal
Carnforth
Caton
Garstang
Abbeystead
Marshaw
Whitewell
Waddington
Sawley
Gisburn
Rimington
Downham
Worston
Pendleton
Hurst Green
Samlesbury
Mellor
Wilpshire
Rishton
Church
Huncoat
Belthorn
Tockholes
Hoddlesden
Helmshore
Edenfield
Waterfoot
Weir
Cornholme
Walsden
Cragg Vale
Ripponden
Rishworth
Oakworth
Haworth
Stanbury
Oxenhope
Cononley
Glusburn
Cowling
Lothersdale
Carleton
Embsay
Thorlby
Rylstone
Cracoe
Hetton
Airton
Calton
Kirkby Malham
Hanlith
Threshfield
Linton
Hebden
Burnsall
Appletreewick
Conistone
Kilnsey
Arncliffe
Litton
Halton Gill
Foxup
Starbotton
Buckden
Hubberholme
Cray
Kidstones
Yockenthwaite
Oughtershaw
Walden Head
West Burton
Aysgarth
Thoralby
Newbiggin
Carpley Green
Marsett
Stalling Busk
Countersett
Burtersett
Gayle
Hawes
Semer Water
Wether Fell
Dodd Fell
PENNINE WAY
INGLEBOROUGH
723
WHITE SCAR CAVES
SIMON FELL
636
PEN-Y-GHENT
694
FOUNTAINS FELL
662
BUCKDEN PIKE
702
GREAT WHERNSIDE
704
Whernside
736
Blea Moor
Cam Fell
Gayle Moor
Wold Fell
CALF TOP
609
RISE HILL
556
CRAG HILL
682
LECK FELL
Scales Moor
Chapel-le-Dale
Ingleborough Common
GAPING GILL
INGLEBOROUGH SHOW CAVE
THE PENNINE BRIDLEWAY
Malham Tarn
MALHAM TARN
THE SETTLE LOOP
MALHAM COVE
KIRKBY FELL
547
Gisburn Forest
Stocks Reservoir
Croasdale Fell
WHITE HILL
544
WARD'S STONE
561
Mallowdale Fell
Tarnbrook Fell
Tarnbrook
Trough of Bowland
WHINS BROW
476
FAIR SNAPE FELL
510
FELL TOP
478
Hawthornthwaite Fell
Bleasdale Moors
Bleasdale
Easington Fell
Burn Moor
Tatham Fells
Catlow Fell
PENDLE HILL
557
PENDLE HERITAGE CENTRE
Longridge Fell
BOULSWORTH HILL
517
KEIGHLEY MOOR
Walshaw Dean Res.
Widdop Res.
Heptonstall Moor
Heptonstall
Forest of Rossendale
THIEVELEY PIKE
449
Anglezarke Moor
Anglezarke Reservoir
WINTER HILL
456
Rivington
Turton Moor
Turton Bottoms
TURTON TOWER
Hollingworth Lake
Rishworth Moor
Soyland Moor
Moss Moor
STANDEDGE VISITOR CENTRE
KEIGHLEY AND WORTH VALLEY RAILWAY
EMBSAY & BOLTON ABBEY STEAM RLY
EAST LANCASHIRE RAILWAY
GRASSINGTON FOLK MUSEUM
CLITHEROE CASTLE MUSEUM
GAWTHORPE HALL
TOWNELEY HALL
BURTON-IN-KENDAL SERVICES (Northbound Only)
LANCASTER(FORTON) SERVICES
CHARNOCK RICHARD SERVICES
RIVINGTON
A65
A59
A56
A646
A682
A666
A680
A671
A6068
A629
M6
M65
M61
M62
B6255
B6479
B6478
B6480
B6160
57
49
43
44
0 1 2 3 4 5 6 miles
0 1 2 3 4 5 6 7 8 9 10 km

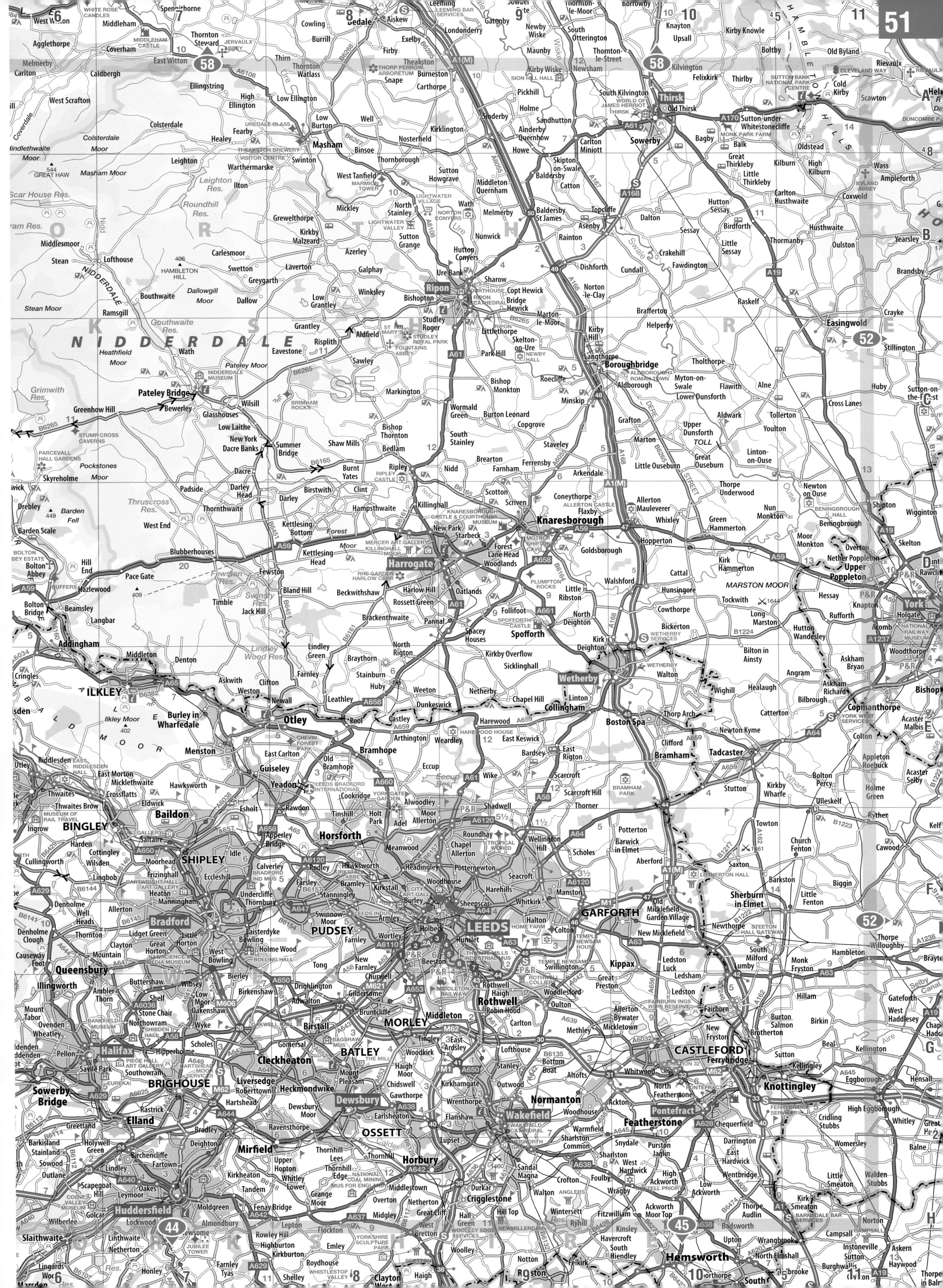

Bedale
Masham
Thirsk
Sowerby
Ripon
Boroughbridge
Easingwold
Pateley Bridge
NIDDERDALE
Knaresborough
Harrogate
Wetherby
Otley
ILKLEY
Addingham
Bolton Abbey
Boston Spa
Tadcaster
York
Upper Poppleton
Copmanthorpe
BINGLEY
Baildon
SHIPLEY
Bradford
Horsforth
LEEDS
PUDSEY
GARFORTH
Queensbury
Halifax
BRIGHOUSE
Cleckheaton
BATLEY
MORLEY
Rothwell
Dewsbury
OSSETT
Wakefield
Normanton
CASTLEFORD
Pontefract
Knottingley
Featherstone
Huddersfield
Elland
Mirfield
Horbury
Hemsworth
Sowerby Bridge
Kippax
Sherburn in Elmet
MARSTON MOOR
HAMBLETON HILLS

NORTH RIDING FOREST PARK
Dalby Forest
Low Dalby
Kirkbymoorside
Helmsley
Pickering
Thornton-le-Dale
Malton
Norton-on-Derwent
Old Malton
Seamer
Easingwold
HOWARDIAN HILLS
HAMBLETON HILLS
Hovingham
Ampleforth
Gilling East
Terrington
Castle Howard
Strensall
Haxby
York
Stamford Bridge
Pocklington
Market Weighton
Driffield
Copmanthorpe
Bishopthorpe
Selby
Barlby
Howden
Goole
Snaith
Carlton
Gilberdyke
Holme-on-Spalding-Moor
North Cave
South Cave
North Ferriby
Humber Bridge
Barton-upon-Humber
Winterton
Thorne
Crowle
Cottingham
Kirk Ella
Anlaby
Hessle
Beverley
Hutton Cranswick
Fridaythorpe
Wetwang
Sledmere
Langtoft
Rillington
Scampston
Flixton
Staxton
Sherburn
YORKSHIRE WOLDS WAY
THE CARRS
NORTH YORKSHIRE
EAST RIDING OF YORKSHIRE
NORTH LINCOLNSHIRE
Read's Island
Redcliff Channel
Goole Fields
Goole Moors
Thorne Waste or Moors
Southfield Reservoir
Aire and Calder Navigation
Dutch River
A64
A19
A1079
A166
A614
A63
A170
A1237
A645
M62
M18
A161
A1077
59
51
45
46
0 1 2 3 4 5 6 miles
0 1 2 3 4 5 6 7 8 9 10 km

Scarborough
South Bay
Cayton Bay
Yons Nab
CLEVELAND WAY
Lebberston
Gristhorpe
Filey Brigg
PLAYDALE FARM PARK
Filey
Folkton
Muston
Filey Bay
Primrose Valley
Hunmanby Moor
Hunmanby
Reighton Sands
Reighton Gap
Reighton
Speeton
KING CHARLES III ENGLAND COAST PATH
Wold Newton
Burton Fleming
Buckton
Bempton
Grindale
Flamborough
FLAMBOROUGH HEAD
Thwing
SEWERBY HALL AND GARDENS
Sewerby
Boynton
Rudston
PRIORY
BAYLE MUSEUM
Bridlington
Bessingby
West Hill
Carnaby
Hilderthorpe
Haisthorpe
BURTON AGNES HALL
Thornholme
BRIDLINGTON ANIMAL PARK
BRIDLINGTON BAY
Kilham
BURTON AGNES MANOR HOUSE
Burton Agnes
Harpham
Fraisthorpe
Lowthorpe
Nafferton
Gransmoor
Great Kelk
Lissett
Barmston
Gembling
Ulrome
Foston on the Wolds
SKIPSEA CASTLE
Skipsea
Brigham
Church End
Beeford
Skipsea Brough
North Frodingham
Dunnington
Rotsea
Hempholme
Bewholme
Atwick
North Cliff
Burshill
Hornsea
Hornsea Mere
HORNSEA MUSEUM
Brandesburton
Baswick Steer
Seaton
HORNSEA FREEPORT
Hornsea Bridge
Rolston
Leven
Leven Canal
Catwick
Sigglesthorne
Goxhill
Mappleton
Eske
Little Hatfield
Routh
Long Riston
Rise
Great Hatfield
Great Cowden
Tickton
Arnold
Withernwick
Weel
Meaux
Skirlaugh
New Ellerby
Marton
West Newton
Aldbrough
East Newton
Woodmansey
Wawne
Old Ellerby
BURTON CONSTABLE HALL
Flinton
Thearne
Swine
Coniston
Garton
Grimston
Dunswell
Bransholme
Sutton on Hull
Thirtleby
Sproatley
Humbleton
Fitling
Hilston
Inglemire
Ganstead
Lelley
Owstwick
Tunstall
Bilton
Elstronwick
Sutton Ings
Stoneferry
Newland
Summergangs
Preston
Burton Pidsea
Roos
North End
Sculcoates
WILBERFORCE HOUSE
West End
Waxholme
Ella
Salt End
Owthorne
Withernsea
Marfleet
STREETLIFE
THE DEEP
Hedon
Rimswell
Haven Side
Burstwick
Halsham
East End
FERENS ART GALLERY
KINGSTON UPON HULL
Paull
Camerton
Thorngumbald
Ryehill
Keyingham
HUMBER
Hollym
Goxhill Haven
Ottringham
Winestead
New Holland
Little Humber
Thorney Crofts
Holmpton
Patrington
Barrow Haven
Out Newton
Cherry Cob Sands
Welwick
Weeton
Goxhill
Barrow upon Humber
South End
East Halton
Sunk Island
Skeffling
Easington
THORNTON ABBEY
Thornton Curtis
North Killingholme
Wootton
Ulceby Skitter
South Killingholme
Immingham
Kilnsea
Ulceby
SPURN DISCOVERY CENTRE
Habrough
ROTTERDAM EUROPOORT
Croxton
Kirmington
Brocklesby
Stallingborough
Grimsby
BARNETBY SERVICES
SPURN
N O R T H
S E A
TA
A165
A1039
B1229
B1255
B1259
B1253
A614
A1038
B1249
B1242
A1035
B1243
A1174
A1033
B1233
A1165
A1105
A63
B1238
B1240
B1239
B1362
B1445
B1206
A1077
A160
A1173
B1211
A180
46
47
6
7
8
9
10
11
A
B
C
D
E
F
G
H

66
CARLETON CASTLE
Bennane Hd.
Poundland
Pinwherry
Bellamore
335 PINDONNAN
Colmonell
Knockdolian
B734
Ballochmorrie
Black Clauchrie
Ballantrae Bay
Heronsford
Glen Tig
Water of Tig
Duisk
Ballantrae
Balkissock
Barrhill
Laggan
Eldrick
A714
Downan Pt.
Auchencrosh
Arecleoch Forest
439 BENERAIRD
B7027
Drumlamford Loch
Dornal
Chirmorrie
Glentrool Village
GLENTROOL VISITOR CENTRE
Glentrool
Forest
Loch Moan
Palgowan
Water of Minnoch
Bargrennan
BELFAST
LARNE
A77
Mark
Glen App
Milleur Pt.
Miltonise
Craig Airie Fell
Loch Maberry
Loch Derry
Polbae
Loch Ochiltree
Clachaneasy
Loch Middle
Kirroughtree Forest
Corsewall Pt.
Barnhills
Portencalzie
257
287
LAGGANGAIRN STANDING STONES
Knowe
North Cairn
South Cairn
Corsewall
B738
Loch Connell
Kirkcolm
Dounan Bay
Mains of Airies
Cairnryan
Penwhirn Res.
Main Water of Luce
Cross Water of Luce
Artfield Fell
244
Carseriggan
Penninghame Forest
Challoch
Ervie
Low Salchrie
B798
The Wig
LOCH RYAN
Braid Fell
Black Loch
Loch Heron
Loch Ronald
213
Knocknain
Slouchnawen Bay
Leswalt
Craigencross
B7043
A77
Innermessan
New Luce
Auchmantle
SOUTHERN UPLAND WAY
Drumphail
205
Shennanton
Benfield
A751
A718
Glenstockadale
Black Loch
CASTLE KENNEDY GARDENS
White Loch
Castle Kennedy
Aird
Tarf Water
A75
B733
Kirkcowan
123
Broadsea Bay
Stranraer
CASTLE OF ST JOHN VISITOR CENTRE
STRANRAER MUSEUM
Whitecairn
Carscreugh
Craighlaw Mains
Knockglass
T H E R H I N S
Soulseat Loch
GLENWHAN GARDENS
GLENLUCE ABBEY
Glenluce
Dernaglar Loch
High Mindork
Spittal
Torhouse
Lochans
Mark
Dunragit
Knock Moss
Black Hd.
B738
182
CASTLE OF PARK
Dunskey Ho.
A77
B7077
Torrs Warren
Whitefield Loch
131
Bladnoch
NW
Awhirk
B7084
Luce Sands
Milton
A747
Fell Loch
Portpatrick
Stoneykirk
Stairhaven
Castle Loch
Auchenmalg
Culmazie
A716
Mochrum Loch
B7005
Port of Spittal Bay
B7042
Culshabbin
Auchenmalg Bay
B7052
Alticry
197
Barrachan
Cairngarroch
Sandhead
KIRKMADRINE STONES
Sandhead Bay
Loch Head
Cairngarroch Bay
CHAPEL FINIAN
Elrig
Money Hd.
B7085
MOTE OF DRUCHTAG
75
Clachanmore
Mochrum
Hole Stone Bay
A747
Airyhassen
Ardwell
Chapel Rossan Bay
Milton Pt.
Drumtroddan
Ardwell Mains
Ardwell Pt.
Logan Mains
Port William
DRUMTRODDAN ST
LOGAN BOTANIC GARDEN
Balgowan Pt.
L U C E B A Y
Monreith Mains
B7021
Mull of Logan
BARSALLOCH FORT
Port Nessock or Port Logan Bay
Barsalloch Pt.
Monreith
Port Logan
Cairnywellan Hd.
B7065
Monreith Bay
Clanyard Bay
Low Clanyard
Drummore
Laggantalluch Hd.
Kirkmaiden
164
Cailliness Pt.
Damnaglaur
B7041
Crammag Hd.
Maryport
Cairngaan
Port Kemin
MULL OF GALLOWAY
0 1 2 3 4 5 6 miles
0 1 2 3 4 5 6 7 8 9 10 km

Castlemaddy
Dundeugh
Kendoon
Glenhoul
Carsfad Loch
GLENKENS
Castlefairn
Wether Hill
Holmhead
Dalmacallan Forest
Wallaceton
Glenmidge
Auldgirth
Corserine
Forrest Lodge
Loch Harrow
Mullwharchar
Merrick
Loch Enoch
Loch Neldricken
Loch Valley
Silver Flowe
Rhinns of Kells
Loch Dungeon
Lochinvar
Lochurr
Bogrie Hill
Dunscore
Sundaywell
Milton
Ellisland Mus & Farm
Millquarter
Earlstoun Loch
St John's Town of Dalry
Bogue
Corriedoo Forest
Drumbuie
Garroch
Glenlee
Bruce's Stone
Trool
Loch Trool
Clatteringshaws Forest
Clatteringshaws Loch
Loch Dee
New Galloway
Balmaclellan
Blackcraig
Knocklearn
Gibbshill
Newtonairds
Holywood
Drumpark
Glenkiln Res.
Irongray
Glenkiln
Glen
Terregles Banks
Shawhead
Newbridge
Lamachan Hill
Ironmacannie
Craig
Corsock
Merkland
Urr Water
Brooklands
Crocketford or Ninemile Bar
Brae
Lochfoot
Lochrutton Loch
Cargenbridge
Raiders Road Forest Drive
Cairn Edward Hill
Bennan Forest
Loch Grannoch
Wild Goat Park
Fell of Fleet
Drumrash
Mossdale
Parton
Auchenreoch Loch
Kirkpatrick Durham
Milton Loch
Milton
Springholm
Beeswing
Loch Arthur
Lochaber Loch
Mabie Forest
Drumcoltran Tower
Stroan Loch
Loch Skerrow
Woodhall Loch
Loch Ken
Crossmichael
Old Bridge of Urr
Clarebrand
Haugh of Urr
Kirkgunzeon
Penkiln Burn
Palnure Burn
Cairnsmore of Fleet
Kirroughtree Visitor Centre
Minnigaff
Creebridge
Newton Stewart
Palnure
Fleet Forest
Lochenbreck Loch
Laurieston
Townhead of Greenlaw
Mote of Urr
Clints of Dromore
Laurieston Forest
Loch Glentoo
Threave Castle
Castle Douglas
Old Buittle Tower
Barhill
Dalbeattie
Long Fell
Big Water of Fleet
Loch Whinyeon
Loch Mannoch
Glengap Forest
Bengray
Glengap
Loch Bargatton
Threave Garden & Estate
Carlingwark Loch
Bridge of Dee
Rhonehouse or Kelton Hill
Gelston
Baltersan
Cree
Causeway End
Gem Rock Museum
Creetown
Wigtown Sands
Wigtown
Bladnoch
Scotland's Book Town
Visitor Centre
Glen
Fleet Valley
NX
Cairnharrow
Carsluith
Carsluith Castle
Cairnholy Cairns
Anwoth
Cardoness Castle
Gatehouse of Fleet
Valleyfield
Ringford
Airieland
Palnackie
Dalbeattie Forest
Drumstinchall
Caulkerbush
Barnbarroch
Orchardton Tower
Sandyhills
Colvend
Kippford or Scaur
Mote of Mark
Rockcliffe
Rough Island
Portling
Mersehead Sands
Galloway Hydro Visitor Centre
Tongland
Broughton House and Garden
Twynholm
Girthon
Bengairn
East Stewartry Coast
Castlehill Pt.
Braehead
Kirkinner
Baldoon Sands
Ravenshall Pt.
Ringdoo Pt.
Fleet Bay
Sandgreen
Barharrow
Whinnieliggate
Auchencairn
Auchencairn Bay
Hestan I.
Whauphill
Islands of Fleet
Knockbrex
Stewartry Museum
Kirkcudbright
St Mary's Isle
Kirkcarswell
Rascarrel
Balcary Pt.
Sorbie
Garlieston
Eggerness Pt.
Wigtown Bay
Kirkandrews
Borgue
Mutehill
Dundrennan
Rascarrel Bay
Orroland
Galloway House Gardens
Borness
Ross
Kirkcudbright Bay
Townhead
Dundrennan Abbey
Netherlaw
Balmae
Port Mary
Abbey Hd.
Borness Pt.
Little Ross
Moor of Ravenstone
Cults
Cruggleton Church and Castle
Bishopton
Whithorn
Priory and Museum
Port Allen
Whithorn Trust Discovery Centre
Portyerrock Bay
Cairn Hd.
Glasserton
Carleton
St Ninian's Chapel
Isle of Whithorn
Castle Bay
Cutcloy
Burrow Head
Solway Firth
Saltom
St Bees Head

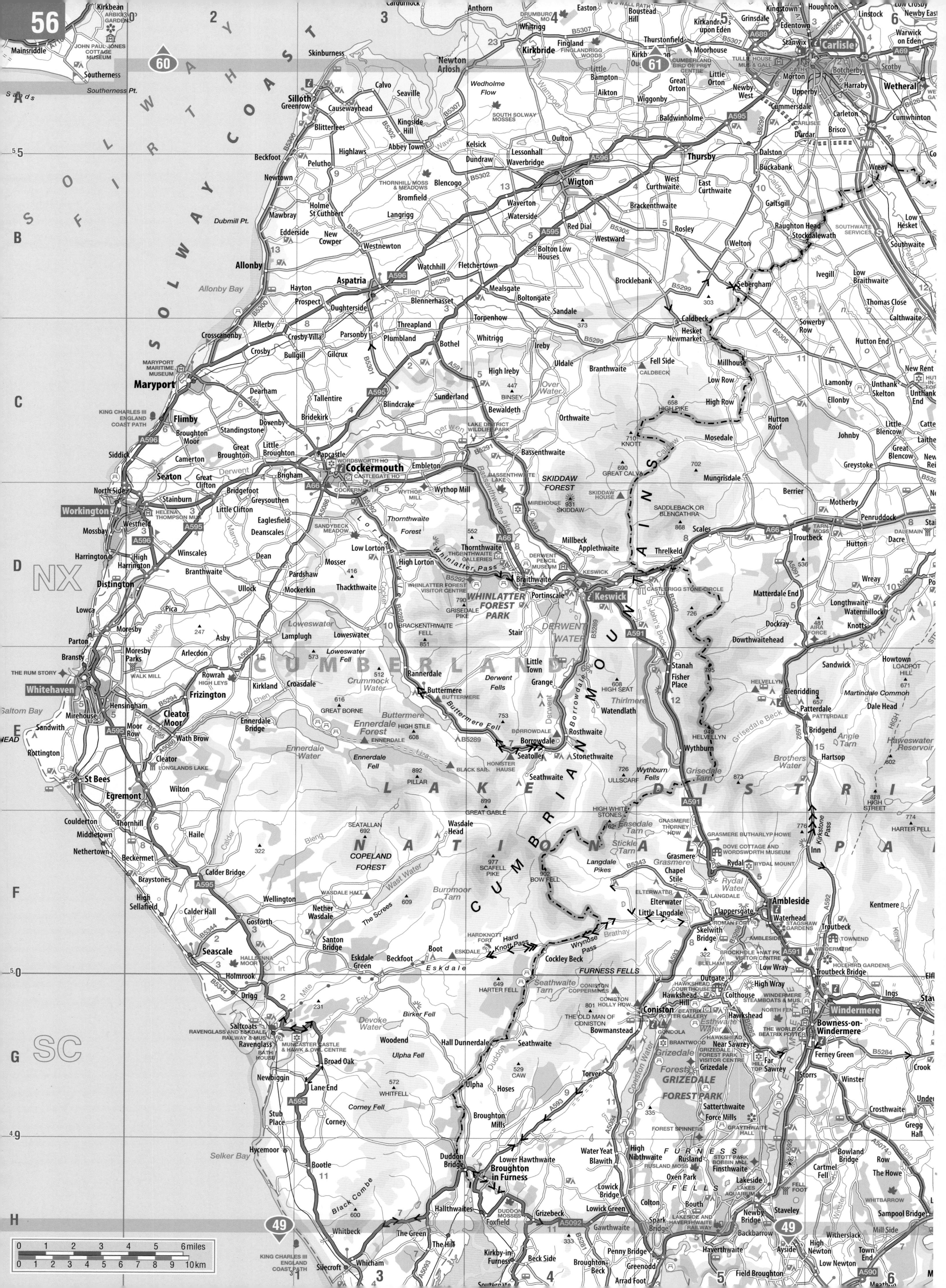
SOLWAY COAST
SOLWAY FIRTH
NX
SC
CUMBERLAND
CUMBRIAN MOUNTAINS
LAKE DISTRICT NATIONAL PARK
Carlisle
Silloth
Wigton
Aspatria
Maryport
Workington
Cockermouth
Keswick
Whitehaven
Cleator Moor
Egremont
St Bees
Seascale
Ravenglass
Broughton in Furness
Coniston
Ambleside
Windermere
Bowness-on-Windermere
Grasmere
Kirkbride
Thursby
Dalston
Caldbeck
Allonby
Flimby
Seaton
Distington
Frizington
Braithwaite
Portinscale
Buttermere
Borrowdale
Seatoller
Rosthwaite
Glenridding
Patterdale
Troutbeck
Penruddock
Hawkshead
Near Sawrey
Far Sawrey
Grizedale
Satterthwaite
Silecroft
Whicham
Millom
Allonby Bay
Selker Bay
Saltom Bay
Dubmill Pt.
Southerness Pt.
Skiddaw Forest
Whinlatter Forest Park
Grizedale Forest Park
Ennerdale Forest
Copeland Forest
Derwent Water
Bassenthwaite Lake
Thirlmere
Ullswater
Coniston Water
Esthwaite Water
Windermere
Crummock Water
Loweswater
Ennerdale Water
Haweswater Reservoir
Burnmoor Tarn
Devoke Water
Seathwaite Tarn
Grisedale Tarn
Easedale Tarn
Stickle Tarn
Wrynose Pass
Hardknott Pass
Kirkstone Pass
Whinlatter Pass
Black Combe
Scafell Pike 977
Helvellyn 949
Skiddaw 931
Great Gable 899
Pillar 892
Saddleback or Blencathra 868
Furness Fells
Ulpha Fell
A595
A596
A66
A591
A593
A592
A5092
M6
0 1 2 3 4 5 6 miles
0 1 2 3 4 5 6 7 8 9 10 km

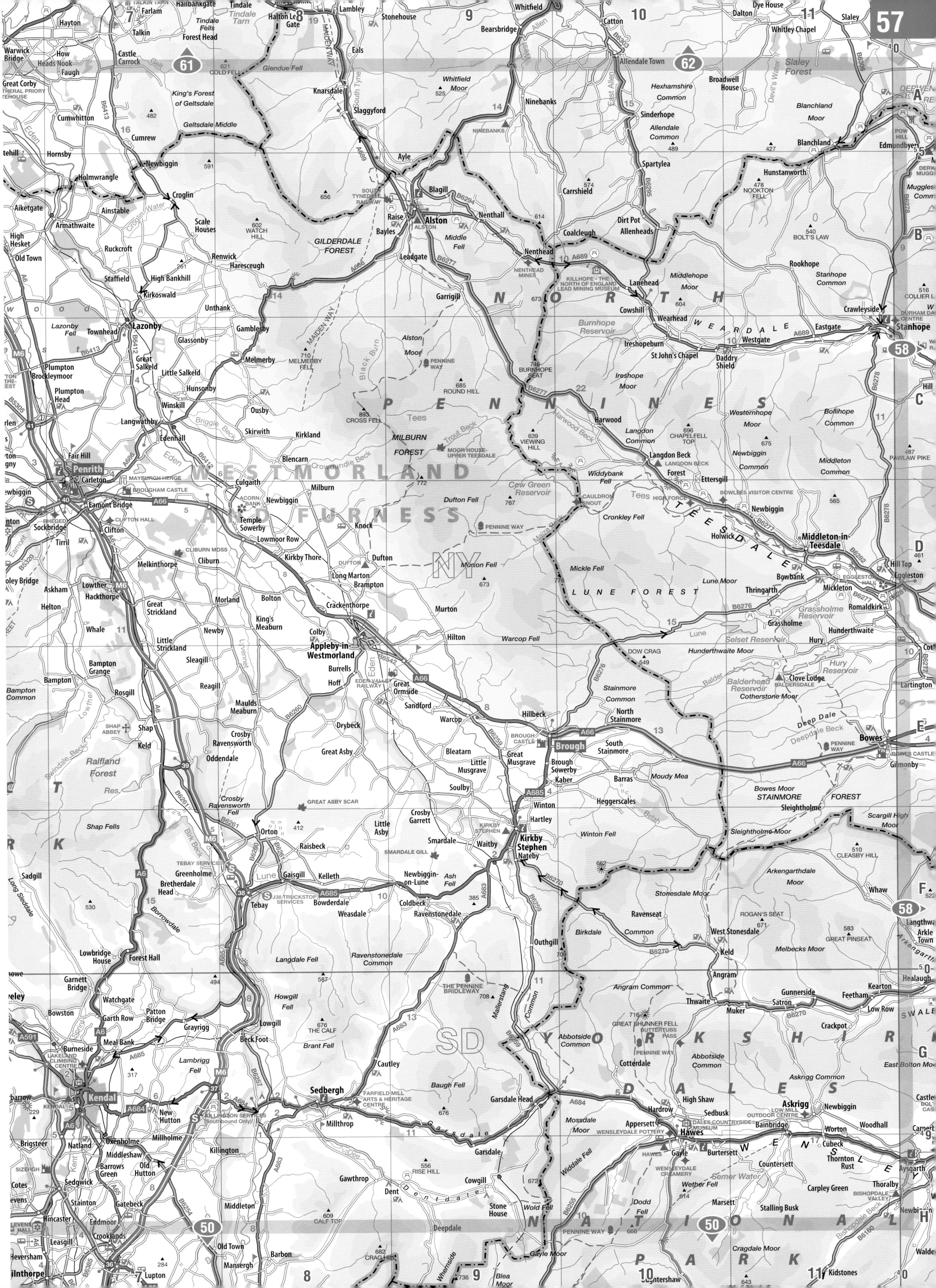
Hayton
Talkin
Farlam
Hallbankgate
Tindale
Tindale Fells
Tindale Tarn
Halton Lea Gate
Lambley
Stonehouse
Whitfield
Bearsbridge
Catton
Dalton
Dye House
Whitley Chapel
Slaley
Slaley Forest
Warwick Bridge
How
Heads Nook
Faugh
Castle Carrock
Cold Fell
Forest Head
Glendue Fell
Eals
Maiden Way
Allendale Town
Whitfield Moor
Knarsdale
Slaggyford
South Tyne
Hexhamshire Common
Broadwell House
Great Corby
Wetheral Priory Gatehouse
King's Forest of Geltsdale
Geltsdale Middle
Cumwhitton
Cumrew
Eden
Ninebanks
Sinderhope
Allendale Common
Blanchland
Blanchland Moor
Edmundbyers
Hornsby
Newbiggin
Holmwrangle
Croglin
Croglin Water
Ayle
Spartylea
Hunstanworth
Nookton Fell
Muggleswick Common
Aiketgate
Armathwaite
Ainstable
Scale Houses
Watch Hill
South Tynedale Railway
Blagill
Carrshield
Nenthall
Raise
Alston
Bayles
Gilderdale Forest
Middle Fell
Dirt Pot
Allenheads
Coalcleugh
Bolt's Law
High Hesket
Old Town
Ruckcroft
Renwick
Haresceugh
Leadgate
Nenthead
Nenthead Mines
Killhope - The North of England Lead Mining Museum
Rookhope
Stanhope Common
Staffield
High Bankhill
Kirkoswald
Garrigill
Lanehead
Middlehope Moor
Collier Law
Cowshill
Wearhead
Crawleyside
Stanhope
Lazonby
Lazonby Fell
Townhead
Unthank
Gamblesby
Glassonby
Maiden Way
Alston Moor
Pennine Way
Burnhope Reservoir
Weardale
Ireshopeburn
Westgate
Eastgate
St John's Chapel
Daddry Shield
Plumpton
Brockleymoor
Great Salkeld
Little Salkeld
Melmerby
Melmerby Fell
Black Burn
Burnhope Seat
Plumpton Head
Hunsonby
Round Hill
Ireshope Moor
Winskill
Ousby
Cross Fell
Pennines
Harwood
Westernhope Moor
Bollihope Common
Langwathby
Edenhall
Brigge Beck
Skirwith
Kirkland
Tees
Milburn Forest
Trout Beck
Moor House-Upper Teesdale
Viewing Hill
Harwood Beck
Langdon Common
Chapelfell Top
Newbiggin Common
Pawlaw Pike
Fair Hill
Penrith
Carleton
Mayburgh Henge
Brougham Castle
Blencarn
Crowdundle Beck
Westmorland and Furness
Widdybank Fell
Langdon Beck
Forest
Ettersgill
Middleton Common
Culgaith
Milburn
Cow Green Reservoir
Cauldron Snout
Bowlees Visitor Centre
High Force
Teesdale
Newbiggin
Eamont Bridge
Acorn Bank
Dufton Fell
Cronkley Fell
Holwick
Middleton-in-Teesdale
Rheged
Sockbridge
Clifton Hall
Clifton
Temple Sowerby
Lowmoor Row
Knock
Pennine Way
Tirril
Cliburn Moss
Cliburn
Kirkby Thore
Dufton
NY
Murton Fell
Mickle Fell
Hill Top
Eggleston
Bowbank
Eggleston Hall Gardens
Lune Moor
Mickleton
Thringarth
Romaldkirk
Melkinthorpe
Long Marton
Brampton
Pooley Bridge
Askham
Lowther
Hackthorpe
Great Strickland
Morland
Bolton
Lune Forest
Helton
Crackenthorpe
Murton
Grassholme Reservoir
Grassholme
Hunderthwaite
Whale
King's Meaburn
Little Strickland
Newby
Colby
Hilton
Warcop Fell
Lune
Selset Reservoir
Hury
Appleby-in-Westmorland
Sleagill
Lyvennet
Dow Crag
Hunderthwaite Moor
Hury Reservoir
Bampton Grange
Burrells
Hoff
Eden Valley Railway
Great Ormside
Balderhead Reservoir
Balder
Clove Lodge
Baldersdale
Cotherstone Moor
Lartington
Bampton
Bampton Common
Rosgill
Reagill
Maulds Meaburn
Sandford
Stainmore Common
Lowther
Shap Abbey
Shap
Crosby Ravensworth
Drybeck
Warcop
Hillbeck
North Stainmore
Deep Dale
Keld
Oddendale
Brough Castle
Brough
South Stainmore
Deepdale Beck
Bowes
Pennine Way
Bowes Castle
Gilmonby
Ralfland Forest
Res.
Great Asby
Bleatarn
Little Musgrave
Great Musgrave
Brough Sowerby
Kaber
Barras
Moudy Mea
Swindale Beck
Soulby
Bowes Moor
Stainmore Forest
Crosby Ravensworth Fell
Great Asby Scar
Winton
Heggerscales
Sleightholme
Scargill High Moor
Shap Fells
Birk Beck
Orton
Little Asby
Crosby Garrett
Kirkby Stephen
Hartley
Winton Fell
Belah
Sleightholme Moor
Raisbeck
Smardale
Waitby
Stephen
Nateby
Cleasby Hill
Tebay Services
Smardale Gill
Sadgill
Greenholme
Bretherdale Head
Lune
Gaisgill
Kelleth
Newbiggin-on-Lune
Ash Fell
Arkengarthdale Moor
Long Sleddale
Tebay
J38 Truckstop Services
Bowderdale
Coldbeck
Stonesdale Moor
Whaw
Borrowdale
Weasdale
Ravenstonedale
Ravenseat
Rogan's Seat
Langthwaite
Arkle Town
Birkdale
Common
West Stonesdale
Great Pinseat
Outhgill
Keld
Melbecks Moor
Arkengarth
Lowbridge House
Forest Hall
Langdale Fell
Ravenstonedale Common
Angram
Healaugh
Kearton
Garnett Bridge
The Pennine Bridleway
Mallerstang
Angram Common
Gunnerside
Feetham
Watchgate
Howgill Fell
Common
Thwaite
Muker
Satron
Low Row
Swaledale
Bowston
Garth Row
Patton Bridge
Grayrigg
The Calf
Great Shunner Fell
Buttertubs Pass
Crackpot
Lowgill
Abbotside Common
Yorkshire
Burneside
Meal Bank
Beck Foot
Brant Fell
SD
Pennine Way
Lakeland Climbing Centre
Lambrigg Fell
Cautley
Cotterdale
Abbotside Common
East Bolton Moor
Baugh Fell
Askrigg Common
Kendal
Sedbergh
Farfield Mill Arts & Heritage Centre
Garsdale Head
Dales
High Shaw
Castle Bolton
New Hutton
Killington Services (Southbound Only)
Millthrop
Mossdale Moor
Hardrow
Sedbusk
Low Mill Outdoor Centre
Askrigg
Newbiggin
Appersett
Wensleydale Pottery
Dales Countryside Museum
Hawes
Bainbridge
Worton
Woodhall
Carperby
Oxenholme
Millholme
Garsdale
Widdale Fell
Burtersett
Wensleydale
Cubeck
Brigsteer
Natland
Middleshaw
Killington
Dee
Rise Hill
Gayle
Wensleydale Creamery
Thornton Rust
Aysgarth
Sizergh
Barrows Green
Old Hutton
Gawthrop
Cowgill
Wether Fell
Semer Water
Countersett
Thoralby
Cotes
Sedgwick
Dent
Dentdale
Carpley Green
Bishopdale Valley
Stainton
Gatebeck
Middleton
Stone House
Wold Fell
Dodd Fell
Marsett
Stalling Busk
Newbiggin
Levens Hall
Hincaster
Endmoor
Calf Top
National
Bishopdale Beck
Leasgill
Crooklands
Deepdale
Pennine Way
Park
Heversham
Old Town
Barbon
Crag Hill
Whernside
Gayle Moor
Cragdale Moor
Walden
Milnthorpe
Lupton
Mansergh
Blea Moor
Oughtershaw
Kidstones
A6
A66
A685
A686
A689
A684
A683
A591
M6
B6412
B6413
B6276
B6277
B6278
B6295
B6303
B6305
B6306
B6259
B6260
B6261
B6270
B6271
B6282
B6254
B6255
B6257
B6160
B6542
B5305
B5320
B6294
58
61
62
50

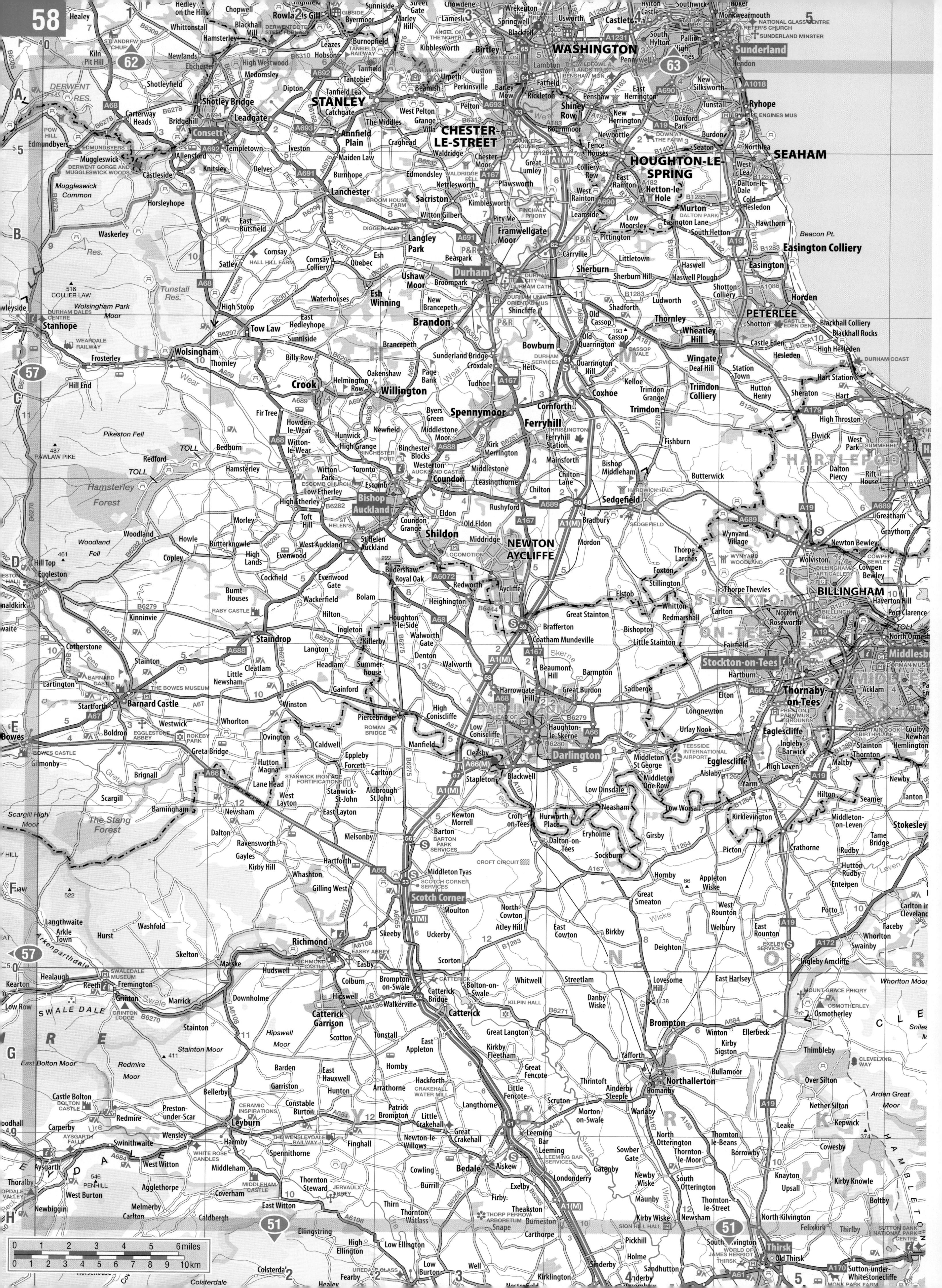
WASHINGTON
Sunderland
STANLEY
CHESTER-LE-STREET
SEAHAM
HOUGHTON-LE-SPRING
Consett
Shotley Bridge
Leadgate
Lanchester
Sacriston
Durham
Easington Colliery
Horden
PETERLEE
Brandon
Crook
Willington
Spennymoor
Ferryhill
Bishop Auckland
Shildon
NEWTON AYCLIFFE
Sedgefield
HARTLEPOOL
BILLINGHAM
STOCKTON-ON-TEES
Stockton-on-Tees
Thornaby-on-Tees
MIDDLESBROUGH
Eaglescliffe
Yarm
Darlington
DARLINGTON
Barnard Castle
Staindrop
Stanhope
Wolsingham
Tow Law
Richmond
Scotch Corner
Catterick
Catterick Garrison
Leyburn
Bedale
Northallerton
Stokesley
Osmotherley
Thirsk
Middleham
Aysgarth
Reeth
Egglescliffe
Croft-on-Tees
Hurworth Place
Brompton
Leeming Bar
Masham
DERWENT RES.
Muggleswick Common
Tunstall Res.
Hamsterley Forest
The Stang Forest
Pikeston Fell
SWALE DALE
Stainton Moor
Redmire Moor
Arden Great Moor
DURHAM COAST
THE BOWES MUSEUM
BEAMISH
DURHAM CATH
CROFT CIRCUIT
TEESSIDE INTERNATIONAL AIRPORT
MOUNT GRACE PRIORY
Beacon Pt.
57
62
63
51
0 1 2 3 4 5 6 miles
0 1 2 3 4 5 6 7 8 9 10 km

NZ
SE
ST HILDA'S PARISH CHURCH
NATIONAL MUS OF THE ROYAL NAVY
Hartlepool Bay
Seaton Carew
Tees Bay
Salt Scar
REDCAR
Coatham
Dormanstown
KIRKLEATHAM OLD HALL MUSEUM
Marske-by-the-Sea
MINIATURE RAILWAY
Saltburn-by-the-Sea
South Bank
Grangetown
Kirkleatham
Yearby
New Marske
Lazenby
KIRKLEATHAM WALLED GARDEN
SALTBURN VALLEY
Brotton
Skinningrove
KING CHARLES III ENGLAND COAST PATH
Boulby
Wilton
Upleatham
Skelton
Carlin How
Loftus
Staithes
Eston
Dunsdale
FOCKETTS WATER MILL
North Skelton
Kilton Thorpe
Easington
Port Mulgrave
Runswick Bay
Normanby
Ormesby
FLATTS LANE WOODLAND
GUISBOROUGH PRIORY
Boosbeck
Lingdale
Hinderwell
Runswick Bay
Kettleness
ORMESBY HALL
Guisborough
Margrove Park
Stanghow
Liverton
Roxby
Newton Mulgrave
Goldsborough
GUISBOROUGH FOREST
Hutton Gate
Charltons
REDCAR AND CLEVELAND
Nunthorpe
Hutton Village
Gisborough Moor
Moorsholm
Scaling
Ellerby
Lythe
Sandsend
Newton under Roseberry
Commondale Moor
Scaling Dam Res.
Mickleby
East Barnby
Sandsend Wyke
SUTCLIFFE GALLERY
Whitby
Saltwick Bay
West Barnby
East Row
Dunsley
Great Ayton
Little Ayton
New Row
Commondale
Danby Low Moor
Lealholm Moor
Ugthorpe
Newholm
WHITBY ABBEY
CAPTAIN COOK MEMORIAL MUSEUM
Easby
Kildale
Kildale Moor
Danby
THE MOORS CENTRE
Stonegate
Ruswarp
Stainsacre
Battersby
Castleton
Ainthorpe
Houlsyke
Lealholm
Aislaby
Briggswath
Sleights
Sneaton
High Hawsker
Ugglebarnby
Kirkby
Great Broughton
Ingleby Greenhow
Westerdale
Low Garth
Street
Glaisdale
Egton
Grosmont
Sneatonthorpe
Raw
Ness Pt.
CLEVELAND WAY
Robin Hood's Bay
OLD COASTGUARD STATION
BOGGLE HOLE
Great Busby
MUSEUM OF VICTORIAN SCIENCE
Egton Bridge
Esk Valley
Littlebeck
Fylingthorpe
Robin Hood's Bay
Old Peak
Westerdale Moor
Glaisdale Moor
Egton High Moor
Beck Hole
Goathland
Ravenscar
Urra
Seave Green
Farndale Moor
Rosedale Moor
Flask Inn
Fylingdales Moor
Chop Gate
COCKAYNE RIDGE
Wake Lady Green
Cockayne
WHEELDALE MOOR ROMAN ROAD
Staintondale
NORTH YORK MOORS NATIONAL PARK
CLEVELAND HILLS
Church Houses
Wheeldale Moor
Harwood Dale Forest
Bilsdale East Moor
Bilsdale West Moor
Thorgill
Rosedale Abbey
Goathland Moor
Saltergate
Harwood Dale
Cloughton Newlands
Cloughton Wyke
Cloughton
PICKERING MOOR
Pickering Forest
Rudland Rigg
Bransdale
Blakey Ridge
Low Mill
ROSEDALE
Langdale Forest
Broxa Forest
Burniston
Fangdale Beck
Cropton Forest
Hartoft End
Stape
Cromer Pt.
East Moors
Spaunton Moor
TOLL
Langdale End
Broxa
Silpho
Suffield
Scalby
SCARBOROUGH
Scalby Ness Rocks
SEA LIFE CENTRE
North Bay
Helmsley Moor
Skiplam Moor
RYEDALE FOLK MUSEUM
Lastingham
Levisham
DALBY FOREST
Staindale Forest
Hackness
Gillamoor
Newton-on-Rawcliffe
Lockton
Wrench Green
Everley
Barrowcliff
Newby
Hawnby
Rievaulx Moor
Fadmoor
Hutton-le-Hole
Spaunton
NORTH RIDING FOREST PARK
Wykeham Forest
ROTUNDA MUSEUM
Scarborough
South
Appleton-le-Moors
Cropton
Low Dalby
NORTH YORKSHIRE MOORS RAILWAY
FORGE VALLEY WOODLANDS
Falsgrave
Carlton
Kirkbymoorside
Keldholme
Sinnington
Wrelton
Aislaby
ST PETER AND ST PAUL CHURCH
DALBY FOREST VISITOR CENTRE
Dalby Forest
East Ayton
Old Byland
Rievaulx
Pockley
Beadlam
Kirkby Mills
Middleton
Sawdon
West Ayton
THE HONEY FARM
Osgodby
CLEVELAND WAY
RIEVAULX ABBEY
HELMSLEY
Welburn
Hutton Buscel
Eastfield
Cold Kirby
Helmsley
Wombleton
Great Edstone
Pickering
PICKERING CASTLE
Ellerburn
Seamer
Scawton
Rye Dale
DUNCOMBE PARK
Marton
Thornton-le-Dale
Wilton
Allerston
Ebberston
Snainton
Ruston
Wykeham
Cayton
DUNCOMBE PARK
Normanby
Sproxton
A1085
A1042
B1269
A174
A66
A1053
A173
A171
A1043
B1292
A172
B1366
B1266
A169
B1410
B1416
B1447
A170
B1257
B1415
B1261
A64
A165
52

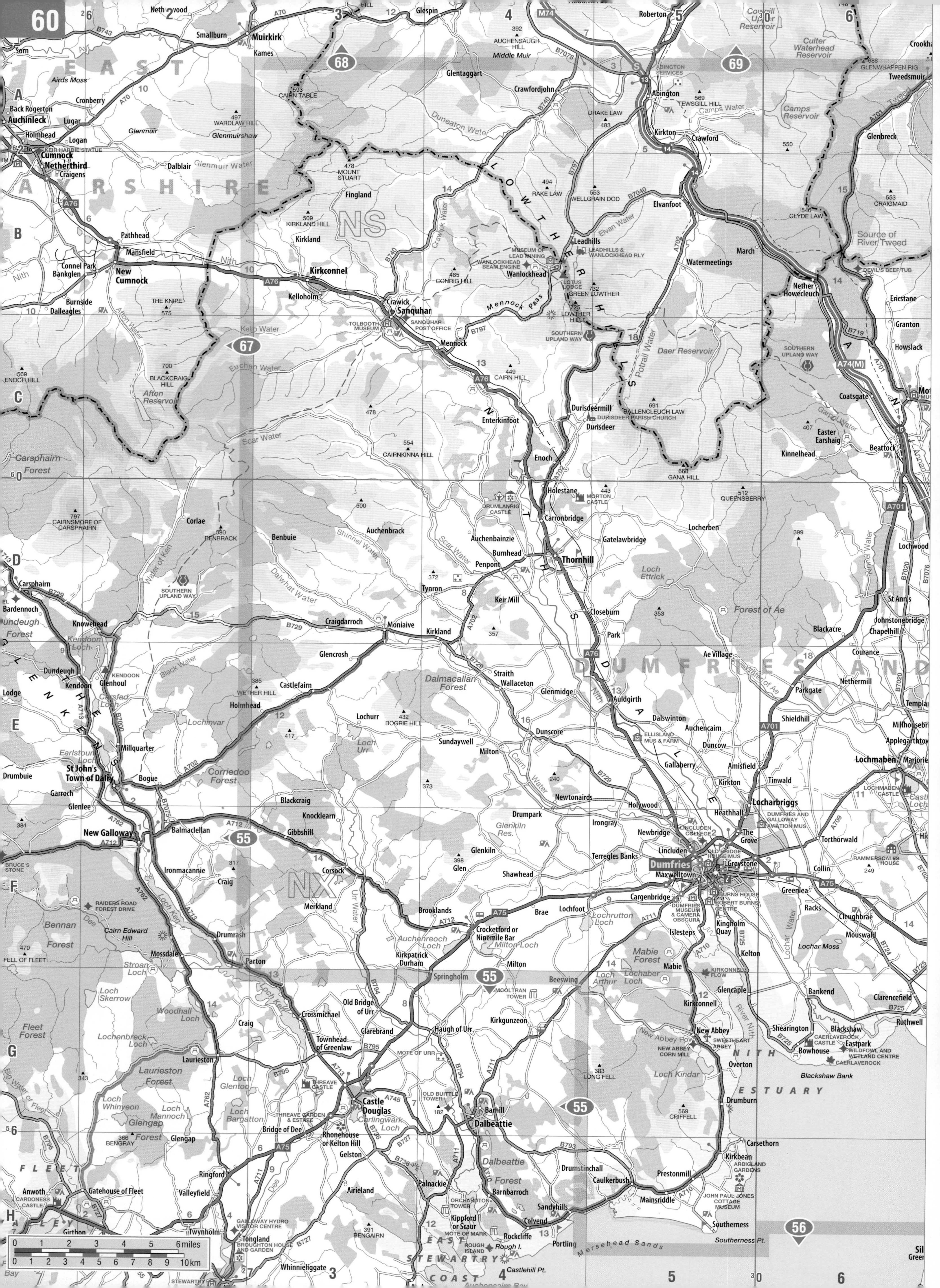
EAST AYRSHIRE
Sorn
Muirkirk
Smallburn
Kames
Airds Moss
Back Rogerton
Auchinleck
Cronberry
Lugar
Holmhead
Logan
Cumnock
Netherthird
Craigens
Dalblair
Glenmuir Water
Glenmuirshaw
Cairn Table
Wardlaw Hill
Glentaggart
Crawfordjohn
Duneaton Water
Middle Muir
Auchensaugh Hill
Glespin
Roberton
Abington
Abington Services
Tewsgill Hill
Camps Water
Camps Reservoir
Drake Law
Kirkton
Crawford
Culter Waterhead Reservoir
Cowgill Upper Reservoir
Glenwhappen Rig
Tweedsmuir
Crookhaugh
Glenbreck
Clyde Law
Craigmaid
Source of River Tweed
Devil's Beef Tub
Mount Stuart
Fingland
Kirkland Hill
Kirkland
NS
Rake Law
Wellgrain Dod
Elvanfoot
Elvan Water
Leadhills
Leadhills & Wanlockhead Rly
Museum of Lead Mining
Wanlockhead Beam Engine
Wanlockhead
Lotus Lodge
Green Lowther
Lowther Hill
LOWTHER HILLS
Mennock Pass
Watermeetings
March
Nether Howecleuch
Ericstane
Granton
Howslack
Southern Upland Way
Pathhead
Mansfield
Connel Park
Bankglen
New Cumnock
Nith
Kirkconnel
Kelloholm
Conrig Hill
Crawick
Sanquhar
Tolbooth Museum
Sanquhar Post Office
Mennock
Burnside
Dalleagles
The Knipe
Afton Water
Kello Water
Euchan Water
Blackcraig Hill
Afton Reservoir
Enoch Hill
Cairn Hill
Potrail Water
Daer Reservoir
Ballencleuch Law
Durisdeermill
Durisdeer
Durisdeer Parish Church
Enterkinfoot
Enoch
Gana Hill
Coatsgate
Easter Earshaig
Kinnelhead
Beattock
Garpol Water
Scar Water
Cairnkinna Hill
Garsphairn Forest
Cairnsmore of Carsphairn
Corlae
Benbrack
Benbuie
Auchenbrack
Shinnel Water
Holestane
Morton Castle
Drumlanrig Castle
Carronbridge
Queensberry
Locherben
Gatelawbridge
Auchenbainzie
Burnhead
Penpont
Thornhill
Loch Ettrick
Lochwood
Tynron
Keir Mill
Closeburn
Park
Forest of Ae
St Ann's
Johnstonebridge
Chapelhill
Carsphairn
Bardennoch
Dundeugh Forest
Knowehead
Water of Ken
Dalwhat Water
Craigdarroch
Moniaive
Kirkland
Blackacre
Courance
Kendoon Loch
Dundeugh
Kendoon
Glenhoul
Black Water
Glencrosh
Wether Hill
Castlefairn
Straith
Wallaceton
Dalmacallan Forest
DUMFRIES AND
NITHSDALE
Ae Village
Water of Ae
Nethermill
Parkgate
Templand
Lodge
Carsfad Loch
Holmhead
Lochinvar
Lochurr
Bogrie Hill
Glenmidge
Auldgirth
Dalswinton
Auchencairn
Shieldhill
Milhousebridge
Applegarthtown
GLENKENS
Millquarter
Earlstoun Loch
Loch Urr
Sundaywell
Milton
Dunscore
Ellisland Mus & Farm
Duncow
Amisfield
Lochmaben
Drumbuie
St John's Town of Dalry
Garroch
Glenlee
Bogue
Corriedoo Forest
Cairn Water
Newtonairds
Gallaberry
Kirkton
Tinwald
Blackcraig
Knocklearn
Gibbshill
Drumpark
Glenkiln Res.
Irongray
Holywood
Heathhall
Locharbriggs
Lochmaben Castle
New Galloway
Balmaclellan
Glenkiln
Glen
Shawhead
Newbridge
Lincluden College
Lincluden
Terregles Banks
The Grove
Dumfries and Galloway Aviation Mus
Torthorwald
Bruce's Stone
Ironmacannie
Craig
Corsock
NX
Dumfries
Maxwelltown
Old Bridge House Mus
Greystone
Rammerscales House
Collin
Raiders Road Forest Drive
Bennan Forest
Cairn Edward Hill
Merkland
Urr Water
Brooklands
Brae
Lochfoot
Lochrutton Loch
Cargenbridge
Burns House
Robert Burns Centre
Dumfries Museum & Camera Obscura
Kingholm Quay
Greenlea
Racks
Cleughbrae
Mouswald
Fell of Fleet
Drumrash
Mossdale
Stroan Loch
Parton
Auchenreoch Loch
Crocketford or Ninemile Bar
Milton Loch
Milton
Islesteps
Mabie Forest
Mabie
Kelton
Lochar Moss
Lochar Water
Loch Skerrow
Kirkpatrick Durham
Springholm
Mcoltran Tower
Beeswing
Loch Arthur
Lochaber Loch
Kirkconnell Flow
Glencaple
Bankend
Clarencefield
Woodhall Loch
Fleet Forest
Lochenbreck Loch
Loch Ken
Old Bridge of Urr
Crossmichael
Craig
Townhead of Greenlaw
Clarebrand
Haugh of Urr
Kirkgunzeon
Mote of Urr
Kirkconnell
New Abbey
Sweetheart Abbey
New Abbey Corn Mill
Shearington
Blackshaw
Caerlaverock Castle
Bowhouse
Eastpark
Wildfowl and Wetland Centre
Caerlaverock
Rothwell
Laurieston
Laurieston Forest
Loch Glentoo
Threave Castle
Long Fell
Loch Kindar
Overton
NITH ESTUARY
Blackshaw Bank
Big Water of Fleet
Loch Whinyeon
Loch Mannoch
Glengap Forest
Bengray
Loch Bargatton
Threave Garden & Estate
Castle Douglas
Carlingwark Loch
Old Buittle Tower
Barhill
Dalbeattie
Criffell
Drumburn
Bridge of Dee
Rhonehouse or Kelton Hill
Gelston
Glengap
Carsethorn
Kirkbean
Arbigland Gardens
FLEET
Ringford
Dalbeattie Forest
Drumstinchall
Caulkerbush
Prestonmill
Anwoth
Cardoness Castle
Gatehouse of Fleet
Valleyfield
Airieland
Palnackie
Barnbarroch
Orchardton Tower
Sandyhills
Mainsriddle
John Paul Jones Cottage Museum
Girthon
Twynholm
Galloway Hydro Visitor Centre
Tongland
Broughton House and Garden
Bengairn
Kippford or Scaur
Mote of Mark
Rough Island
Rough I.
Colvend
Rockcliffe
Portling
Mersehead Sands
Southerness
Southerness Pt.
Castlehill Pt.
EAST STEWARTRY COAST
Whinnieliggate
Stewartry
0 1 2 3 4 5 6 miles
0 1 2 3 4 5 6 7 8 9 10 km

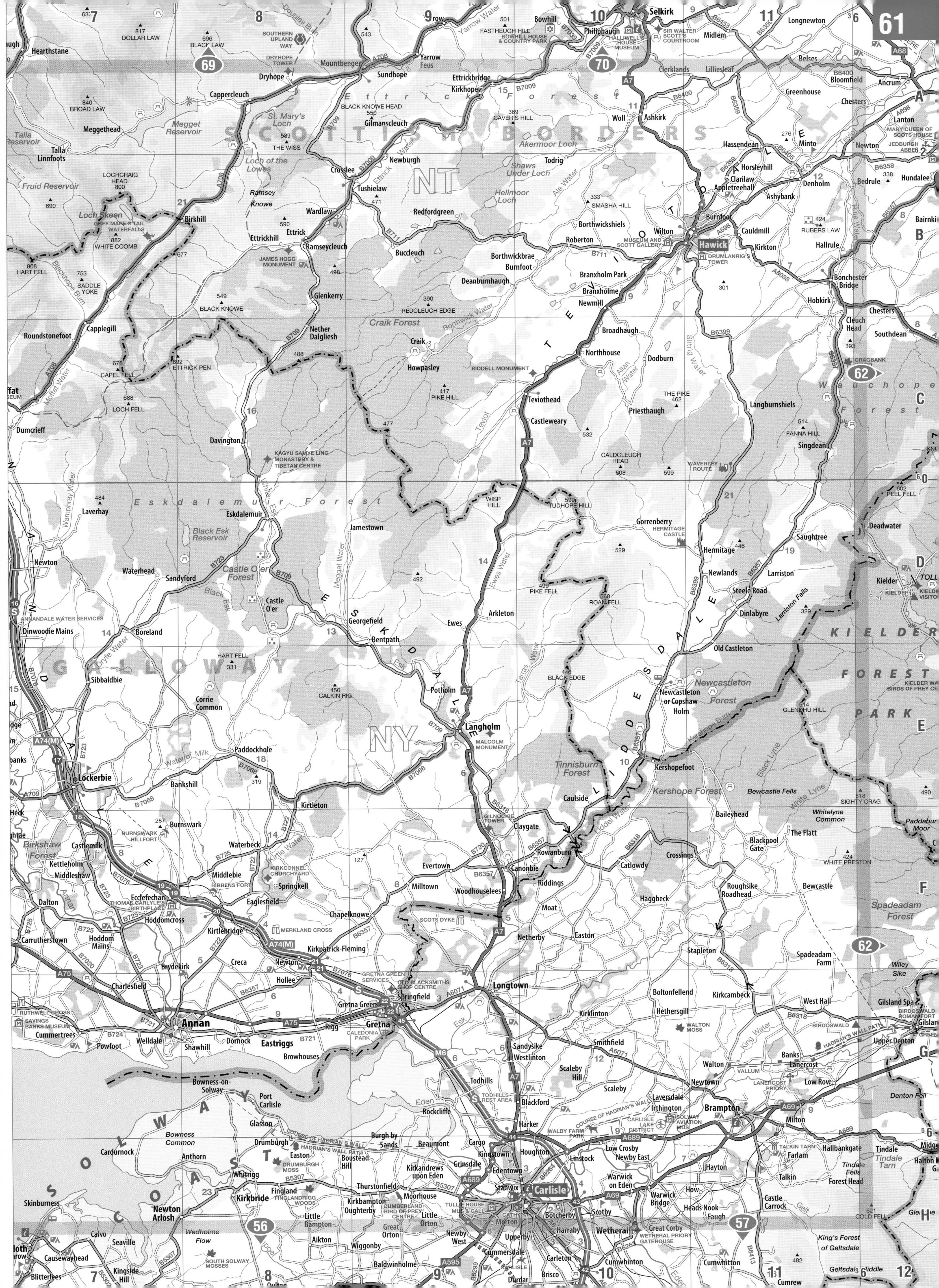
SCOTTISH BORDERS
DUMFRIES AND GALLOWAY
Ettrick Forest
Eskdalemuir Forest
Craik Forest
Castle O'er Forest
KIELDER FOREST PARK
Wauchope Forest
Newcastleton Forest
Kershope Forest
Tinnisburn Forest
Spadeadam Forest
King's Forest of Geltsdale
SOLWAY COAST
NT
NY
TEVIOTDALE
ESKDALE
LIDDESDALE
ANNANDALE
Selkirk
Philiphaugh
Bowhill
FASTHEUGH HILL
BOWHILL HOUSE & COUNTRY PARK
HALLIWELL'S HOUSE MUSEUM
SIR WALTER SCOTT'S COURTROOM
Midlem
Longnewton
Belses
Bloomfield
Ancrum
Lilliesleaf
Clerklands
Greenhouse
Chesters
Lanton
MARY QUEEN OF SCOTS HOUSE
JEDBURGH ABBEY
Minto
Hassendean
Horsleyhill
Clarilaw
Appletreehall
Denholm
Bedrule
Hundalee
Ashybank
Bairnkine
Burnfoot
Cauldmill
Hawick
RUBERS LAW
Hallrule
Kirkton
Wilton
MUSEUM AND SCOTT GALLERY
DRUMLANRIG'S TOWER
Bonchester Bridge
Hobkirk
Chesters
Cleuch Head
Southdean
CRAGBANK
Langburnshiels
FANNA HILL
Singdean
PEEL FELL
Deadwater
Saughtree
Kielder
KIELDER VISITOR
Larriston
Larriston Fells
Steele Road
Dinlabyre
Newlands
Hermitage
HERMITAGE CASTLE
Gorrenberry
WAVERLEY ROUTE
CALDCLEUCH HEAD
THE PIKE
Priesthaugh
Dodburn
Northhouse
Broadhaugh
Newmill
Branxholme
Branxholm Park
Borthwickshiels
Roberton
SMASHA HILL
Borthwickbrae
Burnfoot
Deanburnhaugh
REDCLEUCH EDGE
Craik
Howpasley
RIDDELL MONUMENT
PIKE HILL
Teviothead
Castleweary
WISP HILL
TUDHOPE HILL
PIKE FELL
ROAN FELL
Arkleton
Ewes
Old Castleton
BLACK EDGE
Newcastleton or Copshaw Holm
GLENDHU HILL
Kershopefoot
Bewcastle Fells
SIGHTY CRAG
Whitelyne Common
Baileyhead
The Flatt
Paddaburn Moor
Caulside
Blackpool Gate
Crossings
WHITE PRESTON
Catlowdy
Bewcastle
Roughsike
Roadhead
Haggbeck
Stapleton
Spadeadam Farm
Wiley Sike
Kirkcambeck
West Hall
Gilsland Spa
BIRDOSWALD ROMAN FORT
Upper Denton
Banks
Lanercost
LANERCOST PRIORY
Low Row
Denton Fell
Walton
Newtown
Brampton
Milton
TALKIN TARN
Farlam
Hallbankgate
Tindale
Tindale Tarn
Tindale Fells
Talkin
Forest Head
Castle Carrock
COLD FELL
Geltsdale Middle
Cumrew
Cumwhitton
Heads Nook
Faugh
How
Warwick Bridge
Warwick on Eden
Hayton
Great Corby
WETHERAL PRIORY GATEHOUSE
Wetheral
Scotby
Cumwhinton
Carleton
Brisco
Botcherby
Harraby
Carlisle
Stanwix
Linstock
Low Crosby
Newby East
Houghton
Kingstown
Edentown
Harker
Blackford
TODHILLS REST AREA
Todhills
WALBY FARM PARK
CARLISLE LAKE DISTRICT
SOLWAY AVIATION MUS
Irthington
Laversdale
Scaleby
Scaleby Hill
Smithfield
Hethersgill
WALTON MOSS
Boltonfellend
Kirklinton
Sandysike
Westlinton
Longtown
Netherby
Easton
Moat
Riddings
Canonbie
Rowanburn
Woodhouselees
Claygate
GILNOCKIE TOWER
Milltown
Evertown
SCOTS DYKE
Chapelknowe
Kirkpatrick-Fleming
MERKLAND CROSS
Langholm
MALCOLM MONUMENT
Potholm
Bentpath
Georgefield
CALKIN RIG
Jamestown
Eskdalemuir
KAGYU SAMYE LING MONASTERY & TIBETAN CENTRE
Davington
Black Esk Reservoir
Castle O'er
Sandyford
Waterhead
Boreland
Newton
Laverhay
Dumcrieff
LOCH FELL
CAPEL FELL
ETTRICK PEN
Nether Dalgliesh
Glenkerry
BLACK KNOWE
Capplegill
Roundstonefoot
SADDLE YOKE
HART FELL
WHITE COOMB
GREY MARE'S TAIL WATERFALLS
Loch Skeen
Birkhill
LOCHCRAIG HEAD
Fruid Reservoir
Talla Linnfoots
Talla Reservoir
Meggethead
Megget Reservoir
BROAD LAW
Cappercleuch
St. Mary's Loch
Loch of the Lowes
THE WISS
Hearthstane
DOLLAR LAW
BLACK LAW
SOUTHERN UPLAND WAY
DRYHOPE TOWER
Dryhope
Mountbenger
Yarrow
Yarrow Feus
Sundhope
Ettrickbridge
Kirkhope
BLACK KNOWE HEAD
Gilmanscleuch
CAVER'S HILL
Woll
Ashkirk
Akermoor Loch
Todrig
Shaws Under Loch
Hellmoor Loch
Newburgh
Crosslee
Tushielaw
Redfordgreen
Ramsey Knowe
Wardlaw
Ettrick
Ettrickhill
Ramseycleuch
JAMES HOGG MONUMENT
Buccleuch
Dinwoodie Mains
ANNANDALE WATER SERVICES
Sibbaldbie
HART FELL
Corrie Common
Paddockhole
Lockerbie
Bankshill
Kirtleton
BURNSWARK HILLFORT
Burnswark
Waterbeck
Castlemilk
Birkshaw Forest
Kettleholm
Middleshaw
Middlebie
BIRRENS FORT
KIRKCONNEL CHURCHYARD
Springkell
Ecclefechan
THOMAS CARLYLE'S BIRTHPLACE
Eaglesfield
Hoddomcross
Dalton
Carrutherstown
Hoddom Mains
Kirtlebridge
Brydekirk
Creca
Newton
Hollee
Charlesfield
Springfield
OLD BLACKSMITHS SHOP CENTRE
GRETNA GREEN SERVICES
Gretna Green
Gretna
CALEDONIA PARK
Rigg
Annan
RUTHWELL CROSS
SAVINGS BANKS MUSEUM
Cummertrees
Powfoot
Welldale
Shawhill
Dornock
Eastriggs
Browhouses
Bowness-on-Solway
Port Carlisle
Glasson
Rockcliffe
Bowness Common
Drumburgh
COURSE OF HADRIAN'S WALL
HADRIAN'S WALL PATH
Easton
DRUMBURGH MOSS
Burgh by Sands
Beaumont
Boustead Hill
Cargo
Kirkandrews upon Eden
Grinsdale
Cardurnock
Anthorn
Whitrigg
Fingland
FINGLANDRIGG WOODS
Kirkbride
Thurstonfield
Kirkbampton
Oughterby
Moorhouse
CUMBERLAND BIRD OF PREY CENTRE
Little Orton
Great Orton
Newby West
TULLIE HOUSE MUS & GALL
Morton
Upperby
Cummersdale
Durdar
Skinburness
Newton Arlosh
Little Bampton
Aikton
Wiggonby
Baldwinholme
Calvo
Seaville
Wedholme Flow
SOUTH SOLWAY MOSSES
Causewayhead
Kingside Hill
Blitterlees
Abbeytown

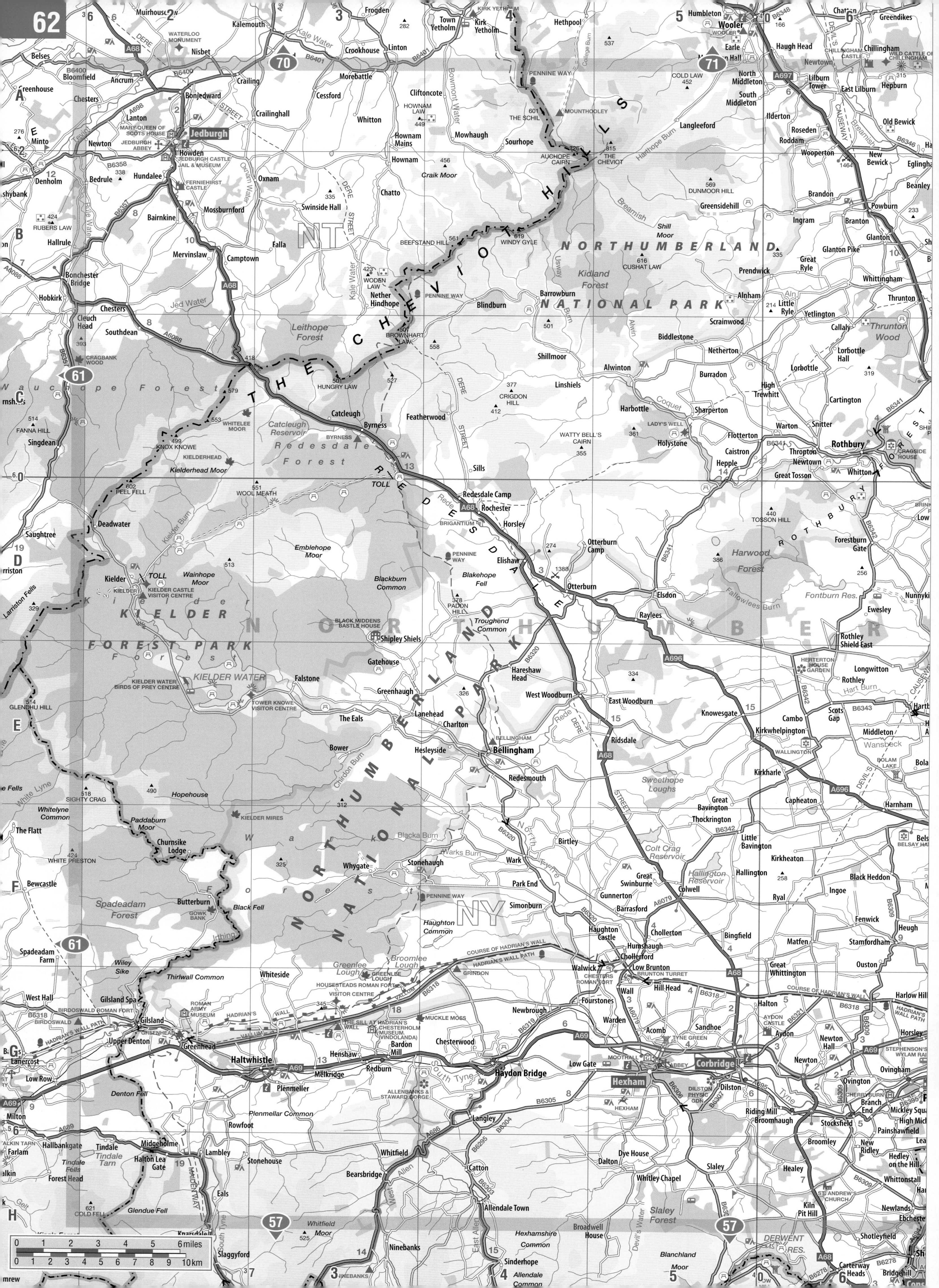

Muirhouse
Kalemouth
Waterloo Monument
Nisbet
Frogden
Town Yetholm
Kirk Yetholm
Hethpool
Humbleton
Wooler
Chatton
Greendikes
Kale Water
Crookhouse
Linton
Earle
Haugh Head
Chillingham
Belses
Bloomfield
Ancrum
Crailing
Morebattle
Cold Law
North Middleton
Lilburn Tower
East Lilburn
Hepburn
Greenhouse
Chesters
Bonjedward
Cessford
Cliftoncote
Hownam Law
Pennine Way
South Middleton
Lanton
Crailinghall
Mounthooley
The Schil
Ilderton
Roseden
Old Bewick
Mary Queen of Scots House
Jedburgh
Jedburgh Abbey
Whitton
Hownam Mains
Mowhaugh
Sourhope
Langleeford
Roddam
Minto
Newton
Howden
Jedburgh Castle Jail & Museum
Auchope Cairn
The Cheviot
Wooperton
New Bewick
Eglingham
Denholm
Bedrule
Hundalee
Hownam
Craik Moor
Ferniehirst Castle
Oxnam
Dunmoor Hill
Brandon
Beanley
Chatto
Greensidehill
Powburn
Mossburnford
Swinside Hall
Bairnkine
Rubers Law
Hallrule
Dere Street
The Cheviot Hills
Breamish
Shill Moor
Ingram
Branton
Glanton
Mervinslaw
Falla
Beefstand Hill
Windy Gyle
Northumberland National Park
Glanton Pike
Camptown
Cushat Law
Great Ryle
Prendwick
Bonchester Bridge
Woden Law
Kidland Forest
Whittingham
Hobkirk
Nether Hindhope
Blindburn
Barrowburn
Alnham
Thrunton
Chesters
Little Ryle
Yetlington
Cleuch Head
Jed Water
Scrainwood
Callaly
Thrunton Wood
Southdean
Leithope Forest
Brownhart Law
Biddlestone
Netherton
Lorbottle Hall
Cragbank Wood
Hungry Law
Shillmoor
Alwinton
Burradon
Lorbottle
Wauchope Forest
Crigdon Hill
Linshiels
High Trewhitt
Cartington
Fanna Hill
Catcleugh
Byrness
Featherwood
Harbottle
Coquet
Sharperton
Singdean
Whitelee Moor
Catcleugh Reservoir
Lady's Well
Holystone
Warton
Snitter
Rothbury
Knox Knowe
Kielderhead
Redesdale Forest
Watty Bell's Cairn
Flotterton
Thropton
Newtown
Cragside House
Kielderhead Moor
Caistron
Hepple
Whitton
Great Tosson
Peel Fell
Wool Meath
Toll
Sills
Redesdale Camp
Rochester
Brigantium
Horsley
Tosson Hill
Rothbury Forest
Deadwater
Saughtree
Kielder Burn
Emblehope Moor
Pennine Way
Otterburn Camp
Harwood Forest
Forestburn Gate
Elishaw
Blakehope Fell
Otterburn
Elsdon
Fallowlees Burn
Fontburn Res.
Kielder
Wainhope Moor
Blackburn Common
Kielder Castle Visitor Centre
Padon Hill
Troughend Common
Raylees
Ewesley
Larriston Fells
Kielder Forest Park
Redesdale
Black Middens Bastle House
Shipley Shiels
Northumberland
Rothley Shield East
Gatehouse
Hareshaw Head
Herterton House Garden
Longwitton
Rothley
Kielder Water
Kielder Water Birds of Prey Centre
Falstone
West Woodburn
East Woodburn
Hart Burn
Glendhu Hill
Tower Knowe Visitor Centre
Greenhaugh
Knowesgate
Cambo
Scots Gap
Middleton
The Eals
Lanehead
Charlton
Ridsdale
Kirkwhelpington
Wansbeck
Bower
Hesleyside
Bellingham
Wallington
Bolam Lake
Redesmouth
Kirkharle
Hopehouse
Sweethope Loughs
Sighty Crag
Whitelyne Common
Capheaton
Great Bavington
Harnham
Kielder Mires
Thockrington
The Flatt
Paddaburn Moor
Blacka Burn
Birtley
Little Bavington
Churnsike Lodge
White Preston
Warks Burn
Kirkheaton
Whygate
Stonehaugh
Wark
Colt Crag Reservoir
Hallington
Black Heddon
Hallington Reservoir
Bewcastle
Park End
Great Swinburne
Colwell
Ingoe
Spadeadam Forest
Butterburn
Gowk Bank
Black Fell
Gunnerton
Ryal
Barrasford
Simonburn
Northumberland National Park
Fenwick
Haughton Common
Haughton Castle
Chollerton
Bingfield
Heugh
Irthing
Humshaugh
Matfen
Stamfordham
Spadeadam Farm
Course of Hadrian's Wall
Broomlee Lough
Greenlee Lough
Hadrian's Wall Path
Grindon
Walwick
Chollerford
Great Whittington
Ouston
Wiley Sike
Thirlwall Common
Whiteside
Housesteads Roman Fort
Chesters Roman Fort
Low Brunton
Brunton Turret
Hill Head
Visitor Centre
Vallum
Wall
Fourstones
Halton
Harlow Hill
West Hall
Gilsland Spa
Roman Army Museum
Newbrough
Warden
Aydon Castle
Gilsland
Birdoswald Roman Fort
Hadrian's Wall
The Sill at Hadrian's Wall
Chesterholm Museum (Vindolanda)
Muckle Moss
Acomb
Sandhoe
Aydon
Horsley
Greenhead
Upper Denton
Bardon Mill
Chesterwood
Tyne Green
Newton Hall
Lanercost
Haltwhistle
Henshaw
Low Gate
Moothall
Abbey
Corbridge
Newton
Ovingham
Low Row
Melkridge
Redburn
Haydon Bridge
South Tyne
Hexham
Dilston
Dilston Physic Gdn
Ovington
Denton Fell
Plenmeller
Allenbanks & Staward Gorge
Tyne
Cherryburn
Branch End
Mickley Square
Milton
Plenmellar Common
Riding Mill
Broomhaugh
Stocksfield
High Mickley
Rowfoot
Langley
Painshawfield
Hallbankgate
Tindale
Midgeholme
Broomley
Farlam
Tindale Fells
Tindale Tarn
Halton Lea Gate
Lambley
Stonehouse
Whitfield
Dalton
Dye House
New Ridley
Hedley on the Hill
Forest Head
Bearsbridge
West Allen
Catton
Slaley
Whitley Chapel
Healey
Whittonstall
Maiden Way
Eals
St Andrew's Church
Glendue Fell
Cold Fell
Allendale Town
Slaley Forest
Newlands
Ebchester
Kiln Pit Hill
Whitfield Moor
Broadwell House
Hexhamshire Common
Shotleyfield
Derwent Res.
Slaggyford
Ninebanks
East Allen
Devil's Water
Sinderhope
Blanchland Moor
Carterway Heads
Bridgehill
Allendale Common
0 1 2 3 4 5 6 miles
0 1 2 3 4 5 6 7 8 9 10 km

NORTHUMBERLAND COAST
NU
NZ
Warenford
Newham
Swinhoe
Fleetham
Benthall
Beadnell Bay
Newstead
Rosebrough
Chathill
Ellingham
Preston
PRESTON TOWER
High Newton-by-the-Sea
Low Newton-by-the-Sea
Brunton
Christon Bank
Embleton Bay
Brownyside
North Charlton
Embleton
Dunstan Steads
Castle Point
DUNSTANBURGH CASTLE
West Ditchburn
South Charlton
Rock
Craster
Dunstan
KING CHARLES III ENGLAND COAST PATH
Rennington
Littlemill
Howick
Littlehoughton
Howick Haven
Shipley
HULNE PRIORY
Titlington
Longhoughton
Boulmer
Boulmer Haven
ALNWICK ABBEY
Denwick
Alnwick
Abberwick
Hawkhill
Broome Park
Lesbury
Lemmington Hall
WILLOWTREE
ALN VALLEY RAILWAY
Bilton
EDLINGHAM CASTLE
Alnmouth
Alnmouth Bay
Edlingham
Shilbottle
High Buston
Low Buston
Birling
Eastfield Hall
Warkworth
Newton-on-the-Moor
Gloster Hill
Amble
Coquet I.
Hazon
Swarland Estate
Guyzance
Hauxley
Brainshaugh
North Togston
Swarland
Acklington
Radcliffe
Togston
Broomhill
Longframlington
Felton
South Broomhill
LONGFRAMLINGTON GARDENS
West Thirston
East Thirston
DRURIDGE BAY
Weldon
Red Row
Hesleyhurst
Eshott
Druridge Bay
West Chevington
Helm
Widdrington
Wingates
Stobswood
Longhorsley
Causey Park Bridge
Widdrington Station
The Scars
Cresswell
Fenrother
Tritlington
Ellington
Ulgham
Lynemouth
Linton
Netherwitton
WOODHORN MUSEUM
Beacon Pt.
Stanton
Hebron
Longhirst
QUEEN ELIZABETH II
Woodhorn
Ashington
Pigdon
Pegswood
Newbiggin-by-the-Sea
Mitford
Bothal
WANSBECK
Hirst
Throphill
Morpeth
Stakeford
North Seaton
Guide Post
Scotland Gate
West Sleekburn
Cambois
Meldon
Molesden
Choppington
Tranwell
Hepscott
East Sleekburn
Clifton
Bedlington Station
Cowpen
Bedlington
BLYTH
Whalton
Nedderton
BEDLINGTON
Bebside
Shilvington
Saltwick
Newsham
East Hartford
New Delaval
Stannington
PLESSEY WOODS
Shankhouse
Ogle
NORTHUMBERLAND COLLEGE ZOO
Nelson Village
New Hartley
Seaton
Seaton Sluice
West Newham
Higham Dykes
Berwick Hill
NORTHUMBERLAND CHEESE COMPANY
Cramlington
SEATON DELAVAL HALL
Hartley
Milbourne
Southfield
East Cramlington
Seaton Delaval
ST MARY'S LIGHTHOUSE
St Mary's or Bait I.
SEATON BURN SERVICES
Brenkley
Seaton Burn
Holywell
Seghill
Dinnington
Annitsford
Ponteland
Earsdon
Dudley
WHITLEY BAY
Dalton
Brunswick Village
Wide Open
Burradon
Backworth
AMSTERDAM
Prestwick
Hazlerigg
Camperdown
Monkseaton
Darras Hall
NEWCASTLE INTERNATIONAL
Killingworth
Shiremoor
Cullercoats
Eachwick
Medburn
High Callerton
Woolsington
Marden
TYNEMOUTH AQUARIUM
TYNEMOUTH CASTLE & PRIORY
Black Callerton
Kenton Bankfoot
Longbenton
STEPHENSON RAILWAY MUSEUM
Tynemouth
Gosforth
North Shields
ARBEIA ROMAN FORT AND MUSEUM
North Walbottle
Westerhope
Kenton
Willington
South Shields
SOUTH SHIELDS MUSEUM & GALLERY
Heddon-on-the-Wall
Throckley
Jesmond
WALLSEND
Tyne Tunnel
THE LEAS AND MARSDEN ROCK
Marsden Bay
Walbottle
Newcastle Upon Tyne
Heaton
Jarrow
Westoe
Harton
Newburn
Byker
Marsden
Wylam
Clara Vale
Scotswood
Walker
Hebburn
SOUTER LIGHTHOUSE
West Wylam
Crawcrook
Ryton
Gateshead
Hedworth
Whiteleas
Cleadon
Whitburn Colliery
Prudhoe
BLAYDON
Dunston
Boldon Colliery
Whitburn
Greenside
Winlaton
Bensham
Pelaw
Coalburns
Whickham
Felling
Boldon
Barlow
Carr Hill
Low Fell
Downhill
Fulwell
High Spen
Highfield
Sunniside
Street Gate
Chowdene
Wrekenton
Hylton Castle
Southwick
Roker
Chopwell
Monkwearmouth
NATIONAL GLASS CENTRE
ST PETER'S CHURCH
SUNDERLAND MINSTER
Rowlands Gill
Byermoor
Marley Hill
Lamesley
Springwell
Usworth
Castletown
Blackhall Mill
Burnopfield
Blackfell
South Hylton
Pallion
Sunderland
Leazes
Kibblesworth
Birtley
WASHINGTON
Hobson
TANFIELD RAILWAY
High Barnes
Hendon
High Westwood
Tanfield
Ouston
Lambton
Pennywell
Medomsley
BEAMISH
Urpeth
Fatfield
New Silksworth
Tantobie
Dipton
Tanfield Lea
Beamish
Perkinsville
Barley Mow
East Herrington
Tunstall
Ryhope
STANLEY
Penshaw
Catchgate
Pelton
Rickleton
Shiney Row
New Herrington
Doxford Park
RYHOPE ENGINES MUS
Leadgate
West Pelton
Grange Villa
The Middles
CHESTER-
Bournmoor
Newbottle
Burdon
Annfield
A1
A697
A1068
A189
A192
A193
A19
A1058
A184
A194(M)
A1231
A690
A1018
A183
A693
A692
A695
A696
A167
A69
B6341
B6347
B1339
B1340
B6345
B1337
B6343
B6524
71
58

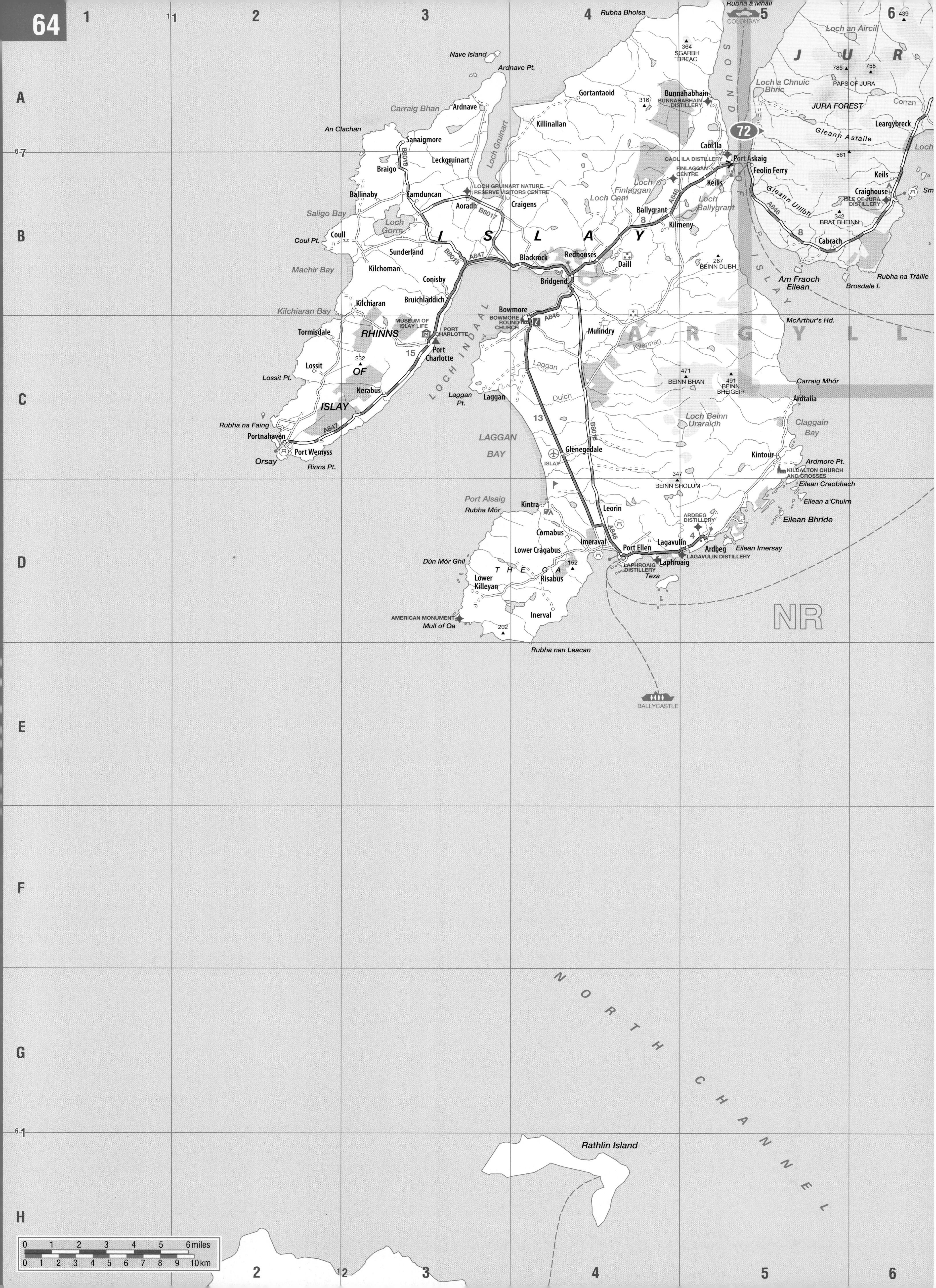

ISLAY
JURA
RHINNS OF ISLAY
ARGYLL
THE OA
NORTH CHANNEL
SOUND OF ISLAY
NR
Rubha Bholsa
Rubha a'Mhàil
COLONSAY
Loch an Aircil
Nave Island
Ardnave Pt.
Ardnave
Carraig Bhan
An Clachan
Sanaigmore
Gortantaoid
Killinallan
Loch Gruinart
316
364 SGARBH BREAC
Bunnahabhain
BUNNAHABHAIN DISTILLERY
785
755
PAPS OF JURA
Loch a Chnuic Bhric
JURA FOREST
Corran
Leargybreck
72
Gleann Astaile
Caol Ila
CAOL ILA DISTILLERY
Port Askaig
Feolin Ferry
FINLAGGAN CENTRE
561
Loch
Braigo
Leckgruinart
Ballinaby
Carnduncan
LOCH GRUINART NATURE RESERVE VISITORS CENTRE
Aoradh
Craigens
Loch Finlaggan
Loch Cam
Keills
Loch Ballygrant
Ballygrant
Kilmeny
Gleann Ullibh
Craighouse
ISLE OF JURA DISTILLERY
342 BRAT BHEINN
Cabrach
Saligo Bay
Loch Gorm
Coull
Coul Pt.
Sunderland
Kilchoman
Machir Bay
Conisby
Blackrock
Redhouses
Daill
Bridgend
267 BEINN DUBH
Am Fraoch Eilean
Brosdale I.
Rubha na Tràille
Kilchiaran
Kilchiaran Bay
Bruichladdich
Bowmore
BOWMORE ROUND CHURCH
MUSEUM OF ISLAY LIFE
PORT CHARLOTTE
Port Charlotte
Tormisdale
Mulindry
Kilennan
McArthur's Hd.
Lossit
232
Lossit Pt.
Nerabus
LOCH INDAAL
Laggan
Laggan Pt.
471 BEINN BHAN
491 BEINN BHEIGEIR
Carraig Mhór
Ardtalla
Duich
Loch Beinn Uraraidh
Claggain Bay
Rubha na Faing
Portnahaven
Port Wemyss
Orsay
Rinns Pt.
LAGGAN BAY
Glenegedale
ISLAY
Kintour
Ardmore Pt.
KILDALTON CHURCH AND CROSSES
Eilean Craobhach
Eilean a'Chuirn
347 BEINN SHOLUM
Port Alsaig
Rubha Mór
Kintra
Leorin
ARDBEG DISTILLERY
Eilean Bhride
Cornabus
Imeraval
Lagavulin
Lower Cragabus
Port Ellen
Ardbeg
Eilean Imersay
LAGAVULIN DISTILLERY
Dùn Mór Ghil
152
LAPHROAIG DISTILLERY
Laphroaig
Texa
Lower Killeyan
Risabus
Inerval
AMERICAN MONUMENT
Mull of Oa
202
Rubha nan Leacan
BALLYCASTLE
Rathlin Island
A846
A847
B8016
B8017
B8018
0 1 2 3 4 5 6 miles
0 1 2 3 4 5 6 7 8 9 10 km

6
7
8
9
10
11
A
B
C
D
E
F
G
H
Lagg
Loch Lesgamaill
Knockrome
Lowlandman's Bay
An Dùnan
na Mile
all Isles
Eilean Mòr
ST CORMAC'S CHAPEL
CHAPEL
Kilmory Bay
Kilmory
Island of Danna
SWEEN
ST COLUMBA'S CAVE
Lochead
Achahoish
Ellary
Clachbreck
Baile Boidheach
Ormsary
Loch Caolisport
Pt. of Knap
Druimdrishaig
Loch nan Torran
Miller's Bay
Cretshengan
CRUACH LAGAIN
Coulaghailtro
Kilberry Hd.
SCULPTURED STONES
Kilberry
Carse Ho.
Dunmore
DUN
Torinturk
Rhu
Loch Stornoway
Ardpatrick
Ardpatrick Ho.
Kilchamaig
Whitehouse
Redhouse
Kennacraig
WEST LOCH TARBERT
Gartnagrenach
Portachoillan
Ardpatrick Pt.
Eilean Traighe
Ronachan Pt.
Clachan
CRUACH NAM FIADH
Erines
STOB ODHAR
Loch Chaorain
Tarbert
West Tarbert
Corranbuie
Barfad
Barmore I.
East Loch Tarbert
CNOC A'BHAILESHIOS
Glenreasdell Mains
Skipness
Claonaig
SKIPNESS CASTLE
Skipness Pt.
Skipness Bay
Claonaig Bay
(Oct-Mar)
(April-Oct)
Kilfinan Bay
Auchalick Bay
Ardmarnock Bay
Glenan Bay
Asgog Loch
Portavadie
Asgog Bay
Kilbride Bay
Ardlamont Ho.
Ardlamont Pt.
Rubha Leathan
Kilfin
Drum
Melldalloch
Auchenlochan
Kames
Millhouse
Tighnabruaich
Port Driseach
Blair's Ferry
Kyles of Bute
KYLES OF BUTE
BEINN BHREAC
Ardentraive
Colintraive
Algaltraig
Ferry
LOCH STRIVEN
Glen More
WINDY HILL
ISLAND OF BUTE
Lamont
Ardyne Pt.
Kames B.
Port B
Rothesay
ROTHESAY CASTLE
Rothe Bay
St Colmac
Ettrick Bay
Straad
Loch Fad
Loch Quien
Scalpsie
Scalpsie Bay
Inchmarnock
Ardscalpsie Pt.
Stravanan Bay
Garroch Hd.
SOUND OF BUTE
AND BUTE
72
Eilean Garbh
West Tarbert Bay
East Tarbert Bay
Tarbert
Gigha Island
Druimyeon More
Ardminish
Ardminish Bay
ACHAMORE GARDENS
Gigalum Island
Cara Island
Tayinloan
SOUND OF GIGHA
SOUND
Loch Ciaran
Balochroy
Crossaig Glen
Loch Garasdale
CRUACH MHIC GOUGAN
Crossaig
Rhunahaorine
BEINN BHREAC
Cour Bay
Cour
CNOC NAN CRAOBH
Carradale Water
CRUACH MHIC-AN T-SAOIR
CRUACH NAN GABHAR
Killean
Beacharr
Grogport
Brackley
Clachaig Water
Muasdale
Carradale
Port Righ
BEINN BHREAC
Amod
Bridgend
Torrisdale Square
Glenacardoch Pt.
Belloch
Glenbarr
Barr Water
BEINN AN TUIRC
Carradale Pt.
Carradale Bay
Cleongart
Bellochantuy Bay
Bellochantuy
Saddell Glen
Saddell
SADDELL ABBEY
A'CHRUACH
Saddell Bay
Killocraw
Lussa Loch
SGREADAN HILL
Ugadale
Tangy Loch
Skeroblingarry
Black Bay
Westport
Kilchenzie
Glenlussa Water
Peninver
Ardnacross Bay
West Darlochan
CAMPBELTOWN
Kilmichael
Low Smerby
Machrihanish Bay
Machrihanish
Trodigal
Campbeltown
CAMPBELTOWN HERITAGE CENTRE
Campbeltown Loch
Island Davaar
DAVAAR ISLAND CAVE PAINTING
Drumlemble
Stewarton
CAMPBELTOWN BUNKHOUSE
Kilkerran
Knocknaha
Kildalloig
ARDROSSAN (May-Sept)
BRODICK (May-Sept, Sat only)
Achinhoan Hd.
Earadale Pt.
BEINN GHUILEAN
THE SLATE
Woodbank
CNOC MOY
BALLYCASTLE
Feochaig
Johnston's Pt.
Rubh'a'Mharaiche
Glen Breackerie
CNOC ODHAR
Conie Glen
North Carrine
Keprigan
Strone Glen
Machariooch
Polliwilline Bay
Southend
Carskiey
Cove Pt.
Brunerican Bay
Port Mean
MULL OF KINTYRE
Rubha Chlachan
Sheep I.
Sanda Island
KINTYRE
KNAPDALE
KILBRANNAN SOUND
Cock of Arran
LOCHRANZA CASTLE
Loch Ranza
Lochranza
LOCHRANZA
Catacol Bay
Catacol
ISLE OF ARRAN DISTILLERY
Millstone Pt.
MEALL NAN DAMH
Thundergay
Sannox
Sannox Bay
Glen Sannox
NORTH
Loch Tanna
Pirnmill
CIR MHÒR
Corrie
BEINN BHARRAIN
BEINN TARSUINN
GOAT FELL
Whitefarland
Imachar
ISLE
ARRAN
OF
ARRAN
NS
ARDROSSAN CAMPBELTOWN (May-Sept Sat only)
BRODICK
BRODICK CASTLE
Glen Rosa
Glen Iorsa
Dougarie
Brodick Bay
Machrie Water
ISLE OF ARRAN HERITAGE MUSEUM
Brodick
Strathwhillan
Auchagallon
Glenloig
A'CHRUACH
Glen Cloy
Machrie Bay
Tormore
MACHRIE MOOR STANDING STONES
66
KING'S CAVE
Balmichael
Clauchlands Pt.
Blairbeg
Margnaheglish
Lamlash
Lamlash Bay
Cordon
Holy Island
Torbeg
Shiskine
Drumadoon Pt.
Blackwaterfoot
Drumadoon Bay
Kilpatrick
KILPATRICK DUN
TIGHVEIN
Kingscross Pt.
Auchencairn
Kingscross
Knockenkelly
Whiting Bay
North Kiscadale
South Kiscadale
Sliddery Water
Glenree
Brown Hd.
CARN BAN
Corriecravie
GLENASHDALE FALLS
Largymore
Largybeg
Kilmory Water
Sliddery
Lagg
Levencorroch
Dippin
Dippin Head
Kilmory
TORRYLINN CAIRN
Bennan
Kildonan
Bennan Hd.
Sound of Pladda
Pladda
A83
A846
A8015
A841
A886
A8003
A844
B8024
B8001
B842
B843
B880
B8000
B875
B878
B881

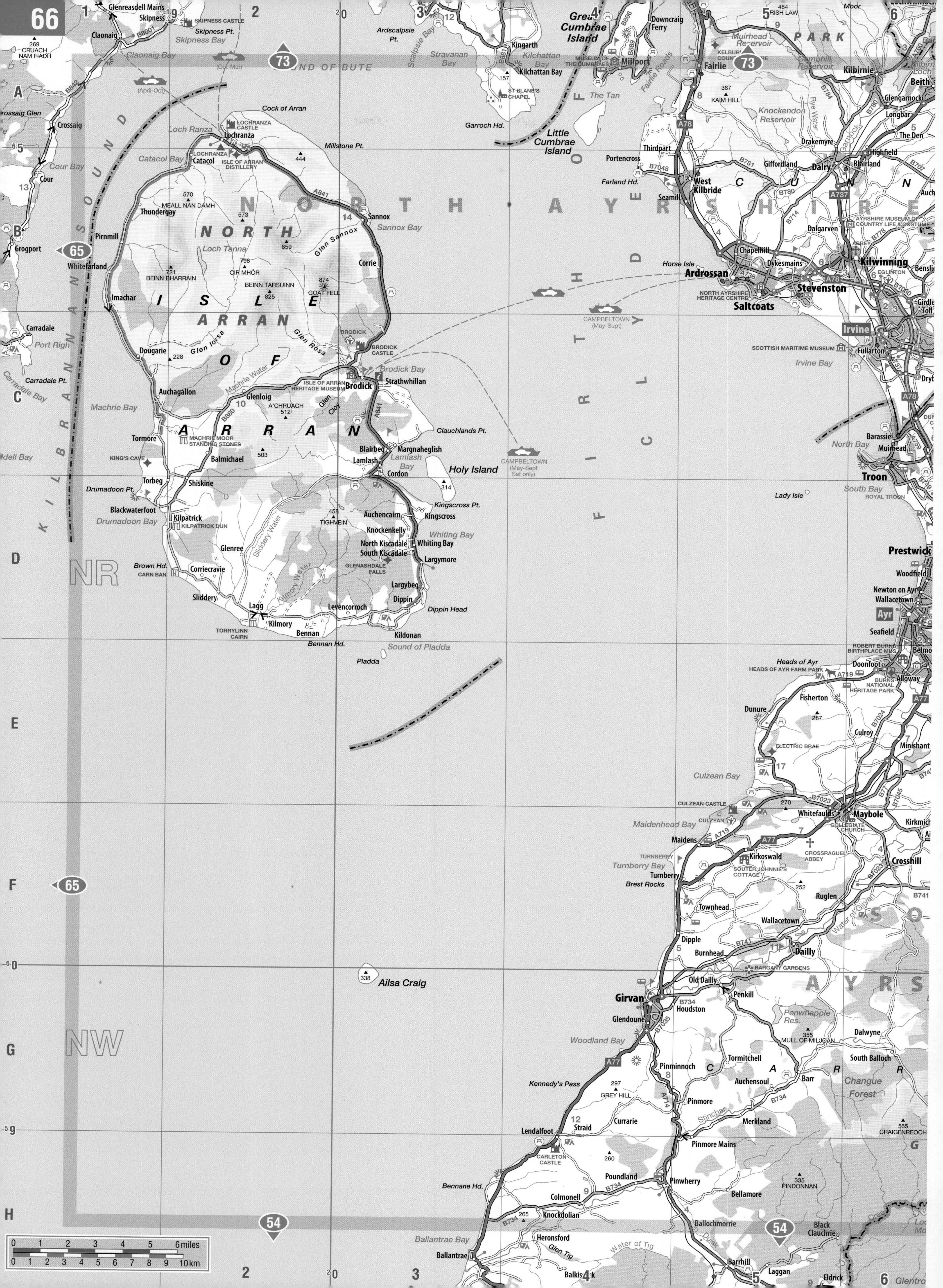

Glenreasdell Mains
Skipness
SKIPNESS CASTLE
Skipness Pt.
Skipness Bay
Claonaig
Claonaig Bay
269 CRUACH NAM FIADH
SOUND OF BUTE
73
(Oct-Mar)
(April-Oct)
Ardscalpsie Pt.
Scalpsie Bay
Stravanan Bay
Kingarth
Kilchattan Bay
ST BLANE'S CHAPEL
Great Cumbrae Island
Millport
MUSEUM OF THE CUMBRAES
Downcraig Ferry
The Tan
Little Cumbrae Island
Garroch Hd.
Fairlie
Fairlie Roads
Muirhead Reservoir
Camphill Reservoir
KELBURN COUNTRY CENTRE
484 RISH LAW
PARK
Kilbirnie
Beith
Glengarnock
Longbar
The Den
387 KAIM HILL
Knockendon Reservoir
Rye Water
Drakemyre
Highfield
Blairland
Dalry
Gifffordland
Thirdpart
Portencross
Farland Hd.
West Kilbride
Seamill
Cock of Arran
Loch Ranza
LOCHRANZA CASTLE
Lochranza
Millstone Pt.
Catacol Bay
Catacol
ISLE OF ARRAN DISTILLERY
444
Crossaig Glen
Crossaig
Cour Bay
Cour
KILBRANNAN SOUND
NORTH AYRSHIRE
570 MEALL NAN DAMH
Thundergay
573
Sannox
Sannox Bay
Glen Sannox
Pirnmill
NORTH
Loch Tanna
859
Grogport
65
Whitefarland
721 BEINN BHARRAIN
798 CIR MHÒR
BEINN TARSUINN 825
874 GOAT FELL
Corrie
Imachar
ISLE OF ARRAN
Horse Isle
Ardrossan
Chapelhill
Dykesmains
Kilwinning
Stevenston
Saltcoats
NORTH AYRSHIRE HERITAGE CENTRE
AYRSHIRE MUSEUM OF COUNTRY LIFE & COSTUME
Dalgarven
EGLINTON
Carradale
Port Righ
Dougarie
228
Glen Iorsa
Glen Rosa
BRODICK
BRODICK CASTLE
Brodick Bay
Brodick
Strathwhillan
ISLE OF ARRAN HERITAGE MUSEUM
CAMPBELTOWN (May-Sept)
Irvine
SCOTTISH MARITIME MUSEUM
Fullarton
Irvine Bay
Carradale Pt.
Carradale Bay
Auchagallon
Machrie Water
Glenloig
A'CHRUACH 512
Glen Cloy
Machrie Bay
Tormore
MACHRIE MOOR STANDING STONES
503
Balmichael
Clauchlands Pt.
Blairbeg
Margnaheglish
Lamlash
Lamlash Bay
Cordon
Holy Island
314
CAMPBELTOWN (May-Sept Sat only)
FIRTH OF CLYDE
Barassie
North Bay
Muirhead
Troon
South Bay
ROYAL TROON
Lady Isle
KING'S CAVE
Torbeg
Shiskine
Drumadoon Pt.
Blackwaterfoot
Drumadoon Bay
Kilpatrick
KILPATRICK DUN
458 TIGHVEIN
Auchencairn
Kingscross Pt.
Kingscross
Knockenkelly
Whiting Bay
North Kiscadale
South Kiscadale
Largymore
Sliddery Water
Glenree
GLENASHDALE FALLS
Prestwick
Woodfield
Brown Hd.
CARN BAN
Corriecravie
NR
Kilmory Water
Largybeg
Dippin
Dippin Head
Sliddery
Lagg
Levencorroch
Kilmory
TORRYLINN CAIRN
Bennan
Kildonan
Bennan Hd.
Sound of Pladda
Pladda
Newton on Ayr
Wallacetown
Ayr
Seafield
ROBERT BURNS BIRTHPLACE MUS.
Heads of Ayr
HEADS OF AYR FARM PARK
Doonfoot
Alloway
BURNS NATIONAL HERITAGE PARK
Fisherton
Dunure
267
Culroy
Minishant
ELECTRIC BRAE
Culzean Bay
CULZEAN CASTLE
270
Whitefaulds
Maybole
COLLEGIATE CHURCH
Maidenhead Bay
CULZEAN
Maidens
Kirkoswald
CROSSRAGUEL ABBEY
Crosshill
TURNBERRY
Turnberry Bay
Turnberry
SOUTER JOHNNIE'S COTTAGE
252
Brest Rocks
Ruglen
Townhead
Wallacetown
Water of Girvan
Dipple
Burnhead
Dailly
BARGANY GARDENS
338
Ailsa Craig
Old Dailly
Penkill
Girvan
Houdston
Glendoune
Penwhapple Res.
355 MULL OF MILJOAN
Dalwyne
NW
Woodland Bay
Pinminnoch
Tormitchell
South Balloch
Barr
Auchensoul
Changue Forest
Kennedy's Pass
297 GREY HILL
Pinmore
Stinchar
Currarie
Straid
Merkland
565 CRAIGENREOCH
Lendalfoot
Pinmore Mains
CARLETON CASTLE
260
Poundland
Pinwherry
335 PINDONNAN
Bennane Hd.
Colmonell
Bellamore
265
Knockdolian
Ballochmorrie
54
Black Clauchrie
Ballantrae Bay
Heronsford
Glen Tig
Water of Tig
Ballantrae
Duisk
Barrhill
Balkissock
Laggan
Eldrick
Glentrool
0 1 2 3 4 5 6 miles
0 1 2 3 4 5 6 7 8 9 10 km

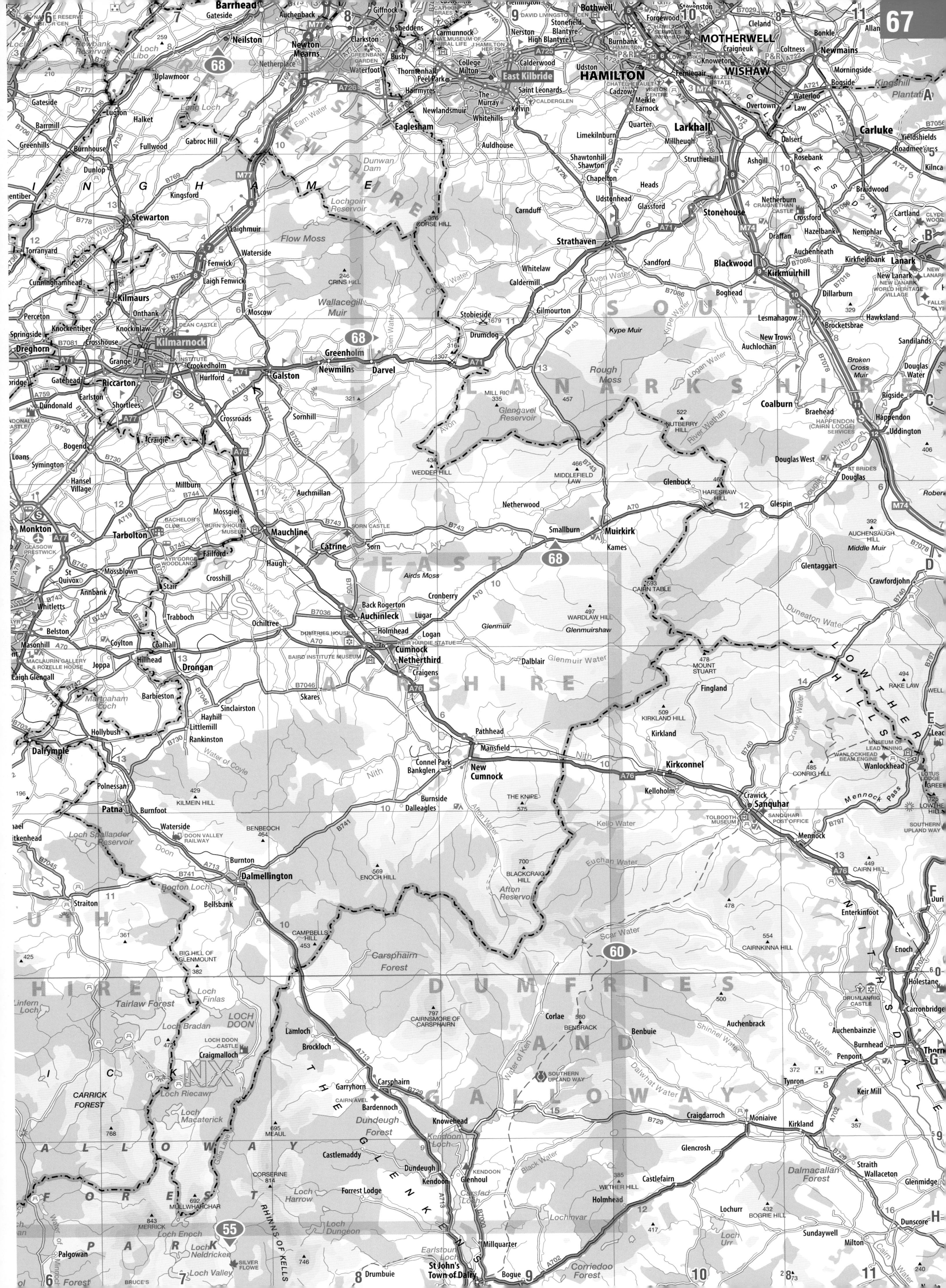
Barrhead
Gateside
Neilston
Auchenback
Giffnock
Newton Mearns
Clarkston
Sheddens
Carmunnock
Busby
Netherplace
Waterfoot
Thorntonhall
Peel Park
College Milton
East Kilbride
Nerston
High Blantyre
Bothwell
Stonefield
Blantyre
Burnbank
Calderwood
Udston
HAMILTON
Forgewood
MOTHERWELL
Cleland
Bonkle
Allan
Newmains
Craigneuk
Coltness
Knoweton
WISHAW
Fernlegair
Chatelherault
Cadzow
Meikle Earnock
Morningside
Bogside
Waterloo
Overtown
Law
Uplawmoor
Loch Libo
Gateside
Lugton
Halket
Long Loch
Harmyres
Newlandsmuir
The Murray
Saint Leonards
Kelvin
Whitehills
Eaglesham
Earn Water
Barrmill
Greenhills
Burnhouse
Fullwood
Gabroc Hill
Dunlop
Auldhouse
Quarter
Larkhall
Limekilnburn
Millheugh
Carluke
Dalserf
Yieldshields
Roadmeet
Kilncadzow
Shawtonhill
Shawton
Chapelton
Strutherhill
Ashgill
Rosebank
Braidwood
Dunwan Dam
Kingsford
Lochgoin Reservoir
Corse Hill
Carnduff
Udstonhead
Heads
Glassford
Stonehouse
Netherburn
Craignethan Castle
Crossford
Cartland
Stewarton
Torranyard
Laighmuir
Flow Moss
Waterside
Strathaven
Hazelbank
Nemphlar
Draffan
Auchenheath
Kirkfieldbank
Lanark
New Lanark
Cunninghamhead
Fenwick
Laigh Fenwick
Crins Hill
Whitelaw
Caldermill
Sandford
Blackwood
Kirkmuirhill
Boghead
Dillarburn
Kilmaurs
Perceton
Onthank
Moscow
Wallacegill Muir
Calder Water
Stobieside
Gilmourton
Lesmahagow
Hawksland
Brocketsbrae
Springside
Knockentiber
Knockinlaw
Dean Castle
Drumclog
Kype Muir
New Trows
Auchlochan
Sandilands
Dreghorn
Crosshouse
Kilmarnock
Grange
Crookedholm
Hurlford
Galston
Greenholm
Newmilns
Darvel
Rough Moss
Broken Cross Muir
Douglas Water
Riccarton
Gatehead
Earlston
Shortlees
Dundonald
Mill Rig
Glengavel Reservoir
Nutberry Hill
Coalburn
Braehead
Rigside
Happendon
Uddington
Crossroads
Sornhill
Bogend
Craigie
Loans
Symington
Hansel Village
Wedder Hill
Middlefield Law
Douglas West
St Brides
Douglas
Glenbuck
Hareshaw Hill
Millburn
Auchmillan
Netherwood
Glespin
Auchensaugh Hill
Middle Muir
Mossgiel
Bachelor's Club
Burns House Museum
Mauchline
Sorn Castle
Sorn
Catrine
Smallburn
Muirkirk
Kames
Monkton
Glasgow Prestwick
Tarbolton
Failford
Ayr Gorge Woodlands
Haugh
Airds Moss
Glentaggart
Crawfordjohn
St Quivox
Mossblown
Annbank
Stair
Crosshill
Lugar Water
Cairn Table
Cronberry
Whitletts
Back Rogerton
Auchinleck
Lugar
Wardlaw Hill
Glenmuir
Glenmuirshaw
Duneaton Water
Trabboch
Ochiltree
Holmhead
Logan
Belston
Dumfries House
Coylton
Masonhill
Coalhall
Baird Institute Museum
Keir Hardie Statue
Cumnock
Netherthird
Dalblair
Glenmuir Water
Maclaurin Gallery & Rozelle House
Joppa
Hillhead
Drongan
Craigens
Mount Stuart
Laigh Glengall
Skares
Fingland
Rake Law
Martnaham Loch
Barbieston
Sinclairston
Hayhill
Littlemill
Rankinston
Kirkland Hill
Kirkland
Lowther Hills
Hollybush
Dalrymple
Pathhead
Mansfield
Museum of Lead Mining
Wanlockhead Beam Engine
Wanlockhead
Water of Coyle
Connel Park
Bankglen
New Cumnock
Nith
Kirkconnel
Conrig Hill
Polnessan
Kilmein Hill
The Knipe
Kelloholm
Crawick
Sanquhar
Tolbooth Museum
Sanquhar Post Office
Mennock Pass
Lowther Hill
Southern Upland Way
Patna
Burnfoot
Burnside
Dalleagles
Afton Water
Kello Water
Mennock
Loch Spallander Reservoir
Waterside
Doon Valley Railway
Benbeoch
Straiton
Burnton
Dalmellington
Enoch Hill
Blackcraig Hill
Euchan Water
Cairn Hill
Bogton Loch
Bellsbank
Afton Reservoir
Enterkinfoot
Campbells Hill
Carsphairn Forest
Scar Water
Cairnkinna Hill
Enoch
Big Hill of Glenmount
Loch Finlas
Tairlaw Forest
Loch Bradan
Loch Doon
Loch Doon Castle
Craigmalloch
Cairnsmore of Carsphairn
Corlae
Benbrack
DUMFRIES AND GALLOWAY
Drumlanrig Castle
Holestane
Carronbridge
Auchenbrack
Auchenbainzie
Lamloch
Brockloch
Benbuie
Shinnel Water
Scar Water
Burnhead
Penpont
Thornhill
Carrick Forest
Loch Riecawr
Garryhorn
Carsphairn
Cairn Avel
Bardennoch
Southern Upland Way
Dalwhat Water
Tynron
Keir Mill
Loch Macaterick
Meaul
Dundeugh Forest
Knowehead
Craigdarroch
Moniaive
Kirkland
Kendoon Loch
The Glenkens
Glencrosh
Castlemaddy
Dundeugh
Kendoon
Glenhoul
Straith
Wallaceton
Glenmidge
Dalmacallan Forest
Corserine
Carsfad Loch
Black Water
Wether Hill
Castlefairn
Loch Harrow
Forrest Lodge
Holmhead
Lochurr
Bogrie Hill
Dunscore
Mullwharchar
Rhinns of Kells
Lochinvar
Merrick
Loch Enoch
Loch Dungeon
Sundaywell
Milton
Palgowan
Loch Neldricken
Millquarter
Loch Urr
Silver Flowe
Earlstoun Loch
Corriedoo Forest
Loch Valley
Drumbuie
St John's Town of Dalry
Bogue
Bruce's
Glentrool Forest
Cairn Water

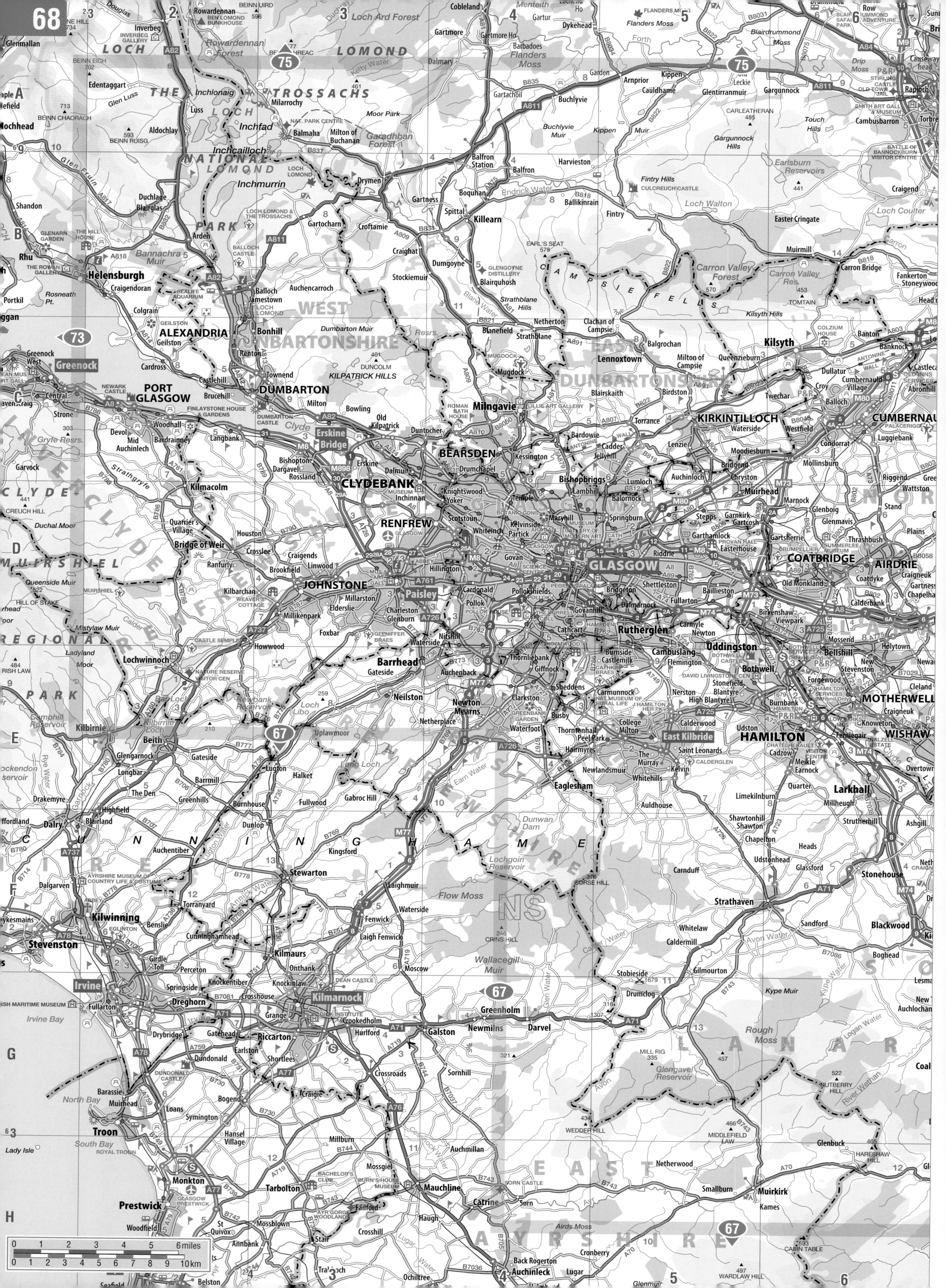
LOCH LOMOND
THE TROSSACHS
THE LOCH LOMOND AND THE TROSSACHS NATIONAL PARK
WEST DUNBARTONSHIRE
EAST DUNBARTONSHIRE
CAMPSIE FELLS
KILPATRICK HILLS
INVERCLYDE
RENFREWSHIRE
CLYDE MUIRSHIEL REGIONAL PARK
EAST RENFREWSHIRE
NORTH LANARKSHIRE
SOUTH LANARKSHIRE
EAST AYRSHIRE
NORTH AYRSHIRE
CUNNINGHAME
Helensburgh
ALEXANDRIA
DUMBARTON
PORT GLASGOW
Greenock
CLYDEBANK
BEARSDEN
Milngavie
RENFREW
JOHNSTONE
Paisley
GLASGOW
Rutherglen
KIRKINTILLOCH
Kilsyth
CUMBERNAULD
COATBRIDGE
AIRDRIE
Bellshill
MOTHERWELL
WISHAW
HAMILTON
East Kilbride
Uddingston
Cambuslang
Barrhead
Newton Mearns
Eaglesham
Strathaven
Larkhall
Lanark
Kilwinning
Stevenston
Irvine
Kilmarnock
Stewarton
Troon
Prestwick
Mauchline
Muirkirk
Auchinleck
Galston
Newmilns
Darvel
Balloch
Drymen
Balfron
Killearn
Strathblane
Lennoxtown
Fintry
Kippen
Buchlyvie
Dalry
Beith
Lochwinnoch
Kilbirnie
Bridge of Weir
Kilmacolm
Erskine Bridge
Irvine Bay
South Bay
North Bay
Lady Isle
Carron Valley Forest
Loch Ard Forest
6 miles
10 km

CLACKMANNANSHIRE
Bridge of Allan
Menstrie
Tillicoultry
Dollar
Alva
Tullibody
Stirling
Cambuskenneth
ALLOA
Clackmannan
Bannockburn
Kincardine
Kincardine Bridge
DENNY
Stenhousemuir
Larbert
GRANGEMOUTH
FALKIRK
Bonnybridge
Bo'ness
Linlithgow
Queensferry Crossing
Queensferry
North Queensferry
Inverkeithing
Rosyth
DUNFERMLINE
Kelty
Lochgelly
Cowdenbeath
Cardenden
Kirkcaldy
Burntisland
Kinghorn
Aberdour
Dalgety Bay
FIFE
FIRTH OF FORTH
Inchkeith
Inchcolm
Cramond I.
Leith
Edinburgh
Portobello
Musselburgh
Kirkliston
Broxburn
Uphall
Winchburgh
Bathgate
Armadale
LIVINGSTON
Whitburn
Blackburn
East Calder
Mid Calder
West Calder
Currie
Balerno
Penicuik
Loanhead
Bonnyrigg and Lasswade
Roslin
Dalkeith
WEST LOTHIAN
MIDLOTHIAN
PENTLAND HILLS REGIONAL PARK
Shotts
Harthill
Fauldhouse
Newmains
Carluke
Lanark
Forth
Carnwath
Biggar
Symington
TINTO HILLS
West Linton
Carlops
Peebles
Innerleithen
UPPER TWEEDDALE
SCOTTISH BORDERS
Broughton
Tweedsmuir
Abington
Douglas
Crawfordjohn
Moorfoot Hills
69
70
76
60
61

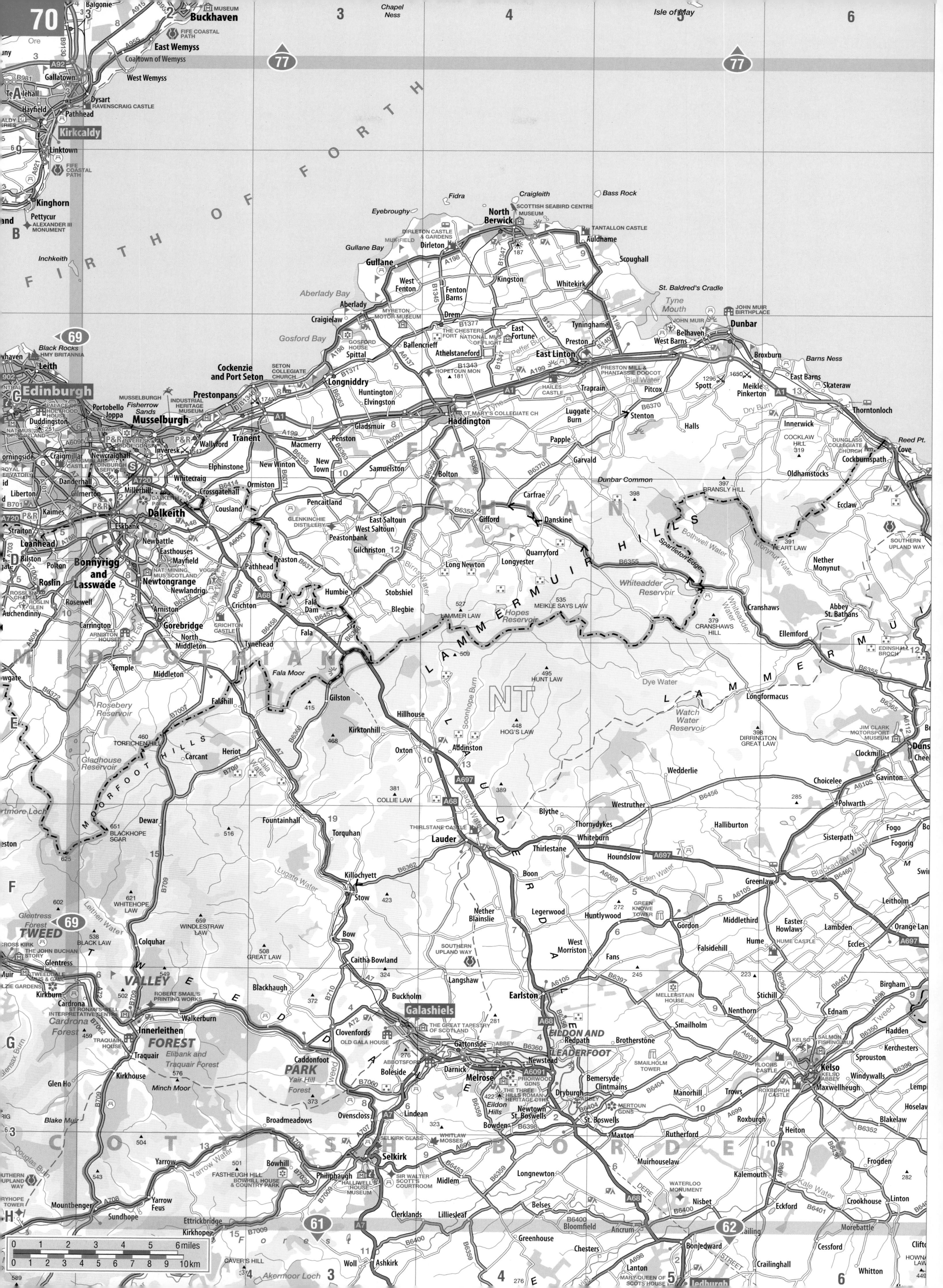

FIRTH OF FORTH
EAST LOTHIAN
MIDLOTHIAN
SCOTTISH BORDERS
LAMMERMUIR HILLS
MOORFOOT HILLS
LAUDERDALE
TWEEDDALE
Buckhaven
East Wemyss
Coaltown of Wemyss
West Wemyss
Gallatown
Dysart
RAVENSCRAIG CASTLE
Pathhead
Kirkcaldy
Linktown
FIFE COASTAL PATH
Kinghorn
Pettycur
ALEXANDER III MONUMENT
Inchkeith
Chapel Ness
Isle of May
Fidra
Craigleith
Bass Rock
Eyebroughy
North Berwick
SCOTTISH SEABIRD CENTRE
TANTALLON CASTLE
Auldhame
Scoughall
DIRLETON CASTLE & GARDENS
Dirleton
Gullane Bay
Gullane
West Fenton
Fenton Barns
Kingston
Whitekirk
Aberlady Bay
Aberlady
Craigielaw
MYRETON MOTOR MUSEUM
Drem
St. Baldred's Cradle
Tyne Mouth
JOHN MUIR BIRTHPLACE
Tyninghame
Belhaven
Dunbar
West Barns
Gosford Bay
Ballencrieff
THE CHESTERS FORT
NATIONAL MUS OF FLIGHT
East Fortune
Athelstaneford
Preston
East Linton
Spittal
HOPETOUN MON
PRESTON MILL & PHANTASSIE DOOCOT
Broxburn
Barns Ness
East Barns
Skateraw
Black Rocks
HMY BRITANNIA
Leith
Edinburgh
Cockenzie and Port Seton
SETON COLLEGIATE CHURCH
Longniddry
Huntington
Elvington
HAILES CASTLE
Traprain
Pitcox
Spott
Meikle Pinkerton
Thorntonloch
Portobello
Joppa
Musselburgh
Fisherrow Sands
Prestonpans
Duddingston
Tranent
Gladsmuir
Haddington
ST MARY'S COLLEGIATE CH
Luggate Burn
Stenton
Halls
Innerwick
COCKLAW HILL
DUNGLASS COLLEGIATE CHURCH
Cockburnspath
Reed Pt.
Cove
Craigmillar
Newcraighall
Inveresk
Wallyford
Macmerry
Penston
Papple
Garvald
Oldhamstocks
Elphinstone
New Winton
New Town
Samuelston
Bolton
Dunbar Common
BRANSLY HILL
Liberton
Danderhall
Gilmerton
Millerhill
Whitecraig
Crossgatehall
Ormiston
Carfrae
Ecclaw
Kaimes
Dalkeith
Cousland
Pencaitland
GLENKINCHIE DISTILLERY
East Saltoun
West Saltoun
Peastonbank
Gifford
Danskine
Straiton
Loanhead
Eskbank
Newbattle
Easthouses
Mayfield
Gilchriston
Quarryford
HEART LAW
SOUTHERN UPLAND WAY
Bilston
Polton
Bonnyrigg and Lasswade
Roslin
NAT MINING MUS SCOTLAND
Newtongrange
Newlandrig
Pathhead
Peaston
Long Newton
Longyester
Nether Monynut
Whiteadder Reservoir
Rosewell
Auchendinny
Crichton
Humbie
Fala Dam
Stobshiel
Blegbie
LAMMER LAW
MEIKLE SAYS LAW
Hopes Reservoir
Cranshaws
Abbey St. Bathans
Carrington
Arniston
Gorebridge
North Middleton
CRICHTON CASTLE
Fala
CRANSHAWS HILL
Ellemford
EDINSHALL BROCH
Temple
Middleton
Tynehead
Fala Moor
HUNT LAW
Dye Water
Longformacus
Rosebery Reservoir
Falahill
Gilston
Watch Water Reservoir
Hillhouse
TORFICHEN HILL
Heriot
Carcant
Kirktonhill
Oxton
Addinston
HOG'S LAW
DIRRINGTON GREAT LAW
JIM CLARK MOTORSPORT MUSEUM
Gladhouse Reservoir
Wedderlie
Clockmill
COLLIE LAW
Choicelee
Gavinton
Westruther
Polwarth
Dewar
BLACKHOPE SCAR
Fountainhall
Torquhan
THIRLSTANE CASTLE
Blythe
Thornydykes
Whiteburn
Lauder
Thirlestane
Halliburton
Fogo
Sisterpath
Fogorig
Houndslow
Boon
Killochyett
Stow
Greenlaw
Eden Water
WHITEHOPE LAW
Leitholm
Glentress Forest
TWEED
WINDLESTRAW LAW
Nether Blainslie
Legerwood
GREEN KNOWE TOWER
Huntlywood
Gordon
Middlethird
Easter Howlaws
Lambden
Orange Lane
BLACK LAW
THE JOHN BUCHAN STORY
Colquhar
Bow
West Morriston
Hume
HUME CASTLE
Eccles
Glentress
GREAT LAW
Caitha Bowland
Falsidehill
Fans
TWEEDDALE MUS & GALL
Langshaw
Stichill
Birgham
VALLEY
Blackhaugh
Buckholm
Earlston
MELLERSTAIN HOUSE
Kirkburn
Cardrona
ROBERT SMAIL'S PRINTING WORKS
Galashiels
Nenthorn
Ednam
ST RONAN'S WELL INTERPRETIVE CENTRE
Walkerburn
THE GREAT TAPESTRY OF SCOTLAND
Smailholm
Hadden
Cardrona Forest
Innerleithen
FOREST
Clovenfords
OLD GALA HOUSE
Gattonside
EILDON AND LEADERFOOT
Redpath
Brotherstone
Kerchesters
TRAQUAIR HOUSE
Elibank and Traquair Forest
Traquair
ABBOTSFORD
Newstead
SMAILHOLM TOWER
FLOORS CASTLE
Kelso
SALMON FISHING MUS
Sprouston
Caddonfoot
PARK
Yair Hill Forest
Boleside
Darnick
Melrose
PRIORWOOD GDNS
Bemersyde
Clintmains
KELSO ABBEY
Windywalls
Kirkhouse
Minch Moor
Glen Ho
THE THREE HILLS ROMAN HERITAGE CTR
Eildon Hills
Dryburgh
Manorhill
Trows
ROXBURGH CASTLE
Maxwellheugh
Blake Muir
Ovenscloss
Lindean
Newtown St. Boswells
MERTOUN GDNS
St. Boswells
Roxburgh
Blakelaw
Broadmeadows
Bowden
WHITLAW MOSSES
Maxton
Rutherford
Heiton
SELKIRK GLASS
Yarrow Water
Yarrow
FASTHEUGH HILL
BOWHILL HOUSE & COUNTRY PARK
Bowhill
Selkirk
Philiphaugh
HALLIWELL'S HOUSE MUSEUM
SIR WALTER SCOTT'S COURTROOM
Midlem
Longnewton
Muirhouselaw
Kalemouth
Frogden
Kale Water
WATERLOO MONUMENT
Nisbet
Crookhouse
Linton
Mountbenger
Yarrow Feus
Sundhope
Clerklands
Lilliesleaf
Belses
Eckford
Ettrickbridge
Kirkhope
Bloomfield
Ancrum
Morebattle
Greenhouse
Chesters
Bonjedward
Cessford
Crailinghall
CAVER'S HILL
Woll
Ashkirk
Akermoor Loch
Lanton
MARY QUEEN OF SCOTS HOUSE
Jedburgh
Whitton
Douglas Burn
NT
0 1 2 3 4 5 6 miles
0 1 2 3 4 5 6 7 8 9 10 km

NORTH SEA
NU
NORTHUMBERLAND COAST
Siccar Pt.
Wheat Stack
FAST CASTLE
ST ABB'S HEAD
St. Abb's Head
Lumsdaine
Coldingham Moor
Northfield
St Abbs
Coldingham Bay
St. Abb's Haven
Grantshouse
Huxton
Coldingham
COLDINGHAM PRIORY
Ale Water
Houndwood
Cairncross
Eye Water
EYEMOUTH MUSEUM
Eyemouth
AYTON CASTLE
Reston
Ayton
Burnmouth
Auchencrow
Prenderguest
Lamberton Beach
Lamberton
Lintlaw
Preston
Chirnside
Chirnsidebridge
Edrom
Foulden
Clappers
Whiteadder Water
FOULDEN TITHE BARN
MANDERSTON
Allanton
Hutton
Paxton
Highfields
Berwick-upon-Tweed
BERWICK-UPON-TWEED BARRACKS & MAIN GUARD
Blackadder West
East Ord
Tweedmouth
Spittal
PAXTON HOUSE
Tweed
Loanend
Prior Park
Sinclair's Hill
Whitsome
Fishwick
UNION SUSPENSION BRIDGE
Horncliffe
Redshin Cove
Scremerston
Horndean
Thornton Park
Murton
Thornton
Leet Water
Ladykirk
NORHAM CASTLE
Swinton
SWINTON KIRK
Norham
West Allerdean
DEVIL'S CAUSEWAY
Cheswick
Simprim
Shoreswood
Shoresdean
Ancroft
Goswick
Grindon
Felkington
Haggerston
Berrington
Beal
South Low
LINDISFARNE
Emmanuel Hd.
Holy Island (Lindisfarne)
LINDISFARNE CASTLE
Castle Pt.
Causeway
Holy Island Sands
Holy Island
HERITAGE CENTRE
LINDISFARNE PRIORY
Shellacres
Duddo
Castle Heaton
Bowsden
Fenham
Guile Pt.
Lennel
Coldstream
HIRSEL
Cornhill-on-Tweed
HEATHERSLAW LIGHT RAILWAY
Etal
HEATHERSLAW CORNMILL
Barmoor Castle
Barmoor Lane End
Lowick
West Kyloe
Kyloe Hills
East Kyloe
Fenwick
Buckton
Farne Islands
Staple Sound
FARNE ISLANDS
Wark
West Learmouth
East Learmouth
Crookham
Branxton
LADY WATERFORD HALL
Ford
Elwick
Ross
Budle Bay
BAMBURGH CASTLE
Holburn
Detchant
Middleton
Inner Sound
Pressen
Flodden
Kimmerston
Hetton Steads
Budle
Bamburgh
Holefield
Downham
Howtel
Milfield
Fenton Town
Nesbit
North Hazelrigg
Belford
Easington
Waren Mill
Glororum
Burton
Mindrum
Pawston
Kilham
Glen
Doddington
South Hazelrigg
Spindlestone
Bradford
Seahouses
KING CHARLES III ENGLAND COAST PATH
Lanton
Newtown
West Horton
East Horton
Mousen
Bellshill
Elford
North Sunderland
Shotton
Westnewton
Coupland
Weetwood Hall
Warenton
ADDERSTONE
Adderstone
Lucker
Beadnell
Kirknewton
Akeld
Chatton
Greendikes
NEWHAM BOG
Newham Hall
Swinhoe
Warenford
Newham
Benthall
KIRK YETHOLM
Humbleton
Fleetham
Town Yetholm
Kirk Yetholm
Hethpool
College Burn
Wooler
Haugh Head
Rosebrough
Newstead
Chathill
Beadnell Bay
Earle
Middleton Hall
Chillingham
CHILLINGHAM CASTLE
WILD CATTLE OF CHILLINGHAM
Ellingham
Preston
High Newton-by-the-Sea
PENNINE WAY
COLD LAW
North Middleton
Newtown
Lilburn Tower
Hepburn
PRESTON TOWER
Brunton
Low Newton-by-the-Sea
South Middleton
East Lilburn
Brownyside
North Charlton
Christon Bank
Embleton Bay
Embleton
Bowmont Water
MOUNTHOOLEY
THE SCHIL
Ilderton
Old Bewick
Dunstan Steads
Castle Point
DUNSTANBURGH CASTLE
Langleeford
Roseden
West Ditchburn
South
Mowhaugh
A1
A1107
A6105
A697
A698
A6112
A1167
B6438
B6355
B6437
B6461
B6460
B6470
B6354
B6525
B6353
B6352
B6351
B6349
B6348
B1342
B1341
B1340
B1339
B6347
62
63

ROSS OF MULL
Loch Scridain
Bunessan
Fionnphort
Baile Mor
Iona Abbey and Cathedral
Kintra
Fidden
Tiraghoil
Erraid
Ardalanish
Uisken
Ardchiavaig
Scoor
Lee
Eorabus
Pennycross
Torrans
Brolass
Carsaig
Carsaig Arches
Malcolm's Pt.
Rubha nam Braithrean
Rubh Ardalanish
Lochbuie
Loch Buie
Kinlochspelve
Barachandroman
Croggan
Laggan
Lord Lovat's Cave
Frank Lockwood's Island
Torran Rocks
NM
FIRTH OF LORN
Garbh Eileach
Garvellachs
Eileach an Naoimh
SCARBA, LUNGA AND THE GARVELLACHS
Eilean Dubh Mor
Lunga
Scarba
Cruach Scarba 449
Gulf of Corryvreckan
Seil
Easdale
Balvicar
Cuan
Cullipool
Luing
Achafolla
Toberonochy
Shuna
Shuna Pt.
Rubha Aird Luing
Arduaine Garden
Kilchoan
Oban
COLONSAY
Kiloran Bay
Balnahard
Kiloran
Kilchattan
Scalasaig
Garvard
Loch Staosnaig
Rubha Dubh
Oronsay
Priory
Dubh Eilean
Eilean nan Ron
Rubh' a' Geadha
Kinuachdrachd
Glengarrisdale Bay
Glendebadel Bay
Ben Garrisdale 365
Corpach Bay
Beinn Bhreac 467
Lealt
Ardlussa
Inverlussa
Lussagiven
Shian Bay
Loch Righ Mòr
Rubh' an t-Sàilein
Loch Tarbert
Tarbert
Rubha Lang-aoinidh
Lagg
Loch Lesgamaill
JURA
Paps of Jura
Jura Forest
Loch a Chnuic Bhric
Gleann Astaile
Leargybreck
Knockrome
An Dùnan
Lowlandman's Bay
Loch na Mile
Keils
Craighouse
Isle of Jura Distillery
Small Isles
Brat Bheinn 342
Gleann Ullibh
Feolin Ferry
Cabrach
Rubha na Tràille
Brosdale I.
Am Fraoch Eilean
McArthur's Hd.
SOUND OF JURA
SOUND OF ISLAY
NR
ISLAY
Rubha Bholsa
Rubha a'Mhail
Sgarbh Breac 364
Nave Island
Ardnave Pt.
Ardnave
Gortantaoid
Bunnahabhain
Bunnahabhain Distillery
Killinallan
Caol Ila
Caol Ila Distillery
Port Askaig
Finlaggan Centre
Keills
Loch Finlaggan
Loch Cam
Ballygrant
Loch Ballygrant
Kilmeny
Loch Gruinart
Leckgruinart
Loch Gruinart Nature Reserve Visitors Centre
Aoradh
Craigens
Blackrock
Redhouses
Daill
Bridgend
Bowmore
Bowmore Round Church
Mulindry
Beinn Dubh 267
Beinn Bhan 471
Beinn Bheigeir 491
Laggan
Laggan Pt.
Port Charlotte
Loch Indaal
Carraig Mhór
Ardtalla
Claggain Bay
Loch Beinn Uraraidh
Ardmore Pt.
Crinan
Loch Crinan
Kilmahumaig
Bellanoch
Gallachoille
Carsaig
Tayvallich
Achanamara
Kilmichael of Inverlussa
Barrahormid
Taynish
Loch Sween
Dunrostan
Cruach Lusach 466
Keills Chapel
Keillmore
New Ulva
Castle Sween
Island of Danna
Lochead
Achahoish
St Columba's Cave
Ellary
Clachbreck
Eilean Mòr
St Cormac's Chapel
Kilmory
Kilmory Bay
Baile Boidheach
Ormsary
Pt. of Knap
Druimdrishaig
Loch Caolisport
Loch nan Torran
Miller's Bay
Cretshengan
Cruach Lagain 264
Coulaghailtro
Kilberry Hd.
Kilberry
Sculptured Stones
Carse Ho.
Dunmore
Loch Stornoway
Ardpatrick
Kilchamaig
Ardpatrick Ho.
Portachoillan
Ardpatrick Pt.
Eilean Traighe
Ronachan Pt.
Clachan
Loch Ciaran
Balochroy
Eilean Garbh
West Tarbert Bay
East Tarbert Bay
Port Ellen
Knapdale
Island Macaskin
Craignish Pt.
Rèisa an t-Sruith
Aird
0 1 2 3 4 5 6 miles
0 1 2 3 4 5 6 7 8 9 10 km

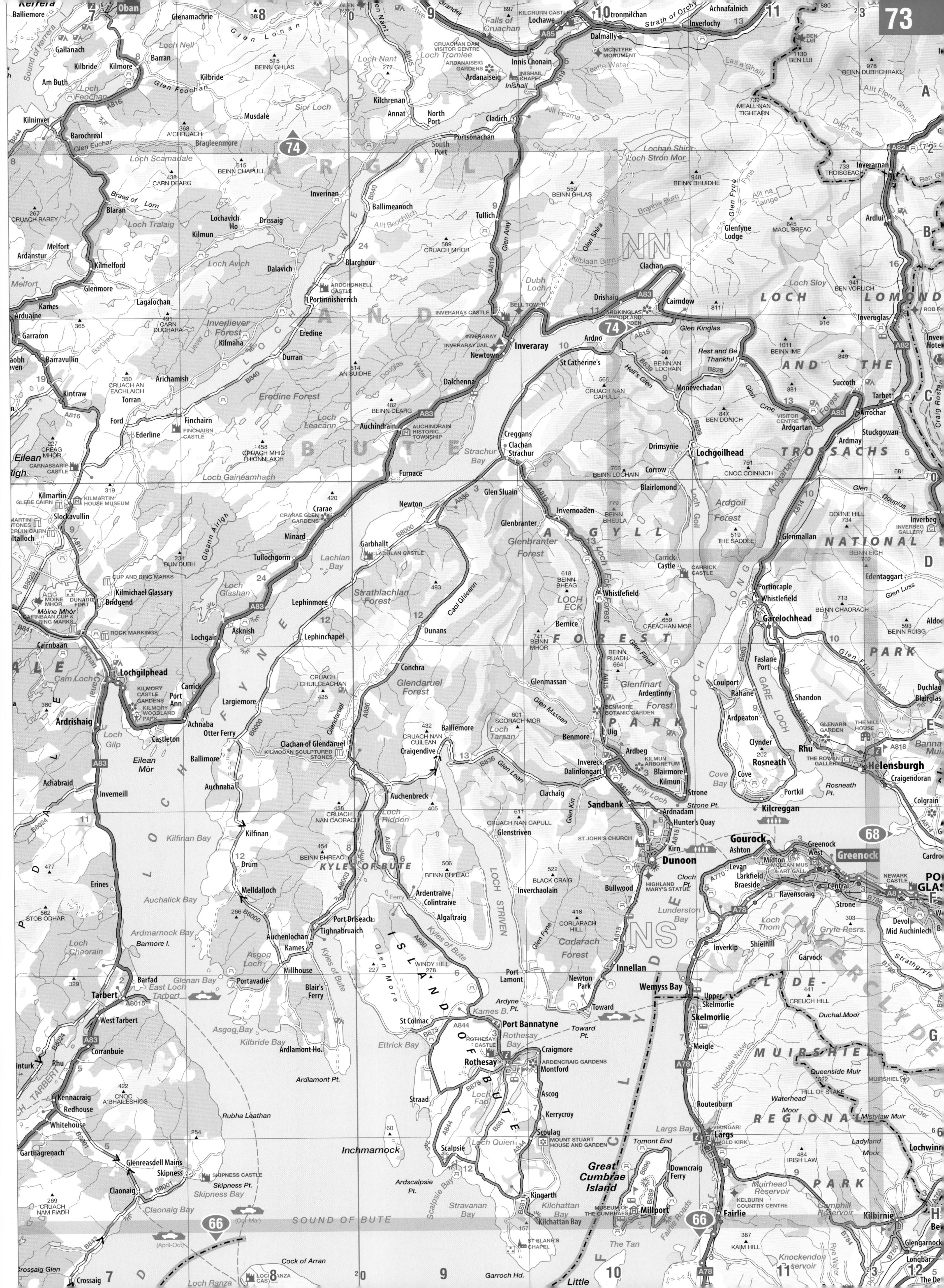
Oban
Balliemore
Glenamachrie
Glen Lonan
Gallanach
Kilbride
Kilmore
Barran
Am Buth
Loch Feochan
Glen Feochan
Kilninver
Barochreal
Musdale
Bragleenmore
Loch Scamadale
Braes of Lorn
Blaran
Loch Tralaig
Melfort
Kilmelford
Glenmore
Ardanstur
Arduaine
Kames
Lagalochan
Garraron
Barravullin
Kintraw
Torran
Ford
Ederline
Finchairn
Kilmartin
Slockavullin
Kilmichael Glassary
Bridgend
Moine Mhor
Cairnbaan
Lochgilphead
Ardrishaig
Castleton
Achnaba
Otter Ferry
Inverneill
Achabraid
Erines
Tarbert
West Tarbert
Corranbuie
Kennacraig
Redhouse
Whitehouse
Gartnagrenach
Claonaig
Skipness
Crossaig
Glen Nant
Falls of Cruachan
Lochawe
Kilchurn Castle
Dalmally
Tyndrum
Strath of Orchy
Achnafalnich
Inverlochy
Ben Lui
Innis Chonain
Ardanaiseig
Inishail
Kilchrenan
Annat
North Port
Cladich
Portsonachan
South Port
Loch Awe
Inverinan
Ballimeanoch
Tullich
Lochavich
Drissaig
Kilmun
Dalavich
Blarghour
Portinnisherrich
Eredine
Durran
Arichamish
Eredine Forest
Inverliever Forest
Kilmaha
Inveraray
Newtown
Dalchenna
Auchindrain
Furnace
Crarae
Minard
Tullochgorm
Lochgair
Asknish
Lephinmore
Lephinchapel
Newton
Garbhallt
Lachlan Castle
Strathlachlan Forest
Largiemore
Ballimore
Auchnaha
Kilfinan
Drum
Melldalloch
Auchenlochan
Tighnabruaich
Kames
Millhouse
Portavadie
Port Driseach
Kyles of Bute
Clachan of Glendaruel
Glendaruel Forest
Conchra
Dunans
Auchenbreck
Balliemore
Craigendive
Ardentraive
Colintraive
Algaltraig
Island of Bute
Port Bannatyne
St Colmac
Rothesay
Craigmore
Montford
Ascog
Kerrycroy
Scoulag
Straad
Scalpsie
Kingarth
Kilchattan Bay
Inchmarnock
Sound of Bute
Loch Fyne
Creggans
Strachur
Glen Sluain
Glenbranter
Glenbranter Forest
Invernoaden
Loch Eck
Whistlefield
Bernice
Glenmassan
Benmore
Uig
Ardbeg
Invereck
Dalinlongart
Clachaig
Sandbank
Kilmun
Blairmore
Strone
Ardnadam
Hunter's Quay
Kirn
Dunoon
Bullwood
Glenstriven
Inverchaolain
Innellan
Toward
Port Lamont
Newton Park
Great Cumbrae Island
Millport
St Catherine's
Ardno
Clachan
Drishaig
Cairndow
Glen Kinglas
Rest and Be Thankful
Monevechadan
Lochgoilhead
Drimsynie
Corrow
Blairlomond
Carrick Castle
Ardgoil Forest
Ardgartan
Arrochar
Tarbet
Succoth
Stuckgowan
Ardmay
Inveruglas
Ardlui
Inverarnan
Glenfyne Lodge
Loch Lomond and the Trossachs National Park
Argyll Forest Park
Glenmallan
Portincaple
Whistlefield
Garelochhead
Faslane Port
Coulport
Rahane
Shandon
Ardpeaton
Clynder
Rosneath
Rhu
Helensburgh
Craigendoran
Kilcreggan
Cove
Portkil
Gourock
Ashton
Greenock
Levan
Larkfield
Braeside
Ravenscraig
Inverkip
Wemyss Bay
Skelmorlie
Meigle
Routenburn
Largs
Fairlie
Kilbirnie
Muirshiel Regional Park
Clyde-Inverclyde
Firth of Clyde
Argyll and Bute
66
68
74

HIGHLAND
BEN NEVIS AND GLEN COE
ARGYLL AND BUTE
MAMORE FOREST
LOCH LINNHE
LYNN OF LORN
LOCH ETIVE
RANNOCH
BLACK MOUNT
Glen Coe
Kinlochleven
Kinlochmore
North Ballachulish
South Ballachulish
Ballachulish
Glencoe
Onich
Corran
Ardgour
Clovullin
Sallachan
Inversanda
Kentallen
Duror
Keil
Appin
Port Appin
Portnacroish
Creagan
South Creagan
Barcaldine
Benderloch
Ledaig
North Connel
Connel
Dunbeg
Oban
Taynuilt
Bonawe
Brochroy
Bridge of Awe
Lochawe
Dalmally
Stronmilchan
Inverlochy
Arrivain
Clifton
Tyndrum
Crianlarich
Inverherive
Bridge of Orchy
Kingshouse Hotel
Altnafeadh
Black Corries Lodge
Inveroran Hotel
Forest Lodge
Achallader
Dalness
Alltchaorunn
Inverarnan
Ardlui
Inveruglas
Tarbet
Arrochar
Succoth
Ardgartan
Lochgoilhead
Carrick Castle
Inveraray
Newtown
Cairndow
Clachan
St Catherine's
Strachur
Creggans
Furnace
Auchindrain
Crarae
Minard
Kilmaha
Dalavich
Portinnisherrich
Kilchrenan
Annat
North Port
Portsonachan
Cladich
Innis Chonain
Ardanaiseig
Musdale
Kilbride
Barran
Inverinan
Ballimeanoch
Tullich
Blarghour
Eredine
Durran
Arichamish
Ford
Ederline
Finchairn
Torran
Luss
Inverbeg
Rowardennan
Inversnaid Hotel
Stronachlachar
Portincaple
Whistlefield
Garelochhead
Glenbranter
Invernoaden
Tullochgorm
Glen Sluain
Newton
Garbhallt
BEN LOMOND
BEN VORLICH
BEN LUI
BEN CRUACHAN
BEN STARAV
BIDEAN NAM BIAN
West Highland Way
A82
A85
A83
A819
A828
A861
A815
A886
B8074
B840
B845
B828
B839
0 1 2 3 4 5 6 miles
0 1 2 3 4 5 6 7 8 9 10 km

Corrour Forest
952 SGOR GAIBHRE
Rannoch Forest
Talla Bheith Forest
81
841 BEINN MHOLACH
515 SRON BHEAG
891 BEINN A'CHUALLAICH
Loch Errochty
Trinafour
Dalchalloch
GLEN ERROCHTY
Tummel Forest
Loch Bhac
LOCH TUMMEL
Falls of the Bruar
CLAN DONNACHAIDH MUSEUM
Calvine
Pitagowan
Blair Atholl
Old Bridge of Tilt
Lude House
Ballentoul
Aldclune
Killiecrankie
Bonskeid House
ATHOLL COUNTRY LIFE
Queen's View
Falls of Tummel
Moulin
Balmore
Loch Faskally
EXPLORER'S GARDEN
Tressait
Tummel Bridge
Dunalastair
Dunalastair Water
Kinloch Rannoch
Craiganor Lodge
Bridge of Ericht
Killichonan
Rannoch Station
Loch Eigheach
LOCH RANNOCH
Carie
Inverhadden
Finnart
Bridge of Gaur
Camghouran
Black Wood of Rannoch
Rannoch Forest
Foss
TUMMEL
Loch Kinardochy
1083 SCHIEHALLION
Allt Mor
780 FARRAGON HILL
Loch Derculich
TAY FOREST PARK
Strathtay
Ballechin
Edradynate
Grandtully
Little Ballinluig
CLUNY HOUSE GARDENS
ST MARY'S CHURCH
LOCH RANNOCH AND GLEN LYON
CARN MAIRG 1042
745 MEALL A'MHUIC
1029 CARN GORM
931 MEALL BUIDHE
Invervar
Camusvrachan
Keltneyburn
CASTLE MENZIES
Weem
Camserney Dull
Appin of Dull
WADE'S BRIDGE
Aberfeldy
DEWAR'S ABERFELDY DISTILLERY
76
Falls of Moness
BOLFRACKS GARDEN
ST FILLAN'S CHURCH & FORTINGALL YEW
Fortingall
Taymouth Castle
PERTH AND KINROSS
Loch an Daimh
Innerwick
Bridge of Balgie
Gallin
907 MEALL BUIDHE
960 STUCHD AN LOCHAIN
Glen Lyon
Pubil
Cashlie
Stronuich Reservoir
Fearnan
Kenmore
THE SCOTTISH CRANNOG CENTRE
Remony
Acharn
Falls of Acharn
Loch Kennard
Glen Cochill
Loch Hoil
Scotston
690 MEALL DEARG
1118
1214 BEN LAWERS
BEN LAWERS
Loch na Lairige
MEALL NAN TARMACHAN 1043
Lawers
LOCH TAY
Ardtalnaig
716 BEINN BHREAC
Garrow
Quaich
Loch Freuchie
Glen Quaich
Cablea
Amulree
Glen Lochay
Kenknock
Carie
Milton Morenish
Morenish
Ardeonaig
888
Gleann a'Chilleine
805 MEALL NAM FUARAN
Corrymuckloch
623 MEALL NAN CAORAICH
NN
FALLS OF LOCHAY AND FISH LIFT
Boreland
MOIRLANICH LONGHOUSE
Finlarig
Killin
Achmore
FALLS OF DOCHART
937 BEINN CHEATHAICH
637
879 CREAG UCHDAG
Almond
Newton
Auchlyne
Auchlyne West Burn
GLEN DOCHART
Lochdochart House
Ardchyle
Ledcharrie
Glen Ogle
931 BEN CHONZIE
Loch Lednock Reservoir
Glen Lednock
Invergeldie
Funtullich
648 MEALL TARSUINN
Loch Turret Reservoir
Glen Turret
Sma' Glen
GLEN ALMOND
Benmore
Portnellan
1174 BEN MORE
1165 STOB BINNEIN
672 SRON MHOR
Dalveich
Lochearnhead
LOCH EARN
St Fillans
Ardtrostan
Dunira
MELVILLE MONUMENT
RIVER EARN
Comrie
Tullybannocher
EARTHQUAKE HOUSE
Ross
Dalginross
Lawers
COMRIE CROFT
FALLS OF TURRET
Ochtertyre
Quoig
Monzie Castle
Monzie
Hosh
Gilmerton
Fowlis Wester
STANDING STONES
GLENTURRET DISTILLERY
Crieff
Madderty
Lochlane
CRIEFF VISITORS' CENTRE
The Balloch
EDINAMPLE FALLS
Edinample
Ardvorlich
852
Braes of Balquhidder
Balquhidder
ROB ROY'S GRAVE
Auchtubh
Monachylemore
Craigruie
LOMOND
Loch Voil
Loch Doine
Inverlochlarig
Ballimore
Strathyre Forest
Strathyre
678
985 BEN VORLICH
Forest of Glenartney
AUCHINGARRICH WILDLIFE & ADVENTURE PARK
Water of Ruchill
Glen Artney
Dalchruin
Tigh-na-Blair
Culloch
Torlum Wood
DRUMMOND CASTLE GARDENS
OLD CHURCH & TOWER
Muthill
INNERPEFFRAY LIBRARY
Kinkell Bridge
STRATHEARN
THE
771
865 STOB A'CHOIN
811 BEINN EACH
Auchnashelloch
Ochtermuthill
Machany Water
533 BEN CLACH
Langside
Tullibardine
TULLIBARDINE CHAPEL
Auchterarder
687 BEINN BHREAC
820 BENVANE
Ardchullarie More
Loch Lubnaig
Kettie Water
STIRLING
Strath Gartney
Glen Finglas Res.
665 UAMH BHEAG
Glenlichorn
Garrick
BLACKHALL ROMAN CAMPS
Gleneagles Hotel
ARDOCH ROMAN CAMP
LOCH KATRINE
THE GREAT TROSSACHS FOREST
The Trossachs
879 BEN LEDI
Anie
Pass of Leny
Leny Ho.
ROB ROY AND TROSSACHS VISITOR CENTRE
BRACKLINN FALLS
Callander
FALLS OF LENY
Kilmahog
Bochastle
Braco
Blackford
STRATHALLAN
Greenloaning
TULLIBARDINE DISTILLERY
Braes of Ogilvie
Glen Eagles
Loch Ard Forest
TROSSACHS PIER COMPLEX
SS SIR WALTER SCOTT
Trossachs Hotel
Brig o'Turk
Coilantogle
BEN VENUE
727
Duncraggan
Lendrick Lodge
THE TROSSACHS
Achray Forest
Loch Venachar
Loch Drunkie
Menteith Hills
Torrie Forest
Loch Rusky
Braes of Doune
Drumvaich
Burn of Cambus
Kinbuck
Ashfield
Balhaldie
Sheriff Muir 1715
Glendevon Resvrs.
543
Kinlochard
Altskeith
Milton
D. MARSHALL LODGE VISITOR CENTRE
Port of Menteith
KILMADOCK INFORMATION & HERITAGE CENTRE
CATHEDRAL
Dunblane
Deanston
Doune
631 BLAIRDENON HILL
721 BEN CLEUCH
648
KING'S SEAT HILL
ELIZABETH
Aberfoyle
Kirkton
Malling
INCHMAHOME PRIORY
Lake of Menteith
Ruskie
Thornhill
Goodie Water
Blair Drummond
Easter Row
BLAIR DRUMMOND SAFARI & ADVENTURE PARK
Pisgah
LEIGHTON LIBRARY
Sunnylaw
Duchray Water
Loch Ard Forest
Cobleland
FLANDERS MOSS
Flanders Moss
Dykehead
Blairdrummond Moss
Bridge of Allan
Blairlogie
Menstrie
Tillicoultry
Gartmore
Forth
Flanders Moss
REST PARK
577 BEINN BHREAC
Drip Moss
Causewayhead
NATIONAL WALLACE MONUMENT
Tullibody
Alva
Fishcross
Devonside
Coalsnaughton
Dalmary
NS
68
Kippen
Arnprior
Cauldhame
Glentirranmuir
Gargunnock
STIRLING CASTLE
OLD TOWN JAIL
Raploch
Cambuskenneth
Cambus
Sauchie
Keilarsbrae
461
Milarrochy
Buchlyvie
CARLEATHERAN 485
SMITH ART GALL & MUSEUM
Stirling
ALLOA
ALLOA TOWER
Moor Park
Touch Hills
Cambusbarron
Torbrex
1314
Fallin
Clackmannan
Kennet
NAT. PARK CENTRE
Balmaha
Buchlyvie Muir
Kippen Muir
Gargunnock
St Ninians
South

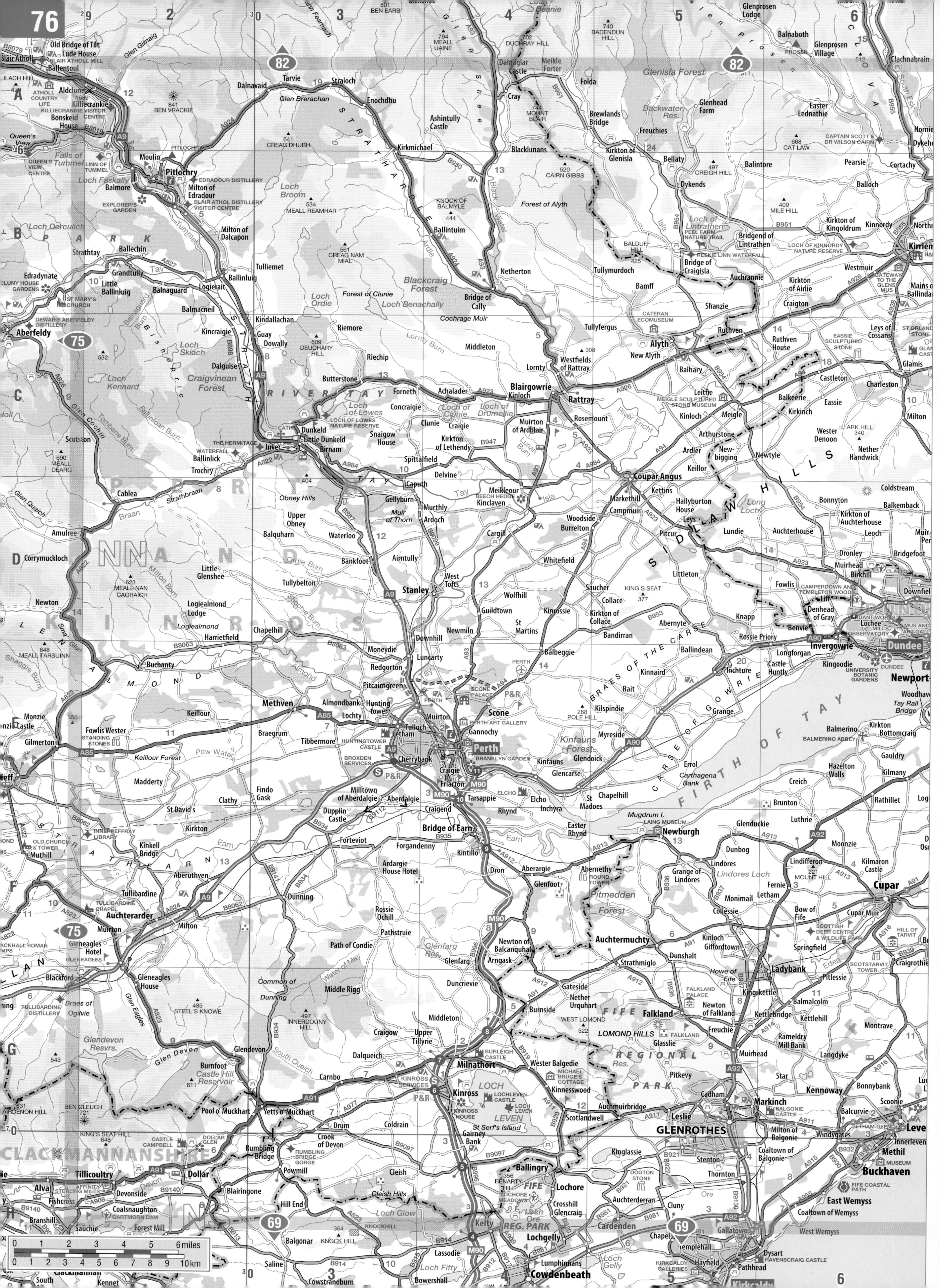

82
801 BEN EARB
Glen Fearnach
794 MEALL UAINE
Glen Shee
702 DUCHRAY HILL
740 BADENDUN HILL
Glenprosen Lodge
Balnaboth
Glenprosen Village
Clachnabrain
Old Bridge of Tilt
Lude House
Blair Atholl
BLAIR ATHOLL MILL
Ballentoul
Glen Girnaig
Tarvie
Straloch
Dalnagiar Castle
Meikle Forter
Glenisla Forest
Dalnavaid
Glen Brerachan
Enochdhu
Cray
Folda
Glenhead Farm
Easter Lednathie
Aldclune
Killiecrankie
ATHOLL COUNTRY LIFE
KILLIECRANKIE VISITOR CENTRE
Bonskeid House
841 BEN VRACKIE
STRATHARDLE
Ashintully Castle
744 MOUNT BLAIR
Brewlands Bridge
Backwater Res.
Queen's View
Falls of Tummel
QUEEN'S VIEW CENTRE
LINN OF TUMMEL
Moulin
PITLOCHRY
Pitlochry
641 CREAG DHUBH
Kirkmichael
Blacklunans
Kirkton of Glenisla
Freuchies
Bellaty
668 CAT LAW
CAPTAIN SCOTT & DR WILSON CAIRN
Loch Faskally
Balmore
EXPLORER'S GARDEN
EDRADOUR DISTILLERY
Milton of Edradour
BLAIR ATHOL DISTILLERY VISITOR CENTRE
Loch Broom
534 MEALL REMHAR
KNOCK OF BALMYLE 444
520 CAIRN GIBBS
497 CREIGH HILL
Balintore
Pearsie
Cortachy
Dykends
Balloch
Forest of Alyth
409 MILE HILL
Loch Derculich
Milton of Dalcapon
Ballintuim
Black Water
Loch of Lintrathen
PEEL FARM NATURE TRAIL
Bridgend of Lintrathen
Kirkton of Kingoldrum
Kinnordy
LOCH OF KINNORDY NATURE RESERVE
Kirriemuir
PARK
Strathtay
Ballechin
561 CREAG NAM MIAL
BALDUFF HILL 425
REEKIE LINN WATERFALL
Bridge of Craigisla
Auchrannie
Westmuir
Edradynate
CLUNY HOUSE GARDENS
Grandtully
Little Ballinluig
Tulliemet
Ballinluig
Netherton
Tullymurdoch
Kirkton of Airlie
ST MARY'S CHURCH
Balnaguard
Logierait
Blackcraig Forest
Forest of Clunie
Loch Ordie
Loch Benachally
Bridge of Cally
Bamff
Shanzie
Craigton
Balmacneil
Kindallachan
Cochrage Muir
CATERAN ECOMUSEUM
DEWAR'S ABERFELDY DISTILLERY
Aberfeldy
75
Bishopric
Kincraigie
Riemore
Tullyfergus
Alyth
Ruthven
Ruthven House
Leys of Cossans
Guay
Dowally
509 DEUCHARY HILL
Lornty Burn
Middleton
308
Westfields of Rattray
New Alyth
EASSIE SCULPTURED STONE
Loch Skiach
532
Dalguise
Riechip
Lornty
Balhary
Glamis
Loch Kennard
Craigvinean Forest
Butterstone
Castleton
Blairgowrie
Kinloch
Rattray
Leitfie
MEIGLE SCULPTURED STONE MUSEUM
Charleston
RIVER TAY
Forneth
Achalader
Loch of Lowes
LOCH OF LOWES NATURE RESERVE
Concraigie
Loch of Clunie
Loch of Drumellie
Balkeerie
Eassie
Clunie
Craigie
Muirton of Ardblair
Rosemount
Kinloch
Meigle
Kirkinch
Glen Cochill
Dunkeld
Little Dunkeld
Snaigow House
Kirkton of Lethendy
River Ericht
Arthurstone
Wester Denoon
ARK HILL 340
Scotston
THE HERMITAGE
WATERFALL
Ballinlick
Inver
Birnam
Spittalfield
Ardler
New-bigging
Newtyle
Nether Handwick
690 MEALL DEARG
Trochry
404
Delvine
Caputh
Keillor
SIDLAW HILLS
Coupar Angus
Kettins
Meikleour
BEECH HEDGE
Kinclaven
Coldstream
Cablea
Strathbraan
Obney Hills
Gellyburn
Murthly
Markethill
Campmuir
Hallyburton House
Long Loch
Bonnyton
Balkemback
Glen Quaich
Upper Obney
Muir of Thorn
Ardoch
Woodside
Burrelton
Leys
Kirkton of Auchterhouse
Amulree
Balquharn
Waterloo
Cargill
Pitcur
Lundie
Auchterhouse
Leoch
Corrymuckloch
NN
Bankfoot
Airntully
Whitefield
Dronley
Bridgefoot
Little Glenshee
623 MEALL NAN CAORAICH
Milton Burn
Tullybelton
Stanley
West Tofts
Littleton
Muirhead
Birkhill
CLATTO
Fowlis
CAMPERDOWN AND TEMPLETON WOODS
Saucher
Collace
KING'S SEAT 377
Downfield
Newton
Logiealmond Lodge
Logiealmond
Wolfhill
Guildtown
Kinrossie
Kirkton of Collace
Knapp
Denhead of Gray
Liff
Harrietfield
Chapelhill
Newmiln
St Martins
Abernyte
Balbeggie
Bandirran
Rossie Priory
Benvie
Invergowrie
VERDANT WORKS
MILLS OBSERVATORY
Dundee
648 MEALL TARSUINN
Downhill
Moneydie
Luncarty
Redgorton
BRAES OF THE CARSE
Ballindean
Longforgan
Kingoodie
UNIVERSITY BOTANIC GARDENS
Buchanty
ALMOND
PERTH
Kinnaird
Inchture
Castle Huntly
Newport-on-Tay
Pitcairngreen
Almondbank
Methven
Hunting-tower
Lochty
SCONE PALACE
P&R
Scone
Rait
288 POLE HILL
Kilspindie
CARSE OF GOWRIE
Grange
Woodhaven
Tay Rail Bridge
Monzie Castle
350
Keillour
Fowlis Wester
STANDING STONES
Braegrum
Tibbermore
HUNTINGTOWER CASTLE
Tulloch
Letham
Muirton
Gannochy
PERTH ART GALLERY
Perth
Myreside
Balmerino
BALMERINO ABBEY
Kirkton
Bottomcraig
Gilmerton
Keillour Forest
Pow Water
BROXDEN SERVICES
Cherrybank
BRANKLYN GARDEN
Kinfauns Forest
Kinfauns
Glendoick
Errol
FIRTH OF TAY
Gauldry
Crieff
Madderty
Findo Gask
Craigie
Friarton
Glencarse
Carthagena Bank
Hazelton Walls
Kilmany
St David's
Clathy
Milltown of Aberdalgie
Aberdalgie
ELCHO
Tarsappie
Rhynd
Elcho
Inchyra
St Madoes
Chapelhill
Creich
Brunton
Rathillet
Dupplin Castle
Craigend
Bridge of Earn
Mugdrum I.
LAING MUSEUM
Easter Rhynd
Newburgh
Glenduckie
Luthrie
INNERPEFFRAY LIBRARY
Kirkton
Earn
Forteviot
Forgandenny
Kintillo
Aberargie
Abernethy
ROUND TOWER
Dunbog
Lindores
Grange of Lindores
Lindores Loch
Lindifferon
221 MOUNT HILL
Moonzie
Kilmaron Castle
OLD CHURCH & TOWER
Muthill
Kinkell Bridge
STRATHEARN
Aberuthven
Ardargie House Hotel
Dron
Glenfoot
Pitmedden Forest
Fernie
Letham
Cupar
Tullibardine
TULLIBARDINE CHAPEL
Auchterarder
Dunning
Rossie Ochill
Monimail
Collessie
Bow of Fife
Cupar Muir
Muirton
Milton
Pathstruie
Newton of Balcanquhal
Auchtermuchty
Kinloch
Giffordtown
SCOTTISH DEER CENTRE & WILDLIFE PARK
HILL OF TARVIT
Gleneagles Hotel
GLENEAGLES
Path of Condie
Glenfarg Res.
Glenfarg
Arngask
Dunshalt
Springfield
Strathmiglo
Howe of Fife
Ladybank
SCOTSTARVIT TOWER
Craigrothie
Blackford
Gleneagles House
Water of May
Common of Dunning
Duncrievie
Gateside
Nether Urquhart
Eden
Pitlessie
Kingskettle
FALKLAND PALACE
Newton of Falkland
Balmalcolm
Kettlebridge
Kettlehill
TULLIBARDINE DISTILLERY
Braes of Ogilvie
Glen Eagles
485 STEEL'S KNOWE
Middle Rigg
497 INNERDOUNY HILL
Middleton
Burnside
WEST LOMOND 522
FIFE
Falkland
LOMOND HILLS
FALKLAND
Freuchie
Rameldry Mill Bank
Montrave
Glendevon Resvrs.
Craigow
Upper Tillyrie
BURLEIGH CASTLE
Glasslie
REGIONAL PARK
Muirhead
Langdyke
543
Glen Devon
Glendevon
Dalqueich
Milnathort
Wester Balgedie
MICHAEL BRUCE'S COTTAGE
Pitkevy
Star
Burnfoot
Castle Hill Reservoir
611
South Queich
Carnbo
KINROSS SERVICES
LOCH LEVEN
LOCHLEVEN CASTLE
Kinnesswood
Cadham
Markinch
Kennoway
Bonnybank
631 BLAIRDENON HILL
BEN CLEUCH 721
Pool o' Muckhart
Yetts o' Muckhart
A91
Kinross
KINROSS HOUSE
St Serf's Island
Scotlandwell
Auchmuirbridge
Leslie
BALGONIE CASTLE
Balcurvie
Scoonie
KING'S SEAT HILL 648
Drum
Coldrain
Gairney Bank
GLENROTHES
Milton of Balgonie
Windygates
LETHAM GLEN
Leven
CLACKMANNANSHIRE
CASTLE CAMPBELL
DOLLAR GLEN
Rumbling Bridge
Crook of Devon
RUMBLING BRIDGE GORGE
Kinglassie
Stenton
Coaltown of Balgonie
Innerleven
Methil
Tillicoultry
Dollar
Powmill
Cleish
Ballingry
356 BENARTY HILL
Lochore
DOGTON STONE
Thornton
METHIL MUSEUM
Buckhaven
Alva
AFFINITY STERLING MILLS
Devonside
Blairingone
Cleish Hills
LOCHORE MEADOWS
Crosshill
Glencraig
Auchterderran
Cluny
Ore
FIFE COASTAL PATH
East Wemyss
Fishcross
Coalsnaughton
GARTMORN DAM
Hill End
Loch Glow
Coaltown of Wemyss
Branshill
Sauchie
Forest Mill
69
KNOCKHILL
364 KNOCK HILL
Kelty
REG. PARK
Cardenden
Lochgelly
Chapel
Gallatown
Templehall
West Wemyss
Balgonar
Lassodie
Dysart
RAVENSCRAIG CASTLE
KIRKCALDY GALLERIES
Hayfield
Pathhead
Saline
Loch Fitty
Lumphinnans
Loch Gelly
Cowdenbeath
Kirkcaldy
Clackmannan
South
Kennet
Cowstrandburn
Bowershall
0 1 2 3 4 5 6 miles
0 1 2 3 4 5 6 7 8 9 10 km

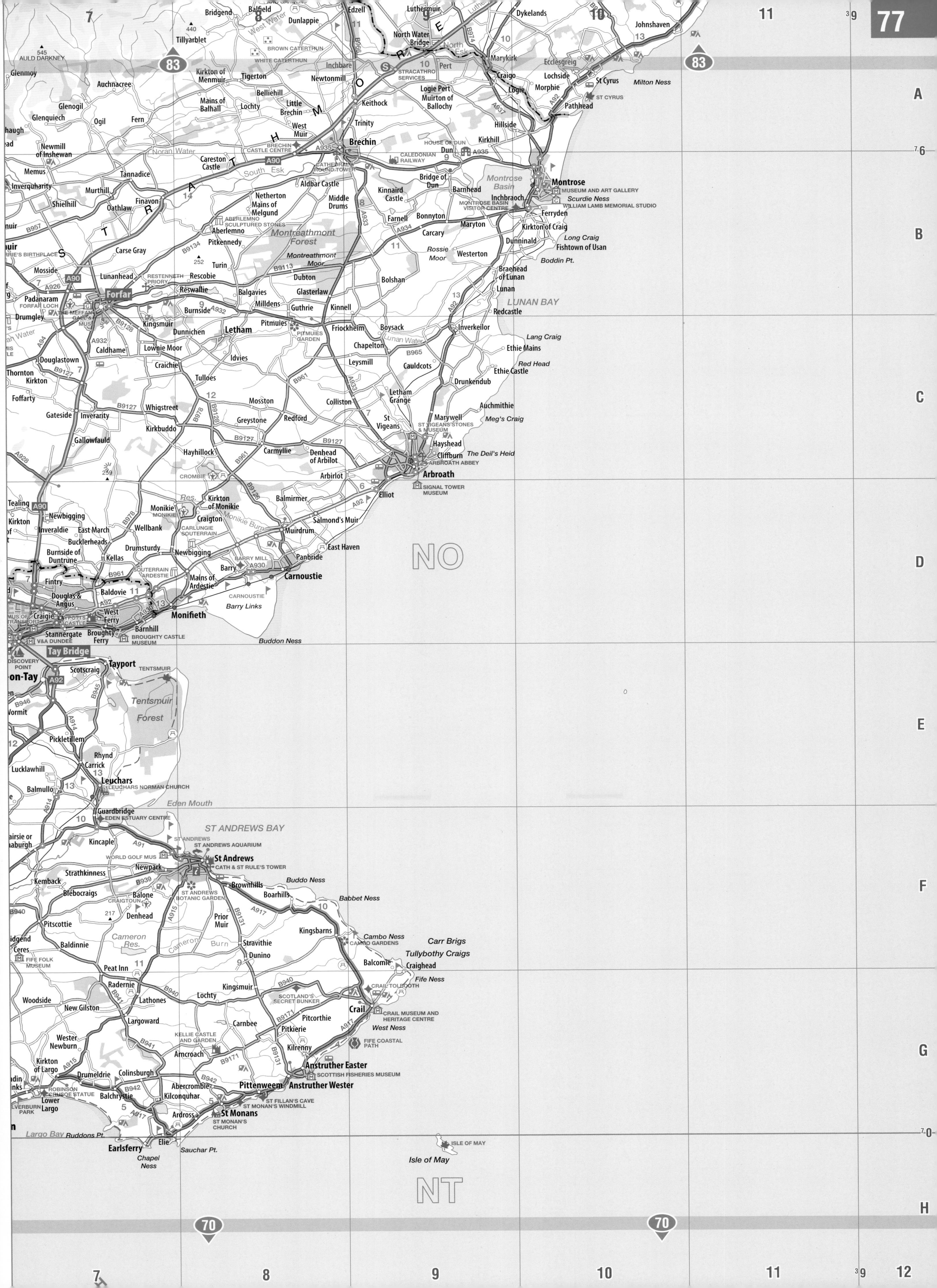
Edzell
Luthermuir
Dykelands
Johnshaven
Bridgend
Balfield
Dunlappie
North Water Bridge
Tillyarblet
Auld Darkney
Brown Caterthun
White Caterthun
Glenmoy
Auchnacree
Kirkton of Menmuir
Tigerton
Inchbare
Stracathro Services
Newtonmill
Pert
Marykirk
Ecclesgreig
Craigo
Lochside
Logie
Morphie
St Cyrus
Milton Ness
Pathhead
Logie Pert
Muirton of Ballochy
Keithock
Bellichill
Mains of Balhall
Lochty
Little Brechin
Glenogil
Glenquiech
Ogil
Fern
West Muir
Trinity
Hillside
Brechin
House of Dun
Dun
Kirkhill
Caledonian Railway
Newmill of Inshewan
Noran Water
Brechin Castle Centre
Careston Castle
Memus
Tannadice
South Esk
Cathedral & Round Tower
Aldbar Castle
Bridge of Dun
Barnhead
Montrose Basin
Montrose
Museum and Art Gallery
Inverquharity
Murthill
Kinnaird Castle
Inchbraoch
Scurdie Ness
Shielhill
Oathlaw
Finavon
Netherton
Mains of Melgund
Middle Drums
Montrose Basin Visitor Centre
William Lamb Memorial Studio
Ferryden
Aberlemno Sculptured Stones
Aberlemno
Farnell
Bonnyton
Maryton
Kirkton of Craig
Montreathmont Forest
Carcary
Dunninald
Long Craig
Fishtown of Usan
Carse Gray
Pitkennedy
Rossie Moor
Westerton
Boddin Pt.
Montreathmont Moor
Turin
Mosside
Lunanhead
Restenneth Priory
Rescobie
Dubton
Bolshan
Braehead of Lunan
Lunan
Padanaram
Forfar
Forfar Loch
Reswallie
Balgavies
Glasterlaw
Lunan Bay
Drumgley
Burnside
Milldens
Guthrie
Kinnell
Redcastle
Kingsmuir
Dunnichen
Letham
Pitmuies
Pitmuies Garden
Friockheim
Boysack
Inverkeilor
Lang Craig
Caldhame
Lownie Moor
Chapelton
Lunan Water
Ethie Mains
Douglastown
Idvies
Leysmill
Cauldcots
Red Head
Craichie
Ethie Castle
Thornton
Kirkton
Tulloes
Drunkendub
Foffarty
Mosston
Colliston
Letham Grange
Auchmithie
Gateside
Inverarity
Whigstreet
Greystone
Redford
St Vigeans
Marywell
Meg's Craig
Kirkbuddo
St Vigeans Stones & Museum
Gallowfauld
Hayshead
Hayhillock
Carmyllie
Denhead of Arbirlot
Cliffburn
The Deil's Heid
Arbroath Abbey
Crombie
Arbirlot
Arbroath
Signal Tower Museum
Tealing
Balmirmer
Elliot
Kirkton of Monikie
Newbigging
Monikie
Craigton
Salmond's Muir
Inveraldie
East March
Wellbank
Carlungie Souterrain
Monikie Burn
Muirdrum
Bucklerheads
Drumsturdy
Newbigging
East Haven
Burnside of Duntrune
Kellas
Panbride
NO
Barry Mill
Barry
Carnoustie
Fintry
Souterrain Ardestie
Mains of Ardestie
Douglas & Angus
Baldovie
Carnoustie
Craigie
West Ferry
Monifieth
Barry Links
Stannergate
Broughty Ferry
Barnhill
Broughty Castle Museum
V&A Dundee
Buddon Ness
Tay Bridge
Discovery Point
Tayport
Tentsmuir
Scotscraig
Tentsmuir Forest
Wormit
Pickletillem
Rhynd
Carrick
Lucklawhill
Balmullo
Leuchars
Leuchars Norman Church
Eden Mouth
Guardbridge
Eden Estuary Centre
St Andrews Bay
Kincaple
St Andrews
St Andrews Aquarium
World Golf Mus
Strathkinness
Newpark
Cath & St Rule's Tower
Kemback
Brownhills
Buddo Ness
Blebocraigs
St Andrews Botanic Garden
Boarhills
Babbet Ness
Craigtoun
Balone
Denhead
Pitscottie
Prior Muir
Kingsbarns
Cambo Ness
Cambo Gardens
Carr Brigs
Tullybothy Craigs
Cameron Res.
Cameron Burn
Stravithie
Dunino
Baldinnie
Ceres
Fife Folk Museum
Balcomie
Craighead
Peat Inn
Fife Ness
Radernie
Kingsmuir
Crail Tolbooth
Woodside
Lathones
Lochty
Scotland's Secret Bunker
Crail
New Gilston
Pitcorthie
Crail Museum and Heritage Centre
Largoward
Carnbee
West Ness
Wester Newburn
Kellie Castle and Garden
Pitkierie
Fife Coastal Path
Kilrenny
Kirkton of Largo
Arncroach
Anstruther Easter
Scottish Fisheries Museum
Drumeldrie
Colinsburgh
Abercrombie
Pittenweem
Anstruther Wester
Robinson Crusoe Statue
Balchrystie
Kilconquhar
Lower Largo
St Fillan's Cave
St Monan's Windmill
Ardross
St Monans
St Monan's Church
Largo Bay
Ruddons Pt.
Elie
Isle of May
Earlsferry
Chapel Ness
Sauchar Pt.
NT
A90
A92
A94
A926
A932
A933
A934
A935
A937
A930
A91
A914
A915
A917
A928
B9134
B9113
B9127
B9128
B961
B965
B966
B974
B978
B957
B946
B945
B939
B940
B941
B942
B9131
B9171
83
70
A
B
C
D
E
F
G
H
7
8
9
10
11
12

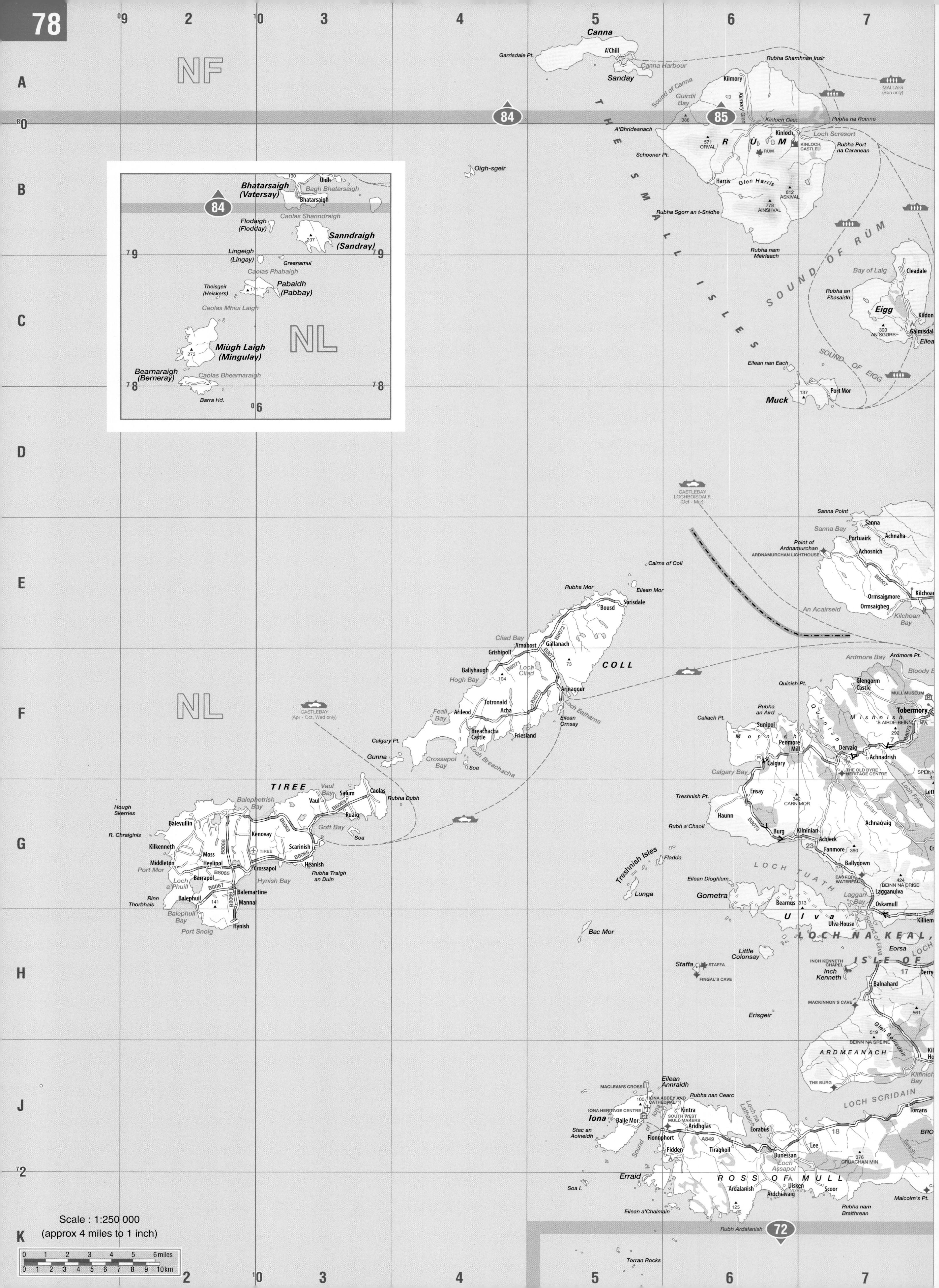
NF
NL
Canna
A'Chill
Garrisdale Pt.
Canna Harbour
Sanday
Sound of Canna
Rubha Shamhnan Insir
Kilmory
Kilmory Glen
Guirdil Bay
MALLAIG (Sun only)
84
85
Kinloch Glen
Rubha na Roinne
A'Bhrideanach
Kinloch
Loch Scresort
KINLOCH CASTLE
Rubha Port na Caranean
RÙM
571 ORVAL
Schooner Pt.
Oigh-sgeir
Harris
Glen Harris
812 ASKIVAL
778 AINSHVAL
Rubha Sgorr an t-Snidhe
THE SMALL ISLES
SOUND OF RÙM
Rubha nam Meirleach
Bay of Laig
Cleadale
Rubha an Fhasaidh
Eigg
393 AN SGURR
Kildon
Galmisdale
SOUND OF EIGG
Eilean nan Each
Muck
Port Mor
Bhatarsaigh (Vatersay)
Uidh
Bagh Bhatarsaigh
Bhatarsaigh
Caolas Shanndraigh
Flodaigh (Flodday)
Sanndraigh (Sandray)
Lingeigh (Lingay)
Greanamul
Caolas Phabaigh
Theisgeir (Heiskers)
Pabaidh (Pabbay)
Caolas Mhiui Laigh
Miùgh Laigh (Mingulay)
Bearnaraigh (Berneray)
Caolas Bhearnaraigh
Barra Hd.
CASTLEBAY LOCHBOISDALE (Oct - Mar)
Sanna Point
Sanna
Sanna Bay
Achnaha
Portuairk
Point of Ardnamurchan
ARDNAMURCHAN LIGHTHOUSE
Achosnich
Cairns of Coll
Eilean Mor
Rubha Mor
Sorisdale
Bousd
Ormsaigmore
Ormsaigbeg
An Acairseid
Kilchoan Bay
Cliad Bay
Arnabost
Gallanach
Grishipoll
COLL
Ballyhaugh
Loch Cliad
Hogh Bay
Arinagour
Totronald
Acha
Feall Bay
Arileod
Loch Eatharna
Eilean Ornsay
Breachacha Castle
Friesland
CASTLEBAY (Apr - Oct, Wed only)
Calgary Pt.
Gunna
Crossapol Bay
Loch Breachacha
Soa
TIREE
Vaul Bay
Salum
Caolas
Vaul
Rubha Dubh
Balephetrish Bay
Ruaig
Hough Skerries
Balevullin
Kenovay
Gott Bay
R. Chraiginis
Kilkenneth
Moss
Scarinish
TIREE
Middleton
Heylipol
Heanish
Port Mor
Crossapol
Rubha Traigh an Duin
Loch a'Phuill
Barrapol
Hynish Bay
Balemartine
Rinn Thorbhais
Balephuil
Mannal
Balephuil Bay
Port Snoig
Hynish
Ardmore Bay
Ardmore Pt.
Quinish Pt.
Glengorm Castle
MULL MUSEUM
Tobermory
Rubha an Aird
Caliach Pt.
Sunipol
Mornish
Penmore Mill
Dervaig
Achnadrish
Calgary
Calgary Bay
THE OLD BYRE HERITAGE CENTRE
Treshnish Pt.
Ensay
342 CARN MOR
Haunn
Achnacraig
Rubh a'Chaoil
Burg
Kilninian
Treshnish Isles
Fladda
Achleck
Fanmore
Ballygown
Eilean Dioghlum
LOCH TUATH
Lunga
Gometra
Laggan Bay
Lagganulva
Bearnus
Oskamull
Ulva
Ulva House
Bac Mor
LOCH NA KEAL
Eorsa
Little Colonsay
Staffa
STAFFA
FINGAL'S CAVE
INCH KENNETH CHAPEL
Inch Kenneth
Balnahard
MACKINNON'S CAVE
Erisgeir
Glen Seilisdeir
ARDMEANACH
THE BURG
Eilean Annraidh
MACLEAN'S CROSS
Rubha nan Cearc
IONA ABBEY AND CATHEDRAL
IONA HERITAGE CENTRE
Iona
Baile Mor
Kintra
SOUTH WEST MULL MAKERS
Aridhglas
Loch na Lathaich
LOCH SCRIDAIN
Torrans
Stac an Aoineidh
Sound of Iona
Fionnphort
Eorabus
A849
Lee
Fidden
Tiraghoil
Bunessan
376 CRUACHAN MIN
Erraid
Loch Assapol
ROSS OF MULL
Soa I.
Ardalanish
Uisken
Scoor
Ardchiavaig
Rubha nam Braithrean
Malcolm's Pt.
Eilean a'Chalmain
Rubh Ardalanish
72
Torran Rocks
Scale : 1:250 000
(approx 4 miles to 1 inch)
miles
km

NG
NH
NM
NN
SOUND OF SLEAT
KNOYDART
LOCH QUOICH
LOCH NEVIS
North Morar
LOCH MORAR
South Morar
LOCH ARKAIG
HIGHLAND
SOUND OF ARISAIG
MORAR, MOIDART AND ARDNAMURCHAN
MOIDART
LOCH SHIEL
LOCH EIL
ARDNAMURCHAN
SUNART
LOCH SUNART
Ardgour
MORVERN
LOCH LINNHE
KINGAIRLOCH
SOUND OF MULL
ISLAND OF MULL
LYNN OF LORN
FIRTH OF LORN
ARGYLL AND BUTE
BENDERLOCH
LOCH ETIVE
Armadale Castle
Ardvasar
Aird of Sleat
Point of Sleat
Mallaig
Glasnacardoch
Morar
Arisaig
Lochailort
Glenfinnan
Kinlocheil
Corpach
Banavie
Fort William
Strontian
Salen
Acharacle
Kilchoan
Tobermory
Lochaline
Craignure
Salen
Oban
Connel
Taynuilt
Dalmally
Port Appin
Kentallen
Ballachulish
Glencoe
Kerrera
Lismore
Seil
Easdale
Luing
Kilmelford
Kilninver
Inverie
Kinloch Hourn
Glen Garry
Invergarry
Gairlochy
Spean Bridge
A830
A861
A82
A828
A85
A816
A849
A884
B8043
B8007
B8044
80
85
74
73
72

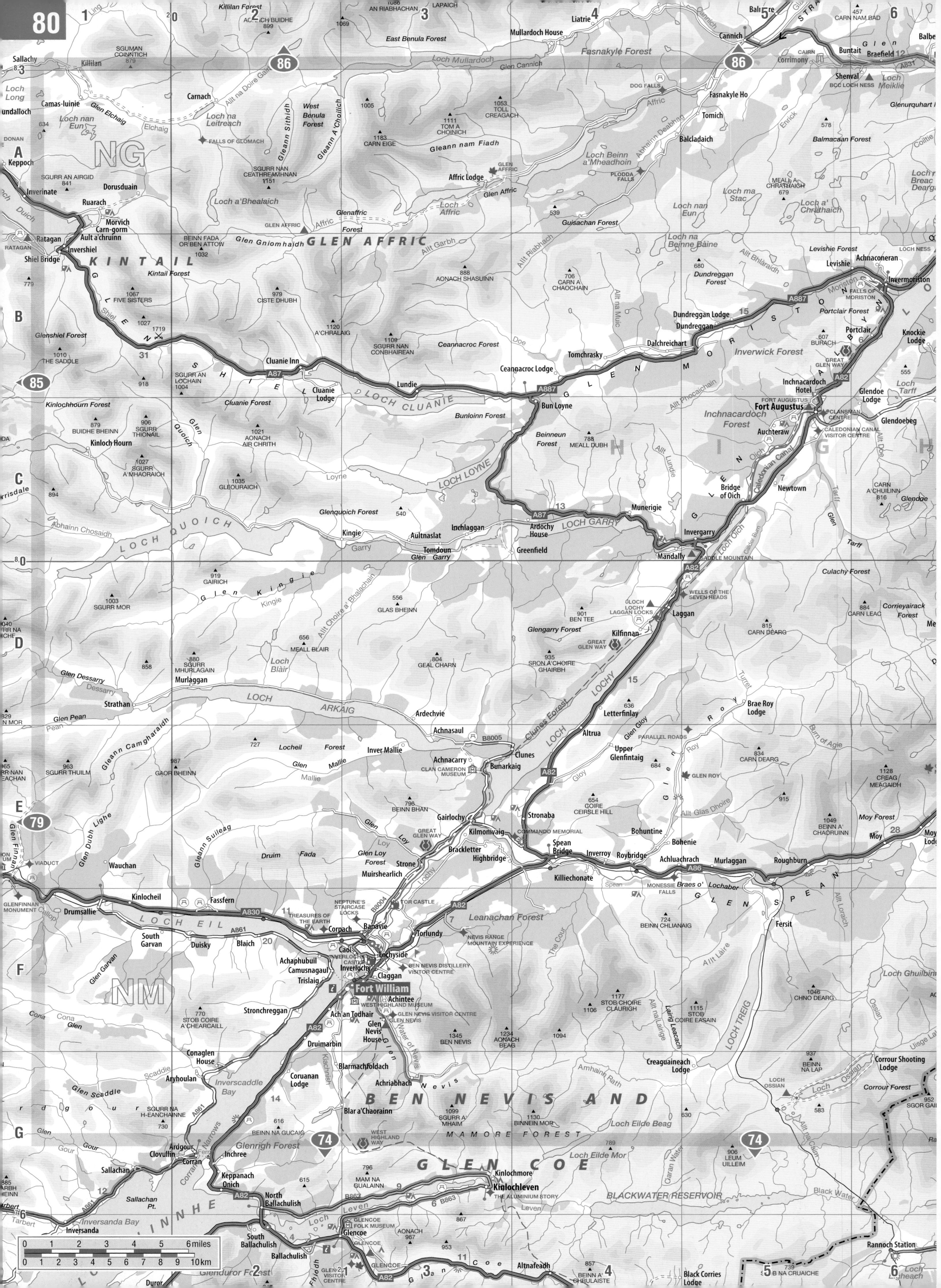

Killilan Forest
AN RIABHACHAN
LAPAICH
Liatrie
Cannich
Mullardoch House
East Benula Forest
Fasnakyle Forest
Loch Mullardoch
Glen Cannich
Corrimony
Buntait
Braefield
Shenval
Loch Meiklie
Glenurquhart
SGUMAN COINNTICH
Sallachy
Killilan
Loch Long
Camas-luinie
Glen Elchaig
Carnach
Loch na Leitreach
West Benula Forest
Gleann Sithidh
Gleann A'Choilich
DOG FALLS
Fasnakyle Ho
Tomich
Balcladaich
Balmacaan Forest
Loch nan Eun
FALLS OF GLOMACH
CARN EIGE
TOM A CHOINICH
TOLL CREAGACH
Gleann nam Fiadh
DONAN
Keppoch
SGURR AN AIRGID
SGURR NAN CEATHREAMHNAN
Dorusduain
Inverinate
Affric Lodge
Glen Affric
Loch Beinn a'Mheadhoin
PLODDA FALLS
Loch ma Stac
MEALL A' CHRATHAICH
Ruarach
Loch a'Bhealaich
Morvich
Carn-gorm
Ault a'chruinn
Ratagan
RATAGAN
Invershiel
Shiel Bridge
Loch Duich
Glenaffric Forest
GLEN AFFRIC
Loch Affric
Loch nan Eun
Guisachan Forest
Loch na Beinne Bàine
Loch a' Chrathaich
BEINN FADA OR BEN ATTOW
Glen Gniomhaidh
KINTAIL
Kintail Forest
AONACH SHASUINN
CARN A' CHAOCHAIN
Dundreggan Forest
Levishie Forest
Levishie
Achnaconeran
LOCH NESS
Invermoriston
FALLS OF MORISTON
FIVE SISTERS
CISTE DHUBH
Glen Shiel
Dundreggan Lodge
Dundreggan
Portclair Forest
Portclair
Knockie Lodge
Glenshiel Forest
THE SADDLE
A'CHRALAIG
SGURR NAN CONBHAIREAN
Ceannacroc Forest
Tomchrasky
Dalchreichart
Inverwick Forest
BURACH
GREAT GLEN WAY
Cluanie Inn
Ceannacroc Lodge
GLEN MORISTON
Loch Tarff
SGURR AN LOCHAIN
A87
A887
A82
Cluanie Lodge
Lundie
Inchnacardoch Hotel
Glendoe Lodge
Kinlochhourn Forest
Cluanie Forest
LOCH CLUANIE
Bun Loyne
Bunloinn Forest
Allt Phocaichain
FORT AUGUSTUS
Fort Augustus
Inchnacardoch Forest
CLANSMAN CENTRE
Glendoebeg
BUIDHE BHEINN
SGURR THIONAIL
Kinloch Hourn
Glen Quoich
AONACH AIR CHRITH
Beinneun Forest
MEALL DUBH
Auchteraw
CALEDONIAN CANAL VISITOR CENTRE
SGURR A'MHAORAICH
GLEOURAICH
LOCH LOYNE
Caledonian Canal
Bridge of Oich
Newtown
CARN A'CHUILINN
Glendoe
Glenquoich Forest
Munerigie
Abhainn Chosaidh
LOCH QUOICH
Kingie
Aultnaslat
Inchlaggan
Ardochy House
LOCH GARRY
Invergarry
Glen Tarff
Tomdoun
Glen Garry
Greenfield
Mandally
SADDLE MOUNTAIN
Loch Oich
GAIRICH
Glen Kingie
Allt Choire a' Bhalachain
Culachy Forest
SGURR MOR
GLAS BHEINN
LOCH LOCHY
LAGGAN LOCKS
WELLS OF THE SEVEN HEADS
Laggan
BEN TEE
CARN LEAC
Corrieyairack Forest
CARN DEARG
Gengarry Forest
Kilfinnan
MEALL BLAIR
SGURR MHURLAGAIN
GEAL CHARN
SRON A'CHOIRE GHAIRBH
Loch Blàir
Murlaggan
Glen Dessarry
Strathan
LOCH ARKAIG
LOCHY
Letterfinlay
Brae Roy Lodge
Glen Pean
Ardechive
Achnasaul
Clunes Forest
Glen Gloy
Glen Roy
PARALLEL ROADS
Altrua
Burn of Agie
Gleann Camgharaidh
Locheil Forest
Inver Mallie
B8005
Upper Glenfintaig
CARN DEARG
SGURR THUILM
GAOR BHEINN
Glen Mallie
Achnacarry
CLAN CAMERON MUSEUM
Bunarkaig
Clunes
GLEN ROY
CREAG MEAGAIDH
BEINN BHAN
COIRE CEIRSLE HILL
Allt Glas Dhoire
Gairlochy
Stronaba
Bohuntine
BEINN A' CHAORUINN
Moy Forest
Glen Dubh Lighe
Gleann Suileag
Glen Loy
GREAT GLEN WAY
Kilmonivaig
COMMANDO MEMORIAL
Spean Bridge
Bohenie
Moy
Glen Finnan
VIADUCT
Wauchan
Druim Fada
Glen Loy Forest
Strone
Brackletter
Highbridge
Inverroy
Roybridge
Achluachrach
Murlaggan
Roughburn
Muirshearlich
Killiechonate
MONESSIE FALLS
Braes o' Lochaber
A86
GLEN SPEAN
GLENFINNAN MONUMENT
Kinlocheil
Fassfern
NEPTUNE'S STAIRCASE LOCKS
TOR CASTLE
Drumsallie
LOCH EIL
A830
TREASURES OF THE EARTH
Corpach
Banavie
B8004
Leanachan Forest
Torlundy
NEVIS RANGE MOUNTAIN EXPERIENCE
BEINN CHLIANAIG
Fersit
South Garvan
A861
Duisky
Blaich
Caol
Lochyside
INVERLOCHY CASTLE
Achaphubuil
Camusnagaul
Inverlochy
BEN NEVIS DISTILLERY VISITOR CENTRE
Claggan
Trislaig
Fort William
Achintee
WEST HIGHLAND MUSEUM
Glen Garvan
NM
Allt Làire
Loch Ghuilbinn
CHNO DEARG
STOB CHOIRE CLAURIGH
STOB COIRE EASAIN
Glen Cona
STOB COIRE A'CHEARCAILL
Stronchreggan
Ach'an Todhair
GLEN NEVIS VISITOR CENTRE
Glen Nevis House
Water of Nevis
BEN NEVIS
AONACH BEAG
Lairig Leacach
LOCH TREIG
Druimarbin
Conaglen House
Blarmachfoldach
Creaguaineach Lodge
BEINN NA LAP
Corrour Shooting Lodge
Aryhoulan
Inverscaddle Bay
Corrour Forest
Achriabhach
Corrour Lodge
Glen Scaddle
SGURR NA H-EANCHAINNE
BEN NEVIS AND
LOCH OSSIAN
Blar a'Chaorainn
SGURR A' MHAIM
BINNEIN MOR
Loch Eilde Beag
BEINN NA GUCAIG
Glenrigh Forest
WEST HIGHLAND WAY
MAMORE FOREST
Ardgour
Clovullin
Corran
Inchree
Corran Narrows
Loch Eilde Mor
LEUM UILLEIM
Sallachan
GLEN COE
MAM NA GUALAINN
Kinlochmore
Keppanach
Onich
Kinlochleven
THE ALUMINIUM STORY
BLACKWATER RESERVOIR
Black Water
Sallachan Pt.
North Ballachulish
B863
Tarbert
Inversanda Bay
Inversanda
LOCH LINNHE
Loch Leven
GLENCOE FOLK MUSEUM
Glencoe
AONACH
South Ballachulish
Ballachulish
GLENCOE
Altnafeadh
BEINN A' CHRULAISTE
Black Corries Lodge
B NA CRUAICHE
Rannoch Station
Loch Laidon
Glenduror Forest
Duror
A82
miles
km

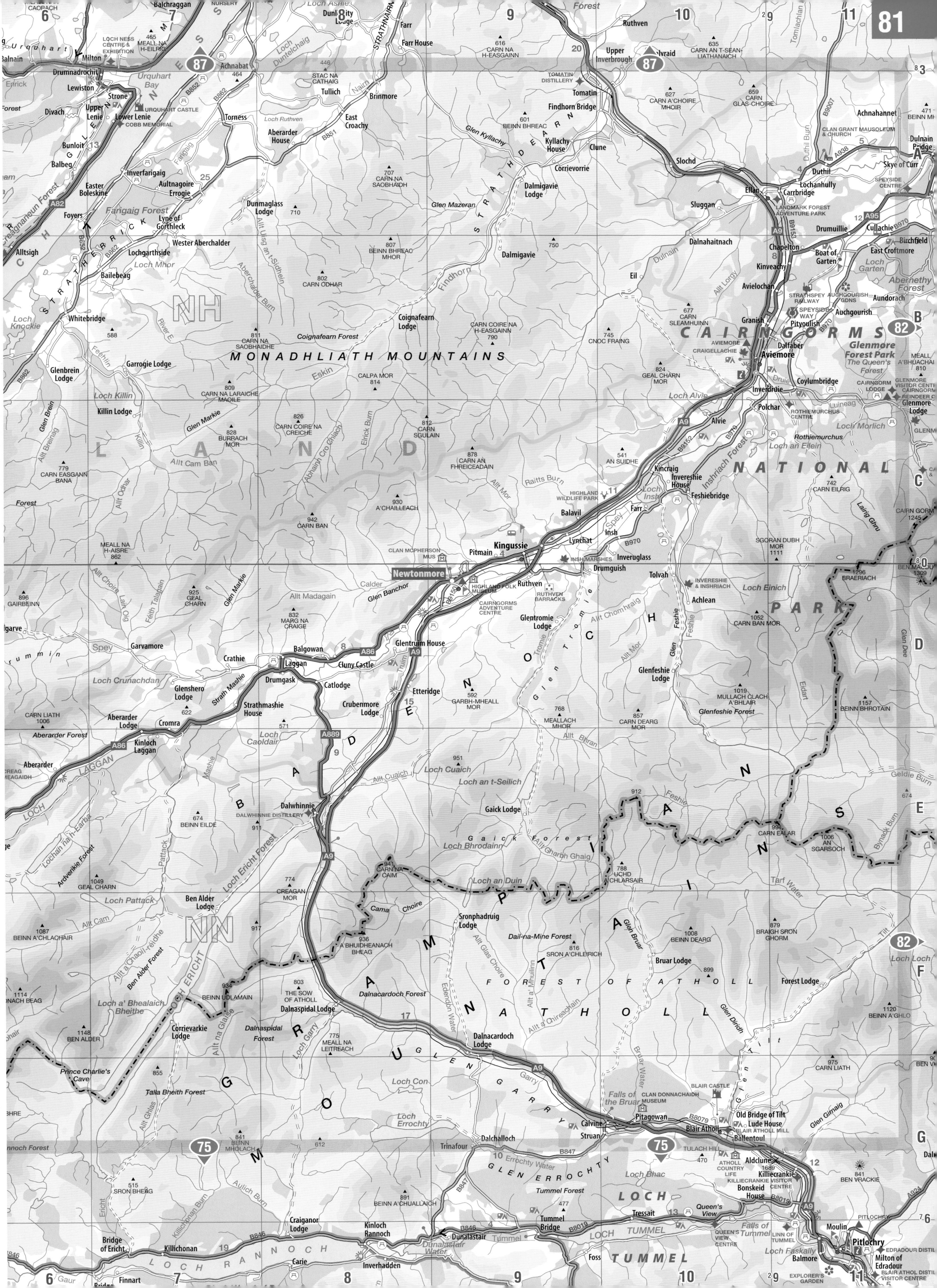

Balchraggan
Loch Ashie
Dunlichity Lodge
STRATHNAIRN
Forest
Ruthven
Farr
Farr House
616 CARN NA H-EASGAINN
635 CARN AN T-SEAN-LIATHANAICH
Milton
LOCH NESS CENTRE & EXHIBITION
465 MEALL NA H-EILRIG
Loch Duntelchaig
87
Achnabat
Upper Inverbrough
Balvraid
Drumnadrochit
464
446 STAC NA CATHAIG
TOMATIN DISTILLERY
Lewiston
Urquhart Bay
Tullich
Tomatin
627 CARN A' CHOIRE MHOIR
659 CARN GLAS-CHOIRE
Strone
URQUHART CASTLE
Brinmore
Divach
Upper Lenie
Lower Lenie
COBB MEMORIAL
Torness
Loch Ruthven
East Croachy
601 BEINN BHREAC
Findhorn Bridge
Achnahannet
CLAN GRANT MAUSOLEUM & CHURCH
Glen Kyllachy
Kyllachy House
Clune
Dulnain Bridge
Bunloit
Aberarder House
Balbeg
Slochd
Duthil
Skye of Curr
Inverfarigaig
707 CARN NA SAOBHAIDH
Corrievorrie
Lochanhully
SPEYSIDE CENTRE
Easter Boleskine
Aultnagoire
Errogie
Dalmigavie Lodge
Ellan
Carrbridge
Sluggan
LANDMARK FOREST ADVENTURE PARK
Foyers
Farigaig Forest
Dunmaglass Lodge
710
Glen Mazeran
Drumuillie
Cullachie
Lyne of Gorthleck
STRATHDEARN
Birchfield
Alltsigh
Wester Aberchalder
807 BEINN BHREAC MHOR
750
Dalnahaitnach
Chapelton
Boat of Garten
East Croftmore
Lochgarthside
Loch Mhor
Dalmigavie
Kinveachy
Loch Garten
Bailebeag
802 CARN ODHAR
Eil
Avielochan
Abernethy Forest
STRATHSPEY RAILWAY
AUCHGOURISH GDNS
Aundorach
NH
Loch Knockie
Whitebridge
SPEYSIDE WAY
Granish
Auchgourish
588
Coignafearn Lodge
677 CARN SLEAMHUINN
Pityoulish
811 CARN NA SAOBHAIDHE
Coignafearn Forest
CARN COIRE NA H-EASGAINN 790
745 CNOC FRAING
CAIRNGORMS
AVIEMORE
82
Dalfaber
Glenmore Forest Park
CRAIGELLACHIE
Aviemore
The Queen's Forest
Garrogie Lodge
MONADHLIATH MOUNTAINS
CALPA MOR 814
824 GEAL CHARN MOR
MEALL A' BHUACHAILLE 810
Glenbrein Lodge
Eskin
809 CARN NA LARAICHE MAOILE
Coylumbridge
CAIRNGORM LODGE
GLENMORE VISITOR CENTRE
REINDEER CENTRE
Loch Killin
Loch Alvie
Inverdruie
Killin Lodge
826 CARN COIRE NA CREICHE
812 CARN SGULAIN
Polchar
Glenmore Lodge
Glen Markie
828 BURRACH MOR
Alvie
ROTHIEMURCHUS CENTRE
Loch Morlich
Glen Brein
Allt Breinag
Rothiemurchus
LAND
Loch an Eilein
878 CARN AN FHREICEADAIN
541 AN SUIDHE
779 CARN EASGANN BANA
Allt Cam Ban
Kincraig
Invereshie House
NATIONAL
Raitts Burn
HIGHLAND WILDLIFE PARK
742 CARN EILRIG
Forest
930 A' CHAILLEACH
Loch Insh
Feshiebridge
Inshriach Forest
Laring Ghru
Balavil
Farr
CAIRN GORM 1245
942 CARN BAN
Lynchat
Insh
MEALL NA H-AISRE 862
CLAN MCPHERSON MUS
Pitmain
Kingussie
B970
SGORAN DUBH MOR 1111
Inveruglass
INSH MARSHES
Drumguish
Newtonmore
Tolvah
1296 BRAERIACH
BEN MACDUI 1309
896 GAIRBEINN
925 GEAL CHARN
Calder
Glen Banchor
HIGHLAND FOLK MUSEUM
Ruthven
RUTHVEN BARRACKS
INVERESHIE & INSHRIACH
Loch Einich
Allt Madagain
CAIRNGORMS ADVENTURE CENTRE
Achlean
PARK
832 MARG NA CRAIGE
Glentromie Lodge
1052 CARN BAN MOR
Garvamore
Spey
Balgowan
Glentruim House
Crathie
Laggan
Cluny Castle
Glen Feshie
Glen Dee
Loch Crunachdan
Drumgask
Catlodge
Glen Tromie
Glenfeshie Lodge
Glenshero Lodge
Strath Mashie
Etteridge
Crubenmore Lodge
592 GARBH-MHEALL MOR
1019 MULLACH CLACH A' BHLAIR
Glenfeshie Forest
1157 BEINN BHROTAIN
CARN LIATH 1006
622
Strathmashie House
768 MEALLACH MHOR
857 CARN DEARG MOR
Aberarder Lodge
Cromra
571
Eidart
Aberarder Forest
Loch Caoldair
Kinloch Laggan
Aberarder
951
Loch Cuaich
Allt Cuaich
Loch an t-Seilich
Geldie Burn
CREAG MEAGAIDH
LOCH LAGGAN
912
Feshie
674
Dalwhinnie
Gaick Lodge
674 BEINN EILDE
DALWHINNIE DISTILLERY
911
994 CARN EALAR
1006 AN SGARSOCH
Bynack Burn
Gaick Forest
Loch Bhrodainn
Allt Gharbh Ghaig
Lochan na h-Earba
Ardverikie Forest
Loch Ericht Forest
941 CARN NA CAIM
788 UCHD A' CHLARSAIR
Tarf Water
1049 GEAL CHARN
774 CREAGAN MOR
Loch an Duin
Loch Pattack
Ben Alder Lodge
Cama' Choire
Sronphadruig Lodge
Glen Bruar
879 BRAIGH SRON GHORM
1087 BEINN A' CHLACHAIR
NN
917
Dail-na-Mine Forest
1008 BEINN DEARG
936 A' BHUIDHEANACH BHEAG
816 SRON A' CHLEIRICH
Bruar Lodge
Loch Loch
Allt a' Chaoil-reidhe
Ben Alder Forest
899
FOREST OF ATHOLL
Forest Lodge
1114 BEINN BHEOIL
803 THE SOW OF ATHOLL
BEINN UDLAMAIN
Loch a' Bhealaich Bheithe
LOCH ERICHT
Dalnaspidal Lodge
Dalnacardoch Forest
ATHOLL
1120 BEINN A' GHLO
1148 BEN ALDER
Corrievarkie Lodge
Dalnaspidal Forest
775 MEALL NA LEITREACH
Dalnacardoch Lodge
Glen Tilt
Prince Charlie's Cave
855
GLEN GARRY
Loch Con
975 CARN LIATH
Talla Bheith Forest
Falls of the Bruar
CLAN DONNACHAIDH MUSEUM
BLAIR CASTLE
Loch Errochty
Calvine
Pitagowan
Old Bridge of Tilt
Lude House
Glen Girnaig
Struan
Blair Atholl
BLAIR ATHOLL MILL
Ballentoul
841 BEINN MHOLACH
612
Trinafour
Dalchalloch
75
TULACH HILL 470
Aldclune
1689 KILLIECRANKIE VISITOR CENTRE
ATHOLL COUNTRY LIFE
Killiecrankie
GLEN ERROCHTY
Loch Bhac
841 BEN VRACKIE
515 SRON BHEAG
Tummel Forest
LOCH
891 BEINN A' CHUALLAICH
477
Bonskeid House
Tressait
Queen's View
Craiganor Lodge
Kinloch Rannoch
Tummel Bridge
QUEEN'S VIEW CENTRE
Falls of Tummel
LINN OF TUMMEL
Moulin
PITLOCHRY
Bridge of Ericht
Killichonan
LOCH TUMMEL
Pitlochry
Dunalastair
Dunalastair Water
Loch Faskally
EDRADOUR DISTILLERY
Milton of Edradour
LOCH RANNOCH
Carie
Foss
TUMMEL
Balmore
Inverhadden
EXPLORER'S GARDEN
BLAIR ATHOL MILL VISITOR CENTRE
Finnart
6 7 8 9 10 11
A B C D E F G

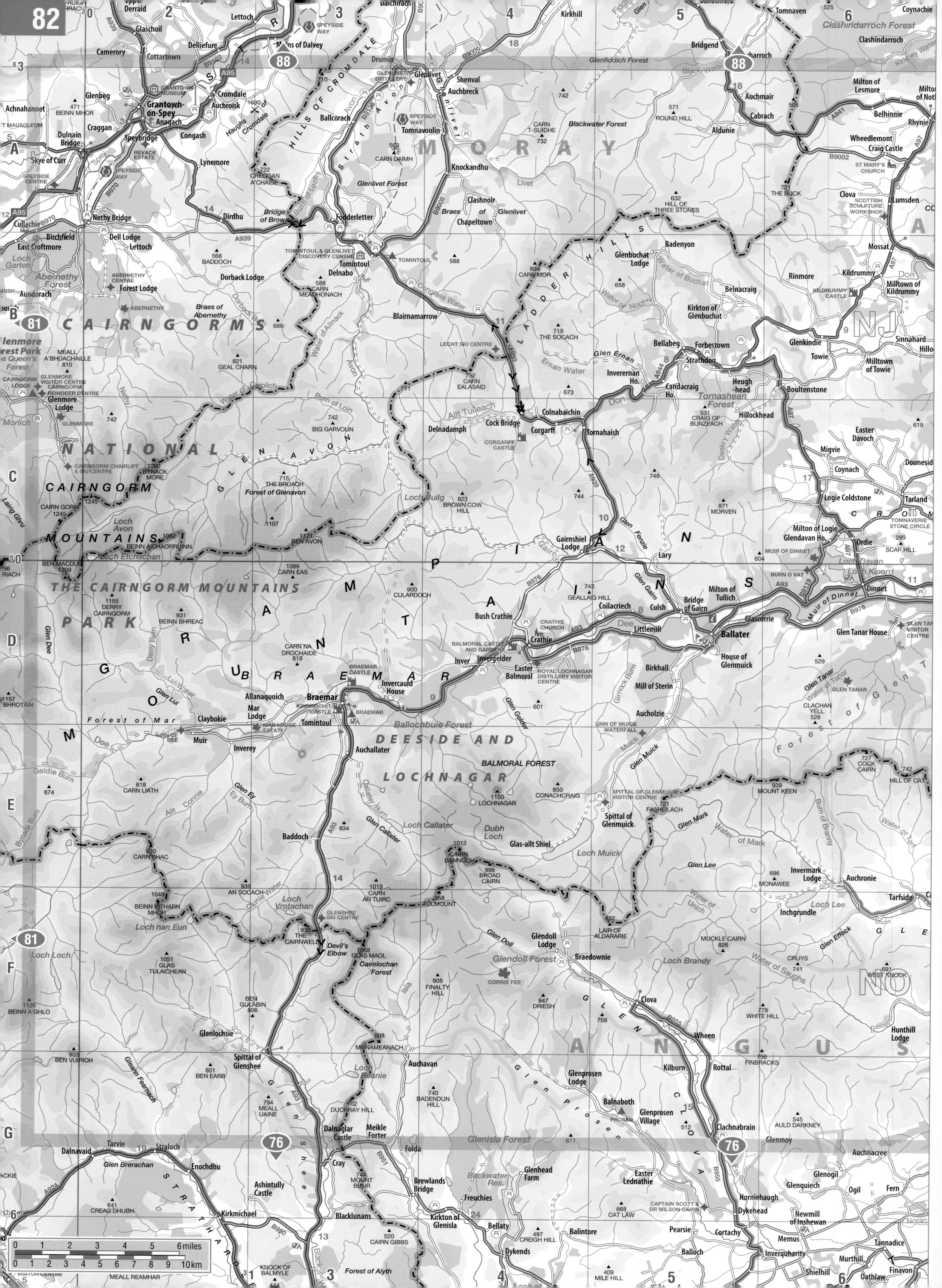

Derraid
Lettoch
Glaschoil
Dalchirach
Kirkhill
Bridgend
Tomnaven
Coynachie
Clashindarroch Forest
Clashindarroch
Camerory
Dellefure
Cottartown
Mains of Dalvey
SPEYSIDE WAY
HILLS OF CROMDALE
Drumin
Glenlivet
GLENLIVET DISTILLERY
Shenval
Auchbreck
Glenfiddich Forest
Black Water
Auchmair
Cabrach
Milton of Lesmore
Belhinnie
Rhynie
GRANTOWN MUSEUM
Grantown-on-Spey
Anagach
Cromdale
Auchroisk
Haughs of Cromdale
Achnahannet
471 BEINN MHOR
Glenbeg
Craggan
Congash
Ballcorach
Strath Avon
Tomnavoulin
CARN T-SUIDHE 732
Blackwater Forest
571 ROUND HILL
Aldunie
Wheedlemont
Craig Castle
MAUSOLEUM
Dulnain Bridge
Speybridge
REVACK ESTATE
569 CARN DAIMH
M O R A Y
ST MARY'S CHURCH
Skye of Curr
Lynemore
722 CREGGAN A' CHAISE
Glenlivet Forest
Knockandhu
Livet
721 THE BUCK
Clova
SCOTTISH SCULPTURE WORKSHOP
Lumsden
SPEYSIDE CENTRE
Nethy Bridge
Dirdhu
Bridge of Brown
Burn of Lochy
Fodderletter
Braes of Glenlivet
Clashnoir
Chapeltown
632 HILL OF THREE STONES
Cullachie
Birchfield
Dell Lodge
Lettoch
East Croftmore
Loch Garten
Abernethy Forest
568 BADDOCH
TOMINTOUL & GLENLIVET DISCOVERY CENTRE
Tomintoul
Delnabo
588
LADDER HILLS
Badenyon
Glenbuchat Lodge
Mossat
Kildrummy
Milltown of Kildrummy
KILDRUMMY CASTLE
Rinmore
804 CARN MOR
658
Water of Buchat
Belnacraig
Water of Nochty
Kirkton of Glenbuchat
Aundorach
Forest Lodge
ABERNETHY CENTRE
Dorback Lodge
588 CARN MEADHONACH
Conglass Water
Braes of Abernethy
CAIRNGORMS
688
Water of Ailnack
Blairnamarrow
718 THE SOCHACH
Bellabeg
Forbestown
Strathdon
Glenkindie
Towie
Sinnahard
Milltown of Towie
Glenmore Forest Park
Queen's Forest
MEALL A'BHUACHAILLE 810
821 GEAL CHARN
LECHT SKI CENTRE
792 CARN EALASAID
Glen Ernan
Ernan Water
Inverernan Ho.
Candacraig Ho.
Heugh-head
Boultenstone
CAIRNGORM LODGE
GLENMORE VISITOR CENTRE
CAIRNGORM REINDEER CENTRE
Glenmore Lodge
Water of Caiplich
711
Burn of Loin
673
Tornashean Forest
531 CRAIG OF BUNZEACH
Hillockhead
Morlich
GLENMORE
742
742 BIG GARVOUN
Allt Tuileach
Delnadamph
Cock Bridge
Colnabaichin
Corgarff
CORGARFF CASTLE
Tornahaish
Deskry Water
Easter Davoch
619
NATIONAL
GLEN AVON
CAIRNGORM CHAIRLIFT & SKI CENTRE
1090 BYNACK MORE
715 THE BRUACH
Forest of Glenavon
749
Migvie
Coynach
Douneside
CAIRNGORM
Loch Builg
823 BROWN COW HILL
744
871 MORVEN
Logie Coldstone
Tarland
Lairig Ghru
CAIRN GORM 1245
1245
Loch Avon
1107
Glen Fenzie
Milton of Logie
Glendavan Ho.
TOMNAVERIE STONE CIRCLE
MOUNTAINS
1082
BEINN A' CHAORRUINN
1171 BEN AVON
Gairnshiel Lodge
Lary
MUIR OF DINNET
604
Ordie
299 SCAR HILL
Loch Etchachan
BEN MACDUI 1309
1089 CARN EAS
Gairn
Loch Davan
Loch Kinord
Dinnet
BURN O VAT
RIACH
THE CAIRNGORM MOUNTAINS
900 CULARDOCH
B976
743 GEALLAIG HILL
Glen Gairn
Milton of Tullich
Bridge of Gairn
Muir of Dinnet
PARK
1155 DERRY CAIRNGORM
931 BEINN BHREAC
Bush Crathie
Coilacriech
Culsh
CRATHIE CHURCH
Crathie
Dee
Littlemill
Glascorrie
Ballater
Glen Tanar House
GLEN TANAR VISITOR CENTRE
Glen Dee
Derry Burn
CARN NA DROCHAIDE 818
BALMORAL CASTLE AND GARDENS
House of Glenmuick
Birkhall
529
Lui Water
Glen Lui
BRAEMAR CASTLE
Invercauld House
Inver
Invergelder
Easter Balmoral
ROYAL LOCHNAGAR DISTILLERY VISITOR CENTRE
Mill of Sterin
Glen Tanar
Water of Tanar
GLEN TANAR
BHROTAIN 1157
Allanaquoich
Braemar
KINDROCHIT CASTLE
BRAEMAR
Mar Lodge
Glen Gelder
601
Girnock Burn
Aucholzie
CLACHAN YELL 526
Forest of Glen Tanar
Forest of Mar
Claybokie
MAR LODGE ESTATE
Tomintoul
Ballochbuie Forest
LINN OF MUICK WATERFALL
LINN OF DEE
Muir
Inverey
Auchallater
DEESIDE AND LOCHNAGAR
BALMORAL FOREST
Glen Muick
727 COCK CAIRN
742 HILL OF CAT
939 MOUNT KEEN
Geldie Burn
674
818 CARN LIATH
Glen Ey
Ey Burn
Allt Connie
Callater Burn
1150 LOCHNAGAR
850 CONACHCRAIG
SPITTAL OF GLENMUICK VISITOR CENTRE
721 FASHEILACH
Burn of Branny
Spittal of Glenmuick
Glen Mark
Water of Mark
Bynack Burn
Glen Callater
Loch Callater
834
Baddoch
Dubh Loch
Glas-allt Shiel
Loch Muick
920 CARN BHAC
1012 CAIRN BANNOCH
998 BROAD CAIRN
Glen Lee
696 MONAWEE
Invermark Lodge
Auchronie
Tarfside
Loch Lee
Inchgrundle
1048 BEINN IUTHARN MHOR
939 AN SOCACH
Clunie Water
Loch Vrotachan
GLENSHEE SKI CENTRE
1019 CARN AN TUIRC
958 TOLMOUNT
Water of Unich
832 LAIR OF ALDARARIE
Loch nan Eun
933 THE CAIRNWELL
Devil's Elbow
1068 GLAS MAOL
Caenlochan Forest
Glen Doll
Glendoll Lodge
Glendoll Forest
Braedownie
MUCKLE CAIRN 826
Glen Effock
Loch Loch
1051 GLAS TULAICHEAN
905 FINALTY HILL
CORRIE FEE
Loch Brandy
CRUYS 741
Water of Saughs
691 WEST KNOCK
1120 BEINN A' GHLO
BEN GULABIN 806
947 DRIESH
Clova
758
B955
778 WHITE HILL
Glenlochsie
808 MONAMENEACH
Wheen
Hunthill Lodge
903 BEN VUIRICH
Spittal of Glenshee
801 BEN EARB
Gleann Fearnach
Glen Shee
Loch Beanie
Auchavan
A N G U S
Glen Prosen
Kilburn
Rottal
756 FINBRACKS
740 BADENDUN HILL
Glenprosen Lodge
794 MEALL UAINE
702 DUCHRAY HILL
Balnaboth
PROSEN
Glenprosen Village
512
GLEN CLOVA
Clachnabrain
545 AULD DARKNEY
Dalnaglar Castle
Meikle Forter
Folda
Glenisla Forest
611
Glenmoy
Dalnavaid
Tarvie
Straloch
Enochdhu
Glen Brerachan
STRATHARDLE
Cray
744 MOUNT BLAIR
Brewlands Bridge
Backwater Res.
Glenhead Farm
Easter Lednathie
Auchnacree
Glenogil
Glenquiech
Ogil
Fern
Ashintully Castle
641 CREAG DHUBH
Kirkmichael
Blacklunans
Freuchies
Kirkton of Glenisla
668 CAT LAW
CAPTAIN SCOTT & DR WILSON CAIRN
Horniehaugh
Dykehead
Newmill of Inshewan
Bellaty
497 CREIGH HILL
Balintore
Pearsie
Cortachy
Memus
Tannadice
520 CAIRN GIBBS
Dykends
Balloch
Inverquharity
Murthill
KNOCK OF BALMYLE
Forest of Alyth
409 MILL HILL
Shielhill
Oathlaw
Finavon
MEALL REAMHAR
VISITOR CENTRE
0 1 2 3 4 5 6 miles
0 1 2 3 4 5 6 7 8 9 10 km
NJ
NO

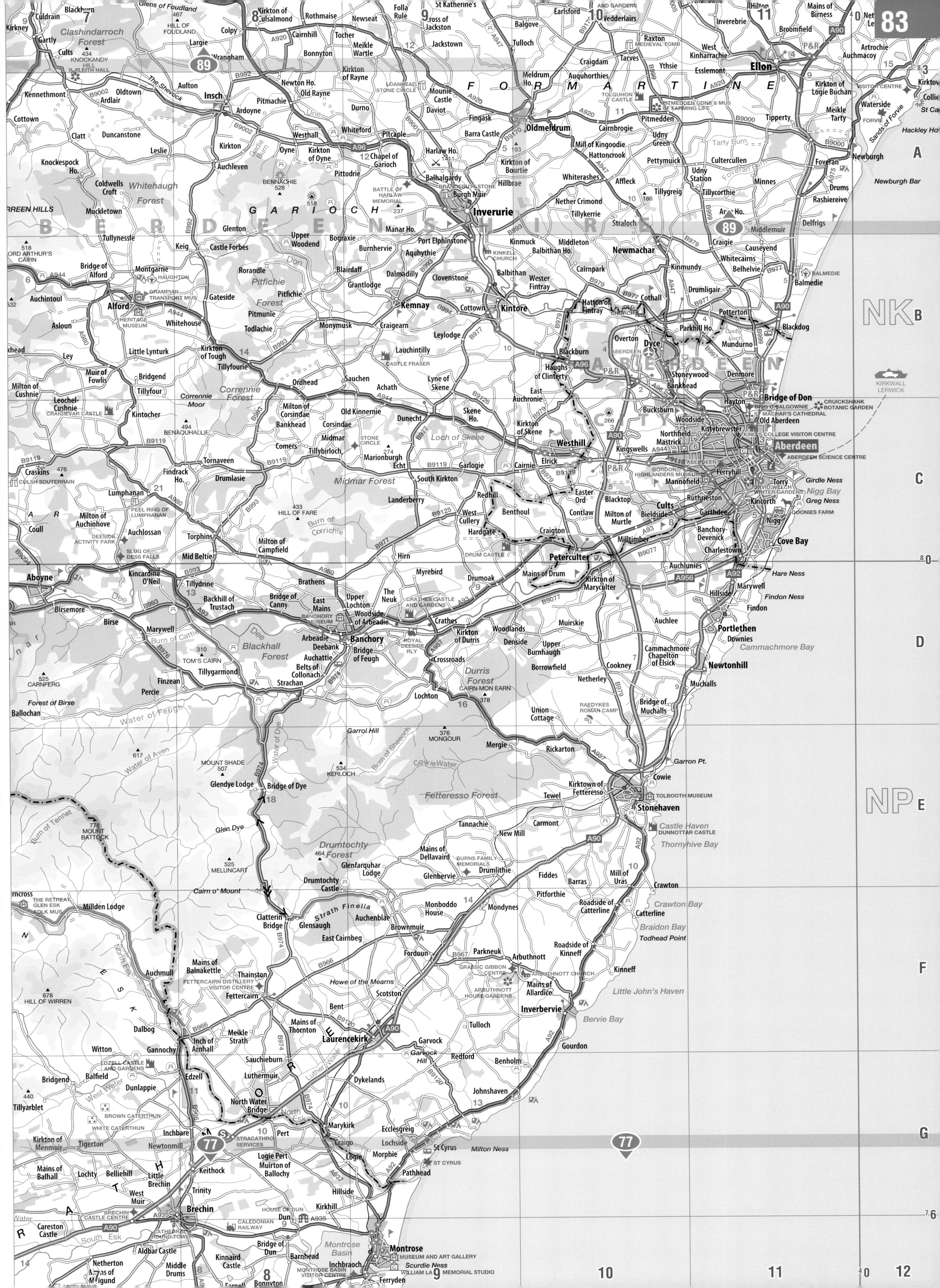
Clashindarroch Forest
Glens of Foudland
HILL OF FOUDLAND
Kirkton of Culsalmond
Rothmaise
Newseat
Folla Rule
St Katherine's
Cross of Jackston
Jackstown
Earlsford
Vedderlairs
Balgove
Tulloch
Raxton
MEDIEVAL TOMB
Inverebrie
Mains of Birness
Broomfield
Artrochie
Auchmacoy
West Kinharrachie
Esslemont
Ellon
Kirkton of Logie Buchan
VISITOR CENTRE
Kirkton
Waterside
FORVIE
Sands of Forvie
Hackley Hd
Newburgh
Newburgh Bar
Foveran
Drums
Rashiereive
Middlemuir
Delfrigs
Kirkney
Culdrain
Gartly
Cults
KNOCKANDY HILL
LEITH HALL
Largie
Colpy
Wrangham
Insch
Aulton
The Shevock
Kennethmont
Oldtown
Ardlair
Ardoyne
Newton Ho.
Old Rayne
Pitmachie
Kirkton of Rayne
LOANHEAD STONE CIRCLE
Mounie Castle
Daviot
Durno
Tocher
Meikle Wartle
Bonnyton
Cairnhill
FORMARTINE
Meldrum Ho.
Craigdam
Tarves
Ythsie
Auquhorthies
TOLQUHON CASTLE
PITMEDDEN GDNS & MUS OF FARMING LIFE
Pitmedden
Tipperty
Oldmeldrum
Cairnbrogie
Udny Green
Tarty Burn
Mill of Kingoodie
Hattoncrook
Pettymuick
Cultercullen
Udny Station
Minnes
Cottown
Clatt
Duncanstone
Leslie
Kirkton
Westhall
Oyne
Kirkton of Oyne
Whiteford
Pitcaple
Chapel of Garioch
Fingask
Barra Castle
Harlaw Ho.
Balhalgardy
BRANDSBUTT STONE
Burgh Muir
Kirkton of Bourtie
Hillbrae
Whiterashes
Affleck
Tillygreig
Tillycorthie
Knockespock Ho.
Auchleven
Pittodrie
BENNACHIE
BATTLE OF HARLAW MEMORIAL
Coldwells Croft
Whitehaugh Forest
Muckletown
GARIOCH
Inverurie
Nether Crimond
Tillykerrie
Straloch
Arnage Ho.
ABERDEENSHIRE
Tullynessle
Glenton
Upper Woodend
Bograxie
Manar Ho.
Port Elphinstone
Kinmuck
Middleton
Balbithan Ho.
Craigie
Causeyend
Whitecairns
Belhelvie
Balmedie
BALMEDIE
LORD ARTHUR'S CAIRN
Keig
Castle Forbes
Burnhervie
Aquhythie
KINKELL CHURCH
Newmachar
Kinmundy
Bridge of Alford
Montgarrie
HAUGHTON
GRAMPIAN TRANSPORT MUS
HERITAGE MUSEUM
Rorandle
Pitfichie Forest
Blairdaff
Grantlodge
Dalmadilly
Clovenstone
Balbithan
Wester Fintray
Cairnpark
Drumligair
Auchintoul
Alford
Gateside
Pitfichie
Pitmunie
Kemnay
Cottown
Kintore
Hatton of Fintray
OLD CHURCH
Cothall
Potterton
Blackdog
Asloun
Whitehouse
Todlachie
Monymusk
Craigearn
Leylodge
Overton
Dyce
Parkhill Ho.
Corby Loch
Mundurno
Ley
Little Lynturk
Kirkton of Tough
Tillyfourie
Lauchintilly
CASTLE FRASER
Blackburn
Haughs of Clinterty
ABERDEEN
Stoneywood
Denmore
Bankhead
Muir of Fowlis
Bridgend
Tillyfour
Sauchen
Achath
Lyne of Skene
Milton of Cushnie
Leochel-Cushnie
CRAIGIEVAR CASTLE
Correnie Moor
Correnie Forest
Ordhead
Milton of Corsindae
Bankhead
Old Kinnernie
Corsindae
Dunecht
Skene Ho.
East Auchronie
Kirkton of Skene
Bucksburn
Woodside
Bridge of Don
Hayton
BRIG O' BALGOWNIE
ST MACHAR'S CATHEDRAL
Old Aberdeen
CRUICKSHANK BOTANIC GARDEN
KIRKWALL LERWICK
Kintocher
BENAQUHALLIE
Midmar
STONE CIRCLE
Marionburgh
Echt
Loch of Skene
Westhill
Kingswells
Northfield
Mastrick
Kittybrewster
KING'S COLLEGE VISITOR CENTRE
Aberdeen
ABERDEEN SCIENCE CENTRE
Tornaveen
Comers
Tillybirloch
Garlogie
Elrick
Cairnie
GORDON HIGHLANDERS MUSEUM
Ferryhill
Craskins
CULSH SOUTERRAIN
Findrack Ho.
Drumlasie
South Kirkton
Midmar Forest
Easter Ord
Mannofield
Torry
DAVID WELCH WINTER GARDENS
Girdle Ness
Nigg Bay
Greg Ness
Lumphanan
PEEL RING OF LUMPHANAN
Milton of Auchinhove
Coull
HILL OF FARE
Burn of Corrichie
Landerberry
Redhill
West Cullery
Benthoul
Blacktop
Contlaw
Milton of Murtle
Cults
Bieldside
Ruthrieston
Kincorth
Garthdee
Nigg
DOONIES FARM
DEESIDE ACTIVITY PARK
Auchlossan
SLUG OF DESS FALLS
Torphins
Mid Beltie
Milton of Campfield
Hardgate
Craigton
Milltimber
Banchory-Devenick
Charlestown
Cove Bay
DRUM CASTLE
Hirn
Peterculter
Auchlunies
Aboyne
Kincardine O'Neil
Tillydrine
Brathens
Myrebird
Drumoak
Mains of Drum
Kirkton of Maryculter
Hare Ness
Marywell
Findon Ness
Hillside
Findon
Birsemore
Backhill of Trustach
Bridge of Canny
East Mains
Upper Lochton
The Neuk
CRATHES CASTLE AND GARDENS
Woodside of Arbeadie
BANCHORY MUSEUM
Crathes
Kirkton of Durris
Woodlands
Muirskie
Auchlee
Portlethen
Downies
Cammachmore Bay
Birse
Marywell
Burn of Cattie
Blackhall Forest
Arbeadie
Deebank
Banchory
Bridge of Feugh
ROYAL DEESIDE RLY
Crossroads
Denside
Upper Burnhaugh
Borrowfield
Cammachmore
Chapelton of Elsick
Cookney
Newtonhill
TOM'S CAIRN
Tillygarmond
Auchattie
Belts of Collonach
Durris Forest
Netherley
Muchalls
CARNFERG
Finzean
Percie
Strachan
Lochton
CAIRN-MON EARN
RAEDYKES ROMAN CAMP
Bridge of Muchalls
Forest of Birse
Ballochan
Union Cottage
Water of Feugh
Garrol Hill
MONGOUR
Mergie
Rickarton
Garron Pt.
Water of Aven
MOUNT SHADE
Water of Dye
KERLOCH
Burn of Sheeoch
Cowie Water
Cowie
Glendye Lodge
Bridge of Dye
Fetteresso Forest
Kirktown of Fetteresso
TOLBOOTH MUSEUM
Tewel
Stonehaven
Burn of Tennet
MOUNT BATTOCK
Glen Dye
Tannachie
Carmont
New Mill
Castle Haven
DUNNOTTAR CASTLE
Thornyhive Bay
Drumtochty Forest
Mains of Dellavaird
BURNS FAMILY MEMORIALS
Drumlithie
MELUNCART
Glenfarquhar Lodge
Glenbervie
Fiddes
Barras
Mill of Uras
Crawton
Cairn o' Mount
Drumtochty Castle
Pitforthie
Roadside of Catterline
Catterline
Crawton Bay
Braidon Bay
Todhead Point
THE RETREAT GLEN ESK FOLK MUS
Millden Lodge
Clatterin Bridge
Strath Finella
Glensaugh
Auchenblae
Monboddo House
Mondynes
East Cairnbeg
Brownmuir
Fordoun
Parkneuk
Arbuthnott
Roadside of Kinneff
Kinneff
North Esk
Auchmull
Mains of Balnakettle
GRASSIC GIBBON CENTRE
ARBUTHNOTT CHURCH
ARBUTHNOTT HOUSE GARDENS
Mains of Allardice
Little John's Haven
HILL OF WIRREN
FETTERCAIRN DISTILLERY VISITOR CENTRE
Thainston
Howe of the Mearns
Fettercairn
Scotston
Inverbervie
Bervie Bay
Bent
Dalbog
Meikle Strath
Mains of Thornton
Laurencekirk
Tulloch
Gourdon
Inch of Arnhall
Witton
Gannochy
EDZELL CASTLE AND GARDENS
Sauchieburn
Garvock
Garvock Hill
Redford
Benholm
Bridgend
Balfield
Edzell
Luthermuir
Dykelands
Johnshaven
West Water
Dunlappie
Tillyarblet
BROWN CATERTHUN
WHITE CATERTHUN
North Water Bridge
Luther Water
Marykirk
Ecclesgreig
Inchbare
Pert
Kirkton of Menmuir
Tigerton
Newtonmill
STRACATHRO SERVICES
Craigo
Lochside
St Cyrus
ST CYRUS
Milton Ness
Logie Pert
Morphie
Mains of Balhall
Lochty
Belliehill
Little Brechin
Keithock
Muirton of Ballochy
Logie
Pathhead
Trinity
Hillside
West Muir
Brechin
BRECHIN CASTLE CENTRE
HOUSE OF DUN
Kirkhill
CALEDONIAN RAILWAY
Dun
Careston Castle
CATHEDRAL ROUND TOWER
South Esk
Bridge of Dun
Montrose Basin
Montrose
MUSEUM AND ART GALLERY
Aldbar Castle
Kinnaird Castle
Barnhead
Scurdie Ness
WILLIAM LAMB MEMORIAL STUDIO
Netherton
Mains of Melgund
Middle Drums
MONTROSE BASIN VISITOR CENTRE
Inchbraoch
Bonnyton
Ferryden
NK
NP
A
B
C
D
E
F
G
7
8
9
10
11
12

Sound of Spuir
Eilean Bhearnaraigh (Berneray)
Ruisigearraidh
Borgh
Baile
Boreray
CAOLAS NA HEARADH
Killegray
Ensay
Cairminis
Srannda
Roghadal
Boirseam
Lingreabhagh
Lingarabay I.
ST CLEMENT'S CHURCH
Langay
Vallay
Renish Pt.
Haskeir I.
Haskeir Eagach
90
Aird a'Mhòrain
Caolas Bheàrnaraigh
Torogay
Groay
Gilsay
Lingay
Scaravay
Veilish Pt.
Lingay
Port nan Long
Vallay
Oronsay
Baile Mhic Phail
Griminish Pt.
Sursay
Tahay
Opsay
Hermetray
Scolpaig
SCOLPAIG TOWER
Vallay Strand
Solas
Greinetobht
Trumaisgearraidh
Malacleit
Baile Mhartainn
Manish Pt.
Hosta
Taigh a Ghearraidh
Loch nan Geireann
Loch Aimhiseaigh
Groatay
Lochportain
Causamul
Aird an Rùnair
Hogha Gearraidh
Baile Raghaill
Glen Drolla
Loch Fada
Rubha Port Scolpaig
MARRIVAL
Loch Sgealtair
Loch nam Madadh (Lochmaddy)
TAIGH CHEARSABHAGH MUS & ARTS CENTRE
Weaver's Pt.
UIG
LOCHMADDY
TARBERT
AN CAOLAS MHONACH
Ceann a Bhaigh
Claddach-Knockline
Loch Scadabhagh
Loch nam Madadh
Rubha nam Plèac
Madadh Gruamach
Paibeil
Baile Mor
CLACH MHOR A CHE STANDING STONES
Cladach Chireboist
Loch Hunna
UIBHIST A TUATH (NORTH UIST)
BARPA LANGASS CAIRN
SOUTH LEE
An t-Aigeach
Waternish Point
Na h-eileanan Monach (Heisker or Monach Islands)
Stockay
Kirkibost Island
Vorogay
Loch Langais
Loch Euphoirt
Rubha Mhic Gille-mhicheil
Clachan na Luib
Loch Euphoirt
Saighdinis
Ceann Iar
Ceann Ear
Teanna Mhachair
Samhla
Càrinis
Loch Caraboist
Loch Obasaraigh
EAVAL
Baile Sear (Baleshare)
Bail Uachdraich
TRINITY TEMPLE
Cairinis
Bail' Iochdrach
Oitir Mhòr
Floddaybeg
Beul an Toim
BENBECULA
Baile Glas
Griomasaigh (Grimsay)
Bagh Mor
Scotbheinn
Floddaymore
Ronay
Baile a Mhanaich
Uachdar
Gramsdal
Flodaigh
Flodday
Baile nan Cailleach
BEINN NA FAOGHLA (BENBECULA)
Rubha na Rodagrich
Maragay Mor
Griminis
Torlum
Loch Uisgeabhagh
Maaey Riabhach
Loch Chreabhagh
Lionacleit
Gualan
Creag Ghoraidh
Rubha Cam nan Gall
Hornish Pt.
Ardivachar Pt.
Iochdar
Aird a Mhachair
Clachan
Bagh nam Faoileann
Fuidhaigh (Wiay)
Loch Bi
Loch a Charnain
Steisay
Sanndabhaig
Gasay
Loch Carnan
Geirinis
OUR LADY OF THE ISLES STATUE
Luirsay Dubh
Stadhlaigearraidh
Loch Sgioport
Dreumasdal
Ornish I.
HOWMORE
Loch Druidibeg
Tobha Mor
LOCH DRUIDIBEG NATURE RESERVE
Moi a'Tuath
NF
Verran I.
Sniseabhal
HECLA
Rubha Rossel
Rubha'Aird-mhicheil
Staoinebrig
Rubha Bhilidh
Ormiclate Castle
Loch Olaigh
BEINN MHOR
Rubha Hellisdale
UIBHIST A DEAS (SOUTH UIST)
SOUTH UIST MACHAIR
Rubha Ardvule
Bornais
Taobh a Thuath Loch Aineort
Loch Cill Donain
Calvay
KILDONAN MUSEUM
Rubha Bolum
Cill Donnain
Unasary
Gearraidh Bhailteas
Minngearraidh
Loch Aineort
FLORA MACDONALD'S BIRTHPLACE
Loch Sniogaiscleit
Aisgernis
STULAVAL
Stuley
Loch Stùlabhal
Dalabrog
Taobh a Tuath Loch Baghasdail
Crois Dughaill
Rubha na Creige Móire
Loch Baghasdail (Lochboisdale)
Cille Pheadair
Loch Baghasdail
Baghasdal
Calvay
Ceann a Deas Loch Baghasdail
Rubha Meall na Hoe
Trosaraidh
Gearraidh na Monadh
Smercleit
Cille Bhrighde
South Glendale
MALLAIG OBAN (Winter only)
Rubha na h-Ordaig
Pol a Charra
Taobh a Chaolais
Ludag
Caolas Eiriosgaigh
Sgeir a'Mhill
Lingeigh (Lingay)
Haunn
Calvay
Am Baile
Bun a'Mhuillin
Hartamul
Fiaraigh (Fiaray)
Caolas Fhiaraigh
Coilleag
Eiriosgaigh (Eriskay)
Scurrival Pt.
Caolas Bharaigh
Eolaigearraidh
CILLE BHARRA
Fuideigh (Fuday)
Stack Is.
Orosay
Traigh Mhòr
Oitir Mhòr
Hellisay
Gighay
Greian Head
Claid
BARRA
BEN CLIAD
Cuidhir
Aird Mhor
Aird Mhidhinis
Bruairnis
Caolas Sheileasaigh
Borve Pt.
Allathasdal
Bagh Shiarabhagh
Baile na Creige
Borgh
Buaile nam Bodach
Fuiay
EILEAN BHARRAIGH (BARRA)
Bruernish Pt.
Doirlinn Hd.
Tangasdal
HEAVAL
Earsairidh
BARRA HERITAGE CENTRE
Bagh a Chaisteil (Castlebay)
Breibhig
Rubha Mor
KIESSIMUL (KISIMUL) CASTLE
TIREE (Apr - Oct, Wed only)
Bhatarsaigh (Vatersay)
Uidh
Bagh Bhatarsaigh
Bhatarsaigh
Muldoanich
OBAN
Flodaigh (Flodday)
Caolas Shanndraigh
78
Sanndraigh (Sandray)
Greanamul
Caolas Phabaigh
WESTERN ISLES
Ard Beag
Trumpan
TRUMPAN CHURCH
BEN GEARY
Ardmore Pt.
Lower Halistra
Upper Halistra
Hallin
Dunvegan Head
LOCH DUNVEGAN
Mingay
Isay
Stein
Galtrigill
Claigan
Borreraig
Uig
BEINN BHREAC
Husabost
An Ceannaich
Loch Pooltiel
Feriniquarrie
Totaig
Lower Milovaig
Glasphein
Oisgill Bay
Upper Milovaig
Lephin
Colbost
DUNVEGAN CASTLE
LIGHTHOUSE
Neist Point
Holmisdale
Glen Dale
Skinidin
Dunvegan
Moonen Bay
HEALABHAL MHOR
Ramasaig
Hoe Rape
Macleod's Tables
Orbost
HEALABHAL BHEAG
Hoe Point
Geodha Mor
MACLEOD'S MAIDENS
Idrigill Point
Canna
A'Chill
Garrisdale Pt.
Oigh-sgeir
Scale : 1:250 000
(approx 4 miles to 1 inch)
6 miles
10 km

8
9
10
11
12
13
91
Fladda-chùain
Eilean Trodday
Rubha Hunish
Rubha na h-Aiseig
Duntulm Castle
Duntulm
Balmacqueen
Kilmaluag
Lub Score
Hungladder
Borneskeitaig
Skye Museum of Island Life
Eilean Flodigarry
Flodigarry
Meall na Suiramach 543
Kilmuir
Flora MacDonald's Memorial
Kilvaxter
Balgown
The Quiraing
Digg
Glashvin
Staffin Bay
Staffin I.
Brogaig
Staffin
Linicro
Totscore
Stenscholl
TROTTERNISH
Kilt Rock
Kilt Rock & Mealt Falls
Kilbride Point
466 Biod Buidhe
Elishader
Loch Mealt
Maligar
Valtos
Ascrib Islands
Idrigill
Uig
Uig Bay
Marishader
Rubha nam Brathairean
Garros
Balnaknock
611 Beinn Edra
Breckrey
Culnaknock
Ru Chorachan
LOCH
Earlish
Lealt
Lealt Falls
Lower Tote
Upper Tote
SNIZORT
Peinlich
Hinnisdal
607 Creag a' Lain
Greshornish Pt.
Lyndale Pt.
Lusta
Kingsburgh
719 The Storr
Old Man of Storr
Lyndale Ho.
Greshornish
Treaslane
Flashader
Suladale
Eyre
TROTTERNISH
Edinbane
The Aird
Kensaleyre
Bernisdale
Haultin
Blackhill
Bearreraig Bay
Holm I.
Loch Leathan
Tote
Glen Bernisdale
Borve
Loch Fada
Skeabost
Carbost
Giant Angus MacAskill Museum
Cruachan Beinn a' Chearcaill 266
Prince Charles's Cave
Lonmore
Uigshader
Drumuie
Achachork
392
Rubha na h Airde Glaise
Roskhill
Glengrasco
Vatten
Shulishadermor
Isle of Skye Candle Company Visitor Centre
Torvaig
Portree
Loch Connan
Harlosh
Ose
Heatherfield
Penifiler
413 Ben Tianavaig
Balmore
417
Glenmore
Loch Duagrich
Mugeary
Camastianavaig
Tianavaig Bay
Holoman Bay
Bracadale
Tarner I.
Ullinish
Struan
Coillore
Conordan
Lower Ollach
Loch Bracadale
Wiay
Upper Ollach
Gedintailor
Battle of the Braes Monument
The Braes
Oronsay
Portnalong
439 Roineval
Narrows of Raasay
Rubha nan Clach
Fiskavaig
444 Ben Lee
Peinchorran
Arnaval 369
Fernilea
Talisker Distillery
Drynoch
Crossal
Loch Sligachan
Gleann Oraid
Carbost
Merkadale
Sconser
Talisker Bay
Talisker
Glamaig 775
Sligachan Hotel
Moll
Eynort
Glen Brittle Forest
Grula
459
445 Beinn Bhreac
Sgurr nan Gillean 964
Glen Sligachan
Loch Ainort
Luib
Dunan
Loch Eynort
Sgurr a' Ghreadaidh 973
736 Marsco
570 Glas Bheinn Mhor
THE CUILLIN HILLS
Glenbrittle
CUILLIN HILLS
Bla Bheinn 928
Bualintur
Glenbrittle House
992 Sgurr Alasdair
924 Sgurr nan Eag
Loch Coruisk
Loch na Creitheach
Camasunary
Strathaird
Kirkibost
Kilmarie
Torrin
Loch Brittle
Rubh an Dunain
Soay Sound
Soay
Loch Scavaig
Ben Meabost 346
Mol-chlach
Elgol
Boat Trips
Glasnakille
Prince Charles's Cave
Rubha na h-Easgainne
Eilean na h-Airde
ISLAND OF SKYE
Island of Rona
125
Eilean Garbh
Eilean Tigh
Garbh Eilean
Caol Rona
Loch a' Sguirr
An Caol
Eilean Fladday
254
Manish Pt.
Torran
Loch Arnish
Arnish
Brochel Castle
Brochel
Glame
385
ISLAND OF RAASAY
Balmeanach
Balachuirn
Oskaig
443 Dun Caan
Raasay
Raasay Ho.
Clachan
Raasay Outdoor Centre
Inverarish
East Suisnish
Eyre
Eyre Point
North Fearns
Rubha na'Leac
Caol Mòr
SOUND OF RAASAY
INNER SOUND
Scalpay
Scalpay Ho.
Guillamon I.
Pabay
Caolas Scalpay
Red Hills
Broadford Bay
Broadford
Corry
Harrapool
Waterloo
Lower Breakish
Upper Breakish
Skulamus
732
Suardal
Kilbride
Strath
301
Heast
Kinloch
Drumfearn
Rubha Suisnish
Loch Eishort
Ord
Dunscaith Castle
Tokavaig
Duisdalemore
Ornsay
Camuscross
Isleornsay
Tarskavaig
Tarskavaig Pt.
Achnacloich
Teangue
Knock Castle
Knock Bay
Ferindonald
Kilbeg
Kilmore
SLEAT
Glen Meadhonach
Armadale Castle
Armadale Gardens
Clan Donald Centre
Armadale Bay
Rubha Charn nan Cearc
280
Calligarry
Ardvasar
Aird of Sleat
Ard Thurinish
SOUND OF SLEAT
Crowlin Islands
Eilean Mór
Eilean na Bà
Longay
NG
Port Erradale
Rubha Bàn
North Erradale
Big Sand
Longa Island
Caolas Beag
Carn Dearg
Peterburn
Aultgrishan
Seana Chamas
Midtown
Brae
Naast
Rubha 'Ard na Bà
Tournaig
Inverewe Garden
Loch Bad a' Chreamh
Londubh
Poolewe
Strath
Gairloch Museum
Gairloch
Smithstown
LOCH GAIRLOCH
Charlestown
Meall an Doirein 420
791 Beinn Airigh Cha
Kerrysdale
Port Henderson
Aird
Badachro
Opinan
Shieldaig
Loch Maree Islands
Eilean Subhainn
South Erradale
Loch Clair
Loch Bad an Sgalaig
Victoria Falls
Talladale
Redpoint
Dubh Loch
Loch Gaineamhach
Flowerdale
675 Baosbheinn Forest
Loch na h-Oidhche
WEST
Shieldaig
624 Beinn Bhreac
Loch a' Bhealaich
Craig
Rubha na Fearn
Fearnmore
Fearnbeg
Arinacrinachd
Loch Torridon
Lower Diabaig
985 Beinn Alligin
Kenmore
Loch a' Chracaich
Cuaig
Ardheslaig
Alligin Shuas
Inveralligin
Rechullin
Torridon Ho.
Torridon Forest
1054 Liathach
86
Fasag
Torridon
Glen Torridon
Upper Loch Torridon
Callakille
Loch Shieldaig
Shieldaig
Balgy
Annat
Lonbain
Loch Gaineamhach
493 Croic-bheinn
Ben-damph Forest
Ben Shieldaig 439
Loch Damh
902 Beinn Damh
993 Maol Chean-dearg
626 Beinn a' Chlachain
Loch nan Eun
Glenshieldaig Forest
Loch Lundie
513
Hartfield House
Applecross Forest
Chapel of St Maelrubha
Applecross Ho.
Applecross Bay
Applecross
896 Beinn Bhan
Loch Coultrie
Bealach na Ba
Camusteel
Camusterrach
Culduie
Ard-dhubh
710 Meall Gorm
Kirkton
Sanachan
Ardarroch
Slumbay
Lochcarron
Attadale Ho.
Attadale
Toscaig
Achintraid
Loch Kishorn
Kishorn I.
Strome Castle
395
Ardaneaskan
Stromemore
Ardnarff
Uags
486 Carn nan Iomairean
Stromeferry
An Dubh-aird
LOCH CARRON
Plockton
Achmore
Port Cam
Duirinish
Drumbuie
Gleann Udalain
Allt-nan-sùgh
Sallachy
Black Is.
Erbusaig
Badicaul
Balmacara Square
Reraig
Auchertyre
Kyle of Lochalsh
Castle Moil
Lochalsh Woodland Garden
Balmacara
Kirkton
Nostie
Ardelve
Kyleakin
Loch Long
Camas-luinie
Bundalloch
Dornie
Eilean Donan Castle
634
LOCH ALSH
Glas Eilean
Totaig
Ardintoul Pt.
Keppoch
Letterfearn
Sgurr na Coinnich 739
Kylerhea Otter Hide
Glen Arroch
Kyle Rhea
Bernera
Galltair
603 Beinn a' Chuirn
Invernate
Loch Duich
Kylerhea
Glenelg
Glenelg Bay
Bernera Barracks
Ratagan
Shiel Bridge
610 Ben Aslak
Eilanreach
Glenelg Brochs
Balvraid
Glen More
779
Sandaig Is.
Upper Sandaig
742 Beinn a' Chapaill
80
Glenshiel Forest
974 Beinn Sgritheall
Beinn nan Caorach 774
1010 The Saddle
Arnisdale
Glen Arnisdale
Rubha Ard Slisneach
Corran
LOCH HOURN
713 Druim Fada
Inverguseran
785 Beinn na Caillich
Barrisdale Bay
Airor
KNOYDART
1020 Ladhar Bheinn
Glen Barrisdale
Gleann na Guiserein
Sandaig
Luinne Bheinn 939
Sandaig Bay
Scottas
Inverie
Gleann an Dubh-Lochain
Inverie Bay
Rubha Shamhnan Insir
Canna Harbour
Kilmory
Sound of Canna
Guirdil Bay
388
Kilmory Glen
Kinloch Glen
Rubha na Roinne
Mallaig (Sun only)
78
571 Orval
RÙM
Kinloch
Kinloch Castle
Loch Scresort
Rubha Port na Caranean
Point of Sleat
79
Rubha Raonuill
Mallaig Heritage Centre
Mallaig
Schooner Pt.
Canna (Sun only)
Harris
Glen Harris
812 Askival
778 Ainshval
Rubha Sgorr an t-Snidhe
Lochboisdale
SOUND OF RÙM
SMALL ISLES
Rubha nam Meirleach
Bay of Laig
Cleadale
522
946 Meall Buidhe
Beinn Bhuidhe 855
Glasnacardoch
LOCH NEVIS
Camusrory
1040 Sgurr na Ciche
Carnach
Kylesknoydart
Stoul
Beoraidbeg
Bracara
Bracorina
Tarbet
Kylesmorar
859
North Morar
Brinacory
Morar
Swordland
LOCH MORAR
Kinlochmorar
829 Carn Mor
Scamadale
Bunacaimb
Portnaluchaig
Letter
Oban
718
A87
A850
A855
A863
A851
A830
A832
A896
A890
A896
B885
B8009
B8036
B883
B8083
B8056
B8021
Kinlochhourn
Glen Dessary

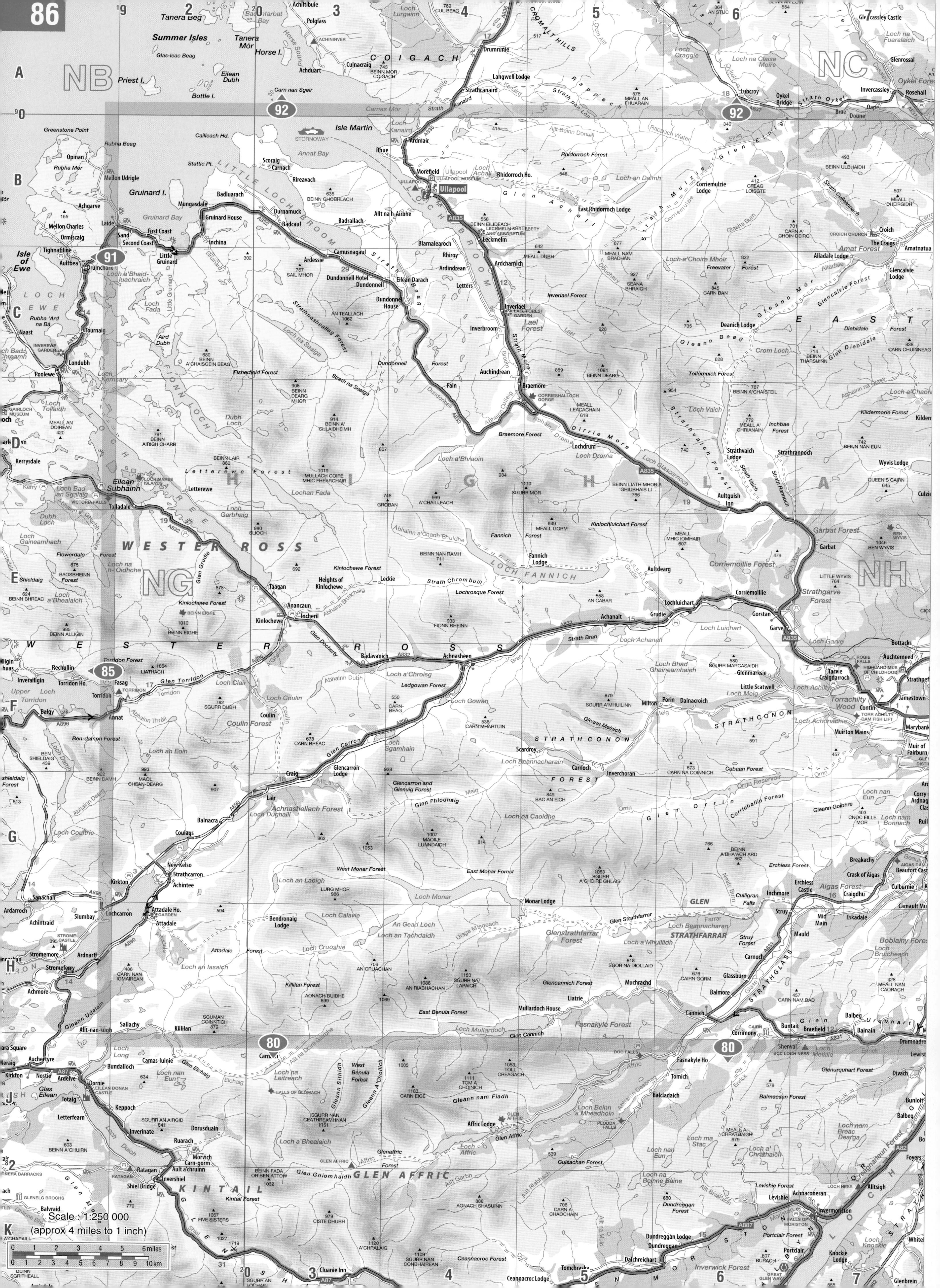
Tanera Beg
Summer Isles
Tanera Mór
Horse I.
Glas-leac Beag
Achiltibuie
Polglass
Achduart
Culnacraig
COIGACH
Loch Lurgainn
CUL BEAG
Drumrunie
CROMALT HILLS
Langwell Lodge
Strathcanaird
Loch Craggie
Loch na Claise Moire
Lubcroy
Oykel Bridge
Strath Oykel
Glencassley Castle
Loch na Fuaralaich
Glenrossal
Invercassley
Rosehall
Oykel Forest
NB
NC
NH
NG
Priest I.
Eilean Dubh
Bottle I.
Carn nan Sgeir
Camas Mòr
Isle Martin
STORNOWAY
Greenstone Point
Cailleach Hd.
Rubha Beag
Opinan
Rubha Mòr
Mellon Udrigle
Stattic Pt.
Annat Bay
Scoraig
Carnach
Rireavach
Gruinard I.
Badluarach
Mungasdale
LITTLE LOCH BROOM
Ardmair
Rhue
Morefield
Ullapool
ULLAPOOL MUSEUM
Loch Kanaird
Rappach Water
Rhidorroch Forest
Rhidorroch Ho.
Loch an Daimh
Glen Achall
East Rhidorroch Lodge
Strath Mulzie
Corriemulzie Lodge
CREAG LOISGTE
BEINN ULBHAIDH
Strath Cuileannach
MEALL DHEIRGIDH
Achgarve
Laide
Mellon Charles
Ormiscaig
Gruinard Bay
Gruinard House
Sand
First Coast
Second Coast
Inchina
Little Gruinard
Durnamuck
Badcaul
Badrallach
Allt na h-Airbhe
BEINN GHOBHLACH
LOCH BROOM
BEINN EILIDEACH
LECKMELM SHRUBBERY AND ARBORETUM
Leckmelm
CARN A' CHOIN DEIRG
CROICH CHURCH
Croich
The Craigs
Amat Forest
Amatnatua
Isle of Ewe
Tighnafiline
Aultbea
Drumchork
Loch a' Bhaid-luachraich
LOCH EWE
Rubha 'Ard na Bà
Naast
Tournaig
INVEREWE GARDEN
Londubh
Poolewe
Loch Fada
Aird Dubh
Camusnagaul
Ardessie
SAIL MHOR
Dundonnell Hotel
Dundonnell
Eilean Darach
Dundonnell House
Strath Beag
Blarnalearoch
Rhiroy
Ardindrean
Letters
Ardcharnich
MEALL DUBH
MEALL NAM BRADHAN
Loch a' Choire Mhoir
Freevater
Forest
SEANA BHRAIGH
CARN BAN
Alladale Lodge
Glencalvie Lodge
Glencalvie Forest
Strathnasheallag Forest
AN TEALLACH
Loch na Sealga
Inverlael
LAEL FOREST GARDEN
Lael Forest
Inverlael Forest
Inverbroom
Deanich Lodge
Gleann Mòr
EAST
Diebidale
Gleann Beag
Crom Loch
BEINN THARSUINN
Glen Diebidale
CARN CHUINNEAG
BEINN A' CHAISGEIN BEAG
FIONN LOCH
Fisherfield Forest
Dundonnell
Forest
Strath na Sealga
Auchindrean
Strath More
BEINN DEARG
Tollomuick Forest
BEINN DEARG MHOR
Fain
Braemore
CORRIESHALLOCH GORGE
MEALL LEACACHAIN
BEINN A' CHAISTEIL
Loch a' Chaorainn
Kildermorie Forest
Kildermorie
GAIRLOCH MUSEUM
Loch Tollaidh
MEALL AN DOIREAN
BEINN A' CHLAIDHEIMH
Dubh Loch
Abhainn Droma
Dirrie More
Braemore Forest
Loch Vaich
MEALL A' GHRIANAIN
Inchbae Forest
BEINN AIRIGH CHARR
Lochdrum
Loch Droma
BEINN NAN EUN
Kerrysdale
BEINN LAIR
Letterewe Forest
MULLACH COIRE MHIC FHEARCHAIR
Loch a' Bhraoin
Loch Glascarnoch
BEINN LIATH MHOR A' GHIUBHAIS LI
Strathvaich Forest
Strathvaich Lodge
Strath Vaich
Strathrannoch
Strath Rannoch
Wyvis Lodge
Kerry
Loch Bad an Sgalaig
Eilean Subhainn
LOCH MAREE ISLANDS
Letterewe
HIGHLAND
Lochan Fada
GROBAN
A' CHAILLEACH
SGURR MOR
Aultguish Inn
QUEEN'S CAIRN
VICTORIA FALLS
Talladale
Dubh Loch
Loch Garbhaig
SLIOCH
Abhainn a' Chadh' Bhuidhe
Fannich
Forest
MEALL GORM
Kinlochluichart Forest
MEALL MHIC IOMHAIR
Garbat Forest
BEN WYVIS
Garbat
Loch Gaineamhach
Flowerdale
Forest
Loch na h-Oidhche
WESTER ROSS
Glen Grudie
BEINN NAN RAMH
Kinlochewe Forest
LOCH FANNICH
Fannich Lodge
Aultdearg
Corriemoillie Forest
LITTLE WYVIS
Strathgarve Forest
Shieldaig
BAOSBHEINN
Forest
BEINN BHREAC
Loch a' Bhealaich
Taagan
Heights of Kinlochewe
Leckie
Strath Chrombuill
Lochrosque Forest
AN CABAR
Lochluichart
Corriemoillie
Kinlochewe Forest
BEINN EIGHE
Anancaun
Incheril
Kinlochewe
Abhainn Bruachaig
Achanalt
Grudie
Gorstan
Garve
BEINN ALLIGIN
Glen Docherty
FIONN BHEINN
Loch Luichart
Loch Achanalt
Strath Bran
Loch Garve
Bottacks
Torridon Forest
LIATHACH
Badavanich
Achnasheen
WESTER ROSS
Loch Bhad Ghaineamhaich
SGURR MARCASAIDH
Glenmarksie
ROGIE FALLS
Auchterneed
Tarvie
Craigdarroch
HIGHLAND MUS OF CHILDHOOD
Strathpeffer
Rechullin
Inveralligin
Torridon Ho.
Fasag
Glen Torridon
Loch Clair
Abhainn Dubh
Loch a' Chroisg
Ledgowan Forest
Upper Loch Torridon
Torridon
TORRIDON
SGURR DUBH
Loch Coulin
Coulin
CARN BEAG
Loch Gowan
SGURR A' MHUILINN
Milton
Porin
Dalnacroich
Little Scatwell
Loch Meig
Loch Achilty
Torrachilty Wood
TORR ACHILTY DAM FISH LIFT
Contin
Jamestown
Balgy
Annat
Abhainn Thrail
Coulin Forest
CARN MHARTUIN
Gleann Meinich
STRATHCONON
Loch Achonachie
Muirton Mains
Marybank
Ben-damph Forest
Loch an Eoin
CARN BREAC
Glen Carron
Loch Sgamhain
Scardroy
Loch Beannacharain
Carnoch
Inverchoran
CARN NA COINNICH
Cabaan Forest
Muir of Fairburn
BEN SHIELDAIG
Loch Damh
BEINN DAMH
MAOL CHEAN-DEARG
Craig
Glencarron Lodge
Glencarron and Glenuig Forest
FOREST
Orrin Reservoir
Corriehallie Forest
Loch nan Eun
Gleann Goibhre
Lair
Achnashellach Forest
Glen Fhiodhaig
BAC AN EICH
Loch na Caoidhe
Glen Orrin
CNOC EILLE MOR
Loch nam Bonnach
Loch Dughaill
Balnacra
Loch Coultrie
Coulags
MAOILE LUNNDAIDH
BEINN A' BHA'ACH ARD
Breakachy
Erchless Forest
Beauly
AIGAS DAM
Beaufort Castle
New Kelso
Strathcarron
Achintee
West Monar Forest
East Monar Forest
SGURR A' CHOIRE GHLAIS
Crask of Aigas
Aigas Forest
Erchless Castle
Kirkton
Loch an Laoigh
LURG MHOR
Loch Monar
Monar Lodge
GLEN
Culligran Falls
Inchmore
Craigdhu
Culburnie
Sanachan
Ardarroch
Achintraid
Slumbay
Lochcarron
Attadale Ho.
Attadale
Bendronaig Lodge
Loch Calavie
An Gead Loch
Loch an Tachdaidh
Uisge Misgeach
Glen Strathfarrar
Loch Beannacharan
STRATHFARRAR
Struy
Mid Main
Eskadale
Camault Muir
STROME CASTLE
Stromemore
Ardnarff
Attadale
Forest
Loch Cruoshie
AN CRUACHAN
Glenstrathfarrar Forest
Loch a' Mhuillidh
SGOR NA DIOLLAID
Struy Forest
Mauld
Carnoch
Boblainy Forest
Loch Bruicheach
Stromeferry
CARN NAN IOMAIREAN
Loch an Iasaich
Killilan Forest
AN RIABHACHAN
SGURR NA LAPAICH
Glencannich Forest
Muchrachd
CAIRN GORM
Glassburn
CARN NAM BAD
MEALL NAN CAORACH
Achmore
AONACH BUIDHE
East Benula Forest
Liatrie
Balmore
STRATHGLASS
Gleann Udalain
Allt-nan-sùgh
Sallachy
Killilan
SGUMAN COINNTICH
Mullardoch House
Loch Mullardoch
Glen Cannich
Fasnakyle Forest
Cannich
Corrimony
Buntait
Glen Braefield
Urquhart
Balbeg
Balnain
Loch Long
Camas-luinie
DOG FALLS
Fasnakyle Ho
Shenval
BCC LOCH NESS
Loch Meiklie
Drumnadrochit
Auchertyre
Nostie
Ardelve
Dornie
EILEAN DONAN CASTLE
Bundalloch
Glen Elchaig
Loch nan Eun
Loch na Leitreach
West Benula Forest
TOM A' CHOINICH
TOLL CREAGACH
Affric
Tomich
Glenurquhart Forest
Lewiston
Divach
Glas Eilean
Totaig
Keppoch
FALLS OF GLOMACH
Gleann Sithidh
Gleann a' Chòmhlaich
CARN EIGE
Gleann nam Fiadh
Balcladaich
Loch Beinn a' Mheadhoin
Balmacaan Forest
Bunloit
Balbeg
Letterfearn
Inverinate
SGURR AN AIRGID
Dorusduain
SGURR NAN CEATHREAMHNAN
Affric Lodge
GLEN AFFRIC
PLODDA FALLS
MEALL A' CHRATHAICH
Loch nam Breac Dearga
BEINN A' CHUIRN
Ruarach
Morvich
Carn-gorm
Loch a' Bhealaich
Glen Affric
Loch Affric
Loch ma Stac
Loch nan Eun
Loch a' Chràthaich
Glenaffric Forest
Guisachan Forest
Invermoriston Forest
Foyers
RATAGAN
Ratagan
Aultachruinn
Invershiel
Loch Duich
Glen Gniomhaidh
GLEN AFFRIC
BEINN FADA OR BEN ATTOW
Allt Garbh
Allt Riabhach
Loch na Beinne Baine
Levishie Forest
LOCH NESS
Alltsigh
Shiel Bridge
KINTAIL
Glen Shiel
Kintail Forest
Levishie
Achnaconeran
Invermoriston
AONACH SHASUINN
CARN A' CHAOCHAIN
Dundreggan Forest
Portclair Forest
FALLS OF MORISTON
Whitefield
FIVE SISTERS
CISTE DHUBH
A' CHRALAIG
SGURR NAN CONBHAIREAN
Ceannacroc Forest
Dundreggan Lodge
Dundreggan
GLENMORISTON
Dalchreichart
Inverwick Forest
Portclair
BURACH
GREAT GLEN WAY
Knockie Lodge
Loch Knockie
Tomchrasky
Ceannacroc Lodge
Cluanie Inn
Glenbrein
Balvraid
GLENELG BROCHS
Glen More
Balvraid
BEINN SGRITHEALL
SGURR AN LOCHAIN
A832
A835
A837
A836
A890
A896
A87
A831
A887
A82
Scale: 1:250 000
(approx 4 miles to 1 inch)
0 1 2 3 4 5 6 miles
0 1 2 3 4 5 6 7 8 9 10 km
91
92
85
80

ND
NJ
Loch Brora
Brora
Golspie
Dunrobin Castle Museum & Gardens
Dornoch
Dornoch Firth
Tarbat Ness
Portmahomack
Tain
Bonar Bridge
Lairg
Ross
Balintore
Shandwick
Alness
Invergordon
Cromarty
Cromarty Firth
Moray Firth
Black Isle
Dingwall
Conon Bridge
Muir of Ord
Beauly
Beauly Firth
Inverness
Nairn
Fortrose
Rosemarkie
Fort George
Forres
Kinloss
Burghead
Burghead Bay
Findhorn
Culbin Forest
Moray
Grantown-on-Spey
Carrbridge
Boat of Garten
Aviemore
Cairngorms National Park
Monadhliath Mountains
Strathdearn
Hills of Cromdale
Tomatin
Loch Ness
The Aird
Glenmore Forest Park
A9
A96
A95
A939
A940
A82
A862
A835
A836
A949
81
88
93

Lossiemouth
Branderburgh
Stotfield
Covesea
Covesea Skerries
Halliman Skerries
LOSSIEMOUTH FISHERIES & COMMUNITY MUSEUM
Burghead
BURGHEAD VISITOR CENTRE
Hopeman
Duffus
Gordonstoun
Cummingston
Roseisle
Roseisle Forest
DUFFUS CASTLE
PALACE OF SPYNIE
Loch Spynie
Lossie Forest
Spynie
Quarrywood
Lower Hempriggs
Newton
Coltfield
Alves
Miltonhill
Elgin
Bishopmill
ELGIN MUSEUM
CATHEDRAL
CASHMERE VISITOR CENTRE
OLD MILLS
MORAY MOTOR MUSEUM
New Elgin
Pittendreich
Miltonduff
Urquhart
Lhanbryde
Leuchars Ho.
Lochhill
Moss of Barmuckity
COXTON TOWER
Lochs Crofts
Mains of Burgie
Monaughty Forest
PLUSCARDEN ABBEY
Barnhill
Califer
Auchtertyre
Foresterseat
Paddockhaugh
BIRNIE CHURCH
Thomshill
Longmorn
Blackhills
MILLBUIES
Dallas Forest
Kellas
Glenlatterach
Briach
Branchill
Dallas
MORAY
Craigroy
365 CAIRN UISH
MILL BUIE
Glen of Rothes
Auchinroath
Newlands
Teindland Forest
Orbliston
Rothes
GLEN GRANT DISTILLERY
Burn of Rothes
Elchies Forest
CARN NA CAILLICHE
Whiteacen
Dandaleith
MACALLAN DISTILLERY
Craigellachie
Archiestown
CARDHU DISTILLERY
Cardow
Upper Knockando
Knockando
Knockando Ho.
Ringorm
SPEYSIDE VISITOR CENTRE
SPEYSIDE COOPERAGE VISITOR CENTRE
Speyview
Charlestown of Aberlour
Milltown of Edinvillie
Carron
Daugh of Kinermony
CARN KITTY
LARIG HILL
Marypark
Bellehiglash
GLENFARCLAS DISTILLERY
CRAGGANMORE DISTILLERY
Advie
Bridge of Avon
Dalchirach
Lettoch
SPEYSIDE WAY
Mains of Dalvey
HILLS OF CROMDALE
Drumin
Cromdale
Auchroisk
Haughs of Cromdale
Ballcorach
Strath Avon
Glenlivet
GLENLIVET DISTILLERY
Shenval
Auchbreck
Tomnavoulin
CARN DAIMH
Knockandhu
Glenlivet Forest
CREGGAN A'CHAISE
Clashnoir
Braes of Chapeltown
Bridge of Brown
Fodderletter
Dirdhu
TOMINTOUL & GLENLIVET DISCOVERY CENTRE
Tomintoul
TOMINTOUL
Delnabo
Dorback Lodge
CARN MEADHONACH
Blairnamarrow
Water of Ailnack
LECHT SKI CENTRE
CAIRNGORMS
NATIONAL
PARK
CARN EALASAID
GEAL CHARN
BIG GARVOUN
Delnadamph
Cock Bridge
Corgarff
CORGARFF CASTLE
Colnabaichin
Tornahaish
THE BRUACH
BROWN COW HILL
BEN AVON
Gairnshiel
Glen Fenzie
Kingston
TUGNET ICE HOUSE
Spey Bay
SCOTTISH DOLPHIN CENTRE
Garmouth
SPEY BAY
Portannachy
Nether Dallachy
Upper Dallachy
Bogmoor
Auchenhalrig
Newlands of Tynet
Mosstodloch
Dipple
Fochabers
FOCHABERS FOLK MUSEUM HERITAGE CENTRE
Braes of Enzie
Speymouth Forest
Ordiequish
Wood of Ordiequish
Inchberry
Mulben
Rosarie Forest
SPEYSIDE WAY
BEN AIGAN
Maggieknockater
Kininvie Ho.
Drummuir Castle
Midtown of Buchromb
BALVENIE CASTLE
GLENFIDDICH DISTILLERY
Dufftown
Milltown of Auchindoun
Kirktown of Mortlach
MEIKLE CONVAL
BEN RINNES
Favillar
Glen Rinnes
Kirkhill
AUCHINDOUN CASTLE
THE SCALP
Glen Fiddich
Ballochford
Bridgend
Glenfiddich Forest
Inverharroch
Auchmair
Cabrach
ROUND HILL
Aldunie
Blackwater Forest
CARN AN T-SUIDHE
HILL OF THREE STONES
LADDER HILLS
Badenyon
Glenbuchat Lodge
Belnacraig
Kirkton of Glenbuchat
CARN MOR
THE SOCACH
Bellabeg
Forbestown
Strathdon
Inverernan Ho.
Candacraig Ho.
Heugh-head
Tornashean Forest
CRAIG OF BUNZEACH
Hillockhead
MORVEN
Portknockie
Findochty
Gordonsburgh
Buckie
Portessie
Buckpool
Rathven
Portgordon
Slackhead
Cairnfield Ho.
Drybridge
Broadley
ST. GREGORY'S CHAPEL
Clochan
Shiel Muir
Craibstone
MILLSTONE HILL
Deerhill
Grange Crossroads
Broadrashes
Forgie
Aultmore
Newmill
Keith
STRATHISLA DISTILLERY
KEITH AND DUFFTOWN RLY
Towiemore
Edintore
Little Pitlurg
Coachford
Drummuir
Glen of Coachford
Balloch Wood
Daugh of Cairnborrow
Cairnborrow
Torry
Haugh of Glass
STRATHBOGIE
Bailiesward
Succoth
Tillathrowie
Tomnaven
Clashindarroch Forest
Clashindarroch
Coynachie
Bridgend
Kirkney
Milton of Lesmore
Belhinnie
Rhynie
Wheedlemont
Craig Castle
ST MARY'S CHURCH
Clova
SCOTTISH SCULPTURE WORKSHOP
Lumsden
CORREEN HILLS
THE BUCK
Mossat
Kildrummy
KILDRUMMY CASTLE
Milltown of Kildrummy
Rinmore
Glenkindie
Towie
Milltown of Towie
Boultenstone
Easter Davoch
Migvie
Coynach
Logie Coldstone
Tarland
CROMAR
TOMNAVERIE STONE CIRCLE
Milton of Logie
Glendavan Ho.
Ordie
Coull
Cullen
Cullen Bay
Logie Hd.
FINDLATER CASTLE
Sandend
Sandend Bay
Portsoy
Redhythe Pt.
Seatown
Lintmill
Fordyce
JOINER'S WORKSHOP
Milton
Kirktown of Deskford
DESKFORD CHURCH
Ardiecow
Berryhillock
Little Toux
Newmills of Boyne
Cornhill
Mains of Edingight
Edingight Ho.
Gordonstown
KNOCK HILL
Finnygaud
Crannoch
Bracobrae
Sillyearn
Davoch of Grange
Knock
Knowes of Elrick
Drumnagorrach
Farmtown
Old Crombie
Knauchland
Marnoch
Milltown of Rothiemay
Mains of Mayen
Yonder Bognie
Bogniebrae
FOURMAN HILL
Ruthven
Cairnie
THE BIN
The Bin Forest
NORDIC SKI CENTRE
Corse of Kinnoir
HUNTLY CASTLE
Huntly
Lessendrum
Drumblade
Corse
Brideswell
Slioch
Thomastown
Denend
Bridgend
Hillhead
Kirkstile
Shanquhar
Culdrain
Blackburn
Gartly
Clashindarroch Forest
Cults
KNOCKANDY HILL
LEITH HALL
Glens of Foudland
HILL OF FOUDLAND
Largie
Kennethmont
Ardlair
Oldtown
Cottown
Clatt
Duncanstone
Leslie
Knockespock Ho.
Coldwells Croft
Whitehaugh Forest
Muckletown
ABERD
Tullynessle
LORD ARTHUR'S CAIRN
Bridge of Alford
Montgarrie
HAUGHTON
GRAMPIAN TRANSPORT MUS.
Alford
HERITAGE MUSEUM
Auchintoul
Asloun
Whitehouse
Sinnahard
Hillockhead
Ley
Little Lynturk
Muir of Fowlis
Bridgend
Tillyfour
Milton of Cushnie
Leochel-Cushnie
CRAIGIEVAR CASTLE
Kintocher
BENAQUHALLIE
Douneside
Craskins
CULSH SOUTERRAIN
Findrack Ho.
Lumphanan
PEEL RING OF LUMPHANAN
Milton of Auchinhove
Auchlossan
Corrennie Moor
Keig
Bainshole
Glendronach Distillery
Hillbrae
Blacklaw
Weachyb
Newmill
Eastern Whyntie
Burn of Loin
Glen Avon
Glen Ernan
Ernan Water
Don
Water of Buchat
Water of Nochty
Deskry Water
Conglass Water
Dorback Burn
Livet
Fiddich
Dullan Water
Black Water
Kirkney Water
Deveron
Isla
Lossie
Spey
Black Burn
Burn of Tulchan
Allt Tuileach
0 1 2 3 4 5 6 miles
0 1 2 3 4 5 6 7 8 9 10 km

Fraserburgh
Kinnaird Head
KINNAIRD HEAD CASTLE & MUS OF SCOTTISH LIGHTHOUSES
Fraserburgh Bay
Rosehearty
Sandhaven
Pittulie
Broadsea
SANDHAVEN MEAL MILL
FRASERBURGH HERITAGE CENTRE
PITSLIGO CASTLE
Cairnbulg Pt.
Inverallochy
MAGGIE'S HOOSIE
St Combs
Inzie Head
Cairnbulg Castle
Troup Hd.
Pennan Hd.
Quarry Hd.
Knock Hd.
Head of Garness
Gamrie Bay
Crovie
Gardenstown
Pennan
Macduff
MACDUFF MARINE AQUARIUM
Banff
BANFF MUSEUM
DUFF HOUSE
Boyndie Bay
Whitehills
Inverboyndie
Longmanhill
Cushnie
Dubford
Towie
New Aberdour
Upper Boyndlie
Mid Ardlaw
Memsie
MEMSIE BURIAL CAIRN
Rathen
Strathellie
Cairness
Loch of Strathbeg
Crimonmogate
Rattray Head
Crimond
Old Rattray
Lonmay
Newburgh
Mormond Hill
New Pitsligo
Strichen
Knowhead
New Byth
Turriff
DELGATIE CASTLE
Delgaty Forest
Cuminestown
Aberchirder
Forglen Ho.
Maud
Mintlaw
ABERDEENSHIRE FARMING MUSEUM
Old Deer
DEER ABBEY
Forest of Deer
Fetterangus
Longside
Peterhead
ARBUTHNOT MUS & ART GALLERY
UGIE SALMON FISH HOUSE
Buchanhaven
Inverugie
INVERUGIE CASTLE
St Fergus
Scotstown Hd.
Rora Moss
Keith Inch
Peterhead Bay
Sandford Bay
Boddam
Buchan Ness
Stirling
Moss of Cruden
Longhaven
North Haven
BULLERS OF BUCHAN
Twa Havens
Cruden Bay
SLAINS CASTLE
Port Erroll
Bay of Cruden
Whinnyfold
B U C H A N
New Deer
Auchnagatt
Fyvie
FYVIE CASTLE
Methlick
HADDO HOUSE AND GARDENS
Tarves
MEDIEVAL TOMB
Ellon
Collieston
Kirktown of Slains
St Catherine's Dub
Hackley Hd. or Forvie Ness
Sands of Forvie
FORVIE
Newburgh
Newburgh Bar
F O R M A R T I N E
Oldmeldrum
TOLQUHON CASTLE
PITMEDDEN GDNS & MUS OF FARMING LIFE
Pitmedden
Udny Green
Udny Station
Inverurie
Kintore
Kemnay
BENNACHIE
G A R I O C H
BATTLE OF HARLAW MEMORIAL
Newmachar
Balmedie
Whitecairns
Dyce
ABERDEEN
Bridge of Don
CRUICKSHANK BOTANIC GARDEN
BRIG O'BALGOWNIE
ST MACHAR'S CATHEDRAL
Old Aberdeen
KING'S COLLEGE VISITOR CENTRE
Aberdeen
ABERDEEN SCIENCE CENTRE
GORDON HIGHLANDERS MUSEUM
Westhill
Girdle Ness
Nigg Bay
Greg Ness
DOONIES FARM
Cults
Bieldside
Milltimber
Loch of Skene
Midmar Forest
CASTLE FRASER
KIRKWALL LERWICK
NK

Fraserburgh
Peterhead
Aberdeen
Rosehearty
Pittulie
Sandhaven
Broadsea
Kinnaird Head
KINNAIRD HEAD CASTLE & MUS OF SCOTTISH LIGHTHOUSES
Fraserburgh Bay
Cairnbulg Pt.
Inverallochy
MAGGIE'S HOOSIE
Cairnbulg Castle
St Combs
Inzie Head
Gowanhill
Strathellie
Rathen
Cairness
Loch of Strathbeg
Crimonmogate
Rattray Head
Old Rattray
Crimond
Blackhill
Lonmay
Nether Park
Longhill
New Leeds
Strichen
Mormond Hill
Newburgh
Memsie
Whitewell
Tyrie
Mid Ardlaw
Coburty
Upper Boyndlie
New Aberdour
Pitblae
Percyhorner
Peathill
SANDHAVEN MEAL MILL
FRASERBURGH HERITAGE CENTRE
PITSLIGO CASTLE
MEMSIE BURIAL CAIRN
Troup Hd.
Pennan Hd.
Quarry Hd.
Pennan
Crovie
Gardenstown
Gamrie Bay
Towie
Dubford
Head of Garness
Macduff
MACDUFF MARINE AQUARIUM
Banff
BANFF MUSEUM
DUFF HOUSE
Knock Hd.
Boyndie Bay
Whitehills
Inverboyndie
Auds
Easter Silverford
West Greenskares
Longmanhill
Cushnie
Minnonie
Windyheads Hill
Nether Glasslaw
Ladysford
Western Culbeuchly
Doune Park
Montcoffer Ho.
Kirktown of Alvah
Keilhill
Netherbrae
Mid Cloch Forbie
Craigmaud
Hillhead of Auchentumb
Gorrachie
Greenlaw
King Edward
The Pole of Itlaw
Fattahead
Hill of Fishrie
New Pitsligo
Knowhead
Milltown of Craigston
Craigston Castle
Plaidy
Fintry
Hill of Mountblairy
Muirden
New Byth
Bonnykelly
Ironside
Adziel
Little Skillymarno
North Ugie Water
Denhead
Leys
Balearn
St Fergus Moss
St Fergus
Scotstown Hd.
North Kirkton
Kirkton
Backfolds
Rora Moss
Hythie
Rora
Lunderton
Kirkton Hd.
Fetterangus
Toux
Forest of Deer
DEER ABBEY
Dunshillock
Woodside
Newseat
Inverugie
INVERUGIE CASTLE
UGIE SALMON FISH HOUSE
Buchanhaven
Torterston
Longside
Flushing
Mintlaw
ADEN
ABERDEENSHIRE FARMING MUSEUM
Old Deer
Stuartfield
Inverquhomery
Hillhead of Cocklaw
ARBUTHNOT MUS & ART GALLERY
Keith Inch
Peterhead Bay
Sandford Bay
Invernettie
Boddam
Buchan Ness
Stirling
Millbreck
Nether Kinmundy
Little Dens
Clola
Blackhill
Millbank
Sandfordhill
Skelmuir
Kinnadie
Mains of Crichie
Crichie
Bulwark
Backhill of Clackriach
Maud
MAUD RAILWAY MUSEUM
New Deer
Culsh
Mains of Fedderate
Oldwhat
Whitestones
Balthangie
Garmond
Cuminestown
Middle Cairncake
Turriff
DELGATIE CASTLE
Forglen Ho.
Muiryfold
Aberchirder
Cranna
Bogton
Clunie
Carnousie
Kirkton
Little Colp
Delgaty Forest
Mill of Muiresk
Hatton Castle
Howe of Teuchar
Rush-head
Darra
Inverkeithny
Auchininna
Birkenhills
Fortrie
Brownhill
Crofts of Inverthernie
Dykeside
Drumblair
Denmoss
Balgaveny
Nether Lenshie
Kirkton of Auchterless
Inverythan
Steinmanhill
Gourdas
Tifty
Lethenty
Monkshill
Cottown
South Millbrex
Crofts of Meikle Ardo
Cairnbanno Ho.
Knaven
Nethermuir
Drymuir
Barrack
Auchnagatt
Mains of Annochie
Backhill of Fortree
Kinknockie
Smallburn
Moss of Cruden
Backhill
Stoneygate
Teuchan
Coldwells
Longhaven
North Haven
BULLERS OF BUCHAN
Twa Havens
Cruden Bay
SLAINS CASTLE
Port Erroll
Bay of Cruden
Auchiries
Hatton
Chapel Hill
Bogbrae
Whinnyfold
Eastertown of Auchleuchries
Muirtack
Toll of Birness
Arthrath
Milton Coldwells
Mains of Inkhorn
Skelmonae
Quilquox
Cairnorrie
Brownhill
Ardo
Backhill
FYVIE CASTLE
Fyvie
Woodhead
Crofts of Haddo
Methlick
Collynie
HADDO
HADDO HOUSE AND GARDENS
Drumwhindle
Ythanbank
Inverebrie
Hilton
Mains of Birness
Nether Leask
Broomfield
Artrochie
Auchmacoy
Ellon
Esslemont
West Kinharrachie
Ythsie
Tarves
Raxton
MEDIEVAL TOMB
Wedderlairs
Earlsford
Barthol Chapel
Balgove
Tulloch
Craigdam
Auquhorthies
Meldrum Ho.
TOLQUHON CASTLE
PITMEDDEN GDNS & MUS OF FARMING LIFE
Pitmedden
Udny Green
Udny Station
Tarty Burn
Tipperty
Kirkton of Logie Buchan
Meikle Tarty
Waterside
VISITOR CENTRE
FORVIE
Sands of Forvie
Kirktown of Slains
Collieston
St Catherine's Dub
Hackley Hd. or Forvie Ness
Newburgh
Newburgh Bar
Foveran
Foveran Burn
Cultercullen
Minnes
Drums
Rashierieve
Delfrigs
Middlemuir
Ardo Ho.
Tillycorthie
Tillygreig
Pettymuick
Affleck
Hattoncrook
Mill of Kingoodie
Cairnbrogie
Oldmeldrum
Barra Castle
Fingask
Kirkton of Bourtie
Hillbrae
Whiterashes
Nether Crimond
Tillykerrie
Straloch
Newmachar
Whitecairns
Causeyend
Belhelvie
BALMEDIE
Balmedie
Kinmundy
Drumligair
Cothall
Potterton
Blackdog
Parkhill Ho.
Corby Loch
Mundurno
Denmore
Bridge of Don
Dyce
Overton
ABERDEEN
Stoneywood
Bankhead
Bucksburn
Hayton
BRIG O'BALGOWNIE
CRUICKSHANK BOTANIC GARDEN
ST MACHAR'S CATHEDRAL
Old Aberdeen
KING'S COLLEGE VISITOR CENTRE
Woodside
Kittybrewster
Northfield
Mastrick
ABERDEEN SCIENCE CENTRE
Kingswells
GORDON HIGHLANDERS MUSEUM
Mannofield
Ferryhill
Torry
DAVID WELCH WINTER GARDENS
Girdle Ness
Nigg Bay
Greg Ness
DOONIES FARM
Ruthrieston
Kincorth
Garthdee
Cults
Bieldside
Banchory-Devenick
Nigg
Cove Bay
Milltimber
Milton of Murtle
Blacktop
Contlaw
Easter Ord
Westhill
Elrick
Kirkton of Skene
Auchronie
East Auchronie
Haughs of Clinterty
Blackburn
Hatton of Fintray
Kintore
Cottown
Balbithan
Wester Fintray
Cairnpark
Balbithan Ho.
Kinmuck
Middleton
KINKELL CHURCH
Port Elphinstone
Inverurie
Burgh Muir
BRANDSBUTT STONE
Balhalgardy
Harlaw Ho.
Pitcaple
Whiteford
Daviot
Durno
Mounie Castle
Kirkton of Rayne
Old Rayne
Newton Ho.
Pitmachie
Ardoyne
Westhall
Kirkton
Oyne
Kirkton of Oyne
Chapel of Garioch
Pittodrie
Auchleven
BENNACHIE
BATTLE OF HARLAW MEMORIAL
GARIOCH
ENSHIRE
Glenton
Upper Woodend
Bograxie
Manar Ho.
Burnhervie
Aquhythie
Dalmadilly
Clovenstone
Blairdaff
Grantlodge
Rorandle
Pitfichie
Pitfichie Forest
Pitmunie
Todlachie
Monymusk
Kemnay
Craigearn
Leylodge
Lauchintilly
CASTLE FRASER
Sauchen
Achath
Lyne of Skene
Skene Ho.
Dunecht
Loch of Skene
Echt
Garlogie
Cairnie
Westhill
Tillyfourie
Ordhead
Corrennie Forest
Milton of Corsindae
Bankhead
Corsindae
Old Kinnernie
Midmar
STONE CIRCLE
Comers
Tillybirloch
Marionburgh
Midmar Forest
Landerberry
South Kirkton
Redhill
West Cullery
Hardgate
Benthoul
Craigton
HILL OF FARE
Burn of Corrichie
Milton of
Drumlasie
Jackstown
Cross of Jackston
Newseat
St Katherine's
Folla Rule
Cromblet
Petty
Rothienorman
Rothiebrisbane
Gordonstown
Badenscoth
Logie Newton
Redhill
Fisherford
Kirkton of Culsalmond
Rothmaise
Cairnhill
Tocher
Meikle Wartle
Bonnyton
Colpy
Wrangham
Aucharnie
Ythanwells
FORMARTINE
BUCHAN
KIRKWALL LERWICK
NK
A90
A98
A947
A948
A950
A952
A981
A920
A96
A944
A93
A975
A97
B9031
B9032
B9033
B9093
B9105
B9107
B9170
B9029
B9030
B9001
B9005
B999
B979
B977
B993
B9119
B9125
B9000
B9002
B992
B9139
B9121
B9025
B9024
83

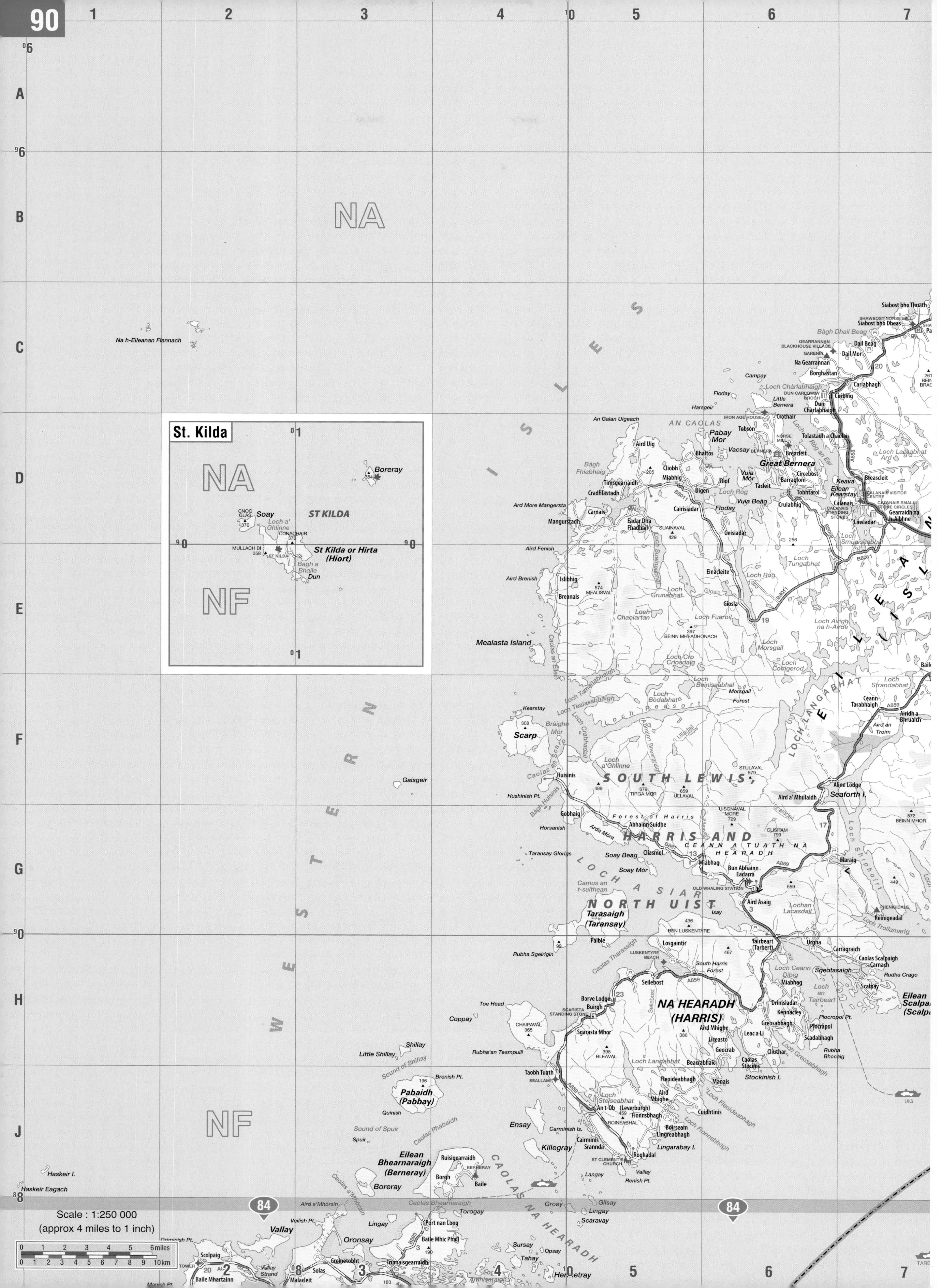

NA
NF
St. Kilda
Boreray
Soay
ST KILDA
St Kilda or Hirta (Hiort)
Loch a' Ghlinne
CONACHAIR
MULLACH BI
Bagh a Bhaile
Dun
Na h-Eileanan Flannach
WESTERN ISLES
EILEAN SIAR
Siabost bho Thuath
Siabost bho Dheas
Bàgh Dhail Beag
Dail Beag
Dail Mor
Na Gearrannan
Borghastan
Carlabhagh
Campay
Floday
Harsgeir
Little Bernera
Crothair
Ciribhig
An Galan Uigeach
AN CAOLAS
Pabay Mor
Tobson
Aird Uig
Bhaltos
Vacsay
Breacleit
Great Bernera
Bàgh Fhiabhaig
Timsgearraidh
Cliobh
Miabhig
Vuia Mor
Riof
Uigen
Loch Rog
Tacleit
Circebost
Barraglom
Tobhtarol
Keava
Eilean Kearstay
Breascleit
Calanais
Gearraidh na h-Aibhne
Linsiadar
Cradhlastadh
Floday
Vuia Beag
Crulabhig
Ard More Mangersta
Carnais
Cairisiadar
Mangurstadh
Eadar Dha Fhadhail
Geisiadar
Aird Fenish
Einacleite
Loch Rog
Aird Brenish
Islibhig
Breanais
MEALISVAL
Loch Grunabhat
Giosla
Loch Fuaroil
BEINN MHEADHONACH
Mealasta Island
Loch Morsgail
Loch Tungabhat
Loch Smuaisabhal
Kearstay
Scarp
Bràighe Mor
Huisinis
Hushinish Pt.
Gaisgeir
Morsgail Forest
Loch Bòdabhat
Loch a'Ghlinne
SOUTH LEWIS,
HARRIS AND
NORTH UIST
TIRGA MOR
ULLAVAL
STULAVAL
Gobhaig
Forest of Harris
Abhainn Suidhe
Horsanish
Arda Mòra
CEANN A TUATH NA HEARADH
UISGNAVAL MORE
CLISHAM
Taransay Glorigs
Soay Beag
Soay Mòr
Cliasmol
Miabhag
Bun Abhainn Eadarra
LOCH A SIAR
Camus an t-suithean
OLD WHALING STATION
Aird Asaig
Tarasaigh (Taransay)
Isay
BEN LUSKENTYRE
Paible
Rubha Sgeirigin
Losgaintir
Tairbeart (Tarbert)
LUSKENTYRE BEACH
South Harris Forest
Seilebost
Aline Lodge
Seaforth I.
Aird a' Mhulaidh
BEINN MHOR
Maraig
Reinigeadal
Loch Trollamarig
Urgha
Carragraich
Caolas Scalpaigh
Carnach
Sgeotasaigh
Rudha Crago
Scalpay
Eilean Scalpay
Toe Head
Borve Lodge
Buirgh
SCARISTA STANDING STONE
NA HEARADH (HARRIS)
Coppay
CHAIPAVAL
Sgarasta Mhor
Aird Mhighe
Liceasto
Leac a Li
Greosabhagh
Kennacley
Plocropol
Drinisiadar
Miabhag
Geocrab
Scadabhagh
Shillay
Little Shillay
Rubha'an Teampuill
BLEAVAL
Loch Langabhat
Beacrabhaic
Caolas Stocinis
Cliuthar
Rubha Bhocaig
Sound of Shillay
Brenish Pt.
Taobh Tuath
Fleoideabhagh
Manais
Stockinish I.
Pabaidh (Pabbay)
Quinish
Aird Mhighe
An t-Ob (Leverburgh)
Fionnsbhagh
Cuidhtinis
Ensay
Sound of Spuir
Spuir
Carminish Is.
Borisearn
Lingreabhagh
Lingarabay I.
Cairminis
Srannda
Killegray
Eilean Bhearnaraigh (Berneray)
Ruisigearraidh
Roghadal
ST CLEMENT'S CHURCH
Langay
Vallay
Renish Pt.
Borgh
Baile
Boreray
Haskeir I.
Haskeir Eagach
CAOLAS NA HEARADH
Aird a'Mhòrain
Caolas Bhearnaraigh
Torogay
Groay
Gilsay
Lingay
Scaravay
Veilish Pt.
Lingay
Port nan Long
Vallay
Oronsay
Baile Mhic Phail
Sursay
Opsay
Tahay
Scolpaig
Greinetobht
Trumaisgearraidh
Baile Mhartainn
Solas
Malacleit
Hermetray
84
Scale : 1:250 000
(approx 4 miles to 1 inch)
6 miles
10km

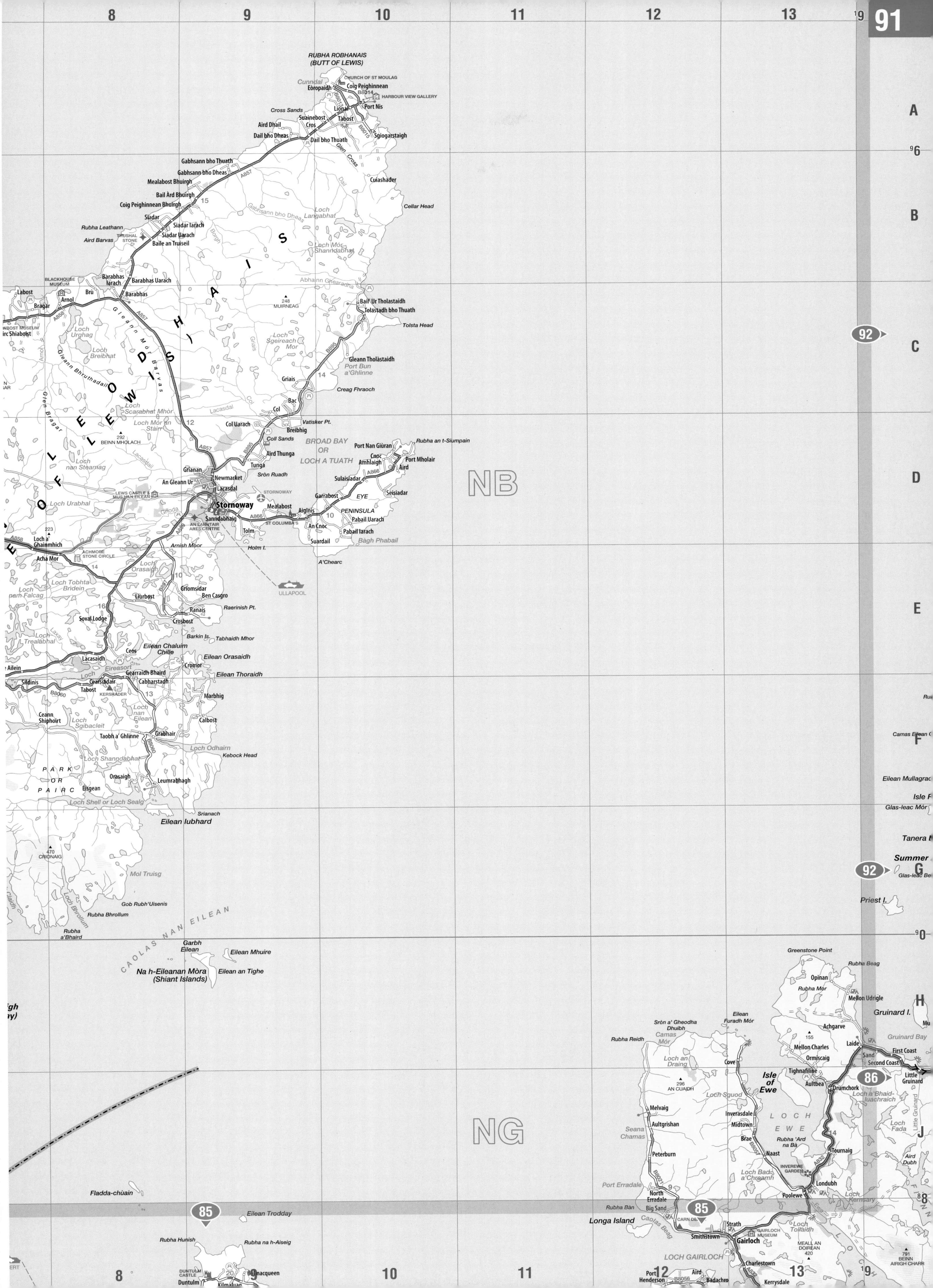
RUBHA ROBHANAIS (BUTT OF LEWIS)
CHURCH OF ST MOULAG
Cunndal
Eòropaidh
Coig Peighinnean
HARBOUR VIEW GALLERY
Lional
Port Nis
Cross Sands
Suainebost
Tabost
Cros
Aird Dhail
Dail bho Dheas
Dail bho Thuath
Sgiogarstaigh
Glen Cross
Gabhsann bho Thuath
Gabhsann bho Dheas
Mealabost Bhuirgh
Bail Àrd Bhuirgh
Coig Peighinnean Bhuirgh
Cuiashader
Cellar Head
Loch Langabhat
Siadar
Siadar Iarach
Siadar Uarach
Rubha Leathann
Aird Barvas
TRUSHAL STONE
Baile an Truiseil
Loch Mòr Shanndabhat
BLACKHOUSE MUSEUM
Labost
Bragar
Arnol
Brù
Barabhas Iarach
Barabhas Uarach
Barabhas
Abhainn Ghearadha
248 MUIRNEAG
Bail' Ur Tholastaidh
Tolastadh bho Thuath
Tolsta Head
Loch Urghag
Loch Breibhat
Gleann Bhruthadail
Gleann Mòr Barvas
Loch Sgeireach Mòr
Gleann Tholàstaidh
Port Bun a'Ghlinne
Griais
Creag Fhraoch
Bac
Col
Col Uarach
Vatisker Pt.
Breibhig
Coll Sands
Loch Scarabhat Mhòr
Loch Mòr an Stairr
292 BEINN MHOLACH
Lacasdal
BROAD BAY OR LOCH A TUATH
Port Nan Giùran
Rubha an t-Siumpain
Cnoc Amhlaigh
Port Mholair
Aird Thunga
Tunga
Aird
Loch nan Stearnag
Sròn Ruadh
Grianan
Newmarket
Sulaisiadar
An Gleann Ur
Lacasdal
NB
LEWS CASTLE & MUS NAN EILEAN
STORNOWAY
Stornoway
Garrabost
EYE PENINSULA
Seisiadar
Loch Urabhal
Mealabost
Aiginis
Sanndabhaig
AN LANNTAIR ARTS CENTRE
ST COLUMBA'S
Pabail Uarach
Pabail Iarach
An Cnoc
Tolm
223
Loch a' Ghainmhich
Suardail
Bàgh Phabail
ACHMORE STONE CIRCLE
Acha Mor
Arnish Moor
Holm I.
A'Chearc
Loch Orasaigh
Loch Tobhta Bridein
ULLAPOOL
Griomsidar
Ben Casgro
Liurbost
Ranais
Raerinish Pt.
Sovat Lodge
Crosbost
Loch Trealabhal
Barkin Is.
Tabhaidh Mhor
Eilean Chaluim Chille
Ceos
Lacasaidh
Eilean Orasaidh
Eireasort
Cromor
Eilean Thoraidh
Gearraidh Bhaird
Sildinis
Cearsiadair
Cabharstadh
Tabost
KERSHADER
Marbhig
Ceann Shiphoirt
Loch Sgibacleit
Loch nan Eilean
Calbost
Taobh a' Ghlinne
Grabhair
Loch Odhairn
Kebock Head
Loch Shanndabhat
PARK OR PAIRC
Orasaigh
Eisgean
Leumrabhagh
Loch Shell or Loch Sealg
Srianach
Eilean Iubhard
470 CRÌONAIG
Mol Truisg
Loch Bhrollum
Gob Rubh'Uisenis
Rubha Bhrollum
Rubha a'Bhaird
CAOLAS NAN EILEAN
Garbh Eilean
Eilean Mhuire
Eilean an Tighe
Na h-Eileanan Mòra (Shiant Islands)
NG
Fladda-chùain
Eilean Trodday
Rubha Hunish
Rubha na h-Aiseig
DUNTULM CASTLE
Duntulm
Kilmaluag
Balmacqueen
Greenstone Point
Rubha Beag
Opinan
Rubha Mòr
Mellon Udrigle
Gruinard I.
Eilean Furadh Mòr
Sròn a' Gheodha Dhuibh
Rubha Reidh
Camas Mòr
Achgarve
155
Laide
Gruinard Bay
Mellon Charles
Ormiscaig
First Coast
Sand
Second Coast
Loch an Draing
Cove
Tighnafiline
Aultbea
Little Gruinard
296 AN CUAIDH
Isle of Ewe
Drumchork
Loch a'Bhaid-luachraich
Loch Sguod
Melvaig
Inverasdale
LOCH EWE
Aultgrishan
Midtown
Seana Chamas
Brae
Rubha 'Ard na Bà
Loch Fada
Peterburn
Naast
Tournaig
Aird Dubh
INVEREWE GARDEN
Loch Bad a'Chreamh
Londubh
Port Erradale
North Erradale
Poolewe
Loch Kernsary
Rubha Bàn
Big Sand
Longa Island
Caolas Beag
CARN DEARG
Strath
Loch Tollaidh
Smithstown
GAIRLOCH MUSEUM
Gairloch
MEALL AN DOIREAN 420
791 BEINN AIRIGH CHARR
LOCH GAIRLOCH
Charlestown
Port Henderson
Aird
Badachro
Kerrysdale
Camas Eilean
Eilean Mullagrach
Glas-leac Mór
Tanera
Summer
Priest I.
92
86
85
A857
A858
A866
B895
B8014
B8015
B8013
B897
B8060
A859
B8021
B8056
A832
B8057
8
9
10
11
12
13
A
B
C
D
E
F
G
H
J

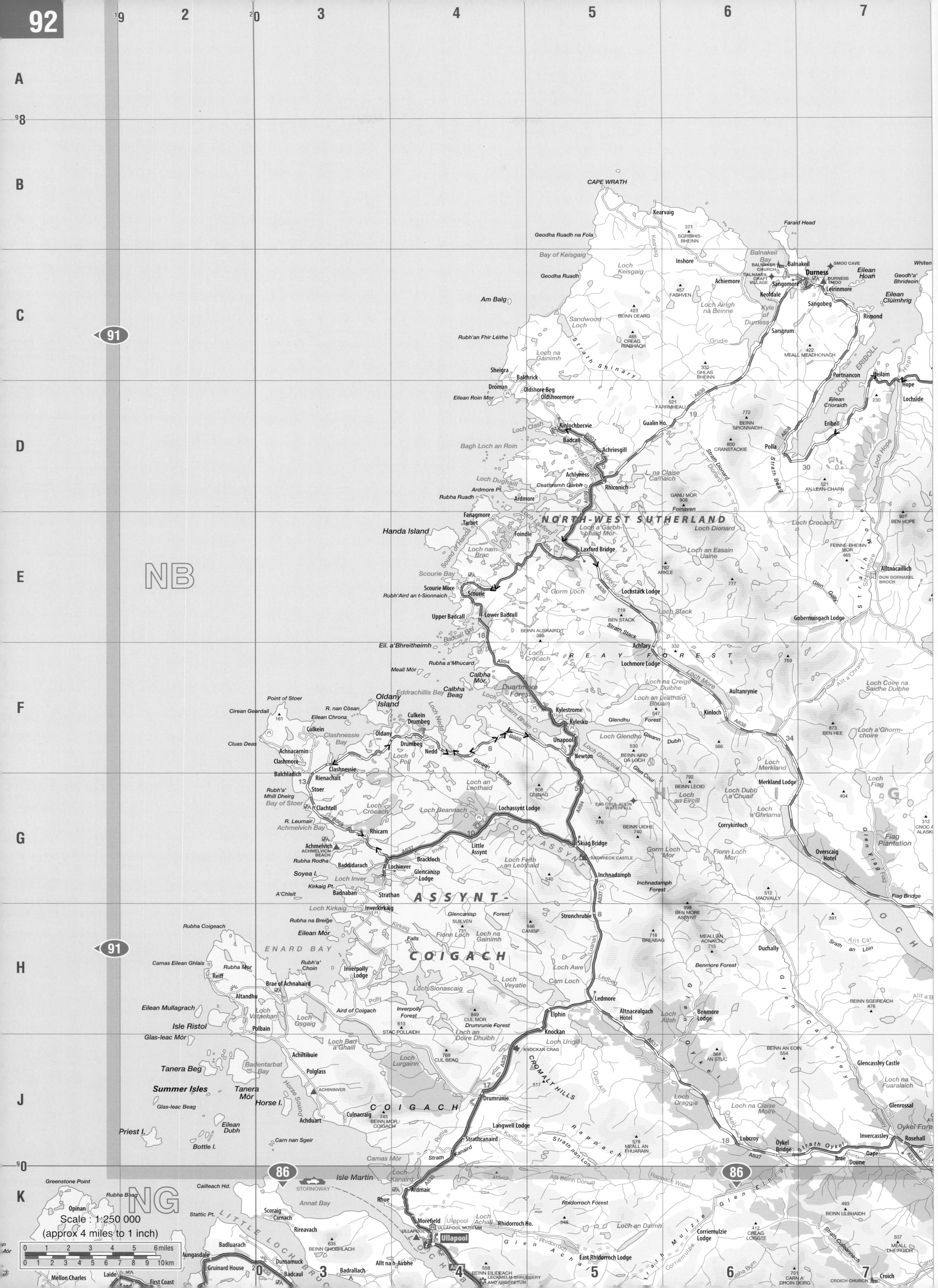
NB
NG
91
86
CAPE WRATH
Kearvaig
Geodha Ruadh na Fola
371 SGRIBHIS-BHEINN
Bay of Keisgaig
Loch Keisgaig
Inshore
Geodha Ruadh
Faraid Head
Balnakeil Bay
BALNAKEIL CHURCH
BALNAKEIL CRAFT VILLAGE
Balnakeil
Durness
SMOO CAVE
DURNESS SMOO
Eilean Hoan
Geodh'a' Bhrideoin
Whiten
Achiemore
457 FASHVEN
Keoldale
Sangomore
Leirinmore
Sangobeg
Eilean Clùimhrig
Am Balg
423 BEINN DEARG
Loch Airigh na Beinne
Kyle of Durness
Rispond
Sandwood Loch
485 CREAG RIABHACH
Grudie
Sarsgrum
Rubh'an Fhir Lèithe
Loch na Gainimh
Strath Shinary
332 GHLAS BHEINN
422 MEALL MEADHONACH
LOCH ERIBOLL
Sheigra
Balchrick
Portnancon
Heilam
Hope
Droman
Oldshore Beg
Oldshoremore
Eilean Roin Mor
521 FARRMHEALL
A838
772 BEINN SPIONNAIDH
Eilean Choraidh
Lochside
Loch Clash
Kinlochbervie
Gualin Ho.
19
Eriboll
Badcall
B801
Bagh Loch an Roin
Achriesgill
800 CRANSTACKIE
Polla
Strath Dionard
Strath Beag
Loch Hope
Achlyness
L. na Claise Carnaich
30
Loch Dughaill
Ardmore Pt.
Ceathramh Garbh
Rhiconich
521 AN LEAN-CHARN
Rubha Ruadh
Ardmore
GANU MOR 908
Foinaven
Fanagmore
Tarbet
NORTH-WEST SUTHERLAND
Loch Crocach
927 BEN HOPE
Handa Island
Sound of Handa
Foindle
Loch a' Garbh-bhaid Mor
Loch Dionard
Loch Laxford
Loch nam Brac
Laxford Bridge
Loch an Easain Uaine
FEINNE-BHEINN MOR 465
787 ARKLE
Alltnacaillich
Scourie Bay
Scourie More
Scourie
Gorm Loch
777
DUN DORNAIGIL BROCH
Rubh'Aird an t-Sionnaich
Lochstack Lodge
Glen Golly
Upper Badcall
Lower Badcall
719 BEN STACK
Loch Stack
Gobernuisgach Lodge
BEINN AUSKAIRD 386
Strath Stack
Badcall Bay
18
Eil. a' Bhreitheimh
Achfary
332
Loch Crocach
REAY FOREST
759
Rubha a' Mhucard
Lochmore Lodge
A894
Meall Mòr
Calbha Mòr
Loch a' Chraisg
Loch More
Allt a' Chràtais
Eddrachillis Bay
Calbha Beag
Duartmore Forest
Loch an Leathaid Bhuain
Aultanrynie
Loch Coire na Saidhe Duibhe
Point of Stoer
Oldany Island
Loch a' Chairn Bhàin
Kylestrome
Kinloch
Cirean Geardail
R. nan Còsan
Kylesku
Glendhu
547 Forest
Eilean Chrona
Culkein Drumbeg
A838
873 BEN HEE
Loch a' Ghorm-choire
161
Clashnessie Bay
Culkein
Loch Nedd
B869
Loch Glendhu
Gleann Dubh
Unapool
566
34
Cluas Deas
Oldany
Drumbeg
Nedd
530 BEINN AIRD DA LOCH
Achnacarnin
8
Newton
Loch Glencoul
Glen Coul
Loch Merkland
Clashmore
Loch Poll
Clashnessie
Gleann Leireag
Merkland Lodge
Balchladich
Rienachait
13
792 BEINN LEOID
Loch Flag
Rubh'a' Mhill Dheirg
Stoer
Loch an Leothaid
808 QUINAG
Loch Dubh a' Chuail
404
Bay of Stoer
EAS COUL AULIN WATERFALL
Loch an Eircill
Clachtoll
Loch Crocach
Loch Beannach
Lochassynt Lodge
Loch a' Ghriama
R. Leumair
Achmelvich Bay
B869
776
BEINN UIDHE 740
Corrykinloch
312 CNOC A' ALASK
Rhicarn
10
LOCH ASSYNT
Skiag Bridge
Gorm Loch Mor
Fionn Loch Mor
Flag Plantation
Achmelvich
ACHMELVICH BEACH
A837
Inver
Little Assynt
ARDVRECK CASTLE
Glen Flag
Rubha Rodha
Baddidarach
Brackloch
Loch Feith an Leothaid
Overscaig Hotel
Lochinver
Glencanisp Lodge
Inchnadamph
Soyea I.
540
Loch Inver
Inchnadamph Forest
Kirkaig Pt.
Badnaban
Strathan
ASSYNT-
512 MAOVALLY
Flag Bridge
A'Chleit
Loch Kirkaig
Inverkirkaig
A837
998 BEN MORE ASSYNT
Glencanisp Forest
Stronchrubie
8
391
Rubha Coigeach
Rubha na Breige
Kirkaig
SUILVEN 731
846 CANISP
718 BREABAG
MEALL AN AONAICH 715
LOCH
Eilean Mòr
Falls
Fionn Loch
Loch na Gainimh
Duchally
Allt Car
Strath an Loin
ENARD BAY
COIGACH
Camas Eilean Ghlais
Rubha Mor
Rubh'a' Choin
Inverpolly Lodge
Loch Awe
Benmore Forest
Reiff
Brae of Achnahaird
Loch Veyatie
Cam Loch
Ledbeg
Glen Oykel
Glen Cassley
Altandhu
Loch Sionascaig
Ledmore
BEINN SGEIREACH 476
Eilean Mullagrach
Polly
Loch Vatachan
Aird of Coigach
Inverpolly Forest
849 CUL MOR
Elphin
Altnacealgach Hotel
Loch Ailsh
Benmore Lodge
Isle Ristol
Loch Osgaig
Polbain
613 STAC POLLAIDH
Drumrunie Forest
Knockan
Glas-leac Mòr
Loch an Doire Dhuibh
Loch Urigill
KNOCKAN CRAG
Loch Bad a' Ghaill
Achiltibuie
769 CUL BEAG
A835
CROMALT HILLS
A837
364 AN STUC
BEINN AN EOIN 554
Glencassley Castle
Tanera Beg
Badentarbat Bay
Loch Lurgainn
Polglass
Loch na Fuaralaich
Summer Isles
Tanera Mòr
Horse Sound
ACHININVER
17
517
Oykel
Horse I.
COIGACH
Drumrunie
Loch Craggie
Loch na Claise Moire
Glenrossal
Glas-leac Beag
Culnacraig
743 BEINN MOR COIGACH
Achduart
Oykel Forest
Eilean Dubh
Priest I.
Carn nan Sgeir
Langwell Lodge
Rappach
578 MEALL AN FHUARAIN
18
Lubcroy
Oykel Bridge
Invercassley
Rosehall
Bottle I.
Runie
Strathcanaird
Kanaird
Strath nan Lon
Strath Oykel
A837
Brae
Oape
Doune
Camas Mòr
Strath
Isle Martin
Loch Kanaird
415
Allt-Beag Donuill
Rappach Water
Greenstone Point
Rubha Beag
Cailleach Hd.
STORNOWAY
Ardmair
Glen Einig
Annat Bay
Rhue
Rhidorroch Forest
Opinan
Static Pt.
Scoraig
Carnach
LITTLE LOCH BROOM
Morefield
Ullapool
Loch Achall
Rhidorroch Ho.
548
Loch an Daimh
Corriemulzie Lodge
412 CREAG LOISGTE
493 BEINN ULBHAIDH
Strath Cuileannach
Scale : 1:250 000
(approx 4 miles to 1 inch)
0 1 2 3 4 5 6 miles
0 1 2 3 4 5 6 7 8 9 10 km
Rireavach
635 BEINN GHOBHLACH
ULLAPOOL MUSEUM
Ullapool
Glen Achall
Strath Mulzie
Corriemulzie
507 MEALL DHEIRGIDH
Mungasdale
Badluarach
East Rhidorroch Lodge
Gruinard House
Durnamuck
Badrallach
Allt na h-Airbhe
558 BEINN EILIDEACH
LECKMELM SHRUBBERY AND ARBORETUM
701 CARN A' CHOIN DEIRG
Croich
CROICH CHURCH
Mellon Charles
Laide
First Coast
Badcaul
A832

8
9
10
11
12
13
14
A
B
C
D
E
F
G
H
J
K
NC
ND
NH
NJ
94
87
Head
Rubha Thormaid
Eilean nan Ron
Strathy Point
Totegan
Strathy Bay
Melvich Bay
Red Pt.
Fresgoe
Sandside Bay
Brims Ness
Spear Hd.
Holborn Hd.
Clardon Hd.
Dunnet Hd.
Briga Hd.
The Thirl
Stromness
St Mary's Chapel
Crosskirk
Scrabster
Thurso Bay
Thurso Castle
Thurso
Thurso East
Millbank
Clardon
Murkle
Castletown
Haimer
Olrig Ho.
Dounreay
Buldoo
Achreamie
Bridge of Forss
Newlands of Geise
Geise
Weydale
Achingills
Ardmore Pt.
Kirtomy Pt.
Armadale Bay
Brawl
Aultiphurst
Baligill
Portskerra
Melvich
Bighouse
Sandside Ho.
Isauld
Reay
Achvarasdal
Cnoc Freiceadain Chambered Cairn
Westfield
Shebster
Lieurary
Buckies
Sordale
Knockdee
Braal Castle
Roadside
Clayock
Calder Mains
Halkirk
Banniskirk Ho.
Strathan
Midfield
Port Vasgo
408 Ben Hutig
West Strathan
Talmine
Skinnet
Midtown
Caol Raineach
Rabbit Is.
Tongue Bay
Skerray
Achtoty
Airdtorrisdale
Torrisdale
Neave I. or Coombe I.
Torrisdale Bay
Farr Pt.
Farr
Strathnaver Museum
Bettyhill
Achina
Kirtomy
Swordly
Armadale
Lednagullin
Strathy
Golval
Loch Akran
Loch Meadie
Bowside Lodge
Strathy Forest
Loch Saorach
Broubster
Loch Thormaid
Shurrery
Loch Calder
A'Mhoine
A838
A836
A897
B871
B873
B874
B870
A9
Coldbackie
Borgie
Invernaver
Leckfurin
Achuvoldrach
Kyle of Tongue
Tongue
Kirkiboll
Castle Varrich
Borgie Forest
Achanlochy Clearance Village
Skelpick
Loch Buidhe Mor
Loch Meala
Achiemore
Loch na Seilge
Upper Bighouse
Craigtown
Dalhalvaig
Shurrery Lodge
Loch Shurrery
Brawlbin
Loch Olginey
Scotscalder Station
Olgrinmore
Harpsdale
Spittal
Mybster
Druim nan Cliar
Ribigill
Loch Craggie
Kinloch Lodge
Achagary
Loch Mor na Caorach
Loch nan Clach
Trantlemore
Trantlebeg
Strath Halladale
Loch Scye
290 Beinn nam Bad Mor
Dorrery
Loch Tuim Ghlais
Loch Caluim
Torran Water
Westerdale
Loch Meadie
Loch na Seilg
Tongue
Loch a' Ghobha-Dhuibh
764 Ben Loyal
527 Beinn Stumanadh
Carnachy
Rhifail
Strathnaver
293 Beinn Rifa-gil
Forsinain
Loch Dubh nan Geodh
Loch Eileanach
Strathmore Lodge
Loch Gaineimh
Little River
Loch an Dherue
Loch Haluim
Loch Loyal Lodge
557 Cnoc nan Cullean
Loch Loyal
Loch Strathy
Loch nam Breac
Loch na Saobhaidhe
280 Sletill Hill
Loch Sletill
Altnabreac Station
Lochmore Cottage
Lochdhu
Loch More
Loch Coulside
Inchkinloch
Loch Syre
Langdale
Syre
Skail
Dalvina Lo.
Forsinard
Forsinard Station
Forsinard Flows
Loch Crocach
221
Loch Ruard
Loch a' Mhuilinn
Loch Sand
Loch Thulachan
Loch Rangag
Rosal Clearance Trail
Loch Druim a' Chliabhain
580 Ben Griam Beg
403
Rimsdale Burn
Dalnawillan Lodge
Rumsdale Water
Loch Meadie
Loch Eileanach
294 Pole Hill
373
Garvault Hotel
509 Ben Griam More
Achentoul Forest
348 Ben Alisky
Loch Bread
Braehungie
Glutt Lodge
Loch Dubh
269 Cnocan Conachreag
Mudale
Naver Forest
Loch nan Clàr
Loch Rimsdale
Badanloch Forest
Loch an Ruathair
Loch Arichlinie
Lochside
438
Knockfin Heights
Houstry
Smerral
Altnaharra
Clebrig
Loch Naver
Loch Truderscaig
Loch an Alltan Fhearna
Loch Badanloch
Badanloch Lodge
Strath Beg
Kinbrace
Achentoul
318 Cnoc Loch Mhadadh
Dunbeath Water
Latheronwheel Ho.
Berriedale Water
Braemore
Balnabruich
Dunbeath
Knockally
473
721 Ben Klibreck
272
Loch Choire Lodge
328
Helmsdale
Loch Choire Forest
Loch Choire
961 Meall nan Con
Strath Vagastie
H
L
A
N
D
438 Cnoc Coire na Pearna
705 Morven
283
Ramscraigs
542
704 Ben Armine
Gorm-loch Beag
Borrobol Forest
Abhainn na Frithe
Borrobol Lodge
Suisgill Burn
517 Cnoc an Eireannaich
Wag
626 Scaraben
Langwell Forest
Borgue
Loch a' Bhealaich
581 Meall a' Bhata
Altanduin
365
Kildonan Burn
Newport
Ceann Leathad nam Bò
Crask Inn
Loch Gaineamhach
718 Creag Mhor
Gorm-loch Mor
387 Creag nam Fiadh
Strath of Kildonan
555 Creag Scalabsdale
Auitibea
Langwell Ho.
Berriedale
Langwell Water
Badbea Clearance Village
422
486
Kildonan Lodge
Baile an Or Goldrush Site
Beinn Dubhain
414
Ben Armine Forest
Tuarie Burn
Strath Skinsdale
Ousdale
Glas-loch Mor
Strath na Seilge
Ben Armine Lodge
Craggie
Craggie Burn
Helmsdale
Torrish
Kilphedir
Eldrable Hill
417
Marrel
Navidale
Ord Point
Timespan Heritage Centre
West Helmsdale
Strath Tirry
461 Meallan Liath Mor
345
Rhian
Shinness
Dalnessie
Black Water
628 Beinn Dhorain
592
Glen Loth
Glen Sletdale
Gartymore
Portgower
Achnairn
Loch Beannach
Brora
Balnacoil
Lothmore
Lothbeg
Lothbeg Pt.
Dalchork
Dalchork Wood
Achnaluachrach
299
West Langwell
Strath Brora
538 Col-Bheinn
Gordonbush
Colaboll
Saval
Allt na Luibe
Loch Brora
Sallachy
Lairg Lodge
Lairg Muir
Loch Craggie
Dalreavoch
Rhilochan
Ben Horn 521
Achrimsdale
East Clyne
West Clyne
Dalchalm
Lairg
Ferrycroft Visitor Centre
323
East Langwell
Farlary
Loch Horn
Clynelish
Clynelish Distillery
Claonel
Gruids
Strath Fleet
Muie
Torroble
Rogart
377 Cagar Feosaig
Brora
Loch Cracail Mor
Ardachu
Pittentrail
Doll
Achany
336
Hector Macdonald Monument
Rogart Station
466 Beinn Lunndaidh
Backies
Dunrobin Castle Museum & Gardens
A839
B864
Shin Forest
Achinduich
Morvich
Golspie
Falls of Shin Visitor Centre
Linsidemore
Culmaily
Torboll Farm
Achnahanat
Loch Laro
Loch Buidhe
Kirkton
Little Torboll
Cambusmore Lodge
Loch Fleet
Inveran
Invershin
Craigton
349 Beinn Domhnaill
Cambusavie Farm
Littleferry
Skelbo
Skelbo Castle
Carbisdale Castle
297
Culrain
Balblair
Airdens
Achvaich
Badninish
Fourpenny
Braelangwell Lodge
Clashcoig
Evelix
Embo
Migdale
Rearquhar
Proncy
Poles
Embo Street
Wester Gruinards
Strathcarron
Bonar Bridge
Gablon

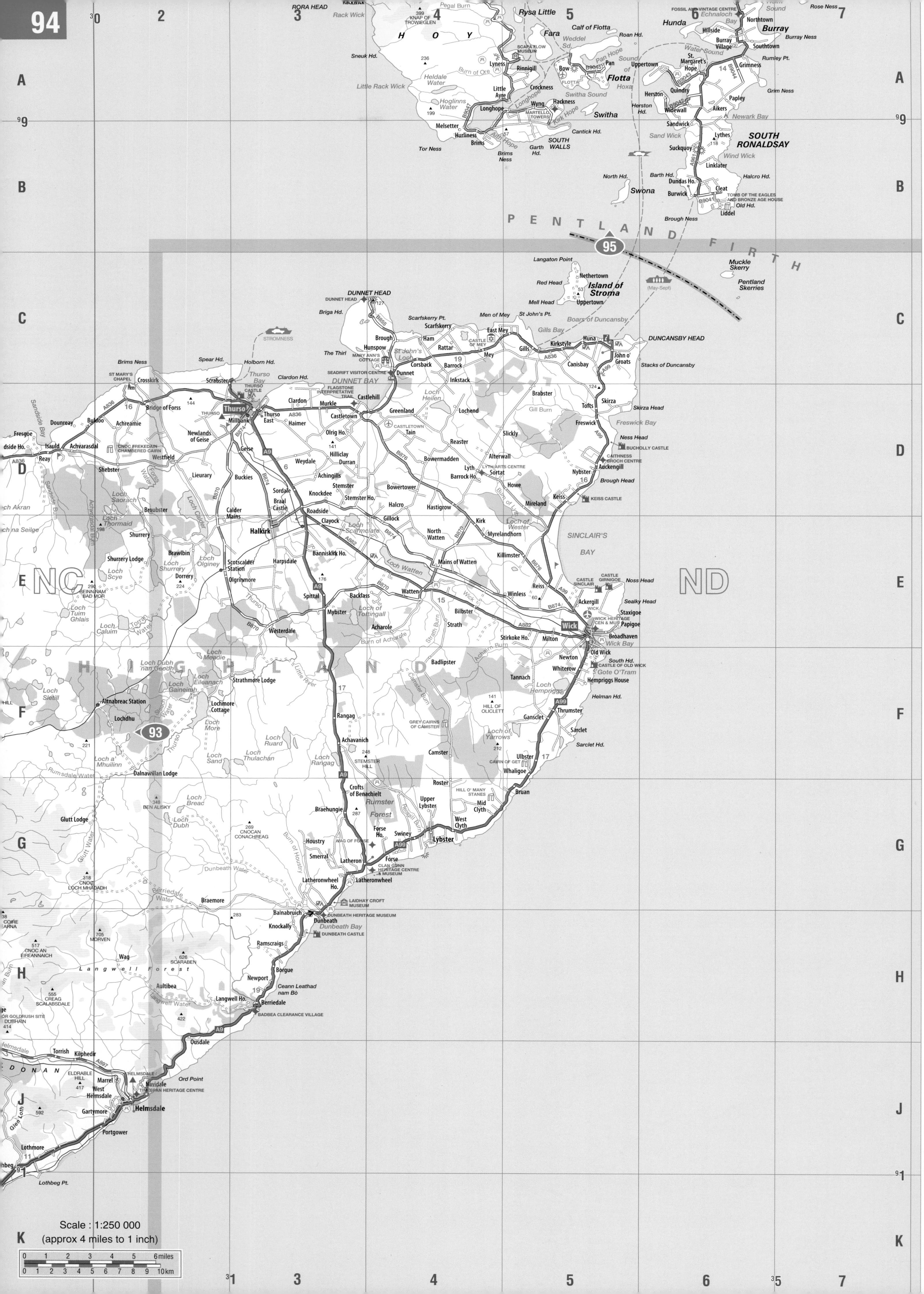
HOY
Rysa Little
Fara
Calf of Flotta
Flotta
Switha
Hunda
Burray
SOUTH RONALDSAY
Swona
PENTLAND FIRTH
Muckle Skerry
Pentland Skerries
Island of Stroma
DUNNET HEAD
DUNCANSBY HEAD
John o' Groats
Stacks of Duncansby
Dunnet Bay
Thurso
Scrabster
Dounreay
Reay
Castletown
Halkirk
Wick
SINCLAIR'S BAY
Keiss
Noss Head
Watten
Lybster
Latheron
Dunbeath
Berriedale
Helmsdale
Langwell Forest
Forse
Whaligoe
Clyth
Dunbeath Bay
Ord Point
Lothbeg Pt.
Altnabreac Station
Morven
HIGHLAND
NC
ND
Scale : 1:250 000
(approx 4 miles to 1 inch)
0 1 2 3 4 5 6 miles
0 1 2 3 4 5 6 7 8 9 10km

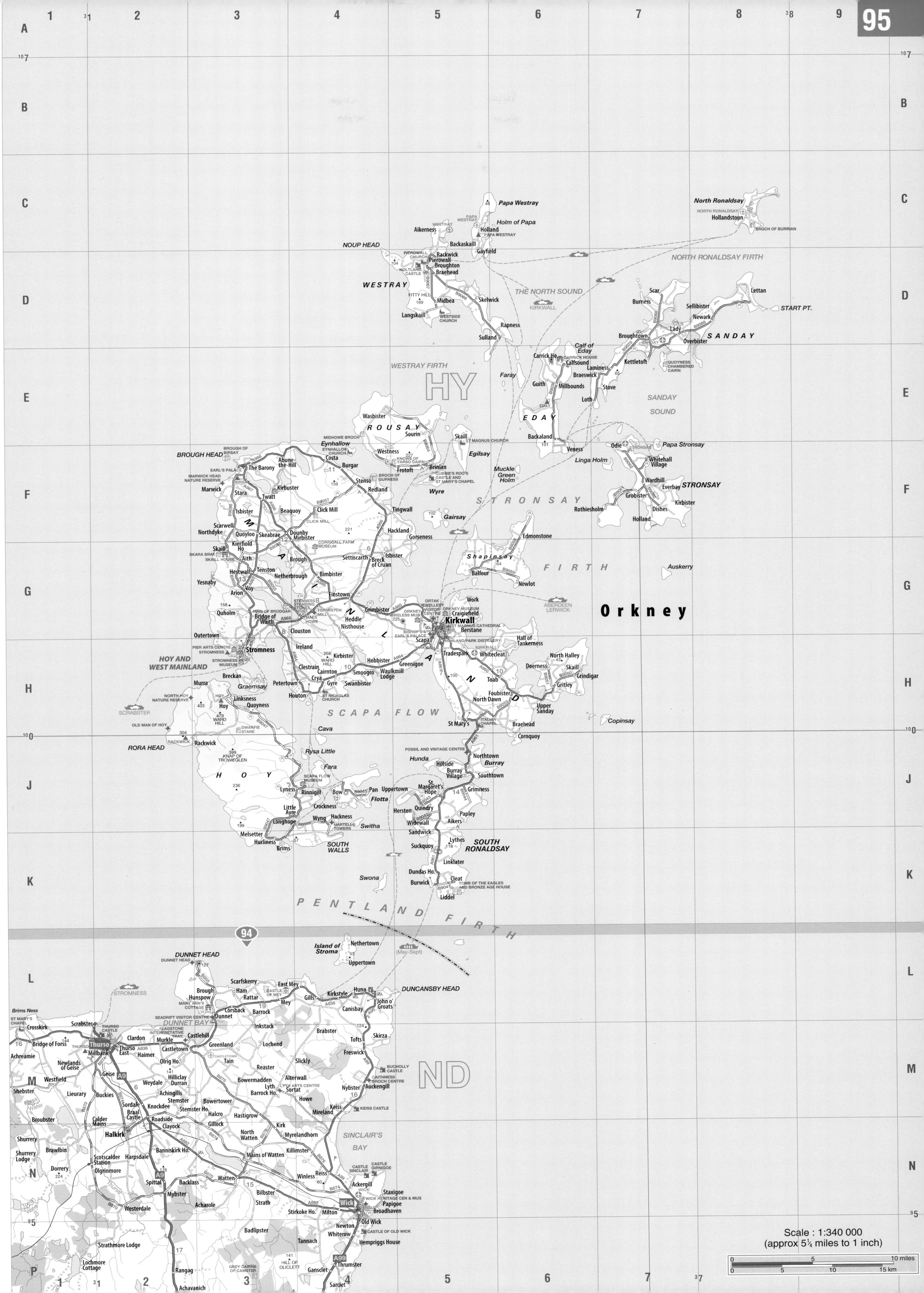
Orkney
HY
ND
Papa Westray
Holm of Papa
North Ronaldsay
Hollandstoun
BROCH OF BURRIAN
NORTH RONALDSAY FIRTH
Aikerness
Holland
Backaskaill
Gayfield
NOUP HEAD
Rackwick
Pierowall
Broughton
Braehead
WESTRAY
Midbea
Skelwick
Langskaill
WESTSIDE CHURCH
Rapness
Sulland
THE NORTH SOUND
Scar
Burness
Lettan
Sellibister
Newark
START PT.
Lady
Overbister
SANDAY
Broughtown
Kettletoft
Calf of Eday
Carrick Ho
Calfsound
Laminess
Braeswick
Stove
WESTRAY FIRTH
Faray
Guith
Millbounds
Loth
SANDAY SOUND
EDAY
Backaland
Veness
Wasbister
ROUSAY
Sourin
Skaill
MIDHOWE BROCH
Eynhallow
Egilsay
Westness
Frotoft
Brinian
Muckle Green Holm
Linga Holm
Odie
Papa Stronsay
Whitehall Village
Wardhill
Everbay
STRONSAY
Grobister
Kirbister
Rothiesholm
Dishes
Holland
BROUGH HEAD
Abune-the-Hill
Costa
The Barony
Burgar
Stenso
Redland
Marwick
Stara
Kirbuster
Wyre
Twatt
Isbister
Beaquoy
Click Mill
Tingwall
STRONSAY
Gairsay
Scarwell
Northdyke
Quoyloo
Skeabrae
Dounby
Mirbister
Hackland
Gorseness
Edmonstone
Skaill
Kierfold Ho
Settiscarth
Isbister
Breck of Cruan
Shapinsay
Balfour
Newlot
FIRTH
Auskerry
Hestwall
Aith
Tenston
Netherbrough
Brough
Bimbister
Yesnaby
Voy
Arion
Finstown
Work
Quholm
Bridge of Waith
Grimbister
Heddle
Nisthouse
Kirkwall
Craigiefield
Berstane
Clouston
Outertown
Scapa
Hall of Tankerness
Stromness
Ireland
HOY AND WEST MAINLAND
Kirbister
Hobbister
Greenigoe
Tradespark
Whitecleat
Deerness
North Halley
Skaill
Grindigar
Gritley
Breckan
Graemsay
Clestrain
Cairnton
Crya
Smoogro
Waulkmill Lodge
Gyre
Swanbister
Toab
Murra
Petertown
Houton
Foubister
North Dawn
Upper Sanday
Linksness
Hoy
Quoyness
SCAPA FLOW
Copinsay
SCRABSTER
OLD MAN OF HOY
St Mary's
Braehead
Cornquoy
RORA HEAD
Rackwick
Cava
Rysa Little
Hunda
Northtown
Burray
Hillside
Burray Village
Southtown
HOY
Fara
Lyness
Rinnigill
Bow
Pan
Uppertown
Flotta
St. Margaret's Hope
Grimness
Herston
Quindry
Little Ayre
Crockness
Longhope
Wyng
Hackness
Switha
Widewall
Papley
Aikers
Sandwick
Melsetter
Hurliness
Brims
SOUTH WALLS
Lythes
SOUTH RONALDSAY
Suckquoy
Linklater
Swona
Dundas Ho.
Burwick
Cleat
Liddel
PENTLAND FIRTH
94
Island of Stroma
Nethertown
Uppertown
DUNNET HEAD
Scarfskerry
Brough
Ham
Rattar
East Mey
Mey
Gills
Huna
Kirkstyle
DUNCANSBY HEAD
John o' Groats
Canisbay
Hunspow
Corsback
Barrock
Dunnet
Brims Ness
Crosskirk
Scrabster
DUNNET BAY
Castlehill
Inkstack
Brabster
Tofts
Skirza
Bridge of Forss
Thurso
Clardon
Murkle
Castletown
Greenland
Lochend
Freswick
Achreamie
Millbank
Thurso East
Haimer
Olrig Ho.
Tain
Slickly
Reaster
Newlands of Geise
Westfield
Geise
Weydale
Hilliclay
Durran
Bowermadden
Alterwall
Lyth
Sortat
Barrock Ho.
Nybster
Auckengill
Shebster
Lieurary
Buckies
Achingills
Stemster
Bowertower
Howe
Stemster Ho.
Mireland
Keiss
KEISS CASTLE
Broubster
Calder Mains
Sordale
Braal Castle
Knockdee
Halcro
Hastigrow
Roadside
Clayock
Gillock
Halkirk
Kirk
North Watten
Myrelandhorn
SINCLAIR'S BAY
Shurrery
Brawlbin
Shurrery Lodge
Banniskirk Ho.
Killimster
Scotscalder Station
Harpsdale
Mains of Watten
Dorrery
Olgrinmore
Reiss
Winless
Ackergill
Spittal
Watten
Backlass
Staxigoe
Mybster
Bilbster
Wick
Papigoe
Strath
Broadhaven
Westerdale
Acharole
Stirkoke Ho.
Milton
Newton
Old Wick
Whiterow
Badlipster
Tannach
Hempriggs House
Strathmore Lodge
Lochmore Cottage
Rangag
Achavanich
Gansclet
Thrumster
Sarclet
Scale : 1:340 000
(approx 5¼ miles to 1 inch)
0 5 10 miles
0 5 10 15 km

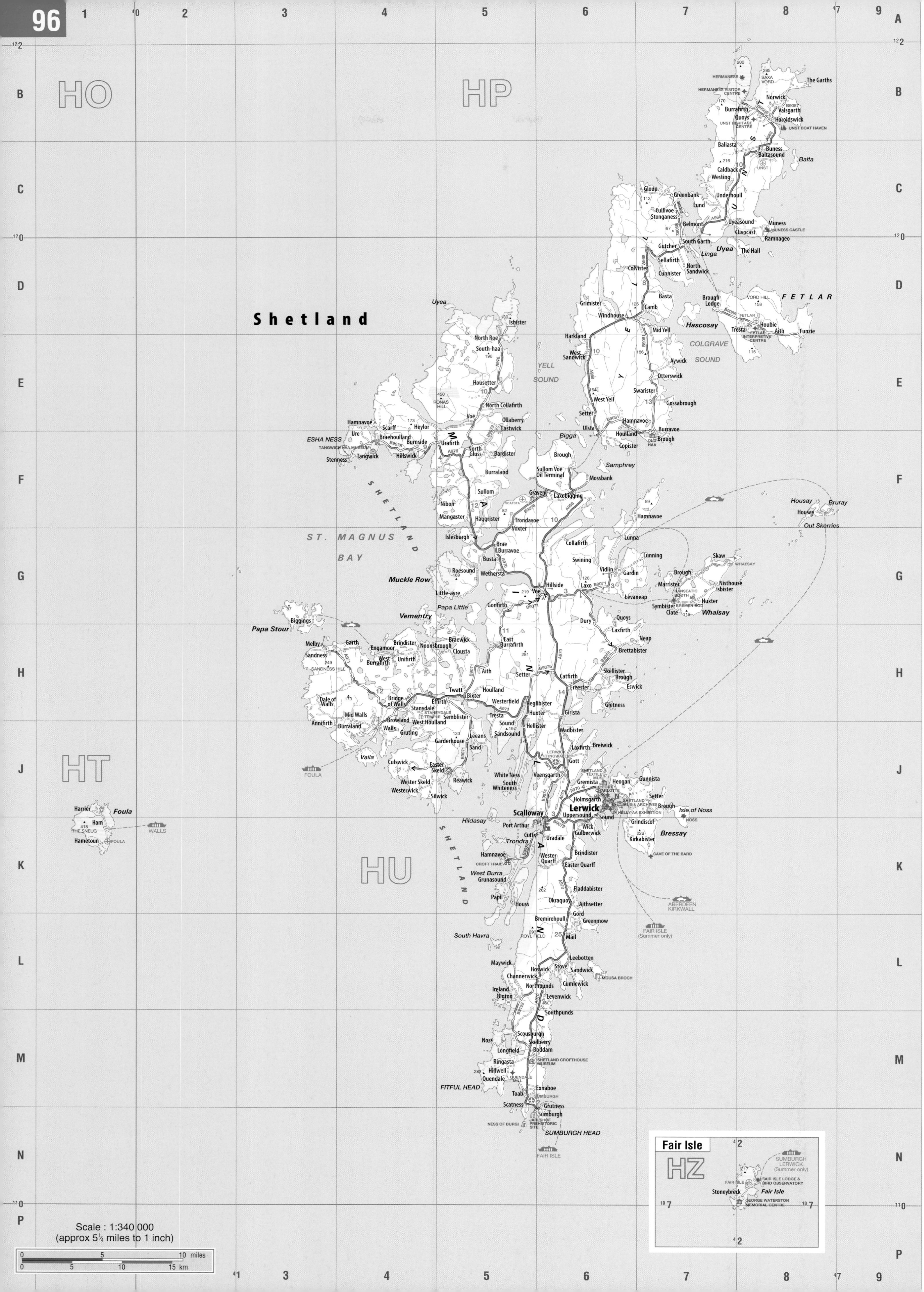
Shetland
HO
HP
HT
HU
HZ
Unst
Yell
Fetlar
Mainland
Uyea
Hascosay
Colgrave Sound
Yell Sound
St. Magnus Bay
Shetland
Muckle Row
Vementry
Papa Little
Papa Stour
Esha Ness
Foula
Vaila
Hildasay
Trondra
West Burra
South Havra
Whalsay
Out Skerries
Housay
Bruray
Isle of Noss
Bressay
Fitful Head
Sumburgh Head
Hermaness
Saxa Vord
The Garths
Norwick
Haroldswick
Baltasound
Balta
Uyeasound
Muness
Gutcher
Mid Yell
Burravoe
Brae
Voe
Sullom Voe Oil Terminal
Walls
Scalloway
Lerwick
Sandwick
Sumburgh
Fair Isle
Stoneybreck
Scale : 1:340 000
(approx 5¼ miles to 1 inch)
0 5 10 miles
0 5 10 15 km

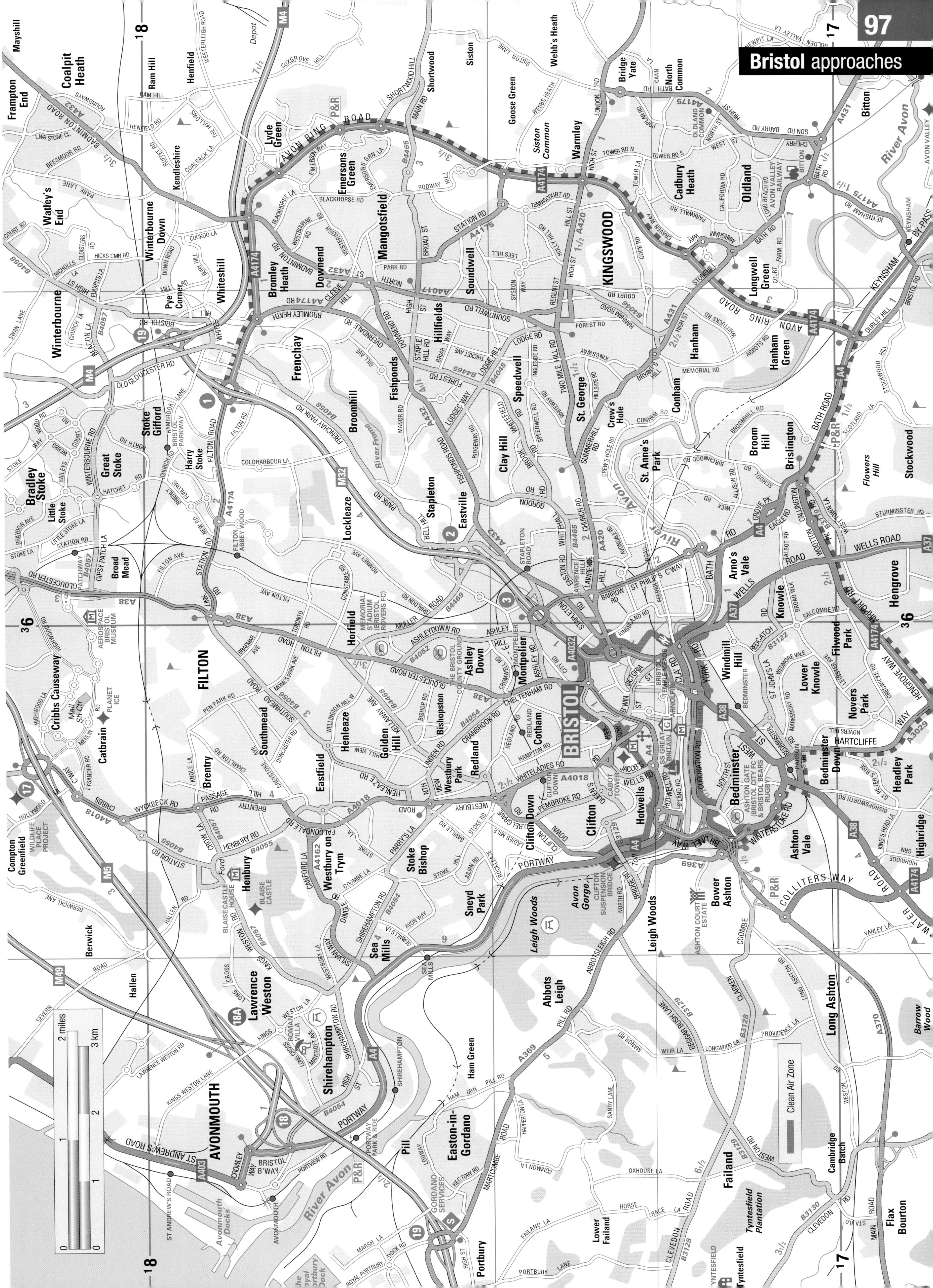
Mayshill
Frampton End
Coalpit Heath
Ram Hill
Henfield
Siston
Webb's Heath
Bridge Yate
North Common
Bitton
Lyde Green
Emersons Green
Mangotsfield
Shortwood
Goose Green
Siston Common
Warmley
Cadbury Heath
Oldland
KINGSWOOD
Soundwell
Downend
Bromley Heath
Hillfields
Fishponds
Frenchay
Winterbourne
Winterbourne Down
Watley's End
Kendleshire
Whiteshill
Pye Corner
Stoke Gifford
Harry Stoke
Bradley Stoke
Little Stoke
Great Stoke
Broomhill
Speedwell
St. George
Crew's Hole
Conham
Hanham
Hanham Green
Longwell Green
Stapleton
Eastville
Lockleaze
Clay Hill
St. Anne's Park
Broom Hill
Brislington
Stockwood
Flowers Hill
FILTON
Broad Mead
Horfield
Ashley Down
Montpelier
Bishopston
Golden Hill
Henleaze
Southmead
Eastfield
Brentry
Westbury Park
Redland
Cotham
BRISTOL
Clifton
Hotwells
Clifton Down
Arno's Vale
Knowle
Windmill Hill
Lower Knowle
Filwood Park
Hengrove
Novers Park
Bedminster
Bedminster Down
Headley Park
Highridge
Ashton Vale
Cribbs Causeway
Catbrain
Compton Greenfield
Henbury
Westbury on Trym
Stoke Bishop
Sneyd Park
Leigh Woods
Avon Gorge
Bower Ashton
Sea Mills
Berwick
Hallen
Lawrence Weston
Shirehampton
AVONMOUTH
Avonmouth Docks
Abbots Leigh
Ham Green
Pill
Easton-in-Gordano
Long Ashton
Barrow Wood
Cambridge Batch
Failand
Lower Failand
Portbury
Flax Bourton
Tyntesfield
Tyntesfield Plantation
River Avon
River Frome
M4
M5
M32
M49
A4
A38
A4174
Clean Air Zone
2 miles
3 km

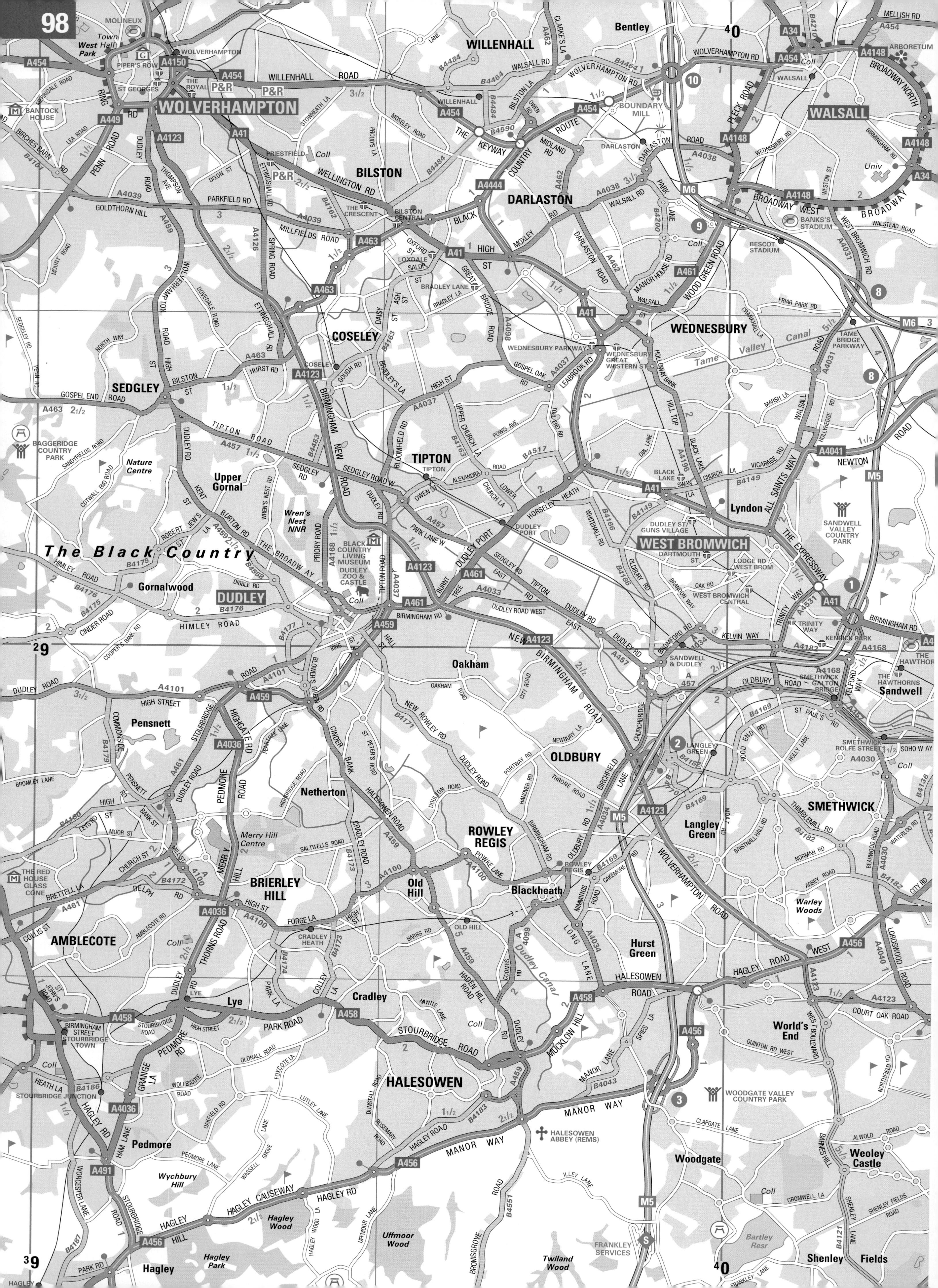
WOLVERHAMPTON
WILLENHALL
Bentley
WALSALL
BILSTON
DARLASTON
WEDNESBURY
COSELEY
SEDGLEY
TIPTON
Upper Gornal
Lyndon
WEST BROMWICH
The Black Country
Gornalwood
DUDLEY
Oakham
OLDBURY
Sandwell
Pensnett
Netherton
ROWLEY REGIS
Langley Green
SMETHWICK
BRIERLEY HILL
Old Hill
Blackheath
AMBLECOTE
Hurst Green
Lye
Cradley
World's End
HALESOWEN
Pedmore
Woodgate
Weoley Castle
Wychbury Hill
Hagley Wood
Uffmoor Wood
Twiland Wood
Hagley Park
Hagley
Shenley Fields
Bartley Resr
Warley Woods
MOLINEUX
BANTOCK HOUSE
BAGGERIDGE COUNTRY PARK
Nature Centre
Wren's Nest NNR
BLACK COUNTRY LIVING MUSEUM
DUDLEY ZOO & CASTLE
Merry Hill Centre
THE RED HOUSE GLASS CONE
SANDWELL VALLEY COUNTRY PARK
BANKS'S STADIUM
BESCOT STADIUM
ARBORETUM
BOUNDARY MILL
WOODGATE VALLEY COUNTRY PARK
HALESOWEN ABBEY (REMS)
FRANKLEY SERVICES
Tame Valley Canal
Dudley Canal
M5
M6
A454
A41
A459
A4123
A461
A456
A458
A4036
A4100
A4101
A4148
A4038
A4037
A4041
A463
A4444
A462
A457
A4034
A4030
A4040
A4150
A449
A491
THE EXPRESSWAY
HAGLEY ROAD
MANOR WAY
HAGLEY CAUSEWAY
BIRMINGHAM NEW ROAD
WOLVERHAMPTON ROAD
29
39
40

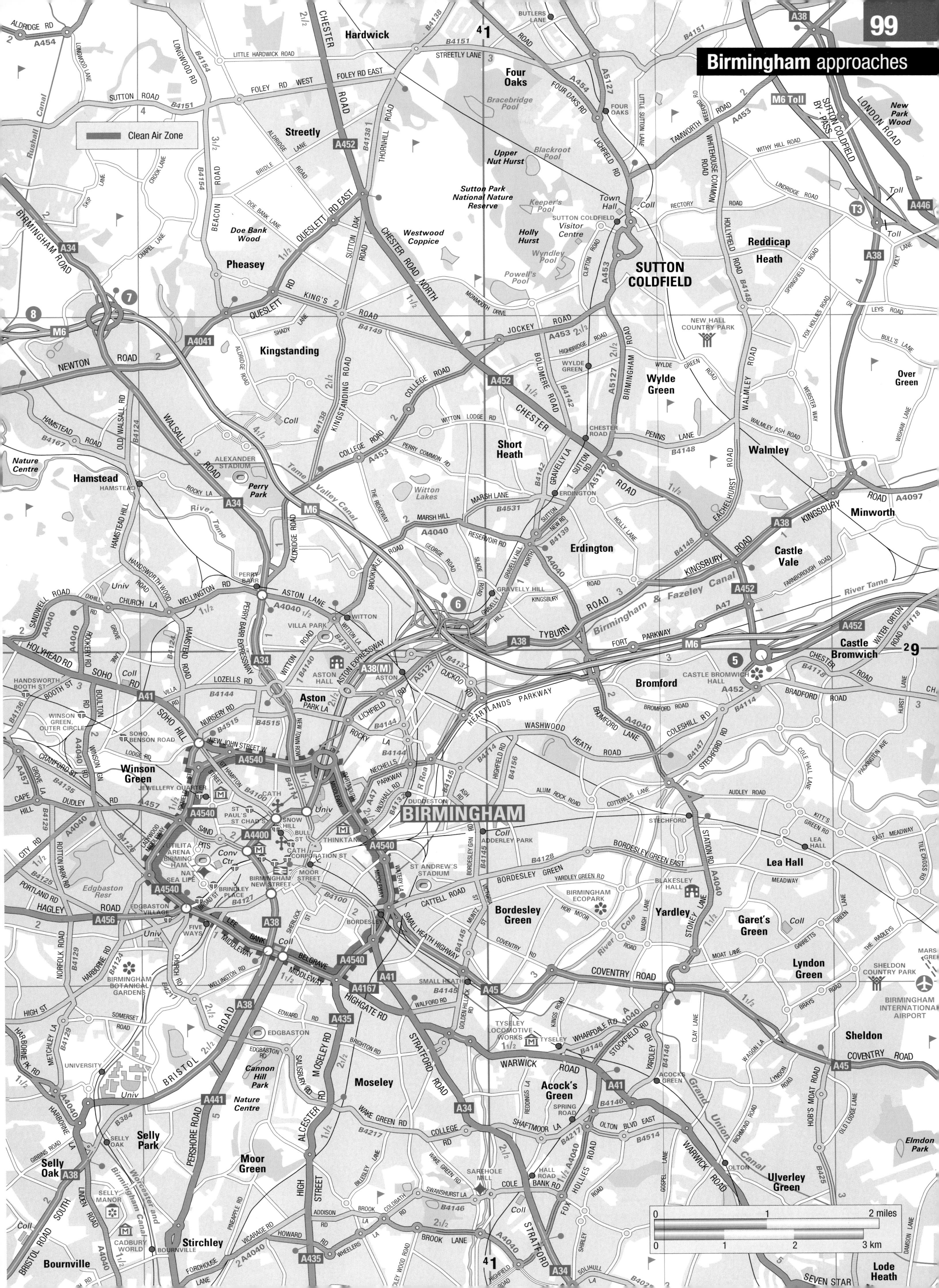
Clean Air Zone
Hardwick
Four Oaks
Bracebridge Pool
Streetly
Blackroot Pool
Upper Nut Hurst
Sutton Park National Nature Reserve
Keeper's Pool
Town Hall
Doe Bank Wood
Westwood Coppice
Holly Hurst
Wyndley Pool
Powell's Pool
Pheasey
SUTTON COLDFIELD
Reddicap Heath
New Park Wood
Kingstanding
New Hall Country Park
Wylde Green
Over Green
Short Heath
Walmley
Nature Centre
Hamstead
Alexander Stadium
Perry Park
Witton Lakes
Minworth
Erdington
Castle Vale
Villa Park
Aston Hall
Castle Bromwich
Aston
Bromford
Castle Bromwich Hall
Winson Green
Jewellery Quarter
BIRMINGHAM
Thinktank
Utilita Arena Birmingham
St Andrew's Stadium
Edgbaston Resr
Lea Hall
Blakesley Hall
Birmingham Ecopark
Bordesley Green
Yardley
Garet's Green
Lyndon Green
Sheldon Country Park
Birmingham International Airport
Birmingham Botanical Gardens
Sheldon
Edgbaston
Tyseley Locomotive Works
Cannon Hill Park
Moseley
Acock's Green
Nature Centre
Selly Park
Selly Oak
Moor Green
Sarehole Mill
Elmdon Park
Ulverley Green
Selly Manor
Cadbury World
Stirchley
Bournville
Lode Heath
0 1 2 miles
0 1 2 3 km

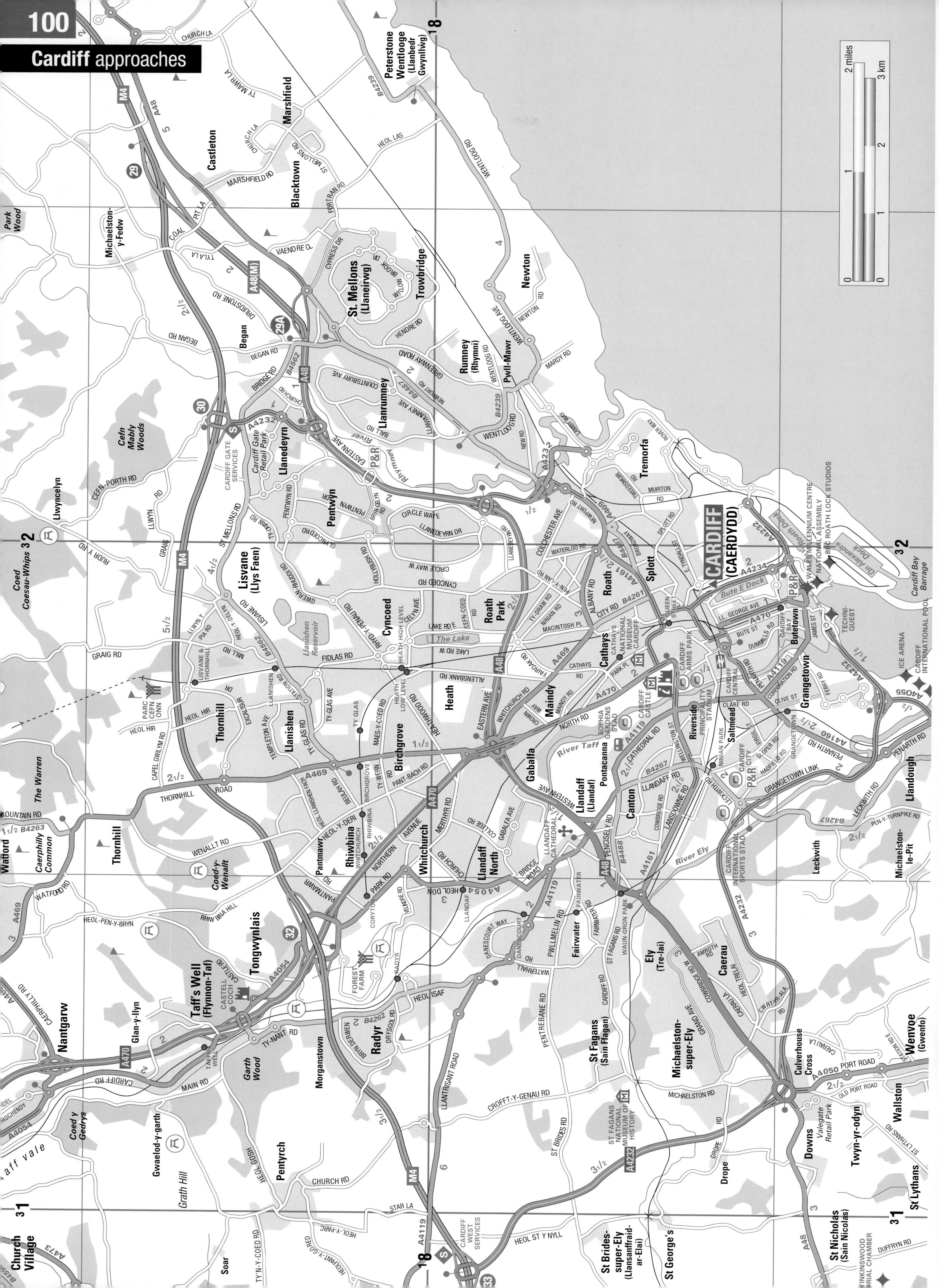
CARDIFF
(CAERDYDD)
Peterstone Wentlooge
Marshfield
Castleton
Blacktown
St. Mellons
(Llaneirwg)
Trowbridge
Newton
Rumney
(Rhymni)
Pwll-Mawr
Llanrumney
Llanedeyrn
Pentwyn
Tremorfa
Splott
Roath
Roath Park
Cyncoed
Lisvane
(Llys Faen)
Thornhill
Llanishen
Heath
Cathays
Maindy
Gabalfa
Birchgrove
Rhiwbina
Whitchurch
Llandaff North
Llandaff
(Llandaf)
Pontcanna
Canton
Riverside
Saltmead
Grangetown
Butetown
Llandough
Leckwith
Michaelston-le-Pit
Ely
(Tre-lai)
Caerau
Fairwater
Radyr
Morganstown
Tongwynlais
Taff's Well
(Ffynnon-Taf)
Nantgarw
Pentyrch
Gwaelod-y-garth
St Fagans
(Sain Ffagan)
Michaelston-super-Ely
Culverhouse Cross
Wenvoe
(Gwenfô)
Wallston
Twyn-yr-odyn
Downs
Drope
St Georges
St Brides-super-Ely
(Llansanffraid-ar-Elái)
St Nicholas
(Sain Nicolas)
St Lythans
Soar
Church Village
Began
Michaelston-y-Fedw
Llwyncelyn
Cefn Mably Woods
Coed Coesau-Whips
The Warren
Watford
Caerphilly Common
Coed-y-Wenallt
Garth Wood
Coed y Gedrys
Grath Hill
Park Wood
Llanishen Reservoir
The Lake
River Taff
River Ely
Rhymney River
Bute E Dock
Roath Dock
Alexandra Dock
Cardiff Bay Barrage
Cardiff Gate Retail Park
Cardiff Gate Services
Cardiff West Services
Valegate Retail Park
Principality Stadium
Cardiff Arms Park
Cardiff Castle
Llandaff Cathedral
Castell Coch
St Fagans National Museum of History
Cardiff International Sports Stadium
Cardiff City Stadium
Ice Arena
Cardiff International Pool
Techniquest
Wales Millennium Centre
National Assembly
BBC Roath Lock Studios
M4
A48(M)
A48
A470
A469
A4232
A4119
A4161
A4160
A4054
A4050
A4055
A4234
A4239
B4562
B4487
B4261
B4267
B4262
29
29A
30
32
33
2 miles
3 km

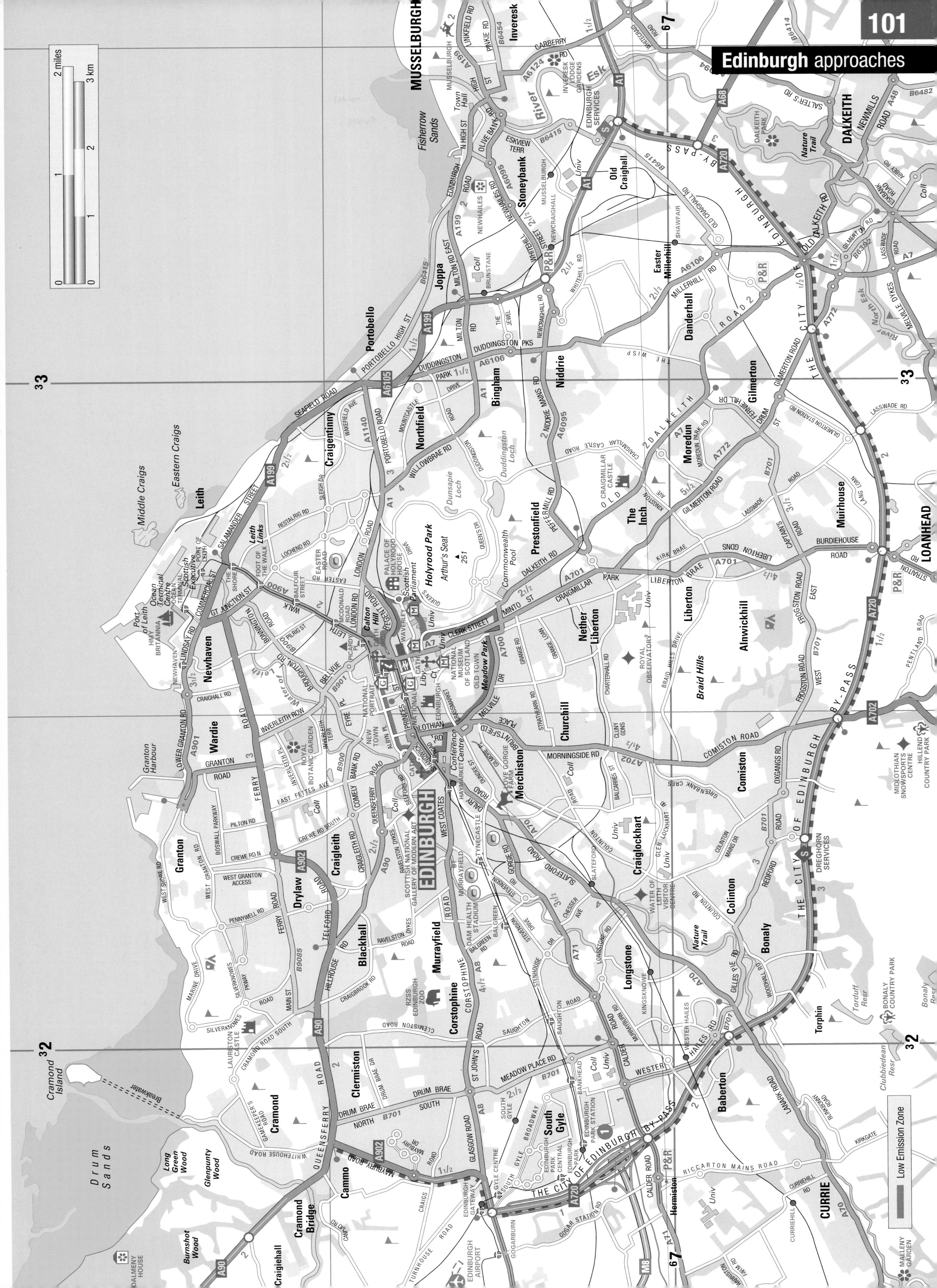
2 miles
3 km
Musselburgh
Inveresk
Fisherrow Sands
Dalkeith
Old Craighall
Stoneybank
Joppa
Portobello
Easter Millerhill
Danderhall
Niddrie
Bingham
Northfield
Craigentinny
Gilmerton
Moredun
The Inch
Prestonfield
Holyrood Park
Arthur's Seat
Dunsapie Loch
Duddingston Loch
Leith
Leith Links
Middle Craigs
Eastern Craigs
Port of Leith
Newhaven
Wardie
Granton Harbour
Granton
Drylaw
Craigleith
Blackhall
Murrayfield
Corstorphine
Cramond Island
Cramond
Cramond Bridge
Clermiston
Cammo
Drum Sands
Long Green Wood
Glenpunty Wood
Burnshot Wood
Craigiehall
Dalmeny House
Edinburgh Airport
South Gyle
Baberton
Hermiston
Currie
Bonaly
Colinton
Longstone
Craiglockhart
Merchiston
Churchill
Comiston
Braid Hills
Liberton
Nether Liberton
Alnwickhill
Muirhouse
Loanhead
Edinburgh
Nature Trail
Torphin
Bonaly Country Park
Clubbiedean Resr
Torduff Resr
Midlothian Snowsports Centre
Hillend Country Park
Dreghorn Services
Edinburgh Services
Malleny Garden
The City of Edinburgh By-Pass
Low Emission Zone
33
32
67

GLASGOW
Moodiesburn
MUIRHEAD
Gartcosh
Chryston
Auchinloch
STEPPS
Craigend
Easterhouse
Swinton
Bargeddie
Muirhead
Birkenshaw
UDDINGSTON
Broomhouse
Newton
Westburn
Flemington
Dechmont Hill
Springboig
Mont Vernon
Robroyston
Balornock
Riddrie
Carntyne
Braidfauld
Clyde Gateway East
CAMBUSLANG
Denniston
Gallowgate
BISHOPBRIGGS
Springburn
Milton
RUTHERGLEN
Castlemilk
Croftfoot
King's Park
Cathcart
Netherlee
Muirend
Firhill
Kelvinside
Pollokshields
Langside
Crossmyloof
Giffnock
Williamwood
Hillpark
Orchard Park
Partick
Ibrox
Govan
Knightswood
Jordanhill
Hillington
Crookston
Priesthill
Nitshill
Cardonald
Maryhill
Glasgow Green
Richmond Park
Tollcross Park
Alexandra Park
Queen's Park
Dawsholm Park
Victoria Park
Bellahouston Park
Pollok Country Park
Rouken Glen Park
Cathkin Braes Country Park
Nature Trail Linn Park
Possil Loch
Nature Reserve
Hogganfield Loch
Frankfield Loch
Bishop Loch
Johnston Loch
Gadloch
River Clyde
White Cart Water
Levern Water
Forth and Clyde Canal
Clyde Tunnel
Celtic Park
Emirates Arena & the Sir Chris Hoy Velodrome
Hampden Park
Ibrox
Firhill Stadium
Scotstoun
Provan Hall
Glasgow Fort
Springburn Museum
Kelvingrove Art Gallery & Museum
Glasgow Botanic Gardens
Riverside Museum
SECC
OVO Hydro
Science Centre
Hagg's Castle
Pollok House
Burrell Collection
Crookston Castle
House for an Art Lover
Holmwood House
Bothwell Castle
David Livingstone Centre
Braehead Shopping Centre
Silverburn Shopping Centre
Waulkmill Glen Reservoir
Dams to Darnley Country Park
Low Emission Zone
2 miles
3 km
M8
M73
M74
M77
M80
A8
A77
A730
A749
A761
A803
A814

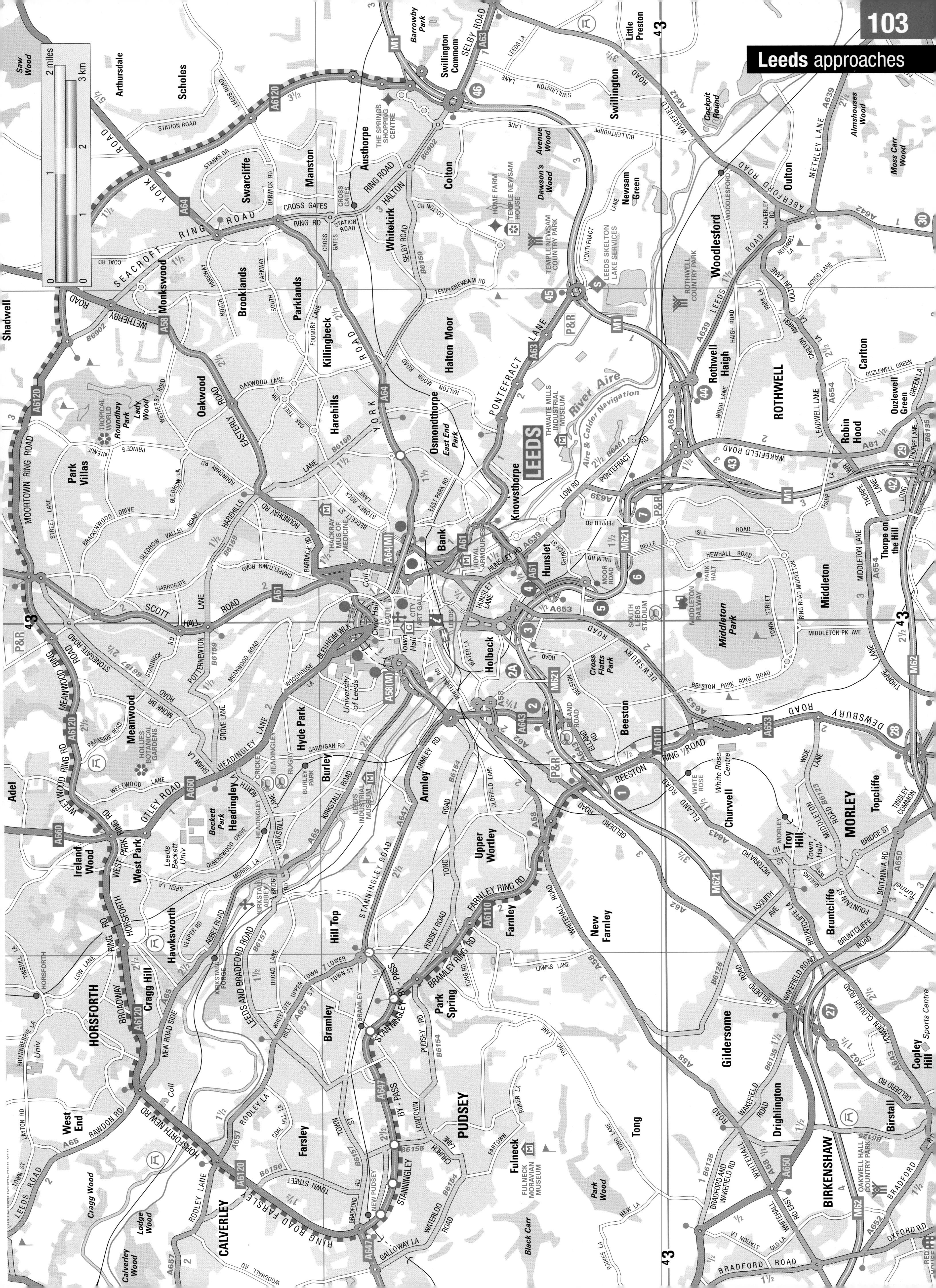
LEEDS
Arthursdale
Scholes
Saw Wood
Barrowby Park
Swillington Common
Little Preston
Swillington
Cockpit Round
Almshouses Wood
Moss Carr Wood
Oulton
Woodlesford
Rothwell Country Park
Newsam Green
Avenue Wood
Dawson's Wood
Temple Newsam Country Park
Temple Newsam House
Home Farm
Leeds Skelton Lake Services
Colton
Austhorpe
The Springs Shopping Centre
Manston
Swarcliffe
Whitekirk
Halton Moor
Killingbeck
Parklands
Brooklands
Monkswood
Shadwell
Oakwood
Harehills
Osmondthorpe
East End Park
Knowsthorpe
Thwaite Mills Industrial Museum
River Aire
Aire & Calder Navigation
Rothwell Haigh
ROTHWELL
Carlton
Oulzewell Green
Robin Hood
Thorpe on the Hill
Middleton
Middleton Park
Middleton Railway
South Leeds Stadium
Hunslet
Holbeck
Cross Flatts Park
Beeston
Bank
Royal Armouries
Thackray Mus of Medicine
Civic Hall
City Art Gall
Town Hall
University of Leeds
Hyde Park
Burley
Burley Park
Headingley
Armley
Leeds Industrial Museum
Upper Wortley
Farnley
New Farnley
Churwell
White Rose Centre
MORLEY
Topcliffe
Tingley Common
Troy Hill
Bruntcliffe
Gildersome
Drighlington
Copley Hill
Birstall
Oakwell Hall Country Park
BIRKENSHAW
Tong
Park Wood
Black Carr
Fulneck Moravian Museum
PUDSEY
Park Spring
Bramley
Hill Top
Farsley
CALVERLEY
Calverley Wood
Lodge Wood
Cragg Wood
West End
HORSFORTH
Cragg Hill
Hawksworth
Kirkstall Abbey
Kirkstall Forge
West Park
Ireland Wood
Leeds Beckett Univ
Beckett Park
Meanwood
Hollies Botanical Gardens
Adel
Park Villas
Tropical World
Roundhay Park
Lady Wood
Moortown Ring Road
Meanwood Ring Road
Weetwood Ring Rd
Ring Road Farsley
Stanningley By-Pass
Farnley Ring Rd
Bramley Ring Rd
Ring Road Beeston
Dewsbury Road
Wakefield Road
Pontefract Lane
York Road
Selby Road
Otley Road
Headingley Lane
Leeds and Bradford Road
Stanningley Road
Kirkstall Road
Harrogate Road
Scott Hall Road
Easterly Road
Roundhay Rd
Aberford Road
Methley Lane
Bradford Road
Ring Road Seacroft
Wetherby Road
A64(M)
A58(M)
A61
A63
A64
A65
A58
A62
A643
A647
A650
A653
A654
A639
A642
A660
A6110
A6120
M1
M62
M621
P&R
2 miles
3 km

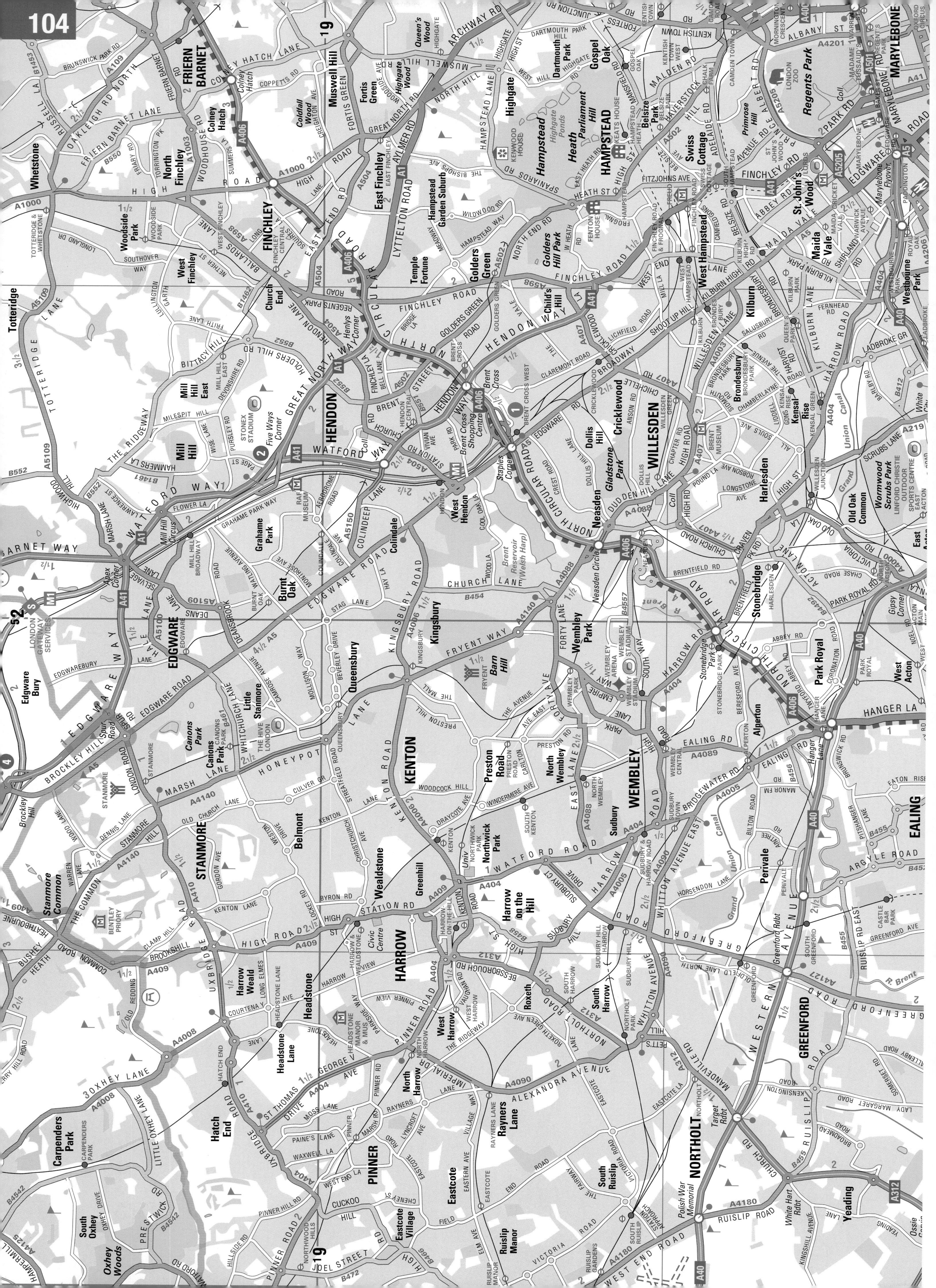
FRIERN BARNET
Colney Hatch
Muswell Hill
Fortis Green
Highgate
Dartmouth Park
Gospel Oak
Kentish Town
Camden Town
MARYLEBONE
Regents Park
Primrose Hill
Swiss Cottage
HAMPSTEAD
Hampstead Heath
Parliament Hill
Belsize Park
Whetstone
North Finchley
FINCHLEY
East Finchley
Hampstead Garden Suburb
Woodside Park
West Finchley
Temple Fortune
Golders Green
Golders Hill Park
West Hampstead
St. John's Wood
Maida Vale
Kilburn
Westbourne Park
Totteridge
Church End
Child's Hill
Mill Hill East
Mill Hill
HENDON
Cricklewood
WILLESDEN
Brondesbury
Kensal Rise
Dollis Hill
Gladstone Park
Harlesden
Old Oak Common
Wormwood Scrubs Park
Grahame Park
West Hendon
Colindale
Burnt Oak
Neasden
Stonebridge
EDGWARE
Edgware Bury
Kingsbury
Queensbury
Wembley Park
Barn Hill
Little Stanmore
Canons Park
KENTON
Preston Road
North Wembley
WEMBLEY
Alperton
Park Royal
West Acton
Stanmore
Belmont
Northwick Park
Sudbury
Perivale
EALING
STANMORE
Stanmore Common
Wealdstone
Greenhill
Harrow on the Hill
HARROW
Harrow Weald
Headstone
Headstone Lane
West Harrow
Roxeth
South Harrow
GREENFORD
North Harrow
Hatch End
Carpenders Park
Rayners Lane
NORTHOLT
Yeading
PINNER
Eastcote
South Ruislip
South Oxhey
Oxhey Woods
Eastcote Village
Ruislip Manor
NORTH CIRCULAR ROAD
WATFORD WAY
EDGWARE ROAD
GREAT NORTH WAY
WESTERN AVENUE
UXBRIDGE ROAD
WATFORD ROAD

PADDINGTON
Mayfair
Pimlico
BATTERSEA
Battersea Park
Clapham Common
Balham
CHELSEA
Hyde Park
Kensington Gardens
Knightsbridge
Upper Tooting
Collier's Wood
Tooting
Earlsfield
Wandsworth Common
WANDSWORTH
Parsons Green
FULHAM
Hurlingham Park
Holland Park
Notting Hill
HAMMERSMITH
Shepherd's Bush
Southfields
Wimbledon Park
WIMBLEDON
MERTON
MORDEN
Morden Hall Park
West Hill
PUTNEY
Putney Heath
BARNES
River Thames
Putney Vale
Wimbledon Common
Crooked Billet
Raynes Park
Bushey Mead
Roehampton
Kingston Vale
Coombe
NEW MALDEN
Richmond Park
East Sheen
Mortlake
CHISWICK
Bedford Park
ACTON
South Acton
Grove Park
North Sheen
RICHMOND
Richmond Hill
Petersham
KINGSTON UPON THAMES
Norbiton
Kew
Gunnersbury Park
Old Deer Park
Syon Park
Ham
TEDDINGTON
Hampton Wick
Hampton Court Park
West Ealing
HANWELL
BRENTFORD
Northfields
St Margarets
TWICKENHAM
ISLEWORTH
Woodlands
HOUNSLOW
Bushy Park
Osterley Park
Norwood Green
Osterley
HESTON
Whitton
Drayton Green
Dormer's Wells
SOUTHALL
North Hyde
Hounslow West
Hounslow Heath
Hanworth Park
HANWORTH
Hampton
FELTHAM
SUNBURY
Hayes Town
Cranford
Ultra Low Emission Zone

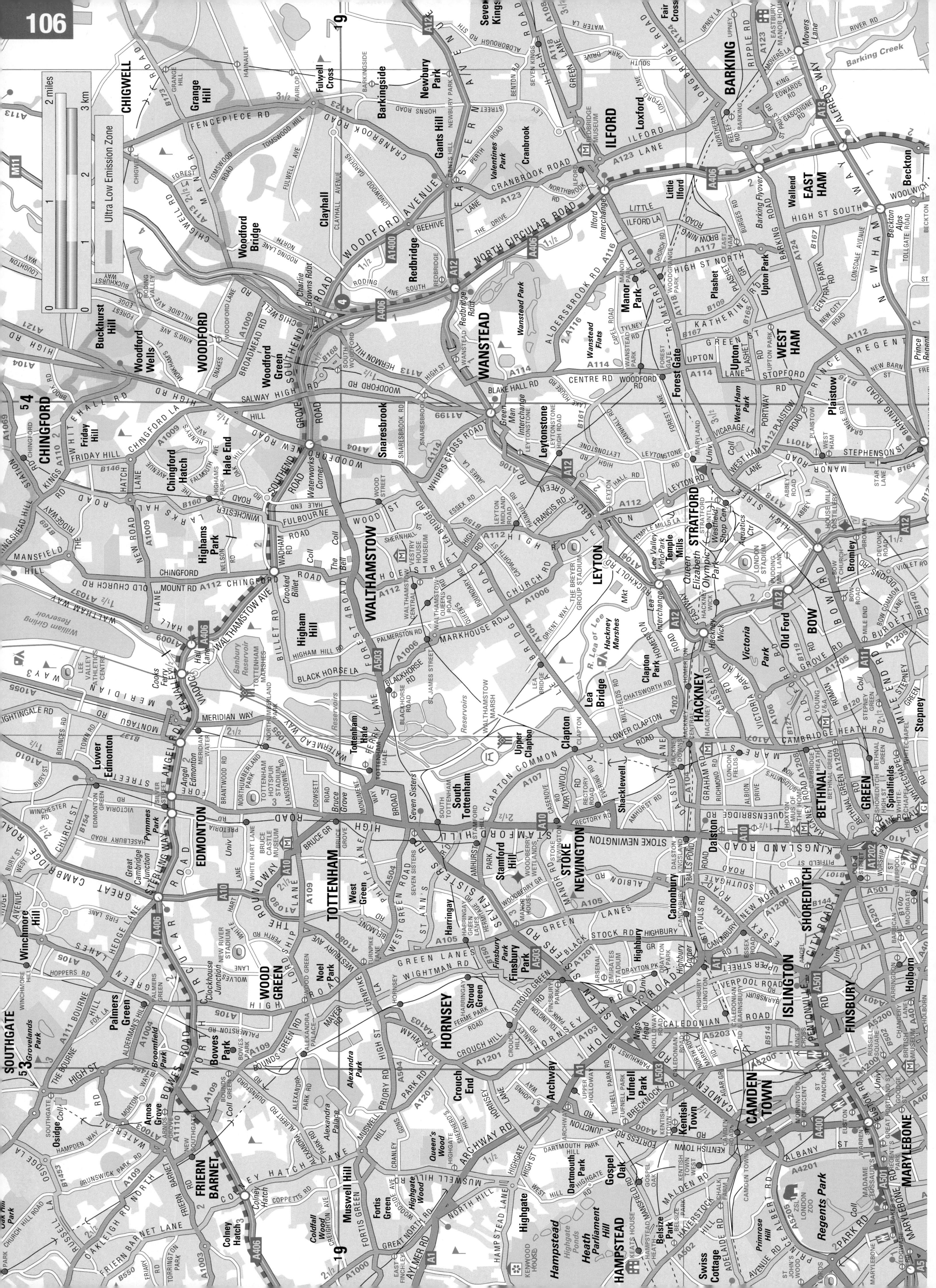
Ultra Low Emission Zone
2 miles
3 km
CHIGWELL
Grange Hill
Fullwell Cross
Barkingside
Newbury Park
Gants Hill
Cranbrook
ILFORD
Loxford
BARKING
Barking Creek
Woodford Bridge
Clayhall
Redbridge
Valentines Park
Charlie Browns Roundabout
Redbridge Roundabout
WANSTEAD
Wanstead Park
Wanstead Flats
Little Ilford
Manor Park
Plashet
Upton Park
EAST HAM
Wallend
Beckton
Beckton Alps
Buckhurst Hill
Woodford Wells
WOODFORD
Woodford Green
Forest Gate
Upton
WEST HAM
West Ham Park
Plaistow
Prince Regent
CHINGFORD
Friday Hill
Chingford Hatch
Hale End
Snaresbrook
Green Man Interchange
Leytonstone
Waterworks Corner
Highams Park
WALTHAMSTOW
Higham Hill
Crooked Billet
LEYTON
STRATFORD
Temple Mills
Queen Elizabeth Olympic Park
Bromley
BOW
Old Ford
Victoria Park
Hackney Wick
Hackney Marshes
Lea Bridge
Clapton Park
Clapton
Upper Clapton
William Girling Reservoir
Cooks Ferry
Banbury Reservoir
Tottenham Hale
Reservoirs
Walthamstow Marsh
Lower Edmonton
Angel Edmonton
EDMONTON
Pymmes Park
Great Cambridge Junction
Seven Sisters
South Tottenham
Stamford Hill
STOKE NEWINGTON
Shacklewell
HACKNEY
Dalston
BETHNAL GREEN
Stepney
Spitalfields
TOTTENHAM
West Green
Bruce Grove
Harringay
Finsbury Park
Canonbury
Highbury
SHOREDITCH
ISLINGTON
FINSBURY
Holborn
Winchmore Hill
Palmers Green
Clockhouse Junction
WOOD GREEN
Noel Park
HORNSEY
Stroud Green
Crouch End
Archway
Tufnell Park
Kentish Town
CAMDEN TOWN
MARYLEBONE
Regents Park
Primrose Hill
SOUTHGATE
Grovelands Park
Bowes Park
Broomfield Park
Arnos Grove
Osidge
Alexandra Park
Alexandra Palace
Queen's Wood
Highgate Wood
Dartmouth Park
Gospel Oak
Belsize Park
Swiss Cottage
Highgate
Muswell Hill
Fortis Green
FRIERN BARNET
Colney Hatch
Coldfall Wood
Hampstead Heath
Parliament Hill
HAMPSTEAD
Kenwood House
NORTH CIRCULAR ROAD
EASTERN AVENUE
WOODFORD AVENUE
CRANBROOK ROAD
ROMFORD ROAD
HIGH STREET NORTH
BARKING ROAD
HOLLOWAY ROAD
SEVEN SISTERS ROAD
STAMFORD HILL
KINGSLAND ROAD
CAMBRIDGE HEATH ROAD
MILE END ROAD
FOREST ROAD
LEA BRIDGE ROAD
GREEN LANES
CALEDONIAN ROAD
CAMDEN ROAD
ARCHWAY ROAD
MUSWELL HILL ROAD
GREAT NORTH ROAD
FRIERN BARNET LANE
A406
A12
A13
A10
A1
A503

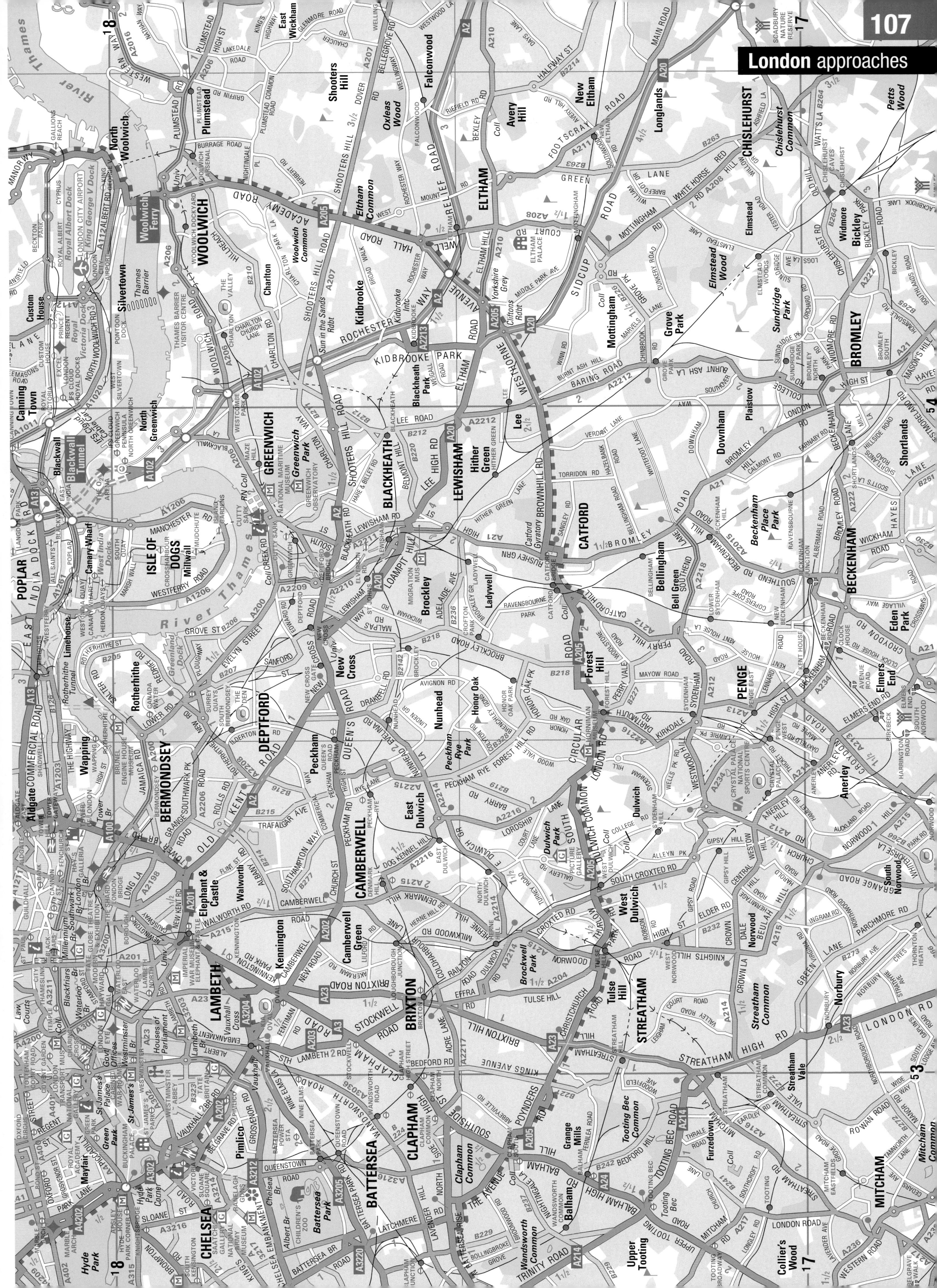
River Thames
North Woolwich
Plumstead
Shooters Hill
East Wickham
Falconwood
Oxleas Wood
Avery Hill
New Eltham
Longlands
CHISLEHURST
Chislehurst Common
Petts Wood
WOOLWICH
Woolwich Ferry
Eltham Common
Woolwich Common
ELTHAM
Charlton
Kidbrooke
Silvertown
Thames Barrier
Custom House
Royal Albert Dock
LONDON CITY AIRPORT
Royal Victoria Dock
Mottingham
Grove Park
Elmstead Wood
Elmstead
Sundridge Park
Widmore
Bickley
BROMLEY
Canning Town
Blackheath Park
Lee
Hither Green
LEWISHAM
BLACKHEATH
GREENWICH
Greenwich Park
North Greenwich
Blackwall
Blackwall Tunnel
Downham
Plaistow
Shortlands
Catford
CATFORD
Bellingham
Bell Green
Beckenham Place Park
BECKENHAM
POPLAR
Canary Wharf
ISLE OF DOGS
Millwall
Limehouse
Rotherhithe
Deptford
DEPTFORD
Brockley
Ladywell
New Cross
Nunhead
Honor Oak
Forest Hill
PENGE
Eden Park
Elmers End
Wapping
BERMONDSEY
Peckham
Peckham Rye Park
East Dulwich
Dulwich
Dulwich Park
Crystal Palace
Anerley
South Norwood
Aldgate
Tower Br
CAMBERWELL
Camberwell Green
Elephant & Castle
Walworth
Kennington
West Dulwich
Norwood
Thornton Heath
LAMBETH
Vauxhall
BRIXTON
Brockwell Park
Tulse Hill
STREATHAM
Streatham Common
Norbury
Streatham Vale
Houses of Parliament
Westminster
Pimlico
CHELSEA
BATTERSEA
Battersea Park
CLAPHAM
Clapham Common
Balham
Grange Mills
Tooting Bec Common
Tooting Bec
Furzedown
MITCHAM
Mitcham Common
Mayfair
Green Park
Hyde Park
Hyde Park Corner
Wandsworth Common
Upper Tooting
Collier's Wood

Liverpool approaches

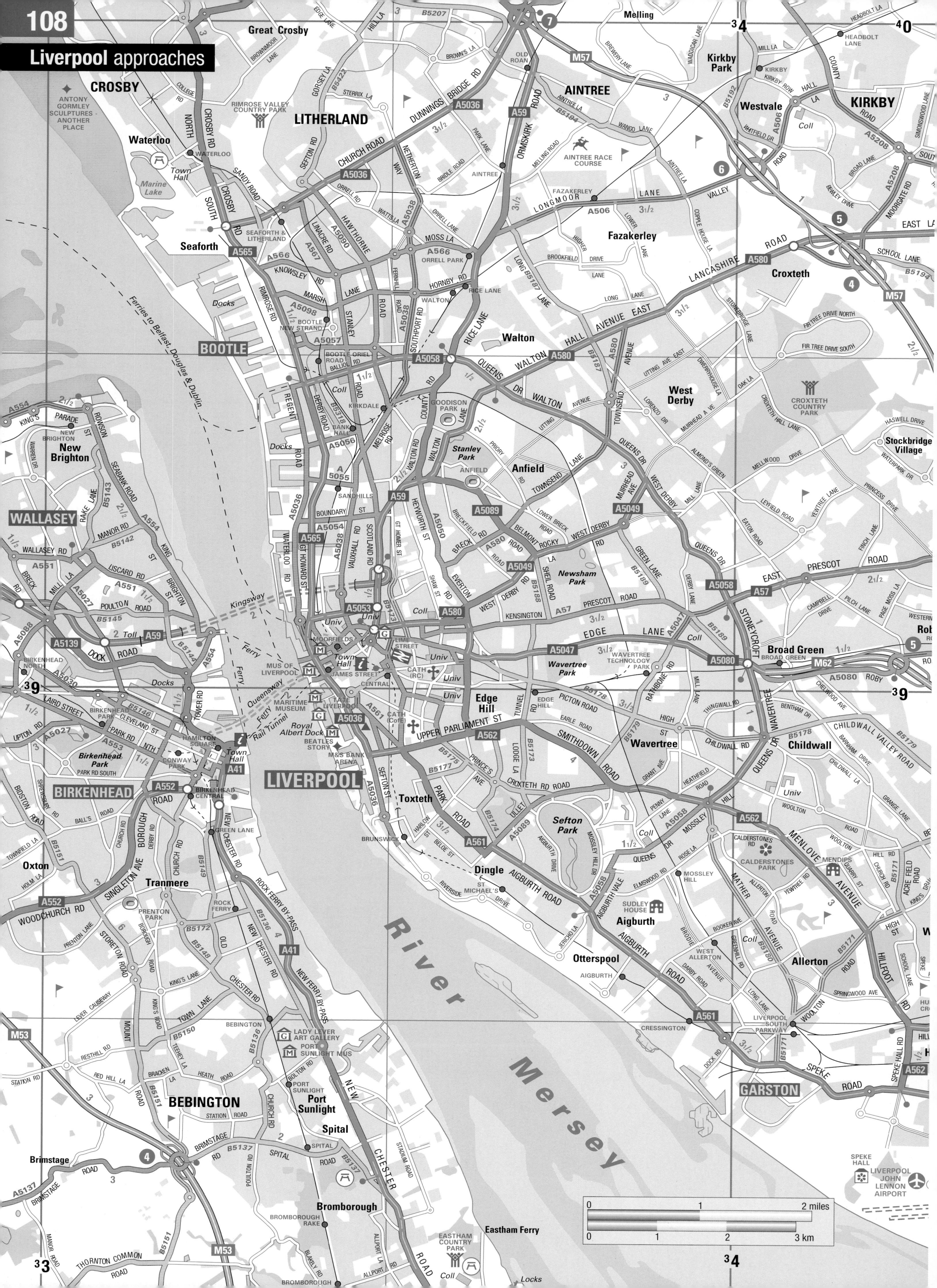

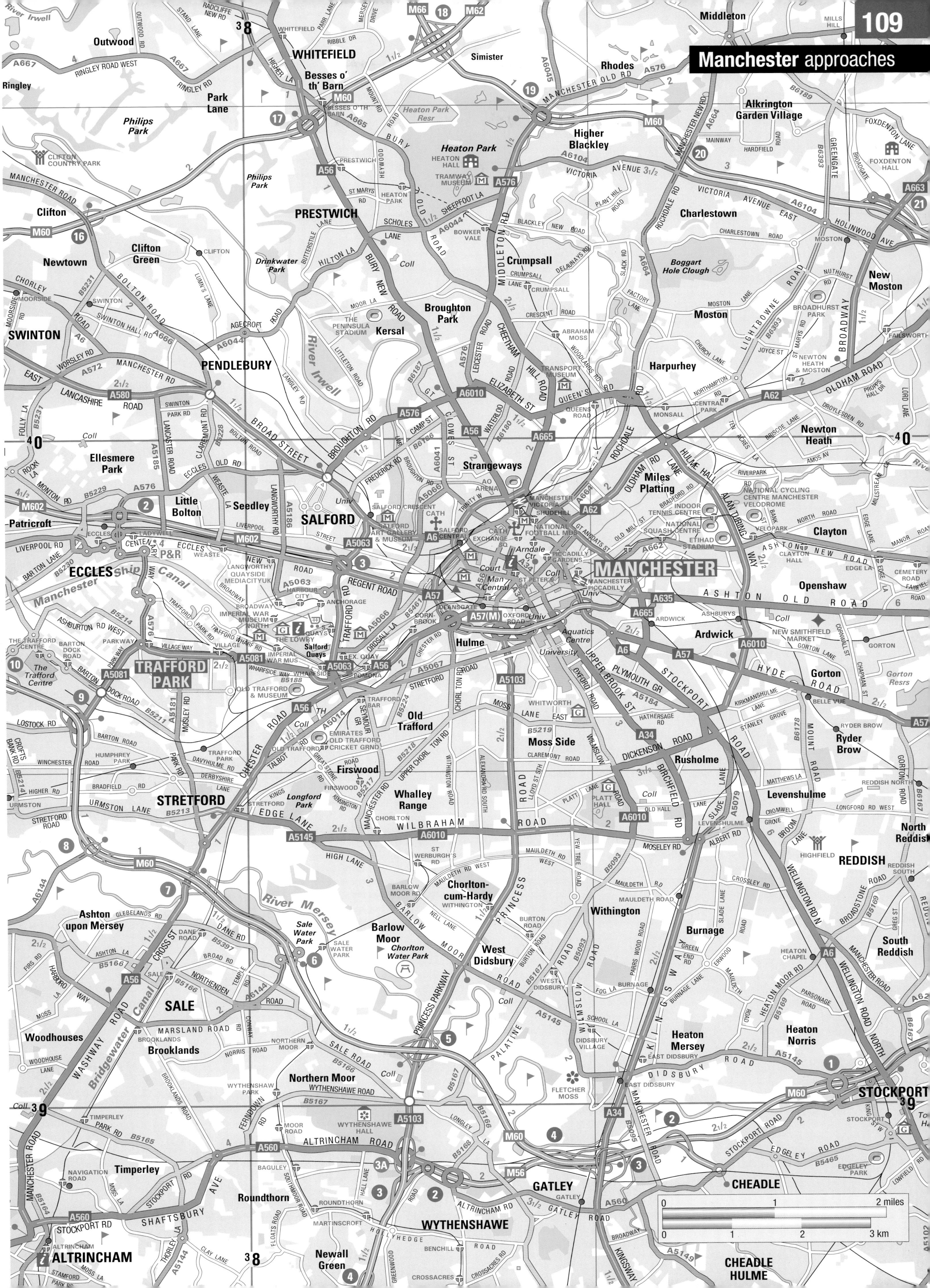
Outwood
WHITEFIELD
Besses o' th' Barn
Simister
Middleton
Rhodes
Ringley
Park Lane
Philips Park
Heaton Park
Higher Blackley
Alkrington Garden Village
Clifton Country Park
Prestwich
Charlestown
Clifton
Clifton Green
Newtown
Drinkwater Park
Crumpsall
Boggart Hole Clough
New Moston
Moston
SWINTON
Kersal
Broughton Park
River Irwell
PENDLEBURY
Harpurhey
Newton Heath
Ellesmere Park
Strangeways
Miles Platting
Little Bolton
Seedley
SALFORD
Clayton
Patricroft
ECCLES
MANCHESTER
Manchester Ship Canal
Openshaw
Ardwick
TRAFFORD PARK
Salford Quays
Hulme
Gorton
The Trafford Centre
Old Trafford
Moss Side
Ryder Brow
Rusholme
Firswood
STRETFORD
Longford Park
Whalley Range
Levenshulme
REDDISH
Chorlton-cum-Hardy
River Mersey
Withington
Ashton upon Mersey
Sale Water Park
Barlow Moor
Burnage
South Reddish
West Didsbury
SALE
Woodhouses
Brooklands
Heaton Mersey
Heaton Norris
Northern Moor
STOCKPORT
Timperley
GATLEY
CHEADLE
Roundthorn
WYTHENSHAWE
ALTRINCHAM
Newall Green
CHEADLE HULME
0 1 2 miles
0 1 2 3 km

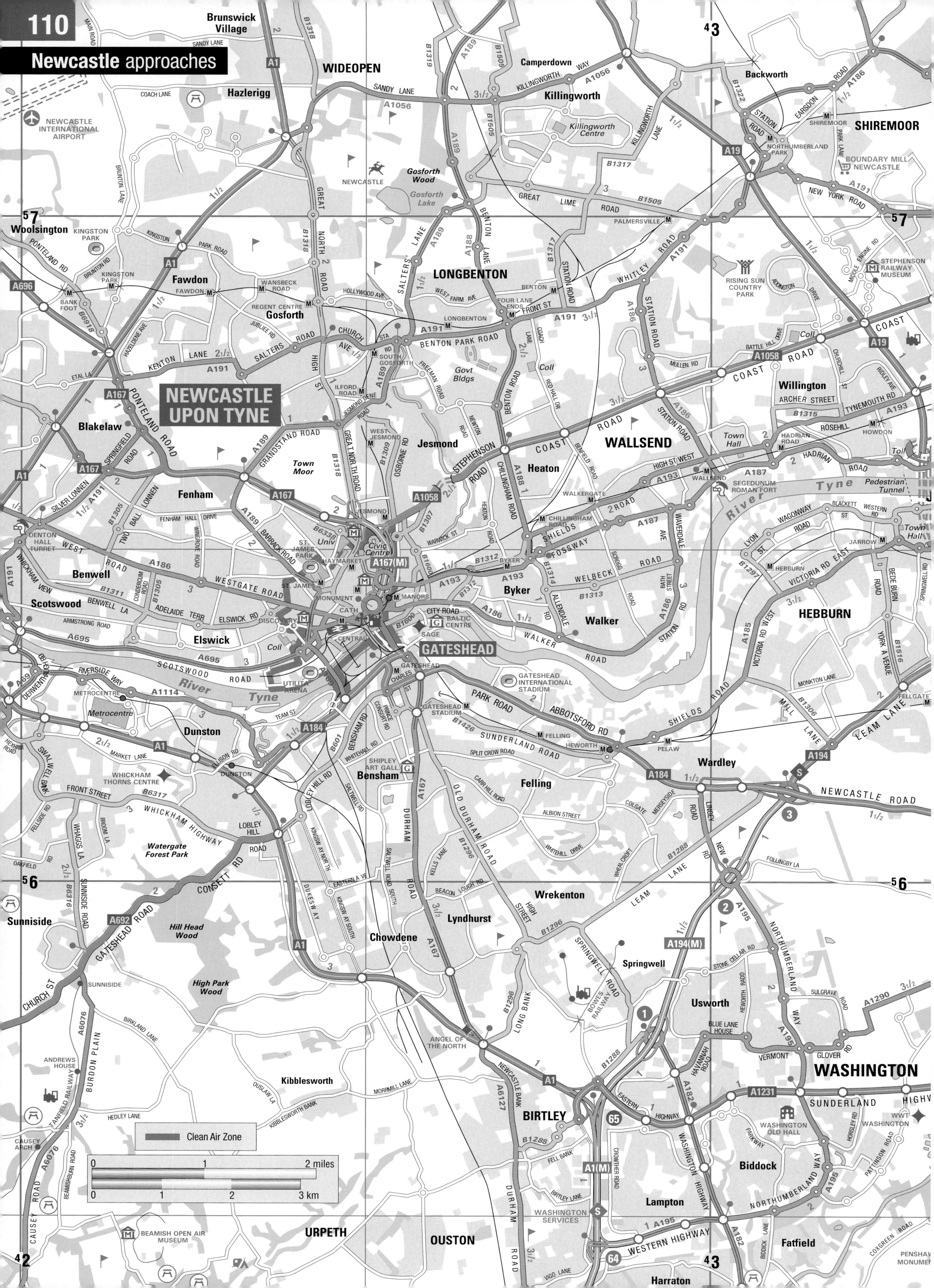
NEWCASTLE UPON TYNE
GATESHEAD
Brunswick Village
WIDEOPEN
Hazlerigg
NEWCASTLE INTERNATIONAL AIRPORT
Camperdown
Killingworth
Killingworth Centre
Backworth
SHIREMOOR
NORTHUMBERLAND PARK
BOUNDARY MILL NEWCASTLE
NEWCASTLE
Gosforth Wood
Gosforth Lake
PALMERSVILLE
Woolsington
KINGSTON PARK
Fawdon
WANSBECK ROAD
LONGBENTON
BENTON
FOUR LANE ENDS
RISING SUN COUNTRY PARK
STEPHENSON RAILWAY MUSEUM
REGENT CENTRE
Gosforth
BANK FOOT
SOUTH GOSFORTH
ILFORD ROAD
Govt Bldgs
Willington
Blakelaw
Town Moor
WEST JESMOND
Jesmond
Heaton
WALLSEND
Town Hall
HADRIAN ROAD
HOWDON
SEGEDUNUM ROMAN FORT
Pedestrian Tunnel
Fenham
JESMOND
WALKERGATE
CHILLINGHAM ROAD
DENTON HALL TURRET
ST. JAMES' PARK
Univ
Civic Centre
HAYMARKET
BYKER
JARROW
Town Hall
HEBBURN
Benwell
ST. JAMES
Byker
Scotswood
MONUMENT
MANORS
CITY ROAD
BALTIC CENTRE
SAGE
Walker
Elswick
DISCOVERY
CENTRAL
Coll
GATESHEAD INTERNATIONAL STADIUM
UTILITA ARENA
River Tyne
METROCENTRE
Metrocentre
GATESHEAD STADIUM
FELLING
HEWORTH
PELAW
FELLGATE
Dunston
DUNSTON
Wardley
WHICKHAM THORNS CENTRE
SHIPLEY ART GALL
Bensham
Felling
LOBLEY HILL
Watergate Forest Park
Wrekenton
Sunniside
Lyndhurst
Hill Head Wood
Chowdene
Springwell
SUNNISIDE
High Park Wood
BOWES RAILWAY
Usworth
BLUE LANE HOUSE
ANGEL OF THE NORTH
VERMONT
WASHINGTON
ANDREWS HOUSE
Kibblesworth
TANFIELD RAILWAY
BIRTLEY
WASHINGTON OLD HALL
WWT WASHINGTON
CAUSEY ARCH
Biddock
Clean Air Zone
0
1
2 miles
0
1
2
3 km
Lampton
WASHINGTON SERVICES
BEAMISH OPEN AIR MUSEUM
URPETH
OUSTON
Fatfield
PENSHAW MONUMENT
Harraton
A1
A167
A189
A191
A193
A184
A1058
A167(M)
A194(M)
A194
A195
A1231
A182
A692
A695
A696
A6076
A19
A1(M)
A6127
A186
A187
A1290
A1114

Dobpark
HUCKNALL
Misk Hill
Long Hill
Watnall Coppice
Beauvale
Ruffs
Hazelgrove
Broomhill
Butler's Hill
Westville
Raceground Hill
Cobbler's Hill
Bestwood Park
Bestwood Village
BESTWOOD
The Warren
Gaunt's Hill
Rise Park
Top Valley
Redhill
Bestwood
TUMBLE TOWN
ARNOLD
CALVERTON
Bonner Hill
Woodborough
Hunger Hill
Lambley
Crocket Beck
Wicketwood Hill
GEDLING
Nuthall
Kimberley
Bulwell
Highbury Vale
Cinderhill
Old Basford
Woodthorpe
Mapperley
Porchester
Gedling
Broxtowe
Aspley
Sherwood
New Basford
Carrington
Mapperley Park
CARLTON
Strelley
Whitemoor
Thorneywood
Bilborough
St. Ann's
NOTTINGHAM
Catstone Hill
Netherfield
Trowell Moor
Radford
Martin's Pond
WOLLATON
Wollaton
New Lenton
GREEN'S MILL & SCIENCE CENTRE
Sneinton
Colwick
WOLLATON HALL
Wollaton Park
CASTLE MUSEUM & GALLERY
The Lake
Holme Pierrepont
HOLME PIERREPONT HALL
NATIONAL WATER SPORTS CENTRE
Bramcore Hills
Nottingham University
Meadows
THE CITY GROUND
TRENT BRIDGE
River Trent
Bramcote
Bassingfield
Gamston
Wilford
WEST BRIDGFORD
NOTTINGHAM CITY AIRPORT
Chilwell
Rylands
Beeston Canal
Grantham Canal
BEESTON
Clifton Grove
Edwalton
Wilford Hill
Sharp Hill
ATTENBOROUGH
ATTENBOROUGH NATURE RESERVE
CLIFTON
Tollerton
The Lake
Clipston
Mill Hill
Brook Hill
Hoe Hill
Manor Park
FRAMEWORK KNITTERS' MUSEUM
Barton in Fabis
RUDDINGTON
Plumtree
Normanton-on-the-Wolds
Fairham Brook
NOTTINGHAM HERITAGE RAILWAY
Ruddington Fields
RUSHCLIFFE
Plumtree Park
British Geological Survey
Thrumpton
THRUMPTON HALL
Gotham Hill
Ruddington Moor
Bradmore
KEYWORTH
Normanton Wolds
Gotham Moor
Bradmore Moor
0 1 2 miles
0 1 2 3 km

SHEFFIELD
ROTHERHAM
ECCLESFIELD
GRENOSIDE
HILLSBOROUGH
Wickersley
Sunnyside
Flanderwell
Listerdale
Dalton Magna
Dalton
Dalton Parva
Brecks
Herringthorpe
Moorgate
Eastwood
Clifton Park
Broom
Canklow
Masbrough
Bradgate
Kimberworth
Jordan
Tinsley
Brinsworth
Catcliffe
Waverley
Treeton
Whiston
Upper Whiston
Morthen
Ulley
Aughton
Aston
Swallownest
Fence
Woodhouse Mill
Woodhouse
Handsworth
Orgreave
Guilthwaite
Wales
Norwood
Killamarsh
Beighton
Sothall
Holbrook
Drakehouse
Hackenthorpe
Waterthorpe
Westfield
Halfway
Moorhole
Owlthorpe
Plumbley
Birley
Highlane
Richmond
Normanton Spring
Frecheville
Ridgeway
Ridgeway Moor
Hollins End
Intake
Gleadless
Lightwood
Manor Estate
Manor Park
Darnall
Greenland
Attercliffe
Brightside
Carbrook
Wincobank
Blackburn
Shiregreen
Pismire Hill
Firth Park
Grimesthorpe
Pitsmoor
Burngreave
Fir Vale
Concord Park
Longley Estate
Parson Cross
Shirecliffe
Parkwood Springs
Owlerton
Wadsley Bridge
Birley Carr
Birley Edge
Oughtibridge
Wadsley
Worrall
Loxley
Malin Bridge
Walkley
Crookesmoor
Steel Bank
Crookes
Tapton Hill
Sandygate
Ranmoor
Fulwood
Greystones
Ecclesall
Brincliffe
Nether Edge
Sharrow
Heeley
Lowfield
Sheffield Park
Arbourthorne
Newfield Green
Meersbrook
Hemsworth
Backmoor
Norton Woodseats
Norton
Jordanthorpe
Gleadless Valley
Meadow Head
Greenhill
Lowedges
Carter Knowle
Millhouses
Abbeydale
Abbeydale Park
Whirlow
Parkhead
Knowle Top
Beeley Wood
Ecclesall Wood
Tinsley Park
Stannington
Brampton en le Morthen
M1
M18
River Rother
River Don
River Sheaf
River Rivelin
Limb Brook
Rother Valley Lake
Gulliver's Valley Resort
Rother Valley
Sheffield Services
Meadowhall Ctr
Botanical Gardens
Clean Air Zone
2 miles
3 km

Town plan symbols

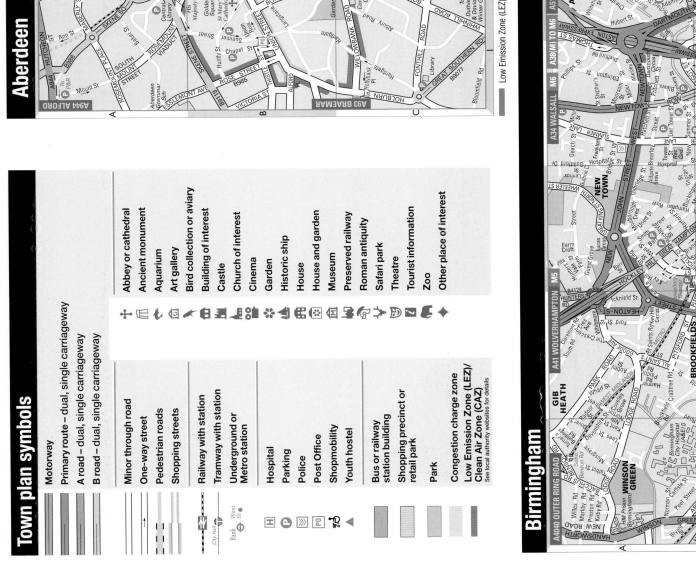

- Motorway
- Primary route – dual, single carriageway
- A road – dual, single carriageway
- B road – dual, single carriageway
- Minor through road
- One-way street
- Pedestrian roads
- Shopping streets
- Railway with station
- Tramway with station
- Underground or Metro station
- Hospital
- Parking
- Police
- Post Office
- Shopmobility
- Youth hostel
- Bus or railway station building
- Shopping precinct or retail park
- Park
- Congestion charge zone
- Low Emission Zone (LEZ)/ Clean Air Zone (CAZ)
  See local authority websites for details
- Abbey or cathedral
- Ancient monument
- Aquarium
- Art gallery
- Bird collection or aviary
- Building of interest
- Castle
- Church of interest
- Cinema
- Garden
- Historic ship
- House
- House and garden
- Museum
- Preserved railway
- Roman antiquity
- Safari park
- Theatre
- Tourist information
- Zoo
- Other place of interest

Aberdeen

0 Miles ¼

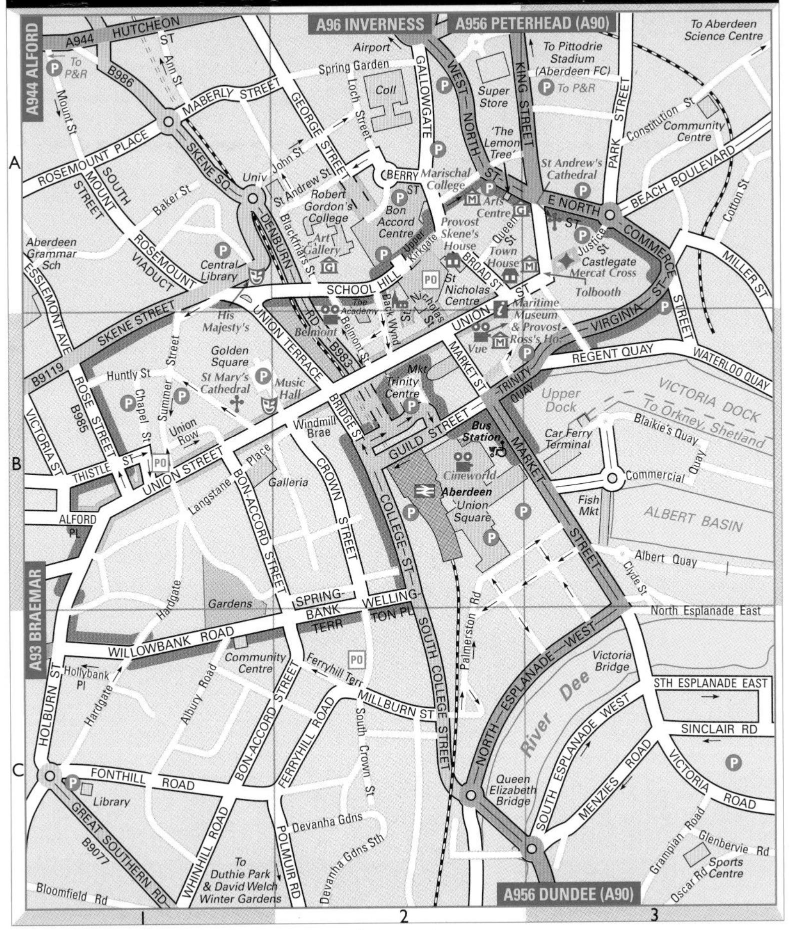

Low Emission Zone (LEZ)/Clean Air Zone (CAZ)

Bath

0 Miles ¼

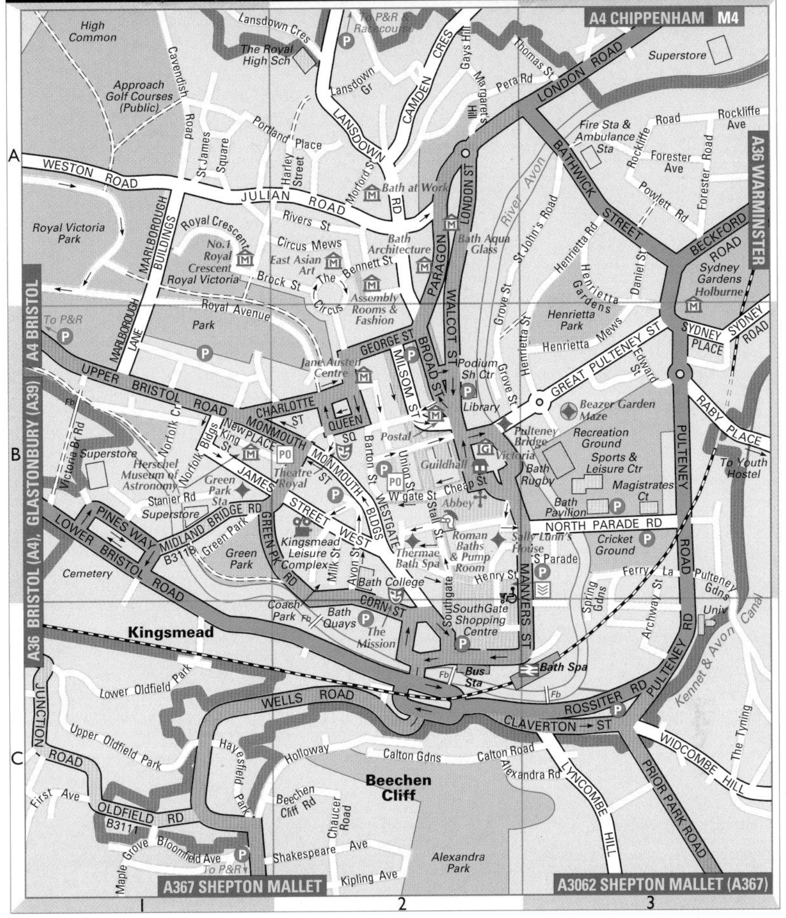

Low Emission Zone (LEZ)/Clean Air Zone (CAZ)

Birmingham

0 Miles ¼

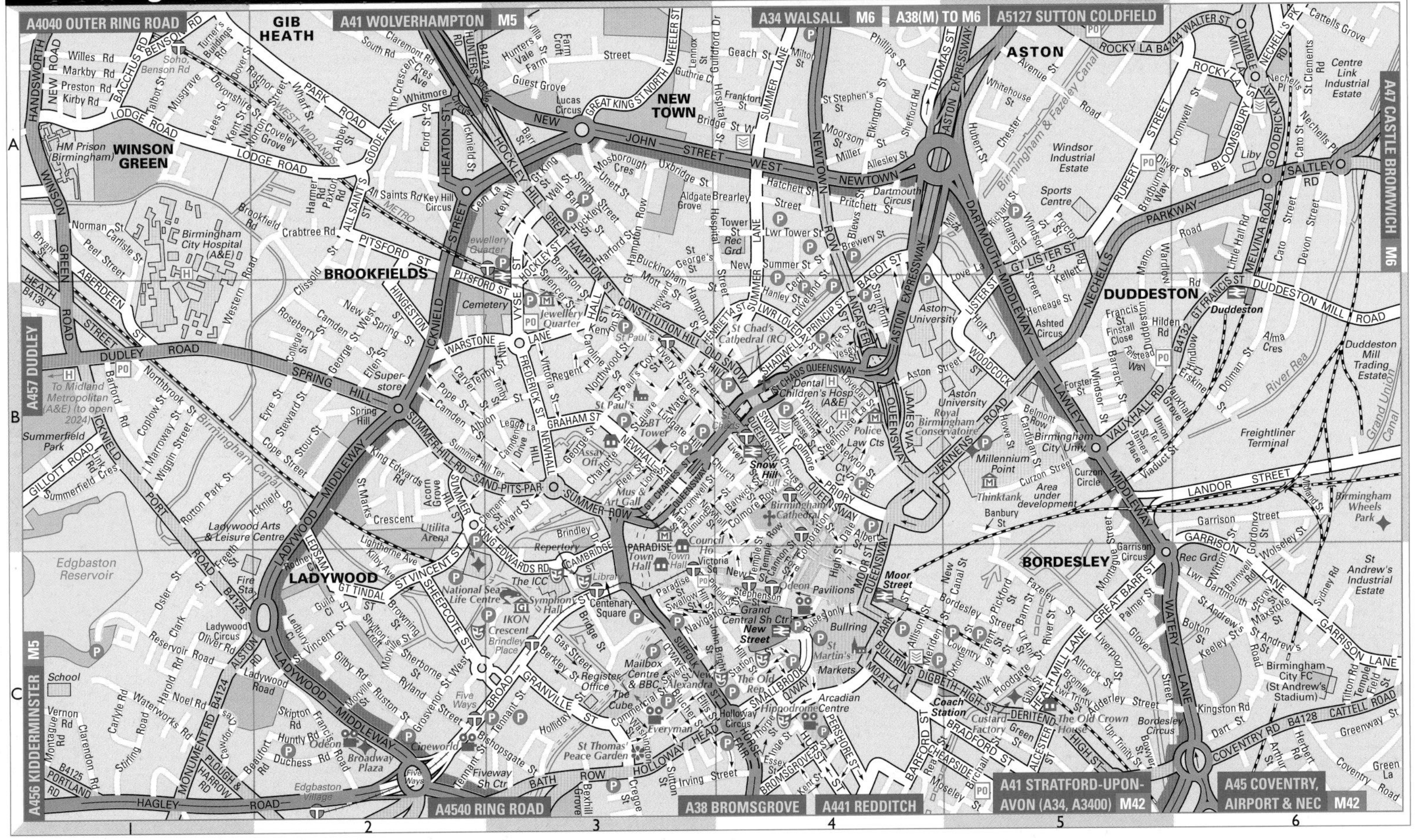

Low Emission Zone (LEZ)/Clean Air Zone (CAZ)

Blackpool

0 Miles ¼

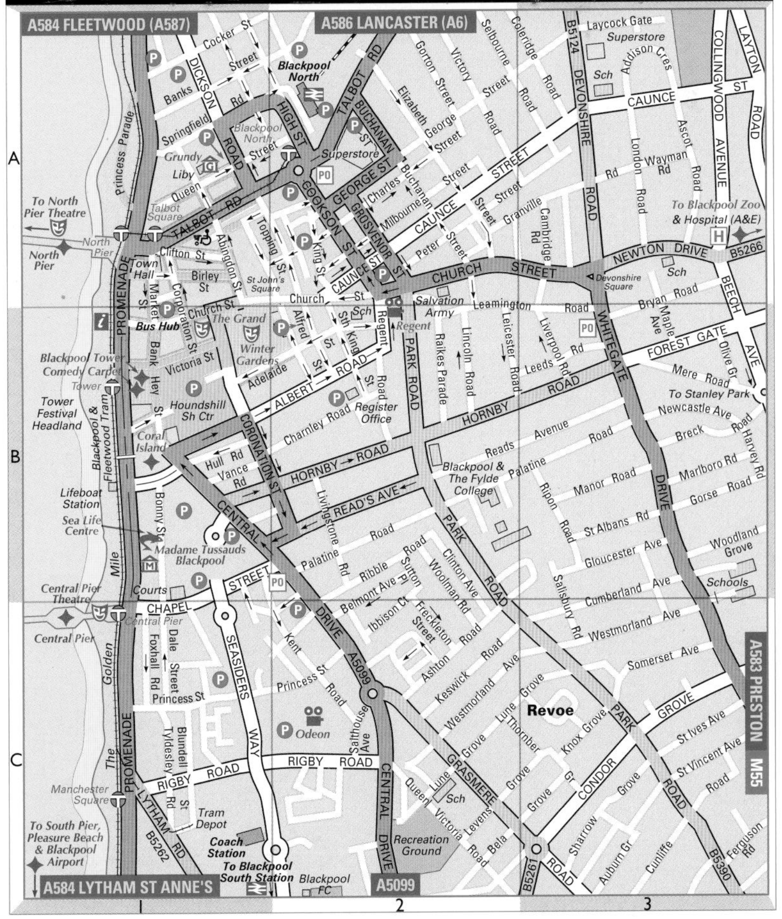

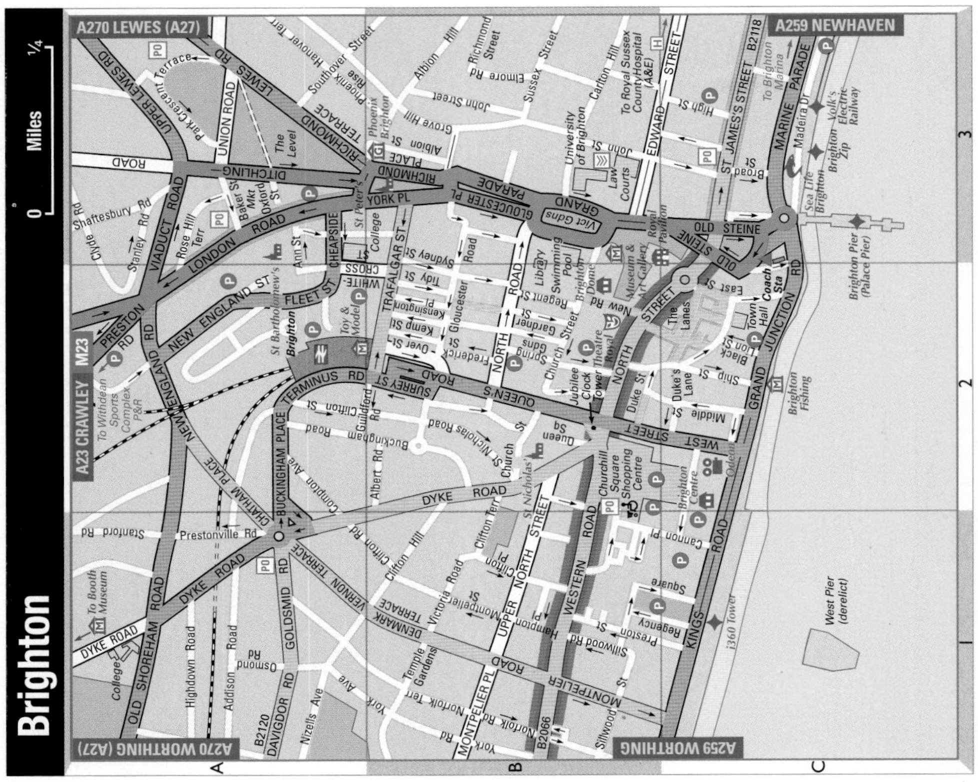

Low Emission Zone (LEZ)/Clean Air Zone (CAZ)

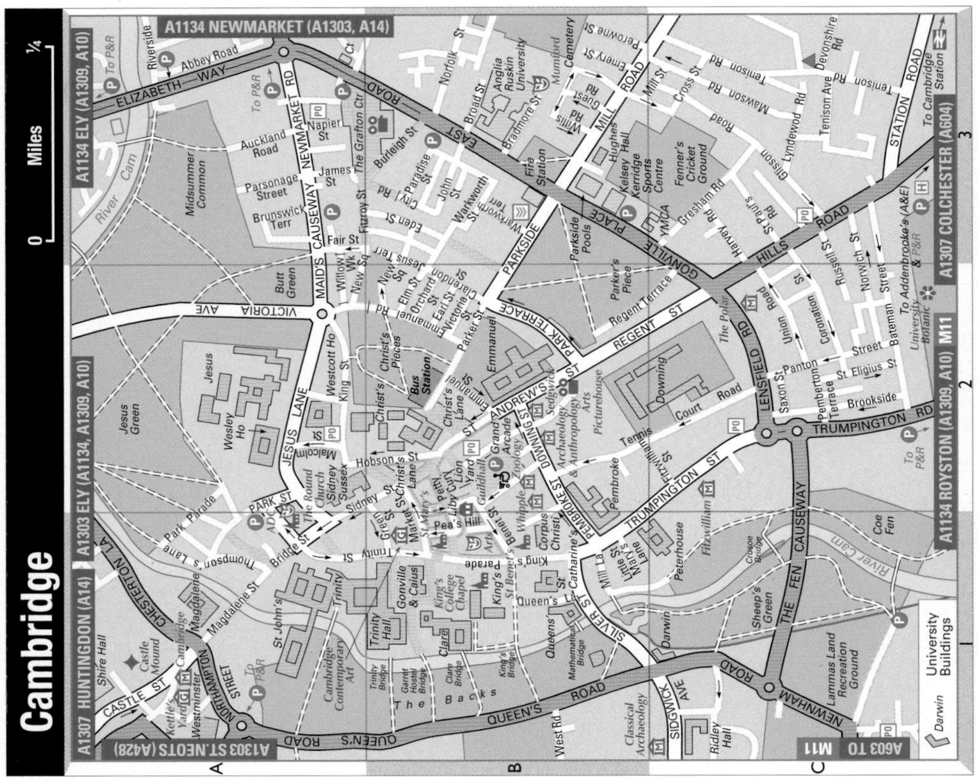

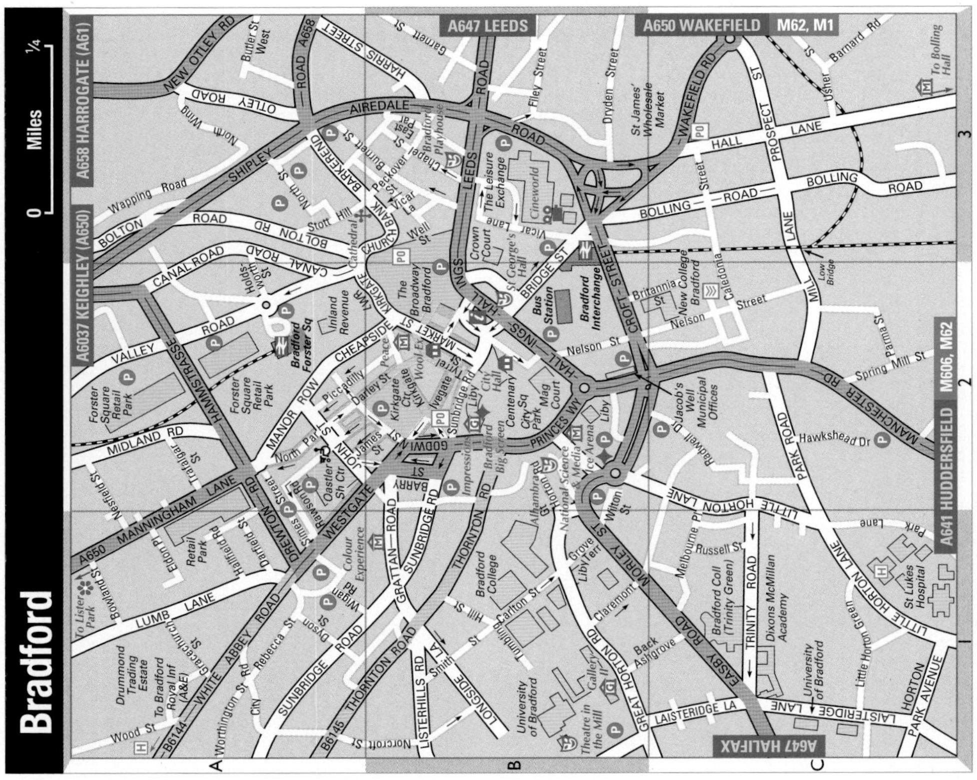

All of the area of the above plan is subject to Clean Air Zone (CAZ) restrictions

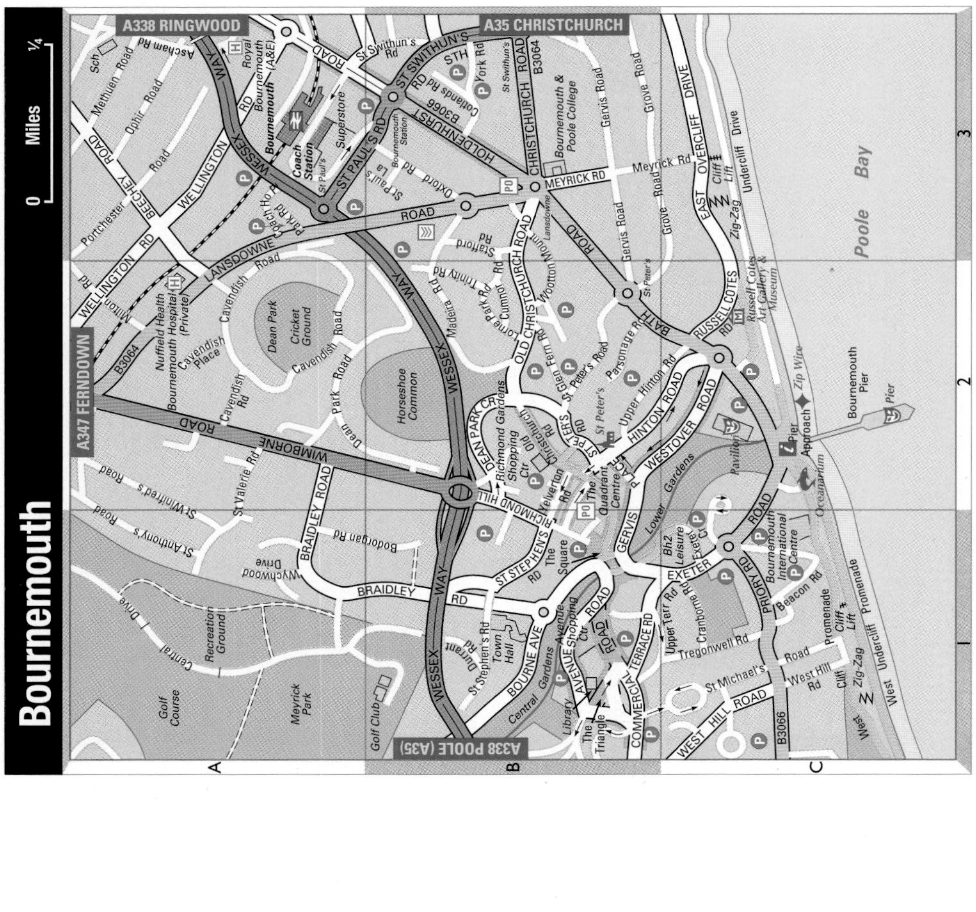

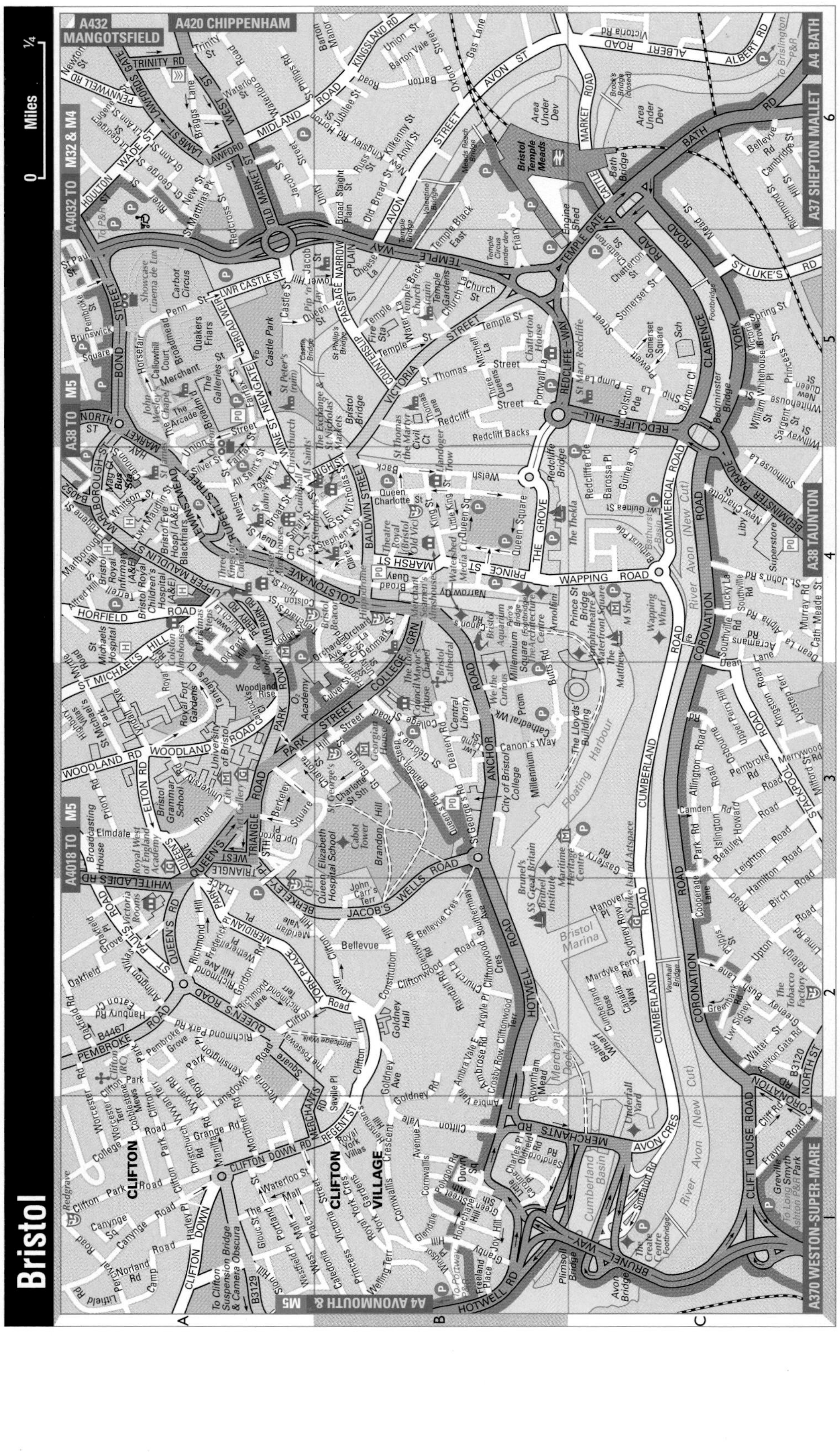

Low Emission Zone (LEZ)/Clean Air Zone (CAZ)

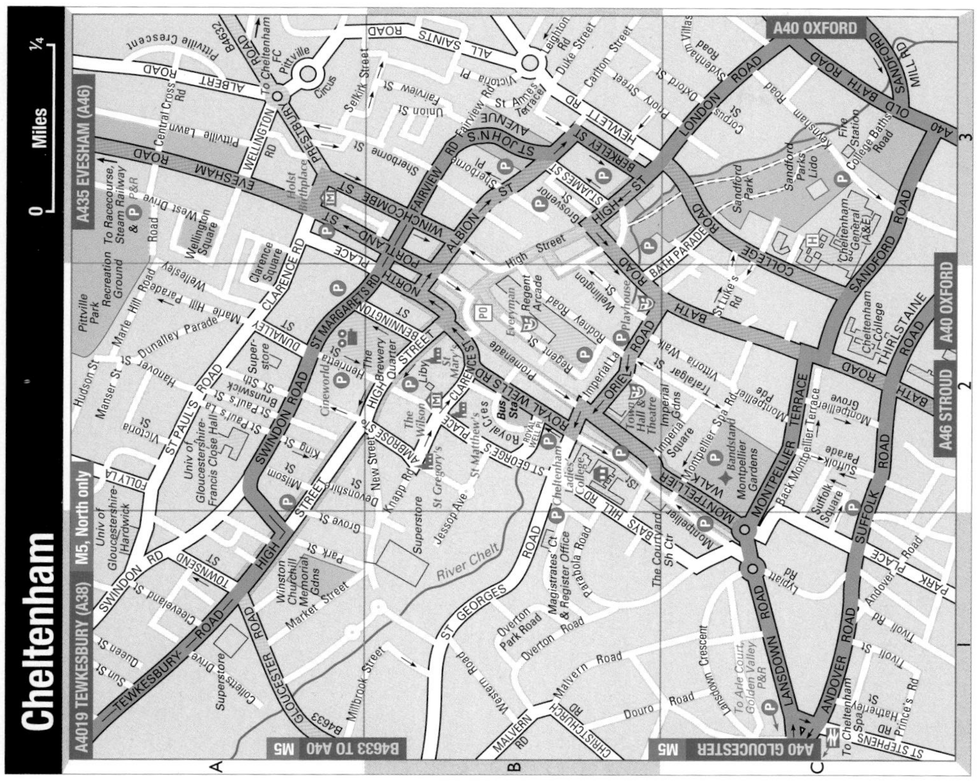
Cheltenham

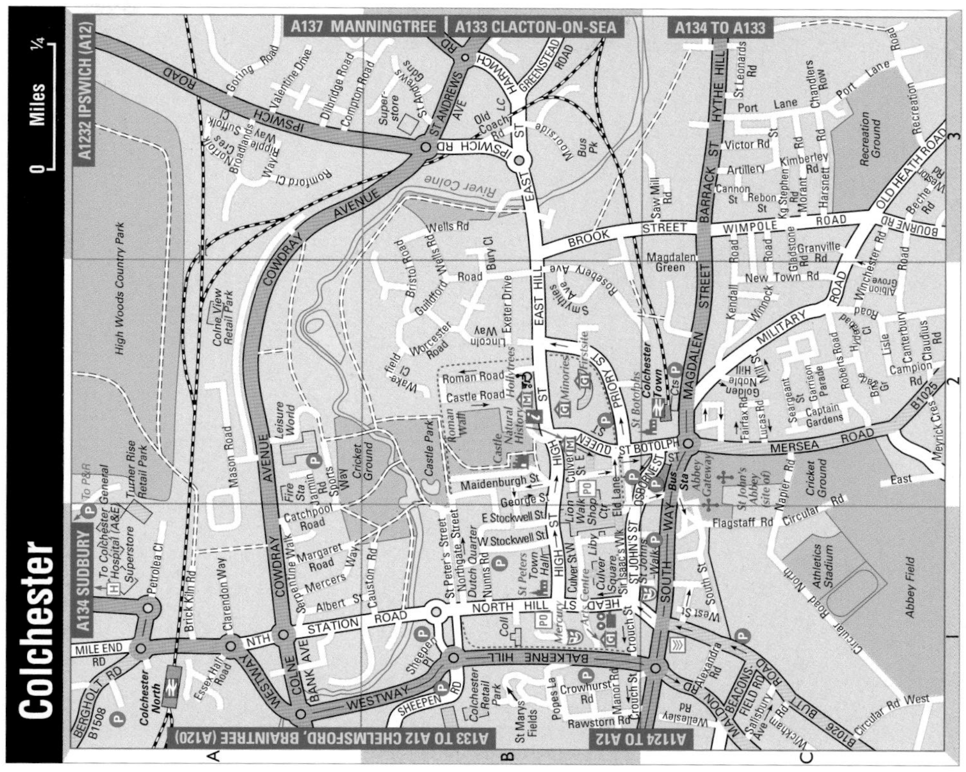
Colchester

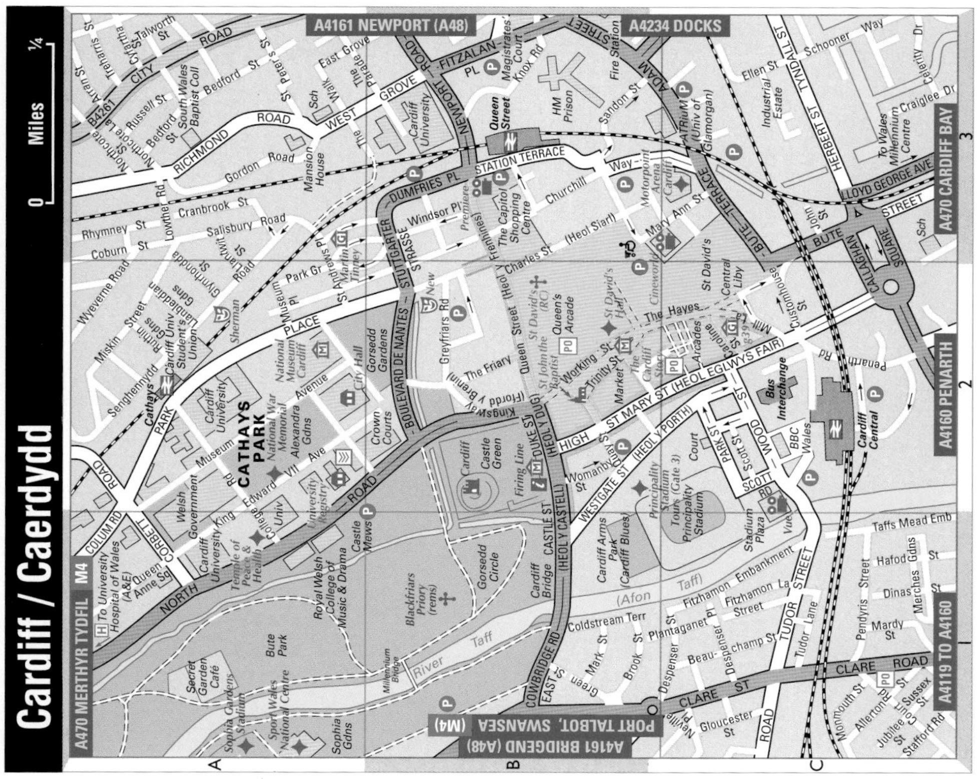
Cardiff / Caerdydd

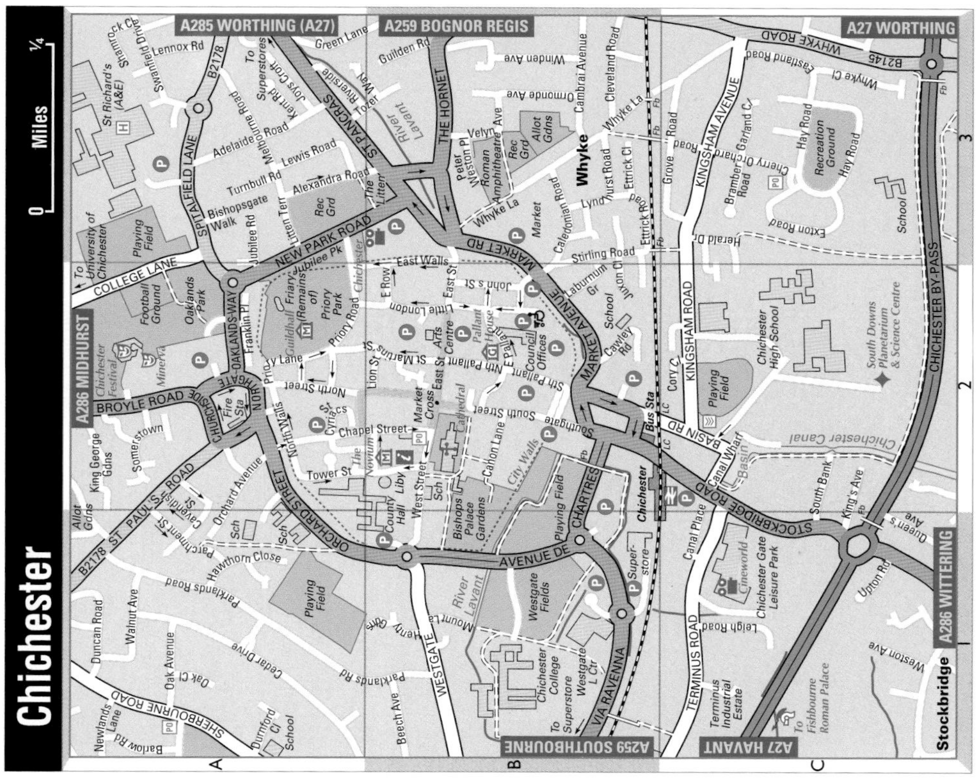
Chichester

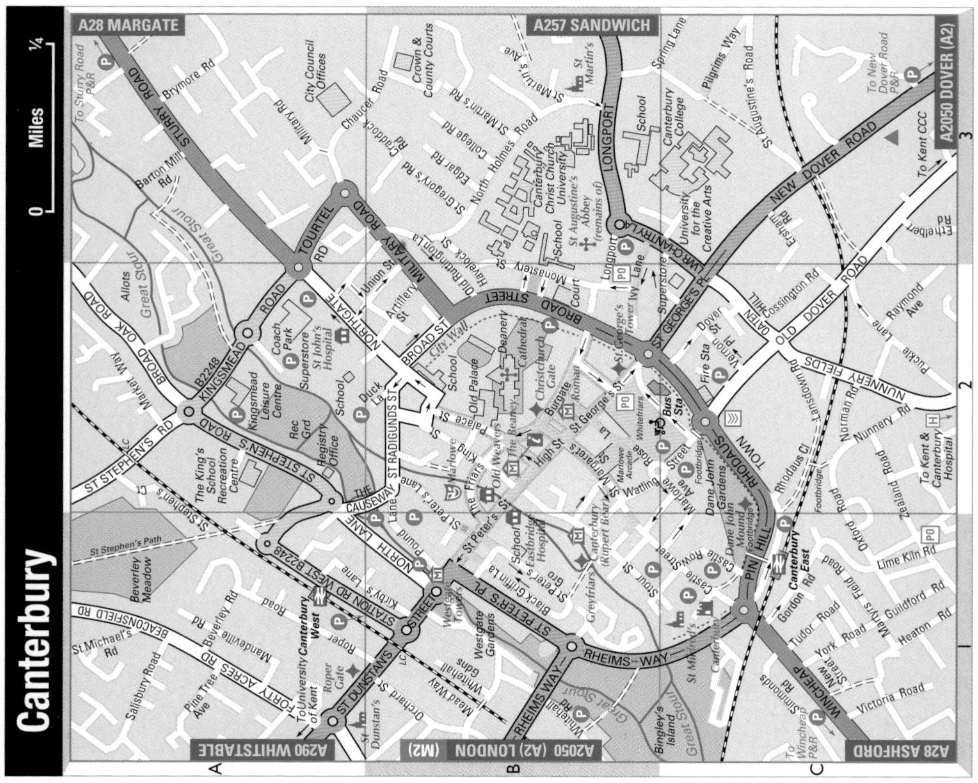
Canterbury

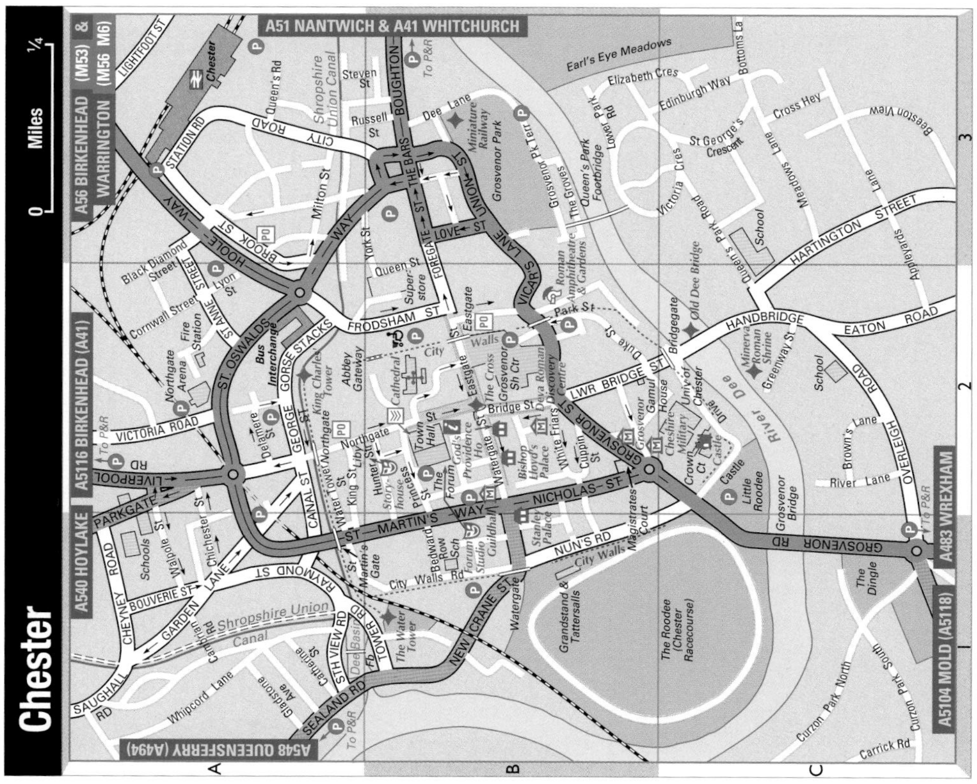
Chester

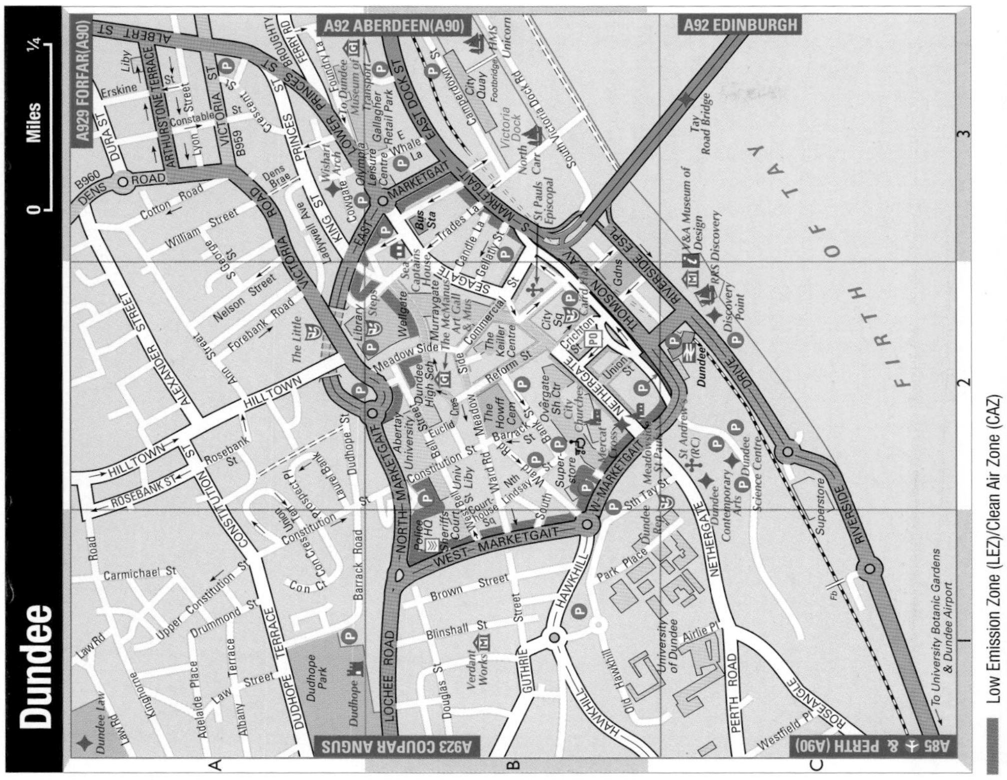
Dundee
Miles
A92 ABERDEEN(A90)
A92 EDINBURGH
A929 FORFAR(A90)
A923 COUPAR ANGUS
A85 & PERTH (A90)
FIRTH OF TAY
Low Emission Zone (LEZ)/Clean Air Zone (CAZ)

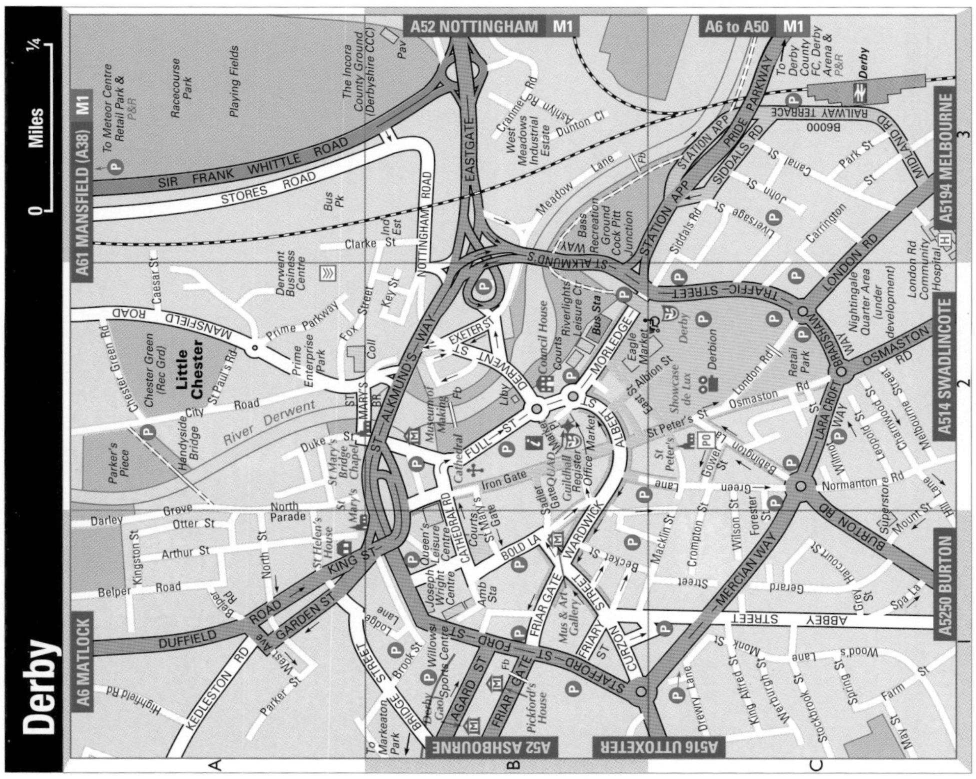
Derby
Miles
A52 NOTTINGHAM M1
A6 to A50 M1
A61 MANSFIELD (A38) M1
A6 MATLOCK
A52 ASHBOURNE
A516 UTOXETER
A5250 BURTON
A514 SWADLINCOTE
A5194 MELBOURNE

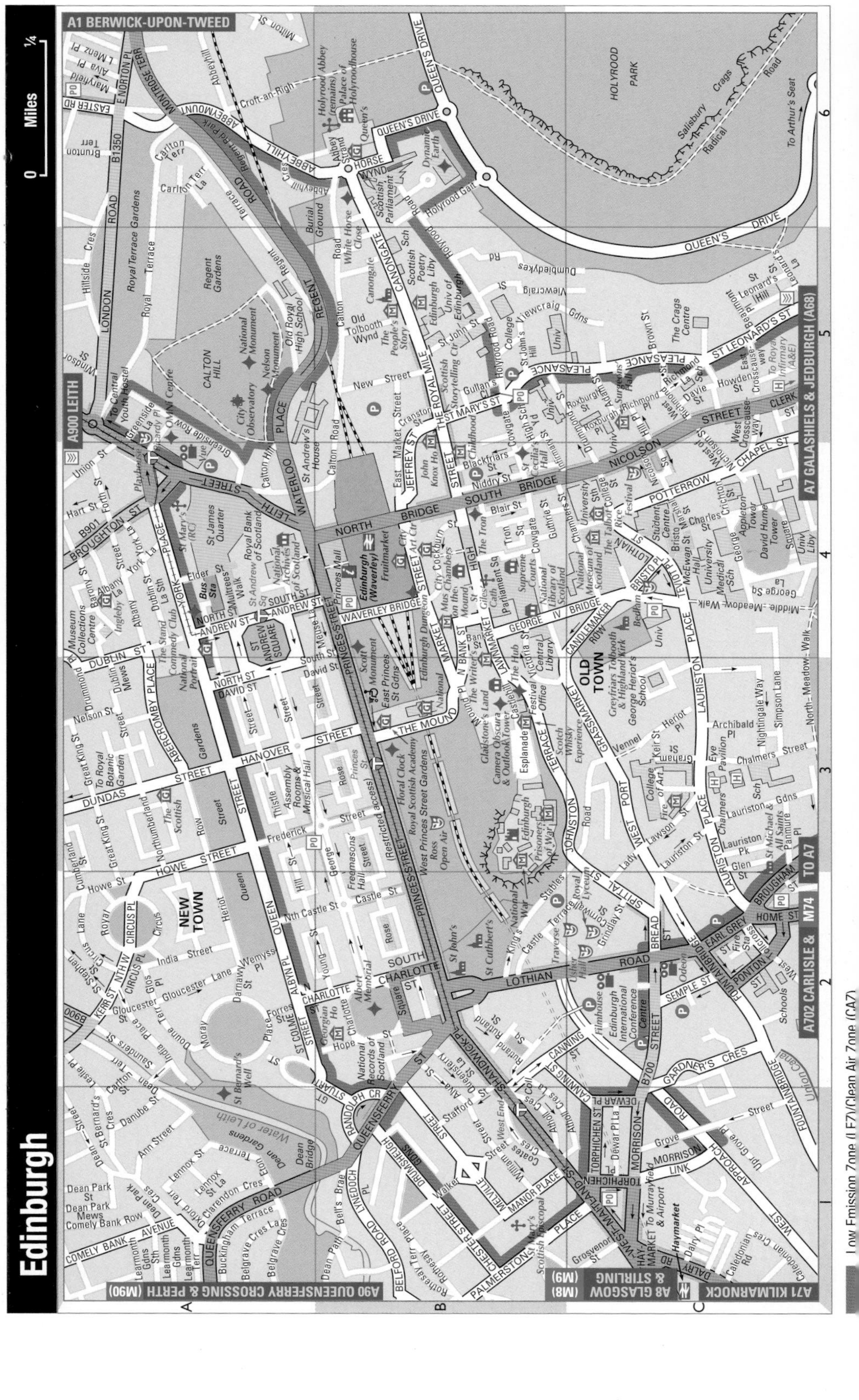
Edinburgh
Miles
A1 BERWICK-UPON-TWEED
A900 LEITH
A7 GALASHIELS & JEDBURGH (A68)
A702 CARLISLE & TO A7 M74
A71 KILMARNOCK
A8 GLASGOW & STIRLING (M8) (M9)
A90 QUEENSFERRY CROSSING & PERTH (M90)
NEW TOWN
OLD TOWN
Low Emission Zone (LEZ)/Clean Air Zone (CAZ)

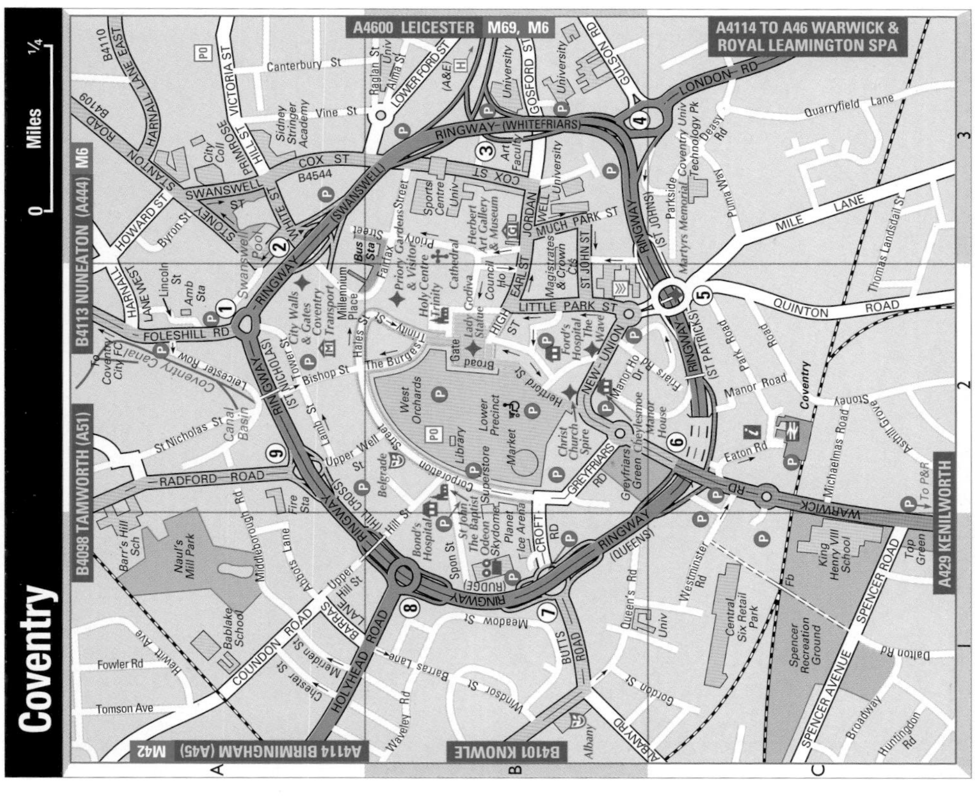
Coventry
Miles
A4600 LEICESTER M69, M6
A4114 TO A46 WARWICK & ROYAL LEAMINGTON SPA
B4113 NUNEATON (A444) M6
B4098 TAMWORTH (A51)
A4114 BIRMINGHAM (A45) M42
B4101 KNOWLE
A429 KENILWORTH

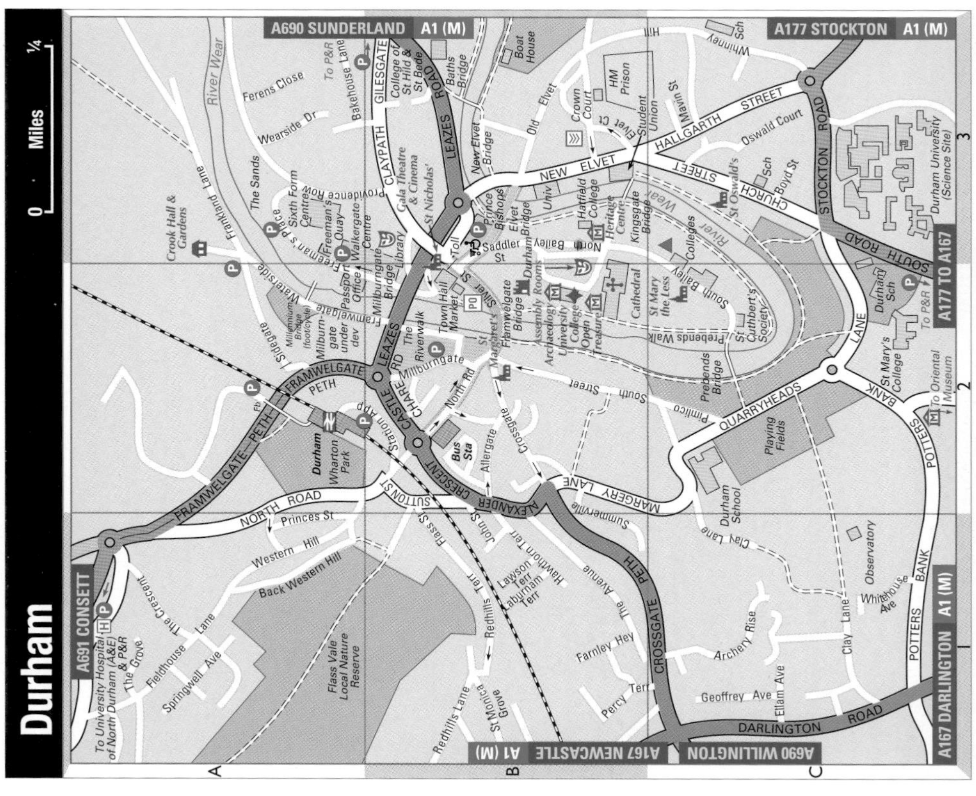
Durham
Miles
A690 SUNDERLAND A1 (M)
A177 STOCKTON A1 (M)
A691 CONSETT
A167 NEWCASTLE A1 (M)
A690 WILLINGTON
A167 DARLINGTON A1 (M)
A177 TO A167

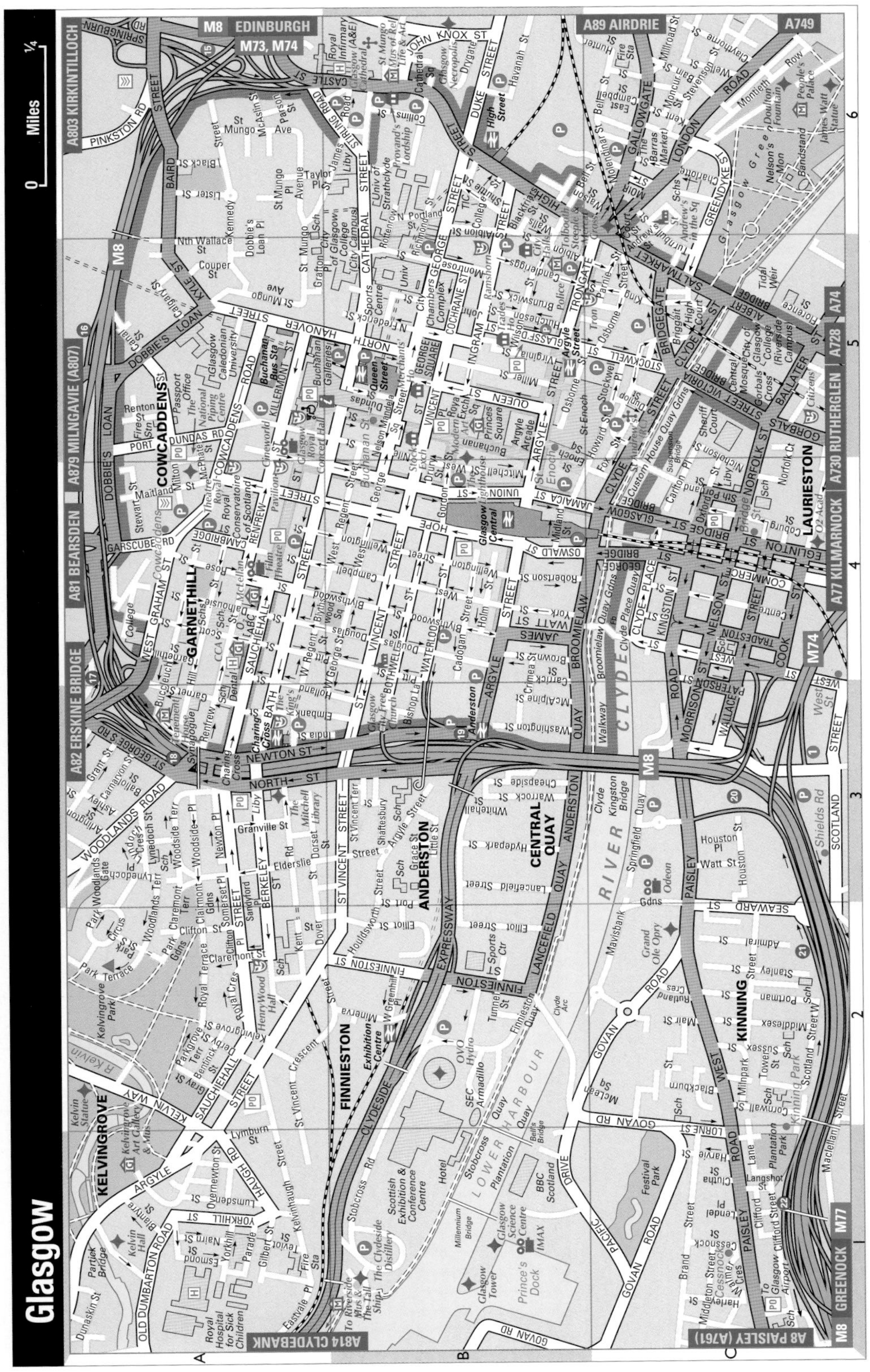
Glasgow

Low Emission Zone (LEZ)/Clean Air Zone (CAZ)

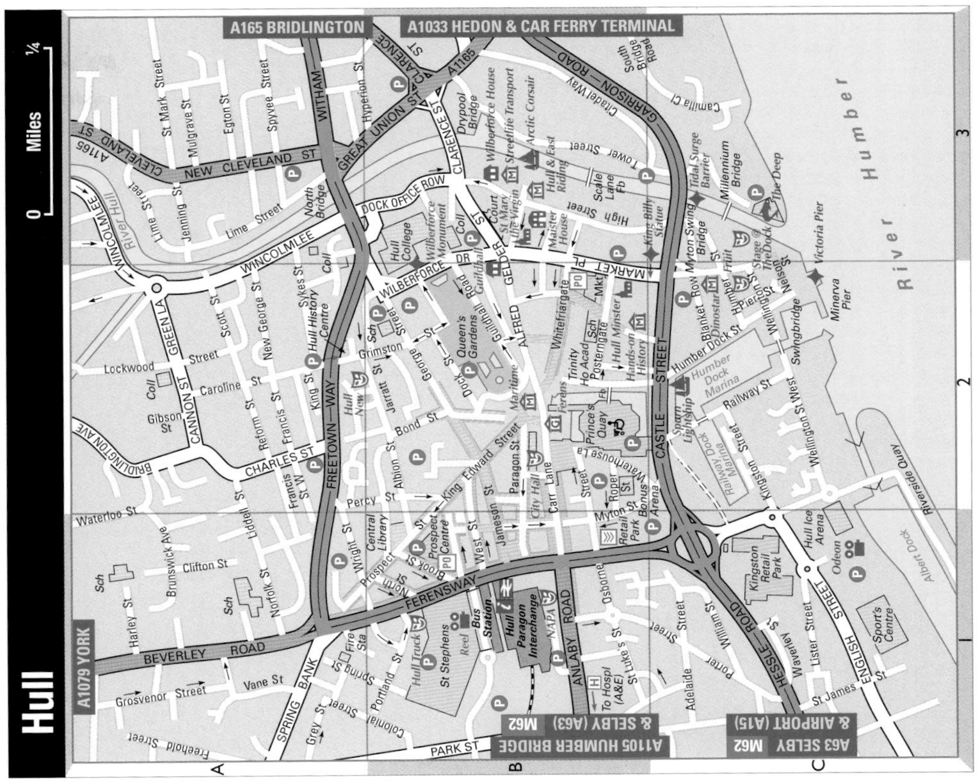
Hull

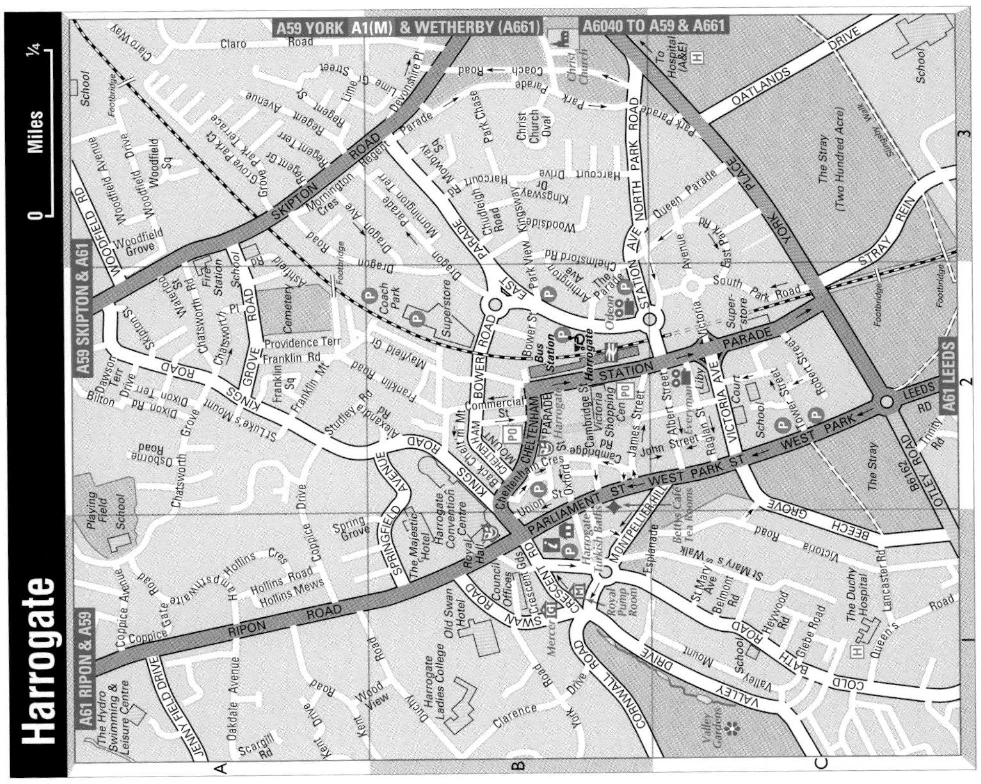
Harrogate

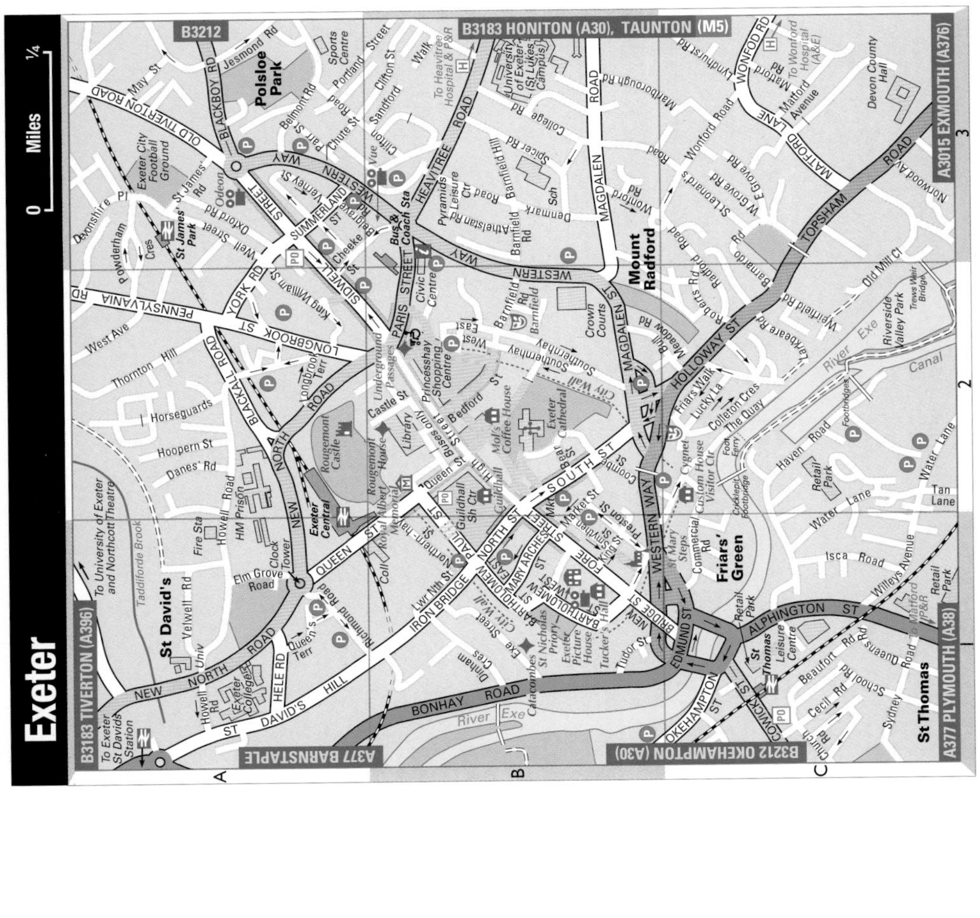
Exeter

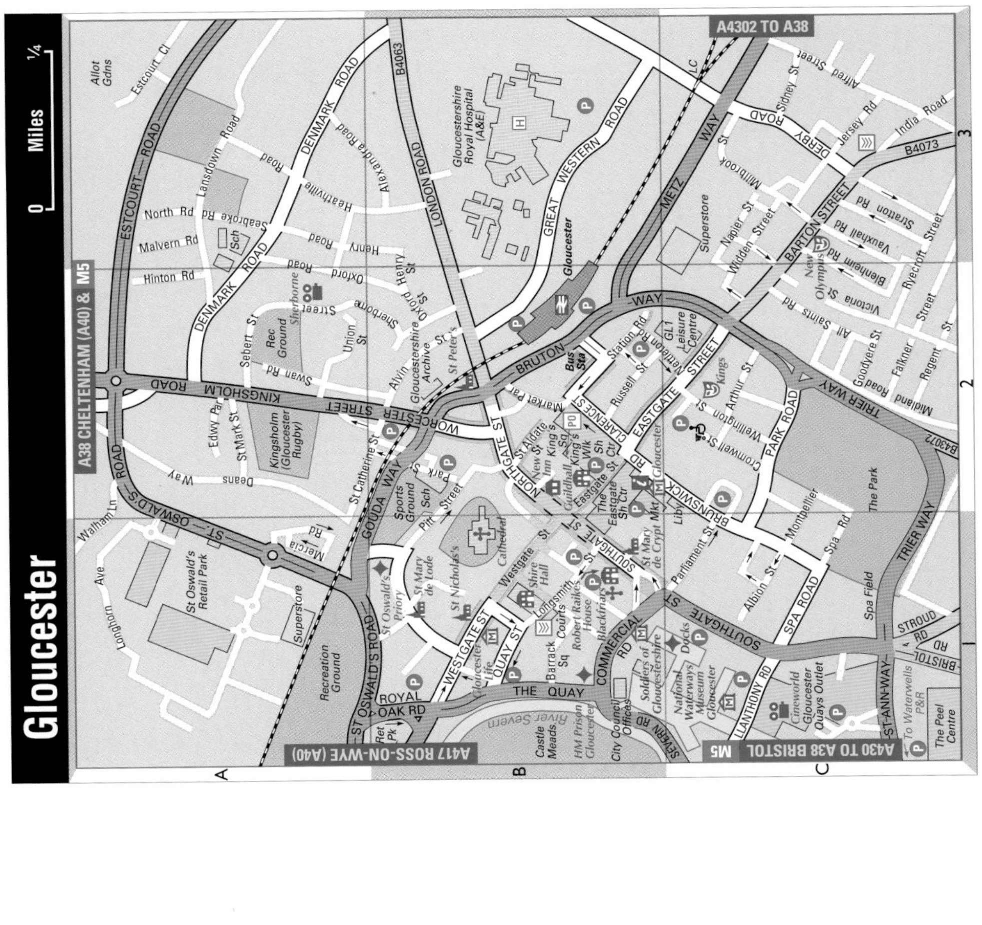
Gloucester

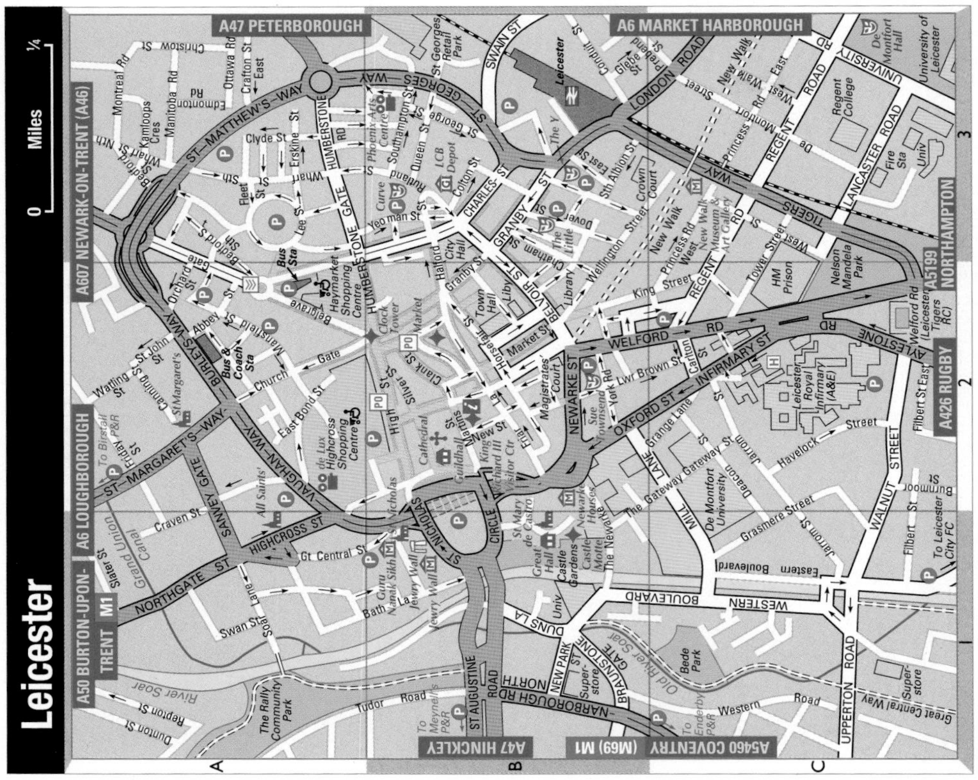
Leicester

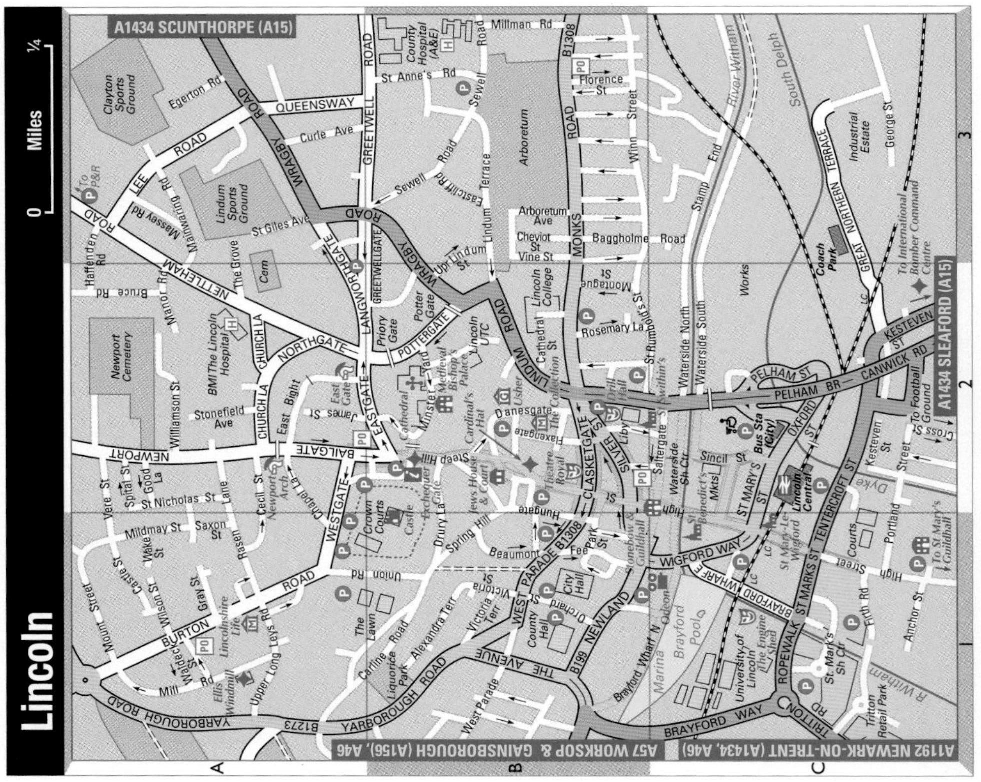
Lincoln

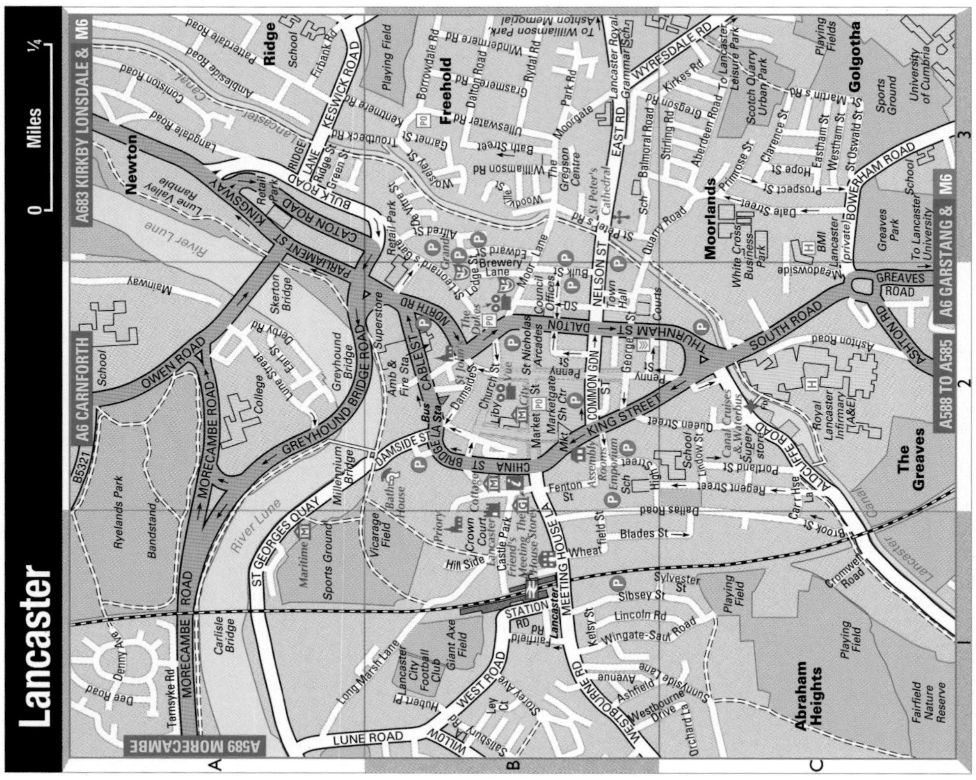
Lancaster

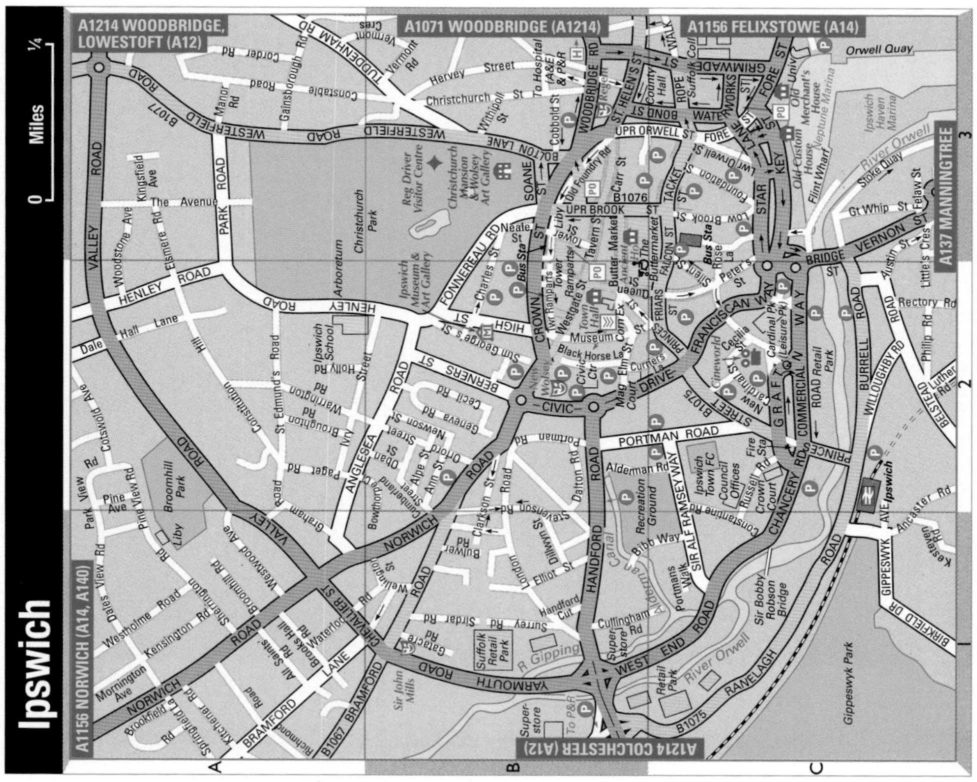
Ipswich

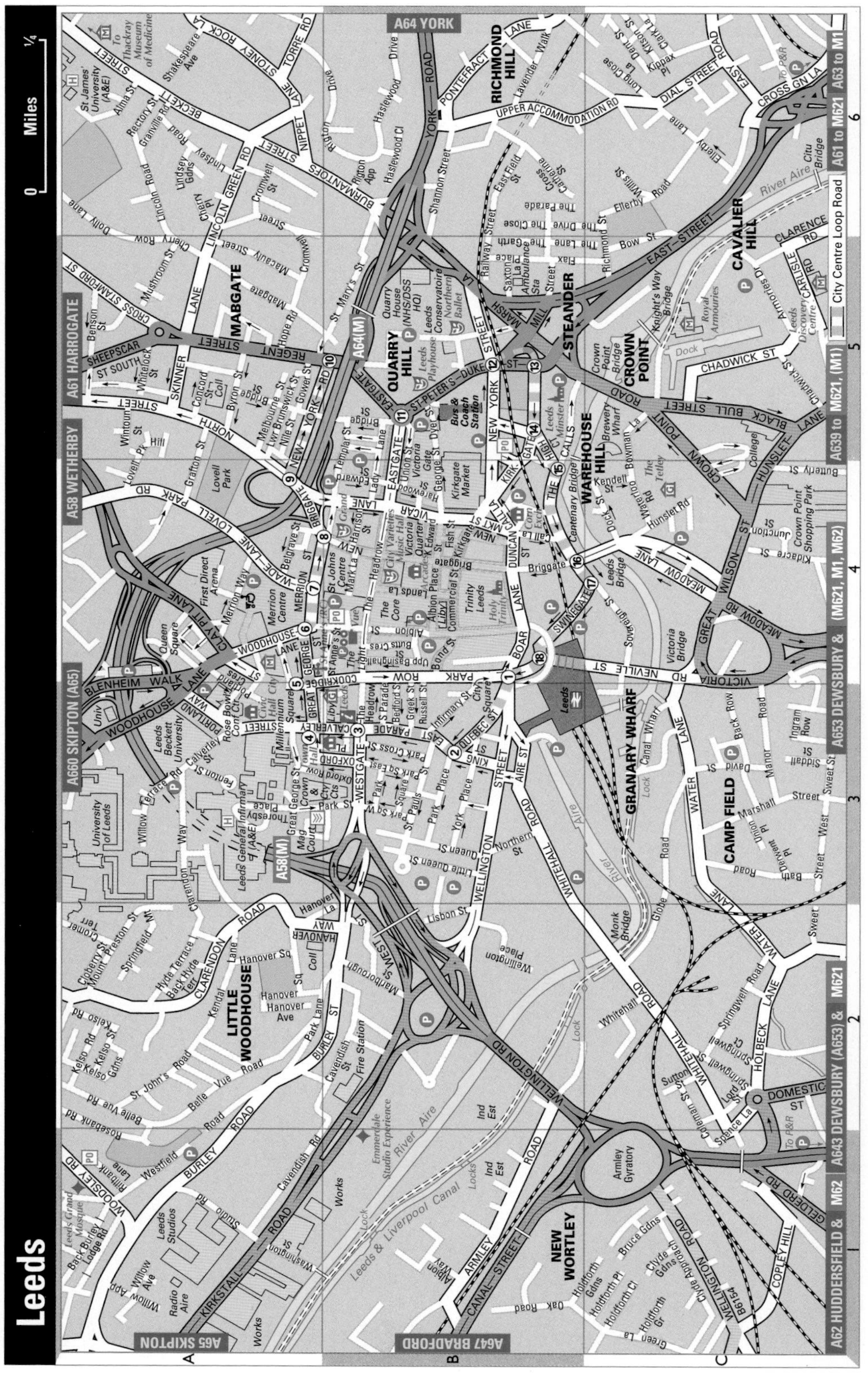
Leeds

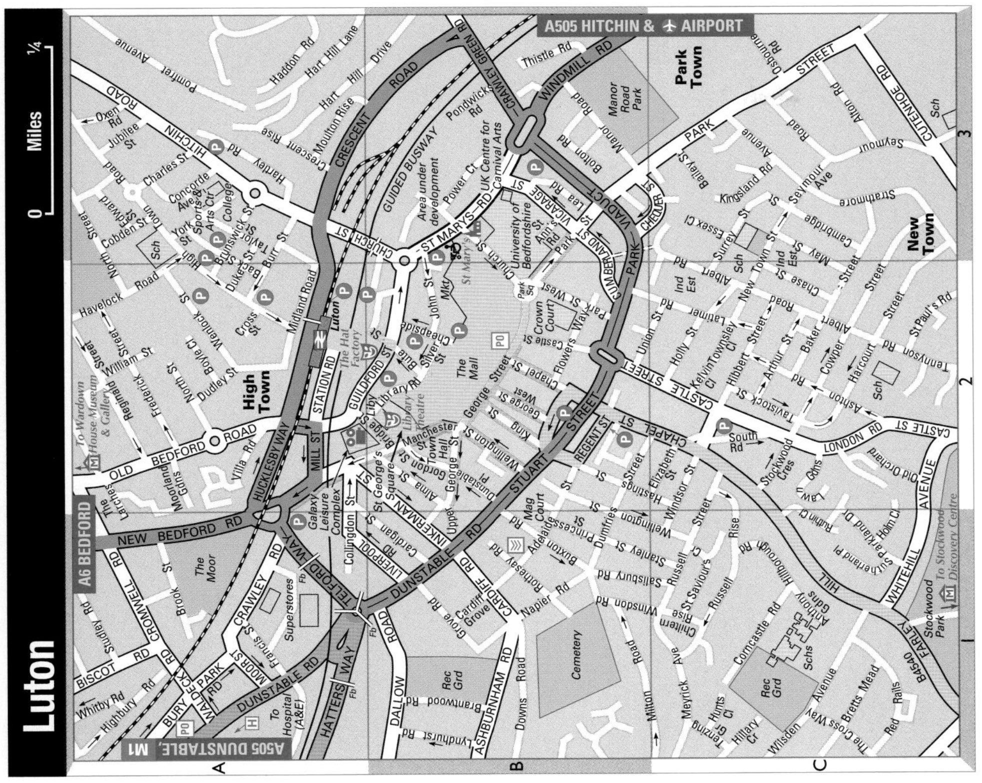
Luton

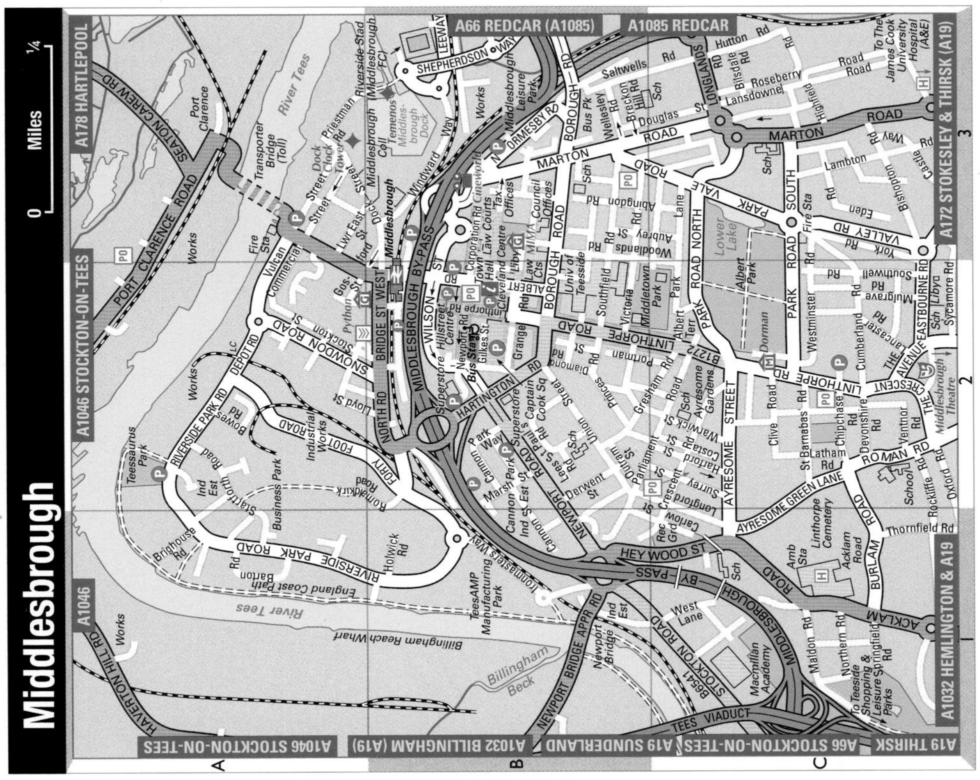
Middlesbrough

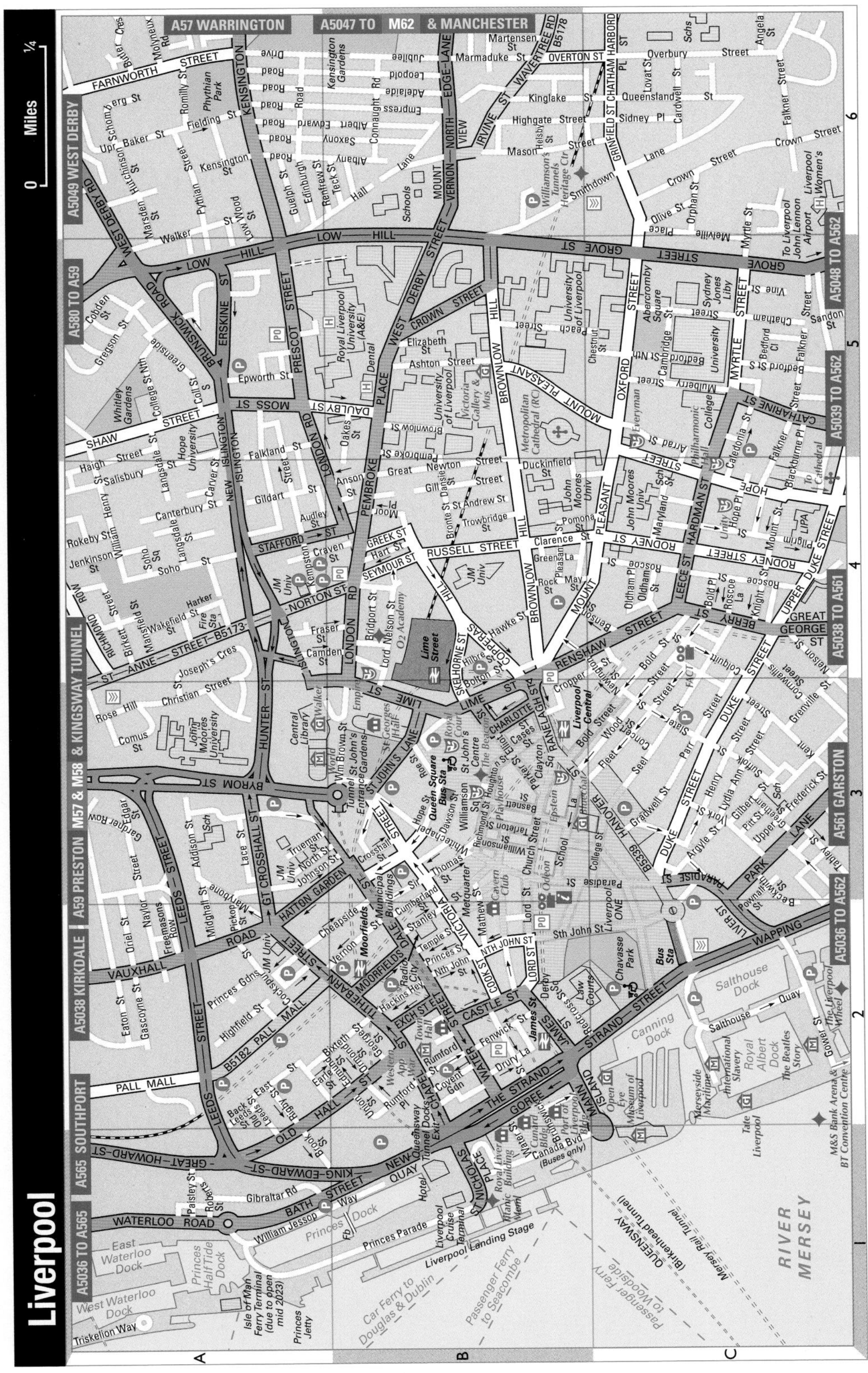
Liverpool

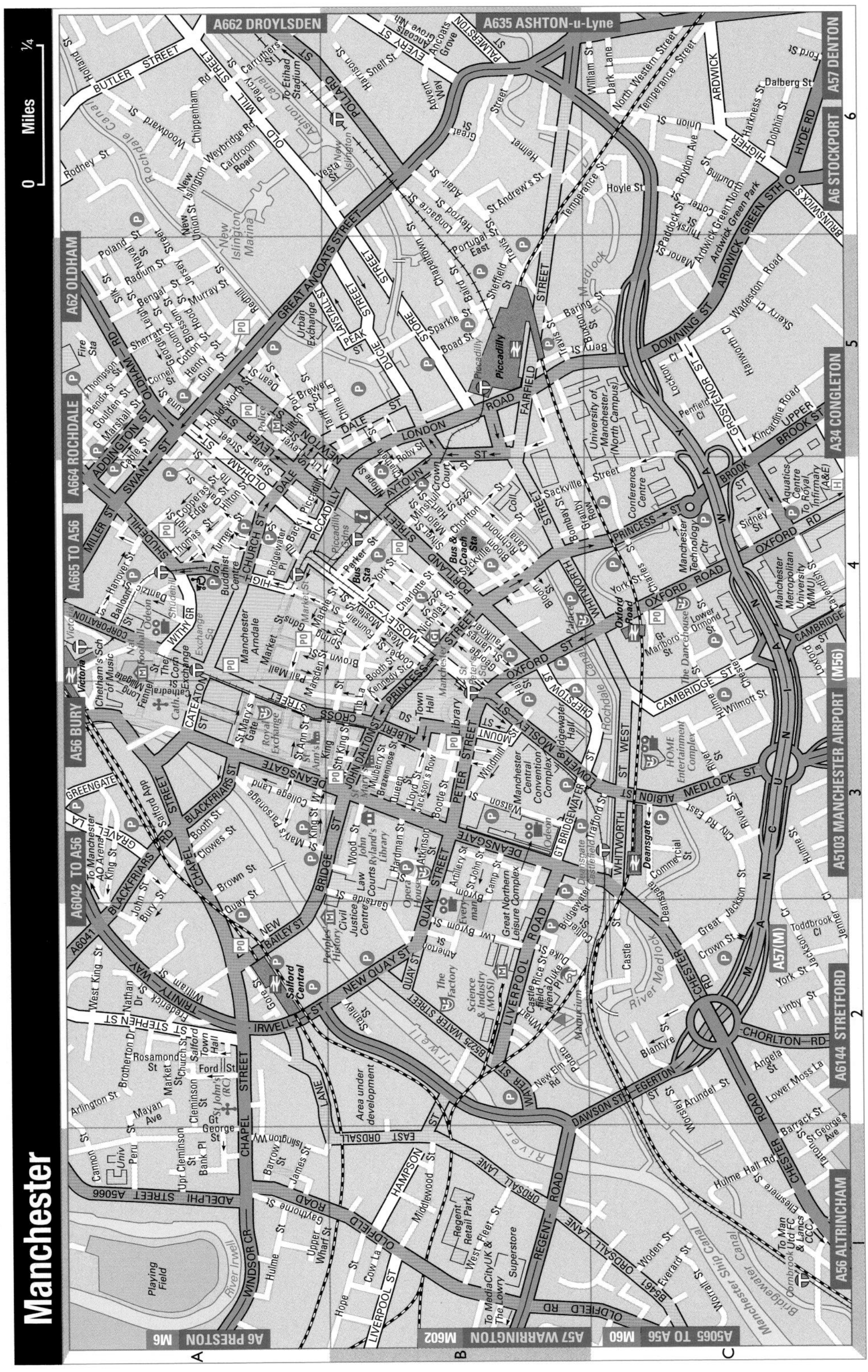
Manchester

REGENT'S PARK
London Zoo
Regent's Park Barracks
Cumberland Gate
St John's Lodge
Capel Manor College
Open Air Theatre
Queen Mary's Gardens
Regent's Park Boating Lake
London Business School
Regents College
Royal College of Physicians
Royal Academy of Music
Madame Tussaud's
Lost Property Office (LT)
Park Square Gardens
Regent's Park
SOMERS TOWN
St Pancras International
King's Cross
British Library
Euston
Euston Square
Euston Tower
Area under development
University College Hosp (A&E)
University College London (UCL)
Petrie Mus
Royal Acad of Dramatic Art (RADA)
Sch of Hygiene & Tropical Med
University of London
British Medical Association
The Brunswick Shopping Centre
The Foundling Museum
Coram's Fields (Children's Playground)
Gt. Ormond St Children's Hosp
Royal London Hosp for Int Medicine
Royal Nat Ear, Nose & Throat Hosp
BLOOMSBURY
British Museum
FITZROVIA
British Telecom Tower
University of Westminster
Wallace Collection
BBC Broadcasting House
All Souls
All Saints
Royal Coll of Nursing
Wigmore Hall
Cent Synagogue
Arch Centre
RIBA
Oxford Circus
Tottenham Court Road
SOHO
Leisure Ctr
Cambridge Circus
Seven Dials
Covent Garden
Royal Opera Ho
London Transport Mus
St Paul's
Freemason's Hall
Oasis Sports Ctr
Marble Arch
Speakers Corner
MAYFAIR
Roosevelt Memorial
Handel/Hendrix Houses
Royal Acad of Arts
London Trocadero
Piccadilly Circus
Eros
National Portrait Gall
National Gall
St Martin-in-the-Fields
TRAFALGAR SQUARE
Nelson's Column
Charing Cross
ST JAMES'S
Arts Council
Crafts Council
Admiralty Arch
The Admiralty
Horse Guards' Parade
Banqueting Ho
Min of Defence
Cabinet Office
Downing St
Foreign & Commonwealth Office
New Scotland Yard
Cenotaph
Treasury
Cabinet War Rooms & Churchill Museum
London Eye Waterloo Pier
London Aquarium
Shrek's Adventure
The London Dungeon
County Hall
Westminster Pier
Embankment Pier
Hungerford Bridge (Rail Bridge)
Golden Jubilee Bridges (Footbridges)
Cleopatra's Needle
Savoy Pier
Victoria Embankment Gdns
HYDE PARK
Diana, Princess of Wales Memorial Walk
7 July Memorial
Achilles Statue
Bandstand
Serpentine Rd
Holocaust Memorial Garden
Apsley House
Wellington Museum
Hyde Park Corner
Wellington Arch
Royal Artillery Memorial
Memorial Gates
GREEN PARK
Constitution Hill Closed to traffic on Sundays
Queen Victoria Memorial
Buckingham Palace
Buckingham Palace Gardens
Queen's Gallery
Royal Mews
Lancaster House
Clarence House
St James's Palace
Marlborough House
The Mall Closed to traffic on Sundays
ST JAMES'S PARK
St. James's Park Lake
Duck Island
Guards Mus & Chapel
Wellington Barracks
Ministry of Justice
Westminster City Hall
Cardinal Place Shopping Centre
Belgrave Square
Westminster Cathedral (RC)
Victoria
Victoria Place Shopping Centre
Westminster Abbey
Westminster School
Jewel Tower
Houses of Parliament
Westminster Hall
Big Ben
Central Hall
Guildhall
Home Office
Dept of Transport (DfT)
WESTMINSTER
Victoria Tower Gardens
Burghers of Calais (Rodin)
Florence Nightingale Museum
St.Thomas' Hospital
Evelina Children's Hosp
Lambeth Pier
Mus of Garden History
Fire Brigade Pier
BELGRAVIA
Old Horticultural Hall
Westminster School Playing Fields
Miles
0
½

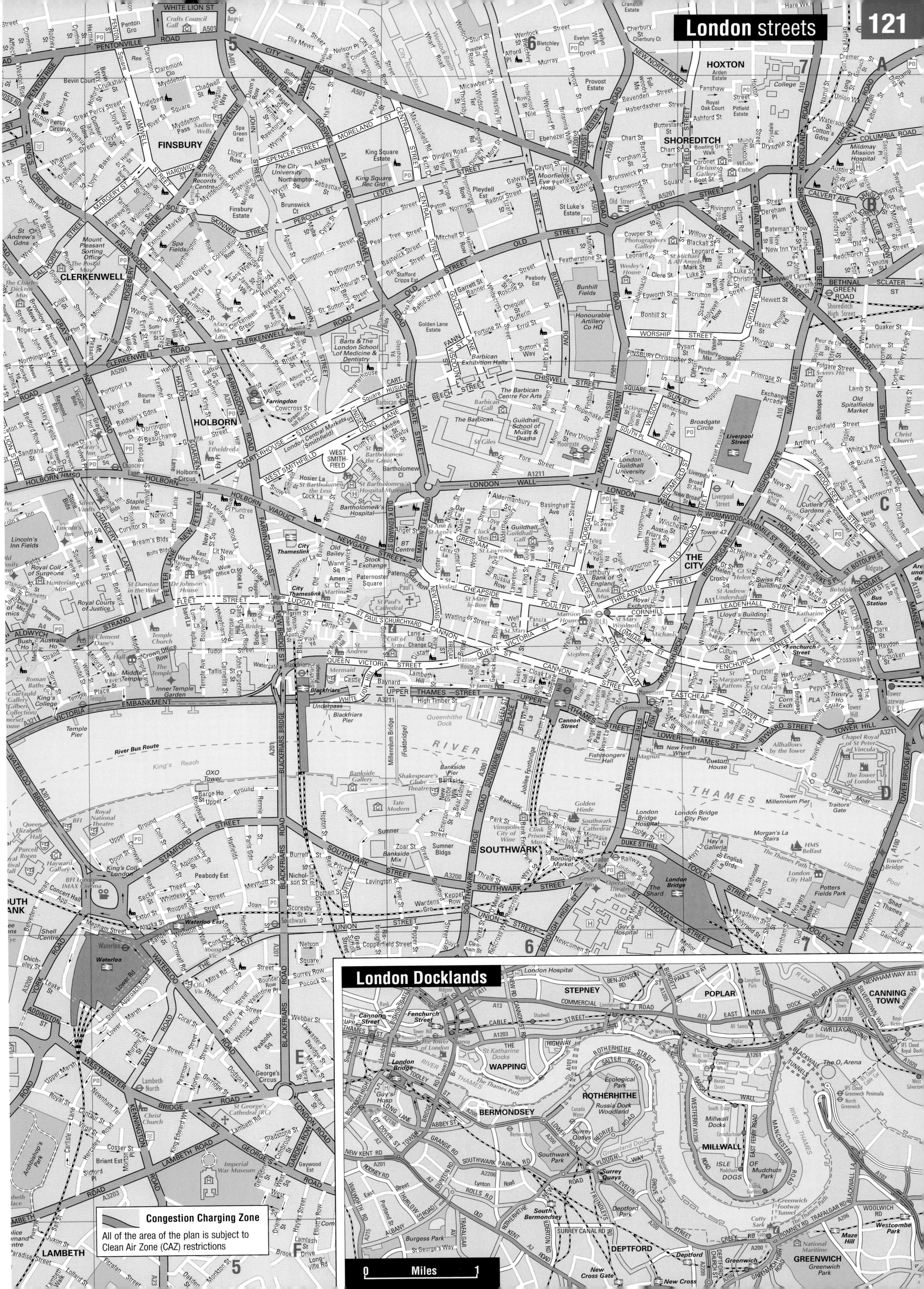
FINSBURY
CLERKENWELL
HOLBORN
HOXTON
SHOREDITCH
THE CITY
SOUTHWARK
LAMBETH
RIVER THAMES
London Docklands
STEPNEY
POPLAR
CANNING TOWN
WAPPING
ROTHERHITHE
BERMONDSEY
MILLWALL
ISLE OF DOGS
DEPTFORD
GREENWICH
Miles
Congestion Charging Zone
All of the area of the plan is subject to Clean Air Zone (CAZ) restrictions

Milton Keynes

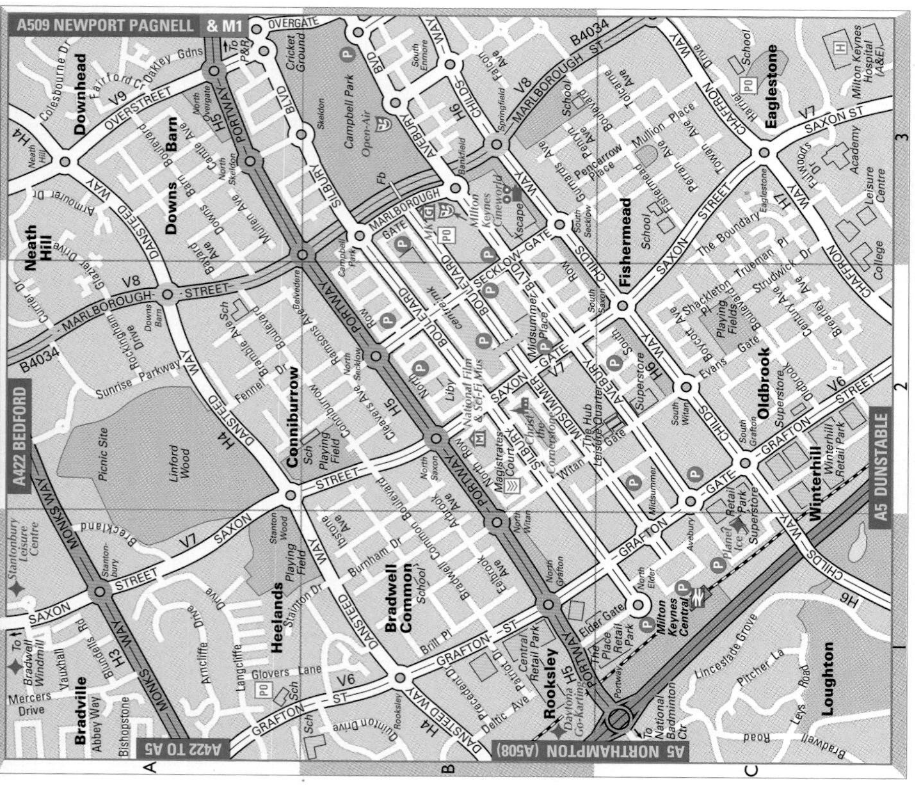

Newcastle upon Tyne

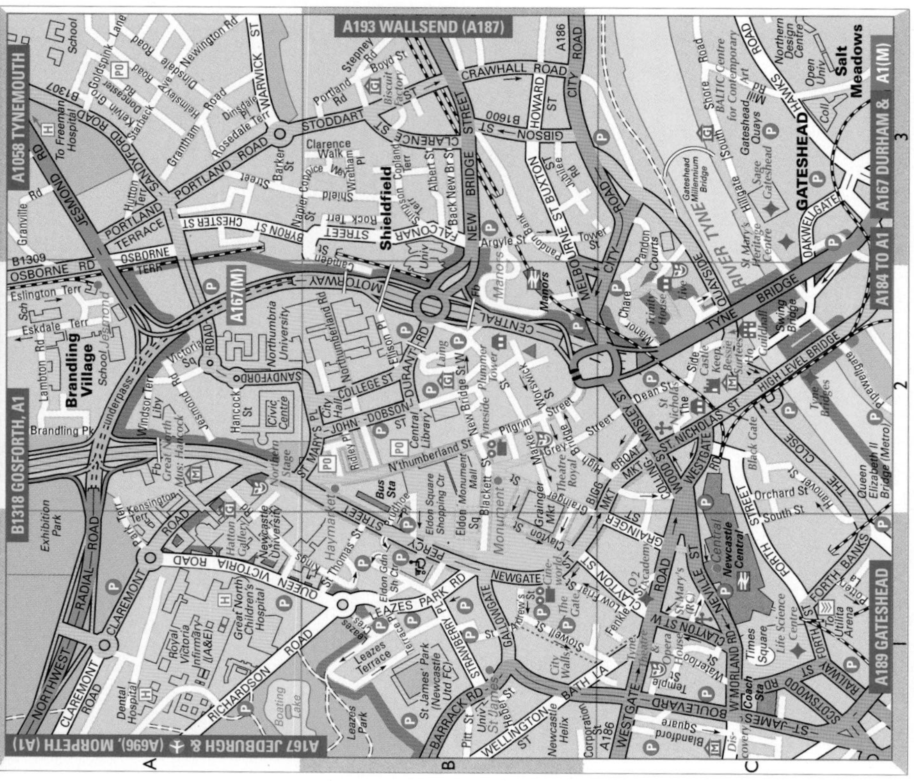

Low Emission Zone (LEZ)/Clean Air Zone (CAZ)

Newport / Casnewydd

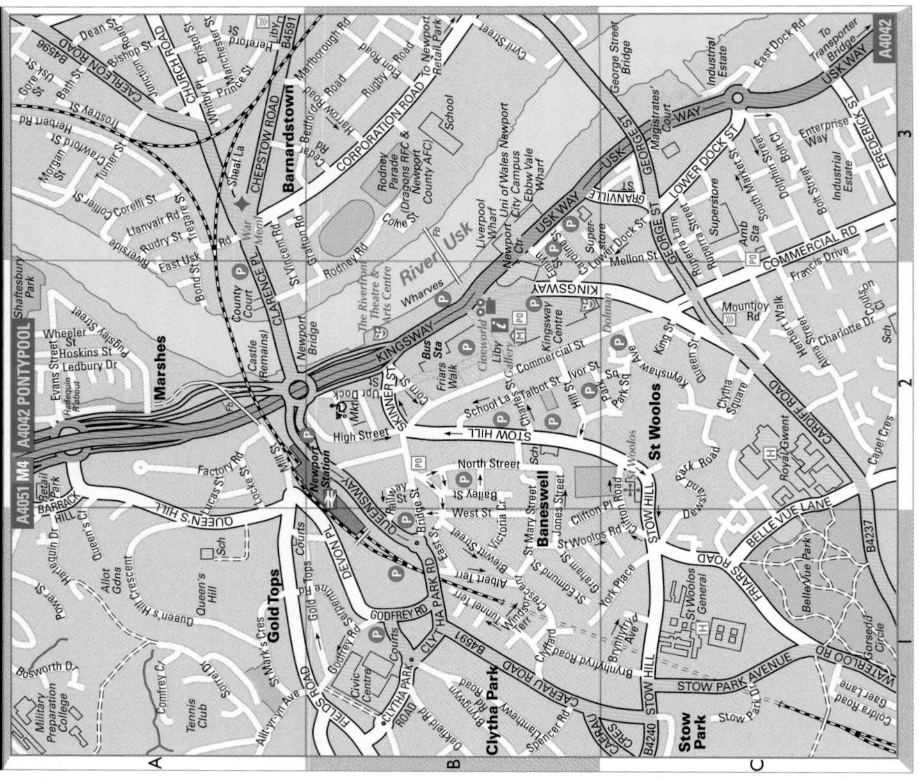

Northampton

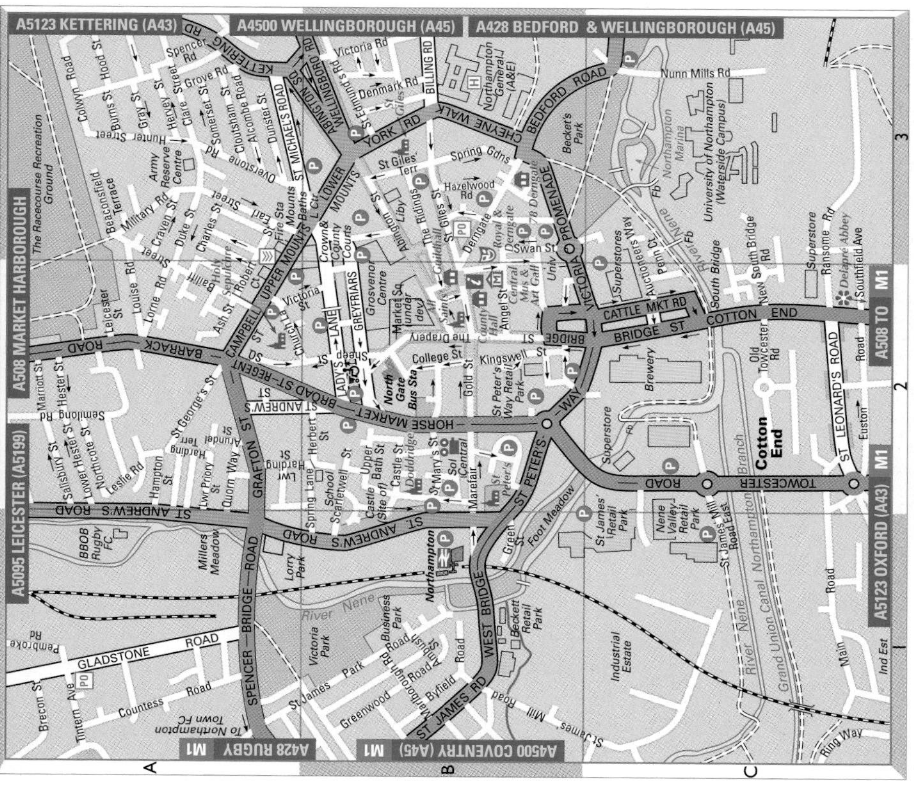

Norwich

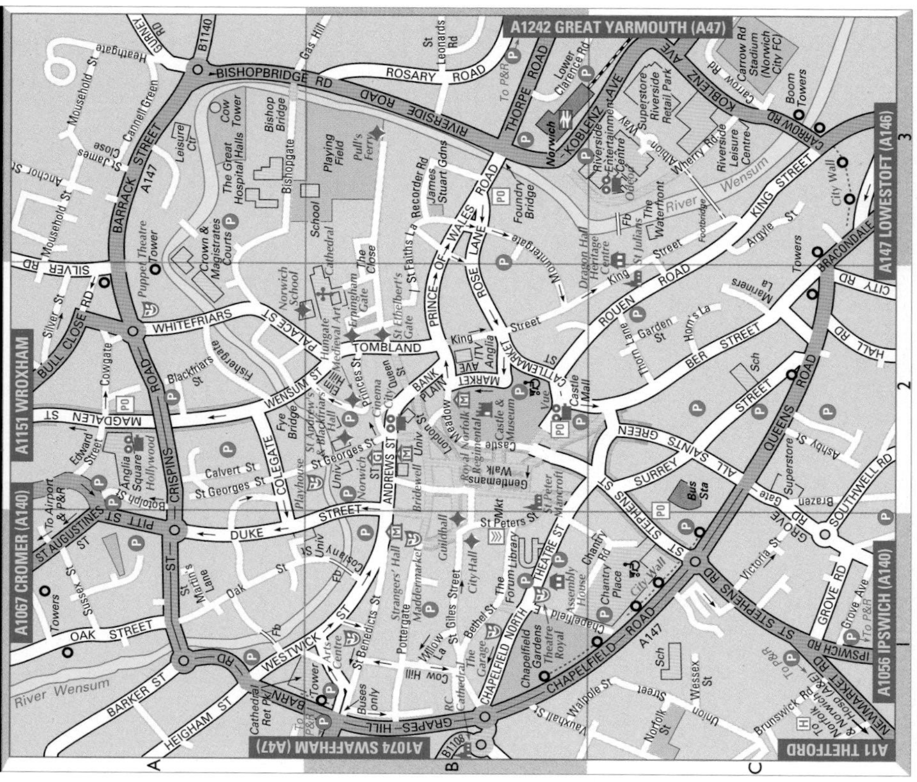

Nottingham

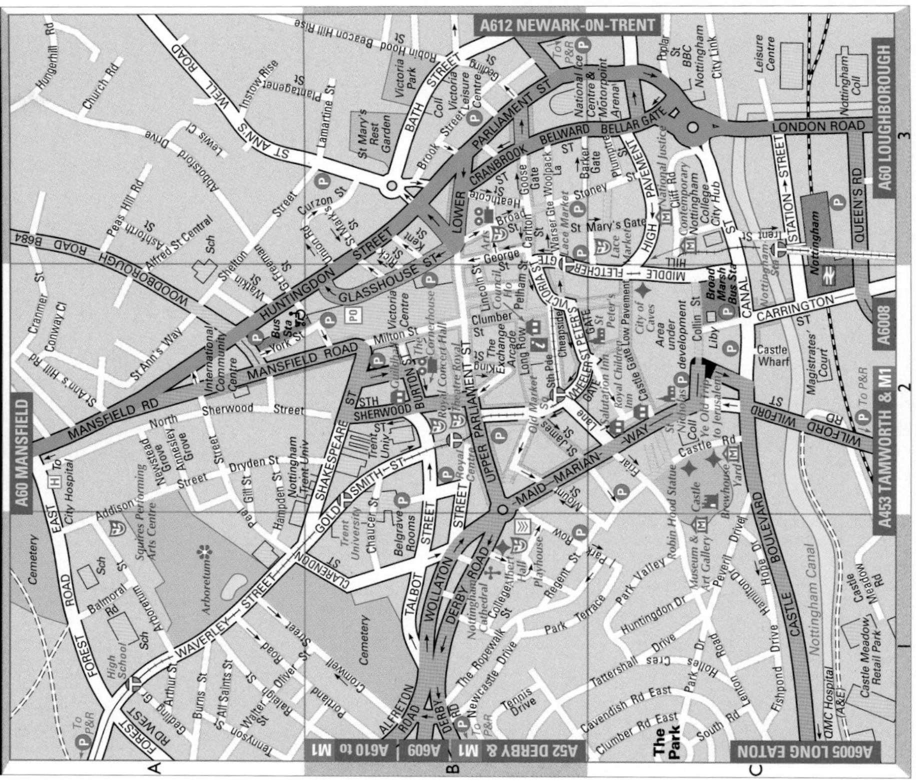

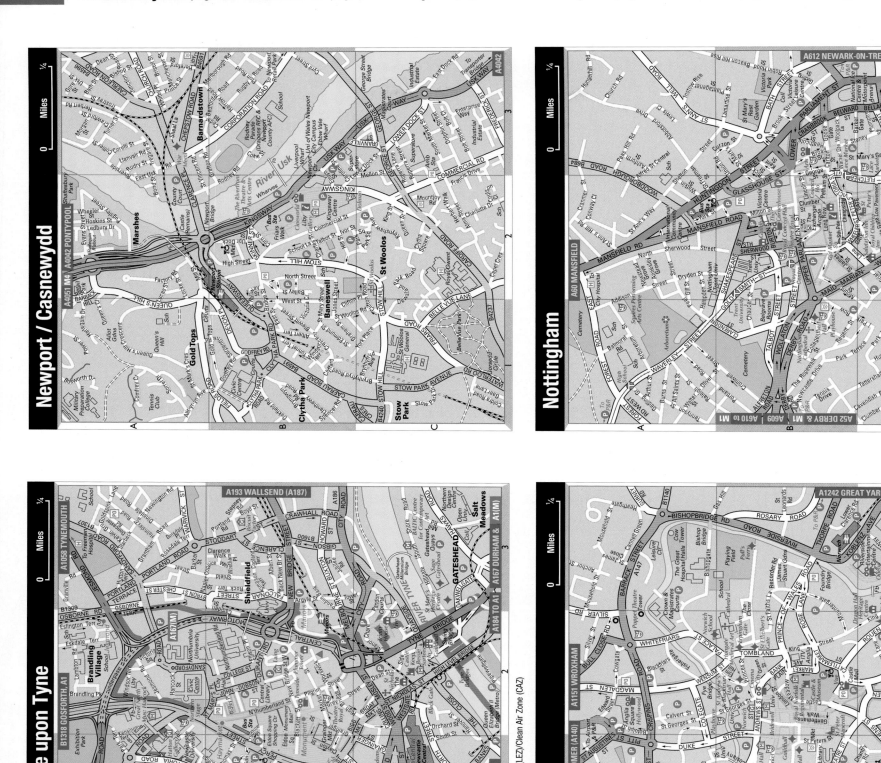

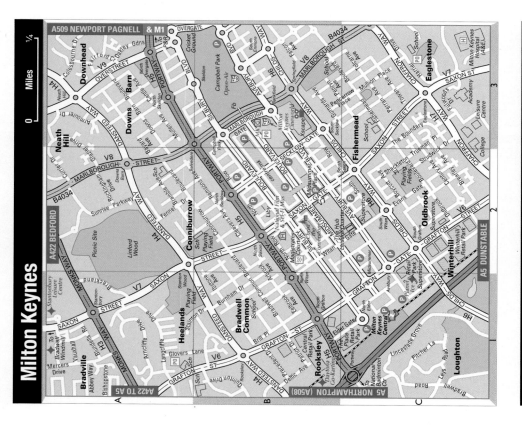

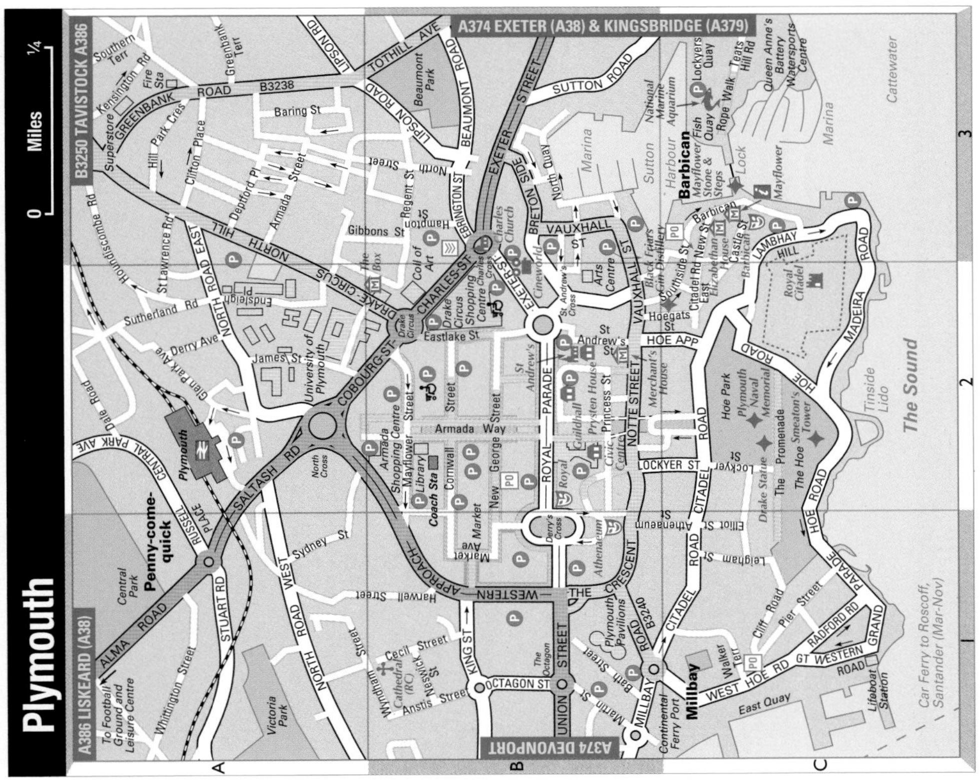
Plymouth
Miles
The Sound

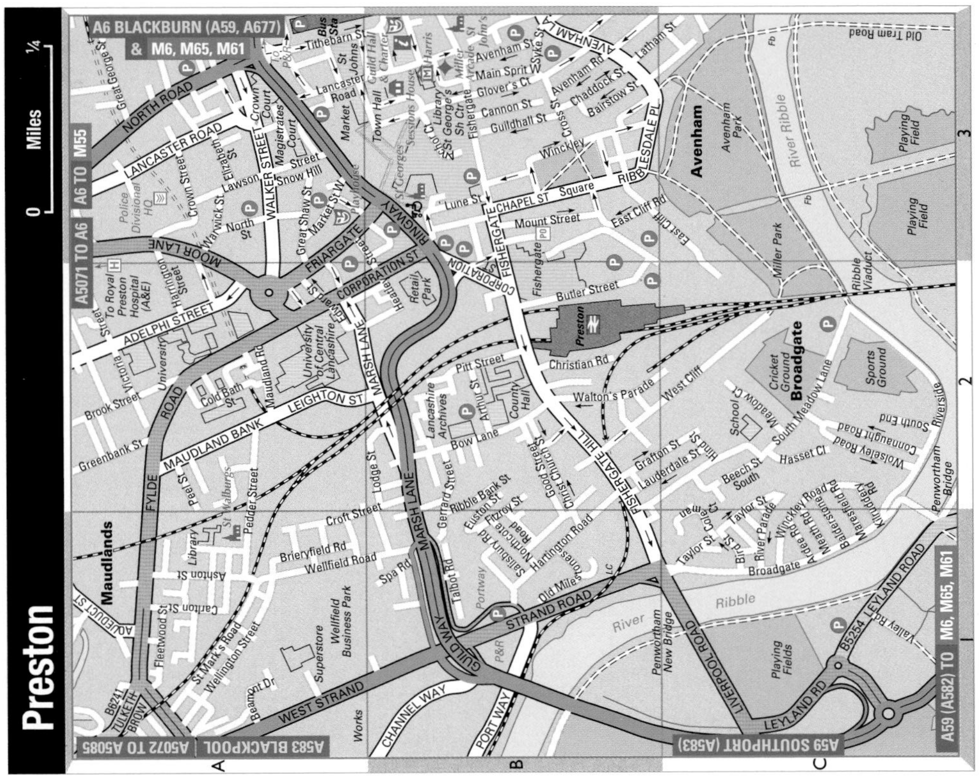
Preston
Miles

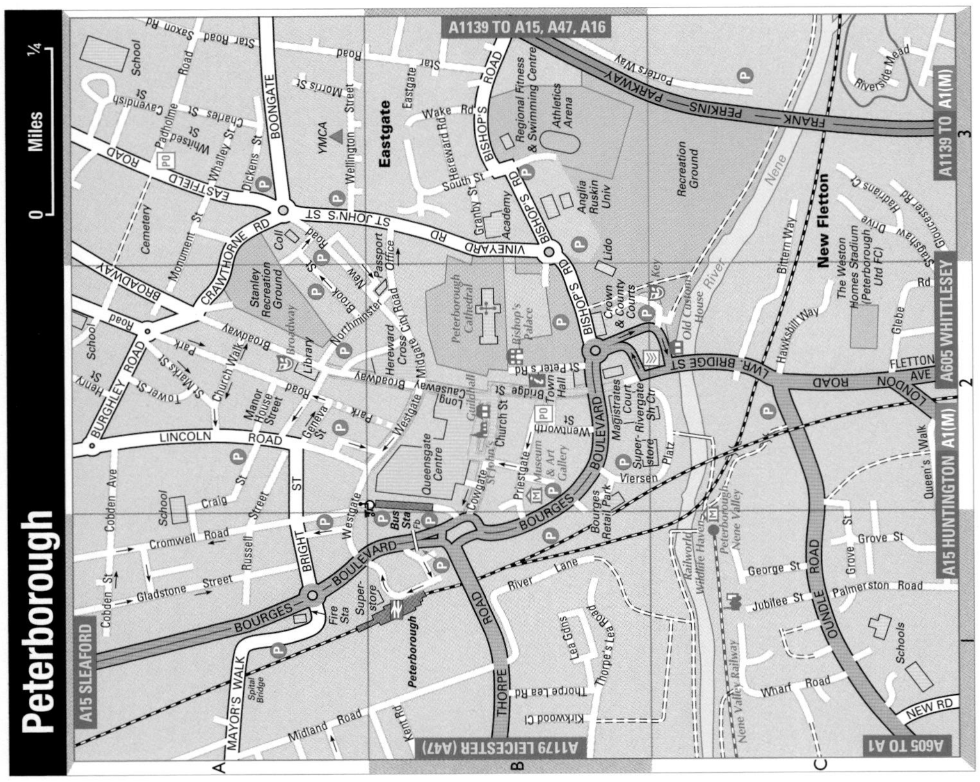
Peterborough
Miles

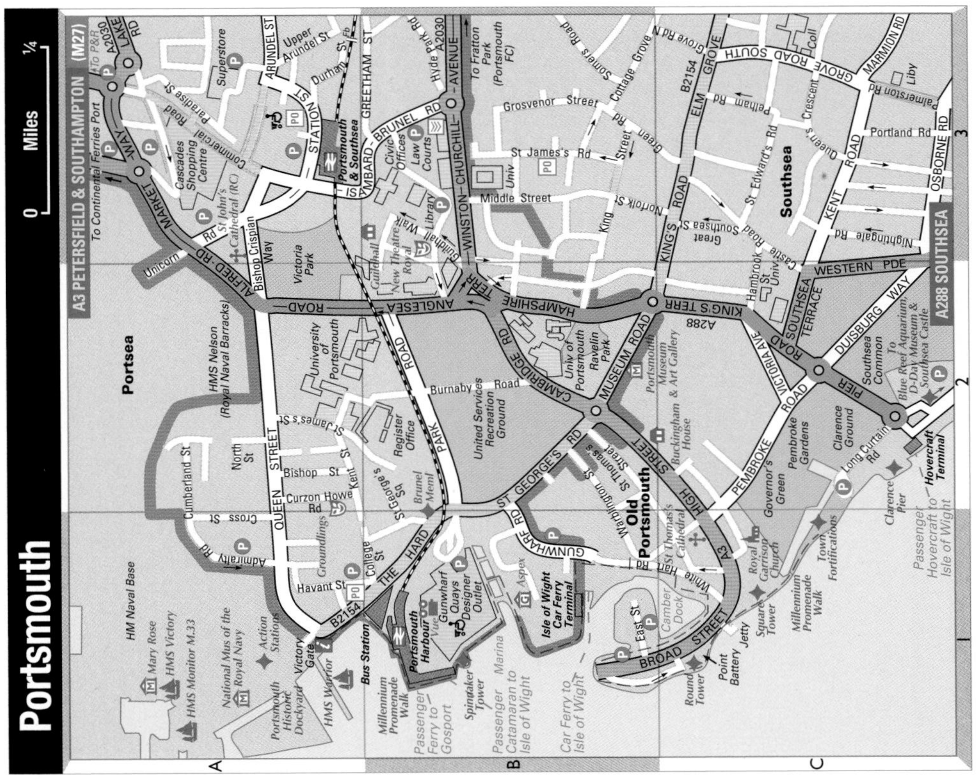
Portsmouth
Miles

Low Emission Zone (LEZ)/Clean Air Zone (CAZ)

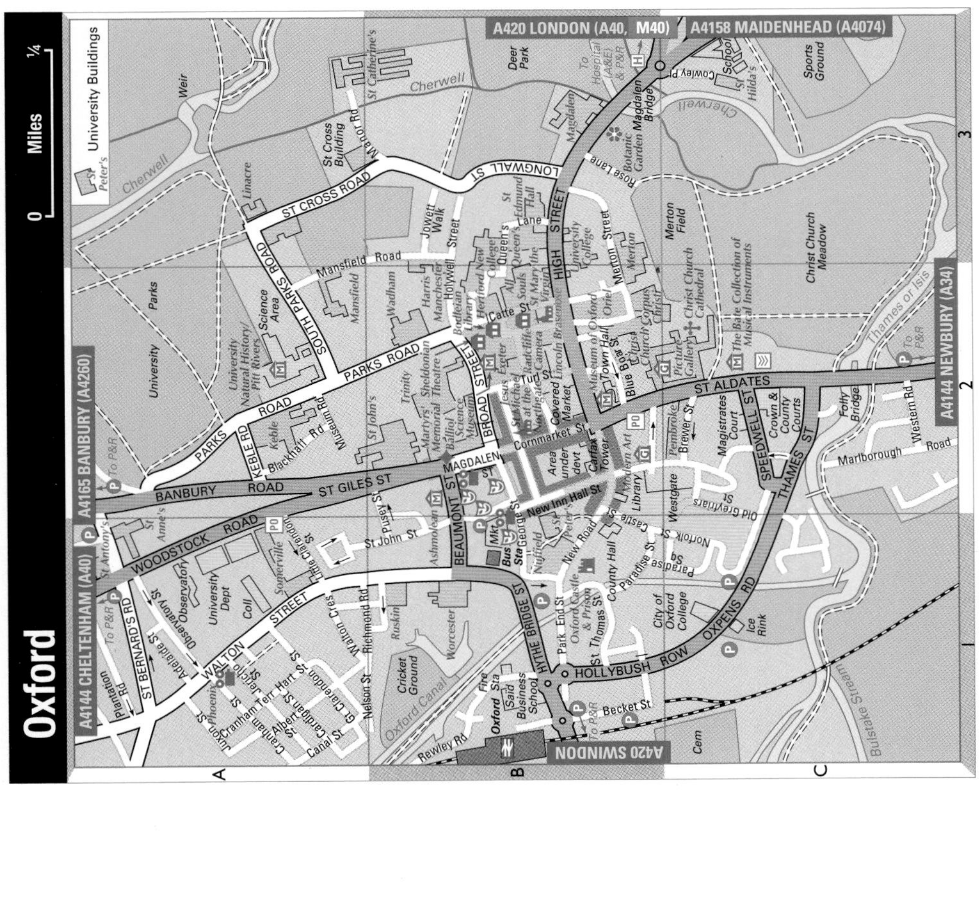
Oxford
Miles
University Buildings

Zero Emission Zone (ZEZ)

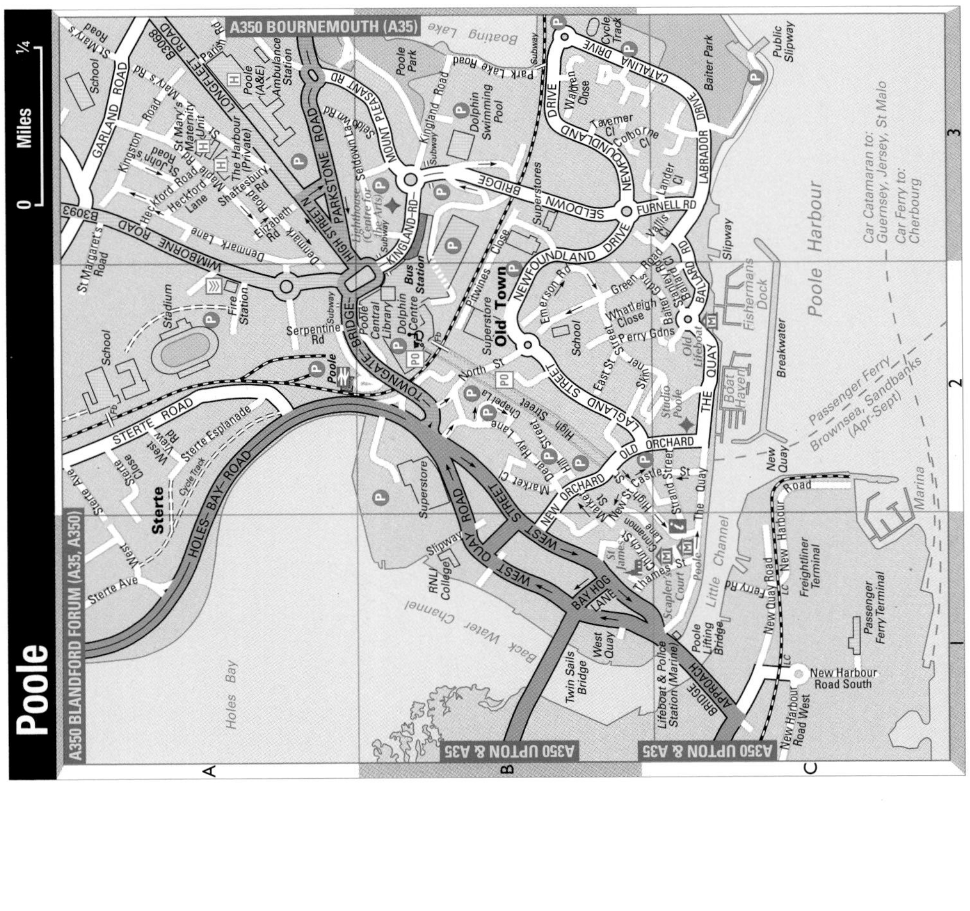
Poole
Miles
Poole Harbour

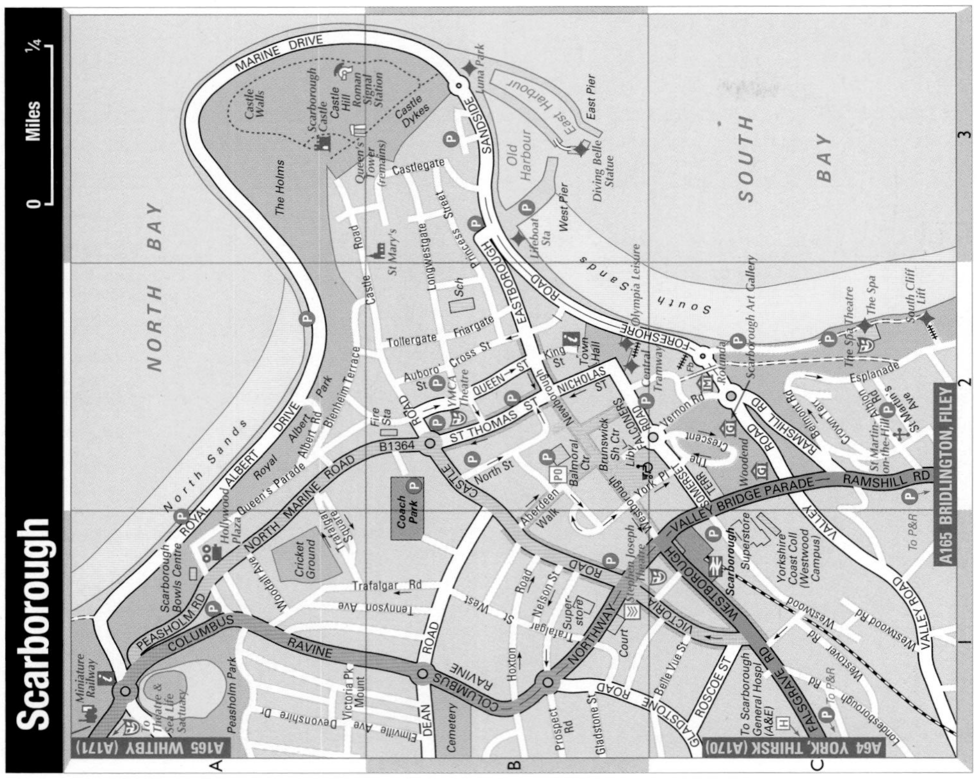

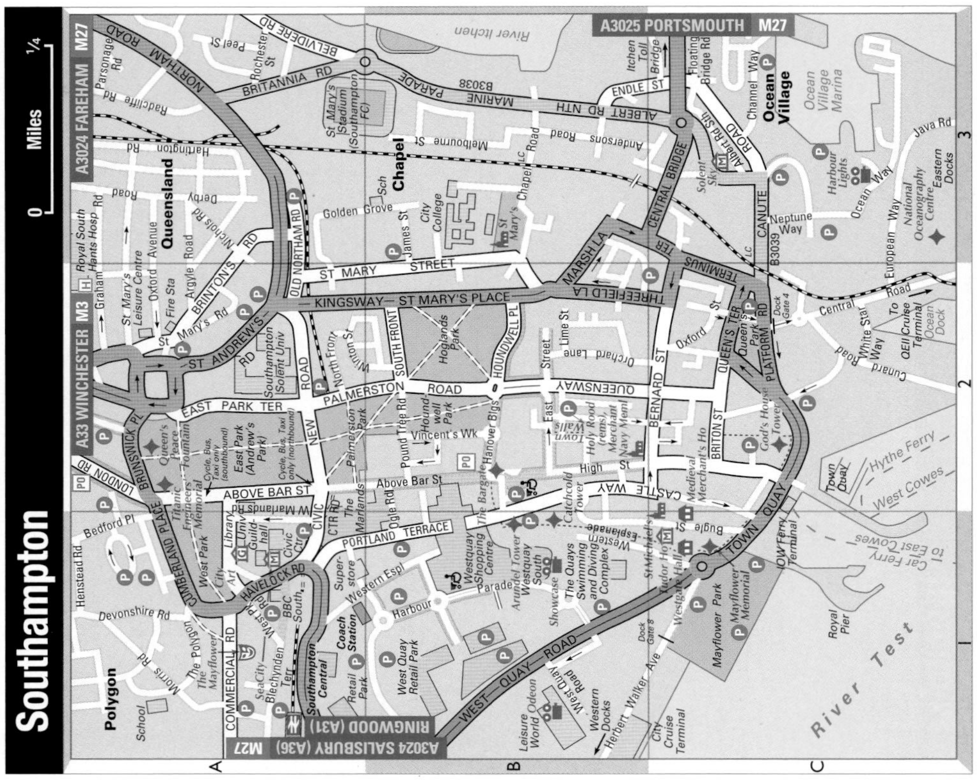

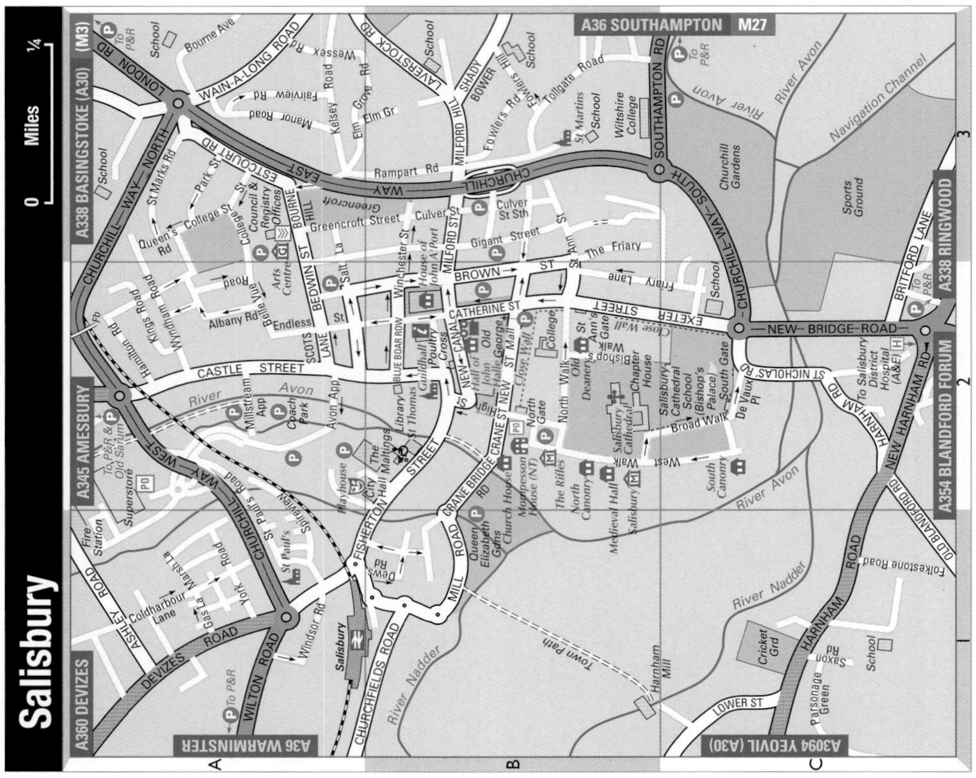

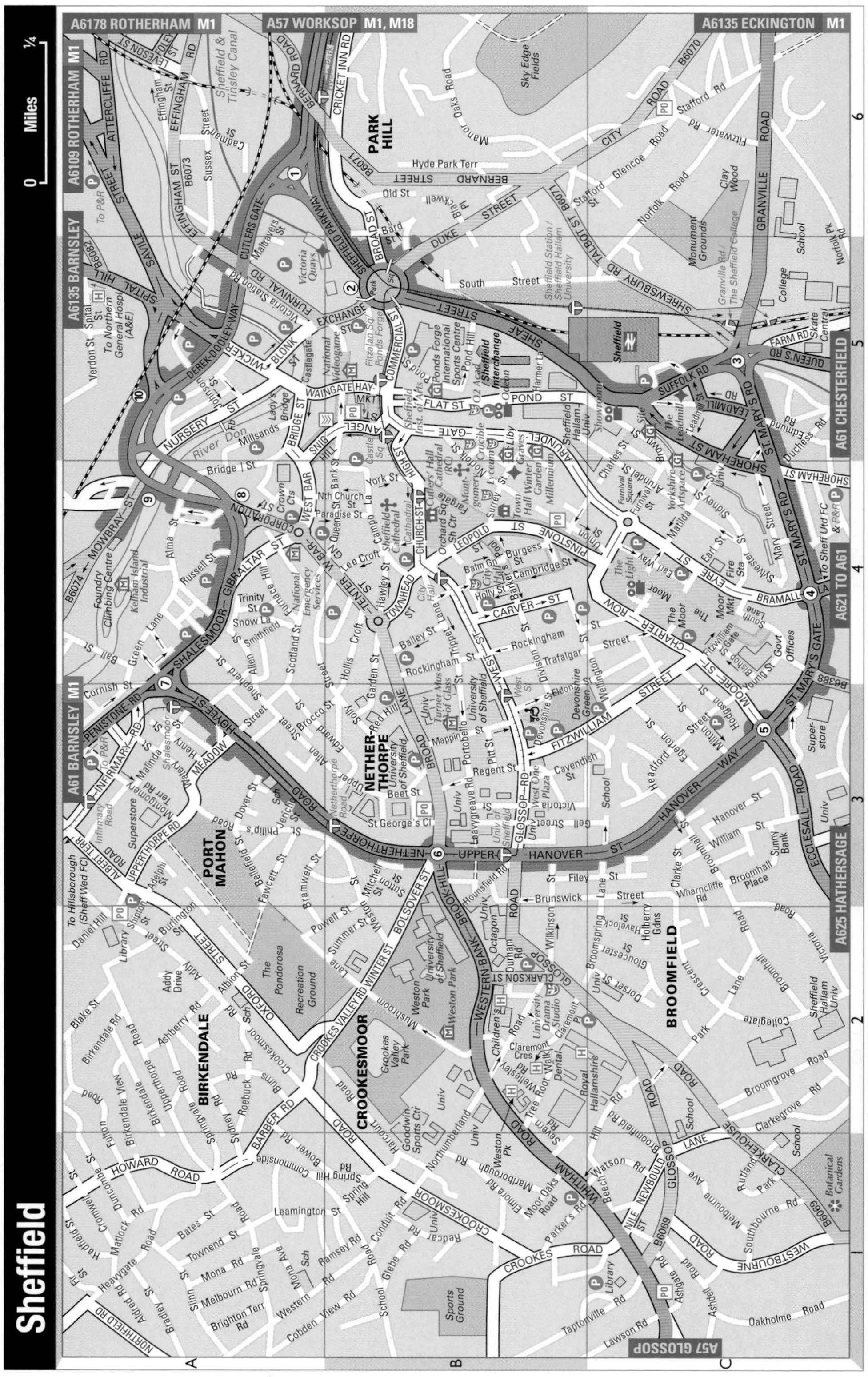

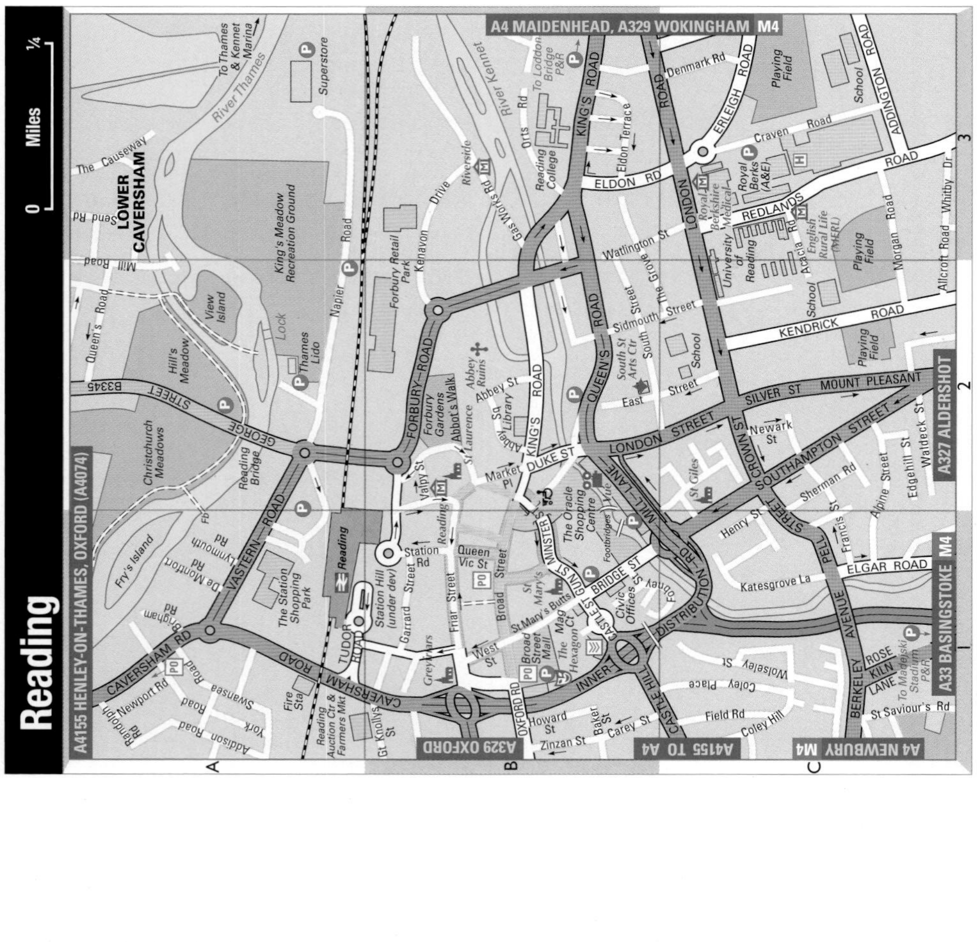

Low Emission Zone (LEZ)/Clean Air Zone (CAZ)

Stratford-upon-Avon

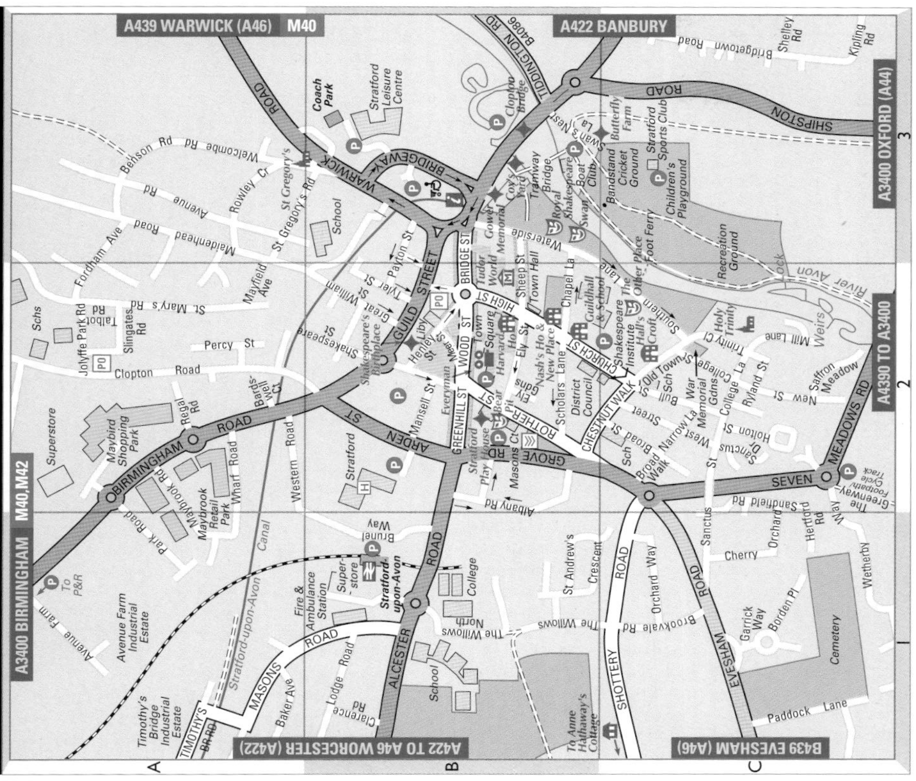

Swindon

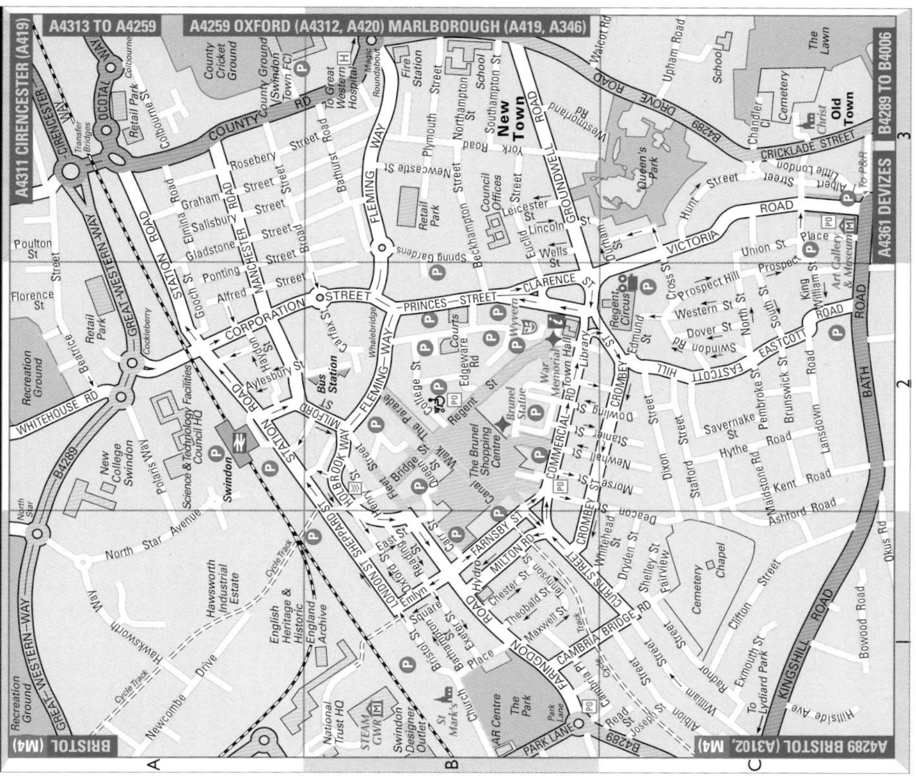

Stoke-on-Trent (Hanley)

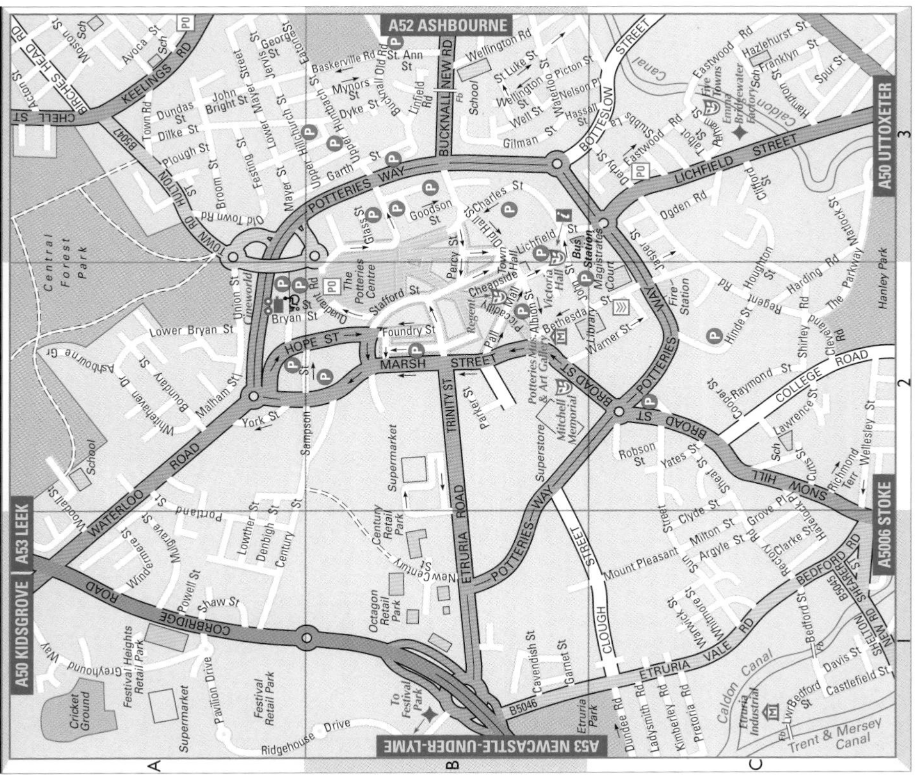

Swansea / Abertawe

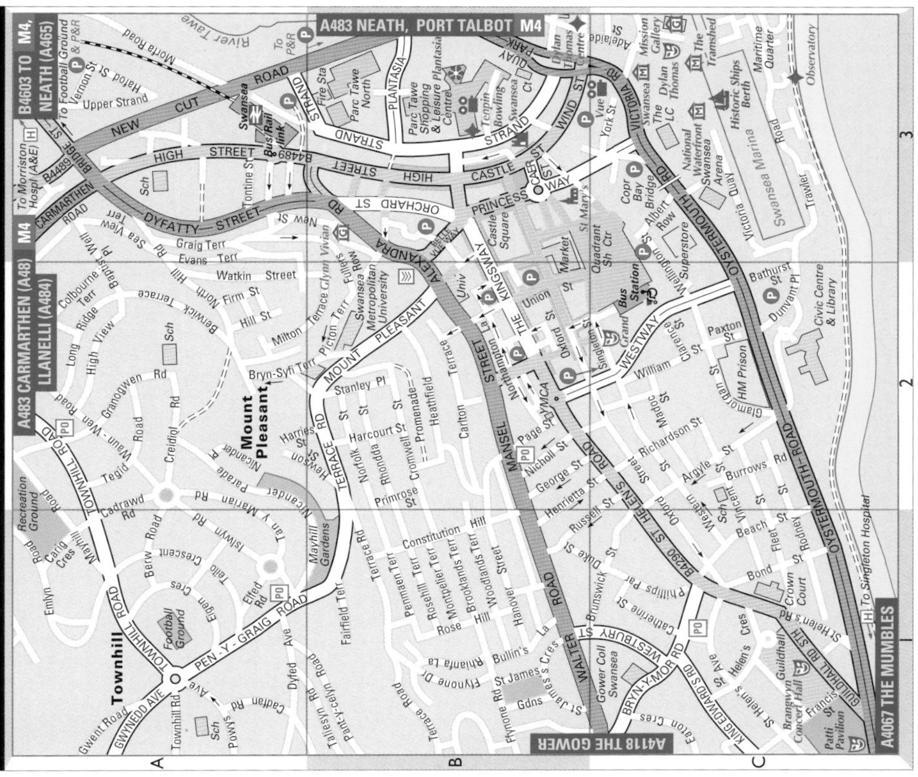

Southend-on-Sea

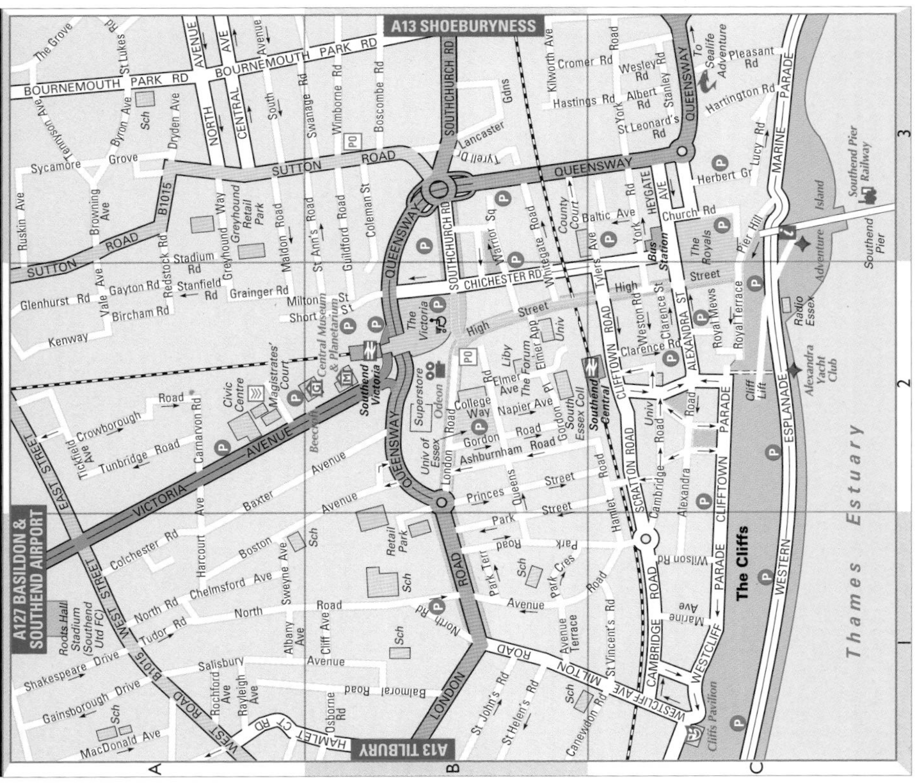

Sunderland

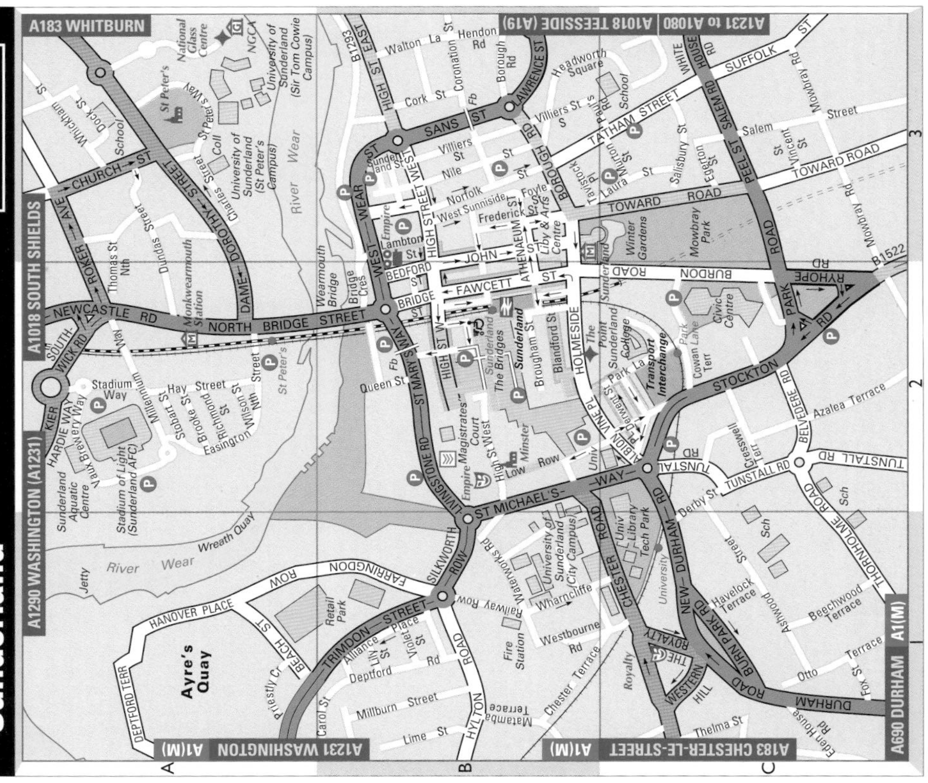

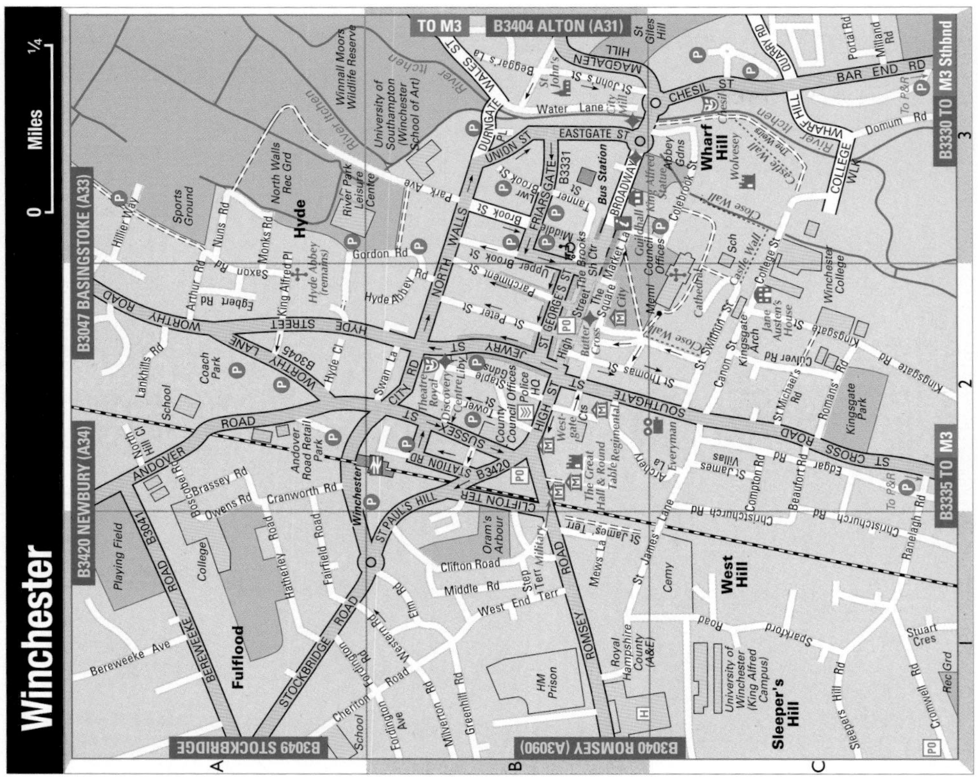
Winchester
B3047 BASINGSTOKE (A33)
B3420 NEWBURY (A34)
TO M3
B3404 ALTON (A31)
B3330 TO M3 Sthbnd
B3335 TO M3
B3049 STOCKBRIDGE
B3040 ROMSEY (A3090)
Miles

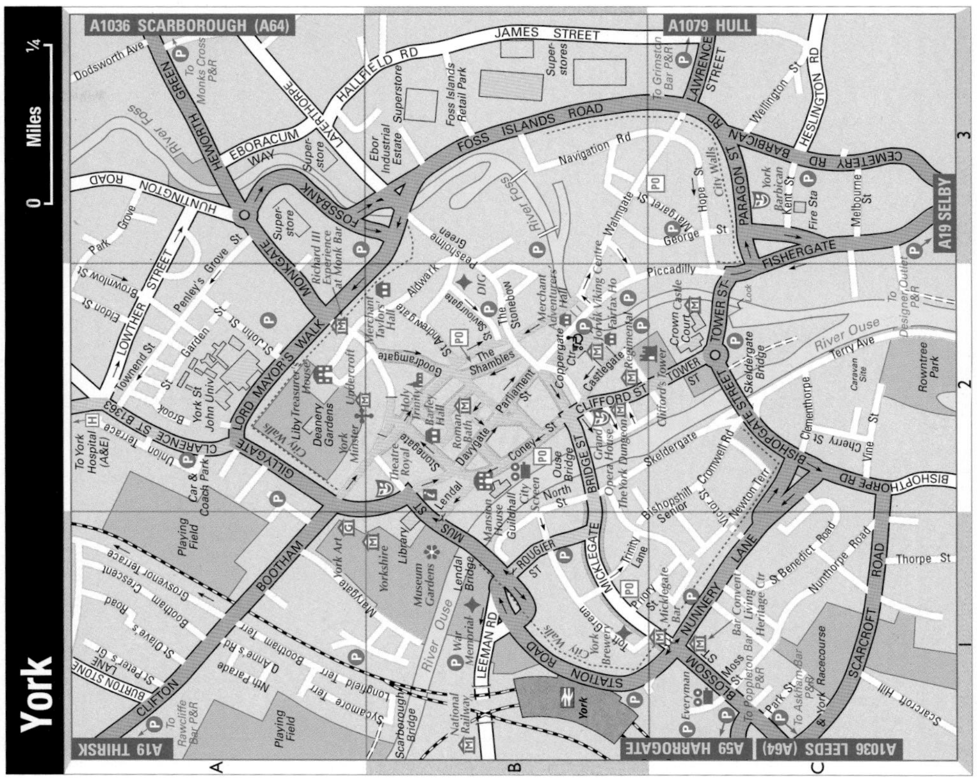
York
A1036 SCARBOROUGH (A64)
A1079 HULL
A19 SELBY
A1036 LEEDS (A64)
A59 HARROGATE
A19 THIRSK
Miles

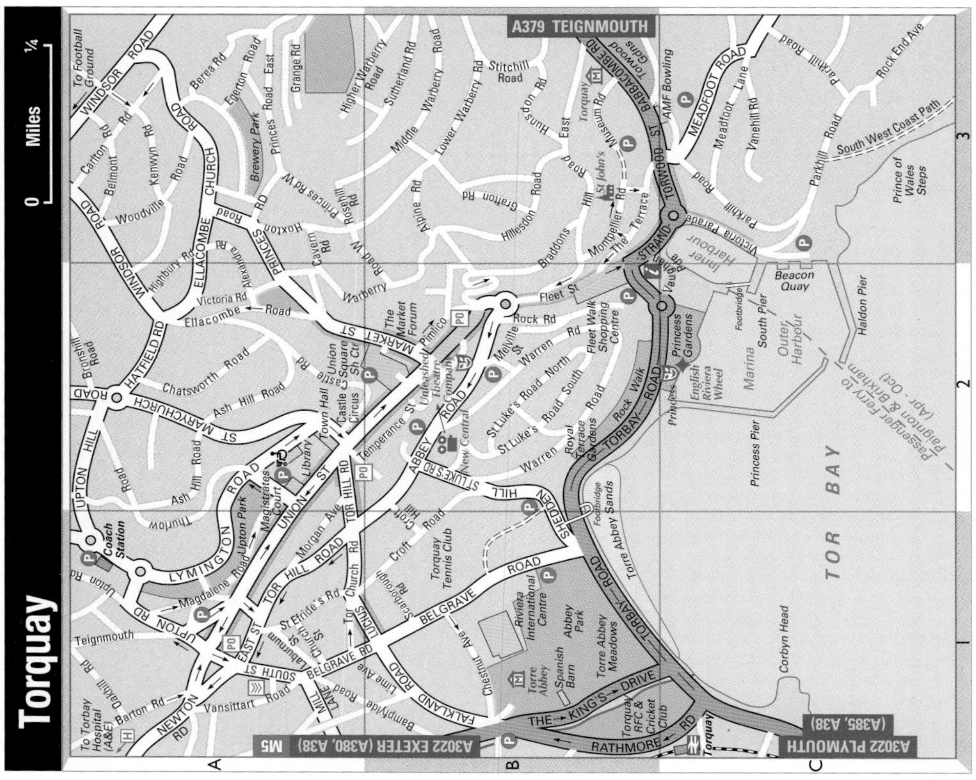
Torquay
A379 TEIGNMOUTH
A3022 PLYMOUTH (A385, A38)
A3022 EXETER (A380, A38) M5
TOR BAY
Miles

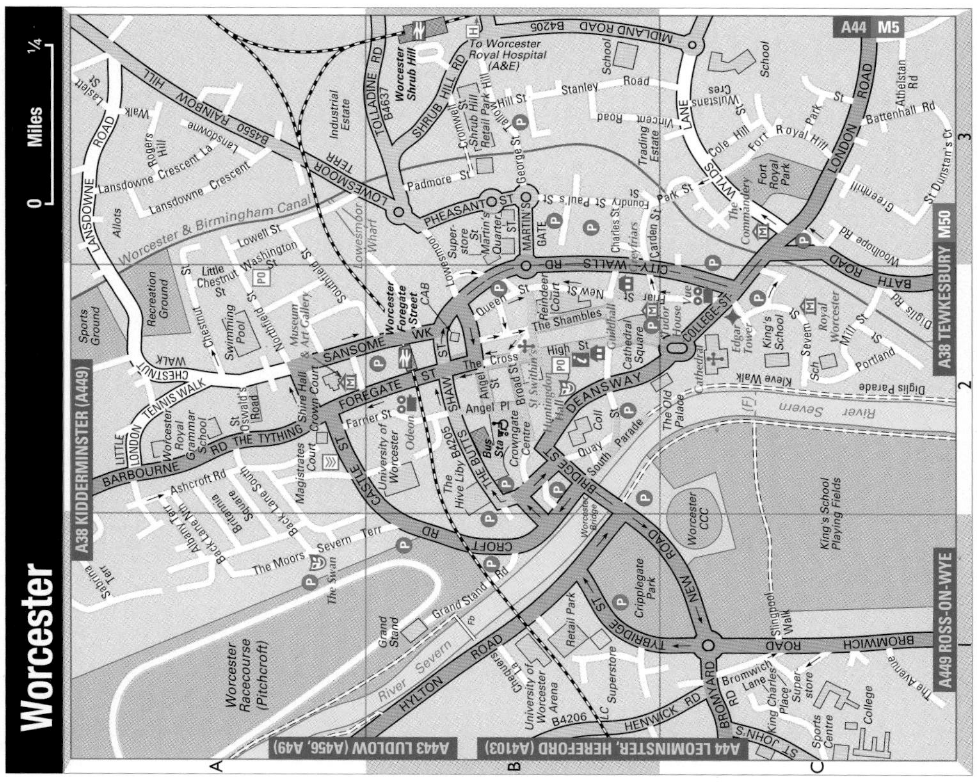
Worcester
A44 M5
A38 TEWKESBURY M50
A449 ROSS-ON-WYE
A44 LEOMINSTER, HEREFORD (A4103)
A443 LUDLOW (A456, A49)
A38 KIDDERMINSTER (A449)
Miles

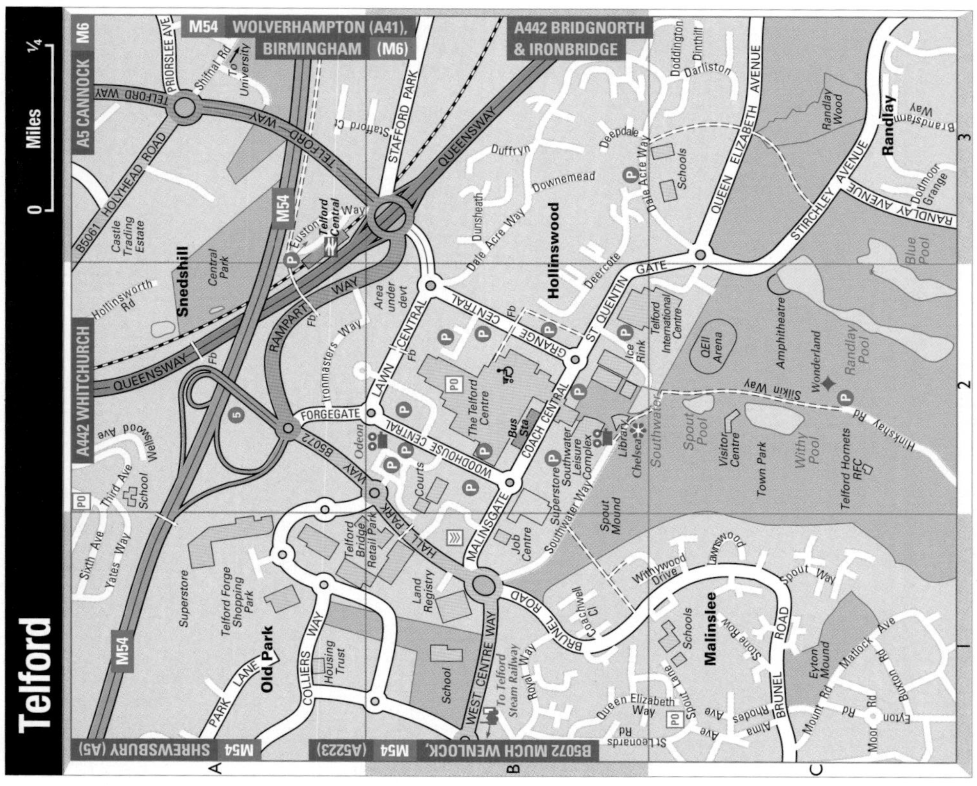
Telford
A5 CANNOCK M6
M54 WOLVERHAMPTON (A41), BIRMINGHAM (M6)
A442 BRIDGNORTH & IRONBRIDGE
B5072 MUCH WENLOCK, M54 (A5223)
M54 SHREWSBURY (A5)
A442 WHITCHURCH
Miles

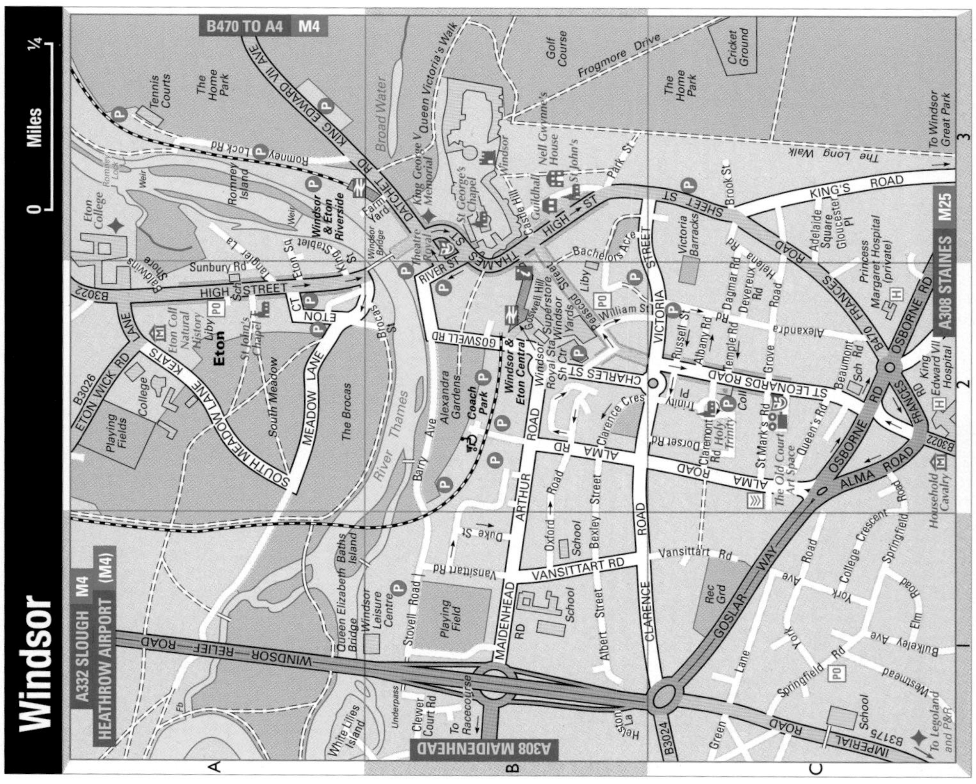
Windsor
B470 TO A4 M4
A308 STAINES M25
A308 MAIDENHEAD
A332 SLOUGH M4 HEATHROW AIRPORT (M4)
Miles

Town plan indexes

Bristol 114

Cambridge 114

Canterbury 115

Cardiff Caerdydd 115

Cheltenham 115

Suffolk Parade C2
Suffolk Rd C1
Suffolk Square C1
Sun St A1
Swindon Rd B2
Sydenham Villas Rd C3
Tewkesbury Rd A1
The Courtyard B1
Thirlstaine Rd C2
Tivoli Rd C1
Tivoli St C1
Town Hall & Theatre B2
Townsend St A1
Trafalgar St C2
Union St B3
University of Gloucestershire (Francis Cl Hall) A2
University of Gloucestershire (Hardwick) A1
Victoria Place B3
Victoria St A2
Vittoria Walk C2
Wellesley Rd A2
Wellington Rd A3
Wellington Square A3
Wellington St B2
West Drive A3
Western Rd B1
Wilson, The B2
Winchcombe St B3
Winston Churchill Meml Gardens A1

Chester 115

Abbey Gateway A2
Appleyards Lane C3
Bars, The B3
Bedward Row B1
Beeston View C3
Bishop Lloyd's Palace B2
Black Diamond St A2
Bottoms Lane C3
Boughton B3
Bouverie St A1
Bus Interchange A2
Bridge St B2
Bridgegate C2
Brook St A3
Brown's Lane C2
Cambrian Rd A1
Canal St A2
Carrick Rd C1
Castle C2
Castle Drive C2
Cathedral B2
Catherine St A1
Cheshire Military Museum C2
Chester A3
Cheyney Rd A1
Chichester St A1
City Rd A3
City Walls B1/B2
City Walls Rd B1
Cornwall St A2
Cross Hey C3
Cross, The B2
Crown Court C2
Cuppin St B2
Curzon Park North C1
Curzon Park South C1
Dee Basin A1
Dee Lane B3
Delamere St A2
Deva Roman Discovery Ctr B2
Dingle, The C1
Duke St B2
Eastgate B2
Eastgate St B2
Eaton Rd C2
Edinburgh Way C3
Elizabeth Crescent B3
Fire Station A2
Foregate St B2
Forum Studio B2
Forum, The B2
Frodsham St B2
Gamul House B2
Garden Lane A1
George St A2
Gladstone Avenue A1
God's Providence House B2
Gorse Stacks A2
Greenway St C2
Grosvenor Bridge C1
Grosvenor Mus B2
Grosvenor Park B3
Grosvenor Pk Terr C1
Grosvenor Shopping Centre B2
Grosvenor St B2
Groves Rd B3
Groves, The B3
Guildhall Mus B1
Handbridge C2
Hartington St C3
Hoole Way A2
Hunter St B2
Information Ctr B2
King Charles' Tower A2
King St A2
Library B2
Lightfoot St A3
Little Roodee C2
Liverpool Rd A2
Love St B3
Lower Bridge St B2
Lower Park Rd B3
Lyon St A2
Magistrates Court B2
Meadows Lane C3
Meadows, The B3
Milton St A3
Minerva Roman Shrine C2
Miniature Railway B3
New Crane St B1
Nicholas St B2
Northgate A2
Northgate Arena A2
Northgate St A2
Nun's Rd B1
Old Dee Bridge C2
Overleigh Rd C2
Park St B2
Police Station B2
Post Office A2/A3
Princess St B2
Queen St B2
Queen's Park Rd C3
Queen's Rd A3
Race Course B1
Raymond St A1
River Lane C2
Roman Amphitheatre & Gardens B2
Roodee (Chester Racecourse), The B1
Russell St A3
St Anne St A2
St George's Cres C3
St Martin's Gate A1
St Martin's Way B1
St Oswalds Way A2
Saughall Rd A1
Sealand Rd A1
South View Rd A1
Stanley Palace B1
Station Rd A3
Steven St A3
Storyhouse B2
Superstore B2
Tower Rd B1
Town Hall B2
Union St B3
University of Chester C2
Vicar's Lane B2
Victoria Crescent C3
Victoria Rd A2
Walpole St A1
Water Tower St A1
Water Tower, The B1
Watergate B1
Watergate St B2
Whipcord Lane A1
White Friars B2
York St B3

Chichester 115

Adelaide Rd A3
Alexandra Rd A3
Arts Centre B2
Ave de Chartres B1/B2
Barlow Rd A1
Basin Rd C2
Beech Avenue B1
Bishops Palace Gardens B2
Bishopsgate Walk A3
Bramber Rd C3
Broyle Rd A2
Bus Station B2
Caledonian Rd B3
Cambrai Avenue B3
Canal Place C1
Canal Wharf C2
Canon Lane B2
Cathedral B2
Cavendish St A1
Cawley Rd B2
Cedar Drive A1
Chapel St A2
Cherry Orchard Rd C3
Chichester B2
Chichester By-Pass C2/C3
Chichester College B1
Chichester Cinema B3
Chichester Festival A2
Chichester Gate Leisure Park C1
Chichester High Sch C2
Churchside A2
Cineworld C1
City Walls B2
Cleveland Rd B3
College Lane A2
Cory Close C2
Council Offices B2
County Hall B2
Duncan Rd A1
Durnford Close A1
East Pallant B2
East Row B2
East St B2
East Walls B3
Eastland Rd C3
Ettrick Close B3
Ettrick Rd B3
Exton Rd C3
Fire Station A2
Football Ground A2
Franklin Place A2
Friary (Rems of) B2
Garland Close C3
Green Lane A3
Grove Rd C3
Guilden Rd B3
Guildhall A2
Hawthorn Close A1
Hay Rd C3
Henty Gardens B1
Herald Drive C3
Hornet, The B3
Information Ctr B2
John's St B2
Joys Croft A3
Jubilee Park A3
Jubilee Rd A3
Juxon Close B1
Kent Rd A3
King George Gdns A2
King's Avenue C2
Kingsham Avenue C3
Kingsham Rd C2
Laburnum Grove B2
Leigh Rd C1
Lennox Rd A3
Lewis Rd A3
Library B2
Lion St B2
Litten Terrace A3
Litten, The A3
Little London B2
Lyndhurst Rd B3
Market B3
Market Avenue B2
Market Cross B2
Market Rd B3
Melbourne Rd A3
Minerva A2
Mount Lane B1
New Park Rd A3
Newlands Lane A1
North Pallant B2
North St A2
North Walls A2
Northgate A2
Novium, The B2
Oak Avenue A1
Oak Close A1
Oaklands Park A2
Oaklands Way A2
Orchard Avenue A1
Orchard St A1
Ormonde Avenue B3
Pallant House B2
Parchment St A1
Parklands Rd A1/B1
Peter Weston Place B3
Police Station C2
Post Office A1/B2/C3
Priory Lane A2
Priory Park A2
Priory Rd A2
Queen's Avenue C1
Riverside A3
Roman Amphitheatre B3
St Cyriacs A2
St Martins' St B2
St Pancras A3
St Paul's Rd A2
St Richard's Hospital (A&E) A3
Shamrock Close A3
Sherbourne Rd A1
Somerstown A2
South Bank C2
South Downs Planetarium & Science Centre C2
South Pallant B2
South St B2
Southgate B2
Spitalfield Lane A3
Stirling Rd B3
Stockbridge Rd C1/C2
Swanfield Drive A3
Terminus Ind Est C1
Tower St A2
Tozer Way A3
Turnbull Rd A3
Upton Rd C1
Velyn Avenue B3
Via Ravenna B1
Walnut Avenue A1
West St B2
Westgate B1
Westgate Fields B1
Westgate Leisure Centre B1
Weston Avenue C1
Whyke Close C3
Whyke Lane B3
Whyke Rd C3
Winden Avenue B3

Colchester 115

Abbey Gateway C2
Albert St A1
Albion Grove C2
Alexandra Rd C1
Artillery St C3
Arts Centre B1
Balkerne Hill B1
Barrack St C3
Beaconsfield Rd C1
Beche Rd C3
Bergholt Rd A1
Bourne Rd C3
Brick Kiln Rd A1
Brigade Grove C2
Bristol Rd B2
Broadlands Way A3
Brook St B3
Bury Close B2
Bus Station B1
Butt Rd C1
Campion Rd C2
Cannon St C3
Canterbury Rd C2
Captain Gardens C2
Castle B2
Castle Park B2
Castle Rd B2
Catchpool Rd A1
Causton Rd B1
Chandlers Row C3
Circular Rd East C2
Circular Rd North C1
Circular Rd West C1
Clarendon Way A1
Claudius Rd C2
Colchester A1
Colchester Camp Abbey Field C1
Colchester Retail Park B1
Colchester Town C2
Colne Bank Avenue A1
Colne View Ret Pk A2
Compton Rd A3
Cowdray Ave A1/A2
Crouch St B1
Crowhurst Rd B1
Culver Square Shopping Centre B1
Culver St East B2
Culver St West B1
Dilbridge Rd A3
East Hill B2
East St B3
East Stockwell St B1
Eld Lane B1
Essex Hall Rd A1
Exeter Drive B2
Fairfax Rd C2
Fire Station A2
Firstsite B2
Flagstaff Rd C1
Garrison Parade C2
George St B2
Gladstone Rd C2
Golden Noble Hill C2
Goring Rd A3
Granville Rd C3
Greenstead Rd B3
Guildford Rd B2
Harsnett Rd C3
Harwich Rd B3
Head St B1
High St B1/B2
High Woods Country Pk A2
Hollytrees B2
Hyderabad Close C2
Hythe Hill C3
Information Ctr B2
Jarmin Rd A2
Kendall Rd C2
Kimberley Rd C3
King Stephen Rd C3
Leisure World A2
Library B1
Lincoln Way B2
Lion Walk Shopping Centre B1
Lisle Rd C2
Lucas Rd C2
Magdalen Green C3
Magdalen St C2
Maidenburgh St B2
Maldon Rd C1
Manor Rd B1
Margaret Rd A1
Mason Rd A2
Mercers Way A1
Mercury B1
Mersea Rd C2
Meyrick Crescent C2
Mile End Rd A1
Military Rd C2
Mill St C2
Minories B2
Moorside B3
Morant Rd C3
Napier Rd C2
Natural History B2
New Town Rd C2
Norfolk Crescent A3
North Hill B1
North Station Rd A1
Northgate St B1
Nunns Rd B1
Odeon B1
Old Coach Rd B3
Old Heath Rd C3
Osborne St B2
Petrolea Close A1
Police Station C1
Popes Lane B1
Port Lane C3
Post Office B1/B2
Priory St B2
Queen St B2
Rawstorn Rd B1
Rebon St C3
Recreation Rd C3
Ripple Way A3
Roberts Rd C2
Roman Rd B2
Roman Wall B2
Romford Close A3
Rosebery Avenue B2
St Andrews Avenue B3
St Andrews Gdns B3
St Botolph St B2
St Botolphs B2
St John's Abbey (site of) C2
St John's St B1
St Johns Walk Shopping Centre B1
St Leonards Rd C3
St Marys Fields B1
St Peter's St B1
St Peters B1
Salisbury Avenue C1
Saw Mill Rd C3
Sergeant St C2
Serpentine Walk A1
Sheepen Place B1
Sheepen Rd B1
Shopmobility B2
Sir Isaac's Walk B1
Smythies Avenue B2
South St C1
South Way C1
Sports Way A2
Suffolk Close A3
Superstore A1
Town Hall B1
Turner Rise Retail Park A2
Valentine Drive A3
Victor Rd C3
Wakefield Close B2
Wellesley Rd C1
Wells Rd B2/B3
West St C1
West Stockwell St B1
Weston Rd C3
Westway A1
Wickham Rd C1
Wimpole Rd C3
Winchester Rd C2
Winnock Rd C2
Worcester Rd B2

Coventry 116

Abbots Lane A1
Albany B1
Albany Rd B1
Alma St B3
Ambulance Station A2
Art Faculty B3
Asthill Grove C2
Bablake School A1
Barras Lane A1/B1
Barr's Hill School A1
Belgrade B2
Bishop St A2
Bond's Hospital B1
Broad Gate B2
Broadway C1
Burges, The B2
Bus Station A3
Butts Radial B1
Byron St A3
Canterbury St A3
Cathedral B3
Central Six Ret Pk C1
Chester St A1
Cheylesmore Manor House B2
Christ Church Spire B2
City College A3
City Walls & Gates A2
Corporation St B2
Council House B2
Coundon Rd A1
Coventry Sta C2
Coventry Transport Museum A2
Coventry University Technology Park C3
Cox St A3
Croft Rd B1
Dalton Rd C1
Deasy Rd C3
Earl St B2
Eaton Rd C2
Fairfax St B3
Fire Station A2
Foleshill Rd A2
Ford's Hospital B2
Fowler Rd A1
Friars Rd C2
Gordon St C1
Gosford St B3
Greyfriars Green B2
Greyfriars Rd B2
Gulson Rd B3
Hales St A2
Harnall Lane East A3
Harnall Lane West A2
Herbert Art Gallery & Museum B3
Hertford St B2
Hewitt Avenue A1
High St B2
Hill St B1
Holy Trinity B2
Holyhead Rd A1
Howard St A3
Huntingdon Rd C1
Information Ctr C2
Jordan Well B3
King Henry VIII Sch C1
Lady Godiva Statue B2
Lamb St A2
Leicester Row A2
Library B2
Lincoln St A2
Little Park St B2
London Rd C3
Lower Ford St B3
Lower Precinct Shopping Centre B2
Magistrates & Crown Courts B2
Manor House Drive B2
Manor Rd C2
Market B2
Martyrs Meml C2
Meadow St B1
Meriden St A1
Michaelmas Rd C2
Middleborough Rd A1
Mile Lane C3
Millennium Place A2
Much Park St B3
Naul's Mill Park A1
New Union B2
Odeon B1
Park Rd C2
Parkside C3
Planet Ice Arena B1
Post Office A3,B2
Primrose Hill St A3
Priory Gardens & Visitor Centre B2
Priory St B3
Puma Way C3
Quarryfield Lane C3
Queen's Rd B1
Quinton Rd C2
Radford Rd A2
Raglan St B3
Ringway (Hill Cross) A1
Ringway (Queens) B1
Ringway (Rudge) B1
Ringway (St Johns) B3
Ringway (St Nicholas) A2
Ringway (St Patricks) C2
Ringway (Swanswell) A2
Ringway (Whitefriars) B3
St John St B2
St John the Baptist B2
St Nicholas St A2
Sidney Stringer Academy A3
Skydome B1
Spencer Avenue C1
Spencer Rec Gnd C1
Spencer Rd C1
Spon St B1
Sports Centre B3
Stoney Rd C2
Stoney Stanton Rd A3
Superstore B2
Swanswell Pool A3
Thomas Landsdail St C2
Tomson Avenue A1
Top Green C1
Tower St A2
Trinity St B2
University B3
Univ Sports Ctr B3
Upper Hill St A1
Upper Well St A2
Victoria St A3
Vine St A3
Wave, The B2
Warwick Rd C2
Waveley Rd B1
West Orchards Shopping Centre B2
Westminster Rd C1
White St A3
Windsor St B1

Derby 116

Abbey St C1
Agard St B1
Albert St B2
Albion St B2
Ambulance Station B1
Arthur St A1
Ashlyn Rd B3
Assembly Rooms B2
Babington Lane C2
Bass Recreation Gd B3
Becket St B1
Belper Rd A1
Bold Lane B1
Bradshaw Way C2
Bradshaw Way Retail Park C2
Bridge St B1
Brook St B1
Burton Rd C1
Bus Station B2
Business Park A3
Caesar St A2
Canal St C3
Carrington St C3
Cathedral B2
Cathedral Rd B1
Charnwood St C2
Chester Green Rd A2
City Rd A2
Clarke St A3
Cock Pitt Junction B3
Council House B2
Courts B1
Cranmer Rd B3
Crompton St C1
Crown & County Courts B2
Curzon St B1
Darley Grove A1
Derbion C2
Derby C3
Derby B2
Derby Gaol B1
Derwent Bsns Ctr A2
Derwent St B2
Drewry Lane C1
Duffield Rd A1
Duke St A2
Dunton Close B3
Eagle Market C2
East St B2
Eastgate B3
Exeter St B2
Farm St C1
Ford St B1
Forester St C1
Fox St A2
Friar Gate B1
Friary St B1
Full St B2
Garden St A1
Gerard St C1
Gower St C2
Green Lane C2
Grey St C1
Guildhall B2
Handyside Bridge A2
Harcourt St C1
Highfield Rd A1
Hill Lane C2
Incora County Ground (Derbyshire CCC), The B3
Information Ctr B2
Iron Gate B2
John St C3
Joseph Wright Ctr B1
Kedleston Rd A1
Key St B2
King Alfred St C1
King St A1
Kingston St A1
Lara Croft Way C2
Leopold St C2
Liversage St C3
Lodge Lane B1
London Rd C2
London Rd Com Hosp C2
Macklin St C1
Mansfield Rd A2
Market B2
Market Place B2
May St C1
Meadow Lane B3
Melbourne St C2
Mercian Way C1
Midland Rd C3
Monk St C1
Morledge B2
Mount St C1
Museum & Art Gallery B1
Mus of Making B2
North Parade A1
North St A1
Nottingham Rd B3
Osmaston Rd C2
Otter St A1
Park St C3
Parker St A1
Pickford's House B1
Police Sta A2, B2
Post Office A1/A2/B1/C2/C3
Pride Parkway C3
Prime Enterprise Park A2
Prime Parkway A2
QUAD B2
Queens Leisure Ctr B1
Racecourse Park A3
Railway Terrace C3
Register Office B2
Riverlights Leisure Centre B2
Sadler Gate B1
St Alkmund's Way B1/B2
St Helens House A1
St Mary's A1
St Mary's Bridge A2
St Mary's Bridge Chapel A2
St Mary's Gate B1
St Paul's Rd A2
St Peter's C2
St Peter's St C2
Showcase De Lux C2
Siddals Rd C3
Sir Frank Whittle Rd A3
Spa Lane C1
Spring St C1
Stafford St B1
Station Approach C3
Stockbrook St C1
Stores Rd A3
Traffic St C2
Wardwick B1
Werburgh St C1
West Avenue A1
West Meadows Industrial Estate B3
Wharf Rd A2
Wilmot St C2
Wilson St C1
Wood's Lane C1

Dundee 116

Abertay University B2
Adelaide Place A1
Airlie Place C1
Albany Terrace A1
Albert St A3
Alexander St A2
Ann St A2
Arthurstone Terr A3
Bank St B2
Barrack Rd A1
Barrack St B2
Bell St B2
Blinshall St B1
Broughty Ferry Rd A3
Brown St B1
Bus Station B3
Caird Hall B2
Camperdown St B3
Candle Lane B3
Carmichael St A1
City Churches B2
City Quay B3
City Square B2
Commercial St B2
Constable St A3
Constitution Cres A1
Constitution Court A1
Constitution St A1/B2
Cotton Rd A3
Courthouse Sq B1
Cowgate A3
Crescent St A3
Crichton St B2
Dens Brae A3
Dens Rd A3
Discovery Point C2
Douglas St B1
Drummond St A1
Dudhope Castle A1
Dudhope St A2
Dudhope Terrace A1
Dundee C2
Dundee Contemporary Arts C2
Dundee High School B2
Dundee Law A1
Dundee Rep C2
Dundee Science Centre C2
Dunhope Park A1
Dura St A3
East Dock St B3
East Marketgait B3
East Whale Lane B3
Erskine St A3
Euclid Crescent B2
Forebank Rd A2
Foundry Lane A3
Gallagher Retail Pk B3
Gellatly St B3
Guthrie St B1
Hawkhill B1
Hilltown A2
HMS Unicorn B3
Howff Cemetery, The B2
Information Ctr B2
Keiller Shopping Centre B2
Keiller Centre, The B2
King St A3
Kinghorne Rd A1
Ladywell Avenue A3
Laurel Bank A2
Law Rd A1
Law St A1
Library A2/A3
Library and Steps Theatre A2
Little Theatre, The A2
Lochee Rd B1
Lower Princes St A3
Lyon St A3
McManus Art Gallery & Museum, The B2
Meadow Side B2
Meadowside St Pauls B2
Mercat Cross B2
Murraygate B2
Nelson St A2
Nethergate B2/C1
North Carr B3
North Lindsay St B2
North Marketgait B2
Old Hawkhill B1
Olympia Leisure Ctr B3
Overgate Shopping Centre B2
Park Place B1
Perth Rd C1
Police Station B1
Post Office B2
Princes St A3
Prospect Place A2
Reform St B2
Riverside Drive C2
Riverside Esplanade C2
Roseangle C1
Rosebank St A2
RRS Discovery C2
St Andrew's C2
St Pauls Episcopal B3
Seagate B2
Sheriffs Court B1
Shopmobility B2
South George St A2
South Marketgait B3
South Tay St B2
South Victoria Dock Road B3
South Ward Rd B2
Tay Road Bridge C3
Thomson Avenue B2
Trades Lane B3
Union St B2
Union Terrace A1
University Library B2
Univ of Dundee B1
Upper Constitution St A1
Verdant Works B1
V&A Museum of Design C2
Victoria Dock B3
Victoria Rd A2
Victoria St A3
Ward Rd B1
Wellgate B2
West Bell St B1
West Marketgait B1/B2
Westfield Place C1
William St A3
Wishart Arch A3

Durham 116

Alexander Cres B2
Allergate B2
Archery Rise C1
Assembly Rooms B2
Avenue, The B1
Back Western Hill A1
Bakehouse Lane A3
Baths Bridge B3
Boat House B3
Boyd St C3
Bus Station B2
Castle Chare B2
Cathedral B2
Church St C3
Clay Lane C1
Claypath B3
College of St Hild & St Bede B3
County Hospital B1
Crescent, The A1
Crook Hall & Gardens A3
Crossgate B2
Crossgate Peth C1
Crown Court B3
Darlington Rd C1
Durham A2
Durham Castle B2
Durham School C2
Durham University (Science Site) C3
Ellam Avenue C1
Elvet Bridge B3
Elvet Court B3
Farnley Hey B1
Ferens Close A3
Fieldhouse Lane A1
Flass St B1
Flass Vale Local Nature Reserve A1
Framwelgate Bridge B2
Framwelgate A2
Framwelgate Peth A2
Framwelgate Waterside A2
Frankland Lane A3
Freeman's Place A3
Freeman's Quay Leisure Centre A3
Gala Theatre & Cinema B3
Geoffrey Avenue C1
Gilesgate B3
Grey College C3
Grove, The A1
Hallgarth St C3
Hatfield College B3
Hawthorn Terrace B1
Heritage Centre B3
HM Prison B3
John St B1
Kingsgate Bridge B3
Laburnum Terrace B1
Lawson Terrace B1
Leazes Rd B2/B3
Library B2
Margery Lane B2
Market B2
Mavin St C3
Millburngate B2
Millburngate Bridge B2
Millennium Bridge (foot/cycle) A2
Mountjoy Research Centre C3
Museum of Archaeology B2
New Elvet B3
New Elvet Bridge B3
North Bailey B3
North End A1
Observatory C1
Old Elvet B3
Open Treasure B2
Oriental Mus C2
Oswald Court C3
Passport Office A2
Percy Terrace B1
Pimlico C2
Police Station B3
Post Office A1/B2
Potters Bank C1/C2
Prebends Bridge C2
Prebends Walk C2
Prince Bishops Shopping Centre B3
Princes St A1
Providence Row A3
Quarryheads Lane C2
Redhills Lane B1
Redhills Terrace B1
Riverwalk, The B2
Saddler St B3
St Cuthbert's Society C2
St Margaret's B2
St Mary the Less C2
St Mary's College C2
St Monica Grove B1
St Nicholas' B3
St Oswald's C3
Sands, The A3
Shopmobility B3
Sidegate A2
Silver St B2
Sixth Form College A3
South Bailey C2
South Rd C3
South St B2
Springwell Avenue A1
Station Approach B2
Stockton Rd C3
Student Union B3
Summerville B1
Sutton St B2
Town Hall B2
Univ Arts Block B3
University Coll B2
Walkergate Centre A3
Wearside Drive A3
Western Hill A1
Wharton Park A2
Whinney Hill C3
Whitehouse Ave C1
YHA C3

Edinburgh 116

Abbey Strand B6
Abbeyhill A6
Abbeyhill Crescent B6
Abbeymount A6
Abercromby Place A3
Adam St C5
Albany Lane A4
Albany St A4
Albert Memorial B2
Albyn Place A2
Alva Place A6
Alva St B1
Ann St A1
Appleton Tower C4
Archibald Place C3
Assembly Rooms & Musical Hall A3
Atholl Crescent B1
Atholl Cres Lane C1
Bank St B4
Barony St A4
Beaumont Place C5
Bedlam C4
Belford Rd B1
Belgrave Crescent A1
Belgrave Cres Lane A1
Bell's Brae B1
Blackfriars St B4
Blair St B4
Bread St C2
Bristo Place C4
Bristo St C4
Brougham St C2
Broughton St A4
Brown St C5
Brunton Terrace A6
Buckingham Terr A1
Burial Ground A6
Bus Station A4
Caledonian Cres C1
Caledonian Rd C1
Calton Hill A4
Calton Hill A5
Calton Rd B4
Camera Obscura & Outlook Tower B3
Candlemaker Row C4
Canning St B2
Canongate B5
Canongate B5
Carlton St A1
Carlton Terrace A6
Carlton Terrace La A6
Castle St B2
Castle Terrace B2
Castlehill B3
Central Library B4
Chalmers Hosp C3
Chalmers St C3
Chambers St C4
Chapel St C4
Charles St C4
Charlotte Square B2
Chester St B1
Circus Lane A2
Circus Place A2
City Art Centre B4
City Chambers B4
City Observatory A5
Clarendon Cres A1
Clerk St C5
Coates Crescent B1
Cockburn St B4
College of Art C3
Comely Bank Ave A1
Comely Bank Row A1
Cornwall St C2
Cowgate B4
Cranston St B5
Crichton St C4
Croft-An-Righ A6
Cumberland St A2
Dalry Place C1
Dalry Rd C1
Danube St A1
Darnaway St A2
David Hume Tower C4
Davie St C5
Dean Bridge A1
Dean Gardens A1
Dean Park Cres A1
Dean Park Mews A1
Dean Park St A1
Dean Path B1
Dean St A1
Dean Terrace A1
Dewar Place C1
Dewar Place Lane C1
Doune Terrace A2
Drummond Place A3
Drummond St C5
Drumsheugh Gdns B1
Dublin Mews A3
Dublin St A4
Dublin St La South A4
Dumbiedykes Rd B5
Dundas St A3
Dynamic Earth B6
Earl Grey St C2
East Crosscauseway C5
East Market St B4
East Norton Place A6
East Princes St Gardens B3
Easter Rd A6
Edinburgh (Waverley) B4
Edinburgh Castle B3
Edinburgh Dungeon B4
Edinburgh International Conference Ctr C2
Elder St A4
Esplanade B3
Eton Terrace A1
Eye Pavilion C3
Festival Office B3
Festival Theatre Edinburgh C4
Filmhouse C2
Fire Station C2
Floral Clock B3
Forres St A2
Forth St A4
Fountainbridge C2
Frederick St A3
Freemasons' Hall B3
Fruitmarket B4
Gardner's Cres C2
George Heriot's School C3
George IV Bridge B4
George Square C4
George Square La C4
George St B3
Georgian House B2
Gladstone's Land B3
Glen St C3
Gloucester Lane A2
Gloucester Place A2
Gloucester St A2
Graham St C3
Grassmarket C3
Great King St A3
Great Stuart B1
Greenside Lane A5
Greenside Row A5
Grindlay St C2
Grosvenor St C1
Grove St C1
Gullan's Close B5
Guthrie St B4
Hanover St A3
Hart St A4
Haymarket C1
Haymarket Sta C1
Heriot Place C3
Heriot Row A2
High School Yard B5
High St B4
Hill Place C5
Hill St A2
Hillside Crescent A5
Holyrood Abbey (Remains) A6
Holyrood Gait B6
Holyrood Park C6
Holyrood Rd B5
Home St C2
Hope St B2
Horse Wynd B6
Howden St C5
Howe St A2
Hub, The B3
India Place A2
India St A2
Infirmary St B4

Ingleby ... A4
Information Ctr ... B4
Jeffrey St ... B4
John Knox Ho ... B4
Johnston Terrace ... C3
Keir St ... C3
Kerr St ... A2
King's Stables Rd ... B2
Lady Lawson St ... C3
Lauriston Gardens ... C3
Lauriston Park ... C3
Lauriston Place ... C3
Lauriston St ... C3
Lawnmarket ... B3
Learmonth Gdns ... A1
Learmonth Terrace ... A1
Leith St ... A4
Lennox St ... A1
Lennox St Lane ... A1
Leslie Place ... A2
London Rd ... A5
Lothian Rd ... B2
Lothian St ... C4
Lower Menz Place ... A6
Lynedoch Place ... B1
Manor Place ... B1
Market St ... B4
Marshall St ... C4
Maryfield ... A6
McEwan Hall ... C4
Medical School ... C4
Melville St ... B1
Meuse Lane ... B4
Middle Mdw Walk ... C4
Milton St ... A6
Montrose Terrace ... A6
Moray Place ... A2
Morrison Link ... C1
Morrison St ... C1
Mound Place ... B3
Mound, The ... B3
Multrees Walk ... A4
Mus Collections Ctr ... A4
Museum of Childhood ... B5
Museum of Edinburgh ... B5
Museum of Fire ... C3
Museum on the Mound ... B4
National Archives of Scotland ... A4
National Museum of Scotland ... C4
National Gallery ... B3
National Library of Scotland ... B4
National Monument ... A5
National Portrait Gallery ... B4
National War Museum ... B3
Nelson Monument ... A5
Nelson St ... A3
New St ... B5
Nicolson Square ... C4
Nicolson St ... C4
Niddry St ... B4
Nightingale Way ... C3
North Bank St ... B3
North Bridge ... B4
North Castle St ... A2
North Charlotte St ... A2
North Mdw Walk ... C3
North St Andrew St ... A4
North St David St ... A3
North West Circus Place ... A2
Northumberland St ... A3
Odeon ... C2
Old Royal High Sch ... A5
Old Tolbooth Wynd ... B5
OMNi Centre ... A4
Oxford Terrace ... A1
Palace of Holyroodhouse ... B6
Palmerston Place ... B1
Panmure Place ... C3
Parliament Square ... B4
People's Story, The ... B5
Picardy Place ... A4
Playhouse ... A4
Pleasance ... C5
Police Station ... A4
Ponton St ... C2
Post Office ... A3/B4/B5/C1/C2/C4
Potterrow ... C4
Princes Mall ... B4
Princes St ... B3
Princes St ... B3
Prisoners of War ... B3
Queen's Gallery ... B6
Queen St ... A2
Queen St Gardens ... A3
Queen's Drive ... B6/C6
Queensferry Rd ... A1
Queensferry St ... B1
Queensferry St La ... B2
Radical Rd ... C6
Randolph Cres ... B1
Regent Gardens ... A5
Regent Rd ... B5
Regent Rd Park ... A6
Regent Terrace ... A5
Richmond Lane ... C5
Richmond Place ... C5
Rose St ... B2
Ross Open Air Theatre ... B1
Rothesay Place ... B1
Rothesay Terrace ... B1
Roxburgh Place ... C5
Roxburgh St ... C5
Royal Bank of Scotland ... A4
Royal Circus ... A2
Royal Lyceum ... C2
Royal Mile, The ... B5
Royal Scottish Academy ... B3
Royal Terrace ... A5
Royal Terr Gardens ... A5
Rutland Square ... B2
Rutland St ... B2
St Andrew Square ... A4
St Andrew Sq ... A4
St Andrew's House ... A4
St Bernard's Cres ... A1
St Bernard's Well ... A1
St Cecilia's Hall ... B4
St Colme St ... A2
St Cuthbert's ... B2
St Giles' ... B4
St James Quarter Shopping Centre ... A4
St John St ... B5
St John's ... B2
St John's Hill ... B5
St Leonard's Hill ... C5
St Leonard's Lane ... C5
St Leonard's St ... C5
St Mary's ... A4
St Mary's Scottish Episcopal ... B1
St Mary's St ... B5
St Michael & All Saints ... C3
St Stephen St ... A2
Salisbury Crags ... C6
Saunders St ... A2
Scotch Whisky Experience ... B3
Scott Monument ... B4
Scottish, The ... A2
Scottish Parliament ... B6
Scottish Storytelling Centre ... B5
Semple St ... C2
Shandwick Place ... B2
Simpson Lane ... C3
South Bridge ... B4
South Charlotte St ... B2
South College St ... C4
South Learmonth Gardens ... A1
South St Andrew St ... A4
South St David St ... A3
Spittal St ... C2
Stafford St ... B1
Stand Comedy Club, The ... A4
Student Centre ... C4
Surgeons' Hall ... C5
Supreme Courts ... B4
Talbot Rice, The ... C4
Teviot Place ... C4
Thistle St ... A3
Tolbooth & Highland Kirk ... C4
Torphichen Place ... C1
Torphichen St ... C1
Traverse Theatre ... B2
Tron Square ... B4
Tron, The ... B4
Union St ... A4
University ... C4
University Library ... C4
Univ of Edinburgh ... B5
Upper Grove Place ... C1
Usher Hall ... C2
Vennel ... C3
Victoria St ... B3
Viewcraig Gardens ... B5
Viewcraig St ... B5
Vue ... A4
Walker St ... B1
Waterloo Place ... A4
Waverley Bridge ... B4
Wemyss Place ... A2
West Approach Rd ... C1
West Crosscauseway ... C5
West End ... B1
West Maitland St ... C1
West of Nicholson St ... C4
West Port ... C3
West Princes Street Gardens ... B3
West Richmond St ... C5
West Tollcross ... C2
White Horse Cl ... B6
William St ... B1
Windsor St ... A5
Writer's Mus ... B4
York Lane ... A4
York Place ... A4
Young St ... B2

Exeter 117

Alphington St ... C1
Athelstan Rd ... B3
Barnardo Rd ... C3
Barnfield Hill ... B3
Barnfield Rd ... B2/B3
Barnfield Theatre ... B2
Bartholomew St E ... B1
Bartholomew St W ... B1
Bear St ... B2
Beaufort Rd ... C1
Bedford St ... B2
Belgrave Rd ... A3
Belmont Rd ... A3
Blackall Rd ... A2
Blackboy Rd ... A3
Bonhay Rd ... B1
Bull Meadow Rd ... C2
Bus & Coach Sta ... B3
Castle St ... B2
Cecil Rd ... C1
Cheeke St ... A3
Church Rd ... C1
Chute St ... A3
City Wall ... B1/B2
Civic Centre ... B2
Clifton Rd ... B3
Clifton St ... B3
Clock Tower ... A1
College Rd ... B3
Colleton Crescent ... C2
Commercial Rd ... C1
Coombe St ... B2
Cowick St ... C1
Crown Courts ... B2
Custom House Visitor Centre ... C2
Cygnet Theatre ... C2
Danes' Rd ... A2
Denmark Rd ... B3
Devon County Hall ... C3
Devonshire Place ... A3
Dinham Crescent ... B1
East Grove Rd ... C3
Edmund St ... C1
Elm Grove Rd ... A1
Exe St ... B1
Exeter Cathedral ... B2
Exeter Central Station ... A1
Exeter City Football Ground ... A3
Exeter College ... A1
Exeter Picture House ... B1
Fire Station ... A1
Fore St ... B1
Friars Walk ... C2
Guildhall ... B2
Guildhall Shop Ctr ... B2
Haven Rd ... C2
Heavitree Rd ... B3
Hele Rd ... A1
High St ... B2
HM Prison ... A2
Holloway St ... C2
Hoopern St ... A2
Horseguards ... A2
Howell Rd ... A1
Information Ctr ... B3
Iron Bridge ... B1
Isca Rd ... C1
Jesmond Rd ... A3
King St ... B1
King William St ... A2
Larkbeare Rd ... C2
Leisure Centre ... C1
Library ... B2
Longbrook St ... A2
Longbrook Terrace ... A2
Lower North St ... B1
Lucky Lane ... C2
Lyndhurst Rd ... C3
Magdalen Rd ... B3
Magdalen St ... B2
Market ... B2
Market St ... B2
Marlborough Rd ... C3
Mary Arches St ... B1
Matford Avenue ... C3
Matford Lane ... C3
Matford Rd ... C3
May St ... A3
Mol's Coffee Ho ... B2
New Bridge St ... B1
New North Rd ... A1/A2
North St ... B1
Northernhay St ... B1
Norwood Avenue ... C3
Odeon ... A3
Okehampton St ... C1
Old Mill Close ... C2
Old Tiverton Rd ... A3
Oxford Rd ... A3
Paris St ... B2
Parr St ... A3
Paul St ... B1
Pennsylvania Rd ... A2
Portland Street ... A3
Post Office ... A3/B2/C1
Powderham Cres ... A3
Preston St ... B1
Princesshay Shopping Centre ... B2
Pyramids Leisure Centre ... B3
Quay, The ... C2
Queen St ... A1
Queen's Terrace ... A1
Queens Rd ... C1
Radford Rd ... C2
Richmond Rd ... A1
Roberts Rd ... C2
Rougemont Castle ... A2
Rougemont Ho ... B2
Royal Albert Memorial Museum ... B2
St David's Hill ... A1
St James' Pk Sta ... A3
St James' Rd ... A3
St Leonard's Rd ... C3
St Mary Steps ... C1
St Nicholas Priory ... B1
St Thomas Sta ... C1
Sandford Walk ... B3
School Rd ... C1
Sidwell St ... A2
Smythen St ... B1
South St ... B2
Southernhay East ... B2
Southernhay West ... B2
Spicer Rd ... B3
Sports Centre ... A3
Summerland St ... A3
Sydney Rd ... C1
Tan Lane ... C2
Thornton Hill ... A2
Topsham Rd ... C3
Tucker's Hall ... B1
Tudor St ... B1
Underground Passages ... B2
Univ of Exeter (St Luke's Campus) ... B3
Velwell Rd ... A1
Verney St ... A3
Vue ... B2
Water Lane ... C1/C2
Weirfield Rd ... C2
Well St ... A3
West Avenue ... A2
West Grove Rd ... C3
Western Way ... A3/B1/B2
Willeys Avenue ... C1
Wonford Rd ... B3/C3
York Rd ... A2

Glasgow 117

Admiral St ... C2
Albert Bridge ... C5
Albion St ... B5
Anderston ... B3
Anderston Quay ... B3
Argyle Arcade ... B5
Argyle St ... A1/A2/B3/B4/B5
Argyle Street ... B5
Arlington St ... A3
Arts Centre ... B3
Ashley St ... A3
Bain St ... C6
Baird St ... A6
Baliol St ... A3
Ballater St ... C5
Barras (Mkt), The ... C6
Bath St ... A3
BBC Scotland ... B1
Bell St ... C6
Bell's Bridge ... B1
Bentinck St ... A2
Berkeley St ... A3
Bishop Lane ... B3
Black St ... A6
Blackburn St ... C2
Blackfriars St ... B6
Blantyre St ... A1
Blythswood Square ... A4
Blythswood St ... B4
Bothwell St ... B4
Brand St ... C1
Breadalbane St ... A2
Bridge St ... C4
Bridge St ... C4
Bridgegate ... C5
Briggait ... C5
Broomielaw ... B4
Broomielaw Quay Gardens ... B3
Brown St ... B4
Brunswick St ... B5
Buccleuch St ... A3
Buchanan Bus Sta ... A5
Buchanan Galleries ... A5
Buchanan St ... B5
Buchanan St ... B5
Cadogan St ... B4
Caledonian Univ ... A5
Calgary St ... A5
Cambridge St ... A4
Canal St ... A5
Candleriggs ... B5
Carlton Place ... C4
Carnarvon St ... A3
Carrick St ... B4
Castle St ... B6
Cathedral Square ... B6
Cathedral St ... B5
Central Mosque ... C5
Ctr for Contemporary Arts ... A4
Centre St ... C4
Cessnock ... C1
Cessnock St ... C1
Charing Cross ... A3
Charlotte St ... C6
Cheapside St ... B3
Cineworld ... A5
Citizens' Theatre ... C5
City Chambers Complex ... B5
City Halls ... B5
City of Glasgow Coll (City Campus) ... B5
City of Glasgow College (Riverside Campus) ... C5
Clairmont Gardens ... A2
Claremont St ... A2
Claremont Terrace ... A2
Claythorne St ... C6
Cleveland St ... A3
Clifford Lane ... C1
Clifford St ... C1
Clifton Place ... A2
Clifton St ... A2
Clutha St ... C1
Clyde Arcade ... B2
Clyde Place ... C4
Clyde Place Quay ... C4
Clyde St ... C5
Clyde Walkway ... C3
Clydeside Distillery, The ... B1
Clydeside Expressway ... B2
Coburg St ... C4
Cochrane St ... B5
College St ... B6
Collins St ... B6
Commerce St ... C4
Cook St ... C4
Cornwall St ... C2
Couper St ... A5
Cowcaddens ... A4
Cowcaddens Rd ... A4
Crimea St ... B3
Custom House Quay Gardens ... C4
Dalhousie St ... A4
Dental Hospital ... A4
Derby St ... A2
Dobbie's Loan ... A4/A5
Dobbie's Loan Pl ... A5
Dorset St ... A3
Douglas St ... B4
Doulton Fountain ... C6
Dover St ... A2
Drury St ... B4
Drygate ... B6
Duke St ... B6
Dunaskin St ... A1
Dunblane St ... A4
Dundas St ... B5
Dunlop St ... C5
East Campbell St ... C6
Eastvale Place ... A1
Eglinton St ... C4
Elderslie St ... A3
Elliot St ... B2
Elmbank St ... A3
Esmond St ... A1
Exhibition Ctr ... B2
Festival Park ... C1
Film Theatre ... A4
Finnieston Quay ... B2
Finnieston St ... B2
Fire Station ... C5
Florence St ... C5
Fox St ... C5
Gallowgate ... C6
Garnet St ... A3
Garnethill St ... A4
Garscube Rd ... A4
George Square ... B5
George St ... B5
George V Bridge ... C4
Gilbert St ... A1
Glasgow Bridge ... C4
Glasgow Cath ... B6
Glasgow Central ... B4
Glasgow City Free Church ... B4
Glasgow Green ... C6
Glasgow Necropolis ... B6
Glasgow Royal Concert Hall ... A5
Glasgow Science Centre ... B1
Glasgow Tower ... B1
Glassford St ... B5
Glebe St ... A6
Gorbals Cross ... C5
Gorbals St ... C5
Gordon St ... B4
Govan Rd ... B1/C1/C2
Grace St ... B3
Grafton Place ... A5
Grand Ole Opry ... C2
Grant St ... A3
Granville St ... A3
Gray St ... A2
Greendyke St ... C6
Grey Eagle St ... B7
Harley St ... C1
Harvie St ... C1
Haugh Rd ... A1
Havanah St ... B6
Henry Wood Hall ... A2
High Court ... C5
High St ... B6
High Street ... B6
Hill St ... A3
Holland St ... A3
Holm St ... B4
Hope St ... A5
Houldsworth St ... B2
Houston Place ... C3
Houston St ... C3
Howard St ... C5
Hunter St ... C6
Hutcheson St ... B5
Hydepark St ... B3
Imax Cinema ... B1
India St ... A3
Information Ctr ... B5
Ingram St ... B5
Jamaica St ... B4
James Watt Statue ... C6
James Watt St ... B4
John Knox St ... B6
John St ... B5
Kelvin Hall ... A1
Kelvin Statue ... A2
Kelvin Way ... A2
Kelvingrove Art Gallery & Mus ... A1
Kelvingrove Park ... A2
Kelvingrove St ... A2
Kelvinhaugh St ... A1
Kennedy St ... A6
Kent Rd ... A2
Killermont St ... A5
King St ... B5
King's, The ... A3
Kingston Bridge ... C3
Kingston St ... C4
Kinning Park ... C2
Kyle St ... A5
Lancefield Quay ... B2
Lancefield St ... B3
Langshot St ... C1
Lendel Place ... C1
Lighthouse, The ... B4
Lister St ... A6
Little St ... B3
London Rd ... C6
Lorne St ... C1
Lower Harbour ... B1
Lumsden St ... A1
Lymburn St ... A1
Lyndoch Crescent ... A3
Lynedoch Place ... A3
Lynedoch St ... A3
Maclellan St ... C1
Mair St ... C2
Maitland St ... A4
Mansell St ... C7
Mavisbank Gdns ... C2
Mcalpine St ... B3
Mcaslin St ... A6
McLean Square ... C2
McLellan Gallery ... A4
McPhater St ... A4
Merchants' Ho ... B5
Middlesex St ... C2
Middleton St ... C1
Midland St ... B4
Miller St ... B5
Millennium Bridge ... B1
Millroad St ... C6
Milnpark St ... C2
Milton St ... A4
Minerva St ... B2
Mitchell St West ... B4
Mitchell Liby, The ... A3
Modern Art Gall ... B5
Moir St ... C6
Molendinar St ... C6
Moncur St ... C6
Montieth Row ... C6
Montrose St ... B5
Morrison St ... C3
Nairn St ... A1
National Piping Centre, The ... A5
Nelson Mandela Sq ... B5
Nelson St ... C4
Nelson's Monument ... C6
Newton Place ... A3
Newton St ... A3
Nicholson St ... C4
Nile St ... B5
Norfolk Court ... C4
Norfolk St ... C4
North Frederick St ... B5
North Hanover St ... B5
North Portland St ... B6
North St ... A3
North Wallace St ... A5
O2 ABC ... A4
O2 Academy ... C4
Odeon ... C3
Old Dumbarton Rd ... A1
Osborne St ... B5/C5
Oswald St ... B4
Overnewton St ... A1
OVO Hydro ... B2
Oxford St ... C4
Pacific Drive ... B1
Paisley Rd ... C3
Paisley Rd West ... C1
Park Circus ... A2
Park Gardens ... A2
Park St South ... A2
Park Terrace ... A2
Parkgrove Terrace ... A2
Parnie St ... C5
Parson St ... A6
Partick Bridge ... A1
Passport Office ... A5
Pavilion Theatre ... A4
Pembroke St ... A3
People's Palace ... C6
Pitt St ... A4/B4
Plantation Park ... C1
Plantation Quay ... B1
Police Museum ... B5
Police Station ... A4/A6
Port Dundas Rd ... A5
Port St ... B2
Portman St ... C2
Post Office ... A3/A5/B4/B5/C4
Prince's Dock ... B1
Princes Square ... B5
Provand's Lordship ... B6
Queen St ... B5
Queen Street ... B5
Ramshorn ... B5
Renfrew St ... A3/A4
Renton St ... A5
Richmond St ... B5
Robertson St ... B4
Rose St ... A4
Rottenrow ... B5
Royal Concert Hall ... A5
Royal Conservatoire of Scotland ... A4
Royal Crescent ... A2
Royal Exchange Sq ... B5
Royal Highland Fusiliers Mus ... A3
West Glasgow Ambulatory Care ... A1
Royal Infirmary ... B6
Royal Terrace ... A2
Rutland Crescent ... C2
St Andrew's in the Square ... C6
St Andrew's (RC) ... C5
St Andrew's St ... C5
St Enoch ... B5
St Enoch Shop Ctr ... B5
St Enoch Square ... B4
St George's Rd ... A3
St James Rd ... B6
St Kent St ... C6
St Mungo Ave ... A5/A6
St Mungo Museum of Religious Life & Art ... B6
St Mungo Place ... A6
St Vincent Crescent ... A2
St Vincent Place ... B5
St Vincent St ... B3/B4
St Vincent Terrace ... B3
Saltmarket ... C5
Sandyford Place ... A3
Sauchiehall St ... A2/A4
SEC Armadillo ... B2
School of Art ... A4
Sclater St ... B7
Scotland St ... C2
Scotland St W ... C2
Scott St ... A4
Scottish Exhibition & Conference Ctr ... B1
Seaward St ... C2
Shaftesbury St ... B3
Sheriff Court ... C5
Shields Rd ... C3
Shopmobility ... A5
Shuttle St ... B6
Somerset Place ... A2
South Portland St ... C4
Springburn Rd ... A6
Springfield Quay ... C3
Stanley St ... C2
Stevenson St ... C6
Stewart St ... A4
Stirling Rd ... B6
Stobcross Quay ... B1
Stobcross Rd ... B1
Stock Exchange ... B5
Stockwell Place ... C5
Stockwell St ... B5
Stow College ... A4
Sussex St ... C2
Synagogue ... A3
Taylor Place ... A6
Tenement House ... A3
Teviot St ... A1
Theatre Royal ... A4
Tolbooth Steeple & Mercat Cross ... C6
Tower St ... C2
Trades House ... B5
Tradeston St ... C4
Transport Mus ... A1
Tron ... C5
Trongate ... B5
Tunnel St ... B2
Turnbull St ... C5
Union St ... B4
Univ of Strathclyde ... B6
Victoria Bridge ... C5
Virginia St ... B5
Wallace St ... C3
Walls St ... B6
Walmer Crescent ... C1
Warrock St ... B3
Washington St ... B3
Waterloo St ... B4
Watson St ... B6
Watt St ... C3
Wellington St ... B4
West Campbell St ... B4
West George St ... B4
West Graham St ... A4
West Greenhill Pl ... B2
West Regent St ... A4
West Regent St ... B4
West St ... C4
West St ... C4
Whitehall St ... B3
Wilkes St ... C7
Wilson St ... B5
Woodlands Gate ... A3
Woodlands Rd ... A3
Woodlands Terrace ... A2
Woodside Place ... A3
Woodside Terrace ... A3
York St ... B4
Yorkhill Parade ... A1
Yorkhill St ... A1

Gloucester 117

Albion St ... C1
Alexandra Rd ... B3
Alfred St ... C3
All Saints Rd ... C2
Alvin St ... B2
Arthur St ... C2
Barrack Square ... B1
Barton St ... C2
Blackfriars ... B1
Blenheim Rd ... C2
Bristol Rd ... C1
Brunswick Rd ... C2
Bruton Way ... B2
Bus Station ... B2
Cineworld ... C1
City Council Offices ... B1
Clarence St ... B2
Commercial Rd ... B1
Courts ... B1
Cromwell St ... C2
Deans Way ... A2
Denmark Rd ... A3
Derby Rd ... C3
Docks ... C1
Eastgate St ... B2
Eastgate, The ... B1
Edwy Parade ... A2
Estcourt Close ... A3
Estcourt Rd ... A3
Falkner St ... C2
GL1 Leisure Centre ... C2
Gloucester Cath ... B1
Gloucester Life ... B1
Gloucester Quays Outlet ... C1
Gloucester Mus ... B2
Gloucester Sta ... B2
Gloucestershire Archive ... B2
Gloucestershire Royal Hospital (A&E) ... B3
Goodyere St ... C2
Gouda Way ... A1
Great Western Rd ... B3
Guildhall ... B2
Heathville Rd ... A3
Henry Rd ... B3
Henry St ... B2
Hinton Rd ... A2
HM Prison Gloucester ... B1
India Rd ... C3
Information Ctr ... B1
Jersey Rd ... C3
King's ... C2
King's Walk Shopping Centre ... B2
Kingsholm (Gloucester Rugby) ... A2
Kingsholm Rd ... A2
Lansdown Rd ... A3
Library ... C2
Llanthony Rd ... C1
London Rd ... B3
Longhorn Avenue ... A1
Longsmith St ... B1
Malvern Rd ... A3
Market ... B2
Market Parade ... B2
Mercia Rd ... A1
Metz Way ... C3
Midland Rd ... C2
Millbrook St ... C3
Montpellier ... C1
Napier St ... C3
National Waterways Mus Gloucester ... C1
Nettleton Rd ... C2
New Inn ... B2
New Olympus ... C3
North Rd ... A3
Northgate St ... B2
Oxford Rd ... A2
Oxford St ... B2
Park & Ride Gloucester ... A1
Park Rd ... C2
Park St ... B2
Park, The ... C2
Parliament St ... C1
Peel Centre, The ... C1
Pitt St ... B1
Police Sta ... B1/C3
Post Office ... B2
Quay St ... B1
Quay, The ... B1
Recreation Gd ... A1/A2
Regent St ... C2
Robert Raikes Ho ... B1
Royal Oak Rd ... B1
Russell St ... B2
Ryecroft St ... C2
St Aldate St ... B2
St Ann Way ... C1
St Catherine St ... A2
St Mark St ... A2
St Mary de Crypt ... B1
St Mary de Lode ... B1
St Nicholas's ... B1
St Oswald's Priory ... B1
St Oswald's Rd ... A1
St Oswald's Ret Pk ... A1
St Peter's ... B2
Seabroke Rd ... A3
Sebert St ... A2
Severn Rd ... C1
Sherborne Cinema ... A2
Sherborne St ... B2
Shire Hall ... B1
Sidney St ... C3
Soldiers of Gloucestershire ... B1
Southgate St ... B1/C1
Spa Field ... C1
Spa Rd ... C1
Sports Ground ... A2/B2
Station Rd ... B2
Stratton Rd ... C3
Stroud Rd ... C1
Superstore ... A1
Swan Rd ... A2
Trier Way ... C1/C2
Union St ... A2
Vauxhall Rd ... C3
Victoria St ... C2
Walham Lane ... A1
Wellington St ... C2
Westgate Retail Pk ... B1
Westgate St ... B1
Widden St ... C2
Worcester St ... B2

Harrogate 117

Albert St ... C2
Alexandra Rd ... B2
Arthington Avenue ... B2
Ashfield Rd ... A2
Back Cheltenham Mount ... B2
Beech Grove ... C1
Belmont Rd ... C1
Bettys Café Tea Rooms ... B2
Bilton Drive ... A2
Bower Rd ... B2
Bower St ... B2
Bus Station ... B2
Cambridge Rd ... B2
Cambridge St ... B2
Cemetery ... A2
Chatsworth Grove ... A2
Chatsworth Place ... A2
Chatsworth Rd ... A2
Chelmsford Rd ... B3
Cheltenham Cres ... B2
Cheltenham Mt ... B2
Cheltenham Pde ... B2
Christ Church ... B3
Christ Church Oval ... B3
Chudleigh Rd ... B3
Clarence Drive ... B1
Claro Rd ... A3
Claro Way ... A3
Coach Park ... B2
Coach Rd ... B3
Cold Bath Rd ... C1
Commercial St ... B2
Coppice Avenue ... A1
Coppice Drive ... A1
Coppice Gate ... A1
Cornwall Rd ... B1
Council Offices ... B1
Crescent Gardens ... B1
Crescent Rd ... B1
Dawson Terrace ... A2
Devonshire Place ... B3
Dixon Rd ... A2
Dixon Terrace ... A2
Dragon Avenue ... B3
Dragon Parade ... B2
Dragon Rd ... B2
Duchy Hosp, The ... C1
Duchy Rd ... B1
East Parade ... B2
East Park Rd ... C3
Esplanade ... B1
Everyman ... B2
Fire Station ... A2
Franklin Mount ... A2
Franklin Rd ... B2
Franklin Square ... A2
Glebe Rd ... C1
Grove Park Court ... A3
Grove Park Terrace ... A3
Grove Rd ... A2
Hampsthwaite Rd ... A1
Harcourt Drive ... B3
Harcourt Rd ... B3
Harrogate ... B2
Harrogate Convention Ctr ... B1
Harrogate Justice Ctr (Magistrates' and County Courts) ... C2
Harrogate Ladies College ... B1
Harrogate Theatre ... B2
Harrogate Turkish Baths ... B1
Heywood Rd ... C1
Hollins Crescent ... A1
Hollins Mews ... A1
Hollins Rd ... A1
Hydro Leisure Centre, The ... A1
Information Ctr ... B1
James St ... B2
Jenny Field Drive ... A1
John St ... B2
Kent Drive ... A1
Kent Rd ... A1
Kings Rd ... A2
Kingsway ... B3
Kingsway Drive ... B3
Lancaster Rd ... C1
Leeds Rd ... C2
Lime Grove ... B3
Lime St ... A3
Mayfield Grove ... B2
Mercer ... B1
Montpellier Hill ... B1
Mornington Cres ... A3
Mornington Terr ... B3
Mowbray Square ... B3
North Park Rd ... B3
Oakdale Avenue ... A1
Oatlands Drive ... C3
Odeon ... B2
Osborne Rd ... A2
Otley Rd ... C2
Oxford St ... B2
Parade, The ... B2
Park Chase ... B3
Park Parade ... B3
Park View ... B2
Parliament St ... B1
Post Office ... B2/C1
Providence Terr ... A2
Queen Parade ... C3
Queen's Rd ... C1
Raglan St ... C2
Regent Avenue ... A3
Regent Grove ... A3
Regent Parade ... A3
Regent St ... A3
Regent Terrace ... A3
Ripon Rd ... A1
Robert St ... C2
Royal Pump Room ... B1
St Luke's Mount ... A2
St Mary's Avenue ... C1
St Mary's Walk ... C1
Scargill Rd ... A1
Skipton Rd ... A3
Skipton St ... A2
Slingsby Walk ... C3
South Park Rd ... C2
Spring Grove ... A1
Springfield Ave ... B1
Station Avenue ... B2
Station Parade ... B2
Stray Rein ... C3
Stray, The ... C2/C3
Studley Rd ... A2
Superstore ... B2/C1
Swan Rd ... B1
Tower St ... C2
Trinity Rd ... C2
Union St ... B2
Valley Drive ... C1
Valley Gardens ... C1
Valley Mount ... C1
Victoria Avenue ... C2
Victoria Rd ... C1
Victoria Shopping Centre ... B2
Waterloo St ... A2
West Park ... C2
West Park St ... C2
Wood View ... A1
Woodfield Avenue ... A3
Woodfield Drive ... A3
Woodfield Grove ... A3
Woodfield Rd ... A3
Woodfield Square ... A3
Woodside ... B3
York Place ... C3
York Rd ... B1

Hull 117

Adelaide St ... C1
Albert Dock ... C1
Albion St ... B2
Alfred Gelder St ... B2
Anlaby Rd ... B1
Arctic Corsair ... B3
Beverley Rd ... A1
Blanket Row ... C2
Bond St ... B2
Bonus Arena ... B2
Bridlington Ave ... A2
Brook St ... B1
Brunswick Ave ... A1
Bus Station ... B1
Camilla Close ... C3
Cannon St ... A2
Caroline St ... A2
Carr Lane ... B2
Castle St ... C2
Central Library ... B1
Charles St ... A2
Citadel Way ... B3
Clarence St ... B3
Cleveland St ... A3
Clifton St ... A1
Colonial St ... B1
Court ... B2
Deep, The ... C3
Dinostar ... C2
Dock Office Row ... B3
Dock St ... B2
Drypool Bridge ... B3
Egton St ... A3
English St ... C1
Ferens Gallery ... B2
Ferensway ... B1
Fire Station ... A1
Francis St ... A2
Francis St West ... A2
Freehold St ... A1
Freetown Way ... A2
Früit Theatre ... C2
Garrison Rd ... B3
George St ... B2
Gibson St ... A2
Great Union St ... A3
Green Lane ... A2
Grey St ... A1
Grimston St ... B2
Grosvenor St ... A1
Guildhall ... B2
Guildhall Rd ... B2
Hands-on History ... B2
Harley St ... A1
Hessle Rd ... C1
High St ... B3
Hull Minster ... B2
Hull Paragon Interchange Station ... B1
Hull & East Riding Museum ... B3
Hull Ice Arena ... C1
Hull City Hall ... B2
Hull College ... B3
Hull History Centre ... A2
Hull New Theatre ... A2
Hull Truck Theatre ... B1
Humber Dock Marina ... C2
Humber Dock St ... C2
Humber St ... C2
Hyperion St ... A3
Information Ctr ... B1
Jameson St ... B1
Jarratt St ... B2
Jenning St ... A3
King Billy Statue ... C2
King Edward St ... B2
King St ... A2
Kingston Retail Pk ... C1
Kingston St ... C2
Liddell St ... A1
Lime St ... A3
Lister St ... C1
Lockwood St ... A2
Maister House ... B3
Maritime Mus ... B2
Market ... B2
Market Place ... B2
Millennium Bridge ... C3
Minerva Pier ... C2
Mulgrave St ... A3
Myton Swing Bridge ... C3
Myton St ... B1
NAPA (Northern Acad of Performing Arts) ... B1
Nelson St ... C2
New Cleveland St ... A3
New George St ... A2
Norfolk St ... A1
North Bridge ... A3
North St ... B1
Odeon ... C1
Old Harbour ... C3
Osborne St ... B1
Paragon St ... B2
Park St ... B1
Percy St ... A2
Pier St ... C2
Police Station ... B1
Porter St ... C1
Portland St ... B1
Post Office ... B1/B2
Posterngate ... B2
Prince's Quay ... B2
Prospect Centre ... B1
Prospect St ... B1
Queen's Gardens ... B2
Railway Dock Marina ... C2
Railway St ... C2
Reel ... B1
Reform St ... A2
Retail Park ... B1
Riverside Quay ... C2
Roper St ... B2
St James St ... C1
St Luke's St ... B1
St Mark St ... A3
St Mary the Virgin ... B3
St Stephens Shopping Centre ... B1
Scale La Footbridge ... B3
Scott St ... A2
South Bridge Rd ... B3
Sport's Centre ... C1
Spring Bank ... A1
Spring St ... B1
Spurn Lightship ... C2
Spyvee St ... A3
Stage @TheDock ... C3
Sykes St ... A2
Tidal Surge Barrier ... C3
Tower St ... B3
Trinity House Acad ... B2
Vane St ... A1
Victoria Pier ... C2
Waterhouse Lane ... B2
Waterloo St ... A1
Waverley St ... C1
Wellington St ... C2
Wellington St West ... C2
West St ... B1
Whitefriargate ... B2
Wilberforce Drive ... B2
Wilberforce Ho ... B3
Wilberforce Monument ... B3
William St ... C1
Wincolmlee ... A3
Witham ... A3
Wright St ... A1

Ipswich 118

Alderman Rd ... B2
All Saints' Rd ... A1
Alpe St ... B2
Ancaster Rd ... C1
Ancient House ... B3

Princes Dock A1
Princes Gardens A2
Princes Jetty A1
Princes Parade B1
Princes St B2
Pythian St A6
Queen Sq Bus Sta. B3
Queensland St C6
QueenswayTunnel (Docks exit) B1
QueenswayTunnel (Entrance) B3
Radio City B2
Ranelagh St B3
Redcross St B2
Renfrew St B6
Renshaw St B4
Richmond Row A4
Richmond St B3
Rigby St A2
Roberts St A1
Rock St B4
Rodney St C4
Roe St B3
Rokeby St A4
Romilly St A6
Roscoe Lane C4
Roscoe St C4
Rose Hill A3
Royal Albert Dock C2
Royal Ct Theatre B3
Royal Liver Building B1
Royal Liverpool Hospital (A&E) [H] B5
Rumford Place B2
Rumford St B2
Russell St B4
St Andrew St B4
St Anne St A4
St Georges Hall B3
St John's Centre B3
St John's Gardens B3
St John's Lane B3
St Joseph's Cres A4
St Minishull St B5
St Nicholas Place B1
Salisbury St A4
Salthouse Dock C2
Salthouse Quay C2
Sandon St C5
Saxony Rd B6
Schomberg St A6
School Lane B2
Seel St C3
Seymour St B4
Shaw St A5
Shopmobility C2
Sidney Place C6
Sir Thomas St B3
Skelhorne St B4
Slater St C3
Smithdown Lane B6
Soho Square A4
Soho St A4
South John St B2
Springfield A4
Stafford St A4
Standish St A3
Stanley St B2
Strand St C2
Strand, The B2
Suffolk St C3
Sydney Jones Liby C5
Tabley St C3
Tarleton St B3
Tate Liverpool Gallery C2
Teck St B6
Temple St B2
Titanic Memorial ✦ B1
Tithebarn St B2
Town Hall B2
Triskelion Wy A1
Trowbridge St B4
Trueman St A3
Union St B2
Unity Theatre C4
University C5
Univ of Liverpool B5
Upper Baker St A6
Upper Duke St C4
Upper Frederick St C3
Vauxhall Rd A2
Vernon St B2
Victoria Gallery & Museum B5
Victoria St B2
Vine St C5
Wakefield St A4
Walker Art Gall A3
Walker St A6
Wapping C2
Water St B1/B2
Waterloo Rd A1
Wavertree Rd B6
West Derby Rd A6
West Derby St B5
Western Approaches War Museum B2
Whitechapel B3
Whitley Gardens A5
William Brown St B3
William Henry St A4
William Jessop Way A1
Williamson Square B3
Williamson St B3
Williamson's Tunnels Heritage Ctr ✦ C6
Wood St B3
World Museum, Liverpool A3
York St C3

London 120

Abbey Orchard St E3
Abchurch Lane D6
Abingdon St E4
Achilles Way D2
Acton St B4
Addington St E4
Air St D3
Albany St B2
Albemarle St D3
Albert Embankment F4
Aldenham St A3
Aldersgate St C6
Aldford St D2
Aldgate ⊖ C7
Aldgate High St C7
Aldwych C4
Allsop Place B1
Amwell St B5
Angel ⊖ A5
Appold St C7
Argyle Square B4
Argyle St B4
Argyll St C3
Arnold Circus B7
Artillery Lane C7
Artillery Row E3
Association of Photographers Gallery B6
Baker St ⊖ B1
Baker St B1
Baldwin's Gardens C5
Baltic St B6
Bank ⊖ C6
Bank Museum C6
Bank of England C6
Bankside D6
Bankside Gall D5
Banner St B6
Barbican ⇌⊖ C6
Barbican Centre for Arts, The C6
Barbican Gall C6
Basil St E1
Bastwick St B6
Bateman's Row B7
Bath St B6
Bayley St C3
Baylis Rd E5
Beak St D3
Bedford Row C4
Bedford Square C3
Bedford St D4
Bedford Way B3
Beech St C6
Belgrave Place E2
Belgrave Square E2
Bell Lane C7
Belvedere Rd E4
Berkeley Square D2
Berkeley St D2
Bernard St B4
Berners Place C3
Berners St C3
Berwick St C3
Bethnal Green Rd B7
Bevenden St B6
Bevis Marks C7
BFI (British Film Institute) D4
BFI London IMAX Cinema D5
Bidborough St B4
Binney St C2
Birdcage Walk E3
Bishopsgate C7
Blackfriars ⇌⊖ D5
Blackfriars Bridge D5
Blackfriars Pas D5
Blackfriars Rd E5
Blandford St C1
Blomfield St C6
Bloomsbury St C3
Bloomsbury Way C4
Bolton St D2
Bond St ⊖ C2
Borough High St E6
Boswell St C4
Bow St C4
Bowling Gn Lane B5
Brad St D5
Bressenden Place E3
Brewer St D3
Brick St D2
Bridge St E4
Britannia Walk B6
British Film Institute (BFI) D4
British Library B3
British Museum C4
Britton St B5
Broad Sanctuary E3
Broadway E3
Brook Drive F5
Brook St D2
Brunswick Place B6
Brunswick Shopping Centre, The B4
Brunswick Square B4
Brushfield St C7
Bruton St D2
Bryanston St C1
BT Centre C6
Buckingham Gate E3
Buckingham Palace E3
Buckingham Pal Rd F2
Bunhill Row B6
Byward St D7
Cabinet War Rooms & Churchill Mus E3
Cadogan Lane E2
Cadogan Place E1
Cadogan Square F1
Caledonian Rd A4
Calshot St A4
Calthorpe St B4
Calvert Avenue B7
Cambridge Circus C3
Camomile St C7
Cannon St D6
Cannon St ⇌⊖ D6
Capel Manor Coll B2
Carey St C4
Carlisle Lane E4
Carlisle Place E3
Carlton Ho Terrace D3
Carmelite St D5
Carnaby St C3
Carter Lane C5
Carthusian St C6
Cartwright Gdns B4
Castle Baynard St D5
Cavendish Place C2
Cavendish Square C2
Caxton Hall E3
Caxton St E3
Central St B6
Chalton St B3
Chancery Lane ⊖ C5
Chapel St E2
Charing Cross ⇌⊖ D4
Charing Cross Rd C3
Charles Dickens Museum, The B4
Charles II St D3
Charles Square B6
Charles St D2
Charlotte Rd B7
Charlotte St C3
Chart St B6
Charterhouse Sq C5
Charterhouse St C5
Cheapside C6
Chenies St C3
Chesham St E2
Chester Square F2
Chesterfield Hill D2
Chiltern St C2
Chiswell St C6
City Garden Row A5
City Rd B6
City Thameslink ⇌ C5
City University, The B5
Claremont Square A5
Clarges St D2
Clerkenwell Close B5
Clerkenwell Green B5
Clerkenwell Rd B5
Cleveland St C3
Clifford St D3
Clink Prison Mus D6
Clock Museum C6
Club Row B7
Cockspur St D3
Coleman St C6
Columbia Rd B7
Commercial St C7
Compton St B5
Conduit St D2
Constitution Hill E2
Copperfield St E5
Coptic St C4
Cornhill C6
Cornwall Rd D5
Coronet St B7
Courtauld Gall D4
Covent Garden ⊖ D4
Covent Garden ✦ D4
Cowcross St C5
Cowper St B6
Cranbourn St D3
Craven St D4
Crawford St C1
Creechurch Lane C7
Cremer St A7
Cromer St B4
Cumberland Gate D1
Cumberland Terr A2
Curtain Rd B7
Curzon St D2
Cut, The E5
D'arblay St C3
Davies St C2
Dean St C3
Deluxe Gallery B7
Denmark St C3
Dering St C2
Devonshire St C2
Diana, Princess of Wales Meml Walk E3
Dingley Rd B6
Dorset St C1
Doughty St B4
Dover St D2
Downing St E4
Druid St E7
Drummond St B3
Drury Lane C4
Drysdale St B7
Duchess St C2
Dufferin St C6
Duke of Wellington Place E2
Duke St C2
Duke St D3
Duke St Hill D6
Duke's Place C7
Duncannon St D4
East Rd B6
Eastcastle St C3
Eastcheap D7
Eastman Dental Hospital [H] B4
Eaton Place E2
Eaton Square E2
Eccleston St E2
Edgware Rd C1
Eldon St C6
Embankment ⊖ D4
Endell St C4
Endsleigh Place B3
Euston ⇌⊖ B3
Euston Rd B3
Euston Square ⊖ B3
Evelina Children's Hospital E4
Eversholt St A3
Exmouth Market B5
Fann St B6
Farringdon ⇌⊖ C5
Farringdon Rd C5
Farringdon St C5
Featherstone St B6
Fenchurch St D7
Fenchurch St ⇌ D7
Fetter Lane C5
Finsbury Circus C6
Finsbury Pavement C6
Finsbury Square B6
Fitzalan St F5
Fitzmaurice Place D2
Fleet St C5
Floral St D4
Florence Nightingale Museum E4
Folgate St C7
Foot Hospital [H] B3
Fore St C6
Foster Lane C6
Foundling Museum, The B4
Francis St F3
Frazier St E5
Freemason's Hall C4
Friday St C6
Gainsford St E7
Garden Row E5
Gee St B6
George St C1
Gerrard St D3
Giltspur St C5
Glasshouse St D3
Gloucester Place C1
Golden Hinde D6
Golden Lane B6
Golden Square D3
Goodge St ⊖ C3
Goodge St C3
Gordon Square B3
Goswell Rd B5
Gough St B4
Goulston St C7
Gower St B3
Gracechurch St D6
Grafton Way B3
Gray's Inn Rd B4
Great College St E4
Great Cumberland Place C1
Great Eastern St B7
Great Guildford St D6
Great Marlborough St C3
Great Ormond St B4
Great Ormond St Children's Hosp [H] B4
Great Percy St B4
Great Peter St E3
Great Portland St ⊖ B2
Great Portland St C2
Great Queen St C4
Great Russell St C3
Great Scotland Yard D4
Great Smith St E3
Great Suffolk St D5
Great Titchfield St C3
Great Tower St D7
Great Windmill St D3
Greek St C3
Green Park ⊖ D3
Green St D2
Greencoat Place F3
Gresham St C6
Greville St B4/C5
Greycoat Hosp Sch E3
Greycoat Place E3
Grosvenor Cres E2
Grosvenor Gardens E2
Grosvenor Place E2
Grosvenor Square D2
Grosvenor St D2
Guards Museum and Chapel E3
Guildhall Art Gallery C6
Guilford St B4
Guy's Hospital [H] D6
Haberdasher St B6
Hackney Rd B7
Half Moon St D2
Halkin St E2
Hall St B5
Hallam St C2
Hampstead Rd B3
Hanover Square C2
Hans Crescent E1
Hanway St C3
Hardwick St B5
Harley St C2
Harrison St B4
Hastings St B4
Hatfields D5
Hay's Galleria D7
Hay's Mews D2
Hayles St F5
Haymarket D3
Hayward Gallery D4
Helmet Row B6
Herbrand St B4
Hercules Rd E4
Hertford St D2
High Holborn C4
Hill St D2
HMS Belfast D7
Hobart Place E2
Holborn ⊖ C4
Holborn C5
Holborn Viaduct C5
Holland St D5
Holmes Museum B1
Holywell Lane B7
Horse Guards' Rd D3
Houndsditch C7
Houses of Parliament E4
Howland St C3
Hoxton Square B7
Hoxton St B7
Hunter St B4
Hunterian Mus C4
Hyde Park D1
Hyde Park Cnr ⊖ E2
Imperial War Museum E5
Inner Circle B2
Ironmonger Row B6
James St C2
James St D4
Jermyn St D3
Jockey's Fields C4
John Carpenter St D5
John St B4
Judd St B4
Kennington Rd E5
King Charles St E4
King St D3
King St D4
King William St C6
King's Coll London D5
King's Cross ⇌ A4
King's Cross Rd B4
King's Cross St Pancras ⊖ A4
King's Rd E2
Kingley St C3
Kingsland Rd B7
Kingsway C4
Kinnerton St E2
Knightsbridge ⊖ E1
Lamb St C7
Lamb's Conduit St C4
Lambeth Bridge F4
Lambeth High St F4
Lambeth North ⊖ E5
Lambeth Palace E4
Lambeth Palace Rd E4
Lambeth Rd E5
Lambeth Walk F4
Lancaster Place D4
Langham Place C2
Leadenhall St C7
Leake St E4
Leather Lane C5
Leicester Sq ⊖ D3
Leicester St D3
Leonard St B6
Lever St B6
Lexington St D3
Lidlington Place A3
Lime St D7
Lincoln's Inn Fields C4
Lindsey St C5
Lisle St D3
Liverpool St C7
Liverpool St ⇌⊖ C7
Lloyd Baker St B5
Lloyd Square B5
Lombard St C6
London Aquarium E4
London Bridge ⇌⊖ D6
London Bridge Hospital [H] D6
London City Hall D7
London Dungeon, The E4
London Guildhall University C6
London Rd E5
London Transport Museum D4
London Wall C6
London Eye ✦ E4
Long Acre D4
Long Lane C5
Longford St B2
Lower Belgrave St E2
Lower Grosvenor Pl E2
Lower Marsh E5
Lower Thames St D6
Lowndes St E2
Ludgate Circus C5
Ludgate Hill C5
Luxborough St C2
Lyall St E2
Macclesfield Rd B6
Madame Tussaud's ✦ B2
Maddox St D2
Malet St C3
Mall, The E3
Manchester Sq C2
Manchester St C2
Mandeville Place C2
Mansell St D7
Mansion House C6
Mansion House ⊖ D6
Maple St C3
Marble Arch ⊖ C1
Marble Arch D1
Marchmont St B4
Margaret St C3
Margery St B5
Mark Lane D7
Marlborough Rd D3
Marshall St C3
Marsham St E3
Marylebone High St C2
Marylebone Lane C2
Marylebone Rd B2
Marylebone St C2
Mecklenburgh Sq B4
Middle Temple La C5
Middlesex St (Petticoat Lane) C7
Midland Rd A3
Minories C7
Monck St E3
Monmouth St C4
Montagu Place C1
Montagu Square C1
Montagu St C4
Montague Place C3
Monument ⊖ D6
Monument St D6
Monument, The ✦ D6
Moor Lane C6
Moorfields C6
Moorfields Eye Hospital [H] B6
Moorgate C6
Moorgate ⇌⊖ C6
Moreland St B5
Morley St E5
Mortimer St C3
Mount Pleasant B5
Mount St D2
Murray Grove A6
Museum of Garden History E4
Museum St C4
Myddelton Square B5
Myddelton St B5
National Gallery D3
National Hospl [H] B4
National Portrait Gallery D3
Neal St C4
Nelson's Column ✦ D4
New Bond St C2/D2
New Bridge St C5
New Cavendish St C2
New Change C6
New Fetter Lane C5
New Inn Yard B7
New North Rd A6
New Oxford St C3
New Scotland Yard E3
New Square C4
Newgate St C5
Newton St C4
Nile St B6
Noble St C6
Noel St C3
North Audley St D2
North Crescent C3
North Row D2
Northampton Sq B5
Northington St B4
Northumberland Avenue D4
Norton Folgate C7
Nottingham Place C2
Obstetric Hosp [H] B3
Old Bailey C5
Old Broad St C6
Old Compton St C3
Old County Hall E4
Old Gloucester St C4
Old King Edward St C6
Old Nichol St B7
Old Paradise St F4
Old Spitalfields Market C7
Old St B6
Old St ⇌⊖ B6
Old Vic E5
Open Air Theatre B2
Operating Theatre Museum D6
Orange St D3
Orchard St C2
Ossulston St A3
Outer Circle B1
Oxford Circus ⊖ C3
Oxford St C2/C3
Paddington St C2
Palace St E3
Pall Mall D3
Pall Mall East D3
Pancras Rd A4
Panton St D3
Paris Garden D5
Park Crescent B2
Park Lane D2
Park Rd B1
Park St D2
Park St D6
Parker St C4
Parliament Square E4
Parliament St E4
Paternoster Square C5
Paul St B6
Pear Tree St B5
Penton Rise B4
Penton St A5
Pentonville Rd A4/A5
Percival St B5
Petticoat Lane (Middlesex St) C7
Petty France E3
Phoenix Place B4
Phoenix Rd A3
Photo Gallery D3
Piccadilly D2
Piccadilly Circus ⊖ D3
Pitfield St B7
Pollock's Toy Museum C3
Polygon Rd A3
Pont St E1
Portland Place C2
Portman Mews C2
Portman Square C2
Portman St C1
Portugal St C4
Postal Mus, The B4
Poultry C6
Primrose St C7
Princes St C6
Procter St C4
Provost St B6
Quaker St B7
Queen Anne St C2
Queen Elizabeth Hall D4
Queen Square B4
Queen St D6
Queen Street Place D6
Queen Victoria St D5
Queens Gallery E3
Radnor St B6
Rathbone Place C3
Rawstorne St B5
Red Lion Square C4
Red Lion St C4
Redchurch St B7
Redcross Way D6
Regency St F3
Regent Square B4
Regent St C3
Regent's Park B2
Richmond Terrace E4
Ridgmount St C3
Rivington St B7
Robert St B2
Rochester Row F3
Ropemaker St C6
Rosebery Avenue B5
Roupell St D5
Royal Academy of Arts D3
Royal Academy of Dramatic Art (RADA) B3
Royal Acad of Music B2
Royal Artillery Memorial ✦ E2
Royal College of Nursing C2
Royal College of Surgeons C4
Royal Festival Hall D4
Royal London Hospital for Integrated Medicine C4
Royal National Theatre D5
Royal National Throat, Nose and Ear Hospital [H] B4
Royal Opera Ho D4
Russell Square B3
Russell Square ⊖ B4
Sackville St D3
Sadlers Wells B5
Saffron Hill C5
St Alban's St D3
St Andrew St C5
St Bartholomew's Hospital [H] C5
St Botolph St C7
St Bride St C5
St George's Circus E5
St George's Rd E5
St Giles High St C3
St James's Palace D3
St James's Park ⊖ E3
St James's St D3
St John St B5
St Margaret St E4
St Mark's Hosp [H] B5
St Martin's Lane D4
St Martin's Le Grand C6
St Mary Axe C7
St Pancras International ⇌ A4
St Paul's ⊖ C6
St Paul's Cath ✝ C6
St Paul's Churchyard C5
St Peter's Hosp [H] D4
St Thomas St D6
St Thomas' Hosp [H] E4
Savile Row D3
Savoy Place D4
Savoy St D4
School of Hygiene & Tropical Medicine C3
Scrutton St B7
Sekforde St B5
Serpentine Rd D1
Seven Dials C4
Seward St B5
Seymour St C1
Shad Thames D7
Shaftesbury Ave D3
Shakespeare's Globe Theatre D6
Shepherd Market D2
Sherwood St D3
Shoe Lane C5
Shoreditch High St B7
Shoreditch High St ⊖ B7
Shorts Gardens C4
Shrek's Adventure ✦ E4
Sidmouth St B4
Silk St C6
Sir John Soane's Museum C4
Skinner St B5
Sloane St E1
Snow Hill C5
Soho Square C3
Somerset House D4
South Audley St D2
South Carriage Dr E1
South Molton St C2
South Place C6
South St D2
Southampton Row C4
Southampton St D4
Southwark ⊖ D5
Southwark Bridge D6
Southwark Bridge Rd D6
Southwark Cath ✝ D6
Southwark St D6
Speakers' Corner D1
Spencer St B5
Spital Square C7
Stamford St D5
Stanhope St B3
Stephenson Way B3
Stock Exchange C5
Stoney St D6
Strand C5
Stratton St D2
Sumner St D5
Sutton's Way B6
Swanfield St B7
Swinton St B4
Tabernacle St B6
Tate Modern D6
Tavistock Place B4
Tavistock Square B3
Tea & Coffee Museum D6
Temple ⊖ D5
Temple Avenue D5
Temple Place D4
Terminus Place E2
Thayer St C2
Theobald's Rd C4
Thorney St F4
Threadneedle St C6
Throgmorton St C6
Tonbridge St B4
Tooley St D7
Torrington Place B3
Tothill St E3
Tottenham Ct Rd B3
Tottenham Ct Rd ⊖ C3
Tottenham St C3
Tower Bridge ✦ D7
Tower Bridge App D7
Tower Bridge Rd E7
Tower Hill D7
Tower Hill ⊖ D7
Tower of London, The D7
Toynbee St C7
Trafalgar Square D3
Trinity Square D7
Trocadero Centre D3
Tudor St D5
Turnmill St C5
Ufford St E5
Union St D5
Univ Coll Hosp [H] B3
University College London (UCL) B3
Univ of London C3
University of Westminster C2
University St B3
Upper Belgrave St E2
Upper Berkeley St C1
Upper Brook St D2
Upper Grosvenor St D2
Upper Ground D5
Upper Montague St C1
Upper St Martin's Lane D4
Upper Thames St D6
Upper Wimpole St C2
Upper Woburn Pl B3
Vere St C2
Vernon Place C4
Vestry St B6
Victoria ⇌⊖ E2
Victoria Emb D4
Victoria Place Shopping Centre F2
Victoria St E3
Villiers St D4
Vincent Square F3
Vinopolis City of Wine D6
Virginia Rd B7
Wakley St B5
Walbrook C6
Wallace Collection C2
Wardour St C3/D3
Warner St B5
Warren St ⊖ B3
Warren St B3
Waterloo ⇌⊖ E5
Waterloo Bridge D4
Waterloo East ⇌ D5
Waterloo Rd E5
Watling St C6
Webber St E5
Welbeck St C2
Wellington Arch ✦ E2
Wellington Mus E2
Wells St C3
Wenlock St A6
Wentworth St C7
West Smithfield C5
West Square E5
Westminster ⊖ E4
Westminster Abbey ✝ E4
Westminster Bridge E4
Westminster Bridge Rd E5
Westminster Cathedral (RC) ✝ E3
Westminster City Hall E3
Westminster Hall E4
Weymouth St C2
Wharf Rd A6
Wharton St B4
Whitcomb St D3
White Cube B7
White Lion Hill D5
White Lion St A5
Whitecross St B6
Whitefriars St C5
Whitehall D4
Whitehall Place D4
Wigmore Hall C2
Wigmore St C2
William IV St D4
Wilmington Square B5
Wilson St C6
Wilton Crescent E2
Wimpole St C2
Windmill Walk D5
Woburn Place B4
Woburn Square B3
Women's Hosp [H] C3
Wood St C6
Woodbridge St B5
Wootton St D5
Wormwood St C7
Worship St B6
Wren St B4
Wynyatt St B5
Young Vic E5
York Rd E4
York St C1
York Terrace East B2
York Terrace West B2
York Way A4

Luton 119

Adelaide St B1
Albert Rd C2
Alma St B2
Alton Rd C3
Anthony Gardens C1
Arthur St C2
Ashburnham Rd B1
Ashton Rd C2
Back St A2
Bailey St C3
Baker St C2
Biscot Rd A1
Bolton Rd B3
Boyle Close A2
Brantwood Rd B1
Bretts Mead C1
Bridge St B2
Brook St A1
Brunswick St A3
Burr St A3
Bury Park Rd A1
Bute St B2
Buxton Rd B2
Cambridge St C3
Cardiff Grove B1
Cardiff Rd B1
Cardigan St A2
Castle St B2/C2
Chapel St C2
Charles St A3
Chase St C2
Cheapside B2
Chequer St C3
Chiltern Rise C1
Church St B2/B3
Cinema A2
Cobden St A3
College A3
Collingdon St A1
Concorde Avenue A3
Corncastle Rd C1
Cowper St C2
Crawley Green Rd B3
Crawley Rd A1
Crescent Rd A3
Crescent Rise A3
Cromwell Rd A1
Cross St A2
Cross Way, The C1
Crown Court B2
Cumberland St B2
Cutenhoe Rd C3
Dallow Rd B1
Downs Rd B1
Dudley St A2
Duke St A2
Dumfries St B1
Dunstable Place B2
Dunstable Rd A1/B1
Edward St A3
Elizabeth St C2
Essex Close C3
Farley Hill C1
Flowers Way B2
Francis St A1
Frederick St A2
Galaxy Leisure Complex A2
George St B2
George St West B2
Gordon St B2
Grove Rd B1
Guildford St A2
Haddon Rd A3
Harcourt St C2
Hart Hill Drive A3
Hart Hill Lane A3
Hartley Rd A3
Hastings St B2
Hat Factory, The B2
Hatters Way A1
Havelock Rd A2
Hibbert St C2
High Town Rd A3
Highbury Rd A1
Hightown Community Sports & Arts Ctr A3
Hillary Crescent C1
Hillborough Rd C1
Hitchin Rd A3
Holly St C2
Holm C1
Hucklesby Way A2
Hunts Close C1
Inkerman St A2
John St B2
Jubilee St A3
Kelvin Close C2
King St B2
Kingsland Rd C3
Larches, The A2
Latimer Rd C2
Lawn Gardens C2
Lea Rd B3
Library B2
Library Rd B2
Library Theatre B2
Liverpool Rd B1
London Rd C2
Luton Station ⇌ A2
Lyndhurst Rd B1
Magistrates Court B2
Mall, The B2
Manchester St B2
Manor Rd B3
Manor Road Park B3
May St C3
Meyrick Avenue C1
Midland Rd A2
Mill St A2
Milton Rd B1
Moor St A1
Moor, The A1
Moorland Gardens A2
Moulton Rise A3
Napier Rd B1
New Bedford Rd A1
New Town St C2
North St A3
Old Bedford Rd A2
Old Orchard C1
Osbourne Rd C3
Oxen Rd A3
Park Square B2
Park St B3/C3
Park St West B2
Park Viaduct B3
Parkland Drive C1
Police Station B1
Pomfret Avenue A3
Pondwicks Rd B3
Post Office A1/B2
Power Court B3
Princess St B1
Red Rails C1
Regent St B2
Reginald St A2
Rothesay Rd B1
Russell Rise C1
Russell St C1
Ruthin Close C1
St Ann's Rd B3
St George's Square B2
St Mary's B3
St Marys Rd B3
St Paul's Rd C2
St Saviour's Cres C1
Salisbury Rd B1
Seymour Avenue C3
Seymour Rd C3
Silver St B2
South Rd C2
Stanley St B1
Station Rd A2
Stockwood Cres C2
Stockwood Park C1
Strathmore Ave C2
Stuart St B2
Studley Rd A1
Surrey St C3
Sutherland Place C1
Tavistock St C2
Taylor St A3
Telford Way A1
Tennyson Rd C2
Tenzing Grove C1
Thistle Rd B3
Town Hall B2
Townsley Close C2
UK Centre for Carnival Arts ✦ B3
Union St B2
University of Bedfordshire B3
Upper George St B2
Vicarage St B3
Villa Rd A2
Waldeck Rd A1
Wardown Ho Mus & Gallery A2
Wellington St B1/B2
Wenlock St A2
Whitby Rd A1
Whitehill Avenue C1
William St A2
Wilsden Avenue C1
Windmill Rd B3
Windsor St C2
Winsdon Rd B1
York St A3

Manchester 119

Adair St B6
Addington St A5
Adelphi St A1
Advent Way B6
Albert Square B3
Albion St C3
Ancoats Grove B6
Ancoats Grove N B6
Angela St C2
Aquatics Centre C4
Ardwick Gn North C5
Ardwick Green Pk C5
Ardwick Gn South C5
Arlington St A2
Artillery St B3
Arundel St C2
Atherton St B2
Atkinson St B3
Aytoun St B4
Back Piccadilly A4
Baird St B5
Balloon St A4
Bank Place A1
Baring St B5
Barrack St C1
Barrow St A1
Bendix St A5
Bengal St A5
Berry St C5
Blackfriars Rd A3
Blackfriars St A3
Blantyre St C2
Bloom St B4
Blossom St A5
Boad St B5
Bombay St B4
Booth St A3
Booth St B4
Bootle St B3
Brazennose St B3
Brewer St A5
Bridge St A3
Bridgewater Hall B3
Bridgewater Place A4
Bridgewater St B2
Brook St C4
Brotherton Drive A2
Brown St A3
Brown St B4
Brunswick St C6
Brydon Avenue C6
Buddhist Centre A4
Bury St A2
Bus & Coach Sta B4
Bus Station B4
Butler St A6
Buxton St C5
Byrom St B3
Cable St A5
Cambridge St C3/C4
Camp St B3
Canal St B4
Cannon St A1
Cardroom Rd A6
Carruthers St A6
Castle St C2
Castlefield Arena B2
Cateaton St A3
Cathedral ✝ A3
Cathedral St A3
Cavendish St C4
Chapel St A1/A3
Chapeltown St B5
Charles St C4
Charlotte St B4
Chatham St B4
Chepstow St B3
Chester Rd C1/C2
Chester St C4
Chetham's Sch of Music A3
China Lane B5
Chippenham Rd A6
Chorlton Rd C2
Chorlton St B4
Church St A2
Church St A4
City Park A4
City Rd East C3
Civil Justice Ctr B2
Cleminson St A2
Clowes St A3
College Land A3
Collier St B2
Commercial St C3
Conference Centre C4
Cooper St B4
Copperas St A4

Nottingham 122

Oxford 123

Peterborough 123

Plymouth 123

Poole 123

Portsmouth 123

Preston 123

Reading 124

Salisbury 124

Scarborough 124

Sheffield 124

Southampton 124

Southend-on-Sea 125

Stoke-on-Trent (Hanley) 125

Stratford-upon-Avon 125

Sunderland 125

Index to road maps of Britain

Abbreviations used in the index

Aberdeen	**Aberdeen City**
Aberds	**Aberdeenshire**
Ald	**Alderney**
Anglesey	**Isle of Anglesey**
Angus	**Angus**
Argyll	**Argyll and Bute**
Bath	**Bath and North East Somerset**
BCP	**Bournemouth, Christchurch and Poole**
Bedford	**Bedford**
Bl Gwent	**Blaenau Gwent**
Blackburn	**Blackburn with Darwen**
Blackpool	**Blackpool**
Borders	**Scottish Borders**
Brack	**Bracknell**
Bridgend	**Bridgend**
Brighton	**City of Brighton and Hove**
Bristol	**City and County of Bristol**
Bucks	**Buckinghamshire**
C Beds	**Central Bedfordshire**
Caerph	**Caerphilly**
Cambs	**Cambridgeshire**
Cardiff	**Cardiff**
Carms	**Carmarthenshire**
Ceredig	**Ceredigion**
Ches E	**Cheshire East**
Ches W	**Cheshire West and Chester**
Clack	**Clackmannanshire**
Conwy	**Conwy**
Corn	**Cornwall**
Cumb	**Cumberland**
Darl	**Darlington**
Denb	**Denbighshire**
Derby	**City of Derby**
Derbys	**Derbyshire**
Devon	**Devon**
Dorset	**Dorset**
Dumfries	**Dumfries and Galloway**
Dundee	**Dundee City**
Durham	**Durham**
E Ayrs	**East Ayrshire**
E Dunb	**East Dunbartonshire**
E Loth	**East Lothian**
E Renf	**East Renfrewshire**
E Sus	**East Sussex**
E Yorks	**East Riding of Yorkshire**
Edin	**City of Edinburgh**
Essex	**Essex**
Falk	**Falkirk**
Fife	**Fife**
Flint	**Flintshire**
Glasgow	**City of Glasgow**
Glos	**Gloucestershire**
Gtr Man	**Greater Manchester**
Guern	**Guernsey**
Gwyn	**Gwynedd**
Halton	**Halton**
Hants	**Hampshire**
Hereford	**Herefordshire**
Herts	**Hertfordshire**
Highld	**Highland**
Hrtlpl	**Hartlepool**
Hull	**Hull**
Invclyd	**Inverclyde**
IoM	**Isle of Man**
IoW	**Isle of Wight**
Jersey	**Jersey**
Kent	**Kent**
Lancs	**Lancashire**
Leicester	**City of Leicester**
Leics	**Leicestershire**
Lincs	**Lincolnshire**
London	**Greater London**
Luton	**Luton**
M Keynes	**Milton Keynes**
M Tydf	**Merthyr Tydfil**
Mbro	**Middlesbrough**
Medway	**Medway**
Mers	**Merseyside**
Midloth	**Midlothian**
Mon	**Monmouthshire**
Moray	**Moray**
N Ayrs	**North Ayrshire**
N Lanark	**North Lanarkshire**
N Lincs	**North Lincolnshire**
N Nhants	**North Northamptonshire**
N Som	**North Somerset**
N Yorks	**North Yorkshire**
NE Lincs	**North East Lincolnshire**
Neath	**Neath Port Talbot**
Newport	**City and County of Newport**
Norf	**Norfolk**
Northumb	**Northumberland**
Nottingham	**City of Nottingham**
Notts	**Nottinghamshire**
Orkney	**Orkney**
Oxon	**Oxfordshire**
Pboro	**Peterborough**
Pembs	**Pembrokeshire**
Perth	**Perth and Kinross**
Plym	**Plymouth**
Powys	**Powys**
Ptsmth	**Portsmouth**
Reading	**Reading**
Redcar	**Redcar and Cleveland**
Renfs	**Renfrewshire**
Rhondda	**Rhondda Cynon Taff**
Rutland	**Rutland**
S Ayrs	**South Ayrshire**
S Glos	**South Gloucestershire**
S Lanark	**South Lanarkshire**
S Yorks	**South Yorkshire**
Scilly	**Scilly**
Shetland	**Shetland**
Shrops	**Shropshire**
Slough	**Slough**
Som	**Somerset**
Soton	**Southampton**
Southend	**Southend-on-Sea**
Staffs	**Staffordshire**
Stirling	**Stirling**
Stockton	**Stockton-on-Tees**
Stoke	**Stoke-on-Trent**
Suff	**Suffolk**
Sur	**Surrey**
Swansea	**Swansea**
Swindon	**Swindon**
T&W	**Tyne and Wear**
Telford	**Telford and Wrekin**
Thurrock	**Thurrock**
Torbay	**Torbay**
Torf	**Torfaen**
V Glam	**The Vale of Glamorgan**
W Berks	**West Berkshire**
W Dunb	**West Dunbartonshire**
W Isles	**Western Isles**
W Loth	**West Lothian**
W Mid	**West Midlands**
W Nhants	**West Northamptonshire**
W Sus	**West Sussex**
W Yorks	**West Yorkshire**
W&F	**Westmorland and Furness**
Warks	**Warwickshire**
Warr	**Warrington**
Wilts	**Wiltshire**
Windsor	**Windsor and Maidenhead**
Wokingham	**Wokingham**
Worcs	**Worcestershire**
Wrex	**Wrexham**
York	**City of York**

How to use the index

Example **Thornton-le-Beans** N Yorks **58** G4

- grid square
- page number
- county or unitary authority

A

Austrey Warks 35 E8
Austwick N Yorks 50 C3
Authorpe Lincs 47 D8
Authorpe Row Lincs 47 E9
Avebury Wilts 17 E8
Aveley Thurrock 20 C2
Avening Glos 16 B5
Averham Notts 45 G11
Aveton Gifford Devon 5 G7
Avielochan Highld 81 B11
Aviemore Highld 81 B10
Avington Hants 10 A4
Avington W Berks 17 E10
Avoch Highld 87 F10
Avon Hants 9 E10
Avon Dassett Warks 27 D11
Avonbridge Falk 69 C8
Avonmouth Bristol 15 D11
Avonwick Devon 5 F8
Awbridge Hants 10 B2
Awhirk Dumfries 54 D3
Awkley S Glos 16 C2
Awliscombe Devon 7 F10
Awre Glos 26 H4
Awsworth Notts 35 A10
Axbridge Som 15 F10
Axford Hants 18 G3
Axford Wilts 17 D9
Axminster Devon 8 E1
Axmouth Devon 8 E1
Axton Flint 42 D4
Aycliff Kent 21 G10
Aycliffe Durham 58 D3
Aydon Northumb 62 G6
Aylburton Glos 16 A3
Ayle Northumb 57 B9
Aylesbeare Devon 7 G9
Aylesbury Bucks 28 G5
Aylesby NE Lincs 46 B6
Aylesford Kent 20 F4
Aylesham Kent 21 F9
Aylestone Leicester 36 E1
Aylmerton Norf 39 B7
Aylsham Norf 39 C7
Aylton Hereford 26 E3
Aymestrey Hereford 25 B11
Aynho W Nhants 28 E2
Ayot St Lawrence Herts 29 G8
Ayot St Peter Herts 29 G9
Ayr S Ayrs 66 D6
Aysgarth N Yorks 58 H1
Ayside W&F 49 A3
Ayston Rutland 36 E4
Aythorpe Roding Essex 30 G2
Ayton Borders 71 D8
Aywick Shetland 96 E7
Azerley N Yorks 51 B8

B

Babbacombe Torbay 5 E10
Babbinswood Shrops 33 B9
Babcary Som 8 B4
Babel Carms 24 E5
Babell Flint 42 E4
Babraham Cambs 30 C2
Babworth Notts 45 D10
Bac W Isles 91 C9
Bachau Anglesey 40 B6
Back of Keppoch Highld 79 C9
Back Rogerton E Ayrs 67 D8
Backaland Orkney 95 E6
Backaskaill Orkney 95 C5
Backbarrow W&F 49 A3
Backe Carms 23 E7
Backfolds Aberds 89 C10
Backford Ches W 43 E7
Backford Cross Ches W 43 E6
Backhill Aberds 89 E10
Backhill Aberds 89 E7
Backhill of Clackriach Aberds 89 D9
Backhill of Fortree Aberds 89 D9
Backhill of Trustach Aberds 83 D8
Backies Highld 93 J11
Backlass Highld 94 E4
Backwell N Som 15 E10
Backworth T&W 63 F9
Bacon End Essex 30 G3
Baconsthorpe Norf 39 B7
Bacton Hereford 25 E10
Bacton Norf 39 B9
Bacton Suff 31 B7
Bacton Green Suff 31 B7
Bacup Lancs 50 G4
Badachro Highld 85 A12
Badanloch Lodge Highld 93 F10
Badavanich Highld 86 F4
Badbury Swindon 17 C8
Badby W Nhants 28 C2
Badcall Highld 92 D5
Badcaul Highld 86 B3
Baddeley Green Stoke 44 G3
Baddesley Clinton Warks 27 A9
Baddesley Ensor Warks 35 F8
Baddidarach Highld 92 G3
Baddoch Aberds 82 E3
Baddock Highld 87 F10
Badenscoth Aberds 89 E7
Badenyon Aberds 82 B5
Badger Shrops 34 F3
Badger's Mount Kent 19 E11
Badgeworth Glos 26 G6
Badgworth Som 15 F9
Badicaul Highld 85 F12
Badingham Suff 31 B10
Badlesmere Kent 21 F7
Badlipster Highld 94 F4
Badluarach Highld 86 B2
Badminton S Glos 16 C5
Badnaban Highld 92 G3
Badninish Highld 87 B10
Badrallach Highld 86 B3
Badsey Worcs 27 D7
Badshot Lea Sur 18 G5
Badsworth W Yorks 45 A8
Badwell Ash Suff 30 B6
Bae Colwyn = Colwyn Bay Conwy 41 C10
Bag Enderby Lincs 47 E7
Bagby N Yorks 51 A10
Bagendon Glos 27 H7
Bagh a Chaisteil = Castlebay W Isles 84 J1
Bagh Mor W Isles 84 C3
Bagh Shiarabhagh W Isles 84 H2
Baghasdal W Isles 84 G2
Bagillt Flint 42 E5
Baginton Warks 27 A10
Baglan Neath 14 B3
Bagley Shrops 33 C10
Bagnall Staffs 44 G3
Bagnor W Berks 17 E11
Bagshot Sur 18 E6
Bagshot Wilts 17 E10
Bagthorpe Norf 38 B3
Bagthorpe Notts 45 G8
Bagworth Leics 35 E10
Bagwy Llydiart Hereford 25 F11
Bail àrd Bhuirgh W Isles 91 B9
Bail' Iochdrach W Isles 84 C3
Bail Uachdraich W Isles 84 B3
Bail' Ur Tholastaidh W Isles 91 C10
Baildon W Yorks 51 F7
Baile W Isles 90 J4
Baile a Mhanaich W Isles 84 C2
Baile Ailein W Isles 91 E7
Baile an Truiseil W Isles 91 B8
Baile Boidheach Argyll 72 F6
Baile Glas W Isles 84 C3
Baile Mhartainn W Isles 84 A2
Baile Mhic Phail W Isles 84 A3
Baile Mor Argyll 78 J5
Baile Mor W Isles 84 B2
Baile na Creige W Isles 84 H1
Baile nan Cailleach W Isles 84 C2
Baile Raghaill W Isles 84 A2
Bailebeag Highld 81 B7
Baileyhead Cumb 61 F11
Bailiesward Aberds 88 E4
Baillieston Glasgow 68 D5
Bainbridge N Yorks 57 G11
Bainsford Falk 69 B7
Bainshole Aberds 88 E6
Bainton E Yorks 52 D5
Bainton Pboro 37 E6
Bairnkine Borders 62 B2
Baker Street Thurrock 20 C3
Baker's End Herts 29 G10
Bakewell Derbys 44 F6
Bala = Y Bala Gwyn 32 B5
Balachuirn Highld 85 D10
Balavil Highld 81 C9
Balbeg Highld 81 A6
Balbeg Highld 86 H7
Balbeggie Perth 76 E4
Balbithan Aberds 83 B9
Balbithan Ho. Aberds 83 B10
Balblair Highld 87 B8
Balblair Highld 87 E10
Balby S Yorks 45 B9
Balchladich Highld 92 F3
Balchraggan Highld 87 G8
Balchraggan Highld 87 H8
Balchrick Highld 92 D4
Balchrystie Fife 77 G7
Balcladaich Highld 80 A4
Balcombe W Sus 12 C2
Balcombe Lane W Sus 12 C2
Balcomie Fife 77 F9
Balcurvie Fife 76 G6
Baldersby N Yorks 51 B9
Baldersby St James N Yorks 51 B9
Balderstone Lancs 50 F2
Balderton Ches W 42 F6
Balderton Notts 46 G2
Baldhu Corn 3 E6
Baldinnie Fife 77 F7
Baldock Herts 29 E9
Baldovie Dundee 77 D7
Baldrine IoM 48 D4
Baldslow E Sus 13 E6
Baldwin IoM 48 D3
Baldwinholme Cumb 56 A5
Baldwin's Gate Staffs 34 A3
Bale Norf 38 B6
Balearn Aberds 89 C10
Balemartine Argyll 78 G2
Balephuil Argyll 78 G2
Balerno Edin 69 D10
Balevullin Argyll 78 G2
Balfield Angus 83 G7
Balfour Orkney 95 G5
Balfron Stirling 68 B4
Balfron Station Stirling 68 B4
Balgaveny Aberds 89 D6
Balgavies Angus 77 B8
Balgonar Fife 69 A9
Balgove Aberds 89 E8
Balgowan Highld 81 D8
Balgown Highld 85 B8
Balgrochan E Dunb 68 C5
Balgy Highld 85 C13
Balhaldie Stirling 75 G11
Balhalgardy Aberds 83 A9
Balham London 19 D9
Balhary Perth 76 C5
Baliasta Shetland 96 C8
Baligill Highld 93 C11
Balintore Angus 76 B5
Balintore Highld 87 D11
Balintraid Highld 87 D10
Balk N Yorks 51 A10
Balkeerie Angus 76 C6
Balkemback Angus 76 D6
Balkholme E Yorks 52 G3
Balkissock S Ayrs 54 A4
Ball Shrops 33 C9
Ball Haye Green Staffs 44 G3
Ball Hill Hants 17 E11
Ballabeg IoM 48 E2
Ballacannel IoM 48 D4
Ballachulish Highld 74 B3
Ballajora IoM 48 C4
Ballaleigh IoM 48 D3
Ballamodha IoM 48 E2
Ballantrae S Ayrs 54 A3
Ballaquine IoM 48 D4
Ballards Gore Essex 20 B6
Ballasalla IoM 48 C3
Ballasalla IoM 48 E2
Ballater Aberds 82 D5
Ballaugh IoM 48 C3
Ballaveare IoM 48 E3
Ballcorach Moray 82 A3
Ballechin Perth 76 B2
Balleigh Highld 87 C10
Ballencrieff E Loth 70 C3
Ballentoul Perth 81 G10
Ballidon Derbys 44 G6
Balliemore Argyll 73 E9
Balliemore Argyll 79 J11
Ballikinrain Stirling 68 B4
Ballimeanoch Argyll 73 B9
Ballimore Argyll 73 E8
Ballimore Stirling 75 F8
Ballinaby Argyll 64 B3
Ballindean Perth 76 E5
Ballingdon Suff 30 D5
Ballinger Common Bucks 18 A6
Ballingham Hereford 26 E2
Ballingry Fife 76 H4
Ballinlick Perth 76 C2
Ballinluig Perth 76 B2
Ballintuim Perth 76 B4
Balloch Angus 76 B6
Balloch Highld 87 G10
Balloch N Lanark 68 C6
Balloch W Dunb 68 B2
Ballochan Aberds 83 D7
Ballochford Moray 88 E3
Ballochmorrie S Ayrs 54 A5
Balls Cross W Sus 11 B8
Balls Green Essex 31 F7
Ballygown Argyll 78 G7
Ballygrant Argyll 64 B4
Ballyhaugh Argyll 78 F4
Balmacara Highld 85 F13
Balmacara Square Highld 85 F13
Balmaclellan Dumfries 55 B9
Balmacneil Perth 76 B2
Balmacqueen Highld 85 A9
Balmae Dumfries 55 E9
Balmaha Stirling 68 A3
Balmalcolm Fife 76 G6
Balmeanach Highld 85 D10
Balmedie Aberds 83 B11
Balmer Heath Shrops 33 B10
Balmerino Fife 76 E6
Balmerlawn Hants 10 D2
Balmichael N Ayrs 66 C2
Balmirmer Angus 77 D8
Balmore Highld 85 D7
Balmore Highld 86 H6
Balmore Highld 87 G11
Balmore Perth 76 B2
Balmule Fife 69 B11
Balmullo Fife 77 E7
Balmungie Highld 87 F10
Balnaboth Angus 82 G5
Balnabruaich Highld 87 E10
Balnabruich Highld 94 H3
Balnacoil Highld 93 H11
Balnacra Highld 86 G2
Balnafoich Highld 87 H9
Balnagall Highld 87 C11
Balnaguard Perth 76 B2
Balnahard Argyll 72 D3
Balnahard Argyll 78 H7
Balnain Highld 86 H7
Balnakeil Highld 92 C6
Balnaknock Highld 85 B9
Balnapaling Highld 87 E10
Balne N Yorks 52 H1
Balochroy Argyll 65 C8
Balone Fife 77 F7
Balornock Glasgow 68 D5
Balquharn Perth 76 D3
Balquhidder Stirling 75 E8
Balsall W Mid 35 H8
Balsall Common W Mid 35 H8
Balsall Hth. W Mid 35 G6
Balscott Oxon 27 D10
Balsham Cambs 30 C2
Baltasound Shetland 96 C8
Balterley Staffs 43 G10
Baltersan Dumfries 55 C7
Balthangie Aberds 89 C8
Baltonsborough Som 8 A4
Balvaird Highld 87 F8
Balvicar Argyll 72 B6
Balvraid Highld 85 G13
Balvraid Highld 87 H11
Bamber Bridge Lancs 50 G1
Bambers Green Essex 30 F2
Bamburgh Northumb 71 G10
Bamff Perth 76 B5
Bamford Derbys 44 D6
Bamford Gtr Man 44 A2
Bampton Devon 7 D8
Bampton Oxon 17 A10
Bampton W&F 57 E7
Bampton Grange W&F 57 E7
Banavie Highld 80 F3
Banbury Oxon 27 D11
Bancffosfelen Carms 23 E9
Banchory Aberds 83 D8
Banchory-Devenick Aberds 83 C11
Bancycapel Carms 23 E9
Bancyfelin Carms 23 E8
Bancyffordd Carms 23 C9
Bandirran Perth 76 D5
Banff Aberds 89 B6
Bangor Gwyn 41 C7
Bangor-is-ycoed = Bangor-on-Dee Wrex 43 H6
Banham Norf 39 G6
Bank Hants 10 D1
Bank Newton N Yorks 50 D5
Bank Street Worcs 26 B3
Bankend Dumfries 60 G6
Bankfoot Perth 76 D3
Bankglen E Ayrs 67 E9
Bankhead Aberdeen 83 B10
Bankhead Aberds 83 C8
Banknock Falk 68 C6
Banks Cumb 61 G11
Banks Lancs 49 G3
Bankshill Dumfries 61 E7
Banningham Norf 39 C8
Banniskirk Ho. Highld 94 E3
Bannister Green Essex 30 F3
Bannockburn Stirling 69 A7
Banstead Sur 19 F9
Bantham Devon 5 G7
Banton N Lanark 68 C6
Banwell N Som 15 F9
Banyard's Green Suff 31 A9
Bapchild Kent 20 E6
Bar Hill Cambs 29 B10
Barabhas W Isles 91 C8
Barabhas Iarach W Isles 91 C8
Barabhas Uarach W Isles 91 B8
Barachandroman Argyll 79 J9
Barassie S Ayrs 66 C6
Baravullin Argyll 79 H11
Barbaraville Highld 87 D10
Barber Booth Derbys 44 D5
Barbieston S Ayrs 67 E7
Barbon W&F 50 A2
Barbridge Ches E 43 G9
Barbrook Devon 6 B6
Barby W Nhants 28 A2
Barcaldine Argyll 74 C2
Barcheston Warks 27 E9
Barcombe E Sus 12 E3
Barcombe Cross E Sus 12 E3
Barden N Yorks 58 G2
Barden Scale N Yorks 51 D6
Bardennoch Dumfries 67 G8
Bardfield Saling Essex 30 F3
Bardister Shetland 96 F5
Bardney Lincs 46 F5
Bardon Leics 35 D10
Bardon Mill Northumb 62 G3
Bardowie E Dunb 68 C4
Bardrainney Invclyd 68 C2
Bardsea W&F 49 B3
Bardsey W Yorks 51 E9
Bardwell Suff 30 A6
Bare Lancs 49 C4
Barfad Argyll 73 G7
Barford Norf 39 E7
Barford Warks 27 B9
Barford St John Oxon 27 E11
Barford St Martin Wilts 9 A9
Barford St Michael Oxon 27 E11
Barfrestone Kent 21 F9
Bargod = Bargoed Caerph 15 B7
Bargoed = Bargod Caerph 15 B7
Bargrennan Dumfries 54 B6
Barham Cambs 37 H7
Barham Kent 21 F9
Barham Suff 31 C8
Barharrow Dumfries 55 D9
Barhill Dumfries 55 C11
Barholm Lincs 37 D6
Barkby Leics 36 E2
Barkestone-le-Vale Leics 36 B3
Barkham Wokingham 18 E4
Barking London 19 C11
Barking Suff 31 C7
Barking Tye Suff 31 C7
Barkingside London 19 C11
Barkisland W Yorks 51 H6
Barkston Lincs 36 A5
Barkston N Yorks 51 F10
Barkway Herts 29 E10
Barlaston Staffs 34 B4
Barlavington W Sus 11 C8
Barlborough Derbys 45 E8
Barlby N Yorks 52 F2
Barlestone Leics 35 E10
Barley Herts 29 E10
Barley Lancs 50 E4
Barley Mow T&W 58 A3
Barleythorpe Rutland 36 E4
Barling Essex 20 C6
Barlow Derbys 45 E7
Barlow N Yorks 52 G2
Barlow T&W 63 G7
Barmby Moor E Yorks 52 E3
Barmby on the Marsh E Yorks 52 G2
Barmer Norf 38 B4
Barmoor Castle Northumb 71 G8
Barmoor Lane End Northumb 71 G9
Barmouth = Abermaw Gwyn 32 D2
Barmpton Darl 58 E4
Barmston E Yorks 53 D7
Barnack Pboro 37 E6
Barnacle Warks 35 G9
Barnard Castle Durham 58 E1
Barnard Gate Oxon 27 G11
Barnardiston Suff 30 D4
Barnbarroch Dumfries 55 D11
Barnburgh S Yorks 45 B8
Barnby Suff 39 G10
Barnby Dun S Yorks 45 B10
Barnby in the Willows Notts 46 G2
Barnby Moor Notts 45 D10
Barnes Street Kent 20 G3
Barnet London 19 B9
Barnetby le Wold N Lincs 46 B4
Barney Norf 38 B5
Barnham Suff 38 H4
Barnham W Sus 11 D8
Barnham Broom Norf 39 E6
Barnhead Angus 77 B9
Barnhill Ches W 43 G7
Barnhill Dundee 77 D7
Barnhill Moray 88 C1
Barnhills Dumfries 54 B2
Barningham Durham 58 E1
Barningham Suff 38 H5
Barnoldby le Beck NE Lincs 46 B6
Barnoldswick Lancs 50 E4
Barns Green W Sus 11 B10
Barnsley Glos 27 H7
Barnsley S Yorks 45 B7
Barnstaple Devon 6 C4
Barnston Essex 30 G3
Barnston Mers 42 D5
Barnstone Notts 36 B3
Barnt Green Worcs 27 A7
Barnton Ches W 43 E9
Barnton Edin 69 C10
Barnwell All Saints N Nhants 36 G6
Barnwell St Andrew N Nhants 36 G6
Barnwood Glos 26 G5
Barochreal Argyll 79 J11
Barons Cross Hereford 25 C11
Barr S Ayrs 66 G5
Barra Castle Aberds 83 A9
Barrachan Dumfries 54 E6
Barrack Aberds 89 D8
Barraglom W Isles 90 D6
Barrahormid Argyll 72 E6
Barran Argyll 79 J11
Barrapol Argyll 78 G2
Barras Aberds 83 E10
Barras W&F 57 E10
Barrasford Northumb 62 F5
Barravullin Argyll 73 C7
Barregarrow IoM 48 D3
Barrhead E Renf 68 E3
Barrhill S Ayrs 54 A5
Barrington Cambs 29 D10
Barrington Som 8 C2
Barripper Corn 2 F5
Barrmill N Ayrs 67 A6
Barrock Highld 94 C4
Barrock Ho. Highld 94 D4
Barrow Lancs 50 F3
Barrow Rutland 36 D4
Barrow Suff 30 B4
Barrow Green Kent 20 E6
Barrow Gurney N Som 15 E11
Barrow Haven N Lincs 53 G6
Barrow-in-Furness W&F 49 C2
Barrow Island W&F 49 C1
Barrow Nook Lancs 43 B7
Barrow Street Wilts 9 A7
Barrow upon Humber N Lincs 53 G6
Barrow upon Soar Leics 36 D1
Barrow upon Trent Derbys 35 C9
Barroway Drove Norf 38 E1
Barrowburn Northumb 62 B4
Barrowby Lincs 36 B4
Barrowcliff N Yorks 59 H11
Barrowden Rutland 36 E5
Barrowford Lancs 50 F4
Barrows Green Ches E 43 G9
Barrows Green W&F 57 H7
Barrow's Green Mers 43 D8
Barry Angus 77 D8
Barry = Y Barri V Glam 15 E7
Barry Island V Glam 15 E7
Barsby Leics 36 D2
Barsham Suff 39 G9
Barston W Mid 35 H8
Bartestree Hereford 26 D2
Barthol Chapel Aberds 89 E8
Barthomley Ches E 43 G10
Bartley Hants 10 C2
Bartley Green W Mid 34 G6
Bartlow Cambs 30 D2
Barton Cambs 29 C11
Barton Ches W 43 G7
Barton Glos 27 F8
Barton Lancs 42 B6
Barton Lancs 49 F5
Barton N Yorks 58 F3
Barton Oxon 28 H2
Barton Torbay 5 E10
Barton Warks 27 C8
Barton Bendish Norf 38 E3
Barton Hartshorn Bucks 28 E3
Barton in Fabis Notts 35 B11
Barton in the Beans Leics 35 E9
Barton-le-Clay C Beds 29 E7
Barton-le-Street N Yorks 52 B3
Barton-le-Willows N Yorks 52 C3
Barton Mills Suff 30 A4
Barton on Sea Hants 9 E11
Barton on the Heath Warks 27 E9
Barton St David Som 8 A4
Barton Seagrave N Nhants 36 H4
Barton Stacey Hants 17 G11
Barton Turf Norf 39 C9
Barton-under-Needwood Staffs 35 D7
Barton-upon-Humber N Lincs 52 G6
Barton Waterside N Lincs 52 G6
Barugh S Yorks 45 B7
Barway Cambs 37 H11
Barwell Leics 35 F10
Barwick Herts 29 G10
Barwick Som 8 C4
Barwick in Elmet W Yorks 51 F9
Baschurch Shrops 33 C10
Bascote Warks 27 B11
Basford Green Staffs 44 G3
Bashall Eaves Lancs 50 E2
Bashley Hants 9 E11
Basildon Essex 20 C4
Basingstoke Hants 18 F3
Baslow Derbys 44 E6
Bason Bridge Som 15 G9
Bassaleg Newport 15 C8
Bassenthwaite Cumb 56 C4
Bassett Soton 10 C3
Bassingbourn Cambs 29 D10
Bassingfield Notts 36 B2
Bassingham Lincs 46 F3
Bassingthorpe Lincs 36 C5
Basta Shetland 96 D7
Baston Lincs 37 D7
Bastwick Norf 39 D10
Baswick Steer E Yorks 53 E6
Batchworth Heath Herts 19 B7
Batcombe Dorset 8 D5
Batcombe Som 16 H3
Bate Heath Ches E 43 E9
Batford Herts 29 G8
Bath Bath 16 E4
Bathampton Bath 16 E4
Bathealton Som 7 D9
Batheaston Bath 16 E4
Bathford Bath 16 E4
Bathgate W Loth 69 D8
Bathley Notts 45 G11
Bathpool Corn 4 D3
Bathpool Som 8 B1
Bathville W Loth 69 D8
Batley W Yorks 51 G8
Batsford Glos 27 E8
Battersby N Yorks 59 F6
Battersea London 19 D9
Battisborough Cross Devon 5 G6
Battisford Suff 31 C7
Battisford Tye Suff 31 C7
Battle E Sus 12 E6
Battle Powys 25 E7
Battledown Glos 26 F6
Battlefield Shrops 33 D11
Battlesbridge Essex 20 B4
Battlesden C Beds 28 F6
Battlesea Green Suff 39 H8
Battleton Som 7 D8
Battram Leics 35 E10
Battramsley Hants 10 E2
Baughton Worcs 26 D5
Baughurst Hants 18 F2
Baulking Oxon 17 B10
Baumber Lincs 46 E6
Baunton Glos 17 A7
Baverstock Wilts 9 A9
Bawburgh Norf 39 E7
Bawdeswell Norf 38 C6
Bawdrip Som 15 H9
Bawdsey Suff 31 D10
Bawtry S Yorks 45 C10
Baxenden Lancs 50 G3
Baxterley Warks 35 F8
Baybridge Hants 10 B4
Baycliff W&F 49 B2
Baydon Wilts 17 D9
Bayford Herts 29 H10
Bayford Som 8 B6
Bayles W&F 57 B9
Baylham Suff 31 C8
Baynard's Green Oxon 28 F2
Bayston Hill Shrops 33 E10
Baythorn End Essex 30 D4
Bayton Worcs 26 A3
Beach Highld 79 F10
Beachampton Bucks 28 E4
Beachamwell Norf 38 E3
Beachans Moray 87 G13
Beacharr Argyll 65 D7
Beachborough Kent 21 H8
Beachley Glos 16 B2
Beacon Devon 7 F10
Beacon End Essex 30 F6
Beacon Hill Sur 18 H5
Beacon's Bottom Bucks 18 B4
Beaconsfield Bucks 18 C6
Beacrabhaic W Isles 90 H6
Beadlam N Yorks 52 A2
Beadlow C Beds 29 E8
Beadnell Northumb 71 H11
Beaford Devon 6 E4
Beal N Yorks 51 G11
Beal Northumb 71 F9
Beamhurst Staffs 35 B6
Beaminster Dorset 8 D3
Beamish Durham 58 A3
Beamsley N Yorks 51 D6
Bean Kent 20 D2
Beanacre Wilts 16 E6
Beanley Northumb 62 B6
Beaquoy Orkney 95 F4
Bear Cross BCP 9 E9
Beardwood Blackburn 50 G2
Beare Green Sur 19 G8
Bearley Warks 27 B8
Bearnus Argyll 78 G6
Bearpark Durham 58 B3
Bearsbridge Northumb 62 H3
Bearsden E Dunb 68 C4
Bearsted Kent 20 F4
Bearstone Shrops 34 B3
Bearwood Hereford 25 C10
Bearwood BCP 9 E9
Bearwood W Mid 34 G6
Beattock Dumfries 60 C6
Beauchamp Roding Essex 30 G2
Beauchief S Yorks 45 D7
Beaufort Bl Gwent 25 G8
Beaufort Castle Highld 87 G8
Beaulieu Hants 10 D2
Beauly Highld 87 G8
Beaumaris = Biwmares Anglesey 41 C8
Beaumont Cumb 61 H9
Beaumont Essex 31 F8
Beaumont Hill Darl 58 E3
Beausale Warks 27 A9
Beauworth Hants 10 B4
Beaworthy Devon 6 G3
Beazley End Essex 30 F4
Bebington Mers 42 D6
Bebside Northumb 63 E8
Beccles Suff 39 F10
Becconsall Lancs 49 G4
Beck Foot W&F 57 G8
Beck Hole N Yorks 59 F9
Beck Row Suff 38 H2
Beck Side W&F 49 A2
Beckbury Shrops 34 E3
Beckenham London 19 E10
Beckermet Cumb 56 F2
Beckfoot Cumb 56 B2
Beckfoot Cumb 56 F3
Beckford Worcs 26 E6
Beckhampton Wilts 17 E7
Beckingham Lincs 46 G2
Beckingham Notts 45 D11
Beckington Som 16 F5
Beckley E Sus 13 D7
Beckley Hants 9 E11
Beckley Oxon 28 G2
Beckton London 19 C11
Beckwithshaw N Yorks 51 D8
Becontree London 19 C11
Bed-y-coedwr Gwyn 32 C3
Bedale N Yorks 58 H3
Bedburn Durham 58 C2
Bedchester Dorset 9 C7
Beddau Rhondda 14 C6
Beddgelert Gwyn 41 F7
Beddingham E Sus 12 F3
Beddington London 19 E10
Bedfield Suff 31 B9
Bedford Bedford 29 C7
Bedham W Sus 11 B9
Bedhampton Hants 10 D6
Bedingfield Suff 31 B8
Bedlam N Yorks 51 C8
Bedlington Northumb 63 E8
Bedlington Station Northumb 63 E8
Bedlinog M Tydf 14 A6
Bedminster Bristol 16 D2
Bedmond Herts 19 A7
Bednall Staffs 34 D5
Bedrule Borders 62 B2
Bedstone Shrops 33 H9
Bedwas Caerph 15 C7
Bedworth Warks 35 G9
Bedworth Heath Warks 35 G9
Beeby Leics 36 E2
Beech Hants 18 H3
Beech Staffs 34 B4
Beech Hill Gtr Man 43 B8
Beech Hill W Berks 18 E3
Beechingstoke Wilts 17 F7
Beedon W Berks 17 D11
Beeford E Yorks 53 D7
Beeley Derbys 44 F6
Beelsby NE Lincs 46 B6
Beenham W Berks 18 E2
Beeny Corn 4 B2
Beer Devon 7 H11
Beer Hackett Dorset 8 C4
Beercrocombe Som 8 B2
Beesands Devon 5 G9
Beesby Lincs 47 D8
Beeson Devon 5 G9
Beeston C Beds 29 D8
Beeston Ches W 43 G8
Beeston Norf 38 D5
Beeston Notts 35 B11
Beeston W Yorks 51 F8
Beeston Regis Norf 39 A7
Beeswing Dumfries 55 C11
Beetham W&F 49 B4
Beetley Norf 38 D5
Begbroke Oxon 27 G11
Begelly Pembs 22 F6
Beggar's Bush Powys 25 B9
Beguildy Powys 33 H7
Beighton Norf 39 E9
Beighton S Yorks 45 D8
Beighton Hill Derbys 44 G6
Beith N Ayrs 66 A6
Bekesbourne Kent 21 F8
Belaugh Norf 39 D8
Belbroughton Worcs 34 H5
Belchamp Otten Essex 30 D5
Belchamp St Paul Essex 30 D4
Belchamp Walter Essex 30 D5
Belchford Lincs 46 E6
Belford Northumb 71 G10
Belhaven E Loth 70 C5
Belhelvie Aberds 83 B11
Belhinnie Aberds 82 A6
Bell Bar Herts 29 H9
Bell Busk N Yorks 50 D5
Bell End Worcs 34 H5
Bell o' th' Hill Ches W 43 H8
Bellabeg Aberds 82 B5
Bellamore S Ayrs 66 H5
Bellanoch Argyll 72 D6
Bellaty Angus 76 B5
Belleau Lincs 47 E8
Bellehiglash Moray 88 E1
Bellerby N Yorks 58 G2
Bellever Devon 5 D7
Belliehill Angus 77 A8
Bellingdon Bucks 28 H6
Bellingham Northumb 62 E4
Belloch Argyll 65 E7
Bellochantuy Argyll 65 E7
Bells Yew Green E Sus 12 C5
Bellsbank E Ayrs 67 F7
Bellshill N Lanark 68 D6
Bellshill Northumb 71 G10
Bellspool Borders 69 G10
Bellsquarry W Loth 69 D9
Belmaduthy Highld 87 F9
Belmesthorpe Rutland 36 D6
Belmont Blackburn 50 H2
Belmont London 19 E9
Belmont S Ayrs 66 D6
Belmont Shetland 96 C7
Belnacraig Aberds 82 B5
Belowda Corn 3 C8
Belper Derbys 45 H7
Belper Lane End Derbys 45 H7
Belsay Northumb 63 F7
Belses Borders 70 H4
Belsford Devon 5 F8
Belstead Suff 31 D8
Belston S Ayrs 67 D6
Belstone Devon 6 G5
Belthorn Blackburn 50 G3
Beltinge Kent 21 E8
Beltoft N Lincs 46 B2
Belton Leics 35 C10
Belton Lincs 36 B5
Belton N Lincs 45 B11
Belton Norf 39 E10
Belton in Rutland Rutland 36 E4
Beltring Kent 20 G3
Belts of Collonach Aberds 83 D8
Belvedere London 19 D11
Belvoir Leics 36 B4
Bembridge IoW 10 F5
Bemersyde Borders 70 G4
Bemerton Wilts 9 A10
Bempton E Yorks 53 B7
Ben Alder Lodge Highld 81 F7
Ben Armine Lodge Highld 93 H10
Ben Casgro W Isles 91 E9
Benacre Suff 39 G11
Benbuie Dumfries 60 D3
Benderloch Argyll 74 D2
Bendronaig Lodge Highld 86 H3
Benenden Kent 13 C7
Benfield Dumfries 54 C6
Bengate Norf 39 C9
Bengeworth Worcs 27 D7
Benhall Green Suff 31 B10
Benhall Street Suff 31 B10
Benholm Aberds 83 G10
Beningbrough N Yorks 51 D11
Benington Herts 29 F9
Benington Lincs 47 H7
Benllech Anglesey 41 B7
Benmore Argyll 73 E10
Benmore Stirling 75 E7
Benmore Lodge Highld 92 H6
Bennacott Corn 6 G1
Bennan N Ayrs 66 D2
Benniworth Lincs 46 D6
Benover Kent 20 G4
Bensham T&W 63 G8
Benslie N Ayrs 66 B6
Benson Oxon 18 B3
Bent Aberds 83 F8
Bent Gate Lancs 50 G3
Benthall Northumb 71 H11
Benthall Shrops 34 E2
Bentham Glos 26 G6
Benthoul Aberdeen 83 C10
Bentlawnt Shrops 33 E9
Bentley E Yorks 52 F6
Bentley Hants 18 G4
Bentley S Yorks 45 B9
Bentley Suff 31 E8
Bentley Warks 35 F8
Bentley Worcs 26 B6
Bentley Heath W Mid 35 H7
Benton Devon 6 C5
Bentpath Dumfries 61 D9
Bents W Loth 69 D8
Bentworth Hants 18 G3
Benvie Dundee 76 D6
Benwick Cambs 37 F9
Beoley Worcs 27 B7
Beoraidbeg Highld 79 B9
Bepton W Sus 11 C7
Berden Essex 29 F11
Bere Alston Devon 4 E5
Bere Ferrers Devon 4 E5
Bere Regis Dorset 9 E7
Berepper Corn 2 G5
Bergh Apton Norf 39 E9
Berinsfield Oxon 18 B2
Berkeley Glos 16 B3
Berkhamsted Herts 28 H6
Berkley Som 16 G5
Berkswell W Mid 35 H8
Bermondsey London 19 D10
Bernera Highld 85 F13
Bernice Argyll 73 D10
Bernisdale Highld 85 C9
Berrick Salome Oxon 18 B3
Berriedale Highld 94 H3
Berrier W&F 56 D5
Berriew Powys 33 E7
Berrington Northumb 71 F9
Berrington Shrops 33 E11
Berrow Som 15 F9
Berrow Green Worcs 26 C4
Berry Down Cross Devon 6 B4
Berry Hill Glos 26 G2
Berry Hill Pembs 22 B5
Berry Pomeroy Devon 5 E9
Berryfield Bucks 28 G4
Berryhillock Moray 88 B5
Berrynarbor Devon 6 B4
Bersham Wrex 42 H6
Berstane Orkney 95 G5
Berwick E Sus 12 F4
Berwick Bassett Wilts 17 D7
Berwick Hill Northumb 63 F7
Berwick St James Wilts 17 H7
Berwick St John Wilts 9 B8
Berwick St Leonard Wilts 9 A8
Berwick-upon-Tweed Northumb 71 E8
Bescar Lancs 43 A6
Besford Worcs 26 D6
Bessacarr S Yorks 45 B10
Bessels Leigh Oxon 17 A11
Bessingby E Yorks 53 C7
Bessingham Norf 39 B7
Bestbeech Hill E Sus 12 C5
Besthorpe Norf 39 F6
Besthorpe Notts 46 F2
Bestwood Nottingham 36 A1
Bestwood Village Notts 45 H9
Beswick E Yorks 52 E6
Betchworth Sur 19 G9
Bethania Ceredig 24 B2
Bethania Gwyn 41 E8
Bethania Gwyn 41 F9
Bethel Anglesey 40 C5
Bethel Gwyn 32 B5
Bethel Gwyn 41 D7
Bethersden Kent 13 B8
Bethesda Gwyn 41 D8
Bethesda Pembs 22 E5
Bethlehem Carms 24 F3
Bethnal Green London 19 C10
Betley Staffs 43 H10
Betsham Kent 20 D3
Betteshanger Kent 21 F10
Bettiscombe Dorset 8 E2
Bettisfield Wrex 33 B10
Betton Shrops 33 E9
Betton Shrops 34 B2
Bettws Bridgend 14 C5
Bettws Mon 25 G9
Bettws Newport 15 B8
Bettws Cedewain Powys 33 F7
Bettws Gwerfil Goch Denb 42 H3
Bettws Ifan Ceredig 23 B8
Bettws Newydd Mon 25 H10
Bettws-y-crwyn Shrops 33 G8
Bettyhill Highld 93 C10
Betws Carms 24 G3
Betws Bledrws Ceredig 23 A10
Betws-Garmon Gwyn 41 E7
Betws-y-Coed Conwy 41 E9
Betws-yn-Rhos Conwy 42 E2
Beulah Ceredig 23 B7
Beulah Powys 24 C6
Bevendean Brighton 12 F2
Bevercotes Notts 45 E10
Beverley E Yorks 52 F6
Beverston Glos 16 B5
Bevington Glos 16 B3
Bewaldeth Cumb 56 C4
Bewcastle Cumb 61 F11
Bewdley Worcs 34 H3
Bewerley N Yorks 51 C7
Bewholme E Yorks 53 D7
Bexhill E Sus 12 F6
Bexley London 19 D11
Bexleyheath London 19 D11
Bexwell Norf 38 E2
Beyton Suff 30 B6
Bhaltos W Isles 90 D5
Bhatarsaigh W Isles 84 J1
Bibury Glos 27 H8
Bicester Oxon 28 F2
Bickenhall Som 8 C1
Bickenhill W Mid 35 G7
Bicker Lincs 37 B8
Bickershaw Gtr Man 43 B9
Bickerstaffe Lancs 43 B7
Bickerton Ches E 43 G8
Bickerton N Yorks 51 D10
Bickington Devon 5 D8
Bickington Devon 6 C4
Bickleigh Devon 4 E6
Bickleigh Devon 7 F8
Bickleton Devon 6 C4
Bickley London 19 E11
Bickley Moss Ches W 43 H8
Bicknacre Essex 20 A4
Bicknoller Som 7 C10
Bicknor Kent 20 F5
Bickton Hants 9 C10
Bicton Shrops 33 D10
Bicton Shrops 33 G8
Bidborough Kent 12 B4
Biddenden Kent 13 C7
Biddenham Bedford 29 D7
Biddestone Wilts 16 D5
Biddisham Som 15 F9
Biddlesden Bucks 28 D3
Biddlestone Northumb 62 C5
Biddulph Staffs 44 G2
Biddulph Moor Staffs 44 G3
Bideford Devon 6 D3
Bidford-on-Avon Warks 27 C8
Bidston Mers 42 C5
Bielby E Yorks 52 E3
Bieldside Aberdeen 83 C10
Bierley IoW 10 G4
Bierley W Yorks 51 F7
Bierton Bucks 28 G5
Big Sand Highld 85 A12
Bigbury Devon 5 G7
Bigbury on Sea Devon 5 G7
Bigby Lincs 46 B4
Biggar S Lanark 69 G9
Biggar W&F 49 C1
Biggin Derbys 44 G5
Biggin Derbys 44 H6
Biggin N Yorks 51 F11
Biggin Hill London 19 F11
Biggings Shetland 96 G3
Biggleswade C Beds 29 D8
Bighouse Highld 93 C11
Bighton Hants 10 A5
Bignor W Sus 11 C8
Bigton Shetland 96 L5
Bilberry Corn 3 C9
Bilborough Nottingham 35 A11
Bilbrook Som 7 B9
Bilbrough N Yorks 51 E11
Bilbster Highld 94 E4
Bildershaw Durham 58 D3
Bildeston Suff 30 D6
Billericay Essex 20 B3
Billesdon Leics 36 E3
Billesley Warks 27 C8
Billingborough Lincs 37 B7
Billinge Mers 43 B8
Billingford Norf 38 C6
Billingham Stockton 58 D5
Billinghay Lincs 46 G5
Billingley S Yorks 45 B8
Billingshurst W Sus 11 B9
Billingsley Shrops 34 G3
Billington C Beds 28 F6
Billington Lancs 50 F3
Billockby Norf 39 D10
Billy Row Durham 58 C2
Bilsborrow Lancs 49 F5
Bilsby Lincs 47 E8
Bilsham W Sus 11 D8
Bilsington Kent 13 C9
Bilson Green Glos 26 G3
Bilsthorpe Notts 45 F10
Bilsthorpe Moor Notts 45 G10
Bilston Midloth 69 D11
Bilston W Mid 34 F5
Bilstone Leics 35 E9
Bilting Kent 21 G7
Bilton E Yorks 53 F7
Bilton Northumb 63 B8
Bilton Warks 27 A11
Bilton in Ainsty N Yorks 51 E10
Bimbister Orkney 95 G4
Binbrook Lincs 46 C6
Binchester Blocks Durham 58 C3
Bincombe Dorset 8 F5
Bindal Highld 87 C12
Binegar Som 16 G3
Binfield Brack 18 D5
Binfield Hth. Oxon 18 D4
Bingfield Northumb 62 F5
Bingham Notts 36 B3
Bingley W Yorks 51 F7
Bings Heath Shrops 33 D11
Binham Norf 38 B5
Binley Hants 17 F11
Binley W Mid 35 H9
Binley Woods Warks 35 H9
Binniehill Falk 69 C7
Binsoe N Yorks 51 B8
Binstead IoW 10 E4
Binsted Hants 18 G4
Binton Warks 27 C8
Bintree Norf 38 C6
Binweston Shrops 33 E9
Birch Essex 30 G6
Birch Gtr Man 44 B2
Birch Green Essex 30 G6
Birch Heath Ches W 43 F8
Birch Hill Ches W 43 E8
Birch Vale Derbys 44 D4
Bircham Newton Norf 38 B3
Bircham Tofts Norf 38 B3
Birchanger Essex 30 F2
Birchencliffe W Yorks 51 H7
Bircher Hereford 25 B11
Birchgrove Cardiff 15 D7
Birchgrove Swansea 14 B3
Birchington Kent 21 E9
Birchmoor Warks 35 E8
Birchover Derbys 44 F6
Birchwood Lincs 46 F3
Birchwood Warr 43 C9
Bircotes Notts 45 C10
Birdbrook Essex 30 D4
Birdforth N Yorks 51 B10
Birdham W Sus 11 E7
Birdholme Derbys 45 F7
Birdingbury Warks 27 B11
Birdlip Glos 26 G6
Birds Edge W Yorks 44 B6
Birdsall N Yorks 52 C4
Birdsgreen Shrops 34 G3
Birdsmoor Gate Dorset 8 D2
Birdston E Dunb 68 C5
Birdwell S Yorks 45 B7
Birdwood Glos 26 G4
Birgham Borders 70 G6
Birkby N Yorks 58 F4
Birkdale Mers 49 H3
Birkenhead Mers 42 D6
Birkenhills Aberds 89 D7
Birkenshaw N Lanark 68 D5
Birkenshaw W Yorks 51 G8
Birkhall Aberds 82 D5
Birkhill Angus 76 D6
Birkhill Borders 61 B8
Birkholme Lincs 36 C5
Birkin N Yorks 51 G11
Birley Hereford 25 C11
Birling Kent 20 E3
Birling Northumb 63 C8
Birling Gap E Sus 12 G4
Birlingham Worcs 26 D6
Birmingham W Mid 35 G6
Birnam Perth 76 C3
Birse Aberds 83 D7
Birsemore Aberds 83 D7
Birstall Leics 36 E1
Birstall W Yorks 51 G8
Birstwith N Yorks 51 D8
Birthorpe Lincs 37 B7
Birtley Hereford 25 B10
Birtley Northumb 62 F4
Birtley T&W 63 H8
Birts Street Worcs 26 E4
Bisbrooke Rutland 36 F4
Biscathorpe Lincs 46 D6
Biscot Luton 29 F7
Bish Mill Devon 7 D6
Bisham Windsor 18 C5
Bishampton Worcs 26 C6
Bishop Auckland Durham 58 D3
Bishop Burton E Yorks 52 F5
Bishop Middleham Durham 58 C4
Bishop Monkton N Yorks 51 C9
Bishop Norton Lincs 46 C3
Bishop Sutton Bath 16 F2
Bishop Thornton N Yorks 51 C8
Bishop Wilton E Yorks 52 D3
Bishopbridge Lincs 46 C4
Bishopbriggs E Dunb 68 D5
Bishopmill Moray 88 B2
Bishops Cannings Wilts 17 E7
Bishop's Castle Shrops 33 G9
Bishop's Caundle Dorset 8 C5
Bishop's Cleeve Glos 26 F6
Bishops Frome Hereford 26 D3
Bishop's Green Essex 30 G3
Bishop's Hull Som 7 D11
Bishop's Itchington Warks 27 C10
Bishops Lydeard Som 7 D10
Bishops Nympton Devon 7 D6
Bishop's Offley Staffs 34 C3
Bishop's Stortford Herts 29 F11
Bishop's Sutton Hants 10 A5
Bishop's Tachbrook Warks 27 B10
Bishops Tawton Devon 6 C4
Bishop's Waltham Hants 10 C4
Bishop's Wood Staffs 34 E4
Bishopsbourne Kent 21 F8
Bishopsteignton Devon 5 D10
Bishopstoke Hants 10 C3
Bishopston Swansea 23 H10
Bishopstone Bucks 28 G5
Bishopstone E Sus 12 F3
Bishopstone Hereford 25 D11
Bishopstone Swindon 17 C9
Bishopstone Wilts 9 B9
Bishopstrow Wilts 16 G5
Bishopswood Som 8 C1
Bishopsworth Bristol 16 E2
Bishopthorpe York 52 E1
Bishopton Darl 58 D4
Bishopton Dumfries 55 E7
Bishopton N Yorks 51 B9
Bishopton Renfs 68 C3
Bishopton Warks 27 C8
Bishton Newport 15 C9
Bisley Glos 26 H6
Bisley Sur 18 F6
Bispham Blackpool 49 E3
Bispham Green Lancs 43 A7
Bissoe Corn 3 E6
Bisterne Close Hants 9 D11
Bitchfield Lincs 36 C5
Bittadon Devon 6 B4
Bittaford Devon 5 F7
Bittering Norf 38 D5
Bitterley Shrops 34 H1
Bitterne Soton 10 C3
Bitteswell Leics 35 G11
Bitton S Glos 16 E3
Biwmares = Beaumaris Anglesey 41 C8
Bix Oxon 18 C4
Bixter Shetland 96 H5
Blaby Leics 36 F1
Black Bourton Oxon 17 A9
Black Callerton T&W 63 G7
Black Clauchrie S Ayrs 54 A5
Black Corries Lodge Highld 74 B5
Black Crofts Argyll 74 D2
Black Dog Devon 7 F7
Black Heddon Northumb 62 F6
Black Lane Gtr Man 43 B10
Black Marsh Shrops 33 F9
Black Mount Argyll 74 C5
Black Notley Essex 30 F4
Black Pill Swansea 14 B2
Black Tar Pembs 22 F4
Black Torrington Devon 6 F3
Blackacre Dumfries 60 D6
Blackadder West Borders 71 E7
Blackawton Devon 5 F9
Blackborough Devon 7 F9
Blackborough End Norf 38 D2
Blackboys E Sus 12 D4
Blackbrook Derbys 45 H7
Blackbrook Mers 43 C8
Blackbrook Staffs 34 B3
Blackburn Aberds 83 B10
Blackburn Aberds 88 E5
Blackburn Blackburn 50 G2
Blackburn W Loth 69 D8
Blackcraig Dumfries 60 E3
Blackden Heath Ches E 43 E10
Blackdog Aberds 83 B11
Blackfell T&W 63 H8
Blackfield Hants 10 D3
Blackford Cumb 61 G9
Blackford Perth 75 G11
Blackford Som 8 B5
Blackford Som 15 G10
Blackfordby Leics 35 D9
Blackgang IoW 10 G3
Blackhall Colliery Durham 58 C5
Blackhall Mill T&W 63 H7
Blackhall Rocks Durham 58 C5
Blackham E Sus 12 C3
Blackhaugh Borders 70 G3
Blackheath Essex 31 F7
Blackheath Suff 31 A11
Blackheath Sur 19 G7
Blackheath W Mid 34 G5
Blackhill Aberds 89 C10
Blackhill Aberds 89 D10
Blackhill Highld 85 C8
Blackhills Highld 87 F12
Blackhills Moray 88 C2
Blackhorse S Glos 16 D3
Blackland Wilts 17 E7
Blacklaw Aberds 89 C6
Blackley Gtr Man 44 B2
Blacklunans Perth 76 A4
Blackmill Bridgend 14 C5
Blackmoor Hants 11 A6
Blackmoor Gate Devon 6 B5
Blackmore Essex 20 A3
Blackmore End Essex 30 E4
Blackmore End Herts 29 G8
Blackness Falk 69 C9
Blacknest Hants 18 G4
Blacko Lancs 50 E4
Blackpool Blackpool 49 F3
Blackpool Devon 5 G9
Blackpool Pembs 22 E5
Blackpool Gate Cumb 61 F11
Blackridge W Loth 69 D7
Blackrock Argyll 64 B4
Blackrock Mon 25 G9
Blackrod Gtr Man 43 A9
Blackshaw Dumfries 60 G6
Blackshaw Head W Yorks 50 G5
Blacksmith's Green Suff 31 B8
Blackstone W Sus 11 C11
Blackthorn Oxon 28 G3
Blackthorpe Suff 30 B6
Blacktoft E Yorks 52 G4
Blacktop Aberdeen 83 C10
Blacktown Newport 15 C8
Blackwall Tunnel London 19 C10
Blackwater Corn 2 E6
Blackwater Hants 18 F5
Blackwater IoW 10 F4
Blackwaterfoot N Ayrs 66 D1
Blackwell Darl 58 E3
Blackwell Derbys 44 E5
Blackwell Derbys 45 G8
Blackwell W Sus 12 C2
Blackwell Warks 27 D9
Blackwell Worcs 26 A6
Blackwood = Coed Duon Caerph 15 B7
Blackwood S Lanark 68 F6
Blackwood Hill Staffs 44 G3
Blacon Ches W 43 F6
Bladnoch Dumfries 55 D7
Bladon Oxon 27 G11
Blaen-gwynfi Neath 14 B4
Blaen-waun Carms 23 D7
Blaen-y-coed Carms 23 D8
Blaen-y-Cwm Denb 32 B6
Blaen-y-cwm Gwyn 32 C3
Blaen-y-cwm Powys 33 C6
Blaenannerch Ceredig 23 B7
Blaenau Ffestiniog Gwyn 41 F9
Blaenavon Torf 25 H9
Blaencelyn Ceredig 23 A8
Blaendyryn Powys 24 E6
Blaenffos Pembs 22 C6
Blaengarw Bridgend 14 B5
Blaengwrach Neath 24 H5
Blaenpennal Ceredig 24 B3
Blaenplwyf Ceredig 32 H1
Blaenporth Ceredig 23 B7
Blaenrhondda Rhondda 14 A5
Blaenycwm Ceredig 32 H4
Blagdon N Som 15 F11
Blagdon Torbay 5 E9
Blagdon Hill Som 7 E11
Blagill W&F 57 B9
Blaguegate Lancs 43 B7
Blaich Highld 80 F2
Blain Highld 79 E9
Blaina Bl Gwent 25 H9
Blair Atholl Perth 81 G10
Blair Drummond Stirling 75 H10
Blairbeg N Ayrs 66 C3
Blairdaff Aberds 83 B8
Blairglas Argyll 68 B2
Blairgowrie Perth 76 C4
Blairhall Fife 69 B9
Blairingone Perth 76 H2
Blairland N Ayrs 66 B6
Blairlogie Stirling 75 H11
Blairlomond Argyll 74 H4
Blairmore Argyll 73 E10
Blairnamarrow Moray 82 B4
Blairquhosh Stirling 68 B4
Blair's Ferry Argyll 73 G8
Blairskaith E Dunb 68 C4
Blaisdon Glos 26 G4
Blakebrook Worcs 34 H4
Blakedown Worcs 34 H4
Blakelaw Borders 70 G6
Blakeley Staffs 34 F4
Blakeley Lane Staffs 44 H3
Blakemere Hereford 25 D10
Blakeney Glos 26 H3
Blakeney Norf 38 A6
Blakenhall Ches E 43 H10
Blakenhall W Mid 34 F5
Blakeshall Worcs 34 G4
Blakesley W Nhants 28 C3
Blanchland Northumb 57 A11
Bland Hill N Yorks 51 D8
Blandford Forum Dorset 9 D7
Blandford St Mary Dorset 9 D7
Blanefield Stirling 68 C4
Blankney Lincs 46 F4
Blantyre S Lanark 68 E5
Blar a'Chaorainn Highld 80 G3
Blaran Argyll 73 B7
Blarghour Argyll 73 B8
Blarmachfoldach Highld 80 G2
Blarnalearoch Highld 86 B4
Blashford Hants 9 D10
Blaston Leics 36 F4
Blatherwycke N Nhants 36 F5
Blawith W&F 56 H4
Blaxhall Suff 31 C10
Blaxton S Yorks 45 B10
Blaydon T&W 63 G7
Bleadon N Som 15 F9
Bleak Hey Nook Gtr Man 44 B4
Blean Kent 21 E8
Bleasby Lincs 46 D5
Bleasby Notts 45 H11
Bleasdale Lancs 50 E1
Bleatarn W&F 57 E9
Blebocraigs Fife 77 F7
Bleddfa Powys 25 B9
Bledington Glos 27 F9
Bledlow Bucks 18 A4
Bledlow Ridge Bucks 18 B4
Blegbie E Loth 70 D3
Blencarn W&F 57 C8
Blencogo Cumb 56 B3
Blendworth Hants 10 C6
Blenheim Park Norf 38 B4
Blennerhasset Cumb 56 B3
Blervie Castle Moray 87 F13
Bletchingdon Oxon 28 G2
Bletchingley Sur 19 F10
Bletchley M Keynes 28 E5
Bletchley Shrops 34 B2
Bletherston Pembs 22 D5
Bletsoe Bedford 29 C7
Blewbury Oxon 18 C2
Blickling Norf 39 C7
Blidworth Notts 45 G9
Blindburn Northumb 62 B4
Blindcrake Cumb 56 C3
Blindley Heath Sur 19 G10
Blisland Corn 4 D2
Bliss Gate Worcs 26 A4
Blissford Hants 9 C10
Blisworth W Nhants 28 C4
Blithbury Staffs 35 C6
Blitterlees Cumb 56 A3
Blo' Norton Norf 38 H6
Blockley Glos 27 E8
Blofield Norf 39 E9
Blofield Heath Norf 39 D9
Bloomfield Borders 61 A11
Blore Staffs 44 H5
Blount's Green Staffs 35 B6
Blowick Mers 49 H3
Bloxham Oxon 27 E11
Bloxholm Lincs 46 G4
Bloxwich W Mid 34 E5
Bloxworth Dorset 9 E7
Blubberhouses N Yorks 51 D7
Blue Anchor Som 7 B9
Blue Anchor Swansea 23 G10
Blue Row Essex 31 G7
Blundeston Suff 39 F11
Blunham C Beds 29 C8
Blunsdon St Andrew Swindon 17 C8
Bluntington Worcs 26 A5
Bluntisham Cambs 29 A10
Blunts Corn 4 E4
Blyborough Lincs 46 C3
Blyford Suff 39 H10
Blymhill Staffs 34 D4
Blyth Northumb 63 E9
Blyth Notts 45 D10
Blyth Bridge Borders 69 F10
Blythburgh Suff 39 H10
Blythe Borders 70 F4
Blythe Bridge Staffs 34 A5
Blyton Lincs 46 C2
Boarhills Fife 77 F8
Boarhunt Hants 10 D5
Boars Head Gtr Man 43 B8
Boars Hill Oxon 17 A11
Boarshead E Sus 12 C4
Boarstall Bucks 28 G3
Boasley Cross Devon 6 G3
Boat of Garten Highld 81 B11
Boath Highld 87 D8
Bobbing Kent 20 E5
Bobbington Staffs 34 F4
Bobbingworth Essex 30 H2
Bocaddon Corn 4 F2
Bochastle Stirling 75 G9
Bocking Essex 30 F4
Bocking Churchstreet Essex 30 F4
Boddam Aberds 89 D11
Boddam Shetland 96 M5
Boddington Glos 26 F5
Bodedern Anglesey 40 B5
Bodelwyddan Denb 42 E3
Bodenham Hereford 26 C2
Bodenham Wilts 9 B10
Bodenham Moor Hereford 26 C2
Bodermid Gwyn 40 H3
Bodewryd Anglesey 40 A5
Bodfari Denb 42 E3
Bodffordd Anglesey 40 C6
Bodham Norf 39 A7
Bodiam E Sus 13 D6
Bodicote Oxon 27 E11
Bodieve Corn 3 B8
Bodinnick Corn 4 F2
Bodle Street Green E Sus 12 E5
Bodmin Corn 4 E1
Bodney Norf 38 F4
Bodorgan Anglesey 40 D5
Bodsham Kent 21 G8
Boduan Gwyn 40 G5
Bodymoor Heath Warks 35 F7
Bogallan Highld 87 F9
Bogbrae Aberds 89 E10
Bogend Borders 70 F6
Bogend S Ayrs 67 C6
Boghall W Loth 69 D8
Boghead S Lanark 68 F6
Bogmoor Moray 88 B3
Bogniebrae Aberds 88 D5
Bognor Regis W Sus 11 E8
Bograxie Aberds 83 B9
Bogside N Lanark 69 E7
Bogton Aberds 89 C6
Bogue Dumfries 55 A9
Bohenie Highld 80 E4
Bohortha Corn 3 F7
Bohuntine Highld 80 E4
Boirseam W Isles 90 J5
Bojewyan Corn 2 F2
Bolam Durham 58 D2
Bolam Northumb 62 E6
Bolberry Devon 5 H7
Bold Heath Mers 43 D8
Boldon T&W 63 G9
Boldon Colliery T&W 63 G9
Boldre Hants 10 E2
Boldron Durham 58 E1
Bole Notts 45 D11
Bolehill Derbys 44 G6
Boleside Borders 70 G3
Bolham Devon 7 E8
Bolham Water Devon 7 E10
Bolingey Corn 3 D6
Bollington Ches E 44 E3
Bollington Cross Ches E 44 E3
Bolney W Sus 12 D1
Bolnhurst Bedford 29 C7
Bolshan Angus 77 B9
Bolsover Derbys 45 E8
Bolsterstone S Yorks 44 C6
Bolstone Hereford 26 E2
Boltby N Yorks 58 H5
Bolter End Bucks 18 B4
Bolton E Loth 70 C4
Bolton E Yorks 52 D3
Bolton Gtr Man 43 B10
Bolton Northumb 63 B7
Bolton W&F 57 D8
Bolton Abbey N Yorks 51 D6
Bolton Bridge N Yorks 51 D6
Bolton-by-Bowland Lancs 50 E3
Bolton-le-Sands Lancs 49 C4
Bolton Low Houses Cumb 56 B4
Bolton-on-Swale N Yorks 58 G3
Bolton Percy N Yorks 51 E11
Bolton Town End Lancs 49 C4
Bolton upon Dearne S Yorks 45 B8
Boltonfellend Cumb 61 G10
Boltongate Cumb 56 B4
Bolventor Corn 4 D2
Bomere Heath Shrops 33 D10
Bon-y-maen Swansea 14 B2
Bonar Bridge Highld 87 B9
Bonawe Argyll 74 D3
Bonby N Lincs 52 H6
Boncath Pembs 23 C7
Bonchester Bridge Borders 61 B11
Bonchurch IoW 10 G4
Bondleigh Devon 6 F5
Bonehill Devon 5 D8
Bonehill Staffs 35 E7
Bo'ness Falk 69 B8
Bonhill W Dunb 68 C2
Boningale Shrops 34 E4
Bonjedward Borders 62 A2
Bonkle N Lanark 69 E7
Bonnavoulin Highld 79 F8
Bonnington Edin 69 D10
Bonnington Kent 13 C9
Bonnybank Fife 76 G6
Bonnybridge Falk 69 B7
Bonnykelly Aberds 89 C8
Bonnyrigg and Lasswade Midloth 70 D2
Bonnyton Aberds 89 E6
Bonnyton Angus 76 D6
Bonnyton Angus 77 B9
Bonsall Derbys 44 G6
Bonskeid House Perth 75 A11
Bont Mon 25 G10
Bont-Dolgadfan Powys 32 E4
Bont-goch Ceredig 32 G2
Bont-newydd Conwy 42 E3
Bont Newydd Gwyn 32 C3
Bont Newydd Gwyn 41 F9
Bontddu Gwyn 32 D2
Bonthorpe Lincs 47 E8
Bontnewydd Ceredig 24 B3
Bontnewydd Gwyn 40 E6
Bontuchel Denb 42 G3
Bonvilston V Glam 14 D6
Booker Bucks 18 B5
Boon Borders 70 F4
Boosbeck Redcar 59 E7
Boot Cumb 56 F3
Boot Street Suff 31 D9
Booth W Yorks 50 G6
Booth Wood W Yorks 50 H6
Boothby Graffoe Lincs 46 G3
Boothby Pagnell Lincs 36 B5
Boothen Stoke 34 A4
Boothferry E Yorks 52 G3
Boothville W Nhants 28 B4
Bootle Cumb 56 H3
Bootle Mers 42 C6
Booton Norf 39 C7
Boquhan Stirling 68 B4
Boraston Shrops 26 A3
Borden Kent 20 E5
Borden W Sus 11 B7
Bordley N Yorks 50 C5
Bordon Hants 18 H5
Bordon Camp Hants 18 H4
Boreham Essex 30 H4
Boreham Wilts 16 G5
Boreham Street E Sus 12 E5
Borehamwood Herts 19 B8
Boreland Dumfries 61 D7
Boreland Stirling 75 D8
Borgh W Isles 84 H1
Borgh W Isles 90 J4
Borghastan W Isles 90 C7
Borgie Highld 93 D9
Borgue Dumfries 55 E9
Borgue Highld 94 H3
Borley Essex 30 D5
Bornais W Isles 84 F2
Bornesketaig Highld 85 A8
Borness Dumfries 55 E9
Borough Green Kent 20 F3
Boroughbridge N Yorks 51 C9
Borras Head Wrex 42 G6
Borreraig Highld 84 C6
Borrobol Lodge Highld 93 G11
Borrowash Derbys 35 B10
Borrowby N Yorks 58 H5
Borrowdale Cumb 56 E4
Borrowfield Aberds 83 D10
Borth Ceredig 32 F2
Borth-y-Gest Gwyn 41 G7
Borthwickbrae Borders 61 B10
Borthwickshiels Borders 61 B10
Borve Highld 85 D9
Borve Lodge W Isles 90 H5
Borwick Lancs 49 B5
Bosavern Corn 2 F2
Bosbury Hereford 26 D3
Boscastle Corn 4 B2
Boscombe BCP 9 E10
Boscombe Wilts 17 H9
Boscoppa Corn 3 D9
Bosham W Sus 11 D7
Bosherston Pembs 22 G4
Boskenna Corn 2 G3
Bosley Ches E 44 F3
Bossall N Yorks 52 C3
Bossiney Corn 4 C1
Bossingham Kent 21 G8
Bossington Som 7 B7
Bostock Green Ches W 43 F9
Boston Lincs 37 A9
Boston Long Hedges Lincs 47 H7
Boston Spa W Yorks 51 E10
Boston West Lincs 46 H6
Boswinger Corn 3 E8
Botallack Corn 2 F2
Botany Bay London 19 B9
Botcherby Cumb 61 H10
Botcheston Leics 35 E10
Botesdale Suff 38 H6
Bothal Northumb 63 E8
Bothamsall Notts 45 E10
Bothel Cumb 56 C3
Bothenhampton Dorset 8 E3
Bothwell S Lanark 68 E6
Botley Bucks 18 A6
Botley Hants 10 C4
Botley Oxon 27 H11
Botolph Claydon Bucks 28 F4
Botolphs W Sus 11 D10
Bottacks Highld 86 E7
Bottesford Leics 36 B4
Bottesford N Lincs 46 B2
Bottisham Cambs 30 B2
Bottlesford Wilts 17 F8
Bottom Boat W Yorks 51 G9
Bottom House Staffs 44 G4
Bottom o' th' Moor Gtr Man 43 A9
Bottom of Hutton Lancs 49 G4
Bottomcraig Fife 76 E6
Botusfleming Corn 4 E5
Botwnnog Gwyn 40 G4
Bough Beech Kent 19 G11
Boughrood Powys 25 E8
Boughspring Glos 16 B2
Boughton Norf 38 E2
Boughton Notts 45 F10
Boughton W Nhants 28 B4
Boughton Aluph Kent 21 G7
Boughton Lees Kent 21 G7
Boughton Malherbe Kent 20 G5
Boughton Monchelsea Kent 20 F4
Boughton Street Kent 21 F7
Boulby Redcar 59 E8
Boulden Shrops 33 G11
Boulmer Northumb 63 B8
Boulston Pembs 22 E4
Boultenstone Aberds 82 B6
Boultham Lincs 46 F3
Bourn Cambs 29 C10
Bourne Lincs 37 C6
Bourne End Bucks 18 C5
Bourne End C Beds 28 D6
Bourne End Herts 29 H7
Bournemouth BCP 9 E9
Bournes Green Glos 16 A6
Bournes Green Southend 20 C6
Bournheath Worcs 26 A6
Bournmoor Durham 58 A4
Bournville W Mid 34 G6
Bourton Dorset 9 A6
Bourton N Som 15 E9
Bourton Oxon 17 C9
Bourton Shrops 34 F1
Bourton on Dunsmore Warks 27 A11
Bourton on the Hill Glos 27 E8
Bourton-on-the-Water Glos 27 F8
Bousd Argyll 78 E5
Boustead Hill Cumb 61 H8
Bouth W&F 56 H5
Bouthwaite N Yorks 51 B7
Boveney Bucks 18 D6
Boverton V Glam 14 E5
Bovey Tracey Devon 5 D9
Bovingdon Herts 19 A7
Bovingdon Green Bucks 18 C5
Bovingdon Green Herts 19 A7
Bovinger Essex 30 H2
Bovington Camp Dorset 9 F7
Bow Borders 70 F3
Bow Devon 6 F6
Bow Orkney 95 J4
Bow Brickhill M Keynes 28 E6
Bow of Fife Fife 76 F6
Bow Street Ceredig 32 G2
Bowbank Durham 57 D11
Bowburn Durham 58 C4
Bowcombe IoW 10 F3
Bowd Devon 7 G10
Bowden Borders 70 G4
Bowden Devon 5 G9
Bowden Hill Wilts 16 E6

C

Castell-Nedd = Neath Neath 14 B3
Castell Newydd Emlyn = Newcastle Emlyn Carms 23 B8
Castell-y-bwch Torf 15 B8
Castellau Rhondda 14 C6
Casterton W&F 50 B2
Castle Acre Norf 38 D4
Castle Ashby W Nhants 28 C5
Castle Bolton N Yorks 58 G1
Castle Bromwich W Mid 35 G7
Castle Bytham Lincs 36 D5
Castle Caereinion Powys 33 E7
Castle Camps Cambs 30 D3
Castle Carrock Cumb 61 H11
Castle Cary Som 8 A5
Castle Combe Wilts 16 D5
Castle Donington Leics 35 C10
Castle Douglas Dumfries 55 C10
Castle Eaton Swindon 17 B8
Castle Eden Durham 58 C5
Castle Forbes Aberds 83 B8
Castle Frome Hereford 26 D3
Castle Green Sur 18 E6
Castle Gresley Derbys 35 D8
Castle Heaton Northumb 71 F8
Castle Hedingham Essex 30 E4
Castle Hill Kent 12 B5
Castle Huntly Perth 76 E6
Castle Kennedy Dumfries 54 D4
Castle O'er Dumfries 61 D8
Castle Pulverbatch Shrops 33 E10
Castle Rising Norf 38 C2
Castle Stuart Highld 87 G10
Castlebay = Bagh a Chaisteil W Isles 84 J1
Castlebythe Pembs 22 D5
Castlecary N Lanark 68 C6
Castlecraig Highld 87 E11
Castlefairn Dumfries 60 E3
Castleford W Yorks 51 G10
Castlehill Borders 69 G11
Castlehill Highld 94 D3
Castlehill W Dunb 68 C2
Castlemaddy Dumfries 67 H8
Castlemartin Pembs 22 G4
Castlemilk Dumfries 61 F7
Castlemilk Glasgow 68 E5
Castlemorris Pembs 22 C4
Castlemorton Worcs 26 E4
Castleside Durham 58 B1
Castlethorpe M Keynes 28 D5
Castleton Angus 76 C6
Castleton Argyll 73 E7
Castleton Derbys 44 D5
Castleton Gtr Man 44 A2
Castleton N Yorks 59 F7
Castleton Newport 15 C8
Castletown Ches W 43 G7
Castletown Highld 87 G10
Castletown Highld 94 D3
Castletown IoM 48 F2
Castletown T&W 63 H9
Castleweary Borders 61 C10
Castley N Yorks 51 E8
Caston Norf 38 F5
Castor Pboro 37 F7
Catacol N Ayrs 66 B2
Catbrain S Glos 16 C2
Catbrook Mon 15 A11
Catchall Corn 2 G3
Catchems Corner W Mid 35 H8
Catchgate Durham 58 A2
Catcleugh Northumb 62 C3
Catcliffe S Yorks 45 D8
Catcott Som 15 H9
Caterham Sur 19 F10
Catfield Norf 39 C9
Catfirth Shetland 96 H6
Catford London 19 D10
Catforth Lancs 49 F4
Cathays Cardiff 15 D7
Cathcart Glasgow 68 D4
Cathedine Powys 25 F8
Catherington Hants 10 C5
Catherton Shrops 34 H2
Catlodge Highld 81 D8
Catlowdy Cumb 61 F10
Catmore W Berks 17 C11
Caton Lancs 49 C5
Caton Green Lancs 49 C5
Catrine E Ayrs 67 D8
Cat's Ash Newport 15 B9
Catsfield E Sus 12 E6
Catshill Worcs 26 A6
Cattal N Yorks 51 D10
Cattawade Suff 31 E8
Catterall Lancs 49 E4
Catterick N Yorks 58 G3
Catterick Bridge N Yorks 58 G3
Catterick Garrison N Yorks 58 G2
Catterlen W&F 57 C6
Catterline Aberds 83 F10
Catterton N Yorks 51 E11
Catthorpe Leics 36 H1
Cattistock Dorset 8 E4
Catton N Yorks 51 B9
Catton Northumb 62 H4
Catwick E Yorks 53 E7
Catworth Cambs 29 A7
Caudlesprings Norf 38 E5
Caulcott Oxon 28 F2
Cauldcots Angus 77 C9
Cauldhame Stirling 68 A5
Cauldmill Borders 61 B11
Cauldon Staffs 44 H4
Caulkerbush Dumfries 60 H5
Caulside Dumfries 61 E10
Caunsall Worcs 34 G4
Caunton Notts 45 G11
Causeway End Dumfries 55 C7
Causeway Foot W Yorks 51 F6
Causeway-head Stirling 75 H10
Causewayend S Lanark 69 G9
Causewayhead Cumb 56 A3
Causey Park Bridge Northumb 63 D7
Causeyend Aberds 83 B11
Cautley W&F 57 G8
Cavendish Suff 30 D5
Cavendish Bridge Leics 35 C10
Cavenham Suff 30 B4
Caversfield Oxon 28 F2
Caversham Reading 18 D4
Caverswall Staffs 34 A5
Cavil E Yorks 52 F3
Cawdor Highld 87 F11
Cawkwell Lincs 46 E6
Cawood N Yorks 52 F1
Cawsand Corn 4 F5
Cawston Norf 39 C7
Cawthorne S Yorks 44 B6
Cawthorpe Lincs 37 C6
Cawton N Yorks 52 B2
Caxton Cambs 29 C10
Caynham Shrops 26 A2
Caythorpe Lincs 46 H3
Caythorpe Notts 45 H10
Cayton N Yorks 53 A6
Ceann a Bhaigh W Isles 84 B2
Ceann a Deas Loch Baghasdail W Isles 84 G2
Ceann Shiphoirt W Isles 91 F7
Ceann Tarabhaigh W Isles 90 F7
Ceannacroc Lodge Highld 80 B4
Cearsiadair W Isles 91 E8
Cefn Berain Conwy 42 F2
Cefn-brith Conwy 42 G2
Cefn Canol Powys 33 B8
Cefn-coch Conwy 41 D10
Cefn Coch Powys 33 C7
Cefn-coed-y-cymmer M Tydf 25 H7
Cefn Cribbwr Bridgend 14 C4
Cefn Cross Bridgend 14 C4
Cefn-ddwysarn Gwyn 32 B5
Cefn Einion Shrops 33 G8
Cefn-gorwydd Powys 24 D6
Cefn-mawr Wrex 33 A8
Cefn-y-bedd Flint 42 G6
Cefn-y-pant Carms 22 D6
Cefneithin Carms 23 E10
Cei-bach Ceredig 23 A9
Ceinewydd = New Quay Ceredig 23 A8
Ceint Anglesey 40 C6
Cellan Ceredig 24 D3
Cellarhead Staffs 44 H3
Cemaes Anglesey 40 A5
Cemmaes Powys 32 E4
Cemmaes Road Powys 32 E4
Cenarth Carms 23 B7
Cenin Gwyn 40 F6
Central Involyd 73 F11
Ceos W Isles 91 E8
Ceres Fife 77 F7
Cerne Abbas Dorset 8 D5
Cerney Wick Glos 17 B7
Cerrigceinwen Anglesey 40 C6
Cerrigydrudion Conwy 42 H2
Cessford Borders 62 A3
Ceunant Gwyn 41 D7
Chaceley Glos 26 E5
Chacewater Corn 3 E6
Chackmore Bucks 28 E3
Chacombe W Nhants 27 D11
Chad Valley W Mid 34 G6
Chadderton Gtr Man 44 B3
Chadderton Fold Gtr Man 44 B2
Chaddesden Derby 35 B9
Chaddesley Corbett Worcs 26 A5
Chaddleworth W Berks 17 D11
Chadlington Oxon 27 F10
Chadshunt Warks 27 C10
Chadwell Leics 36 C3
Chadwell St Mary Thurrock 20 D3
Chadwick End W Mid 27 A9
Chadwick Green Mers 43 C8
Chaffcombe Som 8 C2
Chagford Devon 5 C8
Chailey E Sus 12 E2
Chain Bridge Lincs 37 A9
Chainbridge Cambs 37 E10
Chainhurst Kent 20 G4
Chalbury Dorset 9 D9
Chalbury Common Dorset 9 D9
Chaldon Sur 19 F10
Chaldon Herring Dorset 9 F6
Chale IoW 10 G3
Chale Green IoW 10 G3
Chalfont Common Bucks 19 B7
Chalfont St Giles Bucks 18 B6
Chalfont St Peter Bucks 19 B7
Chalford Glos 16 A5
Chalgrove Oxon 18 B3
Chalk Kent 20 D3
Challacombe Devon 6 B5
Challoch Dumfries 54 C6
Challock Kent 21 F7
Chalton C Beds 29 F7
Chalton Hants 10 C6
Chalvington E Sus 12 F4
Chancery Ceredig 32 H1
Chandler's Ford Hants 10 B3
Channel Tunnel Kent 21 H8
Channerwick Shetland 96 L6
Chantry Som 16 G4
Chantry Suff 31 D8
Chapel Fife 69 A11
Chapel Allerton Som 15 F10
Chapel Allerton W Yorks 51 F9
Chapel Amble Corn 3 B8
Chapel Brampton W Nhants 28 B4
Chapel Choriton Staffs 34 B4
Chapel-en-le-Frith Derbys 44 D4
Chapel End Warks 35 F9
Chapel Green Warks 27 B11
Chapel Green Warks 35 G8
Chapel Haddlesey N Yorks 52 G1
Chapel Head Cambs 37 G9
Chapel Hill Aberds 89 E10
Chapel Hill Lincs 46 G6
Chapel Hill Mon 15 B11
Chapel Hill N Yorks 51 E9
Chapel Lawn Shrops 33 H9
Chapel-le-Dale N Yorks 50 B3
Chapel Milton Derbys 44 D4
Chapel of Garioch Aberds 83 A9
Chapel Row W Berks 18 E2
Chapel St Leonards Lincs 47 E9
Chapel Stile W&F 56 F5
Chapelgate Lincs 37 C10
Chapelhall N Lanark 68 D6
Chapelhill Dumfries 60 D6
Chapelhill Highld 87 D11
Chapelhill N Ayrs 66 B5
Chapelhill Perth 76 D3
Chapelhill Perth 76 E5
Chapelknowe Dumfries 61 F9
Chapelton Angus 77 C9
Chapelton Devon 6 D4
Chapelton Highld 81 B11
Chapelton S Lanark 68 F5
Chapeltown Blackburn 50 H3
Chapeltown Moray 82 A4
Chapeltown S Yorks 45 C7
Chapmans Well Devon 4 B4
Chapmanslade Wilts 16 G5
Chapmore End Herts 29 G10
Chappel Essex 30 F5
Chard Som 8 D2
Chardstock Devon 8 D2
Charfield S Glos 16 B4
Charford Worcs 26 B6
Charing Kent 20 G6
Charing Cross Dorset 9 C10
Charing Heath Kent 20 G6
Charingworth Glos 27 E9
Charlbury Oxon 27 G10
Charlcombe Bath 16 E4
Charlecote Warks 27 C9
Charles Devon 6 C5
Charles Tye Suff 31 C7
Charlesfield Dumfries 61 G7
Charleston Angus 76 C6
Charleston Renfs 68 D3
Charlestown Aberdeen 83 C11
Charlestown Corn 3 D9
Charlestown Derbys 44 C4
Charlestown Dorset 8 G5
Charlestown Fife 69 B9
Charlestown Gtr Man 44 B2
Charlestown Highld 85 A13
Charlestown Highld 87 G9
Charlestown W Yorks 50 G5
Charlestown of Aberlour Moray 88 D2
Charlesworth Derbys 44 C4
Charleton Devon 5 G8
Charlton Hants 17 G10
Charlton Herts 29 F8
Charlton London 19 D11
Charlton Northumb 62 E4
Charlton W Nhants 28 E2
Charlton Som 16 F3
Charlton Telford 34 D1
Charlton W Sus 11 C7
Charlton Wilts 9 B8
Charlton Wilts 16 C6
Charlton Wilts 17 F8
Charlton Worcs 27 D7
Charlton Abbots Glos 27 F7
Charlton Adam Som 8 B4
Charlton-All-Saints Wilts 9 B10
Charlton Down Dorset 8 E5
Charlton Horethorne Som 8 B5
Charlton Kings Glos 26 F6
Charlton Mackerell Som 8 B4
Charlton Marshall Dorset 9 D7
Charlton Musgrove Som 8 B6
Charlton on Otmoor Oxon 28 G2
Charltons Redcar 59 E7
Charlwood Sur 19 G9
Charlynch Som 7 C11
Charminster Dorset 8 E5
Charmouth Dorset 8 E2
Charndon Bucks 28 F3
Charney Bassett Oxon 17 B10
Charnock Richard Lancs 50 H1
Charsfield Suff 31 C9
Chart Corner Kent 20 F4
Chart Sutton Kent 20 G5
Charter Alley Hants 18 F2
Charterhouse Som 15 F10
Charterville Allotments Oxon 27 G10
Chartham Kent 21 F8
Chartham Hatch Kent 21 F8
Chartridge Bucks 18 A6
Charvil Wokingham 18 D4
Charwelton W Nhants 28 C2
Chasetown Staffs 34 E6
Chastleton Oxon 27 F9
Chasty Devon 6 F2
Chatburn Lancs 50 E3
Chatcull Staffs 34 B3
Chatham Medway 20 E4
Chathill Northumb 71 H10
Chattenden Medway 20 D4
Chatteris Cambs 37 G9
Chattisham Suff 31 D7
Chatto Borders 62 B3
Chatton Northumb 71 H9
Chawleigh Devon 7 E6
Chawley Oxon 17 A11
Chawston Bedford 29 C8
Chawton Hants 18 H4
Cheadle Gtr Man 44 D2
Cheadle Staffs 34 A6
Cheadle Heath Gtr Man 44 D2
Cheadle Hulme Gtr Man 44 D2
Cheam London 19 E9
Cheapside Sur 19 F7
Chearsley Bucks 28 G4
Chebsey Staffs 34 C4
Checkendon Oxon 18 C3
Checkley Ches E 43 H10
Checkley Hereford 26 E2
Checkley Staffs 34 B6
Chedburgh Suff 30 C4
Cheddar Som 15 F10
Cheddington Bucks 28 G6
Cheddleton Staffs 44 G3
Cheddon Fitzpaine Som 8 B1
Chedglow Wilts 16 B6
Chedgrave Norf 39 F9
Chedington Dorset 8 D3
Chediston Suff 39 H9
Chedworth Glos 27 G7
Chedzoy Som 15 H9
Cheeklaw Borders 70 E6
Cheeseman's Green Kent 13 C9
Cheglinch Devon 6 B4
Cheldon Devon 7 E6
Chelford Ches E 44 E2
Chell Heath Stoke 44 G2
Chellaston Derby 35 B9
Chellington Bedford 28 C6
Chelmarsh Shrops 34 G3
Chelmer Village Essex 30 H4
Chelmondiston Suff 31 E9
Chelmorton Derbys 44 F5
Chelmsford Essex 30 H4
Chelsea London 19 D9
Chelsfield London 19 E11
Chelsworth Suff 30 D6
Cheltenham Glos 26 F6
Chelveston N Nhants 28 B6
Chelvey N Som 15 E10
Chelwood Bath 16 E3
Chelwood Common E Sus 12 D3
Chelwood Gate E Sus 12 D3
Chelworth Wilts 16 B6
Chelworth Green Wilts 17 B7
Chemistry Shrops 33 A11
Chenies Bucks 19 B7
Cheny Longville Shrops 33 G10
Chepstow = Cas-gwent Mon 15 B11
Chequerfield W Yorks 51 G10
Cherhill Wilts 17 D7
Cherington Glos 16 B6
Cherington Warks 27 E9
Cheriton Devon 7 B6
Cheriton Hants 10 B4
Cheriton Kent 21 H8
Cheriton Swansea 23 G9
Cheriton Bishop Devon 7 G6
Cheriton Fitzpaine Devon 7 F7
Cheriton or Stackpole Elidor Pembs 22 G4
Cherrington Telford 34 C2
Cherry Burton E Yorks 52 E5
Cherry Hinton Cambs 29 C11
Cherry Orchard Worcs 26 C5
Cherry Willingham Lincs 46 E4
Cherrybank Perth 76 E4
Chertsey Sur 19 E7
Cheselbourne Dorset 9 E6
Chesham Bucks 18 A6
Chesham Bois Bucks 18 B6
Cheshunt Herts 19 A10
Cheslyn Hay Staffs 34 E5
Chessington London 19 E8
Chester Ches W 43 F7
Chester-le-Street Durham 58 A3
Chester Moor Durham 58 B3
Chesterblade Som 16 G3
Chesterfield Derbys 45 E7
Chesters Borders 62 A2
Chesters Borders 62 B2
Chesterton Cambs 29 B11
Chesterton Cambs 37 F7
Chesterton Glos 17 B7
Chesterton Oxon 28 F2
Chesterton Shrops 34 F3
Chesterton Staffs 44 H2
Chesterton Warks 27 C10
Chesterwood Northumb 62 G4
Chestfield Kent 21 E8
Cheston Devon 5 F7
Cheswardine Shrops 34 C3
Cheswick Northumb 71 F9
Chetnole Dorset 8 D5
Chettiscombe Devon 7 E8
Chettisham Cambs 37 G11
Chettle Dorset 9 C8
Chetton Shrops 34 F2
Chetwode Bucks 28 F3
Chetwynd Aston Telford 34 D3
Cheveley Cambs 30 B3
Chevening Kent 19 F11
Chevington Suff 30 C4
Chevithorne Devon 7 E8
Chew Magna Bath 16 E2
Chew Stoke Bath 16 E2
Chewton Keynsham Bath 16 E3
Chewton Mendip Som 16 F2
Chicheley M Keynes 28 D6
Chichester W Sus 11 D7
Chickerell Dorset 8 F5
Chicklade Wilts 9 A8
Chicksgrove Wilts 9 A8
Chidden Hants 10 C5
Chiddingfold Sur 18 H6
Chiddingly E Sus 12 E4
Chiddingstone Kent 19 G11
Chiddingstone Causeway Kent 20 G2
Chiddingstone Hoath Kent 12 B3
Chideock Dorset 8 E3
Chidham W Sus 11 D6
Chidswell W Yorks 51 G8
Chieveley W Berks 17 D11
Chignall St James Essex 30 H3
Chignall Smealy Essex 30 G3
Chigwell Essex 19 B11
Chigwell Row Essex 19 B11
Chilbolton Hants 17 H10
Chilcomb Hants 10 B4
Chilcombe Dorset 8 E4
Chilcompton Som 16 F3
Chilcote Leics 35 D8
Child Okeford Dorset 9 C7
Childer Thornton Ches W 42 E6
Childrey Oxon 17 C10
Child's Ercall Shrops 34 C2
Childswickham Worcs 27 E7
Childwall Mers 43 D7
Childwick Green Herts 29 G8
Chilfrome Dorset 8 E4
Chilgrove W Sus 11 C7
Chilham Kent 21 F7
Chilhampton Wilts 9 A9
Chilla Devon 6 F3
Chillaton Devon 4 C5
Chillenden Kent 21 F9
Chillerton IoW 10 F3
Chillesford Suff 31 C10
Chillingham Northumb 71 H9
Chillington Devon 5 G8
Chillington Som 8 C2
Chilmark Wilts 9 A8
Chilson Oxon 27 G10
Chilsworthy Corn 4 D5
Chilsworthy Devon 6 F2
Chilthorne Domer Som 8 C4
Chiltington E Sus 12 E2
Chilton Bucks 28 G3
Chilton Durham 58 D3
Chilton Oxon 17 C11
Chilton Cantelo Som 8 B4
Chilton Foliat Wilts 17 D10
Chilton Lane Durham 58 C4
Chilton Polden Som 15 H9
Chilton Street Suff 30 D4
Chilton Trinity Som 15 H8
Chilvers Coton Warks 35 F9
Chilwell Notts 35 B11
Chilworth Hants 10 C3
Chilworth Sur 19 G7
Chimney Oxon 17 A10
Chineham Hants 18 F3
Chingford London 19 B10
Chinley Derbys 44 D4
Chinley Head Derbys 44 D4
Chinnor Oxon 18 A4
Chipnall Shrops 34 B3
Chippenhall Green Suff 39 H8
Chippenham Cambs 30 B3
Chippenham Wilts 16 D6
Chipperfield Herts 19 A7
Chipping Herts 29 E10
Chipping Lancs 50 E2
Chipping Campden Glos 27 E8
Chipping Hill Essex 30 G5
Chipping Norton Oxon 27 F10
Chipping Ongar Essex 20 A2
Chipping Sodbury S Glos 16 C4
Chipping Warden W Nhants 27 D11
Chipstable Som 7 D9
Chipstead Kent 19 F11
Chipstead Sur 19 F9
Chirbury Shrops 33 F8
Chirk = Y Waun Wrex 33 B8
Chirk Bank Shrops 33 B8
Chirmorrie S Ayrs 54 B5
Chirnside Borders 71 E7
Chirnsidebridge Borders 71 E7
Chirton Wilts 17 F7
Chisbury Wilts 17 E9
Chiselborough Som 8 C3
Chiseldon Swindon 17 D8
Chiserley W Yorks 50 G6
Chislehampton Oxon 18 B2
Chislehurst London 19 D11
Chislet Kent 21 E9
Chiswell Green Herts 19 A8
Chiswick London 19 D9
Chiswick End Cambs 29 D10
Chisworth Derbys 44 C3
Chithurst W Sus 11 B7
Chittering Cambs 29 A11
Chitterne Wilts 16 G6
Chittlehamholt Devon 6 D5
Chittlehampton Devon 6 D5
Chittoe Wilts 16 E6
Chivenor Devon 6 C4
Chobham Sur 18 E6
Choicelee Borders 70 E6
Cholderton Wilts 17 G9
Cholesbury Bucks 28 H6
Chollerford Northumb 62 F5
Chollerton Northumb 62 F5
Cholmondeston Ches E 43 F9
Cholsey Oxon 18 C2
Cholstrey Hereford 25 C11
Chop Gate N Yorks 59 G6
Choppington Northumb 63 E8
Chopwell T&W 63 H7
Chorley Ches E 43 G8
Chorley Lancs 50 H1
Chorley Shrops 34 G2
Chorley Staffs 35 D6
Chorleywood Herts 19 B7
Chorlton cum Hardy Gtr Man 44 C2
Chorlton Lane Ches W 43 H7
Choulton Shrops 33 G9
Chowdene T&W 63 H8
Chowley Ches W 43 G7
Chrishall Essex 29 E11
Christchurch BCP 9 E10
Christchurch Cambs 37 F10
Christchurch Glos 26 G2
Christchurch Newport 15 C9
Christian Malford Wilts 16 D6
Christleton Ches W 43 F7
Christmas Common Oxon 18 B4
Christon N Som 15 F9
Christon Bank Northumb 63 A8
Christow Devon 5 C9
Chryston N Lanark 68 C5
Chudleigh Devon 5 C9
Chudleigh Knighton Devon 5 D9
Chulmleigh Devon 6 E5
Chunal Derbys 44 C4
Church Lancs 50 G3
Church Aston Telford 34 D3
Church Brampton W Nhants 28 B4
Church Broughton Derbys 35 B8
Church Crookham Hants 18 F5
Church Eaton Staffs 34 D4
Church End C Beds 28 E6
Church End C Beds 28 F6
Church End C Beds 29 E8
Church End Cambs 37 E9
Church End Cambs 37 G8
Church End E Yorks 53 D6
Church End Essex 30 D2
Church End Essex 30 F4
Church End Hants 18 F3
Church End Lincs 37 B8
Church End Warks 35 F8
Church End Warks 35 F8
Church End Wilts 17 D7
Church Enstone Oxon 27 F10
Church Fenton N Yorks 51 F11
Church Green Devon 7 G10
Church Green Norf 39 F6
Church Gresley Derbys 35 D8
Church Hanborough Oxon 27 G11
Church Hill Ches W 43 F9
Church Houses N Yorks 59 G7
Church Knowle Dorset 9 F8
Church Laneham Notts 46 E2
Church Langton Leics 36 F3
Church Lawford Warks 35 H10
Church Lawton Ches E 44 G2
Church Leigh Staffs 34 B6
Church Lench Worcs 27 C7
Church Mayfield Staffs 35 A7
Church Minshull Ches E 43 F9
Church Norton W Sus 11 E7
Church Preen Shrops 33 F11
Church Pulverbatch Shrops 33 E10
Church Stoke Powys 33 F8
Church Stowe W Nhants 28 C3
Church Street Kent 20 D4
Church Stretton Shrops 33 F10
Church Town N Lincs 45 B11
Church Town Sur 19 F10
Church Village Rhondda 14 C6
Church Warsop Notts 45 F9
Churcham Glos 26 G4
Churchbank Shrops 33 H8
Churchbridge Staffs 34 E5
Churchdown Glos 26 G5
Churchend Essex 21 B7
Churchend Essex 30 F3
Churchend S Glos 16 B4
Churchfield W Mid 34 F6
Churchgate Street Essex 29 G11
Churchill Devon 6 B4
Churchill Devon 8 D2
Churchill N Som 15 F10
Churchill Oxon 27 F9
Churchill Worcs 26 C6
Churchill Worcs 34 H4
Churchinford Som 7 E11
Churchover Warks 35 G11
Churchstanton Som 7 E10
Churchstow Devon 5 G8
Churchtown Derbys 44 F6
Churchtown IoM 48 C4
Churchtown Lancs 49 E4
Churchtown Mers 49 H3
Churnsike Lodge Northumb 62 F2
Churston Ferrers Torbay 5 F10
Churt Sur 18 H5
Churton Ches W 43 G7
Churwell W Yorks 51 G8
Chute Standen Wilts 17 F10
Chwilog Gwyn 40 G6
Chyandour Corn 2 F3
Cilan Uchaf Gwyn 40 H4
Cilcain Flint 42 F4
Cilcennin Ceredig 24 B2
Cilfor Gwyn 41 G8
Cilfrew Neath 14 A3
Cilfynydd Rhondda 14 B6
Cilgerran Pembs 22 B6
Cilgwyn Carms 24 F4
Cilgwyn Gwyn 40 E6
Cilgwyn Pembs 22 C5
Ciliau Aeron Ceredig 23 A9
Cill Donnain W Isles 84 F2
Cille Bhrighde W Isles 84 G2
Cille Pheadair W Isles 84 G2
Cilmeri = Cilmery Powys 25 C7
Cilmery = Cilmeri Powys 25 C7
Cilsan Carms 23 D10
Ciltalgarth Gwyn 41 F10
Cilwendeg Pembs 23 C7
Cilybebyll Neath 14 A3
Cilycwm Carms 24 E4
Cimla Neath 14 B3
Cinderford Glos 26 G3
Cippyn Pembs 22 B6
Circebost W Isles 90 D6
Cirencester Glos 17 A7
Ciribhig W Isles 90 C6
City London 19 C10
City Powys 33 G8
City Dulas Anglesey 40 B6
Clachaig Argyll 73 E10
Clachan Argyll 72 B6
Clachan Argyll 72 H6
Clachan Argyll 73 E7
Clachan Argyll 74 F4
Clachan Argyll 79 G11
Clachan Highld 85 E10
Clachan W Isles 84 D2
Clachan na Luib W Isles 84 B3
Clachan of Campsie E Dunb 68 C5
Clachan of Glendaruel Argyll 73 E8
Clachan-Seil Argyll 72 B6
Clachan Strachur Argyll 73 C9
Clachaneasy Dumfries 54 B6
Clachanmore Dumfries 54 E3
Clachbreck Argyll 72 F6
Clachnabrain Angus 82 G4
Clachtoll Highld 92 G3
Clackmannan Clack 69 A8
Clacton-on-Sea Essex 31 G8
Cladach Chireboist W Isles 84 B2
Claddach-knockline W Isles 84 B2
Cladich Argyll 74 E3
Claggan Highld 79 G9
Claggan Highld 80 F3
Claigan Highld 84 C7
Claines Worcs 26 C5
Clandown Bath 16 F3
Clanfield Hants 10 C6
Clanfield Oxon 17 A9
Clanville Hants 17 G10
Claonaig Argyll 73 H7
Claonel Highld 93 J8
Clap Hill Kent 13 C9
Clapgate Dorset 9 D9
Clapgate Herts 29 F11
Clapham Bedford 29 C7
Clapham London 19 D9
Clapham N Yorks 50 C3
Clapham W Sus 11 D9
Clappers Borders 71 E8
Clappersgate W&F 56 F5
Clapton Som 8 D3
Clapton-in-Gordano N Som 15 D10
Clapton-on-the-Hill Glos 27 G8
Clapworthy Devon 6 D5
Clara Vale T&W 63 G7
Clarach Ceredig 32 G2
Clarbeston Pembs 22 D5
Clarbeston Road Pembs 22 D5
Clarborough Notts 45 D11
Clardon Highld 94 D3
Clare Suff 30 D4
Clarebrand Dumfries 55 C10
Clarencefield Dumfries 60 G6
Clarilaw Borders 61 B11
Clark's Green Sur 19 H8
Clarkston E Renf 68 E4
Clashandorran Highld 87 G8
Clashcoig Highld 87 B9
Clashindarroch Aberds 88 E4
Clashmore Highld 87 C10
Clashmore Highld 92 F3
Clashnessie Highld 92 F3
Clashnoir Moray 82 A4
Clate Shetland 96 G7
Clathy Perth 76 F2
Clatt Aberds 83 A7
Clatter Powys 32 F5
Clatterford IoW 10 F3
Clatterin Bridge Aberds 83 F8
Clatworthy Som 7 C9
Claughton Lancs 49 E5
Claughton Lancs 50 C1
Claughton Mers 42 D6
Claverdon Warks 27 B8
Claverham N Som 15 E10
Clavering Essex 29 E11
Claverley Shrops 34 F3
Claverton Bath 16 E4
Clawdd-newydd Denb 42 G3
Clawthorpe W&F 49 B5
Clawton Devon 6 G2
Claxby Lincs 46 C5
Claxby Lincs 47 E8
Claxton N Yorks 52 C2
Claxton Norf 39 E9
Clay Common Suff 39 G10
Clay Coton W Nhants 36 H1
Clay Cross Derbys 45 F7
Clay Hill W Berks 18 D2
Clay Lake Lincs 37 C8
Claybokie Aberds 82 E2
Claybrooke Magna Leics 35 G10
Claybrooke Parva Leics 35 G10
Claydon Oxon 27 C11
Claydon Suff 31 C8
Claygate Dumfries 61 F9
Claygate Kent 12 B6
Claygate Sur 19 E8
Claygate Cross Kent 20 F3
Clayhanger Devon 7 D9
Clayhanger W Mid 34 E6
Clayhidon Devon 7 E10
Clayhill E Sus 13 D7
Clayhill Hants 10 D2
Clayock Highld 94 E3
Claypole Lincs 46 H2
Clayton S Yorks 45 B8
Clayton Staffs 34 A4
Clayton W Sus 12 E1
Clayton W Yorks 51 F7
Clayton Green Lancs 50 G1
Clayton-le-Moors Lancs 50 F3
Clayton-le-Woods Lancs 50 G1
Clayton West W Yorks 44 A6
Clayworth Notts 45 D11
Cleadale Highld 78 C7
Cleadon T&W 63 G9
Clearbrook Devon 4 E6
Clearwell Glos 26 H2
Cleasby N Yorks 58 E3
Cleat Orkney 95 K5
Cleatlam Durham 58 E2
Cleator Cumb 56 E2
Cleator Moor Cumb 56 E2
Clebrig Highld 93 F8
Cleckheaton W Yorks 51 G7
Clee St Margaret Shrops 34 G1
Cleedownton Shrops 34 G1
Cleehill Shrops 34 H1
Cleethorpes NE Lincs 47 B7
Cleeton St Mary Shrops 34 H2
Cleeve N Som 15 E10
Cleeve Hill Glos 26 F6
Cleeve Prior Worcs 27 D7
Clegyrnant Powys 32 E5
Clehonger Hereford 25 E11
Cleish Perth 76 H3
Cleland N Lanark 69 E7
Clench Common Wilts 17 E8
Clenchwarton Norf 38 C1
Clent Worcs 34 H5
Cleobury Mortimer Shrops 34 H2
Cleobury North Shrops 34 G2
Cleongart Argyll 65 E7
Clephanton Highld 87 F11
Clerklands Borders 61 A11
Clestrain Orkney 95 H4
Cleuch Head Borders 61 B11
Cleughbrae Dumfries 60 F6
Clevancy Wilts 17 D7
Clevedon N Som 15 D10
Cleveley Oxon 27 F10
Cleveleys Lancs 49 E3
Cleverton Wilts 16 C6
Clevis Bridgend 14 D4
Clewer Som 15 F10
Cley next the Sea Norf 38 A6
Cliaid W Isles 84 H1
Cliasmol W Isles 90 G5
Cliburn W&F 57 D7
Click Mill Orkney 95 F4
Cliddesden Hants 18 G3
Cliff End E Sus 13 E7
Cliffburn Angus 77 C9
Cliffe Medway 20 D4
Cliffe N Yorks 52 F2
Cliffe Woods Medway 20 D4
Clifford Hereford 25 D9
Clifford W Yorks 51 E10
Clifford Chambers Warks 27 C8
Clifford's Mesne Glos 26 F4
Cliffsend Kent 21 E10
Clifton Bristol 16 D2
Clifton C Beds 29 E8
Clifton Derbys 35 A7
Clifton Lancs 49 F4
Clifton N Yorks 51 E7
Clifton Northumb 63 E8
Clifton Nottingham 36 B1
Clifton Oxon 27 E11
Clifton S Yorks 45 C9
Clifton Stirling 74 D6
Clifton W&F 57 D7
Clifton Worcs 26 D5
Clifton York 52 D1
Clifton Campville Staffs 35 D8
Clifton Green Gtr Man 43 B10
Clifton Hampden Oxon 18 B2
Clifton Reynes M Keynes 28 C6
Clifton upon Dunsmore Warks 35 H11
Clifton upon Teme Worcs 26 B4
Cliftoncote Borders 70 H6
Cliftonville Kent 21 D10
Climaen gwyn Neath 24 H4
Climping W Sus 11 D9
Climpy S Lanark 69 E8
Clink Som 16 G4
Clint N Yorks 51 D8
Clint Green Norf 38 D6
Clintmains Borders 70 G5
Cliobh W Isles 90 D5
Clippesby Norf 39 D10
Clipsham Rutland 36 D5
Clipston W Nhants 36 G3
Clipstone Notts 45 F9
Clitheroe Lancs 50 E3
Cliuthar W Isles 90 H6
Clive Shrops 33 C11
Clivocast Shetland 96 C8
Clixby Lincs 46 B5
Clocaenog Denb 42 G3
Clochan Moray 88 B4
Clock Face Mers 43 C8
Clockmill Borders 70 E6
Cloddiau Powys 33 E8
Clodock Hereford 25 F10
Clola Aberds 89 D10
Clophill C Beds 29 E7
Clopton N Nhants 37 G6
Clopton Suff 31 C9
Clopton Corner Suff 31 C9
Clopton Green Suff 30 C4
Close Clark IoM 48 E2
Closeburn Dumfries 60 D4
Closworth Som 8 C4
Clothall Herts 29 E9
Clotton Ches W 43 F8
Clough Foot W Yorks 50 G5
Cloughton N Yorks 59 G11
Cloughton Newlands N Yorks 59 G11
Clousta Shetland 96 H5
Clouston Orkney 95 G3
Clova Aberds 82 A6
Clova Angus 82 F5
Clove Lodge Durham 57 E11
Clovelly Devon 6 D2
Clovenfords Borders 70 G3
Clovenstone Aberds 83 B9
Clovullin Highld 74 A3
Clow Bridge Lancs 50 G4
Clowne Derbys 45 E8
Clows Top Worcs 26 A4
Cloy Wrex 33 A9
Cluanie Inn Highld 80 B2
Cluanie Lodge Highld 80 B2
Clun Shrops 33 G9
Clunbury Shrops 33 G9
Clunderwen Carms 22 E6
Clune Highld 81 A9
Clunes Highld 80 E4
Clungunford Shrops 33 H9
Clunie Aberds 89 C6
Clunie Perth 76 C4
Clunton Shrops 33 G9
Cluny Fife 76 H5
Cluny Castle Highld 81 D8
Clutton Bath 16 F3
Clutton Ches W 43 G7
Clwt-grugoer Conwy 42 F2
Clwt-y-bont Gwyn 41 D7
Clydach Mon 25 G9
Clydach Swansea 14 A2
Clydach Vale Rhondda 14 B5
Clydebank W Dunb 68 C3
Clydey Pembs 23 C7
Clyffe Pypard Wilts 17 D7
Clynder Argyll 73 E11
Clyne Neath 14 A4
Clynelish Highld 93 J11
Clynnog-fawr Gwyn 40 E6
Clyro Powys 25 D9
Clyst Honiton Devon 7 G8
Clyst Hydon Devon 7 F9
Clyst St George Devon 5 C10
Clyst St Lawrence Devon 7 F9
Clyst St Mary Devon 7 G8
Cnoc Amhlaigh W Isles 91 D10
Cnwch-coch Ceredig 32 H2
Coachford Aberds 88 D4
Coad's Green Corn 4 D3
Coal Aston Derbys 45 E7
Coalbrookdale Telford 34 E2
Coalbrookvale Bl Gwent 25 H8
Coalburn S Lanark 69 G7
Coalburns T&W 63 G7
Coalcleugh Northumb 57 B10
Coaley Glos 16 A4
Coalhall E Ayrs 67 E7
Coalhill Essex 20 B4
Coalpit Heath S Glos 16 C3
Coalport Telford 34 E2
Coalsnaughton Clack 76 H2
Coaltown of Balgonie Fife 76 H5
Coaltown of Wemyss Fife 76 H6
Coalville Leics 35 D10
Coalway Glos 26 G2
Coat Som 8 B3
Coatbridge N Lanark 68 D6
Coatdyke N Lanark 68 D6
Coate Swindon 17 C8
Coate Wilts 17 E7
Coates Cambs 37 F9
Coates Glos 16 A6
Coates Lancs 50 E4
Coates Notts 46 D2
Coates W Sus 11 C8
Coatham Redcar 59 D6
Coatham Mundeville Darl 58 D3
Coatsgate Dumfries 60 C6
Cobbaton Devon 6 D5
Cobbler's Green Norf 39 F8
Coberley Glos 26 G6
Cobham Kent 20 E3
Cobham Sur 19 E8
Cobholm Island Norf 39 E11
Cobleland Stirling 75 H8
Cobnash Hereford 25 B11
Coburty Aberds 89 B9
Cock Bank Wrex 42 H6
Cock Bridge Aberds 82 C4
Cock Clarks Essex 20 A5
Cockayne N Yorks 59 G7
Cockayne Hatley C Beds 29 D9
Cockburnspath Borders 70 C6
Cockenzie and Port Seton E Loth 70 C3
Cockerham Lancs 49 D4
Cockermouth Cumb 56 C3
Cockernhoe Green Herts 29 F8
Cockfield Durham 58 D2
Cockfield Suff 30 C6
Cockfosters London 19 B9
Cocking W Sus 11 C7
Cockington Torbay 5 E9
Cocklake Som 15 G10
Cockley Beck W&F 56 F4
Cockley Cley Norf 38 E3
Cockshutt Shrops 33 C10
Cockthorpe Norf 38 A5
Cockwood Devon 5 C10
Cockyard Hereford 25 E11
Codda Corn 4 D2
Coddenham Suff 31 C8
Coddington Ches W 43 G7
Coddington Hereford 26 D4
Coddington Notts 46 G2
Codford St Mary Wilts 16 H6
Codford St Peter Wilts 16 H6
Codicote Herts 29 G9
Codmore Hill W Sus 11 B9
Codnor Derbys 45 H8
Codrington S Glos 16 D4
Codsall Staffs 34 E4
Codsall Wood Staffs 34 E4
Coed Duon = Blackwood Caerph 15 B7
Coed Mawr Gwyn 41 C7
Coed Morgan Mon 25 G10
Coed-Talon Flint 42 G5
Coed-y-bryn Ceredig 23 B8
Coed-y-paen Mon 15 B9
Coed-yr-ynys Powys 25 F8
Coed Ystumgwern Gwyn 32 C1
Coedely Rhondda 14 C6
Coedkernew Newport 15 C8
Coedpoeth Wrex 42 G5
Coedway Powys 33 D9
Coelbren Powys 24 G5
Coffinswell Devon 5 E9
Cofton Hackett Worcs 34 H6
Cogan V Glam 15 D7
Cogenhoe W Nhants 28 B5
Cogges Oxon 27 H10
Coggeshall Essex 30 F5
Coggeshall Hamlet Essex 30 F5
Coggins Mill E Sus 12 D4
Coig Peighinnean W Isles 91 A10
Coig Peighinnean Bhuirgh W Isles 91 B9
Coignafearn Lodge Highld 81 B8
Coilacriech Aberds 82 D5
Coilantogle Stirling 75 G8
Coilleag W Isles 84 G2
Coillore Highld 85 E8
Coity Bridgend 14 C5
Col W Isles 91 C9
Col Uarach W Isles 91 D9
Colaboll Highld 93 H8
Colan Corn 3 C7
Colaton Raleigh Devon 7 H9
Colbost Highld 84 D7
Colburn N Yorks 58 G2
Colby IoM 48 E2
Colby Norf 39 B8
Colby W&F 57 D8
Colchester Essex 31 F7
Colcot V Glam 15 E7
Cold Ash W Berks 18 E2
Cold Ashby W Nhants 36 H2
Cold Ashton S Glos 16 D4
Cold Aston Glos 27 G8
Cold Blow Pembs 22 E6
Cold Brayfield M Keynes 28 C6
Cold Hanworth Lincs 46 D4
Cold Harbour Lincs 36 B5
Cold Hatton Telford 34 C2
Cold Hesledon Durham 58 B5
Cold Higham W Nhants 28 C3
Cold Kirby N Yorks 51 A11
Cold Newton Leics 36 E3
Cold Northcott Corn 4 C3
Cold Norton Essex 20 A5
Cold Overton Leics 36 D4
Coldbackie Highld 93 D9
Coldbeck W&F 57 F9
Coldblow London 20 D2
Coldean Brighton 12 F2
Coldeast Devon 5 D9
Colden W Yorks 50 G5
Colden Common Hants 10 B3
Coldfair Green Suff 31 B11
Coldham Cambs 37 E10
Coldharbour Glos 16 A2
Coldharbour Kent 20 F2
Coldharbour Sur 19 G8
Coldingham Borders 71 D8
Coldrain Perth 76 G3
Coldred Kent 21 G9
Coldridge Devon 6 F5
Coldstream Angus 76 D6
Coldstream Borders 71 G7
Coldwaltham W Sus 11 C9
Coldwells Aberds 89 D11
Coldwells Croft Aberds 83 A7
Coldyeld Shrops 33 F9
Cole Som 8 A5
Cole Green Herts 29 G9
Cole Henley Hants 17 F11
Colebatch Shrops 33 G9
Colebrook Devon 7 F9
Colebrooke Devon 7 G6
Coleby Lincs 46 F3
Coleby N Lincs 52 H4
Coleford Devon 7 F6
Coleford Glos 26 G2
Coleford Som 16 G3
Colehill Dorset 9 D9
Coleman's Hatch E Sus 12 C3
Colemere Shrops 33 B10
Colemore Hants 10 A6
Coleorton Leics 35 D10
Colerne Wilts 16 D5
Cole's Green Suff 31 B9
Coles Green Suff 31 D7
Colesbourne Glos 26 G6
Colesden Bedford 29 C8
Coleshill Bucks 18 B6
Coleshill Oxon 17 B9
Coleshill Warks 35 G8
Colestocks Devon 7 F9
Colgate W Sus 11 A11
Colgrain Argyll 68 B2
Colinsburgh Fife 77 G7
Colinton Edin 69 D11
Colintraive Argyll 73 F9
Colkirk Norf 38 C5
Collace Perth 76 D5
Collafirth Shetland 96 G6
Collaton St Mary Torbay 5 F9
College Milton S Lanark 68 E5
Collessie Fife 76 F5
Collier Row London 20 B2
Collier Street Kent 20 G4
Collier's End Herts 29 F10
Collier's Green Kent 13 C6
Colliery Row T&W 58 B4
Collieston Aberds 89 F10
Collin Dumfries 60 F6
Collingbourne Ducis Wilts 17 F9
Collingbourne Kingston Wilts 17 F9
Collingham Notts 46 F2
Collingham W Yorks 51 E9
Collington Hereford 26 B3
Collingtree W Nhants 28 C4
Collins Green Warr 43 C8
Colliston Angus 77 C9
Collycroft Warks 35 G9
Collynie Aberds 89 E8
Collyweston N Nhants 36 E5
Colmonell S Ayrs 66 H4
Colmworth Bedford 29 C8
Coln Rogers Glos 27 H7
Coln St Aldwyn's Glos 27 H8
Coln St Dennis Glos 27 G7
Colnabaichin Aberds 82 C4
Colnbrook Slough 19 D7
Colne Cambs 37 H9
Colne Lancs 50 E4
Colne Edge Lancs 50 E4
Colne Engaine Essex 30 E5
Colney Norf 39 E7
Colney Heath Herts 29 H9
Colney Street Herts 19 A8
Colpy Aberds 89 E6
Colquhar Borders 70 F2
Colsterdale N Yorks 51 A7
Colsterworth Lincs 36 C5
Colston Bassett Notts 36 B3
Coltfield Moray 87 E14
Colthouse W&F 56 G5
Coltishall Norf 39 D8
Coltness N Lanark 69 E7
Colton Norf 39 E7
Colton N Yorks 51 E11
Colton Staffs 35 C6
Colton W Yorks 51 F9
Colton W&F 56 H5
Colva Powys 25 C9
Colvend Dumfries 55 D11
Colvister Shetland 96 D7
Colwall Green Hereford 26 D4
Colwall Stone Hereford 26 D4
Colwell Northumb 62 F5
Colwich Staffs 34 C6
Colwick Notts 36 A2
Colwinston V Glam 14 D5
Colworth W Sus 11 D8
Colwyn Bay = Bae Colwyn Conwy 41 C10
Colyford Devon 8 E1
Colyton Devon 8 E1
Combe Hereford 25 B10
Combe Oxon 27 G11
Combe W Berks 17 E10
Combe Common Sur 18 H6
Combe Down Bath 16 E4
Combe Florey Som 7 C10
Combe Hay Bath 16 F4
Combe Martin Devon 6 B4
Combe Moor Hereford 25 B10
Combe Raleigh Devon 7 F10
Combe St Nicholas Som 8 C2
Combeinteignhead Devon 5 D10
Comberbach Ches W 43 E9
Comberton Cambs 29 C10
Comberton Hereford 25 B11
Combpyne Devon 8 E1
Combridge Staffs 35 B7
Combrook Warks 27 C10
Combs Derbys 44 E4
Combs Suff 31 C7
Combs Ford Suff 31 C7
Combwich Som 15 G8
Comers Aberds 83 C8
Comins Coch Ceredig 32 G2
Commercial End Cambs 30 B2
Commins Capel Betws Ceredig 24 C3
Commins Coch Powys 32 E4
Common Edge Blackpool 49 F3
Common Side Derbys 45 E7
Commondale N Yorks 59 E7
Commonmoor Corn 4 E3
Commonside Ches W 43 E8
Compstall Gtr Man 44 C3
Compton Devon 5 E9
Compton Hants 10 B3
Compton Sur 18 G5
Compton Sur 18 G6
Compton W Berks 18 D2
Compton W Sus 11 C6
Compton Wilts 17 F8
Compton Abbas Dorset 9 C7
Compton Abdale Glos 27 G7
Compton Bassett Wilts 17 D7
Compton Beauchamp Oxon 17 C9
Compton Bishop Som 15 F9
Compton Chamberlayne Wilts 9 B9
Compton Dando Bath 16 E3
Compton Dundon Som 8 A3
Compton Martin Bath 15 F11
Compton Pauncefoot Som 8 B5
Compton Valence Dorset 8 E4
Comrie Fife 69 B9
Comrie Perth 75 E10
Conaglen House Highld 80 G2
Conchra Argyll 73 E9
Concraigie Perth 76 C4
Conder Green Lancs 49 D4
Conderton Worcs 26 E6
Condicote Glos 27 F8
Condorrat N Lanark 68 C6
Condover Shrops 33 E10
Coney Weston Suff 38 H5
Coneyhurst W Sus 11 B10
Coneysthorpe N Yorks 52 B3
Coneythorpe N Yorks 51 D9
Conford Hants 11 A7
Congash Highld 82 A2
Congdon's Shop Corn 4 D3
Congerstone Leics 35 E9
Congham Norf 38 C3
Congl-y-wal Gwyn 41 F9
Congleton Ches E 44 F2
Congresbury N Som 15 E10
Congreve Staffs 34 D5
Conicaval Moray 87 F12
Coningsby Lincs 46 G6
Conington Cambs 29 B10
Conington Cambs 37 G7
Conisbrough S Yorks 45 C9
Conisby Argyll 64 B3
Conisholme Lincs 47 C8
Coniston E Yorks 53 F7
Coniston W&F 56 G5
Coniston Cold N Yorks 50 D5
Conistone N Yorks 50 C5
Connah's Quay Flint 42 F5
Connel Argyll 74 D2
Connel Park E Ayrs 67 E9
Connor Downs Corn 2 F4
Conon Bridge Highld 87 F8
Conon House Highld 87 F8
Cononley N Yorks 50 E5
Conordan Highld 85 E10
Consall Staffs 44 H3
Consett Durham 58 A2
Constable Burton N Yorks 58 G2
Constantine Corn 2 G6
Constantine Bay Corn 3 B7
Contin Highld 86 F7
Contlaw Aberdeen 83 C10
Conwy Conwy 41 C9
Conyer Kent 20 E6
Conyers Green Suff 30 B5
Cooden E Sus 12 F6
Cooil IoM 48 E3
Cookbury Devon 6 F3
Cookham Windsor 18 C5
Cookham Dean Windsor 18 C5
Cookham Rise Windsor 18 C5
Cookhill Worcs 27 C7
Cookley Suff 39 H9
Cookley Worcs 34 G4
Cookley Green Oxon 18 B3
Cookney Aberds 83 D10
Cookridge W Yorks 51 E8
Cooksbridge E Sus 12 E3
Cooksmill Green Essex 30 H3
Coolham W Sus 11 B10
Cooling Medway 20 D4
Coombe Corn 3 D8
Coombe Corn 6 E1
Coombe Hants 10 B5
Coombe Wilts 17 F8
Coombe Bissett Wilts 9 B10
Coombe Hill Glos 26 F5
Coombe Keynes Dorset 9 F7
Coombes W Sus 11 D10
Coopersale Common Essex 19 A11
Cootham W Sus 11 C9
Copdock Suff 31 D8
Copford Green Essex 30 F6
Copgrove N Yorks 51 C9
Copister Shetland 96 F6
Cople Bedford 29 D8
Copley Durham 58 D1
Coplow Dale Derbys 44 E5
Copmanthorpe York 52 E1
Coppathorne Corn 4 A3
Coppenhall Staffs 34 D5
Coppenhall Moss Ches E 43 G10
Copperhouse Corn 2 F4
Coppingford Cambs 37 G7
Copplestone Devon 7 F6
Coppull Lancs 43 A8
Coppull Moor Lancs 43 A8
Copsale W Sus 11 B10
Copshaw Holm = Newcastleton Borders 61 E10
Copster Green Lancs 50 F2
Copston Magna Warks 35 G10
Copt Heath W Mid 35 H7
Copt Hewick N Yorks 51 B9
Copt Oak Leics 35 D11
Copthorne Shrops 33 D10
Copthorne Sur 12 C2
Copy's Green Norf 38 B5
Copythorne Hants 10 C2
Corbets Tey London 20 C2
Corbridge Northumb 62 G5
Corby N Nhants 36 G4
Corby Glen Lincs 36 C5
Cordon N Ayrs 66 C3
Coreley Shrops 26 A3
Cores End Bucks 18 C6
Corfe Som 7 E11
Corfe Castle Dorset 9 F8
Corfe Mullen Dorset 9 E8
Corfton Shrops 33 G10
Corgarff Aberds 82 C4
Corhampton Hants 10 B5
Corlae Dumfries 67 G9
Corley Warks 35 G9
Corley Ash Warks 35 G8
Corley Moor Warks 35 G8
Cornaa IoM 48 D4
Cornabus Argyll 64 D4
Cornel Conwy 41 D9
Corner Row Lancs 49 F4
Corney Cumb 56 G3
Cornforth Durham 58 C4
Cornhill Aberds 88 C5
Cornhill-on-Tweed Northumb 71 G7
Cornholme W Yorks 50 G5
Cornish Hall End Essex 30 E3
Cornquoy Orkney 95 J6
Cornsay Durham 58 B2
Cornsay Colliery Durham 58 B2
Corntown Highld 87 F8
Corntown V Glam 14 D5
Cornwell Oxon 27 F9
Cornwood Devon 5 F7
Cornworthy Devon 5 F9
Corpach Highld 80 F2
Corpusty Norf 39 B7
Corran Highld 74 A3
Corran Highld 85 H13
Corranbuie Argyll 73 G7
Corrany IoM 48 D4
Corrie N Ayrs 66 B3
Corrie Common Dumfries 61 E8
Corriecravie N Ayrs 66 D2
Corriemoillie Highld 86 E6
Corriemulzie Lodge Highld 86 B6
Corrievarkie Lodge Perth 81 F7
Corrievorrie Highld 81 A9
Corrimony Highld 86 H6
Corringham Lincs 46 C2
Corringham Thurrock 20 C4
Corris Gwyn 32 E3
Corris Uchaf Gwyn 32 E3
Corrour Shooting Lodge Highld 80 G6
Corrow Argyll 74 G4
Corry Highld 85 F11
Corry of Ardnagrask Highld 87 G8
Corrykinloch Highld 92 G6
Corrymuckloch Perth 75 D11
Corrynachenchy Argyll 79 G9
Cors-y-Gedol Gwyn 32 C1
Corsback Highld 94 C4
Corscombe Dorset 8 D4
Corse Aberds 88 D6
Corse Glos 26 F4
Corse Lawn Worcs 26 E5
Corse of Kinnoir Aberds 88 D5
Corsewall Dumfries 54 C3
Corsham Wilts 16 D5
Corsindae Aberds 83 C8
Corsley Wilts 16 G5
Corsley Heath Wilts 16 G5
Corsock Dumfries 60 F3
Corston Bath 16 E3
Corston Wilts 16 C6
Corstorphine Edin 69 C10
Cortachy Angus 76 B6
Corton Suff 39 F11
Corton Wilts 16 G6
Corton Denham Som 8 B5
Coruanan Lodge Highld 80 G2
Corunna W Isles 84 B3
Corwen Denb 33 A6
Coryton Devon 4 C5
Coryton Thurrock 20 C4
Cosby Leics 35 F11
Coseley W Mid 34 F5
Cosgrove W Nhants 28 D4
Cosham Ptsmth 10 D5
Cosheston Pembs 22 F5
Cossall Notts 35 A10
Cossington Leics 36 D2
Cossington Som 15 G9
Costa Orkney 95 F4
Costessey Norf 39 D7
Costock Notts 36 C1
Coston Leics 36 C4
Cote Oxon 17 A10
Cotebrook Ches W 43 F8
Cotehill Cumb 56 A6
Cotes Leics 36 C1
Cotes Staffs 34 B4
Cotes W&F 56 H6
Cotesbach Leics 35 G11
Cotgrave Notts 36 B2
Cothall Aberds 83 B10
Cotham Notts 45 H11
Cothelstone Som 7 C10
Cotherstone Durham 58 E1
Cothill Oxon 17 B11
Cotleigh Devon 7 F11
Cotmanhay Derbys 35 A10
Cotmaton Devon 7 H10
Coton Cambs 29 C11
Coton Staffs 34 B5
Coton Staffs 34 C4
Coton W Nhants 28 A3
Coton Clanford Staffs 34 C4
Coton Hill Shrops 33 D10
Coton Hill Staffs 34 B5
Coton in the Elms Derbys 35 D8
Cott Devon 5 E8
Cottam E Yorks 52 C5
Cottam Lancs 49 F5
Cottam Notts 46 E2
Cottartown Highld 87 H13
Cottenham Cambs 29 B11
Cotterdale N Yorks 57 G10
Cottered Herts 29 F10
Cotteridge W Mid 34 H6
Cotterstock N Nhants 36 F6
Cottesbrooke W Nhants 28 A4
Cottesmore Rutland 36 D5
Cotteylands Devon 7 E8
Cottingham E Yorks 52 F6
Cottingham N Nhants 36 F4
Cottingley W Yorks 51 F7
Cottisford Oxon 28 E2
Cotton Staffs 44 H4
Cotton Suff 31 B7
Cotton End Bedford 29 D7
Cottown Aberds 83 A7
Cottown Aberds 83 B9
Cottown Aberds 89 D8
Cotwalton Staffs 34 B5
Couch's Mill Corn 4 F2
Coughton Hereford 26 F2
Coughton Warks 27 B7
Coulaghailtro Argyll 72 G6
Coulags Highld 86 G2
Coulby Newham Mbro 58 E6
Coulderton Cumb 56 F1
Coulin Highld 86 F3
Coull Aberds 83 C7
Coull Argyll 64 B3
Coulport Argyll 73 E11
Coulsdon London 19 F9
Coulston Wilts 16 F6
Coulter S Lanark 69 G9
Coulton N Yorks 52 B2
Cound Shrops 34 E1
Coundon Durham 58 D3
Coundon W Mid 35 G9
Coundon Grange Durham 58 D3
Countersett N Yorks 57 H11
Countess Wilts 17 G8
Countess Wear Devon 5 C10
Countesthorpe Leics 36 F1
Countisbury Devon 7 B6
County Oak W Sus 12 C1
Coup Green Lancs 50 G1
Coupar Angus Perth 76 C5
Coupland Northumb 71 G8
Cour Argyll 65 D9
Courance Dumfries 60 D6
Court-at-Street Kent 13 C9
Court Henry Carms 23 D10
Courteenhall W Nhants 28 C4
Courtsend Essex 21 B7
Courtway Som 7 C11
Cousland Midloth 70 D2
Cousley Wood E Sus 12 C5
Cove Argyll 73 E11
Cove Borders 70 C6
Cove Devon 7 E8
Cove Hants 18 F5
Cove Highld 91 H13
Cove Bay Aberdeen 83 C11
Cove Bottom Suff 39 H10
Covehithe Suff 39 G11
Coven Staffs 34 E5
Coveney Cambs 37 G10
Covenham St Bartholomew Lincs 47 C7
Covenham St Mary Lincs 47 C7
Coventry W Mid 35 H9
Coverack Corn 3 H6
Coverham N Yorks 58 H2
Covesea Moray 88 A1
Covington Cambs 29 A7
Covington S Lanark 69 G8
Cow Ark Lancs 50 E2
Cowan Bridge Lancs 50 B2
Cowbeech E Sus 12 E5
Cowbit Lincs 37 D8
Cowbridge Lincs 47 H7
Cowbridge Som 7 B8
Cowbridge = Y Bont-Faen V Glam 14 D5
Cowdale Derbys 44 E4
Cowden Kent 12 B3
Cowdenbeath Fife 69 A10
Cowdenburn Borders 69 E11
Cowers Lane Derbys 45 H7
Cowes IoW 10 E3
Cowesby N Yorks 58 H5
Cowfold W Sus 11 B11
Cowgill W&F 57 H9
Cowie Aberds 83 E10
Cowie Stirling 69 B7
Cowley Devon 7 G8
Cowley Glos 26 G6
Cowley London 19 C7
Cowley Oxon 18 A2
Cowleymoor Devon 7 E8
Cowling Lancs 50 H1
Cowling N Yorks 50 E5
Cowling N Yorks 58 H3
Cowlinge Suff 30 C4
Cowpe Lancs 50 G4
Cowpen Northumb 63 E8
Cowpen Bewley Stockton 58 D5
Cowplain Hants 10 C5
Cowshill Durham 57 B10
Cowslip Green N Som 15 E10
Cowstrandburn Fife 69 A9
Cowthorpe N Yorks 51 D10
Cox Common Suff 39 G10
Cox Green Windsor 18 D5
Cox Moor Notts 45 G9
Coxbank Ches E 34 A2
Coxbench Derbys 35 A9
Coxford Norf 38 C4
Coxford Soton 10 C2
Coxheath Kent 20 F4
Coxhill Kent 21 G9
Coxhoe Durham 58 C4
Coxley Som 16 G2
Coxwold N Yorks 51 B11
Coychurch Bridgend 14 D5
Coylton S Ayrs 67 D7
Coylumbridge Highld 81 B11
Coynach Aberds 82 C6
Coynachie Aberds 88 E4
Coytrahen Bridgend 14 C4
Crabadon Devon 5 F8
Crabbs Cross Worcs 27 B7
Crabtree W Sus 11 B11
Crackenthorpe W&F 57 D8
Crackington Haven Corn 4 B2
Crackley Warks 27 A9
Crackleybank Shrops 34 D3
Crackpot N Yorks 57 G11
Cracoe N Yorks 50 C5
Craddock Devon 7 E9
Cradhlastadh W Isles 90 D5
Cradley Hereford 26 D4
Cradley Heath W Mid 34 G5
Crafthole Corn 4 F4
Cragg Vale W Yorks 50 G6
Craggan Highld 82 A2
Craggie Highld 87 H10
Craggie Highld 93 H11
Craghead Durham 58 A3
Crai Powys 24 F5
Craibstone Moray 88 C4
Craichie Angus 77 C8
Craig Dumfries 55 B9
Craig Dumfries 55 C9
Craig Highld 86 G3
Craig Castle Aberds 82 A6
Craig-cefn-parc Swansea 14 A2
Craig Penllyn V Glam 14 D5
Craig-y-don Conwy 41 B9
Craig-y-nos Powys 24 G5
Craiganor Lodge Perth 75 B9
Craigdam Aberds 89 E8
Craigdarroch Dumfries 60 D3
Craigdarroch Highld 86 F7
Craigdhu Highld 86 G7
Craigearn Aberds 83 B9
Craigellachie Moray 88 D2
Craigencross Dumfries 54 C3
Craigend Perth 76 E4
Craigend Stirling 68 B6
Craigendive Argyll 73 E9
Craigendoran Argyll 68 B2
Craigends Renfs 68 D3
Craigens Argyll 64 B3
Craigens E Ayrs 67 E8
Craighat Stirling 68 B3
Craighead Fife 77 G9
Craighlaw Mains Dumfries 54 C6
Craighouse Argyll 72 G4
Craigie Aberds 83 B11
Craigie Dundee 77 D7
Craigie Perth 76 C4
Craigie Perth 76 E4
Craigie S Ayrs 67 C7
Craigiefield Orkney 95 G5
Craigielaw E Loth 70 C3
Craiglockhart Edin 69 C11
Craigmalloch E Ayrs 67 G7
Craigmaud Aberds 89 C8
Craigmillar Edin 69 C11
Craigmore Argyll 73 G10
Craignant Shrops 33 B8
Craigneuk N Lanark 68 D6
Craigneuk N Lanark 68 E6
Craignure Argyll 79 H10
Craigo Angus 77 A9
Craigow Perth 76 G3
Craigrothie Fife 76 F6
Craigroy Moray 87 F14
Craigruie Stirling 75 E7
Craigston Castle Aberds 89 C7
Craigton Aberdeen 83 C10
Craigton Angus 76 B6
Craigton Angus 77 D8
Craigton Highld 87 B9
Craigtown Highld 93 D11
Craik Borders 61 C9
Crail Fife 77 G9
Crailing Borders 62 A2
Crailinghall Borders 62 A2
Craiselound N Lincs 45 C11
Crakehill N Yorks 51 B10
Crakemarsh Staffs 35 B6
Crambe N Yorks 52 C3
Cramlington Northumb 63 F8
Cramond Edin 69 C10
Cramond Bridge Edin 69 C10
Cranage Ches E 43 F10
Cranberry Staffs 34 B4
Cranborne Dorset 9 C9
Cranbourne Brack 18 D6
Cranbrook Devon 7 G9
Cranbrook Kent 13 C6
Cranbrook Common Kent 13 C6
Crane Moor S Yorks 45 B7
Crane's Corner Norf 38 D5
Cranfield C Beds 28 D6
Cranford London 19 D8
Cranford St Andrew N Nhants 36 H5
Cranford St John N Nhants 36 H5
Cranham Glos 26 G5
Cranham London 20 C2
Crank Mers 43 C8
Crank Wood Gtr Man 43 B9
Cranleigh Sur 19 H7
Cranley Suff 31 A8
Cranmer Green Suff 31 A7
Cranmore IoW 10 E2

F

G

Glenhurich Highld 79 E11
Glenkerry Borders 61 B8
Glenkiln Dumfries 60 F4
Glenkindie Aberds 82 B6
Glenlatterach Moray 88 C1
Glenlee Dumfries 55 A9
Glenlichorn Perth 75 F10
Glenlivet Moray 82 A3
Glenlochsie Perth 82 F2
Glenloig N Ayrs 66 C2
Glenluce Dumfries 54 D5
Glenmallan Argyll 74 H5
Glenmarksie Highld 86 F6
Glenmassan Argyll 73 E10
Glenmavis N Lanark 68 D6
Glenmaye IoM 48 E2
Glenmidge Dumfries 60 E4
Glenmore Argyll 73 B7
Glenmore Highld 85 D9
Glenmore Lodge Highld 82 C1
Glenmoy Angus 77 A7
Glenogil Angus 77 A7
Glenprosen Lodge Angus 82 G4
Glenprosen Village Angus 82 G5
Glenquiech Angus 77 A7
Glenreasdell Mains Argyll 73 H7
Glenree N Ayrs 66 D2
Glenridding W&F 56 E5
Glenrossal Highld 92 J7
Glenrothes Fife 76 G5
Glensanda Highld 79 G11
Glensaugh Aberds 83 F8
Glenshero Lodge Highld 81 D7
Glenstockadale Dumfries 54 C3
Glenstriven Argyll 73 F9
Glentaggart S Lanark 69 H7
Glentham Lincs 46 C4
Glentirranmuir Stirling 68 A5
Glenton Aberds 83 A8
Glentress Borders 69 G11
Glentromie Lodge Highld 81 D9
Glentrool Village Dumfries 54 B6
Glentruan IoM 48 B4
Glentruim House Highld 81 D8
Glentworth Lincs 46 D3
Glenuig Highld 79 D9
Glenurquhart Highld 87 E10
Glespin S Lanark 69 H7
Gletness Shetland 96 H6
Glewstone Hereford 26 F2
Glinton Pboro 37 E7
Glooston Leics 36 F3
Glororum Northumb 71 G10
Glossop Derbys 44 C4
Gloster Hill Northumb 63 C8
Gloucester Glos 26 G5
Gloup Shetland 96 C7
Glusburn N Yorks 50 E6
Glutt Lodge Highld 93 F12
Glutton Bridge Staffs 44 F4
Glympton Oxon 27 F11
Glyn-Ceiriog Wrex 33 B8
Glyn-Cywarch Gwyn 41 G8
Glyn Ebwy = Ebbw Vale Bl Gwent 25 H8
Glyn-neath = Glynedd Neath 24 H5
Glynarthen Ceredig 23 B8
Glynbrochan Powys 32 G5
Glyncoch Rhondda 14 B6
Glyncorrwg Neath 14 B4
Glynde E Sus 12 F3
Glyndebourne E Sus 12 E3
Glyndyfrdwy Denb 33 A7
Glynedd = Glyn-neath Neath 24 H5
Glynogwr Bridgend 14 C5
Glyntaff Rhondda 14 C6
Glyntawe Powys 24 G5
Gnosall Staffs 34 C4
Gnosall Heath Staffs 34 C4
Goadby Leics 36 F3
Goadby Marwood Leics 36 C3
Goat Lees Kent 21 G7
Goatacre Wilts 17 D7
Goathill Dorset 8 C5
Goathland N Yorks 59 F9
Goathurst Som 8 A1
Gobernuisgach Lodge Highld 92 E7
Gobhaig W Isles 90 G5
Gobowen Shrops 33 B9
Godalming Sur 18 G6
Godley Gtr Man 44 C3
Godmanchester Cambs 29 A9
Godmanstone Dorset 8 E5
Godmersham Kent 21 F7
Godney Som 15 G10
Godolphin Cross Corn 2 F5
Godre'r-graig Neath 24 H4
Godshill Hants 9 C10
Godshill IoW 10 F4
Godstone Sur 19 F10
Godwinscroft Hants 9 E10
Goetre Mon 25 H10
Goferydd Anglesey 40 B4
Goff's Oak Herts 19 A10
Gogar Edin 69 C10
Goginan Ceredig 32 G2
Golan Gwyn 41 F7
Golant Corn 4 F2
Golberdon Corn 4 D4
Golborne Gtr Man 43 C9
Golcar W Yorks 51 H7
Gold Hill Norf 37 F11
Goldcliff Newport 15 C9
Golden Cross E Sus 12 E4
Golden Green Kent 20 G3
Golden Grove Carms 23 E10
Golden Hill Hants 10 E1
Golden Pot Hants 18 G4
Golden Valley Glos 26 F6
Goldenhill Stoke 44 G2
Golders Green London 19 C9
Goldhanger Essex 30 H6
Golding Shrops 33 E11
Goldington Bedford 29 C7
Goldsborough N Yorks 51 D9
Goldsborough N Yorks 59 E9
Goldsithney Corn 2 F4
Goldsworthy Devon 6 D2
Goldthorpe S Yorks 45 B8
Gollanfield Highld 87 F11
Golspie Highld 93 J11
Golval Highld 93 C11
Gomeldon Wilts 17 H8
Gomersal W Yorks 51 G8
Gomshall Sur 19 G7
Gonalston Notts 45 H10
Gonfirth Shetland 96 G5
Good Easter Essex 30 G3
Gooderstone Norf 38 E3
Goodleigh Devon 6 C5
Goodmanham E Yorks 52 E4
Goodnestone Kent 21 E7
Goodnestone Kent 21 F9
Goodrich Hereford 26 G2
Goodrington Torbay 5 F9
Goodshaw Lancs 50 G4
Goodwick = Wdig Pembs 22 C4
Goodworth Clatford Hants 17 G10
Goole E Yorks 52 G3
Goonbell Corn 2 E6
Goonhavern Corn 3 D6
Goose Eye W Yorks 50 E6
Goose Green Gtr Man 43 B8
Goose Green Norf 39 G7
Goose Green W Sus 11 C10
Gooseham Corn 6 E1
Goosey Oxon 17 B10
Goosnargh Lancs 50 F1
Goostrey Ches E 43 E10
Gorcott Hill Warks 27 B7
Gord Shetland 96 L6
Gordon Borders 70 F5
Gordonbush Highld 93 J11
Gordonsburgh Moray 88 B4
Gordonstoun Moray 88 B1
Gordonstown Aberds 88 C5
Gordonstown Aberds 89 E7
Gore Kent 21 F10
Gore Cross Wilts 17 F7
Gore Pit Essex 30 G5
Gorebridge Midloth 70 D2
Gorefield Cambs 37 D10
Gorey Jersey 11
Gorgie Edin 69 C11
Goring Oxon 18 C3
Goring-by-Sea W Sus 11 D10
Goring Heath Oxon 18 D3
Gorleston-on-Sea Norf 39 E11
Gornalwood W Mid 34 F5
Gorrachie Aberds 89 C7
Gorran Churchtown Corn 3 E8
Gorran Haven Corn 3 E9
Gorrenberry Borders 61 D10
Gors Ceredig 32 H2
Gorse Hill Swindon 17 C8
Gorsedd Flint 42 E4
Gorseinon Swansea 23 G10
Gorseness Orkney 95 G5
Gorsgoch Ceredig 23 A9
Gorslas Carms 23 E10
Gorsley Glos 26 F3
Gorstan Highld 86 E6
Gorstanvorran Highld 79 D11
Gorsteyhill Staffs 43 G10
Gorsty Hill Staffs 35 C7
Gortantaoid Argyll 64 A4
Gorton Gtr Man 44 C2
Gosbeck Suff 31 C8
Gosberton Lincs 37 B8
Gosberton Clough Lincs 37 C7
Gosfield Essex 30 F4
Gosford Hereford 26 B2
Gosforth Cumb 56 F2
Gosforth T&W 63 G8
Gosmore Herts 29 F8
Gosport Hants 10 E5
Gossabrough Shetland 96 E7
Gossington Glos 16 A4
Goswick Northumb 71 F9
Gotham Notts 35 B11
Gotherington Glos 26 F6
Gott Shetland 96 J6
Goudhurst Kent 12 C6
Goulceby Lincs 46 E6
Gourdas Aberds 89 D7
Gourdon Aberds 83 F10
Gourock Invclyd 73 F11
Govan Glasgow 68 D4
Govanhill Glasgow 68 D4
Goveton Devon 5 G8
Govilon Mon 25 G9
Gowanhill Aberds 89 B10
Gowdall E Yorks 52 G2
Gowerton Swansea 23 G10
Gowkhall Fife 69 B9
Gowthorpe E Yorks 52 D3
Goxhill E Yorks 53 E7
Goxhill N Lincs 53 G7
Goxhill Haven N Lincs 53 G7
Goytre Neath 14 C3
Grabhair W Isles 91 F8
Graby Lincs 37 C6
Grade Corn 2 H6
Graffham W Sus 11 C8
Grafham Cambs 29 B8
Grafham Sur 19 G7
Grafton Hereford 25 E11
Grafton N Yorks 51 C10
Grafton Oxon 17 A9
Grafton Shrops 33 D10
Grafton Worcs 26 B2
Grafton Flyford Worcs 26 C6
Grafton Regis W Nhants 28 D4
Grafton Underwood N Nhants 36 G5
Grafty Green Kent 20 G5
Graianrhyd Denb 42 G5
Graig Conwy 41 C10
Graig Denb 42 E3
Graig-fechan Denb 42 G4
Grain Medway 20 D5
Grainsby Lincs 46 C6
Grainthorpe Lincs 47 C7
Grampound Corn 3 E8
Grampound Road Corn 3 D8
Gramsdal W Isles 84 C3
Granborough Bucks 28 F4
Granby Notts 36 B3
Grandborough Warks 27 B11
Grandtully Perth 76 B2
Grange Cumb 56 E4
Grange E Ayrs 67 C7
Grange Medway 20 E4
Grange Mers 42 D5
Grange Perth 76 E5
Grange Crossroads Moray 88 C4
Grange Hall Moray 87 E13
Grange Hill Essex 19 B11
Grange Moor W Yorks 51 H8
Grange of Lindores Fife 76 F5
Grange-over-Sands W&F 49 B4
Grange Villa Durham 58 A3
Grangemill Derbys 44 G6
Grangemouth Falk 69 B8
Grangepans Falk 69 B9
Grangetown Cardiff 15 D7
Grangetown Redcar 59 D6
Granish Highld 81 B11
Gransmoor E Yorks 53 D7
Granston Pembs 22 C3
Grantchester Cambs 29 C11
Grantham Lincs 36 B5
Grantley N Yorks 51 C8
Grantlodge Aberds 83 B9
Granton Dumfries 60 C6
Granton Edin 69 C11
Grantown-on-Spey Highld 82 A2
Grantshouse Borders 71 D7
Grappenhall Warr 43 D9
Grasby Lincs 46 B4
Grasmere W&F 56 F5
Grasscroft Gtr Man 44 B3
Grassendale Mers 43 D6
Grassholme Durham 57 D11
Grassington N Yorks 50 C6
Grassmoor Derbys 45 F8
Grassthorpe Notts 45 F11
Grateley Hants 17 G9
Gratwich Staffs 34 B6
Graveley Cambs 29 B9
Graveley Herts 29 F9
Gravelly Hill W Mid 35 F7
Gravels Shrops 33 E9
Graven Shetland 96 F6
Graveney Kent 21 E7
Gravesend Herts 29 F11
Gravesend Kent 20 D3
Grayingham Lincs 46 C3
Grayrigg W&F 57 G7
Grays Thurrock 20 D3
Grayshott Hants 18 H5
Grayswood Sur 11 A8
Graythorp Hrtlpl 58 D6
Grazeley Wokingham 18 E3
Greasbrough S Yorks 45 C8
Greasby Mers 42 D5
Great Abington Cambs 30 D2
Great Addington N Nhants 28 A6
Great Alne Warks 27 C8
Great Altcar Lancs 42 B6
Great Amwell Herts 29 G10
Great Asby W&F 57 E8
Great Ashfield Suff 30 B6
Great Ayton N Yorks 59 E6
Great Baddow Essex 20 A4
Great Bardfield Essex 30 E3
Great Barford Bedford 29 C8
Great Barr W Mid 34 F6
Great Barrington Glos 27 G9
Great Barrow Ches W 43 F7
Great Barton Suff 30 B5
Great Barugh N Yorks 52 B3
Great Bavington Northumb 62 E5
Great Bealings Suff 31 D9
Great Bedwyn Wilts 17 E9
Great Bentley Essex 31 F8
Great Billing W Nhants 28 B5
Great Bircham Norf 38 B3
Great Blakenham Suff 31 C8
Great Blencow W&F 56 C6
Great Bolas Telford 34 C2
Great Bookham Sur 19 F8
Great Bourton Oxon 27 D11
Great Bowden Leics 36 G3
Great Bradley Suff 30 C3
Great Braxted Essex 30 G5
Great Bricett Suff 31 C7
Great Brickhill Bucks 28 E6
Great Bridge W Mid 34 F5
Great Bridgeford Staffs 34 C4
Great Brington W Nhants 28 B3
Great Bromley Essex 31 F7
Great Broughton Cumb 56 C2
Great Broughton N Yorks 59 F6
Great Budworth Ches W 43 E9
Great Burdon Darl 58 E4
Great Burgh Sur 19 F9
Great Burstead Essex 20 B3
Great Busby N Yorks 58 F6
Great Canfield Essex 30 G2
Great Carlton Lincs 47 D8
Great Casterton Rutland 36 E6
Great Chart Kent 13 B8
Great Chatwell Staffs 34 D3
Great Chesterford Essex 30 D2
Great Cheverell Wilts 16 F6
Great Chishill Cambs 29 E11
Great Clacton Essex 31 G8
Great Cliff W Yorks 51 H9
Great Clifton Cumb 56 D2
Great Coates NE Lincs 46 B6
Great Comberton Worcs 26 D6
Great Corby Cumb 56 A6
Great Cornard Suff 30 D5
Great Cowden E Yorks 53 E8
Great Coxwell Oxon 17 B9
Great Crakehall N Yorks 58 G3
Great Cransley N Nhants 36 H4
Great Cressingham Norf 38 E4
Great Crosby Mers 42 C6
Great Cubley Derbys 35 B7
Great Dalby Leics 36 D3
Great Denham Bedford 29 D7
Great Doddington N Nhants 28 B5
Great Dunham Norf 38 D4
Great Dunmow Essex 30 F3
Great Durnford Wilts 17 H8
Great Easton Essex 30 F3
Great Easton Leics 36 F4
Great Eccleston Lancs 49 E4
Great Edstone N Yorks 52 A3
Great Ellingham Norf 38 F6
Great Elm Som 16 G4
Great Eversden Cambs 29 C10
Great Fencote N Yorks 58 G3
Great Finborough Suff 31 C7
Great Fransham Norf 38 D4
Great Gaddesden Herts 29 G7
Great Gidding Cambs 37 G7
Great Givendale E Yorks 52 D4
Great Glemham Suff 31 B10
Great Glen Leics 36 F2
Great Gonerby Lincs 36 B4
Great Gransden Cambs 29 C9
Great Green Norf 39 G8
Great Green Suff 30 C6
Great Habton N Yorks 52 B3
Great Hale Lincs 37 A7
Great Hallingbury Essex 30 G2
Great Hampden Bucks 18 A5
Great Harrowden N Nhants 28 A5
Great Harwood Lancs 50 F3
Great Haseley Oxon 18 A3
Great Hatfield E Yorks 53 E7
Great Haywood Staffs 34 C6
Great Heath W Mid 35 G9
Great Heck N Yorks 52 G1
Great Henny Essex 30 E5
Great Hinton Wilts 16 F6
Great Hockham Norf 38 F5
Great Holland Essex 31 G9
Great Horkesley Essex 30 E6
Great Hormead Herts 29 F10
Great Horton W Yorks 51 F7
Great Horwood Bucks 28 E4
Great Houghton S Yorks 45 B8
Great Houghton W Nhants 28 C4
Great Hucklow Derbys 44 E5
Great Kelk E Yorks 53 D7
Great Kimble Bucks 28 H5
Great Kingshill Bucks 18 B5
Great Langton N Yorks 58 G3
Great Leighs Essex 30 G4
Great Lever Gtr Man 43 B10
Great Limber Lincs 46 B5
Great Linford M Keynes 28 D5
Great Livermere Suff 30 A5
Great Longstone Derbys 44 E6
Great Lumley Durham 58 B3
Great Lyth Shrops 33 E10
Great Malvern Worcs 26 D4
Great Maplestead Essex 30 E5
Great Marton Blackpool 49 F3
Great Massingham Norf 38 C3
Great Melton Norf 39 E7
Great Milton Oxon 18 A3
Great Missenden Bucks 18 A5
Great Mitton Lancs 50 F3
Great Mongeham Kent 21 F10
Great Moulton Norf 39 F7
Great Munden Herts 29 F10
Great Musgrave W&F 57 E9
Great Ness Shrops 33 D9
Great Notley Essex 30 F4
Great Oakley Essex 31 F8
Great Oakley N Nhants 36 G4
Great Offley Herts 29 F8
Great Ormside W&F 57 E9
Great Orton Cumb 56 A5
Great Ouseburn N Yorks 51 C10
Great Oxendon W Nhants 36 G3
Great Oxney Green Essex 30 H3
Great Palgrave Norf 38 D4
Great Parndon Essex 29 H11
Great Paxton Cambs 29 B9
Great Plumpton Lancs 49 F3
Great Plumstead Norf 39 D9
Great Ponton Lincs 36 B5
Great Preston W Yorks 51 G10
Great Raveley Cambs 37 G8
Great Rissington Glos 27 G8
Great Rollright Oxon 27 E10
Great Ryburgh Norf 38 C5
Great Ryle Northumb 62 B6
Great Ryton Shrops 33 E10
Great Saling Essex 30 F4
Great Salkeld W&F 57 C7
Great Sampford Essex 30 E3
Great Sankey Warr 43 D8
Great Saxham Suff 30 B4
Great Shefford W Berks 17 D10
Great Shelford Cambs 29 C11
Great Smeaton N Yorks 58 F4
Great Snoring Norf 38 B5
Great Somerford Wilts 16 C6
Great Stainton Darl 58 D4
Great Stambridge Essex 20 B5
Great Staughton Cambs 29 B8
Great Steeping Lincs 47 F8
Great Stonar Kent 21 F10
Great Strickland W&F 57 D7
Great Stukeley Cambs 29 A9
Great Sturton Lincs 46 E6
Great Sutton Ches W 43 E6
Great Sutton Shrops 33 G11
Great Swinburne Northumb 62 F5
Great Tew Oxon 27 F10
Great Tey Essex 30 F5
Great Thurkleby N Yorks 51 B10
Great Thurlow Suff 30 C3
Great Torrington Devon 6 E3
Great Tosson Northumb 62 C6
Great Totham Essex 30 G5
Great Totham Essex 30 G5
Great Tows Lincs 46 C6
Great Urswick W&F 49 B2
Great Wakering Essex 20 C6
Great Waldingfield Suff 30 D6
Great Walsingham Norf 38 B5
Great Waltham Essex 30 G3
Great Warley Essex 20 B2
Great Washbourne Glos 26 E6
Great Weldon N Nhants 36 G5
Great Welnetham Suff 30 C5
Great Wenham Suff 31 E7
Great Whittington Northumb 62 F6
Great Wigborough Essex 30 G6
Great Wilbraham Cambs 30 C2
Great Wishford Wilts 17 H7
Great Witcombe Glos 26 G6
Great Witley Worcs 26 B4
Great Wolford Warks 27 E9
Great Wratting Suff 30 D3
Great Wymondley Herts 29 F9
Great Wyrley Staffs 34 E5
Great Wytheford Shrops 34 D1
Great Yarmouth Norf 39 E11
Great Yeldham Essex 30 E4
Greater Doward Hereford 26 G2
Greatford Lincs 37 D6
Greatgate Staffs 35 A6
Greatham Hants 11 A6
Greatham Hrtlpl 58 D5
Greatham W Sus 11 C9
Greatstone on Sea Kent 13 D9
Greatworth W Nhants 28 D2
Greave Lancs 50 G4
Greeba IoM 48 D3
Green Denb 42 F3
Green End Bedford 29 C8
Green Hammerton N Yorks 51 D10
Green Lane Powys 33 F7
Green Ore Som 16 F2
Green St Green London 19 E11
Green Street Herts 19 B8
Greenbank Shetland 96 C7
Greenburn W Loth 69 D8
Greendikes Northumb 71 H9
Greenfield C Beds 29 E7
Greenfield Flint 42 E4
Greenfield Gtr Man 44 B3
Greenfield Highld 80 C4
Greenfield Oxon 18 B4
Greenford London 19 C8
Greengairs N Lanark 68 C6
Greenham W Berks 17 E11
Greenhaugh Northumb 62 E3
Greenhead Northumb 62 G2
Greenhill Falk 69 C7
Greenhill Kent 21 E8
Greenhill Leics 35 D10
Greenhill London 19 C8
Greenhills N Ayrs 67 A6
Greenhithe Kent 20 D2
Greenholm E Ayrs 67 C8
Greenholme W&F 57 F7
Greenhouse Borders 61 A11
Greenhow Hill N Yorks 51 C7
Greenigoe Orkney 95 H5
Greenland Highld 94 D4
Greenlands Bucks 18 C4
Greenlaw Aberds 89 C6
Greenlaw Borders 70 F6
Greenlea Dumfries 60 F6
Greenloaning Perth 75 G11
Greenmount Gtr Man 43 A10
Greenmow Shetland 96 L6
Greenock Invclyd 73 F11
Greenock West Invclyd 73 F11
Greenodd W&F 49 A3
Greenrow Cumb 56 A3
Greens Norton W Nhants 28 D3
Greenside T&W 63 G7
Greensidehill Northumb 62 B5
Greenstead Green Essex 30 F5
Greensted Essex 20 A2
Greenwich London 19 D10
Greet Glos 27 E7
Greete Shrops 26 A2
Greetham Lincs 47 E7
Greetham Rutland 36 D5
Greetland W Yorks 51 G6
Gregg Hall W&F 56 G6
Gregson Lane Lancs 50 G1
Greinetobht W Isles 84 A3
Greinton Som 15 H10
Gremista Shetland 96 J6
Grenaby IoM 48 E2
Grendon N Nhants 28 B5
Grendon Warks 35 E8
Grendon Common Warks 35 F8
Grendon Green Hereford 26 C2
Grendon Underwood Bucks 28 F3
Grenofen Devon 4 D5
Grenoside S Yorks 45 C7
Greosabhagh W Isles 90 H6
Gresford Wrex 42 G6
Gresham Norf 39 B7
Greshornish Highld 85 C8
Gressenhall Norf 38 D5
Gressingham Lancs 50 C1
Gresty Green Ches E 43 G10
Greta Bridge Durham 58 E1
Gretna Dumfries 61 G9
Gretna Green Dumfries 61 G9
Gretton Glos 27 E7
Gretton N Nhants 36 F4
Gretton Shrops 33 F11
Grewelthorpe N Yorks 51 B8
Grey Green N Lincs 45 B11
Greygarth N Yorks 51 B7
Greynor Carms 23 F10
Greysouthen Cumb 56 D2
Greystoke W&F 56 C6
Greystone Angus 77 C8
Greystone Dumfries 60 F5
Greywell Hants 18 F4
Griais W Isles 91 C9
Grianan W Isles 91 D9
Gribthorpe E Yorks 52 F3
Gridley Corner Devon 6 G2
Griff Warks 35 G9
Griffithstown Torf 15 B8
Grimbister Orkney 95 G4
Grimblethorpe Lincs 46 D6
Grimeford Village Lancs 43 A9
Grimethorpe S Yorks 45 B8
Griminis W Isles 84 C2
Grimister Shetland 96 D6
Grimley Worcs 26 B5
Grimness Orkney 95 J5
Grimoldby Lincs 47 D7
Grimpo Shrops 33 C9
Grimsargh Lancs 50 F1
Grimsbury Oxon 27 D11
Grimsby NE Lincs 46 A6
Grimscote W Nhants 28 C3
Grimscott Corn 6 F1
Grimsthorpe Lincs 36 C6
Grimston E Yorks 53 F8
Grimston Leics 36 C2
Grimston Norf 38 C3
Grimston York 52 D2
Grimstone Dorset 8 E5
Grinacombe Moor Devon 6 G3
Grindale E Yorks 53 B7
Grindigar Orkney 95 H6
Grindiscol Shetland 96 K6
Grindle Shrops 34 E3
Grindleford Derbys 44 E6
Grindleton Lancs 50 E3
Grindley Staffs 34 C6
Grindley Brook Shrops 33 A11
Grindlow Derbys 44 E5
Grindon Northumb 71 F8
Grindon Staffs 44 G4
Grindonmoor Gate Staffs 44 G4
Gringley on the Hill Notts 45 C11
Grinsdale Cumb 61 H9
Grinshill Shrops 33 C11
Grinton N Yorks 58 G1
Griomsidar W Isles 91 E8
Grishipoll Argyll 78 F4
Grisling Common E Sus 12 D3
Gristhorpe N Yorks 53 A6
Griston Norf 38 F5
Gritley Orkney 95 H6
Grittenham Wilts 17 C7
Grittleton Wilts 16 C5
Grizebeck W&F 49 A2
Grizedale W&F 56 G5
Grobister Orkney 95 F7
Groby Leics 35 E11
Groes Conwy 42 F3
Groes Neath 14 C3
Groes-faen Rhondda 14 C6
Groes-lwyd Powys 33 D8
Groesffordd Marli Denb 42 E3
Groeslon Gwyn 40 E6
Groeslon Gwyn 41 D7
Grogport Argyll 65 D9
Gromford Suff 31 C10
Gronant Flint 42 D3
Groombridge E Sus 12 C4
Grosmont Mon 25 F11
Grosmont N Yorks 59 F9
Groton Suff 30 D6
Grougfoot Falk 69 C9
Grouville Jersey 11
Grove Dorset 8 G6
Grove Kent 21 E9
Grove Notts 45 E11
Grove Oxon 17 B11
Grove Park London 19 D11
Grove Vale W Mid 34 F6
Grovesend Swansea 23 F10
Grudie Highld 86 E6
Gruids Highld 93 J8
Gruinard House Highld 86 B2
Grula Highld 85 F8
Gruline Argyll 79 G8
Grunasound Shetland 96 K5
Grundisburgh Suff 31 C9
Grunsagill Lancs 50 D3
Gruting Shetland 96 J4
Grutness Shetland 96 N6
Gualachulain Highld 74 C4
Gualin Ho. Highld 92 D6
Guardbridge Fife 77 F7
Guarlford Worcs 26 D5
Guay Perth 76 C3
Guestling Green E Sus 13 E7
Guestling Thorn E Sus 13 E7
Guestwick Norf 39 C6
Guestwick Green Norf 39 C6
Guide Blackburn 50 G3
Guide Post Northumb 63 E8
Guilden Morden Cambs 29 D9
Guilden Sutton Ches W 43 F7
Guildford Sur 18 G6
Guildtown Perth 76 D4
Guilsborough W Nhants 28 A3
Guilsfield Powys 33 D8
Guilton Kent 21 F9
Guineaford Devon 6 C4
Guisborough Redcar 59 E7
Guiseley W Yorks 51 E7
Guist Norf 38 C5
Guith Orkney 95 E6
Guiting Power Glos 27 F7
Gulberwick Shetland 96 K6
Gullane E Loth 70 B3
Gulval Corn 2 F3
Gulworthy Devon 4 D5
Gumfreston Pembs 22 F6
Gumley Leics 36 F2
Gummow's Shop Corn 3 D7
Gun Hill E Sus 12 E4
Gunby E Yorks 52 F3
Gunby Lincs 36 C5
Gundleton Hants 10 A5
Gunn Devon 6 C5
Gunnerside N Yorks 57 G11
Gunnerton Northumb 62 F5
Gunness N Lincs 46 A2
Gunnislake Corn 4 D5
Gunnista Shetland 96 J7
Gunthorpe Norf 38 B6
Gunthorpe Notts 36 A2
Gunthorpe Pboro 37 E7
Gunville IoW 10 F3
Gunwalloe Corn 2 G5
Gurnard IoW 10 E3
Gurnett Ches E 44 E3
Gurney Slade Som 16 G3
Gurnos Powys 24 H4
Gussage All Saints Dorset 9 C9
Gussage St Michael Dorset 9 C8
Guston Kent 21 G10
Gutcher Shetland 96 D7
Guthrie Angus 77 B8
Guyhirn Cambs 37 E9
Guyhirn Gull Cambs 37 E9
Guy's Head Lincs 37 C10
Guy's Marsh Dorset 9 B7
Guyzance Northumb 63 C8
Gwaenysgor Flint 42 D3
Gwalchmai Anglesey 40 C5
Gwaun-Cae-Gurwen Neath 24 G4
Gwaun-Leision Neath 24 G4
Gwbert Ceredig 22 B6
Gweek Corn 2 G6
Gwehelog Mon 15 A9
Gwenddwr Powys 25 D7
Gwennap Corn 2 F6
Gwenter Corn 2 H6
Gwernaffield Flint 42 F5
Gwernesney Mon 15 A10
Gwernogle Carms 23 C10
Gwernymynydd Flint 42 F5
Gwersyllt Wrex 42 G6
Gwespyr Flint 42 D4
Gwithian Corn 2 E4
Gwredog Anglesey 40 B6
Gwyddelwern Denb 42 H3
Gwyddgrug Carms 23 C9
Gwydyr Uchaf Conwy 41 D9
Gwynfryn Wrex 42 G5
Gwystre Powys 25 B7
Gwytherin Conwy 41 D10
Gyfelia Wrex 42 H6
Gyffin Conwy 41 C9
Gyre Orkney 95 H4
Gyrn-goch Gwyn 40 F6

H

Habberley Shrops 33 E9
Habergham Lancs 50 F4
Habrough NE Lincs 46 A5
Haceby Lincs 36 B6
Hacheston Suff 31 C10
Hackbridge London 19 E9
Hackenthorpe S Yorks 45 D8
Hackford Norf 39 E6
Hackforth N Yorks 58 G3
Hackland Orkney 95 F4
Hackleton W Nhants 28 C5
Hackness N Yorks 59 G10
Hackness Orkney 95 J4
Hackney London 19 C10
Hackthorn Lincs 46 D3
Hackthorpe W&F 57 D7
Haconby Lincs 37 C7
Hacton London 20 C2
Hadden Borders 70 G6
Haddenham Bucks 28 H4
Haddenham Cambs 37 H10
Haddington E Loth 70 C4
Haddington Lincs 46 F3
Haddiscoe Norf 39 F10
Haddon Cambs 37 F7
Haddon Ches E 44 F3
Hade Edge W Yorks 44 B5
Hademore Staffs 35 E7
Hadfield Derbys 44 C4
Hadham Cross Herts 29 G11
Hadham Ford Herts 29 F11
Hadleigh Essex 20 C5
Hadleigh Suff 31 D7
Hadley Telford 34 D2
Hadley End Staffs 35 C7
Hadlow Kent 20 G3
Hadlow Down E Sus 12 D4
Hadnall Shrops 33 D11
Hadstock Essex 30 D2
Hady Derbys 45 E7
Hadzor Worcs 26 B6
Haffenden Quarter Kent 13 B7
Hafod-Dinbych Conwy 41 E10
Hafod-lom Conwy 41 C10
Haggate Lancs 50 F4
Haggbeck Cumb 61 F10
Haggerston Northumb 71 F9
Haggrister Shetland 96 F5
Hagley Hereford 26 D2
Hagley Worcs 34 G5
Hagworthingham Lincs 47 F7
Haigh Gtr Man 43 B9
Haigh S Yorks 44 A6
Haigh Moor W Yorks 51 G8
Haighton Green Lancs 50 F1
Hail Weston Cambs 29 B8
Haile Cumb 56 F2
Hailes Glos 27 E7
Hailey Herts 29 G10
Hailey Oxon 27 G10
Hailsham E Sus 12 F4
Haimer Highld 94 D3
Hainault London 19 B11
Hainford Norf 39 D8
Hainton Lincs 46 D5
Hairmyres S Lanark 68 E5
Haisthorpe E Yorks 53 C7
Hakin Pembs 22 F3
Halam Notts 45 G10
Halbeath Fife 69 B10
Halberton Devon 7 E9
Halcro Highld 94 D4
Hale Gtr Man 43 D10
Hale Halton 43 D7
Hale Hants 9 C10
Hale Bank Halton 43 D7
Hale Street Kent 20 G3
Halebarns Gtr Man 43 D10
Hales Norf 39 F9
Hales Staffs 34 B3
Hales Place Kent 21 F8
Halesfield Telford 34 E3
Halesgate Lincs 37 C9
Halesowen W Mid 34 G5
Halesworth Suff 39 H9
Halewood Mers 43 D7
Halford Shrops 33 G10
Halford Warks 27 D9
Halfpenny Furze Carms 23 E7
Halfpenny Green Staffs 34 F4
Halfway Carms 24 E3
Halfway Carms 24 E5
Halfway W Berks 17 E11
Halfway Bridge W Sus 11 B8
Halfway House Shrops 33 D9
Halfway Houses Kent 20 D6
Halifax W Yorks 51 G6
Halket E Ayrs 67 A7
Halkirk Highld 94 E3
Halkyn Flint 42 E5
Hall Dunnerdale Cumb 56 G4
Hall Green W Mid 35 G7
Hall Green W Yorks 51 H9
Hall Grove Herts 29 G9
Hall of Tankerness Orkney 95 H6
Hall of the Forest Shrops 33 G8
Halland E Sus 12 E3
Hallaton Leics 36 F3
Hallatrow Bath 16 F3
Hallbankgate Cumb 61 H11
Hallen S Glos 15 C11
Halliburton Borders 70 F5
Hallin Highld 84 C7
Halling Medway 20 E4
Hallington Lincs 47 D7
Hallington Northumb 62 F5
Halliwell Gtr Man 43 A10
Halloughton Notts 45 G10
Hallow Worcs 26 C5
Hallrule Borders 61 B11
Halls E Loth 70 C5
Hall's Green Herts 29 F9
Hallsands Devon 5 H9
Hallthwaites Cumb 56 H3
Hallworthy Corn 4 C2
Hallyburton House Perth 76 D5
Hallyne Borders 69 F10
Halmer End Staffs 43 H10
Halmore Glos 16 A3
Halmyre Mains Borders 69 F10
Halnaker W Sus 11 D8
Halsall Lancs 42 A6
Halse Som 7 D10
Halse W Nhants 28 D2
Halsetown Corn 2 F4
Halsham E Yorks 53 G8
Halsinger Devon 6 C4
Halstead Essex 30 E5
Halstead Kent 19 E11
Halstead Leics 36 E3
Halstock Dorset 8 D4
Haltham Lincs 46 F6
Haltoft End Lincs 47 H7
Halton Bucks 28 G5
Halton Halton 43 D8
Halton Lancs 49 C5
Halton Northumb 62 G5
Halton W Yorks 51 F9
Halton Wrex 33 B9
Halton East N Yorks 50 D6
Halton Gill N Yorks 50 B4
Halton Holegate Lincs 47 F8
Halton Lea Gate Northumb 62 H2
Halton West N Yorks 50 D4
Haltwhistle Northumb 62 G3
Halvergate Norf 39 E10
Halwell Devon 5 F8
Halwill Devon 6 G3
Halwill Junction Devon 6 F3
Ham Devon 7 F11
Ham Glos 16 B3
Ham Highld 94 C4
Ham Kent 21 F10
Ham London 19 D8
Ham Shetland 96 K1
Ham Wilts 17 E10
Ham Common Dorset 9 B7
Ham Green Hereford 26 D4
Ham Green Kent 13 D7
Ham Green Kent 20 E5
Ham Green N Som 15 D11
Ham Green Worcs 27 B7
Ham Street Som 8 A4
Hamble-le-Rice Hants 10 D3
Hambleden Bucks 18 C4
Hambledon Hants 10 C5
Hambledon Sur 18 H6
Hambleton Lancs 49 E3
Hambleton N Yorks 52 F1
Hambridge Som 8 B2
Hambrook S Glos 16 D3
Hambrook W Sus 11 D6
Hameringham Lincs 47 F7
Hamerton Cambs 37 H7
Hametoun Shetland 96 K1
Hamilton S Lanark 68 E6
Hammer W Sus 11 A7
Hammerpot W Sus 11 D9
Hammersmith London 19 D9
Hammerwich Staffs 35 E6
Hammerwood E Sus 12 C3
Hammond Street Herts 19 A10
Hammoon Dorset 9 C7
Hamnavoe Shetland 96 E4
Hamnavoe Shetland 96 E6
Hamnavoe Shetland 96 F6
Hamnavoe Shetland 96 K5
Hampden Park E Sus 12 F5
Hamperden End Essex 30 E2
Hampnett Glos 27 G7
Hampole S Yorks 45 A9
Hampreston Dorset 9 E9
Hampstead London 19 C9
Hampstead Norreys W Berks 18 D2
Hampsthwaite N Yorks 51 D8
Hampton London 19 E8
Hampton Pboro 37 F7
Hampton Shrops 34 G3
Hampton Worcs 27 D7
Hampton Bishop Hereford 26 E2
Hampton Heath Ches W 43 H7
Hampton in Arden W Mid 35 G8
Hampton Loade Shrops 34 G3
Hampton Lovett Worcs 26 B5
Hampton Lucy Warks 27 C9
Hampton on the Hill Warks 27 B9
Hampton Poyle Oxon 28 G2
Hamrow Norf 38 C5
Hamsey E Sus 12 E3
Hamsey Green London 19 F10
Hamstall Ridware Staffs 35 D7
Hamstead IoW 10 E3
Hamstead W Mid 34 F6
Hamstead Marshall W Berks 17 E11
Hamsterley Durham 58 C2
Hamsterley Durham 63 H7
Hamstreet Kent 13 C9
Hamworthy BCP 9 E8
Hanbury Staffs 35 C7
Hanbury Worcs 26 B6
Hanbury Woodend Staffs 35 C7
Hanby Lincs 36 B6
Hanchurch Staffs 34 A4
Handbridge Ches W 43 F7
Handcross W Sus 12 D1
Handforth Ches E 44 D2
Handley Ches W 43 G7
Handsacre Staffs 35 D6
Handsworth S Yorks 45 D8
Handsworth W Mid 34 F6
Handy Cross Devon 6 D3
Hanford Stoke 34 A4
Hanging Langford Wilts 17 H7
Hangleton W Sus 11 D9
Hanham S Glos 16 D3
Hankelow Ches E 43 H9
Hankerton Wilts 16 B6
Hankham E Sus 12 F5
Hanley Stoke 44 H2
Hanley Castle Worcs 26 D5
Hanley Child Worcs 26 B3
Hanley Swan Worcs 26 D5
Hanley William Worcs 26 B3
Hanlith N Yorks 50 C5
Hanmer Wrex 33 B10
Hannah Lincs 47 E9
Hannington Hants 18 F2
Hannington Swindon 17 B8
Hannington W Nhants 28 A5
Hannington Wick Swindon 17 B8
Hansel Village S Ayrs 67 C6
Hanslope M Keynes 28 D5
Hanthorpe Lincs 37 C6
Hanwell London 19 C8
Hanwell Oxon 27 D11
Hanwood Shrops 33 E10
Hanworth London 19 D8
Hanworth Norf 39 B7
Happendon S Lanark 69 G7
Happisburgh Norf 39 B9
Happisburgh Common Norf 39 C9
Hapsford Ches W 43 E7
Hapton Lancs 50 F3
Hapton Norf 39 F7
Harberton Devon 5 F8
Harbertonford Devon 5 F8
Harbledown Kent 21 F8
Harborne W Mid 34 G6
Harborough Magna Warks 35 H10
Harbottle Northumb 62 C5
Harbury Warks 27 C10
Harby Leics 36 B3
Harby Notts 46 E2
Harcombe Devon 7 G10
Harden W Mid 34 E6
Harden W Yorks 51 F6
Hardenhuish Wilts 16 D6
Hardgate Aberds 83 C9
Hardham W Sus 11 C9
Hardingham Norf 38 E6
Hardingstone W Nhants 28 C4
Hardington Som 16 F4
Hardington Mandeville Som 8 C4
Hardington Marsh Som 8 D4
Hardley Hants 10 D3
Hardley Street Norf 39 E9
Hardmead M Keynes 28 D6
Hardrow N Yorks 57 G10
Hardstoft Derbys 45 F8
Hardway Hants 10 D5
Hardway Som 8 A6
Hardwick Bucks 28 G5
Hardwick Cambs 29 C10
Hardwick N Nhants 28 B5
Hardwick Norf 38 D2
Hardwick Norf 39 G8
Hardwick Notts 45 E10
Hardwick Oxon 27 H10
Hardwick Oxon 28 F2
Hardwick W Mid 35 F6
Hardwicke Glos 26 F6
Hardwicke Glos 26 G4
Hardwicke Hereford 25 D9
Hardy's Green Essex 30 F6
Hare Green Essex 31 F7
Hare Hatch Wokingham 18 D5
Hare Street Herts 29 F10
Hareby Lincs 47 F7
Hareden Lancs 50 D2
Harefield London 19 B7
Harehills W Yorks 51 F9
Harehope Northumb 62 A6
Haresceugh W&F 57 B8
Harescombe Glos 26 G5
Haresfield Glos 26 G5
Hareshaw N Lanark 69 D7
Hareshaw Head Northumb 62 E4
Harewood W Yorks 51 E9
Harewood End Hereford 26 F2
Harford Carms 24 D3
Harford Devon 5 F7
Hargate Norf 39 F7
Hargatewall Derbys 44 E5
Hargrave Ches W 43 F7
Hargrave N Nhants 29 A7
Hargrave Suff 30 C4
Harker Cumb 61 G9
Harkland Shetland 96 E6
Harkstead Suff 31 E8
Harlaston Staffs 35 D8
Harlaw Ho. Aberds 83 A9
Harlaxton Lincs 36 B4
Harle Syke Lancs 50 F4
Harlech Gwyn 41 G7
Harlequin Notts 36 B2
Harlescott Shrops 33 D11
Harlesden London 19 C9
Harleston Devon 5 G8
Harleston Norf 39 G8
Harleston Suff 31 C7
Harlestone W Nhants 28 B4
Harley S Yorks 45 C7
Harley Shrops 34 E1
Harleyholm S Lanark 69 G8
Harlington C Beds 29 E7
Harlington London 19 D7
Harlington S Yorks 45 B8
Harlosh Highld 85 D7
Harlow Essex 29 G11
Harlow Hill N Yorks 51 D8
Harlow Hill Northumb 62 G6
Harlthorpe E Yorks 52 F3
Harlton Cambs 29 C10
Harman's Cross Dorset 9 F8
Harmby N Yorks 58 H2
Harmer Green Herts 29 G9
Harmer Hill Shrops 33 C10
Harmondsworth London 19 D7
Harmston Lincs 46 F3
Harnham Northumb 62 F6
Harnhill Glos 17 A7
Harold Hill London 20 B2
Harold Wood London 20 B2
Haroldston West Pembs 22 E3
Haroldswick Shetland 96 B8
Harome N Yorks 52 A2
Harpenden Herts 29 G8
Harpford Devon 7 G9
Harpham E Yorks 53 C6
Harpley Norf 38 C3
Harpley Worcs 26 B3
Harpole W Nhants 28 B3
Harpsdale Highld 94 E3
Harpsden Oxon 18 C4
Harpswell Lincs 46 D3
Harpur Hill Derbys 44 E4
Harpurhey Gtr Man 44 B2
Harraby Cumb 56 A6
Harrapool Highld 85 F11
Harrier Shetland 96 J1
Harrietfield Perth 76 E2
Harrietsham Kent 20 F5
Harrington Cumb 56 D1
Harrington Lincs 47 E7
Harrington N Nhants 36 G3
Harringworth N Nhants 36 F5
Harris Highld 78 B6
Harrogate N Yorks 51 D9
Harrold Bedford 28 C6
Harrow London 19 C8
Harrow on the Hill London 19 C8
Harrow Street Suff 30 E6
Harrow Weald London 19 B8
Harrowbarrow Corn 4 E4
Harrowden Bedford 29 D7
Harrowgate Hill Darl 58 E3
Harston Cambs 29 C11
Harston Leics 36 B4
Harswell E Yorks 52 E4
Hart Hrtlpl 58 C5
Hart Common Gtr Man 43 B9
Hart Hill Luton 29 F8
Hart Station Hrtlpl 58 C5
Hartburn Northumb 62 E6
Hartburn Stockton 58 E5
Hartest Suff 30 C5
Hartfield E Sus 12 C3
Hartford Cambs 29 A9
Hartford Ches W 43 E9
Hartford End Essex 30 G3
Hartfordbridge Hants 18 F4
Hartforth N Yorks 58 F2
Harthill Ches W 43 G8
Harthill N Lanark 69 D8
Harthill S Yorks 45 D8
Hartington Derbys 44 F5
Hartland Devon 6 D1
Hartlebury Worcs 26 A5
Hartlepool Hrtlpl 58 C6
Hartley Kent 13 C6
Hartley Kent 20 E3
Hartley Northumb 63 F9
Hartley W&F 57 F9
Hartley Westpall Hants 18 F3
Hartley Wintney Hants 18 F4
Hartlip Kent 20 E5
Hartoft End N Yorks 59 G8
Harton N Yorks 52 C3
Harton Shrops 33 G10
Harton T&W 63 G9
Hartpury Glos 26 F4
Hartshead W Yorks 51 G7
Hartshill Warks 35 F9
Hartshorne Derbys 35 C9
Hartsop W&F 56 E6
Hartwell W Nhants 28 C4
Hartwood N Lanark 69 E7
Harvieston Stirling 68 B4
Harvington Worcs 27 D7
Harvington Cross Worcs 27 D7
Harwell Oxon 17 C11
Harwich Essex 31 E9
Harwood Durham 57 C10
Harwood Gtr Man 43 A10
Harwood Dale N Yorks 59 G10
Harworth Notts 45 C10
Hasbury W Mid 34 G5
Hascombe Sur 18 G6
Haselbech W Nhants 36 H3
Haselbury Plucknett Som 8 C3
Haseley Warks 27 B9
Haselor Warks 27 C8
Hasfield Glos 26 F5
Hasguard Pembs 22 F3
Haskayne Lancs 42 B6
Hasketon Suff 31 C9
Hasland Derbys 45 F7
Haslemere Sur 11 A8
Haslingden Lancs 50 G3
Haslingfield Cambs 29 C11
Haslington Ches E 43 G10
Hassall Ches E 43 G10
Hassall Green Ches E 43 G10
Hassell Street Kent 21 G7
Hassendean Borders 61 A11
Hassingham Norf 39 E9
Hassocks W Sus 12 E1
Hassop Derbys 44 E6
Hastigrow Highld 94 D4
Hastingleigh Kent 13 B9
Hastings E Sus 13 F7
Hastingwood Essex 29 H11
Hastoe Herts 28 H6
Haswell Durham 58 B4
Haswell Plough Durham 58 B4
Hatch C Beds 29 D8
Hatch Hants 18 F3
Hatch Wilts 9 B8
Hatch Beauchamp Som 8 B2
Hatch End London 19 B8
Hatch Green Som 8 C2
Hatchet Gate Hants 10 D2
Hatching Green Herts 29 G8
Hatchmere Ches W 43 E8
Hatcliffe NE Lincs 46 B6
Hatfield Hereford 26 C2
Hatfield Herts 29 H9
Hatfield S Yorks 45 B10
Hatfield Worcs 26 C5
Hatfield Broad Oak Essex 30 G2
Hatfield Garden Village Herts 29 H9
Hatfield Heath Essex 30 G2
Hatfield Hyde Herts 29 G9
Hatfield Peverel Essex 30 G4
Hatfield Woodhouse S Yorks 45 B10
Hatford Oxon 17 B10
Hatherden Hants 17 F10
Hatherleigh Devon 6 F4
Hathern Leics 35 C10
Hatherop Glos 27 H8
Hathersage Derbys 44 D6
Hathershaw Gtr Man 44 B3
Hatherton Ches E 43 H9
Hatherton Staffs 34 D5
Hatley St George Cambs 29 C9
Hatt Corn 4 E4
Hattingley Hants 18 H3
Hatton Aberds 89 E10
Hatton Derbys 35 C8
Hatton Lincs 46 E5
Hatton Shrops 33 F10
Hatton Warks 27 B9
Hatton Warr 43 D8
Hatton Castle Aberds 89 D7
Hatton Heath Ches W 43 F7
Hatton of Fintray Aberds 83 B10
Hattoncrook Aberds 89 F8
Haugh E Ayrs 67 D7
Haugh Gtr Man 44 A3
Haugh Lincs 47 E8
Haugh Head Northumb 71 H9
Haugh of Glass Moray 88 E4
Haugh of Urr Dumfries 55 C11
Haugham Lincs 47 D7
Haughley Suff 31 B7
Haughley Green Suff 31 B7
Haughs of Clinterty Aberdeen 83 B10
Haughton Notts 45 E10
Haughton Shrops 33 C9
Haughton Shrops 34 D1
Haughton Shrops 34 E3
Haughton Shrops 34 F2
Haughton Staffs 34 C4
Haughton Castle Northumb 62 F5
Haughton Green Gtr Man 44 C3
Haughton Moss Ches E 43 G8
Haultwick Herts 29 F10
Haunn Argyll 78 G6
Haunn W Isles 84 G2
Haunton Staffs 35 D8
Hauxley Northumb 63 C8
Hauxton Cambs 29 C11
Havant Hants 10 D6
Haven Hereford 25 C11
Haven Bank Lincs 46 G6
Haven Side E Yorks 53 G7
Havenstreet IoW 10 E4
Havercroft W Yorks 45 A7
Haverfordwest = Hwlffordd Pembs 22 E4
Haverhill Suff 30 D3
Haverigg W&F 49 B1
Havering-atte-Bower London 20 B2
Haveringland Norf 39 C7
Haversham M Keynes 28 D5
Haverthwaite W&F 49 A3
Haverton Hill Stockton 58 D5
Hawarden = Penarlâg Flint 42 F6
Hawcoat W&F 49 B2
Hawen Ceredig 23 B8
Hawes N Yorks 57 H10
Hawes' Green Norf 39 F8
Hawes Side Blackpool 49 F3
Hawford Worcs 26 B5
Hawick Borders 61 B11
Hawk Green Gtr Man 44 D3
Hawkchurch Devon 8 D2
Hawkedon Suff 30 C4
Hawkenbury Kent 12 C4
Hawkenbury Kent 13 B7
Hawkeridge Wilts 16 F5
Hawkerland Devon 7 H9
Hawkes End W Mid 35 G9
Hawkesbury S Glos 16 C4
Hawkesbury Warks 35 G9
Hawkesbury Upton S Glos 16 C4
Hawkhill Northumb 63 B8
Hawkhurst Kent 13 C6
Hawkinge Kent 21 H9
Hawkley Hants 10 B6
Hawkridge Som 7 C7
Hawkshead W&F 56 G5
Hawkshead Hill W&F 56 G5
Hawksland S Lanark 69 G7
Hawkswick N Yorks 50 B5
Hawksworth Notts 36 A3
Hawksworth W Yorks 51 E7
Hawksworth W Yorks 51 F8
Hawkwell Essex 20 B5
Hawley Hants 18 F5
Hawley Kent 20 D2
Hawling Glos 27 F7
Hawnby N Yorks 59 H6
Haworth W Yorks 50 F6
Hawstead Suff 30 C5
Hawthorn Durham 58 B5
Hawthorn Rhondda 15 C7
Hawthorn Wilts 16 E5
Hawthorn Hill Brack 18 D5
Hawthorn Hill Lincs 46 G6
Hawthorpe Lincs 36 C6
Hawton Notts 45 G11
Haxby York 52 D2
Haxey N Lincs 45 C11
Hay Green Norf 37 D11
Hay-on-Wye = Y Gelli Gandryll Powys 25 D9
Hay Street Herts 29 F10
Haydock Mers 43 C8
Haydon Dorset 8 C5
Haydon Bridge Northumb 62 G4
Haydon Wick Swindon 17 C8
Haye Corn 4 E4
Hayes London 19 C8
Hayes London 19 E11
Hayfield Derbys 44 D4
Hayfield Fife 69 A11
Hayhill E Ayrs 67 E7
Hayhillock Angus 77 C8
Hayle Corn 2 F4
Haynes C Beds 29 D7
Haynes Church End C Beds 29 D7
Hayscastle Pembs 22 D3
Hayscastle Cross Pembs 22 D4
Hayshead Angus 77 C9
Hayton Aberdeen 83 C11
Hayton Cumb 56 B3
Hayton Cumb 61 H11
Hayton E Yorks 52 E4
Hayton Notts 45 D11
Hayton's Bent Shrops 33 G11
Haytor Vale Devon 5 D8
Haywards Heath W Sus 12 D2
Haywood S Yorks 45 A9
Haywood Oaks Notts 45 G10
Hazel Grove Gtr Man 44 D3
Hazel Street Kent 12 C5
Hazelbank S Lanark 69 F7
Hazelbury Bryan Dorset 8 D6
Hazeley Hants 18 F4
Hazelhurst Gtr Man 44 B3
Hazelslade Staffs 34 D6
Hazelton Glos 27 G7
Hazelton Walls Fife 76 E6
Hazelwood Derbys 45 H7
Hazlemere Bucks 18 B5
Hazlerigg T&W 63 F8
Hazlewood N Yorks 51 D6
Hazon Northumb 63 C7
Heacham Norf 38 B2
Head of Muir Falk 69 B7
Headbourne Worthy Hants 10 A3
Headbrook Hereford 25 C10
Headcorn Kent 13 B7
Headingley W Yorks 51 F8
Headington Oxon 28 H2
Headlam Durham 58 E2
Headless Cross Worcs 27 B7
Headley Hants 18 E2
Headley Hants 18 H5
Headley Sur 19 F9
Headon Notts 45 E11
Heads S Lanark 68 F6
Heads Nook Cumb 61 H10
Heage Derbys 45 G7
Healaugh N Yorks 51 E10
Healaugh N Yorks 58 G1
Heald Green Gtr Man 44 D2
Heale Devon 6 B5
Heale Som 16 G3
Healey Gtr Man 50 H4
Healey N Yorks 51 A7
Healey Northumb 62 H6
Healing NE Lincs 46 A6
Heamoor Corn 2 F3
Heanish Argyll 78 G3
Heanor Derbys 45 H8
Heanton Punchardon Devon 6 C4
Heapham Lincs 46 D2
Hearthstane Borders 69 H10
Heasley Mill Devon 7 C6
Heast Highld 85 G11
Heath Cardiff 15 D7
Heath Derbys 45 F8
Heath and Reach C Beds 28 F6
Heath End Hants 18 E2
Heath End Sur 18 G5
Heath End Warks 27 B9
Heath Hayes Staffs 34 D6
Heath Hill Shrops 34 D3
Heath House Som 15 G10
Heath Town W Mid 34 F5
Heathcote Derbys 44 F5
Heather Leics 35 D9
Heatherfield Highld 85 D9
Heathfield Devon 5 D9
Heathfield E Sus 12 D4
Heathfield Som 7 D10
Heathhall Dumfries 60 F5
Heathrow Airport London 19 D7
Heathstock Devon 8 D1
Heathton Shrops 34 F4
Heatley Warr 43 D10
Heaton Lancs 49 C4
Heaton Staffs 44 F3
Heaton T&W 63 G8
Heaton W Yorks 51 F7
Heaton Moor Gtr Man 44 C2
Heaverham Kent 20 F2
Heaviley Gtr Man 44 D3
Heavitree Devon 7 G8
Hebburn T&W 63 G9
Hebden N Yorks 50 C6
Hebden Bridge W Yorks 50 G5
Hebron Anglesey 40 B6
Hebron Carms 22 D6
Hebron Northumb 63 E7
Heck Dumfries 60 E6
Heckfield Hants 18 E4
Heckfield Green Suff 39 H7
Heckfordbridge Essex 30 F6
Heckington Lincs 37 A7
Heckmondwike W Yorks 51 G8
Heddington Wilts 16 E6
Heddle Orkney 95 G4
Heddon-on-the-Wall Northumb 63 G7
Hedenham Norf 39 F9
Hedge End Hants 10 C3
Hedgerley Bucks 18 C6
Hedging Som 8 B2
Hedley on the Hill Northumb 62 H6
Hednesford Staffs 34 D6
Hedon E Yorks 53 G7
Hedsor Bucks 18 C6
Hedworth T&W 63 G9
Hegdon Hill Hereford 26 C2
Heggerscales W&F 57 E10
Heglibister Shetland 96 H5
Heighington Darl 58 D3
Heighington Lincs 46 F4
Heights of Brae Highld 87 E8
Heights of Kinlochewe Highld 86 E3
Heilam Highld 92 C7
Heiton Borders 70 G6
Hele Devon 6 B4
Hele Devon 7 F8
Helensburgh Argyll 73 E11
Helford Corn 3 G6
Helford Passage Corn 3 G6
Helhoughton Norf 38 C4
Helions Bumpstead Essex 30 D3
Hellaby S Yorks 45 C9
Helland Corn 4 D1
Hellesdon Norf 39 D8
Hellidon W Nhants 28 C2
Hellifield N Yorks 50 D4
Hellingly E Sus 12 E4
Hellington Norf 39 E9
Hellister Shetland 96 J5
Helm Northumb 63 D7
Helmdon W Nhants 28 D2
Helmingham Suff 31 C8
Helmington Row Durham 58 C2
Helmsdale Highld 93 H13
Helmshore Lancs 50 G3
Helmsley N Yorks 52 A2
Helperby N Yorks 51 C10
Helperthorpe N Yorks 52 B5
Helpringham Lincs 37 A7
Helpston Pboro 37 E7
Helsby Ches W 43 E7
Helsey Lincs 47 E9
Helston Corn 2 G5
Helstone Corn 4 C1
Helton W&F 57 D7
Helwith Bridge N Yorks 50 C4
Hemblington Norf 39 D9
Hemel Hempstead Herts 29 H7
Hemingbrough N Yorks 52 F2
Hemingby Lincs 46 E6
Hemingford Abbots Cambs 29 A9
Hemingford Grey Cambs 29 A9
Hemingstone Suff 31 C8
Hemington Leics 35 C10
Hemington N Nhants 37 G6
Hemington Som 16 F4
Hemley Suff 31 D9
Hemlington Mbro 58 E6
Hemp Green Suff 31 B10
Hempholme E Yorks 53 D6
Hempnall Norf 39 F8
Hempnall Green Norf 39 F8
Hempriggs House Highld 94 F5
Hempstead Essex 30 E3
Hempstead Medway 20 E4
Hempstead Norf 39 B7
Hempstead Norf 39 C10
Hempsted Glos 26 G5
Hempton Norf 38 C5
Hempton Oxon 27 E11
Hemsby Norf 39 D10
Hemswell Lincs 46 C3
Hemswell Cliff Lincs 46 D3
Hemsworth W Yorks 45 A8
Hemyock Devon 7 E10
Hen-feddau fawr Pembs 23 C7
Henbury Bristol 16 D2
Henbury Ches E 44 E2
Hendon London 19 C9
Hendon T&W 63 H10
Hendre Flint 42 F4
Hendre-ddu Conwy 41 D10
Hendreforgan Rhondda 14 C5
Hendy Carms 23 F10
Heneglwys Anglesey 40 C6
Henfield W Sus 11 C11
Henford Devon 6 G2
Henghurst Kent 13 C8
Hengoed Caerph 15 B7
Hengoed Powys 25 C9
Hengoed Shrops 33 B8
Hengrave Suff 30 B5
Henham Essex 30 F2
Heniarth Powys 33 E7
Henlade Som 8 B1
Henley Shrops 33 H11
Henley Som 8 A3
Henley Suff 31 C8
Henley W Sus 11 B7
Henley-in-Arden Warks 27 B8
Henley-on-Thames Oxon 18 C4
Henley's Down E Sus 12 E6
Henllan Ceredig 23 B8
Henllan Denb 42 F3
Henllan Amgoed Carms 22 D6
Henllys Torf 15 B8
Henlow C Beds 29 E8
Hennock Devon 5 C9
Henny Street Essex 30 E5
Henryd Conwy 41 C9
Henry's Moat Pembs 22 D5
Hensall N Yorks 52 G1
Henshaw Northumb 62 G3
Hensingham Cumb 56 E1
Henstead Suff 39 G10
Henstridge Som 8 C6
Henstridge Ash Som 8 B6
Henstridge Marsh Som 8 B6
Henton Oxon 18 A4
Henton Som 15 G10
Henwood Corn 4 D3
Heogan Shetland 96 J6
Heol-las Swansea 14 B2
Heol Senni Powys 24 F6
Heol-y-Cyw Bridgend 14 C5
Hepburn Northumb 62 A6
Hepple Northumb 62 C5
Hepscott Northumb 63 E8
Heptonstall W Yorks 50 G5
Hepworth Suff 30 A6
Hepworth W Yorks 44 B5
Herbrandston Pembs 22 F3
Hereford Hereford 26 D2
Heriot Borders 70 E2
Hermiston Edin 69 C10
Hermitage Borders 61 D11
Hermitage Dorset 8 D5
Hermitage W Berks 18 D2
Hermitage W Sus 11 D6
Hermon Anglesey 40 D5
Hermon Carms 23 C8
Hermon Carms 24 F3
Hermon Pembs 23 C7
Herne Kent 21 E8
Herne Bay Kent 21 E8
Herner Devon 6 D4
Hernhill Kent 21 E7
Herodsfoot Corn 4 E3
Herongate Essex 20 B3
Heronsford S Ayrs 54 A4
Herriard Hants 18 G3
Herringfleet Suff 39 F10
Herringswell Suff 30 A4
Hersden Kent 21 E9
Hersham Corn 6 F1
Hersham Sur 19 E8
Herstmonceux E Sus 12 E5
Herston Orkney 95 J5
Hertford Herts 29 G10
Hertford Heath Herts 29 G10
Hertingfordbury Herts 29 G10
Hesket Newmarket Cumb 56 C5
Hesketh Bank Lancs 49 G4
Hesketh Lane Lancs 50 E2
Heskin Green Lancs 49 H5
Hesleden Durham 58 C5
Hesleyside Northumb 62 E4
Heslington York 52 D2
Hessay York 51 D11
Hessenford Corn 4 F4
Hessett Suff 30 B6
Hessle E Yorks 52 G6
Hest Bank Lancs 49 C4
Heston London 19 D8
Hestwall Orkney 95 G3
Heswall Mers 42 D5
Hethe Oxon 28 F2
Hethersett Norf 39 E7
Hethersgill Cumb 61 G10
Hethpool Northumb 71 H7
Hett Durham 58 C3
Hetton N Yorks 50 D5
Hetton-le-Hole T&W 58 B4
Hetton Steads Northumb 71 G9
Heugh Northumb 62 F6
Heugh-head Aberds 82 B5
Heveningham Suff 31 A10
Hever Kent 12 B3
Heversham W&F 49 A4
Hevingham Norf 39 C7
Hewas Water Corn 3 E8
Hewelsfield Glos 16 A2
Hewish N Som 15 E10
Hewish Som 8 D3
Heworth York 52 D2
Hexham Northumb 62 G5
Hextable Kent 20 D2
Hexton Herts 29 E8
Hexworthy Devon 5 D7
Hey Lancs 50 E4
Heybridge Essex 20 B3
Heybridge Essex 30 H5
Heybridge Basin Essex 30 H5
Heybrook Bay Devon 4 G6
Heydon Cambs 29 D11

Heydon Norf 39 C7
Heydour Lincs 36 B6
Heyford Park Oxon 28 F2
Heylipol Argyll 78 G2
Heylor Shetland 96 E4
Heysham Lancs 49 C4
Heyshott W Sus 11 C7
Heyside Gtr Man 44 B3
Heytesbury Wilts 16 G6
Heythrop Oxon 27 F10
Heywood Gtr Man 44 A2
Heywood Wilts 16 F5
Hibaldstow N Lincs 46 B3
Hickleton S Yorks 45 B8
Hickling Norf 39 C10
Hickling Notts 36 C2
Hickling Green Norf 39 C10
Hickling Heath Norf 39 C10
Hickstead W Sus 12 D1
Hidcote Boyce Glos 27 D8
High Ackworth W Yorks 51 H10
High Angerton Northumb 62 E6
High Bankhill W&F 57 B7
High Barnes T&W 63 H9
High Beach Essex 19 B11
High Bentham N Yorks 50 C2
High Bickington Devon 6 D5
High Birkwith N Yorks 50 B3
High Blantyre S Lanark 68 E5
High Bonnybridge Falk 69 C7
High Bradfield S Yorks 44 C6
High Bray Devon 6 C5
High Brooms Kent 12 B4
High Bullen Devon 6 D4
High Buston Northumb 63 C8
High Callerton Northumb 63 F7
High Catton E Yorks 52 D3
High Cogges Oxon 27 H10
High Coniscliffe Darl 58 E3
High Cross Hants 10 B6
High Cross Herts 29 G10
High Easter Essex 30 G3
High Eggborough N Yorks 52 G1
High Ellington N Yorks 51 A7
High Ercall Telford 34 D1
High Etherley Durham 58 D2
High Garrett Essex 30 F4
High Grange Durham 58 C2
High Green Norf 39 E7
High Green S Yorks 45 C7
High Green Worcs 26 D5
High Halden Kent 13 C7
High Halstow Medway 20 D4
High Ham Som 8 A3
High Harrington Cumb 56 D2
High Hatton Shrops 34 C2
High Hawsker N Yorks 59 F10
High Hesket W&F 57 B6
High Hesleden Durham 58 C5
High Hoyland S Yorks 44 A6
High Hunsley E Yorks 52 F5
High Hurstwood E Sus 12 D3
High Hutton N Yorks 52 C3
High Ireby Cumb 56 C4
High Kelling Norf 39 A7
High Kilburn N Yorks 51 B11
High Lands Durham 58 D2
High Lane Gtr Man 44 D3
High Lane Worcs 26 B3
High Laver Essex 30 H2
High Legh Ches E 43 D10
High Leven Stockton 58 E5
High Littleton Bath 16 F3
High Lorton Cumb 56 D3
High Marishes N Yorks 52 B4
High Marnham Notts 46 E2
High Melton S Yorks 45 B9
High Mickley Northumb 62 G6
High Mindork Dumfries 54 D6
High Newton W&F 49 A4
High Newton-by-the-Sea Northumb 71 H11
High Nibthwaite W&F 56 H4
High Offley Staffs 34 C3
High Ongar Essex 20 A2
High Onn Staffs 34 D4
High Roding Essex 30 G3
High Row Cumb 56 C5
High Salvington W Sus 11 D10
High Sellafield Cumb 56 F2
High Shaw N Yorks 57 G10
High Spen T&W 63 H7
High Stoop Durham 58 B2
High Street Corn 3 D8
High Street Kent 12 C6
High Street Suff 30 D5
High Street Suff 31 A11
High Street Suff 31 C11
High Street Green Suff 31 C7
High Throston Hrtlpl 58 C5
High Toynton Lincs 46 F6
High Trewhitt Northumb 62 C6
High Valleyfield Fife 69 B9
High Westwood Durham 63 H7
High Wray W&F 56 F5
High Wych Herts 29 G11
High Wycombe Bucks 18 B5
Higham Derbys 45 G7
Higham Kent 20 D4
Higham Lancs 50 F4
Higham Suff 30 B4
Higham Suff 31 E7
Higham Dykes Northumb 63 F7
Higham Ferrers N Nhants 28 B6
Higham Gobion C Beds 29 E8
Higham on the Hill Leics 35 F9
Higham Wood Kent 20 G2
Highampton Devon 6 F3
Highbridge Highld 80 E3
Highbridge Som 15 G9
Highbrook W Sus 12 C2
Highburton W Yorks 44 A5
Highbury Som 16 G3
Highclere Hants 17 E11
Highcliffe BCP 9 E11
Higher Ansty Dorset 9 D6
Higher Ashton Devon 5 C9
Higher Ballam Lancs 49 F3
Higher Bartle Lancs 49 F5
Higher Boscaswell Corn 2 F2
Higher Burwardsley Ches W 43 G8
Higher Clovelly Devon 6 D2
Higher End Gtr Man 43 B8
Higher Kinnerton Flint 42 F6
Higher Penwortham Lancs 49 G5
Higher Town Scilly 2 C3
Higher Walreddon Devon 4 D5
Higher Walton Lancs 50 G1
Higher Walton Warr 43 D8
Higher Wheelton Lancs 50 G2
Higher Whitley Ches W 43 D9
Higher Wincham Ches W 43 E9
Higher Wych Ches W 33 A10
Highfield E Yorks 52 F3
Highfield Gtr Man 43 B10
Highfield N Ayrs 66 A6
Highfield Oxon 28 F2
Highfield S Yorks 45 D7
Highfield T&W 63 H7
Highfields Cambs 29 C10
Highfields Northumb 71 E8
Highgate London 19 C9
Highlane Ches E 44 F2
Highlane Derbys 45 D8
Highlaws Cumb 56 B3
Highleadon Glos 26 F4
Highleigh W Sus 11 E7
Highley Shrops 34 G3
Highmoor Cross Oxon 18 C4
Highmoor Hill Mon 15 C10
Highnam Glos 26 G4
Highnam Green Glos 26 F4
Highsted Kent 20 E6
Highstreet Green Essex 30 E4
Hightae Dumfries 60 F6
Hightown Ches E 44 F2
Hightown Mers 42 B6
Hightown Green Suff 30 C6
Highway Wilts 17 D7
Highweek Devon 5 D9
Highworth Swindon 17 B9
Hilborough Norf 38 E4
Hilcote Derbys 45 G8
Hilcott Wilts 17 F8
Hilden Park Kent 20 G2
Hildenborough Kent 20 G2
Hildersham Cambs 30 D2
Hilderstone Staffs 34 B5
Hilderthorpe E Yorks 53 C7
Hilfield Dorset 8 D5
Hilgay Norf 38 F2
Hill Pembs 22 F6
Hill S Glos 16 B3
Hill W Mid 35 F7
Hill Brow W Sus 11 B6
Hill Dale Lancs 43 A7
Hill Dyke Lincs 47 H7
Hill End Durham 58 C1
Hill End Fife 76 H3
Hill End N Yorks 51 D6
Hill Head Hants 10 D4
Hill Head Northumb 62 G5
Hill Mountain Pembs 22 F4
Hill of Beath Fife 69 A10
Hill of Fearn Highld 87 D11
Hill of Mountblairy Aberds 89 C6
Hill Ridware Staffs 35 D6
Hill Top Durham 57 D11
Hill Top Hants 10 D3
Hill Top W Mid 34 F5
Hill Top W Yorks 51 H9
Hill View Dorset 9 E8
Hillam N Yorks 51 G11
Hillbeck W&F 57 E9
Hillborough Kent 21 E9
Hillbrae Aberds 83 A9
Hillbrae Aberds 88 D6
Hillbutts Dorset 9 D8
Hillclifflane Derbys 44 H6
Hillcommon Som 7 D10
Hillend Fife 69 B10
Hillerton Devon 7 G6
Hillesden Bucks 28 F3
Hillesley Glos 16 C4
Hillfarance Som 7 D10
Hillhead Aberds 88 E5
Hillhead Devon 5 F10
Hillhead S Ayrs 67 E7
Hillhead of Auchentumb Aberds 89 C9
Hillhead of Cocklaw Aberds 89 D10
Hillhouse Borders 70 E4
Hilliclay Highld 94 D3
Hillingdon London 19 C7
Hillington Glasgow 68 D4
Hillington Norf 38 C3
Hillmorton Warks 28 A2
Hillockhead Aberds 82 B6
Hillockhead Aberds 82 C5
Hillside Aberds 83 D11
Hillside Angus 77 A10
Hillside Mers 42 A6
Hillside Orkney 95 J5
Hillside Shetland 96 G6
Hillswick Shetland 96 F4
Hillway IoW 10 F5
Hillwell Shetland 96 M5
Hilmarton Wilts 17 D7
Hilperton Wilts 16 F5
Hilsea Ptsmth 10 D5
Hilston E Yorks 53 F8
Hilton Aberds 89 E9
Hilton Cambs 29 B9
Hilton Derbys 35 B8
Hilton Dorset 9 D6
Hilton Durham 58 D2
Hilton Highld 87 C10
Hilton Shrops 34 F3
Hilton Stockton 58 E5
Hilton W&F 57 D9
Hilton of Cadboll Highld 87 D11
Himbleton Worcs 26 C6
Himley Staffs 34 F4
Hincaster W&F 49 A5
Hinckley Leics 35 F10
Hinderclay Suff 38 H6
Hinderton Ches W 42 E6
Hinderwell N Yorks 59 E8
Hindford Shrops 33 B9
Hindhead Sur 18 H5
Hindley Gtr Man 43 B9
Hindley Green Gtr Man 43 B9
Hindlip Worcs 26 C5
Hindolveston Norf 38 C6
Hindon Wilts 9 A8
Hindringham Norf 38 B5
Hingham Norf 38 E6
Hinstock Shrops 34 C2
Hintlesham Suff 31 D7
Hinton Hants 9 E11
Hinton Hereford 25 E10
Hinton S Glos 16 D4
Hinton Shrops 33 E10
Hinton W Nhants 28 C2
Hinton Ampner Hants 10 B4
Hinton Blewett Bath 16 F2
Hinton Charterhouse Bath 16 F4
Hinton-in-the-Hedges W Nhants 28 E2
Hinton Martell Dorset 9 D9
Hinton on the Green Worcs 27 D7
Hinton Parva Swindon 17 C9
Hinton St George Som 8 C3
Hinton St Mary Dorset 9 C6
Hinton Waldrist Oxon 17 B10
Hints Shrops 26 A3
Hints Staffs 35 E7
Hinwick Bedford 28 B6
Hinxhill Kent 13 B9
Hinxton Cambs 29 D11
Hinxworth Herts 29 D9
Hipperholme W Yorks 51 G7
Hipswell N Yorks 58 G2
Hirael Gwyn 41 C7
Hiraeth Carms 22 D6
Hirn Aberds 83 C9
Hirnant Powys 33 C6
Hirst N Lanark 69 D7
Hirst Northumb 63 E8
Hirst Courtney N Yorks 52 G2
Hirwaen Denb 42 F4
Hirwaun Rhondda 24 H6
Hiscott Devon 6 D4
Histon Cambs 29 B11
Hitcham Suff 30 C6
Hitchin Herts 29 F8
Hither Green London 19 D10
Hittisleigh Devon 7 G6
Hive E Yorks 52 F4
Hixon Staffs 34 C6
Hoaden Kent 21 F9
Hoaldalbert Mon 25 F10
Hoar Cross Staffs 35 C7
Hoarwithy Hereford 26 F2
Hoath Kent 21 E9
Hobarris Shrops 33 H9
Hobbister Orkney 95 H4
Hobkirk Borders 61 B11
Hobson Durham 63 H7
Hoby Leics 36 D2
Hockering Norf 39 D6
Hockerton Notts 45 G11
Hockley Essex 20 B5
Hockley Heath W Mid 27 A8
Hockliffe C Beds 28 F6
Hockwold cum Wilton Norf 38 G3
Hockworthy Devon 7 E9
Hoddesdon Herts 29 H10
Hoddlesden Blackburn 50 G3
Hoddom Mains Dumfries 61 F7
Hoddomcross Dumfries 61 F7
Hodgeston Pembs 22 G5
Hodley Powys 33 F7
Hodnet Shrops 34 C2
Hodthorpe Derbys 45 E9
Hoe Hants 10 C4
Hoe Norf 38 D5
Hoe Gate Hants 10 C5
Hoff W&F 57 E8
Hog Patch Sur 18 G5
Hoggard's Green Suff 30 C5
Hoggeston Bucks 28 F5
Hogha Gearraidh W Isles 84 A2
Hoghton Lancs 50 G2
Hognaston Derbys 44 G6
Hogsthorpe Lincs 47 E9
Holbeach Lincs 37 C9
Holbeach Bank Lincs 37 C9
Holbeach Clough Lincs 37 C9
Holbeach Drove Lincs 37 D9
Holbeach Hurn Lincs 37 C9
Holbeach St Johns Lincs 37 D9
Holbeach St Marks Lincs 37 B9
Holbeach St Matthew Lincs 37 B10
Holbeck Notts 45 E9
Holbeck W Yorks 51 F8
Holbeck Woodhouse Notts 45 E9
Holberrow Green Worcs 27 C7
Holbeton Devon 5 F7
Holborn London 19 C10
Holbrook Derbys 35 A9
Holbrook S Yorks 45 D8
Holbrook Suff 31 E8
Holburn Northumb 71 G9
Holbury Hants 10 D3
Holcombe Devon 5 D10
Holcombe Som 16 G3
Holcombe Rogus Devon 7 E9
Holcot W Nhants 28 B4
Holden Lancs 50 E3
Holdenby W Nhants 28 B3
Holdenhurst BCP 9 E10
Holdgate Shrops 34 G1
Holdingham Lincs 46 H4
Holditch Dorset 8 D2
Hole-in-the-Wall Hereford 26 F3
Holefield Borders 71 G7
Holehouses Ches E 43 E10
Holemoor Devon 6 F3
Holestane Dumfries 60 D4
Holford Som 7 B10
Holgate York 52 D1
Holker W&F 49 B3
Holkham Norf 38 A4
Hollacombe Devon 6 F2
Holland Orkney 95 C5
Holland Orkney 95 F7
Holland Fen Lincs 46 H6
Holland-on-Sea Essex 31 G9
Hollandstoun Orkney 95 C8
Hollee Dumfries 61 G8
Hollesley Suff 31 D10
Hollicombe Torbay 5 E9
Hollingbourne Kent 20 F5
Hollington Derbys 35 B8
Hollington E Sus 13 E6
Hollington Staffs 35 B6
Hollington Grove Derbys 35 B8
Hollingworth Gtr Man 44 C4
Hollins Gtr Man 44 B2
Hollins Green Warr 43 C9
Hollins Lane Lancs 49 D4
Hollinsclough Staffs 44 F4
Hollinwood Gtr Man 44 B3
Hollinwood Shrops 33 B11
Hollocombe Devon 6 E5
Hollow Meadows S Yorks 44 D6
Holloway Derbys 45 G7
Hollowell W Nhants 28 A3
Holly End Norf 37 E10
Holly Green Worcs 26 D5
Hollybush Caerph 15 A7
Hollybush E Ayrs 67 E6
Hollybush Worcs 26 E4
Hollym E Yorks 53 G9
Hollywood Worcs 35 H6
Holmbridge W Yorks 44 B5
Holmbury St Mary Sur 19 G8
Holmbush Corn 3 D9
Holmcroft Staffs 34 C5
Holme Cambs 37 G7
Holme N Yorks 51 A9
Holme Notts 46 G2
Holme W Yorks 44 B5
Holme W&F 49 B5
Holme Chapel Lancs 50 G4
Holme Green N Yorks 52 E1
Holme Hale Norf 38 E4
Holme Lacy Hereford 26 E2
Holme Marsh Hereford 25 C10
Holme next the Sea Norf 38 A3
Holme-on-Spalding-Moor E Yorks 52 F4
Holme on the Wolds E Yorks 52 E5
Holme Pierrepont Notts 36 B2
Holme St Cuthbert Cumb 56 B3
Holme Wood W Yorks 51 F7
Holmer Hereford 26 D2
Holmer Green Bucks 18 B6
Holmes Chapel Ches E 43 F10
Holmesfield Derbys 45 E7
Holmeswood Lancs 49 H4
Holmewood Derbys 45 F8
Holmfirth W Yorks 44 B5
Holmhead Dumfries 60 E3
Holmhead E Ayrs 67 D8
Holmisdale Highld 84 D6
Holmpton E Yorks 53 G9
Holmrook Cumb 56 G2
Holmsgarth Shetland 96 J6
Holmwrangle Cumb 57 B7
Holne Devon 5 E8
Holnest Dorset 8 D5
Holsworthy Devon 6 F2
Holsworthy Beacon Devon 6 F2
Holt Dorset 9 D9
Holt Norf 39 B6
Holt Wilts 16 E5
Holt Worcs 26 B5
Holt Wrex 43 G7
Holt End Hants 18 H3
Holt End Worcs 27 B7
Holt Fleet Worcs 26 B5
Holt Heath Worcs 26 B5
Holt Park W Yorks 51 E8
Holtby York 52 D2
Holton Oxon 28 H3
Holton Som 8 B5
Holton Suff 39 H9
Holton cum Beckering Lincs 46 D5
Holton Heath Dorset 9 E8
Holton le Clay Lincs 46 B6
Holton le Moor Lincs 46 C4
Holton St Mary Suff 31 E7
Holwell Dorset 8 C6
Holwell Herts 29 E8
Holwell Leics 36 C3
Holwell Oxon 27 H9
Holwick Durham 57 D11
Holworth Dorset 9 F6
Holy Cross Worcs 34 H5
Holy Island Northumb 71 F10
Holybourne Hants 18 G4
Holyhead = Caergybi Anglesey 40 B4
Holymoorside Derbys 45 F7
Holyport Windsor 18 D5
Holystone Northumb 62 C5
Holytown N Lanark 68 D6
Holywell Cambs 29 A10
Holywell Corn 3 D6
Holywell Dorset 8 D4
Holywell E Sus 12 G4
Holywell = Treffynnon Flint 42 E4
Holywell Northumb 63 F9
Holywell Green W Yorks 51 H6
Holywell Lake Som 7 D10
Holywell Row Suff 38 H3
Holywood Dumfries 60 E5
Hom Green Hereford 26 F2
Homer Shrops 34 E2
Homersfield Suff 39 G8
Homington Wilts 9 B10
Honey Hill Kent 21 E8
Honey Street Wilts 17 E8
Honey Tye Suff 30 E6
Honeyborough Pembs 22 F4
Honeybourne Worcs 27 D8
Honeychurch Devon 6 F5
Honiley Warks 27 A9
Honing Norf 39 C9
Honingham Norf 39 D7
Honington Lincs 36 A5
Honington Suff 30 A6
Honington Warks 27 D9
Honiton Devon 7 F10
Honley W Yorks 44 A5
Hoo Green Ches E 43 D10
Hoo St. Werburgh Medway 20 D4
Hood Green S Yorks 45 B7
Hooe E Sus 12 F5
Hooe Plym 4 F6
Hooe Common E Sus 12 E5
Hook E Yorks 52 G3
Hook Hants 18 F4
Hook London 19 E8
Hook Pembs 22 E4
Hook Wilts 17 C7
Hook Green Kent 12 C5
Hook Green Kent 20 E3
Hook Norton Oxon 27 E10
Hooke Dorset 8 E4
Hookgate Staffs 34 B3
Hookway Devon 7 G7
Hookwood Sur 12 B1
Hoole Ches W 43 F7
Hooley Sur 19 F9
Hoop Mon 26 H2
Hooton Ches W 42 E6
Hooton Levitt S Yorks 45 C9
Hooton Pagnell S Yorks 45 B8
Hooton Roberts S Yorks 45 C8
Hop Pole Lincs 37 D7
Hope Derbys 44 D5
Hope Devon 5 H7
Hope = Yr Hôb Flint 42 G6
Hope Highld 92 C7
Hope Powys 33 E8
Hope Shrops 33 E9
Hope Staffs 44 G5
Hope Bagot Shrops 26 A2
Hope Bowdler Shrops 33 F10
Hope End Green Essex 30 F2
Hope Green Ches E 44 D3
Hope Mansell Hereford 26 G3
Hope under Dinmore Hereford 26 C2
Hopeman Moray 88 B1
Hope's Green Essex 20 C4
Hopesay Shrops 33 G9
Hopley's Green Hereford 25 C10
Hopperton N Yorks 51 D10
Hopstone Shrops 34 F3
Hopton Shrops 33 C9
Hopton Shrops 34 C1
Hopton Staffs 34 C5
Hopton Suff 38 H5
Hopton Cangeford Shrops 33 G11
Hopton Castle Shrops 33 H9
Hopton on Sea Norf 39 E11
Hopton Wafers Shrops 34 H2
Hoptonheath Shrops 33 H9
Hopwas Staffs 35 E7
Hopwood Gtr Man 44 B2
Hopwood Worcs 34 H6
Horam E Sus 12 E4
Horbling Lincs 37 B7
Horbury W Yorks 51 H8
Horcott Glos 17 A8
Horden Durham 58 B5
Horderley Shrops 33 G10
Hordle Hants 10 E1
Hordley Shrops 33 B9
Horeb Carms 23 D10
Horeb Carms 23 F9
Horeb Ceredig 23 B8
Horfield Bristol 16 D3
Horham Suff 31 A9
Horkesley Heath Essex 30 F6
Horkstow N Lincs 52 H5
Horley Oxon 27 D11
Horley Sur 12 B1
Hornblotton Green Som 8 A4
Hornby Lancs 50 C1
Hornby N Yorks 58 F4
Hornby N Yorks 58 G3
Horncastle Lincs 46 F6
Hornchurch London 20 C2
Horncliffe Northumb 71 F8
Horndean Borders 71 F7
Horndean Hants 10 C6
Horndon Devon 4 D6
Horndon on the Hill Thurrock 20 C3
Horne Sur 12 B2
Horniehaugh Angus 77 A7
Horning Norf 39 D9
Horninghold Leics 36 F4
Horninglow Staffs 35 C8
Horningsea Cambs 29 B11
Horningsham Wilts 16 G5
Horningtoft Norf 38 C5
Horns Corner Kent 12 D6
Horns Cross Devon 6 D2
Horns Cross E Sus 13 D7
Hornsby Cumb 57 A7
Hornsea E Yorks 53 E8
Hornsea Bridge E Yorks 53 E8
Hornsey London 19 C10
Hornton Oxon 27 D10
Horrabridge Devon 4 E6
Horringer Suff 30 B5
Horringford IoW 10 F4
Horse Bridge Staffs 44 G3
Horsebridge Devon 4 D5
Horsebridge Hants 10 A2
Horsebrook Staffs 34 D4
Horsehay Telford 34 E2
Horseheath Cambs 30 D3
Horsehouse N Yorks 50 A6
Horsell Sur 18 F6
Horseman's Green Wrex 33 A10
Horseway Cambs 37 G10
Horsey Norf 39 C10
Horsford Norf 39 D7
Horsforth W Yorks 51 F8
Horsham W Sus 11 A10
Horsham Worcs 26 C4
Horsham St Faith Norf 39 D8
Horsington Lincs 46 F5
Horsington Som 8 B6
Horsley Derbys 35 A9
Horsley Glos 16 B5
Horsley Northumb 62 D4
Horsley Northumb 62 G6
Horsley Cross Essex 31 F8
Horsley Woodhouse Derbys 35 A9
Horsleycross Street Essex 31 F8
Horsleyhill Borders 61 B11
Horsleyhope Durham 58 B1
Horsmonden Kent 12 B5
Horspath Oxon 18 A2
Horstead Norf 39 D8
Horsted Keynes W Sus 12 D2
Horton Bucks 28 G6
Horton Dorset 9 D9
Horton Lancs 50 D4
Horton S Glos 16 C4
Horton Shrops 33 C10
Horton Som 8 C2
Horton Staffs 44 G3
Horton Swansea 23 H9
Horton W Nhants 28 C5
Horton Wilts 17 E7
Horton Windsor 19 D7
Horton-cum-Studley Oxon 28 G2
Horton Green Ches W 43 H7
Horton Heath Hants 10 C3
Horton in Ribblesdale N Yorks 50 B4
Horton Kirby Kent 20 E2
Hortonlane Shrops 33 D10
Horwich Gtr Man 43 A9
Horwich End Derbys 44 D4
Horwood Devon 6 D4
Hose Leics 36 C3
Hoselaw Borders 71 G7
Hoses W&F 56 G4
Hosh Perth 75 E11
Hosta W Isles 84 A2
Hoswick Shetland 96 L6
Hotham E Yorks 52 F4
Hothfield Kent 20 G6
Hoton Leics 36 C1
Houbie Shetland 96 D8
Houdston S Ayrs 66 G4
Hough Ches E 43 G10
Hough Ches E 44 E2
Hough Green Halton 43 D7
Hough-on-the-Hill Lincs 46 H3
Hougham Lincs 36 A4
Houghton Cambs 29 A9
Houghton Cumb 61 H10
Houghton Hants 10 A2
Houghton Pembs 22 F4
Houghton W Sus 11 C9
Houghton Conquest C Beds 29 D7
Houghton Green E Sus 13 D8
Houghton Green Warr 43 C9
Houghton-le-Side Darl 58 D3
Houghton-le-Spring T&W 58 B4
Houghton on the Hill Leics 36 E2
Houghton Regis C Beds 29 F7
Houghton St Giles Norf 38 B5
Houlland Shetland 96 F7
Houlland Shetland 96 H5
Houlsyke N Yorks 59 F8
Houlton Warks 28 A2
Hound Hants 10 D3
Hound Green Hants 18 F4
Houndslow Borders 70 F5
Houndwood Borders 71 D7
Hounslow London 19 D8
Hounslow Green Essex 30 G3
Housay Shetland 96 F8
House of Daviot Highld 87 G10
House of Glenmuick Aberds 82 D5
Housetter Shetland 96 E5
Houss Shetland 96 K5
Houston Renfs 68 D3
Houstry Highld 94 G3
Houton Orkney 95 H4
Hove Brighton 12 F1
Hoveringham Notts 45 H10
Hoveton Norf 39 D9
Hovingham N Yorks 52 B2
How Cumb 61 H11
How Caple Hereford 26 E3
How End C Beds 29 D7
How Green Kent 19 G11
Howbrook S Yorks 45 C7
Howden Borders 62 A2
Howden E Yorks 52 G3
Howden-le-Wear Durham 58 C2
Howe Highld 94 D5
Howe N Yorks 51 A9
Howe Norf 39 E8
Howe Bridge Gtr Man 43 B9
Howe Green Essex 20 A4
Howe of Teuchar Aberds 89 D7
Howe Street Essex 30 E3
Howe Street Essex 30 G3
Howell Lincs 46 H5
Howey Powys 25 C7
Howgate Midloth 69 E11
Howick Northumb 63 B8
Howle Durham 58 D1
Howle Telford 34 C2
Howlett End Essex 30 E2
Howley Som 8 D1
Hownam Borders 62 B3
Hownam Mains Borders 62 A3
Howpasley Borders 61 C9
Howsham N Lincs 46 B4
Howsham N Yorks 52 C3
Howslack Dumfries 60 C6
Howtel Northumb 71 G7
Howton Hereford 25 F11
Howtown W&F 56 E6
Howwood Renfs 68 D2
Hoxne Suff 39 H7
Hoy Orkney 95 H3
Hoylake Mers 42 D5
Hoyland S Yorks 45 B7
Hoylandswaine S Yorks 44 B6
Hubberholme N Yorks 50 B5
Hubbert's Bridge Lincs 37 A8
Huby N Yorks 51 E8
Huby N Yorks 52 C1
Hucclecote Glos 26 G5
Hucking Kent 20 F5
Hucknall Notts 45 H9
Huddersfield W Yorks 51 H7
Huddington Worcs 26 C6
Hudswell N Yorks 58 F2
Huggate E Yorks 52 D4
Hugglescote Leics 35 D10
Hugh Town Scilly 2 C3
Hughenden Valley Bucks 18 B5
Hughley Shrops 34 F1
Huish Devon 6 E4
Huish Wilts 17 E8
Huish Champflower Som 7 D9
Huish Episcopi Som 8 B3
Huisinis W Isles 90 F4
Hulcott Bucks 28 G5
Hulland Derbys 44 H6
Hulland Ward Derbys 44 H6
Hullavington Wilts 16 C5
Hullbridge Essex 20 B5
Hulme Gtr Man 44 C2
Hulme End Staffs 44 G5
Hulme Walfield Ches E 44 F2
Hulver Street Suff 39 G10
Hulverstone IoW 10 F2
Humber Hereford 26 C2
Humber Bridge N Lincs 52 G6
Humberston NE Lincs 47 B7
Humbie E Loth 70 D3
Humbleton E Yorks 53 F8
Humbleton Northumb 71 H8
Humby Lincs 36 B6
Hume Borders 70 F6
Humshaugh Northumb 62 F5
Huna Highld 94 C5
Huncoat Lancs 50 F3
Huncote Leics 35 F11
Hundalee Borders 62 B2
Hunderthwaite Durham 57 D11
Hundle Houses Lincs 46 G6
Hundleby Lincs 47 F7
Hundleton Pembs 22 F4
Hundon Suff 30 D4
Hundred Acres Hants 10 C4
Hundred End Lancs 49 G4
Hundred House Powys 25 C8
Hungarton Leics 36 E2
Hungerford Hants 9 C10
Hungerford W Berks 17 E10
Hungerford Newtown W Berks 17 D10
Hungerton Lincs 36 C4
Hungladder Highld 85 A8
Hunmanby N Yorks 53 B6
Hunmanby Moor N Yorks 53 B7
Hunningham Warks 27 B10
Hunny Hill IoW 10 F3
Hunsdon Herts 29 G11
Hunsingore N Yorks 51 D10
Hunslet W Yorks 51 F9
Hunsonby W&F 57 C7
Hunspow Highld 94 C4
Hunstanton Norf 38 A2
Hunstanworth Durham 57 B11
Hunsterson Ches E 43 H9
Hunston Suff 30 B6
Hunston W Sus 11 D7
Hunstrete Bath 16 E3
Hunt End Worcs 27 B7
Hunter's Quay Argyll 73 F10
Hunthill Lodge Angus 82 F6
Huntingtower Perth 76 E3
Huntingdon Cambs 29 A9
Huntingfield Suff 31 A10
Huntingford Dorset 9 A7
Huntington E Loth 70 C3
Huntington Hereford 25 C9
Huntington Staffs 34 D5
Huntington York 52 D2
Huntley Glos 26 G4
Huntly Aberds 88 E5
Huntlywood Borders 70 F5
Hunton Kent 20 G4
Hunton N Yorks 58 G2
Hunt's Corner Norf 39 G6
Hunt's Cross Mers 43 D7
Huntsham Devon 7 D9
Huntspill Som 15 G9
Huntworth Som 8 A2
Hunwick Durham 58 C2
Hunworth Norf 39 B6
Hurdsfield Ches E 44 E3
Hurley Warks 35 F8
Hurley Windsor 18 C5
Hurlford E Ayrs 67 C7
Hurliness Orkney 95 K3
Hurn BCP 9 E10
Hurn's End Lincs 47 H8
Hursley Hants 10 B3
Hurst N Yorks 58 F1
Hurst Som 8 C3
Hurst Wokingham 18 D4
Hurst Green E Sus 12 D6
Hurst Green Lancs 50 F2
Hurst Wickham W Sus 12 E1
Hurstbourne Priors Hants 17 G11
Hurstbourne Tarrant Hants 17 F10
Hurstpierpoint W Sus 12 E1
Hurstwood Lancs 50 F4
Hurtmore Sur 18 G6
Hurworth Place Darl 58 F3
Hury Durham 57 E11
Husabost Highld 84 C7
Husbands Bosworth Leics 36 G2
Husborne Crawley C Beds 28 E6
Husthwaite N Yorks 51 B11
Hutchwns Bridgend 14 D4
Huthwaite Notts 45 G8
Huttoft Lincs 47 E9
Hutton Borders 71 E8
Hutton E Yorks 52 D6
Hutton Essex 20 B3
Hutton Lancs 49 G4
Hutton N Som 15 F9
Hutton W&F 56 D6
Hutton Buscel N Yorks 52 A5
Hutton Conyers N Yorks 51 B9
Hutton Cranswick E Yorks 52 D6
Hutton End W&F 56 C6
Hutton Gate Redcar 59 E6
Hutton Henry Durham 58 C5
Hutton-le-Hole N Yorks 59 G8
Hutton Magna Durham 58 E2
Hutton Roof W&F 50 B1
Hutton Roof W&F 56 C5
Hutton Rudby N Yorks 58 F5
Hutton Sessay N Yorks 51 B10
Hutton Village Redcar 59 E6
Hutton Wandesley N Yorks 51 D11
Huxley Ches W 43 F8
Huxter Shetland 96 G7
Huxter Shetland 96 H5
Huxton Borders 71 D7
Huyton Mers 43 C7
Hwlffordd = Haverfordwest Pembs 22 E4
Hycemoor Cumb 56 H2
Hyde Glos 16 A5
Hyde Gtr Man 44 C3
Hyde Hants 9 C10
Hyde Heath Bucks 18 A6
Hyde Park S Yorks 45 B9
Hydestile Sur 18 G6
Hylton Castle T&W 63 H9
Hyndford Bridge S Lanark 69 F8
Hynish Argyll 78 H2
Hyssington Powys 33 F9
Hythe Hants 10 D3
Hythe Kent 21 H8
Hythe End Windsor 19 D7
Hythie Aberds 89 C10

I

Ibberton Dorset 9 D6
Ible Derbys 44 G6
Ibsley Hants 9 D10
Ibstock Leics 35 D10
Ibstone Bucks 18 B4
Ibthorpe Hants 17 F10
Ibworth Hants 18 F2
Ichrachan Argyll 74 D3
Ickburgh Norf 38 F4
Ickenham London 19 C7
Ickford Bucks 28 H3
Ickham Kent 21 F9
Ickleford Herts 29 E8
Icklesham E Sus 13 E7
Ickleton Cambs 29 D11
Icklingham Suff 30 A4
Ickwell Green C Beds 29 D8
Icomb Glos 27 F9
Idbury Oxon 27 G9
Iddesleigh Devon 6 F4
Ide Devon 7 G7
Ide Hill Kent 19 F11
Ideford Devon 5 D9
Iden E Sus 13 D8
Iden Green Kent 12 C6
Iden Green Kent 13 C7
Idle W Yorks 51 F7
Idlicote Warks 27 D9
Idmiston Wilts 17 H8
Idole Carms 23 E9
Idridgehay Derbys 44 H6
Idrigill Highld 85 B8
Idstone Oxon 17 C9
Idvies Angus 77 C8
Iffley Oxon 18 A2
Ifield W Sus 19 H9
Ifold W Sus 11 A9
Iford E Sus 12 F3
Ifton Heath Shrops 33 B9
Ightfield Shrops 34 B1
Ightham Kent 20 F2
Iken Suff 31 C11
Ilam Staffs 44 G5
Ilchester Som 8 B4
Ilderton Northumb 62 A6
Ilford London 19 C11
Ilfracombe Devon 6 B4
Ilkeston Derbys 35 A10
Ilketshall St Andrew Suff 39 G9
Ilketshall St Lawrence Suff 39 G9
Ilketshall St Margaret Suff 39 G9
Ilkley W Yorks 51 E7
Illey W Mid 34 G5
Illingworth W Yorks 51 G6
Illogan Corn 2 E5
Illston on the Hill Leics 36 F3
Ilmer Bucks 28 H4
Ilmington Warks 27 D9
Ilminster Som 8 C2
Ilsington Devon 5 D8
Ilston Swansea 23 G10
Ilton N Yorks 51 B7
Ilton Som 8 C2
Imachar N Ayrs 66 B1
Imeraval Argyll 64 D4
Immingham NE Lincs 46 A5
Impington Cambs 29 B11
Ince Ches W 43 E7
Ince Blundell Mers 42 B6
Ince in Makerfield Gtr Man 43 B8
Inch of Arnhall Aberds 83 F8
Inchbare Angus 83 G8
Inchberry Moray 88 C3
Inchbraoch Angus 77 B10
Incheril Highld 86 E3
Inchgrundle Angus 82 F6
Inchina Highld 86 B2
Inchinnan Renfs 68 D3
Inchkinloch Highld 93 E8
Inchlaggan Highld 80 C3
Inchlumpie Highld 87 D8
Inchmore Highld 86 G6
Inchnacardoch Hotel Highld 80 B5
Inchnadamph Highld 92 G5
Inchree Highld 74 A3
Inchture Perth 76 E5
Inchyra Perth 76 E4
Indian Queens Corn 3 D8
Inerval Argyll 64 D4
Ingatestone Essex 20 B3
Ingbirchworth S Yorks 44 B6
Ingestre Staffs 34 C5
Ingham Lincs 46 D3
Ingham Norf 39 C9
Ingham Suff 30 A5
Ingham Corner Norf 39 C9
Ingleborough Norf 37 D10
Ingleby Derbys 35 C9
Ingleby Lincs 46 E2
Ingleby Arncliffe N Yorks 58 F5
Ingleby Barwick Stockton 58 E5
Ingleby Greenhow N Yorks 59 F6
Inglemire Hull 53 F6
Inglesbatch Bath 16 E4
Inglesham Swindon 17 B9
Ingleton Durham 58 D2
Ingleton N Yorks 50 B2
Inglewhite Lancs 49 E5
Ingliston Edin 69 C10
Ingoe Northumb 62 F6
Ingol Lancs 49 F5
Ingoldisthorpe Norf 38 B2
Ingoldmells Lincs 47 F9
Ingoldsby Lincs 36 B6
Ingon Warks 27 C9
Ingram Northumb 62 B6
Ingrow W Yorks 51 F6
Ings W&F 56 G6
Ingst S Glos 16 C2
Ingworth Norf 39 C7
Inham's End Cambs 37 F8
Inkberrow Worcs 27 C7
Inkpen W Berks 17 E10
Inkstack Highld 94 C4
Inn W&F 56 F6
Innellan Argyll 73 F10
Innerleithen Borders 70 G2
Innerleven Fife 76 G6
Innermessan Dumfries 54 C3
Innerwick E Loth 70 C6
Innerwick Perth 75 C8
Innis Chonain Argyll 74 E4
Insch Aberds 83 A8
Insh Highld 81 C10
Inshore Highld 92 C6
Inskip Lancs 49 F4
Instoneville S Yorks 45 A9
Instow Devon 6 C3
Intake S Yorks 45 B9
Inver Aberds 82 D4
Inver Highld 87 C11
Inver Perth 76 C3
Inver Mallie Highld 80 E3
Inverailort Highld 79 C10
Inveraldie Angus 77 D7
Inveralligin Highld 85 C13
Inverallochy Aberds 89 B10
Inveran Highld 87 B8
Inveraray Argyll 73 C9
Inverarish Highld 85 E10
Inverarity Angus 77 C7
Inverarnan Stirling 74 F6
Inverasdale Highld 91 J13
Inverbeg Argyll 74 H6
Inverbervie Aberds 83 F10
Inverboyndie Aberds 89 B6
Inverbroom Highld 86 C4
Invercassley Highld 92 J7
Invercauld House Aberds 82 D3
Inverchaolain Argyll 73 F9
Invercharnan Highld 74 C4
Inverchoran Highld 86 F5
Invercreran Argyll 74 C3
Inverdruie Highld 81 B11
Inverebrie Aberds 89 E9
Invereck Argyll 73 E10
Inverernan Ho. Aberds 82 B5
Invereshie House Highld 81 C10
Inveresk E Loth 70 C2
Inverey Aberds 82 E2
Inverfarigaig Highld 81 A7
Invergarry Highld 80 C5
Invergelder Aberds 82 D4
Invergeldie Perth 75 E10
Invergordon Highld 87 E10
Invergowrie Perth 76 D6
Inverguseran Highld 85 H12
Inverhadden Perth 75 B9
Inverharroch Moray 88 E3
Inverherive Stirling 74 E6
Inverie Highld 79 B10
Inverinan Argyll 73 B8
Inverinate Highld 85 F14
Inverkeilor Angus 77 C9
Inverkeithing Fife 69 B10
Inverkeithny Aberds 89 D6
Inverkip Invclyd 73 F11
Inverkirkaig Highld 92 H3
Inverlael Highld 86 C4
Inverlochlarig Stirling 75 F7
Inverlochy Argyll 74 E4
Inverlochy Highld 80 F3
Inverlussa Argyll 72 E5
Invermark Lodge Angus 82 E6
Invermoidart Highld 79 D9
Invermoriston Highld 80 B6
Invernaver Highld 93 C10
Inverneill Argyll 73 E7
Inverness Highld 87 G9
Invernettie Aberds 89 D11
Invernoaden Argyll 73 D10
Inveroran Hotel Argyll 74 C5
Inverpolly Lodge Highld 92 H3
Inverquharity Angus 77 B7
Inverquhomery Aberds 89 D10
Inverroy Highld 80 E4
Inversanda Highld 74 B2
Invershiel Highld 80 B1
Invershin Highld 87 B8
Inversnaid Hotel Stirling 74 G6
Inverugie Aberds 89 D11
Inveruglas Argyll 74 G6
Inveruglass Highld 81 C10
Inverurie Aberds 83 A9
Invervar Perth 75 C9
Inverythan Aberds 89 D7
Inwardleigh Devon 6 G4
Inworth Essex 30 G5
Iochdar W Isles 84 D2
Iping W Sus 11 B7
Ipplepen Devon 5 E9
Ipsden Oxon 18 C3
Ipsley Worcs 27 B7
Ipstones Staffs 44 G4
Ipswich Suff 31 D8
Irby Mers 42 D5
Irby in the Marsh Lincs 47 F8
Irby upon Humber NE Lincs 46 B5
Irchester N Nhants 28 B6
Ireby Cumb 56 C4
Ireby Lancs 50 B2
Ireland Orkney 95 H4
Ireland Shetland 96 L5
Ireland's Cross Shrops 34 A3
Ireleth W&F 49 B2
Ireshopeburn Durham 57 C10
Irlam Gtr Man 43 C10
Irnham Lincs 36 C6
Iron Acton S Glos 16 C3
Iron Cross Warks 27 C7
Ironbridge Telford 34 E2
Irongray Dumfries 60 F5
Ironmacannie Dumfries 55 B9
Ironside Aberds 89 C8
Ironville Derbys 45 G8
Irstead Norf 39 C9
Irthington Cumb 61 G10
Irthlingborough N Nhants 28 A6
Irton N Yorks 52 A6
Irvine N Ayrs 66 C6
Isauld Highld 93 C12
Isbister Orkney 95 F3
Isbister Orkney 95 G4
Isbister Shetland 96 D5
Isbister Shetland 96 G7
Isfield E Sus 12 E3
Isham N Nhants 28 A5
Isle Abbotts Som 8 B2
Isle Brewers Som 8 B2
Isle of Whithorn Dumfries 55 F7
Isleham Cambs 30 A3
Isleornsay Highld 85 G12
Islesburgh Shetland 96 G5
Islesteps Dumfries 60 F5
Isleworth London 19 D8
Isley Walton Leics 35 C10
Islibhig W Isles 90 E4
Islington London 19 C10
Islip N Nhants 36 H5
Islip Oxon 28 G2
Istead Rise Kent 20 E3
Isycoed Wrex 43 G7
Itchen Soton 10 C3
Itchen Abbas Hants 10 A4
Itchen Stoke Hants 10 A4
Itchingfield W Sus 11 B10
Itchington S Glos 16 C3
Itteringham Norf 39 B7
Itton Devon 6 G5
Itton Common Mon 15 B10
Ivegill W&F 56 B6
Iver Bucks 19 C7
Iver Heath Bucks 19 C7
Iveston Durham 58 A2
Ivinghoe Bucks 28 G6
Ivinghoe Aston Bucks 28 G6
Ivington Hereford 25 C11
Ivington Green Hereford 25 C11
Ivy Chimneys Essex 19 A11
Ivy Cross Dorset 9 B7
Ivy Hatch Kent 20 F2
Ivybridge Devon 5 F7
Ivychurch Kent 13 D9
Iwade Kent 20 E6
Iwerne Courtney or Shroton Dorset 9 C7
Iwerne Minster Dorset 9 C7
Ixworth Suff 30 A6
Ixworth Thorpe Suff 30 A6

J

Jack Hill N Yorks 51 D8
Jack in the Green Devon 7 G9
Jacksdale Notts 45 G8
Jackstown Aberds 89 E7
Jacobstow Corn 4 B2
Jacobstowe Devon 6 F4
Jameston Pembs 22 G5
Jamestown Dumfries 61 D9
Jamestown Highld 86 F7
Jamestown W Dunb 68 B2
Jarrow T&W 63 G9
Jarvis Brook E Sus 12 D4
Jasper's Green Essex 30 F4
Java Argyll 79 H10
Jawcraig Falk 69 C7
Jaywick Essex 31 G8
Jealott's Hill Brack 18 D5
Jedburgh Borders 62 A2
Jeffreyston Pembs 22 F5
Jellyhill E Dunb 68 C5
Jemimaville Highld 87 E10
Jersey Farm Herts 29 H8
Jesmond T&W 63 G8
Jevington E Sus 12 F4
Jockey End Herts 29 G7
John o' Groats Highld 94 C5
Johnby W&F 56 C6
John's Cross E Sus 12 D6
Johnshaven Aberds 83 G9
Johnston Pembs 22 E4
Johnstone Renfs 68 D3
Johnstonebridge Dumfries 60 D6
Johnstown Carms 23 E9
Johnstown Wrex 42 H6
Joppa Edin 70 C2
Joppa S Ayrs 67 E7
Jordans Bucks 18 B6
Jordanthorpe S Yorks 45 D7
Jump S Yorks 45 B7
Jumpers Green BCP 9 E10
Juniper Green Edin 69 D10
Jurby East IoM 48 C3
Jurby West IoM 48 C3

K

Kaber W&F 57 E9
Kaimend S Lanark 69 F8
Kaimes Edin 69 D11
Kalemouth Borders 70 H6
Kames Argyll 73 B7
Kames Argyll 73 F8
Kames E Ayrs 68 H5
Kea Corn 3 E7
Keadby N Lincs 46 A2
Keal Cotes Lincs 47 F7
Kearsley Gtr Man 43 B10
Kearstwick W&F 50 A2
Kearton N Yorks 57 G11
Kearvaig Highld 92 B5
Keasden N Yorks 50 C3
Keckwick Halton 43 D8
Keddington Lincs 47 D7
Kedington Suff 30 D4
Kedleston Derbys 35 A9
Keelby Lincs 46 A5
Keele Staffs 44 H2
Keeley Green Bedford 29 D7
Keeston Pembs 22 E4
Keevil Wilts 16 F6
Kegworth Leics 35 C10
Kehelland Corn 2 E5
Keig Aberds 83 B8
Keighley W Yorks 51 E6
Keil Highld 74 B2
Keilarsbrae Clack 69 A7
Keilhill Aberds 89 C7
Keillmore Argyll 72 E5
Keillor Perth 76 C5
Keillour Perth 76 E2
Keills Argyll 64 B5
Keils Argyll 72 G4
Keinton Mandeville Som 8 A4
Keir Mill Dumfries 60 D4
Keisby Lincs 36 C6
Keiss Highld 94 D5
Keith Moray 88 C4
Keith Inch Aberds 89 D11
Keithock Angus 77 A9
Kelbrook Lancs 50 E5
Kelby Lincs 36 A6
Keld N Yorks 57 F10
Keld W&F 57 E7
Keldholme N Yorks 59 H8
Kelfield N Lincs 46 B2
Kelfield N Yorks 52 F1
Kelham Notts 45 G11
Kellan Argyll 79 G8
Kellas Angus 77 D7
Kellas Moray 88 C1
Kellaton Devon 5 H9
Kelleth W&F 57 F8
Kelleythorpe E Yorks 52 D5
Kelling Norf 39 A6
Kellingley N Yorks 51 G11
Kellington N Yorks 52 G1
Kelloe Durham 58 C4
Kelloholm Dumfries 60 B3
Kelly Devon 4 C4
Kelly Bray Corn 4 D4
Kelmarsh W Nhants 36 H3
Kelmscot Oxon 17 B9
Kelsale Suff 31 B10
Kelsall Ches W 43 F8
Kelsall Hill Ches W 43 F8
Kelshall Herts 29 E10
Kelsick Cumb 56 A3
Kelso Borders 70 G6
Kelstedge Derbys 45 F7
Kelstern Lincs 46 C6
Kelston Bath 16 E4
Keltneyburn Perth 75 C10
Kelton Dumfries 60 F5
Kelty Fife 69 A10
Kelvedon Essex 30 G5
Kelvedon Hatch Essex 20 B2
Kelvin S Lanark 68 E5
Kelvinside Glasgow 68 D4
Kelynack Corn 2 F2
Kemback Fife 77 F7
Kemberton Shrops 34 E3
Kemble Glos 16 B6
Kemerton Worcs 26 E6
Kemeys Commander Mon 15 A9
Kemnay Aberds 83 B9
Kemp Town Brighton 12 F2
Kempley Glos 26 F3
Kemps Green Warks 27 A8
Kempsey Worcs 26 D5
Kempsford Glos 17 B8
Kempshott Hants 18 F3
Kempston Bedford 29 D7
Kempston Hardwick Bedford 29 D7
Kempton Shrops 33 G9
Kemsing Kent 20 F2
Kemsley Kent 20 E6
Kenardington Kent 13 C8
Kenchester Hereford 25 D11
Kencot Oxon 17 A9
Kendal W&F 57 G7
Kendoon Dumfries 67 H9
Kendray S Yorks 45 B7
Kenfig Bridgend 14 C4
Kenfig Hill Bridgend 14 C4
Kenilworth Warks 27 A9
Kenknock Stirling 75 D7
Kenley London 19 F10
Kenley Shrops 34 E1
Kenmore Highld 85 C12
Kenmore Perth 75 C10
Kenn Devon 5 C10
Kenn N Som 15 E10
Kennacley W Isles 90 H6
Kennacraig Argyll 73 G7
Kennerleigh Devon 7 F7
Kennet Clack 69 A8
Kennethmont Aberds 83 A7
Kennett Cambs 30 B3
Kennford Devon 5 C10
Kenninghall Norf 38 G6
Kenninghall Heath Norf 38 G6
Kennington Kent 13 B9
Kennington Oxon 18 A2
Kennoway Fife 76 G6
Kenny Hill Suff 38 H2
Kennythorpe N Yorks 52 C3
Kenovay Argyll 78 G2
Kensaleyre Highld 85 C9
Kensington London 19 D9
Kensworth C Beds 29 G7
Kensworth Common C Beds 29 G7
Kent Street E Sus 13 E6
Kent Street Kent 20 F3
Kent Street W Sus 11 B11
Kentallen Highld 74 B3
Kentchurch Hereford 25 F11
Kentford Suff 30 B4
Kentisbeare Devon 7 F9
Kentisbury Devon 6 B5
Kentisbury Ford Devon 6 B5
Kentmere W&F 56 F6
Kenton Devon 5 C10
Kenton Suff 31 B8
Kenton T&W 63 G8
Kenton Bankfoot T&W 63 G8
Kentra Highld 79 E9
Kents Bank W&F 49 B3
Kent's Green Glos 26 F4
Kent's Oak Hants 10 B2
Kenwick Shrops 33 B10
Kenwyn Corn 3 E7
Keoldale Highld 92 C6
Keppanach Highld 74 A3
Keppoch Highld 85 F14
Keprigan Argyll 65 G7
Kepwick N Yorks 58 G5
Kerchesters Borders 70 G6
Keresley W Mid 35 G9
Kernborough Devon 5 G8
Kerne Bridge Hereford 26 G2
Kerris Corn 2 G3
Kerry Powys 33 G7
Kerrycroy Argyll 73 G10
Kerry's Gate Hereford 25 E10
Kerrysdale Highld 85 A13
Kersall Notts 45 F11
Kersey Suff 31 D7
Kershopefoot Cumb 61 E10
Kersoe Worcs 26 E6
Kerswell Devon 7 F9
Kerswell Green Worcs 26 D5
Kesgrave Suff 31 D9
Kessingland Suff 39 G11
Kessingland Beach Suff 39 G11
Kessington E Dunb 68 C4
Kestle Corn 3 E8
Kestle Mill Corn 3 D7
Keston London 19 E11
Keswick Cumb 56 D4
Keswick Norf 39 B9
Keswick Norf 39 E8
Ketley Telford 34 D2
Ketley Bank Telford 34 D2
Ketsby Lincs 47 E7
Kettering N Nhants 36 H4
Ketteringham Norf 39 E7
Kettins Perth 76 D5
Kettlebaston Suff 30 C6
Kettlebridge Fife 76 G6
Kettleburgh Suff 31 B9
Kettlehill Fife 76 G6
Kettleholm Dumfries 61 F7
Kettleness N Yorks 59 E9
Kettleshume Ches E 44 E3
Kettlesing Bottom N Yorks 51 D8
Kettlesing Head N Yorks 51 D8
Kettlestone Norf 38 B5
Kettlethorpe Lincs 46 E2
Kettletoft Orkney 95 E7
Kettlewell N Yorks 50 B5
Ketton Rutland 36 E5
Kew London 19 D8
Kew Bridge London 19 D8
Kewstoke N Som 15 E9
Kexbrough S Yorks 45 B7
Kexby Lincs 46 D2
Kexby York 52 D3
Key Green Ches E 44 F2
Keyham Leics 36 E2
Keyhaven Hants 10 E2
Keyingham E Yorks 53 G8
Keymer W Sus 12 E2
Keynsham Bath 16 E3
Keysoe Bedford 29 B7
Keysoe Row Bedford 29 B7
Keyston Cambs 36 H6
Keyworth Notts 36 B2
Kibblesworth T&W 63 H8
Kibworth Beauchamp Leics 36 F2
Kibworth Harcourt Leics 36 F2
Kidbrooke London 19 D11
Kiddemore Green Staffs 34 E4
Kidderminster Worcs 34 H4
Kiddington Oxon 27 F11
Kidlington Oxon 27 G11
Kidmore End Oxon 18 D3
Kidsgrove Staffs 44 G2
Kidstones N Yorks 50 A5
Kidwelly = Cydweli Carms 23 F9
Kiel Crofts Argyll 74 D2
Kielder Northumb 62 D2
Kierfiold Ho Orkney 95 G3
Kilbagie Fife 69 B8
Kilbarchan Renfs 68 D3
Kilbeg Highld 85 H11
Kilberry Argyll 72 G6
Kilbirnie N Ayrs 66 A6
Kilbride Argyll 74 E2
Kilbride Argyll 79 J11
Kilbride Highld 85 F10
Kilburn Angus 82 G5
Kilburn Derbys 45 H7
Kilburn London 19 C9
Kilburn N Yorks 51 B11
Kilby Leics 36 F2
Kilchamaig Argyll 73 G7
Kilchattan Argyll 72 D2
Kilchattan Bay Argyll 66 A4
Kilchenzie Argyll 65 F7
Kilcheran Argyll 79 H11
Kilchiaran Argyll 64 B3
Kilchoan Argyll 72 B6
Kilchoan Highld 78 E7
Kilchoman Argyll 64 B3
Kilchrenan Argyll 74 E3
Kilconquhar Fife 77 G7
Kilcot Glos 26 F3
Kilcoy Highld 87 F8
Kilcreggan Argyll 73 E11
Kildale N Yorks 59 F7
Kildalloig Argyll 65 G8
Kildary Highld 87 D10
Kildermorie Lodge Highld 87 D8
Kildonan N Ayrs 66 D3
Kildonan Lodge Highld 93 G12
Kildonnan Highld 78 C7
Kildrummy Aberds 82 B6
Kildwick N Yorks 50 E6
Kilfinan Argyll 73 F8
Kilfinnan Highld 80 D4
Kilgetty Pembs 22 F6
Kilgwrrwg Common Mon 15 B10
Kilham E Yorks 53 C6
Kilham Northumb 71 G7
Kilkenneth Argyll 78 G2
Kilkerran Argyll 65 G8
Kilkhampton Corn 6 E1
Killamarsh Derbys 45 D8
Killay Swansea 14 B2
Killbeg Argyll 79 G9
Killean Argyll 65 D7
Killearn Stirling 68 B4
Killen Highld 87 F9
Killerby Darl 58 E2
Killichonan Perth 75 B8
Killiechonate Highld 80 E4
Killiechronan Argyll 79 G8
Killiecrankie Perth 76 A2
Killiemor Argyll 78 H7
Killiemore House Argyll 78 J7
Killilan Highld 86 H2
Killimster Highld 94 E5
Killin Stirling 75 D8
Killin Lodge Highld 81 C7
Killinallan Argyll 64 A4
Killinghall N Yorks 51 D8
Killington W&F 57 H8
Killingworth T&W 63 F8
Killmahumaig Argyll 72 D6
Killochyett Borders 70 F3
Killocraw Argyll 65 E7
Killundine Highld 79 G8
Kilmacolm Invclyd 68 D2
Kilmaha Argyll 73 C8
Kilmahog Stirling 75 G9
Kilmalieu Highld 79 F11
Kilmaluag Highld 85 A9
Kilmany Fife 76 E6
Kilmarie Highld 85 G10
Kilmarnock E Ayrs 67 C7
Kilmaron Castle Fife 76 F6
Kilmartin Argyll 73 D7
Kilmaurs E Ayrs 67 B7
Kilmelford Argyll 73 B7
Kilmeny Argyll 64 B4
Kilmersdon Som 16 F3
Kilmeston Hants 10 B4
Kilmichael Argyll 65 F7
Kilmichael Glassary Argyll 73 D7
Kilmichael of Inverlussa Argyll 72 E6
Kilmington Devon 8 E1
Kilmington Wilts 16 H4
Kilmonivaig Highld 80 E3
Kilmorack Highld 86 G7
Kilmore Argyll 79 J11
Kilmore Highld 85 H11
Kilmory Argyll 72 F6
Kilmory Highld 79 D8
Kilmory Highld 85 H8
Kilmory N Ayrs 66 D2
Kilmuir Highld 84 D7
Kilmuir Highld 85 A8
Kilmuir Highld 87 D10
Kilmuir Highld 87 G9
Kilmun Argyll 73 B8
Kilmun Argyll 73 E10
Kiln Pit Hill Northumb 58 A1
Kilncadzow S Lanark 69 F7
Kilndown Kent 12 C6
Kilnhurst S Yorks 45 C8
Kilninian Argyll 78 G6
Kilninver Argyll 79 J11
Kilnsea E Yorks 53 H10
Kilnsey N Yorks 50 C5
Kilnwick E Yorks 52 E5
Kilnwick Percy E Yorks 52 D4
Kiloran Argyll 72 D2
Kilpatrick N Ayrs 66 D2
Kilpeck Hereford 25 E11
Kilphedir Highld 93 H12
Kilpin E Yorks 52 G3
Kilpin Pike E Yorks 52 G3
Kilrenny Fife 77 G8
Kilsby W Nhants 28 A2
Kilspindie Perth 76 E5
Kilsyth N Lanark 68 C6
Kiltarlity Highld 87 G8
Kilton Notts 45 E9
Kilton Som 7 B10
Kilton Thorpe Redcar 59 E7
Kilvaxter Highld 85 B8
Kilve Som 7 B10
Kilvington Notts 36 A3
Kilwinning N Ayrs 66 B6
Kimberworth S Yorks 45 C8
Kimberley Norf 39 E6
Kimberley Notts 35 A11
Kimble Wick Bucks 28 H5
Kimblesworth Durham 58 B3
Kimbolton Cambs 29 B7
Kimbolton Hereford 26 B2
Kimcote Leics 36 G1
Kimmeridge Dorset 9 G8
Kimmerston Northumb 71 G8
Kimpton Hants 17 G9
Kimpton Herts 29 G8
Kinbrace Highld 93 F11
Kinbuck Stirling 75 G10
Kincaple Fife 77 F7
Kincardine Fife 69 B8
Kincardine Highld 87 C9
Kincardine Bridge Falk 69 B8
Kincardine O'Neil Aberds 83 D7
Kinclaven Perth 76 D4
Kincorth Aberdeen 83 C11
Kincorth Ho. Moray 87 E13
Kincraig Highld 81 C10
Kincraigie Perth 76 C2
Kindallachan Perth 76 C2
Kineton Glos 27 F7
Kineton Warks 27 C10
Kinfauns Perth 76 E4
King Edward Aberds 89 C7
King Sterndale Derbys 44 E4
Kingairloch Highld 79 F11
Kingarth Argyll 73 H9
Kingcoed Mon 25 H11
Kingerby Lincs 46 C4
Kingham Oxon 27 F9
Kingholm Quay Dumfries 60 F5
Kinghorn Fife 69 B11
Kingie Highld 80 C3
Kinglassie Fife 76 H5
Kingoodie Perth 76 E6
King's Acre Hereford 25 D11
King's Bromley Staffs 35 D7
King's Caple Hereford 26 F2
King's Cliffe N Nhants 36 F6
King's Coughton Warks 27 C7
King's Heath W Mid 35 G6
Kings Hedges Cambs 29 B11
King's Hill Kent 20 F3
Kings Langley Herts 19 A7
King's Lynn Norf 38 C2
King's Meaburn W&F 57 D8
King's Mills Wrex 42 H6
Kings Muir Borders 69 G11
King's Newnham Warks 35 H10
King's Newton Derbys 35 C9
King's Norton Leics 36 E2
King's Norton W Mid 35 H6
King's Nympton Devon 6 E5
King's Pyon Hereford 25 C11
King's Ripton Cambs 37 H8
King's Somborne Hants 10 A2
King's Stag Dorset 8 C6
King's Stanley Glos 16 A5
King's Sutton W Nhants 27 E11
King's Thorn Hereford 26 E2
King's Walden Herts 29 F8
Kings Worthy Hants 10 A3
Kingsand Corn 4 F5
Kingsbarns Fife 77 F8
Kingsbridge Devon 5 G8
Kingsbridge Som 7 C8
Kingsburgh Highld 85 C8
Kingsbury London 19 C9
Kingsbury Warks 35 F8
Kingsbury Episcopi Som 8 B3
Kingsclere Hants 18 F2
Kingscote Glos 16 B5
Kingscott Devon 6 E4
Kingscross N Ayrs 66 D3
Kingsdon Som 8 B4
Kingsdown Kent 21 G10
Kingseat Fife 69 A10
Kingsey Bucks 28 H4
Kingsfold W Sus 19 H8
Kingsford E Ayrs 67 B7
Kingsford Worcs 34 G4
Kingsforth N Lincs 52 H6
Kingsgate Kent 21 D10
Kingsheanton Devon 6 C4
Kingshouse Hotel Highld 74 B5
Kingside Hill Cumb 56 A3
Kingskerswell Devon 5 E9
Kingskettle Fife 76 G6
Kingsland Anglesey 40 B4
Kingsland Hereford 25 B11
Kingsley Ches W 43 E8
Kingsley Hants 18 H4
Kingsley Staffs 44 H4
Kingsley Green W Sus 11 A7
Kingsley Holt Staffs 44 H4
Kingsley Park W Nhants 28 B4
Kingsmuir Angus 77 C7
Kingsmuir Fife 77 G8
Kingsnorth Kent 13 C9
Kingstanding W Mid 35 F6
Kingsteignton Devon 5 D9
Kingsthorpe W Nhants 28 B4
Kingston Cambs 29 C10
Kingston Devon 5 G7
Kingston Dorset 9 D6
Kingston Dorset 9 G8
Kingston E Loth 70 B4
Kingston Hants 9 D10
Kingston IoW 10 F3
Kingston Kent 21 F8
Kingston Moray 88 B3
Kingston Bagpuize Oxon 17 B11
Kingston Blount Oxon 18 B4
Kingston by Sea W Sus 11 D11
Kingston Deverill Wilts 16 H5
Kingston Gorse W Sus 11 D9
Kingston Lisle Oxon 17 C10
Kingston Maurward Dorset 8 E6
Kingston near Lewes E Sus 12 F2
Kingston on Soar Notts 35 C11
Kingston Russell Dorset 8 E4
Kingston St Mary Som 7 D11
Kingston Seymour N Som 15 E10
Kingston Upon Hull Hull 53 G6
Kingston upon Thames London 19 E8
Kingston Vale London 19 D9
Kingstone Hereford 25 E11
Kingstone Som 8 C2
Kingstone Staffs 35 C6
Kingstown Cumb 61 H9
Kingswear Devon 5 F9
Kingswells Aberdeen 83 C10
Kingswinford W Mid 34 G4
Kingswood Bucks 28 G3
Kingswood Glos 16 B4
Kingswood Hereford 25 C9
Kingswood Kent 20 F5
Kingswood Powys 33 E8
Kingswood S Glos 16 D3
Kingswood Sur 19 F9
Kingswood Warks 27 A8
Kingthorpe Lincs 46 E5
Kington Hereford 25 C9
Kington Worcs 26 C6
Kington Langley Wilts 16 D6
Kington Magna Dorset 9 B6
Kington St Michael Wilts 16 D6
Kingussie Highld 81 C9
Kingweston Som 8 A4
Kininvie Ho. Moray 88 D3
Kinkell Bridge Perth 76 F2
Kinknockie Aberds 89 D10
Kinlet Shrops 34 G3
Kinloch Fife 76 F5
Kinloch Highld 78 B6
Kinloch Highld 85 G11
Kinloch Highld 92 F6
Kinloch Perth 76 C5
Kinloch Perth 76 C4
Kinloch Hourn Highld 80 C1
Kinloch Laggan Highld 81 E7
Kinloch Lodge Highld 93 D8
Kinloch Rannoch Perth 75 B9
Kinlochan Highld 79 E11
Kinlochard Stirling 75 G7
Kinlochbeoraid Highld 79 C11
Kinlochbervie Highld 92 D5

Kinlocheil Highld 80 F1
Kinlochewe Highld 86 E3
Kinlochleven Highld 74 A4
Kinlochmoidart Highld 79 D10
Kinlochmorar Highld 79 B11
Kinlochmore Highld 74 A4
Kinlochspelve Argyll 79 J9
Kinloid Highld 79 C9
Kinloss Moray 87 E13
Kinmel Bay Conwy 42 D2
Kinmuck Aberds 83 B10
Kinmundy Aberds 83 B10
Kinnadie Aberds 89 D9
Kinnaird Perth 76 E5
Kinnaird Castle Angus 77 B9
Kinneff Aberds 83 F10
Kinnelhead Dumfries 60 C6
Kinnell Angus 77 B9
Kinnerley Shrops 33 C9
Kinnersley Hereford 25 D10
Kinnersley Worcs 26 D5
Kinnerton Powys 25 B9
Kinnesswood Perth 76 G4
Kinninvie Durham 58 D1
Kinnordy Angus 76 B6
Kinoulton Notts 36 B2
Kinross Perth 76 G4
Kinrossie Perth 76 D4
Kinsbourne Green Herts 29 G8
Kinsey Heath Ches E 34 A2
Kinsham Hereford 25 B10
Kinsham Worcs 26 E6
Kinsley W Yorks 45 A8
Kinson BCP 9 E9
Kintbury W Berks 17 E10
Kintessack Moray 87 E12
Kintillo Perth 76 F4
Kintocher Aberds 83 C7
Kinton Hereford 25 A11
Kinton Shrops 33 D9
Kintore Aberds 83 B9
Kintour Argyll 64 C5
Kintra Argyll 64 D4
Kintra Argyll 78 J6
Kintraw Argyll 73 C7
Kinuachdrachd Argyll 72 D6
Kinveachy Highld 81 B11
Kinver Staffs 34 G4
Kippax W Yorks 51 F10
Kippen Stirling 68 A5
Kippford or Scaur Dumfries 55 D11
Kirbister Orkney 95 F7
Kirbister Orkney 95 H4
Kirbuster Orkney 95 F3
Kirby Bedon Norf 39 E8
Kirby Bellars Leics 36 D3
Kirby Cane Norf 39 F9
Kirby Cross Essex 31 F9
Kirby Grindalythe N Yorks 52 C5
Kirby Hill N Yorks 51 C9
Kirby Hill N Yorks 58 F2
Kirby Knowle N Yorks 58 H5
Kirby-le-Soken Essex 31 F9
Kirby Misperton N Yorks 52 B3
Kirby Muxloe Leics 35 E11
Kirby Row Norf 39 F9
Kirby Sigston N Yorks 58 G5
Kirby Underdale E Yorks 52 D4
Kirby Wiske N Yorks 51 A9
Kirdford W Sus 11 B9
Kirk Highld 94 E4
Kirk Bramwith S Yorks 45 A10
Kirk Deighton N Yorks 51 D9
Kirk Ella E Yorks 52 G6
Kirk Hallam Derbys 35 A10
Kirk Hammerton N Yorks 51 D10
Kirk Ireton Derbys 44 G6
Kirk Langley Derbys 35 B8
Kirk Merrington Durham 58 C3
Kirk Michael IoM 48 C3
Kirk of Shotts N Lanark 69 D7
Kirk Sandall S Yorks 45 B10
Kirk Smeaton N Yorks 51 H11
Kirk Yetholm Borders 71 H7
Kirkabister Shetland 96 K6
Kirkandrews Dumfries 55 E9
Kirkandrews upon Eden Cumb 61 H9
Kirkbampton Cumb 61 H9
Kirkbean Dumfries 60 H5
Kirkbride Cumb 61 H8
Kirkbuddo Angus 77 C8
Kirkburn Borders 69 G11
Kirkburn E Yorks 52 D5
Kirkburton W Yorks 44 A5
Kirkby Lincs 46 C4
Kirkby Mers 43 C7
Kirkby N Yorks 59 F6
Kirkby Fleetham N Yorks 58 G3
Kirkby Green Lincs 46 G4
Kirkby In Ashfield Notts 45 G9
Kirkby-in-Furness W&F 49 A2
Kirkby la Thorpe Lincs 46 H5
Kirkby Lonsdale W&F 50 B2
Kirkby Malham N Yorks 50 C4
Kirkby Mallory Leics 35 E10
Kirkby Malzeard N Yorks 51 B8
Kirkby Mills N Yorks 59 H8
Kirkby on Bain Lincs 46 F6
Kirkby Overflow N Yorks 51 E9
Kirkby Stephen W&F 57 F9
Kirkby Thore W&F 57 D8
Kirkby Underwood Lincs 37 C6
Kirkby Wharfe N Yorks 51 E11
Kirkbymoorside N Yorks 59 H7
Kirkcaldy Fife 69 A11
Kirkcambeck Cumb 61 G11
Kirkcarswell Dumfries 55 E10
Kirkcolm Dumfries 54 C3
Kirkconnel Dumfries 60 B3
Kirkconnell Dumfries 60 G5
Kirkcowan Dumfries 54 C6
Kirkcudbright Dumfries 55 D9
Kirkdale Mers 42 C6
Kirkfieldbank S Lanark 69 F7
Kirkgunzeon Dumfries 55 C11
Kirkham Lancs 49 F4
Kirkham N Yorks 52 C3
Kirkhamgate W Yorks 51 G8
Kirkharle Northumb 62 E6
Kirkheaton Northumb 62 F6
Kirkheaton W Yorks 51 H7
Kirkhill Angus 77 A9
Kirkhill Highld 87 G8
Kirkhill Midloth 69 D11
Kirkhill Moray 88 E2
Kirkhope Borders 61 A9
Kirkhouse Borders 70 G2
Kirkiboll Highld 93 D8
Kirkibost Highld 85 G10
Kirkinch Angus 76 C6
Kirkinner Dumfries 55 D7
Kirkintilloch E Dunb 68 C5
Kirkland Cumb 56 E2
Kirkland Dumfries 60 B3
Kirkland Dumfries 60 D4
Kirkland W&F 57 C8
Kirkleatham Redcar 59 D6
Kirklevington Stockton 58 F5
Kirkley Suff 39 F11
Kirklington N Yorks 51 A9
Kirklington Notts 45 G10
Kirklinton Cumb 61 G10
Kirkliston Edin 69 C10
Kirkmaiden Dumfries 54 F4
Kirkmichael Perth 76 B3
Kirkmichael S Ayrs 66 F6
Kirkmuirhill S Lanark 68 F6
Kirknewton Northumb 71 G8
Kirknewton W Loth 69 D10
Kirkney Aberds 88 E5
Kirkoswald S Ayrs 66 F5
Kirkoswald W&F 57 B7
Kirkpatrick Durham Dumfries 60 F3
Kirkpatrick-Fleming Dumfries 61 F8
Kirksanton Cumb 49 A1
Kirkstall W Yorks 51 F8
Kirkstead Lincs 46 F5
Kirkstile Aberds 88 E5
Kirkstyle Highld 94 C5
Kirkton Aberds 83 A8
Kirkton Aberds 89 D6
Kirkton Angus 77 C7
Kirkton Angus 77 D7
Kirkton Borders 61 B11
Kirkton Dumfries 60 E5
Kirkton Fife 76 E6
Kirkton Highld 85 F13
Kirkton Highld 86 G2
Kirkton Highld 87 B10
Kirkton Highld 87 F10
Kirkton Perth 76 F2
Kirkton S Lanark 60 A5
Kirkton Stirling 75 G8
Kirkton Manor Borders 69 G11
Kirkton of Airlie Angus 76 B6
Kirkton of Auchterhouse Angus 76 D6
Kirkton of Auchterless Aberds 89 D7
Kirkton of Barevan Highld 87 G11
Kirkton of Bourtie Aberds 89 F8
Kirkton of Collace Perth 76 D4
Kirkton of Craig Angus 77 B10
Kirkton of Culsalmond Aberds 89 E6
Kirkton of Durris Aberds 83 D9
Kirkton of Glenbuchat Aberds 82 B5
Kirkton of Glenisla Angus 76 A5
Kirkton of Kingoldrum Angus 76 B6
Kirkton of Largo Fife 77 G7
Kirkton of Lethendy Perth 76 C4
Kirkton of Logie Buchan Aberds 89 F9
Kirkton of Maryculter Aberds 83 D10
Kirkton of Menmuir Angus 77 A8
Kirkton of Monikie Angus 77 D8
Kirkton of Oyne Aberds 83 A8
Kirkton of Rayne Aberds 83 A8
Kirkton of Skene Aberds 83 C10
Kirkton of Tough Aberds 83 B8
Kirktonhill Borders 70 E3
Kirktown Aberds 89 C10
Kirktown of Alvah Aberds 89 B6
Kirktown of Deskford Moray 88 B5
Kirktown of Fetteresso Aberds 83 E10
Kirktown of Mortlach Moray 88 E3
Kirktown of Slains Aberds 89 F10
Kirkurd Borders 69 F10
Kirkwall Orkney 95 G5
Kirkwhelpington Northumb 62 E5
Kirmington N Lincs 46 A5
Kirmond le Mire Lincs 46 C5
Kirn Argyll 73 F10
Kirriemuir Angus 76 B6
Kirstead Green Norf 39 F8
Kirtlebridge Dumfries 61 F8
Kirtleton Dumfries 61 E8
Kirtling Cambs 30 C3
Kirtling Green Cambs 30 C3
Kirtlington Oxon 27 G11
Kirtomy Highld 93 C10
Kirton Lincs 37 B9
Kirton Notts 45 F10
Kirton Suff 31 E9
Kirton End Lincs 37 A8
Kirton Holme Lincs 37 A8
Kirton in Lindsey N Lincs 46 C3
Kislingbury W Nhants 28 C3
Kites Hardwick Warks 27 B11
Kittisford Som 7 D9
Kittle Swansea 23 H10
Kitt's Green W Mid 35 G7
Kitt's Moss Gtr Man 44 D2
Kittybrewster Aberdeen 83 C11
Kitwood Hants 10 A5
Kivernoll Hereford 25 E11
Kiveton Park S Yorks 45 D8
Knaith Lincs 46 D2
Knaith Park Lincs 46 D2
Knap Corner Dorset 9 B7
Knaphill Sur 18 F6
Knapp Perth 76 D5
Knapp Som 8 B2
Knapthorpe Notts 45 G11
Knapton Norf 39 B9
Knapton York 52 D1
Knapton Green Hereford 25 C11
Knapwell Cambs 29 B10
Knaresborough N Yorks 51 D9
Knarsdale Northumb 57 A8
Knauchland Moray 88 C5
Knaven Aberds 89 D8
Knayton N Yorks 58 H5
Knebworth Herts 29 F9
Knedlington E Yorks 52 G3
Kneesall Notts 45 F11
Kneesworth Cambs 29 D10
Kneeton Notts 45 H11
Knelston Swansea 23 H9
Knenhall Staffs 34 B5
Knettishall Suff 38 G5
Knightacott Devon 6 C5
Knightcote Warks 27 C10
Knightley Dale Staffs 34 C4
Knighton Devon 4 G6
Knighton Leicester 36 E1
Knighton = Tref-y Clawdd Powys 25 A9
Knighton Staffs 34 A3
Knighton Staffs 34 C3
Knightswood Glasgow 68 D4
Knightwick Worcs 26 C4
Knill Hereford 25 B9
Knipton Leics 36 B4
Knitsley Durham 58 B2
Kniveton Derbys 44 G6
Knock Argyll 79 H8
Knock Moray 88 C5
Knock W&F 57 D8
Knockally Highld 94 H3
Knockan Highld 92 H5
Knockandhu Moray 82 A4
Knockando Moray 88 D1
Knockando Ho. Moray 88 D2
Knockbain Highld 87 F9
Knockbreck Highld 84 B7
Knockbrex Dumfries 55 E8
Knockdee Highld 94 D3
Knockdolian S Ayrs 66 H4
Knockenkelly N Ayrs 66 D3
Knockentiber E Ayrs 67 C6
Knockespock Ho. Aberds 83 A7
Knockfarrel Highld 87 F8
Knockglass Dumfries 54 D3
Knockholt Kent 19 F11
Knockholt Pound Kent 19 F11
Knockie Lodge Highld 80 B6
Knockin Shrops 33 C9
Knockinlaw E Ayrs 67 C7
Knocklearn Dumfries 60 F3
Knocknaha Argyll 65 G7
Knocknain Dumfries 54 C2
Knockrome Argyll 72 F4
Knocksharry IoM 48 D2
Knodishall Suff 31 B11
Knolls Green Ches E 44 E2
Knolton Wrex 33 B9
Knolton Bryn Wrex 33 B9
Knook Wilts 16 G6
Knossington Leics 36 E4
Knott End-on-Sea Lancs 49 E3
Knotting Bedford 29 B7
Knotting Green Bedford 29 B7
Knottingley W Yorks 51 G11
Knotts Lancs 50 D3
Knotts W&F 56 D6
Knotty Ash Mers 43 C7
Knotty Green Bucks 18 B6
Knowbury Shrops 26 A2
Knowe Dumfries 54 B6
Knowehead Dumfries 67 G9
Knowes of Elrick Aberds 88 C6
Knowesgate Northumb 62 E5
Knoweton N Lanark 68 E6
Knowhead Aberds 89 C9
Knowl Hill Windsor 18 D5
Knowle Bristol 16 D3
Knowle Devon 6 C3
Knowle Devon 7 F6
Knowle Devon 7 H9
Knowle Shrops 26 A2
Knowle W Mid 35 H7
Knowle Green Lancs 50 F2
Knowle Park W Yorks 51 E6
Knowlton Dorset 9 C9
Knowlton Kent 21 F9
Knowsley Mers 43 C7
Knowstone Devon 7 D7
Knox Bridge Kent 13 B6
Knucklas Powys 25 A9
Knuston N Nhants 28 B6
Knutsford Ches E 43 E10
Knutton Staffs 44 H2
Knypersley Staffs 44 G2
Kuggar Corn 2 H6
Kyle of Lochalsh Highld 85 F12
Kyleakin Highld 85 F12
Kylerhea Highld 85 F12
Kylesknoydart Highld 79 B11
Kylesku Highld 92 F5
Kylesmorar Highld 79 B11
Kylestrome Highld 92 F5
Kyllachy House Highld 81 A9
Kynaston Shrops 33 C9
Kynnersley Telford 34 D2
Kyre Magna Worcs 26 B3

L

La Fontenelle Guern 11
La Planque Guern 11
Labost W Isles 91 C7
Lacasaidh W Isles 91 E8
Lacasdal W Isles 91 D9
Laceby NE Lincs 46 B6
Lacey Green Bucks 18 B5
Lach Dennis Ches W 43 E10
Lackford Suff 30 A4
Lacock Wilts 16 E6
Ladbroke Warks 27 C11
Laddingford Kent 20 G3
Lade Bank Lincs 47 G7
Ladock Corn 3 D7
Lady Orkney 95 D7
Ladybank Fife 76 F6
Ladykirk Borders 71 F7
Ladysford Aberds 89 B9
Laga Highld 79 E9
Lagalochan Argyll 73 B7
Lagavulin Argyll 64 D5
Lagg Argyll 72 F4
Lagg N Ayrs 66 D2
Laggan Argyll 64 C3
Laggan Highld 79 D10
Laggan Highld 80 D4
Laggan Highld 81 D8
Laggan S Ayrs 54 A5
Lagganulva Argyll 78 G7
Laide Highld 91 H13
Laigh Fenwick E Ayrs 67 B7
Laigh Glengall S Ayrs 66 E6
Laighmuir E Ayrs 67 B7
Laindon Essex 20 C3
Lair Highld 86 G3
Lairg Highld 93 J8
Lairg Lodge Highld 93 J8
Lairg Muir Highld 93 J8
Lairgmore Highld 87 H8
Laisterdyke W Yorks 51 F7
Laithes W&F 56 C6
Lake IoW 10 F4
Lake Wilts 17 H8
Lakenham Norf 39 E8
Lakenheath Suff 38 G3
Lakesend Norf 37 F11
Lakeside W&F 56 H5
Laleham Sur 19 E7
Laleston Bridgend 14 D4
Lamarsh Essex 30 E5
Lamas Norf 39 C8
Lambden Borders 70 F6
Lamberhurst Kent 12 C5
Lamberhurst Quarter Kent 12 C5
Lamberton Borders 71 E8
Lambeth London 19 D10
Lambhill Glasgow 68 D4
Lambley Northumb 62 H2
Lambley Notts 45 H10
Lamborough Hill Oxon 17 A11
Lambourn W Berks 17 D10
Lambourne End Essex 19 B11
Lambs Green W Sus 19 H9
Lambston Pembs 22 E4
Lambton T&W 58 A3
Lamerton Devon 4 D5
Lamesley T&W 63 H8
Laminess Orkney 95 E7
Lamington Highld 87 D10
Lamington S Lanark 69 G8
Lamlash N Ayrs 66 C3
Lamloch Dumfries 67 G8
Lamonby W&F 56 C6
Lamorna Corn 2 G3
Lamorran Corn 3 E7
Lampardbrook Suff 31 B9
Lampeter = Llanbedr Pont Steffan Ceredig 23 B10
Lampeter Velfrey Pembs 22 E6
Lamphey Pembs 22 F5
Lamplugh Cumb 56 D2
Lamport W Nhants 28 A4
Lamyatt Som 16 H3
Lana Devon 6 G2
Lanark S Lanark 69 F7
Lancaster Lancs 49 C4
Lanchester Durham 58 B2
Lancing W Sus 11 D10
Landbeach Cambs 29 B11
Landcross Devon 6 D3
Landerberry Aberds 83 C9
Landford Wilts 10 C1
Landford Manor Wilts 10 B1
Landimore Swansea 23 G9
Landkey Devon 6 C4
Landore Swansea 14 B2
Landrake Corn 4 E4
Landscove Devon 5 E8
Landshipping Pembs 22 E5
Landshipping Quay Pembs 22 E5
Landulph Corn 4 E5
Landwade Suff 30 B3
Lane Corn 3 C7
Lane End Bucks 18 B5
Lane End Cumb 56 G3
Lane End Dorset 9 E7
Lane End Hants 10 B4
Lane End IoW 10 F5
Lane End Lancs 50 E4
Lane Ends Lancs 50 D3
Lane Ends Lancs 50 F3
Lane Ends N Yorks 50 E5
Lane Head Derbys 44 E5
Lane Head Durham 58 E2
Lane Head Gtr Man 43 C9
Lane Head W Yorks 44 B5
Lane Side Lancs 50 G3
Laneast Corn 4 C3
Laneham Notts 46 E2
Lanehead Durham 57 B10
Lanehead Northumb 62 E3
Lanercost Cumb 61 G11
Laneshaw Bridge Lancs 50 E5
Lanfach Caerph 15 B8
Langar Notts 36 B3
Langbank Renfs 68 C2
Langbar N Yorks 51 D6
Langburnshiels Borders 61 C11
Langcliffe N Yorks 50 C4
Langdale Highld 93 E9
Langdale End N Yorks 59 G10
Langdon Corn 4 C4
Langdon Beck Durham 57 C10
Langdon Hills Essex 20 C3
Langdyke Fife 76 G6
Langenhoe Essex 31 G7
Langford C Beds 29 D8
Langford Devon 7 F9
Langford Essex 30 H5
Langford Notts 46 G2
Langford Oxon 17 A9
Langford Budville Som 7 D10
Langham Essex 31 E7
Langham Norf 38 A6
Langham Rutland 36 D4
Langham Suff 30 B6
Langhaugh Borders 69 G11
Langho Lancs 50 F3
Langholm Dumfries 61 E9
Langleeford Northumb 62 A5
Langley Ches E 44 E3
Langley Hants 10 D3
Langley Herts 29 F9
Langley Kent 20 F5
Langley Northumb 62 G4
Langley Slough 19 D7
Langley W Sus 11 B7
Langley Warks 27 B8
Langley Burrell Wilts 16 D6
Langley Common Derbys 35 B8
Langley Heath Kent 20 F5
Langley Lower Green Essex 29 E11
Langley Marsh Som 7 D9
Langley Park Durham 58 B3
Langley Street Norf 39 E9
Langley Upper Green Essex 29 E11
Langney E Sus 12 F5
Langold Notts 45 D9
Langore Corn 4 C4
Langport Som 8 B3
Langrick Lincs 46 H6
Langridge Bath 16 E4
Langridge Ford Devon 6 D4
Langrigg Cumb 56 B3
Langrish Hants 10 B6
Langsett S Yorks 44 B6
Langshaw Borders 70 G4
Langside Perth 75 F10
Langskaill Orkney 95 D5
Langstone Hants 10 D6
Langstone Newport 15 B9
Langthorne N Yorks 58 G3
Langthorpe N Yorks 51 C9
Langthwaite N Yorks 58 F1
Langtoft E Yorks 52 C6
Langtoft Lincs 37 D7
Langton Durham 58 E2
Langton Lincs 46 F6
Langton Lincs 47 E7
Langton N Yorks 52 C3
Langton by Wragby Lincs 46 E5
Langton Green Kent 12 C4
Langton Green Suff 31 A8
Langton Herring Dorset 8 F5
Langton Matravers Dorset 9 G9
Langtree Devon 6 E3
Langwathby W&F 57 C7
Langwell Ho. Highld 94 H3
Langwell Lodge Highld 92 J4
Langwith Derbys 45 F9
Langwith Junction Derbys 45 F9
Langworth Lincs 46 E4
Lanivet Corn 3 C9
Lanlivery Corn 4 F1
Lanner Corn 2 F6
Lanreath Corn 4 F2
Lansallos Corn 4 F2
Lansdown Glos 26 F6
Lanteglos Highway Corn 4 F2
Lanton Borders 62 A2
Lanton Northumb 71 G8
Lapford Devon 7 F6
Laphroaig Argyll 64 D4
Lapley Staffs 34 D4
Lapworth Warks 27 A8
Larachbeg Highld 79 G9
Larbert Falk 69 B7
Larden Green Ches E 43 G8
Largie Aberds 88 E6
Largiemore Argyll 73 E8
Largoward Fife 77 G7
Largs N Ayrs 73 H11
Largybeg N Ayrs 66 D3
Largymore N Ayrs 66 D3
Larkfield Invclyd 73 F11
Larkhall S Lanark 68 E6
Larkhill Wilts 17 G8
Larling Norf 38 G5
Larriston Borders 61 D11
Lartington Durham 58 E1
Lary Aberds 82 C5
Lasham Hants 18 G3
Lashenden Kent 13 B7
Lassington Glos 26 F4
Lassodie Fife 69 A10
Lastingham N Yorks 59 G8
Latcham Som 15 G10
Latchford Herts 29 F10
Latchford Warr 43 D9
Latchingdon Essex 20 A5
Latchley Corn 4 D5
Lately Common Warr 43 C9
Lathbury M Keynes 28 D5
Latheron Highld 94 G3
Latheronwheel Highld 94 G3
Latheronwheel Ho. Highld 94 G3
Lathones Fife 77 G7
Latimer Bucks 19 B7
Latteridge S Glos 16 C3
Lattiford Som 8 B5
Latton Wilts 17 B7
Latton Bush Essex 29 H11
Lauchintilly Aberds 83 B9
Lauder Borders 70 F4
Laugharne Carms 23 E8
Laughterton Lincs 46 E2
Laughton E Sus 12 E4
Laughton Leics 36 G2
Laughton Lincs 37 B6
Laughton Lincs 46 C2
Laughton Common S Yorks 45 D9
Laughton en le Morthen S Yorks 45 D9
Launcells Corn 6 F1
Launceston Corn 4 C4
Launton Oxon 28 F3
Laurencekirk Aberds 83 F9
Laurieston Dumfries 55 C9
Laurieston Falk 69 C8
Lavendon M Keynes 28 C6
Lavenham Suff 30 D6
Laverhay Dumfries 61 D7
Laversdale Cumb 61 G10
Laverstock Wilts 9 A10
Laverstoke Hants 17 G11
Laverton Glos 27 E7
Laverton N Yorks 51 B8
Laverton Som 16 F4
Lavister Wrex 42 G6
Law S Lanark 69 E7
Lawers Perth 75 D9
Lawers Perth 75 E10
Lawford Essex 31 E7
Lawhitton Corn 4 C4
Lawkland N Yorks 50 C3
Lawley Telford 34 E2
Lawnhead Staffs 34 C4
Lawrenny Pembs 22 F5
Lawshall Suff 30 C5
Lawton Hereford 25 C11
Laxey IoM 48 D4
Laxfield Suff 31 A9
Laxfirth Shetland 96 H6
Laxfirth Shetland 96 J6
Laxford Bridge Highld 92 E5
Laxo Shetland 96 G6
Laxobigging Shetland 96 F6
Laxton E Yorks 52 G3
Laxton N Nhants 36 F5
Laxton Notts 45 F11
Laycock W Yorks 50 E6
Layer Breton Essex 30 G6
Layer de la Haye Essex 30 G6
Layer Marney Essex 30 G6
Layham Suff 31 D7
Laylands Green W Berks 17 E10
Laytham E Yorks 52 F3
Layton Blackpool 49 F3
Lazenby Redcar 59 D6
Lazonby W&F 57 C7
Le Planel Guern 11
Le Skerne Haughton Darl 58 E4
Le Villocq Guern 11
Lea Derbys 45 G7
Lea Hereford 26 F3
Lea Lincs 46 D2
Lea Shrops 33 E10
Lea Shrops 33 G9
Lea Wilts 16 C6
Lea Marston Warks 35 F8
Lea Town Lancs 49 F4
Leabrooks Derbys 45 G8
Leac a Li W Isles 90 H6
Leachkin Highld 87 G9
Leadburn Midloth 69 E11
Leaden Roding Essex 30 G2
Leadenham Lincs 46 G3
Leadgate Durham 58 A2
Leadgate T&W 63 H7
Leadgate W&F 57 B9
Leadhills S Lanark 60 B4
Leafield Oxon 27 G10
Leagrave Luton 29 F7
Leake N Yorks 58 G5
Leake Commonside Lincs 47 G7
Lealholm N Yorks 59 F8
Lealt Argyll 72 D5
Lealt Highld 85 B10
Leamington Hastings Warks 27 B11
Leamonsley Staffs 35 E7
Leamside Durham 58 B4
Leanaig Highld 87 F8
Leargybreck Argyll 72 F4
Leasgill W&F 49 A4
Leasingham Lincs 46 H4
Leasingthorne Durham 58 D3
Leasowe Mers 42 C5
Leatherhead Sur 19 F8
Leatherhead Common Sur 19 F8
Leathley N Yorks 51 E8
Leaton Shrops 33 D10
Leaveland Kent 21 F7
Leavening N Yorks 52 C3
Leaves Green London 19 E11
Leazes Durham 63 H7
Lebberston N Yorks 53 A6
Lechlade-on-Thames Glos 17 B9
Leck Lancs 50 B2
Leckford Hants 17 H10
Leckfurin Highld 93 D10
Leckgruinart Argyll 64 B3
Leckhampstead Bucks 28 E4
Leckhampstead W Berks 17 D11
Leckhampstead Thicket W Berks 17 D11
Leckhampton Glos 26 G6
Leckie Highld 86 E3
Leckmelm Highld 86 B4
Leckwith V Glam 15 D7
Leconfield E Yorks 52 E6
Ledaig Argyll 74 D2
Ledburn Bucks 28 F6
Ledbury Hereford 26 E4
Ledcharrie Stirling 75 E8
Ledgemoor Hereford 25 C11
Ledicot Hereford 25 B11
Ledmore Highld 92 H5
Lednagullin Highld 93 C10
Ledsham Ches W 42 E6
Ledsham W Yorks 51 G10
Ledston W Yorks 51 G10
Ledston Luck W Yorks 51 F10
Ledwell Oxon 27 F11
Lee Argyll 78 J7
Lee Devon 6 B3
Lee Hants 10 C2
Lee Lancs 50 D1
Lee Shrops 33 B10
Lee Brockhurst Shrops 33 C11
Lee Clump Bucks 18 A6
Lee Mill Devon 5 F7
Lee Moor Devon 5 E6
Lee-on-the-Solent Hants 10 D4
Leeans Shetland 96 J5
Leebotten Shetland 96 L6
Leebotwood Shrops 33 F10
Leece W&F 49 C2
Leechpool Pembs 22 E4
Leeds Kent 20 F5
Leeds W Yorks 51 F8
Leedstown Corn 2 F5
Leek Staffs 44 G3
Leek Wootton Warks 27 B9
Leekbrook Staffs 44 G3
Leeming N Yorks 58 H3
Leeming Bar N Yorks 58 G3
Lees Derbys 35 B8
Lees Gtr Man 44 B3
Lees W Yorks 50 F6
Leeswood Flint 42 F5
Legbourne Lincs 47 D7
Legerwood Borders 70 F4
Legsby Lincs 46 D5
Leicester Leicester 36 E1
Leicester Forest East Leics 35 E11
Leigh Dorset 8 D5
Leigh Glos 26 F5
Leigh Gtr Man 43 B9
Leigh Kent 20 G2
Leigh Shrops 33 E9
Leigh Sur 19 G9
Leigh Wilts 17 B7
Leigh Worcs 26 C4
Leigh Beck Essex 20 C5
Leigh Common Som 8 B6
Leigh Delamere Wilts 16 D5
Leigh Green Kent 13 C8
Leigh on Sea Southend 20 C5
Leigh Park Hants 10 D6
Leigh Sinton Worcs 26 C4
Leigh upon Mendip Som 16 G3
Leigh Woods N Som 16 D2
Leighswood W Mid 35 E6
Leighterton Glos 16 B5
Leighton N Yorks 51 B7
Leighton Powys 33 E8
Leighton Shrops 34 E2
Leighton Som 16 G4
Leighton Bromswold Cambs 37 H7
Leighton Buzzard C Beds 28 F6
Leinthall Earls Hereford 25 B11
Leinthall Starkes Hereford 25 B11
Leintwardine Hereford 25 A11
Leire Leics 35 F11
Leirinmore Highld 92 C7
Leiston Suff 31 B11
Leitfie Perth 76 C5
Leith Edin 69 C11
Leitholm Borders 70 F6
Lelant Corn 2 F4
Lelley E Yorks 53 F8
Lem Hill Worcs 26 A4
Lemmington Hall Northumb 63 B7
Lempitlaw Borders 70 G6
Lenchwick Worcs 27 D7
Lendalfoot S Ayrs 66 H4
Lendrick Lodge Stirling 75 G8
Lenham Kent 20 F5
Lenham Heath Kent 20 G6
Lennel Borders 71 F7
Lennoxtown E Dunb 68 C5
Lenton Lincs 36 B6
Lenton Nottingham 36 B1
Lentran Highld 87 G8
Lenwade Norf 39 D6
Leny Ho. Stirling 75 G9
Lenzie E Dunb 68 C5
Leoch Angus 76 D6
Leochel-Cushnie Aberds 83 B7
Leominster Hereford 25 C11
Leonard Stanley Glos 16 A5
Leorin Argyll 64 D4
Lepe Hants 10 E3
Lephin Highld 84 D6
Lephinchapel Argyll 73 D8
Lephinmore Argyll 73 D8
Leppington N Yorks 52 C3
Lepton W Yorks 51 H8
Lerryn Corn 4 F2
Lerwick Shetland 96 J6
Lesbury Northumb 63 B8
Leslie Aberds 83 A7
Leslie Fife 76 G5
Lesmahagow S Lanark 69 G7
Lesnewth Corn 4 B2
Lessendrum Aberds 88 D5
Lessingham Norf 39 C9
Lessonhall Cumb 56 A4
Leswalt Dumfries 54 C3
Letchmore Heath Herts 19 B8
Letchworth Herts 29 E9
Letcombe Bassett Oxon 17 C10
Letcombe Regis Oxon 17 C10
Letham Angus 77 C8
Letham Falk 69 B7
Letham Fife 76 F6
Letham Perth 76 E3
Letham Grange Angus 77 C9
Lethenty Aberds 89 D8
Letheringham Suff 31 C9
Letheringsett Norf 39 B6
Lettaford Devon 5 C8
Lettan Orkney 95 D8
Letterewe Highld 86 D2
Letterfearn Highld 85 F13
Letterfinlay Highld 80 D4
Lettermorar Highld 79 C10
Lettermore Argyll 78 G7
Letters Highld 86 C4
Letterston Pembs 22 D4
Lettoch Highld 82 B2
Lettoch Highld 87 H13
Letton Hereford 25 A10
Letton Hereford 25 D10
Letton Green Norf 38 E5
Letty Green Herts 29 G9
Letwell S Yorks 45 D9
Leuchars Fife 77 E7
Leuchars Ho. Moray 88 B2
Leumrabhagh W Isles 91 F8
Levan Invclyd 73 F11
Levaneap Shetland 96 G6
Levedale Staffs 34 D4
Leven E Yorks 53 E7
Leven Fife 76 G6
Levencorroch N Ayrs 66 D3
Levens W&F 57 H6
Levens Green Herts 29 F10
Levenshulme Gtr Man 44 C2
Levenwick Shetland 96 L6
Leverburgh = An t-Ob W Isles 90 J5
Leverington Cambs 37 D10
Leverton Lincs 47 H8
Leverton Highgate Lincs 47 H8
Leverton Lucasgate Lincs 47 H8
Leverton Outgate Lincs 47 H8
Levington Suff 31 E9
Levisham N Yorks 59 G9
Levishie Highld 80 B6
Lew Oxon 27 H10
Lewannick Corn 4 C3
Lewdown Devon 4 C5
Lewes E Sus 12 E3
Leweston Pembs 22 D4
Lewisham London 19 D10
Lewiston Highld 81 A7
Lewistown Bridgend 14 C5
Lewknor Oxon 18 B4
Leworthy Devon 6 C5
Leworthy Devon 6 F2
Lewtrenchard Devon 4 C5
Lexden Essex 30 F6
Ley Aberds 83 B7
Ley Corn 4 E2
Leybourne Kent 20 F3
Leyburn N Yorks 58 G2
Leyfields Staffs 35 E8
Leyhill Bucks 18 A6
Leyland Lancs 49 G5
Leylodge Aberds 83 B9
Leymoor W Yorks 51 H7
Leys Aberds 89 C10
Leys Perth 76 D5
Leys Castle Highld 87 G9
Leys of Cossans Angus 76 C6
Leysdown-on-Sea Kent 21 D7
Leysmill Angus 77 C9
Leysters Pole Hereford 26 B2
Leyton London 19 C10
Leytonstone London 19 C10
Lezant Corn 4 D4
Leziate Norf 38 D2
Lhanbryde Moray 88 B2
Liatrie Highld 86 H5
Libanus Powys 24 F6
Libberton S Lanark 69 F8
Liberton Edin 69 D11
Liceasto W Isles 90 H6
Lichfield Staffs 35 E7
Lickey Worcs 34 H5
Lickey End Worcs 26 A6
Lickfold W Sus 11 B8
Liddel Orkney 95 K5
Liddesdale Highld 79 F10
Liddington Swindon 17 C9
Lidgate Suff 30 C4
Lidget S Yorks 45 B10
Lidget Green W Yorks 51 F7
Lidgett Notts 45 F10
Lidlington C Beds 28 E6
Lidstone Oxon 27 F10
Lieurary Highld 94 D2
Liff Angus 76 D6
Lifton Devon 4 C4
Liftondown Devon 4 C4
Lighthorne Warks 27 C10
Lightwater Sur 18 E6
Lightwood Stoke 34 A5
Lightwood Green Ches E 34 A2
Lightwood Green Wrex 33 A9
Lilbourne W Nhants 36 H1
Lilburn Tower Northumb 62 A6
Lilleshall Telford 34 D3
Lilley Herts 29 F8
Lilley W Berks 17 D11
Lilliesleaf Borders 61 A11
Lillingstone Dayrell Bucks 28 E4
Lillingstone Lovell Bucks 28 D4
Lillington Dorset 8 C5
Lillington Warks 27 B10
Lilliput BCP 9 E9
Lilstock Som 7 B10
Lilyhurst Shrops 34 D3
Limbury Luton 29 F7
Limebrook Hereford 25 B10
Limefield Gtr Man 44 A2
Limekilnburn S Lanark 68 E6
Limekilns Fife 69 B9
Limerigg Falk 69 C7
Limerstone IoW 10 F3
Limington Som 8 B4
Limpenhoe Norf 39 E9
Limpley Stoke Wilts 16 E4
Limpsfield Sur 19 F11
Limpsfield Chart Sur 19 F11
Linby Notts 45 G9
Linchmere W Sus 11 A7
Lincluden Dumfries 60 F5
Lincoln Lincs 46 E3
Lincomb Worcs 26 B5
Lincombe Devon 5 F8
Lindal in Furness W&F 49 B2
Lindale W&F 49 A4
Lindean Borders 70 G3
Lindfield W Sus 12 D2
Lindford Hants 18 H5
Lindifferon Fife 76 F6
Lindley W Yorks 51 H7
Lindley Green N Yorks 51 E8
Lindores Fife 76 F5
Lindridge Worcs 26 B3
Lindsell Essex 30 F3
Lindsey Suff 30 D6
Linford Hants 9 D10
Linford Thurrock 20 D3
Lingague IoM 48 E2
Lingards Wood W Yorks 44 A4
Lingbob W Yorks 51 F6
Lingdale Redcar 59 E7
Lingen Hereford 25 B10
Lingfield Sur 12 B2
Lingreabhagh W Isles 90 J5
Lingwood Norf 39 E9
Linicro Highld 85 B8
Linkenholt Hants 17 F10
Linkhill Kent 13 D7
Linkinhorne Corn 4 D4
Linklater Orkney 95 K5
Linksness Orkney 95 H3
Linktown Fife 69 A11
Linley Shrops 33 F9
Linley Green Hereford 26 C3
Linlithgow W Loth 69 C9
Linlithgow Bridge W Loth 69 C8
Linshiels Northumb 62 C4
Linsiadar W Isles 90 D7
Linsidemore Highld 87 B8
Linslade C Beds 28 F6
Linstead Parva Suff 39 H9
Linstock Cumb 61 H10
Linthwaite W Yorks 44 A5
Lintlaw Borders 71 E7
Lintmill Moray 88 B5
Linton Borders 70 H6
Linton Cambs 30 D2
Linton Derbys 35 D8
Linton Hereford 26 F3
Linton Kent 20 G4
Linton N Yorks 50 C5
Linton Northumb 63 D8
Linton W Yorks 51 E9
Linton-on-Ouse N Yorks 51 C10
Linwood Hants 9 D10
Linwood Lincs 46 D5
Linwood Renfs 68 D3
Lionacleit W Isles 84 D2
Lional W Isles 91 A10
Liphook Hants 11 A7
Liscard Mers 42 C6
Liscombe Som 7 C7
Liskeard Corn 4 E3
L'Islet Guern 11
Liss Hants 11 B6
Liss Forest Hants 11 B6
Lissett E Yorks 53 D7
Lissington Lincs 46 D5
Lisvane Cardiff 15 C7
Liswerry Newport 15 C9
Litcham Norf 38 D4
Litchborough W Nhants 28 C3
Litchfield Hants 17 F11
Litherland Mers 42 C6
Litlington Cambs 29 D10
Litlington E Sus 12 F4
Little Abington Cambs 30 D2
Little Addington N Nhants 28 A6
Little Alne Warks 27 B8
Little Altcar Mers 42 B6
Little Asby W&F 57 F8
Little Assynt Highld 92 G4
Little Aston Staffs 35 E6
Little Atherfield IoW 10 F3
Little Ayre Orkney 95 J4
Little-ayre Shetland 96 G5
Little Ayton N Yorks 59 E6
Little Baddow Essex 30 H4
Little Badminton S Glos 16 C5
Little Ballinluig Perth 76 B2
Little Bampton Cumb 61 H8
Little Bardfield Essex 30 E3
Little Barford Bedford 29 C8
Little Barningham Norf 39 B7
Little Barrington Glos 27 G9
Little Barrow Ches W 43 E7
Little Barugh N Yorks 52 B3
Little Bavington Northumb 62 F5
Little Bealings Suff 31 D9
Little Bedwyn Wilts 17 E9
Little Bentley Essex 31 F8
Little Berkhamsted Herts 29 H9
Little Billing W Nhants 28 B5
Little Birch Hereford 26 E2
Little Blakenham Suff 31 D8
Little Blencow W&F 56 C6
Little Bollington Ches E 43 D10
Little Bookham Sur 19 F8
Little Bowden Leics 36 G3
Little Bradley Suff 30 C3
Little Brampton Shrops 33 G9
Little Brechin Angus 77 A8
Little Brickhill M Keynes 28 E6
Little Brington W Nhants 28 B3
Little Bromley Essex 31 F7
Little Broughton Cumb 56 C2
Little Budworth Ches W 43 F8
Little Burstead Essex 20 B3
Little Bytham Lincs 36 D6
Little Carlton Lincs 47 D7
Little Carlton Notts 45 G11
Little Casterton Rutland 36 E6
Little Cawthorpe Lincs 47 D7
Little Chalfont Bucks 18 B6
Little Chart Kent 20 G6
Little Chesterford Essex 30 D2
Little Cheverell Wilts 16 F6
Little Chishill Cambs 29 E11
Little Clacton Essex 31 G8
Little Clifton Cumb 56 D2
Little Colp Aberds 89 D7
Little Comberton Worcs 26 D6
Little Common E Sus 12 F6
Little Compton Warks 27 E9
Little Cornard Suff 30 E5
Little Cowarne Hereford 26 C3
Little Coxwell Oxon 17 B9
Little Crakehall N Yorks 58 G3
Little Cressingham Norf 38 F4
Little Crosby Mers 42 B6
Little Dalby Leics 36 D3
Little Dawley Telford 34 E2
Little Dens Aberds 89 D10
Little Dewchurch Hereford 26 E2
Little Downham Cambs 37 G11
Little Driffield E Yorks 52 D6
Little Dunham Norf 38 D4
Little Dunkeld Perth 76 C3
Little Dunmow Essex 30 F3
Little Easton Essex 30 F3
Little Eaton Derbys 35 A9
Little Eccleston Lancs 49 E4
Little Ellingham Norf 38 F6
Little End Essex 20 A2
Little Eversden Cambs 29 C10
Little Faringdon Oxon 17 A9
Little Fencote N Yorks 58 G3
Little Fenton N Yorks 51 F11
Little Finborough Suff 31 C7
Little Fransham Norf 38 D5
Little Gaddesden Herts 28 G6
Little Gidding Cambs 37 G7
Little Glemham Suff 31 C10
Little Glenshee Perth 76 D2
Little Gransden Cambs 29 C9
Little Green Som 16 G4
Little Grimsby Lincs 47 C7
Little Gruinard Highld 86 C2
Little Habton N Yorks 52 B3
Little Hadham Herts 29 F11
Little Hale Lincs 37 A7
Little Hallingbury Essex 29 G11
Little Hampden Bucks 18 A5
Little Harrowden N Nhants 28 A5
Little Haseley Oxon 18 A3
Little Hatfield E Yorks 53 E7
Little Hautbois Norf 39 C8
Little Haven Pembs 22 E3
Little Hay Staffs 35 E7
Little Hayfield Derbys 44 D4
Little Haywood Staffs 34 C6
Little Heath W Mid 35 G9
Little Hereford Hereford 26 B2
Little Horkesley Essex 30 E6
Little Horsted E Sus 12 E3
Little Horton W Yorks 51 F7
Little Horwood Bucks 28 E4
Little Houghton S Yorks 45 B8
Little Houghton W Nhants 28 C5
Little Hucklow Derbys 44 E5
Little Hulton Gtr Man 43 B10
Little Humber E Yorks 53 G7
Little Hungerford W Berks 18 D2
Little Irchester N Nhants 28 B6
Little Kimble Bucks 28 H5
Little Kineton Warks 27 C10
Little Kingshill Bucks 18 B5
Little Langdale Cumb 56 F5
Little Langdale W&F 17 H7
Little Laver Essex 30 H2
Little Leigh Ches W 43 E9
Little Leighs Essex 30 G4
Little Lever Gtr Man 43 B10
Little London Bucks 28 G3
Little London E Sus 12 E4
Little London Hants 17 G10
Little London Hants 18 F3
Little London Lincs 37 C10
Little London Lincs 37 C8
Little London Norf 39 C7
Little London Powys 32 G6
Little Longstone Derbys 44 E5
Little Lynturk Aberds 83 B7
Little Malvern Worcs 26 D4
Little Maplestead Essex 30 E5
Little Marcle Hereford 26 E3
Little Marlow Bucks 18 C5
Little Marsden Lancs 50 F4
Little Massingham Norf 38 C3
Little Melton Norf 39 E7
Little Mill Mon 15 A9
Little Milton Oxon 18 A3
Little Missenden Bucks 18 B6
Little Musgrave W&F 57 E9
Little Ness Shrops 33 D10
Little Neston Ches W 42 E5
Little Newcastle Pembs 22 D4
Little Newsham Durham 58 E2
Little Oakley Essex 31 F9
Little Oakley N Nhants 36 G4
Little Orton Cumb 61 H9
Little Ouseburn N Yorks 51 C10
Little Paxton Cambs 29 B8
Little Petherick Corn 3 B8
Little Pitlurg Moray 88 D4
Little Plumpton Lancs 49 F3
Little Plumstead Norf 39 D9
Little Ponton Lincs 36 B5
Little Raveley Cambs 37 H8
Little Reedness E Yorks 52 G4
Little Ribston N Yorks 51 D9
Little Rissington Glos 27 G8
Little Ryburgh Norf 38 C5
Little Ryle Northumb 62 B6
Little Salkeld W&F 57 C7
Little Sampford Essex 30 E3
Little Sandhurst Brack 18 E5
Little Saxham Suff 30 B4
Little Scatwell Highld 86 F6
Little Sessay N Yorks 51 B10
Little Shelford Cambs 29 C11
Little Singleton Lancs 49 F3
Little Skillymarno Aberds 89 C9
Little Smeaton N Yorks 51 H11
Little Snoring Norf 38 B5
Little Sodbury S Glos 16 C4
Little Somborne Hants 10 A2
Little Somerford Wilts 16 C6
Little Stainforth N Yorks 50 C4
Little Stainton Darl 58 D4
Little Stanney Ches W 43 E7
Little Staughton Bedford 29 B8
Little Steeping Lincs 47 F8
Little Stoke Staffs 34 B5
Little Stonham Suff 31 B8
Little Stretton Leics 36 E2
Little Stretton Shrops 33 F10
Little Strickland W&F 57 E7
Little Stukeley Cambs 37 H8
Little Sutton Ches W 42 E6
Little Tew Oxon 27 F10
Little Thetford Cambs 37 H11
Little Thirkleby N Yorks 51 B10
Little Thurlow Suff 30 C3
Little Thurrock Thurrock 20 D3
Little Torboll Highld 87 B10
Little Torrington Devon 6 E3
Little Totham Essex 30 G5
Little Toux Aberds 88 C5
Little Town Cumb 56 E4
Little Town Lancs 50 F2
Little Urswick W&F 49 B2
Little Wakering Essex 20 C6
Little Walden Essex 30 D2
Little Waldingfield Suff 30 D6
Little Walsingham Norf 38 B5
Little Waltham Essex 30 G4
Little Warley Essex 20 B3
Little Weighton E Yorks 52 F5
Little Weldon N Nhants 36 G5
Little Welnetham Suff 30 B5
Little Wenlock Telford 34 E2
Little Whittingham Green Suff 39 H8
Little Wilbraham Cambs 30 C2
Little Wishford Wilts 17 H7
Little Witley Worcs 26 B4
Little Wittenham Oxon 18 B2
Little Wolford Warks 27 E9
Little Wratting Suff 30 D3
Little Wymington Bedford 28 B6
Little Wymondley Herts 29 F9
Little Wyrley Staffs 34 E6
Little Yeldham Essex 30 E4
Littlebeck N Yorks 59 F9
Littleborough Gtr Man 50 H5
Littleborough Notts 46 D2
Littlebourne Kent 21 F9
Littlebredy Dorset 8 F4
Littlebury Essex 30 E2
Littlebury Green Essex 29 E11
Littledean Glos 26 G3
Littleferry Highld 87 B11
Littleham Devon 5 C11
Littleham Devon 6 D3
Littlehampton W Sus 11 D9
Littlehempston Devon 5 E9
Littlehoughton Northumb 63 B8
Littlemill Aberds 82 D5
Littlemill E Ayrs 67 E7
Littlemill Highld 87 F12
Littlemill Northumb 63 B8
Littlemoor Dorset 8 F5
Littlemore Oxon 18 A2
Littleover Derby 35 B9
Littleport Cambs 38 G1
Littlestone on Sea Kent 13 D9
Littlethorpe Leics 35 F11
Littlethorpe N Yorks 51 C9
Littleton Ches W 43 F7
Littleton Hants 10 A3
Littleton Perth 76 D5
Littleton Som 8 A3
Littleton Sur 18 G6
Littleton Sur 19 E7
Littleton Drew Wilts 16 C5
Littleton-on-Severn S Glos 16 C2
Littleton Pannell Wilts 17 F7
Littletown Durham 58 B4
Littlewick Green Windsor 18 D5
Littleworth Bedford 29 D7
Littleworth Glos 16 A5
Littleworth Oxon 17 B10
Littleworth Staffs 34 D6
Littleworth Worcs 26 C5
Litton Derbys 44 E5
Litton N Yorks 50 B5
Litton Som 16 F2
Litton Cheney Dorset 8 E4
Liurbost W Isles 91 E8
Liverpool Mers 42 C6
Liverpool Airport Mers 43 D7
Liversedge W Yorks 51 G8
Liverton Devon 5 D9
Liverton Redcar 59 E8
Livingston W Loth 69 D9
Livingston Village W Loth 69 D9
Lixwm Flint 42 E4
Lizard Corn 2 H6
Llaingoch Anglesey 40 B4
Llaithddu Powys 33 G6
Llan Powys 32 E4
Llan Ffestiniog Gwyn 41 F9
Llan-y-pwll Wrex 42 G6
Llanaber Gwyn 32 D2
Llanaelhaearn Gwyn 40 F5
Llanafan Ceredig 24 A3
Llanafan-fawr Powys 24 C6
Llanallgo Anglesey 40 B6
Llanandras = Presteigne Powys 25 B10
Llanarmon Gwyn 40 G6
Llanarmon Dyffryn Ceiriog Wrex 33 B7
Llanarmon-yn-Ial Denb 42 G4
Llanarth Ceredig 23 A9
Llanarth Mon 25 G10
Llanarthne Carms 23 D10
Llanasa Flint 42 D4
Llanbabo Anglesey 40 B5
Llanbadarn Fawr Ceredig 32 G2
Llanbadarn Fynydd Powys 33 H7
Llanbadarn-y-Garreg Powys 25 D8
Llanbadoc Mon 15 B9
Llanbadrig Anglesey 40 A5
Llanbeder Newport 15 B9
Llanbedr Gwyn 32 C1
Llanbedr Powys 25 D8
Llanbedr Powys 25 F9
Llanbedr-Dyffryn-Clwyd Denb 42 G4
Llanbedr Pont Steffan = Lampeter Ceredig 23 B10
Llanbedr-y-cennin Conwy 41 D9
Llanbedrgoch Anglesey 41 B7
Llanbedrog Gwyn 40 G5
Llanberis Gwyn 41 D7
Llanbethêry V Glam 14 E6
Llanbister Powys 25 A8
Llanblethian V Glam 14 D5
Llanboidy Carms 23 D7
Llanbradach Caerph 15 B7
Llanbrynmair Powys 32 E4
Llancarfan V Glam 14 D6
Llancayo Mon 15 A9
Llancloudy Hereford 25 F11
Llancynfelyn Ceredig 32 F2
Llandaff Cardiff 15 D7
Llandanwg Gwyn 32 C1
Llandarcy Neath 14 B3
Llandawke Carms 23 E7
Llanddaniel Fab Anglesey 40 C6
Llanddarog Carms 23 E10
Llanddeiniol Ceredig 24 A2
Llanddeiniolen Gwyn 41 D7
Llandderfel Gwyn 32 B5
Llanddeusant Anglesey 40 B5
Llanddeusant Carms 24 F4
Llanddew Powys 25 E7
Llanddewi Swansea 23 H9
Llanddewi-Brefi Ceredig 24 C3
Llanddewi Rhydderch Mon 25 G10
Llanddewi Velfrey Pembs 22 E6
Llanddewi'r Cwm Powys 25 D7
Llanddoged Conwy 41 D10
Llanddona Anglesey 41 C7
Llanddowror Carms 23 E7
Llanddulas Conwy 42 E2
Llanddwywe Gwyn 32 C1
Llanddyfynan Anglesey 41 C7
Llandefaelog Fach Powys 25 E7
Llandefaelog-tre'r-graig Powys 25 F8
Llandefalle Powys 25 E8
Llandegai Gwyn 41 C7
Llandegfan Anglesey 41 C7
Llandegla Denb 42 G4
Llandegley Powys 25 B8
Llandegveth Mon 15 B9
Llandegwning Gwyn 40 G4
Llandeilo Carms 24 F3
Llandeilo Graban Powys 25 D7
Llandeilo'r Fan Powys 24 E5
Llandeloy Pembs 22 D3
Llandenny Mon 15 A10
Llandevenny Mon 15 C10
Llandewednock Corn 2 H6
Llandewi Ystradenny Powys 25 B8
Llandinabo Hereford 26 F2
Llandinam Powys 32 G6
Llandissilio Pembs 22 D6
Llandogo Mon 15 A11
Llandough V Glam 14 D5
Llandough V Glam 15 D7
Llandovery = Llanymddyfri Carms 24 E4
Llandow V Glam 14 D5
Llandre Carms 24 D3
Llandre Ceredig 32 G2
Llandrillo Denb 32 B6
Llandrillo-yn-Rhos Conwy 41 B10
Llandrindod = Llandrindod Wells Powys 25 B7
Llandrindod Wells = Llandrindod Powys 25 B7
Llandrinio Powys 33 D8
Llandudno Conwy 41 B9
Llandudno Junction = Cyffordd Llandudno Conwy 41 C9
Llandwrog Gwyn 40 E6
Llandybie Carms 24 G3
Llandyfaelog Carms 23 E9
Llandyfan Carms 24 G3
Llandyfriog Ceredig 23 B8
Llandyfrydog Anglesey 40 B6
Llandygwydd Ceredig 23 B7
Llandynan Denb 42 H4
Llandyrnog Denb 42 F4
Llandysilio Powys 33 D8
Llandyssil Powys 33 F7
Llandysul Ceredig 23 B9
Llanedeyrn Cardiff 15 C8
Llanedi Carms 23 F10
Llaneglwys Powys 25 E7
Llanegryn Gwyn 32 E1
Llanegwad Carms 23 D10
Llaneilian Anglesey 40 A6
Llanelian-yn-Rhos Conwy 41 C10
Llanelidan Denb 42 G4
Llanelieu Powys 25 E8
Llanellen Mon 25 G10
Llanelli Carms 23 G10
Llanelltyd Gwyn 32 D3
Llanelly Mon 25 G9
Llanelly Hill Mon 25 G9
Llanelwedd Powys 25 C7
Llanelwy = St Asaph Denb 42 E3
Llanenddwyn Gwyn 32 C1
Llanengan Gwyn 40 H4
Llanerchymedd Anglesey 40 B6
Llanerfyl Powys 32 E6
Llanfachraeth Anglesey 40 B5
Llanfachreth Gwyn 32 C3
Llanfaelog Anglesey 40 C5
Llanfaelrhys Gwyn 40 H4
Llanfaenor Mon 25 G11
Llanfaes Anglesey 41 C8
Llanfaes Powys 25 F7
Llanfaethlu Anglesey 40 B5
Llanfaglan Gwyn 40 D6
Llanfair Gwyn 32 C1
Llanfair-ar-y-bryn Carms 24 E5
Llanfair Caereinion Powys 33 E7
Llanfair Clydogau Ceredig 24 C3
Llanfair-Dyffryn-Clwyd Denb 42 G4
Llanfair Kilgheddin Mon 25 H10
Llanfair-Nant-Gwyn Pembs 22 C6
Llanfair Talhaiarn Conwy 42 E2
Llanfair Waterdine Shrops 33 H8
Llanfair-ym-Muallt = Builth Wells Powys 25 C7
Llanfairfechan Conwy 41 C8
Llanfairpwll-gwyngyll Anglesey 41 C7
Llanfairyneubwll Anglesey 40 C5
Llanfairynghornwy Anglesey 40 A5
Llanfallteg Carms 22 E6
Llanfaredd Powys 25 C7
Llanfarian Ceredig 32 H1
Llanfechain Powys 33 C7
Llanfechan Powys 24 C6
Llanfechell Anglesey 40 A5
Llanfendigaid Gwyn 32 E1
Llanferres Denb 42 F4
Llanfflewyn Anglesey 40 B5
Llanfihangel-ar-arth Carms 23 C9
Llanfihangel-Crucorney Mon 25 F10
Llanfihangel Glyn Myfyr Conwy 42 H2
Llanfihangel Nant Bran Powys 24 E6
Llanfihangel-nant Melan Powys 25 C8
Llanfihangel Rhydithon Powys 25 B8
Llanfihangel Rogiet Mon 15 C10
Llanfihangel Tal-y-llyn Powys 25 F8
Llanfihangel-uwch-Gwili Carms 23 D9
Llanfihangel-y-Creuddyn Ceredig 32 H2
Llanfihangel-y-pennant Gwyn 32 E2
Llanfihangel-y-pennant Gwyn 41 F7
Llanfihangel-y-traethau Gwyn 41 G7
Llanfihangel-yn-Ngwynfa Powys 33 D6
Llanfihangel yn Nhowyn Anglesey 40 C5
Llanfilo Powys 25 E8
Llanfoist Mon 25 G9
Llanfor Gwyn 32 B5
Llanfrechfa Torf 15 B9
Llanfrothen Gwyn 41 F8
Llanfrynach Powys 25 F7
Llanfwrog Anglesey 40 B5
Llanfwrog Denb 42 G4
Llanfyllin Powys 33 D7
Llanfynydd Carms 23 D10
Llanfynydd Flint 42 G5
Llanfyrnach Pembs 23 C7
Llangadfan Powys 32 D6
Llangadog Carms 24 F4
Llangadwaladr Anglesey 40 D5
Llangadwaladr Powys 33 B7
Llangaffo Anglesey 40 D6
Llangain Carms 23 E8
Llangammarch Wells Powys 24 D6
Llangan V Glam 14 D5
Llangarron Hereford 26 F2
Llangasty Talyllyn Powys 25 F8
Llangathen Carms 23 D10
Llangattock Powys 25 G9
Llangattock Lingoed Mon 25 F10
Llangattock nigh Usk Mon 25 H10
Llangattock-Vibon-Avel Mon 25 G11
Llangedwyn Powys 33 C7
Llangefni Anglesey 40 C6
Llangeinor Bridgend 14 C5
Llangeitho Ceredig 24 C3
Llangeler Carms 23 C8
Llangelynin Gwyn 32 E1
Llangendeirne Carms 23 E9
Llangennech Carms 23 F10
Llangennith Swansea 23 G9
Llangenny Powys 25 G9
Llangernyw Conwy 41 D10
Llangian Gwyn 40 H4
Llanglydwen Carms 22 D6
Llangoed Anglesey 41 C8
Llangoedmor Ceredig 22 B6
Llangollen Denb 33 A8
Llangolman Pembs 22 D6
Llangors Powys 25 F8
Llangovan Mon 25 H11
Llangower Gwyn 32 B5
Llangrannog Ceredig 23 A8
Llangristiolus Anglesey 40 C6
Llangrove Hereford 26 G2
Llangua Mon 25 F10
Llangunllo Powys 25 A9
Llangunnor Carms 23 E9
Llangurig Powys 32 H5
Llangwm Conwy 32 A5
Llangwm Mon 15 A10
Llangwm Pembs 22 F4
Llangwnnadl Gwyn 40 G4
Llangwyfan Denb 42 F4
Llangwyfan-isaf Anglesey 40 D5
Llangwyllog Anglesey 40 C6
Llangwyryfon Ceredig 24 A2
Llangybi Ceredig 24 C3
Llangybi Gwyn 40 F6
Llangybi Mon 15 B9
Llangyfelach Swansea 14 B2
Llangynhafal Denb 42 F4
Llangynidr Powys 25 G8
Llangynin Carms 23 E7
Llangynog Carms 23 E8
Llangynog Powys 33 C6
Llangynwyd Bridgend 14 C4
Llanhamlach Powys 25 F7
Llanharan Rhondda 14 C6
Llanharry Rhondda 14 C6
Llanhennock Mon 15 B9
Llanhiledd = Llanhilleth Bl Gwent 15 A8
Llanhilleth = Llanhiledd Bl Gwent 15 A8
Llanidloes Powys 32 G5
Llaniestyn Gwyn 40 G4
Llanifyny Powys 32 G4
Llanigon Powys 25 E9
Llanilar Ceredig 24 A3
Llanilid Rhondda 14 C5
Llanilltud Fawr = Llantwit Major V Glam 14 E5
Llanishen Cardiff 15 C7
Llanishen Mon 15 A10
Llanllawddog Carms 23 D9
Llanllechid Gwyn 41 D8
Llanllowell Mon 15 B9
Llanllugan Powys 33 E6
Llanllwch Carms 23 E8
Llanllwchaiarn Powys 33 F7
Llanllwni Carms 23 C9
Llanllyfni Gwyn 40 E6
Llanmadoc Swansea 23 G9
Llanmaes V Glam 14 E5
Llanmartin Newport 15 C9
Llanmihangel V Glam 14 D5
Llanmorlais Swansea 23 G10
Llannefydd Conwy 42 E2
Llannon Carms 23 F10
Llannor Gwyn 40 G5
Llanon Ceredig 24 B2
Llanover Mon 25 H10
Llanpumsaint Carms 23 D9
Llanreithan Pembs 22 D3
Llanrhaeadr Denb 42 F3
Llanrhaeadr-ym-Mochnant Powys 33 C7
Llanrhian Pembs 22 C3
Llanrhidian Swansea 23 G9
Llanrhos Conwy 41 B9
Llanrhyddlad Anglesey 40 B5
Llanrhystud Ceredig 24 B2
Llanrosser Hereford 25 E9
Llanrothal Hereford 25 G11
Llanrug Gwyn 41 D7
Llanrumney Cardiff 15 C8
Llanrwst Conwy 41 D10
Llansadurnen Carms 23 E7
Llansadwrn Anglesey 41 C7
Llansadwrn Carms 24 E3
Llansaint Carms 23 F8
Llansamlet Swansea 14 B2
Llansannan Conwy 42 F2
Llansannor V Glam 14 D5
Llansantffraed Ceredig 24 B2
Llansantffraed Powys 25 F8
Llansantffraed Cwmdeuddwr Powys 24 B6
Llansantffraed-in-Elvel Powys 25 C7
Llansantffraid-ym-Mechain Powys 33 C8
Llansawel Carms 24 E3
Llansilin Powys 33 C8
Llansoy Mon 15 A10
Llanspyddid Powys 25 F7
Llanstadwell Pembs 22 F4
Llansteffan Carms 23 E8
Llanstephan Powys 25 D8
Llantarnam Torf 15 B9
Llanteg Pembs 22 E6
Llanthony Mon 25 F9
Llantilio Crossenny Mon 25 G10
Llantilio Pertholey Mon 25 G10
Llantood Pembs 22 B6
Llantrisant Anglesey 40 B5
Llantrisant Mon 15 B9
Llantrisant Rhondda 14 C6
Llantrithyd V Glam 14 D6
Llantwit Fardre Rhondda 14 C6
Llantwit Major = Llanilltud Fawr V Glam 14 E5
Llanuwchllyn Gwyn 41 G10
Llanvaches Newport 15 B10

Llanvair Discoed Mon 15 B10
Llanvapley Mon 25 G10
Llanvetherine Mon 25 G10
Llanveynoe Hereford 25 E10
Llanvihangel Gobion Mon 25 H10
Llanvihangel-Ystern-Llewern Mon 25 G11
Llanwarne Hereford 26 F2
Llanwddyn Powys 32 D6
Llanwenog Ceredig 23 B9
Llanwern Newport 15 C9
Llanwinio Carms 23 D7
Llanwnda Gwyn 40 E6
Llanwnda Pembs 22 C4
Llanwnnen Ceredig 23 B10
Llanwnog Powys 32 F6
Llanwrda Carms 24 E4
Llanwrin Powys 32 E3
Llanwrthwl Powys 24 B6
Llanwrtud = Llanwrtyd Wells Powys 24 D5
Llanwrtyd Powys 24 D5
Llanwrtyd Wells = Llanwrtud Powys 24 D5
Llanwyddelan Powys 33 E6
Llanyblodwel Shrops 33 C8
Llanybri Carms 23 E8
Llanybydder Carms 23 B10
Llanycefn Pembs 22 D5
Llanychaer Pembs 22 C4
Llanycil Gwyn 32 B5
Llanycrwys Carms 24 D3
Llanymawddwy Gwyn 32 D5
Llanymddyfri = Llandovery Carms 24 E4
Llanymynech Powys 33 C8
Llanynghenedl Anglesey 40 B5
Llanynys Denb 42 F4
Llanyre Powys 25 B7
Llanystumdwy Gwyn 40 G6
Llanywern Powys 25 E8
Llawhaden Pembs 22 E5
Llawnt Shrops 33 B8
Llawr Dref Gwyn 40 H4
Llawryglyn Powys 32 F5
Llay Wrex 42 G6
Llechcynfarwy Anglesey 40 B5
Llecheiddior Gwyn 40 F6
Llechfaen Powys 25 F7
Llechryd Caerph 25 H8
Llechryd Ceredig 23 B7
Llechrydau Powys 33 B8
Lledrod Ceredig 24 A3
Llenmerewig Powys 33 F7
Llethrid Swansea 23 G10
Llidiad Nenog Carms 23 C10
Llidiardau Gwyn 41 G10
Llidiart-y-parc Denb 33 A7
Llithfaen Gwyn 40 F5
Llong Flint 42 F5
Llowes Powys 25 D8
Llundain-fach Ceredig 23 A10
Llwydcoed Rhondda 14 A5
Llwyn Shrops 33 G8
Llwyn-du Mon 25 G9
Llwyn-hendy Carms 23 G10
Llwyn-têg Carms 23 F10
Llwyn-y-brain Carms 22 E6
Llwyn-y-groes Ceredig 23 A10
Llwyncelyn Ceredig 23 A9
Llwyndafydd Ceredig 23 A8
Llwynderw Powys 33 E8
Llwyndyrys Gwyn 40 F5
Llwyngwril Gwyn 32 E1
Llwynmawr Wrex 33 B8
Llwynypia Rhondda 14 B5
Llynclys Shrops 33 C8
Llynfaes Anglesey 40 C6
Llys-y-frân Pembs 22 D5
Llysfaen Conwy 41 C10
Llyswen Powys 25 E8
Llysworney V Glam 14 D5
Llywel Powys 24 E5
Loan Falk 69 C8
Loanend Northumb 71 E8
Loanhead Midloth 69 D11
Loans S Ayrs 66 C6
Loans of Tullich Highld 87 D11
Lobb Devon 6 C3
Loch a Charnain W Isles 84 D3
Loch a' Ghainmhich W Isles 91 E7
Loch Baghasdail = Lochboisdale W Isles 84 G2
Loch Choire Lodge Highld 93 F9
Loch Euphoirt W Isles 84 B3
Loch Head Dumfries 54 E6
Loch Loyal Lodge Highld 93 E9
Loch nam Madadh = Lochmaddy W Isles 84 B4
Loch Sgioport W Isles 84 E3
Lochailort Highld 79 C10
Lochaline Highld 79 G9
Lochanhully Highld 81 A11
Lochans Dumfries 54 D3
Locharbriggs Dumfries 60 E5
Lochassynt Lodge Highld 92 G4
Lochavich Ho Argyll 73 B8
Lochawe Argyll 74 E4
Lochboisdale = Loch Baghasdail W Isles 84 G2
Lochbuie Argyll 79 J9
Lochcarron Highld 85 E13
Lochdhu Highld 93 E13
Lochdochart House Stirling 75 E7
Lochdon Argyll 79 H10
Lochdrum Highld 86 D5
Lochead Argyll 72 F6
Lochearnhead Stirling 75 E8
Lochee Dundee 76 D6
Lochend Highld 87 H8
Lochend Highld 94 D4
Locherben Dumfries 60 D5
Lochfoot Dumfries 60 F4
Lochgair Argyll 73 D8
Lochgarthside Highld 81 B7
Lochgelly Fife 69 A10
Lochgilphead Argyll 73 E7
Lochgoilhead Argyll 74 G5
Lochhill Moray 88 B2
Lochindorb Lodge Highld 87 H12
Lochinver Highld 92 G3
Lochlane Perth 75 E11
Lochluichart Highld 86 E6
Lochmaben Dumfries 60 E6
Lochmaddy = Loch nam Madadh W Isles 84 B4
Lochmore Cottage Highld 94 F2
Lochmore Lodge Highld 92 F5
Lochore Fife 76 H4
Lochportain W Isles 84 A4
Lochranza N Ayrs 66 A2
Lochs Crofts Moray 88 B3
Lochside Aberds 77 A10
Lochside Highld 87 F11
Lochside Highld 92 D7
Lochside Highld 93 F11
Lochslin Highld 87 C11
Lochstack Lodge Highld 92 E5
Lochton Aberds 83 D9
Lochty Angus 77 A8
Lochty Fife 77 G8
Lochty Perth 76 E3
Lochuisge Highld 79 F10
Lochurr Dumfries 60 E3
Lochwinnoch Renfs 68 E2
Lochwood Dumfries 60 D6
Lochyside Highld 80 F3
Lockengate Corn 3 C9
Lockerbie Dumfries 61 E7
Lockeridge Wilts 17 E8
Lockerley Hants 10 B1
Locking N Som 15 F9
Lockinge Oxon 17 C11
Lockington E Yorks 52 E5
Lockington Leics 35 C10
Lockleywood Shrops 34 C2
Locks Heath Hants 10 D4
Lockton N Yorks 59 G9
Lockwood W Yorks 51 H7
Loddington Leics 36 E3
Loddington N Nhants 36 H4
Loddiswell Devon 5 G8
Loddon Norf 39 F9
Lode Cambs 30 B2
Loders Dorset 8 E3
Lodsworth W Sus 11 B8
Lofthouse N Yorks 51 B7
Lofthouse W Yorks 51 G9
Loftus Redcar 59 E8
Logan E Ayrs 67 D8
Logan Mains Dumfries 54 E3
Loganlea W Loth 69 D8
Loggerheads Staffs 34 B3
Logie Angus 77 A9
Logie Fife 77 E7
Logie Moray 87 F13
Logie Coldstone Aberds 82 C6
Logie Hill Highld 87 D10
Logie Newton Aberds 89 E6
Logie Pert Angus 77 A9
Logiealmond Lodge Perth 76 D2
Logierait Perth 76 B2
Login Carms 22 D6
Lolworth Cambs 29 B10
Lonbain Highld 85 C11
Londesborough E Yorks 52 E4
London Colney Herts 19 A8
Londonderry N Yorks 58 H4
Londonthorpe Lincs 36 B5
Londubh Highld 91 J13
Lonemore Highld 87 C10
Long Ashton N Som 15 D11
Long Bennington Lincs 36 A4
Long Bredy Dorset 8 E4
Long Buckby W Nhants 28 B3
Long Clawson Leics 36 C3
Long Common Hants 10 C4
Long Compton Staffs 34 C4
Long Compton Warks 27 E9
Long Crendon Bucks 28 H3
Long Crichel Dorset 9 C8
Long Ditton Sur 19 E8
Long Drax N Yorks 52 G2
Long Duckmanton Derbys 45 E8
Long Eaton Derbys 35 B10
Long Green Worcs 26 E5
Long Hanborough Oxon 27 G11
Long Itchington Warks 27 B11
Long Lawford Warks 35 H10
Long Load Som 8 B3
Long Marston Herts 28 G5
Long Marston N Yorks 51 D11
Long Marston Warks 27 D8
Long Marton W&F 57 D8
Long Melford Suff 30 D5
Long Newnton Glos 16 B6
Long Newton E Loth 70 D4
Long Preston N Yorks 50 D4
Long Riston E Yorks 53 E7
Long Sight Gtr Man 44 B3
Long Stratton Norf 39 F7
Long Street M Keynes 28 D4
Long Sutton Hants 18 G4
Long Sutton Lincs 37 C10
Long Sutton Som 8 B3
Long Thurlow Suff 31 B7
Long Whatton Leics 35 C10
Long Wittenham Oxon 18 B2
Longbar N Ayrs 66 A6
Longbenton T&W 63 G8
Longborough Glos 27 F8
Longbridge W Mid 34 H6
Longbridge Warks 27 B9
Longbridge Deverill Wilts 16 G5
Longburton Dorset 8 C5
Longcliffe Derbys 44 G6
Longcot Oxon 17 B9
Longcroft Falk 68 C6
Longden Shrops 33 E10
Longdon Staffs 35 D6
Longdon Worcs 26 E5
Longdon Green Staffs 35 D6
Longdon on Tern Telford 34 D2
Longdown Devon 7 G7
Longdowns Corn 2 F6
Longfield Kent 20 E3
Longfield Shetland 96 M5
Longford Derbys 35 B8
Longford Glos 26 F5
Longford London 19 D7
Longford Shrops 34 B2
Longford Telford 34 D3
Longford W Mid 35 G9
Longfordlane Derbys 35 B8
Longforgan Perth 76 E6
Longformacus Borders 70 E5
Longframlington Northumb 63 C7
Longham Dorset 9 E9
Longham Norf 38 D5
Longhaven Aberds 89 E11
Longhill Aberds 89 C9
Longhirst Northumb 63 E8
Longhope Glos 26 G3
Longhope Orkney 95 J4
Longhorsley Northumb 63 D7
Longhoughton Northumb 63 B8
Longlane Derbys 35 B8
Longlane W Berks 17 D11
Longlevens Glos 26 F5
Longley W Yorks 44 B5
Longley Green Worcs 26 C4
Longmanhill Aberds 89 B7
Longmoor Camp Hants 11 A6
Longmorn Moray 88 C2
Longnewton Borders 70 H4
Longnewton Stockton 58 E4
Longney Glos 26 G4
Longniddry E Loth 70 C3
Longnor Shrops 33 E10
Longnor Staffs 44 F4
Longparish Hants 17 G11
Longport Stoke 44 H2
Longridge Lancs 50 F2
Longridge Staffs 34 D5
Longridge W Loth 69 D8
Longriggend N Lanark 69 C7
Longsdon Staffs 44 G3
Longshaw Gtr Man 43 B8
Longside Aberds 89 D10
Longstanton Cambs 29 B10
Longstock Hants 17 H10
Longstone Pembs 22 F6
Longstowe Cambs 29 C10
Longthorpe Pboro 37 F7
Longthwaite W&F 56 D6
Longton Lancs 49 G4
Longton Stoke 34 A5
Longtown W&F 61 G9
Longtown Hereford 25 F10
Longview Mers 43 C7
Longville in the Dale Shrops 33 F11
Longwick Bucks 28 H4
Longwitton Northumb 62 E6
Longwood Shrops 34 E2
Longworth Oxon 17 B10
Longyester E Loth 70 D4
Lonmay Aberds 89 C10
Lonmore Highld 84 D7
Looe Corn 4 F3
Loose Kent 20 F4
Loosley Row Bucks 18 A5
Lopcombe Corner Wilts 17 H9
Lopen Som 8 C3
Loppington Shrops 33 C10
Lopwell Devon 4 E5
Lorbottle Northumb 62 C6
Lorbottle Hall Northumb 62 C6
Lornty Perth 76 C4
Loscoe Derbys 45 H8
Losgaintir W Isles 90 H5
Lossiemouth Moray 88 A2
Lossit Argyll 64 C2
Lostford Shrops 34 B2
Lostock Gralam Ches W 43 E9
Lostock Green Ches W 43 E9
Lostock Hall Lancs 49 G5
Lostock Junction Gtr Man 43 B9
Lostwithiel Corn 4 F2
Loth Orkney 95 E7
Lothbeg Highld 93 H12
Lothersdale N Yorks 50 E5
Lothmore Highld 93 H12
Loudwater Bucks 18 B6
Loughborough Leics 35 D11
Loughor Swansea 23 G10
Loughton Essex 19 B11
Loughton M Keynes 28 E5
Loughton Shrops 34 G2
Lound Lincs 37 D6
Lound Notts 45 D10
Lound Suff 39 F11
Lount Leics 35 D9
Louth Lincs 47 D7
Love Clough Lancs 50 G4
Lovedean Hants 10 C5
Lover Wilts 9 B11
Loversall S Yorks 45 C9
Loves Green Essex 20 A3
Lovesome Hill N Yorks 58 G4
Loveston Pembs 22 F5
Lovington Som 8 A4
Low Ackworth W Yorks 51 H10
Low Barlings Lincs 46 E4
Low Bentham N Yorks 50 C2
Low Bradfield S Yorks 44 C6
Low Bradley N Yorks 50 E6
Low Braithwaite W&F 56 B6
Low Brunton Northumb 62 F5
Low Burnham N Lincs 45 B11
Low Burton N Yorks 51 A8
Low Buston Northumb 63 C8
Low Catton E Yorks 52 D3
Low Clanyard Dumfries 54 F4
Low Coniscliffe Darl 58 E3
Low Crosby Cumb 61 H10
Low Dalby N Yorks 59 H9
Low Dinsdale Darl 58 E4
Low Ellington N Yorks 51 A8
Low Etherley Durham 58 D2
Low Fell T&W 63 H8
Low Fulney Lincs 37 C8
Low Garth N Yorks 59 F8
Low Gate Northumb 62 G5
Low Grantley N Yorks 51 B8
Low Habberley Worcs 34 H4
Low Ham Som 8 B3
Low Hesket W&F 57 B6
Low Hesleyhurst Northumb 62 D6
Low Hutton N Yorks 52 C3
Low Laithe N Yorks 51 C7
Low Leighton Derbys 44 D4
Low Lorton Cumb 56 D3
Low Marishes N Yorks 52 B4
Low Marnham Notts 46 F2
Low Mill N Yorks 59 G7
Low Moor Lancs 50 E3
Low Moor W Yorks 51 G7
Low Moorsley T&W 58 B4
Low Newton W&F 49 A4
Low Newton-by-the-Sea Northumb 63 A8
Low Row Cumb 56 C5
Low Row Cumb 61 G11
Low Row N Yorks 57 G11
Low Salchrie Dumfries 54 C3
Low Smerby Argyll 65 F8
Low Torry Fife 69 B9
Low Worsall N Yorks 58 F4
Low Wray W&F 56 F5
Lowbridge House W&F 57 F7
Lowca Cumb 56 D1
Lowdham Notts 45 H10
Lowe Shrops 33 B11
Lowe Hill Staffs 44 G3
Lower Aisholt Som 7 C11
Lower Arncott Oxon 28 G3
Lower Ashton Devon 5 C9
Lower Assendon Oxon 18 C4
Lower Badcall Highld 92 E4
Lower Bartle Lancs 49 F4
Lower Basildon W Berks 18 D3
Lower Beeding W Sus 11 B11
Lower Benefield N Nhants 36 G5
Lower Boddington W Nhants 27 C11
Lower Brailes Warks 27 E10
Lower Breakish Highld 85 F11
Lower Broadheath Worcs 26 C5
Lower Bullingham Hereford 26 E2
Lower Cam Glos 16 A4
Lower Chapel Powys 25 E7
Lower Chute Wilts 17 F10
Lower Cragabus Argyll 64 D4
Lower Crossings Derbys 44 D4
Lower Cumberworth W Yorks 44 B6
Lower Darwen Blackburn 50 G2
Lower Dean Bedford 29 B7
Lower Diabaig Highld 85 B12
Lower Dicker E Sus 12 E4
Lower Dinchope Shrops 33 G10
Lower Down Shrops 33 G9
Lower Drift Corn 2 G3
Lower Dunsforth N Yorks 51 C10
Lower Egleton Hereford 26 D3
Lower Elkstone Staffs 44 G4
Lower End C Beds 28 F6
Lower Everleigh Wilts 17 F8
Lower Farringdon Hants 18 H4
Lower Foxdale IoM 48 E2
Lower Frankton Shrops 33 B9
Lower Froyle Hants 18 G4
Lower Gledfield Highld 87 B8
Lower Green Norf 38 B5
Lower Hacheston Suff 31 C10
Lower Halistra Highld 84 C7
Lower Halstow Kent 20 E5
Lower Hardres Kent 21 F8
Lower Hawthwaite W&F 56 H4
Lower Heath Ches E 44 F2
Lower Hempriggs Moray 87 E14
Lower Hergest Hereford 25 C9
Lower Heyford Oxon 27 F11
Lower Higham Kent 20 D4
Lower Holbrook Suff 31 E8
Lower Hordley Shrops 33 C9
Lower Horsebridge E Sus 12 E4
Lower Killeyan Argyll 64 D3
Lower Kingswood Sur 19 F9
Lower Kinnerton Ches W 42 F6
Lower Langford N Som 15 E10
Lower Largo Fife 77 G7
Lower Leigh Staffs 34 B6
Lower Lemington Glos 27 E9
Lower Lenie Highld 81 A7
Lower Lydbrook Glos 26 G2
Lower Lye Hereford 25 B11
Lower Machen Newport 15 C8
Lower Maes-coed Hereford 25 E10
Lower Mayland Essex 20 A6
Lower Midway Derbys 35 C9
Lower Milovaig Highld 84 C6
Lower Moor Worcs 26 D6
Lower Nazeing Essex 29 H10
Lower Netchwood Shrops 34 F2
Lower Ollach Highld 85 E10
Lower Penarth V Glam 15 D7
Lower Penn Staffs 34 F4
Lower Pennington Hants 10 E2
Lower Peover Ches W 43 E10
Lower Pexhill Ches E 44 E2
Lower Place Gtr Man 44 A3
Lower Quinton Warks 27 D8
Lower Rochford Worcs 26 B3
Lower Seagry Wilts 16 C6
Lower Shelton C Beds 28 D6
Lower Shiplake Oxon 18 D4
Lower Shuckburgh Warks 27 B11
Lower Slaughter Glos 27 F8
Lower Stanton St Quintin Wilts 16 C6
Lower Stoke Medway 20 D5
Lower Stondon C Beds 29 E8
Lower Stow Bedon Norf 38 F5
Lower Street Norf 39 B9
Lower Street Norf 39 D9
Lower Strensham Worcs 26 D6
Lower Stretton Warr 43 D9
Lower Sundon C Beds 29 F7
Lower Swanwick Hants 10 D3
Lower Swell Glos 27 F8
Lower Tean Staffs 34 B6
Lower Thurlton Norf 39 F10
Lower Tote Highld 85 B10
Lower Town Pembs 22 C4
Lower Tysoe Warks 27 D10
Lower Upham Hants 10 C4
Lower Vexford Som 7 C10
Lower Weare Som 15 F10
Lower Welson Hereford 25 C9
Lower Whitley Ches W 43 E9
Lower Wield Hants 18 G3
Lower Winchendon Bucks 28 G4
Lower Withington Ches E 44 F2
Lower Woodend Bucks 18 C5
Lower Woodford Wilts 9 A10
Lower Wyche Worcs 26 D4
Lowesby Leics 36 E3
Lowestoft Suff 39 F11
Loweswater Cumb 56 D3
Lowford Hants 10 C3
Lowgill Lancs 50 C2
Lowgill W&F 57 G8
Lowick N Nhants 36 G5
Lowick Northumb 71 G9
Lowick Bridge W&F 56 H4
Lowick Green W&F 56 H4
Lowlands Torf 15 B8
Lowmoor Row W&F 57 D8
Lownie Moor Angus 77 C7
Lowsonford Warks 27 B8
Lowther W&F 57 D7
Lowthorpe E Yorks 52 C6
Lowton Gtr Man 43 C9
Lowton Common Gtr Man 43 C9
Loxbeare Devon 7 E8
Loxhill Sur 19 H7
Loxhore Devon 6 C5
Loxley Warks 27 C9
Loxton N Som 15 F9
Loxwood W Sus 11 A9
Lubcroy Highld 92 J6
Lubenham Leics 36 G3
Luccombe Som 7 B8
Luccombe Village IoW 10 G4
Lucker Northumb 71 G10
Luckett Corn 4 D4
Luckington Wilts 16 C5
Lucklawhill Fife 77 E7
Luckwell Bridge Som 7 C8
Lucton Hereford 25 B11
Ludag W Isles 84 G2
Ludborough Lincs 46 C6
Ludchurch Pembs 22 E6
Luddenden W Yorks 50 G6
Luddenden Foot W Yorks 50 G6
Luddesdown Kent 20 E3
Luddington N Lincs 52 H4
Luddington Warks 27 C8
Luddington in the Brook N Nhants 37 G7
Lude House Perth 81 G10
Ludford Lincs 46 D6
Ludford Shrops 26 A2
Ludgershall Bucks 28 G3
Ludgershall Wilts 17 F9
Ludgvan Corn 2 F4
Ludham Norf 39 D9
Ludlow Shrops 26 A2
Ludwell Wilts 9 B8
Ludworth Durham 58 B4
Luffincott Devon 6 G2
Lugar E Ayrs 67 D8
Lugg Green Hereford 25 B11
Luggate Burn E Loth 70 C5
Luggiebank N Lanark 68 C6
Lugton E Ayrs 67 A7
Lugwardine Hereford 26 D2
Luib Highld 85 F10
Lulham Hereford 25 D11
Lullenden Sur 12 B3
Lullington Derbys 35 D8
Lullington Som 16 F4
Lulsgate Bottom N Som 15 E11
Lulsley Worcs 26 C4
Lumb W Yorks 50 G6
Lumby N Yorks 51 F10
Lumloch E Dunb 68 D5
Lumphanan Aberds 83 C7
Lumphinnans Fife 69 A10
Lumsdaine Borders 71 D7
Lumsden Aberds 82 A6
Lunan Angus 77 B9
Lunanhead Angus 77 B7
Luncarty Perth 76 E3
Lund E Yorks 52 E5
Lund N Yorks 52 F2
Lund Shetland 96 C7
Lunderton Aberds 89 D11
Lundie Angus 76 D5
Lundie Highld 80 B3
Lundin Links Fife 77 G7
Lunga Argyll 72 C6
Lunna Shetland 96 G6
Lunning Shetland 96 G7
Lunnon Swansea 23 H10
Lunsford's Cross E Sus 12 E6
Lunt Mers 42 B6
Luntley Hereford 25 C10
Luppitt Devon 7 F10
Lupset W Yorks 51 H9
Lupton W&F 50 A1
Lurgashall W Sus 11 B8
Lusby Lincs 47 F7
Luson Devon 5 G7
Luss Argyll 68 A2
Lussagiven Argyll 72 E5
Lusta Highld 85 C7
Lustleigh Devon 5 C8
Luston Hereford 25 B11
Luthermuir Aberds 83 G8
Luthrie Fife 76 F6
Luton Devon 5 D10
Luton Luton 29 F7
Luton Medway 20 E4
Lutterworth Leics 35 G11
Lutton Devon 5 F6
Lutton Lincs 37 C10
Lutton N Nhants 37 G7
Lutworthy Devon 7 E6
Luxborough Som 7 C8
Luxulyan Corn 4 F1
Lybster Highld 94 G4
Lydbury North Shrops 33 G9
Lydcott Devon 6 C5
Lydd Kent 13 D9
Lydd on Sea Kent 13 D9
Lydden Kent 21 G9
Lyddington Rutland 36 F4
Lyde Green Hants 18 F4
Lydeard St Lawrence Som 7 C10
Lydford Devon 4 C6
Lydford-on-Fosse Som 8 A4
Lydgate W Yorks 50 G5
Lydham Shrops 33 F9
Lydiard Green Wilts 17 C7
Lydiard Millicent Wilts 17 C7
Lydiate Mers 42 B6
Lydlinch Dorset 8 C6
Lydney Glos 16 A3
Lydstep Pembs 22 G5
Lye W Mid 34 G5
Lye Green Bucks 18 A6
Lye Green E Sus 12 C4
Lyford Oxon 17 B10
Lymbridge Green Kent 13 B10
Lyme Regis Dorset 8 E2
Lyminge Kent 21 G8
Lymington Hants 10 E2
Lyminster W Sus 11 D9
Lymm Warr 43 D9
Lymore Hants 10 E1
Lympne Kent 13 C10
Lympsham Som 15 F9
Lympstone Devon 5 C10
Lynchat Highld 81 C9
Lyndale Ho. Highld 85 C8
Lyndhurst Hants 10 D2
Lyndon Rutland 36 E5
Lyne Sur 19 E7
Lyne Down Hereford 26 E3
Lyne of Gorthleck Highld 81 A7
Lyne of Skene Aberds 83 B9
Lyneal Shrops 33 B10
Lyneham Oxon 27 F9
Lyneham Wilts 17 D7
Lynemore Highld 82 A2
Lynemouth Northumb 63 D8
Lyness Orkney 95 J4
Lyng Norf 39 D6
Lyng Som 8 B2
Lynmouth Devon 7 B6
Lynsted Kent 20 E6
Lynton Devon 6 B6
Lyon's Gate Dorset 8 D5
Lyonshall Hereford 25 C10
Lytchett Matravers Dorset 9 E8
Lytchett Minster Dorset 9 E8
Lyth Highld 94 D4
Lytham Lancs 49 G3
Lytham St Anne's Lancs 49 G3
Lythe N Yorks 59 E9
Lythes Orkney 95 K5

M

Mabe Burnthouse Corn 3 F6
Mabie Dumfries 60 F5
Mablethorpe Lincs 47 D9
Macclesfield Ches E 44 E3
Macclesfield Forest Ches E 44 E3
Macduff Aberds 89 B7
Mace Green Suff 31 D8
Macharioch Argyll 65 H8
Machen Caerph 15 C8
Machrihanish Argyll 65 F7
Machynlleth Powys 32 E3
Machynys Carms 23 G10
Mackerel's Common W Sus 11 B9
Mackworth Derbys 35 B9
Macmerry E Loth 70 C3
Madderty Perth 76 E2
Maddiston Falk 69 C8
Madehurst W Sus 11 C8
Madeley Staffs 34 A3
Madeley Telford 34 E2
Madeley Heath Staffs 43 H10
Madeley Park Staffs 34 A3
Madingley Cambs 29 B10
Madley Hereford 25 E11
Madresfield Worcs 26 D5
Madron Corn 2 F3
Maen-y-groes Ceredig 23 A8
Maenaddwyn Anglesey 40 B6
Maenclochog Pembs 22 D5
Maendy V Glam 14 D6
Maentwrog Gwyn 41 F8
Maer Staffs 34 B3
Maerdy Conwy 32 A6
Maerdy Rhondda 14 B5
Maes-Treylow Powys 25 B9
Maesbrook Shrops 33 C8
Maesbury Shrops 33 C9
Maesbury Marsh Shrops 33 C9
Maesgwyn-Isaf Powys 33 D7
Maesgwynne Carms 23 D7
Maeshafn Denb 42 F5
Maesllyn Ceredig 23 B8
Maesmynis Powys 25 D7
Maesteg Bridgend 14 B4
Maestir Ceredig 23 B10
Maesy cwmmer Caerph 15 B7
Maesybont Carms 23 E10
Maesycrugiau Carms 23 B9
Maesymeillion Ceredig 23 B9
Magdalen Laver Essex 30 H2
Maggieknockater Moray 88 D3
Magham Down E Sus 12 E5
Maghull Mers 43 B6
Magor Mon 15 C10
Magpie Green Suff 39 H6
Maiden Bradley Wilts 16 H5
Maiden Law Durham 58 B2
Maiden Newton Dorset 8 E4
Maiden Wells Pembs 22 G4
Maidencombe Torbay 5 E10
Maidenhall Suff 31 D8
Maidenhead Windsor 18 C5
Maidens S Ayrs 66 F5
Maiden's Green Brack 18 D5
Maidensgrave Suff 31 D9
Maidenwell Corn 4 D2
Maidenwell Lincs 47 E7
Maidford W Nhants 28 C3
Maids Moreton Bucks 28 E4
Maidstone Kent 20 F4
Maidwell W Nhants 36 H3
Mail Shetland 96 L6
Main Powys 33 D7
Maindee Newport 15 C9
Mains of Airies Dumfries 54 C2
Mains of Allardice Aberds 83 F10
Mains of Annochie Aberds 89 D9
Mains of Ardestie Angus 77 D8
Mains of Balhall Angus 77 A8
Mains of Ballindarg Angus 77 B7
Mains of Balnakettle Aberds 83 F8
Mains of Birness Aberds 89 E9
Mains of Burgie Moray 87 F13
Mains of Clunas Highld 87 G11
Mains of Crichie Aberds 89 D9
Mains of Dalvey Highld 87 H14
Mains of Dellavaird Aberds 83 E9
Mains of Drum Aberds 83 D10
Mains of Edingight Moray 88 C5
Mains of Fedderate Aberds 89 D8
Mains of Inkhorn Aberds 89 E9
Mains of Mayen Moray 88 D5
Mains of Melgund Angus 77 B8
Mains of Thornton Aberds 83 F8
Mains of Watten Highld 94 E4
Mainsforth Durham 58 C4
Mainsriddle Dumfries 60 H5
Mainstone Shrops 33 G8
Maisemore Glos 26 F5
Malacleit W Isles 84 A2
Malborough Devon 5 H8
Malcoff Derbys 44 D4
Maldon Essex 30 H5
Malham N Yorks 50 C5
Maligar Highld 85 B9
Mallaig Highld 79 B9
Malleny Mills Edin 69 D10
Malling Stirling 75 G8
Malltraeth Anglesey 40 D6
Mallwyd Gwyn 32 D4
Malmesbury Wilts 16 C6
Malmsmead Devon 7 B6
Malpas Ches W 43 H7
Malpas Corn 3 E7
Malpas Newport 15 B9
Malswick Glos 26 F4
Maltby S Yorks 45 C9
Maltby Stockton 58 E5
Maltby le Marsh Lincs 47 D8
Malting Green Essex 30 F6
Maltman's Hill Kent 13 B8
Malton N Yorks 52 B3
Malvern Link Worcs 26 D4
Malvern Wells Worcs 26 D4
Mamble Worcs 26 A3
Manaccan Corn 3 G6
Manafon Powys 33 E7
Manais W Isles 90 J6
Manar Ho. Aberds 83 A9
Manaton Devon 5 C8
Manby Lincs 47 D7
Mancetter Warks 35 F9
Manchester Gtr Man 44 C2
Manchester Airport Gtr Man 44 D2
Mancot Flint 42 F6
Mandally Highld 80 C4
Manea Cambs 37 G10
Manfield N Yorks 58 E3
Mangaster Shetland 96 F5
Mangotsfield S Glos 16 D3
Mangurstadh W Isles 90 D5
Mankinholes W Yorks 50 G5
Manley Ches W 43 E8
Manmoel Caerph 15 A7
Mannal Argyll 78 G2
Mannerston W Loth 69 C9
Manningford Bohune Wilts 17 F8
Manningford Bruce Wilts 17 F8
Manningham W Yorks 51 F7
Mannings Heath W Sus 11 B11
Mannington Dorset 9 D9
Manningtree Essex 31 E8
Mannofield Aberdeen 83 C11
Manor London 19 C11
Manor Estate S Yorks 45 D7
Manorbier Pembs 22 G5
Manordeilo Carms 24 F3
Manorhill Borders 70 G5
Manorowen Pembs 22 C4
Mansel Lacy Hereford 25 D11
Mansell Gamage Hereford 25 D10
Mansergh W&F 50 A2
Mansfield E Ayrs 67 E9
Mansfield Notts 45 F9
Mansfield Woodhouse Notts 45 F9
Mansriggs W&F 49 A2
Manston Dorset 9 C7
Manston Kent 21 E10
Manston W Yorks 51 F9
Manswood Dorset 9 D8
Manthorpe Lincs 36 B5
Manthorpe Lincs 37 D6
Manton N Lincs 46 B3
Manton Notts 45 E9
Manton Rutland 36 E4
Manton Wilts 17 E8
Manuden Essex 29 F11
Maperton Som 8 B5
Maple Cross Herts 19 B7
Maplebeck Notts 45 F11
Mapledurham Oxon 18 D3
Mapledurwell Hants 18 F3
Maplehurst W Sus 11 B10
Maplescombe Kent 20 E2
Mapleton Derbys 44 H5
Mapperley Derbys 35 A10
Mapperley Park Nottingham 36 A1
Mapperton Dorset 8 E4
Mappleborough Green Warks 27 B7
Mappleton E Yorks 53 E8
Mappowder Dorset 8 D6
Mar Lodge Aberds 82 E2
Maraig W Isles 90 G6
Marazanvose Corn 3 D7
Marazion Corn 2 F4
Marbhig W Isles 91 F9
Marbury Ches E 43 H8
March Cambs 37 F10
March S Lanark 60 C5
Marcham Oxon 17 B11
Marchamley Shrops 34 C1
Marchington Staffs 35 B7
Marchington Woodlands Staffs 35 C7
Marchroes Gwyn 40 H5
Marchwiel Wrex 42 H6
Marchwood Hants 10 C2
Marcross V Glam 14 E5
Marden Hereford 26 D2
Marden Kent 12 B6
Marden T&W 63 F9
Marden Wilts 17 F7
Marden Beech Kent 12 B6
Marden Thorn Kent 13 B6
Mardy Mon 25 G10
Marefield Leics 36 E3
Mareham le Fen Lincs 46 F6
Mareham on the Hill Lincs 46 F6
Marehay Derbys 45 H7
Marehill W Sus 11 C9
Maresfield E Sus 12 D3
Marfleet Hull 53 G7
Marford Wrex 42 G6
Margam Neath 14 C3
Margaret Marsh Dorset 9 C7
Margaret Roding Essex 30 G2
Margaretting Essex 20 A3
Margate Kent 21 D10
Margnaheglish N Ayrs 66 C3
Margrove Park Redcar 59 E7
Marham Norf 38 D3
Marhamchurch Corn 4 A3
Marholm Pboro 37 E7
Mariandyrys Anglesey 41 B8
Marianglas Anglesey 41 B7
Mariansleigh Devon 7 D6
Marionburgh Aberds 83 C9
Marishader Highld 85 B9
Marjoriebanks Dumfries 60 E6
Mark Dumfries 54 D4
Mark S Ayrs 54 B3
Mark Som 15 G9
Mark Causeway Som 15 G9
Mark Cross E Sus 12 C4
Mark Cross E Sus 12 E3
Markbeech Kent 12 B3
Markby Lincs 47 E8
Market Bosworth Leics 35 E10
Market Deeping Lincs 37 E7
Market Drayton Shrops 34 B2
Market Harborough Leics 36 G3
Market Lavington Wilts 17 F7
Market Overton Rutland 36 D4
Market Rasen Lincs 46 D5
Market Stainton Lincs 46 E6
Market Warsop Notts 45 F9
Market Weighton E Yorks 52 E4
Market Weston Suff 38 H5
Markethill Perth 76 D5
Markfield Leics 35 D10
Markham Caerph 15 A7
Markham Moor Notts 45 E11
Markinch Fife 76 G5
Markington N Yorks 51 C8
Marks Tey Essex 30 F6
Marksbury Bath 16 E3
Markyate Herts 29 G7
Marland Gtr Man 44 A2
Marlborough Wilts 17 E8
Marlbrook Hereford 26 C2
Marlbrook Worcs 26 A6
Marlcliff Warks 27 C7
Marldon Devon 5 E9
Marlesford Suff 31 C10
Marley Green Ches E 43 H8
Marley Hill T&W 63 H8
Marley Mount Hants 10 E1
Marlingford Norf 39 E7
Marloes Pembs 22 F2
Marlow Bucks 18 C5
Marlow Hereford 33 H10
Marlow Bottom Bucks 18 C5
Marlpit Hill Kent 19 G11
Marlpool Derbys 45 H8
Marnhull Dorset 9 C6
Marnoch Aberds 88 C5
Marnock N Lanark 68 D6
Marple Gtr Man 44 D3
Marple Bridge Gtr Man 44 D3
Marr S Yorks 45 B9
Marrel Highld 93 H13
Marrick N Yorks 58 G1
Marrister Shetland 96 G7
Marros Carms 23 F7
Marsden T&W 63 G9
Marsden W Yorks 44 A4
Marsett N Yorks 57 H11
Marsh Devon 8 C1
Marsh W Yorks 50 F6
Marsh Baldon Oxon 18 B2
Marsh Gibbon Bucks 28 F3
Marsh Green Devon 7 G9
Marsh Green Kent 12 B3
Marsh Green Staffs 44 G2
Marsh Lane Derbys 45 E8
Marsh Street Som 7 B8
Marshall's Heath Herts 29 G8
Marshalsea Dorset 8 D2
Marshalswick Herts 29 H8
Marsham Norf 39 C7
Marshaw Lancs 50 D1
Marshborough Kent 21 F10
Marshbrook Shrops 33 G10
Marshchapel Lincs 47 C7
Marshfield Newport 15 C8
Marshfield S Glos 16 D4
Marshgate Corn 4 B2
Marshland St James Norf 37 E11
Marshside Mers 49 H3
Marshwood Dorset 8 E2
Marske N Yorks 58 F2
Marske-by-the-Sea Redcar 59 D7
Marston Ches W 43 E9
Marston Hereford 25 C10
Marston Lincs 36 A4
Marston Oxon 28 H2
Marston Staffs 34 C5
Marston Staffs 34 D4
Marston Warks 35 F8
Marston Wilts 16 F6
Marston Doles Warks 27 C11
Marston Green W Mid 35 G7
Marston Magna Som 8 B4
Marston Meysey Wilts 17 B8
Marston Montgomery Derbys 35 B7
Marston Moretaine C Beds 28 D6
Marston on Dove Derbys 35 C8
Marston St Lawrence W Nhants 28 D2
Marston Stannett Hereford 26 C2
Marston Trussell W Nhants 36 G2
Marstow Hereford 26 G2
Marsworth Bucks 28 G6
Marten Wilts 17 F9
Marthall Ches E 44 E2
Martham Norf 39 D10
Martin Hants 9 C9
Martin Kent 21 G10
Martin Lincs 46 F5
Martin Lincs 46 G5
Martin Dales Lincs 46 F5
Martin Drove End Hants 9 B9
Martin Hussingtree Worcs 26 B5
Martin Mill Kent 21 G10
Martinhoe Devon 6 B5
Martinhoe Cross Devon 6 B5
Martinscroft Warr 43 D9
Martinstown Dorset 8 F5
Martlesham Suff 31 D9
Martlesham Heath Suff 31 D9
Martletwy Pembs 22 E5
Martley Worcs 26 C4
Martock Som 8 C3
Marton Ches E 44 F2
Marton E Yorks 53 F7
Marton Lincs 46 D2
Marton Mbro 58 E6
Marton N Yorks 51 C10
Marton N Yorks 52 A3
Marton Shrops 33 E8
Marton Shrops 33 C10
Marton Warks 27 B11
Marton-le-Moor N Yorks 51 B9
Martyr Worthy Hants 10 A4
Martyr's Green Sur 19 F7
Marwick Orkney 95 F3
Marwood Devon 6 C4
Mary Tavy Devon 4 D6
Marybank Highld 86 F7
Maryburgh Highld 87 F8
Maryhill Glasgow 68 D4
Marykirk Aberds 83 G8
Marylebone Gtr Man 43 B8
Marypark Moray 88 E1
Maryport Cumb 56 C2
Maryport Dumfries 54 F4
Maryton Angus 77 B9
Marywell Aberds 83 D7
Marywell Aberds 83 D11
Marywell Angus 77 C9
Masham N Yorks 51 A8
Mashbury Essex 30 G3
Masongill N Yorks 50 B2
Masonhill S Ayrs 67 D6
Mastin Moor Derbys 45 E8
Mastrick Aberdeen 83 C10
Matching Essex 30 G2
Matching Green Essex 30 G2
Matching Tye Essex 30 G2
Matfen Northumb 62 F6
Matfield Kent 12 B5
Mathern Mon 15 B11
Mathon Hereford 26 D4
Mathry Pembs 22 C3
Matlaske Norf 39 B7
Matlock Derbys 44 F6
Matlock Bath Derbys 44 G6
Matson Glos 26 G5
Matterdale End W&F 56 D5
Mattersey Notts 45 D10
Mattersey Thorpe Notts 45 D10
Mattingley Hants 18 F4
Mattishall Norf 39 D6
Mattishall Burgh Norf 39 D6
Mauchline E Ayrs 67 D7
Maud Aberds 89 D9
Maugersbury Glos 27 F9
Maughold IoM 48 C4
Mauld Highld 86 H7
Maulden C Beds 29 E7
Maulds Meaburn W&F 57 E8
Maunby N Yorks 58 H4
Maund Bryan Hereford 26 C2
Maundown Som 7 D9
Mautby Norf 39 D10
Mavis Enderby Lincs 47 F7
Maw Green Ches E 43 G10
Mawbray Cumb 56 B2
Mawdesley Lancs 43 A7
Mawdlam Bridgend 14 C4
Mawgan Corn 2 G6
Mawgan Porth Corn 3 C7
Mawla Corn 2 E6
Mawnan Corn 3 G6
Mawnan Smith Corn 3 G6
Mawsley N Nhants 36 H4
Maxey Pboro 37 E7
Maxstoke Warks 35 G8
Maxton Borders 70 G5
Maxton Kent 21 G10
Maxwellheugh Borders 70 G6
Maxwelltown Dumfries 60 F5
Maxworthy Corn 6 G1
May Bank Staffs 44 H2
Mayals Swansea 14 B2
Maybole S Ayrs 66 F6
Mayfield E Sus 12 D4
Mayfield Midloth 70 D2
Mayfield Staffs 44 H5
Mayfield W Loth 69 D8
Mayford Sur 18 F6
Mayland Essex 20 A6
Maynard's Green E Sus 12 E4
Maypole Mon 25 G11
Maypole Scilly 2 C3
Maypole Green Essex 30 F6
Maypole Green Norf 39 F10
Maypole Green Suff 31 B9
Maywick Shetland 96 L5
Meadle Bucks 28 H5
Meadowtown Shrops 33 E9
Meaford Staffs 34 B4
Meal Bank W&F 57 G7
Mealabost W Isles 91 D9
Mealabost Bhuirgh W Isles 91 B9
Mealsgate Cumb 56 B4
Meanwood W Yorks 51 F8
Mearbeck N Yorks 50 C4
Meare Som 15 G10
Meare Green Som 8 B2
Mears Ashby N Nhants 28 B5
Measham Leics 35 D9
Meath Green Sur 12 B1
Meathop W&F 49 A4
Meaux E Yorks 53 F6
Meavy Devon 4 E6
Medbourne Leics 36 F3
Medburn Northumb 63 F7
Meddon Devon 6 E1
Meden Vale Notts 45 F9
Medlam Lincs 47 G7
Medmenham Bucks 18 C5
Medomsley Durham 58 A2
Medstead Hants 18 H3
Meer End W Mid 27 A9
Meerbrook Staffs 44 F3
Meers Bridge Lincs 47 D8
Meesden Herts 29 E11
Meeth Devon 6 F4
Meggethead Borders 61 A7
Meidrim Carms 23 D7
Meifod Denb 42 G3
Meifod Powys 33 D7
Meigle N Ayrs 73 G10
Meigle Perth 76 C5
Meikle Earnock S Lanark 68 E6
Meikle Ferry Highld 87 C10
Meikle Forter Angus 76 A4
Meikle Gluich Highld 87 C9
Meikle Pinkerton E Loth 70 C6
Meikle Strath Aberds 83 F8
Meikle Tarty Aberds 89 F9
Meikle Wartle Aberds 89 E7
Meikleour Perth 76 D4
Meinciau Carms 23 E9
Meir Stoke 34 A5
Meir Heath Staffs 34 A5
Melbourn Cambs 29 D10
Melbourne Derbys 35 C9
Melbourne E Yorks 52 E3
Melbourne S Lanark 69 F9
Melbury Abbas Dorset 9 B7
Melbury Bubb Dorset 8 D4
Melbury Osmond Dorset 8 D4
Melbury Sampford Dorset 8 D4
Melby Shetland 96 H3
Melchbourne Bedford 29 B7
Melcombe Bingham Dorset 9 D6
Melcombe Regis Dorset 8 F5
Meldon Devon 6 G4
Meldon Northumb 63 E7
Meldreth Cambs 29 D10
Meldrum Ho. Aberds 89 F8
Melfort Argyll 73 B7
Melgarve Highld 81 D6
Meliden Denb 42 D3
Melin-y-coed Conwy 41 D10
Melin-y-ddôl Powys 33 E6
Melin-y-grug Powys 33 E6
Melin-y-Wig Denb 42 H3
Melinbyrhedyn Powys 32 F4
Melincourt Neath 14 A4
Melkinthorpe W&F 57 D7
Melkridge Northumb 62 G3
Melksham Wilts 16 E6
Melldalloch Argyll 73 F8
Melling Lancs 50 B1
Melling Mers 43 B6
Melling Mount Mers 43 B7
Mellis Suff 31 A8
Mellon Charles Highld 91 H13
Mellon Udrigle Highld 91 H13
Mellor Gtr Man 44 D3
Mellor Lancs 50 F2
Mellor Brook Lancs 50 F2
Mells Som 16 G4
Melmerby N Yorks 51 B9
Melmerby N Yorks 58 H1
Melmerby W&F 57 C8
Melplash Dorset 8 E3
Melrose Borders 70 G4
Melsetter Orkney 95 K3
Melsonby N Yorks 58 F2
Meltham W Yorks 44 A5
Melton Suff 31 C9
Melton Constable Norf 38 B6
Melton Mowbray Leics 36 D3
Melton Ross N Lincs 46 A4
Meltonby E Yorks 52 D3
Melvaig Highld 91 J12
Melverley Shrops 33 D9
Melverley Green Shrops 33 D9
Melvich Highld 93 C11
Membury Devon 8 D1
Memsie Aberds 89 B9
Memus Angus 77 B7
Menabilly Corn 4 F1
Menai Bridge = Porthaethwy Anglesey 41 C7
Mendham Suff 39 G8
Mendlesham Suff 31 B8
Mendlesham Green Suff 31 B7
Menheniot Corn 4 E3
Mennock Dumfries 60 C4
Menston W Yorks 51 E7
Menstrie Clack 75 H11
Menthorpe N Yorks 52 F2
Mentmore Bucks 28 G6
Meoble Highld 79 C10
Meole Brace Shrops 33 D10
Meols Mers 42 C5
Meonstoke Hants 10 C5
Meopham Kent 20 E3
Meopham Station Kent 20 E3
Mepal Cambs 37 G10
Meppershall C Beds 29 E8
Merbach Hereford 25 D10
Mere Ches E 43 D10
Mere Wilts 9 A7
Mere Brow Lancs 49 H4
Mere Grn. W Mid 35 F7
Mereclough Lancs 50 F4
Mereside Blackpool 49 F3
Mereworth Kent 20 F3
Mergie Aberds 83 E9
Meriden W Mid 35 G8
Merkadale Highld 85 E8
Merkland Dumfries 60 F3
Merkland S Ayrs 66 G5
Merkland Lodge Highld 92 G7
Merley BCP 9 E9
Merlin's Bridge Pembs 22 E4
Merrington Shrops 33 C10
Merrion Pembs 22 G4
Merriott Som 8 C3
Merrivale Devon 4 D6
Merrow Sur 19 F7
Merrymeet Corn 4 E3
Mersham Kent 13 C9
Merstham Sur 19 F9
Merston W Sus 11 D7
Merstone IoW 10 F4
Merther Corn 3 E7
Merthyr Carms 23 D8
Merthyr Cynog Powys 24 E6
Merthyr-Dyfan V Glam 15 E7
Merthyr Mawr Bridgend 14 D4
Merthyr Tudful = Merthyr Tydfil M Tydf 25 H7
Merthyr Tydfil = Merthyr Tudful M Tydf 25 H7
Merthyr Vale M Tydf 14 B6
Merton Devon 6 E4
Merton London 19 D9
Merton Norf 38 F5
Merton Oxon 28 G2
Mervinslaw Borders 62 B2
Meshaw Devon 7 E6
Messing Essex 30 G5
Messingham N Lincs 46 B2
Metfield Suff 39 G8
Metheringham Lincs 46 F4
Methil Fife 76 H6
Methlem Gwyn 40 G3
Methley W Yorks 51 G9
Methlick Aberds 89 E8
Methven Perth 76 E3
Methwold Norf 38 F3
Methwold Hythe Norf 38 F3
Mettingham Suff 39 G9
Mevagissey Corn 3 E9
Mewith Head N Yorks 50 C3
Mexborough S Yorks 45 B8
Mey Highld 94 C4
Meysey Hampton Glos 17 B8
Miabhag W Isles 90 G5
Miabhag W Isles 90 H6
Miabhig W Isles 90 D5
Michaelchurch Hereford 26 F2
Michaelchurch Escley Hereford 25 E10
Michaelchurch on Arrow Powys 25 C9
Michaelston-le-Pit V Glam 15 D7
Michaelston-y-Fedw Newport 15 C8
Michaelstow Corn 4 D1
Michealston-super-Ely Cardiff 15 D7
Micheldever Hants 18 H2
Michelmersh Hants 10 B2
Mickfield Suff 31 B8
Mickle Trafford Ches W 43 F7
Micklebring S Yorks 45 C9
Mickleby N Yorks 59 E9
Mickleham Sur 19 F8
Mickleover Derby 35 B9
Micklethwaite W Yorks 51 E7
Mickleton Durham 57 D11
Mickleton Glos 27 D8
Mickletown W Yorks 51 G9
Mickley N Yorks 51 B8
Mickley Square Northumb 62 G6
Mid Ardlaw Aberds 89 B9
Mid Auchinlech Invclyd 68 C2
Mid Beltie Aberds 83 C8
Mid Calder W Loth 69 D9
Mid Cloch Forbie Aberds 89 C7
Mid Clyth Highld 94 G4
Mid Lavant W Sus 11 D7
Mid Main Highld 86 G7
Mid Urchany Highld 87 G11
Mid Walls Shetland 96 H4
Mid Yell Shetland 96 D7
Midbea Orkney 95 D5
Middle Assendon Oxon 18 C4
Middle Aston Oxon 27 F11
Middle Barton Oxon 27 F11
Middle Cairncake Aberds 89 D8
Middle Claydon Bucks 28 F4
Middle Drums Angus 77 B8
Middle Handley Derbys 45 E8
Middle Littleton Worcs 27 D7
Middle Maes-coed Hereford 25 E10
Middle Mill Pembs 22 D3
Middle Rasen Lincs 46 D4
Middle Rigg Perth 76 G3
Middle Tysoe Warks 27 D10
Middle Wallop Hants 17 H9
Middle Winterslow Wilts 9 A11
Middle Woodford Wilts 17 H8
Middlebie Dumfries 61 F8
Middleforth Green Lancs 49 G5
Middleham N Yorks 58 H2
Middlehope Shrops 33 G10
Middlemarsh Dorset 8 D5
Middlemuir Aberds 89 F9
Middlesbrough Mbro 58 D5
Middleshaw Dumfries 61 F7
Middleshaw W&F 57 H7
Middlesmoor N Yorks 51 B6
Middlestone Durham 58 C3
Middlestone Moor Durham 58 C3
Middlestown W Yorks 51 H8
Middlethird Borders 70 F5
Middleton Aberds 83 B10
Middleton Argyll 78 G2
Middleton Cumb 57 H8
Middleton Derbys 44 F5
Middleton Derbys 44 G6
Middleton Essex 30 E5
Middleton Gtr Man 44 B2
Middleton Hants 17 G11
Middleton Hereford 26 B2
Middleton Lancs 49 D4
Middleton Midloth 70 E2
Middleton N Nhants 36 G4
Middleton N Yorks 51 E7
Middleton N Yorks 59 H8
Middleton Norf 38 D2
Middleton Northumb 62 E6
Middleton Northumb 71 G10
Middleton Perth 76 F4
Middleton Perth 76 C4
Middleton Shrops 33 C9
Middleton Shrops 33 F8
Middleton Shrops 33 H11
Middleton Suff 31 B11
Middleton Swansea 23 H9
Middleton W Yorks 51 G8
Middleton W&F 57 H8
Middleton Warks 35 F7
Middleton Cheney W Nhants 27 D11
Middleton Green Staffs 34 B5
Middleton Hall Northumb 71 H8
Middleton-in-Teesdale Durham 57 D11
Middleton Moor Suff 31 B11
Middleton-on-Leven N Yorks 58 F5
Middleton-on-Sea W Sus 11 D8
Middleton on the Hill Hereford 26 B2
Middleton-on-the-Wolds E Yorks 52 E5
Middleton One Row Darl 58 E4
Middleton Priors Shrops 34 F2
Middleton Quernham N Yorks 51 B9
Middleton St George Darl 58 E4
Middleton Scriven Shrops 34 G2
Middleton Stoney Oxon 28 F2
Middleton Tyas N Yorks 58 F3
Middletown Cumb 56 F1
Middletown Powys 33 D9
Middlewich Ches E 43 F9
Middlewood Green Suff 31 B7
Middlezoy Som 8 A2
Middridge Durham 58 D3
Midfield Highld 93 C8
Midge Hall Lancs 49 G5
Midgeholme Cumb 62 H2
Midgham W Berks 18 E2
Midgley W Yorks 44 A6
Midgley W Yorks 50 G6
Midhopestones S Yorks 44 C6
Midhurst W Sus 11 B7
Midlem Borders 70 H4
Midmar Aberds 83 C8
Midsomer Norton Bath 16 F3
Midton Invclyd 73 F11
Midtown Highld 91 J13
Midtown Highld 93 C9
Midtown of Buchromb Moray 88 D3
Midville Lincs 47 G7
Midway Ches E 44 D3
Migdale Highld 87 B9
Migvie Aberds 82 C6
Milarrochy Stirling 68 A3
Milborne Port Som 8 C5
Milborne St Andrew Dorset 9 E7
Milborne Wick Som 8 B5
Milbourne Northumb 63 F7
Milburn W&F 57 D8
Milbury Heath S Glos 16 B3
Milcombe Oxon 27 E11
Milden Suff 30 D6
Mildenhall Suff 30 A4
Mildenhall Wilts 17 E9
Mile Cross Norf 39 D8
Mile Elm Wilts 16 E6
Mile End Essex 30 F6
Mile End Glos 26 G2
Mile Oak Brighton 11 D11
Milebrook Powys 25 A10
Milebush Kent 20 G4
Mileham Norf 38 D5
Milesmark Fife 69 B9
Milfield Northumb 71 G8
Milford Derbys 45 H7
Milford Devon 6 D1
Milford Powys 33 F6
Milford Staffs 34 C5
Milford Sur 18 G6
Milford Wilts 9 B10
Milford Haven = Aberdaugleddau Pembs 22 F4
Milford on Sea Hants 10 E1
Milkwall Glos 26 H2
Milkwell Wilts 9 B8
Mill Bank W Yorks 50 G6
Mill Common Suff 39 G10
Mill End Bucks 18 C4
Mill End Herts 29 E10
Mill Green Essex 20 A3
Mill Green Norf 39 G7
Mill Green Suff 30 D6
Mill Hill London 19 B9
Mill Lane Hants 18 F4
Mill of Kingoodie Aberds 89 F8
Mill of Muiresk Aberds 89 D6
Mill of Sterin Aberds 82 D5
Mill of Uras Aberds 83 E10
Mill Place N Lincs 46 B3
Mill Side W&F 49 A4
Mill Street Norf 39 D6
Milland W Sus 11 B7
Millarston Renfs 68 D3
Millbank Aberds 89 D11
Millbank Highld 94 D3
Millbeck Cumb 56 D4
Millbounds Orkney 95 E6
Millbreck Aberds 89 D10
Millbridge Sur 18 G5
Millbrook C Beds 29 E7
Millbrook Corn 4 F5
Millbrook Soton 10 C2
Millburn S Ayrs 67 D7
Millcombe Devon 5 G9
Millcorner E Sus 13 D7
Milldale Staffs 44 G5
Millden Lodge Angus 83 F7
Milldens Angus 77 B8
Millerhill Midloth 70 D2
Miller's Dale Derbys 44 E5
Miller's Green Derbys 44 G6
Millgreen Shrops 34 C2
Millhalf Hereford 25 D9
Millhayes Devon 7 F11
Millhead Lancs 49 B4
Millheugh S Lanark 68 E6
Millholme W&F 57 G7
Millhouse Argyll 73 F8
Millhouse W&F 56 C5
Millhouse Green S Yorks 44 B6
Millhousebridge Dumfries 61 E7
Millhouses S Yorks 45 D7
Millikenpark Renfs 68 D3
Millin Cross Pembs 22 E4
Millington E Yorks 52 D4
Millmeece Staffs 34 B4
Millom Cumb 49 A1
Millook Corn 4 B2
Millpool Corn 4 D2
Millport N Ayrs 66 A4
Millquarter Dumfries 55 A9
Millthrop W&F 57 G8
Milltimber Aberdeen 83 C10
Milltown Corn 4 F2
Milltown Derbys 45 F7
Milltown Devon 6 C4
Milltown Dumfries 61 F9
Milltown of Aberdalgie Perth 76 E3
Milltown of Auchindoun Moray 88 D3
Milltown of Craigston Aberds 89 C7
Milltown of Edinvillie Moray 88 D2
Milltown of Kildrummy Aberds 82 B6
Milltown of Rothiemay Moray 88 D5
Milltown of Towie Aberds 82 B6
Milnathort Perth 76 G4
Milner's Heath Ches W 43 F7
Milngavie E Dunb 68 C4
Milnrow Gtr Man 44 A3
Milnshaw Lancs 50 G3
Milnthorpe W&F 49 A4
Milo Carms 23 E10
Milson Shrops 26 A3
Milstead Kent 20 F6
Milston Wilts 17 G8
Milton Angus 76 C6
Milton Cambs 29 B11
Milton Cumb 61 G11
Milton Derbys 35 C9
Milton Dumfries 54 D5
Milton Dumfries 60 E4
Milton Dumfries 60 F4
Milton Highld 86 F6
Milton Highld 86 H7
Milton Highld 87 D10
Milton Highld 87 G8
Milton Highld 94 E5
Milton Moray 88 B5
Milton N Som 15 E9
Milton Notts 45 E11
Milton Oxon 17 B11
Milton Oxon 27 E11
Milton Pembs 22 F5
Milton Perth 76 F2
Milton Ptsmth 10 E5
Milton Stirling 75 G8
Milton Stoke 44 G3
Milton Abbas Dorset 9 D7
Milton Abbot Devon 4 D5
Milton Bridge Midloth 69 D11
Milton Bryan C Beds 28 E6
Milton Clevedon Som 16 H3
Milton Coldwells Aberds 89 E9
Milton Combe Devon 4 E5
Milton Damerel Devon 6 E2
Milton End Glos 17 A8
Milton Ernest Bedford 29 C7
Milton Green Ches W 43 G7
Milton Hill Oxon 17 B11
Milton Keynes M Keynes 28 E5
Milton Keynes Village M Keynes 28 E5
Milton Lilbourne Wilts 17 E8
Milton Malsor W Nhants 28 C4
Milton Morenish Perth 75 D9
Milton of Auchinhove Aberds 83 C7
Milton of Balgonie Fife 76 G6
Milton of Buchanan Stirling 68 A3
Milton of Campfield Aberds 83 C8
Milton of Campsie E Dunb 68 C5
Milton of Corsindae Aberds 83 C8
Milton of Cushnie Aberds 83 B7
Milton of Dalcapon Perth 76 B2
Milton of Edradour Perth 76 B2
Milton of Gollanfield Highld 87 F10
Milton of Lesmore Aberds 82 A6
Milton of Logie Aberds 82 C6
Milton of Murtle Aberdeen 83 C10
Milton of Noth Aberds 83 A7
Milton of Tullich Aberds 82 D5
Milton on Stour Dorset 9 B6
Milton Regis Kent 20 E6
Milton under Wychwood Oxon 27 G9
Miltonduff Moray 88 B1
Miltonhill Moray 87 E13
Miltonise Dumfries 54 B4
Milverton Som 7 D10
Milverton Warks 27 B10
Milwich Staffs 34 B5
Minard Argyll 73 D8
Minchinhampton Glos 16 A5
Mindrum Northumb 71 G7
Minehead Som 7 B8
Minera Wrex 42 G5
Minety Wilts 17 B7
Minffordd Gwyn 32 D3
Minffordd Gwyn 41 C7
Minffordd Gwyn 41 G7
Miningsby Lincs 47 F7
Minions Corn 4 D3
Minishant S Ayrs 66 E6
Minllyn Gwyn 32 D4
Minnes Aberds 89 F9
Minngearraidh W Isles 84 F2
Minnigaff Dumfries 55 C7
Minnonie Aberds 89 B7
Minskip N Yorks 51 C9
Minstead Hants 10 C1
Minsted W Sus 11 B7
Minster Kent 20 D6
Minster Kent 21 E10
Minster Lovell Oxon 27 G10
Minsterley Shrops 33 E9
Minsterworth Glos 26 G4
Minterne Magna Dorset 8 D5
Minting Lincs 46 E5
Mintlaw Aberds 89 D10
Minto Borders 61 A11
Minton Shrops 33 F10
Minwear Pembs 22 E5
Minworth W Mid 35 F7
Mirbister Orkney 95 F4
Mirehouse Cumb 56 E1
Mireland Highld 94 D5
Mirfield W Yorks 51 H8
Miserden Glos 26 H6
Miskin Rhondda 14 C6
Misson Notts 45 C10
Misterton Leics 36 G1
Misterton Notts 45 C11
Misterton Som 8 D3
Mistley Essex 31 E8
Mitcham London 19 E9
Mitchel Troy Mon 25 G11
Mitcheldean Glos 26 G3
Mitchell Corn 3 D7
Mitcheltroy Common Mon 25 H11
Mitford Northumb 63 E7
Mithian Corn 2 D6
Mitton Staffs 34 D4
Mixbury Oxon 28 E3
Moar Orkney 95 H4
Moat Cumb 61 F10
Moats Tye Suff 31 C7
Mobberley Ches E 43 E10
Mobberley Staffs 34 A6
Moccas Hereford 25 D10
Mochdre Conwy 41 C10
Mochdre Powys 33 G6
Mochrum Dumfries 54 E6
Mockbeggar Hants 9 D10
Mockerkin Cumb 56 D2
Modbury Devon 5 F7
Moddershall Staffs 34 B5
Moelfre Anglesey 41 B7
Moelfre Powys 33 C7
Moffat Dumfries 60 C6
Moggerhanger C Beds 29 D8
Moira Leics 35 D9
Mol-chlach Highld 85 G9
Molash Kent 21 F7
Mold = Yr Wyddgrug Flint 42 F5
Moldgreen W Yorks 51 H7

Molehill Green Essex 30 F2
Molescroft E Yorks 52 E6
Molesden Northumb 63 E7
Molesworth Cambs 37 H6
Moll Highld 85 E10
Molland Devon 7 D7
Mollington Ches W 43 E6
Mollington Oxon 27 D11
Mollinsburn N Lanark 68 C6
Monachty Ceredig 24 B2
Monachylemore Stirling 75 F7
Monar Lodge Highld 86 G5
Monaughty Powys 25 B9
Monboddo House Aberds 83 F9
Mondynes Aberds 83 F9
Monevechadan Argyll 74 G4
Monewden Suff 31 C9
Moneydie Perth 76 E3
Moniaive Dumfries 60 D3
Monifieth Angus 77 D7
Monikie Angus 77 D7
Monimail Fife 76 F5
Monington Pembs 22 B6
Monk Bretton S Yorks 45 B7
Monk Fryston N Yorks 51 G11
Monk Sherborne Hants 18 F3
Monk Soham Suff 31 B9
Monk Street Essex 30 F3
Monken Hadley London 19 B9
Monkhopton Shrops 34 F2
Monkland Hereford 25 C11
Monkleigh Devon 6 D3
Monknash V Glam 14 D5
Monkokehampton Devon 6 F4
Monks Eleigh Suff 30 D6
Monk's Gate W Sus 11 B11
Monks Heath Ches E 44 E2
Monks Kirby Warks 35 G10
Monks Risborough Bucks 18 A5
Monkseaton T&W 63 F9
Monkshill Aberds 89 D7
Monksilver Som 7 C9
Monkspath W Mid 35 H7
Monkswood Mon 15 A9
Monkton Devon 7 F10
Monkton Kent 21 E9
Monkton Pembs 22 F4
Monkton S Ayrs 67 D6
Monkton Combe Bath 16 E4
Monkton Deverill Wilts 16 H5
Monkton Farleigh Wilts 16 E5
Monkton Heathfield Som 8 B1
Monkton Up Wimborne Dorset 9 C9
Monkwearmouth T&W 63 H9
Monkwood Hants 10 A5
Monmouth = Trefynwy Mon 26 G2
Monmouth Cap Mon 25 F10
Monnington on Wye Hereford 25 D10
Monreith Dumfries 54 E6
Monreith Mains Dumfries 54 E6
Mont Saint Guern 11
Montacute Som 8 C3
Montcoffer Ho. Aberds 89 B6
Montford Argyll 73 G10
Montford Shrops 33 D10
Montford Bridge Shrops 33 D10
Montgarrie Aberds 83 B7
Montgomery = Trefaldwyn Powys 33 F8
Montrave Fife 76 G6
Montrose Angus 77 B10
Montsale Essex 21 B7
Monxton Hants 17 G10
Monyash Derbys 44 F5
Monymusk Aberds 83 B8
Monzie Perth 75 E11
Monzie Castle Perth 75 E11
Moodiesburn N Lanark 68 C5
Moonzie Fife 76 F6
Moor Allerton W Yorks 51 F8
Moor Crichel Dorset 9 D8
Moor End E Yorks 52 F4
Moor End York 52 D2
Moor Monkton N Yorks 51 D11
Moor of Granary Moray 87 F13
Moor of Ravenstone Dumfries 54 E6
Moor Row Cumb 56 E2
Moor Street Kent 20 E5
Moorby Lincs 46 F6
Moordown BCP 9 E9
Moore Halton 43 D8
Moorend Glos 16 A4
Moorends S Yorks 52 H2
Moorgate S Yorks 45 C8
Moorgreen Notts 45 H8
Moorhall Derbys 45 E7
Moorhampton Hereford 25 D10
Moorhead W Yorks 51 F7
Moorhouse Cumb 61 H9
Moorhouse Notts 45 F11
Moorlinch Som 15 H9
Moorsholm Redcar 59 E7
Moorside Gtr Man 44 B3
Moorthorpe W Yorks 45 A8
Moortown Hants 9 D10
Moortown IoW 10 F3
Moortown Lincs 46 C4
Morangie Highld 87 C10
Morar Highld 79 B9
Morborne Cambs 37 F7
Morchard Bishop Devon 7 F6
Morcombelake Dorset 8 E3
Morcott Rutland 36 E5
Morda Shrops 33 C8
Morden Dorset 9 E8
Morden London 19 E9
Mordiford Hereford 26 E2
Mordon Durham 58 D4
More Shrops 33 F9
Morebath Devon 7 D8
Morebattle Borders 62 A3
Morecambe Lancs 49 C4
Morefield Highld 86 B4
Moreleigh Devon 5 F8
Morenish Perth 75 D8
Moresby Cumb 56 D1
Moresby Parks Cumb 56 E1
Morestead Hants 10 B4
Moreton Dorset 9 F7
Moreton Essex 30 H2
Moreton Mers 42 C5
Moreton Oxon 18 A3
Moreton Staffs 34 D3
Moreton Corbet Shrops 34 C1
Moreton-in-Marsh Glos 27 E9
Moreton Jeffries Hereford 26 D3
Moreton Morrell Warks 27 C10
Moreton on Lugg Hereford 26 D2
Moreton Pinkney W Nhants 28 D2
Moreton Say Shrops 34 B2
Moreton Valence Glos 26 H4
Moretonhampstead Devon 5 C8
Morfa Carms 23 E10
Morfa Carms 23 G10
Morfa Bach Carms 23 E8
Morfa Bychan Gwyn 41 G7
Morfa Dinlle Gwyn 40 E6
Morfa Glas Neath 24 H5
Morfa Nefyn Gwyn 40 F4
Morfydd Denb 42 H4
Morgan's Vale Wilts 9 B10
Moriah Ceredig 32 H2
Morland W&F 57 D7
Morley Derbys 35 A9
Morley Durham 58 D2
Morley W Yorks 51 G8
Morley Green Ches E 44 D2
Morley St Botolph Norf 39 F6
Morningside Edin 69 C11
Morningside N Lanark 69 E7
Morningthorpe Norf 39 F8
Morpeth Northumb 63 E8
Morphie Aberds 77 A10
Morrey Staffs 35 D7
Morris Green Essex 30 E4
Morriston Swansea 14 B2
Morston Norf 38 A6
Mortehoe Devon 6 B3
Mortimer W Berks 18 E3
Mortimer West End Hants 18 E3
Mortimer's Cross Hereford 25 B11
Mortlake London 19 D9
Morton Cumb 56 A5
Morton Derbys 45 F8
Morton Lincs 37 C6
Morton Lincs 46 C2
Morton Lincs 46 F2
Morton Norf 39 D7
Morton Notts 45 G11
Morton S Glos 16 B3
Morton Shrops 33 C8
Morton Bagot Warks 27 B8
Morton-on-Swale N Yorks 58 G4
Morvah Corn 2 F3
Morval Corn 4 F3
Morvich Highld 80 A1
Morvich Highld 93 J10
Morville Shrops 34 F2
Morville Heath Shrops 34 F2
Morwenstow Corn 6 E1
Mosborough S Yorks 45 D8
Moscow E Ayrs 67 B7
Mosedale W&F 56 C5
Moseley W Mid 34 F5
Moseley W Mid 35 G6
Moseley Worcs 26 C5
Moss Argyll 78 G2
Moss Highld 79 E9
Moss S Yorks 45 A9
Moss Wrex 42 G6
Moss Bank Mers 43 C8
Moss Edge Lancs 49 E4
Moss End Brack 18 D5
Moss of Barmuckity Moray 88 B2
Moss Pit Staffs 34 C5
Moss-side Highld 87 F11
Moss Side Lancs 49 F3
Mossat Aberds 82 B6
Mossbank Shetland 96 F6
Mossbay Cumb 56 D1
Mossblown S Ayrs 67 D7
Mossbrow Gtr Man 43 D10
Mossburnford Borders 62 B2
Mossdale Dumfries 55 B9
Mossend N Lanark 68 D6
Mosser Cumb 56 D3
Mossfield Highld 87 D9
Mossgiel E Ayrs 67 D7
Mosside Angus 77 B7
Mossley Ches E 44 F2
Mossley Gtr Man 44 B3
Mossley Hill Mers 43 D6
Mosstodloch Moray 88 C3
Mosston Angus 77 C8
Mossy Lea Lancs 43 A8
Mosterton Dorset 8 D3
Moston Gtr Man 44 B2
Moston Shrops 34 C1
Moston Green Ches E 43 F10
Mostyn Flint 42 D4
Mostyn Quay Flint 42 D4
Motcombe Dorset 9 B7
Mothecombe Devon 5 G7
Motherby W&F 56 D6
Motherwell N Lanark 68 E6
Mottingham London 19 D11
Mottisfont Hants 10 B2
Mottistone IoW 10 F3
Mottram in Longdendale Gtr Man 44 C3
Mottram St Andrew Ches E 44 E2
Mouilpied Guern 11
Mouldsworth Ches W 43 E8
Moulin Perth 76 B2
Moulsecoomb Brighton 12 F2
Moulsford Oxon 18 C2
Moulsoe M Keynes 28 D6
Moulton Ches W 43 F9
Moulton Lincs 37 C9
Moulton N Yorks 58 F3
Moulton Suff 30 B3
Moulton V Glam 14 D6
Moulton W Nhants 28 B4
Moulton Chapel Lincs 37 D8
Moulton Eaugate Lincs 37 D9
Moulton St Mary Norf 39 E9
Moulton Seas End Lincs 37 C9
Mounie Castle Aberds 83 A9
Mount Corn 3 D6
Mount Corn 4 E2
Mount Highld 87 G12
Mount Bures Essex 30 E6
Mount Canisp Highld 87 D10
Mount Hawke Corn 2 E6
Mount Pleasant Ches E 44 G2
Mount Pleasant Derbys 35 D8
Mount Pleasant Derbys 45 H7
Mount Pleasant Flint 42 E5
Mount Pleasant Hants 10 E1
Mount Pleasant W Yorks 51 G8
Mount Sorrel Wilts 9 B9
Mount Tabor W Yorks 51 G6
Mountain W Yorks 51 F6
Mountain Ash = Aberpennar Rhondda 14 B6
Mountain Cross Borders 69 F10
Mountain Water Pembs 22 D4
Mountbenger Borders 70 H2
Mountfield E Sus 12 D6
Mountgerald Highld 87 E8
Mountjoy Corn 3 C7
Mountnessing Essex 20 B3
Mounton Mon 15 B11
Mountsorrel Leics 36 D1
Mousehole Corn 2 G3
Mousen Northumb 71 G10
Mouswald Dumfries 60 F6
Mow Cop Ches E 44 G2
Mowhaugh Borders 62 A4
Mowsley Leics 36 G2
Moxley W Mid 34 F5
Moy Highld 80 E6
Moy Highld 87 H10
Moy Hall Highld 87 H10
Moy Ho. Moray 87 E13
Moy Lodge Highld 80 E6
Moyles Court Hants 9 D10
Moylgrove Pembs 22 B6
Muasdale Argyll 65 D7
Much Birch Hereford 26 E2
Much Cowarne Hereford 26 D3
Much Dewchurch Hereford 25 E11
Much Hadham Herts 29 G11
Much Hoole Lancs 49 G4
Much Marcle Hereford 26 E3
Much Wenlock Shrops 34 E2
Muchalls Aberds 83 D11
Muchelney Som 8 B3
Muchlarnick Corn 4 F3
Muchrachd Highld 86 H5
Muckernich Highld 87 F8
Mucking Thurrock 20 C3
Muckleford Dorset 8 E5
Mucklestone Staffs 34 B3
Muckleton Shrops 34 C1
Muckletown Aberds 83 A7
Muckley Corner Staffs 35 E6
Muckton Lincs 47 D7
Mudale Highld 93 F8
Mudeford BCP 9 E10
Mudeford Dorset 9 E10
Mudford Som 8 C4
Mudgley Som 15 G10
Mugdock Stirling 68 C4
Mugeary Highld 85 E9
Mugginton Derbys 35 A8
Muggleswick Durham 58 B1
Muie Highld 93 J9
Muir Aberds 82 E2
Muir of Fairburn Highld 86 F7
Muir of Fowlis Aberds 83 B7
Muir of Ord Highld 87 F8
Muir of Pert Angus 77 D7
Muirden Aberds 89 C7
Muirdrum Angus 77 D8
Muirhead Angus 76 D6
Muirhead Fife 76 G5
Muirhead N Lanark 68 D5
Muirhead S Ayrs 66 C6
Muirhouselaw Borders 70 H5
Muirhouses Falk 69 B9
Muirkirk E Ayrs 68 H5
Muirmill Stirling 68 B6
Muirshearlich Highld 80 E3
Muirskie Aberds 83 D10
Muirtack Aberds 89 E9
Muirton Highld 87 E10
Muirton Perth 76 E4
Muirton Perth 76 F2
Muirton Mains Highld 86 F7
Muirton of Ardblair Perth 76 C4
Muirton of Ballochy Angus 77 A9
Muiryfold Aberds 89 C7
Muker N Yorks 57 G11
Mulbarton Norf 39 E7
Mulben Moray 88 C3
Mulindry Argyll 64 C4
Mullardoch House Highld 86 H5
Mullion Corn 2 H5
Mullion Cove Corn 2 H5
Mumby Lincs 47 E9
Munderfield Row Hereford 26 C3
Munderfield Stocks Hereford 26 C3
Mundesley Norf 39 B9
Mundford Norf 38 F4
Mundham Norf 39 F9
Mundon Essex 20 A5
Mundurno Aberdeen 83 B11
Munerigie Highld 80 C4
Muness Shetland 96 C8
Mungasdale Highld 86 B2
Mungrisdale W&F 56 C5
Munlochy Highld 87 F9
Munsley Hereford 26 D3
Munslow Shrops 33 G11
Murchington Devon 5 C7
Murcott Oxon 28 G2
Murkle Highld 94 D3
Murlaggan Highld 80 D2
Murlaggan Highld 80 E5
Murra Orkney 95 H3
Murrayfield Edin 69 C11
Murrow Cambs 37 E9
Mursley Bucks 28 F5
Murthill Angus 77 B7
Murthly Perth 76 D3
Murton Durham 58 B4
Murton Northumb 71 F8
Murton W&F 57 D9
Murton York 52 D2
Musbury Devon 8 E1
Muscoates N Yorks 52 A2
Musdale Argyll 74 E2
Musselburgh E Loth 70 C2
Muston Leics 36 B4
Muston N Yorks 53 B6
Mustow Green Worcs 26 A5
Mutehill Dumfries 55 E9
Mutford Suff 39 G10
Muthill Perth 75 F11
Mutterton Devon 7 F9
Muxton Telford 34 D3
Mybster Highld 94 E3
Myddfai Carms 24 F4
Myddle Shrops 33 C10
Mydroilyn Ceredig 23 A9
Myerscough Lancs 49 F4
Mylor Bridge Corn 3 F7
Mynachlog-ddu Pembs 22 C6
Myndtown Shrops 33 G9
Mynydd Bach Ceredig 32 H3
Mynydd-bach Mon 15 B10
Mynydd Bodafon Anglesey 40 B6
Mynydd Isa Flint 42 F5
Mynyddygarreg Carms 23 F9
Mynytho Gwyn 40 G5
Myrebird Aberds 83 D9
Myrelandhorn Highld 94 E4
Myreside Perth 76 E5
Myrtle Hill Carms 24 E4
Mytchett Sur 18 F5
Mytholm W Yorks 50 G5
Mytholmroyd W Yorks 50 G6
Myton-on-Swale N Yorks 51 C10
Mytton Shrops 33 D10

N

Na Gearrannan W Isles 90 C6
Naast Highld 91 J13
Naburn York 52 E1
Nackington Kent 21 F8
Nacton Suff 31 D9
Nafferton E Yorks 53 D6
Nailbridge Glos 26 G3
Nailsbourne Som 7 D11
Nailsea N Som 15 D10
Nailstone Leics 35 E10
Nailsworth Glos 16 B5
Nairn Highld 87 F11
Nalderswood Sur 19 G9
Nancegollan Corn 2 F5
Nancledra Corn 2 F3
Nanhoron Gwyn 40 G4
Nannau Gwyn 32 C3
Nannerch Flint 42 F4
Nanpantan Leics 35 D11
Nanpean Corn 3 D8
Nansledan Corn 3 C7
Nanstallon Corn 3 C9
Nant-ddu Powys 25 G7
Nant-glas Powys 24 B6
Nant Peris Gwyn 41 E8
Nant Uchaf Denb 42 G3
Nant-y-Bai Carms 24 D4
Nant-y-cafn Neath 24 H5
Nant-y-derry Mon 25 H10
Nant-y-ffin Carms 23 C10
Nant-y-moel Bridgend 14 B5
Nant-y-pandy Conwy 41 C8
Nanternis Ceredig 23 A8
Nantgaredig Carms 23 D9
Nantgarw Rhondda 15 C7
Nantglyn Denb 42 F3
Nantgwyn Powys 32 H5
Nantlle Gwyn 41 E7
Nantmawr Shrops 33 C8
Nantmel Powys 25 B7
Nantmor Gwyn 41 F8
Nantwich Ches E 43 G9
Nantycaws Carms 23 E9
Nantyffyllon Bridgend 14 B4
Nantyglo Bl Gwent 25 G8
Naphill Bucks 18 B5
Nappa N Yorks 50 D4
Napton on the Hill Warks 27 B11
Narberth = Arberth Pembs 22 E6
Narborough Leics 35 F11
Narborough Norf 38 D3
Nasareth Gwyn 40 E6
Naseby W Nhants 36 H2
Nash Bucks 28 E4
Nash Hereford 25 B10
Nash Newport 15 C9
Nash Shrops 26 A3
Nash Lee Bucks 28 H5
Nassington N Nhants 37 F6
Nasty Herts 29 F10
Nateby Lancs 49 E4
Nateby W&F 57 F9
Natland W&F 57 H7
Naughton Suff 31 D7
Naunton Glos 27 F8
Naunton Worcs 26 E5
Naunton Beauchamp Worcs 26 C6
Navenby Lincs 46 G3
Navestock Heath Essex 20 B2
Navestock Side Essex 20 B2
Navidale Highld 93 H13
Nawton N Yorks 52 A2
Nayland Suff 30 E6
Nazeing Essex 29 H11
Neacroft Hants 9 E10
Neal's Green Warks 35 G9
Neap Shetland 96 H7
Near Sawrey W&F 56 G5
Neasham Darl 58 E4
Neath = Castell-Nedd Neath 14 B3
Neath Abbey Neath 14 B3
Neatishead Norf 39 C9
Nebo Anglesey 40 A6
Nebo Ceredig 24 B2
Nebo Conwy 41 E10
Nebo Gwyn 40 E6
Necton Norf 38 E4
Nedd Highld 92 F4
Nedderton Northumb 63 E8
Nedging Tye Suff 31 D7
Needham Norf 39 G8
Needham Market Suff 31 C7
Needingworth Cambs 29 A10
Needwood Staffs 35 C7
Neen Savage Shrops 34 H2
Neen Sollars Shrops 26 A3
Neenton Shrops 34 G2
Nefyn Gwyn 40 F5
Neilston E Renf 68 E3
Neinthirion Powys 32 E5
Neithrop Oxon 27 D11
Nelly Andrews Green Powys 33 E8
Nelson Caerph 15 B7
Nelson Lancs 50 F4
Nelson Village Northumb 63 F8
Nemphlar S Lanark 69 F7
Nempnett Thrubwell N Som 15 E11
Nene Terrace Lincs 37 E8
Nenthall W&F 57 B9
Nenthead W&F 57 B9
Nenthorn Borders 70 G5
Nerabus Argyll 64 C3
Nercwys Flint 42 F5
Nerston S Lanark 68 E5
Nesbit Northumb 71 G8
Ness Ches W 42 E6
Nesscliffe Shrops 33 D9
Neston Ches W 42 E5
Neston Wilts 16 E5
Nether Alderley Ches E 44 E2
Nether Blainslie Borders 70 F4
Nether Booth Derbys 44 D5
Nether Broughton Leics 36 C2
Nether Burrow Lancs 50 B2
Nether Cerne Dorset 8 E5
Nether Compton Dorset 8 C4
Nether Crimond Aberds 89 F8
Nether Dalgliesh Borders 61 C8
Nether Dallachy Moray 88 B3
Nether Exe Devon 7 F8
Nether Glasslaw Aberds 89 C8
Nether Handwick Angus 76 C6
Nether Haugh S Yorks 45 C8
Nether Heage Derbys 45 G7
Nether Heyford W Nhants 28 C3
Nether Hindhope Borders 62 B3
Nether Howecleuch S Lanark 60 B6
Nether Kellet Lancs 49 C5
Nether Kinmundy Aberds 89 D10
Nether Langwith Notts 45 E9
Nether Leask Aberds 89 E10
Nether Lenshie Aberds 89 D6
Nether Monynut Borders 70 D6
Nether Padley Derbys 44 E6
Nether Park Aberds 89 C10
Nether Poppleton York 52 D1
Nether Silton N Yorks 58 G5
Nether Stowey Som 7 C10
Nether Urquhart Fife 76 G4
Nether Wallop Hants 17 H10
Nether Wasdale Cumb 56 F3
Nether Whitacre Warks 35 F8
Nether Worton Oxon 27 E11
Netheravon Wilts 17 G8
Netherbrae Aberds 89 C7
Netherbrough Orkney 95 G4
Netherburn S Lanark 69 F7
Netherbury Dorset 8 E3
Netherby Cumb 61 F9
Netherby N Yorks 51 E9
Nethercote Warks 28 B2
Nethercott Devon 6 C3
Netherend Glos 16 A2
Netherfield E Sus 12 E6
Netherhampton Wilts 9 B10
Netherlaw Dumfries 55 E10
Netherley Aberds 83 D10
Netherley Mers 43 D7
Nethermill Dumfries 60 E6
Nethermuir Aberds 89 D9
Netherplace E Renf 68 E4
Netherseal Derbys 35 D8
Netherthird E Ayrs 67 E8
Netherthong W Yorks 44 B5
Netherthorpe S Yorks 45 D9
Netherton Angus 77 B8
Netherton Devon 5 D9
Netherton Hants 17 F10
Netherton Mers 42 B6
Netherton Northumb 62 C5
Netherton Oxon 17 B11
Netherton Perth 76 B4
Netherton Stirling 68 C4
Netherton W Mid 34 G5
Netherton W Yorks 44 A5
Netherton W Yorks 51 H8
Netherton Worcs 26 D6
Nethertown Cumb 56 F1
Nethertown Highld 94 C5
Netherwitton Northumb 63 D7
Netherwood E Ayrs 68 H5
Nethy Bridge Highld 82 A2
Netley Hants 10 D3
Netley Marsh Hants 10 C2
Netteswell Essex 29 G11
Nettlebed Oxon 18 C4
Nettlebridge Som 16 G3
Nettlecombe Dorset 8 E4
Nettleden Herts 29 G7
Nettleham Lincs 46 E4
Nettlestead Kent 20 F3
Nettlestead Green Kent 20 F3
Nettlestone IoW 10 E5
Nettlesworth Durham 58 B3
Nettleton Lincs 46 B5
Nettleton Wilts 16 D5
Neuadd Carms 24 F3
Nevendon Essex 20 B4
Nevern Pembs 22 B5
New Abbey Dumfries 60 G5
New Aberdour Aberds 89 B8
New Addington London 19 E10
New Alresford Hants 10 A4
New Alyth Perth 76 C5
New Arley Warks 35 G8
New Ash Green Kent 20 E3
New Barn Kent 20 E3
New Barnetby N Lincs 46 A4
New Barton N Nhants 28 B5
New Bewick Northumb 62 A6
Newbigging Angus 76 C5
New Bilton Warks 35 H10
New Bolingbroke Lincs 47 G7
New Boultham Lincs 46 E3
New Bradwell M Keynes 28 D5
New Brancepeth Durham 58 B3
New Bridge Wrex 33 A8
New Brighton Flint 42 F5
New Brighton Mers 42 C6
New Brinsley Notts 45 G8
New Broughton Wrex 42 G6
New Buckenham Norf 39 F6
New Byth Aberds 89 C8
New Catton Norf 39 D8
New Cheriton Hants 10 B4
New Costessey Norf 39 D7
New Cowper Cumb 56 B3
New Cross Ceredig 32 H2
New Cross London 19 D10
New Cumnock E Ayrs 67 E9
New Deer Aberds 89 D8
New Delaval Northumb 63 F8
New Duston W Nhants 28 B4
New Earswick York 52 D2
New Edlington S Yorks 45 C9
New Elgin Moray 88 B2
New Ellerby E Yorks 53 F7
New Eltham London 19 D11
New End Worcs 27 C7
New Farnley W Yorks 51 F8
New Ferry Mers 42 D6
New Fryston W Yorks 51 G10
New Galloway Dumfries 55 B9
New Gilston Fife 77 G7
New Grimsby Scilly 2 C2
New Hainford Norf 39 D8
New Hartley Northumb 63 F9
New Haw Sur 19 E7
New Hedges Pembs 22 F6
New Herrington T&W 58 A4
New Hinksey Oxon 18 A2
New Holkham Norf 38 B4
New Holland N Lincs 53 G6
New Houghton Derbys 45 F8
New Houghton Norf 38 C3
New Houses N Yorks 50 B4
New Humberstone Leicester 36 E2
New Hutton W&F 57 G7
New Hythe Kent 20 F4
New Inn Carms 23 C9
New Inn Mon 15 A10
New Inn Pembs 22 C5
New Inn Torf 15 B9
New Invention Shrops 33 H8
New Invention W Mid 34 E5
New Kelso Highld 86 G2
New Kingston Notts 35 C11
New Lanark S Lanark 69 F7
New Lane Lancs 43 A7
New Lane End Warr 43 C9
New Leake Lincs 47 G8
New Leeds Aberds 89 C9
New Longton Lancs 49 G5
New Luce Dumfries 54 C4
New Malden London 19 E9
New Marske Redcar 59 D7
New Marton Shrops 33 B9
New Micklefield W Yorks 51 F10
New Mill Aberds 83 E9
New Mill Herts 28 G6
New Mill W Yorks 44 B5
New Mill Wilts 17 E8
New Mills Ches E 43 D10
New Mills Corn 3 D7
New Mills Derbys 44 D3
New Mills Powys 33 E6
New Milton Hants 9 E11
New Moat Pembs 22 D5
New Ollerton Notts 45 F10
New Oscott W Mid 35 F6
New Park N Yorks 51 D8
New Pitsligo Aberds 89 C8
New Polzeath Corn 3 B8
New Quay = Ceinewydd Ceredig 23 A8
New Rackheath Norf 39 D8
New Radnor Powys 25 B9
New Rent W&F 56 C6
New Ridley Northumb 62 H6
New Road Side N Yorks 50 E5
New Romney Kent 13 D9
New Rossington S Yorks 45 C10
New Row Ceredig 24 A4
New Row Lancs 50 F2
New Row N Yorks 59 E7
New Sarum Wilts 9 A10
New Silksworth T&W 58 A4
New Stevenston N Lanark 68 E6
New Street Staffs 44 G4
New Street Lane Shrops 34 B2
New Swanage Dorset 9 F9
New Totley S Yorks 45 E7
New Town E Loth 70 C3
New Tredegar = Tredegar Newydd Caerph 15 A7
New Trows S Lanark 69 G7
New Ulva Argyll 72 E6
New Walsoken Cambs 37 E10
New Waltham NE Lincs 46 B6
New Whittington Derbys 45 E7
New Wimpole Cambs 29 D10
New Winton E Loth 70 C3
New Yatt Oxon 27 G10
New York Lincs 46 G6
New York N Yorks 51 C7
Newall W Yorks 51 E7
Newark Orkney 95 D8
Newark Pboro 37 E8
Newark-on-Trent Notts 45 G11
Newarthill N Lanark 68 E6
Newbarns W&F 49 B2
Newbattle Midloth 70 D2
Newbiggin Cumb 56 G2
Newbiggin Durham 57 D11
Newbiggin N Yorks 57 G11
Newbiggin N Yorks 57 H11
Newbiggin W&F 49 C2
Newbiggin W&F 56 D6
Newbiggin W&F 57 B7
Newbiggin W&F 57 D8
Newbiggin-by-the-Sea Northumb 63 E9
Newbiggin-on-Lune W&F 57 F9
Newbigging Angus 77 D7
Newbigging Angus 77 D7
Newbigging S Lanark 69 F9
Newbold Derbys 45 E7
Newbold Leics 35 D10
Newbold on Avon Warks 35 H10
Newbold on Stour Warks 27 D9
Newbold Pacey Warks 27 C9
Newbold Verdon Leics 35 E10
Newborough Anglesey 40 D6
Newborough Pboro 37 E8
Newborough Staffs 35 C7
Newbottle T&W 58 A4
Newbottle W Nhants 28 E2
Newbourne Suff 31 D9
Newbridge Caerph 15 B8
Newbridge Ceredig 23 A10
Newbridge Corn 2 F3
Newbridge Corn 4 E4
Newbridge Dumfries 60 F5
Newbridge Edin 69 C10
Newbridge Hants 10 C1
Newbridge IoW 10 F3
Newbridge Pembs 22 C4
Newbridge Green Worcs 26 E5
Newbridge-on-Usk Mon 15 B9
Newbridge on Wye Powys 25 C7
Newbrough Northumb 62 G4
Newbuildings Devon 7 F6
Newburgh Aberds 89 C9
Newburgh Aberds 89 F9
Newburgh Borders 61 B9
Newburgh Fife 76 F5
Newburgh Lancs 43 A7
Newburn T&W 63 G7
Newbury W Berks 17 E11
Newbury Park London 19 C11
Newby Lancs 50 E4
Newby N Yorks 50 B3
Newby N Yorks 58 E6
Newby N Yorks 59 G11
Newby W&F 57 D7
Newby Bridge W&F 56 H5
Newby East Cumb 61 H10
Newby West Cumb 56 A5
Newby Wiske N Yorks 58 H4
Newcastle Mon 25 G11
Newcastle Shrops 33 G8
Newcastle Emlyn = Castell Newydd Emlyn Carms 23 B8
Newcastle-under-Lyme Staffs 44 H2
Newcastle Upon Tyne T&W 63 G8
Newcastleton or Copshaw Holm Borders 61 E10
Newchapel Pembs 23 C7
Newchapel Powys 32 G5
Newchapel Staffs 44 G2
Newchapel Sur 12 B2
Newchurch Carms 23 D8
Newchurch IoW 10 F4
Newchurch Kent 13 C9
Newchurch Lancs 50 F4
Newchurch Mon 15 B10
Newchurch Powys 25 C9
Newchurch Staffs 35 C7
Newcott Devon 7 F11
Newcraighall Edin 70 C2
Newdigate Sur 19 G8
Newell Green Brack 18 D5
Newenden Kent 13 D7
Newent Glos 26 F4
Newerne Glos 16 A3
Newfield Durham 58 C3
Newfield Highld 87 D10
Newford Scilly 2 C3
Newfound Hants 18 F2
Newgale Pembs 22 D3
Newgate Norf 39 A6
Newgate Street Herts 19 A10
Newhall Ches E 43 H9
Newhall Derbys 35 C8
Newhall House Highld 87 E9
Newhall Point Highld 87 E10
Newham Northumb 71 H10
Newham Hall Northumb 71 H10
Newhaven Derbys 44 G5
Newhaven E Sus 12 F3
Newhaven Edin 69 C11
Newhey Gtr Man 44 A3
Newholm N Yorks 59 E9
Newhouse N Lanark 68 D6
Newick E Sus 12 D3
Newingreen Kent 13 C10
Newington Kent 20 E5
Newington Kent 21 E10
Newington Kent 21 H8
Newington Notts 45 C10
Newington Oxon 18 B3
Newington Shrops 33 G10
Newland Glos 26 H2
Newland Hull 53 F6
Newland N Yorks 52 G2
Newland Worcs 26 D4
Newlandrig Midloth 70 D2
Newlands Borders 61 D11
Newlands Highld 87 G10
Newlands Moray 88 C3
Newlands Northumb 62 H6
Newland's Corner Sur 19 G7
Newlands of Geise Highld 94 D2
Newlands of Tynet Moray 88 B3
Newlands Park Anglesey 40 B4
Newlandsmuir S Lanark 68 E5
Newlot Orkney 95 G6
Newlyn Corn 2 G3
Newmachar Aberds 83 B10
Newmains N Lanark 69 E7
Newmarket Suff 30 B3
Newmarket W Isles 91 D9
Newmill Borders 61 B10
Newmill Corn 2 F3
Newmill Moray 88 C4
Newmill of Inshewan Angus 77 A7
Newmills of Boyne Aberds 88 C5
Newmiln Perth 76 D4
Newmilns E Ayrs 67 C8
Newnham Cambs 29 C11
Newnham Glos 26 G3
Newnham Hants 18 F4
Newnham Herts 29 E9
Newnham Kent 20 F6
Newnham W Nhants 28 C2
Newnham Bridge Worcs 26 B3
Newpark Fife 77 F7
Newport Devon 6 C4
Newport E Yorks 52 F4
Newport Essex 30 E2
Newport Highld 94 H3
Newport IoW 10 F4
Newport = Casnewydd Newport 15 C9
Newport Norf 39 D11
Newport = Trefdraeth Pembs 22 C5
Newport Telford 34 D3
Newport-on-Tay Fife 77 E7
Newport Pagnell M Keynes 28 D5
Newpound Common W Sus 11 B9
Newquay Corn 3 C7
Newsbank Ches E 44 F2
Newseat Aberds 89 D10
Newseat Aberds 89 E7
Newsham N Yorks 51 A9
Newsham N Yorks 58 E2
Newsham Northumb 63 F9
Newsholme E Yorks 52 G3
Newsholme Lancs 50 D4
Newsome W Yorks 44 A5
Newstead Borders 70 G4
Newstead Northumb 71 H10
Newstead Notts 45 G9
Newthorpe N Yorks 51 F10
Newton Argyll 73 D9
Newton Borders 62 A1
Newton Bridgend 14 D4
Newton Cambs 29 D11
Newton Cambs 37 D10
Newton Cardiff 15 D8
Newton Ches W 43 E8
Newton Ches W 43 F7
Newton Ches W 43 G8
Newton Derbys 45 G8
Newton Dorset 9 C6
Newton Dumfries 61 D7
Newton Dumfries 61 F8
Newton Gtr Man 44 C3
Newton Hereford 25 E10
Newton Hereford 26 C2
Newton Highld 87 E10
Newton Highld 87 G10
Newton Highld 92 F5
Newton Highld 94 F5
Newton Lancs 49 F4
Newton Lancs 50 B1
Newton Lancs 50 D2
Newton Lincs 36 B6
Newton Moray 88 B1
Newton N Nhants 36 G4
Newton Norf 38 D4
Newton Northumb 62 G6
Newton Notts 36 A2
Newton Perth 75 D11
Newton S Lanark 68 D5
Newton S Lanark 69 G8
Newton S Yorks 45 B9
Newton Staffs 34 C6
Newton Suff 30 D6
Newton Swansea 14 C2
Newton W Loth 69 C9
Newton Warks 35 H11
Newton Wilts 9 B11
Newton W&F 49 B2
Newton Abbot Devon 5 D9
Newton Arlosh Cumb 61 H7
Newton Aycliffe Durham 58 D3
Newton Bewley Hrtlpl 58 D5
Newton Blossomville M Keynes 28 C6
Newton Bromswold N Nhants 28 B6
Newton Burgoland Leics 35 E9
Newton by Toft Lincs 46 D4
Newton Ferrers Devon 4 G6
Newton Flotman Norf 39 F8
Newton Hall Northumb 62 G6
Newton Harcourt Leics 36 F2
Newton Heath Gtr Man 44 B2
Newton Ho. Aberds 83 A8
Newton Kyme N Yorks 51 E10
Newton-le-Willows Mers 43 C8
Newton-le-Willows N Yorks 58 H3
Newton Longville Bucks 28 E5
Newton Mearns E Renf 68 E4
Newton Morrell N Yorks 58 F3
Newton Mulgrave N Yorks 59 E8
Newton of Ardtoe Highld 79 D9
Newton of Balcanquhal Perth 76 F4
Newton of Falkland Fife 76 G5
Newton on Ayr S Ayrs 66 D6
Newton on Ouse N Yorks 51 D11
Newton-on-Rawcliffe N Yorks 59 G9
Newton-on-the-Moor Northumb 63 C7
Newton on Trent Lincs 46 E2
Newton Park Argyll 73 G10
Newton Poppleford Devon 7 H9
Newton Purcell Oxon 28 E3
Newton Regis Warks 35 E8
Newton Reigny W&F 57 C6
Newton St Cyres Devon 7 G7
Newton St Faith Norf 39 D8
Newton St Loe Bath 16 E4
Newton St Petrock Devon 6 E3
Newton Solney Derbys 35 C8
Newton Stacey Hants 17 G11
Newton Stewart Dumfries 55 C7
Newton Tony Wilts 17 G9
Newton Tracey Devon 6 D4
Newton under Roseberry Redcar 59 E6
Newton upon Derwent E Yorks 52 E3
Newton Valence Hants 10 A6
Newtonairds Dumfries 60 E4
Newtongrange Midloth 70 D2
Newtonhill Aberds 83 D11
Newtonhill Highld 87 G8
Newtonmill Angus 77 A9
Newtonmore Highld 81 D9
Newtown Argyll 73 C9
Newtown Ches W 43 E8
Newtown Corn 2 G6
Newtown Cumb 56 B2
Newtown Cumb 61 G11
Newtown Derbys 44 D3
Newtown Devon 7 D6
Newtown Glos 16 A3
Newtown Glos 26 E6
Newtown Hants 10 B2
Newtown Hants 10 C4
Newtown Hants 10 C1
Newtown Hants 10 C5
Newtown Hants 10 D3
Newtown Hants 17 E11
Newtown Hereford 26 D3
Newtown Highld 80 C5
Newtown IoM 48 E3
Newtown IoW 10 E3
Newtown Northumb 62 C6
Newtown Northumb 71 G8
Newtown Northumb 71 H9
Newtown BCP 9 E9
Newtown = Y Drenewydd Powys 33 F7
Newtown Shrops 33 B10
Newtown Staffs 44 F4
Newtown Staffs 44 F3
Newtown Wilts 9 B8
Newtown Linford Leics 35 E11
Newtown St Boswells Borders 70 G4
Newtown Unthank Leics 35 E10
Newtyle Angus 76 C5
Neyland Pembs 22 F4
Niarbyl IoM 48 E2
Nibley S Glos 16 C3
Nibley Green Glos 16 B4
Nibon Shetland 96 F5
Nicholashayne Devon 7 E10
Nicholaston Swansea 23 H10
Nidd N Yorks 51 C9
Nigg Aberdeen 83 C11
Nigg Highld 87 D11
Nigg Ferry Highld 87 E10
Nightcott Som 7 D7
Nilig Denb 42 G3
Nine Ashes Essex 20 A2
Nine Mile Burn Midloth 69 E10
Nine Wells Pembs 22 D2
Ninebanks Northumb 57 A9
Ninfield E Sus 12 E6
Ningwood IoW 10 F2
Nisbet Borders 70 H5
Nisthouse Orkney 95 G4
Nisthouse Shetland 96 G7
Niton IoW 10 G4
Nitshill Glasgow 68 D4
No Man's Heath Ches W 43 H8
No Man's Heath Warks 35 E8
Noak Hill London 20 B2
Noblethorpe S Yorks 44 B6
Nobottle W Nhants 28 B3
Nocton Lincs 46 F4
Noke Oxon 28 G2
Nolton Pembs 22 E3
Nolton Haven Pembs 22 E3
Nomansland Devon 7 E7
Nomansland Wilts 10 C1
Noneley Shrops 33 C10
Nonikiln Highld 87 D9
Nonington Kent 21 F9
Noonsbrough Shetland 96 H4
Norbreck Blackpool 49 E3
Norbridge Hereford 26 D4
Norbury Ches E 43 H8
Norbury Derbys 35 A7
Norbury Shrops 33 F9
Norbury Staffs 34 C3
Nordelph Norf 38 E1
Norden Gtr Man 44 A2
Norden Heath Dorset 9 F8
Nordley Shrops 34 F2
Norham Northumb 71 F8
Norley Ches W 43 E8
Norleywood Hants 10 E2
Norman Cross Cambs 37 F7
Normanby N Lincs 52 H4
Normanby N Yorks 52 A3
Normanby Redcar 59 E6
Normanby-by-Spital Lincs 46 D4
Normanby by Stow Lincs 46 D2
Normanby le Wold Lincs 46 C5
Normandy Sur 18 F6
Norman's Bay E Sus 12 F5
Norman's Green Devon 7 F9
Normanstone Suff 39 F11
Normanton Derby 35 B9
Normanton Leics 36 A4
Normanton Lincs 46 H3
Normanton Notts 45 G11
Normanton Rutland 36 E5
Normanton W Yorks 51 G9
Normanton le Heath Leics 35 D9
Normanton on Soar Notts 35 C11
Normanton-on-the-Wolds Notts 36 B2
Normanton on Trent Notts 45 F11
Normoss Lancs 49 F3
Norney Sur 18 G6
Norrington Common Wilts 16 E5
Norris Green Mers 43 C6
Norris Hill Leics 35 D9
North Anston S Yorks 45 D9
North Aston Oxon 27 F11
North Baddesley Hants 10 C2
North Ballachulish Highld 74 A3
North Barrow Som 8 B5
North Barsham Norf 38 B5
North Benfleet Essex 20 C4
North Bersted W Sus 11 D8
North Berwick E Loth 70 B4
North Boarhunt Hants 10 C5
North Bovey Devon 5 C8
North Bradley Wilts 16 F5
North Brentor Devon 4 C5
North Brewham Som 16 H4
North Buckland Devon 6 B3
North Burlingham Norf 39 D9
North Cadbury Som 8 B5
North Cairn Dumfries 54 B2
North Carlton Lincs 46 E3
North Carrine Argyll 65 H7
North Cave E Yorks 52 F4
North Cerney Glos 27 H7
North Charford Wilts 9 C10
North Charlton Northumb 63 A7
North Cheriton Som 8 B5
North Cliff E Yorks 53 E8
North Cliffe E Yorks 52 F4
North Clifton Notts 46 E2
North Cockerington Lincs 47 C7
North Coker Som 8 C4
North Collafirth Shetland 96 E5
North Common E Sus 12 D2
North Connel Argyll 74 D2
North Cornelly Bridgend 14 C4
North Cotes Lincs 47 B7
North Cove Suff 39 G10
North Cowton N Yorks 58 F3
North Crawley M Keynes 28 D6
North Cray London 19 D11
North Creake Norf 38 B4
North Curry Som 8 B2
North Dalton E Yorks 52 D5
North Dawn Orkney 95 H5
North Deighton N Yorks 51 D9
North Duffield N Yorks 52 F2
North Elkington Lincs 46 C6
North Elmham Norf 38 C5
North Elmshall W Yorks 45 A8
North End Bucks 28 F5
North End E Yorks 53 F8
North End Essex 30 G3
North End Hants 17 E11
North End Lincs 37 A8
North End N Som 15 E10
North End Ptsmth 10 D5
North End Som 8 B1
North End W Sus 11 D10
North Erradale Highld 91 J12
North Fambridge Essex 20 B5
North Fearns Highld 85 E10
North Featherstone W Yorks 51 G10
North Ferriby E Yorks 52 G5
North Frodingham E Yorks 53 D7
North Gluss Shetland 96 F5
North Gorley Hants 9 C10
North Green Norf 39 G8
North Green Suff 31 B10
North Greetwell Lincs 46 E4
North Grimston N Yorks 52 C4
North Halley Orkney 95 H6
North Halling Medway 20 E4
North Hayling Hants 10 D6
North Hazelrigg Northumb 71 G9
North Heasley Devon 7 C6
North Heath W Sus 11 B9
North Hill Cambs 37 H10
North Hill Corn 4 D3
North Hinksey Oxon 27 H11
North Holmwood Sur 19 G8
North Howden E Yorks 52 F3
North Huish Devon 5 F8
North Hykeham Lincs 46 F3
North Johnston Pembs 22 E4
North Kelsey Lincs 46 B4
North Kelsey Moor Lincs 46 B4
North Kessock Highld 87 G9
North Killingholme N Lincs 53 H7
North Kilvington N Yorks 58 H5
North Kilworth Leics 36 G2
North Kirkton Aberds 89 C11
North Kiscadale N Ayrs 66 D3
North Kyme Lincs 46 G5
North Lancing W Sus 11 D10
North Lee Bucks 28 H5
North Leigh Oxon 27 G10
North Leverton with Habblesthorpe Notts 45 D11
North Littleton Worcs 27 D7
North Lopham Norf 38 G6
North Luffenham Rutland 36 E5
North Marden W Sus 11 C7
North Marston Bucks 28 F4
North Middleton Midloth 70 E2
North Middleton Northumb 62 A6
North Molton Devon 7 D6
North Moreton Oxon 18 C2
North Mundham W Sus 11 D7
North Muskham Notts 45 G11
North Newbald E Yorks 52 F5
North Newington Oxon 27 E11
North Newnton Wilts 17 F8
North Newton Som 8 A1
North Nibley Glos 16 B4
North Oakley Hants 18 F2
North Ockendon London 20 C2
North Ormesby Mbro 58 D6
North Ormsby Lincs 46 C6
North Otterington N Yorks 58 H4
North Owersby Lincs 46 C4
North Perrott Som 8 D3
North Petherton Som 8 A1
North Petherwin Corn 4 C3
North Pickenham Norf 38 E4
North Piddle Worcs 26 C6
North Poorton Dorset 8 E4
North Port Argyll 74 E3
North Queensferry Fife 69 B10
North Radworthy Devon 7 C6
North Rauceby Lincs 46 H4
North Reston Lincs 47 D7
North Rigton N Yorks 51 E8
North Rode Ches E 44 F2
North Roe Shetland 96 E5
North Runcton Norf 38 D2
North Sandwick Shetland 96 D7
North Scale W&F 49 C1
North Scarle Lincs 46 F2
North Seaton Northumb 63 E8
North Shian Argyll 74 C2
North Shields T&W 63 G9
North Shoebury Southend 20 C6
North Shore Blackpool 49 F3
North Side Cumb 56 D2
North Side Pboro 37 F8
North Skelton Redcar 59 E7
North Somercotes Lincs 47 C8
North Stainley N Yorks 51 B8
North Stainmore W&F 57 E10
North Stifford Thurrock 20 C3
North Stoke Bath 16 E4
North Stoke Oxon 18 C3
North Stoke W Sus 11 C9
North Street Hants 10 A5
North Street Kent 21 F7
North Street Medway 20 D5
North Street W Berks 18 D3
North Sunderland Northumb 71 G11
North Tamerton Corn 6 G2
North Tawton Devon 6 F5
North Thoresby Lincs 46 C6
North Tidworth Wilts 17 G9
North Togston Northumb 63 C8
North Tuddenham Norf 38 D6
North Walbottle T&W 63 G7
North Walsham Norf 39 B8
North Waltham Hants 18 G2
North Warnborough Hants 18 F4
North Water Bridge Angus 83 G8
North Watten Highld 94 E4
North Weald Bassett Essex 19 A11
North Wheatley Notts 45 D11
North Whilborough Devon 5 E9
North Wick Bath 16 E2
North Willingham Lincs 46 D5
North Wingfield Derbys 45 F8
North Witham Lincs 36 C5
North Woolwich London 19 D11
North Wootton Dorset 8 C5
North Wootton Norf 38 C2
North Wootton Som 16 G2
North Wraxall Wilts 16 D5
North Wroughton Swindon 17 C8
Northacre Norf 38 F5
Northallerton N Yorks 58 G4
Northam Devon 6 D3
Northam Soton 10 C3
Northampton W Nhants 28 B4
Northaw Herts 19 A9
Northbeck Lincs 37 A6
Northborough Pboro 37 E7
Northbourne Kent 21 F10
Northbridge Street E Sus 12 D6
Northchapel W Sus 11 B8
Northchurch Herts 28 H6
Northcott Devon 6 G2
Northdown Kent 21 D10
Northdyke Orkney 95 F3
Northend Bath 16 E4
Northend Bucks 18 B4
Northend Warks 27 C10
Northenden Gtr Man 44 C2
Northfield Aberdeen 83 C11
Northfield Borders 71 D8
Northfield E Yorks 52 G6
Northfield W Mid 34 H6
Northfields Lincs 36 E6
Northfleet Kent 20 D3
Northgate Lincs 37 C7
Northhouse Borders 61 C10
Northiam E Sus 13 D7
Northill C Beds 29 D8
Northington Hants 18 H2
Northlands Lincs 47 G7
Northlea Durham 58 A5
Northleach Glos 27 G8
Northleigh Devon 7 G10
Northlew Devon 6 G4
Northmoor Oxon 17 A11
Northmoor Green or Moorland Som 8 A2
Northmuir Angus 76 B6
Northney Hants 10 D6
Northolt London 19 C8
Northop Flint 42 F5
Northop Hall Flint 42 F5
Northorpe Lincs 37 B8
Northorpe Lincs 37 D6
Northorpe Lincs 46 C2
Northover Som 8 B4
Northover Som 15 H10
Northowram W Yorks 51 G7
Northport Dorset 9 F8
Northpunds Shetland 96 L6
Northrepps Norf 39 B8
Northstowe Cambs 29 B11
Northtown Orkney 95 J5
Northway Glos 26 E6
Northwich Ches W 43 E9
Northwick S Glos 16 C2
Northwold Norf 38 F3
Northwood Derbys 44 F6
Northwood IoW 10 E3
Northwood Kent 21 E10
Northwood London 19 B7
Northwood Shrops 33 B10
Northwood Green Glos 26 G4
Norton E Sus 12 F3
Norton Glos 26 F5
Norton Halton 43 D8
Norton Herts 29 E9
Norton IoW 10 F2
Norton Mon 25 G11
Norton Notts 45 E9
Norton Powys 25 B10
Norton S Yorks 51 H11
Norton Shrops 33 G10
Norton Shrops 34 E1
Norton Shrops 34 E3
Norton Stockton 58 D5
Norton Suff 30 B6
Norton W Nhants 28 B3
Norton W Sus 11 D8
Norton W Sus 11 E7
Norton Wilts 16 C5
Norton Worcs 26 C5
Norton Worcs 27 D7
Norton Bavant Wilts 16 G6
Norton Bridge Staffs 34 B4
Norton Canes Staffs 34 E6
Norton Canon Hereford 25 D10
Norton Corner Norf 39 C6
Norton Disney Lincs 46 G2
Norton East Staffs 34 E6
Norton Ferris Wilts 16 H4
Norton Fitzwarren Som 7 D10
Norton Green IoW 10 F2
Norton Hawkfield Bath 16 E2
Norton Heath Essex 20 A3
Norton in Hales Shrops 34 B3
Norton-in-the-Moors Stoke 44 G2
Norton-Juxta-Twycross Leics 35 E9
Norton-le-Clay N Yorks 51 B10
Norton Lindsey Warks 27 B9
Norton Malreward Bath 16 E3
Norton Mandeville Essex 20 A2
Norton-on-Derwent N Yorks 52 B3
Norton St Philip Som 16 F4
Norton sub Hamdon Som 8 C3
Norton Woodseats S Yorks 45 D7
Norwell Notts 45 F11
Norwell Woodhouse Notts 45 F11
Norwich Norf 39 E8
Norwick Shetland 96 B8
Norwood Derbys 45 D8
Norwood Hill Sur 19 G9
Norwoodside Cambs 37 F10
Noseley Leics 36 F3
Noss Shetland 96 M5
Noss Mayo Devon 4 G6
Nosterfield N Yorks 51 A8
Nostie Highld 85 F13
Notgrove Glos 27 F8
Nottage Bridgend 14 D4
Nottingham Nottingham 36 B1
Nottington Dorset 8 F5
Notton W Yorks 45 A7
Notton Wilts 16 E6
Nounsley Essex 30 G4
Noutard's Green Worcs 26 B4
Novar House Highld 87 E9
Nox Shrops 33 D10
Nuffield Oxon 18 C3
Nun Hills Lancs 50 G4
Nun Monkton N Yorks 51 D11
Nunburnholme E Yorks 52 E4
Nuncargate Notts 45 G9
Nuneaton Warks 35 F9
Nuneham Courtenay Oxon 18 B2
Nunney Som 16 G4
Nunnington N Yorks 52 B2
Nunnykirk Northumb 62 D6
Nunsthorpe NE Lincs 46 B6
Nunthorpe Mbro 59 E6
Nunthorpe York 52 D2
Nunton Wilts 9 B10
Nunwick N Yorks 51 B9
Nupend Glos 26 H4
Nursling Hants 10 C2
Nursted Hants 11 B6
Nutbourne W Sus 11 C9
Nutbourne W Sus 11 D6
Nutfield Sur 19 F10
Nuthall Notts 35 A11
Nuthampstead Herts 29 E11
Nuthurst W Sus 11 B10
Nutley E Sus 12 D3
Nutley Hants 18 G3
Nutwell S Yorks 45 B10
Nybster Highld 94 D5
Nyetimber W Sus 11 E7
Nyewood W Sus 11 B7
Nymet Rowland Devon 6 F6
Nymet Tracey Devon 7 F6
Nympsfield Glos 16 A5
Nynehead Som 7 D10
Nyton W Sus 11 D8

O

Oad Street Kent 20 E5
Oadby Leics 36 E2
Oak Cross Devon 6 G4
Oakamoor Staffs 35 A6
Oakbank W Loth 69 D9
Oakdale Caerph 15 B7
Oake Som 7 D10
Oaken Staffs 34 E4
Oakenclough Lancs 49 E5
Oakengates Telford 34 D3
Oakenholt Flint 42 E5
Oakenshaw Durham 58 C3
Oakenshaw W Yorks 51 G7
Oakerthorpe Derbys 45 G7
Oakes W Yorks 51 H7
Oakfield Torf 15 B9
Oakford Ceredig 23 A9
Oakford Devon 7 D8
Oakfordbridge Devon 7 D8
Oakgrove Ches E 44 F3
Oakham Rutland 36 E4
Oakhanger Hants 18 H4
Oakhill Som 16 G3
Oakhurst Kent 20 F2
Oakington Cambs 29 B11
Oaklands Herts 29 G9
Oaklands Powys 25 C7
Oakle Street Glos 26 G4
Oakley Bedford 29 C7
Oakley Bucks 28 G3
Oakley Fife 69 B9
Oakley Hants 18 F2
Oakley Oxon 18 A4
Oakley BCP 9 E9
Oakley Suff 39 H7
Oakley Green Windsor 18 D6
Oakley Park Powys 32 G5
Oakmere Ches W 43 F8
Oakridge Glos 16 A6
Oakridge Hants 18 F3
Oaks Shrops 33 E10
Oaks Green Derbys 35 B7
Oaksey Wilts 16 B6
Oakthorpe Leics 35 D9
Oakwoodhill Sur 19 H8
Oakworth W Yorks 50 F6
Oape Highld 92 J7
Oare Kent 21 E7
Oare Som 7 B7
Oare W Berks 18 D2
Oare Wilts 17 E8
Oasby Lincs 36 B6
Oathlaw Angus 77 B7
Oatlands N Yorks 51 D9
Oban Argyll 79 J11
Oban Highld 79 C11
Oborne Dorset 8 C5
Obthorpe Lincs 37 D6
Occlestone Green Ches W 43 F9
Occold Suff 31 A8
Ochiltree E Ayrs 67 D8
Ochtermuthill Perth 75 F11
Ochtertyre Perth 75 E11
Ockbrook Derbys 35 B10
Ockham Sur 19 F7
Ockle Highld 79 D8
Ockley Sur 19 H8
Ocle Pychard Hereford 26 D2
Octon E Yorks 52 C6
Octon Cross Roads E Yorks 52 C6
Odcombe Som 8 C4
Odd Down Bath 16 E4
Oddendale W&F 57 E7
Odder Lincs 46 E3
Oddingley Worcs 26 C6
Oddington Glos 27 F9
Oddington Oxon 28 G2
Odell Bedford 28 C6
Odie Orkney 95 F7
Odiham Hants 18 F4
Odstock Wilts 9 B10
Odstone Leics 35 E9
Offchurch Warks 27 B10
Offenham Worcs 27 D7
Offham E Sus 12 E2
Offham Kent 20 F3
Offham W Sus 11 D9
Offord Cluny Cambs 29 B9
Offord Darcy Cambs 29 B9
Offton Suff 31 D7
Offwell Devon 7 G10
Ogbourne Maizey Wilts 17 D8
Ogbourne St Andrew Wilts 17 D8
Ogbourne St George Wilts 17 D9
Ogil Angus 77 A7
Ogle Northumb 63 F7
Ogmore V Glam 14 D4
Ogmore-by-Sea V Glam 14 D4
Ogmore Vale Bridgend 14 B5
Okeford Fitzpaine Dorset 9 C7
Okehampton Devon 6 G4
Okehampton Camp Devon 6 G4
Okraquoy Shetland 96 K6
Old W Nhants 28 A4
Old Aberdeen Aberdeen 83 C11
Old Alresford Hants 10 A4
Old Arley Warks 35 F8
Old Basford Nottingham 35 A11
Old Basing Hants 18 F3
Old Bewick Northumb 62 A6
Old Bolingbroke Lincs 47 F7
Old Bramhope W Yorks 51 E8
Old Brampton Derbys 45 E7
Old Bridge of Tilt Perth 81 G10
Old Bridge of Urr Dumfries 55 C10
Old Buckenham Norf 39 F6
Old Burghclere Hants 17 F11
Old Byland N Yorks 59 H6
Old Cassop Durham 58 C4
Old Castleton Borders 61 D11
Old Catton Norf 39 D8
Old Clee NE Lincs 46 B6
Old Cleeve Som 7 B9
Old Clipstone Notts 45 F10
Old Colwyn Conwy 41 C10
Old Coulsdon London 19 F10
Old Crombie Aberds 88 C5
Old Dailly S Ayrs 66 G5
Old Dalby Leics 36 C2
Old Deer Aberds 89 D9
Old Denaby S Yorks 45 C8
Old Edlington S Yorks 45 C9
Old Eldon Durham 58 D3
Old Ellerby E Yorks 53 F7
Old Felixstowe Suff 31 E10
Old Fletton Pboro 37 F7
Old Glossop Derbys 44 C4
Old Goole E Yorks 52 G3
Old Hall Powys 32 G5
Old Heath Essex 31 F7
Old Heathfield E Sus 12 D4
Old Hill W Mid 34 G5
Old Hunstanton Norf 38 A2
Old Hurst Cambs 37 H8
Old Hutton W&F 57 H7
Old Kea Corn 3 E7
Old Kilpatrick W Dunb 68 C3
Old Kinnernie Aberds 83 C9
Old Knebworth Herts 29 F9
Old Langho Lancs 50 F3
Old Laxey IoM 48 D4
Old Leake Lincs 47 G8
Old Malton N Yorks 52 B3
Old Micklefield W Yorks 51 F10
Old Milton Hants 9 E11
Old Milverton Warks 27 B9
Old Monkland N Lanark 68 D6
Old Netley Hants 10 D3
Old Philpstoun W Loth 69 C9
Old Quarrington Durham 58 C4
Old Radnor Powys 25 C9
Old Rattray Aberds 89 C10
Old Rayne Aberds 83 A8
Old Romney Kent 13 D9
Old Sodbury S Glos 16 C4
Old Somerby Lincs 36 B5
Old Stratford W Nhants 28 D4
Old Thirsk N Yorks 51 A10
Old Town Northumb 62 D4
Old Town Scilly 2 C3
Old Town W&F 50 A1
Old Town W&F 57 B6
Old Trafford Gtr Man 44 C2
Old Tupton Derbys 45 F7
Old Warden C Beds 29 D8
Old Weston Cambs 37 H6
Old Whittington Derbys 45 E7
Old Wick Highld 94 E5
Old Windsor Windsor 18 D6
Old Wives Lees Kent 21 F7
Old Woking Sur 19 F7
Old Woodhall Lincs 46 F6
Oldany Highld 92 F4
Oldberrow Warks 27 B8
Oldborough Devon 7 F6
Oldbury Shrops 34 F3
Oldbury W Mid 34 G5
Oldbury Warks 35 F9
Oldbury-on-Severn S Glos 16 B3
Oldbury on the Hill Glos 16 C5
Oldcastle Bridgend 14 D5
Oldcastle Mon 25 F10
Oldcotes Notts 45 D9
Oldfallow Staffs 34 D5
Oldfield Worcs 26 B5
Oldford Som 16 F4
Oldham Gtr Man 44 B3
Oldhamstocks E Loth 70 C6
Oldland S Glos 16 D3
Oldmeldrum Aberds 89 F8
Oldshore Beg Highld 92 D4
Oldshoremore Highld 92 D5
Oldstead N Yorks 51 A11
Oldtown Aberds 83 A7
Oldtown of Ord Aberds 88 C6
Oldway Swansea 23 H10
Oldways End Devon 7 D7
Oldwhat Aberds 89 C8
Olgrinmore Highld 94 E2
Oliver's Battery Hants 10 B3
Ollaberry Shetland 96 E5
Ollerton Ches E 43 E10
Ollerton Notts 45 F10

Rhodiad Pembs 22 D2
Rhondda Rhondda 14 B5
Rhonehouse or Kelton Hill Dumfries 55 D10
Rhoose = Y Rhws V Glam 14 E6
Rhos-fawr Gwyn 40 G5
Rhos-goch Powys 25 D8
Rhos-hill Pembs 22 B6
Rhos-on-Sea Conwy 41 B10
Rhos-y-brithdir Powys 33 C7
Rhos-y-garth Ceredig 24 A3
Rhos-y-gwaliau Gwyn 32 B5
Rhos-y-llan Gwyn 40 G4
Rhos-y-Madoc Wrex 33 A9
Rhos-y-meirch Powys 25 B9
Rhosaman Carms 24 G4
Rhosbeirio Anglesey 40 A5
Rhoscefnhir Anglesey 41 C7
Rhoscolyn Anglesey 40 C4
Rhoscrowther Pembs 22 F4
Rhosesmor Flint 42 F5
Rhosgadfan Gwyn 41 E7
Rhosgoch Anglesey 40 B6
Rhoshirwaun Gwyn 40 H3
Rhoslan Gwyn 40 F6
Rhoslefain Gwyn 32 E1
Rhosllanerchrugog Wrex 42 H5
Rhosmaen Carms 24 F3
Rhosmeirch Anglesey 40 C6
Rhosneigr Anglesey 40 C5
Rhosnesni Wrex 42 G6
Rhosrobin Wrex 42 G6
Rhossili Swansea 23 H9
Rhosson Pembs 22 D2
Rhostryfan Gwyn 40 E6
Rhostyllen Wrex 42 H6
Rhosybol Anglesey 40 B6
Rhu Argyll 73 E11
Rhu Argyll 73 G7
Rhuallt Denb 42 E3
Rhuddall Heath Ches W 43 F8
Rhuddlan Ceredig 23 B9
Rhuddlan Denb 42 E3
Rhue Highld 86 B3
Rhulen Powys 25 D8
Rhunahaorine Argyll 65 D8
Rhuthun = Ruthin Denb 42 G4
Rhyd Gwyn 41 F8
Rhyd Powys 32 E5
Rhyd-Ddu Gwyn 41 E7
Rhyd-moel-ddu Powys 33 H6
Rhyd-Rosser Ceredig 24 B2
Rhyd-uchaf Gwyn 32 B5
Rhyd-wen Gwyn 32 D3
Rhyd-y-clafdy Gwyn 40 G5
Rhyd-y-fro Neath 24 H4
Rhyd-y-gwin Swansea 14 A2
Rhyd-y-meirch Mon 25 H10
Rhyd-y-meudwy Denb 42 G4
Rhyd-y-pandy Swansea 14 A2
Rhyd-y-sarn Gwyn 41 F8
Rhyd-yr-onen Gwyn 32 E2
Rhydaman = Ammanford Carms 24 G3
Rhydargaeau Carms 23 D9
Rhydcymerau Carms 23 C10
Rhydd Worcs 26 D5
Rhydding Neath 14 B3
Rhydfudr Ceredig 24 B2
Rhydlewis Ceredig 23 B8
Rhydlios Gwyn 40 G3
Rhydlydan Conwy 41 E10
Rhydness Powys 25 D8
Rhydowen Ceredig 23 B9
Rhydspence Hereford 25 D9
Rhydtalog Flint 42 G5
Rhydwyn Anglesey 40 B5
Rhydycroesau Powys 33 B8
Rhydyfelin Ceredig 32 H1
Rhydyfelin Rhondda 14 C6
Rhydymain Gwyn 32 C4
Rhydymwyn Flint 42 F5
Rhyl = Y Rhyl Denb 42 D3
Rhymney = Rhymni Caerph 25 H8
Rhymni = Rhymney Caerph 25 H8
Rhynd Fife 77 E7
Rhynd Perth 76 E4
Rhynie Aberds 82 A6
Rhynie Highld 87 D11
Ribbesford Worcs 26 A4
Ribblehead N Yorks 50 B3
Ribbleton Lancs 50 F1
Ribchester Lancs 50 F2
Ribigill Highld 93 D8
Riby Lincs 46 B5
Riby Cross Roads Lincs 46 B5
Riccall N Yorks 52 F2
Riccarton E Ayrs 67 C7
Richards Castle Hereford 25 B11
Richings Park Bucks 19 D7
Richmond London 19 D8
Richmond N Yorks 58 F2
Rickarton Aberds 83 E10
Rickinghall Suff 38 H6
Rickleton T&W 58 A3
Rickling Essex 29 E11
Rickmansworth Herts 19 B7
Riddings Cumb 61 F10
Riddings Derbys 45 G8
Riddlecombe Devon 6 E5
Riddlesden W Yorks 51 E6
Riddrie Glasgow 68 D5
Ridge Dorset 9 F8
Ridge Hants 10 C2
Ridge Wilts 9 A8
Ridge Green Sur 19 G10
Ridge Lane Warks 35 F8
Ridgebourne Powys 25 B7
Ridgehill N Som 15 E11
Ridgeway Cross Hereford 26 D4
Ridgewell Essex 30 D4
Ridgewood E Sus 12 E3
Ridgmont C Beds 28 E6
Riding Mill Northumb 62 G6
Ridleywood Wrex 43 G7
Ridlington Norf 39 B9
Ridlington Rutland 36 E4
Ridsdale Northumb 62 E5
Riechip Perth 76 C3
Riemore Perth 76 C3
Rienachait Highld 92 F3
Rievaulx N Yorks 59 H6
Rift House Hrtlpl 58 C5
Rigg Dumfries 61 G8
Riggend N Lanark 68 C6
Rigsby Lincs 47 E8
Rigside S Lanark 69 G7
Riley Green Lancs 50 G2
Rileyhill Staffs 35 D7
Rilla Mill Corn 4 D3
Rillington N Yorks 52 B4
Rimington Lancs 50 E4
Rimpton Som 8 B5
Rimswell E Yorks 53 G9
Rinaston Pembs 22 D4
Ringasta Shetland 96 M5
Ringford Dumfries 55 D9
Ringinglow S Yorks 44 D6
Ringland Norf 39 D7
Ringles Cross E Sus 12 D3
Ringmer E Sus 12 E3
Ringmore Devon 5 G7
Ringorm Moray 88 D2
Ring's End Cambs 37 E9
Ringsfield Suff 39 G10
Ringsfield Corner Suff 39 G10
Ringshall Herts 28 G6
Ringshall Suff 31 C7
Ringshall Stocks Suff 31 C7
Ringstead N Nhants 36 H5
Ringstead Norf 38 A3
Ringwood Hants 9 D10
Ringwould Kent 21 G10
Rinmore Aberds 82 B6
Rinnigill Orkney 95 J4
Rinsey Corn 2 G4
Riof W Isles 90 D6
Ripe E Sus 12 E4
Ripley Derbys 45 G7
Ripley Hants 9 E10
Ripley N Yorks 51 C8
Ripley Sur 19 F7
Riplingham E Yorks 52 F5
Ripon N Yorks 51 B9
Rippingale Lincs 37 C6
Ripple Kent 21 G10
Ripple Worcs 26 E5
Ripponden W Yorks 50 H6
Rireavach Highld 86 B3
Risabus Argyll 64 D4
Risbury Hereford 26 C2
Risby Suff 30 B4
Risca = Rhisga Caerph 15 B8
Rise E Yorks 53 E7
Riseden E Sus 12 C5
Risegate Lincs 37 C8
Riseholme Lincs 46 E3
Riseley Bedford 29 B7
Riseley Wokingham 18 E4
Rishangles Suff 31 B8
Rishton Lancs 50 F3
Rishworth W Yorks 50 H6
Rising Bridge Lancs 50 G3
Risley Derbys 35 B10
Risley Warr 43 C9
Risplith N Yorks 51 C8
Rispond Highld 92 C7
Rivar Wilts 17 E10
Rivenhall End Essex 30 G5
River Bank Cambs 30 B2
Riverhead Kent 20 F2
Rivington Lancs 43 A9
Roa Island W&F 49 C2
Roachill Devon 7 D7
Road Green Norf 39 F8
Roade W Nhants 28 C4
Roadhead Cumb 61 F11
Roadmeetings S Lanark 69 F7
Roadside Highld 94 D3
Roadside of Catterline Aberds 83 F10
Roadside of Kinneff Aberds 83 F10
Roadwater Som 7 C9
Roag Highld 85 D7
Roath Cardiff 15 D7
Roberton Borders 61 B10
Roberton S Lanark 69 H8
Robertsbridge E Sus 12 D6
Roberttown W Yorks 51 G7
Robeston Cross Pembs 22 F3
Robeston Wathen Pembs 22 E5
Robin Hood W Yorks 51 G9
Robin Hood's Bay N Yorks 59 F10
Roborough Devon 4 E6
Roborough Devon 6 E4
Roby Mers 43 C7
Roby Mill Lancs 43 B8
Rocester Staffs 35 B7
Roch Pembs 22 D3
Roch Gate Pembs 22 D3
Rochdale Gtr Man 44 A2
Roche Corn 3 C8
Rochester Medway 20 E4
Rochester Northumb 62 D4
Rochford Essex 20 B5
Rock Corn 3 B8
Rock Northumb 63 A8
Rock W Sus 11 C10
Rock Worcs 26 A4
Rock Ferry Mers 42 D6
Rockbeare Devon 7 G9
Rockbourne Hants 9 C10
Rockcliffe Cumb 61 G9
Rockcliffe Dumfries 55 D11
Rockfield Highld 87 C12
Rockfield Mon 25 G11
Rockford Hants 9 D10
Rockhampton S Glos 16 B3
Rockingham N Nhants 36 F4
Rockland All Saints Norf 38 F5
Rockland St Mary Norf 39 E9
Rockland St Peter Norf 38 F5
Rockley Wilts 17 D8
Rockwell End Bucks 18 C4
Rockwell Green Som 7 D10
Rodborough Glos 16 A5
Rodbourne Swindon 17 C8
Rodbourne Wilts 16 C6
Rodbourne Cheney Swindon 17 C8
Rodd Hereford 25 B10
Roddam Northumb 62 A6
Rodden Dorset 8 F5
Rode Som 16 F5
Rode Heath Ches E 44 G2
Rodeheath Ches E 44 F2
Roden Telford 34 D1
Rodhuish Som 7 C9
Rodington Telford 34 D1
Rodley Glos 26 G4
Rodley W Yorks 51 F8
Rodmarton Glos 16 B6
Rodmell E Sus 12 F3
Rodmersham Kent 20 E6
Rodney Stoke Som 15 F10
Rodsley Derbys 35 A8
Rodway Som 15 H8
Rodwell Dorset 8 G5
Roe Green Herts 29 E10
Roecliffe N Yorks 51 C9
Roehampton London 19 D9
Roesound Shetland 96 G5
Roffey W Sus 11 A10
Rogart Highld 93 J10
Rogart Station Highld 93 J10
Rogate W Sus 11 B7
Rogerstone Newport 15 C8
Roghadal W Isles 90 J5
Rogiet Mon 15 C10
Rogue's Alley Cambs 37 E9
Roke Oxon 18 B3
Roker T&W 63 H10
Rollesby Norf 39 D10
Rolleston Leics 36 E3
Rolleston Notts 45 G11
Rolleston-on-Dove Staffs 35 C8
Rolston E Yorks 53 E8
Rolvenden Kent 13 C7
Rolvenden Layne Kent 13 C7
Romaldkirk Durham 57 D11
Romanby N Yorks 58 G4
Romannobridge Borders 69 F10
Romansleigh Devon 7 D6
Romford London 20 C2
Romiley Gtr Man 44 C3
Romsey Hants 10 B2
Romsey Town Cambs 29 C11
Romsley Shrops 34 G3
Romsley Worcs 34 H5
Ronague IoM 48 E2
Rookhope Durham 57 B11
Rookley IoW 10 F4
Rooks Bridge Som 15 F9
Roos E Yorks 53 F8
Roosebeck W&F 49 C2
Rootham's Green Bedford 29 C8
Rootpark S Lanark 69 E8
Ropley Hants 10 A5
Ropley Dean Hants 10 A5
Ropsley Lincs 36 B5
Rora Aberds 89 C10
Rorandle Aberds 83 B8
Rorrington Shrops 33 E9
Roscroggan Corn 2 E5
Rose Corn 3 D6
Rose Ash Devon 7 D6
Rose Green W Sus 11 E8
Rose Grove Lancs 50 F4
Rose Hill E Sus 12 E3
Rose Hill Lancs 50 F4
Rose Hill Suff 31 D8
Roseacre Kent 20 F4
Roseacre Lancs 49 F4
Rosebank S Lanark 69 F7
Rosebrough Northumb 71 H10
Rosebush Pembs 22 D5
Rosecare Corn 4 B2
Rosedale Abbey N Yorks 59 G8
Roseden Northumb 62 A6
Rosefield Highld 87 F11
Rosehall Highld 92 J7
Rosehaugh Mains Highld 87 F9
Rosehearty Aberds 89 B9
Rosehill Shrops 34 B2
Roseisle Moray 88 B1
Roselands E Sus 12 F5
Rosemarket Pembs 22 F4
Rosemarkie Highld 87 F10
Rosemary Lane Devon 7 E10
Rosemount Perth 76 C4
Rosenannon Corn 3 C8
Rosewell Midloth 69 D11
Roseworth Stockton 58 D5
Roseworthy Corn 2 F5
Rosgill W&F 57 E7
Roshven Highld 79 D10
Roskhill Highld 85 D7
Roskill House Highld 87 F9
Rosley Cumb 56 B5
Roslin Midloth 69 D11
Rosliston Derbys 35 D8
Rosneath Argyll 73 E11
Ross Dumfries 55 E9
Ross Northumb 71 G10
Ross Perth 75 E10
Ross-on-Wye Hereford 26 F3
Rossett Wrex 42 G6
Rossett Green N Yorks 51 D9
Rossie Ochill Perth 76 F3
Rossie Priory Perth 76 D5
Rossington S Yorks 45 C10
Rosskeen Highld 87 E9
Rossland Renfs 68 C3
Roster Highld 94 G4
Rostherne Ches E 43 D10
Rosthwaite Cumb 56 E4
Roston Derbys 35 A7
Rosyth Fife 69 B10
Rothbury Northumb 62 C6
Rotherby Leics 36 D2
Rotherfield E Sus 12 D4
Rotherfield Greys Oxon 18 C4
Rotherfi eld Peppard Oxon 18 C4
Rotherham S Yorks 45 C8
Rothersthorpe W Nhants 28 C4
Rotherwick Hants 18 F4
Rothes Moray 88 D2
Rothesay Argyll 73 G9
Rothiebrisbane Aberds 89 E7
Rothienorman Aberds 89 E7
Rothiesholm Orkney 95 F7
Rothley Leics 36 D1
Rothley Northumb 62 E6
Rothley Shield East Northumb 62 D6
Rothmaise Aberds 89 E6
Rothwell Lincs 46 C5
Rothwell N Nhants 36 G4
Rothwell W Yorks 51 G9
Rothwell Haigh W Yorks 51 G9
Rotsea E Yorks 53 D6
Rottal Angus 82 G5
Rotten End Suff 31 B10
Rottingdean Brighton 12 F2
Rottington Cumb 56 E1
Roud IoW 10 F4
Rough Close Staffs 34 B5
Rough Common Kent 21 F8
Rougham Norf 38 C4
Rougham Suff 30 B6
Rougham Green Suff 30 B6
Roughburn Highld 80 E5
Roughlee Lancs 50 E4
Roughley W Mid 35 F7
Roughsike Cumb 61 F11
Roughton Lincs 46 F6
Roughton Norf 39 B8
Roughton Shrops 34 F3
Roughton Moor Lincs 46 F6
Roundhay W Yorks 51 F9
Roundstonefoot Dumfries 61 C7
Roundstreet Common W Sus 11 B9
Roundway Wilts 17 E7
Rous Lench Worcs 27 C7
Rousdon Devon 8 E1
Routenburn N Ayrs 73 G10
Routh E Yorks 53 E6
Row Corn 4 D1
Row W&F 56 H6
Row Heath Essex 31 G8
Rowanburn Dumfries 61 F10
Rowardennan Stirling 74 H6
Rowde Wilts 16 E6
Rowen Conwy 41 C9
Rowfoot Northumb 62 G2
Rowhedge Essex 31 F7
Rowhook W Sus 11 A10
Rowington Warks 27 B9
Rowland Derbys 44 E6
Rowlands Castle Hants 10 C6
Rowlands Gill T&W 63 H7
Rowledge Sur 18 G5
Rowlestone Hereford 25 F10
Rowley E Yorks 52 F5
Rowley Shrops 33 E9
Rowley Hill W Yorks 44 A5
Rowley Regis W Mid 34 G5
Rowly Sur 19 G7
Rowney Green Worcs 27 A7
Rownhams Hants 10 C2
Rowrah Cumb 56 E2
Rowsham Bucks 28 G5
Rowsley Derbys 44 F6
Rowstock Oxon 17 C11
Rowston Lincs 46 G4
Rowton Ches W 43 F7
Rowton Shrops 33 D9
Rowton Telford 34 D2
Roxburgh Borders 70 G6
Roxby N Lincs 52 H5
Roxby N Yorks 59 E8
Roxton Bedford 29 C8
Roxwell Essex 30 H3
Royal Leamington Spa Warks 27 B10
Royal Oak Darl 58 D3
Royal Oak Lancs 43 B7
Royal Tunbridge Wells Kent 12 C4
Royal Wootton Bassett Wilts 17 C7
Roybridge Highld 80 E4
Roydhouse W Yorks 44 A6
Roydon Essex 29 H11
Roydon Norf 38 C3
Roydon Norf 39 G6
Roydon Hamlet Essex 29 H11
Royston Herts 29 D10
Royston S Yorks 45 A7
Royton Gtr Man 44 B3
Rozel Jersey 11
Ruabon = Rhiwabon Wrex 33 A9
Ruaig Argyll 78 G3
Ruan Lanihorne Corn 3 E7
Ruan Minor Corn 2 H6
Ruarach Highld 80 A1
Ruardean Glos 26 G3
Ruardean Woodside Glos 26 G3
Rubery Worcs 34 H5
Ruckcroft W&F 57 B7
Ruckhall Hereford 25 E11
Ruckinge Kent 13 C9
Ruckland Lincs 47 E7
Ruckley Shrops 33 E11
Rudbaxton Pembs 22 D4
Rudby N Yorks 58 F5
Ruddington Notts 36 B1
Rudford Glos 26 F4
Rudge Shrops 34 F4
Rudge Som 16 F5
Rudgeway S Glos 16 C3
Rudgwick W Sus 11 A9
Rudhall Hereford 26 F3
Rudheath Ches W 43 E9
Rudley Green Essex 20 A5
Rudry Caerph 15 C7
Rudston E Yorks 53 C6
Rudyard Staffs 44 G3
Rufford Lancs 49 H4
Rufforth York 51 D11
Rugby Warks 35 H11
Rugeley Staffs 34 D6
Ruglen S Ayrs 66 F5
Ruilick Highld 87 G8
Ruishton Som 8 B1
Ruisigearraidh W Isles 90 J4
Ruislip London 19 C7
Ruislip Common London 19 C7
Rumbling Bridge Perth 76 H3
Rumburgh Suff 39 G9
Rumford Corn 3 B7
Rumney Cardiff 15 D8
Runcorn Halton 43 D8
Runcton W Sus 11 D7
Runcton Holme Norf 38 E2
Rundlestone Devon 5 D6
Runfold Sur 18 G5
Runhall Norf 39 E6
Runham Norf 39 D10
Runham Norf 39 E11
Runnington Som 7 D10
Runsell Green Essex 30 H4
Runswick Bay N Yorks 59 E9
Runwell Essex 20 B4
Ruscombe Wokingham 18 D4
Rush Green London 20 C2
Rush-head Aberds 89 D8
Rushall Hereford 26 E3
Rushall Norf 39 G7
Rushall W Mid 34 E6
Rushall Wilts 17 F8
Rushbrooke Suff 30 B5
Rushbury Shrops 33 F11
Rushden Herts 29 E10
Rushden N Nhants 28 B6
Rushenden Kent 20 D6
Rushford Norf 38 G5
Rushlake Green E Sus 12 E5
Rushmere Suff 39 G10
Rushmere St Andrew Suff 31 D9
Rushmoor Sur 18 G5
Rushock Worcs 26 A5
Rusholme Gtr Man 44 C2
Rushton Ches W 43 F8
Rushton N Nhants 36 G4
Rushton Shrops 34 E2
Rushton Spencer Staffs 44 F3
Rushwick Worcs 26 C5
Rushyford Durham 58 D3
Ruskie Stirling 75 G9
Ruskington Lincs 46 G4
Rusland W&F 56 H5
Rusper W Sus 19 H9
Ruspidge Glos 26 G3
Russell's Water Oxon 18 C4
Russel's Green Suff 31 A9
Rusthall Kent 12 C4
Rustington W Sus 11 D9
Ruston N Yorks 52 A5
Ruston Parva E Yorks 53 C6
Ruswarp N Yorks 59 F9
Rutherford Borders 70 G5
Rutherglen S Lanark 68 D5
Ruthernbridge Corn 3 C9
Ruthin = Rhuthun Denb 42 G4
Ruthrieston Aberdeen 83 C11
Ruthven Aberds 88 D5
Ruthven Angus 76 C5
Ruthven Highld 81 D9
Ruthven Highld 87 H11
Ruthven House Angus 76 C6
Ruthvoes Corn 3 C8
Ruthwell Dumfries 60 G6
Ruyton-XI-Towns Shrops 33 C9
Ryal Northumb 62 F6
Ryal Fold Blackburn 50 G2
Ryall Dorset 8 E3
Ryarsh Kent 20 F3
Rydal W&F 56 F5
Ryde IoW 10 E4
Rye E Sus 13 D8
Rye Foreign E Sus 13 D7
Rye Harbour E Sus 13 E8
Rye Park Herts 29 G10
Rye Street Worcs 26 E4
Ryecroft Gate Staffs 44 F3
Ryehill E Yorks 53 G8
Ryhall Rutland 36 D6
Ryhill W Yorks 45 A7
Ryhope T&W 58 A5
Rylstone N Yorks 50 D5
Ryme Intrinseca Dorset 8 C4
Ryther N Yorks 52 F1
Ryton Glos 26 E4
Ryton N Yorks 52 B3
Ryton Shrops 34 E3
Ryton T&W 63 G7
Ryton-on-Dunsmore Warks 27 A10

S

Sabden Lancs 50 F3
Sacombe Herts 29 G10
Sacriston Durham 58 B3
Sadberge Darl 58 E4
Saddell Argyll 65 E8
Saddington Leics 36 F2
Saddle Bow Norf 38 D2
Saddlescombe W Sus 12 E1
Sadgill W&F 57 F6
Saffron Walden Essex 30 E2
Sageston Pembs 22 F5
Saham Hills Norf 38 E5
Saham Toney Norf 38 E5
Saighdinis W Isles 84 B3
Saighton Ches W 43 F7
St Abbs Borders 71 D8
St Abb's Haven Borders 71 D8
St Agnes Corn 2 D6
St Agnes Scilly 2 D2
St Albans Herts 29 H8
St Allen Corn 3 D7
St Andrews Fife 77 F8
St Andrew's Major V Glam 15 D7
St Anne Ald 11
St Annes Lancs 49 G3
St Ann's Dumfries 60 D6
St Ann's Chapel Corn 4 D5
St Ann's Chapel Devon 5 G7
St Anthony-in-Meneage Corn 3 G6
St Anthony's Hill E Sus 12 F5
St Arvans Mon 15 B11
St Asaph = Llanelwy Denb 42 E3
St Athan V Glam 14 E6
St Aubin Jersey 11
St Austell Corn 3 D9
St Bees Cumb 56 E1
St Blazey Corn 4 F1
St Boswells Borders 70 G4
St Brelade Jersey 11
St Breock Corn 3 B8
St Breward Corn 4 D1
St Briavels Glos 16 A2
St Bride's Pembs 22 E3
St Brides Major V Glam 14 D4
St Bride's Netherwent Mon 15 C10
St Brides-super-Ely V Glam 14 D6
St Brides Wentlooge Newport 15 C8
St Budeaux Plym 4 F5
St Buryan Corn 2 G3
St Catherine Bath 16 D4
St Catherine's Argyll 73 C10
St Clears = Sanclêr Carms 23 E7
St Cleer Corn 4 E3
St Clement Corn 3 E7
St Clements Jersey 11
St Clether Corn 4 C3
St Colmac Argyll 73 G9
St Columb Major Corn 3 C8
St Columb Minor Corn 3 C7
St Columb Road Corn 3 D8
St Combs Aberds 89 B10
St Cross South Elmham Suff 39 G8
St Cyrus Aberds 77 A10
St David's = Tyddewi Pembs 22 D2
St David's Perth 76 E2
St Day Corn 2 E6
St Dennis Corn 3 D8
St Devereux Hereford 25 E11
St Dogmaels Pembs 22 B6
St Dogwells Pembs 22 D4
St Dominick Corn 4 E5
St Donat's V Glam 14 E5
St Edith's Wilts 16 E6
St Endellion Corn 3 B8
St Enoder Corn 3 D7
St Erme Corn 3 D7
St Erney Corn 4 F4
St Erth Corn 2 F4
St Ervan Corn 3 B7
St Eval Corn 3 C7
St Ewe Corn 3 E8
St Fagans Cardiff 15 D7
St Fergus Aberds 89 C10
St Fillans Perth 75 E9
St Florence Pembs 22 F5
St Genny's Corn 4 B2
St George Conwy 42 E2
St George's V Glam 14 D6
St Germans Corn 4 F4
St Giles Lincs 46 E3
St Giles in the Wood Devon 6 E4
St Giles on the Hth. Devon 6 G2
St Harmon Powys 24 A6
St Helen Auckland Durham 58 D2
St Helena Warks 35 E8
St Helen's E Sus 13 E7
St Helens IoW 10 F5
St Helens Mers 43 C8
St Helier Jersey 11
St Helier London 19 E9
St Hilary Corn 2 F4
St Hilary V Glam 14 D6
Saint Hill W Sus 12 C2
St Illtyd Bl Gwent 15 A8
St Ippollytts Herts 29 F8
St Ishmael's Pembs 22 F3
St Issey Corn 3 B8
St Ive Corn 4 E4
St Ives Cambs 29 A10
St Ives Corn 2 E4
St Ives Dorset 9 D10
St James South Elmham Suff 39 G9
St Jidgey Corn 3 C8
St John Corn 4 F5
St John's IoM 48 D2
St John's Jersey 11
St John's Sur 18 F6
St John's Worcs 26 C5
St John's Chapel Durham 57 C10
St John's Fen End Norf 37 D11
St John's Highway Norf 37 D11
St John's Town of Dalry Dumfries 55 A9
St Judes IoM 48 C3
St Just in Roseland Corn 3 F7
St Just Corn 2 F2
St Katherine's Aberds 89 E7
St Keverne Corn 3 G6
St Kew Corn 3 B9
St Kew Highway Corn 3 B9
St Keyne Corn 4 E3
St Lawrence Corn 3 C9
St Lawrence Essex 20 A6
St Lawrence IoW 10 G4
St Leonard's Bucks 28 H6
St Leonards Dorset 9 D10
St Leonards E Sus 13 F6
Saint Leonards S Lanark 68 E5
St Levan Corn 2 G2
St Lythans V Glam 15 D7
St Mabyn Corn 3 B9
St Madoes Perth 76 E4
St Margaret South Elmham Suff 39 G9
St Margaret's Hereford 25 E10
St Margarets Herts 29 G10
St Margaret's at Cliffe Kent 21 G10
St. Margaret's Hope Orkney 95 J5
St Mark's IoM 48 E2
St Martin Corn 4 F3
St Martins Corn 2 G6
St Martin's Jersey 11
St Martins Perth 76 D4
St Martin's Shrops 33 B9
St Mary Bourne Hants 17 F11
St Mary Church V Glam 14 D6
St Mary Cray London 19 E11
St Mary Hill V Glam 14 D5
St Mary Hoo Medway 20 D5
St Mary in the Marsh Kent 13 D9
St Mary's Jersey 11
St Mary's Orkney 95 H5
St Mary's Bay Kent 13 D9
St Maughans Mon 25 G11
St Mawes Corn 3 F7
St Mawgan Corn 3 C7
St Mellion Corn 4 E4
St Mellons Cardiff 15 C8
St Merryn Corn 3 B7
St Mewan Corn 3 D8
St Michael Caerhays Corn 3 E8
St Michael Penkevil Corn 3 E7
St Michael South Elmham Suff 39 G9
St Michael's Kent 13 C7
St Michaels Worcs 26 B2
St Michael's on Wyre Lancs 49 E4
St Minver Corn 3 B8
St Monans Fife 77 G8
St Neot Corn 4 E2
St Neots Cambs 29 B8
St Newlyn East Corn 3 D7
St Nicholas Pembs 22 C3
St Nicholas V Glam 14 D6
St Nicholas at Wade Kent 21 E9
St Ninians Stirling 68 A6
St Osyth Essex 31 G8
St Osyth Heath Essex 31 G8
St Ouens Jersey 11
St Owens Cross Hereford 26 F2
St Paul's Cray London 19 E11
St Paul's Walden Herts 29 F8
St Peter Port Guern 11
St Peter's Jersey 11
St Peter's Kent 21 E10
St Petrox Pembs 22 G4
St Pinnock Corn 4 E3
St Quivox S Ayrs 67 D6
St Ruan Corn 2 H6
St Sampson Guern 11
St Stephen Corn 3 D8
St Stephen's Corn 4 C4
St Stephens Corn 4 F5
St Stephens Herts 29 H8
St Teath Corn 4 C1
St Thomas Devon 7 G8
St Tudy Corn 4 D1
St Twynnells Pembs 22 G4
St Veep Corn 4 F2
St Vigeans Angus 77 C9
St Wenn Corn 3 C8
St Weonards Hereford 25 F11
Saintbury Glos 27 E8
Salcombe Devon 5 H8
Salcombe Regis Devon 7 H10
Salcott Essex 30 G6
Sale Gtr Man 43 C10
Sale Green Worcs 26 C6
Saleby Lincs 47 E8
Salehurst E Sus 12 D6
Salem Carms 24 F3
Salem Ceredig 32 G2
Salen Argyll 79 G8
Salen Highld 79 E9
Salesbury Lancs 50 F2
Salford C Beds 28 E6
Salford Gtr Man 44 C2
Salford Oxon 27 F9
Salford Priors Warks 27 C7
Salfords Sur 19 G9
Salhouse Norf 39 D9
Saline Fife 69 A9
Salisbury Wilts 9 B10
Sallachan Highld 74 A2
Sallachy Highld 86 H2
Sallachy Highld 93 J8
Salle Norf 39 C7
Salmonby Lincs 47 E7
Salmond's Muir Angus 77 D8
Salperton Glos 27 F7
Salph End Bedford 29 C7
Salsburgh N Lanark 69 D7
Salt Staffs 34 C5
Salt End E Yorks 53 G7
Saltaire W Yorks 51 F7
Saltash Corn 4 F5
Saltburn Highld 87 E10
Saltburn-by-the-Sea Redcar 59 D7
Saltby Leics 36 C4
Saltcoats Cumb 56 G2
Saltcoats N Ayrs 66 B5
Saltdean Brighton 12 F2
Salter Lancs 50 C2
Salterforth Lancs 50 E4
Salterswall Ches W 43 F9
Saltfleet Lincs 47 C8
Saltfleetby All Saints Lincs 47 C8
Saltfleetby St Clements Lincs 47 C8
Saltfleetby St Peter Lincs 47 D8
Saltford Bath 16 E3
Salthouse Norf 39 A6
Saltmarshe E Yorks 52 G3
Saltney Flint 43 F6
Salton N Yorks 52 B3
Saltwick Northumb 63 F7
Saltwood Kent 21 H8
Salum Argyll 78 G3
Salvington W Sus 11 D10
Salwarpe Worcs 26 B5
Salwayash Dorset 8 E3
Sambourne Warks 27 B7
Sambrook Telford 34 C3
Samhla W Isles 84 B2
Samlesbury Lancs 50 F1
Samlesbury Bottoms Lancs 50 G2
Sampford Arundel Som 7 E10
Sampford Brett Som 7 B9
Sampford Courtenay Devon 6 F5
Sampford Peverell Devon 7 E9
Sampford Spiney Devon 4 D6
Sampool Bridge W&F 56 H6
Samuelston E Loth 70 C3
Sanachan Highld 85 D13
Sanaigmore Argyll 64 A3
Sanclêr = St Clears Carms 23 E7
Sancreed Corn 2 G3
Sancton E Yorks 52 F5
Sand Highld 86 B2
Sand Shetland 96 J5
Sand Hole E Yorks 52 F4
Sand Hutton N Yorks 52 D2
Sandaig Highld 85 H12
Sandal Magna W Yorks 51 H9
Sandale Cumb 56 B4
Sandbach Ches E 43 F10
Sandbank Argyll 73 E10
Sandbanks BCP 9 F9
Sandend Aberds 88 B5
Sanderstead London 19 E10
Sandfields Glos 26 F6
Sandford Devon 7 F7
Sandford Dorset 9 F8
Sandford IoW 10 F4
Sandford N Som 15 F10
Sandford S Lanark 68 F6
Sandford Shrops 34 B1
Sandford W&F 57 E9
Sandford on Thames Oxon 18 A2
Sandford Orcas Dorset 8 B5
Sandford St Martin Oxon 27 F11
Sandfordhill Aberds 89 D11
Sandgate Kent 21 H8
Sandgreen Dumfries 55 D8
Sandhaven Aberds 89 B9
Sandhead Dumfries 54 E3
Sandhills Sur 18 H6
Sandhoe Northumb 62 G5
Sandholme E Yorks 52 F4
Sandholme Lincs 37 B9
Sandhurst Brack 18 E5
Sandhurst Glos 26 F5
Sandhurst Kent 13 D6
Sandhurst Cross Kent 13 D6
Sandhutton N Yorks 51 A9
Sandiacre Derbys 35 B10
Sandilands Lincs 47 D9
Sandilands S Lanark 69 G7
Sandiway Ches W 43 E9
Sandleheath Hants 9 C10
Sandling Kent 20 F4
Sandlow Green Ches E 43 F10
Sandness Shetland 96 H3
Sandon Essex 20 A4
Sandon Herts 29 E10
Sandon Staffs 34 B5
Sandown IoW 10 F4
Sandplace Corn 4 F3
Sandridge Herts 29 G8
Sandridge Wilts 16 E6
Sandringham Norf 38 C2
Sandsend N Yorks 59 E9
Sandside Ho. Highld 93 C12
Sandsound Shetland 96 J5
Sandtoft N Lincs 45 B11
Sandway Kent 20 F5
Sandwell W Mid 34 G6
Sandwich Kent 21 F10
Sandwick Orkney 95 K5
Sandwick Shetland 96 L6
Sandwick W&F 56 E6
Sandwith Cumb 56 E1
Sandy C Beds 29 D8
Sandy Carms 23 F9
Sandy Bank Lincs 46 G6
Sandy Haven Pembs 22 F3
Sandy Lane Wilts 16 E6
Sandy Lane Wrex 33 A9
Sandycroft Flint 42 F6
Sandyford Dumfries 61 D8
Sandyford Stoke 44 G2
Sandygate IoM 48 C3
Sandyhills Dumfries 55 D11
Sandylands Lancs 49 C4
Sandypark Devon 5 C8
Sandysike Cumb 61 G9
Sangobeg Highld 92 C7
Sangomore Highld 92 C7
Sanna Highld 78 E7
Sanndabhaig W Isles 84 D3
Sanndabhaig W Isles 91 D9
Sannox N Ayrs 66 B3
Sanquhar Dumfries 60 C3
Santon N Lincs 46 A3
Santon Bridge Cumb 56 F3
Santon Downham Suff 38 G4
Sapcote Leics 35 F10
Sapey Common Hereford 26 B4
Sapiston Suff 38 H5
Sapley Cambs 29 A9
Sapperton Glos 16 A6
Sapperton Lincs 36 B6
Saracen's Head Lincs 37 C9
Sarclet Highld 94 F5
Sardis Carms 23 F10
Sarn Bridgend 14 C5
Sarn Powys 33 F8
Sarn Bach Gwyn 40 H5
Sarn Meyllteyrn Gwyn 40 G4
Sarnau Carms 23 E8
Sarnau Ceredig 23 A8
Sarnau Gwyn 32 B5
Sarnau Powys 25 E7
Sarnau Powys 33 D8
Sarnesfield Hereford 25 C10
Saron Carms 23 C8
Saron Carms 24 G3
Saron Denb 42 F3
Saron Gwyn 40 E6
Saron Gwyn 41 D7
Sarratt Herts 19 B7
Sarre Kent 21 E9
Sarsden Oxon 27 F9
Sarsgrum Highld 92 C6
Satley Durham 58 B2
Satron N Yorks 57 G11
Satterleigh Devon 6 D5
Satterthwaite W&F 56 G5
Satwell Oxon 18 C4
Sauchen Aberds 83 B8
Saucher Perth 76 D4
Sauchie Clack 69 A7
Sauchieburn Aberds 83 G8
Saughall Ches W 42 E6
Saughtree Borders 61 D11
Saul Glos 26 H4
Saundby Notts 45 D11
Saundersfoot Pembs 22 F6
Saunderton Bucks 18 A4
Saunton Devon 6 C3
Sausthorpe Lincs 47 F7
Saval Highld 93 J8
Savary Highld 79 G9
Savile Park W Yorks 51 G6
Sawbridge Warks 28 B2
Sawbridgeworth Herts 29 G11
Sawdon N Yorks 59 H10
Sawley Derbys 35 B10
Sawley Lancs 50 E3
Sawley N Yorks 51 C8
Sawston Cambs 29 D11
Sawtry Cambs 37 G7
Saxby Leics 36 D4
Saxby Lincs 46 D4
Saxby All Saints N Lincs 52 H5
Saxelbye Leics 36 C3
Saxham Street Suff 31 B7
Saxilby Lincs 46 E2
Saxlingham Norf 38 B6
Saxlingham Green Norf 39 F8
Saxlingham Nethergate Norf 39 F8
Saxlingham Thorpe Norf 39 F8
Saxmundham Suff 31 B10
Saxon Street Cambs 30 C3
Saxondale Notts 36 B2
Saxtead Suff 31 B9
Saxtead Green Suff 31 B9
Saxthorpe Norf 39 B7
Saxton N Yorks 51 F10
Sayers Common W Sus 12 E1
Scackleton N Yorks 52 B2
Scadabhagh W Isles 90 H6
Scaftworth Notts 45 C10
Scagglethorpe N Yorks 52 B4
Scaitcliffe Lancs 50 G3
Scalasaig Argyll 72 D2
Scalby E Yorks 52 G4
Scalby N Yorks 59 G11
Scaldwell W Nhants 28 A4
Scale Houses W&F 57 B7
Scaleby Cumb 61 G10
Scaleby Hill Cumb 61 G10
Scales Lancs 49 F4
Scales W&F 49 B2
Scales W&F 56 D5
Scalford Leics 36 C3
Scaling Redcar 59 E8
Scallastle Argyll 79 H9
Scalloway Shetland 96 K6
Scalpay W Isles 90 H7
Scalpay Ho. Highld 85 F11
Scalpsie Argyll 73 H9
Scamadale Highld 79 B10
Scamblesby Lincs 46 E6
Scamodale Highld 79 D11
Scampston N Yorks 52 B4
Scampton Lincs 46 E3
Scapa Orkney 95 H5
Scapegoat Hill W Yorks 51 H6
Scar Orkney 95 D7
Scarborough N Yorks 59 H11
Scarcliffe Derbys 45 F8
Scarcroft W Yorks 51 E9
Scarcroft Hill W Yorks 51 E9
Scardroy Highld 86 F5
Scarff Shetland 96 E4
Scarfskerry Highld 94 C4
Scargill Durham 58 E1
Scarinish Argyll 78 G3
Scarisbrick Lancs 43 A6
Scarning Norf 38 D5
Scarrington Notts 36 A3
Scartho NE Lincs 46 B6
Scarwell Orkney 95 F3
Scatness Shetland 96 M5
Scatraig Highld 87 H10
Scawby N Lincs 46 B3
Scawsby S Yorks 45 B9
Scawton N Yorks 51 A11
Scayne's Hill W Sus 12 D2
Scethrog Powys 25 F8
Scholar Green Ches E 44 G2
Scholes W Yorks 44 B5
Scholes W Yorks 51 F9
Scholes W Yorks 51 G7
School Green Ches W 43 F9
Scleddau Pembs 22 C4
Sco Ruston Norf 39 C8
Scofton Notts 45 D10
Scole Norf 39 H7
Scolpaig W Isles 84 A2
Scone Perth 76 E4
Sconser Highld 85 E10
Scoonie Fife 76 G6
Scoor Argyll 78 K7
Scopwick Lincs 46 G4
Scoraig Highld 86 B3
Scorborough E Yorks 52 E6
Scorrier Corn 2 E6
Scorton Lancs 49 E5
Scorton N Yorks 58 F3
Scotbheinn W Isles 84 C3
Scotby Cumb 61 H10
Scotch Corner N Yorks 58 F3
Scotforth Lancs 49 D4
Scothern Lincs 46 E4
Scotland Gate Northumb 63 E8
Scotlandwell Perth 76 G4
Scots' Gap Northumb 62 E6
Scotsburn Highld 87 D10
Scotscalder Station Highld 94 E2
Scotscraig Fife 77 E7
Scotston Aberds 83 F9
Scotston Perth 76 C2
Scotstoun Glasgow 68 D4
Scotstown Highld 79 E11
Scotswood T&W 63 G7
Scottas Highld 85 H12
Scotter Lincs 46 B2
Scotterthorpe Lincs 46 B2
Scottlethorpe Lincs 37 C6
Scotton Lincs 46 C2
Scotton N Yorks 51 D9
Scotton N Yorks 58 G2
Scottow Norf 39 C8
Scoughall E Loth 70 B5
Scoulag Argyll 73 H10
Scoulton Norf 38 E5
Scourie Highld 92 E4
Scourie More Highld 92 E4
Scousburgh Shetland 96 M5
Scrabster Highld 94 C2
Scrafield Lincs 47 F7
Scrainwood Northumb 62 C5
Scrane End Lincs 37 A9
Scraptoft Leics 36 E2
Scratby Norf 39 D11
Scrayingham N Yorks 52 C3
Scredington Lincs 37 A6
Scremby Lincs 47 F8
Scremerston Northumb 71 F9
Screveton Notts 36 A3
Scrivelsby Lincs 46 F6
Scriven N Yorks 51 D9
Scrooby Notts 45 C10
Scropton Derbys 35 B7
Scrub Hill Lincs 46 G6
Scruton N Yorks 58 G3
Sculcoates Hull 53 F6
Sculthorpe Norf 38 B4
Scunthorpe N Lincs 46 A2
Scurlage Swansea 23 H9
Sea Palling Norf 39 C10
Seaborough Dorset 8 D3
Seacombe Mers 42 C6
Seacroft Lincs 47 F9
Seacroft W Yorks 51 F9
Seadyke Lincs 37 B9
Seafield S Ayrs 66 D6
Seafield W Loth 69 D9
Seaford E Sus 12 G3
Seaforth Mers 42 C6
Seagrave Leics 36 D2
Seaham Durham 58 B5
Seahouses Northumb 71 G11
Seal Kent 20 F2
Sealand Flint 42 F6
Seale Sur 18 G5
Seamer N Yorks 52 A6
Seamer N Yorks 58 E5
Seamill N Ayrs 66 B5
Searby Lincs 46 B4
Seasalter Kent 21 E7
Seascale Cumb 56 F2
Seathorne Lincs 47 F9
Seathwaite Cumb 56 E4
Seathwaite W&F 56 G4
Seatoller Cumb 56 E4
Seaton Corn 4 F4
Seaton Cumb 56 C2
Seaton Devon 8 F1
Seaton Durham 58 A4
Seaton E Yorks 53 E7
Seaton Northumb 63 F9
Seaton Rutland 36 F5
Seaton Burn T&W 63 F8
Seaton Carew Hrtlpl 58 D6
Seaton Delaval Northumb 63 F9
Seaton Ross E Yorks 52 E3
Seaton Sluice Northumb 63 F9
Seatown Aberds 88 B5
Seatown Dorset 8 E3
Seave Green N Yorks 59 F6
Seaview IoW 10 E5
Seaville Cumb 56 A3
Seavington St Mary Som 8 C3
Seavington St Michael Som 8 C3
Sebergham Cumb 56 B5
Seckington Warks 35 E8
Second Coast Highld 86 B2
Sedbergh W&F 57 G8
Sedbury Glos 15 B11
Sedbusk N Yorks 57 G10
Sedgeberrow Worcs 27 E7
Sedgebrook Lincs 36 B4
Sedgefield Durham 58 D4
Sedgeford Norf 38 B3
Sedgehill Wilts 9 B7
Sedgley W Mid 34 F5
Sedgwick W&F 57 H7
Sedlescombe E Sus 13 E6
Sedlescombe Street E Sus 13 E6
Seend Wilts 16 E6
Seend Cleeve Wilts 16 E6
Seer Green Bucks 18 B6
Seething Norf 39 F9
Sefton Mers 42 B6
Seghill Northumb 63 F8
Seifton Shrops 33 G10
Seighford Staffs 34 C4
Seilebost W Isles 90 H5
Seion Gwyn 41 D7
Seisdon Staffs 34 F4
Seisiadar W Isles 91 D10
Selattyn Shrops 33 B8
Selborne Hants 10 A6
Selby N Yorks 52 F2
Selham W Sus 11 B8
Selhurst London 19 E10
Selkirk Borders 70 H3
Sellack Hereford 26 F2
Sellafirth Shetland 96 D7
Sellibister Orkney 95 D8
Sellindge Kent 13 C9
Sellindge Lees Kent 13 C10
Selling Kent 21 F7
Sells Green Wilts 16 E6
Selly Oak W Mid 34 G6
Selmeston E Sus 12 F4
Selsdon London 19 E10
Selsey W Sus 11 E7
Selsfield Common W Sus 12 C2
Selsted Kent 21 G9
Selston Notts 45 G8
Selworthy Som 7 B8
Semblister Shetland 96 H5
Semer Suff 30 D6
Semington Wilts 16 E5
Semley Wilts 9 B7
Send Sur 19 F7
Send Marsh Sur 19 F7
Senghenydd Caerph 15 B7
Sennen Corn 2 G2
Sennen Cove Corn 2 G2
Sennybridge = Pont Senni Powys 24 F6
Serlby Notts 45 D10
Sessay N Yorks 51 B10
Setchey Norf 38 D2
Setley Hants 10 D2
Setter Shetland 96 E6
Setter Shetland 96 H5
Setter Shetland 96 J7
Settiscarth Orkney 95 G4
Settle N Yorks 50 C4
Settrington N Yorks 52 B4
Seven Kings London 19 C11
Seven Sisters Neath 24 H5
Sevenhampton Glos 27 F7
Sevenoaks Kent 20 F2
Sevenoaks Weald Kent 20 F2
Severn Beach S Glos 15 C11
Severn Stoke Worcs 26 D5
Severnhampton Swindon 17 B9
Sevington Kent 13 B9
Sewards End Essex 30 E2
Sewardstone Essex 19 B10
Sewardstonebury Essex 19 B10
Sewerby E Yorks 53 C7
Seworgan Corn 2 F6
Sewstern Leics 36 C4
Sezincote Glos 27 E8
Sgarasta Mhor W Isles 90 H5
Sgiogarstaigh W Isles 91 A10
Shabbington Bucks 28 H3
Shackerstone Leics 35 E9
Shackleford Sur 18 G6
Shade W Yorks 50 G5
Shadforth Durham 58 B4
Shadingfield Suff 39 G10
Shadoxhurst Kent 13 C8
Shadsworth Blackburn 50 G3
Shadwell Norf 38 G5
Shadwell W Yorks 51 F9
Shaftesbury Dorset 9 B7
Shafton S Yorks 45 A7
Shalbourne Wilts 17 E10
Shalcombe IoW 10 F2
Shalden Hants 18 G3
Shaldon Devon 5 D10
Shalfleet IoW 10 F3
Shalford Essex 30 F4
Shalford Sur 19 G7
Shalford Green Essex 30 F4
Shallowford Devon 6 B6
Shalmsford Street Kent 21 F7
Shalstone Bucks 28 E3
Shamley Green Sur 19 G7
Shandon Argyll 73 E11
Shandwick Highld 87 D11
Shangton Leics 36 F3
Shankhouse Northumb 63 F8
Shanklin IoW 10 F4
Shanquhar Aberds 88 E5
Shanzie Perth 76 B5
Shap W&F 57 E7
Shapwick Dorset 9 D8
Shapwick Som 15 H10
Shardlow Derbys 35 B10
Shareshill Staffs 34 E5
Sharlston W Yorks 51 H9
Sharlston Common W Yorks 51 H9
Sharnbrook Bedford 28 C6
Sharnford Leics 35 F10
Sharoe Green Lancs 49 F5
Sharow N Yorks 51 B9
Sharp Street Norf 39 C9
Sharpenhoe C Beds 29 E7
Sharperton Northumb 62 C5
Sharpness Glos 16 A3
Sharpthorne W Sus 12 C2
Sharrington Norf 38 B6
Shatterford Worcs 34 G3
Shaugh Prior Devon 4 E6
Shavington Ches E 43 G10
Shaw Gtr Man 44 B3
Shaw W Berks 17 E11
Shaw Wilts 16 E5
Shaw Green Lancs 49 H5
Shaw Mills N Yorks 51 C8
Shawbury Shrops 34 C1
Shawdon Hall Northumb 62 B6
Shawell Leics 35 G11
Shawford Hants 10 B3
Shawforth Lancs 50 G4
Shawhead Dumfries 60 F4
Shawhill Dumfries 61 G8
Shawton S Lanark 68 F5
Shawtonhill S Lanark 68 F5
Shear Cross Wilts 16 G5
Shearington Dumfries 60 G6
Shearsby Leics 36 F2
Shebbear Devon 6 F3
Shebdon Staffs 34 C3
Shebster Highld 93 C13
Sheddens E Renf 68 E4
Shedfield Hants 10 C4
Sheen Staffs 44 F5
Sheepscar W Yorks 51 F9
Sheepscombe Glos 26 G5
Sheepstor Devon 5 E6
Sheepwash Devon 6 F3
Sheepway N Som 15 D10
Sheepy Magna Leics 35 E9
Sheepy Parva Leics 35 E9
Sheering Essex 30 G2
Sheerness Kent 20 D6
Sheet Hants 11 B6
Sheffield S Yorks 45 D7
Sheffield Bottom W Berks 18 E3
Sheffield Green E Sus 12 D3
Shefford C Beds 29 E8
Shefford Woodlands W Berks 17 D10
Sheigra Highld 92 C4
Sheinton Shrops 34 E2
Shelderton Shrops 33 H10
Sheldon Derbys 44 F5
Sheldon Devon 7 F10
Sheldon W Mid 35 G7
Sheldwich Kent 21 F7
Shelf W Yorks 51 G7
Shelfanger Norf 39 G7
Shelfield W Mid 34 E6
Shelfield Warks 27 B8
Shelford Notts 36 A2
Shellacres Northumb 71 F7
Shelley Essex 20 A2
Shelley Suff 31 E7
Shelley W Yorks 44 A6
Shellingford Oxon 17 B10
Shellow Bowells Essex 30 H3
Shelsley Beauchamp Worcs 26 B4
Shelsley Walsh Worcs 26 B4
Shelthorpe Leics 35 D11
Shelton Bedford 29 B7
Shelton Norf 39 F8
Shelton Notts 36 A3
Shelton Shrops 33 D10
Shelton Green Norf 39 F8
Shelve Shrops 33 F9
Shelwick Hereford 26 D2
Shenfield Essex 20 B3
Shenington Oxon 27 D10
Shenley Herts 19 A8
Shenley Brook End M Keynes 28 E5
Shenley Church End M Keynes 28 E5
Shenleybury Herts 19 A8
Shenmore Hereford 25 E10
Shennanton Dumfries 54 C6
Shenstone Staffs 35 E7
Shenstone Worcs 26 A5
Shenton Leics 35 E9
Shenval Highld 80 A6
Shenval Moray 82 A4
Shepeau Stow Lincs 37 D9
Shephall Herts 29 F9
Shepherd's Green Oxon 18 C4
Shepherd's Port Norf 38 B2
Shepherdswell Kent 21 G9
Shepley W Yorks 44 B5
Shepperdine S Glos 16 B3
Shepperton Sur 19 E7
Shepreth Cambs 29 D10
Shepshed Leics 35 D10
Shepton Beauchamp Som 8 C3
Shepton Mallet Som 16 G3
Shepton Montague Som 8 A5
Shepway Kent 20 F4
Sheraton Durham 58 C5
Sherborne Dorset 8 C5
Sherborne Glos 27 G8
Sherborne St John Hants 18 F3
Sherbourne Warks 27 B9
Sherburn Durham 58 B4
Sherburn N Yorks 52 B5
Sherburn Hill Durham 58 B4
Sherburn in Elmet N Yorks 51 F10
Shere Sur 19 G7
Shereford Norf 38 C4
Sherfield English Hants 10 B1
Sherfield on Loddon Hants 18 F3
Sherford Devon 5 G8
Sheriff Hutton N Yorks 52 C2
Sheriffhales Shrops 34 D3
Sheringham Norf 39 A7
Sherington M Keynes 28 D5
Shernal Green Worcs 26 B6
Shernborne Norf 38 B3
Sherrington Wilts 16 H6
Sherston Wilts 16 C5
Sherwood Green Devon 6 D4
Shettleston Glasgow 68 D5
Shevington Gtr Man 43 B8
Shevington Moor Gtr Man 43 A8
Shevington Vale Gtr Man 43 B8
Sheviock Corn 4 F4
Shide IoW 10 F3
Shiel Bridge Highld 80 B1
Shieldaig Highld 85 A13
Shieldaig Highld 85 C13
Shieldhill Dumfries 60 E6
Shieldhill Falk 69 C7
Shieldhill S Lanark 69 F9
Shielfoot Highld 79 E9
Shielhill Angus 77 B7
Shielhill Invclyd 73 F11
Shifford Oxon 17 A10
Shifnal Shrops 34 E3
Shilbottle Northumb 63 C7
Shildon Durham 58 D3
Shillingford Devon 7 D8
Shillingford Oxon 18 B2
Shillingford St George Devon 5 C10
Shillingstone Dorset 9 C7
Shillington C Beds 29 E8
Shillmoor Northumb 62 C4
Shilton Oxon 27 H9
Shilton Warks 35 G10
Shilvington Northumb 63 E7
Shimpling Norf 39 G7
Shimpling Suff 30 C5
Shimpling Street Suff 30 C5
Shincliffe Durham 58 B3
Shiney Row T&W 58 A4
Shinfield Wokingham 18 E4
Shingham Norf 38 E3
Shingle Street Suff 31 D10
Shinner's Bridge Devon 5 E8
Shinness Highld 93 H8
Shipbourne Kent 20 F2
Shipdham Norf 38 E5
Shipham Som 15 F10
Shiphay Torbay 5 E9
Shiplake Oxon 18 D4
Shipley Derbys 35 A10
Shipley Northumb 63 B7
Shipley Shrops 34 F4
Shipley W Sus 11 B10
Shipley W Yorks 51 F7
Shipley Shiels Northumb 62 D3
Shipmeadow Suff 39 G9
Shippea Hill Sta. Cambs 38 G2
Shippon Oxon 17 B11
Shipston-on-Stour Warks 27 D9
Shipton Glos 27 G7
Shipton N Yorks 52 D1
Shipton Shrops 34 F1
Shipton Bellinger Hants 17 G9
Shipton Gorge Dorset 8 E3
Shipton Green W Sus 11 D7
Shipton Moyne Glos 16 C5
Shipton on Cherwell Oxon 27 G11
Shipton Solers Glos 27 G7
Shipton-under-Wychwood Oxon 27 G9
Shiptonthorpe E Yorks 52 E4
Shirburn Oxon 18 B3
Shirdley Hill Lancs 42 A6
Shirebrook Derbys 45 F9
Shiregreen S Yorks 45 C7
Shirehampton Bristol 15 D11
Shiremoor T&W 63 F9
Shirenewton Mon 15 B10
Shireoaks Notts 45 D9
Shirkoak Kent 13 C8
Shirl Heath Hereford 25 C11
Shirland Derbys 45 G7
Shirley Derbys 35 A8
Shirley London 19 E10
Shirley Soton 10 C3
Shirley W Mid 35 H7
Shirrell Heath Hants 10 C4
Shirwell Devon 6 C4
Shirwell Cross Devon 6 C4
Shiskine N Ayrs 66 D2
Shobdon Hereford 25 B11
Shobnall Staffs 35 C8
Shobrooke Devon 7 F7
Shoby Leics 36 D2
Shocklach Ches W 43 H7
Shoeburyness Southend 20 C6
Sholden Kent 21 F10
Sholing Soton 10 C3
Shoot Hill Shrops 33 D10
Shop Corn 3 B7
Shop Corn 6 E1
Shop Corner Suff 31 E9
Shore Mill Highld 87 E10
Shoreditch London 19 C10
Shoreham Kent 20 E2
Shoreham-By-Sea W Sus 11 D11
Shoresdean Northumb 71 F8
Shoreswood Northumb 71 F8
Shoreton Highld 87 E9
Shorncote Glos 17 B7
Shorne Kent 20 D3
Short Heath W Mid 34 E5
Shortacombe Devon 4 C6
Shortgate E Sus 12 E3
Shortlanesend Corn 3 E7
Shortlees E Ayrs 67 C7
Shortstown Bedford 29 D7
Shorwell IoW 10 F3
Shoscombe Bath 16 F4
Shotatton Shrops 33 C9
Shotesham Norf 39 F8
Shotgate Essex 20 B4
Shotley Suff 31 E9
Shotley Bridge Durham 58 A1
Shotley Gate Suff 31 E9
Shotleyfield Northumb 58 A1
Shottenden Kent 21 F7
Shottermill Sur 11 A7
Shottery Warks 27 C8
Shotteswell Warks 27 D11
Shottisham Suff 31 D10
Shottle Derbys 45 H7
Shottlegate Derbys 45 H7
Shotton Durham 58 C5
Shotton Flint 42 F6
Shotton Northumb 71 G7
Shotton Colliery Durham 58 B4
Shotts N Lanark 69 D7
Shotwick Ches W 42 E6
Shouldham Norf 38 E2
Shouldham Thorpe Norf 38 E2
Shoulton Worcs 26 C5
Shover's Green E Sus 12 C5
Shrawardine Shrops 33 D10
Shrawley Worcs 26 B5
Shrewley Common Warks 27 B9
Shrewsbury Shrops 33 D10
Shrewton Wilts 17 G7
Shripney W Sus 11 D8
Shrivenham Oxon 17 C9
Shropham Norf 38 F5
Shrub End Essex 30 F6
Shucknall Hereford 26 D2
Shudy Camps Cambs 30 D3
Shulishadermor Highld 85 D9
Shurdington Glos 26 G6
Shurlock Row Windsor 18 D5
Shurrery Highld 93 D13
Shurrery Lodge Highld 93 D13
Shurton Som 7 B11
Shustoke Warks 35 F8
Shute Devon 7 F7
Shute Devon 8 E1
Shutford Oxon 27 D10
Shuthonger Glos 26 E5
Shutlanger W Nhants 28 C4
Shuttington Warks 35 E8
Shuttlewood Derbys 45 E8
Siabost bho Dheas W Isles 90 C7
Siabost bho Thuath W Isles 90 C7
Siadar W Isles 91 B8
Siadar Iarach W Isles 91 B8
Siadar Uarach W Isles 91 B8
Sibbaldbie Dumfries 61 E7
Sibbertoft W Nhants 36 G2
Sibdon Carwood Shrops 33 G10
Sibford Ferris Oxon 27 E10
Sibford Gower Oxon 27 E10
Sible Hedingham Essex 30 E4
Sibsey Lincs 47 G7
Sibson Cambs 37 F6
Sibson Leics 35 E9
Sibthorpe Notts 45 H11
Sibton Suff 31 B10
Sibton Green Suff 31 A10
Sicklesmere Suff 30 B5
Sicklinghall N Yorks 51 E9
Sid Devon 7 H10
Sidbury Devon 7 G10
Sidbury Shrops 34 G2
Sidcot N Som 15 F10
Sidcup London 19 D11
Siddick Cumb 56 C2
Siddington Ches E 44 E2
Siddington Glos 17 B7
Sidemoor Worcs 26 A6
Sidestrand Norf 39 B8
Sidford Devon 7 G10
Sidlesham W Sus 11 E7
Sidley E Sus 12 F6
Sidlow Sur 19 G9
Sidmouth Devon 7 H10
Sigford Devon 5 D8
Sigglesthorne E Yorks 53 E7
Sighthill Edin 69 C10
Sigingstone V Glam 14 D5
Signet Oxon 27 G9
Silchester Hants 18 E3
Sildinis W Isles 91 F7
Sileby Leics 36 D1
Silecroft Cumb 49 A1
Silfield Norf 39 F7
Silian Ceredig 23 A10
Silk Willoughby Lincs 37 A6
Silkstone S Yorks 44 B6
Silkstone Common S Yorks 44 B6
Silloth Cumb 56 A3
Sills Northumb 62 C4
Sillyearn Moray 88 C5
Siloh Carms 24 E4
Silpho N Yorks 59 G10
Silsden W Yorks 50 E6
Silsoe C Beds 29 E7
Silver End Essex 30 G5
Silverburn Midloth 69 D11
Silverdale Lancs 49 B4
Silverdale Staffs 44 H2
Silvergate Norf 39 C7
Silverhill E Sus 13 E6
Silverley's Green Suff 39 H8
Silverstone W Nhants 28 D3
Silverton Devon 7 F8
Silvington Shrops 34 H2
Silwick Shetland 96 J4
Simmondley Derbys 44 C4
Simonburn Northumb 62 F4
Simonsbath Som 7 C6
Simonstone Lancs 50 F3
Simprim Borders 71 F7
Simpson M Keynes 28 E5
Simpson Cross Pembs 22 E3
Sinclair's Hill Borders 71 E7
Sinclairston E Ayrs 67 E7
Sinderby N Yorks 51 A9
Sinderhope Northumb 57 A10
Sindlesham Wokingham 18 E4
Singdean Borders 61 C11
Singleborough Bucks 28 E4
Singleton Lancs 49 F3
Singleton W Sus 11 C7
Singlewell Kent 20 D3
Sinkhurst Green Kent 13 B7
Sinnahard Aberds 82 B6
Sinnington N Yorks 59 H8
Sinton Green Worcs 26 B5
Sipson London 19 D7
Sirhowy Bl Gwent 25 G8
Sisland Norf 39 F9
Sissinghurst Kent 13 C6
Sisterpath Borders 70 F6
Siston S Glos 16 D3
Sithney Corn 2 G5
Sittingbourne Kent 20 E5
Six Ashes Staffs 34 G3
Six Hills Leics 36 C2
Six Mile Bottom Cambs 30 C2
Sixhills Lincs 46 D5
Sixpenny Handley Dorset 9 C8
Sizewell Suff 31 B11
Skail Highld 93 E10
Skaill Orkney 95 E5
Skaill Orkney 95 G3
Skaill Orkney 95 H6
Skares E Ayrs 67 E8
Skateraw E Loth 70 C6
Skaw Shetland 96 G7
Skeabost Highld 85 D9
Skeabrae Orkney 95 F3
Skeeby N Yorks 58 F3
Skeffington Leics 36 E3
Skeffling E Yorks 53 H9
Skegby Notts 45 F8
Skegness Lincs 47 F9
Skelberry Shetland 96 M5
Skelbo Highld 87 B10
Skelbrooke S Yorks 45 A9
Skeldyke Lincs 37 B9
Skellingthorpe Lincs 46 E3
Skellister Shetland 96 H6
Skellow S Yorks 45 A9
Skelmanthorpe W Yorks 44 A6
Skelmersdale Lancs 43 B7
Skelmonae Aberds 89 E8
Skelmorlie N Ayrs 73 G10
Skelmuir Aberds 89 D9
Skelpick Highld 93 D10
Skelton E Yorks 52 G3
Skelton N Yorks 58 F1
Skelton Redcar 59 E7
Skelton W&F 56 C6
Skelton York 52 D1
Skelton-on-Ure N Yorks 51 C9
Skelwick Orkney 95 D5
Skelwith Bridge W&F 56 F5
Skendleby Lincs 47 F8
Skene Ho. Aberds 83 C9
Skenfrith Mon 25 F11
Skerne E Yorks 52 D6
Skeroblingarry Argyll 65 F8
Skerray Highld 93 C9
Skerton Lancs 49 C4
Sketchley Leics 35 F10
Sketty Swansea 14 B2
Skewen Neath 14 B3
Skewsby N Yorks 52 B2
Skeyton Norf 39 C8
Skiag Bridge Highld 92 G5
Skibo Castle Highld 87 C10
Skidbrooke Lincs 47 C8
Skidbrooke North End Lincs 47 C8
Skidby E Yorks 52 F6
Skilgate Som 7 D8
Skillington Lincs 36 C4
Skinburness Cumb 61 H7
Skinflats Falk 69 B8
Skinidin Highld 84 D7
Skinnet Highld 93 C8
Skinningrove Redcar 59 D8
Skipness Argyll 73 H7
Skippool Lancs 49 E3
Skipsea E Yorks 53 D7
Skipsea Brough E Yorks 53 D7
Skipton N Yorks 50 D5
Skipton-on-Swale N Yorks 51 B9
Skipwith N Yorks 52 F2
Skirbeck Lincs 37 A9
Skirbeck Quarter Lincs 37 A9
Skirlaugh E Yorks 53 F7
Skirling Borders 69 G9
Skirmett Bucks 18 C4
Skirpenbeck E Yorks 52 D3
Skirwith W&F 57 C8
Skirza Highld 94 D5
Skulamus Highld 85 F11
Skullomie Highld 93 C9
Skyborry Green Shrops 25 A9
Skye of Curr Highld 82 A1
Skyreholme N Yorks 51 C6
Slackhall Derbys 44 D4
Slackhead Moray 88 B4
Slad Glos 26 H5
Slade Devon 6 B4
Slade Pembs 22 E4
Slade Green London 20 D2
Slaggyford Northumb 57 A8
Slaidburn Lancs 50 D3
Slaithwaite W Yorks 44 A4
Slaley Northumb 62 H5
Slamannan Falk 69 C7
Slapton Bucks 28 F6
Slapton Devon 5 G9
Slapton W Nhants 28 D3
Slatepit Dale Derbys 45 F7
Slattocks Gtr Man 44 B2
Slaugham W Sus 12 D1
Slaughterford Wilts 16 D5
Slawston Leics 36 F3
Sleaford Hants 18 H5
Sleaford Lincs 46 H4
Sleagill W&F 57 E7
Sleapford Telford 34 D2
Sledge Green Worcs 26 E5
Sledmere E Yorks 52 C5
Sleightholme Durham 57 E11
Sleights N Yorks 59 F9
Slepe Dorset 9 E8
Slickly Highld 94 D4
Sliddery N Ayrs 66 D2
Sligachan Hotel Highld 85 F9
Slimbridge Glos 16 A4
Slindon Staffs 34 B4
Slindon W Sus 11 D8
Slinfold W Sus 11 A10
Sling Gwyn 41 D8
Slingsby N Yorks 52 B2
Slioch Aberds 88 E5
Slip End C Beds 29 G7
Slip End Herts 29 E9
Slipton N Nhants 36 H5
Slitting Mill Staffs 34 D6
Slochd Highld 81 A10
Slockavullin Argyll 73 D7
Sloley Norf 39 C8
Sloothby Lincs 47 E8
Slough Slough 18 D6
Slough Green W Sus 12 D1
Sluggan Highld 81 A10
Slumbay Highld 85 E13
Slyfield Sur 18 F6

T

Y

Z